# THE AMERICAN LANGUAGE
## SUPPLEMENT I

# SUPPLEMENT I

# T H E

## *American Language*

AN INQUIRY

INTO THE DEVELOPMENT OF ENGLISH

IN THE UNITED STATES

BY

# H.   L.   Mencken

1977

ALFRED A. KNOPF

NEW YORK

THIS IS A BORZOI BOOK,
PUBLISHED BY ALFRED A. KNOPF, INC.

COPYRIGHT *1945 by Alfred A. Knopf, Inc. All rights reserved. No part of this book may be reproduced in any form without permission in writing from the publisher, except by a reviewer who may quote brief passages in a review to be printed in a magazine or newspaper. Manufactured in the United States of America and distributed by Random House, Inc. Published in Canada by Random House of Canada, Limited.*

Published August 20, 1945
Reprinted Ten Times
Twelfth Printing, August 1977

# PREFACE

Since the fourth edition of "The American Language" was published in April, 1936, it has been reprinted eight times (not to mention an English edition and one in Braille, in fourteen volumes, for the use of the blind), and in consequence I have had a chance to correct some of the more embarrassing errors in the earlier printings; but the size of the volume has made it impracticable to attempt any considerable addition of new matter, and in consequence there is a formidable arrearage of material awaiting working up. It has poured in from numerous and varied sources. For one thing, there has been a sharp increase in the professional literature of the subject, culminating in the launching in 1939 of the monumental "Linguistic Atlas of the United States and Canada," and the completion in 1944 of " A Dictionary of American English on Historical Principles," which was barely getting under way when my fourth edition was published. Meanwhile, the publication of the third volume of Richard H. Thornton's "American Glossary" (the first two volumes had appeared in 1912) was finished in *Dialect Notes* in 1939, and that intermittent journal and the more regular *American Speech* (begun in 1925) continued to print many valuable papers on American speechways, laid under heavy contribution here. Nor was all the work of exploration and mapping done by Americans, for in 1939 H. W. Horwill brought out at Oxford his "Anglo-American Interpreter," the first attempt at an English-American dictionary on a comprehensive scale, and Eric Partridge continued his studies of English borrowings of American slang. In the latter field the American, W. J. Burke, published an excellent bibliography in 1939, under the title of " The Literature of Slang," and Lester V. Berrey and Melvin Van den Bark followed in 1942 with " The American Thesaurus of Slang," which went far beyond the late Maurice H. Weseen's "Dictionary of American Slang" of 1934. There appeared also a number of books dealing with various other special phases of the subject — for example, Robert L. Ramsay and Frances Guthrie Emberson's " Mark Twain Lexicon " in 1938, Satoshi Ichiya's " King's English or President's English " in 1939, Charles Carpenter Fries's " American English Grammar " in 1940, Colonel Elbridge Colby's " Army Talk " in 1942, and Harold Wentworth's " American Dialect Dictionary " in 1944.

I have given diligent study to all this literature, and in addition have accumulated a large body of observations from other sources. Ever since the publication of my first edition in 1919 I have had clipping bureaus supply me with everything printed on the subject in the newspapers of the United States, Great Britain and the British dominions and colonies, and until the outbreak of World War II my gleanings also included many contributions from non-English-speaking countries, especially Germany and Japan. Finally, I have been in constant correspondence with interested persons, many of them professional philologians but most of them lay inquirers like myself, in all parts of the world, and from them I have received a great deal of extremely useful matter, most of it unprinted. Not a few excellent suggestions have come from blind readers of the Braille edition before mentioned. I have given credit to all these helpers at appropriate places in the text, but to some I owe debts so heavy that they should be mentioned again here — for example, to Dr. Louise Pound of the University of Nebraska, whose early work put the study of current American English on its legs, and whose interest in my book has been of fundamental value at all of its stages; to the Right Rev. J. B. Dudek, chancellor of the Roman Catholic diocese of Oklahoma City and Tulsa, whose wide learning includes a mass of philological knowledge that he has been generous enough, at every turn, to place at my disposal; to Allen Walker Read, late of the staff of " A Dictionary of American English," from whose invaluable investigations of the history of the language I have borrowed often and copiously; to Fred Hamann of Pekin, Ill., who turned over to me a large body of very useful material, otherwise unobtainable; to Don Bloch of the United States Fish and Wildlife Service, Department of the Interior, for many contributions of the same sort; to P. E. Cleator of Wallasey (Cheshire), who has favored me with many clippings missed by the English clipping bureaus, and has otherwise lent a sturdy hand to my labors; to my old friend H. W. Seaman of Norwich, an English journalist of extensive American experience, a dili-

gent and perspicacious student of the popular speech of both countries, and hence my constant (and amiably willing) referee on questions of disputed usage; to Professor D. W. Brogan of Cambridge
University, another Briton with a wide and deep knowledge of
American speechways; to Dr. Joseph M. Carrière of the University
of Virginia, who has led me to sources that I'd certainly have missed
without his open-handed aid; to Dr. Atcheson L. Hench of the same
university, who has made me free of his large and valuable accumulations and given me generous help otherwise; and to the late F. H.
Tyson of Hong Kong, who began to send me a steady stream of
useful material (largely from the English colonial papers) in 1923,
and whose widow, after his lamented death in 1942, made me a
present of his extraordinarily rich collection. I am indebted too to
the editors and publishers of "A Dictionary of American English,"
"Webster's New International," *American Speech, Dialect Notes,
Words, Word Study, American Notes and Queries*, the *Writer's
Monthly* and a large number of other books and periodicals for permission to quote from them, in some cases frequently and at length.
Finally, I owe thanks to a number of librarians who have supplied
me with material and helped me to solve problems, and especially to
the ladies of the Pratt Library, Baltimore; to Wilmer Ross Leech
of the New York Public Library, and to my old and much esteemed
colleague, Edgar Ellis, librarian of the Baltimore *Sunpapers*. My
secretary, Mrs. Rosalind C. Lohrfinck, has labored on this book, as
she labored on the fourth edition of "The American Language,"
with such diligence and intelligence that any acknowledgment of
her aid must seem meagre, and I am in debt, too, to her sister, Mrs.
Clare Crump, who helped me greatly while Mrs. Lohrfinck was dis-
abled by illness.

This Supplement is not a new edition of "The American Language," and repeats only a small and inconsiderable amount of the
matter in the fourth edition thereof. My first plan was to revise that
work as I had done thrice before, and so make a fifth edition, but it
quickly appeared that if I tried to get all the new material into it
I'd have a volume of forbidding bulk, probably running to 2,000
pages. I was thus forced to resort to the present Supplement, only
to discover that even a Supplement of the same size as the fourth edition would not contain the whole of my accumulations. Thus I
must offer it in two volumes. The present one covers the ground

of "The American Language," fourth edition, through Chapter VI. The second, to follow, if all goes well, in about a year, will cover Chapters VII to XIII — The Pronunciation of American, American Spelling, The Common Speech, Proper Names in America, American Slang, and The Future of the Language —, and also the appendix on Non-English Dialects in America. In addition, I hope to add a second appendix on various subjects not hitherto discussed, for example, the language of gesture, that of children, cattle brands, hog and other animal calls, and American prose style.

The plan adopted for both Supplements is simple, and I hope it will turn out to be workable. It follows precisely the order of my fourth edition, and each section of it is hooked to that work by identical headings. But it is not necessary for the reader to have the fourth edition before him, nor even to have read it, in order to make his way, for the new matter here presented is almost always self-contained and I have included in brackets, wherever they seemed useful, explanatory catch-lines or quotations. The figures at the beginnings of sections all refer to pages of the fourth edition. There are numerous cross-references, but I have not tried to include them in all cases where terms discussed in one place are also mentioned elsewhere, for the reader interested in finding every reference to a given term may do so readily by consulting the List of Words and Phrases. The arrangement is generally chronological, but whenever it has seemed conducive to clarity and coherence to group material from different periods I have not hesitated to do so. As in all the editions of "The American Language," I have presented my bibliographical and other documentary material with the text. There is, I believe, a certain prejudice against footnotes, especially when they are numerous, but I am convinced that it is not shared by the readers of such books as this one. On the contrary, I have learned by the thousands of communications with which I have been favored that they find somewhat elaborate annotations useful and attractive. Moreover, I have had to provide a critical apparatus for the enlightenment of later (and, I hope, far more competent) students of this or that phase of American speech, inasmuch as a large part of the material I present comes from obscure sources, and some of it is quite inaccessible without guidance. I have called attention, from time to time, to the great gaps in the existing knowledge of the subject, and I am in hopes that enough volunteers to fill them will appear soon or late. There is room here for the labors of a whole herd of nascent Ph.D.'s. I trust that all readers of the present volume will bear in mind that, like "The American Language," it does not pretend to be a lexicon. I have sought to put together, not a complete list of American words and phrases, but simply a collection of interesting and perhaps instructive specimens, with a commentary. I have not hesitated to use nonce-words when they illustrated a tendency. Various works that will cover more thoroughly some of the areas I explore are now in progress — for example, the before-mentioned "Linguistic Atlas of the United States and Canada," a dictionary of American place-names by Dr. George A. Stewart, Jr., and a shorter version of "A Dictionary of American English," but covering a much wider field, by Dr. M. M. Mathews, a member of its staff.

The literature of the subject was so meagre at the time I published my first edition in 1919 that I got a comprehensive bibliography of it into less than seventeen pages, and even so had room for many books and papers that bore upon American speechways only indirectly. During the years that have passed since then that literature has become so vast that an adequate account of it would half fill a book as large as this one. A brief history of "The American Language," down to and including the fourth edition, is given in the preface thereof. Here I seize the chance to answer a question that reaches me frequently, to wit, What aroused my interest in the subject, and when did I print my earliest discussions of it? The answer to the first part is that I began to observe American speechways as a young newspaper reporter, working in the police-courts of Baltimore at the turn of the century, and that I was urged to a more systematic study by a chance encounter with a file of *Dialect Notes* in the Enoch Pratt Free Library of the same city, probably about 1905. *Dialect Notes* had been set up in 1890, but it was still moving very slowly (as it is still moving very slowly), and its second volume had got only to Part IV. What it lacked in bulk, however, was more than made up for by the industry and learning of its pioneer contributors — for example, A. F. Chamberlain, E. S. Sheldon, O. F. Emerson, C. H. Grandgent, E. H. Babbitt, George Hempl, Albert Matthews, George T. Flom, Clark S. Northrup, J. M. Manly, M. D. Learned, and Francis J. Child, who were joined after a while by Louise Pound and her students. I was a steady customer of *Dialect Notes* after my discovery of its riches, and it presently sent me to

such early works as John S. Farmer's " Americanisms Old and New,"
1889; M. Schele de Vere's " Americanisms: The English of the New
World," 1872, and J. R. Bartlett's " Glossary of Words and Phrases
Usually Regarded as Peculiar to the United States," second edition,
1859. When, in 1910, the Baltimore *Evening Sun* was launched, and
I was set to doing a daily article for its editorial page, I began experimenting with an occasional discussion of the common speech of the
country, and by October was engaged upon an effort to expound its
grammar. These inquiries brought a pleasant response from the
readers of the paper, who took to sending me additional material,
and I soon began that huge accumulation of notes and commentaries
which still engulfs me. In August, 1913, I printed my first magazine
article on the subject, and it was presently followed by others. When,
in 1917, the United States entered World War I, and free speech was
suspended in the department of public affairs, then my main interest,
I sought release from my bonds and exercise for my curiosity in that
of language. The result was the first edition of " The American
Language," completed just as the war ended. When it was published
in March, 1919, it brought in a large number of suggestions from
other persons interested in the subject, and the second edition naturally followed in 1921. There was a third in 1923, after which I had
to shelve the book on account of the heavy work thrown upon me
by the launching of the *American Mercury*. But fresh materials kept
on piling up, and when, at the end of 1933, I resigned my editorship
of the magazine, I resumed work upon the book, and in 1936 the
fourth edition was published. It ran to 809 pages; for the first edition
374 had sufficed. Corrected from time to time, it is still in print.

As I close this preface new material continues to come in. I have
made arrangements for the preservation of it on my departure for
parts unknown, and it will be available to any other investigator who
cares to use it. Thus I am still glad to have more. It should be addressed to me at 1524 Hollins street, Baltimore-23.

Baltimore, 1945                                    H. L. M.

# Table of Contents

## I. THE TWO STREAMS OF ENGLISH

## II. THE MATERIALS OF INQUIRY

## III. THE BEGINNINGS OF AMERICAN

## IV. THE PERIOD OF GROWTH

## V. THE LANGUAGE TODAY

## LIST OF WORDS AND PHRASES

## INDEX

With reference to footnote 1 on page 5, Mr. Julian Boyd of Princeton, New Jersey, has pointed out that John Adams, writing on September 11, 1785, to Mr. Dumas and Mr. Short concerning the Treaty with Prussia, said: "I will not disguise from you, what I should advise you to reserve from others with some discretion, that, old as I am, I hope to live to see the day when the American language will be understood and respected in every Court in Europe. . . ."

# ABBREVIATIONS

To save space some of the books referred to frequently in the text are cited by the following catch-words and abbreviations:

AL4  The American Language, by H. L. Mencken; fourth ed.; New York, 1936.

Baker  A Popular Dictionary of Australian Slang, by Sidney J. Baker; second ed.; Melbourne, n.d.

Barrère  Argot and Slang, by A. Barrère; London, 1887.

Bartlett  A Glossary of Words and Phrases Usually Regarded as Peculiar to the United States, by John Russell Bartlett; New York, 1848; second ed., Boston, 1859; third ed., Boston, 1860; fourth ed., Boston, 1877.

Bentley  A Dictionary of Spanish Terms in English, by Harold W. Bentley; New York, 1932.

Berrey and Van den Bark  The American Thesaurus of Slang, by Lester V. Berrey and Melvin Van den Bark; New York, 1942.

Boucher  Boucher's Glossary of Archaic and Provincial Words; a Supplement to the Dictionaries of the English Language, Particularly Those of Dr. Johnson and Dr. Webster, . . . by the late Rev. Jonathan Boucher, . . . edited jointly by the Rev. Joseph Hunter and Joseph Stevenson; London, Part I, 1832; Part II, 1833.

Bristed  The English Language in America; in Cambridge Essays, Contributed by Members of the University; London, 1855.

Burke  The Literature of Slang, by W. J. Burke; New York, 1939.

Cairns  British Criticisms of American Writings, by William B. Cairns; Madison, Wis., 1918.

Clapin  A New Dictionary of Americanisms, by Sylva Clapin; New York, n.d.

College Standard  The College Standard Dictionary, abridged from the Standard Dictionary by Frank H. Vizetelly; New York, 1922.

Concise Oxford  The Concise Oxford Dictionary of Current English, adapted by H. W. Fowler and F. G. Fowler, third ed., revised by H. W. Fowler and H. G. Le Mesurier; Oxford, 1934.

DAE  A Dictionary of American English on Historical Principles, edited by Sir William Craigie and James R. Hulbert; four vols.; Chicago, 1938–44.

Dunglison  Americanisms, in the *Virginia Literary Museum and Journal of Belles Lettres, Arts, Sciences, &c.*, signed Wy and supposed to be by Robley Dunglison; Charlottesville, Va., 1829–30.

Farmer  Americanisms Old and New, by John S. Farmer; London, 1889.

Farmer and Henley  Slang and Its Analogues, by John S. Farmer and W. E. Henley; seven vols.; London, 1890–1904.

Grose   A Classical Dictionary of the Vulgar Tongue, by Francis Grose; London, 1785; new edition edited by Eric Partridge; London, 1931.

Horwill   A Dictionary of Modern American Usage, by H. W. Horwill; Oxford, 1935.

Humphreys   Glossary appended to The Yankey in England, by David Humphreys; n.p., 1815.

Jespersen   A Modern English Grammar, by Otto Jespersen; three vols.; Heidelberg, 1922–27.

Joyce   English As We Speak It In Ireland, by P. W. Joyce; second ed.; London, 1910.

Krapp   The English Language in America, by George Philip Krapp; two vols.; New York, 1925.

LA   Linguistic Atlas of the United States; Linguistic Atlas of New England, by Hans Kurath, Miles L. Hanley, Bernard Bloch, Guy S. Lowman, Jr., and Marcus L. Hansen; Providence, R. I., 1939.

Leonard   The Doctrine of Correctness in English Usage, 1700–1800, by Sterling Andrus Leonard; Madison, Wis., 1929.

Maitland   The American Slang Dictionary, by James Maitland; Chicago, 1891.

Marryat   A Diary in America, by Frederick Marryat; three vols.; London, 1839.

Mathews   The Beginnings of American English, by M. M. Mathews; Chicago, 1931.

NED   A New English Dictionary on Historical Principles, edited by Sir James A. H. Murray, Henry Bradley, W. A. Craigie, and C. T. Onions; ten vols.; Oxford, 1888–1928.[1]

NED Supplement   A New English Dictionary on Historical Principles; Introduction, Supplement and Bibliography; edited by Sir James A. H. Murray, Henry Bradley, William A. Craigie and C. T. Onions; Oxford, 1933.

Nevins   American Social History as Recorded by British Travelers, compiled and edited by Allan Nevins; New York, 1923.

Partridge   A Dictionary of Slang and Unconventional English, by Eric Partridge; second ed.; New York, 1938.

Pickering   A Vocabulary or Collection of Words and Phrases Which Have Been Supposed to be Peculiar to the United States of America, by John Pickering; Boston, 1816.

Schele de Vere   Americanisms: The English of the New World, by M. Schele de Vere; New York, 1871; second edition, 1872.

Sherwood   Gazetteer of the State of Georgia, by Adiel Sherwood; third ed.; 1837.

Shorter Oxford   The Shorter Oxford English Dictionary on Historical Principles, prepared by William Little, H. W. Fowler and J. Coulson, and revised and edited by C. T. Onions; two vols.; Oxford, 1933.

Thornton   An American Glossary, by Richard H. Thornton; two vols.; Philadelphia, 1912. Vol. III published serially in *Dialect Notes*, 1931–39.

Ware   Passing English of the Victorian Era, by J. Redding Ware; London, n.d.

Warfel   Noah Webster, Schoolmaster to America, by Harry R. Warfel; New York, 1936.

---

[1] This work is often referred to as the OED or OD (Oxford Dictionary), but it seems to me to be preferable to use an abbreviation of its actual title.

Warrack  A Scots Dialect Dictionary, by Alexander Warrack; London, 1911.

Webster 1806  A Compendious Dictionary of the English Language, by Noah Webster; New Haven, 1806.

Webster 1828  An American Dictionary of the English Language, by Noah Webster; New York, 1828.

Webster 1852  An American Dictionary of the English Language, by Noah Webster; revised and enlarged by Chauncey A. Goodrich; Springfield, Mass., 1852.

Webster 1934  Webster's New International Dictionary of the English Language, edited by William Allan Neilson, Thomas A. Knott and Paul W. Carhart; Springfield, Mass., 1934.

Weekley  An Etymological Dictionary of Modern English, by Ernest Weekley; New York, 1921.

Weseen  A Dictionary of American Slang, by Maurice H. Weseen; New York, 1934.

Wright  Dictionary of Obsolete and Provincial English, by Thomas Wright; London, 1857.

Wyld  A History of Modern Colloquial English, by Henry Cecil Wyld; London, 1920.

In some cases the authors whose principal works are listed above are also the authors of other works. All references to the latter are in full.

# THE AMERICAN LANGUAGE
## SUPPLEMENT I

# THE TWO STREAMS OF ENGLISH

## 1. THE EARLIEST ALARMS

4. [By 1754 literary London was already sufficiently conscious of the new words arriving from the New World for Richard Owen Cambridge . . . to be suggesting that a glossary of them would soon be in order.] Cambridge's suggestion is reprinted in " British Recognition of American Speech in the Eighteenth Century," by Allen Walker Read,[1] and it is from that reprint that I take the following extract:

> I wish such a work had been published in time enough to have assisted me in reading the following extract of a letter from one of our colonies. . . . " The *Chippeways* and *Orundaks* [2] are still very troublesome. Last week they *scalped* one of our Indians; but the *Six Nations* continue firm; [3] and at a meeting of *sachems* it was determined to *take up the hatchet* and *make the war-kettle boil*.[4] The French desired to *smoke the calumet of peace*,[5] but the *half king* would not consent. They offered the *speech-belt*, but it was refused.[6] Our governor

[1] *Dialect Notes*, Vol. VI, Pt. VI, 1933, pp. 313–334.

[2] The *Chippewas*, or Ojibwa Indians were of the Algonquian race and held a large territory at the head of the Great Lakes. They were warlike, and fought against the Americans in the colonial wars, in the Revolution and in the War of 1812. The few that survive are now caged on reservations in the upper lakes country. They first appear in American records in 1671, when they were called *Chipoës*. The *Orundaks* were apparently inhabitants of the Adirondack region.

[3] The Six Nations were the Mohawks, Oneidas, Onondagas, Cayugas, Senecas and Tuscaroras. They came from the St. Lawrence region, but by 1700 had more or less control of a territory stretching from Hudson's Bay to what is now North Carolina, and from Connecticut to the Mississippi. Most of them took the English side in the Revolution and were settled in Canada after it was over.

[4] For these phrases see the List of Words and Phrases.

[5] *Calumet* was not an Indian word, but came from a French dialect word signifying a pipe. Robert Beverley, in his History and Present State of Virginia, 1705, said: " This *calumet* is used in all their important transactions. However, it is nothing but a large tobacco pipe made of red, black or white marble." The colonists soon dropped the French word and used *pipe of peace* instead.

[6] The *speech-belt* was a belt of *wampum* (beads used as ornament, and also as currency). The DAE's first (and only) example of its use is credited to George Washington, 1753, but it must have been familiar to the colonists long before then.

has received an account of their proceedings, together with *a string of wampum and a bundle of skins to brighten the cabin*." . . . A work of this kind, if well executed, cannot fail to make the fortune of the undertaker.[1]

Read's paper, just cited, is a valuable review of the impact of Americanisms upon the English in the Eighteenth Century, and I have made further use of it in what follows. He undertook a diligent search, not only of the more obvious English literature of the time, but also of many obscure books and periodicals. In the *Connoisseur* for 1760 [2] he found a brief humorous sketch showing that the English were beginning to find a certain pungency in such American locutions as *sachem, wampum, war-whoop* and *to scalp*, and a little while later references to them multiplied. In the 1780s, says Read, John Wilkes was greatly struck by the American sense of *cleared*, relating to woodland, and in 1794 Thomas Cooper, in his " Some Information Respecting America," was explaining that it meant " the small trees and shrubs grubbed up, and the larger trees cut down about two feet from the ground." The American delight in *cleared* land rather amazed these Englishmen, for in their own country forests were cherished, and one of the standing English objections to Scotland was that it was almost bare of trees. Dr. Johnson, as everyone knows, hated all things American, and it was hardly to be expected that he would admit any Americanism into his Dictionary of the English Language (1755); nevertheless, according to Edmund Malone, he quoted an American-born author, Charlotte Lennox, as authority for the use of two words,[3] one of which, *talent*, had a satellite adjective, *talented*, that was to be de-

1 Cambridge (1717–1802) was a Londoner, educated at Eton and Oxford. After 1751 he lived at Twickenham and was one of the intimates of Horace Walpole. His Scribleriad, a mock-heroic poem, appeared in 1751.

2 The *Connoisseur* belonged to the second flight of English essay periodicals, and was founded by George Colman the elder in 1754. It ran on until 1756, and, like the *Spectator* before it, was reprinted as a book. There was a third edition of that book in three volumes in 1760, containing some new matter. Read's citation comes from this new matter. The *Connoisseur* was contemporaneous with Samuel Johnson's *Rambler* (1750–52); the *Adventurer* (1752–54), to which he also contrib-

uted; the *World* (1753–56), to which Chesterfield and Walpole contributed; the *Idler* (1758–60), also Johnson's; and the *Citizen of the World* (1760), written by Goldsmith.

3 La Lennox was born in 1720 in New York, where her father was the royal lieutenant-governor. She went to England at 15 and married there. Johnson knew her and esteemed her. The novel he quoted from was The Female Quixote, 1752. She also wrote Henrietta, 1758; Sophia, 1761; and Euphemia, 1790, but she is best known for her Shakespeare Illustrated, in which she reprinted some of the sources of Shakespeare's plays and argued that they were better than the plays. Johnson, who agreed, wrote a dedication for the book.

nounced as a vile and intolerable Americanism when it began to be used toward the end of the century.[1] Johnson himself once condescended to use an Americanism in the *Idler* [2] to wit, *tomahawk*, but he at least had the decency to change it into *tom-ax*. In 1756, a year after his Dictionary was published, he was sneering in a review in the *London Magazine* at the " mixture of the American dialect " in Lewis Evans's " Geographical, Historical, Philosophical and Mechanical Essays," [3] and calling it " a tract [4] of corruption to which every language widely diffused must always be exposed." " Johnson," says Read, " probably was offended by such of Evans's words as *portage, statehouse, creek, gap, upland, spur* (glossed as ' *spurs* we call little ridges jetting out from the principal chains of mountains, and are of no long continuing '), *branch, back of,* or *fresh* (noun)."

But not all Englishmen of that era were as hostile to American speechways as Johnson. I have heard of none, in the Eighteenth Century, who actually praised American neologisms, but there were some, at least, who noted with approval that most educated Americans used very few of them. Thus Sir Herbert Croft, Bart., in 1797:

[The] natives write the language particularly well, considering they have no dictionary yet, and how insufficient Johnson's is. Washington's speeches seldom exhibited more than a word or two, liable to the least objection; and, from the style of his publications, as much, or more accuracy may be expected from his successor, Adams.[5]

1 *Talented* was actually quite sound in English, but it had dropped out of use. S. T. Coleridge argued against it in his Table-Talk so late as July 8, 1832. " I regret," he said, " to see that vile and barbarous vocable, *talented*, stealing out of the newspapers into the leading reviews and most respectable publications of the day. Why not *shillinged, farthinged, tenpenced,* &c? The formation of a participle passive from a noun is a license that nothing but a very peculiar felicity can excuse. If mere convenience is to justify such attempts upon the idiom, you cannot stop till the language becomes, in the proper sense of the word, corrupt. Most of these pieces of slang come from America." Coleridge seems to have overlooked *moneyed* (or *monied*), used by Marlowe, Bacon, Clarendon and Wordsworth.

2 No. 40, 1759.
3 Philadelphia, 1755.
4 A variant of *trace,* and already becoming obsolete in Johnson's time.
5 In Croft's fling at Johnson, and perhaps also in his praise of American writings, there was more than a little self-interest, for he had announced a dictionary of his own in 1788, and hoped to find a large market for it in America. Down to Johnson's death in 1788 he and the lexicographer were on good terms, and he contributed the life of Edward Young to the Lives of the Poets. In this he achieved a slavish imitation of Johnson's thunderous style. Croft was a graduate of Oxford and a clergyman. In 1780 he published a novel in letter form called Love and Madness, and in it he used certain letters by Thomas Chatterton, obtained under what amounted to false

The *Monthly Review*, which is described by William B. Cairns [1] as "always kindly toward America," praised the contents of "Addresses and Recommendations of the States," issued by Congress, as "pieces of fine, energetic writing and masterly eloquence." It would be, it said, "a curious speculation for the philosophical inquirer to account for the perfections to which the English language has been carried in our late colonies, amidst the distresses, the clamors and horrors of war." [2] Benjamin Franklin's writings were nearly always praised by the English reviewers, but Franklin had spent so much time in England that he wrote like an Englishman, and was himself dubious about most Americanisms. Paine also got a pretty good press, probably on the score of his English birth, though his atheism alarmed the more orthodox reviewers, but even the friendly *Monthly* protested that many of his words and phrases were "such as have not been used by anybody before, and such as we would not advise anybody to use again." Jefferson was also cried down because of his free-thinking, but even more because of his free use of such Americanisms as *to belittle*.[3] Most of the English travelers before 1800 reported that the Americans, at least of the educated class, spoke English with a good accent. Indeed, one of them, Nicholas Cresswell,[4] declared that they spoke it better than the English. But this favorable verdict was mainly grounded on the discovery that there were no marked dialects in America. "Accustomed as he was to the diversity of dialect in his own island," says Read, "the Englishman found a principal subject of comment in the purity and uniformity of English in America." [5] This was before the Oxford dialect of today had appeared in England, and there was but little uniformity of pronunciation, even in the court circles of London.

4. [The first all-out attack on Americanisms came in 1781 from a Briton living in America, and otherwise ardently pro-American. He was John Witherspoon, president of Princeton, a member of the Con-

---

pretenses from the poet's sister, Mrs. Newton. For this he was roundly denounced by Southey in the *Monthly Review*. Nothing came of his projected dictionary. When he died in 1816 it existed only as 200 volumes of manuscript.
1 British Criticisms of American Writings, 1783–1815; Madison, Wis., 1918, p. 21.

2 Nov., 1783.
3 This one, incidentally, was apparently his own invention. The DAE's first example comes from his Notes on Virginia, written in 1781–2. See *Belittle*, by W. J. Burke, *American Speech*, April, 1932, p. 318.
4 In his journal for July 19, 1777.
5 British Recognition of American Speech, *op. cit.*, p. 322.

tinental Congress, and a signer of the Declaration of Independence.] His observations were printed in the *Pennsylvania Journal and Weekly Advertiser* of Philadelphia on May 9, 16, 23 and 30, 1781, under the general heading of " The Druid." He began by admitting that " the vulgar in America speak much better than the vulgar in Great Britain, for a very obvious reason, *viz.*, that being much more unsettled, and moving frequently from place to place, they are not so liable to local peculiarities either in accent or phraseology. There is a greater difference in dialect," he went on, " between one county and another in Britain than there is between one state and another in America." But in sharp dissent from some of the Englishmen lately quoted, he argued that " gentlemen and scholars " in the new Republic were much less careful and correct in their " public and solemn discourses " than the corresponding dignitaries of the Old Country. He coined the word *Americanism* [1] to designate the novelties they affected, and explained that he did not mean it to be opprobrious but simply desired it to be accepted as " similar in its formation and signification to the word *Scotticism*." " There are many instances," he explained, " in which the Scotch way is as good, and some in which every person who has the least taste as to the propriety or purity of a

[1] At all events, his specific claim to its invention has never been challenged, and the NED allows it, though fixing the date, erroneously, as *c.* 1794 instead of 1781. The word was adopted by Noah Webster in 1809 and by John Pickering in 1816. In 1836 it appeared in the *Southern Literary Messenger*, then edited by Poe. The first occurrence of *American*, applied to the English of the United States, was apparently in the Georgia records of 1740, where it appeared as *American dialect*. Webster made it *American tongue* in his Dissertations on the English Language in 1789, and fours years later Dr. William Thornton made it *American language* in his Cadmus; or, a Treatise on the Elements of Written Language. This book was published in Philadelphia, and was awarded the Magellanic Gold Medal of the American Philosophical Society. See American Projects for an Academy to Regulate Speech, by Allen Walker Read, *Proceedings of the Modern Language Association*, Dec., 1936, p. 1142. *American language* appeared in the debates in Congress in 1802, and by 1815 the *North American Review* was using it. The DAE lists no example of its use between 1822 and 1872, but no doubt it appeared with some frequency. It is to be found in the Rev. John Mason Peck's Guide to Emigrants, 1831 (John Mason Peck and the American Language, by Elrick B. Davis, *American Speech*, Oct., 1926, p. 25), and in *Harper's Magazine*, Aug., 1858, p. 336, col. 1, in an anonymous article entitled Vagabondizing in Belgium: " In an instant I was by her side and speaking to her in her own language — the *American language*." It thus had a long history behind it when I used it for the title of my first edition in 1919. In late years the English, after long resistance, have begun to use it. See, for example, a headline in the *Literary Supplement* of the London *Times*, May 15, 1937, p. 371.

language in general must confess that it is better than that of England, yet speakers and writers must conform to custom." He then proceeded to list Americanisms in seven classes, the first of which included " ways of speaking peculiar to this country." Of these ways he presented twelve examples, as follows:

1. The United States, or *either* of them. This is so far from being a mark of ignorance, that it is used by many of the most able and accurate speakers and writers, yet it is not English. The United States are thirteen in number, but in English *either* does not signify one of many, *but one or the other* of two. I imagine *either* has become an adjective pronoun by being a sort of abbreviation of a sentence where it is used adverbially, *either the one or the other*. It is exactly the same with *ekateros* in Greek, and *alteruter* in Latin.

2. This is to *notify* the publick; or the people had not been *notified*. By this is meant *inform* and *informed*. In English we do not *notify* the person of the thing, but *notify* the thing to the person. In this instance there is certainly an impropriety, for *to notify* is just saying, by a word of Latin derivation, *to make known*. Now if you cannot say this is to make the public known, neither ought you to say this is to *notify* the public.

3. *Fellow countrymen*. This is a word of very frequent use in America. It has been heard in public orations from men of the first character, and may be daily seen in newspaper publications. It is an evident tautology, for the last word expresses fully the meaning of both. If you open any dictionary you will find the word *countryman* signifies one born in the same country. You may say *fellow citizens, fellow soldiers, fellow subjects, fellow Christians*, but not *fellow countrymen*.

4. These things were ordered delivered to the army. The words *to be* are omitted. I am not certain whether this is a local expression or general in America.

5. I wish we could *contrive* it to Philadelphia. The words *to carry it, to have it carried*, or some such, are wanting. It is a defective construction; of which there are but too many that have already obtained in practice, in spite of all the remonstrances of men of letters.

6. We may *hope* the assistance of God. The word *for* or *to receive* is wanting. In this instance *hope*, which is a neuter verb, is turned into an active verb, and not very properly as to the objective term *assistance*. It must be admitted, however, that in some old English poets, *hope* is sometimes used as an active verb, but it is contrary to modern practice.

7. I do not consider myself equal to this task. The word *as* is wanting. I am not certain whether this may not be an English vulgarism, for it is frequently used by the renowned author of " Common Sense," [1] who is an Englishman born; but he has so happy a talent of adopting the blunders of others, that nothing decisive can be inferred from his practice. It is, however, undoubtedly an Americanism, for it is used by authors greatly superior to him in every respect.

8. Neither to-day *or* to-morrow. The proper construction is, either the one *or* the other, neither the one *nor* the other.

9. A *certain* Thomas Benson. The word *certain*, as used in English, is an indefinite, the name fixes it precisely, so that there is a kind of contradiction in

---

1 *i.e.*, Thomas Paine. Common Sense had been published on Jan. 9, 1776.

the expression. In England they would say a certain person *called* or *supposed* to be Thomas Benson.

10. Such bodies are *incident* to these evils. The evil is incident or ready to fall upon the person, the person liable or subject to the evil.

11. He is a very *clever* man. She is quite a *clever* woman. How often are these phrases to be heard in conversation! Their meaning, however, would certainly be mistaken when heard for the first time by one born in Britain. In these cases Americans generally mean by *clever* only goodness of disposition, worthiness, integrity, without the least regard to capacity; nay, if I am not mistaken, it is frequently applied where there is an acknowledged simplicity or mediocrity of capacity. But in Britain, *clever* always means capacity, and may be joined either to a good or bad disposition. We say of a man, he is a *clever* man, a *clever* tradesman, a *clever* fellow, without any reflection upon his moral character, yet at the same time it carries no approbation of it. It is exceeding good English, and very common to say, He is a *clever* fellow, but I am sorry to say it, he is also a great rogue. When *cleverness* is applied primarily to conduct and not to the person, it generally carries in it the idea of art or chicanery not very honourable; for example — Such a plan I confess was very *clever*, *i.e.*, sly, artful, well contrived, but not very fair.

12. I was quite *mad* at him, he made me quite *mad*. This is perhaps an English vulgarism, but it is not found in any accurate writer, nor used by any good speaker, unless when poets or orators use it as a strong figure, and, to heighten the expression, say, he was *mad* with rage.

Looking back from the distance of more than a century and a half, it seems rather strange that Witherspoon should have been able to amass so few " ways of speaking peculiar to this country." Of the twelve that he listed, Nos. 5, 6 and 10 have long since vanished, No. 11 is pretty well played out, and Nos. 1 and 8 are still belabored by the American schoolma'am.[1] The others remain sound American to this day. *To notify* did not, in fact, originate in America, but was in use in England in the Fifteenth Century, though by the end of the Seventeenth it had dropped out there; since then it has been an Americanism. *Fellow countrymen* must have been a novelty in Witherspoon's time, for the DAE's first example is taken from his denunciation of it, but it is now in perfectly good usage. So is the omission of *to be* in " These things were ordered delivered to the army," though purists may often restore it; and so, again, is the omission of *as* from " I do not consider myself equal to this task." Witherspoon's objection to the use of *certain* before a full name was mere pedantry. There may be, in fact, more than one Thomas Benson; indeed, there may be more than one Franklin D. Roosevelt. *Mad*, in England, is commonly

---

1 *Schoolma'am*, incidentally, is itself an Americanism. The DAE's first example of it is dated 1844, but it is no doubt older. *Schoolmarm* is traced to 1848.

used to designate what we call *crazy*, but it is by no means unknown in the sense of *angry*. The NED traces it in that sense to the Fourteenth Century and says that it is the ordinary word for *angry* in some of the English dialects. But it is much more commonly heard in the United States than in England, and most Englishmen regard it as an Americanism.

Witherspoon's second category of errors consisted of "vulgarisms in England and America" and his third of "vulgarisms in America only." Among the former he listed *an't* (now *ain't*), *can't*, *han't* (now *haven't*),[1] *don't*, *shouldn't*, *wouldn't*, *couldn't*, *knowed* for *knew*, *see* for *saw*, *this here*, *that there*, *drownded*, *gownd*, *fellar*, *waller* for *wallow*, *winder* for *window*, *on 'em* for *of 'em*, *lay* for *lie*, *thinks* in the first person singular, *has* for *have*, *as* following *equally*, *most highest*, *had fell*, *had rose*, *had spoke*, *had wrote*, *had broke*, *had threw*, *had drew*, *sat out* for *set out*, and *as how*. Most of these are common vulgarisms, discussed in Chapter IX of AL4. The astonishing thing is that Witherspoon reported them in use by "gentlemen and scholars" in America. "There is great plenty," he said, "to be found everywhere in writing and conversation. They need very little explication, and indeed would scarcely deserve to be mentioned in a discourse of this nature were it not for the circumstance . . . that scholars and public persons are at less pains to avoid them here than in Britain." Apparently the American politicians of those days, encountered by Witherspoon in the New Jersey constitutional convention, in the Continental Congress and on the stump, were as careless of their parts of speech as those of today — and no doubt as calculatingly so. As for *can't*, *don't*, *shouldn't*, *wouldn't* and *couldn't*, they are obviously quite sound in both English and American. As for *ain't*, it is apparently coming into countenance in the United States, even among pedagogues.

Witherspoon's list of "vulgarisms in America only" was thus set forth in the second of his "Druid" papers:

1. I have not done it yet, but am just *going to*. This is an imperfect construction; it wants the words *do it*. Imperfect constructions are the blemish of

---

1 H. C. Wyld shows in A History of Modern Colloquial English; London, 1920, p. 161, that *can't*, *han't*, *shan't*, *couldn't*, *isn't*, etc., were in common use in England. Swift noted them in his Polite Conversation, 1712. *An't* is traced by the DAE to 1723; the NED carries it back to 1706 in England. *Ain't* had begun to supplant it before Witherspoon's day. It is probable that the word he gives as *han't* was really pronounced *haint*. In that form it still survives in the dialect of Appalachia.

the English language in general, and rather more frequent in this country than in England.

2. It is *partly all* gone, it is *mostly all* gone. This is an absurdity or barbarism, as well as a vulgarism.

3. This is the weapon with which he defends himself when he is *attacted,* for *attacked;* or according to the abbreviation, *attack'd.*

4. As I told *Mr.* ——, for as I told *you.* I hope *Mr.* —— is well this morning — What is *Mr.* ——'s opinion upon this subject? This way of speaking to one who is present in the third person, and as if he were absent, is used in this country by way of respect. No such thing is done in Britain, except that to persons of very high rank, they say *your Majesty, your Grace, your Lordship;* yet even there the continuance of the discourse in the third person is not customary.

5. I have been *to* Philadelphia, for *at* or *in* Philadelphia; I have been *to* dinner, for I have *dined.*

6. Walk *in* the house, for *into* the house.

7. You *have no right* to pay it, where right is used for what logicians would call the correlative term obligation.

8. A *spell* of sickness, a long *spell,* a bad *spell.* Perhaps this word is borrowed from the sea dialect.

9. *Every* of these states, *every* of them, *every* of us; for *every one.* I believe the word *every* is used in this manner in some old English writers, and also in some old laws, but not in modern practice. The thing is also improper, because it should be *every one* to make it strictly a partitive and subject to the same construction as some of them, part of them, many of them, &c., yet it must be acknowledged that there is no greater impropriety, if so great, in the vulgar construction of *every* than in another expression very common in both countries, *viz., all of them.*

At the end of this list Witherspoon charged, as in the case of the other list, that even the worst barbarisms on it were affected in his day by Americans of condition. He ascribed this habit to a desire to avoid "bombast and empty swelling," and though he did not say so, I suspect again that a desire to curry favor with voters may have had something to do with it. The first of his caveats has certainly not disposed of the elision he condemns: "I have not done it yet, but I am just *going to*" is perfectly good American idiom at this moment. So is "I have been *to* Philadelphia." So is the free use of *spell* to designate a stretch of time or action. The DAE traces the latter, in the form of "a *spell* of weather," to 1705: it was not encountered in England until 1808. In the more general sense, as in "I'll continue a *spell*," it goes back to 1745, and in the form of "a *spell* of sickness" to 1806. It must be remembered that the DAE's examples do not always show the first actual use; all they indicate is the first *printed* use encountered by its searchers. The forms denounced by Witherspoon in his fourth and ninth counts are now extinct, but those mentioned in his second and seventh still survive in the vulgar speech, and so does *attacted* or *attackted*.

His fourth list, devoted to "local phrases or terms," shows that, despite his statement that the Americans of his time were not "liable to local peculiarities either in accent or phraseology," there were still differences in regional dialect. He offers, unfortunately, but seven examples, so his list is not very illuminating. Three are ascribed to New England or "the northern parts": the use of *considerable* as a general indicator of quality or quantity, the use of *occasion* as a substitute for *opportunity*, and the use of *to improve* in such a sentence as "He *improved* the horse for ten days," meaning he rode it. The DAE says that this use of *considerable* is old in English, and the NED cites an example from Hobbes's "Leviathan," 1651. But the Americans seem to have employed the adjective much more freely than the English, and may have originated its application to material things, as in *considerable snow* and *considerable money*. Combined with *of*, as in *considerable of a shock*, it appears to be clearly American. The other New Englandisms that Witherspoon mentions survive only in rural dialects. He offers two specimens of "improprieties" from the South and two from the middle colonies. The former are *raw salad* for *salad* and the verb *to tote*, which he spells *tot*. *Raw salad* does not appear in the DAE, but *to tote* goes back to the Seventeenth Century, and is still in wide use. It is, in fact, a perfectly good word. Witherspoon's two examples from the middle colonies are *chunk*, in the sense of a half-burned piece of wood, and *once in a while* in the sense of occasionally, as in "He will *once in a while* get drunk." *Chunk* is but little used in English, but it is very familiar in American, and in many senses indicating a thick object. *Once in a while* for *occasionally* was apparently a novelty in Witherspoon's day, for the DAE's first example of it is taken from his denunciation of it. It is still somewhat rare in English, but in American it has long been perfectly sound idiom.

Witherspoon's fifth category of Americanisms is made up of "common blunders through ignorance." The first is the misuse of *eminent* for *imminent*, and he follows with the misuse of *ingenious* for *ingenuous*, *successfully* for *successively*, *intelligible* for *intelligent*, *confisticate* for *confiscate*, *fictious* for *fictitious*, *susceptive* for *susceptible*, *veracity* for *credibility*, *detect* for *dissect*, *scrimitch* for *skirmish*, *duplicit* as an adjective from *duplicity*, and *rescind* for *recede*. Most of these must have been rarely encountered among educated persons, even in Witherspoon's day. He says specifically, however, that one of them, the substitution of *veracity* for *credibility*, was " not a blunder in conversation, but in speaking and writing." The example he gives is " I have some doubt of the *veracity* of this fact." Well, why not? *Veracity* has been used as a synonym of *truth* by some of the best English authors, including Samuel Johnson. In fact, the NED's second definition of it is " agreement of statement or report with the actual fact or facts; accordance with truth; correctness, accuracy." As for *scrimitch*, it is obviously only a bad reporting of *scrimmage*, not a manhandling of *skirmish*. In the precise sense of skirmish it goes back in English to the Fifteenth Century. In America it was in common use during the Revolution, and since the post-Civil War period it has been made familiar as a football term, often used figuratively in the general speech. Witherspoon, in fact, had a bad ear, and not only missed many salient Americanisms, but reported others that probably did not exist. He was archetypical of the academic bigwigs of his day, and showed many of the weaknesses that have since marked the American schoolma'am.

His sixth class of improprieties consists of " cant phrases introduced into public speaking or composition." Most of them are what we would now call slang, *e.g., to take in* (to swindle), *to bilk, to bite* (to swindle), *quite the thing, not the thing, to bamboozle, to sham Abraham*. All of these save *to sham Abraham* (a sailor's locution, meaning to pretend illness) are now in common use, and not one of them originated in America. Witherspoon, always prissy, reproved Johnson for admitting *to bamboozle* to the Dictionary, but he was nevertheless intelligent enough to see that the fate of a word is not determined by lexicographers, but by public opinion. " It is first," he said, " a cant phrase; secondly, a vulgarism; thirdly, an idiom of the language. Some expire in one or other of the two first [*sic*] stages; but if they outlive these they are established forever. . . . I think *topsy-turvy* and *upside-down* have very nearly attained the same privilege."

He was right about both. *Topsy-turvy*, as a matter of fact, had been in familiar use in England since the early Sixteenth Century, and today not even the most fanatical purist would think of questioning it. *Upside-down* is two centuries older, and quite as respectable. It appeared in the Coverdale Bible, 1535, and occurs five times in the

Authorized Version.[1] It was used by Chaucer, Gower, Spenser and Addison, and got into the Encyclopedia Britannica ten years after Witherspoon discussed it.

His seventh and last category comprises " personal blunders, that is to say, effects of ignorance and want of precision in an author, which are properly his own and not reducible to any of the heads above mentioned." [2] These throw a revealing light upon the sad state of American writing in 1781, but have little to do with the subject of Americanisms. His examples are:

  1. The members of a popular government should be continually *availed* of the situation and condition of every part.
  2. A degree of dissentions and oppositions under some circumstances, and a political lethargy under others, *impend* certain ruin to a free state.
  3. I should have let your performance sink into *silent disdain.*
  4. He is a man of most *accomplished* abilities.
  5. I have a *total* objection against this measure.
  6. An *axiom* as well established as any Euclid ever demonstrated.

Witherspoon hints that he found these in the political writing of the time. All they show is that when the primeval American politicians tried to imitate the bow-wow manner of their elegant opposite numbers in England, they sometimes came to grief. In fact, they still do. No. 6, I suspect, was introduced mainly to show off Witherspoon's own learning. It must have been a considerable satisfaction for a president of Princeton to be able to inform a non-academic publicist that Euclid " never demonstrated axioms, but took them for granted." [3]

Witherspoon's account of the Americanisms prevailing in his day must be received with some caution, for he was a Scotsman and had never lived in London. Wyld shows in " A History of Modern Colloquial English " that not a few of the words, phrases and pronunciations that he denounced in America were commonly heard in the best English society of the time. Mathews, below cited, reprints two letters from readers that appeared in the *Pennsylvania Journal* in

1 II Kings XXI, 13; Psalms CXLVI, 9; Isaiah XXIV, 1; XXIX, 16; Acts XVII, 6.
2 In his first article, published May 9, 1781, he promised to close his discussion with " technical terms introduced into the language," and at the end of his fourth article, published May 30, he renewed that promise,

but The Druid did not proceed any further.
3 I am indebted here to M.M.Mathews, who reprints the four Druid papers in full in Chapter II of The Beginnings of American English; Chicago, 1931, a little book that is indispensable to every serious student of American speechways.

June, 1781, commenting upon the " Druid " articles. The first, published June 20, was signed X and included the following additional list of alleged Americanisms:

*Manured* for *inured.*
*Bony-fidely* for *bona fide.*
*Scant-baked* and *slack-baked,* meaning deficient in understanding.
*Sarten* for *certainly.*
*Nice* for *handsome.*
*E'en amost* and *e'en just* for *almost.*
*Tarnal* for *eternal.*
*Grand* for *excellent.*
*Keount* for *count.*
*Keow* for *cow.*
*Darn* for *d——d.*
*To swear e'en amost like a woodpile.*
*Power* for *multitude.*

To these the writer appended a " speech said to have been made by a member of an important public body, soon after the evacuation of Ticonderoga," as follows:

General Clear behaved with great *turpitude* at the *vacation* of *Ty;* Gen. Burgoyne shot *language* at our people, thinking thereby to *intimate* them; but it only served to *astimate* them, for they took up the very *dientical language,* and shot it back again at the *innimy* and did great *persecution;* for their wounds *purified* immediately.

This anticipation of the later struggles of colored preachers with hard words (a favorite subject of American humor in the 1850–1900 period) is scarcely, of course, worth recording, save perhaps as an indicator of the primitiveness of philological discussion in that era. It is, indeed, not at all impossible that the whole communication was intended to be a sort of burlesque of Witherspoon. *Manured* for *inured* is not listed in the DAE, and probably was never in use. Nor does the DAE list *bony-fidely, scant-baked* or *slack-baked. Sarten,* as an illiterate or dialectical form of *certain,* goes back to the Fifteenth Century, and still survives in the speech of Appalachia.[1] *Nice* for *handsome* is encountered in many English dialects, and *tarnal* lives on in various American dialects.[2] *Grand* in the sense of excellent is now

1 *Cf.* John Fox, Jr.'s Hell fer *Sartain,* 1897.
2 For example, see Cape Cod Dialect, II, by George Davis Chase, *Dialect Notes,* 1904, p. 428; A List of Words From Northwest Arkansas, by Joseph William Carr and Rupert Taylor, the same, 1907, p. 208; A Central Connecticut Word-List, by William E. Mead and George D. Chase, the same, 1905, p. 22. See also The English Language in America, by George Philip Krapp; New York, 1925, Vol. I, p. 118. In his second volume, p.

almost good American; set beside *swell*, indeed, it takes on a certain elegance. *Power*, in the sense of a multitude, was used by Thomas Fuller in "The Worthies of England," *c.* 1661, and retained such respectability in England until 1803 that it appeared in "Thaddeus of Warsaw," published in that year by the refined lady author, Jane Porter. As for *a'most*, Wyld shows [1] that it was commonly heard in England, even in good society, in the early Eighteenth Century. It was listed without objection in a work on phonology published by one Jones, a Welshman, in 1701. Many other words in which *l* follows *a*, at that time, dropped the *l*, for example, *almanac, falter, falcon*, and the proper nouns, *Talbot, Walter* and *Falmouth*.

The second letter to the *Pennsylvania Journal* on Witherspoon's "Druid" papers was signed Quercus, and consisted mainly of frank spoofing of the learned and rev. grammarian on his own failings in English. There were, in fact, many slips in his four articles, especially misplacings of *only*, as in "The poor man *only* meant to say," and a certain shakiness in number, as in "The scholars . . . write all their *life* afterward." Good Witherspoon, in truth, was not only the first American writer on "correct" English, but also a shining exemplar of the failings of the whole fraternity, now so numerous, for it is a lamentable fact that but one book on "good" writing has ever been written by an author of any recognized capacity as a writer. That exception was by Ambrose Bierce — and his "Write It Right," published in 1909, was so pedantic and misleading as to be worse than most of the treatises of the pedagogues.

7. [John Adams wrote to the president of Congress from Amsterdam on September 5, 1780, suggesting that Congress set up an academy for "correcting, improving and ascertaining the English language."] This was not the first proposal of the sort. In the January 1774, issue of the *Royal American Magazine*, a writer signing himself An American published a short article suggesting the organization of what he called the Fellows of the American Society of Language. Krapp hazards the opinion that An American was probably Adams, and I am inclined to agree. Most of the text of the letter is given in AL4, p. 8. The rest follows:

---

168, Krapp discusses the change of *e* to *a* in such words as (e)*ternal*, *clerk, Derby* and *sergeant*. Dr. Louise Pound has demonstrated that *tarnal* was probably the mother of *darn*. See Chapter VI, Section 8.

1 A History of Modern Colloquial English, p. 175.

I conceive that such a society might easily be established, and that great advantages would thereby accrue to science, and consequently America would make swifter advances to the summit of learning. It is perhaps impossible for us to form an idea of the perfection, the beauty, the grandeur, and sublimity to which our language may arrive in the progress of time, passing through the improving tongues of our rising posterity, whose aspiring minds, fired by our example and ardor for glory, may far surpass all the sons of science who have shone in past ages, and may light up the world with new ideas bright as the sun.[1]

Adams's letter to the president of Congress, omitting the first paragraph, was as follows:

Most of the nations of Europe have thought it necessary to establish by public authority institutions for fixing and improving their proper languages. I need not mention the academies in France, Spain, and Italy, their learned labors, nor their great success. But it is very remarkable, that although many learned and ingenious men in England have from age to age projected similar institutions for correcting and improving the English tongue, yet the government have never found time to interpose in any manner; so that to this day there is no grammar nor dictionary extant of the English language which has the least public authority; and it is only very lately that a tolerable dictionary has been published, even by a private person, and there is not yet a passable grammar enterprised by any individual.

The honor of forming the first public institution for refining, correcting, improving, and ascertaining [2] the English language, I hope is reserved for congress; they have every motive that can possibly influence a public assembly to undertake it. It will have a happy effect upon the union of the States to have a public standard for all persons in every part of the continent to appeal to, both for the signification and pronunciation of the language. The constitutions of all the States in the Union are so democratical that eloquence will become the instrument for recommending men to their fellow-citizens, and the principal means of advancement through the various ranks and offices of society.

In the last century Latin was the universal language of Europe. Correspondence among the learned, and indeed among merchants and men of business, and the conversation of strangers and travellers, was generally carried on in that dead language. In the present century, Latin has been generally laid aside, and French has been substituted in its place, but has not yet become universally established, and, according to present appearances, it is not probable that it will. English is destined to be in the next and succeeding centuries more generally the language of the world than Latin was in the last or French is in the present age. The reason of this is obvious, because the increasing population in America, and their universal connection and correspondence with all nations will, aided by the influence of England in the world, whether great or small, force their

1 Dr. Arthur M. Schlesinger of Harvard informs me that this letter was also printed in the *New-Hampshire Gazette*, April 22, 1775. It was addressed To the Literati of America.

2 Adams borrowed this phrase from Swift's Proposal for Correcting, Improving and Ascertaining the English Tongue, in a Letter to the Lord High Treasurer of Great Britain, Feb. 22, 1711/12.

language into general use, in spite of all the obstacles that may be thrown in their way, if any such there should be.

It is not necessary to enlarge further, to show the motives which the people of America have to turn their thoughts early to this subject; they will naturally occur to congress in a much greater detail than I have time to hint at. I would therefore submit to the consideration of congress the expediency and policy of erecting by their authority a society under the name of " the American Academy for refining, improving, and ascertaining the English Language." The authority of congress is necessary to give such a society reputation, influence, and authority through all the States and with other nations. The number of members of which it will consist, the manner of appointing those members, whether each State shall have a certain number of members and the power of appointing them, or whether congress shall appoint them, whether after the first appointment the society itself shall fill up vacancies, these and other questions will easily be determined by congress.

It will be necessary that the society should have a library consisting of a complete collection of all writings concerning languages of every sort, ancient and modern. They must have some officers and some other expenses which will make some small funds indispensably necessary. Upon a recommendation from congress, there is no doubt but the legislature of every State in the confederation would readily pass a law making such a society a body politic, enable it to sue and be sued, and to hold an estate, real or personal, of a limited value in that State.[1]

Despite this ardent advocacy of an academy " for refining, improving and ascertaining the English language " in America, Adams does not seem to have joined the Philological Society that was organized in New York in 1788, with substantially the same objects. But Noah Webster, the lexicographer, was a member of it, and indeed the boss of it. It got under way on March 17 and apparently blew up early in 1789, after he had moved to Boston. Its only official acts of any importance, so far as the surviving records show, were to recommend his immortal spelling-book " to the use of schools in the United States, as an accurate, well-digested system of principles and rules," and to take part in a " grand procession " in New York in July, " to celebrate the adoption of the Constitution by ten States." Webster was told off to prepare a record of the society's participation in the latter, and wrote the following:

The Philological Society

The secretary bearing a scroll, containing the principles of a *Federal* language.

[1] I am indebted for both the anonymous article and Adams's signed letter to Mathews, pp. 40–43. The latter is also to be found in The Works of John Adams, edited by Charles Francis Adams; Boston, 1852; Vol. VII, pp. 249 *ff*.

Vice-president and librarian, the latter carrying Mr. Horne Tooke's treatise on language, as a mark of respect for the book which contains a new discovery, and as a mark of respect for the author, whose zeal for the American cause, during the late war, subjected him to a prosecution.[1]

Josiah Ogden Hoffman, Esq., the president of the society,[2] with a sash of blue and white ribbons. The standard-bearer, Mr. William Dunlap,[3] with the arms of the society, *viz.* – argent three tongues, gules, in chief. emblematical of *language*, the improvement of which is the object of the institution. Chevron, or, indicating firmness and support; an *eye*, emblematical of *discernment*, over a pyramid or rude mountain, sculptured with Gothic, Hebrew and Greek letters. The Gothic on the *light* side, indicating the *obvious* origin of the American language from the Gothic. The Hebrew and Greek upon the reverse or *shade* of the monument, expressing the remoteness and *obscurity* of the connection between these languages and the modern. The *crest*, a cluster of cohering magnets, attracted by a key in the center, emblematical of *union* among the society in acquiring *language*, the *key* of knowledge, and clinging to their *native* tongue in preference to a *foreign* one. The *shield*, ornamented with a branch of the oak, from which is used the *gall* used in making ink, and a sprig of *flax*, from which paper is made, supported on the dexter side by Cadmus, in a robe of Tyrian purple, bearing in his right hand leaves of the rush or flag, *papyrus*, marked with Phoenician characters, representing the introduction of letters into Greece and the origin of writing. On the sinister side, by Hermes, or Taaut, the inventor of letters and god of eloquence, grasping his caduceus or wand. Motto – *Concedat laurea linguae*, expressive of the superiority of *civil* over *military* honors. The flag, embellished with the Genius of America, crowned with a wreath of 13 plumes, ten of them starred, representing the ten States which have ratified the

---

1 The book was The Diversions of Purley, published in 1786. It had much influence upon Webster, who greatly admired it. Born in 1736, Horne added the name of Tooke to his patronymic in compliment to William Tooke, of Purley, his frequent benefactor. He got into trouble in 1777 for printing an advertisement soliciting funds for the Americans " murdered by the king's troops at Lexington and Concord." He served a year in the King's Bench prison and had to pay fines and costs amounting to £1,000. He died in 1812.

2 Hoffman (1766–1837) was one of the salient figures in the New York of his day. The descendant of a Baltic German who immigrated in 1657, he was connected with many of the rich families of the town, and was himself a leader in its fashionable society. He was a successful lawyer, and was a member of the State legislature in 1791–95 and again in 1797,

attorney-general of the State in 1798–1801, and recorder of New York City in 1808–15. He was a Loyalist during the Revolution, became a Federalist afterward, and opposed the War of 1812. His daughter Matilda was betrothed to Washington Irving, but died before they could be married. Two of his sons attained prominence – Charles Fenno as a poet and novelist, and Ogden as a lawyer and politician.

3 Dunlap (1766–1839), a native of Perth Amboy, N. J., studied painting under Benjamin West in London, but on his return to the United States devoted himself mainly to the theatre. He wrote plays and managed the Park Theatre in New York. Late in life he returned to painting and became one of the founders of the National Academy of Design. He also did a great deal of writing, and is perhaps best remembered for his History of the American Theatre, 1832.

Constitution. Her right hand pointing to the Philological Society, and in her left a standard with a pedant, inscribed with the word, CONSTITUTION. The members of the society in order, clothed in black.[1]

It is easy here to discern the hand of Webster, who had a deft talent for what is now known as public relations counselling or publicity engineering. The Philological Society was not the first organization of its sort to be projected in America, nor was the " American Academy for refining, improving and ascertaining the English language " suggested by Adams in his letter to the president of Congress in 1780, nor the American Society of Language proposed by An American (as I have noted, probably also Adams) in 1774. So early as 1721 Hugh Jones, professor of mathematics at William and Mary College, had adumbrated something of the sort in " An Accidence to the English Tongue," the first English grammar produced in America.[2] But nothing came of this, and it was not until the end of the century that any active steps were taken toward getting such a project under way.[3] They resulted, in 1806, in the introduction of a bill in Congress incorporating a National Academy or National Institution, one of the purposes of which was to nurse and police the language, but that bill collided with a rising tenderness about States' rights, and soon died in committee, though it was supported by John Adams's son, John Quincy, then a Senator from Massachusetts. The projectors, however, did not despair, and in 1820 they organized an American Academy of Language and Belles Lettres in New York, with John Quincy Adams as president. Its objects were thus set forth in the first article of its constitution:

To collect, interchange and diffuse literary intelligence; to promote the purity and uniformity of the English language; to invite a correspondence with

1 I am indebted for this to The Philological Society of New York, by Allen Walker Read, *American Speech*, April, 1934, pp. 133 and 134. See also his The Constitution of the Philological Society of 1788, *American Speech*, Feb., 1941, pp. 71 and 72.

2 American Projects for an Academy to Regulate Speech, by Allen Walker Read, *Publications of the Modern Language Association*, Dec., 1936, p. 1141.

3 There were, however, several local academies which occasionally showed

some interest in language. One was the American Philosophical Society of Philadelphia, the heir and assign of Franklin's Junto of 1727. Another was the Connecticut Academy of Arts and Sciences of New Haven, of which Webster was a member. He joined it at some time before 1799 and in 1804 made over to it 50 cents for every 1,000 copies of his spelling-book printed in Connecticut. But both organizations were much more interested in the sciences than in letters.

distinguished scholars in other countries speaking this language in common with ourselves; to cultivate throughout our extensive territory a friendly intercourse among those who feel an interest in the progress of American literature, and, as far as may depend on well meant endeavors, to aid the general cause of learning in the United States.[1]

There was but little indication here of a design to set up American standards. As a matter of fact, the academy was quite willing to accept English authority, and when it appointed a committee on Americanisms that committee was instructed " to collect throughout the United States a list of words and phrases, whether acknowledged corruptions or words of doubtful authority, which are charged upon us as bad English, with a view to take the best practical course for promoting the purity and uniformity of our language." Its corresponding secretary and chief propagandist, William S. Cardell,[2] made this plain in a letter to Thomas B. Robertson, Governor of Louisiana, on October 12, 1821:

Without any dogmatical exercise of authority, if such words as *lengthy, to tote* and *to approbate* [3] should be published as doubtful or bad they would generally fall into disuse.

A formidable party of big-wigs supported the academy, including James Madison, former President of the United States; John Marshall, Chief Justice of the Supreme Court (who contributed $100 to its funds); Joseph Story and Brockholst Livingston, Associate Justices; Charles Carroll of Carrollton (who also contributed $100); Dr. John Stearns, founder of the State Medical Society of New York; John Trumbull, the last survivor of the Hartford Wits; John Jay, Chancellor James Kent, Daniel Webster, Henry Clay, William B. Astor, William Wirt, General Winfield Scott and various governors, senators, ambassadors, judges, congressmen and college presidents, but there were also some opponents, and one of them was Webster, though he consented grudgingly to being elected a corresponding

1 Here again I am in debt to Read. The constitution of the academy is reprinted in full in his American Projects for an Academy to Regulate Speech, just cited, pp. 1154-56.

2 Cardell (1780-1828) was a native of Norwich, Conn., and after 1816 devoted himself to teaching English and French. He was the author of a number of books, including Essay on Language; New York, 1825; and Elements of English Grammar; New York, 1826. He also wrote a very successful story for boys, Jack Halyard.

3 All of them denounced by the English critics of the time as Americanisms that were barbaric, immoral and against God.

member.[1] " Such an institution," he wrote to Cardell, apparently in 1820, " would be of little use until the American public should have a dictionary which should be received as a standard work." This standard work, of course, was already in progress in Webster's studio, but it was not to be published until 1828. Before it came out he launched a plan of his own for a sort of joint standing committee of American and English scholars to consider " such points of difference in the practise of the two countries as it is desirable to adjust," but when he appointed Dr. Samuel Lee, professor of Arabic at Cambridge, to take charge of it in England the dons of the two universities refused to have anything to do with it. Others who opposed the American Academy of Language and Belles Lettres were Edward Everett, then editor of the *North American Review*, and Thomas Jefferson. Read suggests that " sectional jealousy, Boston against New York," may have influenced Everett. Jefferson was offered the honorary presidency of the Academy, but refused it. When he was then elected an honorary member he wrote to Cardell from Monticello, January 27, 1821:

There are so many differences between us and England, of soil, climate, culture, productions, laws, religion and government, that we must be left far behind the march of circumstances, were we to hold ourselves rigorously to their standard. If, like the French Academicians, it were proposed to *fix* our language, it would be fortunate that the step were not taken in the days of our Saxon ancestors, whose vocabulary would illy express the science of this day. Judicious neology can alone give strength and copiousness to language, and enable it to be the vehicle of new ideas.

" Clearly," says Read, " Jefferson was not sympathetic to the aims of an academy." But though this one soon petered out, efforts to revive it in one form or another continued for years, and those efforts culminated, in 1884, in the launching of plans for what is now the American Academy of Arts and Letters, with the National Institute of Arts and Letters as its farm or antechamber.[2]

Among the members of the Philological Society of 1788 was Sam-

1 A full list of the first members — honorary, resident and corresponding — is in The Membership of Proposed American Academies, by Allen Walker Read, *American Literature*, May 1935, pp. 145 ff.

2 There is a history of the whole matter in Read's paper, just cited, including some curious details. In another paper, Suggestions for an Academy in England in the Latter Half of the Eighteenth Century, *Modern Philology*, Nov., 1938, pp. 145 ff, he deals with similar schemes in England. His inquiries into the obscure literature of such projects have thrown much light upon the subject.

uel Mitchill, a famous character of the era. This Mitchill, whose name
was erroneously spelled Mitchell in my earlier editions, was a scien-
tifico in general practise, and in his later years was called the Nestor
of American science. Born on Long Island in 1764, he took his degree
in medicine at Edinburgh, and on his return to the United States became professor of chemistry, natural history and philosophy at Columbia. In 1796 he undertook a geological tour of New York State
that got him a lot of notice, and a year later he and two associates
set up the *Medical Repository*, the first American medical journal.
He joined the faculty of the College of Physicians and Surgeons when
it was organized in 1807, and was at different times professor of natural history, of botany and of materia medica. He was an enlightened
physician for his time, but succumbed to some of the crazes that
characterized it. Fielding H. Garrison says,[1] for example, that he was
one of those who, following Lavoisier's discovery of the physiological function of oxygen, " were carried away by their imaginations to
the extent of attributing diseases either to lack or excess of oxygen,
or to some fine-spun modification of this theory." Mitchill's interests
and activities were by no means confined to the physical sciences. He
also took a hand in politics, and after service in the New York Legislature and the national House of Representatives, was elected a
United States Senator in 1804. He was likewise engrossed by language
problems and by pedagogy, and one of his projects was the Americanization of the classical nursery rhymes, which he regarded as too
monarchical in tendency for the children of a free democracy.
Among other changes he advocated the following revision of " Sing
a Song of Sixpence ":

> And when the pie was opened
> The birds they were songless;
> Now, wasn't that a funny dish
> To set before the Congress! [2]

Of all the early American savants to interest themselves in the language of the country the one destined to be the most influential was
Webster. A penetrating and amusing account of him is to be found
in " Noah Webster, Schoolmaster to America," by Harry R. Warfel.[3] There was nothing of the traditional pedagogue about him —

1 An Introduction to the History of
Medicine, fourth ed.; Philadelphia,
1929, p. 330.
2 For this I am indebted to Mr. Henry

Burnell Shafer of Haddon Heights,
N. J.
3 New York, 1936.

no sign of caution, policy, mousiness. He launched his numerous reforms and innovations with great boldness, and defended them in a forthright and often raucous manner. Frequently traveling in the interest of his spelling-book,[1] he got involved in controversies in many places, and was belabored violently by a long line of opponents. Moreover, he took a hand in political, medical, economic and theological as well as philological disputes, and made a convenient target every time bricks were flying. Not many men have ever been more sure of themselves. It was almost impossible for him to imagine himself in error, and most of his disquisitions were far more pontifical than argumentative in tone. He had no respect for dignity or authority, and challenged the highest along with the lowest. Once he even went to the length of upbraiding the sacrosanct Washington — for proposing to send to Scotland for a tutor for the Custis children. When it came to whooping up his spelling-book he was completely shameless, and did not hesitate to demand encomiums from Washington, Jefferson and Franklin. Franklin responded with a somewhat equivocal letter and Washington with a frankly evasive one, but the franker Jefferson, though inclined to support the Websterian reforms, did not like Webster, and not only refused to help him but once denounced him as " a mere pedagogue, of very limited understanding and very strong prejudices and party passion." [2] Jeremy Belknap, founder of the Massachusetts Historical Society,[3] sneered at him as " No-ur Webster eskwier junier, critick and coxcomb general of the United States "; Samuel Campbell, one of his many publishers, called him " a pedantic grammarian, full of vanity and ostentation," and William Cobbett, while in Philadelphia in 1797, publishing *Porcupine's Gazette*, denounced him as a " spiteful viper," a " prostitute wretch," a " demagogue coxcomb," a " toad in the service of sans-culottism," a " great fool and barefaced liar," and a " rancorous villain." [4] Webster responded to these assaults in like terms. " His snarling wit," says Warfel, " lacked the salt of Franklin's good humor

1 It first appeared in 1783, as the first part of his Grammatical Institute of the English Language, published at Hartford. It was the most successful book ever brought out in America, and is still in print. The New International Encyclopedia says that 62,000,000 copies had been sold by 1889.

2 Letter to James Madison, Aug. 12, 1801.

3 Belknap (1744–98) was a New Hampshireman and a Congregational clergyman. He was one of the earliest of American antiquarians.

4 Warfel, p. 234.

and of Francis Hopkinson's rollicking fun. He had taken the nation
for his scholars, and he used old-fashioned browbeating tactics." [1]

But the fact remains that he was often right, and that not a few of
the strange doctrines he preached so violently, at least in the field of
language, gradually won acceptance. He came upon the scene at a
time when there was a rising, if still inarticulate, rebellion against the
effort to police English from above, and he took a leading hand in
shaping and directing it. " The prevailing view of language in the
Eighteenth Century," say Sterling Andrus Leonard in " The Doctrine
of Correctness in English Usage, 1700–1800," [2] " was that English
could and must be subjected to a process of classical regularizing.
Where actual usage was observed and recorded — even when the
theory was promulgated that usage is supreme — this was, in general,
done only to reform and denounce the actual idiom." Webster's natural prejudices, I believe, ran the same way, for he was not only a
pedagogue but also a Calvinist, and not only a Calvinist but also a
foe of democracy.[3] Indeed, all his attacks upon authority were no
more than arguments against the other fellow's and in favor of his
own. But he was far too shrewd to believe, like Johnson and most of
the other English lexicographers and grammarians, that language
could really be brought under the yoke. He had observed in his native
New England that it was a living organism with a way of life of its
own — that its process of evolution was but little determined by
purely rational considerations. Thus, when he came to write his own
books, he knew that the task before him was predominantly one of
reporting rather than of philosophizing, of understanding before ad-
monition. He saw clearly that English was undergoing marked
changes in America, both in vocabulary and in pronunciation, and,
though he might protest now and then, he was in general willing to
accept them. The pronunciations he adopted were those of the educated class in New England, and he offered no resistance to American
neologisms in vocabulary, provided only they were not what his Puritan soul regarded as " low." When, after the publication of his trial-
balloon Dictionary of 1806, he was taken to task for admitting into it
such apparent barbarisms of the New World as *customable* and *dece-*

---

1 p. 189.
2 Madison, Wis., 1929, p. 14. This is a
very valuable book and presents a
great deal of matter not otherwise
accessible.

3 His blistering opinion of democratic
government, set forth in a letter to
the New York *Spectator* for Aug.
1837, is reprinted by Warfel, pp.
425–27.

*dent*,[1] he defended them in a letter to Thomas Dawes, dated New Haven, August 5, 1809. " Such local terms exist," he wrote, " and will exist, in spite of lexicographers or critics. Is this *my* fault? And if local terms exist, why not explain them? Must they be left unexplained because they are local? This very circumstance renders their insertion in a dictionary the more necessary, for, as the faculty of Yale College [2] have said in approbation of this part of my work, how are such words to be understood without the aid of a dictionary? " And as in vocabulary, so in pronunciation. Great Britain, he wrote in the opening essay of his " Dissertations on the English Language," [3] " is at too great a distance to be our model, and to instruct us in the principles of our own tongue. . . . Within a century and a half North America will be peopled with a hundred millions of men, *all speaking the same language.*[4] . . . Compare this prospect, which is not visionary, with the state of the English language in Europe, almost confined to an island and to a few millions of people; then let reason and reputation decide how far America should be dependent on a transatlantic nation for her standard and improvements in language." [5] " The differences in the language of the two countries," he added in 1800,[6] " will continue to multiply, and render it necessary that we should have dictionaries of the American language." His standard of pronunciation, says Warfel,[7] " was ' general custom,' [8] or, to use the more recent phrase, ' standard usage.' In this choice of cur-

---

1 Neither of these was actually an Americanism. The former, according to the NED, has been used in England since 1529 and the latter since 1599. But both had attained to wider acceptance on this side of the ocean.

2 Led by Timothy Dwight.

3 Boston, 1789. The book was dedicated to Benjamin Franklin.

4 This was a good prophecy. The United States, Canada and the British West Indies actually reached 100,000,000 population, taken together, about 1912, which was a century and a third after 1789.

5 pp. 20–22.

6 In an anonymous advance puff of his 1806 dictionary in the New Haven newspapers, June 4, written (like many another such sly boost) by himself.

7 p. 65.

8 His own words in his Dissertations, p. 24, are "the general practise of the nation." On p. 167 he quotes with approval the following from a Dissertation on the Influence of Opinions on Language and of Language on Opinions by the German Hebrew scholar, Johann David Michaelis (1717–91), professor of oriental languages at Göttingen: "Language is a democratical state where all the learning in the world does not warrant a citizen to supersede a received custom till he has convinced the whole nation that this custom was a mistake. Scholars are not so infallible that everything is to be referred to them." Michaelis was one of the first to study the Bible scientifically.

rent speech, rather than the university, dictionary or stage, as his source of correctness, he anticipated by nearly a century and a half the innovations of the National Council of Teachers of English." " Common practise, even among the unlearned," declared Webster in the preface to his " Dissertations," " is generally defensible on the principles of analogy and the structure of the language.[1] . . . The most difficult task now to be performed by the advocates of *pure English* is to restrain the influence of men learned in Greek and Latin but ignorant of their own tongue." [2]

" Dissertations on the English Language " still makes excellent reading, and it is surprising that no literary archeologist has ever reprinted it. The book was begun while Webster was on one of his early tours of the States, trying to induce their legislatures to give him copyright on his " Grammatical Institute of the English Language," which included his spelling-book.[3] He says in his preface:

> While I was waiting for the regular sessions of the legislatures . . . I amused myself in writing remarks on the English language, without knowing to what purpose they would be applied. They were begun in Baltimore in the Summer of 1785; and at the persuasion of a friend, and the consent of the Rev. Dr. Allison, . . . they were read publicly to a small audience in the Presbyterian church. They were afterward read in about twenty of the large towns between Williamsburg in Virginia and Portsmouth in New Hampshire. These public readings were attended with various success; the audiences were generally small, but always respectable; and the readings were probably more useful to myself than to my hearers. I everywhere availed myself of the libraries and conversation of learned men, to correct my ideas and collect new materials.[4]

Webster was convinced that " several circumstances render a future separation of the American tongue from the English necessary and unavoidable," but, rather curiously, he thought that the greater changes would occur in English. Indeed, he believed that " the vicinity of the European nations, with the uninterrupted communication in peace and the changes of dominion in war, are gradually assimilating their respective languages." This was a bad guess, nor has time yet borne out his prediction that English and American would eventually become mutually unintelligible, though he based it upon sound premises:

> Numerous local causes, such as a new country, new associations of people, new combinations of ideas in arts and science, and some intercourse with tribes

1 p. viii.         4 pp. ix and x.
2 p. ix.
3 There was no country-wide copyright until 1790.

wholly unknown to Europe, will introduce new words into the American tongue. These causes will produce, in a course of time, a language in North America as different from the future language of England as the modern Dutch, Danish and Swedish are from the German, or from one another — like remote branches of a tree springing from the same stock, or rays of light shot from the same center and diverging from each other in proportion as their distance from the point of separation.[1]

Webster was no philologian, in the modern sense; indeed, scientific philology was barely getting on its legs in the days of his early activity.[2] It was thus no wonder that he leaned overheavily, in his etymological speculations, upon Holy Writ, and argued gravely that the original language of mankind must have been what he called Chaldee, *i.e.*, what is now known as Biblical Aramaic. But despite this naïveté he was shrewd enough to see the relationship between such apparently disparate languages as Greek, Latin, English, French and Russian before their descent from a common ancestry was generally understood, and in particular he had the acumen to recognize English as a Germanic language, despite its large admixture of Latin and French terms. He hints, in his "Dissertations,"[3] that it was a study of Horne Tooke's "The Diversions of Purley"[4] that convinced him of this last. He was a diligent student of the other English writers on language in his day, and saw that the overwhelming majority of them were quacks.[5] "They seem not to consider," he said, "that grammar is formed on language, and not language on grammar." In his ponderous introduction to his American Dictionary[6] he aired his knowledge of the principal foreign languages, such as it was, at length, and in his preface he described his method of study. "I spent ten years," he said, "in the comparison of radical words, and in forming a synopsis of the principal words in twenty languages, arranged in classes under their primary elements or letters. The result has been to open what are to me new views of language, and to unfold what appear to be the genuine principles on which these languages are constructed." Nor was all this show of learning mere *blague*. "In 1807," says Warfel, "Webster had mastered twelve languages. Steadily, as grammars and dictionaries were made available, he penetrated the secrets of new languages or dialects. By 1813 he had

1 pp. 22 and 23.
2 *Cf.* Warfel, pp. 345 *ff.*
3 p. 38.
4 The first volume was published in 1786.

5 The best account of their speculations is in Leonard, lately cited.
6 New York, 1828. This introduction ran to nearly 70,000 words.

learned twenty: Chaldaic, Syriac, Arabic, Samaritan, Hebrew, Ethiopic, Persian, Irish (Hiberno Celtic), Armoric, Anglo-Saxon, German, Dutch, Swedish, Danish, Greek, Latin, Italian, Spanish, French, Russian, and, of course, English. Later he added Portuguese, Welsh, Gothic and the early dialects of English and German. . . . He was not only America's first eminent lexicographer, but also her first notable comparative philologist." [1]

11. [Webster dedicated his " Dissertations " to Franklin but Franklin delayed acknowledging the dedication until the last days of 1789, and then ventured upon no approbation of Webster's linguistic Declaration of Independence.] According to Warfel, Webster first met Franklin in Philadelphia early in 1786, when he called upon the sage to ask for permission to deliver one of his lectures on language at the University of Pennsylvania, of whose board of trustees Franklin was then president. Franklin seems to have been but little impressed by Webster's plan to set up a purely American standard of speech, but the two found a common ground in the matter of simplified spelling. Eighteen years before, in 1768, Franklin himself had published " A Scheme for a New Alphabet and a Reformed Mode of Spelling," [2] and was still very much interested in the subject. On

1 p. 348. I should add that a high philological authority, Dr. Franklin Edgerton, professor of Sanskrit and comparative philology at Yale, does not agree with this. In his Notes on Early American Work in Linguistics, *Proceedings of the American Philosophical Society*, 1943, p. 26, Edgerton speaks disdainfully of Webster's " Chaldee " etymologies, which were retained in his Dictionary until his death in 1843, and indeed until 1864, when they were finally eliminated " by C. A. F. Mahn, a German scholar who was then put in charge of the etymological department of the work." " Even the relative isolation of American scholarship from Europe," says Edgerton, " hardly excuses such astounding ignorance in Webster, writing forty years after Sir William Jones, twenty after Schlegel, a dozen after Bopp, and half a dozen or more after the first volume of Jacob Grimm." Jones (1746–94) first called

attention to the similarity between the grammatical structures of Sanskrit, Greek and Latin in 1796. Franz Bopp (1791–1867) published Über das Conjugationssystem der Sanskritsprache in Vergleichung mit jenem der griechischen, lateinischen, persischen und germanischen Sprache in 1816, and his Analytical Comparison of the Sanskrit, Greek, Latin and Teutonic Languages (in English) in 1820. Jacob Grimm (1785–1863) published the first part of his Deutsche Grammatik in 1819 and the second in 1822. August Wilhelm von Schlegel (1767–1845) began publishing his *Indische Bibliothek* in 1823. The first really scientific philologian to rise in America was W. D. Whitney (1827–94). He was a child in arms when the first edition of Webster's American Dictionary appeared in 1828.

2 It is reprinted in Franklin's Works, edited by John Bigelow; New York, 1887-8; Vol. IV, pp. 198 *ff*.

May 24, 1786, Webster sent him an outline of a scheme of his own, and Franklin replied: " Our ideas are so nearly similar that I make no doubt of our easily agreeing on the plan." They had frequent palavers on the subject in 1787, but could never come to terms. They remained, however, on a friendly footing, and Franklin's delay in acknowledging the dedication of the " Dissertations " was due only to his last and very painful illness. He wrote on December 26, 1789, and died on April 17, 1790.

Despite his advocacy of a reform in spelling Franklin was by no means in favor of American independence in language; on the contrary, he was something of a purist, and accepted the dicta of the English authorities without cavil. Thus he was very cautious in his letter to Webster, and had praise only for " your zeal for preserving the purity of our language, both in its expressions and pronunciation, and in correcting the popular errors several of our States are continually falling into with respect to both." Franklin then proceeded to list some of those " errors," for example, *to improve* in the sense of to employ, *to notify* (a person), *to advocate*, *opposed to* and *to progress*. Of the first he said:

> When I left New England in the year '23 this word had never been used among us, as far as I know, but in the sense of ameliorated or made better, except once in a very old book of Dr. Mather's, entitled " Remarkable Providences." As that eminent man wrote a very obscure hand I remember that when I read that word in his book, used instead of the word *imployed*, I conjectured that it was an error of the printer, who had mistaken a too short *l* in the writing for an *r*, and a *y* with too short a tail for a *v;* whereby *imployed* was converted into *improved*.[1]
>
> But when I returned to Boston, in 1773, I found this change had obtained favor, and was then become common, for I met with it often in perusing the newspapers, where it frequently made an appearance rather ridiculous. Such, for instance, as the advertisement of a country-house to be sold, which had been many years *improved* as a tavern; [2] and, in the character of a deceased country gentleman, that he had been for more than 30 years *improved* as a justice-of-peace. The use of the word *improved* is peculiar to New England, and not to be met with among any other speakers of English, either on this or the other side of the water.

1 Franklin was probably wrong in this surmise. Increase Mather's Essay for the Recording of Illustrious Providences (the title was commonly reduced to Remarkable Providences) was not published until 1684, and the DAE shows that *to improve* in the sense here dealt with was used in the Connecticut records so early as 1640. The same authority shows that Franklin himself used it in 1789!

2 In this sense of to occupy the DAE traces the verb to the Connecticut records of 1647.

*To improve,* in the sense that Franklin complained of, has now become obsolete, but it continued in respectable usage long enough to be admitted to Webster's American Dictionary in 1828. It still survived, indeed, in the edition of 1852, edited nine years after his death by his son-in-law, Chauncey A. Goodrich. He also gave his imprimatur to *to notify, to advocate, opposed to,* and *to progress,* and all of them are now in perfectly good usage. *To notify* (as in "The police were *notified*") is not actually an Americanism, but it is much oftener encountered in this country than in England, and most Englishmen take it to be native here. The DAE's first example of its use in America is dated 1697. *To advocate* is also English, and was used by Milton, but it dropped out in England in the Eighteenth Century, and in Webster's day it was one of the "Americanisms" chiefly belabored by English purists. *Opposed to* and *to progress* have much the same history. Of the latter the NED says:

Common in England *c.* 1590–1670, usually stressed like the substantive. In 18th c. obs. in England, but app. retained (or formed anew) in America, where it became very common, *c.* 1790, with stress *progréss.* Thence readopted in England after 1800 (Southey 1809); but often characterized as an Americanism, and much more used in America than in Great Britain in sense in which ordinary English usage says *go on, proceed.*

After Franklin's death in 1790 Webster published his letter in the *American Mercury* (New York), and used it as a text for fourteen articles on language.[1] There was little sign in these articles of Franklin's influence; they were radical rather than cautious. In one of them Webster actually argued for the use of *them* in such phrases as *them horses.* Such expressions, he said, "may be censured as vulgar, but I deny that they are ungrammatical." He then went on to deny that they were even vulgar:

As far as records extend we have positive proof that these phrases were originally correct. They are not vulgar corruptions; they are as old as the language we speak, and nine-tenths of the people still use them. In the name of common sense and reason, let me ask, what other warrant can be produced for *any* phrase in *any* language? Rules, as we call them, are all formed on established practise and on nothing else. If writers have not generally admitted these phrases into their works it is because they have embraced a false idea that they

1 The pertinent parts of the letter are reprinted by Mathews. It appears in full in The Writings of Benjamin Franklin, edited by A. H. Smyth; New York, 1905–07; Vol. X, pp. 75 *ff.*

are not English. But many writers *have* admitted them and they are *correct English*.

In his last article, printed August 30, 1790, Webster included the following exposition and defence of his general position:

Much censure has been thrown upon the writer of these remarks by those who do not comprehend his design, for attempting to make innovations in our language. *His vanity prompts him to undertake something new,* is the constant remark of splenetic and ill-natured people. But any person who will read my publications with a tolerable share of candor and attention will be convinced that my principal aim has been to check *innovations,* and bring back the language to its purity and original simplicity. In doing this I am sometimes obliged to call in question authorities which have been received as genuine and the most respectable, and this has exposed me to the charge of *arrogance.* I have, however, the satisfaction to find the ground I have taken is defensible; and that the principles for which I contend, though violently opposed at first, have afterwards been believed and adopted.[1]

At this time, in all probability, Webster was already at work upon his first dictionary, but it did not appear until 1806.[2] The reception it got was certainly not altogether cordial; in fact, there were denunciations of it before it actually came out.[3] Webster, always ready for a row, defended it both before and after publication. On June 4, 1800 he inserted a puff in the New Haven papers describing it as " a small dictionary for schools " and announcing that enlarged revisions, " one for the counting-house " and the other " for men of science," would follow, but it was actually a very comprehensive work for its time and listed 5,000 more words than Johnson's dictionary of 1755. His qualifications for the task of compiling it are thus rehearsed by Warfel:

1. " He had literally taken all knowledge for his province, and he had achieved distinction as a contributor in many departments," *e.g.,* law, medicine, economics and theology.

2. " In every essay he took time to define carefully each important term he used. . . . Fuzzy thinking, arising from fuzzy terminology, had led astray peo-

---

1 I am indebted for these extracts to Warfel, pp. 201 and 202.

2 It issued from Sidney's Press at New Haven on Feb. 11, and made a volume of 408 pages, plus a 21-page preface. The original price was $1.50. The full title was A Compendious Dictionary of the English Language.

3 Some of the most bitter were launched by Joseph Dennie, editor of the *Gazette of the United States* and the *Port Folio* in Philadelphia. This Dennie was a Bostonian, a graduate of Harvard, and a violent Anglomaniac. He studied law but after 1795 devoted himself to journalism. In 1799 he was private secretary to Timothy Pickering, then Secretary of State. He died in 1812. *Cf.* Warfel, pp. 289–323.

ple and legislators alike. From the day he entered the newspaper scribbling contest in 1782 until his death he was writing definitions to help his countrymen think straight."

3. He "delighted in etymological investigations."

4. His "curiosity was fortified by the scholar's greatest asset, patience." [1]

But the best proof of his qualifications lay in the work itself. It was full of the author's crotchets and prejudices, and many of its proposed reforms in spelling were so radical and so grotesque that even their author later abandoned them, but despite all these deficiencies it showed wide learning and hard common sense, and so it opened the way for the large American Dictionary of 1828. In all the years since its first publication there has been no working dictionary of English, of any value whatsoever, that does not show something of its influence. There are plain tracks of it even in the Concise Oxford Dictionary of the brothers Fowler.[2]

11. [In 1801 a savant using the *nom de plume* of Aristarcus delivered an attack on Webster in a series of articles contributed to the *New England Palladium* and reprinted in the *Port Folio* of Philadelphia.] There were three of these articles, and they were admirably summarized by Leon Howard in *American Speech* in 1930.[3] The author, who has never been identified, objected to various real and imaginary Americanisms, among them, *spry, lengthy, illy, sauce* (in the sense of a vegetable), *caucus, to wait on* (in the sense of to wait for), and the use of *grand* and *elegant* as intensives of all work. Howard, in his commentary, shows that some of these were not Americanisms, but had been in use in England for many years. *Spry* is listed by the NED as "current in English dialects, but more familiar as an Americanism"; the DAE, however, does not give it at all. The NED's first example is dated 1746, and is from an English dialect source; the first American example is dated 1789. The NED lists *sauce*, in the sense of a vegetable or salad, as "chiefly U.S.," but its first quotation is from an English book of 1629, and it finds no use of the word in America until 1705. It says, following Bartlett,[4] that *long-sauce* is used (or *was* used) in the United States to designate beets, carrots and parsnips, and *short-sauce* to designate potatoes, turnips, onions,

1 pp. 306–308.

2 Oxford, 1911; revised in 1929 and 1934.

3 Towards a Historical Aspect of American Speech Consciousness, April, pp. 301–05. I am indebted to Howard for much of what follows.

4 A Glossary of Words and Phrases Usually Regarded as Peculiar to the United States; second ed., Boston, 1859, p. 255. Hereafter referred to as Bartlett.

pumpkins, etc. The DAE's first example of *long-sauce* is dated 1809, and its first of *short-sauce* is dated 1815. *Garden-sauce* is traced to 1833. In the sense of stewed or preserved fruit, as in *apple-sauce*, *sauce* is undoubtedly an Americanism: the DAE's first example is dated 1801. The word was then almost universally pronounced *sass*, as it is to this day by rustics. *Cranberry-sauce* is even older, for it is found in John Adams's diary, April 8, 1767. *To wait on* is a hawking term, used of a hawk circling above the head of a falconer, waiting for a bird to be flushed, but it has been used in England in the sense of to wait for since the Seventeenth Century. In that sense it is now reduced to dialectical usage in this country,[1] but in the sense of to court it still enjoys some vogue, especially in the South, and in that sense the DAE calls it an Americanism, tracing it to 1877. *Grand* and *elegant*, as mellifluous intensives, seem to be genuinely American, and many of the English travelers of the early days marked their prevalence. The DAE does not list *grand*, but the NED's first example comes from John Pickering's " Vocabulary or Collection of Words and Phrases Which Have Been Supposed to be Peculiar to the United States," 1816. *Elegant* is traced by the DAE to 1764. The NED, whose first example is from Bartlett's first edition of his Glossary, 1848, hints that it may owe something to the influence of the Irish *iligant*. But this surmise is probably only a hazard inspired by the date of Bartlett's book, which came out before the close of the great Irish immigration to the United States. *Caucus* and *lengthy* are discussed elsewhere.

Howard suggests that the motive behind Aristarcus's onslaught upon Americanisms and upon Webster's effort to set up independent standards of speech in the United States was largely political. " The organ which placed its stamp of approval upon the papers, in reprinting them prominently," he says, " was notoriously Federalistic and pro-British; and although Webster was definitely an opponent of Jefferson democracy and strongly Federalistic in his sympathies, he had attacked Alexander Hamilton during the previous year." Like most of the other Englishmen and Anglomaniacs who wrote against Americanisms in his time, Aristarcus objected to them on the idiotic ground that they were unnecessary. In his first article [2] he stated his case as follows:

1 The DAE reports, on the authority of the *Transactions of the American Philological Association*, 1886, that it was still in use among the Pennsylvania Germans in that year.
2 *Port Folio*, Nov. 21, 1801.

A language, arrived at its zenith, like ours, and copious and expressive in the extreme, requires no introduction of new words. On the contrary, it is incumbent on literary men to guard against impurities, and chastise with critical lash all useless innovations. The decline of taste in a nation always commences when the language of its classical authors is no longer considered as authority. Colloquial barbarisms abound in all countries, but among no civilized peoples **are** they admitted with impunity into books, since the very admission would subject the writer to ridicule in the first instance and to oblivion in the second.

Now, in what can a Columbian dictionary differ from an English one, but in these barbarisms? Who are the Columbian authors who do not write in the English language and spell in the English manner, except Noah Webster, Junior, Esq.? The embryo dictionary then [1] must either be a dictionary of pure English words, and in that case superfluous, as we already possess the admirable lexicon of Johnson, or else must contain vulgar, provincial words, unauthorized by good writers, and in this case must surely be the just object of ridicule and censure. If the Connecticut lexicographer considers the retaining of the English language as a badge of slavery, let him not give us a Babylonish dialect in its stead, but adopt at once the language of the aborigines. . . . If he will persist, in spite of common sense, to furnish us with a dictionary which we do not want, in return for his generosity I will furnish him with a title for it. Let, then, the projected volume of foul and unclean things bear his own Christian name, and be called " Noah's Ark."

The doctrine that the English language was already complete and sufficient and thus needed no enrichment from Yankee sources persisted among Englishmen and Anglomaniacs for a generation after Aristarcus's time. Captain Basil Hall, who ventured into the American wilds in 1827 and 1828 and published an account of his sufferings on his return home,[2] went so far in urging it as to visit Webster in New Haven and tackle him in person.

" But surely," argued Hall, " such innovations are to be deprecated."

" I don't know that," replied old Noah. " If a word becomes universally current in America, where English is spoken, why should it not take its station in the language? "

" Because," replied Hall loftily, " there are words enough already."

## 2. THE ENGLISH ATTACK

13. [There is an amusing compilation of some of the earlier English diatribes against American speechways in William B. Cairns's

1 *i.e.*, Webster's trial-balloon dictionary of 1806, announced some time before this.

2 Travels in North American in the Years 1827–28; 3 vols.; Edinburgh and London, 1829.

" British Criticisms of American Writing, 1783–1815."] [1] More out of the same barrel are in Allen Walker Read's " British Recognition of American Speech in the Eighteenth Century," [2] in the same author's " Amphi-Atlantic English," [3] and in John Pickering's " Vocabulary or Collection of Words and Phrases Which Have Been Supposed to be Peculiar to the United States of America." [4] Pickering, as we shall see in Section 4 of the present chapter, was inclined to acquiesce in the objections raised by British reviewers to the new words and phrases that were crowding into the American language of his time, but he was honest enough to quote those reviewers when they were idiotic as well as when, by his standards, they were more or less plausible, as, for example, when the *Annual Review* denounced the use of *appellate* in *appellate court*,[5] the *British Critic* argued that *have arrived* should always be *are arrived*,[6] the *Eclectic Review* sneered at *avails* in the sense of the proceeds of property sold,[7] and the *Edinburgh* frowned upon *governmental*.[8] Not infrequently Pickering adopted the pawky device of showing that a locution complained of by one review was used by another, as, for example, *derange*, which the *British Critic* disapproved,[9] but the *Edinburgh* employed without apology.[10] This device was especially effective against an American imitator of the English — the intensely Anglomaniacal *Monthly Review* of Boston. When it called *presidential* a " barbarism," Pickering showed that the word had been used by the *Quarterly Review*,[11] which surpassed all others in its animosity to America.

Cairns's valuable monograph is mainly devoted to English criticism of American publications, but Read, in his two papers, also gives

1 Cited in Section 1 of this chapter, p. 4. Cairns (1867–1932) was a scholar who deserves to be remembered. He was educated at the University of Wisconsin, became assistant professor of American literature there in 1901, was made full professor in 1917, and served in that chair until his death. His contributions to the history of American letters were original and valuable.
2 Cited on pp. 1 ff.
3 *English Studies* (Amsterdam, Holland), Oct., 1935, pp. 161–78.
4 Boston, 1816. Hereafter cited as Pickering.

5 1808, p. 241.
6 Vol. VIII, p. 606.
7 The word is perfectly good English, and is traced by the NED to *c.* 1449.
8 Vol. II, p. 184.
9 Vol. V, p. 97.
10 Vol. I, pp. 356 and 376.
11 Jan., 1814, p. 497. The *Quarterly* was then edited by William Gifford, perhaps the most ferocious American-eater that England has ever produced. There is some account of him in AL4, pp. 19 and 79.

some account of the observations on the spoken language made by English travelers. Cairns's conclusion is that the majority of the English and Scotch reviewers " were disposed to be fair, though they were unable to restrain the expression of their own feeling of superiority, and were likely to adopt a paternal, if not patronizing manner. The extremists of both sorts — those whose political conservatism led to bitterness in literary as in other judgments, and those whose liberalism led to absurd praise — were relatively few in number, but they were highly conspicuous; their articles were likely to be longer and to contain more quotable passages than the judicious estimates of the relatively unimportant literary work which America was at this time producing." Most of the more eminent English literati of the post-revolutionary period, observes Cairns, took little interest in that work, and seldom so much as mentioned it. " Gibbon's published letters," he says, " discuss American political affairs, but contain no literary references." Johnson was against everything American, but Boswell was indifferent. So was Crabbe. Cowper was much more interested in the theological uproars which engaged the citizens of the new Republic than in their contributions to beautiful letters. Blake's poem, " America," published in 1793, had a lot to say about soldiers and politicians, but nothing about literati. Coleridge met Washington Allston [1] at Rome in 1806, and the two became friends, but Cairns says that the author of " The Ancient Mariner " " never refers to Allston's poetical works." Wordsworth also knew Allston, but apparently thought of him as a painter only, not as a writer. Scott admired Irving's " Knickerbocker's History of New York " and Freneau's " Eutaw Springs " and had kind words for Charles Brockden Brown, but that is about as far as he went. Byron was delighted to hear that he was read in America, and wrote in his journal that " to be popular in a rising and far country has a kind of posthumous feel," [2] but there is no record that he ever lent (or gave) a hand to an American author or an American book. And so on down to Southey and Landor. Landor admired some of

[1] Allston (1779-1843) was both a writer and a painter. He was a South Carolinian, but grew up in New England. In 1801 he became a pupil at the Royal Academy, London, of which another American, Benjamin West, was then the president. He spent four years in Rome. In 1809 he returned to the United States, and devoted the rest of his life to painting and writing. His poem, The Sylphs of the Seasons, was published in 1813, and his novel, Monaldi, in 1841.

[2] 1815. Quoted by Cairns, p. 14.'

the American politicoes of his time, and proposed to dedicate one of his books to James Madison, but he showed no interest in either American literature or American *Kultur* in general, and when Southey sent him a bitter protest against this dedication,[1] he replied complacently, " I detest the American character as much as you do." Only Shelley seems to have discovered anything of genuine merit in American literature, and his discovery was limited to the novels of the aforesaid Charles Brockden Brown.[2]

Of the English and Scotch reviews of the time, Cairns says that those most constantly anti-American were the *European Magazine and London Review*, the *Anti-Jacobin Review*, the *Edinburgh*, the *Quarterly*, and the *Monthly Mirror*, and that those which showed most friendliness were the *Monthly*, the *Literary Magazine and British Review*, the *Eclectic*, the *Scot's Magazine* and the *Bee* of Edinburgh, the last-named a weekly. The *Anti-Jacobin* and the *Quarterly* were not only hostile, but also scurrilous. Both were edited, at different times, by the William Gifford lately mentioned. The *Anti-Jacobin* specialized in reviling George Washington and the *Quarterly* in spreading scandal about Thomas Jefferson. The former, in 1788, denounced Washington as not only guilty of " the horrid crime of rebellion, which nothing but repentance can efface," but also of the still worse infamy of deism. The latter propagated the fable that Jefferson maintained a harem of Negro mistresses at Monticello, and derived a large revenue from the sale of their (and his) children. In addition it accused Americans in general of a long list of incredible offenses against sound morals, among them, employ-

1 The Americans, wrote Southey in 1812, " have in the course of twenty years acquired a distinct national character for low and lying knavery, and so well do they deserve it that no man ever had any dealings with them without having proofs of its truth." Twenty-eight years later, in his Table-Talk for May 28, 1830, he showed a much more friendly spirit. " I deeply regret," he said, " the anti-American articles of some of the leading reviews. The Americans regard what is said of them in England a thousand times more than they do anything said of them in any other country. The Americans are excessively pleased with any

kind or favourable expressions, and never forgive or forget any slight or abuse. It would be better for them if they were a trifle thicker-skinned."
2 Brown (1771–1810) wrote seven of them, all now forgotten save by literary archeologists. Brought up in Philadelphia under Quaker influences, he succumbed to the English radicals of the time, and was regarded as an advanced thinker. He was the first professional author that America ever produced. For his relations with Shelley see Shelley and the Novels of Brown, by Melvin Solve, in Fred Newton Scott Anniversary Papers; Chicago, 1929, pp. 141–56.

ing naked Negro women to wait upon them at table, and kidnapping Scotsmen, Welshmen and Hollanders and selling them into slavery.[1] On the literary front both reviews were implacably contemptuous of American writing, and to their diatribes they commonly added flings at the whole of American civilization. Thus the *Quarterly* in two reviews [2] quoted by Cairns:

> No work of distinguished merit in any branch has yet been produced among them. . . . The founders of American society brought to the composition of their nation few seeds of good taste, and no rudiments of liberal science.

The English who toured America in the post-revolutionary period were, on the whole, more favorable in their comments, both upon the spoken and written speech of the new Republic and upon its institutions, than the English and Scotch reviewers. Even after the turn of the century they seem to have been generally friendly: it was only in the years following the War of 1812 that they took over the job of denouncing everything American. They noticed, of course, the strange neologisms that had appeared on this side of the water, and sometimes they were shocked by them, but in the main they showed a tolerant spirit, and were pleased to discover that the dialectical differences between the speech of various parts of the country were less marked than those familiar to them in Britain. This fact had been noted, indeed, before the Revolution — for example, by William Eddis, who came to America in 1769 and stayed until 1777. In a letter written on June 8, 1770 he said:

> In England almost every county is distinguished by a peculiar dialect; even different habits and different modes of thinking discriminate inhabitants whose local situation is not far remote. But in Maryland and throughout the adjacent provinces it is worthy of observation that a striking similarity of speech uni-

[1] "We owe to the *Quarterly*," said N. P. Willis in the preface to Pencillings by the Way; London, 1835, "every spark of ill-feeling that has been kept alive between England and America for the last twenty years. The sneers, the opprobrious epithets of this bravo in literature have been received, in a country where the machinery of reviewing was not understood, as the voice of the English people, and an animosity for which there was no other reason has been thus periodically fed and exasperated. I conceive it to be my duty as a literary man — I *know* it is my duty as an American — to lose no opportunity of setting my heel on the head of this reptile of criticism." The *Quarterly* still survives, but is no longer the power that it once was. W. E. Gladstone once described it as "the food which is served up for the intellectual appetites of the highest classes." See *Every Saturday* (Boston), Aug. 4, 1866, p. 128, for an account of its skulduggeries in that era.

[2] Nov., 1809, and Jan., 1814.

versally prevails, and it is strictly true that the pronunciation of the generality of the people has an accuracy and elegance that cannot fail of gratifying the most judicious ear. . . . The language of the immediate descendants of a promiscuous ancestry is perfectly uniform and unadulterated, nor has it borrowed any provincial or national accent from its British or foreign parentage. . . . This uniformity of language prevails not only on the coast, where Europeans form a considerable mass of the people, but likewise in the interior parts, where population has made but slow advances, and where opportunities seldom occur to derive any great advantages from an intercourse with intelligent strangers.[1]

Testimony to the same effect was offered by Nicholas Cresswell, whose journal in America ran from 1774 to 1777. He said:

No county or colonial dialect is to be distinguished here, except it be the New Englanders',[2] who have a sort of whining cadence that I cannot describe.[3]

Nevertheless, the English travelers of the time noted that American speech was not quite identical with any form of English speech —that it made use of many words not heard in England, and was also developing certain peculiarities of pronunciation and intonation. "There are few natives of the United States," wrote the editor of the London edition of David Ramsay's "History of the American Revolution" in 1791, quoting an unnamed "penetrating observer," "who are altogether free from what may be called *Americanisms*,[4] both in their speech and their writing. In the case of words of rarer use they have framed their own models of pronunciation, as having little access to those established among the people from whom they have derived their language." The more naïve travelers were sometimes astonished to discover that familiar objects had acquired new names in America. Thus Richard Parkinson, in "A Tour in America, 1798–1800":[5]

It was natural for me to enquire what they kept their cows and horses on during the Winter. They told me — their horses on *blades* and their cows on *slops*. . . . [*Blades*] turned out to be blades and tops of Indian corn, and the *slops* were the same that are put into the *swill*-tub in England and given to hogs, composed of broth, dish-washings, cabbage-leaves, potato-parings, etc.[6]

1 Letters From America, Historical and Descriptive; London, 1792, pp. 59–61. For this extract I am indebted to Read's British Recognition of American Speech in the Eighteenth Century, before cited.
2 Other reports on the early emergence of the New England twang are in Read, just cited, pp. 325–27.
3 The Journal of Nicholas Cresswell;

New York, 1824, p. 271. Here again I am indebted to Read.
4 Read suggests that the "penetrating observer" was probably John Witherspoon, who invented the term *Americanism* in 1781. See the footnote on p. 5.
5 London, 1805, Vol. I, pp. 39–40.
6 Both words seem to be Americanisms. The DAE's first example of

Read lists some of the other novelties remarked by English travelers — *lengthy* and *to advocate* by Henry Wamsey in 1794; [1] *to loan, to enterprise, portage, immigration* and *boatable* by Thomas Twining in 1796, [2] and *fork* (of a road) by Thomas Anburey shortly before 1789. [3] Most of these terms are discussed in other places. *Boatable,* an obvious coinage to designate streams too shallow to be called *navigable,* is traced by the DAE to 1683, when it was used by William Penn. *To loan,* in the sense of to lend, goes back in England to the Sixteenth Century and probably even beyond, but the NED marks it "now chiefly U.S." The DAE's first American example is dated 1729; it is now in such wide use in the United States that it has appeared in the text of laws, though purists still frown upon it. *To enterprise* seems to have died out. The DAE does not list it, and it is marked "archaic" by the NED, though John Ruskin used it in "Fors Clavigera" so recently as 1871.

13. [The famous sneer of Sydney Smith.] This gibe rankled in American bosoms for many years, and was still often cited, always with indignation, during the 90s of the last century, when I was first becoming aware of literary atrocities. It was printed in the first issue of the *Edinburgh Review* for 1820, as a sort of postscript to a review of Adam Seybert's "Statistical Annals of the United States," [4] and, in accordance with the custom of the magazine, appeared anonymously, but its authorship was generally known and Smith acknowledged it when his reviews were reprinted in his Works in 1839. [5] It is usually quoted only in part, [6] so I here give the whole of it:

The Americans are a brave, industrious and acute people; but they have, hitherto, given no indications of genius, and made no approaches to the heroic, either in their morality or character. They are but a recent offset, indeed, from England; and they should make it their chief boast, for many generations to come, that they are sprung from the same race with Bacon and Shakespeare and Newton. Considering their numbers, indeed, and the favorable circumstances

---

*slops* is from Parkinson, but the NED does not find it in England until 1815. The DAE traces *blades* to 1724.

1 An Excursion to the United States of North America in the Summer of 1794; Salisbury (England), 1796, p. 214.

2 Travels in America One Hundred Years Ago; New York, 1894, p. 167.

3 Travels Through the Interior Parts of America; London, 1789, Vol. II, p. 197.

4 Philadelphia, 1818.

5 In three volumes. They included not only his reviews, but also his Peter Plymley Letters on the subject of Catholic emancipation (1807), and a number of his speeches and sermons. There was an edition in one volume; Philadelphia, 1858.

6 As, for example, in AL4, p. 13, n. 1.

in which they have been placed, they have yet done marvellously little to assert the honor of such a descent, or to show that their English blood has been exalted or refined by their republican training and institutions.

Their Franklins and Washingtons, and all the other sages and heroes of their Revolution, were born and bred subjects of the King of England, — and not among the freest or most valued of his subjects. And since the period of their separation, a far greater proportion of their statesmen and artists and political writers have been foreigners than ever occurred before in the history of any civilized and educated people. During the thirty or forty years of their independence, they have done absolutely nothing for the sciences, for the arts, for literature or even for the statesman-like studies of politics or political economy. Confining ourselves to our own country, and to the period that has elapsed since they had an independent existence, we should ask where are their Foxes, their Burkes, their Sheridans, their Windhams, their Horners, their Wilberforces? — where their Arkwrights, their Watts, their Davys? — their Robertsons, Blairs, Smiths, Stewarts, Paleys, and Malthuses? — their Porsons, Parrs, Burneys, or Bloomfields? — their Scotts, Rogers's, Campbells, Byrons, Moores, or Crabbes? — their Siddons's, Kembles, Keans, or O'Neils? — their Wilkies, Lawrences, Chantrys? — or their parallels to the hundred other names that have spread themselves over the world from our little island in the course of the last thirty years, and blest or delighted mankind by their works, inventions or examples? In so far as we know, there is no such parallel to be produced from the whole annals of this self-adulating race.

In the four quarters of the globe, who reads an American book? or goes to an American play? or looks at an American picture or statue? What does the world yet owe to American physicians or surgeons? What new substances have their chemists discovered? or what old ones have they analyzed? What new constellations have been discovered by the telescopes of Americans? What have they done in the mathematics? Who drinks out of American glasses? or eats from American plates? or wears American coats or gowns? or sleeps in American blankets? Finally, under which of the old tyrannical governments of Europe is every sixth man a slave, whom his fellow-creatures may buy and sell and torture?

When these questions are fairly and favorably answered, their laudatory epithets may be allowed; but till that can be done, we would seriously advise them to keep clear of superlatives.

There was enough truth in this to make it sting, and it kept on stinging long after all truth had vanished from it. It was not Smith's first essay on America, nor his last. He had tackled the subject in 1818, in the form of a review of four books by English travelers, and he was to return to it in 1824. In the former article he said:

Literature the Americans have none — no native literature, we mean. It is all imported. They had a Franklin, indeed; and may afford to live half a century on his fame. There is, or was, a Mr. Dwight, who wrote some poems; and his baptismal name was Timothy.[1] There is also a small account of Virginia by

1 Dwight (1752–1817) was a clergyman and president of Yale from 1795 until his death. His grandson, also Timothy, was president from 1886 to 1899. The elder Dwight, who was the grandson of Jonathan Ed-

Jefferson, and an epic by Joel Barlow;[1] and some pieces of pleasantry by Mr. Irving. But why should the Americans write books when a six weeks' passage brings them, in their own tongue, our sense, science and genius, in bales and hogsheads? Prairies, steamboats, grist-mills, are their natural objects for centuries to come. Then, when they have got to the Pacific Ocean — epic poems, plays, pleasures of memory and all the elegant gratifications of an ancient people who have tamed the wild earth, and set down to amuse themselves. — This is the natural march of human affairs.

In his 1824 *Edinburgh* article Smith referred to the uproar that his sneers of 1820 had kicked up in the United States, but professed to believe (with obvious disingenuousness) that it was his 1818 article that was complained of. Thus:

It is rather surprising that such a people, spreading rapidly over so vast a portion of the earth, and cultivating all the liberal and useful arts so successfully, should be so extremely sensitive and touchy as the Americans are said to be. We really thought at one time they would have fitted out an armament against the *Edinburgh* and *Quarterly Reviews*, and burnt down Mr. Murray's and Mr. Constable's shops, as we did the American Capitol. We, however, remember no other anti-American crime of which we were guilty, than a preference of Shakespeare and Milton over Joel Barlow and Timothy Dwight. That opinion we must still take the liberty of retaining. There is nothing in Dwight comparable to the finest passages of " Paradise Lost," nor is Mr. Barlow ever humorous or pathetic, as the great bard of the English stage is humorous and pathetic. We have always been strenuous advocates for, and admirers of, America — not taking our ideas from the overweening vanity of the weaker part of the Americans themselves, but from what we have observed of their real energy and wisdom.

As a matter of fact, Smith's attitude toward the United States was generally friendly, and in all of his articles he set up contrasts, always favorable to America, between American ways and institutions and

---

wards, was reckoned one of the Hartford Wits, but he was a gloomy fellow and clung resolutely to the Puritanism of his ancestors. His principal poems were The Conquest of Canaan, 1785; Greenfield Hill, 1794; and The Triumph of Infidelity, 1788. They survive today only as literary fossils.

[1] Another of the Hartford Wits. His chief poems were The Vision of Columbus, 1787; Hasty Pudding, 1796; and The Columbiad, 1807. Barlow (1754–1812), finding poetry unremunerative, took to land speculation, and in 1788 went to France as agent of the Scioto Company. He made a fortune there by trading in French securities, but simultaneously became converted to radicalism and was made a French citizen during the French Revolution. On his return to America he moderated his ideas, was appointed consul to Algiers, and later became minister to France. In 1812 he followed Napoleon to Russia to negotiate a trade treaty, was overtaken by the retreat from Moscow, and died in Poland. He was one of the backers of Robert Fulton, the pioneer of the steamboat.

those of England.¹ But after 1840 his friendliness vanished, for by that time he had inherited £50,000 from his brother, an Indian nabob, and had invested a substantial part of it in American State bonds. When the States, following the panic of 1837, began to repudiate those bonds, he yielded himself to moral indignation of a very high voltage, and in 1843 he published a volume called "Letters on American Debts" which was for years a favorite textbook of all the more extreme varieties of English Americophobes. Most of the bonds he held appear to have been issued by Pennsylvania, and it is probable that he really lost only the interest on them, for in the end the principal was repaid. But maybe he also owned a few of Mississippi, Michigan and Florida, which repudiated both principal and interest.

17. [John Pickering said, so late as 1816, that "in this country we can hardly be said to have any authors by profession."] ² He added:

> The works we have produced have, for the most part, been written by men who were obliged to depend upon other employments for their support, and who could devote to literary pursuits those few moments only which their thirst for learning stimulated them to snatch from their daily avocations. Our writings, therefore, though not deficient in ability, yet too frequently want that *finishing*, as artists term it, which is to be acquired only by long practise in writing, as in other arts; and this is a defect which, with scholars accustomed to highly-finished productions, can only be compensated by an extraordinary degree of merit in the *substance* of a work.

This was already something of an exaggeration, for Irving's "Knickerbocker" had been published in 1809, the *North American Review* had been set up in 1815, and the *Federalist*, the writings of Franklin, Jefferson, Paine and Jonathan Edwards and all the novels of Charles Brockden Brown were behind Pickering as he wrote. But the great burgeoning was still ahead. In 1817 came Bryant's "Thanatopsis"; in 1818, the poems of Samuel Woodworth, including "The Old Oaken Bucket"; in 1819, Irving's "Sketch-Book"; in 1820, Cooper's "Precaution"; in 1821, "The Spy"; in 1822, "Bracebridge Hall"; in 1823, three Cooper novels, and in 1824,

---

1 He also protested occasionally againstthe high-handed way in which the British government dealt with the United States. Thus in his 1818 article: "The vice of impertinence has lately crept into our Cabinet, and the Americans have been treated with ridicule and contempt. But they are becoming a little too powerful, we take it, for this cavalier sort of management, and are increasing with a rapidity which is really no matter of jocularity to us, or the other powers of the Old World."

2 On p. v of the preface to his *Vocabulary*.

" Tales of a Traveler " and the début of several lady poets who were destined to enchant not only Americans but also a wide circle in England.[1] By 1828 so much progress had been made that Noah Webster was able to say in the preface to his American Dictionary that one of his aims in preparing it was to call attention to the writings of various American authors. He went on:

> I do not indeed expect to add celebrity to the names of Franklin, Washington, Adams, Jay, Madison, Marshall, Ramsay, Dwight, Smith, Trumbull, Hamilton, Belknap, Ames, Mason, Kent, Hare, Silliman, Cleaveland, Walsh, Irving, and many other Americans distinguished by their writings or by their science; but it is with pride and satisfaction that I can place them, as authorities, on the same page with those of Boyle, Hooker, Milton, Dryden, Addison, Ray, Milner, Cowper, Davy, Thomson and Jameson.

It will be noted that Webster omitted Cooper, who had published seven novels by 1828, and that he also overlooked Jefferson, Paine, Edwards, Paulding, Bryant, Halleck, Schoolcraft, Audubon, Ticknor and Edward Everett, not to mention Poe, whose " Tamerlane and Other Poems " had come out *pianissimo* in 1827. Some of the names he listed so proudly are now forgotten by all save pedagogues, *e.g.*, Ramsay, Belknap, Hare, Cleaveland and Walsh.

23. [After 1824, when the *North American Review* gave warning that if the campaign of abuse went on it would " turn into bitterness the last drops of good-will toward England that exists in the United States," even *Blackwood's* became somewhat conciliatory.] [2] But this letting up did not last. Toward the end of the 30s the English reviews began again to belabor all things American, and especially American books, and during the decade following they had the enthusiastic support of a long line of English travelers, headed by Frances Trollope and Charles Dickens.[3] During the 50s

1 A book that gives all such dates in a clear and convenient way is Chronological Outlines of American Literature, by Selden L. Whitcomb; New York, 1894. In an introduction to this work Brander Matthews says: " It would be possible to maintain the thesis that American literature began in 1809 with the publication of Irving's Knickerbocker's History of New York."

2 *Blackwood's* began as the *Edinburgh Monthly Magazine* in 1817. Its name was changed to the still surviving form with its seventh issue. It appeared too late to be included in Cairns's report on the anti-American diatribes of the British reviews, 1783–1815.

3 An excellent account of the reports of these pilgrims, with copious extracts, is in American Social History as Recorded by British Travelers, by Allan Nevins; New York, 1923. Other useful books on the same theme are As Others See Us, by John Graham Brooks; New York,

*Harper's Magazine* made frequent protests against the unfairness of the current English notices of new American books. In October, 1851, for example, it took the London *Athenaeum* to task for a grossly prejudiced notice of Henry Theodore Tuckerman's " Characteristics of Literature,"[1] and complained that it was " systematically cold to American writers." The month following[2] *Harper's* quoted and denounced a patronizing and idiotic review of Francis Parkman's " History of the Conspiracy of Pontiac."[3] In 1864 Tuckerman struck back in " America and Her Commentators," a well documented and **very** effective counterblast, but now so far forgotten that the Cambridge History of American Literature does not so much as mention it. To this day the English reviewers are generally wary of American books, and seldom greet them with anything properly describable as cordiality. In particular, they are frequently denounced on the ground that the Americanisms which spatter them are violations of the only true enlightenment.[4]

### 3 . AMERICAN " BARBARISMS "

24. [Captain Thomas Hamilton, in his " Men and Manners in America, 1833,[5] reported that even Americans " of the better orders " assumed " unlimited liberty in the use of *expect, reckon, guess* and *calculate* " and perpetrated " other conversational anomalies with remorseless impunity."] Nearly every other English traveler of the first half of the century was likewise upset by the prevalence of the verbs mentioned. For example, John Palmer, who, in his " Journal of Travels in the United States of North America and in Lower Canada "; London, 1819, put his report into the following

---

1908, and The English Traveler in America, 1785–1835, by Jane Louise Mesick; New York, 1922. All three works include bibliographies, and Brooks also lists French and German books.

1 Published in two series; Philadelphia, 1849 and 1851.
2 Literary Notices, p. 857.
3 Two volumes; Boston, 1851.
4 See AL4, pp. 29 and 30.
5 Edinburgh, 2 vols. There was a re-

print in Philadelphia the same year. Hamilton was a younger brother to Sir William Hamilton (1788–1856), the Scottish philosopher, and a son and grandson of distinguished medical men. Born in Edinburgh in 1789, he died in 1842. He is best remembered as the author of Cyril Thornton, a novel, 1827, very popular in its day. His Men and Manners in America was translated into French and twice into German.

imaginary dialogue between himself and " a New England man settled in Kentucky " as an innkeeper: [1]

*On arriving at the tavern door the landlord makes his appearance.*
*Landlord.* Your servant, gentlemen. This is a fine day.
*Answer.* Very fine.
*Landlord.* You've got two *nice creatures;* [2] they are *right elegant* [3] matches.
*Answer.* Yes, we bought them for matches.
*Landlord.* They cost a *heap* [4] of dollars (*a pause and a knowing look*) —
200, I *calculate.*
*Answer.* Yes, they cost a good sum.
*Landlord. Possible!* [5] (*A pause*). Going westward to Ohio, gentlemen?

[1] pp. 129–30. Palmer made his tour with two companions, and on the ship coming from Liverpool to New York they found that William Cobbett, in flight from the English police, was a fellow-passenger. Palmer admitted that his dialogue was " not a literal copy," but added that it embraced " most of the frequent and improper applications of words used in the back country, with a few New England phrases." He offered it as " a specimen of the worst English you can possibly hear in America."

[2] *Creature,* in its English sense, of course, took in horses and cattle, but its special application to them seems to have been an Americanism. It was almost always pronounced *critter.* In the sense of a horse or mule the DAE calls it " chiefly Southern " and traces it to 1782. It was listed as *crittur* in the glossary appended to David Humphreys' *Yankey in England,* 1815. In that printed in the *Virginia Literary Museum and Journal of Belles Lettres, Arts, Science, &c.,* in Dec., 1829, and usually ascribed to Robley Dunglison it was accompanied by the following note: " Much employed in New England for horses, oxen, &c.; this extensive signification is probably obtained from Ireland. In Virginia the word is often restricted to the horse." It does not appear in P. W. Joyce's *English As We Speak It In Ireland;* 2nd ed.; London and Dublin, 1910.

[3] As we have seen, p. 32, the use of

*elegant* as a counter-adjective in the sense of the more recent *swell* was marked by many of the other English travelers of the period. " The epithet is used," reported Morris Birkbeck in Notes of a Journey in America; London, 1818, " on every occasion of commendation but that to which it is appropriate in the English language." Birkbeck said that he had heard *elegant mill, orchard* and *tanyard.* The DAE, which traces the vogue of the word to 1764, adds *elegant fireworks, flannel* and *potatoes,* 1772–1822, and Thornton adds *elegant lighthouse, eightday clock, mare, coffin, schoolhouse, parasol, real estate, lodgings, man, hogs, steamboat, bacon, corn, whiskey,* and *cement,* 1765–1824.

[4] This use of *heap* in the sense of much or many was not actually an Americanism — the NED lists English examples from 1661 to 1884 — but the word was commoner in the United States. In the *Virginia Literary Museum* glossary it is described as Southern and Western. It does not appear in Pickering, but it is listed by Adiel Sherwood in his Gazetteer of the State of Georgia, 1837. *Heap sight* is a true Americanism, but it did not appear until half a century later.

[5] The DAE quotes one Todd as reporting that in 1835 *O my* and *possible* were " universal interjections in America." *Possible* does not appear in Humphreys, 1815; Pickering, 1816, or Dunglison, 1829.

*Answer.* We are going to Philadelphia.

*Landlord.* Philadelphia, ah! That's a *dreadful* [1] large place, three or four times as *big* [2] as Lexington.

*Answer.* Ten times as large.

*Landlord.* It is, by George! what a *mighty heap* of houses. (*A pause*). But I *reckon* [3] you were not *reared* [4] in Philadelphia.

*Answer.* Philadelphia is not our native place.

*Landlord.* Perhaps *away up* [5] in Canada?

*Answer.* No, we are from England.

*Landlord. Is it possible!* Well, I *calculated* you were from abroad. (*Pause*). How long have you been from the *old country?* [6]

*Answer.* We left England last March.

---

1 *Dreadful* as an adverb was certainly no stranger to English, though it may have been more often used in America. Humphreys, 1815, listed it as "used often, as, very, excessively, even as it regards beauty, goodness, etc." Bartlett, in 1848, grouped it with *awful, powerful, monstrous, mighty, almighty* and *all-fired* as in common use in the South and West.

2 *Big* had become the favorite adjective of magnitude in the United States, and at a later date also came to signify fine or excellent.

3 Humphreys, in his glossary, 1815, noted under *calculate* that it was "used frequently in an improper sense, as *reckon, guess.*" *Reckon* occurs in many English dialects and is not unknown in the standard speech. In 1871 Benjamin Jowett put it into the mouth of Socrates in his translation of the Dialogues of Plato. But it was in much wider use in the America of 1800–75 than it has ever been in England, and it is still heard often in the South.

4 Why Palmer should have underscored *reared* I do not know. It is actually much more English than American, and Shakespeare used it in A Midsummer Night's Dream, 1590. The more usual American term is *raised*, which the NED calls "chiefly U.S." *To raise*, at one time, was also used in England, but the DAE says that it "became obsolete in British usage about 1800." It was denounced by the *North American Review* in 1818 as "a provincialism ... not to be found in any correct writer" ... and "confined al-

most exclusively to Virginia, and perhaps some of the neighboring states." It was denounced again by Sherwood, who said primly in his Gazetteer of Georgia, 1837: "We raise horses, cattle and swine, but not human beings." In his American Dictionary of 1828 Noah Webster said of it: "In New England it is never applied to the breeding of the human race, as it is in the Southern States. In the North we say to *raise* wheat and to *raise* horses or cattle, but not to *raise* men, though we may say to *raise* a sickly child." But Dunglison in the *Virginia Literary Museum*, 1829, gave "I was *raised* in Virginia" without comment, and the term is now in general use in the United States. "The writers of grammars and rhetorics," says Mathews, p. 140, "have for over a century voiced their unanimous disapproval of *raise* ... and have commended *rear* for use in connection with 'the breeding of the human race' ... [But] a large number of people have never heard of the distinction ... and have used *raise* with peaceful and pleasurable results in places where, according to the rhetorics, *rear* should have been employed."

5 This is a true Americanism. The DAE, overlooking Palmer, takes its first example from The Letters of Major Jack Downing, 1834.

6 The DAE's first example is dated 1796. At first the term was applied only to England, but after the Civil War it began to be used by immigrants from other countries.

*Landlord.* And in August here you are in *Kentuck.* Well, I should have *guessed* you had been in the state some years; you speak almost as good English as we do.[1]

Hamilton was one of the most amiable of the English travelers of the first half of the century, and described his adventures in the United States, says Nevins, "in a spirit of picturesque enjoyment rather than of censure. . . . Only rarely do we catch a captious accent in his book." But he nevertheless found American English somewhat disconcerting, and in addition to noting the pestiferous prevalence of *to expect, to reckon, to guess* and *to calculate,* recorded the fact that he was vastly puzzled by *hollow-ware, spider* (in the sense of a skillet or frying-pan) and *fire-dog. Hollow-ware* was not actually an Americanism, despite the fact that it appeared strange to him. But *spider,* in the sense noted, seems to have originated in this country, and the DAE's first example is dated 1790. Regarding *fire-dog,* in the sense of andiron, there has been some dispute. The DAE does not call the term an Americanism, but its first example, dated 1792, precedes by three-quarters of a century the first English example so far unearthed. In a catalogue of the exhibits of furniture and objects of arts at the Paris Exhibition of 1867 is the following:

M. Morisot is one of the most eminent of the Paris manufacturers of fenders, if so we are to term those indispensable necessaries that suit only the fireplaces of France and which resembled the ancient *fire-dogs* of England.[2]

*Fender* may be an Americanism, though this is also uncertain. The DAE's first example, dated 1647, antedates the first recorded Eng-

1 Following this dialogue, pp. 130–31, Palmer lists the following "other words and sayings that are peculiar to the United States or differently applied to what they are in England":

*Smart.* Clever, active, industrious.
*Sick.* Unwell; they never use the word *ill.*
*Log.* A trunk of a tree when felled and the branches off.
*Right away.* Straight along.
*Hwich, hwen,* etc. Sometimes used for *which, when,* etc.
*Madam.* The word spoken at full (except in the cities) [*i.e.,* not reduced to *ma'am.*]
*Improved.* Occupied.
*Ingen.* Indian.

*Nigger.* Negro.
*Lengthy.* Long.
*Progressing.* Passing.
*Tote.* Pull.
*Boss.* Master.
*Chunk.* A small horse.
*Tarnation.* Annoying or excessive.
*Awful.* Unpleasant, very.
*Trade.* Barter.

All these words are discussed at other places in the present Supplement. See the List of Words and Phrases.

2 The *Art Journal* Catalogue of the Paris Universal Exhibition, edited by S. C. Hall. F. S. A.; London, 1868, p. 122. For this I am indebted to Mrs. James W. Craig, of Scituate, Mass.

lish example by forty-one years. In the sense of a fire-screen the word is undoubtedly American, and also in the sense of a bumper or cowcatcher. The English usually call an automobile *fender* a *mud-guard* or *wing*.

25. [Captain Frederick Marryat, in " A Diary in America " (1839), observed that " it is remarkable how very debased the language has become in a short period in America," and then proceeded to specifications.] This was the same Captain Marryat who wrote " Mr. Midshipman Easy," " Jacob Faithful," " Peter Simple " and various other nautical tales, and has been declared by at least one critic [1] to have been, " excepting Walter Scott, the only [English] novelist of his period who might lay claim to eminence." He had put in twenty-four years in the English Navy, and had served against the United States in the War of 1812, but the new Republic interested him greatly, and he came out in 1837 to have a look at it. His observations were recorded in two books, both published in the United States.[2] What he had to say about American speechways was in his first book, under the heading of " Remarks, &c. &c. — Language." It is reprinted in full by Mathews, and in part by Nevins, but it is sufficiently interesting to be summarized here, with annotations. Marryat refused to countenance the common boast of the Americans of his time that they spoke better English than the English: their speech, he argued, was actually a gallimaufry of all the dialects of England, and the fact that this heterogenous mixture had been " collected and bound up " in a dictionary by Noah Webster did not suffice to make it, in his judgment, a *Kultursprache*. Every Americanism that he investigated, he said, turned out to be either

---

1 Harold Child, in The Cambridge History of English Literature; New York, 1916, p. 278.
2 A Diary in America, With Remarks on Its Inhabitants; New York, 1839, and Second Series of a Diary in America; Philadelphia, 1840. I am informed by Dr. P. I. Nixon, of San Antonio, Tex., that Marryat is also credited in the Southwest with the authorship of a book called Travels and Adventures of Monsieur Violet in California, Sonora and Western Texas, published in 1849, but there is no record that he was ever in that region and he had died in England

in 1848. Dr. Nixon says (private communication, July 15, 1937): " Raines, in his Bibliography of Texas, dismisses the book with this comment: ' A sensational story, with a strange mixture of truth and falsehood; the truth borrowed from Gregg's Commerce of the Prairies and Kendall's Santa Fé Expedition; the falsehoods being original, perhaps.' " A Narrative of the Texan Santa Fé Expedition, by George W. Kendall (1809–67) was published in 1841, and Commerce of the Prairies, by Josiah Gregg (1806–50) in 1844.

" a provincialism of some English county, or else obsolete English." [1]
" The upper class of the Americans," he went on, " do not speak
or pronounce English according to our standard; they appear to
have no exact rule to guide them, probably from the want of any
intimate knowledge of Greek or Latin. You seldom hear a derivation from the Greek pronounced correctly, the accent being generally laid upon the wrong syllable. In fact, everyone appears to be
independent, and pronounces just as he pleases. But it is not for me to
decide the very momentous question as to which nation speaks the
best English. The Americans generally improve upon the inventions
of others; probably they may have improved upon our language.
. . . Assuming this principle of improvement to be correct, it must
be acknowledged that they have added considerably to our dictionary; but . . . this being a point of too much delicacy for me to decide upon I shall just submit to the reader the occasional variations,
or improvements, as they may be, which met my ears during my
residence in America, as also the idiomatic peculiarities, and having
done so, I must leave him to decide for himself." And then:

I recollect once talking to one of the first men in America, who was nar-
rating to me the advantages which might have accrued to him if he had followed up a certain speculation, when he said, " Sir, if I had done so I should
not only have *doubled* and *trebled*, but I should have *fourbled*, and *fivebled*
my money." [2]

The Americans dwell upon their words when they speak — a custom arising,
I presume, from their cautious, calculating habits; and they have always more or
less of a nasal twang. I once said to a lady: " Why do you drawl out your words
in that way? " " Well," she replied, " I'll drawl all the way from Maine to
Georgia rather than *clip* my words as you English people do."

Many English words are used in a different sense from that which we attach
to them; for instance, a *clever* person in America means an amiable, good-
tempered person, and the Americans make the distinction by saying, " I mean
*English clever*." Our *clever* is represented by the word *smart*.

The verb *to admire* is also used in the East instead of the verb *to like*. " Have
you ever been at Paris? " " No; but I should *admire* to go." [3] . . .

1 His own evidence showed that this
was far from true.
2 Neither the NED nor the DAE records these picturesque verbs, but
Webster's New International, 1934,
lists *fourble* as a noun in the sense
of a stand of oil-well pipe of four
lengths.
3 The DAE's first American example
of *to admire* in this sense is from
one of the letters of Benjamin Franklin, *c.* 1770. The word was first recorded in England in 1645, but soon
afterward was reduced to dialect, as
indeed it has been reduced in the
United States. Pickering defined it
as " to like very much; to be very
fond of " and said of it: " This verb
is much used in New England in expressions like the following: ' I
should *admire* to go to such a place;
I should *admire* to have such a thing,

The word *ugly* is used for cross, ill-tempered. " I did feel so *ugly* when he said that." [1]

*Bad* is used in an odd sense; it is employed for awkward, uncomfortable, sorry:

" I did feel so *bad* when I read that " — awkward.

" I have felt quite *bad* about it ever since " — uncomfortable.

" She was so *bad* I thought she would cry " — sorry.

And as *bad* is tantamount to *not good* I have heard a lady say: " I don't feel *at all good* this morning." [2]

*Mean* is occasionally used for ashamed. " I never felt so *mean* in my life." [3]

The word *handsome* is oddly used. " We reckon this very *handsome* scenery, sir," said an American to me, pointing to the landscape. [4]

" I *consider* him very truthful " is another expression. " He *stimulates* too much." " He dissipates *awfully*." [5]

---

&c.' It is never thus used by the English; and among us it is confined to the language of conversation."

1 The DAE says that *ugly* was used in this sense in England before it has been found in America. It is recorded by Dunglison, who calls it a New Englandism. Pickering does the same, and says that it and the compound *ugly-tempered* " are both heard only among the illiterate." In my youth in Maryland *ugly* was widely used in the sense of ill-tempered, especially as applied to horses.

2 The DAE's first example of the use of *bad* in the sense of sorry is from Marryat's book, and it does not record the other senses at all. Witherspoon, Pickering and Dunglison all overlooked them, as did Humphreys.

3 Witherspoon, Pickering, Humphreys and Dunglison all overlooked *mean*, and the DAE's first example is from Marryat. The DAE defines it, in *to feel mean*, as " to be ashamed, feel guilty; to feel ill or uncomfortable," and marks it an Americanism. It was used in both senses by Mark Twain in Sketches Old and New. Webster's New International calls it " colloq. U.S.," and notes also a slang meaning, as in " He pitches a *mean* curve."

4 The DAE calls *handsome* an Americanism in two senses — " of any aspect of a landscape; satisfying to the eye; of pleasing appearance," and as used in the phrase *to do the handsome thing*. Its first example of the

former is dated 1773, and of the latter 1796. Pickering says of the word in the former sense: " An obliging correspondent observes that [it] ' is here applied to almost everything,' and then adds (though in rather too strong terms) that ' in England it is used only in reference to the human countenance.' " He says that the *Quarterly Review* noted it as an Americanism in a review of the record of the Lewis and Clarke expedition. Dunglison said of it in 1829: " *Handsome* is more extensively used in this country than in England. There they would rarely or never speak of a *handsome* garden, although the term is now more extensively applied there than formerly." Harriet Martineau said in her Society in America; London, 1838, Vol. III, p. 83: " [The Americans] say . . . that Webster made a *handsome* speech in the Senate; that a lady talks *handsomely* (eloquently); that a book sells *handsomely*. A gentleman asked me in the Catskill Mountains whether I thought the sun *handsomer* there than at New York."

5 No other observer of American usage reports *to stimulate* in this sense. Probably Marryat heard it as a nonce-word, or imagined it. Pickering, in 1816, called *awful*, in the sense of disagreeable, ugly, a New Englandism, and noted its use as a general intensive. " In New England," he said, " many people would call a disagreeable medicine

And they are very fond of using the noun as a verb, as — " I *suspicion* that's a fact," " I *opinion* quite the contrary." [1]

The word *considerable* is in considerable demand in the United States. In a work in which the letters of the party had been given to the public as specimens of good style and polite literature, it is used as follows: " My dear sister, I have taken up the pen early this morning, as I intend to write *considerable*." [2]

The word *great* is oddly used for fine, splendid. " She's the *greatest* gal in the whole Union." [3]

But there is one word which we must surrender up to the Americans as their *very own*, as the children say. I will quote a passage from one of their papers: " The editor of the Philadelphia *Gazette* is wrong in calling *absquatiated* a Kentucky phrase. (He may well say phrase instead of word.) It may prevail there, but its origin was in South Carolina, where it was a few years since regularly derived from the Latin, as we can prove from undoubted authority. By the way, there is a little corruption in the word as the *Gazette* uses it: *absquatalized* is the true reading." Certainly a word worth quarreling about! [4]

---

*awful;* an ugly woman, an *awful*-looking woman; a perverse, ill-natured child that disobeys its parents would be said to behave *awfully,* &c. This word, however, is never used except in conversation, and is far from being so common in the seaports now as it was some years ago." He added that John Lambert, in Travels Through Lower Canada and the United States of America; London, 1810, Vol. II, p. 505, reported that to " the country people of Vermont and other New England States . . . everything that creates surprise is *awful:* What an *awful* wind! *awful* hole! *awful* hill! *awful* mouth! *awful* nose! &c." The DAE calls *awful,* in the general sense of very unpleasant or disagreeable, an Americanism and traces it to 1809. In the sense of very great, without any connotation of the unpleasant, it is also an Americanism, but seems to have come in later, for the DAE's first example is dated 1842. Bartlett says that this second sense, in his time, was " peculiar to the West."

1 *To suspicion* still survives in the vulgar speech, but *to opinion* must have been rare, for no other observer records it.

2 In this situation *considerable* is traced by the DAE to 1722 and called an Americanism. Followed by *of* it was also in wide use, and that use was confined to the United States. Witherspoon, 1781, says that

*considerable of* was then peculiar to " the Northern parts." Theodoric Romeyn Beck, in his Notes on Mr. Pickering's Vocabulary, 1829, says that the locution was "formerly used in a similar way in England," and notes that it had appeared in the bitterly anti-American *Quarterly Review* in a review of a book by Southey. Dunglison marks it "New England."

3 The DAE records no use of *great* in this way before Marryat, but lists another and earlier peculiarly American use of *great,* as a noun, in " Sloop sunk at Boston and spoiled a *great* of our English goods," 1724. This use seems to survive in dialect. Sherwood, 1837, said of *great* as an intensive: " This word is used variously — *great* Christian for pious man; *great* horse is applied to a small pony, meaning a horse of good qualities and bottom; *great* plantation, a fertile one." Pickering did not note it. *Gal* is apparently an Americanism. It was listed as an " impropriety " in an American grammar-book published in 1795, but the NED's earliest English example, marked " vulgar or dial.", is dated 1842. It is listed by Humphreys, 1815, and Sherwood, 1837.

4 There were various early forms of the word — *absquatulate, absquatalize, absquatiate, absquattle, absquatelate, absquatilate, absquotulate, absquotilate* — ; of these, *absquatulate*

" Are you cold, miss? " I said to a young lady, who pulled the shawl closer over her shoulders. " *Some*," was the reply.[1]

The English *what?*, implying that you did not hear what was said to you, is changed in America to the word *how?* [2]

Like all the other English travelers of his time Marryat noted the large use of *guess, reckon* and *calculate* in America. " Each term," he said, " is said to be peculiar to different States, but I found them used everywhere, one as often as the other." [3]

He gave a dialogue showing how *to guess* was used, following the lines of that offered by Henry Bradshaw Fearon in 1818. He noted the tendency in America for technical words and phrases to enter into the general speech by metaphor. For example:

In the West, where steam navigation is so abundant, when they ask you to drink they say, " Stranger, will you *take in wood?* " — the vessels taking in wood to keep the steam up, and the person taking in spirits to keep *his* steam up.

finally prevailed. Mathews, in The Beginnings of American English, p. 114, defines it as meaning to go away. It is not listed by the early writers on Americanisms, and seems to have been relatively new at the time Marryat noted it.

1 Pickering says that the free use of *some* in America was borrowed from the Scotch, and quotes the *Monthly Magazine*, May, 1800, in proof. He marks it " New England " and " used chiefly by the illiterate." He gives these specimens: He is *some* better than he was; it rains *some*; it snows *some*. The DAE's first example of its use as an adjective is dated 1845. It survives in full vigor, and has given rise to two very familiar locutions, *going some* and *and then some*.

2 There seems to be an impression that *how* was borrowed from the Indians, but there is no evidence that they ever used it in the sense of *what*. According to John Bradbury, whose Travels in the Interior of America in the Years 1809, 1810 and 1811 was published in 1817, it signified, among them, *come on* or *let us begin*, and according to George Catlin, writing c. 1837, it was " their word for *yes*." The DAE marks it an Americanism in the sense of " an interrogative used in asking for the repetition of something not quite understood," but traces it no further back than Marryat. In the form of a simple greeting, also an Americanism, it is traced to 1817.

3 *To guess*, as we shall see, was not an Americanism, but it survived in America after it had become obsolete in England, and is now listed by the NED as " U.S. colloq." The DAE runs it back to 1805, in American use, in the sense of to suppose, expect, judge, or believe after consideration, and to 1816 in the sense of to purpose, intend or expect. Thornton's examples extend from 1812 to 1869. Pickering quoted an example from John Lambert's Travels Through Lower Canada and the United States; London, 1810. *To reckon*, said Pickering, was " used in some of the Southern States," Dunglison, 1829, ascribed it to Virginia. On Sept. 30, 1844 the following appeared in the *Spirit of the Times* (Philadelphia): " The New Englander *guesses*, the Virginians and Pennsylvanians *think*, the Kentuckian *calculates*, the man from Alabama *reckons*." In American Speech and Foreign Listeners, *American Speech*, Dec., 1940, pp. 448–49, John T. Krumpelmann showed that this was lifted from A Night on the Banks of the Tennessee, *Blackwood's*

The roads in the country being cut through woods, and the stumps of the trees left standing, the carriages are often brought up by them. Hence the expression, " Well, I am *stumped* this time." [1]

I heard a young man, a farmer in Vermont, say, when talking about another having gained the heart of a pretty girl, " Well, how he contrived to *fork* into her young affections [2] I can't tell, but I've a mind to *put my whole team on,* and see if I can't *run him off the road.*"

The old phrase of *straining at a gnat and swallowing a camel* [3] is, in the Eastern States, rendered *straining at a gate and swallowing a saw mill.*

*To strike* means to attack. " The Indians have *struck* on the frontier." " A rattlesnake *struck* at me." [4]

*To make tracks* — to walk away. " Well, now, I shall *make tracks* " — from footprints in the snow.[5]

*Clear out, quit* and *put* — all mean be off. " Captain, now, you *hush* or *put* " — that is, " either hold your tongue or be off." Also " Will you *shut,* mister? ", *i.e.,* will you shut your mouth, *i.e.,* hold your tongue? [6]

*Curl up* — to be angry — from the panther and other animals when angry raising their hair.[7] " Raise my *dander* up," from the human hair, and a nasty idea.[8] *Wrathy* is another common expression.[9] Also, " savage as a meat-ax." [10]

---

*Magazine,* Sept., 1844, pp. 278 *ff,* and that the *Blackwood* paper was a translation of the second chapter of George Howard's Esq. Brautfahrt, by Charles Sealsfield (Karl Postl), published in German at Stuttgart in 1843. Sealsfield (1793–1864) was an Austrian priest who came to the United States in 1822, and wrote several books on his travels.

1 An early, and now obsolete use of *to stump,* in the sense of to challenge, is noted by Humphreys. The DAE traces it to 1766, and calls it an Americanism. In the sense of to confuse or baffle the verb is traced to 1828, and in that of to electioneer to 1838. In both these latter senses it is also an Americanism. So is the noun *stump* in the sense of hustings: the DAE traces it to 1775.

2 *To fork* is not listed by the DAE, but *to fork on,* in the sense of " to appropriate to one's self," is in A Collection of College Words and Phrases, by B. H. Hall; Cambridge, Mass., 1851.

3 Matthew XXIII, 24.

4 In this sense *to strike* is listed by none of the lexicons as an Americanism.

5 The DAE lists this as an Americanism. Its first example is from J. P. Kennedy's Swallow Barn, 1832.

6 *To clear out* is a nautical term. The DAE's first example of its use in a non-nautical sense is dated 1792. In that sense it is an Americanism. The NED lists *to quit,* in the sense of making off, as " dial. and U.S." The DAE's first example of it is dated 1833. The NED lists *to put,* in the same sense, as " obs. exc. U.S. colloq.", but the DAE finds no trace of it before Marryat's example. Save in the phrase *he put off* it is seldom heard today. *To shut,* without *up,* is not listed by any of the authorities. Probably Marryat actually heard *to shut up.*

7 Whether or not this is an Americanism I do not know. No authority so lists it.

8 *Dander* is found in various English dialects. Its origin is uncertain, but it may come from *dandruff.*

9 The DAE calls *wrathy* an Americanism, and traces it to 1828. In Baltimore, in the 80s, it was in common use among boys, but was always pronounced *rossy.*

10 One of the grotesque tropes characteristic of American in the days of the great Western migration. The DAE's first example is from C. A. Davis's Letters of Jack Downing (not to be confused with those of Seba Smith), 1834.

Here are two real American words — *sloping*, for slinking away; *splunging,*
like a porpoise.[1]

In the Western States, where the raccoon is plentiful, they use the abbreviation *coon* when speaking of people. When at New York I went into a hair-
dresser's shop [2] to have my hair cut, there were two young men from the West,
one under the barber's hands, the other standing by him. " I say," said the one
who was having his hair cut, " I hear Captain M—— is in the country." " Yes,"
replied the other, " so they said. I should like to see the *coon*."

" I'm a *gone coon* " implies " I am distressed — or ruined — or lost." [3]

But one of the strangest perversions of the meaning of a word which I ever
heard of is in Kentucky, where sometimes the word *nasty* is used for *nice*. For
instance, of a rustic dance in that State a Kentuckian said to an acquaintance of
mine, in reply to his asking the name of a very fine girl, " That's my sister,
stranger; and I flatter myself that she shows the *nastiest* ankle in all Kentuck."
. . . From the constant rifle practice in that State a good shot or a pretty shot
is termed also a *nasty* shot, because it would make a *nasty* wound: *ergo,* a nice or
pretty ankle becomes a nasty one.[4]

The term for all baggage, especially in the South or West, is *plunder*. This
has been derived from the buccaneers, who for so long a time infested the
bayores,[5] and creeks near the mouth of the Mississippi, and whose luggage was
probably very correctly so designated.[6] . . .

The gamblers on the Mississippi use a very refined phrase for cheating —
*playing the advantages over him*. But, as may be supposed, the principal terms
used are those which are borrowed from trade and commerce. The rest, or
remainder, is usually termed the *balance*. " Put some of those apples into a dish,
and the *balance* into the storeroom."

When a person has made a mistake, or is out in his calculations, they say,
" You *missed a figure* that time." . . .

There is sometimes in American metaphors an energy which is very remarkable. " Well, I reckon that, from the teeth to the toenail, there's not a

1 *To slope*, in this sense, has not been
traced before Marryat, but the
DAE presents later examples. It
does not list *to splunge*, nor does
Pickering.
2 Seldom so called in America after
1800, when the term began to be
supplanted by *barber-shop*. The
usual English form is *barber's-shop*.
3 Marryat then proceeds to tell the
familiar story about the *coon* that,
on being treed by a famous hunter,
cried " Don't shoot! I'll come
down." He makes the hunter Captain Martin Scott, of the United
States Army; usually he is David
Crockett. The abbreviation *coon* for
*raccoon* is traced by the DAE to
1742. Its first example of the application of the term to a human being
is from W. G. Simms's Guy Rivers,
1834. It also appeared in A. B. Long-

street's Georgia Scenes, 1835. Apparently its use to designate a Negro
did not come in until the 80s.
4 Marryat's explanation here is hardly
convincing. *Nasty* is but one of
many derogatory adjectives that
Americans have used, by trope, in
commendatory senses. The DAE
quotes the *Knickerbocker Magazine*, 1834, as explaining that *to sling
a nasty foot* then meant to dance
exceedingly well, and that " she is
a *nasty*-looking girl " meant that she
was " a splendid woman." In later
days *mean* and *wicked* have been
widely used in the same sense.
5 *i.e.*, bayous.
6 Here again Marryat fails as an ety-
mologist. It is more probable that,
in the sense of baggage, the word
was borrowed from the Dutch. The
DAE's first example is dated 1805.

human of a more conquering nature than General Jackson." One *gentleman* said to me, " I wish I had all hell boiled down to a pint, just to pour down your throat." [1]

27. [After 1850 the chief licks at the American dialect were delivered, not by English travelers, most of whom had begun by then to find it more amusing than indecent, but by English pedants who did not stir from their cloisters.] The first traveler to show a genuine liking for all things American seems to have been Lady Emmeline Stuart Wortley, who published " Travels in the United States " in 1851. She met many notables during her stay in 1850, including Agassiz, William H. Prescott the historian, N. P. Willis, and President Zachary Taylor, and gushed over all of them. She was naturally astonished to hear that Prescott, despite " The Conquest of Mexico " and " The Conquest of Peru," had never visited either country, but insisted that he was nevertheless " one of the most agreeable people " she had ever encountered, and " as delightful as his own delightful books." Taylor gave her a cordial reception at the White House, advised her to visit St. Louis, which he described as " altogether perhaps the most interesting town in the United States," and bade her farewell in a manner which she thus recounted:

> The President insisted most courteously on conducting us to our carriage, and bareheaded he handed us in, standing on the steps till we drove off, and cordially reiterating many kind and friendly wishes for our prosperous journey, and health, and safety.

Lady Emmeline not only refrained from denouncing the speech of Americans; she actually praised their habit, then in full tide, of giving grandiloquent sobriquets to their cities. New Bedford, Mass., she reported, was called the *City of Palaces*. She went on:

> Philadelphia is the *City of Brotherly Love,* or the *Iron City.* Buffalo, the *Queen City of the Lakes;* New Haven, the *City of Elms,* &c. I think the American imagination is more florid than ours. I am afraid matter-of-fact John Bull, if he attempted such a fanciful classification, would make sad work of it. Perhaps we should have Birmingham the *City of Buttons* or *Warming-pans;* Nottingham, the *City of Stockings;* Sheffield, the *City of Knives and Forks,* and so forth.[2]

---

1 Marryat was here making contact with tall talk, which was to flourish in the South and West after his visit. There are specimens of it in Richard H. Thornton's American Glossary; Philadelphia, 1912, Vol. II, pp. 969 ff.

2 The DAE traces *City of Brotherly*

*Love* to 1799; it is a translation, of course, of the Greek *Philadelphia. City of Elms* is not traced beyond 1843. Cincinnati began to call itself the *Queen City* in the 1830s; when Buffalo adopted *Queen City of the Lakes* I do not know.

Lady Emmeline's encomiums were so grateful to the fevered national gills that *Harper's Magazine* gave over four pages in its issue for August, 1851, to extracts from her book. But in part, at least, that appreciation may have been inspired by the fact that Harper & Brothers had just brought out an American edition of it.

29. [*Slanguage.*] In AL4, on the strength of a suggestion in *American Speech*,[1] I noted that this term was apparently " invented in 1925 or thereabout." Dr. William R. Williams, of New York, tells me that it is really much older. He says that it occurred in Edward E. Rice's " Evangeline," a great stage success of the 80s. One of the characters in that piece was a young girl who made heavy use of the current slang in saucing her father. He turned to the audience and said sadly, " Such *slanguage* from a daughter! " *Slanguage* is not listed by Partridge, but it is used in England.[2] The related *slangwhanger* and its congeners are Americanisms, traced by the DAE to 1807. *Slangwhanger* is defined as " a low, noisy, ranting talker or writer." In his brief section on " American Dialects " in " The English Language,"[3] William C. Fowler, professor of rhetoric at Amherst, put it among " very low expressions, mostly political."

## 4. THE ENGLISH ATTITUDE TODAY

30. [The English war upon Americanisms is in progress all the time, but it naturally has its pitched battles and its rest-periods between.] The rest-periods, of course, tend to coincide with the times when it is politic, on grounds remote from the philological, to treat the Yankee barbarian with a certain amount of politeness. Such a time, as historians will recall, came in 1917, and lasted until the first mention of the repayment of war debts, when the genial if oafish Uncle Sam was supplanted by the horrendous Uncle Shylock. It came again in 1943, when American troops began pouring into England in large force, and the fear of invasion, so lively during the first years of World War II, was allayed at last. The Ministry of Information and the Board of Education celebrated this happy deliverance by bringing out jointly a pamphlet by Louis MacNeice, entitled " Meet the U. S. Army." This pamphlet was circulated

1 Feb., 1930, p. 250.
2 And also in Ireland. On Oct. 9, 1926 The American *Slanguage* appeared as the heading on a letter in the *Irish Statesman* (Dublin).
3 Revised ed.: New York, 1855, p. 122.

wholesale, not only among the English soldiery but also among school children. Its title showed a graceful concession to an American vulgarism that more than one English pedagogue had reviled in the past, and in the text there were many more. Thus its message in the department of speech, as summarized with approval by the London *Times:*

American speech, coinage, games and food are discussed in turn. If they seem strange to us, our own equivalents will look equally odd to Americans, and for just as good — or sometimes better — reasons. If some people in Britain consider American slang too flamboyant, to the ears of some of our visitors our own may be " flat, hackneyed, monotonous and colorless." [1]

The *Times*, ordinarily, deals with American speechways much less blandly. In normal times, indeed, it seldom mentions them save to sneer at them, and in its *Literary Supplement* it adverts to the unpleasant subject frequently.[2] " The very language of most American writers of imaginative literature," it said on Jan. 3, 1929, " is fast approaching the stage of being only a form of English." But in wartime this forthright attitude is considerably ameliorated, as it is in the other great organs of British opinion. Thus the somewhat malicious Baltimore *Evening Sun* was able to note in 1940 [3] that all these organs, including the *Times*, had grown " a good deal cagier " than usual " about denouncing certain expressions as horrid Americanisms," and that the *Times* itself had lately achieved the extraordinary feat of belaboring *to check up on* without " any mention of America." [4] Yet even in war-time it occasionally blurts out its low opinion

1 Aug. 3, 1943.
2 See AL4, pp. 29 ff.
3 The King's English, editorial page, Feb. 12.
4 The DAE overlooks this verb-phrase, but it is almost surely an Americanism, for the much more comprehensive NED does not list it, and it is not in Partridge. The DAE also omits *to check out*, meaning to leave a hotel, and the nouns, *check-up* and *check-off*, the latter in the sense of the deduction of a worker's union dues from his pay. It traces *to pass in one's checks* to 1869, *to hand* them in to 1870, and *to cash* them in to 1880. Berrey and Van den Bark, in their American Thesaurus of Slang; New York, 1942, define *to check up on* as to in-

vestigate, to examine. They also list *to check out, to check in* and *to check up with*. Partridge lists *to cash, pass* or *hand in one's checks*, calls all three forms Americanisms, and says they began to creep into English *c.* 1875. He adds that during World War I the English soldiers used *to get one's checks* in the sense of to be killed, and also in that of " to receive one's discharge, especially from a medical board." He says that *to take check* was formerly used in England in the sense of to be offended, but indicates that it is now obsolete. So is *to check up* or *to check it up* in the sense of to enter a theatre on some other person's discarded pass-out check. Partridge says that the English busmen have

of the American way of talking and writing, though usually with the addition of a disarming corollary. " To describe the language in which the American language is now written as almost a foreign language," it said on April 5, 1941, " is to make no reference to slang. American slang — that amazing blend of flexibility and sense of absurdity — has always had as many admirers in England as it could desire and more unsuccessful imitation than it deserves." The Edinburgh *Scotsman*, another ardent guardian of English linguistic purity, qualifies and abates its dudgeon, in times of national peril, in much the same way. Thus, when an anonymous reader took space in its columns on Nov. 6, 1941, to denounce *by and large, to contact, to demote* and *O.K.*,[1] it printed an article the same day saying that " it can be argued that these expressions are useful currency; they present definite nuances and inflections and make possible a certain informality of mood or approach which is not otherwise attainable. And they have a certain historical significance and even dignity, in virtue of their association with a restless, changeable and disturbing age." In this article there was no mention of their American origin. The same prudence is visible, when the Hun is at the gate, on lower levels. Thus when Commander Reginald Fletcher, M.P. (now Lord Winster), private secretary to the First Lord of the Admiralty, undertook in 1941 to confute and confuse " the people who say that Germany will be out of oil next week or will crack next month " by hurling at them a derisive " Oh, yeah! ", a columnist in the London *Sunday Mercury* [2] backed into his denunciation of the infamy in the following very graceful manner:

---

been using *checker* in the sense of an inspector since *c.* 1925. It is much older in the United States, though the DAE does not list it. Berrey and Van den Bark show that *checker* is used in the sense of an employer's spy or spotter in many industries. It is also used by deep-sea fishermen to designate a fish-pen on deck, and by gamblers to designate a silver dollar. *Checker-upper* is used in two senses — that of a superintendent and that of a chronic dissenter, or no-man.

1 Of *O.K.* he said: " From the slang of the American bargee it has ad-

vanced to the favor of the diplomatist." There is, of course, no such thing as an American *bargee:* we call him a *bargeman. By and large* is an old nautical phrase which seems to have come into general use in the United States in the pre-Civil War era. *To demote* is traced by the DAE to *c.* 1891 and marked an Americanism. It does not list *to contact*, but there can be little doubt that it originated in the United States.

2 English is Good Enough, Nov. 9, 1941.

I have every respect for most Americans; I think the graphic descriptive vigor of much American prose has an animating effect upon the English language; but the nasal American intonation — and " Oh, yeah! " is a typical example of it — is vile.

The same device was used by a writer signing himself Argus, in the Falkirk *Herald* five months later: [1]

> The writer does not despise the American language (for it cannot be termed the King's English). It has virility and vividness; it is easy to speak. But the writer does lament that there are Britons who taint our language with phraseology which belongs to another, the New World; that our boys no longer say " Stand and deliver! " but " Stick 'em up! "; that *so long* [2] and *O.K.* have replaced the British *cheerio* and *all right*. . . . One charge against Americanism can be brought, maintained, and even proved. . . . The American has the greatest appreciation of the individual who is " different." So they make their language different, distinct from our own by calling a waistcoat a *vest*, a lift an *elevator*, the pavement the *sidewalk*, and so on.

But in times of peace and security the British critics of American speech seldom condescend to pull their punches in this way; on the contrary, they lay about them in a berserk and all-out manner, and commonly couple flings at the American character with their revilings of the American language. " Every few years," says D. W. Brogan,

> someone sounds the clarion and fills the fife, calling us on to man the breaches and repel the assailing hordes of Americanisms that threaten the chastity of the pure well of English undefiled. Sometimes the invaders intend to clip off the strong verbs, sometimes they threaten to enrich our language with new and horrid words. Whatever they do, or threaten to do, it must be resisted.[3]

1 Casual Comments, April 8, 1942. Falkirk is a sizeable town in Scotland, midway between Edinburgh and Glasgow. On July 22, 1298 it was the scene of a battle in which the celebrated William Wallace, leading the Scots, was defeated by an English army under King Edward I. The Scots of today, though no right-thinking Englishman admits that they speak English, are commonly fervent defenders of it against American influence.

2 The DAE hesitates to call *so long* an Americanism, but the first English example is dated 1865, and Walt Whitman was using the phrase in his 1860 edition of Leaves of Grass.

3 The Conquering Tongue, London

*Spectator*, Feb. 5, 1943, reprinted in *Encore*, Sept., 1943, p. 351. Brogan is professor of political science at Cambridge, but his interests are by no means confined to that lugubrious discipline. He spent some time at Harvard and knows the United States well, and a large part of his writing is devoted to explaining Americans to Britons and vice versa. His books include Government of the People: a Study of the American Political System; London, 1933; U.S.A.: An Outline of the Country, Its People and Institutions; London, 1941; The English People: Impressions and Observations; New York, 1943, and The American Character; New York, 1944.

It is a pity that no literary pathologist has ever investigated and reported at length on the ebb and flow of this resistance during the past several generations, as Pickering, Cairns and Read have reported on its manifestations in the era between the Revolution and the Civil War.[1] The material is rich and instructive, and my files bulge with it, but I have space here only for a few specimens. The first real blast of the modern era was probably that delivered by the Very Rev. Henry Alford, D.D., dean of Canterbury, in his " Plea for the Queen's English " in 1863.[2] Alford set the tone of nearly all the objurgations that have followed, for he began by describing American as a debased and barbaric form of English, and then proceeded to a denunciation of the " character and history " of the Republic — " its blunted sense of moral obligation and duty to man; its open disregard of conventional right when aggrandisement is to be obtained; and I may now say, its reckless and fruitless maintenance of the most cruel and unprincipled war in the history of the world." This was before Gettysburg, and most Englishmen of the dean's class were looking forward hopefully to the break-up and ruin of the United States, with certain pleasant benefits to British trade, not to mention what then appeared to be British military and naval security. That hope was soon to perish, and there ensued a period of uneasy politeness, but when the *Alabama* claims began to threaten the British treasury there was a sharp revival of moral indignation, and *Punch* expressed the prevailing English view when it said:

If the pure well of English is to remain undefiled no Yankee should be allowed henceforth to throw mud into it. It is a form of verbal expectoration that is most profane, most detestable.[3]

By 1870 the rage against the loutish and depraved American had gone so far that it was possible for the *Medical Times and Gazette* (London) to allege quite seriously that the medical journals of the United States were written in a slang so outlandish that no decent

1 There is some discussion of the reaction of later British travelers to American speechways in Nevins, but his book is mainly devoted to other matters. There is more in As Others See Us, by John Graham Brooks; New York, 1908. The subject is barely alluded to in The American Impact on Great Britain, 1898–1914, by Richard Heathcote Heindel; Philadelphia, 1940, otherwise a very valuable work.
2 For the history of this book, and of the attempt of an American, G. Washington Moon, to refute it, see AL4, p. 27, n. 2.
3 I borrow this quotation from an article by James Thurber in the *New Yorker*, May 13, 1939, p. 49.

English medical man could be expected to understand it,[1] and in 1871 it seemed quite rational to his English readers when John Ruskin let go with:

> You have felt, doubtless, at least those of you who have been brought up in any habit of reverence, that every time I have used an American expression, or aught like one, there came upon you a sense of sudden wrong — the darting through you of acute cold. I meant you to feel that: for it is the essential function of America to make us feel like that.

Sharp-shooting went on through the 70s and 80s, culminating in a violent attack with all arms after Grover Cleveland's Venezuela message of December 17, 1895, but when the possible effects thereof began to be pondered there appeared a more conciliatory spirit, and during the uneasy years before World War I the Americano began to be cherished as an Anglo-Saxon brother, and not much was heard about the villainousness of either his character or his speech.[2] The war itself brought a return to Bach, and by two routes. First, the American and English troops, coming into contact in France, found that intercommunication was impeded by harsh differences in speech-ways, and, in the manner of simple-minded men at all times and everywhere, laid those differences to moral deficiencies. Second, the American movie, which began to invade England on a large scale at the end of the war, introduced so many Americanisms, especially on the level of slang, that the guardians of the King's English were aroused to protest. But even more influential in reviving the old indignation against everything American was the sinister talk of war debts that began in 1920 and led up to Calvin Coolidge's derisive, " Well, they hired the money, didn't they? " in 1925. It was at this time that Uncle Sam became Uncle Shylock, and every fresh Americanism an insult to the English language. A climax was reached in 1927, when a group of American literati, traveling at the expense of the Commonwealth Fund and Thomas W. Lamont, went to London

1 Jan. 8 and June 4, 1870. I am indebted for this reference, and for the one following, to Dr. Richard H. Heindel.

2 There were, however, stalwarts who kept up the clamour, Kaiser or no Kaiser. Thus, when Percival Pollard published his Their Day in Court, in 1910, a reviewer for the *Academy* (May 28, p. 511), in a generally favorable notice of it, added: " It is unfortunate for Mr. Pollard that he should be an American because, do as he will, he is unable to get rid of the vulgarities which attach to American methods of thinking and American methods of writing." As a matter of fact, Pollard had an English father and a German mother, and was born at Greifswald in Pomerania.

to confer with a similar committee of Britishers upon the present state and future prospects of the common tongue, with special reference to the unhappy differences between English and American usage.[1] The English newspapers reported the deliberations of the conference in some detail, and it brought forth a good deal of editorial comment, some no worse than patronizing but the rest downright vitriolic. In AL4, p. 33, there are some extracts from an article in the *New Statesman*[2] in which Americans were warned in no weasel terms to keep hands off the mother-tongue. "Why," demanded the author, "should we offer to discuss the subject at all with America? . . . From time to time we may adopt this [American] word or that, or sometimes a whole vivid phrase. But for all serious lovers of the English language it is America that is the only dangerous enemy." I add a few more strophes of this diatribe, not given in AL4: [3]

[1] The first proposal that such a conference be held came from the American side in March, 1922. It was signed by Robert Underwood Johnson, representing the American Academy of Arts and Letters, and the following academic dignitaries: John Livingston Lowes, head of the English department at Harvard; Fred Newton Scott, professor of rhetoric at the University of Michigan; James W. Bright, then professor of English literature at the Johns Hopkins; Charles H. Grandgent, professor of Romance languages at Harvard; Charles G. Osgood, chairman of the department of English at Princeton, and John M. Manly, professor of English at Brown. This proposal was addressed to Arthur J. Balfour (then only a knight), Sir Henry Newbolt and Dr. Robert Bridges, the last-named Poet Laureate and founder of the Society for Pure English. After seven months a favorable reply was received, but nothing came of it and the meeting of 1927 was actually arranged by Bridges and Henry S. Canby, the latter then editor of the *Saturday Review of Literature*. The American delegates who made the trip were Canby, Lowes, Johnson, Scott, George Philip Krapp, Louise Pound,

Kemp Malone, Leonard Bacon and William A. Craigie, then in the United States as editor of the Dictionary of American English. Those representing the British Isles were Balfour (by now an earl); Newbolt, president of the Royal Society for Literature; Sir Frederic Kenyon, director of the British Museum; Sir Israel Gollancz, secretary of the British Academy; Sir John Reith, chairman of the British Broadcasting Corporation; Dr. Dover Wilson, of the British Association; John C. Squire, editor of the London *Mercury*; George Bernard Shaw, John Buchan (later Lord Tweedsmuir), Dr. F. S. Boas, and John C. Bailey, editor of the *Literary Supplement* of the London *Times*. See the International Council For Speech, by Kemp Malone, *American Speech*, April, 1928, pp. 261–75. The letters exchanged in 1922 were printed in the *Literary Review* of the New York *Herald Tribune*, Dec. 16, 1922, p. 330.

[2] June 25, 1927.

[3] It was reprinted in full by Dr. Malone in the article just cited, *American Speech*, April, 1928. Parts of it were reprinted in Words Across the Sea, by Doris Fox Benardete, *New Republic*, June 12, 1929, p. 102.

After sitting for two days the conference decided to form an International Council as " an investigating body which will consider facts as to disputed usage and other questions of language in the various English-speaking countries, and give the results of its investigations the widest publicity; in short, will maintain the traditions and foster the development of our common tongue. The Council is to consist of one hundred members — fifty from the United States and fifty from the British Empire. . . . Its proposed composition is palpably absurd. The English language proper belongs to the people who dwell south of Hadrian's Wall, east of the Welsh hills and north of the English Channel. . . . We may do what we please with it, and we cannot submit to any sort of foreign dictation or even influence about it without destroying it. An authoritative Council to decide doubtful questions which must inevitably arise from time to time might be very useful indeed, but such a body ought not to include more than one Scotchman and one Irishman; and it should certainly not include even a single American.

In the course of the somewhat timorous deliberations of the conference Dr. Canby permitted himself the blasphemy of speaking of Anglicisms as well as of Americanisms. This slip was seized upon with ferocity by the *New Statesman* writer, and denounced as follows:

What Dr. Canby meant by it, presumably, was some usage which his own country had not adopted. His point of view, at any rate, was clear enough. He claimed for America a right equal to our own to decide what is English and what is not! That is a claim which we cannot too emphatically repudiate. . . , The English language is our own. . . . We cannot admit that it contains " Anglicisms " — because that admission would imply that it belongs to everybody who uses it — including Negroes and Middle-Westerners and Americanized Poles and Italians. That is the fundamental point. "Anglicisms" are English *tout court*. On the question of what words and idioms are to be used or to be forbidden we cannot afford any kind of compromise or even discussion with the semi-demi-English-speaking populations of overseas. Their choice is to accept our authority or else make their own language.

The other English commentators upon the conference were somewhat less violent than this *New Statesman* brother, but all of them, however polite, were more or less unfriendly, and all of them dealt with the American language as something strange and hostile. " The differences in vocabulary, the meanings attached to words, their spelling, and so on are always very great and are becoming so marked," said a writer in the *Nation and Athenaeum*,[1] " that the result promises or threatens to produce over there a new form of the language." To which the London *Times* added: [2] " Without offense it may be said that no greater assaults are made on the common lan-

1 June 25, 1927.         2 June 20, 1927.

guage than in America. . . . The question is, . . . how far the disruptive process can be stayed." Nor was there any more favorable response to the stated purpose of the conference from colonial newspapers and pedagogues. The Canadian and Australian commentators sneered at it, and the South-Africa-born Professor J. R. R. Tolkien of Oxford wrote in "The Year's Work in English Studies": [1] "Whatever may be the special destiny and peculiar future splendor of the language of the United States, it is still possible to hope that our fate may be kept distinct." Nothing more was ever heard of the proposed General Council on English, with its membership of fifty Britons and fifty Americans. The Commonwealth Fund withdrew its support, Lamont turned to forms of the uplift less loathsome, and the hundred immortals were never actually appointed. [2]

It was during this period that the English antipathy to American translations of foreign books broke forth into one of the fiercest of its recurring outbursts. The *casus belli* was a version of the Italian plays of Luigi Pirandello in two volumes, one being translated by Dr. Arthur Livingston, an American, and the other by Edward Storer, an Englishman. Dr. Livingston, professor of Romance languages at Columbia, was an Italian scholar of the highest eminence, and the qualifications of Mr. Storer were considerably less conspicuous, but the English reviewers, with few exceptions, denounced Livingston in their reviews and at the same time whooped up Storer. Their chief objection to Livingston was that, in cases where English and American usage differed, he preferred the forms and locutions of his own country, and did not try to write like an Englishman. Thus the uproar was summed up by Ernest Boyd, himself a translator of long experience:

In one London weekly a reviewer cites *right away* indignantly, and asks: "Why not *at once?*" The London correspondent of the New York *Bookman* declares that *candies* does not strike an English reader as Italian, but *sweets* does!

1 Vol. VI, 1927.
2 Dr. Malone noted, in the *American Speech* article lately cited, that there was no American response to the English onslaught. It was not, in fact, until two years later that any notice of it was taken in the United States, and that notice then got no further than a brief series of letters in the *New Republic*. On June 26, 1929 George E. G. Catlin contributed one

in which he observes shrewdly that the English objection to American speechways is not always "a genuine philological one, but quite frequently is symbolical" of deeper aversions. "Sometimes," he said, "it is merely an expression of anti-Americanism which, unable to declare itself directly, breaks out like a rash in unexpected places."

Another critic wonders if the expression *a man made over* means anything to an American, doubts it, but concludes triumphantly that it is certainly meaningless to English ears. Nobody condescends to explain how it is closer to the original Italian, French, Polish, Russian, or whatever the text may be, to say: "Come off it, old bean!" rather than "Quit your kiddin', buddy!"; *top hole* instead of *O.K.;* or "I shall let my flat in Gower Street this Autumn," rather than "I shall rent my apartment on 12th Street this Fall." An English locution is *ipso facto* not only more familiar to an English reader, but, it seems, also nearer the text. Yet, the fact actually is that more people from Continental Europe speak American than speak English! [1]

Boyd, in his article, hinted that business rivalry had something to do with the English antipathy to American translations — an ever-recurring *leit motif* in the symphony of moral indignation. He said:

Pirandello is not the only Continental author of importance whose existence in English is due to American enterprise. There are many others: André Gide, Pío Baroja, Pérez de Ayala, Henri Céard, Jacinto Benavente, Ladislas Reymont, Carl Spitteler, Hauptmann, Blasco Ibáñez, Azorín, Eça de Queiroz, Heinrich Mann, Thomas Mann, C. F. Ramuz, Jakob Wassermann. The list might be greatly extended, especially if one adds to it the writers such as Gobineau, Hamsun, Maupassant, Werner von Heidenstam, and Romain Rolland, who would have been abandoned after a volume or two had been tried, but for the support of American publishers and readers.

As the 20s faded there was an abatement of ardor in the English discovery and running down of American barbarisms. The passage of the Cinematograph Films Act in 1927, putting a high duty on American movie films and requiring every British exhibitor to show a certain number of English-made films after September 30, 1928, running up to 20% from 1935 onward, gave a considerable reassurance to the guardians of the national language, and they were unaware as yet that the American talkie would soon overwhelm them. But there was still some lust for battle left in them, and on occasion they performed in the traditionally hearty manner. When, early in 1930, I contributed an article on Americanisms to the London *Daily Express* [2] and ventured in it to hint that the worst had already come, I was belabored right zealously in many newspapers, including the *Express* itself.[3] Its chosen gladiator was James Douglas, then editor

---

1 Translations, *Saturday Review of Literature*, Dec. 26, 1925, p. 442. An interesting comparative study of the English and American translations of Lion Feuchtwanger's Die Geschwister Oppenheim, 1933, is in American and English Translations of The Oppermanns, by Edmund E. Miller, *American Speech*, Oct., 1935, pp. 180–83.

2 What America Is Doing to Your Language, Jan. 15.

3 See AL4, p. 31.

of its Sunday edition and later director of the London *Express* Newspapers, Ltd. He took the strange line of arguing that the talkies were having virtually no effect on English speech. " It is not true to say," he said, " that ' the Englishman is talking and writing more and more American.' American dialects and slang find us curiously un-imitative." [1] But other contributors to the discussion were a good deal less complacent, and one of them said:

> One must admit that we write and speak Americanisms. So long as Yankee-isms came to us insidiously we absorbed them carelessly. They have been a valuable addition to the language — as nimble coppers are a valuable addition to purer currency. But the talkies have presented the American language in one giant meal, and we are revolted.[2]

I was the unwitting cause of another uproar in 1936, when the *Daily Express* reprinted some long extracts from an article that I had written for the *Yale Review*.[3] In that article I argued that the in-creasing adoption of American words and phrases in England was a natural and inevitable process, and that they got in simply because England had " nothing to offer in competition with them — that is, nothing so apt or pungent, nothing so good." There was the usual flood of protests from indignant Englishmen, whereupon the *Express* fanned the flames by printing some more extracts from my article, including the following:

> Confronted by novelty, whether in object or in situation, the Americans always manage to fetch up a name for it that not only describes it but also illuminates it, whereas the English, since the Elizabethan stimulant oozed out of them, have been content merely to catalogue it.[4]

Typical of the protests was a letter signed Hilda Coe,[5] beginning as follows:

> I began to read Mr. Mencken's article in the hope that it would clear away some of my English dislike of Americanisms. But I found instead a school-masterly style, lamentably dull. Mr. Mencken gives the impression that he has

1 You Are Wrong About the Mother Tongue, Jan. 18, 1930. Mr. Douglas was kind enough to grant that my article had been written in very fair English. He found " only one vul-garism " in it, to wit, the phrase *on American motion.* " But that," he said, " is not an Americanism. It is merely bad English." *On* (or at all events, *upon*) *his motion* is actually ancient in English, though the NED marks it " now archaic."

2 Words That We Borrow, by Jame-son Thomas, Jan. 21, 1930.
3 The American Language, Spring, 1936. The *Daily Express* extracts ap-peared on June 5, 1936, and were headed Boloney!
4 This appeared under the heading of More Boloney, June 10, 1936.
5 *Daily Express,* June 6, 1936.

revised his work until he has revised all the life out of it. He is even glad to make use of an old English cliché — *to run the gauntlet*. From him I learn only what I knew before, that we owe to America a few individual words, examples of which are *gee, darn, nerts* and *oh, yeah*. They have less liveliness and vigor than the rude remarks of a small boy, and America — still very young — has the small boy's impudent pride in them.

" Most Americanisms," said another correspondent, " are merely examples of bad grammar, like *going some place else*. Many others are vulgar and lazy misrepresentations of recognized English words." This charge that Americanisms are largely only good old English terms, taken over either without any change at all or with debasements in form or meaning suggested by American uncouthness, is one that appears very often in English discourses on the repellant subject. In 1935, for example, a correspondent signing himself W. G. Bloom informed the London *Daily Telegraph* [1] that " many so-called American colloquialisms " were " only emigrants returning to England." Thus he specified:

> *Too true* is to be found in Shakespeare, and so is *to beat it*. In Cowper *tell the world* appears, and Byron gives us *and all that. Son-of-a-gun*, while savouring of Arizona, is to be found in " The Ingoldsby Legends," and *to bite the dust* is in " The Adventures of Gil Blas."

A year later, when Sir George Philip Langton, a justice of the Probate, Divorce and Admiralty Division of the High Court, rebuked a lawyer for using the American *to bluff* in an argument,[2] one of the

[1] Homing Emigrants, March 11, 1935.

[2] Langton was a bitter critic of Americanisms and would not tolerate them in his court. He was a man of curious misfortunes. Once he sat too late in his chambers and was locked up in the Law Courts, and had to wait while a passing office-boy, hailed from a window, found someone with the keys. " The observant office-boy," said the *Eastern Daily Press* (Norwich), Aug. 14, 1942, " received a judicial 5s " for his pains. In 1942 the learned justice did a vanishing act while on holiday in the West of England, and the police used bloodhounds in an effort to find him. Four days later his body was found in the river Parret. The coroner's jury brought in what the English call an *open verdict* — that is to say, it refused to make an official guess as to how he had come by his death. He was not the only English judge to forbid the use of Americanisms in his presence. Another was Mr. Justice Humphreys, who, when a lawyer read a document saying that an agreement had been *reached*, roared from the bench: " We do not want these horrible things to get into our language! " (London dispatch to the New York *Herald Tribune*, Nov. 3, 1937). In England agreements are *arrived at*, or *concluded*, and decisions are not *reached* but *taken*. I am indebted here to Mr. William S. Pfriender of Glendale, L. I. Less decorous Americanisms are often slapped down by English judges. Even more often they set their catchpolls to guffawing by pretending that they don't know the meaning of such terms. Thus the London *Sunday Express* reported on Feb. 21, 1937 that Mr. Justice Clauson, in the

London newspapers assured its readers that the verb was actually sound and old English, and went on to argue that the game of *poker*, from which it had been borrowed, was English too.[1] Again, a contributor to the London *Morning Post*, in 1936, claimed *bee-line* and *come-uppance* for old England, and even questioned the American origin of *cracker*, in the sense of what the English call (or used to call) a *biscuit*.[2] The recognized authorities, unhappily, do not agree with these patriots. *Too true*, of course, is not an Americanism at all, and neither is *and all that*. It is possible that *to tell the world* may be found in Cowper, but Partridge says that its latter-day vogue originated in the United States, and that it was not until 1930 or 1931 that it was "anglicized as a colloquialism." Partridge says that *to beat it* is also of American origin, and he does not list *to bite the dust* as an English phrase. The NED gives the latter, but its first example is from William Cullen Bryant's translation of the Iliad, 1870. The NED lists two English forerunners, *to bite the sand*, 1718, and *to bite the ground*, 1771, but both are obviously less picturesque than *to bite the dust*, which has about it a strong suggestion of the plainsman, and probably arose during the great movement into the West, though the DAE omits it. The history of *son-of-a-gun*, like that of the allied *son-of-a-bitch*, is obscure, and neither seems to be ancient.[3] They are not listed in Grose, but Partridge says that *son-of-a-bitch* is to be found in "The Triumph of Wit," 1712. Admiral W. H. Smyth, in "The Sailor's Word-Book,"[4] says that *son-of-a-gun* is a nautical term, and that it was "originally applied to boys born afloat, when women were permitted to accompany their husbands to sea" — that is, in the British Navy. "One admiral," he adds, "declared that he literally was thus cradled, under the breast of a gun-carriage." Partridge says that the term dates from the early Eighteenth Century, but gives no reference earlier than 1823, and Farmer and Henley's earliest quotation is dated 1830. *Bee-line* and *come-uppance* seem to be indubitable Americanisms. The first is traced by the DAE to *c.* 1845, and the second to 1859. As for *cracker* in the

---

Chancery Division, had raised a laugh by alleging that he was baffled by *sez you*, used by the poet, Osbert Sitwell, and on Nov. 29, 1938 the London *Telegraph and Post* reported that Mr. Justice Merriman, in the Divorce Division, had got another by saying of *hangover:* "I won't yield to the temptation of asking what it is."

1 The Origin of *Bluff, John o' London's Weekly*, April 4, 1936, p. 33.
2 Americanese, Aug. 27, 1936.
3 See Chapter VI, Section 8.
4 London, 1867.

sense of a small hard biscuit, *e.g.*, a *soda-cracker*, it is traced to 1739 in America, but only to 1810 in England, and the NED marks it "now chiefly in U.S." *Graham-cracker* goes back to the early 80s and *soda-cracker* to 1863, and the DAE marks both Americanisms. It does not list *animal-cracker*, but that is probably one also.

The British discussions of the origin of such terms are seldom profitable, for they are carried on, in the main, by writers who are patriots rather than etymologists, and what they have to say often reduces itself to a feeble and ill-natured complaint against all things American.[1] Those who avoid a show of bogus learning and devote themselves frankly and whole-heartedly to damning the abominable Yankee and his gibberish are much more amusing. They had a field-day in 1935 when the 100% British Cunard White Star Line, in its advertising (in London) of the first sailing of the *Queen Mary*, offered prospective passengers *one-way* and *round-trip* tickets instead of *single* and *return* tickets. The uproar over this ignominious concession to American terminology became so heated that news of it was cabled to the United States.[2] "Is the *Queen Mary*," asked the Manchester *Guardian* gravely, "to be a British or an American vessel?"[3] There was another pother in 1938, when Sydney F. Markham, M.P.,[4] in a speech in the House of Commons, expressed the waggish hope that King George and Queen Mary, then about to embark on their American tour, would not come home speaking American instead of English.[5] The subject was tender at the time,

1 Often they reveal their amateur status by condemning as an Americanism a word or phrase that is actually quite sound English. I take an example from Ireland, the home of bulls, where a Dublin judge in 1935 rebuked a lawyer for using *to kill time*. "This hideous colloquialism," said a reproving writer in the Dublin *Evening Mail* (Jottings by a Man About Town, July 22, 1935), "no doubt originated in Chicago, where gangsters occupy their time by killing it, and one another. The appearance of such expressions in our courts is an alarming reminder that the American language is rapidly shouldering out English and Irish in the Free State." *To kill time* is listed by the NED without any indication that it is not kosher English.

2 English Resent Yankee Lingo in *Queen Mary* Ads, Baltimore *Sun*, Dec. 28, 1935.
3 Dec. 27, 1935.
4 Markham is a member of the Labor party, and the author of a history of Socialism. He was private secretary to the Prime Minister during J. Ramsay Macdonald's term in that office, and was chosen to complete the official life of King Edward VII.
5 Associated Press dispatch from London, Nov. 8, 1938. In the course of the same speech he said: "It may be that the Commissioner of Works will in time label this lobby (pointing to the House's *aye*-lobby) the *sez-you*-lobby, and that lobby (pointing to the *no*-lobby) the *include-me-out*-lobby."

for King Edward VIII, whom George had succeeded only two years before, had been more than once accused of a traitorous and unmanly liking for Americanisms. But the new king and queen somehow escaped contamination, and both still speak English, the latter with a touch of Scots accent. Such doubts and dubieties, before the outbreak of World War II and even down to the fateful event of Pearl Harbor, produced a great deal of indignant writing about the American language. In 1937 there was a heavy outbreak of it,[1] with Cosmo Hamilton denouncing the " slick Americanisms . . . that belong to the worst illiteracy of a foreign tongue "; Lord Plender protesting against the Americanization of English newspaper headlines; [2] William Powell damning " the gibberish of morons " produced by "immigrations of South Europeans, many of whom were backward and illiterate "; [3] and Pamela Frankau taking space in the London *Daily Sketch* [4] to arraign all " victims to the American craze " as enemies of the true, the good and the beautiful. Their enthusiasm for *oke* and *scram*, for " I'll *call you back* " instead of " I'll *ring again*," and for various other such " nonsensical " Americanisms was plain evidence, to her mind, of spiritual collapse and deterioration. She continued:

It goes with the professed admiration of meaningless poetry, incomprehensible pictures, ugly fashions and uncomfortable furniture. It is the refuge of the intellectual coward who trumpets his affection for everything modern in case he be thought old-fashioned. . . . We have a perfectly good language of our own. We owe no syllable of it to America.[5]

1 " The outcry against the pollution of our well of pure English by Americanisms," said a writer in the London *Tatler*, Oct. 6, 1937, " has yet once again become very clamant."

2 In a speech to the boys of King's School, Rochester. The London *Sunday Dispatch*, June 27, 1937, poked fun at his lordship by heading its report of his remarks: Hot For Good Books, He Slams Slouch Scribes.

3 Americanisms, Glasgow *Daily Record and Mail*, June 30, 1937.

4 Snob-stuff From U.S.A., Oct. 25, 1937.

5 Unhappily, La Frankau's indignation led her into the usual forensic excesses. For example, she told of an American who produced a " howl of delight " at a party by demanding of her, " Are you giving me a *ham steer*? " Whether her ears actually heard this as *ham steer* or her delicacy prevented her reporting *bum steer* I do not know. *Bum*, of course, means only the backside in England, and is thus a naughty word. The poor lady also fell into the error of denouncing *serviette* as an Americanism for a table-napkin. The NED shows that it was in common use in Scotland so long ago as the Fifteenth Century. It was introduced into England from France early in the Nineteenth Century, but " has come to be considered vulgar." It is seldom heard in the United States.

At the time this moral rebellion against Americanisms was going on in England there were also repercussions in the colonies and dominions, and especially in Canada. In January, 1937, a learned Englishman by the name of C. Egerton Lowe, described as " of Trinity College, London," turned up in Toronto with a warning that American influence was corrupting the pure English that the Canadians (at all events, in Ontario) formerly spoke. He was denounced with some asperity in the Detroit *Free Press,* just across the border,[1] but he found a certain amount of support among those he was seeking to save, and soon he was joined in his crusade by Mr. Justice A. Rives Hall, of the Canadian Court of Appeal, who was heard from on the subject several times during the months following.[2] The learned judge took the line of denouncing my AL4,[3] and appeared to be convinced that my specimens of the American vulgar speech, presented in Chapter IX thereof, had been offered as examples of tony American usage, and even as goals for all aspiring Americanos to aim at. He said:

> To support his argument Mencken has ransacked the Bowery and the haunts of Chicago gunmen, isolated valleys in the mountains of the South, mining camps and Western saloons, dives on the Mexican border, the training camps of pugilists, and the slums in which are congregated unassimilated foreigners for words and phrases never heard in England and seldom if ever used in polite or educated circles in the United States.

Mr. Justice Hall was still laboring the revolting subject so late as 1939,[4] but whether or not his direful admonitions had any effect I do not know. In the Motherland, by that time, many erstwhile viewers with alarm had retreated into a sort of despair, for the flood of Americanisms pouring in through the talkies and the comic-strips had been reinforced by a fashion, suddenly raging among English columnists, for imitating Walter Winchell, and, among other journalists of low aesthetic visibility, for borrowing the iconoclastic jargons of *Variety* and *Time.* This new menace was attacked by J. B. Firth in the London *Daily Telegraph,* by A. E. Wilson in the London *Star,* by St. John Ervine in the London *Observer,* and by various other orthodox literati, most of them several cuts higher than the lady novelists, old subscribers and other such persons who

1 Good Morning, by Malcolm W. Bingay, Jan. 21, 1937.
2 Montreal *Daily Star,* March 13, 1937; Montreal *Gazette,* May 5.
3 Published in April, 1936.
4 Montreal *Star,* March 15, 1939.

had carried on the holy war of 1937. Thus Ervine described the English imitators of what he called American tabloids:

> Bright young gents who cannot compose a grammatical sentence flourish on these shameless sheets, shameless not only for the way in which they are written, but for what is written in them; and they have the impertinence to claim that the style they inflict on their readers is the style we should all use. . . .
>
> The American tabloid reporter has to communicate with an extraordinary diversity of alien readers, great numbers of whom can scarcely read their native language, and can only spell their way through the easiest English phrases. The paradoxical fact about American journalism of this sort is that in attempting to make their sentences as plain as possible, so that the most elementary alien reader shall understand them, the reporters have produced a hybrid language which is often incomprehensible to many Americans.[1]

But whether comprehensible to Americans or not, it was plainly having a considerable success in England, and many Englishmen, while still disliking it violently, apparently came to the dismayed conclusion that the time was too late for halting it. This defeatist faction, indeed, had been heard from off and on for some years past, and in 1932 Ellis Healey was reporting in the Birmingham *Gazette* [2] that " a definitely American flavor " had already appeared in " the more progressive " English newspapers and even in " the more modern " English magazines; worse, he was playing with the resigned thought that " in about fifty years " England might be only " a moral colony of America." A year or so later Lieut. R. N. Tripp, R.N., joined in the melancholy foreboding. " If the public would just listen, wonderingly, to the American language," he said, " and refrain from speaking it or writing it, all would be well. Unfortunately, they will not." [3] Naturally enough, there was some effort to track down the agent or agencies chiefly responsible, and in 1935 a smart pedagogue, A. Noxon, headmaster of Highfield College, Leigh, found a convenient goat in the British Broadcasting Corporation. " It is high time," he wrote to the Southend *Standard*,[4]

> that protest was made against the increasingly wretched example set by the B.B.C. in broadcasting during the Children's Hour the most horrible American slang for the benefit of children who, naturally imitative, quickly pick up all the atrocities which are broadcast for their benefit(?). Schoolmasters have a difficult enough job already to teach decent English to their pupils. What chance have they when every cinema fills their ears with ungrammatical Americanisms?

1 Debasing Our Speech, London *Observer*, Jan. 30, 1938.
2 The Invasion From U.S.A., April 11.
3 Slushy Talk: the American Invasion, London *Morning Post*, Oct. 26, 1933.
4 Broadcasting and American Slang, Oct. 31, 1935.

Nor was it only school children who picked up these barbaric words and phrases, for in 1936 a writer signing himself Ochiltree was reporting in the Glasgow *Evening Times:*

> Only those people who know the latest American slang are considered to be up-to-date and smart in some circles, just as in others the bright Mayfair wits are thought to be those who strain their brains to find successors to *marvellous, darling, bogus, too utterly utter, shame-making,* and the series of other idiotic words that are ridden to death rapidly.[1]

In 1938 Stephen Williams summed up the situation in the London *Evening Standard.*[2] " I seldom hear English spoken," he said, " in the streets of London. I hear constantly the kind of bastard American culled from the films." To which Cecil G. Calvert, an actor, added a few days later: [3] " What is the use of sending a boy or girl to one of our universities to learn English? When they come to make their way in the world they will find that it is obsolete. Children who are supposed to be taught the English language at our board schools [4] go from them to the cinema, and the horrible distortion of our language that they hear there becomes their everyday speech." A female contributor to the London *Evening News* presently confirmed all this with two anecdotes, as follows:

> An American, coming over to England for the first time, was struck by the fact that English children in the streets of London and elsewhere talked exactly the same as children in the United States. An American impressario came to this country to make films. He was anxious to secure a crowd of English-speaking children, but he utterly failed to find English children who could talk English, and he had to abandon that part of his programme altogether.[5]

The objection here, of course, was primarily to American slang, though not many of the Britons who wrote to the newspapers on the subject differentiated clearly between it and more decorous American speech. Many of them, in fact, denounced *sidewalk, elevator* and *candy-store* quite as vigorously as they denounced *sez you, nert* and *oh, yeah.* The special case of slang will be discussed in Chapter

---

1 Slang and Language, April 13, 1935. *Bogus,* here listed as a Mayfair invention, is actually an Americanism. The DAE calls it " of obscure origin " and traces it to 1839. The NED calls it " a cant word of U.S." *Shame-making* is not listed in any dictionary of English or American slang. It must have had a very short life.

2 Shakespeare as She is Spoke, July 26, 1938.

3 London *Evening Standard,* July 29, 1938.

4 The English equivalent of the American public schools.

5 A Serious Woman's Diary, Dec. 14, 1938.

XI of Volume II: here it is in order to remark that not *all* English-men, even at the height of one of the recurrent alarms, were un-qualifiedly against *all* Americanisms. There were, in fact, not a few who rose to defend them, or, at all events, to explain and condone them, and among those defenders were men and women of authority, *e.g.*, William Archer, Robert Bridges, Richard Aldington, G. K. Chesterton, Virginia Woolf and Sir John Foster Fraser. There is some account in AL4 [1] of the earlier writings in that direction; there have been many reinforcements in later years. " We have to admit," said a staff contributor to the Manchester *Evening News* in 1936,[2] " the intense vitality and colorful expressiveness of the American tongue, no matter what the purists may say. . . . American makes plain English sound a tortuous and poverty-stricken language. It is no idle fancy of the younger generation which seizes on the American idiom to express something which would need a lot more words in English." A few months later Wilfred R. Childe, lecturer in English at Leeds University, said much the same thing in an address to the Annual Army Educational Conference,[3] and presently there was in progress an earnest if somewhat mild defense of certain American-isms under fire from chauvinists. Even the Manchester *Guardian*, ordinarily at least 150% British, took a hand in this counter-attack when Dr. Henry Albert Wilson, Bishop of Chelmsford, denounced *to release* in his diocesan paper. " Why," asked the *Guardian*, " is *released*, in the sense of a film's being freed for general exhibition, ' an abominable Americanism '? It seems to convey a perfectly plain meaning in a perfectly plain way." His Lordship had hinted to his customers that they might be safer post-mortem if they used *pre-pared* instead, but the *Guardian* would have none of it. *Released*, it argued, " does not mean the same thing as *prepared*, for a film might be and sometimes is prepared long before it is released." [4] But this was a debate about a single word, and not altogether significant. The London *Times*, even more truculently British than the *Guard-ian*, went the whole hog (as Abraham Lincoln was fond of saying) in its obituary of John V. A. Weaver, the American poet, in 1938 His books in vulgar American — " In American," " More Ameri-

---

1 Pp. 44–48.
2 To-night, by Tempus, March 24.
3 Americanisms and Slang, *Catholic Herald* (Manchester edition), June 19, 1936.

4 An English Paper Deplores a Bishop for Deploring, Baltimore *Evening Sun* (editorial page), Nov 6, 1936.

can" and so on—offered proof, it allowed, that "the American language is a separate and living tongue, capable of beauty and poetry in itself. These vernacular American poems have something of the same freshness, robustness and beauty of ' The Canterbury Tales.' " [1] A few more specimens of English approval must content us. The first was by a Cambridge double-first [2] in 1938:

> Are there really people who think that English is still the exclusive property of those born (in comfortable circumstances) in these little islands? Surely we ought to regard the American influence of the films as a vitalizing power of enormous benefit to us all as Englishmen. America has given us, admittedly, a good deal of rubbishy slang through the medium of the talkies; but the rubbish perishes very rapidly, whether it be American or English; and the talking film has actually opened up for us an enormous range of neat phrasing, vivid simile and picturesque metaphor which every year tend to enrich our speech rather than impoverish it.[3]

Next came A. Witcomb Jenkins in *Answers:*

> Americanisms are often extremely useful additions to our language. Many of them are clear, vivid, brief and picturesque. There's imagination in them. They hit off a situation with uncanny accuracy. . . . There is no two-word phrase in English for " I *commute*," which in the States means, "I live out of town and come in every day with a season-ticket." And an American doesn't waste his breath saying, "Second turning on the right after you get to the next corner." He says, tersely, "Two blocks on." [4]

Finally the Professor Brogan who was quoted some time back went overboard in the grand manner in 1943:

> There is nothing surprising in the constant reinforcement, or, if you like, corruption of English by American. And there is every reason to believe that it has increased, is increasing and will not be diminished. If American could influence English a century ago, when the predominance of the Mother Country in wealth, population and prestige was secure, and when most educated Americans were reverentially colonial in their attitude to English culture, how can it be prevented from influencing English today, when every change has been a change of weight to the American side? That the balance of linguistic power is upset is hard to doubt. Of the 200,000,000 people speaking English, nearly seven-tenths live in the United States,[5] and another tenth in the British Dominions are

1 June 17, 1938. What the *Times* had to say of Weaver's poems in American at the time of their publication in the early 20s—if, indeed, it said anything at all—I do not know.
2 Defined by the NED as one who takes " a place in the first class in each of two final examinations in different subjects " at an English university.
3 Quoted in English Films and the

U. S. Market, by Campbell Dixon, London *Daily Telegraph*, April 11, 1938.
4 Oh! What Slanguage!, July 23, 1938.
5 When I called attention to the same fact in 1930 (What America is Doing to Your Language, London *Daily Express*, Jan. 15) I was lambasted with great energy. See AL4, pp. 31 and 32.

as much influenced by American as by English English. Nor is this all. As an international language, it is American that the world increasingly learns. . . .

To understand what is happening to the language in whose ownership and control we are now only minority shareholders is an object of curiosity worthy of serious persons. It is also an object worthy of less serious persons, for the study of American is rich in delights and surprises.[1]

Five months later the *Times* called for an armistice in the ancient war. " There is urgent need," it said, " for surmounting what some-one has called the almost insuperable barrier of a common language. It would never do for Great Britain and America to think they understand, yet miss, the point of each other's remarks just now. Both versions of the common language must be correctly understood by both peoples." It then went on to commend a school set up in London to teach Americanisms to British officers and Anglicisms to Americans, and paused to recall, perhaps with a touch of nostalgia, the ill humors of days now (perhaps only transiently) past:

" English as she is spoke " by foreigners has always been a popular touch in comedy. It was an old device when Shakespeare wrote the English of that fine theoretical and practical soldier, the Welsh Fluellen.[2] By the time of the Restoration the Dutch were sharing the honors with the Irish, who lasted until the latter part of the Victorian era, when they yielded first place to the French. Then came the Americans. The Briton who could not raise a laugh by pretending to talk American was either a great fool or a very dull dog.[3]

34. [There has been a steady emission of English-American glossaries since the earliest days. . . . The first seems to have been that of the Rev. Jonathan Boucher, probably drawn up before 1800, but not published until 1832. . . . It was followed by that of David Humphreys, one of the Hartford Wits, printed as an appendix to his play, " The Yankey in England," in 1815.] The Hartford Wits had an enormous reputation in their time, but survive today only as ghosts in treatises on American literature. Humphreys was one of the first of the long line of jobholding literati that was to reach its full effulgence in Henry Van Dyke and Robert Underwood Johnson. He was born at Derby, Conn., on July 10, 1752, and was the son of a clergyman named Daniel Humphrey; he himself added the final *s* to the family name. He was graduated from Yale in 1774, and after teaching school for two years entered the Revolutionary Army. He had a creditable record as a soldier, and in 1780 became military sec-

1 The Conquering Tongue, London        3 Two Peoples and One Tongue,
   *Spectator*, Feb. 5, 1943, pp. 120–21.        June 29, 1943.
2 A character in Henry V.

retary to George Washington, with the rank of major. After the Revolution he went into politics and held various offices at home and abroad, both elective and appointive. When, in 1802, Jefferson retired him at last, he was minister to Spain. In 1797 he married the daughter of an English banker at Lisbon. On his return to private life he went into sheep-raising in Connecticut and set up a woolen mill. He died in 1818.[1]

His play, "The Yankey in England," was one of two that he wrote, the other being "The Widow of Malabar." It was apparently designed for an English audience, but there is no record that it was ever played in London. The glossary was added because Humphreys feared that the talk of Doolittle, the Yankey of his title, might be unintelligible without it.[2] There are very few actual Americanisms in it. Indeed, among its 275 items, I can find but nineteen, to wit, *to boost*, 1815;[3] *breadstuffs*, 1793; *to calculate* (in the sense of to suppose or expect), 1805; *cent*, 1783; *cuss*, 1775; *cussed;*[4] *darned*, 1806;[5] *fortino* or *fortizno* (for aught I know);[6] *forzino* (far as I know), c. 1870;[7] *gal*, 1795; *to guess* (in the sense of to think or suppose), 1732; *gum* (foolish talk, nonsense);[8] *to improve* (to employ), 1640; *lengthy*, 1689; *Sabbaday*, c. 1772; *slim* (sick), 1815;[9] *to spark it* (to engage in what is now called *petting* or *necking*), 1787; *spook*, 1801;

1 An interesting contemporary account of him is in Anecdotes of Colonel Humphreys, *Monthly Magazine and American Review*, June, 1800, pp. 472–75.

2 It is reprinted in full in Mathews, pp. 57–61. He also reprinted it in *Dialect Notes*, Vol. V., Part IX, 1926, pp. 375–82.

3 The dates are those of the earliest examples in the DAE. That of *to boost* is the date of the play's publication. The word was apparently just coming in at the time.

4 Discussed in Chapter VI, Section 8.

5 Humphreys describes *darned* as "old English," but the NED's early examples are all American.

6 I suspect that Humphreys invented this monstrosity. The DAE's first example comes from his glossary, and its second, obviously borrowed therefrom, from Bartlett's, 1848. Bartlett says: "This remarkable specimen of clipping and condensing a phrase approaches the Indian method of forming words. The word is very common through New England, Long Island, and the rest of New York." But he confused it with *forzino*, the next term on the Humphreys list.

7 Or *farzino*. The DAE throws no light on either form, and Thornton, Clapin, Farmer and most of the other American lexicographers ignore them. Schele de Vere describes a third form, *farziner*, as "a violent corruption of *as far as I know* throughout New England, and in parts of New York, but confined to the most ignorant classes and rapidly disappearing." Schele was too optimistic. I have heard *farzino* in Maryland within the last few years.

8 Humphreys so defines the word, but the DAE does not list it.

9 Here again the DAE's first example is from Humphreys himself.

*to stump* (to challenge or dare), 1766. Of these nearly half are now obsolete.

The rest of Humphreys's list is a monument to his faulty observation and lack of common sense, though it seems to have been taken seriously in his day, and Bartlett was relying on it so late as 1848. Scores of the pronunciations he sets down were at least as common in England as in America, for example, *ort* for *ought*, *biled* for *boiled*, *darter* for *daughter*, *hoss* for *horse*, and *kittle* for *kettle*. Not a few were in perfectly good usage in both countries and remain so to this day, for example, *pritty* for *pretty*, *strait* for *straight*, *vittles* for *victuals*, *dubble* for *double*, *blud* for *blood*, *cumfort* for *comfort*, and *fokes* for *folks*. Even *close* for *clothes* was hardly peculiar to America, or to the class represented by Doolittle the Yankey. Finally, Humphreys was apparently unaware, despite his English wife, that such clipped forms as *cute* for *acute* and *potecary* for *apothecary* were common in England, and that *to argufy* for *to argue* was anything but a novelty. Worse, he failed to list certain actual Americanisms that occurred in his play, as Mathews notes, for example, *to pluck up stakes*, 1640 (later, *to pull up stakes*); *as fine as a fiddle*, 1811; and *to rain pitchforks*.[1]

*To guess* was not actually an Americanism, for Shakespeare, Chaucer, Wycliffe and Gower had used it, but it seems to have dropped out of use in England in the Eighteenth Century, and was either preserved or revived in America. Its constant use by Americans in the sense of to believe or suppose was remarked by nearly all the early English travelers. It was, at the start, confined to New England, and in 1815 the *Massachusetts Spy* alleged that a Southerner, though he made free with *reckon* and *calculate*, " would as soon . . . blaspheme as *guess*," but it went along with the pioneers on the great movement into the West, and soon moved into the South. Some of the English travelers illustrated its use with dialogues, for example, Henry Bradshaw Fearon, who offered the following in his " Sketches of America ": [2]

1 The DAE's first example of this is from Humphreys himself. It apparently did not appear in England until the middle of the century.

2 London, 1818. The subtitle is *A Narrative of a Journey of Five Thousand Miles Through the Eastern and Western States*. There was a second edition the same year and a third in 1819. Fearon was sent out in 1817 by 39 English heads of families " to ascertain whether any and what part of the United States would be suitable for their residence." He reached New York Aug. 6, and sailed for home May 10, 1818. The post-Napo-

Q. What is your name?
A. William Henry ——, I *guess*.
Q. Is your wife alive?
A. No, she is dead, I *guess*.
Q. How long have you been married?
A. Thirty years, I *guess*.

Fearon mentioned various other Americanisms in his book. He thought it necessary, for example, to explain that *cracker* was the American name for what the English call a *biscuit*. He also gave some attention to *caucus*, but more to the thing itself than to the word. This, explained Sydney Smith, in reviewing his book for the *Edinburgh,* was

the cant word of the Americans for the committees and party meetings in which the business of the elections is prepared – the influence of which he seems to consider as prejudicial. To us, however, it appears to be nothing more than the natural, fair, and unavoidable influence which talent, popularity and activity always must have upon such occasions. What other influence can the leading characters of the democratic party in Congress possibly possess? Bribery is entirely out of the question – equally so is the influence of family and fortune. What then can they do, with their *caucus* or without it, but recommend? And what charge is it against the American government to say that those members of whom the people have the highest opinion meet together to consult whom they shall recommend for President, and that their recommendation is successful in their different States? Could any friend to good order wish other means to be employed, or other results to follow?

Humphreys' glossary was followed in 1816 by John Pickering's "Vocabulary or Collection of Words and Phrases Which Have Been Supposed to be Peculiar to the United States of America, to Which is Prefixed an Essay on the Present State of the English Language in the United States," the first really competent treatise on the subject.[1] Pickering, who was the son of Timothy Pickering, Postmaster-General, Secretary of War and Secretary of State under Washington, was himself apparently trained for a political career, but he preferred scholarship. Dr. Franklin Edgerton, professor of Sanskrit and comparative philology at Yale, says that he was "one

leonic depression was on in England at the time, and he says in his preface that emigration had "assumed a totally new character; it was no longer merely the poor, the idle, the profligate, or the wholly speculative who were proposing to quit their native country, but men also of capital, of industry, of sober habits and regular pursuits." Despite the recentness of the War of 1812 he was politely received.

[1] It was published in Boston and makes a volume of 207 pp. It has never been reprinted, but copies are still occasionally encountered in the second-hand book-stores.

of the two greatest general linguists of the first half of the Nineteenth Century in America," [1] the other being Peter Stephen Du
Ponceau (1760–1844). Born at Salem, Mass., in 1777, he survived
until 1846. Says Edgerton:

> He was an excellent classical scholar, and prepared what has been called
> " the best Greek-English dictionary before Liddell and Scott." In 1814 he de-
> clined the newly founded Eliot professorship of Greek at Harvard (to which
> Edward Everett was then appointed); he had previously declined the professor-
> ship of Hebrew at the same institution. Even while working on his Greek dic-
> tionary he found time to go deeply into the American Indian languages. He
> reprinted John Eliot's "Indian Grammar" (1822), Jonathan Edwards, Jr.'s
> "Observations on the Language of the Muhhekaneew (Mohegan) Indians"
> (1823), Roger Williams's "Key to the Indian Language" (1827), Josiah Cotton's
> "Vocabulary of the Massachusetts Indians" (1830), and Rasles's (or Râle's)
> "Dictionary of the Abnaki Language" (1833), all with linguistic notes and
> comments of his own. He wrote the article on Indian languages of North America
> for the Encyclopaedia Americana (1831). Particularly interesting is his early
> "Essay on a Uniform Orthography for the Indian Languages of North America"
> (1820), which is nothing more or less than a start toward an international pho-
> netic alphabet. It is, of course, crude and rudimentary when judged by modern
> standards. But it is highly creditable to Pickering that he saw what was needed.
> His alphabet was adopted by missionary societies, and it exerted an important
> and useful influence. . . .
> [He] was a founder and the first president of the American Oriental Society,
> the organization of which in 1842 is an important landmark in American lin-
> guistics as well as in oriental studies. His presidential address at his first annual
> meeting is a remarkable performance. It is a very competent summary of current
> learning in all oriental fields, from Northern Africa to the Pacific islands. Its
> sources were almost wholly European, since this country then had virtually no
> original or creative scholarship in oriental fields. There was little more than
> some rather conventional Hebrew learning, chiefly associated with the training
> of clergymen.

Pickering's Vocabulary was prepared in 1815 as a paper for a meeting of the American Academy of Arts and Sciences of Boston, of
which he was president, and was published in its *Memoirs*,[2] but the
circulation of the *Memoirs* was so limited that he reissued it in June
of the next year, with extensive additions, as a book. He says in his
preface that he began to note and record Americanisms during a
residence in London, where he served as secretary to Rufus King,

1 Notes on Early American Work in
Linguistics, *Proceedings of the
American Philosophical Association*,
July, 1943, p. 27.
2 Allen Walker Read says in American Projects for an Academy to
Regulate Speech, *Publications of the*
*Modern Language Association*, Dec.,
1936, p. 1150, that the academy usually devoted itself to " practical
matters in geology, agriculture,
mathematics and the like ": the
Pickering paper was something of ᴧ
novelty for it.

the American minister, from the end of 1799 to the Autumn of 1801.
But he did not attempt a formal collection, he goes on, until

a few years ago, when, in consequence of a decided opinion of some friends that
a work of the kind would be generally acceptable,[1] I began to reduce into order
the few materials I possessed, and to make such additions to them as my leisure
would permit. The present volume is the result of that labor, for labor it may
be called. To those persons, indeed, who have never undertaken to make such
a collection and to investigate, compare and cite the numerous authorities which
a work of this nature demands, the present volume will, perhaps, not appear to
have been a very arduous task. But when the reader shall have examined it, and
have observed the various citations, and the continual references to dictionaries
and glossaries, he will be able to form some judgment of the time and pains it
must have cost me.

This boast of diligence is well borne out by the book, which, for a
pioneer work, is unusually comprehensive. Pickering not only de-
pended upon his own collectanea for its substance; he also made
drafts upon Witherspoon, and got a great deal of material from the
denunciations of Americanisms in the British reviews of the time.
On the whole, he was in sympathy with their protests, and his book
was mainly devoted to supporting them. He gave next to no attention to the loan words from the Indian languages that had been taken
into American [2] but confined himself to the new coinages from English material and to the changes in meaning that had overtaken some
of the terms of standard English. Thus he stated his position:

The language of the United States has perhaps changed less than might have
been expected, when we consider how many years have elapsed since our ancestors brought it from England; yet it has in so many instances departed from
the English standards that our scholars should lose no time in endeavoring to
restore it to its purity, and to prevent future corruption. . . . As a general
rule we should avoid all those words which are noticed by English authors of
reputation as expressions with which *they are unacquainted;* for though we
might produce some English authority for such words, yet the very circumstance of their being thus noticed by well educated *Englishmen* is a proof that
they are not in use at this day in England, and, of course, ought not to be used
elsewhere by those who would speak *correct English.*

The italics are Pickering's. The most bitter denunciations of the
British reviews did not daunt him, and he even professed to believe

1 One of these friends, it would appear, was the Peter Du Ponceau
lately mentioned. In 1935 Dr. Julian
P. Boyd, then librarian of the Historical Society of Pennsylvania and
now (1944) librarian of Princeton,
discovered a long run of letters from
Pickering to Du Ponceau in the His-

torical Society's collection, all of
them dealing with language. So far
they have not been published.
2 The only ones he listed were *barbecue, caucus, hominy, moccasin,
netop, papoose, samp, squaw* and
*succotash.*

that there was no real anti-American feeling in them. Thus his defense of them:

> We see the same critics censure the Scotticisms of their Northern brethren, the peculiarities of the Irish, and the provincial corruptions of their own English writers. We cannot therefore be so wanting in liberality as to think that when deciding upon the literary claims of Americans they are governed by prejudice or jealousy. . . . It is to be regretted that the reviewers have not pointed out *all* the instances which have come under their notice of our deviations from the *English* standard. This would have been doing an essential service to our literature, and have been the most effectual means of accomplishing what those scholars appear to have so much at heart – the preservation of the English language in its purity, wherever it is spoken.

Again the italics are Pickering's. A few pages further on, as if uneasily aware that his Anglomania may have carried him a bit too far, he hastened to add in a footnote:

> The reader will not infer from these remarks that *our right* to make new words is here meant to be denied. We, as members of that great community or family which speaks the English language have undoubtedly, as well as other members, a right to make words and to propose them for adoption into our common language. But unless those who are the final arbiters in the case – that is, the body of the learned and polite of this whole community wherever they shall be – shall sanction such new terms it will be presumptuous in the authors of them to attempt to force them into general use. . . . That a radical change in the language of a people so remote from the source of it as we are from England is not an imaginary supposition will be apparent from the alterations which have taken place among the nations of Europe; of which no instance, perhaps, is more striking than the gradual change and final separation, of the languages of Spain and Portugal, notwithstanding the vicinity and frequent intercourse of the people of those two countries.

Rather curiously, Pickering was not greatly concerned about the actual novelties invented in America; in fact, he believed that their production was falling off. " It has been asserted," he said, " that we have discovered a much stronger propensity than the English to add new words to the language, and the little animadversion which, till within a few years, such new-coined words have met with among us seems to support that opinion. The passion for these senseless novelties, however, has for some time past been declining." This was written just as the great movement into the West was beginning, and the pages following will show how much in error Pickering was about the future course of American. His dominant fear in 1816, it appears, was not of new words, but of old ones preserved in America after their abandonment in England, and of new meanings attached to words still surviving.

> Our greatest danger now is that we shall continue to use antiquated words which were brought to this country by our forefathers nearly two centuries ago (some of which, too, were at that day *provincial* words in England), and that we shall affix a new *signification* to words which are still used in that country solely in their original sense. Words of these descriptions having long formed a part of the language, we are not led to examine critically the authority on which their different significations rest; but those which are *entirely* new, like strangers on their first appearance, immediately attract attention, and induce us to inquire into their pretensions to the rank they claim.[1]

Pickering's Vocabulary runs to more than 500 terms, and some of his discussions of them are of considerable length: he gives, for example, nearly five pages to *to advocate*. This verb was frowned upon by Benjamin Franklin, who asked Noah Webster, in a letter of December 26, 1789, to use his authority " in reprobating " it, but Webster admitted it to his American Dictionary of 1828 — and supported it with a number of examples from high English sources. It was, in fact, not an American invention, but had been used in England long before the English reviewers began to denounce its use by such Americans as Alexander Hamilton and John Quincy Adams. Pickering quoted at length from a discussion of it in the Rev. Henry J. Todd's edition of Johnson's Dictionary, " with numerous corrections and additions," [2] as follows:

> *To advocate, v.a.* [Lat. *advoco;* Fr. *avocasser*]. To plead, to support, to defend. Mr. Boucher [3] has remarked that though this verb has been said to be an improvement on the English language, which has been discovered by the United States of America since their separation from Great Britain, it is a very common and old Scottish word, which, indeed it is, both as an active and neuter verb. But Mr. Boucher has been misled in this literary concession which he has made to the Americans, for it is also an old English word, employed by one of our finest and most truly manly writers; and if the Americans affect to plume themselves on *this pretended improvement of our language* let them as well as their abetters withdraw the unfounded claim to discovery in turning to the prose writings of Milton. In the dictionaries of the Sixteenth and Seventeenth

1 Pickering's introductory essay, but not his preface, is reprinted in full in Mathews, pp. 65 *ff*.
2 The Cambridge History of English Literature, Vol. X; New York and Cambridge, 1913, p. 516, says that the Todd revision was brought out in four volumes in 1818, but the first volume, at least, must have appeared earlier, for Pickering was quoting it in 1816. It increased Johnson's vocabulary to 58,000 words.
3 The Rev. Jonathan Boucher, author of a Glossary of Archaic and Provincial Words. For an account of him see AL4, p. 35, n. 1.

Centuries, however, as in the Latin of Thomas, the Spanish of Minsheu, the Italian of Florio, and the French of Cotgrave, *advoco, advogar, avocare* and *advocasser* are rendered, not *to advocate* but *to play the advocate*.

Todd then quoted Milton: " Parliament . . . thought this petition worthy, not only of receiving but of voting to a commitment, after it had been *advocated*," [1] and Burke: " This is the only thing distinct and sensible that has been *advocated*." [2] Todd's sneer at imaginary American inventors of the term got under Pickering's skin, despite his general willingness to accept British admonitions docilely, and he hastened to enter a plea of not guilty:

Mr. Todd seems to suppose that the Americans " affect to plume themselves on this pretended improvement of our language," and he then, in a tone which the occasion seemed hardly to require, calls upon them as well as their " abetters," to " withdraw their unfounded claim to discovery." I was not aware that the Americans did " plume themselves " upon this word. We did, indeed, believe it to be a word not in use among Englishmen, because they themselves have considered it as a word *invented* by us, and have censured it as one of the faults of our writers. The truth is that although most Americans have adopted it, yet some of our writers who have been particularly attentive to their style have (whether there is any merit in this or not, let scholars judge) avoided using it. Nor would they probably have felt themselves warranted in employing this, any more than they would many other ancient words (the word *freshet*, for example) [3] because it is to be found in Milton or Burke, unless it were also *in general use at the present day* among Englishmen.

To this, as an afterthought, he added the following in the brief supplement that followed his vocabulary:

If the Americans have not a right to " plume themselves " on this word as a " discovery," they may justly claim the merit (if there is any in the case) of *reviving* it.

*To advocate* is now perfectly good English on both sides of the water, though Robert Southey led a belated attack upon it so late as 1838. So is *to belittle*, though when Thomas Jefferson used it in his " Notes on the State of Virginia," 1781–82, the *European Magazine and London Review* let go with a veritable tirade against it. [4] Pickering sought to get rid of it by pretending that only Jefferson used it seriously. It was " sometimes heard here," he said primly, " in *conver-*

1 Animadversions Upon the Remonstrants' Defense Against Smectymnuus; London, 1641.
2 Speech on the reform of representation in Parliament, *c.* 1767. Pickering gives the date as 1782.
3 *Freshet*, in the sense of a flood

caused by melting snow or excessive rainfall, is probably an Americanism. The DAE's first example is dated 1638. The NED's first is later.
4 This curious denunciation is printed in full in AL4, p. 14. The *Quarterly Review* also denounced the word.

*sation;* but in *writing* it is, I believe, peculiar to that gentleman." This imbecility was echoed by Dr. Robley Dunglison, in his treatise on Americanisms in the *Virginia Literary Museum,* 1829. *Belittle,* he opined, was " not an Americanism, but an individualism." Noah Webster, in his American Dictionary of 1828, described it as " rare in America, not used in England," but it was already lodged firmly on this side of the water and was soon making progress on the other, and today it is everywhere accepted as a perfectly sound word.

Pickering's list included a number of terms that are now obsolete, for example, *to admire* (in the sense of to be pleased),[1] *alone* (as in " the *alone* God "),[2] *applicant* (in the sense of a diligent student),[3] *brief* (in the sense of prevalent, as of an epidemic disease),[4] *citess* (a female citizen, borrowed from the French *citoyenne*),[5] *to compromit* (in the sense of to involve by indiscretion, to compromise, to imperil),[6] *docity* (described by Pickering as " a low word, used in some part of the United States to signify quick comprehension "),[7] *to doxologize* (defined by Webster as " to give glory to God "), *to happify* (to make happy),[8] *to improve* (in the sense of to occupy),[9] *to missionate, publishment, redemptioner,*[10] *releasement,* and *to squale*

1 Mark Twain used it in Sketches Old and New, 1864, but it is now heard only in rustic speech, and seldom there.

2 Not listed in the DAE. Pickering says that in his day it was " often heard from our pulpits," but notes that it had come from England, where it was obsolete.

3 The DAE's first American example is dated 1809. It apparently appeared in England before this, but quickly passed out.

4 The DAE's first example is from the *New England Courant* of April 9/16, 1722. The word is in Thomas Wright's Dictionary of Obsolete and Provincial English; London 1857. Wright says that it comes from the Anglo-Norman, whatever that may be. The NED gives a quotation from Shakespeare's King John, 1595, but throws some doubt upon it. Its first unmistakable quotation is dated 1706.

5 The DAE's only quotations are from Pickering himself and from a review in the *British Critic,* 1796, which he quotes. He says that the *British Critic* called the word an American coinage, and declared that it was better than *citizeness.* It did not last long.

6 Jefferson used the word as early as 1787, and it was admitted by Noah Webster to his American Dictionary of 1828. The DAE's last example is dated 1879.

7 It was provincial in England. The DAE does not list it.

8 *To doxologize* and *to happify* are not listed in the DAE. The latter appears in Dunglison.

9 Traced by the DAE to the Connecticut probate records of 1647. Pickering says that, in his time, it was " in constant use in all parts of New England."

10 This word, which arose at the close of the Eighteenth Century, went out with the disappearance of the redemptioners themselves. They were immigrants who paid for their passage to America by binding themselves to service for a term of years.

(" to throw a stick, or other thing, with violence, and in such a manner that it skims along the ground ").[1] Some of the terms listed by Pickering, in fact, were so little used, even in his day, that Noah Webster, in a letter to him, professed to be unfamiliar with them, *e.g., brash* (brittle and easily split, as of wood),[2] *clitchy* (clammy, sticky, glutinous),[3] *docity, kedge* (brisk, in good health and spirits), *to quackle* (to choke or suffocate), *rafty* (rancid), *to slat* (to throw down with violence), *to squale,* and *to squat* (to squeeze or press).[4] But a much larger number of Pickering's terms survive in the speech of today, *e.g., accountability, to americanize, to appreciate* (to raise in value), *appellate* (of a court), *authority* (in the sense of a person or group), *backwoodsman, balance* (remainder), *betterments, bookstore, dutiable, to energize, to evoke, Fall* (for *Autumn*), *governmental, gunning* (for what the English call *shooting*), *to heft, immigrant* (as the newcomer is seen from the receiving end), *influential, lean-to, mad* (angry), *nationality, to obligate, passage* (of a legislative act), *caucus, census, checkers* (the English call the game *draughts*), *chore, clapboard, to consider* (without *as* following), *constitutionality, corn* (maize) *creek* (an inland brook), *to debark, to deed* (to convey by deed), *to demoralize, departmental, to deputize, to locate, poorly* (ill), *presidential, to progress, to solemnize, squatter, stockholder* and *to systematize.* Many of these, of course, were not actually American inventions, but most of them were in greater vogue in this country than in England, and not a few were denounced violently by the English purists of the time, *e.g., appellate, balance, dutiable, influential, to obligate, caucus, to debark, to demoralize, presidential,* and *to progress. Appellate,* in the sense in which it is used in Article III, Section 2 of the Constitution, 1788, was employed by Blackstone in the first volume of his " Commentaries on the Laws of England " in 1765, and was used again by Burke in " Reflections

1 Pickering lists this as a New England provincialism. It is not recorded in the DAE.

2 The NED traces *brash* in this sense to 1566, but says that it is "now chiefly U.S." Pickering said the term was used "in some parts of New England," and Dunglison, in 1829, marked it "New England." It is now used universally by workmen dealing with wood, *e.g.,* carpenters and cabinet-makers.

3 Pickering hazards the guess that this

word may be a variant of the Devonshire dialect term, *clatchy,* meaning the same. The NED traces *to clitch,* in the sense of to stick, to adhere, to *c.* 1325, but it apparently vanished into dialect soon after 1400. The NED prints a note from a correspondent who says that *to clitch,* not *to clatch,* still survives in the West of England.

4 I take this Webster list from Mathews.

on the Revolution in France," 1790, but so late as 1808 the *Annual Review* denounced John Marshall for using it in his "Life of Washington." Pickering, ordinarily disposed to yield to English censure, defended it by quoting an unnamed correspondent as follows:

If *appellate*, in the sense in which it is employed in the Constitution, has not found its way into English dictionaries, it has found its way into English minds. . . . The word is intelligible to every scholar, and is pointed, useful and sonorous.[1]

*Balance*, in the sense of remainder, is apparently a genuine Americanism. The DAE's first example is dated 1788, and by the turn of the century the word was in general use. The purists, however, continued to belabor it. Noah Webster, writing to Pickering in 1817, said that its use was "forced, and not warranted by any good principle," and so late as 1876 Richard Grant White, in "Words and Their Uses,"[2] was calling it "an abomination," and denying patriotically that it was an Americanism. The reviewer of the *Monthly Anthology* (published in Boston, 1803–11) censured Marshall for using *dutiable* in his "Life of Washington," 1804–07, but the DAE shows that it was used in England fifteen years before it was heard in the debates of Congress, 1789. It was, however, so much more frequently in use in America than in England that it came to be thought of as an Americanism, and it strikes most Englishmen as such to this date. *Influential* belongs to the same category. It has been traced back to *c*. 1734 in England, and Johnson admitted it to his dictionary, but it was used only seldom, and when it began to appear frequently in American books and newspapers it was mistaken for an Americanism, and denounced as such. *To obligate* is even older in English: the NED's first example is from one of Robert South's sermons, 1692. But it began to go out in England as it came into vogue in this country, and the NED lists it as "not now in good use." The DAE's first example is from no less a dignitary than George Washington, 1753, but so recently as 1927 George Bernard Shaw was commenting tartly upon its use by Woodrow Wilson.[3] The *Monthly Anthology*, in its review of Webster's first dictionary of 1806, denounced it as "unnecessary" and without "respectable support," and the *British Critic*, in noticing a book in which it was used by an Oxford don, called it "a low colloquial inaccuracy." The same *British Critic* deplored the use of *to debark* by Washington, and called it "a Gallicism . . .

1 It was listed in Todd's revision of Johnson's Dictionary.

2 Boston, new ed., p. 94.

3 See AL4, p. 40, n. 2.

without rational ground of preference for melody or force " to a
" genuine English word," to wit, *disembark*. The DAE passes over
*to debark* as obviously English, and the NED traces it to 1654. *To
demoralize* was introduced into American, in the form of *demoraliz-
ing*, by Webster in 1794, and he entered the infinitive in his dictionary of 1806. It is said to have been his only original contribution to the
American vocabulary. The *Edinburgh Review* sneered at it when
it appeared, as *demoralization*, in a book by an English lady publicist,
Miss Helen Maria Williams (1762–1827), and it got some thwacks
from other English reviews, but it continued to flourish in this great
Republic, and is still flourishing today. Pickering thought that it had
been " adopted from France since the revolution " there. " It is used,"
he said, " by some English writers, but not as often as by us. It is not
in any of the dictionaries, except Mr. Webster's." One finds it hard
to believe that so logical and necessary a word as *presidential* should
have been denounced, but it is a fact. The *Monthly Anthology* called
it a " barbarism," and the *North American Review* agreed. " English
writers," said Pickering, " have sometimes used it, but only in speaking of American affairs." So late as 1876 Richard Grant White was
arguing that it was " not a legitimate word " and pleading for the
substitution of *presidental*. The DAE's first example is dated 1799,
but in all probability it is older. *To progress*, according to the NED,
was in common use in England in the Seventeenth Century, but then
became obsolete there. It was " retained (or formed anew) in America, where it became very common, *c*. 1790." It was readopted by
the English after 1800, but is still " characterized as an Americanism,
and is much more used in America than in Great Britain." The DAE's
first example is from Franklin, 1789: it comes from his letter of December 26 to Noah Webster, in which he described it as " most awkward and abominable " and asked Webster to use his authority to
" reprobate " it. The *Monthly Anthology* for August, 1808, censured Marshall for using it in his " Life of Washington." Pickering,
writing in 1815, said that it had had " extraordinary currency for
the last twenty or thirty years, notwithstanding it has been condemned by the English, and by the best American writers." He noted
that it was in Johnson's Dictionary, 1755, but also noted that it was
marked " not used." In 1876 Richard Grant White was still hot
against it, even in the form of *progressive*.

The rest of the words on the Pickering list may be noticed briefly.

*Accountability, authority* (in the collective sense), *to energize, to evoke, Fall, gunning, to heft, lean-to, mad* (angry), *nationality, passage* (of a legislative act), *census, checkers, chore, clapboard, to deputize, poorly, to solemnize* and *to systematize* were not, of course, American inventions, but most of them were in wider use in this country than in England, and some are still regarded as Americanisms by Englishmen, notably *Fall, gunning, checkers* and *clapboard*. Of the genuine Americanisms, *to americanize* has been traced to 1797, *to appreciate* (in value) to 1778, *backwoodsman* to 1784 (*backwoods* goes back to 1742), *betterments* (in real property) to 1785, *bookstore* to 1763, *governmental* to 1744, *immigrant* to 1789, *constitutionality* to 1787, *to deed* to 1806, and *to locate* (on land) to 1652. *To americanize* was listed in Noah Webster's dictionary of 1806, but Pickering, writing in 1815, said that he had never encountered it in either writing or conversation. It had been used, as a matter of fact, by John Jay in 1797 and by Jefferson in 1801. Rather curiously, *americanization* did not appear until the middle of the Nineteenth Century. *To appreciate* (to raise in value) is traced by the DAE to 1778, but when Webster listed it in his dictionary the *Monthly Anthology* alleged that it was " only admitted into genteel company by inadvertence." It seems to be going out, and the DAE's last example is dated *c.* 1889. In the sense of to rise in value (intransitive) it goes back to 1779. The corresponding noun, *appreciation*, was used by John Adams in 1777, and is still sound American. Pickering says that in his time *backwoodsman* was applied " by the people of the commercial towns to those who inhabit the territory westward of the Allegany [*sic*] [1] mountains." The word was commonly used, he adds, " as a term of reproach (and that, only in the familiar style) to designate those people who, being at a distance from the sea and entirely *agricultural*, are considered as either hostile or indifferent to the interests of the commercial states." " Thirty years ago," said a writer in *Niles' Register* in 1818, " the heart of Pennsylvania was con-

---

[1] The spelling of this Indian word is variable. The Pennsylvania town, river and college are *Allegheny*, the mountains are the *Alleghanies*, and the New York village is *Allegany*. Webster, in his American Dictionary of 1828, preferred *Allegany* for the mountains, and *Alleganean* for a denizen thereof, but the latter word is now commonly written

*Alleghanian*. The form *Alleghenian* is also recorded. There are various derivatives, *e.g.*, *alleghany hell-bender* (a bird), *alleghany plum* (*Prunus alleghaniensis*), *alleghany-vine* (*Adlumia cirrhosa*), and *allegany-skiff*. *To alleghany*, in the West, once meant to induce the Indians to neglect paying for trade-goods.

sidered as the *backwoods*, and appeared as distant to the citizens of the Atlantic border as the Mississippi does now."

Pickering says that *betterments*, in the sense of " the improvements made on new lands, by cultivation, the erection of buildings, etc.," was first used in Vermont, and the DAE's first example, dated 1785, actually comes from that State. From Vermont it spread to New Hampshire, and then to Massachusetts. Webster omitted it from his first dictionary of 1806, but included it in his American Dictionary of 1828. It was noted as an Americanism by Edward Augustus Kendall in his " Travels Through the Northern Parts of the United States in 1806–08," [1] and when it was embodied in the titles of *betterment acts* it took on official standing. *Book-store*, of course, was one of the new words that followed the transformation of the English *shop* (for a retail establishment) to *store* — a very characteristic Americanism, still often remarked by English travelers. The DAE's first example of this use of *store* is dated 1721 and comes from the *American Weekly Mercury* of March 16. " What are called *shops* in England," observed Thomas Anburey in his " Travels Through the Interior Parts of America " in 1789 [2] " are here denominated *stores*." Pickering says that the word was similarly used in Canada and the West Indies. *To keep store*, also an Americanism, is traced by the DAE to 1752, but *store-clothes* is not found before 1840, and *store-teeth* not before 1891. *Storekeeper* in the American sense goes back to 1741 and *storekeeping* to 1774. *Book-store* is first recorded in 1763 (in Boston), *drug-store* in 1819 (in Louisville), and *grocery-store* in 1774 (in Pennsylvania).

*Governmental* seems to have appeared in the South in 1744, but by 1796 it had spread to New England. The ever-watchful *Monthly Anthology* denounced it as a barbarism, and Noah Webster excluded it from his dictionary of 1806, but he admitted it to his American Dictionary of 1828, and ascribed it to Alexander Hamilton. When it was used by William Belsham (1752–1827) in his " Memoirs of George the Third," the *Edinburgh Review* condemned it, along with *liberticidal* and *royalism*, as " innovations " of a " thirsty reformer," and declined to give up the English language to his " ravages." Pickering discusses *immigrant, immigration* and *to immigrate* at some length. He says that they were first used by Jeremy Belknap (1744–

---

1 Three vols. New York, 1809, Vol.    2 Two vols. London, 1789, Vol. II,
III, p. 160.                                      p. 357.

98) in his "History of New Hampshire," 1784–92, but the DAE's first example of *immigrant*, apparently the oldest of the three words, comes from an "American Geography," by one Morse, published in 1789. In the United States it is usual to employ *immigrant* to designate an incoming wanderer and *emigrant* to designate one leaving. In England it seems to be more common to use *emigrant* in both cases, maybe under the influence of the French *émigré*. When John Marshall's "Life of Washington" was brought out in England *immigrations*, in "The immigrations from England continued to be very considerable," was changed to *emigrations*. It is rather astonishing that *constitutionality* did not appear in England before it was used by Alexander Hamilton in 1787, but such seems to have been the case. The NED's first example of its English use is dated 1801. *Constitutionalist* goes back to 1766 in England, sixteen years before it is recorded in America, and *constitutional* to 1682. *Constitutionally*, in the political sense, has been traced to 1756. The DAE classes *constitutional-amendment. constitutional-lawyer* and *constitutional-convention* as Americanisms. The first is first recorded in 1854, the second in 1830 and the third in 1843. *To deed*, defined by Webster as to give or transfer by deed, is listed by Pickering as "a low word, used colloquially, but rarely, except by illiterate people." "None of our writers," he continued, "would employ it. It need hardly be observed that it is not in the English dictionaries." But J. Fenimore Cooper was using it by 1845, and it is today reasonably respectable. So with *to locate*, which goes back to 1652 in America, but did not appear in England until 1837.

One of the indubitable Americanisms that was attacked with violence by the English reviewers, but all in vain, was *lengthy*.[1] Albert Matthews has traced it to 1689, and by the end of the Eighteenth Century it was in common use in the United States. The searchers for the NED found ten examples in the writings of Jefferson between 1782 and 1786, and others in those of Washington, Hamilton, Franklin and John Adams. "This word," says Pickering, "has been very common among us, both in writing and in the language of conversation, but it has been so much ridiculed by Americans as well as Englishmen that in *writing* it is now generally avoided.[2] Mr. Webster has

[1] See AL4, pp. 15, 119 and 223.
[2] There was evidence against Pickering here. John Davis, in his Travels of Four Years and a Half in the United States of America, 1798, 1799, 1800, 1801 and 1802; London, 1802, said "it is frequently used by the *classical* writers of the New World."

admitted it to his dictionary [1] but (as need hardly be remarked) it is not in any of the *English* ones. It is applied by us, as Mr. Webster justly observes, chiefly to writings or discourses. Thus we say, a *lengthy* pamphlet, a *lengthy* sermon, etc. The English would say a *long* or (in the more familiar style) a *longish* sermon." Pickering then undertakes to show how, by the use of *diffuse, lengthened, prolonged, extended, extensive* and *prolix, lengthy* might be avoided. He was, of course, wasting his energy. The word not only got firm lodgment in America; it also penetrated England, and in a little while many of the best writers were using it, notably Southey, Bentham, Scott, Dickens, and George Eliot, sometimes as a conscious Americanism but oftener not.

Pickering gave some attention to certain changes in the use of prepositions that had arisen in America, for example, the use of *at* before *auction* in place of the English *by*. He recorded, under *averse*, that American writers formerly followed this word with *to*, but had begun to substitute *from*, apparently under the prodding of John Witherspoon and other such policemen of the national speech. But he added a sensible defense of *averse to* from George Campbell's "The Philosophy of Rhetoric," 1776, as follows:

> The words *averse* and *aversion* are more properly construed with *to* than with *from*. The examples in favor of the latter preposition are beyond comparison outnumbered by those in favor of the former. The argument from etymology is here of no value, being taken from the use of another language. If, by the same rule, we were to regulate all nouns and verbs of Latin original our present syntax would be overturned.

Pickering also discussed the American use of *to* instead of the English *at* or *in* in such phrases as "I have been *to* Philadelphia." Witherspoon had denounced this practise in 1781, but it had survived, and in the vulgar speech it had produced such forms as *to home*. The latter have disappeared, but "I have been *to* Philadelphia" is today sound American.

The other early glossaries of Americanisms were of much less value than Pickering's painstaking work. On March 18, 1829, Dr. Theodoric Romeyn Beck (1791–1855) read a paper on Pickering before the Albany Institute, and it was printed in the *Transactions* of the Institute for 1830. Mathews reprints it in full, but there is little in it of any value. Beck, who was a New York physician and peda-

1 Of 1806.

gogue, was inclined, like Pickering, to believe that Americans should follow English precept and example in their speechways, though he protested against the " overwhelming ridicule and contempt " with which the English reviewers greeted every fresh Americanism. " This, however," he went on, " is merely an objection to the *man-ner*. The *matter* of their animadversions deserves more serious consideration." His brief and far from persuasive contribution to the subject was followed by a series of articles in the *Virginia Literary Museum and Journal of Belles Lettres, Arts, Sciences, &c*. on December 16 and 30, 1829 and January 6, 1830. Their author was Dr. Robley Dunglison, an Englishman educated in Germany, who had been brought out by Thomas Jefferson in 1824 to be professor of medicine in the University of Virginia. In 1833 he moved to the University of Maryland and in 1836 to Jefferson Medical College, Philadelphia. He was a competent medical man, and Fielding H. Garrison says of him that he " compiled an excellent medical dictionary and wrote an amazing array of textbooks on nearly every subject except surgery." [1] But his vast energy was not exhausted by this professional diligence, and Allen Walker Read adds that " he wrote on almost any conceivable subject." The glossary which constitutes the bulk of his three articles has been reprinted by Read [2] and also by Mathews. " His sport," says Read, " was that of many a later man: the proving that many so-called Americanisms are distinctly of British origin." But he also made some useful contributions to the subject. He was, for example, the first lexicographer to list the word *blizzard*, and his entry of it in his glossary is the first example unearthed by the searchers for the DAE. He is also credited with the DAE's first example of *to cavort* (in the American sense of to prance, to act up, to cut monkey-shines), *to hornswoggle, to mosey, retiracy* and *sockdolager*. Finally, he recorded a number of words that seem to have been of short life, for they are not recorded by subsequent lexicographers, *e.g., coudeript* (credited to Kentucky and defined as " thrown into fits "), *givy* (a Southernism signifying muggy weather), and *mollagausauger* (" a stout fellow ").

Another early glossary of Americanisms was that of the Rev.

[1] An Introduction to the History of Medicine; fourth ed.; Philadelphia, 1929, p. 443. Dunglison's son, also a physician, published a memoir of him in 1870.

[2] Dunglison's Glossary (1829–1830), *Dialect Notes*, Vol. V, Part X, 1927, pp. 422–32.

Adiel Sherwood, first published in his " Gazetteer of the State of Georgia " in 1827 and much extended in a third edition of 1837. Mathews reprinted it in *Dialect Notes* in 1927 [1] and also in " The Beginnings of American English " in 1931. It is mainly interesting because of its indications of the prevailing vulgar pronunciations of the South in the 30s, *e.g.*, *arter* for *after*, *axd* for *asked*, *blather* for *bladder*, *bess* for *best*, *becase* for *because*, *beyant* for *beyond*, *crap* for *crop*, *fare* for *far*, *gimme* for *give me*, *gal* for *girl*, *hit* for *it*, *inimy* for *enemy*, *mounting* for *mountain*, *queshton* for *question*, *sacer* for *saucer*, *umberillo* for *umbrella* and *year* for *here*, but it also shows some other curiosa, *e.g.*, the use of *to assign* for *to sign*, *Baptises* for *Baptists*, *done said*, *done did*, *flitter* for *fritter*, *to get shet of*, *hadn't ought*, *to lay* for *to lie*, *mighty* and *monstrous* as general intensives, *prasbattery* for *presbytery*, *plunder* for goods and effects, *sparrow-grass* for *asparagus*, *smart chance* for good deal, and *to use* for to feed. The DAE's first example of *bodaciously*, in the sense of wholly, is from Sherwood. " It will be seen," he said in his brief introduction, " that many of our provincialisms are borrowed from England."

The first attempt at a dictionary of Americanisms on a really comprehensive scale was made by John Russell Bartlett in 1848, with his " Glossary of Words and Phrases Usually Regarded as Peculiar to the United States." Bartlett, who was a Rhode Islander, born in 1805 and surviving until 1886, began life as a bank clerk in Providence and was later a partner in a publishing house in New York, but he attained to considerable reputation as a bibliographer and antiquarian and also dabbled in ethnology. His glossary, beginning as a volume of 412 pages, was expanded to 524 when it was reissued in 1859, and reached 813 with its fourth and last edition in 1877. From his first edition onward he supported his entries, whenever possible, with illustrative quotations, but most of them, unfortunately, were not dated. In the preface to his fourth edition he discussed the origin of new Americanisms, and defended his listing of what critics had apparently denounced as ephemeral slang. The novelties of his time, he said, came chiefly from the following sources: first, the jargon of the stock market, rapidly adopted by the whole business community; second, the slang of the " colleges and higher schools ";

1 Vol. V, Part X, pp. 415–21. It was omitted from Sherwood's fourth edition; Macon and Atlanta, 1860.

third, the argot " of politicians, of the stage, of sportsmen, of Western boatmen, of pugilists, of the police, of rowdies and roughs, of thieves, of work-shops, of the circus, of shopkeepers, workmen, etc." Many of these neologisms had only short lives, but Bartlett insisted sensibly that they should be listed nevertheless, if only for the sake of the record. " Sometimes," he said, " these strange words have a known origin, but of the larger number no one knows whence they come. Slang is thus the source whence large additions are made to our language." [1]

The " Glossary of Supposed Americanisms " of Dr. Alfred L. Elwyn, which appeared in 1859, was chiefly devoted to showing that most of the 465 terms it listed were English provincialisms or archaisms, but he also listed a few words and phrases picked up in Pennsylvania. Elwyn, under *ball*, offered one of the early descriptions of baseball. He called it *bat and ball*, said that it was played in his youth, and hazarded the guess that it might be " an imperfect form of cricket," though calling it, in the same breath, " a Yankee invention." He defined *lynching*, with polite ingenuity, as " a Western mode of arranging social grievances," and said that " in new countries " it seemed to be " absolutely necessary, as, without it, there would be no hope of ridding society of those who are a nuisance." " It is," he went on, " a rough expression of the moral sense, and frequently well directed." M. Schele de Vere's " Americanisms: The English of the New World," which followed in 1871, was not arranged in vocabulary form, but included a great deal of matter not in previous works, especially a learned and valuable discussion of loan-words. Freiherr Maximilian von Schele, the son of a Swedish officer in the Prussian service and of a French mother, took his Ph.D. at Bonn in 1841 and his J.U.D. at Greifswald in 1842. He came to America soon afterward and studied Greek at Harvard. In 1844 he was recommended for the chair of modern languages at the University of Virginia by Henry Wadsworth Longfellow and others, and there, save for four years service in the Confederate Army during the Civil War, he taught French, Spanish, Italian, German and Anglo-Saxon until 1895, when he retired to Washington. After coming to America he added his mother's maiden name, de Vere, to his patro-

[1] Bartlett should not be confused with John Bartlett (1820–1905), the Boston publisher who, in 1855, brought out a volume of Familiar Quotations that, with revisions by other hands, is still a standard work.

nymic, but he was always known at Charlottesville as Schele. He was one of the founders of the American Philological Association in 1869, published a number of books on language, and served on the staff of the Standard Dictionary, 1893–95. He died in 1898. A second edition of his " Americanisms " was published in 1872, but since then it has not been reprinted.[1] For seventeen years afterward no contribution of any importance was made to the subject save Bartlett's fourth edition of 1877. Then, in 1889, John S. Farmer brought out " Americanisms Old and New," a stout volume of 564 double-column pages, listing about 5000 terms. Farmer was a busy compiler and lexicographer, and is chiefly remembered for the monumental " Slang and Its Analogues: Past and Present " which he began to publish in London in 1890. This ambitious undertaking, which was enriched with dated quotations on the plan of the New English Dictionary, ran to seven quarto volumes and was completed in 1904. Beginning with the second volume in 1891 the name of William E. Henley the poet was associated with that of Farmer on the title page, and in consequence the work is commonly referred to as Farmer and Henley. In 1905 Farmer brought out a one-volume abridgment for general circulation, with the quotations omitted and no mention of the numerous profane and obscene terms listed in the seven-volume edition. His " Americanisms Old and New " contains many dated quotations from American newspapers, mainly of the year 1888. It shows but little dependence upon its predecessors in the field, and is, in the main, a workmanlike and valuable work, but Farmer occasionally fell into error in his definitions — for example, in that of *to get back at* — , and, as Burke says, sometimes betrayed a certain British insularity. His preface made it plain that the impact of Americanisms upon English speechways was already powerful in 1888. He said:

Latterly, for good or ill, we have been brought face to face with what has been grandiloquently called "The Great American Language," oftentimes in its baldest form, and on its most repulsive side. The works, also, of the popular exponents of " American humour," itself an article as distinct in type as is the

1 Schele's own copy of the book, with many corrections and additions, is in the University of Virginia library. Dr. Atcheson L. Hench gave an account of it in a paper read before the Present-Day English Section of the Modern Language Association at Philadelphia, Dec. 29, 1934. Unhappily, that paper has not been printed, but Dr. Hench has courteously permitted me to see it. Schele's notes were apparently made in 1872–75. Dr. Hench calls attention to the fact that copies of the first edition of 1871 are extremely scarce; in fact, he has never seen one, and neither have I.

American character, have made the English people familiar with transatlantic words, phrases, turns cf expression, and constructions, most of which, strange of sound and quaint in form, are altogether incomprehensible. Their influence is daily gaining ground — books in shoals, journals by the score, and allusions without stint are multiplying on every hand. American newspapers, too, humorous and otherwise, circulate in England by hundreds of thousands weekly — all this and a good deal else is doing its work in popularizing American peculiarities of speech and diction to an extent which, a few years since, would have been deemed incredible. Even our own newspapers, hitherto regarded as models of correct literary style, are many of them following in their wake; and, both in matter and phraseology, are lending countenance to what at first sight appears a monstrously crude and almost imbecile jargon; while others, fearful of a direct plunge, modestly introduce the uncouth bantlings with a saving clause. The phrase, " as the Americans say," might in some cases be ordered from the type-foundry as a logotype, so frequently does it do introduction duty.

Whatever Farmer's distaste, as a patriotic Englishman, for this " monstrously crude and almost imbecile jargon," he was too good a philologian to believe that it could be stayed. On the contrary, he believed that the English of England, in the long run, would have to take in much of it, and that the preponderance of population in the United States would eventually force American speechways upon the language as a whole. He said:

Purists may object, and cry out in alarm concerning sacrilegious innovation, but on going to the root of the matter this tendency is found to be not altogether void of satisfaction when regarded as indicative of the vitality and creative vigor still enshrined in our speech. Language, like everything else, is progressive; there is no spoken language a thousand years old.

Farmer seems to have been a somewhat mysterious fellow, and the reference-books neglect him. Said G. Alexander Legman in *Notes and Queries,* May 23, 1942:

His productive period was from about 1885 to 1914. The name Farmer is not a pseudonym, as he appeared in court in 1890 to defend his work against a charge of obscenity brought against his printer. He was a frequent contributor to *Notes and Queries,* which referred to him as " Dr. Farmer." He was known as an eccentric and believed in spiritualism, on which he published several books. These meagre oddments of information are all that seems to be known of a fine scholar whose published work totals more than thirty volumes.

His works, beside those mentioned, included " A New Basis of Belief in Immortality," " 'Twixt Two Worlds," " Ex Oriente Lux," " Musa Pedestris " (1896), and " The Public School Word Book " (1900). After his " Americanisms Old and New " came Sylva Clapin's " New Dictionary of Americanisms," a third-rate compilation, but valuable because of the inclusion of a number of Canadian terms.

Finally, in 1912, appeared the two volumes of Richard Harwood Thornton's "American Glossary," and the lexicography of Americanisms was put on a firm and scientific foundation at last.

Thornton was an Englishman, born in Lancashire, September 6, 1845. His name does not appear in any of the standard reference books, and the only printed account of him that I know of is a brief sketch by the Rev. E. H. Clark, published in *Dialect Notes* in July, 1939. By this it appears that he was the son of a Methodist clergyman who, at the time of his birth, was a classical tutor in the Wesleyan Theological Institution at Disbury. It is possible, though I have no evidence for it, that he was related to the Dr. William Thornton (1762–1828) who was awarded the Magellanic Gold Medal of the American Philosophical Society of Philadelphia in 1793 for a treatise on phonetics in which Americans were thus exhorted:

> You have corrected the dangerous doctrines of European powers; correct now the languages you have imported, for the oppressed of various nations knock at your gates, and desire to be received as your brethren. . . . The American language will thus be as distinct as the government, free from all the follies of unphilosophical fashion, and resting upon truth as its only regulator.[1]

Richard H. Thornton got only a secondary school education, though he seems to have had some grounding in Latin, Greek, French and German. He passed the Oxford entrance examination in 1862, but was too poor to go to the university. Instead he got a job with a business house in London and there he remained until 1871. During this time he also tackled Italian and seems to have acquired a fair reading knowledge of it. In 1871, seeing only poor prospects in London, he immigrated to Canada, and in 1874 came to the United States. In 1876 he entered Columbia Law School at Washington,

[1] I take this from American Projects for an Academy to Regulate Speech, by Allen Walker Read, *Publications of the Modern Language Association*, Dec., 1936, p. 1142. Thornton's book, published in Philadelphia in 1793, was called Cadmus, or, a Treatise on the Elements of Written Language. He was a native of Tortola, one of the Virgin Islands belonging to England. He had come to the United States a little while before and presently set up practise as an architect, though he had no professional training. In 1793 he submitted plans for the Capitol at Washington and they were approved by George Washington. His design survives in the central part of the building. He served as one of the commissioners of the District of Columbia until 1802, and after that was Commissioner of Patents until his death. He was mentioned by James Boswell in a letter of July 28, 1793, and was denounced by a Scot, James Adams, for proposing "a plan of abolishing our language, . . . noticed by a philosophical society."

and was graduated therefrom in 1878. He was then admitted to the bar in Philadelphia, but soon moved to Williamsport, Pa., the home of his wife, Martha Sproul, married in 1877. In 1884 he went to Portland, Ore., as the first dean of the Oregon Law School, and there, save for several trips to England, he remained until his death on January 7, 1925. He was naturalized in 1881. On November 3, 1923 the University of Oregon gave him the degree of doctor of laws.

When he began work on his " American Glossary " does not seem to be known, but it must have been before 1907, for in that year he was in London pursuing inquiries with respect to it. Its format, without doubt, was suggested by that of the NED, which had begun to appear in 1888. Thornton acknowledged in his preface his debt to Bartlett, to Farmer and to Albert Matthews,[1] but the chief burden of assembling his extraordinarily copious materials lay upon his own shoulders. He undertook the herculean task of reading the *Congressional Globe* from the beginning to 1863, and also got together an immense mass of citations from newspapers, magazines and books. He endeavored to unearth dated quotations showing the use of every one of the 3700 terms he listed, and in many cases he found and presented a large number — in that of *Yankee*, no less than sixty. Nothing on so comprehensive a scale or following so scientific a method had been undertaken before, and Thornton's first two volumes, issued in 1912, remain indispensable to this day. Indeed, the DAE would have been impossible without them, and it shows its debt to them on almost every page. Unhappily, the author could find no publisher for his work in the United States, and had to take it to London. There it was brought out in an edition of 2000 by a small firm, Francis & Company. Once it was in type Lippincott, the Philadelphia publisher, took 250 sets of the sheets and issued them with his imprint, but they sold only slowly and so late as 1919 the small edition was still not exhausted. It was never reissued.[2] Meanwhile, Thornton kept on accumulating materials, and during World War I he tried to find a publisher willing to bring out a third volume or backers willing to stake it. In this he was unsuccessful, so he turned

---

1 A Boston antiquary, born in 1860, whose diligent and valuable work entered into the NED, the DAE and other dictionaries, and greatly enriched the files of learned journals. Unhappily, he never collected it

2 I am indebted here to the late J. Jefferson Jones, chief of the Lippincott editorial department.

over his MS., in 1919, to Dr. Percy W. Long, then editor of *Dialect Notes*, who deposited it in the Widener Library at Harvard. There it remained until 1931, six years after Thornton's death, when its publication was begun serially in *Dialect Notes*, with prefaces by Dr. Long and Sir William Craigie and the editorial assistance of Mrs. Louise Hanley, wife of Dr. Miles L. Hanley, then secretary and treasurer of the American Dialect Society. It was the expectation at the time that the publication of the volume would be completed by the end of 1933, but the chronic financial difficulties of the Dialect Society got in the way, and the last of the material was not actually worked off until July, 1939 — eight years after the beginning. The instalments were so paged that they could be cut out of *Dialect Notes* and bound together, but there has never been a reprint in book form. For the following brief reminiscence of Thornton I am indebted to Lewis A. McArthur of Portland, author of the well-known and excellent " Oregon Geographic Names ":

> Professor Thornton lived in Portland during the '90s. He was a great friend of my father. He was dean of the University of Oregon Law School, where my father, who was a lawyer, gave certain lecture courses. I used to see a good deal of him, as he was frequently at our home. I was a small boy then and it seemed to me that he was the oldest man I had ever seen. He had a sort of Old Testament beard and looked as though he was a grandfather of Confucius.
>
> Despite the fact that Professor Thornton looked formidable to me when I was small, I remember that I was often interested in his talks with my father about English words. They both had an unusual knowledge of the business. I have a notion that perhaps that is one of the reasons I have been attracted to the subject.
>
> Professor Thornton subsequently dropped out of sight. He returned to Portland a few years later and was given an honorary degree by the University of Oregon. I saw the old gentleman paddling along Fifth street in Portland in the Fall of 1924 in a pair of carpet slippers. He died in January, 1925.

### 5. THE POSITION OF THE LEARNED

It will be noted that nearly all the investigators of American speech-ways mentioned so far were either amateurs or foreigners, and that more than one of them was both. The earlier native *Gelehrte* of the language faculty, with the massive exceptions of Webster and Pickering, disdained the subject as beneath their notice, and even Pickering, as we have seen, discussed it with distaste. Beginning with Lindley Murray (1745–1826) and running down to Richard Grant

White (1821–85) and Thomas S. Lounsbury (1838–1915), the more influential of its accepted expositors threw themselves into a mighty effort, not to describe and study the language of their country, but to police and purify it, and most of them accepted without challenge the highly artificial standards set up by English pedants of the Eighteenth Century.[1] By a curious irony it fell to Murray's fate to be more influential in England than in America, and it would not be absurd to argue that he was responsible beyond all others for the linguistic lag visible in the Mother Country to this day, but it is not to be forgotten that he also had a great deal of weight at home, and was the *Stammvater* of the dismal pedagogues who still expound " correct English " in our schools and colleges.[2] From these pedagogues the investigation of the living speech of 140,000,000 Americans has seldom got any effective assistance. All the contributions from the English faculty that have gone into the files of *Dialect Notes* and *American Speech* and into such enterprises as the Dictionary of American English and the Linguistic Atlas of the United States and Canada have come from an extremely small minority, scattered among the general as sparsely as raisins in an orphanage cake. There is, of course, nothing really singular in this lack of professional keenness, for it is to be observed in the United States in other similar groups. Of the 175,000 physicians and surgeons in the country, probably not 5000 have ever added anything, however little, to the sum of medical knowledge, and among lawyers the ratio of legal scholars to legal hewers of wood and drawers of water is even smaller. But the percentage of actual students of the language among teachers of English seems to be the smallest of all, and even the members of this minority commonly eschew the speech of their own country. Four-fifths of those who write at all devote themselves to " literary " rabbinism,[3] and many of the rest waste themselves upon

---

1 White and Lounsbury are dealt with at some length in AL4, pp. 61 ff.

2 Murray was born in Lancaster county, Pa., in 1745. Trained as a lawyer, he went into business and made a comfortable fortune during the Revolution. In 1784 he moved to England, where he died in 1826. His Grammar of the English Language Adapted to the Different Classes of Learners first appeared in 1795. It ran through hundreds of editions.

In 1804 he published a spelling-book that became a formidable rival to Webster's.

3 This depressing business was thus described by the late Dr. Otto Heller (1863–1941), of Washington University, in a paper entitled The Pseudo-Science of Literature, *Proceedings of the Conference on the Association of American Universities*, 1936, pp. 78–88: " Collating all existing versions and variants of lit-

the current philological crazes — in recent years, upon the study of the mysterious entities called phonemes, and the high-falutin but hollow pseudo-science of semantics.[1] These sombre studies exhaust the brethren, and they have no time or energy left for the investigation of the language they all speak. So far as I can make out, the American Dialect Society, though it was launched by men of high professional reputation and influence and has the support of such men (and women) to this day, has never had more than a few hundred members, and at last accounts the circulation of the interesting and valu-

---

erary monuments or compositions; 'fixing' the authentic text; making 'standard' editions; ferreting out analogies and parallels and tracing sources; annotating; recovering writing lost or missing; excavating literary ruins or fragments; disinterring works and parts of works deservedly buried alive by their authors; disclosing guarded privacies." The typical " study " is a laborious tracking down of the sources of some work that no one ever reads, or the tracing of the relations between two authors, one of them usually a nonentity, and sometimes both. Dr. Heller admitted in his paper that such humorless inquiries occasionally unearth more or less useful knowledge, but noted sadly that the pedants who engage in them usually " content themselves with the mechanical preliminaries."

[1] Semantics is a new name for semasiology, the study of the meaning of words. Its masterpiece is the discovery, announced with a great fanfare, that a given word often means different things to different people, and that words worked to death by ignoramuses, *e.g., democracy*, commonly take on emotional overtones that quite obliterate their historical meaning. All this, of course, was known to the Greeks, but it seems new and thrilling to the sort of person to whom it seems new and thrilling. Of late the professors of semantics have divided into two factions. The first, led by metaphysicians, lifts the elemental business of communicating ideas to the level of

a baffling and somewhat sinister arcanum standing midway between the geometry of the fourth dimension and the Freudian rumble-bumble; the other, led by popularizers, converts it into a club for use upon the skulls of enemies of the current New Deals. The study of phonemes is based upon the revolutionary discovery that there are speech elements smaller than words. Unhappily, no two professors of the new mystery seem to be in agreement as to just what a phoneme is. Their differences were described at length by Dr. W. Freeman Twaddell of the University of Wisconsin in On Defining the Phoneme, *Language* (supplement), March, 1935. He favored getting rid of the difficulty by calling a phoneme " an abstractional fictitious unit." "We shall have many a headache," added Dr. Arthur G. Kennedy of Stanford University in Recent Trends in English Linguistics, *Modern Language Quarterly*, June, 1940, p. 177, speaking of the analogous morpheme, " before the grammarians, more particularly the philosophical linguists, succeed in straightening out the matter of definitions." Dr. Kennedy reported that he had also got news of morphonemes, tonemes, enthymemes, glossemes, graphemes, noemes, philosophemes, tagmemes, taxemes, archimorphemes and phonomorphemes. Such monstrosities are hardly more than evidences of the ancient scholastic belief that giving a thing a new name is equivalent to saying something about it.

able *American Speech* [1] was stated (probably somewhat generously) to be 520.[2] The surveys of the Linguistic Atlas are being made by students rather than by teachers, with an Austrian-born professor of German in charge of them, and the DAE was edited by a Scotsman imported for the purpose. Some of the chief defects in the DAE, to be noted presently, are to be blamed on the fact that the far-flung and almost innumerable teachers of English of the country failed nearly unanimously to give it any help.

The Modern Language Association, which includes in its membership virtually all the scientifically-trained language teachers of the country,[3] has had a Present-Day English section since 1924, but its activities have been of a very moderate degree of virulence, to say the least, and I judge by the names appearing on its modest programs that it has recruited few philologues who were not already at work for *Dialect Notes* and *American Speech*. Nor have all its lucubrations had to do with American English. The Linguistic Society of America, organized in 1924, also gives an occasional glance to the subject,[4] but the papers in point that are presented at its meetings are seldom printed in its organ, *Language*,[5] which is devoted principally to languages more interesting to its members than American English, *e.g.*, Hittite and Old Church Slavonic.[6] In 1941 a pro-

1 Vol. I, No. 1 was dated Oct., 1925. It was a monthly at $4 a year until Sept., 1927. Then it became a bi-monthly at $3. Between Aug., 1932 and Feb., 1933 it was suspended. In the latter month it became a quarterly at $4 a year, and has so continued.

2 When *American Speech* was launched, with Dr. Louise Pound as editor, it started off promisingly, and by April, 1926 had 1469 paid subscribers. But in 1929 and 1930 the circulation dropped to an average of 550, and by October of the latter year it had got down to 329. There was a slight revival afterward and it reached 570 at the end of 1932, but soon afterward it dropped again. I am indebted here to Mr. Robert S. Gill, of the Williams and Wilkins Company, Baltimore, its publishers from the start to 1930, and to Mr. H. E. Buchholz of Warwick and York, Baltimore, its publishers from

then until the end of 1932, when it was taken over by the Columbia University Press, with Dr. William Cabell Greet as editor.

3 As of Nov. 21, 1942 it had 3925 members.

4 At its second annual meeting, at Chicago in Dec., 1925, it approved the work of the aforesaid Present-Day English section. See Notes and Quotes, *American Speech*, Aug., 1926, p. 620.

5 Vol. I, No. 1 was dated March, 1925.

6 Since 1928 the society has been conducting Linguistic Institutes in Summer at various universities. In June, 1944, for example, there was one at the University of Wisconsin. The lectures listed offered instruction in General Linguistics, Phonetics, Vulgar Latin, Syriac, Sanskrit, Hittite, Old Norse, Old High German, the American Indian languages, Old Spanish, Anglo-Saxon, Polish, Portuguese, Russian and Greek, but

posal was made to widen the scope of the American Dialect Society by changing its name to the English Language Society of America, but it was rejected by the members at a meeting in Indianapolis on December 30. The society, however, has been hospitable, ever since its organization in 1889,[1] to scholars working in regions outside its own special field, and the files of *Dialect Notes* are rich with the contributions of such students of general American speechways as Albert Matthews, M. M. Mathews, Allen Walker Read and Dr. Louise Pound and her pupils, and of such specialists in non-English languages as J. Dynely Prince (Dutch) and George T. Flom (Norwegian). In 1943 it issued a circular entitled "Needed Research in American English" in which the whole subject was admirably surveyed, and excellent suggestions were made to willing investigators. By 1917 *Dialect Notes* had printed 26,000 examples of American dialect terms and phrases, and had accumulated almost as many more. The publication of a Dialect Dictionary of the United States thus suggested itself, and plans for it were undertaken in 1926.[2] Unhappily, they were delayed inordinately by the Dialect Society's lack of support, leading to recurrent financial crises, and when, in 1941, Dr. Harold Wentworth, then of West Virginia University, projected, at the suggestion of Dr. Louise Pound, a dialect dictionary of his own, and applied for the use of the society's files, it was found that they had been lost. The equivalent of a court martial, set up to inquire into this catastrophe, found that the cards had been stored for years in a room in Warren House at Harvard, that the university authorities, having other uses for the space they occupied, moved them out, and that after that they vanished. Harvard put the blame on the officers of the society, and the officers denied that they were responsible, so nothing came of the investigation, nor were the cards recovered. Simultaneously, the society made a narrow escape from bankruptcy. The membership, in 1941, dropped to 38, with three unpaid, and there was an accumulated debt of

there was only one course dealing with American English, and that was confined to its pronunciation. For the original plans see The Linguistic Institute of the Linguistic Society of America, *American Speech*, Feb., 1928, pp. 171–72.

1 It is probable that the current vogue of the dialect novel had something to do with its launching. For the first time the riches of American dialect were being systematically explored. The resultant reports were often anything but accurate, but they at least directed attention to the subject.

2 The American Dialect Dictionary, by Percy W. Long, *American Speech*, May, 1926, pp. 439–42.

$868.12. Part of this debt was shouldered by Dr. Miles L. Hanley, of the University of Wisconsin, the secretary and treasurer, and the balance was raised through the efforts of Dr. Pound, Mr. Read and others. In 1941 the society was reorganized, and by the end of 1942 it had 231 members, the annual dues had been raised from $1 to $2, and a receipt and release were in hand from the long-suffering printers of *Dialect Notes*. Dr. Pound was elected president, Dr. Harry Morgan Ayres of Columbia became vice-president, and Dr. Atcheson L. Hench of the University of Virginia secretary-treasurer. A year later Ayres succeeded Dr. Pound, Dr. Kemp Malone of the Johns Hopkins became vice-president, and Read followed Hench as secretary-treasurer. At the end of 1943 Ayres retired and was succeeded by Malone. Read, who had gone into the Army, was forced by his military duties to resign soon afterward, and Dr. George P. Wilson was appointed in his place. Thus the society stands in the first years of its second half-century, rejuvenated and indeed rein-carnated. It is still small, but its members include all the American philologians who are really interested in American English, and it has more ambitious plans than ever before.

The two great events in the study of the American language since the publication of AL4 in 1936 have been the appearance of the first volume of " A Linguistic Atlas of the United States and Canada " in 1939 and the completion of " A Dictionary of American English on Historical Principles " in 1944. The origin, plan and early history of the dictionary are given in AL4, pp. 56 *ff*, and need not be re-hearsed here.[1] When it was announced that Dr. William A. Craigie, one of the editors of the monumental " New English Dictionary on Historical Principles," had been engaged to edit it, I permitted my-self, in a newspaper article, a chauvinistic sniff,[2] for it was impos-sible for me to imagine a British don getting to really close grips with the wayward speech of this great Republic. It is still impossible for me to imagine it, but I should add at once that Sir William (he was knighted in 1928) made a gallant attempt, and that the result is a dictionary which, whatever its deficiencies, is at least enormously better than anything that preceded it. It leans heavily upon the

---

[1] It was at first called The Historical Dictionary of American English, but the change in title was made in 1935, before publication began.

[2] The American Language, Chicago *Tribune*, April 12, 1925. This article was printed simultaneously in a num-ber of other newspapers, *e.g.*, the New York *World*.

pioneer work of Thornton, but it shows a much wider sweep, and, what is more important, a higher degree of accuracy and a greatly superior technical competence.[1] On every page there is evidence that the editing was directed by a first-rate professional lexicographer. Sir William's long years of service on the NED equipped him as no American of his trade was equipped, and when he got to Chicago in 1925 he assembled a staff of highly competent Americans, including Dr. M. M. Mathews, Dr. Catherine Sturtevant, Allen Walker Read and Dr. Woodford A. Heflin, which remedied the deficiencies in his own first-hand knowledge of the subject. In 1935 they were reinforced by Dr. James R. Hulbert, professor of English in the University of Chicago, who became co-editor. Sir William brought with him a large mass of material that had been gathered for the NED but not used, and he presently set up classes in lexicography at the University of Chicago, and put his students to work. From the great body of American professors of English and from Americans in general he seems to have got relatively little help. Even the names of many of the contributors to *Dialect Notes* and *American Speech* are missing from his list of acknowledgments. His predecessors and colleagues of the NED were a great deal better served. In their first volume, published in 1888, they recorded their debt to a list of volunteers ranging from philologians of the first eminence to country clergymen with time on their hands. One of these volunteers actually sent in 165,000 quotations, and another 136,000. Many Americans also took a hand. One of them, the Rev. J. Pierson, of Ionia, Mich., contributed 46,000, and another, the Rev. B. Talbot, of Columbus, O., 16,600. But both clergy and laity seem to have ignored the appeals of the DAE.[2]

1 The frequent slips of Thornton are discussed by Allen Walter Read in The Policies of the Dictionary of American English, *Dialect Notes*, July–Dec., 1938, p. 641.

2 There were, of course, brilliant exceptions, notably Albert Matthews, who placed his extensive collections at the disposal of the editors; Herbert Horwill, author of Modern American Usage; Oxford, 1935, who lent them the dated quotations he had used in the preparation of that work; and C. W. Ernst of Boston, whose valuable notes, now in the Harvard library, were open to them. They also had the loan, from the American Dialect Society, of the materials for the third volume of Thornton's Glossary. In *American Speech*, in 1930 (The Historical Dictionary of American English in the Making, p. 37), Floy Perkinson Gates called attention to the difficulties caused by the lack of a more general response. " The chief concern at present," he said, " is the fact that the material on hand is not sufficient for the needs. More examples of the use of concrete words asso-

Work was begun soon after Dr. Craigie's arrival in Chicago,[1] and the first half dozen years were devoted to collecting materials. Then the difficult task of editing was begun, and in 1936 the first fascicle, running from *A* to *Baggage*, was published by the University of Chicago Press. The first volume, ending with *Corn Patch*, was finished in 1938; the second, ending with *Honk*, in 1940; the third, ending with *Record*, in 1942; and the fourth, completing the work, in 1943. The whole fills 2552 large double-column pages, beautifully printed by the university printers and substantially bound in maroon cloth, with gilt stamping. The father of the enterprise was the late John M. Manly (1865–1940), a native of Alabama who took his Ph.D. at Harvard in 1890, was head of the English department at the University of Chicago from 1929 to 1933, and made his chief mark as an editor of Chaucer. It was he, apparently, who induced the General Education Board, the American Council of Learned Societies and the University of Chicago to supply the necessary funds — about $350,000 for the editing and $70,000 for printing and promotion.[2] The print order was for 2500 copies, of which all but about 100 had been sold before the last volume was published. The price was fixed at $100 for the four volumes, but subscribers in advance got a substantial discount, and with review and presentation copies and dealers' profits counted out, the total receipts were but $120,000.[3] Unhappily, the plates of the earlier sections were destroyed before the work was completed, so a reprint was impossible, but plans are now afloat to reset the four volumes at the conclusion of World

---

ciated with the objects and activities of everyday America, and more instances of indigenous phrases, must be supplied. An examination of the material filed under the caption *back*, for instance, has shown that of the two hundred words collected, only one-tenth are ideally illustrated, while about one-fifth are represented by single quotations, or are without any first class historical evidence." But this alarm brought no onrush of volunteers. A direct appeal for "more coöperation in this work," saying that " it is necessary to emphasize again the need for all the outside help that can be given," was made by Sir William Craigie in *American Speech* in February, 1931,

and two years later, in July, 1933, Dr. Louise Pound attempted to arouse interest with an article in the *American Mercury*, but these efforts were likewise in vain.

1 His appointment had been hailed by the Chicago *Tribune* on Oct. 18, 1924 in an immortal headline: Midway Signs / Limey Prof. to / Dope Yank Talk.

2 In the later stages contributions were also made by the Rockefeller Foundation and by Mrs. Ruth Swift Maguire, a sister to Harold H. Swift, chairman of the university's board of trustees.

3 I take these figures from American English, Springfield (Mass.) *Republican*, Feb. 4, 1944.

War II and its sequelae.[1] After the publication of the first volume in 1936 Sir William returned to England, and thereafter his editing was carried on at long distance, with Dr. Hulbert in charge on the ground.[2]

The DAE lists about 26,000 terms and is by no means restricted to those originating in the United States. It also includes many words that, while old in English, have acquired new meanings in this country, or have come into wider use than in England, or have survived after becoming obsolete there. All save a few entries are supported by illustrative quotations, with dates, and whenever a word or phrase has a history in England the date of the first quotation in the NED is noted. Such are the " historical principles " of the title of the work. It must be manifest that the quotations, in many and perhaps most instances, do not show the actual age of the term: all they show is the date of its first appearance in print, or, more accurately, the date of the first appearance discovered by the dictionary's searchers. But this is a defect visible in all " historical " dictionaries, including the massive NED. It can be remedied more or less by the accumulation of new material, and in the case of the NED an attempt was made to push the histories back in time by a Supplement issued in 1933, five years after the main work was completed. But in the majority of cases the history of a given word or phrase must remain incomplete, for it would be impossible to read *all* the printed matter in English, and allowance must be made for the fact that a considerable body of it has disappeared altogether, and for the more important fact that many terms have a history before they are recorded in print, and that others are never recorded at all. There is no way to get round these difficulties, and the most a lexicographer can do is to be as diligent as possible. The editors of the DAE did not spare hard work, and the result is an extremely valuable dictionary, despite its defects. Its indispensability to the student of the national speech is well demonstrated by the number of times it is quoted in the present

---

1 Dictionary of American English, by Dorothea Kahn, *Christian Science Monitor* (Boston), April 1, 1944.

2 Talking United States, *Time*, Feb. 7, 1944. " Throughout the long printing process," says this *Time* article, " two sets of every proof went to Sir William. He corrected and returned both. Sometimes he did his final editing on proofs, a practise which unnerves typesetters. The mangling got so bad that the press almost lost its staff, and had to serve an ultimatum on the editors. To keep himself sane during his long devotion to thousands of little cards Co-Editor Hulbert refreshed himself with detective stories."

volume. Unhappily, some of the limitations that the editors set for themselves forced the omission of interesting and useful matter. They did not undertake to investigate American slang after 1875 or the American vocabulary in general after 1900, though they made exceptions in the cases of a few terms. Moreover, they gave relatively little attention to etymology, and avoided the indication of speech levels (always a vexatious business) whenever possible. But for all these lacks the DAE remains an impressive monument to the scholarship of its editors. Going through it page by page, I find occasional evidence that the chief of them was a foreigner, and hence a stranger to the national *Sprachgefühl*, but against that misfortune must be set the fact that he was an expert lexicographer whose personal prestige (especially after he was knighted in 1928), overcame at least to some extent the prevailing prejudice against the serious study of American speechways.[1]

As the successive fascicles of the DAE were published they were reviewed at length in the philological press, and many excellent suggestions were made for additions and improvements. Some of those who were active in this work of criticism and renovation were John A. Kouwenhoven of Bennington College, J. Louis Kuethe of the Johns Hopkins, and Miles L. Hanley of the University of Wisconsin. An elaborate review of the first two fascicles, running from *A* to *Blood*, printed by Dr. Hanley in *Dialect Notes* in July, 1937, raised

---

1 The Anglomaniacal Boston *Transcript* was among the first American newspapers to succumb. In Dec., 1924, soon after Sir William's appointment was announced, it published an editorial (reprinted in the Washington *Post*, Dec. 10) containing the following: " The dictionary marks a stage in American history, the recognition virtually official that there is such a thing as American English, a language and not a dialect. Sovereign states do not talk dialects, but possess a language. There will be some to rebel at this idea, as they have rebelled hitherto, now with perfect right, and now with too strong an academic slant." In other words, the American language became respectable the moment a British authority gave it his countenance. On Jan. 22, 1937, after the publication of the first fascicle of the dictionary, the London *Spectator* followed with: " Now after eleven years of labor this first part disposes once for all of transatlantic bickering, fear of contamination, and the hot suspicion that the American language was something wickedly thought up as a hoax by Mr. Mencken in his Baltimore den." Finally, L. H. Robbins wrote in the New York *Times Magazine*, Oct. 6, 1940, p. 11: "American English has been a long while in making the grade to respectability. Noah Webster boosted it, Richard H. Thornton gave it a hand, H. L. Mencken went to bat for it, and still certain classrooms and editoral offices figured that to write United States is sort of low-down, or something. The new dictionary may help to smear that dull notion."

a considerable pother, for it not only criticized severely the general plan of the dictionary, but also accused the editors of failing to give Thornton sufficient credit for their copious borrowings from him. This attack was met by Allen Walker Read, of the dictionary staff, in *Dialect Notes* for July–December, 1938. In *American Speech* for April, 1939, Dr. Hanley withdrew his general criticisms as "presumptuous and probably wrong-headed," but stuck to his contention that Thornton had been treated badly. On this point, fortunately, it is possible to disagree without rancor. So early as 1930, in a paper in *American Speech*,[1] Sir William Craigie had made specific acknowledgment of the dictionary's debt to Thornton and testified to "the great value of his labors," and in the preface to the first volume, dated 1938, he was given thanks for "frequently" supplying the work with "its earliest instances, as well as the illustration of many colloquialisms and rarer uses." For the rest, it seems to me that it may be taken as obvious that every dictionary must depend heavily on earlier workers in its special field.

The limitations set by the plan of the DAE have left the way open for further work in this field. It is very weak in slang and vulgar English, even for the period before 1875, and its 1900 deadline bars out a vast number of picturesque words and phrases on all levels. The average reader is bound to be critical of a lexicon of Americanisms, however meritorious otherwise, which omits such terms as *blurb, highbrow, jitney, flivver, rubberneck, boob, gob* (sailor) and *leatherneck*, and shows a considerable discretion in dealing with profanity and other loose language. There is, beside, the objection to its high cost, and the fact that no more copies are obtainable. To supply something at once more comprehensive, less burdened with historical apparatus, and salable at a more moderate price the University of Chicago Press has undertaken a " Dictionary of Americanisms," with the competent Dr. M. M. Mathews as editor. It will include every sort of Americanism save the most transient slang, and will bring the record up to the time of publication. It will also deal with etymologies and pronunciations, omitted by the DAE. How long it will take to complete this project remains to be seen.[2] Meanwhile, Allen Walker Read, another of the collaborators of Sir Wil-

1 The Progress of the Historical Dictionary of American English, p. 260.
2 It was announced by the University of Chicago Press on March 19, 1944.

See Lexicography at Chicago, by M. M. Mathews, *American Scholar*, Summer, 1944, pp. 369-71.

liam Craigie, continues at work upon his projected "Historical Dictionary of Briticisms," announced in 1938.[1] It will be devoted to "words found in England but not in America," *e.g., cinema, rook, squirearchy, pub, corn law, bloody* (as an expletive), *woolsack, beefeater, furze* and *hear, hear,* and will be fortified by dated quotations of the sort made familiar by Thornton, the NED and the DAE. Various other special dictionaries are also in progress. One is "A Dictionary of American English Grammar," by Dr. Janet Rankin Aiken of Columbia, and another is "A Dictionary of American Criminal Argots" by Dr. D. W. Maurer of the University of Louisville.[2] The need for special works confined to relatively small areas of space or time was admirably set forth by Sir William Craigie in Tract No. LVIII of the Society for Pure English.[3] He is himself engaged upon "A Dictionary of the Older Scottish Tongue," and other enterprises of the sort, dealing with American English, will probably follow soon or late. There is plenty of room, despite the DAE, for intensive studies, *inter alia,* of English in colonial America, of the novelties introduced into the language by the great movement into the West, of American trade argots, and of American slang.

The Linguistic Atlas of the United States and Canada is on a grandiose scale, and if it is ever completed will run to scores of large folio volumes, at a cost beyond the means of all save a small number of the richer libraries and private students. The first section, dealing with New England, began to appear in 1939 and was completed in 1943. It consists of three volumes, each in two parts, and the six immense books are made up of no less than 734 double-page maps. Along with the first volume, in 1939, there appeared a quarto "Handbook of the Linguistic Geography of New England," by Dr. Hans Kurath of Brown University. Dr. Kurath with Dr. Miles L. Hanley, formerly secretary and treasurer of the American Dialect Society, as his chief aide, has been in charge of the project since it was launched in 1929, and into it they and their collaborators have put an immense amount of hard work. The funds have been found by the American Council of Learned Societies, which also helped to finance the DAE, and grants in aid have been made by the Rockefeller Foundation, the Carnegie Corporation, the General Education

---

1 Plans for a Historical Dictionary of Briticisms, *American Oxonian,* July, 1938, pp. 186–90.

2 *Studies in Linguistics* (New Haven), April, 1943, pp. 1 and 3.
3 Oxford, 1941

Board, and various colleges and universities.[1] The atlas, in its early stages, attracted more attention from professional philologians than the DAE, but as the work has gone on its burdens have been thrown upon a relatively small group, made up mainly of associates and students of Dr. Kurath. I called attention in AL4 [2] to the fact that four of the seven men principally engaged upon it in 1936 had non-English surnames. Dr. Kurath himself is a native of Austria, but came to the United States in early life, and was educated at the Universities of Wisconsin, Texas and Chicago, the last-named of which made him Ph.D. in 1920. After teaching German at Texas, Northwestern and Ohio State, he became professor of the Germanic languages and general linguistics and chairman of the department of Germanic languages at Brown in 1932. Since 1942 he has been chairman of the university's division of modern languages. He reports in Jacques Cattell's " Dictionary of American Scholars " [3] that his chief interests are " American English; linguistic geography; American pronunciation; linguistic geography of New England; speech areas, settlement areas and culture areas in the United States." He is a man of indomitable energy, and is carrying on a vast work with a good deal less than an excess of help.[4]

The Linguistic Atlas attempts to record dialectal variations, not only in pronunciation but also in vocabulary. Thus Map No. 235 shows that the common round or littleneck clam (*Venus mercenaria*) is usually called a *quahog* along the New England coast, but that in

1 The American Council of Learned Societies, organized in 1919, is made up of representatives of the principal humanistic organizations of the United States, *e.g.*, the American Philosophical Society, the American Historical Association, the American Economic Association, the American Political Science Association, the American Oriental Society, the American Sociological Society, the Medieval Academy of America, the American Anthropological Association, the Linguistic Society of America, and the Modern Language Association.

2 p. 58, n. 2.

3 Lancaster, Pa., 1942.

4 The first linguistic atlas was Sprach-atlas des Deutschen Reiches, begun in 1876 and completed in 1926. In 1902–08 Jules Gilliéron and E. Edmont brought out an Atlas linguistique de la France, recording, for 638 localities, the dialectal forms of more than 2,000 words and phrases. There are also atlases for Italy and Italian Switzerland and for Japan, the former edited by Karl Jaberg and Jacob Jud and the latter by M. Tojo. Before World War II others were under way for the Slovak, Flemish and other dialects, and one covering the whole civilized world had been projected. See Linguistic Geography and the American Atlas, by Robert J. Menner, *American Speech*, Oct., 1933, pp. 3–7.

some places it is spoken of as a *round, hard, hardshell* or *hen* clam.[1]
Similarly, the soft or long-neck clam (*Mya arenaria*) is sometimes
called a *long,* or *soft-shell,* or *sand,* or *steaming* clam, or simply a
*clam.* Many other familiar terms show equally curious local variations. The common *lightning-bug* remains a *lightning-bug* until it
comes into the Boston *Sprachgebiet,* where it becomes a *fire-fly.*
*June-bug,* which is in wide use to the southward, is seldom encountered in New England, but *fire-bug* is recorded.[2] *Faucet* is the usual
New England name for the kitchen water-tap, but *spigot* seems to
be coming in from the southward, and *cock* and *tap* are also recorded.
A wooden spigot in a cider barrel is sometimes called a *spile.* The
towel used for drying dishes is usually a *dish-towel,* but in various
places it is a *cup-towel,* a *wiping-towel,* a *dish-cloth,* a *wiping-cloth,*
a *wiper,* a *dish-wiper* or a *cup-wiper.* Sometimes such variants appear in clusters on the maps, and sometimes they are scattered, probably in response to migrations. The lingering strength of Puritan
prudery is shown in the survival of a number of grotesque euphemisms for *bull,* e.g., *gentleman cow, top cow, cow critter, seed ox,*
*male animal, he-cow, roarer,* or *the beast, the brute, the sire, the male,*
*the masculine, the old man, the gentleman, the master* or *the he.*
Similarly, a stallion is sometimes a *sire,* a *male horse,* a *seed horse,* a
*stock horse,* a *top horse,* a *he-horse* or simply a *horse,* a ram is a *buck,*
a *sire,* a *male* or a *gentleman sheep,* and a boar is a *seed* or *top hog,*
a *gimlet pig,* a *borer,* a *sire* or a *stock hog.* The DAE neglects such
forms, and as a result the LA makes a novel and useful contribution
to the study of the American vocabulary.

But its chief stress is on pronunciations, and in that field it is considerably more interesting to the professional phonologist than to the
layman. This is mainly because it uses " a finely graded phonetic
alphabet based on that of the International Phonetic Association " —
an alphabet so extensive that no less than nineteen pages of the accompanying handbook are needed to explain it. How many separate
symbols and combinations of symbols are in it I have not attempted

1 *Quahog,* borrowed from the Pequot
Indian *p'quaughhaug,* is traced by
the DAE to 1799, but is probably
older. It has variants in *cohog,* traced
to 1788, and *pooquaw,* traced to 1848.
The field workers for the LA found
*pooquaw* surviving on Nantucket.

2 *Lightning-bug* is traced by the DAE
to 1778 and marked an Americanism. It is avoided in polite speech in
England because *bug,* there, signifies a bed-bug. But *June-bug* survives in various English dialects.

to determine, but the number must run to hundreds. More, it is used differently by the different field workers, and even by the same field worker at different times, and in consequence the lay student of the maps is confronted by a mass of strange characters that are frequently unintelligible and sometimes almost maddening. The truth is that the sounds of American speech are so numerous that it is next to impossible to represent all of them with complete accuracy by printed symbols. They vary not only in every pair of individuals, but also in the same individual at different times. The hopeful phonologists, however, do not despair of getting them on paper, and in consequence there is a constant effort to improve and augment the International Phonetic Alphabet, leading to the incessant invention of new symbols and combinations, many of them baffling even to phonologists. Even in its simplest form the IPA is almost as unilluminating to the layman as so much Mongolian, as anyone may discover by examining it in *American Speech*, where it is printed on the inside cover of every issue, along with an exposition that does not explain. It is dealt with a good deal more understandably in " A Pronouncing Dictionary of American English," by John S. Kenyon and Thomas A. Knott,[1] but even Kenyon and Knott fall very far short of making its interpretation facile.[2]

### 6. THE VIEWS OF WRITING MEN

" American authors," said Alexis de Tocqueville in 1835,[3] " may truly be said to live more in England than in their own country, since they constantly study the English writers and take them every day for their models. But such is not the case with the bulk of the population, which is more immediately subjected to the peculiar causes acting upon the United States. It is not then to the written, but to the spoken language that attention must be paid if we would detect the modifications which the idiom of an aristocratic people may undergo

[1] Springfield, Mass., 1944.
[2] Its difficulties are discussed in What Symbols Shall We Use?, by Leonard Bloomfield and George M. Bolling, *Language*, June, 1927, pp. 123–29.
[3] De la démocratie en Amérique; Paris, 1835, Vol. II, Book I, Chapter XVI. Translated as The Republic of the United States of America and Its Political Institutions, Reviewed and Examined, by Henry Reeves, with notes and a preface by John C. Spencer; New York, 1858. I am indebted here to Mr. Frank W. Buxton, editor of the Boston *Herald*.

when it becomes the language of a democracy." [1] Toqueville's visit
to the United States was made in 1831, and his remarks about American writers were certainly true for their time.[2] The two then principally admired and influential, Washington Irving and James Fenimore Cooper, were both regarded by their contemporaries, and
with sound reason, as Anglomaniacs. Cooper, to be sure, had been
moved, three years before, to protest (anonymously) against the
venomous and incessant English revilings of all things American,
including American speechways, but he seems to have regretted his
contumacy, for in " The American Democrat," which followed in
1838, he sneered at Americanisms in the best manner of the English
reviewers.[3] As for Irving, he never ceased to be subservient to English precept and example.[4] The revolt against both, as against English
libel and invective, was left to lesser men, the most effective of whom,
James K. Paulding, had been Irving's collaborator in *Salmagundi* in
1807, and had brought out a second series all his own in 1819. Paulding, a New Yorker from Dutchess county, in the heart of the Hudson Valley Little England, nevertheless took the American side in
the War of 1812, and hastened into print with a " Diverting History
of John Bull and Brother Jonathan " that must have had a powerful

1 The superior importance of the
spoken language, often overlooked
by writers on the subject, was
stressed again nearly a century later
by another French observer, Dr. A.
G. Feuillerat, professor of French
at Yale, in A Dictionary of the
American Language, *Yale Review*,
June, 1929, p. 830. " It is," he said,
" the most vital part of the language,
the one that will in the end impose
its laws when American civilization,
having severed all links from English civilization, may eventually desire to assert itself in the adoption
of a truly national mode of expression."

2 It is hardly necessary to add that
they were also true for the time immediately preceding. The neologisms of Joel Barlow (1754–1812),
noted in AL4, p. 16, were mainly
grotesque inventions that showed
no essentially American color. See
A Historical Note on American
English, by Leon Howard, *American Speech*, Sept., 1927, pp. 497–99.

Those of Philip Freneau (1752–1832)
were hardly more significant. See
Philippic Freneau, by S. B. Hustvedt,
*American Speech*, Oct., 1928, pp.
1–18. Those used by David Humphreys (1752–1818) have been discussed in Section 4 of this chapter.

3 Cooper also discussed the differences
between English and American
usage in Gleanings in Europe; London, 1836. See Cooper's Notes on
Language, by Robert E. Spiller,
*American Speech*, April, 1929, pp.
294–300.

4 In a postscript to the first English
edition of The Sketch Book, 1820,
he spoke of the English as " a public
which he has been accustomed, from
childhood, to regard with the highest feelings of awe and reverence,"
and added that he was " full of so-
licitude to deserve their approbation." I am indebted here to Conservatism in American Speech, by
George H. McKnight, *American
Speech*, Oct., 1925, p. 5.

effect at the time, for it remained in print until 1835 and was brought out again in 1867. This last edition had a preface by William I. Paulding, a son of the author. The younger man was apparently somewhat upset by the bitterness of his pa's satire, and sought to apologize for it as follows:

> He wrote in an atmosphere of acerbity, about matters then really of almost national [*sic!*] concern, though at the present day they can scarcely be made to appear in that light. He looked upon the whole detracting tribe [1] as mercenary calumniators of an entire people, with no claim to either courtesy or grace; and pitched upon the individual subjects of attack rather as types of the the different styles of the British objector than from any personal feeling or knowledge of the parties.

This, of course, was poppycock. Paulding's savage thrusts were aimed at easily recognized offenders, and he must have known some of them well enough. Thirteen years later, in 1825, he returned to the attack with a still more devastating buffoonery, this time under the title of " John Bull in America, or, The New Munchhausen." Here he singled out individual travelers so plainly that even his dunderhead son, writing forty-two years later, could not escape identifying them, *e.g.*, Thomas Ashe, Richard Parkinson and William Faux, to whom Thomas Hamilton was added in a new edition in 1837. The book still makes excellent reading, for it is a burlesque full of broad humors, with no squeamish pulling of punches. In his preface Paulding suggests waggishly that the author was probably William Gifford, editor of the *Quarterly Review* and grand master of all the English America-haters. Throughout he very adroitly parodies Gifford's condescending style, and is full of other devices that make the thing a capital example of a kind of writing that has been curiously little practised in the United States. Paulding, of course, got some help in his counterattack — from Edward Everett, from Timothy Dwight, from Robert Walsh,[2] and even from the timorous Cooper — but for twenty years he bore most of the burden and heat of the day. Everett (1794–1865) was a convert to the cause of American independence in speech, and had no truck with it until he vis-

---

1 *i.e.*, the English travelers who had begun to support the reviewers in reviling all things American.

2 Walsh (1784–1859) was a Baltimorean, and edited various magazines from 1811 to 1837. From 1845 to 1851 he was American consul at Paris. In 1819 he published An Appeal From the Judgments of Great Britain, an answer to the anti-American philippics of the *Quarterly Review*.

ited England in 1815, and then proceeded to Göttingen to take his doctorate. Says Allen Walker Read:

In his early years he imbibed the cultural colonialism that prevailed in Boston, but this he lost upon becoming acquainted with England. He became a leader in defense of the right of Americans to develop new words and to retain old ones, and held that in point of fact the state of English in America was sounder than that in England. He rebutted vigorously the attacks of small-minded British critics.[1]

Everett had several encounters with Gifford in London and stood up to him boldly, even to the extent of criticizing the English of the *Quarterly* itself. He was unfavorably impressed, not only by the multiplicity of English provincial dialects, but also by the accepted speech of the higher circles of London, and sneered impartially at the language of " a stout Lancashire yeoman " who shined his shoes in Liverpool and that of the royal Duke of Sussex. When, on returning home, he became editor of the *North American Review*, he denounced one of the slanderous English travelers of the time as a " miscreant " and another as a " swindler." Even when, in 1841, he was made American minister to England, he resisted stoutly the notorious tendency of that exalted post to make its incumbents limber-kneed, and came back in 1845 still convinced that American English was better than British English. He was the first, in fact, to suggest a dictionary of Briticisms. In one of his last publications, the " Mount Vernon Papers " of 1860, he quoted David Hume's prophecy to Edward Gibbon in 1767: " Our solid and increasing establishments in America . . . promise a superior stability and duration to the English language," and added: " What a contrast between these sensible remarks . . . and the sneers of English tourists and critics on the state of the English language as written and spoken in America." [2]

Cooper, as I have noted, blew both hot and cold — and not so briskly hot as cold. According to his biographer, Robert E. Spiller, the purpose of " Notions of the Americans," which was published in London in 1828 and in Philadelphia a little later in the same year, was twofold: " the misinformed and prejudiced criticism of the English must be silenced, and the slavish mental dependence of the Amer-

[1] Edward Everett's Attitude Towards American English, *New England Quarterly*, March, 1939, pp. 112–29.

[2] I am indebted here to Read, just cited.

ican mind upon British opinion must be brought to an end." [1] But he was so faint-hearted that he withheld his name from the book and ascribed it instead to an anonymous " traveling bachelor," seeking to make it appear that this bachelor was an Englishman. In " The American Democrat," which followed ten years later, he forgot altogether the denunciations of American speechways by the English, and devoted himself mainly to drawing up an indictment on his own account. In part he said:

> The common faults of American language are an ambition of effect, a want of simplicity, and a turgid abuse of terms. To these may be added ambiguity of expression. Many perversions of significations also exist, and a formality of speech, which, while it renders conversation ungraceful, and destroys its playfulness, seriously weakens the power of the language, by applying to ordinary ideas words that are suited only to themes of gravity and dignity.
>
> While it is true that the great body of the American people use their language more correctly than the mass of any other considerable nation, it is equally true that a smaller proportion than common attain to elegance in this accomplishment, especially in speech. Contrary to the general law in such matters, the women of the country have a less agreeable utterance than the men, a defect that great care should be taken to remedy, as the nursery is the birth-place of so many of our habits. . . .
>
> *Creek*, a word that signifies an *inlet* of the sea, or of a lake, is misapplied to running streams, and frequently to the *outlets* of lakes.[2] A *square* is called a *park;*[3] *lakes* are often called *ponds;*[4] and arms of the sea are sometimes termed *rivers.*[5]
>
> In pronunciation, the faults are still more numerous, partaking decidedly of provincialisms. The letter *u*, sounded like double *o* or *oo*, or like *i*, as in

1 Fenimore Cooper, Critic of His Times; New York, 1931, Ch. X. I am indebted here to Mr. F. Reed Alvord, of Hamilton, N. Y.

2 The American use of *creek* to designate any small stream had been remarked by various earlier commentators on American English, including Pickering, Theodoric Romeyn Beck, and Robley Dunglison. The DAE's first example is dated 1638. It is usually pronounced *crick*.

3 *Square*, in the sense of a small city park, is not an Americanism. The DAE traces it to 1698 in Philadelphia, but the NED finds an English example eleven years older. But *public square* seems to be of American origin, though the DAE, which traces it to 1786, does not so mark it. *Square*, in the sense of a city block or of the distance between one street and the next, apparently originated in Philadelphia, where William Penn laid out the city in rectangles — the first time this was done in America, and possibly in the world. All the other early American cities, at least in their older parts, have many crooked streets.

4 The use of *pond*, in England, is confined with few exceptions to artificial bodies of water, but it began to be applied to natural lakes in America so early as 1622, and in the name of Walden *Pond* it is familiar in that meaning to all readers of Thoreau.

5 The misapplication of *river* to arms of the sea is quite as common in England as in America; the lower Thames, for example, is actually an inlet of the North Sea, and is often called, more properly, an *estuary*.

vir*too*, for*tin*, for*tinate;* and *ew*, pronounced also like *oo*, are common errors. This is an exceedingly vicious pronunciation, rendering the language mean and vulgar. *New*, pronounced as *noo*, is an example,[1] and *few*, as *foo;* the true sounds are *nu* and *fu*, the *u* retaining its *proper* soft sound, and not that of *oo.* . . .[2]

False accentuation is a common American fault. *Ensign* (insin) is called en*syne*, and *engine* (injin), eng*yne.* Indeed, it is a common fault of narrow associations to suppose that words are to be pronounced as they are spelled.[3]

Many words are in a state of mutation, the pronunciation being unsettled even in the best society, a result that must often arise where language is as variable and undetermined as the English. To this class belong *clerk, cucumber* and *gold*, which are often pronounced as spelt, though it were better and more in conformity with polite usage to say *clark, cow*cumber (not cow*cum*ber), and *goold.*[4] For *looten*ant (lieutenant) there is not sufficient authority, the true pronunciation being *levten*ant. By making a familiar compound of this word, we see the uselessness of attempting to reduce the language to any other laws than those of the usages of polite life, for they who affect to say *looten*ant, do not say *lootenant-co-lo-nel*, but *iootenant-kurnel.*[5]

The polite pronunciation of *either* and *neither* is *i-ther* and *ni-ther*, and not *eether* and *neether.*[6] This is a case in which the better usage of the language has respected derivations, for *ei*, in German, is pronounced as in *height* and *sleight*, *ie* making the sound of *ee*. We see the arbitrary usages of the English, however, by comparing these legitimate sounds with those of the words *lieutenant colonel*, which are derived from the French, in which language the latter word is called *co-lo-nel*.

Cooper, always a snob, then proceeded to a discussion of the true inward and glorious meaning of *gentleman*, at that time laboring under derisory suspicions in the new Republic. He said:

1 A long and interesting discussion of the *u*-sound in American speech is in The English Language in America, by George Philip Krapp; New York, 1925, Vol. II, pp. 155 ff. Krapp shows that a *y*-sound, in American usage is seldom heard after *l* or *r*. After *d, t, th, n, sh, s* and *z* the current practice varies, with *y* the most marked in the Boston area and the South. Noah Webster was violently against it, and advocated the simple *u* in even *few*, making it rhyme with *zoo*.

2 Here Cooper, who was certainly no phonologist, is apparently trying to say that the *u* should be preceded by the *y*-sound, as in *pure* and *beauty*.

3 Where Cooper heard the pronunciation he denounced, or what his authority was for those he recommended, I do not know. *Injine* for

*engine* survives in the common speech of today, but certainly not *injin*, which is reserved for *Indian*. I have never heard *ensign* with the accent on the second syllable. In the common speech the first is heavily accented, and the second is drawn out. In the Navy the first is also accented, but the second is clipped.

4 These were all Eighteenth Century pronunciations, surviving in England. *Clark* survives to this day. *Cowcumber* is still occasionally heard in the United States, especially among rustics. In the early days *cucumber* was often so spelled. The DAE's first example is dated 1685, and its last (not consciously dialectical) 1742.

5 *Leftenant* is still the usual English pronunciation of *lieutenant*.

6 For *either* and *neither* see AL4, p. 341.

The word has a positive and limited signification. It means one elevated above the mass of society by his birth, manners, attainments, character, and social conditions. As no civilized society can exist without these social differences, nothing is gained by denying the use of the term. If *blackguards* were to be called *gentlemen*, and *gentlemen blackguards*, the difference between them would be as obvious as it is today. The word *gentleman* is derived from the French *gentilhomme*, which originally signified one of noble birth. This was at a time when the characteristics of the condition were never found beyond a caste. As society advanced, ordinary men attained the qualifications of nobility, without that of birth, and the meaning of the word was extended. It is now possible to be a *gentleman* without birth, though, even in America, where such distinctions are purely conditional, they who have birth, except in extraordinary instances, are classed with *gentlemen*. To call a laborer, one who has neither education, manners, accomplishments, tastes, associations, nor any one of the ordinary requisites, a *gentleman*, is just as absurd as to call one who is thus qualified a *fellow*. The word must have some especial signification, or it would be synonymous with *man*. One may have *gentlemanlike* feelings, principles and appearance, without possessing the liberal attainments that distinguish the *gentleman*. Least of all does money alone make a *gentleman*, though, as it becomes a means of obtaining the other requisites, it is usual to give it a place in the claims of the class. Men may be, and often are, very rich, without having the smallest title to be deemed *gentlemen*. A man may be a distinguished *gentleman*, and not possess as much money as his own footman.

This word, however, is sometimes used instead of the old terms, *sirs*, *my masters*, &c., &c., as in addressing bodies of men. Thus we say *gentlemen* in addressing a public meeting, in compliance, and as, by possibility, some *gentlemen* may be present. This is a license that may be tolerated, though he who should insist that all present were, as individuals, *gentlemen*, would hardly escape ridicule.

What has just been said of the word *gentleman* is equally true with that of *lady*. The standard of these two classes, rises as society becomes more civilized and refined; the man who might pass for a gentleman in one nation, or community, not being able to maintain the same position in another.

The inefficiency of the effort to subvert things by names, is shown in the fact that, in all civilized communities, there is a class of men, who silently and quietly recognize each other as *gentlemen;* who associate together freely and without reserve, and who admit each other's claims without scruple or distrust. This class may be limited by prejudice and arbitrary enactments, as in Europe, or it may have no other rules than those of taste, sentiment and the silent laws of usage, as in America.

The same observations may be made in relation to the words *master* and *servant*. He who employs laborers, with the right to command, is a *master*, and he who lets himself to work, with an obligation to obey, a *servant*. Thus there are *house*, or *domestic servants*, *farm servants*, *shop servants*, and various other *servants;* the term *master* being in all these cases the correlative.

In consequence of the *domestic servants* of America having once been Negro slaves, a prejudice has arisen among the laboring class of the whites, who not only dislike the term *servant*, but have also rejected that of *master*. So far has this prejudice gone, that in lieu of the latter, they have resorted to the use of

the word *boss,* which has precisely the same meaning in Dutch! ¹ How far a
subterfuge of this nature is worthy of a manly and common sense people, will
admit of question.

A similar objection may be made to the use of the word *help,* which is not
only an innovation on a just and established term, but which does not properly
convey the meaning intended. They who aid their masters in the toil may be
deemed *helps,* but they who perform all the labor do not assist, or help to do
the thing, but they do it themselves. A man does not usually hire his cook to
*help* him cook his dinner, but to cook it herself. Nothing is therefore gained,
while something is lost in simplicity and clearness, by the substitution of new
and imperfect terms for the long established words of the language. In all cases
in which the people of America have retained the *things* of their ancestors,
they should not be ashamed to keep the *names.*

The love of turgid expressions is gaining ground, and ought to be corrected.
One of the most certain evidences of a man of high breeding is his simplicity
of speech; a simplicity that is equally removed from vulgarity and exaggeration.
He calls a spade a *spade.* His enunciation, while clear, deliberate and dignified,
is totally without strut, showing his familiarity with the world, and, in some
degree, reflecting the qualities of his mind, which is polished without being
addicted to sentimentalism, or any other bloated feeling. He never calls his wife
his *lady,* but his *wife,* and he is not afraid of lessening the dignity of the human
race by styling the most elevated and refined of his fellow creatures *men* and
*women.* He does not say, in speaking of a dance, that " the attire of the *ladies*
was exceedingly elegant and peculiarly becoming at the late assembly," but that
" the *women* were well dressed at the last ball; " nor is he apt to remark " that
the Rev. Mr. G. —— gave us an elegant and searching discourse the past *Sabbath,*"
but that " the parson preached a good sermon last *Sunday.*" ²

Cooper's plea for " simplicity of speech, . . . totally without strut
. . . or any other bloated feeling," had little effect upon his contemporaries, or indeed upon himself. All of them were still under
the influence of the Johnsonian or bow-wow style of the Eighteenth
Century, and not many of them attempted to make any use of the
new and vivid native vocabulary that was flourishing about them.
Bryant, born in 1794 and surviving until 1878, was essentially a con-
formist,³ and after he became editor of the New York *Evening Post*

1 *Boss* is obviously derived from the
Dutch *baas,* but though it must have
been familiar, at least in New York,
in the Seventeenth Century, it did
not come into general use until the
Nineteenth. The DAE's first example is dated 1806. It was propagated
by the proletarian self-assertion that
preceded the opening of the first
Century of the Common Man, with
Jackson's election in 1828.

2 *Sabbath* for *Sunday* was an inherit-
ance from the Puritans. It survived
generally until after the Civil War,
and is still used by some of the ultra-
pious. Cooper's chapter On Language is reprinted in full in Mathews,
pp. 123–29.

3 In 1868 he became president of a
primeval National Institute of Letters, Arts and Sciences which proposed, among other things, to police
the language. The chairman of its
executive committee was the im-

he drew up a list of terms prohibited to his staff which included some
of the Americanisms denounced by the English reviewers, *e.g.*, *reliable, balance, standpoint, bogus, lengthy, to jeopardize, to donate* and
*to progress* — all of them now perfectly sound American, and even
sound English. This *Index* was imitated in many other American
newspaper offices, and its blight is not altogether thrown off to this
day.[1] The younger Americans of the classical period showed but
little more interest in the evolving national speechways, and Joseph
Warren Beach was hardly guilty of hyperbole when he called them
" cultivated and anemic writers milk-fed upon the culture of England." [2] Mamie Meredith has directed attention to the fact that Emerson, in the seclusion of his diaries, was not above a certain bold ex-
perimentation in words,[3] but in his published work he wrote like a
university-trained Englishman — to be sure, like one of unusual
originality and force, but still like an Englishman. It may be true, as
Oliver Wendell Holmes said, that " The American Scholar," 1837,
was " the intellectual declaration of independence " of America, but
if so the independence it declared was a good deal more in ideas than
in speech. Poe and Melville delighted in strange words, but very few
of them came out of the rising American vocabulary of their time.
In a list of 180 terms found in Melville before the earliest dates of their
recording from other sources, compiled by James Mark Purcell in
1941,[4] only a small number are properly describable as Americanisms:

placable pedant, Richard Grant
White. John Bigelow described the
project as one designed " to throw
the French Academy into the
shade." See American Projects for
an Academy to Regulate Speech, by
Allen Walker Read, *Publications of
the Modern Language Association*,
Dec., 1936, pp. 1141–79.

1 I should add in fairness that some of
the other words that Bryant banned
belonged to the worst newspaper
jargon of the time, and probably de-
served to be frowned upon, *e.g.*,
*above* and *over* for *more than*, *casket* for *coffin*, *claimed* for *asserted*,
*decease* as a verb, *devouring element*
for *fire*, *to inaugurate* for *to begin*, *in
our midst*, *juvenile* for *boy*, *lady* for
*wife*, *to loan* for *to lend*, *Mrs. Governor*, *ovation*, *party* for *person*, *posted*

for *informed*, *rendition* for *performance*, *Rev.* without the *the*, *to
state* for *to say*, and *on the tapis*. But
he also prohibited such terms as *to
beat* for *to defeat*, *to collide*, *to graduate* for *to be graduated*, *House* for
*House of Representatives*, *humbug*,
*loafer*, *rowdy* and *on yesterday*. *On
yesterday* still appears every day in
the *Congressional Record*, and the
rest are in impeccable American use.
2 The Outlook for American Prose;
Chicago, 1926, p. 21.
3 Emersonian        Unconventionalities,
*American Speech*, Oct., 1936, p. 272.
4 Melville's Contribution to English,
*Publications of the Modern Lan-
guage Association*, Sept., 1941, pp.
797–808. Under the same title Purcell corrected a few errors in *American Speech*, Oct., 1943, p. 211. See

the overwhelming majority are either borrowings from or adaptations of the argot of English sailors, or nonce-words of no significance, and usually of very small ingenuity. As for Poe, a similar study published by J. H. Neumann in 1943 [1] shows even rarer inventions of any substance, and none that reveal genuinely American influence or have got into the common store. Poe had a weakness for the grandiloquent, and was thus fond of such monsters as *circumgyratory, concentralization, paragraphism* and *supremeness,* but his actual vocabulary was relatively small; indeed, Robert L. Ramsay estimates that in his poetry it was limited to between 3,100 and 3,200 words.[2] He is often credited with *tintinnabulation,* which occurs in " The Bells," 1831, but it is really no more than an obvious derivative of a Latin loan traced by the NED to 1398.[3] Poe used the phrase *American language* in " The Rationale of Verse," and denounced Noah Webster, in " Fifty Suggestions," as " more English than the English —*plus Arabe qu'en Arabie,*" but his other discussions of language, in " Marginalia " and elsewhere, showed that he was a rigid purist, and could imagine no standards for American English save those in favor in England. Nor could Hawthorne,[4] or Thoreau, or Longfellow, or Holmes.

Whitman, the precise contemporary of Melville, was more language-conscious than any of the other writers so far mentioned, and it fitted into his romantic confidence in democracy to praise the iconoclastic and often uncouth American speechways of his time. Two formal treatises on the subject survive, beside a number of

---

also Some Americanisms in Moby Dick, by William S. Ament, *American Speech,* June, 1932, pp. 365–67.

1 Poe's Contributions to English, *American Speech,* Feb., 1943, pp. 73–74.

2 Review of A Concordance of the Poetical Works of Edgar Allan Poe, by Brandford A. Booth and Claude E. Jones; Baltimore, 1941, in *American Speech,* April, 1942, p. 112. Ramsay handles this concordance roughly; it is, in fact, of very small value. It should be remembered that Poe's poetical output was not large, and that this fact may reduce his apparent vocabulary.

3 Six other derivatives are run back

by the NED to dates earlier than 1831: *tintinnabulatory* to 1827, *tintannabulism* to 1826, *tintinnabulant* to 1812, *tintinnabulous* to 1791, *tintinnabulary* to 1787 and *tintinnabular* to 1767.

4 Hawthorne may have been the author of three articles on " correct English " which appeared in the *American Magazine of Useful and Entertaining Knowledge,* June and Sept., 1835, and June, 1836. This magazine was published by S. G. Goodrich, for whom he had worked off and on since *c.* 1828. He was its editor in 1836 at $500 a year. I am indebted here to Mr. John H. Kouwenhoven of New York.

notes and reports of conversations. In November, 1885, he contributed a paper to the *North American Review* under the title of " Slang
in America," and three years later he included it in " November
Boughs." [1] Thirty years before, in the period of " Leaves of Grass,"
he prepared a lecture entitled " An American Primer," and at various
times afterward he seems to have devoted himself to its revision. But
it was apparently never delivered, and the manuscript did not get
into print until 1904, twelve years after his death, when it was published in the *Atlantic Monthly* by his faithful retainer, Horace Traubel.[2] Both the paper and the lecture, like all of Whitman's prose
writings, are somewhat vague and flowery, but their central purpose
remains plain enough, to wit, to make war upon the old American
subservience to Eighteenth Century English pedantry, and open the
way for the development of a healthy and vigorous autochthonous
language in the United States. In " Slang in America " he said:

> Language, be it remember'd, is not an abstract construction of the learn'd,
> or of dictionary-makers, but is something arising out of the work, needs, ties,
> joys, affections, tastes of long generations of humanity, and has its bases broad
> and low, close to the ground. Its final decisions are made by the masses, people
> nearest the concrete, having most to do with actual land and sea.

He labored this theme in many conversations with Traubel in
Mickle street, and once said:

> I sometimes think the " Leaves " is only a language experiment — that it is
> an attempt to give the spirit, the body, the man, new words, new potentialities
> of speech — an American, a cosmopolitan (the best of America is the best
> cosmopolitanism) range of self-expression. The new world, the new times, the
> new peoples, the new vistas, need a tongue according — yes, what is more, will
> have such a tongue — will not be satisfied until it is evolved.

To which may be added the following from " An American
Primer ":

1 Philadelphia, 1888.
2 April, pp. 460 *ff.* Traubel says that
he found an alternative title in Whitman's papers, to wit, The Primer of
Words: for American Young Men
and Women, for Literati, Orators,
Teachers, Musicians, Judges, Presidents, &c. He adds: " Whitman told
me that when the idea of the American Primer first came to him it was
for a lecture. He wrote at this thing
in the early 50s — even as far along
as 1856–57. And there is evidence that
he made brief additions to it from
time to time in the ten years that followed. But after 1855, when he succeeded in issuing the first edition of
Leaves of Grass, some of his old
plans were abandoned — this lecture
scheme with others — , and certain
new plans were formulated. The
Primer was thenceforth, as a distinct
project, held in abeyance." An
American Primer was reprinted in
an edition of 500 copies; Boston,
1904.

The words continually used among the people are, in numberless cases, not words used in the dictionaries by authority. There are just as many words in daily use, not inscribed in the dictionary, and seldom or never in print. Also, the forms of grammar are never persistently obeyed, and cannot be. The Real Dictionary will give all words that exist in use, the bad words as well as any. The Real Grammar will be that which declares itself a nucleus of the spirit of laws, even violating them if necessary.

But these bold words found little realization in Whitman's actual practise. His prose certainly fell very far short of colloquial ease. In his early days he wrote the dingy, cliché-laden journalese of the era, and after his discovery of Carlyle he indulged himself in a heavy and sometimes absurd imitation of the Scotsman's gnarled and tortured style. Not many specimens of the popular speech that he professed to admire ever got into his writings, either in prose or in verse. He is remembered for a few, *e.g.*, *yawp* and *gawk*, but for a few only.[1] His own inventions were mainly cacophonous miscegenations of roots and suffixes, *e.g.*, *scientism, presidentiad, civilizee, venerealee, erysipalite, to memorandize, diminute* (adjective), *omnigenous, aidancy, poemet* and *infidelistic*, and not one of them has ever gained any currency. Moreover, more than half his innovations were simply borrowings from finishing-school French, with a few examples of Spanish and Italian added for good measure. Dr. Louise Pound, in a study of his French loans,[2] suggests that he must have picked them up during his brief newspaper days in New Orleans, but it is hard to believe that they were used with any frequency by journalistic colleagues who actually knew French. Most of them were what Dr. Pound, in another place, describes as " social words," which is to say, pearls from the vocabulary of the primeval society editors of his time, *e.g.*, *coiffeur, restaurateur, mon cher, mélange, rapport, faubourg, début, distingué, morceau, bijouterie, résumé, ensemble, insouciance, cortège, haut ton, soirée, ennui, aplomb, douceur* and *éclat*.[3] A number of these have been naturalized, but I doubt that Whitman had anything to do with the process. Nor did he succeed any better with his Spanish and Italian favorites, *e.g.*, *camerado, libertad, Americano,*

---

1 *Yawp*, the most famous, is commonly supposed to have been his invention, but the DAE traces it to 1835, when it was used by J. H. Ingraham in The South-West. *Gawk* has been in use in England since the early Eighteenth Century.

2 Walt Whitman and the French Language, *American Speech*, May, 1926, p. 425.

3 Poe had a weakness for terms of the same sort, *e.g.*, *recherché, outré, dégagé* and *littérateur*. See The French of Edgar Allan Poe, by Edith Philips, *American Speech*, March, 1927, pp. 270–74.

*romanza* and *cantabile*. Like Poe, he was fond of airing foreign words that struck him as tony, but like Poe again, he wrote a stiff and artificial English, and seldom showed any command of the vernacular riches that he professed to admire.[1]

Of the lesser American writers who flourished in the era running from the publication of " Thanatopsis " in 1817 to that of " Leaves of Grass " in 1855, only the professed humorists showed any active interest in American speechways. N. P. Willis, like J. K. Paulding, resented the gross libels of all things American in the current English reviews and travel books, and sought revenge in 1835, in his " Pencillings By the Way," by giving the English a dose of their own medicine. This work, which still repays reading, is an impudent and often satirical picture of the English life of the time, especially on the more pretentious intellectual levels, and in it there are some effective hits, as when, for example, Willis compliments the second Lord Grenville, who had visited America, on speaking " American English . . . with all the careless correctness and fluency of a vernacular tongue, [and without] a particle of the cockney drawl, half Irish and half Scotch, with which many Englishmen speak." " Pencillings By the Way " made a considerable uproar in England, and was attacked violently by the *Quarterly Review*,[2] but it seems to have been read, and there was an English reprint so recently as 1943.[3] It would be, however, an exaggeration to call Willis an advocate of American independence in speech; on the contrary, he wrote in what he regarded as the best English fashion of the period, and disdained the neologisms that were beginning to show themselves in the work of the popular humorists. His own contributions to the vocabulary were such banalities as *biggerness, haughty culture* (for *high cul-*

1 His unhappy efforts to devise new words of English material are described in Walt Whitman's Neologisms, by Louise Pound, *American Mercury*, Feb., 1925, pp. 199–201. Dr. Pound apparently includes *sit*, the infinitive of the verb used as a noun, as one of them. It was actually borrowed from the argot of printers, and is listed in Charles T. Jacobi's Printers' Vocabulary as an abbreviation of *situation*. Whitman's writings on language are well summarized in Walt Whitman and the American Language, by Leon How-

ard, *American Speech*, Aug., 1930, pp. 441–51. In A Study of Whitman's Diction, *University of Texas Studies in English*, No. 16, 1936, pp. 115–24, Rebecca Coy shows that the Americanisms in Leaves of Grass are not numerous.

2 The savagely anti-American Gifford had retired as editor in 1824 and died in 1826, but his heirs and assigns were carrying the torch.

3 In a series called Live Books Resurrected, edited by L. Stanley Jast. It was reviewed in the London *Times Literary Supplement*, May 15, 1943.

*ture*), *other-people-ness*, *un-get-about-able*, *superfinery*, *whirlsated* (confused), *Caesar-or-nobody-dom* and *to brickify*. He was denounced for these confections by a reviewer in *Putnam's Monthly* twenty years after the appearance of " Pencillings By the Way." [1] But the same reviewer revealed the prissy standards still prevailing in the American reviews by denouncing him likewise, but quite irrationally, for " the recurring substitution of a passive verb, with a preposition and the objective case of the actor, instead of the usual active verb with the actor in the nominative — thus: ' That was repeatedly heard *by me* ' instead of ' I repeatedly heard that.' " No one, as yet, has searched the American reviews of the pre-Civil War era, as the English reviews have been searched by Pickering, Cairns and Read, but some light upon their position with regard to American English is to be found in a paper by Read, dealing, *inter alia*, with their treatment of the early American dictionaries.[2] On the appearance of Noah Webster's first dictionary in 1806, it was generally denounced for its inclusion of Americanisms, and the same treatment was given to the works of John Elliott, Caleb Alexander, William Woodbridge and the American Samuel Johnson, Jr., for somewhat less conspicuous offendings. Both the *American Review* and the *Monthly Anthology* protested bitterly against the listing of *composuist*, a substitute for *composer*, then " much used " according to Pickering, " at some of our colleges," but now happily obsolete. The *Monthly Magazine* laid down the doctrine that, save for a few " technical and scientific terms, . . . any other species of American words are manifest corruptions, and to embalm these by the lexicographic process would only be a waste of time and abuse of talents." Rather curiously, two eminent pedagogues of the time took the other line. One was Jeremiah Atwater, president of Middlebury College in Vermont, who declared that " local words are always with propriety inserted in dictionaries, especially when marked as being local." The other was Timothy Dwight, president of Yale, already mentioned as giving aid and comfort to Paulding. He drew up, in 1807, and not only signed himself but had nine members of his faculty sign, a letter to Webster saying:

1 Feb., 1855, p. 213.
2 The Development of Faith in the Dictionary in America, read before the Present Day English section of the Modern Language Association at Philadelphia, Dec. 29, 1934. So far as I am aware this paper has not been published, but I have had access to it by the courtesy of the author.

The insertion of local terms in your small dictionary we approve. No good reason can be given why a person who meets with words of this kind should not be able to find their meaning in a dictionary — the only place where they can usually be found at all.

It was not, however, such scholastic bigwigs as Webster and Dwight who forced the seasoning of American writing with the pungent herbs of the vernacular, nor was it such literary rebels as Paulding and Whitman; it was the lowly humorists whose buffooneries began to appear in the newspapers soon after the War of 1812, and whose long line culminated in James Russell Lowell and Samuel L. Clemens. The first of them whose work got between covers was Seba Smith, who published his " Letters of Major Jack Downing " in 1830. Of him Will D. Howe has said:

> Almost immediately after his graduation from Bowdoin College in 1818 he began to contribute a series of political articles in the New England dialect to the papers of Portland, Maine. These illustrated fairly well the peculiarities of New England speech and manners, and doubtless had a great influence in encouraging similar sketches in other parts of the country. Smith was in several ways a pioneer. He led the way for " The Biglow Papers " and all those writings which have exploited back-country New England speech and character. He anticipated, in the person of Jack Downing, confidant of Jackson, David Ross Locke's Petroleum V. Nasby, confidant of Andrew Johnson. He was the first in America, as Finley Peter Dunne, with his Mr. Dooley, is the latest, to create a homely character and through him to make shrewd comments on politics and life.[1]

Smith was imitated at once by Charles A. Davis, who borrowed not only his method and manner but also his Jack Downing, and in a little while he had a long stream of followers — Augustus Baldwin Longstreet, Charles Henry Smith (Bill Arp), George W. Bagby, George W. Harris (Sut Lovengood), Joseph G. Glover, Frances Miriam Whitcher (the Widow Bedott), Samuel G. Goodrich (Peter Parley), Benjamin P. Shillaber (Mrs. Partington), Thomas C. Haliburton (Sam Slick),[2] Charles G. Halpine (Private Miles O'Reilly),

---

1 The Cambridge History of American Literature; New York, 1918; Vol. II, p. 151. See also American Idiom in the Major Downing Letters, by Ernest E. Leisy, *American Speech*, April, 1933, pp. 78–79.

2 Haliburton was not an American, but a Nova Scotian, and his Sam Slick, the Yankee clock peddler, was depicted with British bias. He was frequently accused of misrepresentations, not only in character but also in speech. Said an anonymous writer in *Putnam's Monthly*, Aug., 1854, p. 227: " He writes tales and sketches of American life on purpose for the English market. He knows about as much of genuine Yankee character as one half the comic actors who attempt to per-

Charles G. Leland (Hans Breitmann), Henry W. Shaw (Josh Billings), David R. Locke (Petroleum V. Nasby), Charles Farrar Browne (Artemus Ward), Mortimer Thompson (Philander Doesticks),[1] and George H. Derby (John Phoenix). Most of these created characters which, like Smith's Major Downing, were their spokesmen, and as humorists multiplied their characters began to represent many national types — the Southern cracker, the Western frontiersman, the Negro, the Irishman, the German, as well as the New Englander. The result was a steady infiltration of the new American words and ways of speech, and the laying of foundations for a genuinely colloquial and national style of writing.[2] The first masterpiece of this national school was Lowell's "The Biglow Papers," Series I of which appeared in 1848. Lowell not only attempted to depict with some care the peculiar temperament and point of view of the rustic New Englander; he also made an extremely successful effort to report

---

sonate it in the stage, *i.e.,* he knows a few enormous exaggerations and nothing more. His representations, however, are received in England as the true thing, and nine out of ten of the current slang expressions which the English ascribe to Yankees are taken from his books, never having been heard of in Yankee land. They strike a New Englander as oddly as they do John Bull himself, and are most likely inventions of the author." Haliburton, who was a judge in Nova Scotia from 1828 to 1856, contributed his first Sam Slick sketches to the *Nova Scotian* of Halifax in 1835. Collections of them were brought out in 1837, 1838 and 1840. Despite their prejudiced tone they were widely reprinted in American newspapers.

1 A study of words invented by Thompson or borrowed by him from the popular speech of his time is in Q. K. Philander Doesticks, P. B., Neologist, by J. Louis Kuethe, *American Speech*, April, 1937. In it he is credited with introducing *gutter-snipe, forty-rod, baggage-smasher, brass-knuckles, bucksaw, citified, muley-cow, hot stuff* and various other now familiar Americanisms. On the appearance of the

DAE it turned out that Thompson had been anticipated in some of these, but in other cases his priority was maintained. In some instances the DAE's first examples are from his writings.

2 Some of these humorists, notably Browne and Leland, had considerable successes in England, and, as R. H. Heindel says in The American Impact on Great Britain, 1898–1914; Philadelphia, 1940, p. 305, "broke down the resistance to Americanisms." But that breaking down, of course, was only partial and only transitory. The English reviewers, in the main, sneered at them, despite their popularity. In *Every Saturday* (Boston), July 10, 1869, p. 52, is a reprint of a curious attack on Leland's German dialect verses from an unnamed English review. It dismisses them loftily as "written in the jargon of a German clown who has half learned English" and actually undertakes to translate one of the most famous of them, Han's Breitmann's Barty, into orthodox English! A good account of the early humorists, with special reference to their sources, is in Native American Humor (1800–1900), by Walter Blair; New York, 1937.

Yankee speech.[1] His brief prefatory treatise on its peculiarities of pronunciation, though it included a few observations that had been made long before him by Witherspoon, was the first to deal with the subject with any approach to comprehensiveness, and in his introduction to Series II he expanded this preliminary note to a long and interesting essay, with a glossary of nearly 200 terms. In that essay he said:

> In choosing the Yankee dialect I did not act without forethought. It had long seemed to me that the great vice of American writing and speaking was a studied want of simplicity, that we were in danger of coming to look on our mother-tongue as a dead language, to be sought in the grammar and dictionary rather than in the heart, and that our only chance of escape was by seeking it at its living sources among those who were, as Scottowe says of Major-General Gibbons, "divinely illiterate." . . . Whether it be want of culture, for the highest outcome of that is simplicity, or for whatever reason, it is certain that very few American writers or speakers wield their native language with the directness, precision and force that are common as the day in the mother country. We use it like Scotsmen, not as if it belonged to us, but as if we wished to prove that we belonged to it, by showing our intimacy with its written rather than with its spoken dialect. And yet all the while our popular idiom is racy with life and vigor and originality, bucksome (as Milton used the word) to our new occasions, and proves itself no mere graft by sending up new suckers from the old root in spite of us. . . . The first postulate of an original literature is that a people should use their language instinctively and unconsciously, as if it were a living part of their growth and personality, not as the mere torpid boon of education or inheritance. Even Burns contrived to write very poor verse and prose in English. Vulgarisms are often only poetry in the egg.[2]

Unhappily, Lowell labored under the delusion that he had sufficiently excused the existence of any given Americanism when he had proved that it was old English, and so a large part of his essay was given over to that popular but vain exercise. But despite his folly in this respect and his timorousness in other directions [3] he did a great service to the common tongue of the country, and must be

1 The significance of The Biglow Papers as a philological document was quickly recognized. Said an anonymous writer in *Putnam's Monthly*, May, 1853, p. 554: "This is an unmistakably American performance. . . . It is a valuable repository of the dialectic peculiarities of New England."

2 In the Policies of the Dictionary of American English, *Dialect Notes*, July–Dec., 1938, p. 630. Allen Walker Read called this essay "probably the most important discussion of American English in the Nineteenth Century."

3 He permitted himself, for example, to denounce slang on the ground that it "is always vulgar," and he thought it worth while to defend Hosea Biglow at some length against the idiotic charge of "speaking of sacred things familiarly."

numbered among its true friends.[1] His writing in his own person, however, showed but little sign of it: he gradually developed a very effective prose style, but it did not differ materially from that of his New England contemporaries. The business of introducing the American language to good literary society was reserved for Clemens — and, as everyone knows, Clemens had a long, long wait below the salt before it ever occurred to any of the accepted authorities of his generation that he was not a mere zany like Browne and Locke, but a first-rate artist. Unless my records are in error, the first academic dignitary to admit formally that he belonged at the head of the table was the late William Lyon Phelps, who did so in "Essays on Modern Novelists" in 1910, just as old Mark departed this earth for bliss eternal.[2] Since then his importance has come to be generally recognized, even by the authors of school and college " literature " books, though a number of the heirs and converts to the standards of the Haircloth Age, notably Van Wyck Brooks, have continued to hack away at him. In 1929 the members of the English department of the Graduate School of the University of Missouri, led by Dr. Robert L. Ramsay and Miss (later Dr.) Frances Guthrie Emberson, undertook an exhaustive study of his vocabulary, and nine years later it was completed. It bears the title of " A Mark Twain Lexicon " and is a very interesting and valuable work,[3] for it shows that Mark not only made free use of the swarming Ameri-

1 Speech was not the main theme of his On a Certain Condescension in Foreigners, 1869, but that famous essay did not altogether overlook it. The Englishman coming to America, he said in it, felt himself " defrauded, nay, even outraged" because he found " a people speaking what he admits to be something like English, and yet so very different from (or, as he would say, to) those he left at home. . . . 'How am I vulgar?' asks the culprit, shudderingly. 'Because thou art not like unto Us,' answers Lucifer, Son of the Morning, and there is no more to be said. . . . We did not pronounce the diphthong *ou* as they did, and we said *eether* and not *eyther*, following therein the fashion of our ancestors, who unhappily could bring over no English better than Shakespeare's."

2 I hailed the marvel in The Greatest of American Writers, *Smart Set*, June, 1910, pp. 153–54. It was an astonishing event indeed, and without a parallel until May, 1944, when the empurpled illuminati of the American Academy of Arts and Letters discovered at last that Theodore Dreiser was an important American novelist, and paid him $1,000 in cash, apparently as an indemnity for 44 years' lofty neglect of him.

3 *University of Missouri Studies*, Jan. 1, 1938. Dr. Emberson's Mark Twain's Vocabulary: A General Survey was published in the same series, July 1, 1935. In 1930 the Mark Twain Society of Webster Groves. Mo., published A Vocabulary Study of The Gilded Age, by Alma Borth Martin. It is of small value and is defaced by a donkeyish foreword by Hamlin Garland.

canisms (and especially the Westernisms) of his time, but also contributed a number of excellent inventions to the store. In a long preliminary note there is a detailed study of his use of both sorts cf words and phrases. He was the first American author of world rank to write a genuinely colloquial and native American; there is little if any trace in his swift and vivid prose of classical English example. He had a magnificent artistry, and few other Americans have written so well, but, once he had thrown off the journalese of his first years, he achieved his effects without any resort to the conventional devices. Drs. Ramsay and Emberson, in an elaborate preface to their lexicon, attempt a detailed analysis of his vocabulary. They show that of the 7802 words they list as characteristic no less than 2329 appear to be Americanisms, with 2743 others possibly deserving that classification. Unhappily, their study was made before the publication of the DAE was begun, but it is highly probable that a reëxamination of the materials today would produce relatively little change in these figures, for of all the authors listed in the DAE's bibliography Mark Twain occupies by far the largest space — more than Bret Harte, the runner-up,[1] and a great deal more than Cooper, Holmes, Howells, Lowell or the whole corps of early humorists.[2] Save for "Personal Recollections of Joan of Arc," a calculated *tour de force*, somewhat toilsomely out of character, there is not a book of his that did not yield something to the DAE's searchers, and some of his major books yielded rich stores. "The flavor of his style," say Ramsay and Emberson, "is always racy of the American soil, and it owes this quality largely to the prodigious store of native phrases and idioms which he employs." Nor did he employ them without deliberate purpose. He was, in fact, always very language-conscious, and wrote upon the subject not infrequently. So early as 1872, in "Roughing It," he was testifying to his delight in "the vigorous new vernacular of the occidental plains and mountains," and in a prefatory note to "Huckleberry Finn," in 1884, he showed a pardonable pride in his grasp of it by warning his readers that what

[1] So far as I know, there is no study in English of Harte's vocabulary. In German there is Die Verwendung der Mundart bei Bret Harte, by Heinrich Kessler, *Beiträge zur Erforschung der Sprache und Kultur Englands und Amerikas*, Vol. V, No. 2, 1928.

[2] An anonymous reviewer of the DAE in the *Pathfinder* (Washington), Feb. 28, 1944, says that Mark "contributed more American words [to it] than any other writer, while Emerson stuck closely to English usage and contributed none."

followed attempted to differentiate between " the Missouri negro dialect, the extremest form of the backwoods Southwestern dialect, the ordinary Pike County dialect, and four modified varieties of this last." [1] " The shadings," he said, " have not been done in a haphazard fashion, or by guesswork, but painstakingly, and with the trustworthy guidance and support of personal familiarity with these several forms of speech." There was a chapter, " Concerning the American Language," crowded out of " A Tramp Abroad " in 1880, which antedated all the enormous accumulation of latter-day writing on the subject. In it he said:

> Our changed conditions and the spread of our people far to the South and far to the West have made many alterations in our pronunciation, and have introduced new words among us and changed the meaning of many old ones. . . . A nation's language is . . . not simply a manner of speech obtaining among the educated handful; the manner obtaining among the vast uneducated multitude must be considered also. . . . English and American are separate languages. . . . When I speak my native tongue in its utmost purity an Englishman can't understand me at all.[2]

Mark's influence upon the development of American prose was very large, but most of his immediate contemporaries fought against it. One of those who followed him, though somewhat gingerly and at a safe distance, was Howells, who came out in the Editor's Study of *Harper's Magazine*, in January, 1886, for American autonomy in speech. " Languages, while they live," he said, " are perpetually changing. God apparently meant them for the common people, . . . and the common people will use them freely, as they use other gifts of God. On their lips our continental English will differ more and more from the insular English, and we believe that this is not deplorable, but desirable. . . . We have only to leave our studies, editorial or other, and go into the shops and fields to find the ' spacious times of great Elizabeth ' again." [3] The spirit of the time, how-

---

1 An attempt to sort out some of these dialects is made in Mark Twain and American Dialect, by Katherine Buxbaum, *American Speech*, Feb., 1927, pp. 233–36.

2 Concerning the American Language was included in The Stolen White Elephant; Boston, 1882. On July 20, 1879, Mark had written in his London note-book: " One must have a play-book at an English play — the English accent is so different one cannot understand or follow the actors. The same in ordinary conversation which one tries to hear."

3 Howells's own prose, as he advanced in life, showed some concession to American idiom, but he never quite got over his fear of vulgarity. See Conservatism in American Speech, by George H. McKnight, *American Speech*, Oct., 1925, pp. 7 and 8, and my Prejudices: First Series; New York, 1919, especially p. 58.

ever, was against this yielding to the national speech habits, and most of its other salient writers were not only careful conformists to English precept and example in their writing but abject colonials otherwise. A ludicrous but by no means untypical example was Henry Van Dyke, D.D., LL.D., D.C.L., a Presbyterian pastor turned poet, pedagogue and literary politician, whose influence throughout the 1890–1910 period was enormous, and not only enormous but also incredible, for it is impossible to find anything in his numerous books, pamphlets and pronunciamentoes worth reading today.[1] When, in 1923, there was a conference of English and American professors of English at Columbia University, he seized the opportunity to declare that " the proposal to make a new American language to fit our vast country may be regarded either as a specimen of American humor or as a serious enormity." [2] The assembled birchmen gave him a hearty round of applause, and one of them, Dr. Fred Newton Scott, of the University of Michigan, leaped up to denounce my burlesque translation of the Declaration of Independence into the American vulgate,[3] which he took quite seriously, as a crime against humanity, fit " for the hair shirt and the lash, or tears of shame and self-abasement." [4] Needless to say, the learned pastor had the en-

[1] After being graduated from the Princeton Theological Seminary Van Dyke pastored a church at Newport, R. I., and was then elevated to the pulpit of the Brick Presbyterian in New York. In 1900 he became professor of English literature at Princeton. In 1913 his services to the Anglo-Saxon *Kultur* were rewarded with the post of minister to the Netherlands and Luxemburg. After this service he returned to Princeton, where he remained until 1923. He was a D.D. of Princeton, Harvard and Yale, and an Oxford D.C.L. He was one of the first ornaments of the national letters drafted for the National Institute of Arts and Letters and rose to be its president. Later he became a member of its upper chamber, the American Academy, along with Brander Matthews, Robert Underwood Johnson, George W. Cable, T. R. Lounsbury, William M. Sloane, Henry Cabot Lodge, Owen Wister, Hamlin Garland, Paul Elmer More, John H.

Finley and other such immortals. He died in 1933.

[2] Van Dyke Scoffs at Ideas of New Language in U. S., New York *Tribune*, June 4. The statement was discussed at length in the newspapers during the month following, and most of them appeared to agree with Van Dyke. Some of their editorials were summarized in a Daily Editorial Digest then current, printed in a number of papers, *e.g.*, the Roanoke (Va.) *World-News*, July 4; the Washington *Star*, July 3; the Salt Lake City *Deseret News*, July 6; and the Oklahoma City *Oklahoman*, July 6.

[3] The American Language, 3rd ed.; New York, 1923, pp. 398–402.

[4] Scott, who died in 1930, was a completely humorless man and an almost archetypical pedagogue. He was a delegate to the unfortunate London conference of 1927. He professed rhetoric at Ann Arbor for more than forty years and also taught journalism, though he knew no more about

thusiastic support of his colleagues of the American Academy of Arts and Letters. A year or two later seven of them joined him in publishing "Academy Papers: Addresses on Language Problems," a series of earnest pleas for a rigid yielding to English standards, with bitter flings at all the current American authors guilty of stooping to the use of Americanisms. The most idiotic chapter in this preposterous volume was by Van Dyke himself: in it he denounced Carl Sandburg with Calvinistic rancor, and said of "The Spoon River Anthology" (including "Ann Rutledge"!) that "to call it poetry is to manhandle a sacred word."[1] Brander Matthews, who was one of the contributors, had been an eager student of American speechways in the days before World War I,[2] but the sound of the bugles filled him with colonial doubts that there could ever be any essential difference between the English of England and that of this great self-governing Dominion.[3]

The outbreak of World War II brought on another upsurge of colonialism, but this time it exhibited a certain weakness, and few authors of any dignity or authority were actively associated with it: indeed, its leaders were mainly writers of palpable trash. Nevertheless, it will probably keep on showing itself in the more or less beautiful letters of the country for a long while to come. After all, England is still the fount of honor for America, and almost the only native literati who disdain English approval altogether are those to whom it is plainly sour grapes. But there has certainly been a considerable im-

---

it than a child. He was also an author, and his bibliography includes Memorable Passages from the Bible, 1906; Selections from the Old Testament, 1910; Paragraph Writing, 1893; Introduction to Literary Criticism, 1899; Aphorisms for Teachers of English Composition, 1905; and A Brief English Grammar, 1905.

1 Academy Papers appeared as a book in 1925. It consisted of discourses delivered before the Academy on the Blashfield Foundation between 1916 and 1925. I reviewed it in the *American Mercury*, Jan., 1926, pp. 122–23, and reprinted my review in Prejudices: Sixth Series; New York, 1927, pp. 155–59. The other contributors to the volume were Paul Elmer More, Bliss Perry, Paul Shorey, Brander Matthews, Robert Under-

wood Johnson, William M. Sloane and W. C. Brownell.

2 His writings on the subject are in his Americanisms and Briticisms, Etc.; New York, 1892; Parts of Speech; New York, 1901; The American of the Future; New York, 1909; and Essays on English; New York, 1921.

3 In 1936 Mr. Samuel L. M. Barlow of New York took me politely to task for ascribing a war-time Anglomania to Matthews, and on March 8, 1938 Arthur Guiterman denounced me for it in the New York *Times*. Unhappily, I find myself constrained to stand upon the evidence presented in AL4, pp. 65–66. Certainly Matthews made no effort, while the band was playing, to challenge the silly rantings of Van Dyke, Scott and company.

provement in independence and self-respect since the days when
Lowell could write:

> You steal Englishmen's books and think Englishmen's thought;
> With their salt on her tail your wild eagle is caught;
> Your literature suits its each whisper and motion
> To what will be thought of it over the ocean.[1]

The whole swing of American style, for a quarter century past,
has been toward greater and greater freedom in the use of essentially
national idioms. The tart admonitions of English purists — as, for
example, in the *Literary Supplement* of the London *Times* — are no
longer directed solely or even mainly to writers who need apology
at home: the offenders now include many of the best we have yet
produced. And they begin to get the understanding and approval of
a larger and larger faction of intelligent Englishmen.[2]

### 7. THE POLITICAL FRONT

79. [William Gifford, the bitterly anti-American editor of the
*Quarterly Review*, is authority for the story that at the close of the
Revolution certain members of Congress proposed that the use of
English be formally prohibited in the United States, and Hebrew
substituted for it.] This charge appeared in the *Quarterly* in January, 1814, in the course of a review of " Inchiquen, the Jesuit's Letters, . . . Containing a Favorable View of the Manners, Literature
and State of Society of the United States," brought out by Charles
Jared Ingersoll in 1810.[3] The review was a furious (and, at least in
some part, apt and effective) onslaught upon the whole American
scheme of things, and included the following: [4]

1 A Fable for Critics, 1848.
2 " The usage of the leading American writers of the period of Lowell and Holmes," says H. W. Horwill in American Variations, *S. P. E. Tract No. XLV*, 1936, " was more closely akin to that of the English writers of their day than is that of Twentieth Century American writers to their contemporaries in England. English readers today have greater need of a glossary for Theodore Dreiser than their fathers and grandfathers had for Nathaniel Hawthorne. Possibly the ambition of so many American writers of the present generation to emancipate themselves from Old World models has something to do with this."
3 Ingersoll (1782–1862) was a son of Jared Ingersoll (1750–1822), one of the framers of the Constitution. He studied law, spent some time in the diplomatic service and in Congress, and wrote a tragedy produced in Philadelphia and a history of the War of 1812.
4 p. 528.

Nor have there been wanting projects . . . for getting rid of the English language, not merely by barbarizing it — as when they *progress* a bill,[1] *jeopardize* a ship,[2] *guess* a probability, proceed by *grades*,[3] hold a *caucus*, *conglaciate* a wave,[4] etc., when the president of Yale College talks of a *conflagrative* brand,[5] and President Jefferson of *belittling* the productions of nature [6] — but by abolishing the use of English altogether, and substituting a new language of their own. One person indeed had recommended the adoption of Hebrew, as being ready made to their hands, and considering the Americans, no doubt, as the " chosen people " of the new world.[7]

In 1934 Allen Walker Read called attention to evidence [8] that Gifford had probably lifted this tale from the Marquis de Chastellux,[9] who served as a major-general under Rochambeau during the Revolution and on his return to France after Yorktown published an ac-

1 *To progress*, as a matter of fact, was never used as a transitive verb in the United States. As an intransitive it had flourished in England from *c*. 1590 to *c*. 1670, but had then been dropped, and it seems to have been reinvented in America. Benjamin Franklin disliked it and the English reviewers denounced it, but it made its way, and was included in Webster's American Dictionary of 1828. It is now used in England, but not often.

2 An Old English verb, revived in America and later readopted by the English. Pickering said in 1816 that it was " often seen in the debates of Congress, as they are reported in the newspapers," but added primly: " It is hardly necessary to remark that it is not in any of the dictionaries." But Webster admitted it to his dictionary in 1828, though marking it " useless " [*to jeopard* could be used instead], and by 1834 Sir Henry Taylor was using it in the second part of *Philip Van Artevelde*. By 1864 the great English philologian, W. W. Skeat, was using it.

3 The English reviewers frequently denounced the large use of *grade* in America, where it had got the meaning of military rank by 1806, of the slope of a road by 1808, and of a division in a school by 1835. But the English have since used it, though they still prefer *level-crossing* to *grade-crossing*.

4 *To conglaciate*, in the sense of to freeze, was not actually an Americanism. The NED traces it in English use to 1640, and it does not appear in any dictionary of Americanisms.

5 *Conflagrative* was not an Americanism. Thackeray used it in 1848 and Carlyle in 1865. The NED traces *to conflagrate* in English use to 1657. The noun, *conflagration*, goes back to 1555.

6 Jefferson first used *to belittle* in his Notes on Virginia, 1781–82, and seems to have invented it.

7 The *Quarterly's* diatribe was answered by Timothy Dwight in Remarks on the Review of Inchiquen's Letters; Boston, 1815. He denied formally that any such proposal had ever been made.

8 The Philological Society of New York, 1788, *American Speech*, April, 1934, p. 131.

9 Voyages dans l'Amérique sententrionale dans les années 1780, 1781 et 1782; Paris, 1786. There seems to have been a private print of at least part of this record at Newport, R. I., n.d. A second edition was published in Paris in 1788. Chastellux (1734–88) also wrote other books, one of them a discussion of the question whether the discovery of America had been profitable or unprofitable to Europe. (He decided that it had been profitable). On the strength of his De la félicité publique; Paris, 1772, which

count of his observations in America. In Volume II of that work, p. 203, there was the following passage:

> The Americans . . . testify more surprise than peevishness at meeting with a foreigner who does not understand English. But if they are indebted for this opinion to a prejudice of education, a sort of national pride, that pride suffered not a little from the reflection, which frequently occurred, of the language of the country being that of their oppressors. Accordingly they avoided these expressions, *You speak English; You understand English well;* and I have often heard them say *You speak American well; the American is not difficult to learn.* Nay, they have carried it even so far as seriously to propose introducing a new language, and some persons were desirous, for the convenience of the public, that the Hebrew should be substituted for the English. The proposal was that it should be taught in the schools and made use of in all public acts. We may imagine that this project went no further, but we may conclude from the mere suggestion that the Americans could not express in a more energetic manner their aversion for the English.[1]

The substitution of Greek for Hebrew in this legend was apparently made by Charles Astor Bristed, a grandson of the original John Jacob Astor. This was done in the essay, " The English Language in America," that he contributed to a volume of " Cambridge Essays " in 1855.[2] But Bristed's reference to the matter, I suppose, was intended to be jocular, for he reported that Congress had rejected the proposal on the ground that " it would be more convenient for us to keep the language as it is, and make the English speak Greek." Eight years before this another writer, this time a German named Franz Loher, had alleged in a book that, in Pennsylvania at least, an effort had been made to displace English with German.[3] He said:

> In the State Assembly, not long after the conclusion of peace, a motion was made to establish the German language as the official and legal language of Pennsylvania. . . . When the vote was taken on this question — whether the prevailing language in the Assembly, in the courts, and in the official records of

was praised by Voltaire, he was elected a member of the French Academy. His book on America was severely criticized in France.

1 I take this translation from Travels in North America in the Years 1780, 1781 and 1782, by the Marquis de Chastellux, "translated from the French by an English gentleman who resided in America at that period"; London, 1787; Vol. II, pp. 265–66. There is another translation, by Robert Withington, in The Marquis de Chastellux on Language and Peace, *New England Quarterly,* (Orono, Maine), June, 1943, pp. 316–

19. Withington says: "It is, perhaps, worth observing that apparently no attempt was made to use French as an alternative to English, though it was even then the 'diplomatic' language, replacing an earlier Latin for international communication."

2 There is a summary of the essay, with extracts, in AL4, pp. 69–71. Bristed (1820–74) spent several years at Trinity College, Cambridge. He wrote half a dozen books, but all of them are forgotten.

3 Geschichte und Zustande der Deutschen in Amerika; Cincinnati, 1847, pp. 194–98.

Pennsylvania should be German — there was a tie. Half voted for the introduction of the German language. . . . Thereupon the Speaker of the Assembly, a certain Muhlenberg, cast the deciding vote in favor of the English language.

This Muhlenberg was Frederick Augustus Conrad (1750–1801), twice Speaker of the Pennsylvania House and later the first Speaker of the House of Representatives at Washington, 1789–91 and again in 1793–95. The story was afloat for a long while, and many German-Americans believed it; indeed, there were those who execrated the memory of Muhlenberg, who was the son of the founder of Lutheranism in America, for killing so fine a chance to make the language of their Fatherland, and not English, the language of their adopted country. Finally, in 1931, Otto Lohr tracked the tale down to 1813, and discovered, as might have been expected, that it was a fable based upon a misunderstanding. The time was 1794 and the scene was Philadelphia, where Congress was in session. The proposal before it was not to make German the language of the United States, but simply to provide for the publication of some of the laws in a German translation, for the accommodation of immigrants — in Virginia, not Pennsylvania — who had not yet learned English. The whole story was later unearthed by Theodore G. Tappert and printed in the *Lutheran* of Philadelphia.[1] A petition from the Virginia Germans, it appeared, was received on January 9, 1794, and on March 20 it was referred to a committee of three members, one of whom was John Peter Gabriel Muhlenberg (1746–1807), a brother to the speaker. The committee brought in a favorable report on April 1, but it was laid on the table. On December 1 a new committee was appointed, and on December 23 it likewise brought in a favorable report. This one was discussed by the House committee of the whole on January 13, 1795, and rejected by a vote of 41 ayes to 42 noes. It is possible that the Speaker cast the deciding vote, and that the story told by Loher thus originated, but it is not certain, for there is no record of a roll-call. In 1795 the project was again revived, but apparently it failed again, for an act of March 3 of that year, providing for the printing of the laws, made no mention of an edition in German.[2]

1 Language and Legislation, Nov. 15, 1939, pp. 11–19.
2 Summaries of the Tappert paper are in German the National Language, by W. L. Werner, *American Notes* and *Queries*, July, 1942, p. 64, and in The Official German Language Legend, by the same, *American Speech*, Dec., 1942, p. 246.

Such translations of State laws, however, had already appeared in two of the States, Pennsylvania and Maryland — in the former in 1776, 1778, 1785, 1786 and 1787, and in the latter in 1787. The Germans of Pennsylvania were extraordinarily tenacious of their mother-tongue, and even to this day, as everyone knows, thousands of their descendants still speak it. In 1753, thirty-six years after the beginning of their great influx, Benjamin Franklin wrote to an English friend, Peter Collinson:

> Advertisements, intended to be general, are now printed in Dutch [i.e., German] and English. The signs in our streets have inscriptions in both languages, and in some places only German. They begin of late to make their bonds and other legal instruments in their own language, which (though I think it ought not to be) are allowed good in our courts, where German business so increases that there is continued need of interpreters; and I suppose in a few years they will also be necessary in the Assembly, to tell one half of our legislators what the other half say.[1]

French continued as an active rival to English in Louisiana long after the American flag was run up in 1803. Indeed, its use is still permitted in the courts of the State, though it has been seldom if ever used for some years. The first State constitution, adopted in 1812, was promulgated in both English and French, and it provided that both languages should be used in the publication of the laws. A new constitution, adopted in 1868, abolished the use of French,[2] but another, adopted in 1879, permitted the Legislature, at its discretion, to publish the laws in French for the convenience of the French-speaking parishes. Under that discretion they were so published until 1915 or 1916. In New Orleans, of course, English was the language of the courts, but a French newspaper of the city, *L'Abeille*, lived for years on the revenue derived from printing new laws in French. When French was dropped *L'Abeille* fell upon evil days, and was eventually absorbed into the *Times-Democrat*.[3] In California and Texas, in the early days, the laws were printed in both English

1 May 9, 1732. The letter is printed in full in Franklin's Complete Works; New York, 1887, pp. 297–98. I borrow this reference from Read.

2 At that time it was still spoken in New Orleans almost as much as English. Said Albert D. Richardson in The Field, the Dungeon and the Escape; Hartford, 1865, p. 47: "The French Quarter is more un-American even than the famous German portion of Cincinnati known as Over the Rhine. Here you may stroll for hours, 'a straggler from another civilization,' hearing no word of your native tongue, seeing no object to remove the impression of an ancient French city."

3 I am indebted here to my old friend and colleague, Marshall Ballard, editor of the New Orleans *Item*.

and Spanish, and in New Mexico Spanish is still used. On April 18, 1842, after the beginning of German immigration into Texas, the State Legislature ordained that the laws be printed in German also, and in 1858 it added Norwegian.[1] In 1853 a writer in *Gleason's Pictorial* reported that the laws of California were being printed, not only in English and Spanish, but also in Chinese, but this seems to have been a false report.[2] In New Mexico, until 1941, the Legislature was bilingual and the laws were printed in both English and Spanish.[3] Spanish is still permitted in the justices' courts, the probate court and the district courts of the State, though it has been abolished in the United States district court. There are many Mexicans in New Mexico who cannot speak English, and when they face a jury which includes members who know little or no Spanish it is necessary to employ interpreters for them. I am informed by Mr. Brian Ború Dunne of Santa Fé that these interpreters are not always of ideal competence. He says:

In an embezzlement case in the district court of the First Judicial District, the late and brilliant A. B. Renehan, lawyer of Santa Fé, asked, in addressing the jury: "Who killed Cock Robin?" The interpreter translated this outburst thus: "Quien mató à Cock *Robinson?*" Mr. Renehan, who was a Spanish scholar, mildly corrected: "I said, 'who killed Cock *Robin!*'" But the interpreter failed to get it and repeated: "Quien mató à Cock *Robinson?*"

Mr. Dunne continues:

At political meetings it is customary to call for an interpreter, and the sentences of the so-called orators are usually interpreted between commas thus: "Ladies and Gentlemen, *señores y señoras*, it gives me great pleasure, *me da mucho gusto*, this evening, *estate noche*, to speak to you, *di hablar a Ustedes.*" Visitors hearing this strange arrangement for the first time usually leave the hall in convulsions, but it is a God-send to reporters who are unfamiliar with shorthand, for it gives them plenty of time to take notes.[4]

The English tried to wipe out Dutch in New York after the conquest of the colony in 1664, but it carried on an underground existence for many years, and so late as the second half of the Eighteenth Century an English observer was reporting that it was "still so

---

1 State Laws in Other Languages, by Richard F. Burges, *American Notes and Queries*, Dec., 1943, p. 144.
2 State Laws in Other Languages, by M. J. P., *American Notes and Queries*, Oct., 1943, p. 102.
3 *American Notes and Queries*, Feb., 1944, p. 173.

4 On Oct. 25, 1943 the Associated Press reported from Yuma, Arizona, that a magistrate there, J. T. Hodges, had that day tried and sentenced three successive prisoners in an Indian language, in English, and in Spanish.

much used in some counties that the sheriffs find it difficult to obtain persons sufficiently acquainted with the English tongue to serve as jurors in the courts of law." [1] Dutch, indeed, was the first language in some of the remoter parts of the Hudson valley until our own time, and also in parts of New Jersey. In Baltimore, down to World War I, there were actually public schools, the so-called German-English schools, in which German was used in the teaching of the elements.

81. [In 1923 bills making the American language official (but never clearly defining it) were introduced in the Legislatures of Illinois, North Dakota, Minnesota and other States. At the same time the Hon. Washington Jay McCormick, then a Republican member of the House of Representatives from Montana, offered a similar bill in Congress.] The text of this bill, along with a statement in support of it by its author, is given in AL4, pp. 81 and 82. It was dealt with jocosely by most of the newspapers that noticed it at all, but a few discussed it more seriously — for example, the Portland *Oregonian*, which said:

> Notwithstanding the obvious chauvinism of the movement, more might be said in its behalf if it were practicable to designate specifically, as the Montana congressman would do, which are the " words and phrases generally accepted as being in good use by the people of the United States." Right here the difficulty lies. Neither in the United States nor in England is there an equivalent of the French academy as a recognized arbiter of propriety in diction. With certain not very well-defined exceptions, language is with us largely a matter of individual preference. In attempting to separate the sheep from the goats by statutory enactment it is likely that Mr. McCormick has attempted more than he is likely to be able to perform.[2]

The McCormick bill died in the files of the House judiciary committee, but others substantially like it were offered in the Legislatures of various States. One of them was signed by Governor Len Small of Illinois on June 19, 1923, and went upon the books of the State as Chapter 127, Section 178 of the Acts of the Legislature of that year (albeit with considerable revision). The text of it is given in AL4, pp. 82 and 83.[3] Its father was a legislator bearing the ancient Irish name of Ryan, and the Chicago papers, then in the midst of their

1 Bilingualism in the Middle Colonies, by Allen Walker Read, *American Speech*, April, 1937, p. 97.
2 The " American " Language (editorial), March 1, 1923.
3 A few days before this the Legislature designated the American cardinal (*Cardinalis cardinalis*) as the State bird, and a little while later designated a song called Illinois, with words by C. H. Chamberlain to the tune of Baby Mine, as the State song.

gory battle with Mayor Big Bill Thompson, professed to see the same Anglophobia in it that prompted his Honor's historic warning to King George V. The *News*, when the new law was published, headed a sneering article on it " Illinois State Assembly Adopts Menckenese as Official Language," and then proceeded to the astonishing disclosure that " the term *American language* was first substituted for *English* by the Germans during the war, because of their hatred of all things English." [1] The New York *Sun*, rather less upset by Big Bill, had thus commented on the act while it was still before the Legislature:

> There was a time in American life when it was possible to be both well-fed and 100% American by ordering *liberty-cabbage;* in these saner times *sauerkraut* is to be found on the bill-of-fare. Giving a new tag to our language would be just such an adventure in hair-splitting.[2]

The proposed Minnesota law of 1923, introduced in the State House of Representatives on March 8 by two rural legislators, was reported favorably by the committee on education on April 6, but got no further. It ran as follows:

> *Section 1.* That the official language of the State and people of Minnesota is hereby defined and declared to be the American language.
> *Section 2.* That all laws and parts of laws of this State, including the rules and regulations of the several departments thereof, wherein the printing, speaking, reading, writing or knowledge of the English language is set forth as a requirement for any purpose or use, hereby are amended to the extent of substituting in the text for the word *English* the word *American.*

This bill was supported with great vigor by John M. Leonard of St. Paul, president of the American Foundation and founder and business manager of *Hail! Columbia*, " America's foremost patriotic magazine," [3] and it also had the countenance of the Hon. Magnus Johnson, who said a year later: " There will be a day in the near future when there will be only one language in this ᴄountry — the

---

1 July 25, 1923. The DAE traces *American language* to a debate in Congress in 1802, and Allen Walker Read runs it back to 1793. See p. 5, footnote.
2 We Still Understand English (editorial), April 9, 1923.
3 Leonard was not the first advocate of the reform in Minnesota. In May, 1920, a St. Paul man named A. J. Roberts launched the *American Language National Magazine*, and

announced his candidacy for the City Council. It was his hope, he said, to become commissioner of education later on, in order " to boost for the American language and American literature in the bearing that these subjects have toward citizenship, Americanization and loyalty to the United States and American principles." What fate befell this aspiration I do not know.

American," [1] but, as I have said, it failed of passage. Despite this set-back the movement continued active in the upper Middle West. In 1927 the Hon. Andrew W. Mellon, then Secretary of Treasury, re-vived the hopes of its proponents by ordering that the redemption call for the Second Liberty Loan be printed in the American lan-guage, and in February, 1934 they got another lift from the Hon. Fred A. Britten of Chicago, who moved in the national House of Representatives that the members of the American *corps diplo-matique* be instructed to carry on their legerdemain in the same. "When an American envoy," he declared, "begins to *lawf* and *cawf* and ape the British, he ought to be brought home and kept here until he speaks the language as we speak it in the United States." [2] Early in 1937 a State senator of North Dakota by the name of the Hon. William A. Thatcher introduced a resolution declaring that American, not English, should be the language of that State there-after, but though it seems to have been passed by the Senate, it was killed in the House of Representatives. [3] So the crusade rested until June 3, 1940, when the Hon. Claude D. Pepper of Florida, in the course of a speech advocated all-out aid to the English and their allies, nevertheless gave formal notice that a resolution he had intro-duced to that effect was "set down in the American language, in black and white." A month later the Rochester (N. Y.) Central Trades and Labor Council came to the bat with the following:

*Whereas,* Since the independence of this country was established we have used a language that carried a misnomer, known as the English language; and

*Whereas,* We believe no foreign name should be connected with our lan-guage;

*Therefore, be it resolved,* That our representatives in Congress be petitioned to enact a law to the effect, henceforth the language we speak is to be known as the American or United States language. [4]

1 Speech before the Swedish-Ameri-can League at Duluth, reported in the St. Paul *Dispatch*, June 25, 1924. "By next Spring," commented the *Dispatch* maliciously, "the colleges will be conferring honorary degrees in letters upon Ring Lardner, and then the glory of the American lan-guage will be complete. It is ac-cordingly a great pleasure to find in Senator Johnson a champion of it. Through him we may hope for its early acceptance as the national tongue."

2 Diplomats Should be Understood (editorial), San Antonio *News*, Feb. 15, 1934.

3 North Dakota's Language (edi-torial), Minneapolis *Evening Trib-une*, Feb. 11, 1937. I am indebted here to Mr. James D. Gronan, secre-tary of state of North Dakota, and to Mr. E. J. Conrad, president of the Capital Publishing Company of Bis-marck.

4 Associated Press dispatch from Rochester, July 12, 1940. I am in-debted for the text of the resolution

Then there was another armistice until April 20, 1944, when the Hon. Edwin B. Roscoe of Passaic, a member of a Model Legislature sponsored in New Jersey by the Y.M.C.A., introduced a bill at the year's opening session at Trenton providing that "the official language of the State of New Jersey shall be hereafter known as the American language instead of the English language." What became of this measure I do not know.

## 8. FOREIGN OBSERVERS

86. [From an early day the peculiarities of American have attracted the attention of Continental philologians, and especially of the Germans]. Among the pioneer writings on the subject were "Die englische Philologie in Nordamerika," by Dr. Felix Flügel, in *Gersdorf's Repertorium*, 1852;[1] "Woordenboek van Americanismen," by M. Keijzer; Gorinchem (Holland), 1854; and "Wörterbuch der Americanismen," by Friedrich Köhler; Leipzig, 1866. The Keijzer book was based on the first edition of John Russell Bartlett's "Glossary of Words and Phrases Usually Regarded as Peculiar to the United States"; Boston, 1848, and that of Köhler on Bart-

to Mr. James H. Faulkner, secretary of the Central Trades and Labor Council.

[1] Flügel, who survived until 1904, was the son of a well-known German lexicographer, Johann Gottfried Flügel (1788–1855), whose Vollständiges englisch-deutsches und deutsch-englisches Wörterbuch; Leipzig, 1830, maintained its authority for many years. Johann came out to the United States in 1810 and remained nine years. On his return to Germany with a sound knowledge of American English he became professor of English in the University of Leipzig. In 1838 he was appointed American consul in Leipzig, and during his later years was a corresponding member of many American learned societies. His son, Felix, was also a lexicographer of some distinction, and after Johann's death brought out many editions of his dictionary under the new title of Praktisches Wörterbuch der englischen und deutschen Sprache: the fourteenth was published at Leipzig in 1883. Felix married Pauline Mencken, sister to Burkhard L. Mencken, grandfather of the present writer, and they had a son, Ewald, who followed in the family line. Ewald was born in Leipzig in 1863 and was educated there and at Freiburg. He took his Ph.D. in philology in 1885, and was *privat dozent* at Leipzig until 1892, when he was called to the chair of English philology in the new Leland Stanford University. He remained there until his death in 1914. He was editor of *Anglia* after 1889, edited the Chaucer Lexicon of the London Chaucer Society; London, 1891, and was president of the Pacific Coast branch of the American Philological Association in 1901–02. His numerous publications included "Die nordamerikanische Litteratur," published in 1907.

lett's third edition of 1860.[1] Nor was it only in Western Europe that the growing differences between standard English and American were noted in that era. In 1858 Czar Alexander II of Russia ordered that "the American language" be included in the curriculum of the Russian military academies,[2] and in 1861 a memorial of the Chinese Prince Kung Ts'in, petitioning his brother, the Emperor Hsien-fung, to establish a Foreign Office on Western lines, asked that men be appointed to its staff who were familiar with English, French and American.[3] The first American appointed was William A. P. Martin (1827–1916), an American Presbyterian missionary who had gone out to China in 1850 and lived to be the first president of the Imperial University at Peking.

During the years between the first two World Wars the Germans printed a large number of guides to and studies of American English and there were frequent discussions of it in such learned journals as *Anglia, Neueren Sprachen, Anglistische Studien,* the *Archiv für das Studium der neueren Sprachen und Literaturen,* the *Giessener Beiträge zur Erforschung der Sprach und Kultur Englands und Nordamerikas,* the *Neuphilologische Monatsschrift,* and the *Zeitschrift für französischen und englischen Unterricht.* Much of this discussion, of course, consisted only of reviews and summaries of American or English writings on the subject, but there were also some publications embodying original contributions — for example, "Die Volkssprache im Nordosten der Vereinigten Staaten von Amerika," by Johann Alfred Heil; Breslau, 1927; "Amerikanisches Englisch," by Hermann U. Meysenbug; Ettlingen and Leipzig, 1929; "A Glossary of Americanisms," by Dr. H. Mutschmann; Tartu-Dorpat, 1931, and numerous monographs by Dr. Heinrich Spies, Dr. Georg Kartzke and Dr. Walther Fischer. Some of these books and papers are noted in AL4, pp. 85 ff, and others are listed below.[4] There was also a large

---

[1] Flügel had reviewed Bartlett's first edition in the *Archiv für das Studium der neueren Sprachen und Literaturen* in 1848.

[2] *Harper's Magazine,* Jan., 1859, p. 274.

[3] For this I am indebted to Dr. Richard H. Heindel.

[4] Die amerikanische Sprache, by Georg Kartzke, *Archiv für das Studium der neueren Sprachen und Literaturen,* 1921, pp. 181–98; Die amerikanische Sprache, by Johannes Hoops, *Englische Studien,* 1923; Das amerikanische Englisch, by C. M. Bratter, *Vossische Zeitung,* Feb. 23, 1923; Zur amerikanischen Intonation, by Fritz Karpf, *Die neueren Sprachen,* Sept., 1926; Amerikanisches und Britisches Englisch, by W. Franz (in Festschrift Friedrich Kluge zum 70. Geburtstage), 1926; Neue Amerikanismen, by Ed. O. Paget, *Die neueren Sprachen,* 1927; Die amerikanische Sprache, by

popular literature on the subject, mainly in pamphlet form.[1] One
of the most curious items thereof was *Paustians lustige Sprachzeit-
schrift für Forthildung, Nachhilfe und Unterhaltung,* a serial published at Hamburg which undertook to teach foreign languages
and foreign ways in a painless and even joyous manner by repro-
ducing and expounding comic stories and pictures from foreign
publications. On April 25, 1938, for example, it printed on its first
page a drawing from the *New Yorker,* and explained the phrase
*I guess,* which occurred in the legend beneath, thus: " *ai gess,* ameri-
kanisch für *I think = ich glaube, denke, meine.*" There was also a
considerable interest in American English in Italy before the Italian
entrance into World War II,[2] and likewise, though to a less extent,
in France, Belgium, Russia, Holland and the Scandinavian countries.[3]
In Holland the lead in American studies has been taken by Dr. R. W.
Zandvoort of The Hague, editor of *English Studies* (Amsterdam),
who said in 1934:

> Since the Great War it has become increasingly difficul for European teach-
> ers and scholars to ignore the fact that different norms of English usage are

Arnold Schröer, *Kölnische Zeitung,*
Sept. 13, 1927; Amerikanisches Englisch, by Walther Fischer (in his
Hauptfragen der Amerikakunde, pp.
68 *ff*); Bielefeld; a chapter of the
same title in his Handbuch der
Amerikakunde; Frankfurt a. M.,
1931; Die Erforschung des amerikanischen Englisch, by the same (in
Festschrift für Hermann Hirt, Vol.
II), 1936; Sprachliche Neubildungen
in der englischen Gegenwartslitera-
tur, by Hans Marcus, *Neuphilologische Monatsschrift,* July–Aug.,
1937; Zur Biologie des ameri-
nischen Englisch, by Ph. Aronstein,
*Leuvensche Bijdragen,* Jan., 1934;
Amerikanisches Englisch, by F. L.
Sack; Bern, 1935; Das amerikanische
Idiom, by Sigillum, *Berliner Tage-
blatt,* May 31, 1935. The discussion
of American speechways in German
guide-books for immigrants has not
been sufficiently investigated. They
were numerous before the Civil
War. One of them, Der amerikanische Dollmetscher; New York,
1844, is described in *College Topics*
(University of Virginia), Nov. 11,
1936, p. 3. (I take this reference

from *American Speech,* April, 1938,
p. 142).
1 For example, The American Language, in America of Today (No. 3
of the English section of Langen-
scheidt's Fremdsprachliche Lektüre;
Berlin, n.d.); Uncle Sam and His
English (No. 32 of the same; Berlin,
n.d.); Spoken American, by S. A.
Nock and H. Mutschmann; Leipzig
and Berlin, 1931. All these are in
English, with German glosses.
2 Some of its fruits were La lingua
americana, by L. F. Biondi, *Corriere
della Sera* (Milan), Oct. 16, 1928;
Cosi si parla in America, by Carlo
Rosetti; Milan, 1937; Slang, by L.
Krasnick, Milan, 1938.
3 For Russia see AL4, p. 88. From
France came an intelligent article,
Une nouvelle langue: l'Américain,
by Alfred Obermann, *Le Mois*
(Paris), Feb. 1, 1937, pp. 165–74, (I
am indebted here to the Rev. Dr.
Donald Grey Barnhouse of Phila-
delphia), and from Belgium La
langue américaine, by F. Peeters,
*Revue de l'université de Bruxelles,*
Dec., 1929, pp. 164–91.

being evolved in another hemisphere, and that these norms are beginning to encroach on territory where hitherto Standard Southern English has held undisputed sway. . . . So long as the attitude of educated Americans towards their own form of speech was expressed in the words of Richard Grant White that " just in so far as it deviates from the language of the most cultivated society in England it fails to be English " there was no need for Continental language teachers to take American English seriously. But with its world-wide dissemination through business, literature, the talking film, the gramophone record, on one hand, and the growing determination of Americans to assert their independence in matters of speech on the other, the situation is taking on a different aspect.[1]

Dr. Zandvoort reported that, at the time he wrote, the majority of Netherlands university pundits, like their opposite numbers in the United States, were still disposed to look down their noses at American English, but that Americanisms were being picked up in large number by their students and that a demand for their consideration in university courses was in the making. Unhappily, the practical difficulty of giving instruction in two forms of the same language was a serious one, especially since Dutch *Gymnasium* students, by the time they came to English, were already more or less worn out by hard drilling in French, German, Latin and Greek. But Dr. Zandvoort and his fellow advocates of American refused to be daunted. " We look upon American English," he said, " not as a mere lapse from ' good ' English, but as a legitimate development, autonomous within its own domain, and from the European point of view subordinate to British English for historical and practical reasons only."

How the Russians, in 1930, solemnly debated substituting American for English in their schools, on the ground that American is " more democratic " and also more " alive and picturesque," is set forth in AL4, p. 88. But it was the Japanese who, in the days before Pearl Harbor, took the liveliest interest in American peculiarities of speech, and showed the keenest understanding of their significance. Their philologians, headed by Dr. Sanki Ichikawa, professor of English in Tokyo Imperial University, discussed the subject frequently, at considerable length and with great acumen, both in *Studies in English Literature*, published by Tokyo University, and in pamphlets and books. In this work they were given active aid by Western teachers of English resident in Japan, including several Englishmen.

1 Standards of English in Europe,
*American Speech*, Feb., 1934, pp.
3–10.

Among the latter was H. E. Palmer, linguistic adviser to the Japanese Ministry of Education, who, when he brought out " A Dictionary of English Pronunciation " in 1926, included " With American Variants " in its title, and listed hundreds of them.[1] Palmer noted that some of the Americans in Japan managed to achieve a passable imitation of the standard English pronunciation, but for every one who did so, he said, there were " about ten " whose speech remained unmistakably American. Another Englishman in Japan who took cognizance of such differences was Thomas R. G. Lyell, lecturer in English at Waseda University and the Tokyo Foreign Language School, whose " Slang, Phrase and Idiom in Colloquial English and Their Use," listed many Americanisms.[2] There were also a large number in " English Influence on Japanese," by Professor Ichikawa,[3] and yet more in " An Introduction to the Study of Loan-Words in Modern Japanese," by Sawbay Arakawa.[4] In 1930 G. Tomita brought out " English and American of Today," [5] which not only discussed the differences between the English and American vocabularies, but also gave an account of the grammar of vulgar American. Finally, Satoshi Ichiya, a well-known Japanese journalist, set English and American in direct apposition in " King's English or President's English?," [6] and decided that the Japanese had better learn American. Ichiya, who wrote in English, was educated at the University of London, and confessed to a nostalgic attachment to English speechways, but he concluded that " in an academic discussion of this nature it is not right to allow one's personal sentiment to carry away with it one's sense of truth." He went on:

Owing partly to the nearness of the United States to Japan, as compared with Great Britain, and partly to the larger number of American teachers of English in Japanese schools, English in Japan has more of an American flavor than a British. Also, a large number of different American periodicals and books — far more than British publications — which are read by a great many people here, including the British themselves, evidently exert a constant influence upon the English used in this country. . . .

1 This useful work was written in collaboration with J. Victor Martin, also resident in Japan, and F. G. Blandford. It was published in Cambridge, England, but Palmer's preface was dated Tokyo.

2 The first edition of this book, which was addressed to Japanese, was published in Tokyo in 1931. A second edition appeared in 1936.

3 *Studies in English Literature*, April, 1928, pp. 165–208.

4 Tokyo, 1932. This work is in Japanese.

5 Tokyo. This work, like the foregoing, is in Japanese.

6 Kobe, n.d.

American-English is spoken by a large majority — at least two-thirds — of the English-speaking people of the world, . . . and its claim is growing year after year with the continued increase in the wealth, influence and population of the United States. . . . Common sense teaches us the wisdom of deciding for the majority where the question concerned is that of greater utility.

Ichiya noted that there was some prejudice against American speechways in Japan because of " the increasing haughtiness of the United States as a nation, and the bombastic utterances and idiotic and vulgar behavior of many irresponsible Americans both at home and abroad who are pleased to call themselves 100% American," but he hastened to assure his Japanese readers that " the majority are not like that. As a matter of fact, real Americans are as refined as any other cultured nationals; they are much freer from a foolish snobbery than some so-called ' cultured ' Englishmen. It is indeed impossible to dislike such Americans or their speech." [1]

As in Germany, there is a considerable popular literature on the English language, with notes on American variants. In the days before World War II all the stewards and waiters on the Japanese Pacific liners were provided with more or less illuminating handbooks instructing them in the mysteries of English idiom, with special attention to the idioms of Americans. That of the Nippon Yusen Kaisha (Japan Mail Steamship Company) included the following:

Although Americans speak English they often use words which are different from those the passengers from London and other British ports use. For example, Americans like to call the first-class cabins *staterooms*, but English people say *first-class cabin, second-class*, etc. A London passenger brings a *portmanteau, Gladstone* and *hold-all*, but the American would call the same things *trunk, suit-case, grip* and *rug-strap*.

To this was appended a list of variants, in part as follows:

| English | American |
|---|---|
| walking-stick | cane |
| waterproof | raincoat |
| galoshes | rubbers, or overshoes |
| boots | shoes |
| boot-laces | shoe-strings |
| braces | suspenders |
| waistcoat | vest |
| stud | collar-button |
| postcard | postal-card |
| lift | elevator |

[1] When AL4 was published in 1936 one of the most searching and intelligent reviews it received (and by no means a wholly favorable one) was by H. Shigemi, *Studies in English Literature* (Tokyo), Oct., 1937.

# THE MATERIALS OF INQUIRY

## 1. THE HALLMARKS OF AMERICAN

There are frequent efforts by philologians both professional and amateur to frame a character for American English, with results that show some conflict. " The characteristic American word," said the New York *Times* in 1944, [1] " must be something short, sinewy, native to the soil of American life — *creek, pone, squaw,* or something in the rudely fantastic line, like *calaboose* or *gerrymander.* The most un-American words, in theory, would be the long bookish, Latin polysyllables." Almost precisely a year before, Dr. Jacques Barzun of Columbia had taken a diametrically opposite line in the *Saturday Review of Literature.*[2] " Once upon a time," he said, " American speech was known for its racy, colloquial creations — *barnstorm, boom, boost, bulldoze, pan out, splurge* and so on. Now it is the flaccid polysyllable that expresses the country's mind. Pioneer has yielded to pedant, and one begins to wonder whether the German word-order had better not be adopted to complete the system." There seems to be an irreconcilable difference here over a fundamental matter, but, as in many similar cases, that seeming may be only seeming. What the *Times* had in mind, obviously, was the pungent, iconoclastic, everyday speech of the American people, whereas what fevered Dr. Barzun was the artificial pseudo-English that schoolma'ams, whether in step-ins or pantaloons, try to foist upon their victims, and the even worse jargon that Dogberries in and out of office use for their revelations to the multitude. The extent of that dichotomy was well described by Dr. George H. McKnight in *American Speech* so long ago as 1925.[3] On the one hand, there is a

1 Topics of the Times, editorial page, Feb. 24. The author was Simeon Strunsky.
2 How to Suffocate the English Language, Feb. 13, p. 3.
3 Conservatism in American Speech, Oct., 1925, pp. 1–17.

force making for something almost approaching anarchy in language, a constant upsurge of innovation, some of it close to barbaric, from the levels where the laws of the pedants and precisians do not run; and on the other hand there is a persistent effort to break the national gabble to rigid rules, and, what is worse, to adorn it with inventions springing, not from the field and workshop, but from the study. Nor is this the whole story, for even the common speech has its curious conservatism, its liking for an occasional archaism in the midst of novelty. But the issue of the struggle in the past shows what may be looked for hereafter. The schoolma'am still fights on, but she is plainly fighting a losing battle, and many of her guiding grammarians have become so well aware of it that they have begun to throw up their hands. Said McKnight:

> The rule of the grammar and the spelling-book and the dictionary are not over. Better English weeks still support the old régime, to abandon which entirely, indeed, would mean anarchy. But a wealth of fresh words and phrases, products of new conditions of life, are being made to enrich an older language. The "rude and busteous" elements in uncultivated speech are being assimilated to form a re-invigorated form of speech.

That these "rude and busteous" elements are more potent in America than in England seems to be generally recognized. The fact, to be sure, is denied occasionally in England, but only in moments of patriotic exaltation and by American-haters of the extreme wing. So long ago as 1835 Tocqueville tried to account for the superior energy and fecundity of American speech in that era by an appeal to the political theories then prevailing, and so recently as 1940 Dr. Harold Whitehall of the University of Indiana made an attempt in the light of the ideology of today. Said Tocqueville:

> The most common device used by democratic peoples to make an innovation in language consists in giving a new meaning to an expression already in use. This method is simple, prompt and convenient; no learning is needed to use it, and ignorance rather facilitates the process, but that process is dangerous to the language. When a democratic people doubles the meaning of a word in this way they sometimes make its old significance as ambiguous as its new one.

This shrewd anticipation of what the current fuglemen of semantics are whooping up as a revolutionary discovery was supported by an excellent discussion of the democratic liking for general ideas, most of them beautifully vague, and for terms of corresponding muzziness to designate them. Said Tocqueville:

These abstract terms enlarge and obscure the thoughts they are intended to convey. They render speech more succinct, but the underlying idea less clear. With regard to language democratic peoples prefer obscurity to painstaking.

Finally,

When men, no longer restrained by the effect of ranks, meet on terms of constant intercourse — when caste is destroyed and all the classes of society are intermixed — all the words of a language are mingled. Those which are unsuitable to the majority perish; the remainder form a common store, from which everyone chooses nearly at random.[1]

Dr. Whitehall, like Tocqueville, seeks a political cause for the present state of American English, and finds it in the Industrial Revolution. He says:

In its literate, written form, American English is a pruned and regimented language. But so, for that matter, is the equivalent British English. Wherever distinction may lie, it is not here. Both owe their present form to the effects of authoritarianism working upon bourgeois credulity. Both have succumbed to a vicious purism that is no older than the Industrial Revolution. . . . Modern Received Standard English, for all its social pretensions, is nothing more than a transmogrified middle-class dialect, and Beacon Hill quite legitimately plays hands-across-the-sea to Mayfair. In language, as in politics and society, the " new men " finally prevailed.

But this authoritarianism, says Whitehall, despite its powerful support by popular education, has never succeeded in quite breaking the free spirit of American English.

Its spoken forms have always veered so sharply from its most elevated literary form that they could develop almost untrammeled. American colloquial speech, constantly modified and enriched by the changing patterns of American life, has served the modern American literary language as an inexhaustible reservoir. By contrast, the equivalent influence of British colloquial English has been a thin, attenuated stream. Of all the differences between the two national languages, this is the most significant.[2]

More than one observer has noted the likeness between the situation of American English today and that of British English at the end of the Sixteenth Century. The Englishmen of that time had not yet come under the yoke of grammarians and lexicographers, and they were thus free to mold their language to the throng of new ideas that naturally marked an era of adventure and expansion. Their situation closely resembled that of the American pioneers who

1 The quotations are all from Part II, Book I, Chapter XVI of De la démocratie en Amérique.     2 America's Language, *Kenyon Review* (Gambier, O.), Spring, 1940, pp. 212–25.

swarmed into the West following the War of 1812, and they met its linguistic needs with the same boldness. By a happy accident, they had at hand a group of men who could bring to the business of word-making a degree of ingenuity and taste running far beyond the common; above all, they had the aid and leading of a really first-rate genius, Shakespeare. The result was a renovation of old ways of speech and a proliferation of new and useful terms that has had no parallel, to date, save on this side of the Atlantic. Standard English, in the Eighteenth Century, succumbed to pedants whose ignorance of language processes was only equalled by their impudent assumption of authority, and, as Dr. Whitehall says, their influence still survives more or less, even in the United States. But here the national spirit, as everyone knows, has resisted stoutly, and the schoolma'am who carries the torch of Samuel Johnson has certainly not prevailed against it. The following description of what was going on in Shakespeare's time, by an English scholar, George Gordon, might well be used as a description of the situation in the United States today:

> The first quality of Elizabethan English . . . is its power of hospitality, its passion for free experiment, its willingness to use every form of verbal wealth, to try anything. They delighted in novelties, and so exultingly that prudent word-fearing men became alarmed. The amusing thing is that even the alarmists were unable to deny themselves the very contraband they denounced; in this matter of language they were all smugglers. Thanks to this generous and unlicensed traffic we discover a quite astonishing number of words, introduced, apparently, by the Elizabethans, which today we could not do without. We observe also — what is not without some practical interest for us — the impossibility of predicting, of any new words at any given moment, which of them were going to last.[1]

Mr. Gordon gives some curious examples, from Shakespeare and other writers of the time, of neologisms that have come to seem so necessary and so commonplace that we could hardly imagine English without them, *e.g., scientific, idiom, prolix, figurative, obscure, delineation, dimension, audacious, conscious, jovial, rascality, to effectuate, negotiation* and *artificiality.* Shakespeare himself either invented or introduced to good literary society a large number, *e.g., aerial, auspicious, assassination, bare-faced, bump, clangor, countless, critic, disgraceful, to dwindle, fretful, gloomy, gnarled, hunch-*

1 Shakespeare's English, *S. P. E. Tracts,* No. XXIX; Oxford, 1928.

*backed, ill-starred, laughable, pedant, seamy* and *sportive.* Like all the other writers of his time, he made extremely free with prefixes and suffixes, and disregarded altogether the irrational rule, still maintained by the less intelligent sort of pedagogues, that they must agree in origin with the roots they modify, *i.e.,* Greek with Greek, Latin with Latin, and so on. He employed *dis-, re-* and *en-* with the utmost daring, and made frequent and effective use of the old English suffixes *-full, -less* and *-y.* Word-making was in the air, along with phrase-making, and there was emulation and imitation of one writer by another,[1] and, as in any other such natural process, a high percentage of failure and wastage, with only a minority surviving. A great many of the novelties of the time, says Gordon,

were made quite casually. It was easy enough; a man once started could turn them out forever. Shakespeare made them and forgot them, coining *disgraceful,* for example, at the beginning of his career, and never using it again. But there was more than casual fertility in the matter. . . . The reason why so many adjectives were made was partly, no doubt, because they were needed, but still more because they were fancied: because Golding[2] and Spenser, among others, had deliberately cultivated them, and because Shakespeare and all the other young expression-hunters of the 1590s had Golding's Ovid and Spenser's poems in their heads. It is amusing to see how smartly they borrow each other's finds; how Golding's *heedless* and *careless,* for example, reappear inevitably in Spenser and Shakespeare, and Sackvill's *luckless* in all three; or how Spenser and Marlowe almost dispute by their nimbleness as connoisseurs the Shakespearian paternity of *gloom.* For they were collectors as well as inventors, and hunted words and verbal patterns as bibliophiles hunt first editions.

There was some ostentation in Lowell's saying that " our ancestors could bring over no English better than Shakespeare's," but it is a fact that the first immigrants brought in the precise attitude toward word-making that was the mark of his time. " The American language," says a recent Irish observer,[3] " developed its distinctive note because it was three thousand miles away from Europe, and began its course four years after Shakespeare died." The long arm of the Eighteenth Century pedants reached out to police it, but the

---

1 Thomas Heywood launched *to diapason, sonance, moechal,* and *obdure* in The Rape of Lucrece, 1608, and was censured for it nearly three centuries later by John Addington Symonds in the Mermaid edition of his plays.

2 Arthur Golding (*c.* 1536–*c.* 1605) published a translation of the first four books of Ovid's Metamorphoses

in 1565, and followed them two years later with the remaining eleven. Despite his interest in one of the least inhibited of Roman poets, Golding was a strict Puritan, and also translated some of the writings of John Calvin.

3 The American Language, by Sean O Faolain, *Irish Times* (Dublin), April 1, 1944.

wide and thin dispersal of population hobbled their effort, and when the great Western trek began there was enough of the Elizabethan spirit left to flower again. This spirit was given a powerful reinforcement by the appearance of Webster's American Dictionary in 1828, for until it provided Americans with a standard of their own they were necessarily more or less dependent upon the authority of Samuel Johnson, who was not only bitterly hostile to everything American but also the grand master of all the pedantic quacks of his time. No eminent lexicographer was ever more ignorant of speech-ways than he was. In his dictionary of 1755 he thundered idiotically against many words that are now universally recognized as sound English, *e.g.*, *to wabble, to bamboozle*, and *touchy*. *To wabble* he described as " low, barbarous," and *to bamboozle* and *touchy* as " low," and at other times he denounced *to swap, to coax, to budge, fib, banter, fop, fun, stingy, swimmingly, row* (in the sense of a disturbance), *chaperon* and *to derange*. Thus Sir John Hawkins, editor of his Collective Edition of 1787: [1]

> He would not allow the verb *derange*, a word at present much in use, to be an English word. " Sir," said a gentleman who had some pretensions to literature, " I have seen it in a book." " Not in a *bound* book," said Johnson; " *disarrange* is the word we ought to use instead of it."

The NED's first example of *to derange* is from Adam Smith's " The Wealth of Nations," 1776. In the United States the verb acquired the special meaning, now obsolete, of to remove from office, and was so used by George Washington. *To bamboozle* had been under fire before Johnson tackled it. It was used by Colley Cibber in " She Wou'd and She Wou'd Not " in 1702, but eight years later Jonathan Swift was listing it in the *Tatler* [2] among corruptions introduced into English by " some pretty fellow " and " now struggling for the vogue," along with *banter, sham, mob, bubble* and *bully*. Dr. John Arbuthnot, one of Swift's intimates, used it in 1712 in his political satire, " The History of John Bull," but it remained below the salt until the end of the Eighteenth Century, and Grose listed it as slang in 1785. Not until toward the middle of the Nineteenth Century did it come into general usage in England. In America it got into circu-

---

1 Apothegms, Sentiments, Opinions   2 No. 230.
and Occasional Reflections of Samuel Johnson in Vol. XI.

lation at about the same time, and presently the perfect participle took on the special meaning of drunk, never used in England and now obsolete here. The NED says that its origin is unknown, but that it was probably borrowed from the cant of rogues. It has been ascribed to the gipsies, but does not occur in any vocabulary of their language that I am aware of. *Banter*, noun and verb, is equally mysterious. Swift, in " A Tale of a Tub," 1710, says that it was " first borrowed from the bullies in White Friars, then fell among the footmen, and at last retired to the pedants." Samuel Pepys had used it in his diary, December 24, 1667, and John Locke had mentioned it in his " Essay Concerning Human Understanding " in 1690, and by 1700 it had worked its way into respectable society, but Swift and Johnson continued to denounce it. Its origin, like that of *to bamboozle*, is unknown, and the NED is uncertain whether the noun or the verb appeared first. In the United States, early in the Nineteenth Century, it acquired a number of special meanings, unknown in England. First, as a verb, it came to signify to haggle, to bargain, and in that sense is traced by the DAE to 1793. Then, after the turn of the century, it came to signify a challenge or to challenge. In the original sense of to chaff, to make fun of, to provoke by ridicule, it is now perfectly sound English.

*To budge* is old in English, and was in good usage in the Seventeenth Century, but for some reason unknown the purists of the Eighteenth took a dislike to it, and their opposition was so effective that the word was listed as slang by Grose in 1785. Its origin remains in dispute. Weekley derives it from a French verb, *bouger*, meaning to stir, but admits that " this etymology is rather speculative." Apparently it did not come from the old English noun, *budge*, meaning a kind of fur, which is traced by the NED to 1382. That noun was originally spelled *bugee, bugeye, bogey, buge* or *bogy*, and did not acquire its present spelling until *c.* 1570. In Virginia, early in the Nineteenth Century, *budge* picked up the special meaning of nervous irritation or fidgetiness, and in that sense the DAE traces it to 1824. Miss Ellen Glasgow used it in her novel, " The Deliverance," in 1904, but apparently it has not made any progress elsewhere in the United States. *Chaperon*, a loan from the French, originally had the meaning of a hood or cap, and in that sense is traced by the NED to *c.* 1380. In its present figurative sense of a duenna it appeared in 1720 or thereabout,[1] and was soon in good usage, though the pedants denounced it for years afterward — mainly, I gather, because they mistook it for a recent importation from the French, and were against all loan-words. *To coax*, in the modern sense of to wheedle or blandish, is traced by the NED to 1663, but in other senses it is older. It seems to have come originally from a noun, *cokes*, signifying a fool, but that is uncertain. It has no special American meanings, but when the first *coachers* appeared in baseball, *c.* 1890,[2] they were often called *coaxers* by the fans, to whom *coacher* (later reduced to *coach*) and *to coach* were novelties, though the DAE shows that *coach* had been used in football, as a conscious loan from English, so early as 1871.

That *fib*, *fop*, and *fun* were once under fire may seem incredible today, but it is a fact. *Fib*, in the sense of a venal falsehood, was used by Dryden, Defoe and Goldsmith. Perhaps its disrepute in the Eighteenth Century arose from the fact that it had, as a verb, acquired the sense of to beat, and was used in that sense by the criminals of the time. Grose gives this specimen of their jargon: "to *fib* the cove's quarron in the rumpad for the lour in his bung," and translates it thus: "to beat the fellow in the highway for the money in his purse." The origin of the word is unknown, but the NED suggests that it may be a shortened form of *fible-fable*, a reduplication of *fable*. Weekley, dissenting, inclines to think that it is a thinned form of *fob*, an old English word signifying an imposter. The origin of *fop* is equally uncertain, though all authorities agree that it may be related to the German verb *foppen*, meaning to fool. In the sense of a fool it is traced by the NED to *c.* 1440. It did not acquire the special meaning of a person overattentive to his dress until the end of the Seventeenth Century. Johnson's effort to put it down was in vain, and it is now perfectly good English. Derivatives of the word in its earlier sense were used by Shakespeare, Greene and the Foxe who wrote the once celebrated "Book of Martyrs," and derivatives in the present sense were used by Hume, Fielding, Evelyn and Addison. *Fun*, though it seems commonplace today, is a relatively

---

1 A writer in *Notes and Queries*, 1864, p. 280, quoted by the NED, says that it "means that the experienced married woman shelters the youthful débutante as a hood shelters the face."

2 An Historical Dictionary of Baseball Terminology, by Edward J. Nichols; State College, Pa., 1939, p. 15.

recent word. It appeared toward the end of the Seventeenth Century in the sense of a cheat or hoax, and in that meaning was listed by the mysterious B. E. in his " Dictionary of the Canting Crew," 1698. Grose testifies that it was still thieves' cant so late as 1785, but it had also acquired a more innocent significance by 1727, when Swift used it.

*Row,* in the sense of a violent disturbance or commotion, is traced by the NED to 1787, but it is undoubtedly older. The NED calls it " a slang or colloquial word of obscure origin," but Weekley thinks it is a back-formation from *rouse,* which, in the sense of a carousal or drinking-bout, was used by Shakespeare in " Hamlet," 1601. *Row* was used by Byron without any apparent sense of its vulgarity in 1820, and by Dickens in 1837. It is now in good usage, though Webster 1934 still marks it " colloquial." *Stingy,* in the sense of avaricious, mean, close-fisted, was something of a novelty in Johnson's day, and his dislike for it seems to have worked against its adoption, but by the end of the Eighteenth Century it had forced its way into the language, and today not even the most extravagant pedant would question it. Weekley says that it is apparently derived from *stinge,* a dialectical form of *sting.* The softening of the g is a phenomenon not infrequently encountered in English.[1] *To swap,* in the sense of to exchange, goes back to the end of the Sixteenth Century, and the NED says that it was " probably orig. a horsedealer's term." It has always been in more general use in the United States than in England, and it occurs in one of the most famous of American sayings — Abraham Lincoln's " Don't *swap* horses crossing a stream." *Swimmingly* goes back to 1622, when it appeared in one of the plays of Fletcher and Massinger, and *touchy* to 1605. Why the Eighteenth Century purists disliked them I do not know: they are both sound English today. So is *to wabble* (or *wobble*), which is traced by the NED to 1657, when it was used by Richard Ligon in describing the gait of the cockroaches of the West Indies.[2] *To wabble* is derived by the NED from a Middle High German verb, *wabblen,* signifying to move restlessly, but Weekley prefers to relate it to the Middle English *quappen,* meaning to tremble.

Johnson and Swift, of course, were not the only illuminati of their time to fling themselves against new words that were destined to flour-

---

1 For example, in *dingy,* which seems to be derived from *dung.*

2 A True and Exact History of the Island of Barbadoes; London, p. 62.

ish in America and gradually make their way in England. Another was Horace Walpole, who, in a letter dated February 4, 1759, took William Robertson to task for using *interference* in his "History of Scotland." [1] In this letter Walpole indicates that he thought Robertson coined the word, and it is possible that he did, for the NED's first example of it, from Edmund Burke, is dated 1783. Thus Walpole:

> If the accent is laid where it should be, on the second syllable, it forms an un-couth-sounding word; if on the third syllable a short-cut is made long. In most places *intervention* will express *interference;* in others, *intermeddling*.[2]

Walpole also objected to *stripped piecemeal*, to *independency* and to *paction*, the last-named a Scotch form of *compact*. Thomas Gray, author of the Elegy, was another furious purist; indeed, his dudgeon was aroused not only by neologisms, but also by various words that had been long in use, and by writers of the first chop. In 1741, for example, he wrote to Richard West denouncing John Dryden's use of *beverage, roundelay, ireful, disarray, wayward, furbished, smouldering, crone* and *beldam*. Gray admitted that Shakespeare and Milton had "enriched" the language with "words of their own composition or invention," but argued that "the affectation of imitating Shakespeare may be carried too far." The NED traces *roundelay* to 1573, *beldam(e)* to *c.* 1440, *crone* and *disarray* to *c.* 1386, *furbished* to 1382, *wayward* to *c.* 1830, *beverage* to *c.* 1325, and *ireful* to *c.* 1300.

The authority of Johnson continued in both England and America for more than half a century after the first edition of his Dictionary appeared in 1755.[3] Other dictionaries came out during that time, but they were all poor things, and it was not until the publication of Webster's Compendious Dictionary in 1806 that the Great Cham was ever really challenged. The Rev. H. J. Todd's two revisions of the Johnson dictionary of 1755, in 1818 and 1827, showed a dispo-

---

1 London, 1759. Robertson (1721–93) was historiographer-royal for Scotland and principal of Edinburgh University. He also wrote a History of America; London, 1777, in which he used *to derange*.

2 Horace Walpole and Wm. Robertson, by W. Forbes Gray, London *Times Literary Supplement*, March 14, 1942, p. 132.

3 The effects of that authority are hard to realize today. "In modern times," said George Campbell sadly, in The Philosophy of Rhetoric, 1776, "the privilege of coining tropes is almost confined to poets and orators." For Campbell see pp. 50 n and 97 n of AL4. He was a very sensible man and his book was the best thing of its sort that had appeared in English up to its time.

sition to break away from his implacable dogmatism, but it remained for Webster to deliver the fatal blow to him in 1828, when the first edition of the *American* Dictionary, the father of all the Websters of today, was published. But the effect of the *American* Dictionary, though it was to be felt eventually in England, was chiefly noticeable at the start in the United States only, and down to the middle of the Nineteenth Century the majority of the English learned continued to hold to Johnson's doctrine that the English language was already copious enough and ought to be protected against change and novelty. All the more respectable English writers stuck to the vocabulary that he had approved, and kept within hailing distance of his orotund and menacing style.[1] When Thomas Carlyle began printing " Sartor Resartus " in *Fraser's Magazine*, in 1833, the pother it made was produced by its strange words and disregard of Johnsonian " elegance " more than by the ideas in it. Although " Sketches by Boz," " The Ingoldsby Legends "[2] and " The Yellowplush Papers " were only 'round the corner, the paralyzing influence of Johnson still prevailed in England, and Carlyle was taken to task by even his friend John Sterling, whose life he was later to write, for the saucy liberties he was taking with what was still regarded as sound English. Thus Sterling wrote to him:

First as to the language.[3] A good deal of this is positively barbarous. *Environment, vestural, stertorous, visualized, complected*, and others to be found, I think, in the first twenty pages, — are words, so far as I know, without any authority; some of them contrary to analogy; and none repaying by their value the disadvantage of novelty. To these must be added new and erroneous locutions: *whole other tissues* for *all the other*, and similar uses of the word *whole;*

1 I am not forgetting, of course, Jeremy Bentham and S. T. Coleridge. Bentham not only invented a number of words that still survive, *e.g., to minimize, self-regarding, international, dynamic*, and *unilateral;* he also argued formally in favor of neologisms. See Notes on Jeremy Bentham's Attitude to Word-Creation, by Graham Wallas, *S. P. E. Tract No. XXXI*, 1928, pp. 333–34. But he used such words sparingly and his writing in general was quite orthodox. Coleridge ran to somewhat wilder novelties, *e.g., protoplast, accrescence, extroitive, to coadunate, to potenziate, ultracrepidated, expectability, novellish, in-*teradditive, *desynonymizative, chilographic, to pantisocratize, poematic*, and *athanasiophagus*. See Coleridge's Critical Terminology, by J. Isaac, in Essays and Studies by Members of the English Association; Oxford, 1936, pp. 86–104. But these were technical terms, and in his ordinary writing Coleridge was safely Johnsonian.

2 R. H. Barham, the author thereof (1788–1845), was a great lover of neologisms and used many of them in the Legends. In particular, he was fond of Americanisms. Into The Lay of St. Odille he introduced, for example, *tarnation*, and *Jim Crow.*

3 *i.e.,* of Sartor Resartus.

*orients* for *pearls; lucid* and *lucent* employed as if they were different in meaning; *hulls* perpetually for *coverings*, it being a word hardly used, and then only for the husk of a nut; "to insure a man of misapprehension;" *talented*, a mere newspaper and hustings word, invented, I believe, by O'Connell.[1]

Of these, Carlyle seems to have actually invented *environment*. *Stertorous* had been used by medical writers since the beginning of the century, and *visualized* was in Coleridge before it got into Carlyle. The English, to this day, dislike *complected* as a substitute for *complexioned*, but it was already in wide use in the United States before Carlyle used it; indeed, the DAE calls it an Americanism and traces it to 1806. *Vestural* was another of Carlyle's inventions, but *talented* was apparently introduced to England by the elder Bulwer-Lytton, who used it in his novel, "Falkland," in 1827. It was for long regarded by Englishmen as an Americanism, and damned as such by many of them; and so late as 1886 an American writer on the language [2] was alleging that it had been transplanted to England by Dickens in "American Notes," 1842, but for this American origin there is no evidence, and the DAE does not list it as an Americanism. Carlyle's bold use of *hulls* as a trope for clothes found no imitators in England, but Emerson used it in "The Sovereignty of Ethics" in 1878. Carlyle's attempt to differentiate between *lucid* and *lucent* seems to have failed, for the NED defines the first, in one sense, as "bright, shining, luminous," and the other as "shining, bright, luminous," and both, in another and more familiar sense, as "clear." Its first example of *lucent* is from Keats's "The Eve of St. Agnes," 1820, but it carries *lucid* back to 1620. The use of *orient* to designate a pearl seems to have been original with Carlyle, but the gem had been called *pearl of orient* so far in the past as *c.* 1440. Browning, following Carlyle, used *orient* in "Sordello" in 1840. Even T. B. Macaulay, one of the most enlightened Englishmen of the mid-century, took an occasional hand in the vain and irrational effort to put down neologians. On April 18, 1842, for example, he wrote to Macvey Napier to denounce the aforesaid *talented*. "Such a word," he said primly, "it is proper to avoid: first, because it is not wanted; secondly, because you never did hear it from those who speak very good English." But Southey and Coleridge had both used it, and in that very year 1842 it was being used by the immensely correct and

1 Sterling's letter is reprinted in Contemporary Comments, by E. H. Lacon-White; London, 1931, p. 325.

2 A. Cleveland Coxe, in Americanisms in England, *Forum*, Oct., 1886.

elegant Edward B. Pusey in " A Letter to the Archbishop of Canterbury on Some Circumstances Connected With the Present Crisis in the English Church." [1]

Such attempts to force the language into a strait-jacket all came to grief in America, though the schoolma'am was to continue her shrewish dos and don'ts for a long while afterward. To this day, in fact, she clings to the doctrine that there is such a thing as " correct English," that its principles have been laid down for all time by the English purists, and that she is under a moral obligation to inculcate it. But not many American grammarians above the level of writers of school texts subscribe to any such ideas. They have learned by their studies that every healthy language has ways of its own, and that those of vernacular American are very far from those of Johnsonese English. From the early Nineteenth Century onward the speech of the United States has been marked by a disdain of rules and precedents, and an eager search for novelties, and it seems destined to go on along that path as far into the future as we can see. Said Dr. Robert C. Pooley in his presidential address to the National Council of Teachers of English in 1941:

American English may be derided by conservative critics for the readiness with which neologisms become accepted and flash overnight to all parts of our land, but the fact itself is a sign of health. The purpose of a language is to communicate; if a new word or a new phrase carries with it a freshness of meaning, a short cut to communication, it is a desirable addition to our tongue, no matter how low its source or how questionable its etymology. We need not fear word creation as harmful; what we must fear is crystallization, the preservation of a conventional vocabulary by a limited minority who resent the normal steady changes which inevitably must take place within a language. . . .

We are a youthful nation, exuberant and perhaps sometimes a little rowdy. But there is promise and hope in the exuberance of youth; we see in our language a lively imagination, a picturesque freshness, and a readiness to accept change which are characteristic of youth. We need not fear exuberance. What we must fear and guard against is senility, the complacency of old age, which is content with things as they are and mockingly derisive of change.[2]

To what extent this youth theory is sound I do not profess to judge; it is heard often, and seems to have many adherents. Dr. Pooley, in his paper, called attention to the tendency to mass hysteria which unquestionably exists in the Republic, whether it be due to

[1] Macaulay's letter is in The Life and Letters of Lord Macaulay, by G. Otto Trevelyan; New York, 1877, Vol. II, p. 100.

[2] One People, One Language, *English Journal*, Feb., 1942, pp. 110-20.

adolescence or to senility, and showed some of its unhappy consequences in the field of spoken and written communication.

## 2. WHAT IS AN AMERICANISM?

97. [John Pickering was the first to attempt to draw up a schedule of Americanisms.] When I wrote this I somehow forgot John Witherspoon, though I was, of course, familiar with his papers in the *Pennsylvania Journal and Weekly Advertiser* in 1781, and had in fact summarized them on pp. 4 *ff* of AL4. There is more about them on pp. 4 *ff* of the present Supplement. The other early writers on the subject did not attempt to define categories of Americanisms.[1] Even Noah Webster, though he had probably formulated ideas as to their nature, omitted all discussion of them from his "Dissertations on the English Language," 1789, and it was not until he came to the preface of his American Dictionary of 1828, that he undertook any formal consideration of them. In that preface, which is still worth reading in full,[2] he said:

> Language is the expression of ideas; and if the people of one country cannot preserve an identity of ideas they cannot retain an identity of language. Now, an identity of ideas depends materially upon the sameness of things or objects with which the people of the two countries are conversant. But in no two portions of the earth, remote from each other, can such identity be found. Even physical objects must be different. But the principal differences between the people of this country and of all others arise from different forms of government, different laws, institutions and customs.
>
> Thus the practice of hawking and hunting, the institution of heraldry, and the feudal system of England originated terms which formed, and some of which now form, a necessary part of the language of that country; but in the United States many of these terms are no part of our present language, — and they can-

1 One of them, the Rev. Jonathan Boucher, alleged in the preface to his Glossary of Archaic and Provincial Words; second ed.; London, 1832, p. xlix, that the only additions the Americans had made to the English vocabulary were "such as they have adapted either from naval or mercantile men, with whom, on their first settlement, they were principally connected, or else from the aboriginal inhabitants," but the evidence offered by a poem from his hand, printed in the same volume, was strongly against him. This poem bore the title of Absence, a Pastoral Drawn From the Life, From the Manners, Customs and Phraseology of Planters (or, so to Speak more Pastorally, of the Rural Swains) Inhabiting the Banks of the Potomac, in Maryland. It is reprinted by Allen Walker Read in Boucher's Linguistic Pastoral of Colonial Maryland, *Dialect Notes*, Dec., 1933, pp. 353–60. There is an account of Boucher in AL4, p. 35, n. 1, and another in Read's paper just mentioned.

2 It was reprinted in *Encore*, July, 1943, pp. 90–95.

not be, for the things which they express do not exist in this country. They can be known to us only as obsolete or as foreign words. On the other hand, the institutions in this country which are new and peculiar give rise to new terms or to new applications of old terms, unknown to the people of England; which cannot be explained by them and which will not be inserted in their dictionaries, unless copied from ours. Thus the terms *land-office; land-warrant; location of land; consociation* of churches; *regent* of a university; *intendant* of a city; *plantation, senate, congress, court, assembly, escheat,* &c. are either words not belonging to the language of England, or they are applied to things in this country which do not exist in that.[1] No person in this country will be satisfied with the English definitions of the words *congress, senate* and *assembly, court,* &c., for although these are words used in England, yet they are applied in this country to express ideas which they do not express in that country. With our present constitution of government, *escheat* can never have its feudal sense in the United States.

But this is not all. In many cases, the nature of our governments, and of our civil institutions, requires an appropriate language in the definition of words, even when the words express the same thing as in England. Thus the English dictionaries inform us that a *justice* is one deputed by the *king* to do right by way of judgment — he is a *lord* by his office — *justices* of the peace are appointed by the *king's commission* — language which is inaccurate in respect to this officer in the United States. So *constitutionally* is defined by Todd or·Chalmers as *legally,* but in this country the distinction between *constitution* and *law* requires a different definition.

1 *Land-office* is traced by the DAE to 1681, when such an office existed in Maryland, but the term did not come into wide use until after the Revolution, when the distribution of public lands to the soldiers began. The waggish derivative, *land-office business,* in its figurative sense, probably arose during the rush to the West, but the DAE does not trace it beyond 1865, when it was used by Mark Twain. *Land-warrant* is traced by the DAE to 1742, *location* (in the sense of "locating or fixing the bounds of a tract or area of land") to 1718, *consociation* (now obsolete) to 1644, *regent* to 1813, and *selectman* to 1635. The use of *intendant* to designate a city official analogous to a mayor is traced by the DAE to 1789, but the word is now abandoned and forgotten. *Plantation,* to the English, means either a colony overseas or an area that has been planted to some useful crop (more especially, trees). In this country it began to take on the sense of a farm in the Seventeenth Century. It is still used in that sense in the South, as *ranch* is used in the Far West. The upper houses of some of the colonial legislatures were called *senates,* and the name was given to that of Congress by the Constitution, 1787. *Congress* was used to designate a gathering of legislators representing more than one colony so early as 1711. When the Continental *Congress* was set up in 1774 the word was always preceded by *the,* but the *the* began to be dropped so early as the year following. It was revived by Woodrow Wilson in 1913. Presidents Harding, Coolidge and Hoover ordinarily omitted it, but it was revived again by Franklin D. Roosevelt. The word, of course, is not an Americanism, though its special meaning is. Neither is *assembly,* but *general assembly,* to designate a legislature, has not been found in English before 1619, the date of the DAE's first American example. In England *escheat* means the lapsing of an intestate decedent's land to the crown; in the United States it means its lapsing to the State Treasury.

The other lexicographers of the Webster era attempted no categories of Americanisms: this was true alike of David Humphreys, whose glossary of 1815 has been noticed, and of Theodoric Romeyn Beck, whose " Notes on Mr. Pickering's Vocabulary " was published in 1830. Robley Dunglison, in the articles headed " Americanisms " that he contributed to the *Virginia Museum* in 1829–30, contented himself with setting up two classes — " old words used in a new sense," and " new words of indigenous origin." He excluded old words preserved or revived in America in their original sense, for, as he said, " if fashion induces the people of Great Britain to neglect them, we have the right to oppose the fashion and to retain them: they are English words." Also, he frowned upon native inventions that were not absolutely essential. " Those," he said, " which have been employed to express a state of things not previously existing, which have arisen from the peculiarities of the government or people," were " allowable," but " those which have occurred wantonly and unnecessarily . . . ought to be rejected." James Fenimore Cooper, in his chapter " On Language " in " The American Democrat," 1838, showed much the same spirit: he was so busy rebuking Americans for faulty pronunciations and the misuse of the word *gentleman* that he neglected to lay down the areas in which they were free to exercise their fancy. The English travelers who roved the country between the Revolution and the Civil War, denouncing Americanisms as vulgar and heathenish, were similarly negligent about defining them, and it remained for William C. Fowler, in his brief chapter on " American Dialects " in " The English Language," 1850, to attempt the first classification of them after Pickering.[1] John

[1] It is given in AL4, pp. 98 and 99. A reviewer in *Harper's Magazine* in 1855 alleged that it was really drawn up by G. W. Gibbs, a professor at Yale, " whose studies in the department of comparative philology entitle the productions of his pen on this subject to peculiar respect." Fowler, who married Noah Webster's widowed daughter, Harriet Webster Cobb, in 1825, has been rather neglected by American literary historians. He was professor of rhetoric at Amherst and introduced the study of Anglo-Saxon there some years before Francis J. Child began teaching it at Harvard.

He gave his father-in-law help with the checking and proofreading of the American Dictionary, 1828, and after the lexicographer's death in 1843 quarreled violently with another son-in-law, Chauncey A. Goodrich, for control of it. In this combat he suffered defeat. " Goodrich," says Warfel, p. 418, " was quietly foxlike, while Fowler was brusque, pompous, and leonine in his rages." Fowler's English Language, first published in 1850, was the accepted American authority on linguistics until the appearance of William Dwight Whitney's Language and the Study of Language in

Russell Bartlett followed in 1859,[1] John S. Farmer in 1889,[2] Sylva Clapin in 1902,[3] Richard H. Thornton in 1912,[4] and Gilbert M. Tucker in 1921.[5] Alfred L. Elwyn did not set up categories of Americanisms in his " Glossary of Supposed Americanisms," published in 1859,[6] nor did Schele de Vere in his " Americanisms: the English of the New World," nor did James Maitland in " The American Slang Dictionary," [7] nor did Brander Matthews in his " Americanisms and Briticisms," [8] nor did George Philip Krapp in " The English Language in America." [9] The editors of " A Dictionary of American English," when they brought out their first volume in 1938, con-

---

1867, and even afterward it maintained a high place as a college textbook. It was commonly called Fowler's English Grammar. The revised edition of 1855 was a tome of 754 pages.

1 Bartlett's list is given in AL4, p. 98.
2 Farmer's list is given in AL4, p. 100.
3 Clapin was a Canadian, and had published earlier a Dictionnaire canadien-français; Montreal, 1894, in which some attention was paid to Americanisms. In an appendix to his New Dictionary of Americanisms were reprinted four magazine articles on Americanisms and slang — Americanisms, by a mysterious Dr. Aubrey (possibly a pseudonym), *Leisure Hour* (London), 1887, pp. 827-29; Wild Flowers of English Speech in America, by Edward Eggleston, *Century Magazine*, 1894, pp. 848-56; The Philology of Slang, by E. B. Tylor, *Macmillan's Magazine*, 1874, pp. 502-13; and The Function of Slang, by Brander Matthews, *Harper's Monthly*, July, 1893, pp. 304-12 (reprinted in Parts of Speech; New York, 1901, pp. 185-213). Clapin's classification of Americanisms is in AL4, p. 100.
4 Thornton's list is given in AL4, pp. 100 and 101.
5 American English, New York, 1921. Tucker's list is given in AL4, p. 101.
6 Elwyn's list is made up almost wholly of English dialect words in use in America, and he leans heavily upon J. T. Brockett's Glossary of North Country Words; third ed.; Newcastle and London, 1846.

7 Chicago, 1891.
8 First published in *Harper's Magazine*, 1891, pp. 214-22; republished in Americanisms and Briticisms, With Other Essays on Other Isms; New York, 1892, pp. 1 ff.
9 Two vols.; New York, 1925. In the Chapter on Vocabulary in Vol. I Krapp discussed Americanisms at great length, but did not undertake a formal classification of them. He was greatly inclined to pooh-pooh them. " Professor Krapp," said Dr. John M. Manly, in a review of his book in the *New Republic*, Jan. 20, 1926, " maintains that the vocabulary of English has remained practically unchanged during its three hundred years of existence in America. This attitude of course involves a very summary treatment of new words and phrases and new meanings of old words and phrases. . . . Any American who has tried to travel or shop in England . . . will testify that the whole phraseology of common life is different in the two countries, and any American scholar who has written for British periodicals or books will testify to a constant sense of the difference between British and American usage in what is commonly called literary English." But despite his obsession, Krapp's writings on the subject are very valuable. They are listed in Bibliography of the Writings of George Philip Krapp, by Elliott V. K. Dobbie, *American Speech*, Dec., 1934, pp. 252-54.

tented themselves with saying in their preface that "the different types of words and phrases" listed in it could "be more readily ascertained by inspection than by any attempt at classification," but their chief, Sir William Craigie, went into rather more detail in a paper published in 1940.[1] After excluding loan-words, the topographical terms derived from them, and "composite names of plants and trees, animals, birds and fishes, of the type *black alder, black bear, black bass*, &c.," he listed the following categories:

1. Words showing "the addition of new senses to existing words and phrases."
2. "New derivative forms and attributive collocations or other compounds."
3. "Words not previously in use, and not adapted from other languages of the American continent."

Finally there is H. W. Horwill, who distinguishes nine classes of Americanisms in his "Dictionary of Modern American Usage," [2] as follows:

1. "Words whose meaning in America is entirely different from their meaning in England; as *billion, present, ruby type, solicitor*."
2. "Words whose general meaning is the same in both countries, but which, in America, have acquired a specific meaning in addition; as *brotherhood, commute, dues, fit, homestead, senior*."
3. "Words whose normal use has, in America, been extended to cover certain adjacent territory; as *freight, graduate, hunt*."
4. "Words that, in America, have acquired different shades of meaning and therefore carry different implications; as *jurist, politics*."
5. "Words that retain in America a meaning now obsolete in England; as *apartment, citizen, conclude, tardy, thrifty, town*."
6. "Words that, in America, have acquired a figurative meaning not in current use in England; as *gridiron, knife, pork, stripe, timber*."
7. "Words that, in America, commonly take the place of synonyms that are more generally used in England; as *faucet* (for *tap*), *hog* (for *pig*), *line* (for *queue*), *mail* (for *post*), *two weeks* (for *fortnight*)."
8. "Words of slightly varying form, of which one form is preferred in America and another in England; as *aluminum* (*aluminium*), *acclimate* (*acclimatize*), *candidacy* (*candidature*), *deviltry* (*devilry*), *telegrapher* (*telegraphist*)."
9. "Words that, in America, go to form compounds unknown in England; as *blue, night, scratch, thumb*."

It will be noted that Horwill does not mention loan-words. Some of the differences he lists will be discussed in Chapter VI, Section 2.

1 The Growth of American English,     2 Oxford, 1935, p. vi.
I, *S. P. E. Tracts, No. LVI;* Oxford.
1940, p. 204.

# III

# THE BEGINNINGS OF AMERICAN

## I. THE FIRST LOAN-WORDS

104. [The earliest Americanisms were probably words borrowed bodily from the Indian languages — words, in the main, indicating natural objects that had no counterparts in England.] Most of these came from the Indian languages of the Algonquian group. This group was only one of nearly sixty known to exist north of the Rio Grande, but the Indians who spoke it covered most of the region invaded by the first settlers, and out of it came the native personages who most dramatically appealed to the colonial imagination, for example, King Philip, Pontiac, Tecumseh and Pocahontas. In 1902 the late Alexander F. Chamberlain, professor of anthropology at Clark University, compiled a list of 132 words borrowed from Algonquian dialects, of which 36 survive in the American of today.[1] The latter were the following, to each of which I have appended the date of the first example of its use given by the DAE:

| | |
|---|---|
| Caribou, 1610. | Muskellunge, or maskinouge, 1794 |
| Caucus, 1745. | Opossum, 1610. |
| Chinquapin, 1676. | Papoose, 1634. |
| Chipmunk, 1841. | Pecan, 1778. |
| Hickory, 1634. | Pemmican, 1804. |
| Hominy, 1629. | Persimmon, 1612. |
| Mackinaw, 1827. | Podunk, 1666. |
| Menhaden, 1643. | Poke (plant), 1634. |
| Moccasin, 1612. | Pone, 1612. |
| Moose, 1613. | Porgy (fish), 1775. |
| Mugwump, 1832. | Powwow, 1624. |

1 *Journal of American Folk-Lore*, 1902, pp. 240–67. Chamberlain was an Englishman who received his early education in Canada. He got his Ph.D. at Clark in 1892, and remained there as a teacher until his death in 1914. He was one of the founders of the American Folk-Lore Society and editor of its *Journal* from 1900 to 1908. He contributed many papers to other scientific journals and was the author of two books on the child and a volume of poems. He took a hand in local politics in Worcester, Mass., and in 1905 was an alderman of the town and chairman of the Democratic city committee.

Raccoon, 1608.
Sachem, 1622
Scuppernong, 1825.
Skunk, 1634.
Squash, 1643.
Squaw, 1634.
Succotash, 1751.

Tammany, 1771.
Terrapin, 1672.
Toboggan, 1829.
Tomahawk, 1612.
Totem, 1609.
Wigwam, 1628.
Woodchuck, 1674.

Some of these, *e.g.*, *chipmunk*, *mugwump* and *Tammany*, are probably materially older than the DAE's first examples. The other words on Chamberlain's list have either become obsolete or survive only in dialects. Some specimens follow, with the dates of the DAE's first examples:

Apishamore ("used in the West for a saddle-blanket made of buffalo-calf skins"), 1830.
Cantico (a dance or jollification, surviving until 1867), 1670.
Carcajou (a wolverine), 1744.
Cashaw or cushaw (a squash), 1698.
Chebacco (a fishing-boat), 1835.
Chebog (a name for the menhaden), not listed in DAE.
Chogset (a New England name for the blue perch), 1842.
Cisco (a Great Lakes fish resembling the herring), 1848.
Cockarouse (a chief or leader, surviving until 1743), 1624.
Cohosh (the baneberry), 1796.
Hackmatack (an evergreen tree), 1792.
Killhag, or culheag (an animal trap made of logs), 1784.
Kinnikinnick (a mixture of tobacco with other dried leaves), 1817.
Kiskitomas (the hickory nut), 1810.
Mananosay, or maninose (the soft clam), 1843.
Manito, or manitou (a deity), 1671.
Maycock, or macock (a squash or melon), 1588.
Mocuck, or mocock (a basket in which maple-sugar is kept), 1822.
Moonack (the woodchuck), 1666.
Musquash (a muskrat), 1616.
Namaycush (a Great Lakes trout), 1787.
Netop (a friend or crony), 1643.
Nocake (parched corn), 1634.
Peag (shell used as ornament or money), 1648.
Pembina (the wild cranberry), 1824.
Pocosin (a swamp), 1634.
Poccoon (a plant yielding pigment), *c.* 1618.
Quahog, or quahaug (a hard clam), 1799.
Quickhatch (the wolverine), 1743.
Roanoke (a Virginia name for wampum), 1624.
Sagakomi (a substitute for tobacco), 1703.
Sagamite (a gruel made of hominy), 1698.
Sagamore (a chief), 1613.
Samp (corn porridge), 1643.
Sannup (a married male Indian), 1628.

Scuppaug, or scup (a marine fish), 1807.

Seawan (shell beads), 1627.

Squantersquash (an early name for the squash, obsolete by the middle of the Seventeenth Century), 1634.

Squantum (a spirit), 1630.

Squeteague, or suittee (the weakfish), 1803.

Supawn (corn-meal mush), 1780.

Tamarack (the red larch), 1805.

Tuckahoe (an edible root), 1612.

Tuckernuck (a picnic), not listed.

Wabash (to cheat, once used in the West), 1859.

Wampum (shell money), 1647.

Wangan (a boat), 1848.

Wapatoo, or wappatoo (a bulbous root), 1805.

Wauregan (good, fine, showy), 1643.

Weequash (to spear eels by night), 1792.

Wendigo (a fabulous giant), not listed.

Werowance (in Maryland and Virginia, a chief), 1588.

Whiskey-jack, or whiskey-john (in Canada and parts of the Northwest, a blue-jay: the word is a corruption of the Cree *wisketjan*), 1839.

In this case, as in that of the surviving Algonquian loans, some of the DAE's dates probably fall considerably short of showing the earliest use of the words. "The Indian elements in American English," said Chamberlain in his paper, "is much larger than is commonly believed to be the case. . . . In the local speech of New England, especially among the fishermen of its coasts and islands, many words of Algonquian origin, not familiar to the general public, are still preserved, and many more were once current, but have died out within the last 100 years."

The etymologies of the early Indian loan-words are sometimes obscure: [1] the DAE is often content to ascribe them to " an Algonquian source," which is hardly illuminating. Some of them, *e.g.*, *caribou*, *mackinaw* and *toboggan*, seem to have come into colonial English by way of Canadian French. Webster 1934 suggests that *caribou* may be derived from a Micmac word, *khalibu*, signifying pawer or scratcher. Weekley spells the Indian word *kaleboo*, and says that it referred to the fact that " the deer shovels away the snow with its hoofs to get at the moss on which it feeds." Some sense of the French associations of *caribou* must have lingered into the Eighteenth Cen-

---

[1] The best easily accessible authority is Webster 1934. Its etymologies in this field were prepared by Joseph Coy Green, associate professor of history and politics at Princeton and now an official of the State Department. See A Gallery of Philologists: Joseph Coy Green, by John Pomfret, *Word Study*, May, 1939, pp. 2–4.

tury, for in 1744 a writer quoted by the DAE spelled the plural *cariboux*. Early variants were *caribo*, *carraboo* and *carriboo*. The etymology of *caucus*, which is most likely not of Indian origin, is discussed in Chapter IV. *Chinquapin* is applied to both the dwarf chestnut of the region east of the Mississippi (*Castanae pumila*) and the giant *Castanopsis chrysophalla* of the Pacific Coast. The former is hardly more than a shrub, but the latter is an evergreen that may reach a height of 150 feet. There are also several minor varieties of *chinquapin*, not to mention a *chinquapin oak* and a *chinquapin perch*. *Chipmunk* is related by Webster to the Ojibway *atchitamon*, meaning a squirrel and referring to the animal's habit of coming down a tree head first. The DAE's first example is from Cooper's " The Deerslayer." Soon afterward the word appeared in the *Knickerbocker Magazine* as *chipmuck*, and the latter form survived into the 80s. *Hickory*, according to Webster, comes from *pawcohiccora*, a word used by the Indians of Virginia to designate a dish made of the pounded nuts. The early colonists spelled it *pokickery* or *pohickery* and applied it to the tree, and presently it was shortened to *hiccory* and *hickery* and finally became *hickory*. It has produced many derivatives, *e.g.*, *hickory-nut*, *-stick*, *-shirt*, *-shad*, *-elm*, *-borer*, *-pine* and *-pole*. *Hickory* was also the name of a strong cotton cloth formerly much in use for making worktrousers and shirts. The *hickory* tree is a native of North America, but has been introduced into Europe. Its genus includes the pecan.

*Hominy*, according to the DAE, is derived from an Algonquian word, *rockahominy;* Webster 1934 says that the form prevailing among the Virginia Indians was *rokahamen*, a compound of three words — *rok*, meal; *aham*, pounded; and *mem*, grain; Weekley says that the original was *rockahomonie*, " of which the first element means maize." In the DAE's first quotation, from John Smith, *milke homini* is described as " bruized Indian corne pounded, and boiled thicke, and milke for the sauce." Smith added: " but boiled with milke the best of all." Among the other early spellings were *omine*, *homine*, *homminy* and *homonoy*. The later settlers used lye water to soften the hulls of the grain, and by 1821 *lye-hominy* was recorded. Many other obvious derivatives have been in use at different times, *e.g.*, *hominy-sifter*, *-pot*, *-bread*, *-bean*, *-mill*, *-cake*, *-grits*, *-block* (a sort of pestle), and *-mortar*. A traveler of 1746 recorded that the name of *great hominy* was given to a dish which included meat or fowl. Some of the early settlers used cider instead of water for cooking hominy. *Mackinaw*, which entered American by way of the Canadian French word *mackinac*, is derived by the DAE from the Ojibway *mitchimakinak*, meaning a large turtle. The same word provided the names of the Strait of Mackinac and the Michigan island, country, fort and town. *Mackinaw* was applied in the 20s to the gaudy blankets which the government provided for the Indians of the vicinity, and soon afterward was used to designate a gun and a boat. The *mackinaw jacket*, so called because it was made of blanket material in loud designs, apparently did not appear until toward the end of the Nineteenth Century. *Menhaden* was borrowed from the Indians of the lower New England coast and according to Webster 1934 appeared in the Massachusetts dialect as *munnoquoh-teau*, meaning that which enriches the soil. The Indians buried one of the fish in each hill of corn, and the custom was borrowed by the settlers. Roger Williams, in 1643, called the fish a *munnawhat-teaug* and described it as somewhat like a herring. It has many other names, *e.g.*, *bunker, marshbanker, mosbanker, mossbonker, mossy-bunker, skippaug, Long Island herring, American sardine, pogy, bony fish, bugfish, bughead, fatback, yellowtail, savega, greentail, Sam Day, mud shad* and *shadine*. It is still taken for fertilizer, and also yields an oil and a cattle food. Its young are often canned under the guise of sardines.

*Moccasin* comes from a New England Indian word variously rendered by the early chronicles as *mockasin, mockison,* and *mogasheen.* Weekley says that there were different forms in different dialects, and Webster 1934 cites *mohkisson* and *mocussin.* The object designated, a soft-soled shoe, seems to have been borrowed by the settlers along with the word: they quickly found by experience that it was better suited for wilderness travel than their leather boots. The name was eventually transferred to a flower and a snake. *Moose* was apparently borrowed from the Passamaquoddy Indians of the Maine coast, but there were analogous forms in other dialects. The spelling, in the early days, included *mus, moos* and even *mouse.* The original Indian word seems to have had some reference to the animal's habit of stripping off the bark of trees for food. A number of derivatives are listed in the dictionaries, *e.g.*, *moose-berry, -bird, -bush, -deer, -elm, -flower, -maple, -tick* and *-wood,* along with such obvious forms as *moose-hunter, -hide, -meat, -horn, -skin, -tongue* and *-yard. Mug-*

*wump* is discussed in Chapter IV, Section 2. *Muskellunge* is the name of a pike much sought by sportsmen in the Great Lakes region. The DAE says that the name comes from the Ojibway word *mash-kinoje* and Webster agrees. Its variants include *muschilongue, muskalonge, muskanounge* and *muskinunge*. *Opossum* is from a word that occurred in different Indian dialects as *apasum* and *wabassim*. On its first appearance in American records it was written *apossoun*, but *opassum* and *opposum* soon followed. The shortened form, *possown*, appeared by 1613, and *possum*, which is in almost universal use today, followed in 1666. *To play possum* is traced by the DAE to 1822, and *to possum* to 1846. During the great movement into the West the pioneers sometimes called *persimmon-beer possum-toddy*. It is a part of American folklore that the colored people are extraordinarily fond of *possum* meat; the DAE records, on the authority of a traveler of 1824, that one of their favorite dishes in that era was *possum fat and hominy*. *Papoose* comes from a word signifying a suckling baby in all the Algonquian dialects. *Pecan* comes from one meaning any hard-shelled nut, and may have reached American English by way of Spanish. In the early days, it was spelled *peccane, pecanne, peccan, pecaun, pekaun* or *pecon*. *Pemmican*, from the Cree word *pimmikkan*, meaning fat, was brought in by the movement into the West, and is not recorded before the time of the Lewis and Clark expedition. *Persimmon*, from an Indian word reported to to have been *pasiminan* or *pasimenan*, has been traced by J. Louis Kuethe, in its present form, to 1676.[1] Some of the early spellings were *posimon, parsimmon, pursimond* and *putchamin*. *Persimmon-beer* is recorded in 1737. During the early years of the Nineteenth Century a number of phrases embodying *persimmon* were in wide use, *e.g.*, *a huckleberry to a persimmon* and *to bring down the persimmon*, but they are now obsolete. *Poke*, from the Indian word *uppowoc*, was first applied to the tobacco plant, but has since been transferred to the skunk cabbage, to a plant whose berries are used in dyeing, to a species of hellebore, and to various common weeds. The DAE traces *pokeberry* to 1774, *pokeroot* to 1687 and *pokeweed* to 1751.

*Pone*, most often encountered in *cornpone*, is derived from an Algonquian word signifying anything baked. John Smith, in 1612, wrote

1 *Baltimore Oriole* and *Persimmon*,
  *American Speech*, Oct., 1940, p. 334.

it *ponap*, but it had acquired its present spelling before the end of the Seventeenth Century. The DAE's first example of *cornpone* comes from Bartlett, 1859, but it must be much older. *Pone*, in the regions where it is still in common use, signifies especially a bread made in small oval loaves, flat on the bottom and rounded on the top. *Porgy* (or *porgee, pargie, pogy,* or *paugie*) is listed as an Indian loanword by Chamberlain, but the DAE marks it " of obscure origin " and Webster intimates that it may be derived from the Spanish *pargo*, designating the same fish. *Powwow* comes from the Indians of the New England coast: it first appeared as *powah*, but had acquired its present spelling by 1744. It was applied, at first, to an Indian medicine man, and was then transferred to a ceremonial rite by the Indians, and finally to any of their meetings. It began to be used to designate a meeting of whites early in the Nineteenth Century, and today usually has the special significance of a political palaver. The earliest meaning of the term is still preserved in the Pennsylvania German region, where a *powwow-man* (or *-woman*) designates a witchdoctor. This use was also common in New England in the early days, and the DAE records that a *powwower* was fined £5 in Massachusetts in 1646. The DAE says that *raccoon* is derived from the Algonquian word *arakunem*, signifying a creature that scratches with its hands. *Sachem*, like *powwow* and *wigwam*, has been preserved in the argot of politics, and especially in that of Tammany Hall. Webster derives it from *sachimau* and says that it also gave rise to *sagamore*, of the same meaning (*i.e.*, a chief), now almost vanished from American speech, though it survives in proper names. *Scuppernong*, the name of one of the principal varieties of American grapes, comes from an Indian word, *askuponong*, signifying the place of the magnolias. It first appeared in American use as a proper name for a river and lake in North Carolina, and was later applied to the grapes growing in the vicinity. *Skunk* is derived by Weekley from an Algonquian word *sengankw* or *segongw*, the original significance of which was apparently " he who urinates." It is applied to several species of the genus *Mephitis*, all of them characterized by the ejection of a foulsmelling secretion when disturbed. The word has been transferred to various animals and plants, *e.g.*, *skunk-cabbage* (or *-weed*), *skunkbird, skunk-bear, skunk-duck, skunk-current, skunk-grape* and *skunkspruce*. Its application as a pejorative to human beings is traced by the DAE to 1840. It also appears as a verb, signifying to defeat an opponent (*e.g.*, in a card game), to slink from danger, and to evade a debt. A noun derived from this verb, *skunker*, is also known, though the DAE does not list it. *Squash* is a shortened form of a Narragansett Indian word which Weekley gives as *asquutasquash*, the original significance of which seems to have been any fruit or vegetable eaten green. It appeared in the early chronicles as *isquotersquash* and *squantersquash*, but had acquired its present form by 1683. Its derivatives include *squash-bug, -beetle, -borer* and *-vine*.

*Squaw*, in its various Indian forms, signified any woman, but the early settlers seem to have given it the special significance of a wife. It was applied in the course of time to womanish men. Its derivatives include *squaw man* (the white consort of an Indian woman), *Squaw Winter*, and *squaw-ax, -berry, -bush, -cabbage, -corn, -fish, -flower, -huckleberry, -root, -vine* and *-weed*. *Succotash*, derived by the DAE from the Narragansett *misickquatash*, signifying an ear of corn, designates an American dish invented by the Indians and borrowed by the white settlers of New England. It apparently came into popularity relatively late, for the DAE's first example of its use is dated 1751. True *succotash* consists of corn and lima beans, but I have encountered it with mashed potatoes substituted for the beans. *Terrapin*, in its original Indian form, meant little turtle, and the DAE indicates that it was first borrowed by the whites in Virginia. In the early days it was variously spelled *terrapine, tarapin, tarapen* and *turpin*, but the modern spelling appeared so early as 1738. The *diamond-backed terrapin*, so called because of the markings on its carapace, is not recorded before Bartlett's fourth edition of his Glossary, 1877, but it must be much older. There is a legend in Maryland that *terrapin* were so plentiful on the Eastern Shore of the State in the early days that a law had to be passed forbidding the planters to feed them to their slaves more than twice a week. *Toboggan* came into American English through the Canadian French *tobagan*, a borrowing from the Micmac Indian *tobakun*, signifying a sled made of skins. The sport of *tobogganing* is first recorded by the DAE in 1856. *Tomahawk* was picked up by the settlers of both New England and Virginia in the earliest days; it seems to have come from a word common to all the Indian languages of the Eastern seaboard. *Totem*, now in universal use by anthropologists to signify an animal or plant associated with a given group of savages, and supposed to exercise some sort of influence over

them, is said by F. W. Hodge,[1] quoted by the DAE, to be derived
"from the term *ototeman* of the Chippewa and other cognate Algonquian dialects." It goes back to 1609, and *totemism* followed in
1791, but *totem-pole* appeares to be a relatively late addition to the
American vocabulary. *Wigwam* is derived by the DAE from the
Ojibway *wigiwam*, signifying a dwelling-place. The DAE notes that,
though its use by the Indians seems to have been restricted to the
East, it has been applied by whites to Indian habitations in the West
also. The Western Indians actually used *tipi*, from which *tepee* is
derived, or *hogán*, which is still in use among the Navahos. *Woodchuck* is an example of folk etymology, for it has nothing to do with
either *wood* or *chuck*. It comes, according to Webster, from the
Algonquian *wejack*. In recent years the more common name for the
animal (*Marmota monax*) has been *ground-hog*, which the DAE
traces to 1784. But the first known example of *Ground-Hog Day* (*i.e.,*
*Candlemas Day*, February 2) comes from Schele de Vere, 1871.

The Indian loans in American English are by no means confined
to terms borrowed from the languages of Indians inhabiting the present territory of the United States. Through the Spanish a great many
Nahuatl words from Mexico have come in, and not a few of them
have gone over into British English. In a paper published in 1938 [2]
Dr. George Watson of the University of Chicago listed a large number, *e.g., chili*, traced in print by the DAE to 1836; [3] *chocolate*, in English use, to 1604; *tomato*, traced to the same year; *avocado* (pear),
mentioned by George Washington in his diary in 1751; *ocelot*, a
Western leopard (*Felix pardalis*); *jalap*, in use by 1682; *coyote*, traced
by the DAE to 1834; *chicle*, the basis of chewing-gum; and *tamale*,
traced to 1854. In addition, there are many Nahuatl words that are
familiar in the Southwest, though relative strangers (save in cowboy
tales and movies) to the rest of the country, *e.g., mesquite, mescal,
tequila, sapota* and *peyote*. From the West Indian dialects, also
through the Spanish, have come a number of words, *e.g., canoe* and
*tobacco*. To these etymologists commonly add *barbecue*, which they
derive from the Spanish *barbacoa*, itself a loan from a Haitian dialect
But this Spanish *barbacoa* originally indicated a sleeping-bench ele-

[1] Handbook of American Indians North of Mexico; Washington, 1907-10.
[2] Nahuatl Words in American Eng-lish, *American Speech*, April, 1938, pp. 108-21.
[3] *Chili sauce* is traced to 1882 and *chili con carne* to 1895.

vated on stilts, not a device for roasting meat, and there has always been some difficulty about accounting for the change in meaning. In 1937 Dr. J. M. Carrière, a leading authority upon the French of the New World, suggested that *barbecue* may not come from the Spanish word at all, but may derive from a Canadian word, *barboka*, derived from a Western Indian language and signifying a frame for roasting or smoking meat.[1] He showed that *barboka* was reported by a French traveler of 1770 in the exact sense of the American *barbecue*. "The word *barbacoa*," he said, "never had in Mexico . . . , as far as recorded evidence can show, the meaning of a social entertainment at which animals are roasted whole. . . . It must have been taken over by the early American settlers in the Mississippi valley, where it was an old word among the French population." But this was written before the appearance of the first volume of the DAE. In that volume evidence is presented that *barbecue* was in American use in the sense of a roasted animal by 1709, and in the sense of a social gathering by 1733. It is thus hardly likely that the word came from the French of the Mississippi valley; it is easier to believe that it came from the Spanish, and acquired its special American meaning soon after it was used in the original sense of a sleeping arrangement by William Dampier in his "New Voyage Round the World" in 1697. Indeed, it apparently acquired that meaning, at least in the West Indies, before Dampier's time, for Edmund Hickeringill had used the verb *to barbecue*, in the sense of to roast, in his "Jamaica View'd" in 1661.

*Canoe* was picked up from the Indians of the West Indies by Columbus's sailors. It seems to come from a Haitian word, *canoa*, and was taken without change into Spanish, where it remains *canoa* to this day, as it does in Italian.[2] Like *maize*, it appears in English for the first time in Eden's "Decades," 1555, where its form it still *canoa*. During its first two centuries as an English word it was spelled *cannoa*, *canoae*, *canow*, *canowe*, *cannoe*, *cannew*, *conow*, *connue*, *connou*,

1 Indian and Creole *Barboka*, American *Barbecue*, *Language*, April–June, 1937, pp. 148–50.

2 This is the etymology favored by the NED and by Webster's New International. In Nov., 1942 Epsy Colling printed the following caveat in *College English*, p. 136: "When Columbus, writing his journal in Latin, had occasion to mention the boats of the Indians, he used the word *scapha*. Some careless scribe changed the *scapha* to *canoa*, and, as the error remained undetected, Indian boats came to be called *canoas*. When the Englishman reached the Spanish Main . . . he taught the word to the Indians." *Scapha* is defined by Cassell's Latin Dictionary as "a small boat, a skiff."

*cannou, cannowe, caano, canoo* and *canot,* but by the end of the Eighteenth Century the present form became fixed. At the start it was restricted in meaning to a craft made of a hollowed tree-trunk, but after a while it came to mean any sort of savage vessel operated by paddles. In the course of time the more limited American sense of a small craft sharp at both ends, made of bark, canvas or some other light material and operated by paddles, supplanted the various English senses, and at present the English use the word exactly as Americans do. The familiar American phrase, *to paddle one's own canoe,* is traced by the DAE to 1828. *Canoeing* as a sport did not arise until after the Civil War: it was launched by the publication of John MacGregor's book, " A Thousand Miles in the *Rob Roy Canoe,*" in 1866.[1] The DAE's first reference to a *canoe-club* in the United States is dated 1872. By that time *canoeists* were already numerous on the rivers and lakes of the East. Said a writer in *Harper's Magazine* in 1880: [2]

When MacGregor published his account of the *Rob Roy's* voyage he established *canoeing* as a Summer pastime. The idea was not new; it was older than authentic history; but he gave it an overhauling and brushing up that brought it out in a form that was wonderfully attractive. The *Rob Roy* was so diminutive that her captain was able to transport her on horseback, but what she accomplished made her quite as famous as any ship in her Majesty's navy. The English *canoe-fleet* was soon numbered by hundreds. The *Rob Roy* was superseded, as a sailing *canoe,* by the *Nautilus,* and many voyages, under an endless variety of conditions, have since been accomplished. *Canoe-clubs* were organized, and in an incredibly brief time *canoeing* became in Great Britain a national pastime.

Its introduction in the United States may be said to have·taken place in 1870, when the New York *Canoe-Club* was founded by William L. Allen. The Indian birch and dug-out, it is true, belong to the *canoe* group, but they are, at best, rude craft, unfit for general cruising, and had long before gone into disuse, and come to be valued only as relics of an uncivilized condition. Americans have enthusiastically adopted the pastime, and it is only a question of time when *canoes* will be as frequently seen on our bays, lakes, and rivers as sail and row boats. . . .

Long cruises have been made by Americans. The *Kleine Fritz* (A. H. Siegfried) has followed the course of the Mississippi from the extreme head-waters to Rock Island, Ill.; the *Maria Theresa* (N. H. Bishop) has cruised by inland waters from Lansingburg, N. Y., to the mouth of the Suwannee river; the *Bubble* (Charles E. Chase) in 1878 cruised from New York to Quebec by connecting

1 MacGregor (1825–92) was a Scotsman and was called to the English bar in 1851, but spent most of his life traveling. He heard about the *canoe* on a visit to America, and started out on a long cruise on the inland waterways of Europe in the *Rob Roy* in 1865. Later he made voyages in the North Sea countries and along the river Jordan.

2 The Cruising *Canoe* and Its Outfit, by C. E. Chase, Sept., pp. 395 *ff.*

waterways, thence by portage, through the Valley of the Chaudière, to the head-waters of and down the Connecticut river, to and through Long Island Sound, to New York. Mr. C. H. Farnham has recently completed a Canadian voyage embracing the Saguenay, its tributaries, and other water-courses. In 1879 Mr. Frank Zihler made a cruise of about 1200 miles, from Racine, Wis., to New Orleans. Many less extended cruises have been made, and clubs have been organized in the larger cities.

" A *canoe*," according to a recent official and technical definition, " is a boat sharp at both ends, not more than thirty-six inches beam, and which can be effectively propelled by a double-bladed paddle; but a *canoe* may be propelled either by a double or single bladed paddle, or by one or more sails. No other means of propulsion shall be used."

The author of this article distinguished between various types of *canoes* as follows:

The *Herald* and *English canoes* are reflections of the birch; the *Nautilus*, of the whale-boat; the *Rob Roy* of the racing shell; and the *Shadow*, the combination of all.

*Canoe* hatched the usual derivatives before 1800. The DAE traces *canoe-tree* (a tree suitable for making a canoe) to 1638, *canoe-place* (a landing place for canoes) to 1653, *canoeload* to 1691, *canoeing* to 1752, *canoeman* to 1755, and *canoewood* to 1762. Its first example of *to canoe* is dated 1794, but the verb undoubtedly arose much earlier. *Canoeist* is traced to 1879, *canoe-racing* to 1879 and *canoer* to 1898.

105. [Finally, new words were made by translating Indian terms, whether real or imaginary — for example, *war-path*, *war-paint*, *pale-face*, *big-chief*, *medicine-man*, *pipe-of-peace*, *fire-water* and *to bury the hatchet* — , and by using the word *Indian* as a prefix.] Many of the former class naturally had to do with war, for it was predominantly as an enemy in the field that most Americans, down to the end of the Nineteenth Century, were conscious of Indians. The DAE traces *war-dance* to 1711, *war-dress* to 1724, *war-whoop* to 1725, *war-path* to 1755, *war-hatchet* to 1760, *war-club* and *war-belt* to 1776, *war-party* to 1792, *war-eagle* to 1821, *war-paint* and *to go upon the war-path* to 1826, and *war-trail* to 1840. The first examples of the last three come from Cooper, who was also the first, apparently, to use *pale-face* (1821). *War-drum* was recorded in England so long ago as 1593, and *war-cry* seems to have been in English use in South America before it appeared in the present United States. The DAE does not list *big-chief*, but it traces *big-medicine* to 1846, and records various other

words and phrases embodying *medicine* to the 1790–1860 era, *e.g.*, *bad medicine* to 1815, *medicine-man* to 1806, *medicine-dance* to 1808, and *to make medicine* to 1805. *Pipe-of-peace* is traced to 1705, *Great Spirit* to 1790, *fire-water* to 1817, and *to bury the hatchet* to 1754. The last-named seems to have been preceded by *to bury the ax* (1680) and *to lay down the hatchet* (1724). Many such terms, once much more familiar than they are today, were introduced by the reports of the Lewis and Clark expedition of 1804–1806, *e.g.*, *to make medicine*.[1] Of compounds embodying *Indian* the DAE lists more than eighty, of which the earliest seems to be *Indian-hemp*, 1619. Among the others that arose before the end of the Seventeenth Century were *Indian-field*, 1634; *-meal*, 1635; *-harvest*, 1642; *-purchase*, 1642; *-trade*, 1644; *-arrow*, 1654; *-bread*, 1654; *-land*, 1658; *-deed*, 1664; *-war*, 1668; *-dog*, 1672; *-claim*, 1674; *constable*, 1682; *-conveyance*, 1683; *-title*, 1683; and *-preacher*, 1699.[2] It used to be assumed that *Indian Summer* must have been one of the earliest of these compounds, but in 1902 Albert Matthews produced evidence that it was actually relatively recent.[3] Mr. Matthews summed up his contentions as follows:

that the term *Indian Summer* first made its appearance in the last decade of the Eighteenth Century; that during the next decade the expression *second Summer*[4] was used, indicating that there was no generally accepted designation for the supposed spell of peculiar weather in Autumn; that this spell itself was first noticed shortly before 1800; that the term *Indian Summer* became established about twenty years after its earliest appearance; that it was first employed in Western Pennsylvania; that it had spread to New England by 1798, to New York by 1809, to Canada by 1821, and to England by 1830; that the term is not merely an Americanism, but has become part of the English language in its widest sense, having actually supplanted in England expressions which had there been in vogue for centuries, and is now heard among English-speaking people throughout the world; that it has been adopted by the poets; that it has often

1 An account of the neologisms thus launched is in Lewis and Clark: Linguistic Pioneers, by Elijah Criswell, *University of Missouri Studies*, April 1, 1940.
2 *Honest Injun*, meaning honestly, truly, is traced by the DAE to 1875, but is probably older. Other terms in *Indian-*, with the dates of the DAE's earliest examples, are *-agent*, 1766; *-blanket*, 1765; *-country*, 1715; *-dance*, 1705; *-doctor*, 1724; *-fashion*, 1751; *-fighter*, 1832; *-file*, 1758; *-mound*, 1791; *-reservation*, 1821;

and *-sign*, 1812. The last-named, as a schoolboys' term, is discussed by Peter Tamony in *Indian Sign*, San Francisco *News Letter and Wasp*, July 21, 1939, p. 9.
3 The Term *Indian Summer*, *Monthly Weather Review*, Jan. and Feb., 1902.
4 The DAE offers the following quotation from Travels in America, by Thomas Ashe; London, 1808: "The Autumn [in Kentucky] is distinguished by the name of *Second summer*."

been employed in a beautiful figurative sense, as applied to the declining years of a man's life; and that it has given rise to much picturesque, if also some flamboyant writing.

Subsequent inquiries have forced a modification of some of these conclusions. Matthews fixed the date of the earliest appearance of the term as 1794, but the searchers for the DAE found that it was used by the famous St. John de Crèvecoeur (1731–1813), in 1778, in a paper describing the season as " a short interval of smoke and mildness." In its figurative sense, designating the closing days of life, the term was used by De Quincey in 1830, but it is still regarded as an Americanism in England and it would be an exaggeration to say that it is in common use. Perhaps the main reason for this last is that the English climate offers nothing comparable to the balmy, smoky weather that usually prevails along the Atlantic coast of the United States from the end of October until the onset of Winter. But in the main Matthews was clearly right. Why the term should have been so late in appearing no one knows. It was not listed by John Pickering in his Vocabulary of 1816, and Noah Webster did not admit it to his American Dictionary of 1828. There is, in fact, no mention of it in any of the early writers on Americanisms brought together by Mathews in " The Beginnings of American English." Regarding the origin of the term there is considerable difference of opinion, and the DAE contents itself with recording some of the guesses. C. B. Brown, in his translation of Volney's " Tableau du climat et du sol des États-Unis," 1804, suggested that the season probably owes its name " to its being predicted by the natives to the first emigrants, who took the early frosts as the signal of Winter." But the " first emigrants," as we have seen, never spoke of *Indian Summer*, though they undoubtedly marked its appearance and character. The Rev. James Freeman (1759–1835), in his " Sermons on Particular Occasions," 1812, said that the term was " derived from the natives, who believe that it is caused by a wind which comes immediately from the court of the great and benevolent god Cautantowwit," and William Faux, in his " Memorable Days in America," 1823, hazarded the guess that the brush-fires common during Indian Summer were lighted by the Indians to pen up game, and that the colonists thus named the season after them. Philip Doddridge, in his " Notes on the Indian Wars," 1824, suggested that *Indian Summer* was so called " because it afforded the Indians another opportunity of visiting the settlements with their destructive warfare," and Dr. Harry Morgan Ayres, in 1942, offered the theory that it got its name because the early settlers associated the word *Indian* with a concept of bogusness.[1] Said Ayres:

> In Europe, where the phenomenon is less striking than with us, it had long been known as *St. Martin's Summer*. . . . To Englishmen, unlike other Europeans, the name *St. Martin* suggested something false, a sham or imitation, for the dealers in cheap jewelry were gathered in the parish of St. Martin-de-Grand in London. . . . For English-speaking folk, though clearly this was not the reason the name was given to it,[2] the gentle hazy weather of late Autumn was indeed a *St. Martin's Summer*, an imitation and a sham.
>
> The first of our American forefathers, then, whoever he or quite possibly she was, that may have said, " 'Tis but an *Indian* kind of Summer after all, as false and fickle as they," [3] was only following the early habit among them of characterising by the term *Indian* whatever in the New World looked something like the real thing was but not. *Indian-corn* is not wheat. An *Indian-barn* is a hole in the ground.[4] There were *Indian-beans, Indian-cucumbers, Indian-hemp, Indian-paintbrushes, Indian-pipes, Indian-tea*, . . . *Indian* this and *Indian* that, and so most appropriately, by a happy and enduring stroke of creative language, *Indian Summer*.

The brief *Indian Summer* of England usually begins at Martinmas, November 11, hence its name. Sometimes it is called *St. Luke's Summer*, because St. Luke's day falls on October 18, or *All Hallow's Summer*, because All Saints' day (preceded by Hallowe'en) falls on November 1.[5] It is certainly possible, as Ayres surmises, that the concept of fraudulence attaching to *St. Martin's* in the minds of English immigrants of the Eighteenth Century may have suggested the

1 *Indian Summer, American Speech,* Oct., 1942, pp. 210 and 211.

2 The NED traces *St. Martin's Summer* to 1591.

3 Cf. *Indian-gift* and *Indian-giver.* The former, defined by the DAE as " a gift for which the giver expects a return; a revoked gift," is traced by it to 1764. There is another example from the same year in a letter from Nathaniel Ames to a Dr. Mather, March 26: " We Americans well know what is meant by an *Indian gift* — that is, to make a present but expect more in return than we give." This letter is in The Essays, Humor and Poems of Nathaniel Ames, Father and Son, with notes by Sam. Briggs; Cleveland, O., 1891, p. 25. The DAE's first example of *Indian-giver* is from Bartlett's first edition of 1848. In recent years the significance of *Indian-gift* as one "for which the giver expects a return " has rather passed out, and the term now usually means one which the giver takes back.

4 Traced by the DAE to 1634; defined by a writer of a century later as a hole in the ground " lined and covered with bark, and then with dirt."

5 *Indian Summer,* by J. E. T. Horne, London *Daily Telegraph,* Oct. 10, 1936. *Indian* — or *St. Martin's* — *Summer,* by Grace Tyers, Melbourne *Herald,* April 21, 1936. Miss Tyers says that in Australia, where *Indian Summer* comes in Spring, it has no name. She suggests the *Australian Summerette,* or *Easter's Little Summer.*

substitution of *Indian*. On the exact duration and nature of *Indian Summer* there seems to be no agreement among meteorologists. John R. Weeks, then the weather man at Baltimore, proposed in 1938 that it be defined as " a mild period of five or more days with no daily mean temperature below 40 degrees and with no rain on any day," [1] but it would be quite as rational to define it as a period of ten, or fifteen or thirty or even more days during which the *average* daily temperature is above 40, regardless of an occasional drop below or an occasional rain. Mr. Weeks called attention to the fact that in the Baltimore-Washington area *Indian Summer* often runs on until beyond Christmas; he showed, indeed, that it had included Christmas nine times during the 66 years from 1872 to 1938. The Gazetteer of the State of New York for 1813 described *Indian Summer* as beginning " about the last of October " and extending " into December, with occasional interruptions by Eastern storms." " Warm periods in January," said Weeks in the paper just cited, " when snow and ice melt and ice gorges sometimes cause floods in Northern rivers, were, in the early days, called by many *Indian Summer*, but now they are universally called the *January thaw*." *False Spring* is a premature burst of balmy weather in March or April: it may be followed by *onion snow* — " one that falls after the onions are planted." In Missouri a belated touch of Winter is called *Blackberry* or *Snowball Winter*, in North Carolina *Dogwood Winter*, in Canada *Squaw Winter*, and in Nebraska *Indian Winter*.[2]

The use of real or supposed Indian terms by Tammany and by various fraternal organizations, sometimes as translations, is familiar to most Americans. The DAE's first example of *sachem* in the Tammany sense is dated 1786. The Improved Order of Red Men, which is claimed to be an offshoot of the colonial Sons of Liberty from which Tammany is also alleged to be sprung,[3] carries on all its mysterious business in an argot largely made up of Indian and pseudo-

1 *Indian Summer* in Maryland, Baltimore *Evening Sun*, editorial page, Dec. 20, 1938.
2 Notes on American Weather Terms, by Mamie Meredith, *American Speech*, Aug., 1931, p. 466; *Blackberry Winter* and *Snowball Winter*, by M. S. Dearing, *American Speech*, Feb., 1932, p. 233; *Blackberry Winter*, by Vance Randolph, *American Speech*, Feb., 1932, p. 239; and

*Onion Winter*, by Mary Mielenz, *American Speech*, Oct., 1937, p. 237.
3 This claim, like that of the Freemasons to descent from the trades unions of King Solomon's time, has been disputed by cynics. The present order seems to have been organized in Baltimore during the Winter of 1833–34. It has about half a million members.

Indian terms. Its chief national dignitary is the *great incohonee*, and he is supported by two *great sagamores*, a *great keeper of wampum* (treasurer), and a *great tocakon* and a *great minewa* (guards). The head of a State-wide jurisdiction is a *great sachem*, and in his suite are two *great sagamores*, a *great sannap* and a *great mishinewa*. Of these terms, only *sachem, sagamore, wampum* and *sannap* (or *sannup*) are listed by the DAE; the last-named is defined, rather curiously, as "an Indian brave who is married." A lodge is called a *tribe* and its head is a *sachem*. Tribal jurisdictions are *hunting-grounds*, a meeting-place is a *wigwam* or *tepee*, a member is a *warrior*, and a nonmember is a *pale-face*. The brethren reckon time in terms of their own. Their calendar runs back to the year 1 G.S.D. (great sun of discovery), *i.e.*, to 1492, the year of the discovery of America. A minute is a *breath*, an hour is a *run*, a day is a *sun*, a night is a *sleep*, a month is a *moon*, and a year is a *great sun*. All the months have names supposed to be of Indian origin, *e.g.*, *Cold Moon* for January, *Plant Moon* for April, *Corn Moon* for September and *Beaver Moon* for December. The funds of a tribe are *wampum:* they are reckoned in *fathoms* (dollars), *feet* (ten cents) and *inches* (cents). A speech or report is a *talk* or *long talk*, to organize a meeting is *to kindle the council fire*, the gavel is a *tomahawk*, to adjourn is *to quench the fire* to carry on business is *to follow the hunt*, to take a vote is *to twig*, and to wrong a brother is *to cross the path*.[1] The Red Men have a female auxiliary called the *Degree of Pocahontas*, but the word *squaw* is frowned upon.

The names of two American Indian groups, the Mohawks and the Apaches, have acquired special meanings in British English and French, respectively. *Mohawk* (or *mohock*) is traced by the NED to 1711 and defined as "one of a class of aristocratic ruffians who infested the streets of London at night in the early years of the Eighteenth Century." The *Gentleman's Magazine*, in 1768, said that they had been so called because they mauled passersby "in the same cruel manner which the *Mohawks*, one of the Six Nations of Indians, might be supposed to do." *Apache*, of similar origin, was introduced to the French vocabulary in the early years of the Twentieth Century by Émile Darsy, then a reporter on *Le Figaro*. Paris was beset at the time by great gangs of rowdies and sometimes they staged sanguinary

1 Revised Red Men Illustrated; Chicago, 1928.

battles. M. Darsy, an ardent reader of the Western fiction of the time, tried the experiment of giving these gangs the names of Indian groups, and after failing to make *Sioux, Pawnee, Comanche* and various others stick, scored a ten-strike with *Apache*, which was adopted at once by M. Lepine, then prefect of police, and soon became a generic name for all the gangs. On the outbreak of World War I they were rounded up by the Army and put into the forefront of the fray, and not many of their members survived to the armistice. But *apache* remained in use to designate any ruffian, and in 1924 it was formally admitted to the language by the French Academy.[1] During the war or soon afterward *apache-dancers* began to appear in the United States. They always came in pairs, a man and a woman, and were dressed in costumes supposed to be those of the Paris *apaches* and their doxies. In the dance they performed the man always handled the woman in a violent manner, sometimes swinging her about him by her hair. They were displaced eventually by the less febrile *adagio-dancers*.

108. [The contributions of the New Amsterdam Dutch during the half century of their conflicts with the English included *cruller, coleslaw, cookey, stoop, sleigh, span* (of horses), *dope, spook, to snoop, pit* (as in *peach-pit*), *waffle, hook* (a point of land), *scow, boss* and *Santa Claus.*] The NED says that *Santa Claus* comes from *Sante Klaas,* a dialect form of *Sint Klaas,* meaning St. Nicholas, the patron saint of children; the DAE gives its source as *Sinterklaas,* "a corruption of *Sant Nikolaas.*" All authorities agree that both the name and the gift-bearing old fellow it designates were introduced to America by the Dutch of the New York region. The Puritans knew nothing of either, and neither did the more genial English settlers of the Southern colonies. All the NED's examples of *Santa Claus* are either American or relate to America; the usual English name for the saint is *Father Christmas,* which is traced by the NED to *c.* 1800,[2] but even *Father Christmas* did not attain to any general popularity in England until Queen Victoria, married in 1840, had children on her knee, and her German husband introduced them to the Christmas delights of his native land. The DAE's first example of *Santa Claus* comes from

1 *Apaches* in the Dictionary, New York *Times* (editorial), Aug. 17, 1924.
2 At Random, London *Observer,* Oct. 31, 1937: "*Father Christmas* is al-ready in the shops." But *Santa Claus* seems to be used occasionally. Headline in London *Daily Telegraph,* Dec. 27, 1938: "*Santa Claus* Did Not Forget."

J. Fenimore Cooper's " The Pioneers," 1823.[1] The Dutch did not bring in the *Christmas tree,* which had to wait for the Germans. There is a legend that the first one in America was set up at Wooster, Ohio, in 1847, by August Imgard, a recent immigrant from Wetzler in Hesse,[2] but that legend has been challenged by claimants for other pioneers and places, *e.g.,* Rochester, N. Y., 1840 and Philadelphia, 1834.[3] On January 6, 1842 the Rev. Theodore Ledyard Cuyler [4] wrote from Philadelphia:

> On Thursday evening we had our annual soiree at the school. The parents were invited . . . and altogether we mustered about 160 or 170. Everything was genteel. . . . We had a large *Christmas-tree,* which was a great attraction and novelty — it was decorated with the coats of arms of the boys, fanciful designs, and ribands, and looked beautiful.[5]

The most famous of American Christmas verses, beginning " 'Twas the night before Christmas," were written by Clement C. Moore in 1822, but they do not mention either *Santa Claus* or a *Christmas-tree,* though a tree is always shown in the modern illustrated editions for children. The title of the poem is " A Visit From *St. Nicholas,*" which is the way the saint seems to have been designated before *Santa Claus* became general. It was first printed in the Troy *Sentinel,* Dec. 23, 1823, but did not become generally known until Moore re-printed it in his " Poems " in 1844.

Schreiber, lately cited, says that even in Germany the *Christmas tree* is not really ancient. The first on record was set up in Strass-burg in 1604. It had reached Berlin by 1780, and in 1841 Queen Victoria and the Prince Concert had a tree in Windsor Castle. The first trees offered for sale at Christmas were on display in New York in 1851. By 1941 the trade in them, and in the associated Christmas

1 Under *St. Nicholas* the DAE prints a reference to *Santa Claus* dated 1773, but it comes from Esther Single-ton's Social New York Under the Georges, which was not published until 1902. H. W. Longfellow used the form *Santiclaus* in Outre-Mer, 1834 (first page of the section headed Note-Book).

2 The First American *Christmas-Tree,* by William I. Schreiber, *American-German Review,* Dec., 1943, p. 4.

3 Philadelphia Christmas Tree, *American-German Review,* June, 1944, p. 38. In this article the credit for set-ting up the first tree is given to Dr. Constantin Hering, born in Oschatz near Leipzig, who arrived in the United States in Jan., 1833, and prac-tised medicine in Philadelphia until his death in 1880.

4 Cuyler was a Presbyterian, born in 1822 and surviving until 1909. He was a popular pastor in Brooklyn from 1860 to 1890.

5 Trees Everywhere in the Forties?, *American-German Review,* April, 1944, p. 31.

greens, amounted to $25,000,000 for the country as a whole. President Franklin D. Roosevelt began growing trees for the Christmas market at Hyde Park during his time as Governor of New York, and continued in the business after he entered the White House. The Germans, of course, know nothing of *Santa Claus:* their name for the saint who brings presents at Christmas is *Belsnickel,* and that name is retained by the Pennsylvania Germans.[1] The American *Kriss-kring'l* or *Kriss-Kingle,* now obsolete, arose from a misunderstanding of the German *Christkindlein* or *Christkind'l,* which means, not St. Nicholas, but the Child in the Manger.[2] *Christmas-garden,* like *Christmas-tree,* is borrowed from the German. The DAE does not list it. *Krisskring'l,* in the form of *Kriss Kringle,* is traced to 1830 and marked an Americanism.[3] *Santa Claus* is always pronounced *Santy Claws* in the United States, with the *a* in *Santy* that of *pants.* To many American children the saint is not *Santa Claus* at all, but simply *Santy,* and they think of his wife as *Mrs. Santy.*

*Boss* has been discussed in Chapter 1, Section 6. It must have come into American English from the Dutch of the New York area much before 1806, the date of the DAE's first example, which is from Washington Irving. The verb *to boss* is not traced beyond 1856, but it also must be older. Neither term, however, is listed by Witherspoon or Pickering. The original Dutch form, *baas,*[4] is used in South African English precisely as we use *boss. Coleslaw* comes from the Dutch *koolsla,* which is made up of *kool,* meaning cabbage, and *sla,* a shortened form of *salade,* meaning salad. It is traced by the DAE to 1794. Folk etymology frequently converts it into *cold slaw. Cookey*

---

1 A Dictionary of the Non-English words of the Pennsylvania-German Dialect, by M. B. Lambert; Lancaster, Pa., 1924, p. 16. Lambert says that it is made up of *Pelz,* fur and *Nikolaus.* It is accented on the first syllable.

2 An anonymous article, The American Language, in *Putnam's Magazine,* Nov., 1870, p. 523, says that at that time, among American children in general, *Kriss-Kingle* was "only subordinate to *Santa Claus* as a designation for that obese personage who, in their philosophy, stands far beyond king or kaiser." *Kriss-Kingle* was still in wide use in the Baltimore of my childhood, 1885–90.

3 St. Nicholas is the patron saint, not only of children, but also of scholars, travelers, sailors, pawnbrokers and the Russian Orthodox Church. He flourished somewhere in the Eastern Mediterranean region in the Fourth Century and is said to have taken part in the Council of Niceae. His feast-day, December 6, was assimilated to Christmas during the Middle Ages.

4 Defined in Kramer's Nieuw Engelsch Woordenboek, edited by F. P. H. Prick van Wely; Gouda, 1921, as meaning master, foreman. It is used in Dutch in many figurative senses, *e.g.,* to designate a jolly fellow, a big baby, a shrewish wife.

(or *cookie* or *cooky*) comes from the Dutch *koekje*, a small cake, and seems to have been borrowed independently in the Scotch Lowlands. The DAE's first example of its American use is dated 1786. *Cruller* is apparently related to the Dutch verb *krullen*, to curl or crisp. The DAE traces it to 1805, but it is probably older. *Dope* is derived by the DAE from a Dutch word, *doop*, signifying a sauce, but no such meaning for *doop* is recorded in any of the Dutch dictionaries at hand. The true meaning of the word is a baptism or christening. Weekley believes that *dope* really comes from the corresponding verb, *doopen*, which has the sense of to dip, and Webster agrees. The history of the term in the United States remains to be worked out. The DAE traces it, in the meaning of "a preparation, mixture or drug, especially one that is harmful," to 1872, in that of opium to 1895, in that of a thick lubricant or other substance to 1876, and in that of inside knowledge to 1901, but these dates are hardly to be accepted as final. The word, as everyone knows, has acquired an enormous currency in the United States, and has picked up various other significances, *e.g.*, a fool. It is also in wide use in England; in Australia, according to Partridge, it has acquired the meaning of a heavy drinker.[1] In the argots of American industry it is used to indicate any liquid or semi-liquid material of a composition unknown to the workman, and thus has hundreds of significances. Its derivatives, *dope-fiend*, *dope-peddler*, *dope-sheet*, *dopester*, *to dope* and *to dope out* are also in frequent use.

*Pit*, in the sense of the hard seed of a fruit, as in *peach-pit* and *cherry-pit*, is not recorded before Bartlett listed it in 1848, but it is no doubt older. The DAE derives it from an identical Dutch word of the same meaning; perhaps it was helped into American by its resemblance to *pip*, traced by the NED to the late Eighteenth Century. *Scow* was borrowed from the Dutch, as the DAE shows, so early as 1669: the original form was *schouw*. *Sleigh*, from the Dutch *slee*, is traced by the DAE to 1703; in the early days it was spelled *slay*, *slae* and *sley*. *To snoop*, from the Dutch verb *snoepen*, meaning to eat sweets on the sly, is traced by the DAE, in its American sense of to pry or spy, to 1832. Bartlett, so late as his 1877 edition, records the earlier sense of "to clandestinely eat dainties or other victuals which have been put aside." "A servant who goes slyly into a dairy-

---

1 Baker, however, does not list it.

room and drinks milk from a pan," he says, " or a child who makes free with the preserves in the cupboard is said to be *snooping*." He added that the term was then " peculiar to New York." It is now in general use, and indicates any sort of surreptitious prowling. Thus Mark Twain in " A Connecticut Yankee at King Arthur's Court," 1889: " They always put in the long absence *snooping* around, . . . though none of them had any idea where the Holy Grail really was." *Span*, in the sense of a harnessed pair of horses, came from an identical Dutch word, with cognates in other Germanic languages, which apparently meant, originally, a yoke of oxen. Its verb, *spannen*, meant to stretch. To South African English it has given a number of derivative loans, *e.g.*, *to outspan*, to unharness. Webster 1852 said:

> A *span* of horses consists of two, usually of about the same color, and otherwise nearly alike, which are usually harnessed side by side. The word signifies properly the same as yoke, when applied to horned cattle, from buckling or fastening together. But in American *span* always implies resemblance in color at least, it being an object of ambition with gentlemen and with teamsters to unite two horses abreast that are alike.

The DAE traces *span* to 1769. Webster 1828 recorded a verb, *to span*, meaning to agree in color and size, but it seems to have dropped out. Neither noun nor verb was ever taken into British English. *Spook*, in the sense of a spectre, is from an identical Dutch word of the same meaning. The NED runs it back to 1801 in American use, but it is probably older. By the middle of the century it had been adopted by the English, who produced a number of derivatives, *e.g.*, *spookery*, *spookiness*, *spookish*, *spookism*, *spookology* and *spooky*, of which only the last is listed by the DAE.[1] *Stoop*, from the Dutch *stoep*, is traced to 1735 in American use. It means, ordinarily, the front steps of a house, but once had the additional meaning of a small porch with benches. *Waffle*, from the Dutch *wafel*, is not recorded by the DAE before 1817, but it is obviously much older, for *waffle-party* is recorded for 1808, *waffle-iron* for 1794, and *waffle-frolic* for 1744. *Waffle-iron* is a direct translation of the Dutch *wafelijzer*. Schele de Vere, in his " Americanisms," directs attention to a number of Dutch geographical terms that survive in the vicinity of New

---

[1] It is possible that *spook* was helped into American English by the German *spuk*, of the same meaning. A writer in *Harper's Magazine*, Aug., 1853, p. 201, reported that it was then in common use in the vicinity of Strasburg, Va., where the people spoke " scarcely anything but German."

York, sometimes anglicized out of recognition, *e.g.*, *kil*, a channel, as in *Kill van Kull*, *Catskill*, *Schuylkill* and *Fishkill;* *hoek*, a bend or corner, as in *Kinderhook* and *Sandy Hook;* and *gat*, a pass in a channel, as in *Barnegat* and *Hell-Gate* (*Helle-Gat*);[1] to which may be added *fly*, a swamp, traced by the DAE to 1675. Schele de Vere also lists many Dutch terms still surviving in his time (1871) in the New York area only, *e.g.*, *overslaugh*, a sand bar; *noodleje*, a noodle; *fetticus*, a salad; *rolliche*, a sort of sausage; and *hoople*, a child's rolling hoop.[2] A very large number of Dutch words were taken into English before the migration to America began, *e.g.*, *pickle*, *sled*, *spool*, *deck*, *hoist*, *bulwark*, *to loiter*, *freebooter*, *wagon*, *isinglass*, *luck*, *spatter* and *frolic*. Many of these were nautical or military.[3] The American use of *dominie* to indicate a clergyman (it exists in Scots English but only in the sense of a schoolmaster) and of *bush* to indicate wild land was probably influenced by the Dutch *dominee* and *bosch*. How *filibuster*, a Dutch loan, has been changed in meaning in the United States is discussed in Chapter IV, Section 2. *Hunky-dory*, an Americanism that has puzzled etymologists, is probably derived from the Dutch *honk*, signifying a goal in a game. Said an anonymous writer in *Putnam's Magazine* in 1870:[4]

The incipient manhood of New Amsterdam used this word in its plays, saying of one who had reached base that he was *honk*. Their American successors adopted it. . . . It found its way into the slang dialect, and through the medium

1 Washington Irving, in A History of New York . . . by Diedrich Knickerbocker; New York, 1809, Ch. IV: " Certain mealy-mouthed men of squeamish consciences, who are loath to give the Devil his due, have softened [this] into *Hurlgate*, forsooth! "

2 To these might be added *boonder*, to brush away; *pease*, disgusted; *grilly*, chilly; *plock*, to settle down; *sluck*, to swallow; *blummie*, a flower; *blickie*, a tin pail; and *speck*, fat. In the Dutch colony in Wisconsin, " I am *fees* of that " is used to indicate repugnance — a translation of the Dutch " Ik ben er *vies* van." See *Fiesty* and *Fiesty* Again, *American Speech*, April, 1943, p. 111. In the much larger Dutch colony of Michigan there are many more such borrowings, *e.g.*, *advokat* (egg-nog),

*voorzinger* (front-singer), *hutspot* (a combination of potatoes and some green), *balkenbry* (a pork loaf), *erwten soep* (pea soup), and *boerenjongens* (a drink made of brandy and raisins). A number are listed in Dutch Survivals in Holland, Michigan, by Peter Veltman, *American Speech*, Feb., 1940, pp. 80–83.

3 See A History of Foreign Words in English, by Mary S. Serjeantson; London, 1935, pp. 170–79. Also, A Dictionary of the Low-Dutch Element in the English Vocabulary, by J. F. Bense; the Hague, 1926–   ; Niederländisches Lehngut im Mittelenglischen, by J. M. Toll; Halle, 1926, and The Influence of Low Dutch on the English Vocabulary, by E. C. Llewellyn; Oxford, 1936.

4 The American Language, Nov., p. 522.

of the daily papers was widely disseminated. . . . With the anomalous affix *dory* (probably coined by some euphoniously-inspired member of the genus " Mose ") it now holds a high position in the public favor. . . . From the same Dutch roots come the word *hunker*, meaning, in political parlance, one who clings to the homestead, or to old principles.

Efforts have been made to find a Japanese source for *hunky-dory*, but they are far from persuasive. They were probably suggested by the fact that one of the first Japanese to visit the United States, an acrobat, was reputed to have an American vocabulary of but two words — *olrite* (all right) and *hunky-dory*. Today one term, *O.K.*, would suffice. The elegant euphemism *cuspidor* is commonly ascribed by lexicographers to the Portuguese *cuspidiera*, but it may actually come from the Dutch *kwispedoor* or *kwispeldoor*, of the same meaning.[1] It is not, unhappily, an Americanism, though it had a much greater vogue in this country than in Britain. In 1875 Mark Twain, in one of the chapters of " Old Times on the Mississippi " (later to become "Life on the Mississippi"), contributed to the *Atlantic Monthly*, told of " a *cuspidor* with the motto ' In God We Trust,' " and in 1892, in " The Quality of Mercy," William Dean Howells spoke with quite natural pride of " a nickel-plated *cuspidor*." In those innocent days the word was sometimes spelled *cuspidore* or *cuspadore*, but *cuspidor* was approved by the spellingbooks in use at Harvard, Yale and Princeton.

110. [Perhaps the most notable of all the contributions of Knickerbocker Dutch to American is the word *Yankee*.] The etymology adopted in AL4, to wit, that *Yankee* comes from *Jan* and *kees*, signifying *John Cheese*, is not approved by the DAE, but it has the support of Dr. Henri Logeman of the University of Ghent, and it seems likely to stand. In its original form the term was *Jan Kaas*, and in that form it has been a nickname for a Hollander, in Flanders and Germany, for a great many years. In the days of the buccaneers the English sailors began to use it to designate a Dutch freebooter, and in this sense it became familiar in New York. Presently the New York Dutch, apparently seizing upon its opprobrious significance, began to apply it to the English settlers of Connecticut, who were regarded at the time as persons whose commercial enterprise ran far beyond their moral scruples. A little while later it came into general

---

1 I am indebted here to Miss Ernestine Evans, who picked up news of *kwispedoor* in the United Press office in Berlin.

use in the colonies to designate a disliked neighbor to the northward, and there was a time when the Virginians applied it to Marylanders. In the end the New Englanders saw in it a flattering tribute to their cunning, and so not only adopted it themselves, but converted it into an adjective signifying excellence. The DAE's first printed example of *Yankee*, then spelled *Yankey*, is dated 1683, at which time the term still meant a pirate, and was applied as a proper name to one of the Dutch commanders in the West Indies. By the middle of the Eighteenth Century it had come to mean a New Englander, and by the Revolutionary period the English were using it to designate any American. During the Civil War, as everyone knows, the Southerners used it, usually contemptuously, of all Northerners,[1] and in consequence its widened meaning became restricted again, but in World War I it underwent another change, and since then, though they objected at first, even Southerners have got used to being called *Yankees*, e.g., by the English. The shortened form *Yank* is traced by the DAE to 1778. The adjective *yankee*, signifying good or superior, had a vogue in the Boston area at the beginning of the Eighteenth Century, but soon passed out of use, and has not been found in print for many years. *To yankee*, a verb signifying to cheat, followed a century later, but is also now obsolete. So is *yankee* as the name of a drink made of whiskey sweetened with molasses, recorded for 1804, but forgotten by the Civil War era.[2]

Many derivatives are listed by the DAE, e.g., *Yankee-trick*, traced to 1176; *-land*, to 1788; *-ism*, to 1792; *-like*, to 1799; *-phrase*, to 1803; *-notions*, to c. 1851; *ish*, to 1830; *-dialect* to 1832; *-peddler*, to 1834; *-made* and *-clock*, to 1839; *-dom*, to 1843; *-grit*, to 1865; *-twang*, to 1866; *to catch a Yankee* (to catch a tartar), to 1811 and *to play Yankee* (to reply to a question by asking one), to 1896. *Yankee Doodle* as the name of a song is traced to 1767. Its history was detailed at length in a report by the late O. G. T. Sonneck, then chief of the

---

1 The Field, the Dungeon and the Escape, by Albert Richardson; Hartford, Conn., 1865, p. 90: " The Southern politicians and newspapers have persuaded the masses that the *Yankees* (a phrase which they no longer apply distinctly to New Englanders, but to every person born in the North) mean to subjugate them, but are arrant cowards, who may easily be frightened away." After the war the pejorative usually appeared as *damyankee*, and that form still survives in the South.

2 *Yankee beverage*, at the same period, was the name of a drink made of vinegar, water and molasses, apparently on the theory that a true Yankee would not waste whiskey on a guest.

music division in the Library of Congress, in 1909.[1] In the same document he discussed at length the various etymologies proposed for *Yankee*. Dr. Logeman also deals with some of them in the paper lately cited.[2] Said Sonneck:

> The word gradually came to fascinate the historian of words until about 1850 fascination reached its climax. Since then the craze has subsided, yet any number of explanations are still current and proposed as facts, usually on the presumption that embellished reiteration of statements correctly or incorrectly quoted produces facts.

Some of the etymologies still floating about are the following:

1. That *Yankee* is derived from the name of the *Yankos*, a tribe of Massachusetts Indians. In their language *Yanko* meant invincible, and they transferred it to the New Englanders on being defeated in battle by them. Unfortunately, no such tribe is recorded by the early historians, nor is any word resembling *Yanko* found in any known Indian dialect.

2. That *Yankee* comes from *yonokie*, an Indian word signifying silent, and was bestowed upon the whites satirically because they seemed very garrulous to the reticent Indians. No such word can be found.[3]

3. That *Yankee* comes from a Cherokee word *eankkle*, signifying coward, and was bestowed upon the New Englanders by the Virginians on the failure of the former to lend aid in a Cherokee war. No such word is in the Cherokee language.

4. That *Yankee* was derived from the adjective *yankee*. The latter word was made popular among the Harvard students of *c.* 1713 by a farmer of Cambridge named Jonathan Hastings, who used it so often, *e.g.,* in *yankee horse, yankee cider,* etc., that he acquired *Yankee* as a nickname.

5. That *Yankee* represents an Indian attempt to pronounce the word *English*. The Indians, in fact, did not use *English*, but had a much different word of their own to designate Englishmen.

6. That it represents an Indian attempt to pronounce the French *Anglaise*. See No. 5.

7. That it is a Lincolnshire dialect word meaning gaiters or leggings made of undressed leather, and was brought in by the immigrants from that region.

8. That it is a Scots dialect word, *yankie*, signifying "a sharp, clever, forward woman." [4]

1 Report on The Star-Spangled Banner, Hail Columbia, America, and *Yankee Doodle;* Washington, 1909.
2 The Etymology of *Yankee*, in Studies in English Philology . . . in Honor of Frederick Klaeber; Minneapolis, 1929, pp. 403–13.
3 Washington Irving gave this etymology circulation in Knickerbocker's History of New York, 1809, but his explanation differed somewhat from the usual one. "The simple aborigines," he said, "for a while contemplated these strange folk in utter astonishment; but, discovering that they wielded harmless though noisy weapons, and were a lively, ingenious race of men, became very friendly . . . and gave them the name of *yanokies* . . . a waggish appellation, since shortened into the familiar epithet of *Yankees*."
4 I take this definition from A Scots Dialect Dictionary, by Alexander Warrack; London, 1911.

9. That it is from a Scots word, *yanking*, signifying "active, forward, pushing." [1]

10. That it is from *Janke*, a diminutive of the Dutch given-name *Jan*. But, as Logeman shows, the Dutch diminutive for *Jan* is actually *Jantje*. "This *Janke*," he says, "is most likely, like the famous *Peterkin* of 'Hohenlinden' fame, nothing but the product of the brain of the author, who fondly imagined he was using a Dutch name."

11. That *Yankee* comes from the aforesaid *Jantje*.

12. That it comes from the Dutch *janker*, signifying, "howler, yelper, whiner, squaller." [2]

13. That it comes from the Swedish *enka*, a widow, and was applied to the English because they had either been banished from England or had left "for political or religious reasons." [3]

14. That it comes from the Danish *janke* (pronounced *yank-keh*), a word used to designate "the savage habit some mothers have of jerking or lifting unruly babies by their hands or wrists." [4]

15. That it comes from the Dutch *jonkheer*.[5]

16. That it comes from the Persian word *janghe* or *jenghe*, meaning a war-like man or a swift horse.

The last etymology, though it has been taken seriously, was actually proposed as a hoax. It first appeared in the *Monthly Anthology and Boston Review* for 1810,[6] where it was presented in the form of a letter allegedly copied from "the *Connecticut Herald*, a paper printed in New Haven," and signed W. It was intended to be a burlesque upon the philological writings of Noah Webster, and the *Monthly Anthology* pretended to be "credibly informed" that it was "from the pen of N—— W——, jun., Esq." himself. It was as follows:

As the origin of the word *Yankee* has been a subject of much inquiry, and no satisfactory account of it appears to have been given, I send you the following history of the word.

*Yankee* appears to have been used formerly by some of our common farmers

1 Here again the definition is War-rack's.

2 The definition is from Kramer's Nieuw Engelsch Woordenboek; Gouda, 1921.

3 This suggestion was made by Mr. Paul E. Hansen, of Napa county, Calif.; private communication, Nov. 23, 1939. He called attention to the fact that the Swedes settled in Delaware in 1627, before the first recorded appearance of *Yankee*.

4 I am indebted here to a correspondent whose name, unhappily, has been lost in the illimitable mazes of my notes.

5 I am indebted here to Mr. Valdemar Viking of Red Bank, N. J. He says: "*Jonkheer* is a title of respect reserved for the aristocracy, but it would not be surprising if it had been bestowed in a jocular or derisive manner on the Dutch pirates by their fellows of other nationalities. The buccaneers, as a body, may even have applied this honorific to all the Dutch settlers, and in time it might easily have become a nickname for any inhabitant of the Hudson valley and the New England colonies."

6 Vol. VIII, pp. 244–45. I am indebted for this to Dr. J. M. Carrière of the University of Virginia.

in its genuine sense. It was an epithet descriptive of excellent qualities — as a *Yankee horse* — that is a horse of high spirit and other good properties. I am informed that this use of the word has continued in some parts of New England till within a short period.

In the course of my inquiries I have discovered what I presume to be the same word in the Persian language, in which the whole family of words is preserved. It is a fact well known that the people of Europe, from whom we descended, are the posterity of the tribes which emigrated from the ancient Media, and northern part of Persia — and if not known, it is a fact capable of being proved. In the Persian language, let it be observed that in the place of our *y* authors write letters whose powers correspond nearly to the English *j* and *ch*, as in *joy* and *chess*. Thus the word which we write *yoke*, which the Latins wrote *jugum* and the Greeks *zeugus*, and which without the final article would be *jug* and *zeug*, the Persians write *chag*, and it may be equally well written *jag*; for throughout the Persian these sounds are used promiscuously in words from the same root. Hence we see the name of the Asiatic river *Yenesei* written also *Jenesei*, and we write the word, from our Indians, *Gennesee*. Thus also the name of the great Asiatic conqueror is written *Genghis Khan* or *Jenghis Khan*, and Tooke [1] writes it *Tschingis Khan*. Thus *Jenghis* is not his name, but a title.

Now in the Persian language, *Janghe* or *Jenghe* — that is, *Yankee* — signifies "a warlike man, a swift horse; also, one who is prompt and ready in action, one who is magnanimous." This is the exact interpretation as given in the lexicon. The word is formed from *jank*, *jenk*, battle, contest, war; and this from a like word signifying the fist, the instrument of fighting; like *pugna*, from *pugnus*, the fist. In Persian *jankidan* (*yankidan*) is to commence or carry on war.

We hence see the propriety of the use of *yankee* as applied to a high spirited, warlike horse.

The word *Yankee* thus claims a very honorable parentage; for it is the precise title assumed by the celebrated Mongolian khan, *Jenghis;* and in our dialect his titles, literally translated, would be *Yankee King*, that is, *Warlike Chief*.

This is not the only instance in which one of the oldest words in the language has lost its dignity. We have many popular words which have never found admission into books, that are among the oldest words ever formed. I can prove some of them to have been used before the dispersion of men; for they are found in Asia, Africa and Europe, among nations which could have no intercourse after that event.

New Haven, March 2, 1810.

It will be noted that *Jan Kaas*, to English ears, must have seemed like a plural. "The loss of the *s*," says Logeman, "cannot cause the slightest difficulty; . . . the change would be on a par with that in *Chinee*, *pea* and *cherry*, from *Chinese*, *pease* and *cherries*." [2] Mr. H. de Groot of Los Angeles tells me that when he was a boy in Holland

---

1 See Tooke's View of the Russian Empire, Vol. I, 409.
2 Logeman's paper was summarized, with the addition of other matter, in On the Origin of *Yankee Doodle,* by Harold Davis, *American Speech,* April, 1938, pp. 93–96. Davis also published Origin of *Yankee* Is Not Clear in the Boston *Herald,* July 2, 1938, a letter embodying the same material.

a popular juvenile book was " De Zoon van den Berendooder " (The Son of the Bear-Killer), and that in it the plural of *Yankee* was given as *Yankeezen*. This indicates that the Dutch author thought of the second element of *Yankee* as *kees*, which Logeman describes as " a dialect form of *Kaas*," for the plural of *kees* is *keezen*.

Many of the early loans from the French, *e.g.*, *caribou* and *to-boggan*, had been borrowed in turn, as we have seen, from the Indian languages. To these, perhaps, *bayou* may be added, for it seems to have been influenced by the Choctaw *bayuk*, a small stream. But there were also direct borrowings, *e.g.*, *chowder* (from *chaudière*, a kettle or pot), traced by the DAE to 1751; [1] *batteau*, traced to 1717; *calumet* (a tobacco pipe), to 1705; *carryall* (from *cariole*, by folk-etymology), to 1714; *gopher* (possibly from *gaufre*, a honeycomb, though this is doubted by the DAE), to 1791; *levee*, to 1719; *portage*, to 1698; and *prairie*, to 1773.[2] Most of these came in along the Canadian border, but others were picked up in the West or South, *e.g.*, *voyageur*, *bagasse*, and *crevasse*. Those of the latter class are mainly unrecorded before the Nineteenth Century, though they were probably in local use before. A number of French terms found in proper names, *e.g.*, *sault*, meaning rapids in a river, were taken over in the West, and the later colonists made large use of a French suffix for town names, to wit, *-ville*, that had been used very rarely in England. *Buc-caneer*, from the French *boucanier*, is chiefly associated with American history, and in consequence it is sometimes reckoned an Americanism, but the DAE shows that it was in use in England seventy-five years before its first recorded appearance in America. A number of familiar terms came into American from the Spanish by way of Louisiana French, *e.g.*, *calaboose*, which the DAE traces to 1792, and *quadroon*, which is discussed in Chapter VI. Direct loans from the Spanish were very rare before 1800; indeed, I can find none that were not anticipated in English use, though they may have been borrowed independently here. Even *mosquito*, *palmetto*, *banjo* and *key* belong

---

1 Says Steven T. Byington in *American Speech*, April, 1944, p. 122: " The word makes its appearance in Boston in 1751. Nova Scotia (then including New Brunswick) was ceded to England by the Treaty of Utrecht in 1713. Thenceforth it received English settlers; these lived peaceably among the Acadians, who were not deported until 1755. It was natural that these settlers should pick up from their French neighbors a bit of French cookery, with its name. And of course these Englishmen of Nova Scotia had friendly relations with New England."

2 For compounds in *prairie-* see AL4, p. 151.

to that category. *Banjo* is traced by the DAE to 1774 and marked an Americanism, but it was preceded by the West Indian *banshaw*, and both represent corruptions of the Spanish *bandurria*. Such familiar Spanish loans as *lasso, mustang, plaza, corral, canyon, bronco* and *ranch*, now almost as thoroughly American as *ambulance-chaser* or *to hitch-hike*, did not come in until after the beginning of the movement into the West. The early Americans, in fact, had very little contact with the Spaniards; they knew the Dutch and French much better. Of the early Germans they knew still less, for the Germans had a numerous colony only in Pennsylvania, and there they kept to themselves. It is commonly assumed by lexicographers that *sauerkraut, smearcase* and *noodle* are American loans from the German, but the evidence is not too clear. Two of them, *sauerkraut* and *noodle*, are recorded in England before their first apparent appearance in print in America, and *smearcase* may have been borrowed from the Dutch. All the other German words in the American vocabulary seem to have come in after the War of 1812.

Very few words were borrowed from the languages of the Negro slaves, even in the South. *Buckra*, meaning a white man, is derived from an African word, *makana* or *mbakana*, of the same meaning, by Webster 1934, and traced to 1795 in white American use by the DAE, which notes that it was reported from the island of Antigua about six years earlier. Save in a few areas it never spread from Negro speech to that of the whites, and at the present day it is unknown to most Americans.[1] *Cooter*, a name applied to a box turtle (*Costudo carolina*) in the Carolinas, is derived from an African word, *kuta* or *nkuda*, by the DAE, but is not traced before 1832. *Goober*, a Southern name for the peanut, is derived by Webster from the African *nguba*, but the DAE's first example of its printed use is dated so late as 1848. *Gumbo*, the common Southern name for *Abelmoschus exculentus*, is derived by the DAE from an Angolan word, *kingombo*, and traced to 1805. In the sense of a Negro patois of French both the DAE and Webster 1934 say that it may be derived from a quite different word, *nkombo*, used by the tribes of the Congo region. The

---

[1] The African etymology of *buckra* has been challenged by Mr. Albert Wehde of Chicago (private communication), who says that it is more likely derived from an identical **word** in the language of the Indians of the Mosquito Coast, now a part of Nicaragua. Mr. Wehde, who lived on the coast in the 90s, suggests that the word got to Jamaica during the days of the buccaneers, and from Jamaica reached the American coast.

original significance of the latter was a runaway slave. *Okra*, another name for the gumbo, is derived by Webster from *nkruman*, a loan from the Tshi people of Africa. *Gumbo* has produced a number of derivatives, *e.g.*, *gumbo-ball*, a kind of harlequinade, traced by the DAE to 1835; *gumbo-box*, a drum, derived from *nkumbi*, of the same meaning, and traced to 1861; *gumbo limbo*, a small tree found in Florida; and *gumbo-soup*, traced to 1832. In 1939 Dwight L. Bolinger suggested that *bozo*, which has puzzled the etymologists, may be derived from *bozal*, "a term applied in the African slave trade to a Negro recently brought from the country of his origin." This term also had the sense of a halter, and *bozo* exists in Cuban Spanish in that significance.[1] *Voodoo* seems to be derived from the African *vodu*, but it got into American English from the French of Haiti, and on its first appearance in print was spelled *vaudoux*. *Hoodoo* is a later form. *Juba* is listed by Webster as "perhaps of Bantu origin," but its etymology remains to be worked out. It apparently did not get into the general American vocabulary until the rise of the minstrel show, *c.* 1830.

But if the African languages thus left but little sediment in the common language of the United States, they undoubtedly had a considerable influence upon the dialect of the Southern Negroes, not only in phonology and syntax, but also in vocabulary. This is especially true in the remoter backwaters, for example, the Sea Islands of Georgia, where the local Negro dialect, called Gullah, is almost unintelligible to a visiting Northerner. Dr. Lorenzo D. Turner of Fisk University, who has a working knowledge of the principal West African languages, reports that no less than 6,000 African words survive among the Gullah-speaking Negroes. Most of them are personal names and all save a few of the remainder are used only in speaking to other Gullahs; in their dealings with the local whites the Negroes make a larger use of what they take to be English. But even in this polite dialect, says Dr. Turner, there are many African words that white observers have mistaken for debased forms of English words.[2]

1 *Bozo, American Speech*, Oct., 1939, pp. 238–39.
2 Dr. Turner has kindly given me access to outlines of lectures he gave before the American Dialect Society at Columbia University in Dec., 1938, the Linguistic Club at Yale a few weeks earlier, and the University of Wisconsin in July, 1943. His observations are summarized at some length in The Myth of a Negro Past, by Melville J. Herskovits; New York, 1941, pp. 276 *ff.*

## 2. NEW WORDS OF ENGLISH MATERIAL

The first English-speaking colonists in America found an immediate need for a large number of new words — some to designate the new objects that were presented to their sight, and some to describe the novel conditions and operations that marked their new life. Not a few of these necessary neologisms, as we have just seen, were taken from the Indian languages or from the tongues of other immigrants, but the great majority were made of English material — sometimes by giving an old English word a new meaning, but more often by arranging common English elements in new combinations. A number of examples are give in AL4, pp. 113 *ff*, and there are many more in the DAE. Some of these combinations go back to the Seventeenth Century — *e.g.*, *snow-shoe*, traced by the DAE to 1666; *salt-meadow*, to 1656, and *selectman*, to 1635 — but the majority date from the century following, and especially from the era of burgeoning national self-consciousness following the Revolution. It was not until the beginning of the great movement into the West that the American language really began to flower, but it was already showing many signs of a lush vitality before 1800. I turn to the letter *B* in the DAE and find the following examples of compounds made of English material during the Eighteenth Century:

back-country, 1755
back-settlement, 1759
back-taxes, 1788
backwoods, 1784
bake-oven, 1777
bale-cloth, 1797
ball-ground, 1772
barn-swallow, 1790
bay-vessel, 1789
bear-hunter, 1765

beef-cattle, 1776
beef-packer, 1796
bee-tree, 1782
bell-horse, 1775
blue-laws, 1781
breadstuff, 1793
breech-clout, 1757
broom-corn, 1781
broom-straw, 1785
buck-shot, 1775

I turn to the letter *S* and find:

salt-lick, 1751
sheathing-paper, 1790
sheet-iron, 1776
shingle-roof, 1749
ship-channel, 1775
ship-canal, 1798
shooting-iron, 1787
shot-gun, 1776

shower-bath, 1785
sink-hole, 1749
smoke-house, 1759
smoking-tobacco, 1796
snow-plow, 1792
spoon-victuals, 1777
spring-house, 1755
stamping-ground, 1786

These are only a few specimens, taken almost at random. Among the new names for natural objects there are many more, most of them meant to be descriptive. Under *G*, for example, I find:

| | |
|---|---|
| gall-berry, 1709 | green-snake, 1709 |
| garden-flea, 1790 | grizzly-bear, 1791 |
| garter-snake, 1775 | ground-hog, 1784 |
| german-corn (rye), 1741 | ground-pea, 1769 |
| glass-snake, 1736 | ground-squirrel, 1709 |
| gray-eagle, 1778 | gum-swamp, 1799 |

And under *S:*

| | |
|---|---|
| shagbark, 1751 | sourwood, 1709 |
| shortleaf-pine, 1796 | spice-wood, 1756 |
| slippery-elm, 1748 | sugar-maple, 1731 |
| snap-bean, 1775 | sweet-potato, 1750 |

And these at random:

| | |
|---|---|
| blue-grass, 1751 | clingstone (peach), 1705 |
| blue-jay, 1709 | lightning-bug, 1778 |
| butternut, 1741 | pond-lily, 1748 |
| canvasback (duck), 1782 | tree-frog, 1738 |
| cat-bird, 1709 | |

Under *blue-* the DAE lists scores of such coinages, and under *black-* and *white-* almost as many. Some of the natural objects encountered by the first settlers, *e.g.*, the *bear*, the *beaver* and the *eagle*, were more or less strange to them, and that strangeness stimulated their word-making proclivities, and thus enriched their vocabulary. In a paper in *American Speech* in 1935 [1] Allen Walker Reed listed a large number of Americanisms in *bear-* dating from the Eighteenth Century, *e.g.*, *bear-skin*, 1647; *bear's oil*, 1674; *bear's fat* and *bear-venison*, 1709; *bear-hunter*, 1765; *bear-ham*, 1766; *bear-bacon* and *bear's meat*, 1772; *bear-fat*, 1780; *bear-steak*, 1788; and *bear-ground*, 1797. The term was also used in a figurative sense, as in *bear-grass*, 1750. The new political and social conditions under which the settlers lived also suggested a large number of new compounds, some of which survive to this day, *e.g.*, *statehouse, selectman, best-room, leaf-tobacco, hoe-cake, frame-house, spinning-bee, State's attorney, land-office, worm-fence, hay-scales, drygoods, bottom-land,* and *double-house.* Lieut. Thomas Anburey, of the British Army, who surrendered with Burgoyne at Saratoga on October 17, 1777, and spent several years

1 The Bear in American Speech, Oct.,
pp. 195–202.

as a prisoner in America, thought it necessary, when he came to write of his adventures for his fellow Britons, to explain the meaning of *fence-rails*.[1] The DAE does not claim the compound as an Americanism, but its first example goes back to 1733, and the NED does not list it at all. *Fencing-stuff*, signifying material used for making fences, has been traced to 1644; *fence-viewer*, an official appointed to inspect fences, to 1661; *fencing-rail* to 1780, and *under fence* to 1796; but *on the fence* (in the political sense), *fence-law, fence-rider, fence-row, fence-war* and *fencing-wire* belong to the Nineteenth Century. All of them are Americanisms, and so, apparently, is *fence-corner*. The DAE traces *worm-fence* to 1652, *rail-fence* to 1649, and *snake-fence* to 1805. *Back-log* is traced by the DAE to 1684. It is still a stranger to the English, and when it appeared in an English edition of Henry A. Wallace's " The Century of the Common Man " in 1944, a correspondent of the London *Times Literary Supplement* demanded to know what it meant.[2]

*Statehouse* used to be credited by etymologists to the Dutch *stadhuis*, but in 1902 Albert Matthews produced evidence that it was in use in Virginia in 1638,[3] and had reached Maryland by 1662, and that it did not appear in New York until 1671. The DAE traces *best-room* to 1719, *leaf-tobacco* to 1637, *hoe-cake* to 1774, *frame-house* (in the early form of *framed-house*) to 1639, *spinning-bee* to 1679, *State's attorney* to 1779, *land-office* to 1681, *hay-scales* to 1773, *dry-goods* to 1701, *bottom-land* to 1728, and *double-house* to 1707. The second element of *spinning-bee* may have been invented by some ingenious Americano, for etymologists have been unable to find any trace of it in the vocabulary of England. The NED suggests it may embody " an allusion to the social character of the insect," but the DAE rejects this as lacking evidence. The first *spinning-bee*, according to the DAE, seems to have been recorded in 1769, but the term was still a novelty at that time, and it was not until after the Revolution that it came into general use. After the War of 1812 there was a great proliferation of *bees*, especially in the new West. Whenever a

1 Travels Through the Interior Parts of America; London, 1789; Vol. II, p. 323. I am indebted here to The Comment of British Travelers on Early American Terms Relating to Agriculture, by Allen Walker Read, *Agricultural History*, July, 1933, pp. 99 ff.

2 This correspondent was answered by Bernard Aylwin in *Back-Log, Times Literary Supplement*, April 8, 1944, p. 175.

3 The Term *State-House, Dialect Notes*, Vol. II, Pt. VI, 1902, pp. 199–224.

pioneer had a job in hand that was too much for him and his family, the neighbors pitched in to help, and there was usually a jollification when the work was over. The DAE traces *husking-bee* to 1816, *apple-bee* (for paring and cutting up apples preparatory to drying them) to 1827, *quilting-bee* to 1832, *logging-bee* and *raising-bee* (for raising the frame of a new house) to 1836, *pigeon-picking-bee* to 1841, *paring-bee* (a new name for an *apple-bee*) to 1845, *cellar-digging-bee* and *sewing-bee* to 1856, and *spelling-bee* to 1875. All of them are probably older, especially *spelling-bee*. The simple word *bee*, without a prefix, was also used to signify a donation-party for a pastor, and sometimes that party included repairs to his house. In this sense the DAE traces the word to 1823. *Bee-line* is also an Americanism, traced to *c.* 1845.

Many of the early American terms had to do with food, *e.g., buck-wheat-cake*, first recorded in John Adams's diary, September 21, 1774; *corn-bread*, 1796; *spoon-victuals*, 1777; *johnny-cake*, 1739; *bread-stuffs*, first recorded in a report by Thomas Jefferson, December 16, 1793; and *hog-and-hominy*, 1792. The inventor of the *buckwheat-cake*, though immortal, remains unknown. Buckwheat was being grown for human food in Pennsylvania so early as 1698, and was then sometimes called *French wheat;* in the South it seems to have been used, in the first half of the Eighteenth Century, only as hog and poultry food, or as a crop to be plowed in to enrich the soil. In parts of Appalachia, to this day, it is eaten much more extensively than wheat. *Johnny-cake* had acquired the variant form of *journey-cake* by 1754,[1] and in consequence Noah Webster surmised that this may have been the original term, and that it signified a hard loaf baked for use on a journey. The DAE suggests that both *johnny-cake* and *journey-cake* may have been corruptions of *jonokin*, traced to 1675, but no one seems to know precisely what a *jonokin* was, and there is no actual evidence for the derivation. It is much more plausible to accept an etymology given by Will H. Loudermilk, in his " History of Cumberland " (Maryland), 1878:

---

[1] In 1780 a Moravian bishop, Reichel by name, made a journey from the Moravian headquarters at Lititz, Pa., to the outpost at Salem, N. C. On June 8 he recorded in his diary that he had made his first acquaintance with a *journey-cake*. The diary was in German, but he entered the word in English. Records of the Moravians in North Carolina, edited by Adelaide Fries; Vol. IV, p. 1894. For this I am indebted to Dr. George T. Harrell, Jr., of Duke University.

A favorite article of diet amongst these (Shawnese) Indians was a cake made of maise beaten as fine as the means at command would permit. This was mixed with water, and baked upon a flat stone which had been previously heated in the fire. The trappers followed the Indians' example in the baking of *Shawnee-cakes,* as they called them, and the lapse of a few years was sufficient to corrupt the term into that of *johnny-cake,* so familiar throughout the South, and in common use at this day.[1]

It is possible that *breadstuffs* was invented by Jefferson, for the first recorded use of it was in his report of 1793. It was first noted as an Americanism by one of the watchful English critics in a review of John Marshall's " Life of Washington," 1804–1807, in the *Annual Review.* Jefferson defined it in his report as " bread-grains, meals and bread." Said Pickering in 1816:

It has probably been more readily allowed among us because we do not, like the English, use the word *corn* as a general name for all sorts of grain. . . . A friend has favored me with the following remarks on it: " *Breadstuffs* is American. In Jamaica they have a term for the esculent roots, &c. substituted for bread, *viz., breadkind.* Some generic name is wanting here in these cases, analogous to *lumber,* which is the term used for the whole class of rough wooden materials."

The early Americans, counting out a relatively small class of intelligentsia, largely clerical, were a far from elegant folk, and their rowdy personal habits were naturally reflected in their vocabulary. The DAE traces *tarring and feathering* to 1774, *gouging* (" the action of squeezing or pushing out a person's eye ") to the same year, *Lynch's law* to 1782, and *rough-and-tumble* to 1792. Thomas Hutchinson's diary for 1774 indicates that *tarring and feathering* was already so well established a practise by that time that regular committees were formed to carry it on, and that they objected when volunteers undertook it. *Gouging* reached its highest development among the boatmen of the Western rivers after the beginning of the movement across the Alleghanies, but it was already practised before the Revolution, along with biting, butting and scratching. " To perform the horrid operation," said Isaac Weld, an English traveler toward the end of the century, " the combatant twists his forefingers in the sidelocks of his adversary's hair, and then applies his thumbs to the bottom of the eye, to force it out of the socket." [2] There is, unhappily, some

1 I am indebted for this to *Johnnycake* by J. Louis Kuethe, *American Speech,* Oct., 1935, p. 202.
2 Travels Through the States of North America, 1795–97; London,

1799. Weld was not the first to take news of *gouging* to England. It was already entered in 1785 in Grose's Classical Dictionary of the Vulgar Tongue. Grose, with probably un-difference of opinion among etymologists regarding the identity of the man who served *Lynch's law* (and its progeny, *lynch-law, lynching, lyncher, lynching-bee* and *to lynch*) as eponym. Dr. James Elbert Cutler, in an extremely painstaking and valuable study of lynching, published in 1905,[1] came to the conclusion, supported by impressive documentation, that its father was Colonel Charles Lynch (1736–96), a Quaker magistrate and militia-officer of Bedford county, Virginia, but the DAE says that the practise was " named after Captain William Lynch (1742–1820) of Pittsylvania county, Virginia, and later of Pendleton district, South Carolina." Local tradition at Lynchburg, Va., which was founded in 1786 by Charles Lynch's younger brother, John, supports the former theory, but it should be said that an interview with Richard Venable, an aged and much respected citizen of Prince Edward county, published in *Harper's Magazine* in 1859,[2] gave some countenance, on the strength of personal recollection, to the latter.

Charles and John Lynch were the sons of Charles L. Lynch, an Irishman who came out to Virginia early in the Eighteenth Century, married Sarah Clark, the daughter of a Quaker to whom he was indentured, and acquired with her lands along the upper waters of the James river. Their son Charles settled on this land, and became one of the principal inhabitants of Bedford county. He was appointed a justice of the peace in 1766, and was disowned by his fellow Quakers for taking the oath of office. In 1769 he was elected to the Virginia Legislature, in 1769 and 1774 he signed the two Williamsburg protests against English taxation, in 1776 he served in the Virginia constitutional convention, and in 1778 he became a colonel in the State militia. In 1781 Governor Thomas Jefferson sent him to the aid of General Nathanael Greene in North Carolina, and he took part in all of the subsequent Southern operations until the surrender of Cornwallis. The activities which attached his name to summary justice went on in 1780. Bedford county, at that time, had a considerable population of Loyalists, and some of them engaged in violence; worse, the county,

---

conscious humor, defined it as " to squeeze out a man's eye with the thumb, a cruel practice used by the *Bostonians* in America." Similarly, he defined *tarring and feathering* as " a punishment lately inflicted by the good people of Boston on any person convicted or suspected of loy-

alty." " Such delinquents," he explained, " being stripped naked, were daubed all over with tar, and after put into a hogshead of feathers."

1 Lynch Law: An Investigation Into the History of Lynching in the United States; New York, 1905.

2 Lynch Law, May, 1859, pp. 794–98.

then still a wild region, was ravaged by bands of robbers. Lynch and his fellow magistrates managed to arrest some of these outlaws, but the business of punishing them presented difficulties, for the only court in Virginia authorized to try felonies was at Williamsburg, and a prisoner dispatched to Williamsburg was commonly rescued along the way either by Loyalists or by English troops. Lynch and his colleagues of the local magistrates' court — William Preston, Robert Adams, Jr., and James Callaway — thereupon decided to set up a rump court of their own, and proceeded to try their prisoners. This proceeding, of course, was unlawful, but they kept strictly to legal forms in their trials, and after inflicting heavy fines on some of the offenders and corporal punishment on others, they managed to put down the prevailing lawlessness. There is no evidence that they ever inflicted the death penalty save once, and that was in the case of a Negro slave convicted of poisoning his master's wife. After the Revolution some of the victims of their extra-legal justice entered suits against the four magistrates for damages, and in October, 1782 the Virginia Legislature passed an act holding them harmless, on the ground that their measures, while perhaps " not strictly warranted by law," were " justifiable from the imminence of the danger."

Until recent years a tree under which Lynch and his brother magistrates were supposed to have held their court stood in the yard of a house near Altavista, Va. The Colonial Dames of Lynchburg made a pious pilgrimage to it in June, 1922, and a Lynchburg lawyer, H. C. Featherston, read them a paper on the life and times of Lynch and the cradle-days of *lynching*.[1] The founder, of the science, of course, was what later came to be called a *vigilante*, not a lyncher in the current sense. He always gave his prisoners fair and public trials. The subsequent history of the word is largely the history of *lynching* itself, which is set forth comprehensively in Dr. Cutler's book, aforesaid.[2] The testimony in favor of the Pittsylvania county Lynch as the father of *lynching*, as given by the ancient Venable to a contributor to *Harper's Magazine* in 1859, was in part as follows:

I knew Mr. Lynch well — as well as a stripling could be expected to know a dignified and venerable gentleman. He was for many years the senior and presiding justice of the county court of Pittsylvania, whose terms he attended with

1 Women Visit *Lynch* Tree, Lynchburg *News*, July 30, 1922.
2 See also Rope and Faggot by Walter White; New York, 1929, and the

article on Charles Lynch in the Dictionary of American Biography (by John C. Wylie); Vol. XI; New York, 1933.

remarkable punctuality. Our war, like all wars, was an *alma nutrix* of depredations and felonies. The prices paid by both armies for fine horses rendered that species of property particularly insecure; and contemporaneously with, or rather in advance of, the Southern invasion by Cornwallis, an organized band of horse thieves had established posts and dépôts from far away North through Virginia into the Carolinas. They were headed by a man of some notoriety, fitted by nature to shine in any office or profession. He was said to be a man of strikingly handsome face and elegant person, of most courtly manners, and easy, graceful conversation. His life was a mystery, and so his fate remains, I believe. He was known as Captain Perkins, and his name was as perfect a terror in the nursery as was that of the Douglas when English nurses were wont to quiet their babies with the lullaby:

> Hush ye, hush ye, little pet ye;
> The Black Douglas shall not get ye!

These thieves were frequently arrested, often *flagrante delictu*. They would be committed, examined by a bench of justices, and remanded to Williamsburg for final trial. Even before the occupation of the country by the English, the distance of the court rendered the attendance of witnesses uncertain; and when they appeared to prosecute they would be confronted with any number of contradicting witnesses the occasion might require — men, too, of equal or superior appearance of respectability to themselves, thoroughly instructed as to what they should swear, and as thoroughly capable of strictly obeying their instructions.

The conviction of these outlaws being thus rendered next to impossible, sufferers had become averse to add the cost of time and money to the loss of property, even before the enemy entered the country. The advent of the British troops gave a new impulse to the operations of this gang by bringing the market to the seller, by rendering the chance even of transporting the criminals to Williamsburg more than doubtful, and making the sessions of the court itself very uncertain. The horse-thieves, when they and their guard would be intercepted, were always ready to take English bounty, and being, for the most part, young, wiry, active fellows, acquainted with all the highways, and still better with all the by-ways of the country, they were gladly enlisted in that service, while their guards would, probably, be held prisoners of war. As long as the escape of these miscreants was attributable only to the imperfection of the criminal jurisprudence — was, in other words, the fault of the law — no one thought of overstepping the barrier which that law interposed.

But when a state of things existed which enhanced the evil ten-fold, and took away even the semblance of a remedy, the cry of a whole community suffering under the accumulation of pillage and fire from the enemy, and the loss by theft of what property they could hide from that enemy, came up to the only tribunal to which they could look for relief, the only tribunal, in fact, which might be said to have been left possessed of vitality — the county magistracy — a body of men who, at that time, would have compared favorably with Rome's proud *patres conscripts* in the purest days of that republic.

In obedience to this call for relief, and impelled by this stern necessity, the justices of Pittsylvania county were summoned specially to be in attendance at one of the regular terms of their court — a majority, perhaps the whole bench, being present. The presiding justice, Mr. Lynch, having plainly but forcibly reminded them of the extraordinary condition of the country, the entire insecurity of life and property, and the complete suspension of the administration of justice, exactly when stringent laws required most vigorous enforcing, submitted a proposition that in consideration of the fact that the criminal court at Williamsburg had ceased to exist, at least in so far as related to the border counties, the county court of Pittsylvania should undertake to try finally all cases of murder and felony occurring within that county which were required to be sent to the court at Williamsburg for trial, by the words of the law. That in such trials the accused should have the same rights as to the impaneling the jury, the preëmptory challenge, the challenge for cause, etc.; the same rights as to all pleadings, general and special; as to the summoning and compelling the attendance of their witnesses, and the cross-examination of witnesses for the Commonwealth, and of being heard by counsel, as were secured to them by the law giving jurisdiction of their cases exclusively to the court at Williamsburg. In short, he simply proposed to change the forum. The plan was adopted and recommended to the neighboring counties, by some of which it was also adopted. As may be imagined, the effect was felt at once. A few were caught, tried, and hung — hanging was the legal penalty then — the rest sought a more congenial clime. The gang was dispersed in fact.

Mr. Lynch was a man of enlarged mind, great decision of character, fixedness, almost sternness of purpose, but most eminently a law-loving and law-abiding man. He had thoroughly counted the cost, and carefully weighed the consequences; he took his position with full knowledge of its responsibility, and maintained it with firmness and dignity. He continued to preside over the county court long after it had laid down the powers it had so bravely assumed; and he carried to the grave the love and veneration of all good men.

It will be noted that the two traditions, save in the matter of the identity of the eponymic Lynch, are virtually identical. It is highly probable that they are grounded upon historical facts, and that Southwestern Virginia is thus entitled to public veneration, not only for the invention of *lynching*, but also for the launching of its name.

The free way in which the Elizabethan English interchanged the parts of speech was brought in as a natural language process by the early English colonists, continued to be practised during the whole colonial period, and is still one of the hallmarks of American English. The New Englanders had made a verb of *scalp* before the end of the Seventeenth Century, and early in the century following they followed with *to tomahawk. To top*, in the sense of to remove the top of a growing tobacco plant, is traced by the DAE to 1688, and *to tote*, which may or may not be a noun turned verb, to 1677. The true origin of the latter remains mysterious. The DAE calls it " of obscure origin," the NED marks it " origin unascertained," and Webster 1934 follows it with " origin uncertain." Noah Webster, in his American Dictionary of 1828, credited " they say " with two irreconcilable etymologies, but did not choose between them. The first was to the effect that the word was of African origin, and had been brought in by the slaves; the other sought to identify it with *tolt*, an old English law term derived from the Latin *tollere* through the medieval Latin *tolta* and the Anglo-French *tolte*. That term, which is traced by the NED to 1294 and is still in use, is a noun signifying a writ employed to remove a case from a court-baron to a county court. The latter etymology was adopted by Dunglison in the vocabulary of Americanisms that he contributed to the *Virginia Literary Museum* in 1829,[1] and Sherwood declared for substantially the same origin in his " Gazetteer of Georgia " in 1837. " *Tote*," he said, " is from the Latin *tollit*, he carries. It became *tolt* in English, and then as *holpe* fell to *hope*, so has *tolt* to *tote*." [2] The later etymologists, both professional and amateur, have continued to speculate about the word. Weekley, in " An Etymological Dictionary of Modern English," suggests that it may be derived from an old French verb, *tauter*, meaning to move a heavy object by means of rollers or otherwise. " The existence of an OF word in Virginia," he says, " would not be unnatural." In 1935 one J. Windsor of Reading wrote to the London *Daily Express*,[3] saying that he believed it came from " one of the West African tribal languages." " In Sierra Leone," he continued, " it is indicative of the method adopted by native carriers when they carry packages on their heads. It is also used by the Kroo boys [4] who man the ships." This African etymology was supported by Nathaniel Tillman, of Atlanta University, in *American Speech* in 1942.[5] He said:

> In a conversation with a friend, a Negro missionary from Portuguese West Africa, I learned that among his tribe *oku-tuta* means to carry something a long way. The root *-tuta* may be the parent of *tote*. . . . The abbreviation might be of Negro origin, an adaptation by speakers of different dialects. Or it might be a shortening by the labor bosses who heard the longer word from slaves. The further simplification to a monosyllable might likewise occur in the speech of the Negroes by analogy with the short English words used by the whites in communication with the workers; or it might be the result of the practise of the whites to use only the basic, or stressed syllable of a word taken from the dialects.

1 Reprinted by Mathews in The Beginnings of American English, pp. 99 ff.

2 Unfortunately for Sherwood, there is no evidence that *hope* is derived from *holpe*. *Holp* is an archaic inflection of *help*, and *help* and *hope* come down to us from quite different Old English words.

3 These Names Make News, March 22.

4 A *Kroo boy* is a native sailor, usually hailing from the coast of Liberia. He speaks a jargon called *Kroo English* or *trade English*.

5 A Possible Etymology of *Tote*, April, pp. 128 and 129.

Mr. Tillman called attention to the fact that the DAE's first recorded use of the word in writing is from the South. Witherspoon, in his pioneer treatise on Americanisms, 1781, listed it as prevailing " in some of the Southern States," and Webster, in his Compendious Dictionary of 1806 marked it " Virginia." But it had spread to New England by 1769, as the DAE shows, though Pickering, in 1816, said that it was still " much more used in the Southern than in the Northern States." Dunglison, in 1829, said that it was then " common in Massachusetts and in the Southern States." " Its early spread in New England, its general use throughout the cotton section of the South, and its survival still in Southern folk-speech," says Tillman, " seems to indicate a geographical distribution that coincides with the slave trade in this country."

*Tote,* in the sense of to carry, occurs in various American combinations, *e.g., to tote fair,* traced by the DAE to 1866; *tote-road,* traced to *c.* 1862; *tote-bag, tote-load, tote-team, pistol-toter* and *gun-toter.* Some of these have been made more or less familiar to the English by American movies and talkies. *Tote* as a shortened form of *totalizer* or *totalization* is a Briticism, little used in the United States, where the *tote system* of betting on races is usually called *pari-mutuel.* The word occurs in various senses in English and Scotch dialects, *e.g.,* signifying to bulge (Somerset), fat or large (Gloucestershire), and a boy's game resembling leapfrog (Norfolk), but its etymology in all such cases is obscure. It was formerly used in England as a short form of *total abstainer,* but in that sense appears to have passed out.

Half a dozen other early terms may be worth noticing, though some of them are not certainly of American origin. They are *bobolink, bootee, bundling, sophomore, Jimson-weed* and *harmonica.* The DAE calls *bobolink* an Americanism and the NED's first example is from America, but it has a decidedly English sound and may have been borrowed from some English dialect. Among the recorded forms are *boblincon, bob-on-linkhorn, bob-a-linkum, boblink, bob-a-link bob-o-link* and *bob-o'-linck.* The DAE and the NED agree that the term probably arose by onomatopoeia, and the former calls it " an imitation of the metallic clinking note of the bird," *i.e.,* the reed- or rice-bird (*Dolichonyx oryzivorus*). The DAE's first example is from the writings of John Adams, 1774. He used it in a figurative sense in speaking of a foppish young man. *Reed-bird,* in England, is the name of a quite different bird. In AL4, p. 12, I described *bootee* as "now obsolete," but that was an error, for a revival of it had begun at the time I wrote. The DAE defines the original *bootee* as " a half boot or high shoe, covering the ankle but not the leg " and traces it to 1799. *Bootees* were issued to the Federal troops during the Civil War, but soon afterward they began to disappear, and with them their name, though it was still listed by the Century Dictionary in 1889. The revived *bootee* is defined in " The Language of Fashion," by Mary Brooks Picken,[1] as " a boot having a short leg; for men, usually made with elastic gore over ankle or with laced front; for infants, usually knitted and tiny or half-leg length." I am informed by a correspondent [2] that the modern *bootee* is " usually knitted or crocheted, and is used for very small babies. It is used by some mothers with strings, and by some alone. It is usually white, pink or pale blue in color, and made of a fine quality wool yarn. It comes about half-way to the knees, and usually has a drawstring at the ankle, so that the baby can't kick it off." Sometimes *bootee* is spelled *bootie*.[3]

The art of *bundling* was not an American invention, and the DAE does not mark the term an Americanism, but both art and word flourished in this country more luxuriantly than in the British Isles. The DAE's definition is " the practice of unmarried couples (partly undressed) occupying the same bed " and its first American example is dated 1781. That example comes from Samuel Peters's " General History of Connecticut," [4] a work remembered today mainly because in it the author printed a list of ferocious Connecticut Blue Laws that have been denounced by other historians as imaginary,[5] but are still generally accepted as authentic. Peters says that bundling, in 1781,

1 New York, 1939, p. 11.
2 Miss Ruth Wilson, of New York.
3 Cf. an advertisement of the May Company in the Baltimore *Sunday Sun*, rotogravure section, Nov. 28, 1943.
4 The DAE overlooks an earlier example cited by Peters, from Travels Through the Middle Settlements in North America in the years 1759 and 1760, by Andrew Burnaby; London, 1775. Burnaby was an English clergyman.
5 See The True Blue Laws of Connecticut and New Haven and the

False Blue Laws Invented by the Rev. Samuel Peters, by J. Hammond Trumbull; Hartford, 1876. Trumbull (1821-97) was a well-known antiquarian and was especially interested in Indian place-names and the Indian languages. From 1863 until his death he was librarian of the Watkinson Library at Hartford. In 1874 he was president of the American Philological Association. He was State librarian of Connecticut 1854-56 and secretary of state 1861-65.

had prevailed in New England since " the first settlement in 1634," but that it went on " only in cold seasons of the year." [1] The NED's first example of *to bundle* comes, as I have noted, from his book, but the practise seems to have existed in the remoter parts of Britain, especially Wales, some time before he wrote. It attracted, however, but little attention from the primeval sociologists of the time, and Grose did not mention it in the first edition of his " Classical Dictionary of the Vulgar Tongue," 1785. But soon afterward news of it began to reach England from America, and when his third edition appeared in 1796 Grose defined it as follows:

> A man and woman sleeping in the same bed, he with his small clothes and she with her petticoats on; an expedient practised in America on a scarcity of beds, where, on such an occasion, husbands and parents frequently permitted travelers to bundle with their wives and daughters.

To this Partridge adds the following gloss in the edition of Grose that he brought out in 1931:

> In America the practise, strangely enough, prevailed only in New England, but it existed also in Wales, *c.* 1870. In Cumberland and Westmoreland the word was applied to another practise — that of a betrothed couple going to bed together in their clothes.

It was in this latter sense that the word was chiefly used in America. The chief authority on it is Henry Reed Stiles, who published " *Bundling:* Its Origin, Progress and Decline in America " in 1871. Stiles, who was a medical man, was a native of New York, but came of a long line of Connecticut ancestry, and always thought of himself as " truly a Connecticut man." He had first referred to *bundling* in a book called " History and Genealogies of Ancient Windsor, Conn.," published in 1859, in the following words:

> Then came war,[2] and young New England brought from the long Canadian campaigns stores of loose camp vices and recklessness, which soon flooded the land with immorality and infidelity. The church was neglected, drunkenness fearfully increased, and social life was sadly corrupted. *Bundling* — that ridiculous and pernicious custom which prevailed among the young to a degree which we can scarcely credit — sapped the fountain of morality and tarnished the escutcheons of thousands of families.

1 Peters (1735–1826) wrote a number of other books, and was a man of celebrity in his time. In 1794 he was elected Episcopal Bishop of Connecticut, but was never consecrated. He later moved to New York and there died in poverty and obscurity. 2 *i.e.*, the French and Indian War of 1754.

These words, said Stiles in the preface to his later work, produced
" a bussing around my ears. Divers good sons of Connecticut winced
under the soft impeachment of having a *bundling* ancestry, and inti-
mated that my sketch of society in the olden times was somewhat
overdrawn." He thereupon decided to amass proofs of his statement,
and the result was " *Bundling:* Its Origin, Progress and Decline." In
that book he showed that there were references to *bundling* in the
French romances of the Fourteenth Century, and that it had been reported by travelers, not only in Britain, but also in Holland, Switzerland and among various savage tribes. Stiles believed and argued that,
in the early days, *bundling* was quite innocent, and quoted the following in substantiation from Peters:

> People who are influenced more by lust than a serious faith in God, who is too
> pure to behold iniquity with approbation, ought never to *bundle*. If any man,
> thus a stranger to the love of virtue, of God, and the Christian religion, should
> *bundle* with a young lady in New England, and behave himself unseemly towards
> her, he must first melt her into passion, and expel Heaven, death and Hell from
> her mind, or he will undergo the chastisement of Negroes turned mad – if he
> escape with life it will be owing to the parents flying from their bed to
> protect him.

But with " the increased laxity of public morals," said Stiles, *bundling* was " more frequently abused," and its " pernicious effects became constantly more apparent, and more decidedly challenged the attention of the comparatively few godly men who endeavored to stem
and to control the rapidly widening current of immorality which
threatened to overwhelm the land." One of these godly men was the
celebrated Jonathan Edwards, who " thundered his anathemas upon
it." The *bundlers*, however, went on *bundling*, and the Revolution
only augmented the saturnalia that had begun with the French and
Indian War. " Not before the close of that struggle," said Stiles, " may
the custom be said to have received its death-blow, and even then it
*died hard*." The italics are his. He believed that two non-theological
events had most to do with exterminating it in New England. The
first was the " improved condition of the people after the Revolution,
enabling many to live in larger and better warmed houses," and the
second was the appearance, in an almanac in 1785 or thereabout, of a
satirical ballad against *bundling* which had a wide circulation and
produced " such a general storm of banter and ridicule that no girl
had the courage to stand up against it, and continue to admit her lovers
to her bed." This ballad, printed by Stiles in full, ridiculed the theory

that petticoats or even full clothing were sufficient protection against an infidel swain, and closed with the following sad story:

> A *bundling* couple went to bed
> With all their clothes from foot to head;
> That the defense might seem complete
> Each one was wrapped in a sheet.
> But oh, this *bundling's* such a witch
> The man of her did catch the itch,
> And so provoked was the wretch
> That she of him a bastard catch'd.

Stiles's book was reprinted in 1928 by A. Monroe Aurand, Jr., who added a great deal of interesting new matter.[1] Mr. Aurand, who is an authority upon Pennsylvania German antiquities, has also published three pamphlets upon the subject.[2] He says, challenging Partridge, that bundling was widespread among the Pennsylvania Germans in the early days, and is not unknown in their remoter settlements today. He suggests that the episode described in Ruth III, 6–13 may offer a primeval example of the practise.[3]

*Sophomore*, designating a second-year student in a four-year college course, is probably an Americanism, though the evidence is not altogether convincing. The DAE's first example is from a Latin document of Harvard, dated 1654. By 1684 it was appearing in the Harvard records as an English word, but it is recorded in England only four years later, with every sign of being in familiar university use. It had bred the adjective *sophomoric* by 1837, and *sophomorical* by 1839, in each case in the United States. It seems to have been extended to second-year students in high-schools during the 90s, and has since been used to designate even post-freshmen in kindergartens. *Freshmen*, which the DAE traces in American use to 1682, again at Harvard, is not an Americanism: the NED records it in England so early as 1596, and it is still in use there. *Junior* and *senior*, however, are both credited to American English by the DAE; the first is traced to *c.* 1764 and the second to 1741. In *American Speech* in 1930 Dr. Louise Pound published a curious note upon the difficulties that American students have with *sophomore*.[4] She said:

1 Harrisburg, Pa., The Aurand Press, 1928.
2 Slants on the Origin of *Bundling* in the Old World; Harrisburg, 1938; Little Known Facts About *Bundling* in the New World; Harrisburg, 1938; eleventh printing, 1943; and *Bundling* Prohibited: Pennsyl- vania History, Folk-lore and Sociology; Harrisburg, 1929. See also The Art of *Bundling*, by Dana Doten; New York, 1938.
3 Slants on the Origin of *Bundling*, just cited, pp. 11 *ff.*
4 *Sophomore*, April, p. 270.

The word seems peculiarly unable to get itself pronounced by high-school and college students. The tendency to syncopate the middle syllable is not a new one, for *sophmore* occurs in the diary of Nathaniel Ames, a second year student at Yale in 1758. But much happens to the word besides syncopation. Many speakers say *sothamore* or *sothmore*, . . . like those who say *syntheny* for *symphony*, or *nimth* for *nymph*. The contrary substitution, *f* for *th*, is that common among children, as *fum* for *thumb* or *fred* for *thread*. A few speakers . . . say *southamore* or *southmore*. . . . Further, many speakers that I once tested (six in a group of about thirty) said *solphomore* or *solphmore*. . . . When I first heard the intrusive *l* I found it as hard to give credence to it as I did to the inserted *r* of *langridge* for *language* or *sandridge* for *sandwich*. Still another frequent pronunciation (and spelling) is *sopamore* or *sopmore*.

*Campus* is marked an Americanism by the DAE and traced to 1774. All its early examples are taken from a classical monograph on the term by Albert Matthews.[1] Matthews surmises that the term may have been introduced by John Witherspoon, and with this the DAE agrees. At all save a few colleges, *e.g.*, Harvard, it has displaced the earlier *yard*.

*Jimson-weed* or *Jimpson-weed* is a degenerate form of *Jamestown-weed*, which the DAE traces to 1687. The plant (*Datura stramonium*) was discovered growing at Jamestown in Virginia by the English settlers who landed there in 1607, but they seem to have been unaware of the kick in it until 1676, when Nathaniel Bacon's rebellion reduced them to short commons and they ate it. What happened was thus described by Robert Beverley in his " History and Present State of Virginia," 1705: [2]

This being an early Plant, was gather'd very young for a boil'd salad, by some of the Soldiers sent thither, to pacifie the troubles of Bacon; and some of them ate plentifully of it, the effect of which was a very pleasant Comedy; for they turned natural Fools upon it for several Days. One would blow a Feather in the Air; another would dart straws at it with much Fury; and another stark naked was sitting up in a Corner, like a Monkey grinning and making Mows at them; a Fourth would fondly kiss and paw his Companions, and snear in their Faces, with a Countenance more antik than any in a Dutch Droll. In this frantik Condition they were confined, lest they in their Folly should destroy themselves; though it was observed that all their Actions were full of Innocence and Good Nature. Indeed, they were not very cleanly; for they would have wallow'd in their own Excrements, if they had not been prevented. A Thousand such simple Tricks they play'd and after Eleven Days, return'd themselves again, not remembering anything that had pass'd.

1 The Use at American Colleges of the Word *Campus. Publications of the Colonial Society of Massachusetts*, Vol. III, 1900, pp. 3-9.

2 Vol. II, p. 24.

The poisonous alkaloids in the *Jimson-weed* are hyoscyamine, atropine and scopolamine, all of which have important medical uses. The dried leaves, seeds and flowers are a constituent of many proprietary powders for the relief of asthma. Burned for their smoke, which the sufferer inhales, they help him by dilating and drying his bronchial tubes.[1] In view of the wide distribution of the weed it is surprising that so few cases of poisoning are reported.[2]

The *harmonica* was invented in 1762 by Benjamin Franklin who first called it the *armonica* (from the Italian *armonico*, harmonious), but had changed its name by 1765. It was no more than an improvement of the *musical glasses* mentioned in an oft-quoted passage in "The Vicar of Wakefield,"[3] which had been introduced to England by an Irishman named Richard Pockrich in 1744. Their original inventor seems to have been an anonymous German of the Seventeenth Century. Franklin heard them played in London in 1760 or thereabouts, and resolved to improve them. In their crude form they consisted simply of goblets filled with different amounts of water, and the musical notes produced by rubbing the rims of these goblets varied according to the height of the water in them. Franklin substituted a series of revolving glass basins operated by a treadle. Below them was a trough full of water, and as they revolved they picked it up. Musical notes were then produced by touching their wet rims. This contrivance was superior to the old *musical glasses* in two particulars: the glass basins were of fixed tonality, and more than one tone could be produced at the same time. The new instrument interested Mozart and Beethoven so much that both wrote pieces for it, and it produced virtuosi in Marianna Davies and Marianna Kirchgessner, but it is now forgotten. The modern *harmonica* or *mouth-organ* was invented in 1829 by a Viennese named Damien. It is a reed instrument and bears no sort of relation to the *musical glasses*.[4]

1 A Manual of Pharmacology, by Torald Sollmann; 6th ed.; Philadelphia, 1942, p. 366.

2 The symptoms, which may be very alarming, are described at length in Stramonium Poisoning, by John D. Hughes and James A. Clark, *Journal of the American Medical Association*, June 17, 1939, pp. 2500–02. See also Mandrakes in the Bible, Literature, and Pharmacology, by David I. Macht, *American Druggist*, Dec., 1933.

3 London, 1766, Ch. IX: "They would talk of nothing but high life and high-lived company, with other fashionable topics, such as pictures, taste, Shakespeare, and the *musical glasses*."

4 I am indebted here to Mr. D. F. Munro of Lexington, Mo.

## 3. CHANGED MEANINGS

Many common English words were given new meanings by the English colonists in America, *e.g., store, shop, corn, rock, cracker, block, creek, spell, lumber, college, city, boot, shoe, bluff* and *bureau Store,* in the sense of a retail establishment, began to be substituted for the English *shop* early in the Eighteenth Century, and by 1741, as the DAE shows, had bred *store-keeper.* To the English, *store* means primarily a large establishment, corresponding roughly to what we call a warehouse,[1] but they have been using the word in the American sense, to designate a coöperative retail store, since about 1850, and in later years they show a tendency to adopt it in the form of *department-store.* Contrariwise, there has been an increasing use of the English *shop* in the United States, not infrequently in the elegant form of *shoppe.* The DAE traces *book-store* to 1763, *grocery-store* to 1774, *hardware-, shoe-* and *drygoods-store* to 1789, *to keep store* to 1752, *store-book* to 1740, and *storekeeping* to 1774, but most of its first examples of the other familiar derivatives of *store* are later, *e.g., store-clothes,* 1840; *store-cheese,* 1863; *store-boy,* 1845; *store-front,* 1880; *store-window,* 1896; *store-hours,* 1857; *store-street,* 1879; and *store-teeth,* 1891. In some of these cases a more intensive search of the smaller and more remote newspapers would undoubtedly turn up much earlier examples.

*Corn,* in the American sense, is known to the English only as an odd Americanism; they use the word to designate any sort of edible grain, but especially wheat, as in *Corn Laws.* They commonly call our corn *maize,* which was its first name in America. The early Spaniards borrowed both the grain and its name from the Indians of the West Indies, and the English colonists took over both from the Spaniards. The first occurrence of the word in English found by the searchers for the NED is in Richard Eden's translation, published in London in 1555, of Peter Martyr's " De Rebus Oceanicis et Novo Orbe Decades," which had come out in Spain, in Latin, thirty years earlier. The word appears in Eden's translation as *mazium,* described

1 " In England," says Horwill, " *store* has normally much the same meaning as *storehouse.*" He quotes the following from Some Impressions of the United States, by E. A. Freeman; London, 1883, p. 63: " In the early settlements a shop was really a *store* in a sense which it hardly is now on either side of the ocean."

as " a kynde of grayne." [1] His book, which he called " The Decades of the Newe Worlde or West India, Conteyning the Navigations and Conquests of the Spaniards, with Particular Description of the Most Ryche and Large Landes and Islandes Lately Found in the West Ocean," was designed to arouse English interest in the new discoveries and to encourage English adventurers to attempt to seize land along the American coast. He was supported in both purposes by Richard Hakluyt, whose " Principall Navigations, Voiages and Discoveries of the English Nation " came out in 1589, and by Samuel Purchas, whose " Purchas, His Pilgrimage," followed in 1613. Hakluyt's book was republished in three volumes in 1600, and in the third of them *maize* appeared as *maiz*, which was then, and is still, its Spanish form. In Purchas it was made *mais*. Other forms recorded before 1700 were *maith, maix, mass, maze, mayis, mahiz, mayze* and *maes*, but by 1683 William Penn was spelling the word *maize* in his " Brief Account of the Province of Pennsylvania," and *maize* it has been ever since. The DAE shows that it began to drop out of use in America so early as 1629, being supplanted by *corn*.[2] To distinguish this New World corn from the grains which were called *corn* in England the latter were called *English corn*. To help in the differentiation *maize* was often called *Indian corn*, and indeed it sometimes is to this day, but by the middle of the Eighteenth Century simply *corn* usually sufficed.

At present the word is always understood, in the United States, to mean *maize*. Such derivatives as *corn-pone, -field, -hill, -husk, -crib, -crop, -cultivator, -fed, pop-, sweet-, -starch* and *-whiskey* all relate

---

1 Martyr was an Italian whose real name was Pierto Martire di Anghiera; he was born at Arona in 1457 or thereabout. As a young man he went to Rome and there became secretary to the governor of the city. In 1487 the Spanish ambassador, Count Tendilla, induced him to go to Madrid. He entered the church in 1494 and was made tutor to the children of Ferdinand and Isabella. After some experience in the Spanish diplomatic service he became dean of the cathedral at Granada in 1505 and royal chronicler in 1520. He was also a member of the Council for the Indies. His book was an attempt to bring into one volume all that was known in the early Sixteenth Century about America. He died in 1526. He is not to be confused with that other Peter Martyr (1500–1562) who was born at Zürich, became an Augustinian friar, renounced Catholicism, married a nun, became professor of theology at Oxford, and survives in history as a salient figure of the Reformation.

2 But an American *Maize* Products Company is still listed in the Manhattan telephone directory (1944).

to *maize*, not to any other grain,[1] and so does the familiar American phrase, *to acknowledge the corn*. The DAE traces *corn-field* to 1608, *-ground* to 1622, *-stalk* to 1645, *-basket* to 1648, *-land* to 1654, *-snake* to 1676, *-crib* to 1687, *sweet-* to 1646, *-blade* to 1688, *-house* to 1699, *-husk* to 1712, *-hill* to 1751, *-row* to 1769, *-patch* to 1784, *-cake* to 1791, *-fed* to 1793, *-bread* to 1796, *-country* to 1817, *-shelter* to 1819, *-grower* to 1831, *-pipe* to 1832, *-dodger* to 1834, *to acknowledge the corn* to 1840, *-bottoms* and *-whiskey* to 1843, *-juice* to c. 1846, *-worm* to 1849, *pop-*, to 1851, *-barn* to 1852, *-State* to 1853, *-starch* to 1857, and *-Belt* to 1882. All these save the first half dozen are probably materially older. The American colonists took to *corn* at once, and borrowed not only the Indian method of growing it — by planting an alewife or other fish in every row, for fertilizer — but also some of the Indian ways of preparing it for the table, *e.g.*, by making hominy. But the English at home did not like it, and in John Gerard's " Herball, or Generall Historie of Plants," enlarged and amended by Thomas Johnson; London, 1638, a favorite authority of the time, it was denounced as unfit for human food. " The bread which is made thereof," said Gerard-Johnson, " is meanly white, without bran; it is hard and dry as bisket is, and hath in it no clamminess at all; for which cause it is of hard digestion, and yieldeth to the body little or no nourishment; it slowly descendeth and bindeth the belly, as that doth which is made of millet or panick [an Italian variety of millet]." When John Winthrop, Jr., governor of Connecticut, went to England in 1662 to obtain a new charter for the colony, he was elected a member of the Royal Society and got upon friendly terms with Robert Boyle, the chemist. At Boyle's suggestion he prepared

---

1 Says Edgar J. Goodspeed in his preface to The Goodspeed Parallel New Testament: the American Translation and the King James Version; Chicago, 1943: " Differences of meaning have . . . grown up in different parts of the English-speaking world since Tyndale's day. What he called a *corn-field* we call a *wheat-field*, and his account of the disciples plucking the ears of *corn* conjures up a wholly false picture before the American mind; they were picking ears of wheat. King James's *corn of wheat*, of course, means a grain of wheat. Neither of them ever saw what we understand by a *corn-field*." I add the following from What Does *Corn* Mean? by W. Beach Thomas, London *Spectator*, Oct. 9, 1936, p. 584: " Possibly the much quoted *corn in Egypt* refers to barley. . . . Corn began as a generic name for a group of edible grains; but it was also adopted as a specific name for the standard grain of the country: for wheat in England, for oats in Scotland, for maize in America. . . . Does it, in our generic use, include rye? " The NED says that it does — and also barley and rice.

a long memorandum upon the growing, milling and uses of *corn* (including the preparation of a malt for brewing), and it was deposited in the Royal Society's archives. There, save for a few extracts, it remained unprinted until 1937, when Fulmer Mood unearthed it and printed it in full in the *New England Quarterly*.[1] Winthrop defended *corn* stoutly against the ignorant sneers of Gerard and Johnson. But the English, to this day, do not like it.[2]

*Rock*, to an Englishman, commonly signifies a stone of large size, and the Pilgrims so used it when they named *Plymouth Rock* in 1620. But the colonists apparently began to apply it to small stones during the Eighteenth Century, though the DAE's first example of *to throw a rock* is dated no earlier than 1817. A year before this Pickering recorded in his Vocabulary that " in New England we often hear the expression of *heaving rocks* for *throwing stones*." Some of the early American writers on speech tried to restore *rock* to its original English meaning, but in vain. Webster omitted it, in the American sense, from his dictionaries, and Sherwood, in his " Gazetteer of the State of Georgia," denounced it as follows:

> He threw a *rock* at me. *Stone* is the proper word. There are rocks, stones and pebbles; the first are large and unmanagable by the hand; the second, the stones, are smaller and can be thrown. David slung a *stone* at Goliath, but it would have required Sampson [*sic*] to have cast a rock.

*Cracker*, to indicate what the English commonly call a *biscuit*, is traced by the DAE to 1739. In recent years *biscuit*, in the English sense, has been borrowed in America, as in *National Biscuit Company*, and simultaneously the English have begun to make increasing use of *cracker*, which first appeared in England so long ago as 1810.[3] The word seems to come from the verb *to crack*, and probably was suggested by the cracker's crispness. *Block*, in the sense of a group of houses, is sometimes used in England, as in *block of shops*, but perhaps only as a conscious Americanism.[4] The DAE's first Ameri-

1 March, pp. 121–33.
2 Some Nebraska terms in *-corn* are discussed by Mamie Meredith in *Squaw Patch, Squaw Corn, Calico Corn, Yankee Corn, Tea Wheat, Sandy Wheat*, American Speech, Aug., 1932, pp. 420–22. *Squaw-corn* is traced by the DAE to 1824 and *calico-corn* to 1849. *Yankee-corn* is not listed. Miss Meredith also mentions *Pawnee-corn*.

3 The difference between the English *biscuit* and the American *biscuit* is discussed at length by Horwill.
4 The more usual term seems to be *parade* of shops. I find " Fine *Parade* of Freehold Shops " in a real-estate advertisement in the London *Telegraph*. *Business-block* is unknown to the English.

can example is dated 1796, but the NED does not report the term in English use until fifty-five years later. In the sense of the whole mass of buildings between four streets it goes back to 1815 in the United States, and is still exclusively American.[1] It is also American in the sense of the distance from one street to the next, as in " a *block* further on," and " he walked ten *blocks*." In this last sense the DAE traces it to 1843. South of the Mason and Dixon Line, in my boyhood, it was common to use *square* to designate the distance from one street to the next, but I don't think the term ever had much currency in New York. The DAE traces it to 1827. *Square* was also used in the South to designate the area marked off by four streets, and in that sense was employed by Thomas Jefferson in 1776. In Australia *block* means a portion of public land — roughly, what we call a *section*. It has given rise to a common derivative, *back-blocks*, signifying the back country.

*Creek*, in England, means a tidal inlet of the ocean or of some large river, but in America it began to designate any small stream so long ago as 1637, and, along with *run* and *branch*, has since pretty well obliterated the English *brook*.[2] It is still occasionally used in the United States in the English sense, as in *Curtis creek* (Maryland), and *Deep creek* (Virginia), but the English never use it in the more usual American sense. The use of *spell* in various familiar phrases, *e.g.*, *spell of sickness*, is apparently indigenous to America. *Spell of work* is old in English, but the first known examples of *spell of weather*, *spell of sickness*, *cold-spell*, *rainy-spell* and *hot spell* are American, and so is the first recorded use of *spell* standing alone, as an indicator of " a time or while." [3] *Lumber*, in England, means articles left lying about and taking up needed room, and in this sense it survives in America in a few compounds, *e.g.*, *lumber-room*; in the sense of timber it is an Americanism, traced by the DAE to the Seventeenth Cen-

---

1 The editor of Karl Baedeker's The United States; London, 1909, thought it necessary to list and define *block* in this sense for the information of English travelers. It was not included, however, in the list of Americanisms with English equivalents in A Short Guide to Great Britain, issued by the War and Navy Departments for the guidance of American soldiers in England, 1943.
2 In Topographical Terms From Vir-

ginia, II, *American Speech*, April, 1940, p. 168, George Davis McJimsey quotes the following from a Virginia document of 1637: " Up towards the head of the maine *Creek* over small *creekes* or brookes. . . ." See also *Runs, Creeks* and *Branches* in Maryland, by J. Louis Kuethe, *American Speech*, Dec., 1935, pp. 256–59.
3 See p. 9.

tury. In this American sense, says the DAE, it " undoubtedly arose from the fact that ship masts, sawed timber, barrel staves, etc., as important but bulky commodities, once blocked or *lumbered* up roads, streets and harbors of various towns." In England *college* ordinarily means one of the constituent corporations of a university, though sometimes it is also applied to a preparatory school; in the United States, since the Seventeenth Century, it has been applied to any degree-giving institution short of university rank.[1] In England *city* is restricted, says Horwill, to " a large and important town, or one that contains a cathedral "; in America it has been applied since the early Eighteenth Century to much smaller places.[2] *Boot*, in England, means what Americans, since the Seventeenth Century, have been calling a *shoe;* for our *boot*, signifying footgear covering the leg as well as the foot, the English commonly use other terms, *e.g., Wellington*.[3] *Bootblack*, traced by the DAE to 1817; *boot-brush*, to 1866, *bootee* (a half boot), to 1799; *bootlegger*, to 1889; and *to bootlick*, to 1845, are all marked Americanisms by the DAE, but they originally referred to the American *boot*, not the English. *Bureau*, to an Englishman, means an article of furniture including a writing desk — what we ordinarily call a *secretary;* in the United States it means a chest of drawers for holding linens. The English use it occasionally in our sense of a government or other office, but not often: they prefer *office*. But they use *bureaucrat* and *bureaucracy* just as we do.

Many English zoölogical and botanical terms were misapplied by the early colonists to species generally resembling what they had been familiar with in England, but actually not identical. The cases of *partridge, rabbit, beech, hemlock, lark, laurel, swallow* and *bay* are discussed in AL4, pp. 123 and 124.[4] The list might be greatly lengthened. For two curious instances I am indebted to Mr. Theodore W. Bozarth of Mount Holly, N. J. He says:

> The European *robin* (*Erythacus rubecola*) is a member of the warbler family, but the settlers gave its name to a bird (*Planesticus migratorus*) that be-

1 There is an interesting discussion of its early uses in America in On the Use of the Words *College* and *Hall* in the United States, by Albert Matthews, *Dialect Notes*, Vol. II, Part II, 1900, pp. 91–114.

2 Not infrequently it is embodied in their names, as in *Ellicott City*, Md., with 1216 inhabitants; *Dow City*, Iowa, with 588; *Filer City*, Mich.,

with 408; and *Lee City*, Ky., with 152.

3 The American trade term for a low shoe is *Oxford*. *Slipper* designates a topless foot-covering that does not lace. I am indebted here to Mr. Charles H. Jaggard of Woodstown, N. J.

4 All save *rabbit* are also dealt with by Horwill.

longs to the thrush family and is second-cousin to the mocking-bird. In 1920 the Postoffice Department pictured both the English and the American types of *mayflower* on its Pilgrim Tercentenary stamps. To quote from " A Description of United States Postage Stamps," published by it in 1933, p. 31: " The border at the left of the picture presents a vertical row of hawthorn blossoms (the British *mayflower*); the border at the right contains a row of trailing arbutus (the American *mayflower*, which tradition says was named by the Pilgrims after their ship)."

The impact of a new landscape upon the early colonists caused them to abandon a number of English topographical terms, *e.g., moor*, and to make heavy use of others that were rare or dialectical in England, *e.g., run* and *branch*. They also invented many quite new ones, usually devised by giving familiar English words new meanings, *e.g., divide* and *bluff*. The NED's first example of *bluff* in the sense of a promontory is dated 1737 and comes from John Wesley's diary. The DAE, on the authority of a contemporary document printed in the *South Carolina Historical and General Magazine* for July, 1929, carries its history back to 1687, and gives four more examples antedating Wesley, including the one from Francis Moore, 1735, quoted in AL4, p. 3. It says that the word was used only rarely before 1700, and then mainly in the region of Savannah. The noun is plainly a derivative of the adjective *bluff*, meaning presenting a bold and more or less perpendicular front. This adjective, which was applied to ships' bows that were blunt and nearly vertical, has a history in English going back to the beginning of the Seventeenth Century, and was apparently borrowed, like many other English sea-terms, from a Dutch prototype, *blaf*, now obsolete. As I recorded in AL4, p. 3, *bluff* as a noun has the distinction of being the first Americanism sneered at by an English purist.[1] But though he called it " barbarous " in 1735, it was used without apology by the eminent English geologist, Sir Charles Lyell, in the first volume of his " Principles of Geology " in 1830, and by 1842 it was appearing in a poem by Tennyson. It has never, however, become as familiar in England as it is in the United States, and there is no English parallel to our frequent use of it in geographical names, *e.g., Council Bluffs* and *Bluff City* (applied to both Memphis, Tenn., and Hannibal, Mo.). It had emerged from the Savannah area by the middle of the Eighteenth Century, and when the movement into the West began it enjoyed a large increase in

[1] The Moore just mentioned. His sneer was in A Voyage to Georgia, Begun in the Year 1735; London, 1744, p. 24.

use. By 1807 a traveler beyond the Alleghanies was explaining that " by *bluffs* in the Western country is understood high steep banks which come close to and are washed at their base by the rivers." Whether the other American *bluff*, in the sense of bluster or pretense, derives from the adjective or the noun I do not know: probably it owes something to both. It seems to have first appeared in the game of poker, but by 1852, as the DAE shows, it had come into general use as a verb. Its use as a noun probably preceded this, and by 1850 both *bluffer* and *bluffing* had appeared.

## 4. ARCHAIC ENGLISH WORDS

The notion that American English is fundamentally only an archaic form of British English has been propagated diligently by two groups of writers on language: first, Americans who seek to establish the truth of Lowell's saying that " our ancestors, unhappily, could bring over no English better than Shakespeare's," and second, Englishmen who deny Americans any originality whatsoever in speech, and seek to support their denial by showing that every new Americanism that pops up was used centuries ago by Chaucer, Spenser or Gower. The latter enterprise has been sometimes carried to extravagant lengths; indeed, it would not surprise me to find a correspondent of the London *Times* or Manchester *Guardian* reporting, with a mingling of patriotic satisfaction and moral indignation, that he had found even *duck-soup* and *hitch-hike* in a state paper of the age of Henry VII. But despite all this absurdity, it remains an undoubted fact that there is a recognizable substratum of archaic English, or of English faded into the dialects, in the American vocabulary, and that it includes a number of terms that other watchful Englishmen have denounced as American barbarisms. Ready examples are *to guess, to advocate, to notify, to loan,* and *mad* for *angry.* Nearly all the early English travelers noted the use of *to guess* in America, especially in New England — not in the sense of to conjecture or suppose, but, as the NED says, " with playful moderation of statement, in reference to what the speaker regards as a fact or a secure inference." But, as we have seen in Chapter I, Section 4, this distortion of the original meaning of the verb was by no means an American invention, for the NED finds it so used in no less respectable an English book than John

Locke's " Some Thoughts of Education," published in 1692. It passed out of English use during the Eighteenth Century, and though Byron revived it in 1814 and Scott in 1818, it is now unused in England save as a conscious Americanism.[1]

*To notify*, as in " The policy were *notified*," is not in common use in England, where the word is more often employed in such forms as " The appointment was *notified* in the newspapers," but what is now the American practise is traced by the NED, in English use, to 1440, though it has been rare since about 1700. *To loan* has been traced by the DAE, in American use, to 1729, and in recent years it has been worked so heavily that it strikes Englishmen as a very typical Americanism, but the NED traces it to *c.* 1200, and it appears in one of the acts of Henry VIII. Since the middle of the Eighteenth Century, however, the English have preferred *to lend*. *Mad* for *angry* is now regarded by the English as another characteristic Americanism, but the NED traces it in English use to *c.* 1300 and it survives in a number of English dialects. So with *sick* for *ill*. The NED traces it to the King Alfred translation of Boëthius's " De Consolatione Philosophiae," *c.* 888, but it began to be displaced by *ill* in the Fifteenth Century, and the English now regard the latter as more chaste and elegant, and have given *sick* the special sense of nauseated. In that sense it is not found in English use before 1614. In many compounds the original (and now American) sense survives, *e.g.*, *sickness, sick-bed, sick-allowance, sick-bay, sick-room, sick-leave, sick-rate* and *sick* (noun).

The list of such old English terms still alive in American might be greatly lengthened, and it would include many other words and phrases that have been denounced as abominable Americanisms, from time to time, by English purists, *e.g.*, *to progress, patch* (of land), *clever* (in the sense of good-natured and obliging), *druggist, gotten, gap* (a break in a range of hills), *to wilt, deck* (of cards), *shoat*, and *Fall* (for Autumn).[2] But, as the late George Philip Krapp argued

---

1 See The Chaucerian-American *I Guess*, by Stuart Robertson, *Modern Language Notes*, Jan., 1933, pp. 37–40.

2 A number of others are listed in American English, by M. J. C. Meikeljohn, London *Spectator*, Aug. 6, 1927, pp. 212–13. Said Daniel Drake in Pioneer Life in Kentucky; Cincinnati, 1860, p. 128 (speaking of Kentucky *c.* 1795–1800): " The *Fall*, as we always called it, not less than Spring and Summer, brought its sylvan scenes and pleasures; but do not for a moment suppose that the foreign adjective (*sylvan*) I have just employed was a word of those days, or that *Autumn* and *forest* made a part of our vocabulary. All was rudely vernacular, and I knew not

effectively in a paper published in 1927,[1] it is easy to overestimate the size and importance of this archaic element in American speech. It is largest in the dialect of certain remote communities, notably that of the mountaineers of Appalachia, but even in such communities it is smaller than is commonly assumed. The theory that the English brought to America by the early colonists underwent a sort of freezing here was first propagated, according to Krapp, by A. J. Ellis, a distinguished English philologian of the last century.[2] It was apparently suggested to him by the well-known fact that the Old Norse of *c.* 1000 has survived with relatively little change in Iceland. But, as Krapp shows, Ellis appears to have been densely ignorant of the history of the English settlements in America, and ascribed to them a cultural isolation that never approached in completeness the isolation of the Norwegians in Iceland. Krapp goes on:

> One of the most striking characteristics of American cultural development is the fact that it has taken place under the stimulus of an astonishing number of contacts with the outer world, British and otherwise. The American community has not been segregated, unadulterated, merely self-perpetuating. Relations with the parent country have never been discontinued. Through the appeal of literature they have been growing stronger and stronger from generation to generation. American English and British English are not identical, but they are and always have been equal citizens in the cosmopolitan world of the English language. The absurdity of describing American English as the archaic speech of an isolated community may be realized by considering what might have happened if the conditions favoring isolation had been present. If migration to New England had ceased in the year 1700, if New England had remained after that time a separate state, severed not only from Europe but from the rest of America, it is not improbable that something approximating the language of Dryden might still be heard in New England. But Dryden's speech is forever lost in the medley of later voices that sound more loudly in our ears.

---

then the meaning of that word. We spoke a dialect of old English, in queer pronunciation, and abominable grammar."

1 Is American English Archaic?, *Southwest Review,* Summer, pp. 292–303.

2 In his On Early English Pronunciation, brought out at intervals from 1869 to 1889. Ellis was born in 1814 and died in 1890. He was also a mathematician and a writer on musical theory.

# IV

# THE PERIOD OF GROWTH

## 1. A NEW NATION IN THE MAKING

Though the American language had begun its dizzy onward march even before the Revolution, it did not begin to show the vigor and daring which mark it today until after the beginning of the Nineteenth Century. Its chief riches, at all times since, have come out of argot and slang, and American slang, says Krapp in the paper quoted at the end of the last chapter, was " the child of the new nationalism, the spirit of joyous adventure that entered American life after the close of the War of 1812." He goes on:

> One will search earlier colonial literature in vain for any flowering of those verbal ingenuities which ornament the colloquial style of Americans so abundantly in the first great period of Western expansion, and which have ever since found their most favorable conditions along the shifting line of the frontier.

In support of his thesis he quotes the following from F. J. Turner's well-known book, " The Frontier in American History ": [1]

> That coarseness and strength combined with acuteness and inquisitiveness; that practical, inventive turn of mind, quick to find expedients; that masterful grasp of material things, lacking in the artistic but powerful to effect great ends; that restless, nervous energy; that dominant individualism, working for good and for evil, and withal that buoyancy and exuberance which comes with freedom — these are traits of the frontier, or traits called out elsewhere because of the existence of the frontier.

The old American frontier, of course, had vanished by the end of the Nineteenth Century, but it is not to be forgotten that, to the immigrants who poured in after 1850, even the slums of the great Eastern cities presented what were reasonably describable as frontier conditions, and that there are still cultural, if not geographic frontiers

[1] New York, 1920. Turner (1861–1932) was professor of history at Wisconsin from 1889 to 1910 and at Harvard from 1910 to 1924. In his later years he was a research associate at the Henry E. Huntington Library.

at Hollywood and Miami, not to mention Oklahoma, Nevada and Mississippi. From 1814 to 1861 the influence of the great open spaces was immediate and enormous, and during those gay, hopeful and melodramatic days all the characteristics that mark American English today were developed — its disdain of all scholastic rules and precedents, its tendency toward bold and often bizarre tropes, its rough humors, its not infrequent flights of what might almost be called poetic fancy, its love of neologisms for their own sake. In recent years most of these neologisms come from the East, and not a few of them show a somewhat painful artfulness, but during the half century before the Civil War the great reservoir of them was the West, which then still included a large part of the South, and they showed a gaudy innocence. Said a shrewd and well-informed observer, Dr. Thomas Low Nichols: [1]

> The language, like the country, has a certain breadth and magnitude about it. A Western man " sleeps so sound it would take an earthquake to wake him." He is in danger " pretty considerable much " because somebody is " down on him," [2] like " the whole Missouri on a sandbar." He is a " gone coon." [3] He is down on all " cussed varmints," [4] gets into an " everlasting fix," and holds that " the longest pole knocks down the persimmons." A story " smells rather tall." . . .[5]

In the Southwest is found the combination of Western and Southern character and speech. The Southwestern man was " born in old Kaintuck, raised in

1 Forty Years of American Life, 1821–1861; London, 1864; reprinted, London, 1874; New York, 1937. Nichols (1815–1901) was a New Englander by birth, and had a large hand in the numerous " reform " movements that racked the country before the Civil War. He was, in turn, a water curist, a vegetarian, a spiritualist, an advocate of free love, and a pacifist. In the end he became a convert to Catholicism. He left the country for England in 1861 because he was opposed to the military coercion of the South. Despite his vagaries his book is a fair and illuminating picture of the American *Kultur* of his time. Say Stanley J. Kunitz and Howard Haycraft in American Authors, 1600–1900; New York, 1938, p. 565: " With republication in 1937, it has come into its own as an excellent piece of autobiography and social history." Long extracts from its discussion of speech are reprinted in Tall Talk in America Sixty Years Ago, by Mamie Meredith, *American Speech*, April, 1929, pp. 290–93.

2 The DAE traces *down on*, in the sense of to show disapproval or dislike of, to 1851, and marks it an Americanism. *To down* (in the sense of to gulp or swallow hastily) is also an Americanism, and so are *to be down sick*, traced by the DAE to 1745; *down cellar*, to 1805; *down river*, to 1853; *down country*, to 1823; *down East*, to 1825; *down grade*, to 1872; *down South*, to 1835; *down town*, to 1835.

3 The DAE's first example is from Marryat, 1839: " In the Western States . . . 'I'm a *gone coon*' implies 'I'm distressed — or ruined — or lost.' "

4 *Cussed* is discussed in Chapter VI, Section 8. *Varmint* is not an Americanism.

5 More examples of Western talk from Nichols are in AL4, p. 137.

Mississippi, is death of a b'ar, and smartly on a painter [1] fight." He " walks on water, out hollers the thunder, drinks the Mississippi," " calculates " that he is " the genuwine article," and that those he don't like " ain't worth shucks." [2] He tells of " a fellow so poor and thin he had to lean up agin a saplin' to cuss." He gets " as savage as a meat ax." He " splurges [3] about," and " blows up like a steamboat."

The Southerner is " mighty glad to see you." He is apt to be " powerful lazy " and " powerful slow "; [4] but if you visit him where he has located himself, he'll " go for you to the hilt agin creation." When people salute each other at meeting, he says they are " howdyin' [5] and civilizin' each other." He has " powerful nice corn." The extreme of facility is not as easy as lying, but " as easy as shootin'." A man who has undressed has " shucked himself." To make a bet with a man is to " size his pile.". . . Most Yankeeisms can be found in the districts of England from which the country was first settled. The colloquialisms of the South and West are more original. Miners, gamblers, and all sorts of adventurers, attracted by gold to California and the Rocky Mountains, have invented new forms of expression.

" American humor," says Nichols, " consists largely of exaggeration, and of strange and quaint expressions." That it differs in this respect from English humor, which tends toward understatement, has been frequently noted, and this difference extends to the popular speech of both countries. Said an Associated Press correspondent in London in 1944, in a dispatch dealing with the current English slang: [6]

You don't say some one gives you a *pain in the neck;* you just remark, " He's not *my cup of tea.*" To answer whether a bomb which caused extensive damage took any lives the Londoner will say cautiously, " A *decent few.*". . . An Englishman takes a *poor view* of something he disapproves. Soldiers who get fresh with girls are *saucy.*

" Much that seems droll to English readers in the extravagances of Western American," says Nichols, " is very seriously intended. The man who described himself as ' squandering about permiscuous ' had no idea that his expression was funny. When he boasted of his sister that ' she slings the nastiest ankle in old Kentuck ' he only intended to say that she was a good dancer." However much this may have been true in the earliest days, among the loutish fur-trappers and mountain-men who constituted the first wave of pioneers, it had ceased to be so by the time the new West began to develop recorders

1 *i.e.,* a panther.
2 Traced by the DAE to 1843. From *corn-shuck.*
3 Traced to 1830 as a noun and to 1844 as a verb. It is an Americanism.
4 The use of *powerful* as a general intensive goes back to the 1820s.
5 *Howdy* and to *howdy* are Americanisms.
6 Londoner's Slang Intrigues Yank Forces in England, by Hal Boyle, Boston *Traveler,* June 2, 1944.

of its speech. From that time onward the naïve but spontaneous hyperboles of those who bore the burden and heat of the day were reinforced by the deliberate inventions of a more sophisticated class, and Western " tall talk " began to take on the character of a distinct and well-recognized *genre*. The identity of its first recorders has been forgotten, but I suspect that some of them were professional humorists, for by the end of the 40s the stars of the craft were beginning to turn from the New England Yankee to the trans-Alleghany American, often a Southerner and usually only theoretically literate. Joseph G. Baldwin's " The Flush Times of Alabama and Mississippi " (then a true frontier country) appeared in 1853, and only a few years later one of the most popular of the humorists, George H. Derby (John Phoenix), a lieutenant in the Topographical Engineers of the Army, made a visit to Oregon. The discovery of gold in California attracted not only fortune-seekers but also journalists, and out of their ranks came a large number of satirical historians of the rise of Western civilization, with Mark Twain, in the end, overshadowing all the rest. It was these wags, I believe, who really made " tall talk " the fearful and wonderful thing that it became during the two pre-war decades, though no doubt its elements were derived from authentic folk-speech. Thornton printed some specimens in the appendix to the second volume of his glossary, and many others have been exhumed in late years by other cultural explorers. It was, said William F. Thompson in 1934,[1]

a form of utterance ranging in composition from striking concoctions of ingeniously contrived epithets, expressing disparagement or encomium, to wild hyperbole, fantastic simile and metaphor, and a highly bombastic display of oratory, employed to impress the listener with the physical prowess or general superiority of the speaker or of his friends.

It survives more or less in Western fiction, and there are even traces of it remaining in real life,[2] but the best of it belongs to the era of its first burgeoning. B. A. Botkin, in his " Treasury of American Folklore," [3] gives some specimens of the wild and woolly neologisms it produced, *e.g., to absquatulate, angeliferous, bodaciously, boliterated, to exflunct, to obflisticate, to ramsquaddle, ringtailed roarer, ripstaver* and *screamer. To absquatulate*, meaning to depart stealthily, is traced by the DAE to 1833, and *bodaciously*, meaning completely,

1 Frontier Tall Talk, *American Speech*, Oct., 1934, p. 187.
2 Tall Talk of the Texas Trans-Pecos, by Haldeen Braddy, *American Speech*, April, 1940, pp. 220–22.
3 New York, 1944, p. 273.

to 1837. *To absquatulate* was once in wide use, but began to drop out during the Civil War, when *to skedaddle* supplanted it. The DAE suggests that it may be a blend of *to abscond* and *to squat,* but that seems hardly likely. The earliest recorded example of *bodaciously* is in Sherwood's " Gazetteer of the State of Georgia," third edition, 1837, but in the form of *body-aciously* it was used by James Hall in his "Legends of the West," second edition, 1832. *To exflunct,* meaning to beat, appeared in the East in the early 30s, but when it crossed the mountains it was changed into the more satisfying *to exfluncticate, to exflunctificate, to explunctify* and *to explunciticate. To obflisticate,* meaning to eclipse or obliterate, is traced by the DAE to 1832, and Botkin records *to obflusticate* and *to obfusticate* as variants. *To ramsquaddle,* which is not listed by the DAE, seems to have been a synonym for *to exflunct. Ringtailed roarer,* meaning a big and hearty fellow, is traced to 1830; *ripstaver,* meaning a person of consequence, to 1833, and *screamer,* meaning a strong man, to 1831. Many other similar coinages of the period might be added. *Rip-roaring,* now almost standard American, is traced by the DAE to 1834, and *rip-snorter* to 1840. Whether or not *teetotal* is an Americanism is not certain, but it seems to be very probable. The DAE's first example is dated 1837, three years later than the date of the first English example, but Thornton finds *teetotaciously* in 1833, and the DAE offers *tetotally* (soon to become *teetotally*) in the letters of the celebrated Parson Weems, 1807.[1] *Ramstugious,* meaning wild, is traced by the DAE to 1847; *to cohogle,* meaning to deceive, to 1829; *conbobberation,* a disturbance, to 1835; *to explaterate,* to talk at length, to 1831; *to honeyfogle,* to cheat, to 1829; *to hornswoggle,* also to cheat, to the same year;[2] and *rambunctious,* uncontrollable, to 1835. A number of other inventions of the era, not listed by the DAE, are given by Mathews in his chapter on Western and Southern Vernacular, *e.g., blustiferous,* blustering; *clamjamphrie,* rubbish; *clodpolish,* awkward;

1 Says Bristed, p. 71: "The infinite variety of Western phraseology embraces every sort of expression from the clumsiest vulgarity to the most poetic metaphor; from unintelligible jargon to pregnant sententiousness. Sometimes it luxuriates in elongation of words and reduplication of syllables, as if the mother-English were not sufficiently strong and expressive, — *cantankerous* for *rancorous,* *salvagerous* for *savage.* The barbarous cant word *teetotal* was doubtless thus coined by some Western speaker at a ' temperance' meeting."

2 Said a (presumably reverend) writer in the *Church Standard* of Sydney, Australia, Nov. 27, 1936: "So far as we are concerned, the only American coinage which has left us breathless with admiration is *hornswoggle.*"

*to cornuck,* to throw into fits; *to explicitrize,* to censure; *killnifer-ously,* fondly; *monstracious* and *monstropolous,* huge; *peedoodles,* a nervous disorder; *to puckerstopple,* to embarrass; and to *rampoose,* to go on a rampage.

Some of the Western terms of the 1812–1861 era remain mysterious to lexicographers, *e.g., bogus* and *burgoo.* Webster 1934 marks *bogus* " origin uncertain " and the DAE marks it " of obscure origin." Efforts have been made to connect it with the French *bagasse,* meaning the refuse left after sugar-cane is crushed, but there is no plausible evidence for that derivation. Nor is there any evidence for the theory, occasionally propounded by amateur etymologists, that it was borrowed from the name of a man named *Bogus.*[1] A verb, *to bogue,* meaning to go around, was in use before the Revolution, but no one has ever succeeded in connecting it with *bogus.* The noun is traced to 1823 by Thornton, and he shows that it then signified an apparatus for making counterfeit money. By 1839, as the DAE records, it was being applied to the money thus made, and by *c.* 1849 it had become an adjective with the general sense of not genuine. *Burgoo* is not an American invention, but was borrowed originally from the argot of British sailors, to whom it meant a thick oatmeal porridge. In that sense it was in American use so early as 1787. How it came to be used to designate a meat and vegetable stew is not known. It was in use in that sense in the West by the early 50s, and since then it has been generally associated with Kentucky. Arthur H. Deute, a culinary authority,[2] says that a *burgoo* is composed of a mixture of rabbit or squirrel meat, chicken, beef, salt pork, potatoes, string beans, onions, lima beans, corn, okra, carrots and tomatoes, and is made in two pots, the meats in a small one and the vegetables in a large. When both have cooked sufficiently the meats are added to the vegetables, the two are well stirred together, and the *burgoo* is ready. " Remember," adds Deute, " it is not a soup. It is a stew." Perhaps *shivaree* should be added here, though it may not be a Western term. All the etymologists appear to be agreed that it is a naturalized form of the French *charivari.* It signifies, primarily, a rowdy serenade of a newly-married couple, but it is also used to designate any noisy demonstra-

1 A suggestion that it may have been introduced by immigrants from Ireland, Wales or England appears in *American Notes and Queries,* Sept., 1942, p. 88.

2 Pages From the Notebook of a Gourmet, Chicago *Daily News,* May 4, 1944, p. 21.

tion. The DAE's first example is from Baynard R. Hall's " The New Purchase," 1843. An earlier form, *sherrivarrie*, is traced to 1805.[1] The *shivaree* still survives in many rural areas, East and West. In the West it is sometimes called a *belling* or a *warmer*,[2] and in New England it is variously known as a *serenade, horning, rouser, wake-up, belling, jamboree, tin-pan shower, skimmelton, shivaree* or *callithumpian*.[3] Bartlett said in the first edition of his Glossary, 1848, that *callithumpian* had been used, " in New York as well as other parts of the country," to designate a noisy parade on New Year's eve, but that such parades were going out of fashion.[4]

*Stogy*, in the sense of a crude cigar, made with a simple twist at the mouthward end instead of a fashioned head, is not traced by the DAE beyond 1893, but it must be very much older. It is a shortened form of *conestoga*, the name of a heavy covered wagon with broad wheels, much in use in the early days for transport over the Alleghanies. This name came from that of the Conestoga valley in Lancaster county, Pennsylvania, which came in turn from that of a tribe of Iroquois Indians, extinct before the Revolution. The term *Conestoga-wagon* seems to have been in use in Pennsylvania before 1750, but it was apparently but little known to the country at large until after 1800. Many of the Conestoga wagoners were Pennsylvanians, and they prepared the tobacco of Lancaster county for smoking on their long trips by rolling it into what soon came to be known as *conestogies* and then *stogies*. When the commercial manufacture of these pseudo-cigars began I have been unable to learn: it is now centered, not in Pennsylvania, but at Wheeling, W. Va. The *Conestoga-wagon* survived until my own boyhood. I have seen whole fleets lined up in Howard street, Baltimore, laden with butter and eggs from the Pennsylvania German country. My father made a round

1 *Sherrivarrie* is not to be confused with *sherry-vallies*, meaning, according to Bartlett, " pantaloons made of thick velvet or leather, buttoned on the outside of each leg, and generally worn over other pantaloons." Bartlett says that the word comes from the French *chevalier*, but the DAE derives it from a Polish word, *szarawary*, meaning loose trousers. If this etymology is sound, then *sherry-vallies* seems to be the only Polish loan made by American English. The DAE traces it to 1778, and it seems to have been picked up from Polish volunteers during the Revolution. It was becoming obsolete by the time Bartlett listed it in 1848.

2 *Belling* the Bridal Couple in Pioneer Days, by Mamie Meredith, *American Speech*, April, 1933, pp. 22–24.

3 *Serenade* in New England, by Miles L. Hanley, *American Speech*, April, 1933, pp. 24–26.

4 See *Callithumpians*, by Louise Pound, *American Speech*, Oct., 1942, p. 213.

trip in one immediately after the Civil War, and was a week on the road from Baltimore to Lancaster and return. The covered-wagon of the Western pioneer was often a *Conestoga*.

## 2. THE EXPANDING VOCABULARY

Taking one with another, the pioneers who trekked westward during the half century between the War of 1812 and the Civil War stood a good deal closer, humanly speaking, to the Okies of latter times than to the heroic figures who commonly represent them in historical fiction and the movies. They were not, perhaps, as vicious as the Puritans of early New England, but by the same token they lacked almost altogether the cultural aptitudes and propensities that, in the Puritans, even Calvinism could not kill. Most of them were bankrupt (and highly incompetent) small farmers or out-at-heel city proletarians, and the rest were mainly chronic nomads of the sort who, a century later, were to rove the country in caricatures of automobiles. Very few settled down in the areas that were their first goals. If they headed, at the start, for Kentucky or Ohio, they were presently moving on to Indiana or Illinois, and after that they proceeded doggedly and irrationally to even wilder and less hospitable regions. How the last wave of them was finally brought up by the Pacific on the coast of Oregon is magnificently described in a memorable novel by H. L. Davis, by title " Honey in the Horn." [1] In the case of multitudes, there was but little more sign of intelligent purpose in their painful wanderings than in the migrations of Norwegian lemmings. They simply pressed on and on, sweating in Summer, freezing in Winter, and hoping always for a miracle over the ever-receding horizon. When they halted it was not because they had actually found Utopia; it was simply because they had become exhausted. There ensued, commonly, a desperate struggle with the climate, the Indians, the local Mammalia and Insectivora and an endless series of plagues and pestilences, and if, by some chance mercy of their sanguinary God, they managed to survive and an organized community arose, it was quickly afflicted by a fresh scourge of money-lenders, theologians, patent-medicine quacks and politicians. The loutish humor

1 New York, 1935. The Oklahoma backwash was dealt with sentimentally in Grapes of Wrath, by John Steinbeck; New York, 1939, and more realistically in Prairie City, by Angie Debo; New York, 1944.

of these poor folks was their Freudian reply to the intolerable hard-
ships of their existence. They had to laugh to escape going crazy –
and not infrequently the remedy did not work. It was not in such relatively civilized centers as Cincinnati and St. Louis that the " tall talk "
of the West developed, nor was it in such transplanted New Yorks
and Bostons that the racier new words and phrases of the era were
coined; it was along the rivers, in the mountains and among the lonely
and malarious settlements of the prairies. There was thus very little
verbal subtlety in them, for subtlety is the monopoly of classes that
were only sparsely represented in the westward advance. But they
were often extremely pungent and picturesque, and like every other
trait of the rude but really autochthonous trans-Alleghany culture they soon had repercussions in the East.

It was a time, along the seaboard, of ardent but vain efforts to set
up a series of Alexandrias *in partibus infidelium*. Not only Boston,
but also New Haven, New York, Philadelphia, Baltimore and Charleston had its caste of austere and hopeful Brahmins, and they laid
down the law with humorless assurance, convinced that an almost
celestial light was in them. They knew precisely what was right and
what was wrong, not only in such gross and public matters as speech,
but also in the most minute details of private conduct. Reformers of a
thousand varieties swarmed the land, whooping up their new arcana
and passing the hat. The " gifted " female began to emerge from the
seraglio – Margaret Fuller, Lydia Sigourney, Lucretia Mott, all the
bad lady poets praised by Poe, all the vestals of elegance and decorum
assembled by *Godey's Lady's Book*.[1] The effort of one and all was
to polish and refine the country; they frowned, like William Jennings
Bryan in 1926, upon the suggestion that *Homo americanus* was a
mammal. But all their hard striving went for naught, for the West
was fast devouring the East, and a true Century of the Common Man
was beginning. The tide turned with Jackson's first election in 1828,
but it took the Brahmins almost a full generation to realize what had
happened to them. By the time the fumes of the Civil War cleared
away the whole American empire, from the rocks of Maine to the
Golden Gate, was far, far closer to a mining-camp in its way of life
and habit of thought than to the grove of Academe. Emerson had
shrunk to a wraith almost as impalpable as his own Transcendental-

1 *Godey's* was established in 1830. All
three of the pythonesses mentioned
were born between 1790 and 1810.

ism, and the reigning demigod was a river boatman and rail splitter of the West. Of all the evangelists of Better Things who had flourished since 1800 only Noah Webster left any permanent mark upon the American people. He taught them how to spell — a faculty that they were not to lose until the emergence of pedagogy as a learned profession, cradled at Teachers College, Columbia. But he taught them nothing else.[1]

A glance through the DAE is sufficient to show how luxuriantly the new American language bloomed during this gaudy era. Hundreds and perhaps even thousands of terms that are now inextricably of its essence were then hatched by ingenious men — to the horror, I have no doubt, of all the " madmen, madwomen, men with beards, Dunkers, Muggletonians, Come-outers, Agrarians, Seventh-Day Baptists, Quakers, Abolitionists, Calvinists, Unitarians and philosophers " sneered at by Emerson,[2] and perhaps to the equal horror of Emerson himself, but to the delight of the populace that these visionaries were bent on saving. They contributed nothing to the store themselves, and the populace itself contributed no more, but on the other side of the ideational fence were plenty of antinomians well fitted by talent and taste for the job — the journalists of the new penny press, the humorists who came from their ranks, the great class of itinerant traders and schemers, the politicians who roared from 10,000 stumps. I turn to the letter *S* and find the DAE listing the following common coins of American speech as born in the period under review:

| | |
|---|---|
| saloon (drinking-place), 1841 | score, to (to castigate), 1812 |
| salt (sailor), 1840 [3] | Scotch-whiskey, 1848 [4] |
| sassy, 1831 | scraper (for making roads), 1823 |
| saw-buck (a $10 bill), 1850 | scratch, to (a ticket), 1841 |
| saw-log, 1831 | scrawny, 1833 |
| say, to have the, 1838 | scrod, 1856 |
| scare up, to, 1841 | sea-food, 1836 |
| school commissioner, 1838 | season-ticket, 1820 |
| school-teaching, 1846 | secession (of a State), 1830 |
| scoot, to, 1841 | seckel-pear, 1817 |

1 The influence of Webster is well presented by Warfel, especially p. 76 *ff*. There is more in The Development of Faith in the Dictionary in America, by Allen Walker Read, a paper read before the Present-Day English section of the Modern Language Association at Philadelphia, Dec. 29, 1934.

2 He was speaking of a congress of reformers of all wings, held in Boston in 1840.

3 Not recorded in England before 1877. Possibly invented by Richard Henry Dana, from whose Two Years Before the Mast the first American example comes.

4 Not recorded in England until 1855.

secretary (book-case with writing-desk), 1815
second table, 1850
section (quarter or district), 1814
seed-store, 1833
self-culture, 1837
self-made man, 1832
semi-monthly, 1851
semi-occasional, 1850
send-off, 1856
set (as in *all set*), 1844
seventeen-year locust, 1844
seven-up, 1836
sewing-circle, 1846
sewing-machine, 1847
sewing-society, 1842
shad-bellied, 1832
shakes (ague), 1825
sheepnose (apple), 1817
sheet-music, 1857 [1]
shell (racing-boat), 1858
shell out, to, 1833
shell-road, 1840
sheriff's sale, 1817
shine, to cut a, 1819
shine off, to take the, 1834
shine to, to take a, 1840
shingle (a doctor's sign), 1842
shingle, to (to cut the hair short), 1857
ship, to (by land), 1857 [2]
shirt on, to keep one's, 1854
shirt-bosom, 1852 [3]
shoe-bench, 1841
shoe-findings, 1836
shoe-peg, 1854
shook (a bundle of staves or other wooden objects), 1819
shooting, as sure as, 1853
short (a broker who sells for future delivery securities he does not yet own), 1849
show-window, 1855
shuck, to (corn), 1834 [4]
shucks (exclamation), 1847

shut down, to (to close a factory), 1850 [5]
side-show, 1855
side-track, 1840
side-wheel, 1845
sight, not by a damned (or darned), 1834
sight-draft, 1850
silent-partner, 1828
silk, as fine as, 1836
simon-pure, 1840
single-track, 1838
sis (for *sister*), 1835
six-shooter, 1853
skeeter (mosquito), 1852
split, full, 1834
splurge, 1830
sponge-cake, 1805
spool-cotton, 1839
sport (a gamester), 1859
spots off, to knock the, 1861
spot, to (to recognize), 1848
spread-eagle (bombastic), 1858
spring-chicken, 1845
spring-fever, 1859
sprouts, course of, 1851
squally, to look (to be threatening), 1814
square-meal, 1850
square-thing, *c.* 1860
squirt (a contemptible person), 1843
stag-dance, 1843
stag-party, 1856
stall, to (come to a halt), 1807
stand, old, 1847
stand from under, to, 1857
standee, 1856
star-spangled banner, 1814
state-bank, 1815
state-line, 1817
State's evidence, 1831
State-university, 1831
station-agent, 1855
stay put, to, *c.* 1848
stick at, to shake a, 1818

---

1 Not recorded in England until 1881.
2 In England *to ship* is commonly restricted to transportation by water.
3 The English always use *shirt-front*.
4 Apparently *to shuck* was not used

with reference to oysters until the 70s. The DAE does not list *oyster-shucker*.
5 The noun *shutdown* is not found by the DAE before 1884.

still-hunt, 1836
stock-car, 1858
stock-grower, 1837
stock-raising, 1800
stone-bruise, 1805
stool-pigeon (used to catch crim-
    inals), 1836
stop off, to, 1855
stop over, to, 1857
store-clothes, 1840
stovepipe-hat, 1855
stranger (as a form of address), 1817
street-railroad, 1859

stub one's toe, to, 1846
sucker (an easy victim), 1836
sugar-cured, 1851
Summer-complaint, 1847
Summer-hotel, 1852
Summer-resort, 1854
sure-enough, *c.* 1846
sure-thing, 1853
sweat, to (to force to confess), 1824
swell-front (house), 1848
swell-head, 1845
switch, to (railroad), 1861 [1]
swivel-chair, 1860

The boldness of trope so often marked in the neologisms of un-
schooled and uninhibited men will be noted in many of these, *e.g.,*
*saw-buck, send-off, shad-bellied, to keep one's shirt on, to slop over,*
*soft-soap, stag-party, swell-head* and *spread-eagle,* and also the frequent brutal literalness, *e.g., shakes, smash-up, spitball, standee, store-*
*clothes* and *sure-thing.* There is apparent likewise, in the coinages
of the era, a great fondness for harsh debasements of more seemly
words, *e.g., to scoot, scrawny, slick, to snoop, slather* and *to smooch.*
The NED surmises that *to scoot* may be derived from a sailor's verb,
*to scout,* signifying to go away hurriedly, but adds that in its current
meaning it was " apparently imported into general British use from
the United States." The DAE relates it to *to skeet,* an obsolete variant
of *to skate,* but that is in a somewhat different sense. It is traced, in
its commoner meaning, to 1841. *Scrawny* is first recorded in 1833,
and the DAE suggests that it may have been derived from *scranny,*
though for this there is no evidence. *Slick,* which comes, like *sleek,*
from a Middle English *slike,* is old in England, but it seems to have
dropped out of use there and was revived in the United States early
in the Nineteenth Century. Most of the phrases in which it occurs,
*e.g., as slick as a whistle* (or *as grease,* or *as molasses*), *to slick down,*
*to slick up* and *to slick off,* are unquestionably Americanisms. *Slather,*
marked " origin unknown " by the DAE, is not recorded before 1876,
when Mark Twain used it in " Tom Sawyer," but it is probably
considerably older. *To smooch,* meaning to dirty, is old in English,
but has been almost exclusively in American use since the early
Nineteenth Century. It apparently comes from *to smutch* or *to*
*smudge. To smouch,* meaning to pilfer, is also an English archaism

1 The English use *to shunt.*

revived in the United States. Mark Twain used it so often that Ramsay and Emberson call it one of his favorite words.

The period under review was rich in uncouth neologisms of the class of *shebang, shenanigan, shindig, to skedaddle, skeezicks, skookum, slambang, slangwhanger, slantidicular, slumgullion, sockdolager, splendiferous* and *spondulicks,* many of which survive. *Shebang,* which is of uncertain origin but may be related to the Irish *shebeen,* an unlicensed drinking-place, came into great popularity during the Civil War, but it is probably older. *Shenanigan,* which also has an Irish smack, belongs to the same period. *Shindig* was used in the South, before the Civil War, in the literal sense of a blow on the shins, but it soon took on the wider meaning of a rowdy party, and may have been influenced by *shindy.* Whether or not *shindy* is American is not certain. It is recorded as sailor's slang in England in 1821, but did not come into general use there until after it had become widely adopted in America. *To cut a shindy* and *to kick up a shindy* are both marked Americanisms by the DAE. *To skedaddle* has long mystified etymologists. Webster 1864 sought to relate it to a Danish or Swedish word, said to have been picked up from Scandinavian settlers in the Northwest, but the DAE says that no likely original can be found. The theory that it is of Greek origin, noted in AL4, p. 165, n. 4, still crops up at intervals in the newspapers, but there is no evidence for it.[1] The word has been recorded in English dialect use in the sense of to spill milk, but it is difficult to connect this sense with the American meaning of to flee precipitately. Moreover, the English *skedaddle* has not been traced beyond 1862, by which time the American *skedaddle* was already in wide use. It came into popularity at the beginning of the Civil War, but it had probably got into the vocabulary some time before.

*Skeezicks,* originally meaning a good-for-nothing but later used mainly in playful and affectionate senses, is traced by the DAE to 1850: its origin is unknown. *Skookum* seems to have been borrowed from the Chinook dialect of the Northwest, in which it signified powerful, but Berrey and Van den Bark list it as now synonymous with *scrumptious, splendiferous, hotsy-totsy* and *hunky-dory.* *Skookum-house,* in the West, is a name for the jail on an Indian reser-

---

1 An interesting discussion of this and other etymologies is in Bartlett's fourth edition, 1877.

vation, and in the argot of American criminals it is sometimes used for any jail. *Slam Bang* was used in the 30s to designate one of the factions of the Democratic party, and there is every reason for believing that the term was an American invention. The DAE traces *slambanging*, in the sense of making a noisy tumult, to 1843. *Slangwhanger* was used by Irving, in the sense of a bitterly partisan political journalist, in 1807, but by the time Pickering brought out his Vocabulary in 1816 it had come to mean also a demagogic orator. It was denounced by the *Monthly Review* as an abhorrent Americanism in its review of the English edition of Irving's "Salmagundi." *Slantidicular*, from *slanting* and *perpendicular*, is traced by the DAE to 1832. Bartlett dismissed it as "a factitious vulgarism," and it is now obsolete. *Slumgullion*, of unknown etymology, came into use during the California gold rush to signify a muddy residue left after sluicing gravel, but its meaning was soon extended to include anything disgusting, especially food or drink. Among American tramps it is now used as a synonym for *mulligan*, the name of a stew made of any comestibles they can beg or steal. Not infrequently it is shortened to *slum*. The DAE traces *slumgullion* to 1850 and *slum* to 1874, and marks them both Americanisms. *Sockdolager* originally meant a knock-down blow, but has now come to signify anything large or overwhelming. Berrey and Van den Bark list it as synonymous with *corker, whopper, lollapaloosa* [1] and *topnotch*, but note that it is still used by prize-fighters in its original sense. It has lately acquired a variant, *sockeroo*. The DAE traces it to 1830. Bartlett suggests that it is "probably a perversion in spelling and pronunciation of *doxology*, a stanza sung at the close of religious services, and as a signal of dismissal," and the DAE hands on this guess, but no evidence is offered to support it. *Splendiferous*, first encountered by the searchers for the DAE in R. M. Bird's once famous "Nick of the Woods," 1837, is now reduced to consciously whimsical usage, along with its congeners, *splendacious, grandiferous, supergobsloptius* and *scrumptious*. [2] *Spondulicks*, often spelled *spondulix*, is traced by Thornton

1 The DAE traces *corker* to 1835–37, but omits *lollapaloosa*. It also omits *humdinger* and *peacherina*, but traces *peach* in the sense of a pretty girl to 1865 and in the sense of anything meritorious to 1896. Its first example of *lulu* is dated 1889, and of *crackerjack* 1897.

2 The DAE does not list *splendacious*, *grandiferous* and *supergobsloptious*, but traces *scrumptious* to 1830. A long list of such terms is in Terms of Approbation and Eulogy in American Dialect Speech, by Elsie L. Warnock, *Dialect Notes*, Vol. IV, Part I, 1913, pp. 18–20.

to 1857 and by the DAE to a year earlier. It is marked " origin uncertain."

Not a few of the characteristic coinages of the era have became
obsolete. I have mentioned *slantidicular,* and to it may be added
*spizarinctum, sposhy, to squinch, to squiggle, squirtish, to squizzle,
smidgeon, snollygoster, to sqush, savagerous,* and the expletive *swow.
Spizarinctum,* meaning specie or hard money, is traced by the DAE
to 1845, and may have been suggested by *specie.* The last recorded
example is dated 1872. *Sposhy,* meaning soft or wet, flourished in the
40s, but is now no more: it had a noun, *sposh,* signifiying mud or
slush, that has also gone to word heaven. *To squinch,* possibly suggested by *to squint,* meant originally to screw up the eyes, but soon
acquired the general meaning of to squeeze or pinch. The DAE traces
it to 1835. *To squiggle,* meaning to squirm like an eel, was listed by
Pickering in 1816 as " used in some parts of New England, but only
in very familiar conversation." I have heard it in recent years, but
it is no longer in common use. *Squirtish,* meaning given to display,
is traced by the DAE to 1847, but the last example is dated 1851, so
it seems to have had a short life. During that short life, however, it
produced a variant, *squirty. To squizzle* seems to have had the meaning of to explode, but one of the DAE's examples indicates that it
was also used in place of *to sizzle. Smidgeon* (or *smidgen, smitchin*
or *smidgin*) meant a small part of anything. The DAE traces it to
1845 and it still apparently survives in the dialect of Appalachia. A
*snollygoster,* apparently confined to the South, was a political job-
seeker, defined by " a Georgia paper," quoted by the DAE, as " a
fellow who wants office, regardless of party, platform or principles,
and who, whenever he wins, gets there by the sheer force of monumental talknophical assumacy." *To sqush,* obviously a form of *to
squash,* is traced to 1837, and was used by Mark Twain in " Huckleberry Finn." The DAE says that *savagerous* was a blend of *savage*
and *dangerous,* but its first example, dated 1835, is spelled *servigrous,*
and its second, dated 1837, is spelled *savagarous,* whereas it offers
no example of *savagerous* before 1843, so the etymology is left in
some doubt. Bartlett, in the fourth edition of his Dictionary, 1877,
marked *savagerous* " a low word " and " Southern," and Schele de
Vere, in 1872, also credited it to the South, but it seems to have been
in general use until *c.* 1870. " I *swow*," which came in before 1800,
was one of a long list of euphemistic oaths in wide use after the turn

of the century, but now extinct, *e.g.*, " I *swan, snore, swowgar, swad, swamp* and *vum.*"

So far, the letter *S* only. The reader who gives himself the pleasure of searching the four volumes of the DAE will find corresponding riches elsewhere, but here I must confine myself to a few surviving Americanisms of the period. It is indeed astonishing how many of the common coins of American speech date from it. Consider, for example, the terms in *dead-*, *horse-*, and *ice-*. *Dead-broke* is traced by the DAE to 1851, *deadhead* to 1843, *to get the deadwood on* to 1851, and *dead-beat* to 1863. *Dead letter* is not marked an Americanism, but the first recorded American example is nearly seventy years earlier than the first English example. *Dead right* and *dead wrong*, it appears, may have originated in England, but if so they were quickly put to much wider use in the United States, and most Englishmen now think of them as Americanisms. The figurative use of *deadline* (as in newspaper men's argot) is clearly American, and so are *dead to rights, on the dead-run* and *dead-house*. Of the common terms in *horse-*, all marked Americanisms by the DAE, *horse-sense* is traced to 1832,[1] *horse-swapping* to 1800, *horse-trading* to 1826, and *horse-thief* to 1768. *Man on horseback* is an Americanism, and was apparently first applied to General Grant in 1879. So is the phrase *hold your horses*, which the DAE traces to *c.* 1846. *Horse-car*, now obsolete, is first recorded in 1833. *Horse-show*, traced to 1856, may be an Americanism also. There was a *horse-show* at Springfield, Mass., in 1858, and two years later *Harper's Magazine* was praising the term as " good because it is descriptive," though noting that *show* had become somewhat vulgarized by *minstrel-show*.[2] The English were aware of *iced-cream* (borrowed from Italy) so early as 1688, but the first appearance of *ice-cream*, in 1744, was in America. The DAE traces *ice-breaker* to 1833, *ice-box* to 1855, *ice-cart* to 1842, *ice-chest* to 1841, *ice-company* to 1834, *ice-cream freezer* to 1854, *ice-cream saloon* to 1849, *ice-dealer* to 1851, *ice-pitcher* to 1865 and *ice-wagon* to 1873, and marks them all Americanisms. But *ice-man* is not recorded until 1870, *ice-pick* not until 1879, *iced-tea* not until 1886, and *ice-cream soda* not until 1887.

1 It does not refer, of course, to the intelligence of the horse, which is one of the stupidest animals on earth. The term originated, I fancy, among horse-traders, and had reference to smartness at their science.

2 Aug., 1860, p. 411.

The stately word *anesthesia* appeared in Nathan Bailey's " Dictionarium Britannicum " in 1721, defined as " a defect of sensation, as in paralytic or blasted persons," but it was Oliver Wendell Holmes the elder who launched it in the meaning of an insensitiveness to pain produced by a drug. This was on November 20, 1846, in a letter to W. T. G. Morton, the discoverer of ether *anesthesia*, and in the same letter Holmes proposed *anesthetic* as a designation for the drug itself. Both words have gone into the vocabularies of all civilized languages.[1] The Morse *telegraph*, first used in 1844, did not introduce the word to the world, for it had been used in England since the late Eighteenth Century to designate various other contrivances for transmitting messages. Nor is *telegrapher* an Americanism, though the English prefer *telegraphist*. But *telegram*, first recorded in 1852, seems to be an American invention, as is *cablegram*, first recorded in 1868. The latter, at the start, was denounced by purists as barbarous, but it quickly made its way. *Telephone* was introduced by Alexander Graham Bell in 1876: his first patent was issued on March 7 of that year. The verb *to telephone* is traced by the DAE to 1880; when *to phone* came in is not clear, but it was probably soon afterward. The introduction of photography in the early 40s brought on a curious combat between *photographer* and *photographist*, parallel to that between *telegrapher* and *telegraphist*. The DAE's first example of *photographist* in American use is dated 1861, but the word actually appeared in *Sartain's Magazine* (Philadelphia) so early as 1852.[2] It survived until the 70s, but was then completely supplanted by *photographer*.

A few miscellaneous examples of words and phrases first recorded during the period under review: *blood and thunder* is traced by the DAE to 1857, *ripsnorter* to 1840, *to back and fill* to 1848, *to back down* to 1849, *way back* to 1855, *way down* to 1851, *way off* to 1853, *way over* to 1850, *way up* to 1850, *way-station* to 1849, *bulletin-*

1 Morton (1819–68) was a dentist. On Oct. 16, 1846 he administered ether to a patient undergoing, at the Massachusetts General Hospital, an operation for the removal of a tumor on the jaw. By 1848 Holmes's *anesthesia* and *anesthetic* were being used by Sir James Young Simpson (1811–70), the Scottish surgeon who had introduced the use of chloroform in obstetrics in 1847. Holmes spelled the words *anaesthetic* and *anaesthesia*, the form still preferred in England.

2 Jan., p. 94.

*board* to 1852, *chewing-gum* to 1864,[1] *close shave* to 1856,[2] *the whole kit and biling* to 1859,[3] *cow-catcher* to 1838,[4] *go-aheadativeness* to 1846,[5] *to discombobulate* (originally *to discombobberate*, and then *to discomboborate* and *to discomboberate*) to 1837, *caboose* (of a train) to 1862, *to raise Cain* to 1840, *dicker* to 1833, *to face the music* to 1850, *to flunk* to 1843, *level best* to 1851, *ornery* to 1830, *all-around* to 1856, *played out* to 1859, *walking-papers* to 1825, *to go the whole hog* to 1829, *whole-hearted* to 1840, *surprise-party* to 1859, *to locomote* to 1834, *to boost* to 1815,[6] *buddy* to 1852,[7] *in cahoots* to 1829, *to crawfish* to 1848, *to donate* to 1845, *to fill the bill* to 1860, *grab-bag* to 1855, *A to izzard* to 1835, *bridal-tour* to 1856, *one-horse* (in the general sense of petty) to 1854, *to be mustered in* to 1848, *packinghouse* (for meats) to 1853, *pilot-house* to *c.* 1846, *extra* (of a newspaper) to 1842, *firecracker* to 1848, *wharf-rat* to 1837, and *quick on the trigger* to 1808.

*Blizzard* appears to have been set afloat by the first wave of Western pioneers, though it did not acquire its present significance until after the Civil War. Its origin has long entertained speculative lexicographers, and various fanciful etymologies are still cherished, but what seems to be its true history has been established in a characteristically thorough paper by Allen Walker Read.[8] The first recorded appearance of the word was in the list of Americanisms contributed by Dunglison to the *Virginia Museum* in 1829. Dunglison there defined it as " a violent blow, perhaps from *blitz* (German: *lightning*)" and ascribed it to Kentucky. It next turned up, in the sense of a rifle shot, in David Crockett's autobiography, 1834, and a year later

1 *American Speech*, Oct., 1942, p. 207, runs it back to 1854, when the gum was apparently a novelty, for the Chicago *Daily Democrat*, Oct. 25, described it as " a new and superior preparation of spruce gum."
2 *American Speech*, just cited, finds an example in 1834.
3 *Whole kit* is recorded in England in 1785. By 1861 *whole kit and biling* had become *and boodle*, and by 1888 *and caboodle*. *Caboodle* was first recorded by Bartlett in 1848.
4 In those early days it was sometimes called a *horse-catcher*. The English locomotives have never been equipped with *cow-catchers*. Nor with *cabs*.

5 *Go-ahead* as an adjective is traced to 1839, and as a noun to 1840.
6 Its subsequent history is recorded in *Boost*, by Klara H. Collitz, *American Speech*, Sept., 1926, pp. 661–72.
7 *Buddy* is discussed in The Southwestern World Box, by T. M. P., *New Mexico Quarterly*, Nov., 1932, p. 340.
8 The word *Blizzard*, *American Speech*, Feb., 1928, pp. 191–217. The late Frank H. Vizetelly printed a far from effective criticism of this paper in *American Speech*, Aug., 1928, pp. 489–90, and Read replied in *Blizzard* Again, *American Speech*, Feb., 1930, pp. 232–35.

he used it in the sense of a crushing retort in his " Tour to the North and Down East." By 1846, as the DAE shows, it was used to signify a cannon shot and during the Civil War it came to mean a volley of musketry. Whether or not it originated by onomatopoeia is not known, but the possibility is suggested by various English dialect words in *bliz-*, all of them signifying some sort of violent action, and by the German *blitz*. But where and when was it first applied to a severe snowstorm, with high wind? Read, it seems to me, presents conclusive evidence that this transfer occurred in the village of Estherville, Iowa, and that the first appearance of the term in its now common sense was probably in the pioneer village newspaper, the *Northern Vindicator*, some time during the early Spring of 1870.[1] The *Northern Vindicator* had been established in 1868 by O. C. Bates and E. B. Northrup, and Bates was the editor from the start until 1871. He was very fond of the neologisms of the time, *e.g.*, *lallygag*, and seems to have devised a number of his own, *e.g.*, *baseballism*, *weatherist* and *weatherology*. Whether or not he was the first to apply *blizzard* to a storm is not known — he may have picked it up from a town character known as Lightning Ellis — but he gave it a heavy play after Estherville was snowed in on March 14, 1870, and ever thereafter that storm was spoken of locally as the *March blizzard* or the *great blizzard*. " The swiftness of the spread of *blizzard* after the adoption of the meaning storm," says Read, " is truly a phenomenon. The preparation for it through the earlier uses is the only explanation." Bates's successors in the editorship of the *Northern Vindicator* continued to use it, and in a little while it had spread to other Iowa papers, and was presently in wide use all over the Upper Middle West. During the Winter of 1880–81, which saw a long succession of severe storms, it reached the rest of the country and even England. Soon afterward the discussion of its etymology began, and there has been wrangling over it ever since. But Read's paper remains unanswered, and probably unanswerable.

One of the characteristic inventions of pre-Civil War days was the *guyascutus*, an imaginary animal that still survives in American folklore, though memory of its ecology and morphology has begun to

---

1 Estherville is now a town of 5,000 people. It is in the northwestern part of the State, seventy miles from Fort Dodge. The *Vindicator*, now the *Vindicator and Republican*, a semi-weekly, is still its principal newspaper.

fade.[1] Its original name seems to have been *guyanousa*, and under that name it was described by an anonymous contributor to the *Knickerbocker Magazine* in 1846.[2] He depicted it as " a monster of gigantic proportions," inhabiting " the tallest branches of the poplar " in " the disputed territory of Penobscot " in Maine.[3] He recorded that men of vision who alleged that they had captured a specimen were going about the country offering to show it in a tent, but that as soon as a paying crowd of yokels was assembled they would rush out from its supposed den yelling " The *gyanousa* am loose! ", and the customers would flee for their lives, leaving the gate-money behind. This tale [4] reached far-away Oregon before the end of 1846, and was retold in the *Oregon Spectator*,[5] with the name of the beast changed to *guiaskuitas* and the scene of the swindle transferred to the South. In those early days various other variations of the name were recorded, *e.g., guyanosa, gyascutus, guyastacutus, sidewinder, lunkus, stone-eater, ricaboo racker, sidehill gouger* (or *dodger*, or *badger*, or *sauger*), *prock, gwinter* and *cute-cuss* or *cuter-cuss*, and the habits of the bearer were described differently by different authorities. When, in 1855, George H. Derby (John Phoenix) visited Oregon, he sent the San Francisco *Herald* an account of the *guyascutus,* and attempted to differentiate between it and the *prock.* This account was purportedly from the pen of " Dr. Herman Ellenbogen,

1 Such monsters, of course, go back to the infancy of humanity. The *basilisk*, the *phoenix*, the *dragon* and the *sea-serpent* will be recalled. There have been many others.

2 Adventures of a Yankee Doodle; Chapter VI: The *Guyanousa;* July, 1846, pp. 36–38. Randall V. Mills suggests in Frontier Humor in Oregon and Its Charicteristics, *Oregon Historical Quarterly*, Dec., 1942, p. 355, that the author may have been George P. Burnham, a forgotten humorist of the period. I am indebted to Miss Nellie P. Pipes, of the Oregon Historical Society, Portland, for the Mills paper.

3 The territory east of the Penobscot river had been occupied by the British during the War of 1812, and they hung on to it for years afterward. In 1839 the dispute over it almost

brought on another war. In 1842 it was restored to the United States by the Ashburton treaty, but the ratifications of the two governments did not follow until some time afterward.

4 In its essence it was not new. Some time before 1846 Burnham and another humorist of the time named Francis A. Durivage, in a book called Stray Subjects Arrested and Bound Over, told of a yokel who, on a visit to Boston, saw the sign *Littel's Living Age* on the publisher's door, and insisted upon seeing the creature. He would not leave until one of the publisher's goons rushed out yelling that the *age* was loose.

5 The *Guiaskuitas*, by an Ox Driver, Oct. 16. I am indebted here to Mills, already cited, p. 354.

naturalist for Governor Stevens' Exploring Expedition." [1] It gave the *prock*, or *sidehill sauger*, the name of *perockius Oregoniensis* and described it as having shoulder joints capable of dislocation at will, so that it could shorten its legs on one side and thus graze upon steep hillsides with comfort. The *gyascutus* (*gyascutus Washingtoniensis*) was said to be a harmless rodent subsisting on " the roots of the *Camissis exculenta*,[2] which its powerful nails permit it to dig with facility." " Dr. Ellenbogen " proceeded:

> This extraordinary animal is about three feet in height and nine in extreme length, its corrugated tail being about one foot. Its back is covered with a shield composed of scales, or rather plates, of an osseous substance, imposed upon a pachydermatous hide, forming a flexible but secure armor, and having along the dorsal plates a row of short and powerful horns, slightly recurved, which extend from the shoulders to the loins.[3]

But in the East the *prock* and the *gyascutus* apparently remained identical, and the chief mark of the combined creature was its curious development of the legs on one side. A savant native to Vermont thus described it in the Haverhill (Mass.) *Gazette* in 1944: [4]

> During my boyhood on a Vermont farm the *gyascutus* or *cute cuss*, was not a rare barnyard animal. He or the female of the species, *gyascuta*, which we affectionately called the *cuter cuss*, were as necessary as the cow to most Vermont farmers. Indeed, without the *gyascutus*, dairy farming in Vermont would have been restricted to the narrow lowlands, the riverside meadows that probably do not account for more than one-tenth of one per cent. of Vermont's acreage. . . .
>
> Obviously, the ordinary cow cannot clamber over Vermont pastures. The early settlers, bringing cows from other States, quickly learned this, and for several years a problem worse than the Indians . . . was that of getting cows to and from pasture. It took two men for each cow and the task was comparable to teaching her to go up and down a ladder.
>
> But the *gyascutus* had legs shorter on one side than on the other, so it could circumambulate the Vermont hills with the greatest ease. The Vermonters immediately understood they must have cows with the *gyascutus's* running gear, so they domesticated the creature and by interbreeding developed a new breed of cattle. Today, as all Americans should know, all Vermont calves are born with legs shorter on one side than the other. . . .

1 Isaac Ingalls Stevens (1818–62) was a West Pointer who served with distinction in the Mexican War. In 1852 he resigned from the Army to become governor of the new Washington Territory. On the outbreak of the Civil War he returned to the Army, and by 1862 had become a major-general. He was killed at Chantilly on Sept. 1 of that year.

2 Perhaps *Camassia esculenta*, the wild hyacinth.

3 Here again I am indebted to Mills.

4 A *Cuter Cuss For a Pet*, March 18, p. 4. The author was William H. Heath, editor of the *Gazette*.

Some *gyascutuses*, or *gyuscuti*, survived in an unadulterated state even as recently as the period of my boyhood. They were cherished by the farmers as evidence of Providence's concern for their welfare. We recall one especially affectionate *gyascuta* that was strongly attached to us in our early youth. How many times we have trudged to school in tears at the sight of the *cuter cuss's* attempts to follow us on a road made for legs of equal length.[1]

On March 8, 1944, at a press conference in Baltimore, the Hon. Gerald L. K. Smith, head of the American First party and former chaplain to the Hon. Huey P. Long, denounced the Hon. Franklin D. Roosevelt as " the great *girasticutam*," and explained that he meant that the President wanted to be " the above all man of all above-allers — the President of the world or something of that sort." [2] Challenged by various specialists in pathophilology, including the present writer, because of his apparent ignorance of the name and nature of the *guyascutus*, he replied that his *girasticutam* was not a *guyascutus* at all, but an invention of his own. Writing from his Kremlin in Detroit, he said:

When real Americans create words they do not bother with thick books like dictionaries or with cynical word surgeons like Mencken. We have a science all our own. For instance, I was taught as a boy in Wisconsin that Chicago is three-sevenths chicken, two-thirds cat and one-half goat, as follows:

Chi — *chicken*
Ca  — *cat*
Go  — *goat*

Thus I created the word *girasticutam* because it sounds like the fourth term. Broken down scientifically, it is as follows:

Gi — the first two sevenths of *giraffe*
Ra — the first one-third of *rabbit*
St — the last two-fifths of *ghost*
Ic — the middle half of *tick*
Ut — the last two-thirds of *gut*
Am — the last two-thirds of *ram*.[3]

This somewhat improbable etymology for *girasticutam* matches those that have been proposed for *guyascutus*. Webster 1934 dismisses the latter as " quasi New Latin, an arbitrary coinage," but the DAE is silent on the subject. The theory that the word comes from *Gyas scutos*, the name of the buckler worn by Gyas, the companion

1 Mr. Heath, in March, 1944, asked his father in Vermont to search the attic of the family homestead " for an old snapshot of the female of the species that was a pet of my boyhood." Unfortunately, it could not be found.

2 Gerald Smith Says *Girasticutam*, Baltimore *Evening Sun*, March 18, 1944.

3 Created *Girasticutam*, Smith says; Gives Recipe, Baltimore *Evening Sun*, March 31, 1944.

of Aeneas, seems to have been launched by the aforesaid "Dr. Ellen-bogen" in 1855. Gyas took a hand in the boat-race which marked the funeral orgies of Anchises, the father of Aeneas: his buckler was made of the scaly hide of a mythical monster. Mills, in the paper I have quoted, suggests that *guyascutus* may have come from *hyas cultus*, a phrase in the Chinook jargon meaning very worthless, and a writer in the Cleveland *Plain Dealer* once sought to derive it from *gyre*, signifying a circular course, and *astichous*, signifying out of line or not arranged in rows.[1] I myself once pointed to a possible eponym in Gehazi, mentioned in II Kings V, 20–27, as an ambulance-chaser employed by the prophet Elisha, and remembered for the fact that he tried to shake down a Syrian general named Naaman, who came to Elisha's office to be cured of leprosy, and was punished by being afflicted with the disease himself.[2] The etymology of *prock* is equally mysterious. The DAE presents a quotation from the New Orleans *Picayune* of September 8, 1840, showing that the creature was already known at that time, and that its "discovery" was credited to one Kock, owner of a museum in St. Louis. All these animals, whatever they were called, had one character in common: their legs were longer on one side than on the other, and they could thus graze on steep hillsides. The name *sidewinder* and the various forms in *side-hill* plainly refer to this.

The *guyascutus* quickly entered into the florid mythology of the Northwest, and "The *guyascutus* am (or is) loose" became a popular catch-phrase, signifying that skulduggery was abroad. The beast is now a part of the Paul Bunyan legend, and Charles Edward Brown, in his "Paul Bunyan Natural History,"[3] thus describes it:

[It is] about the size of a white-tailed deer. Has ears like a rabbit and teeth like a mountain lion. It has telescopic legs which enable it to easily graze on hills. It has a long tail which it wraps around rocks when its legs fail to tele-scope together. It feeds on rocks and lichens, the rocks enabling it to digest the tough and leathery lichens. It is never seen except after a case of snake-bite.

*Gyastacutas*, as Thornton shows on the authority of H. H. Riley,[4] was also used in the 50s to designate a drum used by the callithumpian bands of the period. This drum, says Riley, was made of "a nail-

1 Misunderstood Beast, April 8, 1944.
2 Associated Press dispatch from Baltimore, March 16, 1944.
3 Madison, Wis., 1935. Reprinted in A Treasury of American Folklore,
by B. A. Botkin; New York, 1944, p. 64.
4 Puddleford and Its People; New York, 1854, p. 94.

keg with a raw hide strained over it. . . . Inside of the keg, attached
to the center of this drumhead, a string hung, with which the instrument was worked by pulling in the string and letting fly." There
were many other mythical beasts in those days, and the memory of
some of them survives today, especially in the Northwest. The *argo-
pelter*, according to Brown, lives in the hollows of trees, and amuses
itself by throwing chunks of wood at passing lumbermen. The *flitter-
bick* is a flying squirrel of such rapid flight that when it hits an ox
between the eyes the blow is sufficient to kill. The *gumberoo* is a
creature larger than a bear, with a hide so tough that it turns bullets.
The *hodag* is a ferocious animal known to have killed and eaten man:
it has formidable horns and claws and sleeps by leaning against a
tree. The *lufferlang* has triple-jointed legs and a bushy tail springing
from the middle of its back. The *rumptifusel*, which is large and bellicose, rests by wrapping its thin body about a tree. The *shagamaw*
has the fore legs of a bear and the hind legs of a moose, and is given
to devouring the clothing of lumbermen. The *tripodero* has tripod
legs and its beak is like the barrel of a gun, with a sight at the end.
The *gillygaloo* is a bird that lays square eggs. The *goofus* is another
that flies backward. The *pinnacle-grouse* has only one wing. The
*hoop-snake* sticks its tail into its mouth and rolls along at high speed.[1]
Other strange creatures are reported by other scientists, notably the
*milamo*, a super-crane so large that it can swallow earthworms as
thick as inner tubes; the *wiffle-poofle*, a cross between an eel and a
gila monster; the *club-tailed glyptodont*, a ferocious variety of kangaroo;[2] the *squonk*, a pathological monstrosity, for it is covered with
warts and moles, and weeps constantly in self-pity; the *splinter-cat*,
which feeds on raccoons; the *billdad*, which has the hind legs of a
kangaroo, webbed feet, and a bill like a hawk, and the *cactus-cat*,
which has sharp knives attached to its forelegs, and gets drunk on the
fermented sap of the cactus.[3]

The list of such fabulous creatures, nearly all of them apparently
dating from the 1841–1861 period, might be lengthened almost endlessly. The *kiamuck*, mentioned in association with the *guyascutus* in

1 The DAE traces *hoop-snake* to 1840.
2 I take these from Tall Tales From
   Texas, by Mody C. Boatwright;
   Dallas, Texas, 1934, quoted by Botkin, pp. 638–43.
3 Here I am indebted to Fearsome

Creatures of the Lumberwoods,
With a Few Desert and Mountain
Beasts, by William T. Cox; Washington, 1911, quoted by Botkin, pp.
648–50

1869,[1] but without any description of its habits, appears to be extinct and forgotten, but many other survive, at least as names, *e.g.*, the *phillyloo-bird*,[2] the *galliwampus*, the *swamp-gahoon*, the *hicklesnifter*, the *willopus-wallopus*, the *cattywampus*, the *hidebehind*, the *bim-bam*, the *kankagee*, the *swamp-swiver*, the *tree-squeak*, the *whiffen-paff*, the *screbonil*, the *bowger*, the *whangdoodle* [3] and the *whiffle-cat*.[4]

From Maine comes news of two extinct creatures, the *gazerium* and the *snydae*. Both, according to Richard G. Kendall, a specialist in unearthly zoölogy highly esteemed in that great State, were found only along the Kennebec river, and were favorite delicacies of the Kennebec Indians and the early white settlers. Kendall says that the *gazerium* resembled a shrimp, but had two legs forward and only one aft, and that it fed chiefly upon the *snydae*, which were minute forms of marine life. The *snydae*, in turn, fed upon the eggs of the *gazerium*, so the two species gradually exterminated each other. He adds:

> The Kennebecs usually cooked the *gazerium* in deep fat. It tasted something like a French fried potato, with just a hint of the flavor of cocktail sauce imparted to it by its diet of *snydae*.[5]

The marvellous tricks and habits of such creatures are frequently discussed by other newspaper scientificos. A few weeks after Kendall's monograph on the *gazerium* and *snydae* appeared in Portland, Maine, a contributor to the eminent *Oregonian* of the other Portland wrote learnedly about the *sidehill gouger, ricaboo racker,* or *lunkus,*

1 Southwestern Slang, by Socrates Hyacinth, *Overland Monthly*, Aug., 1869, quoted by Mathews, p. 160.
2 Or *philamaloo-bird*. See Fields For Collectors, *Dialect Notes*, Vol. V, Part V, 1922, p. 188.
3 The DAE's first example of *whang-doodle* is from the New York *Times*, 1861. It was supposed to devote itself, like the *squonk*, to lamentation, and was one of the favorite animals of Col. Henry Watterson, who mentioned it frequently in the Louisville *Courier-Journal*. Sydney Porter (O. Henry, 1867–1910) was very fond of such creatures, and in one of his stories, Heart of the West, defined the *galliwampus* as a mammal with fins on its back and eighteen toes. He also mentioned the *hickle-*

snifter, the *willopus-wallopus* and the *bim-bam*. See O. Henry's Linguistic Unconventionalities, by Margaret Cannell, *American Speech*, Dec., 1937, p. 279.
4 The *shite-poke* is not imaginary. It is the common green heron, *Butorides virescens*. *Shite-poke* is traced by the DAE to 1832. Early alternative names were *poke*, and *skouk*, both recorded in 1794, and *chalk-line* and *fly-up-the-creek*, both recorded in 1844. One of the authorities cited by the DAE says that *shite-poke* was borrowed from the Dutch *schyte-poke*. It is legendary throughout the *shite-poke's* territory that it lives on excrement.
5 Journal of a Journeyman, Portland *Press Herald*, March 20, 1944.

of that section — obviously identical with the *guyascutus*, or, at all events, closely analogous.[1] It had, however, a faculty that the Eastern *guyascutus* apparently lacked: it could, when pursued, turn itself inside out, and so escape in an opposite direction. Nor is the record of such marvels complete, even to this day. So recently as March 8, 1944, Harry Gwynn Morehouse of Trenton, N. J., announced the discovery of a hitherto unknown one in the mangrove swamps surrounding Princeton University. He gave it the name of the *glyco-benphene*, and sent me a colored picture of it. The picture shows a reptile with red legs, a yellow body, and blue scales along its backbone. It is engaged in constant warfare, says Morehouse, with a dragon-like enemy, the *hychlorothene*, but so far he has been unable to obtain an accurate portrait of the latter. In 1939 the United Press reported from Glastonbury, Conn., that a mysterious beast said to resemble a lion, a cougar, a panther, and a boar was terrifying the people there, and that some learned man among them had given it the name of the *glawackus*.[2] In November, 1944, a similar creature roved the vicinity of Frizzleburg, Md., and was reported to have fought and routed a bull.

In two other fields of word-making the period from 1800 to the Civil War was especially productive, to wit, in those of drinking terms and political terms. Perhaps a majority of the former, still in constant use by American boozers, date from it, but for the sake of convenience I shall consider all American drinking terms, of whatever date, together. Here the DAE offers a great deal less help than it should, for its editors seem to have been somewhat shy of the rich and inspiring vocabulary of bibbing. Indeed, they do not list *rickey*, *fizz* and *sour* at all, which is almost like discussing political terms without mentioning *graft* and *buncombe*. *Cooler*, which the DAE traces to 1840, is defined lamely as " a cooling, spirituous drink," and in the first quotation, taken from the New Orleans *Picayune*, there is an

1 The *Sidehill Gouger* Again, April 9, 1944, editorial page. I am indebted for this reference to Mr. Lewis A. McArthur of Portland.

2 *American Speech*, Oct., 1939, p. 238. Perhaps the *sooner-dog* should be added here — a hound so bellicose that it would sooner fight than eat. The DAE does not list the term. *Sooner*, signifying a person who oc- cupied government land before it was thrown open for settlement, came in at the time of the opening of Oklahoma in 1889. The *ring-tailed roarer* was not a beast, but a man. Schele de Vere defined him as " a specially fine fellow of great size and strength." The DAE traces the term to 1830.

effort to connect it with the *julep*. This is an absurdity, for every American schoolboy should know that a *cooler*, save when it is concocted obscenely of Scotch whiskey, contains, must contain and always has contained lemon juice, which would be as out of place in a *julep* as catsup or gasoline. The true father of the *mint-julep* is the *smash*, which the DAE traces, in the form of *brandy-smash*, to 1850, though it is unquestionably very much older. The DAE's first example of *mint-julep* is dated 1809, and comes from the writings of Washington Irving, who was the first American writer of flag rank to mention other eminent American drinks, e.g., the *sherry-cobbler* and the *stone-fence*, the latter now virtually obsolete. *Julep*, of course, is not an Americanism, for the NED traces it to *c.* 1400, and shows that it came from the Spanish and Portuguese *julepe* by the way of the French. But the English *julep* of those early days was only a sweet and harmless chaser used to wash down unpleasant medicines, whereas the *julep* of today is something quite else again, and the honest NED marks it " U. S." [1]

Eric Partridge, in his " Slang Today and Yesterday," [2] says that *rickey* arose in America about 1880, but makes no attempt upon its etymology. Many older bartenders allege that it was invented by a Washington colleague of the Golden Age and named after a client named Jim Rickey, a Kentucky colonel, but the encyclopedias are as prudishly silent about this colonel as they are about his once famous comrade-in-arms, Col. William Campbell Preston Breckenridge. Charles V. Wheeler, in his valuable " Life and Letters of Henry William Thomas, Mixologist," [3] says that the scene of the invention was Hancock's bar at 1234 Pennsylvania avenue, but does not give the date. He says that the *rickey* was " originally made of whiskey," and that is why the title *gin-ricky* was specified at times. Albert Stevens Crockett, a high authority on bar life in America, agrees with this in general, but differs radically in particular. He says that Col. Rickey's given name was Joe, not Jim, and that he was actually a Texan, " though some have claimed Kentucky as his spot of origin." He was

[1] The old and extremely bitter controversy over the spirituous content of the *julep* need not be gone into here. In Kentucky and its spiritual dependencies Bourbon is always used, but in the Maryland Free State it would be an indecorum verging upon indecency to use anything save rye whiskey. There is every reason to believe that in the first *juleps* the motive power was supplied by brandy.

[2] Second ed.; London, 1935, p. 457.

[3] Second edition; Washington, 1939, p. 7.

a lobbyist in Washington, and usually used Shoomaker's, not Hancock's, bar in Pennsylvania avenue for operating upon congressmen and other public officials. The lime, in those days, was a novelty to bartenders, though it had been used for many years by sailors as an antiscorbutic. One day, when the colonel appeared at Shoomaker's, the bartender who always served him squeezed a lime into a tall glass, added cracked ice, poured in a jigger of gin, hosed the mixture from a seltzer-siphon, and shoved it before the colonel. "The colonel," says Crockett, "took a deep one, and liked it. Coming up for air, he smacked his lips, said the current equivalent of 'Oh, boy!', gulped what was left, and demanded another. The bartender thereupon christened the drink the *gin-rickey* in honor of his patron. The *rum-rickey* and the *rye-rickey* came later." [1] The standard *rickey* of today is made of any ardent spirits (including applejack), lime juice and soda-water. There are also quack rickeys containing syrups and even some that are decorated with slices of orange or pineapple, but they are not served in bars of any tone. The addition of sugar converts a *rickey* into a *Tom Collins*, which is supposed to have been named after its inventor, a distinguished bartender of that name, and the substitution of Holland gin for dry gin makes a *Tom Collins* a *John Collins*.[2] The use of Scotch whiskey and the substitution of ginger-ale for soda-water produces a *Mamie Taylor*, which is described by the Maestro Duffy just cited as "a popular Summer drink." It is actually almost undrinkable. But the use of genuine ginger-*beer* in-

---

[1] Private communication, March 18, 1944. Mr. Crockett first gave this piece of history to the world in In Memoriam, *American Mercury*, Feb., 1930, pp. 229–34, an important contribution to bar-lore. There is more such stuff in his Ghosts of the Old Waldorf; New York, 1929. I am also indebted here to Samuel Hopkins Adams and to the late Charles J. Rosebault. In a one-act dramatic sketch entitled One Evening on Newspaper Row, published by the Gridiron Club, Washington, in 1930, Col. Rickey is made to describe himself as a Missourian. One of the characters says: "Come on, fellows, let's go round to Shoomaker's and try that new drink that Joe Rickey has just invented."

Rickey says: "To a jigger of rye whiskey in a tall glass I add the juice of a lime, cracked ice, and fill it up with seltzer water." Another character says: "I want a *Rickey* right now." A third says: "That's a good name for it. I want a *Rickey*, too." The date is not given but seems to be *c.* 1885.

[2] The Official Mixer's Manual, by Patrick Gavin Duffy; New York, 1934, p. 233. Who John Collins was I do not know. Sidney J. Baker, author of A Popular Dictionary of Australian Slang; Melbourne, n.d., tells me that the *John Collins* was known in Australia so long ago as 1865, but he does not list it in his dictionary.

stead of ginger-*ale* [1] produces something that is magnificent, whether it be based upon gin, rum, rye whiskey or Bourbon.[2]

As I have noted, the DAE omits all mention of the *fizz* and the *sour*. It also overlooks the *fix*, the *skin*, the *shrub* and the *daisy*. The NED likewise passes over the *fizz, sour, skin, fix* and *daisy*, but defines the *shrub* as " a prepared drink made with the juice of orange or lemon (or other acid fruit), sugar, and rum (or other spirit)," and traces it in English use to 1747. The modern American *shrub* shows substantially the same formula, but its preparation has been considerably elaborated, and no conscientious bartender undertakes to mix it impromptu. To make even the simplest *shrub*, indeed, takes half an hour, and the best professional opinion favors laying it away for from a few days to six weeks, to ripen.[3] The *flip*, like the *shrub*, is of English origin and is listed in Johnson's Dictionary, 1755; the NED defines it as " a mixture of beer and spirits sweetened with sugar and heated with a hot iron," and traces it to 1695. But the American *flip* of today shows a considerable improvement upon this nauseous concoction. Save in the case of the *ale-flip* it contains no malt liquor, and when it is desired to serve it hot the heat is supplied, not by a hot iron, but by hot water. Moreover, a beaten egg has been added. Thus the American *flip*, though it borrows its name from an English progenitor, is essentially a national invention. It arose at some time after the Civil War, for the DAE's examples, which go back to 1722 and run down to 1869, mention the hot iron, and its definition is substantially identical with that of the NED. The NED calls the *sling* an American drink, the NED Supplement traces it to *c*. 1793, and the DAE carries it back to 1768. In its simplest form it is a mixture of some sweetened hard liquor and either hot or cold water, but imaginative bartenders sometimes add lemon peel and bitters.[4]

The *sour* is simply a mixture of a hard liquor, sugar, lemon and/or lime juice, and chopped ice, and is usually served strained. There are

1 Ginger-*beer* is fermented like any other beer, but ginger-*ale* is mixed in a vat.

2 Who invented this masterpiece I do not know, and so far as I am aware it has no name. I was introduced to it by Joseph Hergesheimer, *c*. 1925. Ginger-*beer* is not easily come by in America, but a few of the better purveyors stock the excellent English brand of Schweppes.

3 The Official Mixer's Manual, before cited, p. 272, and Wehman Bros.' Bartenders' Guide; New York, 1912, p. 63.

4 The Official Mixer's Manual, before cited, p. 271. Mark Twain mentioned the *gin-sling* in Innocents Abroad, 1869, p. 429.

fancy forms that contain liqueurs and even eggs, but they are not favored by connoisseurs. In my early days the *sour* was in great request among bibuli as a morning pick-up: it was supposed to allay the gastritis that so often beset them. This theory has been exploded by the advance of medical science, and they now use the alkaline salts of sodium, magnesium, bismuth and aluminum. The *fix* is substantially an unstrained *sour*, the *fizz* is the same with soda-water, and the *daisy* is a *fizz* with the addition of a dash of grenadine, maraschino, or something of the sort. The DAE traces the *sherry-cobbler* to 1841 and calls it an American invention. The NED says that the origin of *cobbler* " appears to be lost." " Various conjectures," it adds, " are current, *e.g.*, that it is short for *cobbler's punch*, and that it ' patches up ' the drinkers." But *cobbler's punch*, which is defined as " a warm drink of beer or ale with the addition of spirit, sugar and spice," is traced only to 1865, and may have been borrowed from the American *cobbler*. The term has also been used in the United States to designate a fruit pie made in a deep pan, with a crust on top but not on the bottom. The modern *sherry-cobbler* consists of sherry, sugar and cracked ice, with no addition of malt liquor or spice. The *sangaree*, which is essentially a cobbler to which grated nutmeg has been added, is apparently not an American invention. The NED prints a quotation from the *Gentleman's Magazine*, 1736, showing that one Gordon, a publican in the Strand, in London, then claimed to be its father. He made it of madeira, not sherry, and apparently spiced it. The NED says that the word comes from the Spanish *sangria*, meaning bleeding. Francis Grose, in his " Classical Dictionary of the Vulgar Tongue," 1783, says that *rack-punch*[1] was formerly called *sangaree* " in bagnios."

The *cocktail*, to multitudes of foreigners, seems to be the greatest of all the contributions of the American way of life to the salvation of humanity, but there remains a good deal of uncertainty about the etymology of its name and even some doubt that the thing itself is of American origin. The NED is content to say of it that " the real origin appears to be lost " and the DAE is significantly silent on the subject. Of the numerous etymologies that I have accumulated, the only ones showing any plausibility whatsoever are the following:

1 *Rack-punch* was based on arrack. Richard Steele said in the *Guardian*, 1713, that it was sometimes laced with brandy and gunpowder.

1. That the word comes from the French *coquetier*, an egg-cup, and was first used in New Orleans soon after 1800.

2. That it is derived from *coquetel*, the name of a mixed drink known in the vicinity of Bordeaux for centuries, and introduced to America by French officers during the Revolution.

3. That it descends from *cock-ale*, a mixture of ale and the essence of a boiled fowl, traced by the NED to *c.* 1648 in England.

4. That its parent was a later *cock-ale* meaning a mixture of spirits and bitters fed to fighting-cocks in training.

5. That it comes from *cock-tailed*, meaning " having the tail cocked so that the short stump sticks up like a cock's tail."

6. That it is a shortened form of *cock-tailings*, the name of a mixture of tailings from various liquors, thrown together in a common receptacle and sold at a low price.

7. That in " the days of cock-fighting, the spectators used to toast the cock with the most feathers left in its tail after the contest," and " the number of ingredients in the drink corresponded with the number of feathers left."

For the first etymology the only authority I know of is an anonymous writer in the *Roosevelt Review,* the house-organ of the Roosevelt Hotel, New Orleans.[1] He says that the father of the *cocktail* was Antoine Amédée Peychaud, an apothecary who came to New Orleans from Santo Domingo after the native uprising of 1795, and opened a pharmacy at what is now 437 rue Royale. He goes on:

Peychaud, like most of the Dominguois, was extremely sociable, and his pharmacy became a rendezvous for his fellow Masons after lodge meetings. To them he served the customary *brandy-toddy,* but in his individual style. To the toddy of sugar, water and cognac he added bitters which he compounded by a secret formula brought from Santo Domingo, and instead of serving the drink in the regular brandy tumbler he used the double-ended egg-cup, the *coquetier* (ko-kay-tay). The name was soon given to the highly-flavored drink, but guests who did not speak French called it a *cocktay,* and presently the usage of the world had it the now familiar *cocktail.*[2]

1 The *Cocktail,* America's Drink, Was Originated in New Orleans, April, 1943, pp. 30 and 31.

2 Peychaud was the inventor of the *Peychaud bitters,* still popular. In his cocktails he used Sazerac brandy, made by Sazerac du Forge et Fils of Limoges, and so they came to be called *Sazeracs.* In 1859 one John B. Schiller opened a Sazerac Coffee House at 13 Exchange alley. In 1870 Thomas H. Handy became proprietor of the place and changed its name to the Sazerac House. Simultaneously he substituted rye whiskey for brandy in the cocktail. It is still popular, but with the formula varying. In the Official Mixer's Manual, by Duffy, p. 125, the ingredients given are rye whiskey, Peychaud bitters, absinthe, sugar and lemon peel; in The Savoy Cocktail Book, by Harry Craddock; New York, 1930, they are rye or Canadian whiskey, Angostura or Peychana (*sic*) bitters, absinthe, sugar and lemon peel; in The Barkeeper's Manual, by Raymond E. Sullivan; fourth ed., Baltimore, n.d., p. 8, they are brandy, anisette, Peychard's (*sic*) bitters and

The authority for the second etymology is a French writer named Marcel Boulenger, who printed an article in *Le Figaro Hebdomadaire* (Paris) in 1925 arguing for the abandonment of *cocktail* by the French,[1] and the restoration of *coquetel*. He said that its priority had been supported in a paper read before the Académie de Médecine by a Dr. Tardieu, who cited the case of an actor who had died after drinking a *coquetel au veronal*.[2] The third etymology has the imprimatur of Peter Tamony, well-known as a writer on the American vocabulary. He says:

> During the Seventeenth and Eighteenth Centuries a drink called *cock-ale* was popular in England. It was made by flavoring a cask of new ale with a red cock — the older the better — which had been pounded to a pulp and steeped in sack. The cock, together with a quantity of raisins, mace and cloves, was sacked in canvas, put in the ale, and allowed to infuse for a week or ten days. The result was bottled, and aged until used. Is it any wonder that lexicographers since the Seventeenth Century have defined *cock-ale* as a " pleasant drink, said to be provocative "?[3]

This allegation that *cock-ale* was " provocative " was duly noted by Grose in 1785. The NED lists the term, and says that the concoction consisted of " ale mixed with the jelly or minced meat of a boiled cock, besides other ingredients." Tamony is also disposed to give some credit to the fourth etymology that I have listed. I gave it in AL4 on the authority of William Henry Nugent,[4] but repeat it here in Tamony's words:

absinthe; in Life and Letters of Henry William Thomas, Mixologist; p. 42, they are rye whiskey, anisette, absinthe and Peychaud bitters; in Cheerio, by Charles; New York, 1930, p. 17, they are an unnamed whiskey, absinthe, syrup, unnamed bitters and mint; and in the *Roosevelt Review* article they are rye or Bourbon, vermouth, unnamed bitters, orange bitters, absinthe and sugar. Obviously, mixologists differ almost as much as etymologists. *Sazerac* is not listed by the DAE. An early example of its use is in Remembrances of the Mississippi, by T. B. Thorpe, *Harper's Magazine*, Dec., 1855, p. 37, col. 1.

1 The word has got into practically all modern languages, including Japanese (English Influence on Japanese, by Sanki Ichikawa; Tokyo, 1928, p. 166), and C. K. Ogden includes it among the fifty "international words" taken into Basic English. (The System of Basic English; New York, 1934, p. 134).

2 A translation of part of Boulenger's article, made for the Kansas City *Star*, was published in the Baltimore *Evening Sun* (editorial page), Feb. 11, 1926. In George Washington: the Image and the Man; New York, 1936, p. 377, W. E. Woodward records a story to the effect that the *coquetel* was brought to America by French officers stationed at a Connecticut port. I am indebted here to Mr. Cary F. Jacobs, of Smith College.

3 Origin of Words: *Cocktail*, San Francisco *News Letter and Wasp*, Aug. 4, 1939, p. 9.

4 P. 149, n. 1. Nugent printed it in Cock Fighting Today, *American Mercury*, May, 1929, p. 80.

Prior to a match [a fighting-cock] was trained and conditioned much as boxers are today. It was long ago recognized that a proper diet was important, and food, especially that given for three or four days before a match, was carefully prepared. One of the preparations, known as *cock-bread-ale*, was made of fine white bread mixed with ale or wine or any other spirits that were handy, and an infusion of roots and herbs. The tonic quality of this mixture was highly valued. In time it came to be more or less standard, and its name was shortened to *cock-ale*.

Cockers appear to have sampled these mixtures before adding them to the dough, and when they were found of benefit to man as well as beast it appears that they were added to the ordinary potations of the day. Being a rude sort of bitters, *cock-ale* added tang and taste to poorly brewed or distilled grog, and thus had something to do with the standardization and popularity of mixed drinks.[1]

An English correspondent, Mr. Henry Irvine, sends me the following in support of the fifth etymology: [2]

When *cocktails* under that name became really popular in England, which was not until some time after the establishment of *American-bars*, we had no doubt as to the derivation. To us it was a short drink that *cocked your tail*, using the same metaphor as *to keep your tail up*. If you exhibited a sporting dog of the setter type, which tends to carry its tail low except in action, the show photographer would tell you *to cock that dog's tail*. . . . A *cocktail* was therefore what I suppose today would be called a *pepper-upper*.

This, of course, was only speculation at a long distance in time, for the DAE traces *cocktail* in American use to 1806, and Partridge says that it reached England *c.* 1870, but it should be added that the NED traces *cocktail*, applied to horses, to 1769, and *cock-tail proud* to 1600. The sixth etymology has no authority save an ingenious suggestion by Mr. William S. Gleim, of Rohrerstown, Pa.[3] He writes:

In many English taverns the last of the liquor drawn from barrels of ardent spirits, otherwise the *cock-tailings*,[4] were thrown together in a common receptacle. This mixture was sold to topers at a reduced price, so, naturally, they would call for *cocktails*. The word was evidently imported to describe our popular drink composed of several liquors. I know of one saloon in Phila-

1 Origin of Words: *Cocktail*, before cited. Tamony says that mixed drinks were by no means an American invention. In the Sixteenth Century, he reports, the Germans had concoctions called the *cow's-tail*, the *calf's neck*, the *stamp-in-the-ashes*, the *crowing-cock* and the *swell-nose*, and during the same period the English had the *Humpty-Dumpty*, the *knock-down* and the *Old Pharaoh*. Grose defines a *Humpty-Dumpty* as " ale boiled with brandy," and a *knock-me-down* as a "strong ale or beer." He omits the *Old Pharaoh*, but defines a *Pharaoh* of unstated age as " strong malt liquor."

2 Private communication, Jan. 9, 1938.

3 Private communication, Feb. 23, 1938.

4 From *cock*, a valve or spigot, and *tailings*, dregs or leavings.

delphia where the bartender saved all hard drinks that were not entirely consumed by the customers. These remainders were poured into a demijohn, which when full, would be taken to a nearby auction-room and sold as *cocktails* to the highest bidder.

The seventh etymology is taken from a statement made in court by an English solicitor, Thomas Bagley, in 1937, and cabled to the United States by the alert United Press. It sounds very fishy. A *cocktail* today consists essentially of any hard liquor, any milder diluent, and a dash of any pungent flavoring. The DAE's first example of the use of the word, dated 1806, shows that it was then compounded of " spirits of any kind, sugar, water, and bitters." A later quotation, 1833, defines it as " composed of water, with the addition of rum, gin, or brandy, as one chooses — a third of the spirits to two-thirds of the water; add bitters, and enrich with sugar and nutmeg." Bartlett, in his second edition of 1859, gave only the bare word *cocktail* and said it then consisted of " brandy or gin mixed with sugar and a very little water," but by the time he came to his fourth edition of 1877 he was listing no less than seven varieties — the *brandy*, the *champagne*, the *gin*, the *Japanese*, the *Jersey*, the *soda* and the *whiskey*. He did not, however, give their formulae. When the *Martini*, the *Bronx*, the *old-fashioned*, the *sidecar*, the *Daiquiri*, the *orange blossom*, the *Alexander*, the *Dubonnet*, the *Manhattan* and the other popular *cocktails* of today were invented I do not know: the DAE lists only the *Manhattan* and traces it only to 1894. The principal manuals for bartenders list hundreds: in the Savoy *Cocktail* Book there are actually formulae for nearly 700. I have myself invented eleven, and had nine named after me. William Warren Woollcott [1] and I once employed a mathematician to figure out how many could be fashioned of the *materia bibulica* ordinarily available in a first-rate bar. He reported that the number was 17,864,392,788. We tried 273 at random, and found them all good, though some, of course, were better than others.

In the Gothic Age of American drinking as of American word-making, between the Revolution and the Civil War, a great many fantastic drinks were invented, and some of them were given equally fantastic names, *e.g.*, *horse's neck*, *stone-fence* (or *stone-wall*), *brandy-crusta*, *brandy-champarelle*, *blue-blazer*, *locomotive*, *bishop*

[1] Author of "I Am a One Hundred Per Cent. American, Goddam!"    See Chapter VII of my Heathen Days; New York, 1943.

and *stinkibus*. Of these, the DAE passes over all save the *stone-fence*, which it describes as a mixture of whiskey and cider and traces to 1843. As a gesture, perhaps, of appeasement it adds the *switchel*, a banal drink of molasses and water, usually flavored with ginger and vinegar [1] but sometimes with rum, which it traces to 1790; the *anti-fogmatic, i.e.*, any sort of hard liquor " taken on the pretext of counter-acting the effects of fog," which it traces to 1789; [2] the *timber-doodle*, first recorded (by Charles Dickens in his " American Notes ") in 1842; the *hold-fast*, 1844; and the *eggnog*, which it marks an Ameri-can invention and traces to *c*. 1775. Bartlett, less inhibited, adds many more, *e.g.*, the *bald-face*, the *black-jack*, the *bust-head*, the *ching-ching*, the *deadbeat*, the *deacon*, the *floater*, the *fiscal agent*, the *knickerbocker*, the *moral suasion*, the *pine-top*, the *phlegm-cutter*, the *ropee*, the *shambro*, the *silver-top*, the *snap-neck*, the *split-ticket*, the *stagger-juice*, and the *vox populi*.[3] The touring Englishmen of those days always marked such grotesque drink-names, and when they got home spread the news of them. Some of these Columbuses, it appears, embellished the list with outlandish inventions of their own, for in 1868 an American writing in *Tinsley's Magazine* (Lon-don) was protesting against the practice.[4] " Genuine American drinks," he said, " have names strange enough; but the fact that cer-tain decoctions are called *brandy-smashes, mint-juleps* and *sherry-cobblers* scarcely justifies the invention of the Haymarket *corpse-reviver*, or of Mr. George Augustus Sala's *that thing* and *that other thing*." The fashion for such names began to pass out after the Civil War, and the new drinks of the 1865–1900 era, the Golden Age of American drinking, were largely eponymous and hence relatively decorous, *e.g.*, *rickey* and *John Collins. The high-ball* came in about 1895, and the DAE's first example is dated 1898. It was, of course, simply the English *whiskey-and-soda*, which had been familiar to American visitors to England for many years.[5] The etymology of

---

1 It survives in the more backward sec-tions of New Jersey as the *belly-whistle*. See Jerseyisms by F. B. Lee, *Dialect Notes*, Vol. I, Part VII, 1894, p. 328.

2 It also lists the *fog-cutter*, which it traces to 1833.

3 These are from his fourth edition of 1877. The list was shorter in his second edition of 1859. *Angel-teat* is missing.

4 English Hotels, by an American; re-printed in *Every Saturday* (Boston), May 30, 1868, p. 691.

5 *Soda-water* seems to have been in-vented in the Eighteenth Century, and in 1802 an English doctor quoted by the NED said that it had " long been used " in England. But the *whiskey-and-soda* was called *whis-key-and-water* down to the middle of the Nineteenth Century. Even

*high-ball* remains obscure. Some authorities say that it was borrowed from the argot of railroad men, to whom a *high-ball* means a signal from a conductor to an engineer to go ahead. Others say that it originated from the fact that *ball*, in the 90s, was common bartender's slang for a glass, and the glass used for a *high-ball* was naturally taller than that used for an old-time straight whiskey. There is also some dispute about the identity of the bartender who introduced the *high-ball* to the United States. It has been claimed for an unnamed member of the faculty of the Parker House in Boston, but Patrick Gavin Duffy, in his "Official Mixer's Manual," says that he himself shoved the first across the bar in 1895, and adds that the New York *Times* has allowed his priority.[1] The *high-ball* came in on the heels of *Scotch whiskey*, which was but little drunk in America before 1895.[2] It quickly became enormously popular, and it has retained its popularity ever since. During Prohibition days the custom arose of substituting ginger-ale for soda-water, especially in rye *high-balls*, but it has never been approved by either high-toned bartenders or enlightened boozers.

Many generic names for alcoholic stimulants, some of them racy and amusing, have been current in the United States since the Gothic Age, *e.g.*, *nose-paint, milk of the wild cow, belly-wash, hog-wash, tangle-foot, sheep-dip, snake medicine, red-eye, gum-tickler, phlegm-cutter, gall-breaker, coffin-varnish* and *bug-juice*.[3] There are also generic names for various kinds and classes of drinks, *e.g.*, *joy-water* and *fire-water* for whiskey; *foolish-water* and *bubble-water* for champagne; *Jersey lightning* for apple-jack; *prairie oyster* for a drink with an egg in it; *red-ink* and *Dago-red* for red wine; and *hard liquor* for

---

*brandy-and-water* was in use, and the NED's first example of *brandy-and-soda* is dated 1871.

1 Mr. Duffy was bartender at the old Ashland House in New York for twelve years, and there had the honor of serving many eminent men, including J. Pierpont Morgan the elder, E. H. Sothern, James J. Corbett, Edwin Booth and Oscar Wilde. Once he actually served William Jennings Bryan, though Bryan's order was for Apollinaris. From the Ashland House he moved to the St. James.

2 The English did not begin to use

*Scotch whiskey* before the middle of the last century. Before that it was simply *whisky*.

3 Some of these were Southern. Says Bell Irvin Wiley in The Plain People of the Confederacy; Baton Rouge (La.), 1944, pp. 26–27: "The potency of Confederate liquor, as well as the esteem in which it was held, were reflected by nicknames applied to it by the campaign-hardened butternuts; among the appellations were: *How Come You, Tanglefoot, Rifle Knock-Knee, Bust Skull, Old Red Eye*, and *Rock Me to Sleep, Mother*."

any kind of distilled stuff.[1] The DAE traces *snake-medicine* to 1865, when it appeared in the chaste pages of *Harper's Magazine. Nose-paint* is first recorded in 1881, but is probably much older. *Smile*, as a euphemism for a drink, goes back to 1850; *stick*, in the sense of a slug of liquor, to 1854; *to set 'em up* to 1851; *pony* to 1849; *finger* to 1856; *jigger* to 1836; *snifter* to 1848;[2] *shot-in-the-neck*, the predecessor of *shot-in-the-arm*, to 1851; and *long drink* to 1828.[3] *Jim-jams*, which is marked an Americanism by the DAE, is traced to 1852. *Straight* is also an Americanism, first recorded in 1862: the English use *neat*. Whether or not *soft-drink* is another remains to be determined. The first known English example antedates the first American example, but further investigation may establish American priority. The DAE's earliest example of *schooner* is from Bartlett's fourth edition of 1877, but the term must be considerably older. *To rush the growler*, traced to 1888, is also older. *To rush the can* is not listed, nor are *bucket* (or *scuttle*) *of suds, chaser, hooker, nip, pick-me-up, on a binge, brannigan, slug* (though *to slug up* is traced to 1856), *water-wagon, to spike* (a drink), *hang-over* (in the alcoholic sense), *dark-brown taste, morning after, kick, katzenjammer, bung-starter,*[4] *keg-drainer, bar-rail, souse, stew, bun* or *jitters*. Some of these may be omitted by the DAE on the ground that they have come in since 1900 and others on the ground that they are also used in England, but probably not many. It traces *bracer* to 1829, *eye-opener* to 1818, *on a bender* to 1846, *on a bat* to 1848, *to liquor up* to 1850, *to set 'em up*

---

1 The Englishman calls it *spirits.* What we call *hard cider* is *rough cider* to him. Many more such terms are listed in Poppings of the Corks, by Jean DeJournette, *Esquire*, April, 1934, pp. 36–87.

2 Writing in the *Colver Magazine*, July, 1943, p. 24, William Feather offered the following on the authority of F. O. Richey: " (1) A *snifter* is a light drink, not greatly exceeding a sniff or smelling of the liquor. (2) A *swish* is a drink long enough to wet the lips and require the wiping of the lips with a handkerchief or the back of the hand. (3) A *swig* is a drink deep enough to exhaust some of the air in the bottle. When the bottle is removed from the lips the air makes a gurgling sound, rushing into the bottle to fill the void. (4) A

*snort* is when you hold onto the bottle so long that when you take it down you give a snort to get the fumes out of your lungs." I am indebted here to Mr. Fred Hamann.

3 A *Long-Drink* and the American Chesterfield, by Kenneth Forward, *American Speech*, Dec., 1939, p. 316.

4 The English call a *bung-starter* a *beer-mallet*. Says H. W. Seaman (private communication): " In March, 1935, this implement was used by a boy named Stoner to dispatch an old man named Rattenbury. Throughout the trial at the Old Bailey the word *beer-mallet* was used. If the thing had happened in America it would certainly have been called the *Bung-Starter* Mystery."

to 1851, *family entrance* to 1881, *barrel-house* to 1883, *bust-head* to 1863, and *red-eye* to 1819, and marks them all Americanisms. Its first example of *booze-fighter* is from a poem by Carl Sandburg, 1916: the term is actually much older. So is *booze-fight*, which is run back no further than 1922.[1] It does not list *booze-h'ister* at all, nor *hooch*, though it has *hoochino*, which the authority it quotes describes as "the name of firewater in Alaska." *Frappé*, applied to a very cold drink, is said by a newspaper lexicographer to have been introduced by Henry Wadsworth Longfellow in 1848, but for this I have been unable to find any evidence.

Prohibition increased enormously the number of American boozers, both relatively and absolutely, and made the whole nation booze-conscious, and as a result its everyday speech was peppered with terms having to do with the traffic in strong drink, *e.g., bootlegger, bathtub-gin, rum-runner, bone-dry, needle-beer* [2] and *jake* (Jamaica ginger). A number of earlier terms for the cruder varieties of whiskey, *e.g., forty-rod* (traced to "The Witches of New York," by Mortimer N. Thomson (Philander Doesticks) 1858, and defined by him as "warranted to kill at forty rods"),[3] *tarantula-juice* (traced by the DAE to 1861), *white-mule*,[4] *squirrel-whiskey*,[5] and *panther-sweat* [6] were revived, and such novelties as *depth-bomb* and *third-*

---

1 *Booze* is an old word in English. The NED traces it, in the form of *bouse*, to *c.* 1300. Weekley suggests that it may have been reintroduced, from the analogous Dutch *buizen* or the German *bausen*, in the Sixteenth Century. Efforts have been made to relate it to the Arabic *buzeh*, meaning sweetmeats, but in vain. In England *booze* means ale or beer, not wine or spirits. An English working-man calls his favorite pub his *boozer*.

2 *Near-beer* appeared in 1920, but did not last long. It continued to be brewed, but before it reached the consumer it was usually converted into *needle-beer*.

3 Q. K. Philander Doesticks, P.B., by J. Louis Kuethe, *American Speech*, April, 1937, p. 115.

4 The designation of Southern corn-whiskey, fresh from the still. It is white in color and is said to have the power of a mule's kick. Only native Southerners of at least the second

generation can drink it with any relish.

5 *Squirrel-whiskey* was first heard of in the early part of the Nineteenth Century. A familiar etymology seeks to account for it on the ground that a man who drank it commonly ran up a tree like a squirrel. I think it is much more likely that it got its name by the fact that squirrels were often drowned in the open-air mash-tubs used by moonshiners and then distilled along with the fermented mash. In the Appalachian mountain stills, to this day, the tubs show a high density of dead squirrels, rabbits, possums, coons, woodrats, birds, lizards, bull-frogs and insects.

6 *Sweat* was actually in use, but it was perhaps more common to couple *panther* with the vulgar name of another saline secretion. See II Kings XVIII 27 and Isaiah XXXVI, 12.

*rail*[1] were added. Denatured alcohol from which some effort had been made to remove the (usually) poisonous denaturant acquired the special name of *smoke*, and this was also applied to alcohol in combination with some waxy substance, sold for heating purposes. The user of such high exhilarants was called a *smoke-eater*. The Prohibitionists, throughout the Thirteen Years, kept on using their old favorite, *rum*, to designate all alcoholic drinks, including even beer.[2] Its employment went back to the days before the distillation of whiskey became general, when rum was actually the chief tipple of American dipsomaniacs. Some of its derivatives date from the Eighteenth Century. The DAE traces *rum-dealer* to 1860, *rummery* to 1851, *rum-mill* to *c.* 1849, *rum-hole* to 1836, *rummy* to 1834, *rum-seller* to 1781, *rum-guzzler* to 1775, *rum-house* to 1739 and *rum-shop* to 1738. I can't find *rum-blossom* in any of the American vocabularies of slang save that of Berrey and Van den Bark, who do not date it, but *rum-bud*, which may have preceded it, is listed by Bartlett and credited to Dr. Benjamin Rush, who died in 1813. *Speak-easy* is not listed by the DAE, and may not be an Americanism, for though it is missing from P. W. Joyce's "English as We Speak It In Ireland,"[3] it is said by other authorities to be a term of long standing in that country. In 1922 M. A. M. Tasker said in the London *Sunday Times*:

> I well remember, more than fifty years ago, the definition of a *spake-aisy* shop as a place where illicit whiskey was sold. The explanation was accompanied by a rather irreverent reference to St. Patrick, in the following terms:
> > No wonder that the saint himself
> > To take a drop was willin',
> > For his mother kept a *spake-aisy* shop
> > In the town of Enniskillen.[4]

1 The vocabulary of the boozers in a theoretically dry community is dealt with by Vance Randolph in Wet Words in Kansas, *American Speech*, June, 1929, pp. 385–89.

2 Oliver Wendell Holmes protested against this misuse in The Autocrat of the Breakfast-Table, 1858: "Sir, I repudiate the loathsome vulgarism as an insult to the first miracle."

3 Second ed.; Dublin, 1910.

4 *Speak-Easy*, March 25, 1928. On May 7, 1938 Eric Partridge suggested in the London *Times Literary Supplement* that the term "may have been suggested by the English *speak-softly-shop*, a significant underworld term for a smuggler's house at which liquor could be inexpensively obtained." Partridge traced this English term to 1823. Thornton lists *speak-easy*, but without attempting to trace it in American usage. He says that it "seems to belong to Philadelphia" — on what ground, I do not know. The NED Supplement calls it "U. S. slang" and traces it to 1889, but it is undoubtedly much older. Partridge, in his Dictionary of Slang and Unconventional English; second ed., 1938, says that it was anglicized about 1925. The DAE traces *blind-tiger* to 1883 and *blind-pig* to 1887.

The wild boozing of Prohibition days gave hard service to the large répertoire of American synonyms for *drunk*, and brought in a number of new ones. In the main, however, old ones were preferred, *e.g.*, *cock-eyed, pifflicated, boozed-up, paralyzed, orey-eyed, soused, corned* and *stewed*. The English have a great many terms of the same sort,[1] and some of them have been borrowed in this country, *e.g.*, *half seas over*, but Americans have also been rolling their own since an early day. Benjamin Franklin was apparently the first to attempt to list them. This he did in the *New England Courant* in 1722, when he was but sixteen years old. His list included only nineteen terms, but fifteen years later, after he had moved to Philadelphia and become publisher of the *Pennsylvania Gazette*, he expanded it to 228 terms and printed it again in his paper. A few months later it was reprinted in the *South Carolina Gazette* of Charleston, in which he also had an interest. His purpose in compiling it, as he explained in a preface, was to issue a warning against drunkenness, which was then very prevalent in the colonies, as it was in England. This vice, he said, " bears no kind of similitude with any sort of virtue, from which it might possibly borrow a name, and is therefore reduced to the wretched necessity of being expressed by distant round-about phrases, and of perpetually varying those phrases as often as they come to be well understood to signify plainly that *a man is drunk*." At the end of his list he said: " The phrases in this dictionary are not (like most of our terms of art) borrowed from foreign languages, neither are they collected from the writings of the learned in our own, but gathered wholly from the modern tavern-conversation of tipplers." Whether he meant by this to indicate that they were all of American origin is not clear, but Edward D. Seeber has shown that, of his 228 terms, 90 are not to be found in either the NED or the English Dialect Dictionary.[2] Some of the latter are pungent and picturesque, *e.g.*, *bewitched, been to Barbados*,[3] *cramped, curved, got a brass eye, frozen, flushed, has his flag out, gold-headed, had a kick in the*

---

1 For a list of them see Slang and Its Analogues, by John S. Farmer and W. E. Henley; London, 1891, Vol. II, p. 327. An earlier one is to be found in the *Gentleman's Magazine*, 1770, pp. 559 and 560, reprinted in the *Gentleman's Magazine* Library: Dialect, Proverbs and Word-Lore, edited by George Laurence Gomme; Boston, n.d., pp. 142 *ff.*

2 Franklin's Drinkers Dictionary Again, *American Speech*, Feb., 1940, pp. 103–05. The full text is to be found in The Drinkers Dictionary, by Cedric Larson, *American Speech*, April, 1937, pp. 87–92. It was Seeber who unearthed the earlier dictionary of 1722.

3 Where much of the American rum of the time came from.

*guts, has bet his kettle, muddy, nimptopsical, oiled, pigeon-eyed, ragged* and *as stiff as a ring-bolt*. At least one is still in use today, to wit, *stewed*. There are also some good ones among those that Franklin apparently borrowed from England,[1] *e.g., afflicted, in his airs, buzzey, bungey, cherubimical, cherry-merry, disguised, dipped his bill, seen the devil, wet both eyes, fears no man, fuzzled, glaized, top-heavy, loose in the hilt, juicy, lordly, lappy, limber, moon-eyed, overset,*[2] *raddled, seafaring, in the suds, staggerish, in a trance* and *out of the way*. Here, again, there have been survivals, *e.g., boozy, cock-eyed, fuddled, jagged, muddled, mellow, has a skin full, soaked,* and *half seas over*.[3]

A little while back, I noted some of the early American names, all of them in *rum*, for drinking place. Others of different pattern are listed in AL4, p. 292. The DAE traces *café* to 1893, *buffet* to 1890, *sample-room* to 1869 and *exchange* to 1856, all euphemisms for *bar-room*, which goes back to 1807, or *saloon*, which is traced to 1841. During the last gory battle against Prohibition, in 1930 and 1931, most of the wet leaders of the country sought to convince waverers by promising that, in case of repeal, the old-time saloon should not be revived.[4] When an overwhelming (and somewhat unexpected) victory followed in 1932, and it appeared that the triumphant antinomians of the country demanded its restoration exactly as it was, with the traditional brass rail, the mirror behind the bar and even some-

---

1 He was a diligent borrower, and at least a third of the maxims in Poor Richard's Almanac were lifted from various English authors, especially Pope.

2 Obviously, a printers' term.

3 For some modern terms see The Vocabulary of Drinking, by Richard Connell, *Encore*, Feb., 1942, pp. 62–64; Slang Synonyms for *Drunk*, by Manuel Prenner, *American Speech*, Dec., 1928, pp. 102 and 103; More Slang Words for *Drunk*, by the same, the same, Aug., 1929, p. 441; *Drunk* Again, by Lowry Axley, the same, p. 440; *Drunk* in Slang — Addenda, by Manuel Penner, *American Speech*, Feb., 1941; The Elegant Eighties, by E. A. Powell, *Atlantic Monthly*, Aug., 1938, especially p. 219, and Berrey and Van den Bark's American Thesaurus of Slang; New York, 1942, pp. 122 ff. A graduated list of terms for *drunk*, ranging from *joyous, lightsome*, etc. to *dead drunk*, from the *Monthly Magazine or British Register*, July 1, 1816, is reprinted in *American Notes and Queries*, May, 1944, pp. 24 and 25, with a gloss by R. P. Breaden. Thomas Nash's list of " the eight kinds of drunkennesse " in his Pierce Penilesse His Svpplication to the Diuell, 1592, is reprinted in the *Quarterly Journal of Studies of Alcohol*, Dec., 1943, and in Tonics and Sedatives, *Journal of the American Medical Association*, Feb. 26, 1944. Other compilations are listed in Burke, pp. 151–52.

4 This promise was made, for example, by Al Smith and by Governor Albert C. Ritchie of Maryland.

thing resembling the free-lunch of happy memory, there arose a need to invent new and mellifluous names for it. So far as I know there is not a single undisguised *saloon* in the United States today. They are all *taverns*,[1] *cocktail-lounges, taprooms, beer-stubes* or the like. Some are even called *bars, lounge-bars* or *cocktail-bars*, but *saloon* seems to be definitely out.[2] The snobbish English *saloon-bar* never got a lodgment in this country, and neither did *bar-parlour, snug* or *pub*.[3] Nor are our wets familiar with such English names for drinks as *pint-of-bitter*,[4] *gin-and-French*, and *audit ale*. *Bitter* is an abbreviation of *bitter-beer*, which is of rather indefinite meaning, but signifies, in general, a beer containing a reasonable sufficiency of hops. *Gin-and-French* (sometimes *gin-and-it*) [5] is a mixture of dry gin and French vermouth, differing from a *dry Martini* in containing rather more vermouth, and no ice. *Audit-ale* is a strong ale that used to be brewed in the English universities for drinking on audit-day, when the students had to settle their college accounts. A writer in the London *Morning Post* said of it in 1936 [6] that it is brewed " from beer instead of from water," though how this is accomplished he did not explain. " Some Oxford colleges," he continued, " are now the only places where *audit-ale* is brewed. It is drunk there, as is fitting, only on rare occasions." Two other English drinks are seldom drunk in this country, though neither can be said to be unknown. They are *half-and-half* and *shandygaff*. The former is defined by the NED as " a mixture of two malt liquors, especially ale and porter," and traced to 1756. The latter is defined as " a mixture of beer and ginger-beer " and

1 The DAE shows that, from 1817 onward, *tavern* was in use in the United States to designate a hotel or inn. In England there is a sharper distinction. *Tavern*, which is now little used, means a drinking place with no sleeping accommodation; *inn*, according to English Inns, by Thomas Burke; London, 1944, means a place " forbidden to allow itself to be used for tippling or as a place of idle resort."

2 That is, save in the more elegant form of *salon*. At the Biltmore Hotel, Los Angeles, the principal drinking-spot is called the *salon d'apéritif*.

3 In an English *pub* the *saloon-bar*, or *lounge*, is the toniest part of the establishment. All drinks cost a bit more there than in other parts. The *private-bar*, also somewhat exclusive, is supposed to be reserved for patrons with particular business to discuss, but in pubs which have no separate *ladies'-bar* it is commonly used also by women. The *public-bar* is for any and all.

4 I am informed by Mr. F. MacCarthy of Watertown, Mass., that at Oxford and Cambridge the students use *can* and *half a can* instead of *pint* and *half pint*. Whether or not this shows American influence I do not know.

5 I am indebted here to Mr. Harris Booge Peavey of Maplewood, N. J.

6 *Audit-ale*, June 11.

traced to 1853. The late F. H. Tyson, of Hong Kong, informed me that in that colony *shandygaff* was often compounded of ale and ginger-ale, and sometimes even of lager-beer and bottled lemonade. I have myself drunk more than one horn of *half-and-half* (always pronounced *arf-'n-arf*, in deference to the English) compounded of beer and porter, or beer and brown stout. *Black velvet* is a mixture of porter and champagne.

So much for the vocabulary of bacchanalia in the Republic. The American contributions to that of politics have been almost as lush and impressive, and many of them go back likewise to the period between the War of 1812 and the Civil War. A shining example is *O.K.*, without question the most successful of all Americanisms, old or new. The long battle over its etymology, described at length in AL4, pp. 205 *ff*, came to a dramatic end on July 19, 1941, when Allen Walker Read published in the *Saturday Review of Literature* an article [1] which, for the first time, brought forward a body of evidence that was new, sound and precisely to the point. That evidence was to the effect that *O.K.* made its first appearance in print in the New York *New Era* on March 23, 1840, that it was then part of the name of the Democratic *O.K.* Club, an organization of supporters of Martin Van Buren for a second term in the White House, and that it was an abbreviation of *Old Kinderhook*, the name of the Hudson Valley village in which he had been born in 1782. The association of *Kinderhook* with his name was by no means new. He had been known to his political enemies since the early days of the Albany Regency as the *Kinderhook Fox*, and to his followers as the *Sage, Magician* or *Wizard* of *Kinderhook*, and it was thus natural for one of the rowdy clubs which supported him in New York to call itself after the little town. Who thought of reducing the name to *O.K.* is not known but it was in accord with the liking for secrecy and mystification that marked the politics of the time. The Democratic *O.K.* Club held its first recorded meeting in the house of Jacob Colvin, at 245 Grand street, on March 24, 1840, and the new name caught on at once. It was brief, it had a masculine and even bellicose ring, and it was mysterious enough to have a suggestion of the sinister. By the next day *O.K.* had become a sort of slogan among the other Locofocos of the city, the lower orders of whom had been masquerading for some time past under similar dark and puzzling names, *e.g.*, *Butt-enders, Roar-*

[1] The Evidence on *O.K.*, pp. 3–11.

*ers, Huge Paws, Ringtails* and *Ball-rollers*. On March 27, when the New York Whigs ventured to hold a meeting in Masonic Hall, a gang of Locofocos, using *O.K.* as their war-cry, raided it and tried to break it up. "About 500 stout, strapping men," said the New York *Herald* the next morning, "marched three and three, noiselessly and orderly. The word *O.K.* was passed from mouth to mouth, a cheer was given, and they rushed into the hall upstairs, like a torrent." The gang was headed, added the *Daily Express*, "by Custom House officers and a Locofoco street inspector." Naturally enough, the meaning of *O.K.* provoked speculation, and at once the anti-Locofoco newspapers began to print derisory interpretations. On May 27 the *New Era*, in reporting the appearance of an *O.K.* breast-pin, stated categorically that the term was "significant of the birthplace of Martin Van Buren, *Old Kinderhook*," but that did not shut off the rising flood of rival etymologies. One of these, appearing in the *Herald* on March 30, was to have the curious fate of being accepted gravely, in one form or another, for a full century. It was as follows:

> A few years ago some person accused Amos Kendall to General Jackson of being no better than he should be. "Let me examine the papers," said the old hero. "I'll soon tell you whether Mr. Kendall is right or wrong." The general did so and found everything right. "Tie up them papers," said the general. They were tied up. "Mark on them *O.K.*," continued the general. *O.K.* was marked on them. "By the eternal," said the good old general, taking his pipe from his mouth, "Amos is *oll kurrect* and no mistake." [1]

This tale was circulated by the other anti-Locofoco papers, and soon even the Democrats, at least outside New York, were believing it, sometimes with fantastic variations. To this day it is a tradition in Tennessee that Jackson, while serving as clerk of the court in that State, marked *O.K.* on legal papers approved by the judges. Investigation has discovered the following in the records of Sumner county:

> Wednesday the 6th of October 1790.
> Andrew Jackson, Esqr. proved a bill of Sale from Hugh McGary to Kasper Mansker for a negro man which is *O.R.*

[1] Kendall (1789–1869) was, like Van Buren, a devoted follower of Jackson, and perhaps the most influential member of his Kitchen Cabinet. He was made Postmaster General in 1835 and founded the tradition that the holder of that office should be a practical politician. In 1845 he became interested in the Morse electric telegraph and made a fortune promoting it.

How anyone could have ever mistaken this *O.R.* (order recorded) for *O.K.* is hard to imagine. In *American Speech* for April, 1941 [1] Woodford A. Heflin printed a photographic facsimile of the page in the court docket; only the briefest examination of it was enough to show that the letters are *O.R.* Moreover, Mr. Heflin showed that the entry is not in the handwriting of Jackson, but in that of Daniel Smith, the actual clerk of the court. Jackson, as a matter of fact, was never its clerk, though he served as public prosecutor.[2] Various other jocose etymologies for *O.K.* were suggested during the year following its first appearance in the New York *New Era,* for the term seized the fancy of the country, and was soon in wide use. So early as December 18, 1840, a Philadelphia music publisher named George Willig was copyrighting " The *O.K.* Quick Step," " composed and arranged for the piano-forte and especially dedicated to the citizens of Richmond, Va., by Jos. K. Opl." Willig's son, George, Jr., operated a music publishing business in Baltimore, and before the end of 1840 he brought out an " *O.K.* Gallopade," " dedicated to the Whig ladies of the United States by John H. Hewitt." [3] It will be noted by this dedication that *O.K.,* at least outside New York, had already lost its exclusively Democratic significance. On April 2 the New York *Daily Express,* referring to the fact that the *O.K.* boys who raided the Whig meeting were overcome and expelled, said that it was an Arabic word which, read backward, came to *kicked out.*[4] On April 11, after an election in Connecticut in which the Democrats had been bested by the Whigs, the *Express* reported that *O.K.*

1 *O.K.* – But What Do We Know About It?, pp. 89–95.

2 Two other examples from the same docket, one antedating the Jackson entry, are given by the DAE under *O.R.*

3 I am indebted here to Mr. Arthur A. Houghton, Jr., curator of the rare book collection in the Library of Congress and custodian of the early copyright records. He could find no trace of the *O.K.* Gallopade, but he unearthed the *O.K.* Quick Step. Whether or not the former was earlier than the latter cannot be established. I have a copy of the *O.K.* Gallopade, which was entered for copyright, in accordance with the law of the time, " in the clerk's office of the District Court of Maryland." Mr. Charles Zimmerman, the present clerk of the court, made a search of its records, but could find no trace of this entry. See *O.K.,* 1840, by H. L. Mencken, *American Speech,* April, 1942, p. 126.

4 This attempt at humor seems to have taken the public fancy. A year later it was retailed in Adventures in Texas, Chiefly in the Spring and Summer of 1840, by William L. McCalla; Philadelphia, 1841, p. 120. See *Kayoed:* American Slang, by Albert Matthews, *Notes and Queries,* July 30, 1938, p. 82.

meant *Old Konnecticut.* Says Read, from whom I have taken the foregoing:

> Another Whig version, soon current, was *out of kash, out of kredit, out of karacter* and *out of klothes.* Some months later a congressman from Illinois, on the floor of the House of Representatives, offered the interpretation *orful kalamity.*[1]

Many efforts have been made, both before and since the appearance of the Read paper in the *Saturday Review,* to trace O.K. beyond 1840, but so far they have produced no convincing evidence. In 1911 a contributor to *Notes and Queries*[2] reported that he had found it in the will of one Thomas Cumberland, dated December 8, 1565 and entered in the Archdeaconry Court records in London, but it is highly probable that the letters were only the initials of the scrivener. Again, Albert Matthews reported in *American Speech* in 1941[3] the discovery of O.K. in books by Gabriel Harvey and Thomas Nashe, published in London in 1593 and 1596 respectively, but, as he pointed out, it was used as a noun and in some unknown sense that manifestly had nothing to do with the modern sense.[4] Yet again, there is a report of its occurrence in a Massachusetts muster-roll of 1757,[5] but an investigation by Matthews has revealed, as Read says, that the alleged O.K. "is not O.K. at all, but an ill-written *Att.,* standing for *Attestation* or *Attested by.*"[6] Once more, there is its apparent appearance in a letter from John Richardson to John Porteous, dated Oswego, N. Y., September 23, 1789, a copy of which is in the Public Archives of Canada at Ottawa.[7] The passage refers to the building of a schooner, and in the transcript is as follows:

1 On Nov. 21, 1840 the once famous Mrs. Anne Newport Royall printed in her weekly paper, the *Huntress* (Washington), a paragraph from some unnamed newspaper saying: "The ladies, God bless them, have decided that O.K. means *only kissing.*" For this I am indebted to Mr. Cedric Larson of the Library of Congress.

2 June 10. I take this from Read.

3 A Note on O.K., Dec., 1941, p. 256.

4 Nashe applied it, in Have With You to Saffron Walden; London, 1596, (Vol. III, p. 48 of his Works, edited by Ronald B. McKerrow; London, 1910), to Henry Nichols, one of his numerous antagonists in the Marprelate controversy. The passage follows: "Martin is Guerra, Brown a brone-bill, & Barrow a wheelbarrow; Ket a knight, H.N. an o.k." The meaning is unfathomable. I am indebted here to Dr. Mary Parmenter.

5 Ulster Scots and Blandford Scouts, by S. G. Wood; Boston, 1928, pp. 382–83. Massachusetts Archives, Vol. XCX, p. 552.

6 See also the Heflin paper, before cited, pp. 92 and 93.

7 Labeled Letters of John Richardson, 1789–1799, Copied From Originals That Were in the Possession of H. R. Howland, Buffalo, N. Y., Oct. 1, 1909.

Her floor Timbers, Keel, Keelson, Stern and Lower futtocks are *O.K.* The Transoms, Stern Post, upper port of stern, Upper Futtocks, Top Timbers, Stern Timbers, Beams and Knees are all red cedar.

Unhappily, I have had no access to the original letter, but it seems to me to be highly likely that the word here transcripted as *O.K.* must be really *oak*, and in that judgment the Ontario Historical Society acquiesces, for it makes the word *oak* in a print of two Richardson letters [1] in its *Papers and Records.*[2] Finally, there is the apparent presence of *O.K.* in the travel diary of William Richardson, who made a journey from Boston to New Orleans in 1815.[3] This diary was published privately by William Bell Wait, president of the Valve Pilot Corporation of New York, in 1938.[4] The entry is that for February 21, 1815, and appears in the printed diary as follows: " Arrived at Princeton, a handsome little village, *o.k.* and at Trenton where we dined at 1 P.M." A reference to the original manuscript [5] shows that this transcription is not quite accurate. What Richardson actually wrote was: " Arrived at Princeton, a handsome little village, 15 Mil. from N. Brunswick *o k*, & at Trenton, where we dined at 1 P.M." The passage shows three corrections and as it originally stood was apparently as follows: " We this day dined in Princeton, a handsome little village, 15 Mil. from N. Brunswick, & Arrived & at Trenton, where we dined at 1 P.M." " We this day dined " is struck out and " Arrived at " written above it, and " & Arrived " is struck out

1 My attention was first called to the letter of Sept. 23, 1789 by Mr. A. J. H. Richardson, of the Public Archives of Canada (no relative of the writer), in January, 1942. I made diligent efforts to track down the original, but despite the courteous aid of Mrs. Elleine H. Stones, chief of the Burton Historical Collection in the Detroit Public Library, and of Mr. Robert W. Bingham, director of the Buffalo Historical Society, was unable to do so.

2 Vol. VI, 1905, p. 27.

3 The two Richardsons were apparently not related. William (1791–1867) was a Boston business man, twenty-four years old at the time of his journey. John was a Scotsman, born in 1755. At the age of eighteen he came out to America to enter the employ of the great fur-trading firm of Phyn, Ellice & Company at Schenectady. During the Revolution he served on a British privateer of which he was part owner. Afterward he returned to the Phyn-Ellice service. Porteus, to whom his letter was addressed, was a fellow-employé. I am indebted here to Mr. A. J. H. Richardson.

4 Travel Diary of William Richardson From Boston to New Orleans by Land, 1815; New York, 1938. Richardson began his trip on Feb. 17, 1815. He returned to Boston by sea, arriving home Aug. 24. On Oct. 24 of the same year he set out on a second journey, and again kept a diary. It was published by Mr. Wait as Journal From Boston to the Western Country and Down the Ohio and Mississippi Rivers to New Orleans, 1815–1816; New York, 1940.

5 Mr. Wait kindly sent me a photostat.

and *o k* inserted above. What, precisely, did the author mean? Thus the reply of Heflin:

> To answer this satisfactorily, it is first necessary to reconstruct the words that have been scratched out to see if *ok* stands for anything deleted. This I have done with the aid of Miss Mary Charlotte Lane, a competent decipherer of handwriting at the University of Chicago. The passage, we believe, was originally written in two stages. The first went as follows: " *We this day dined in* Princeton, a handsome little village, 15 miles from N. Brunswick, *& arrived*." At this point Mr. Richardson, who evidently was writing up his journal some hours after the events had occurred, suddenly realized that he had dined at Trenton instead of at Princeton. So he went back and crossed out " We this day dined in " and wrote in above these words " Arrived at." Then, returning to the end of his unfinished sentence, he observed that " & arrived " was now redundant; so he crossed the words out, and set an " *ok* " above them. The second stage of the writing then followed: " & at Trenton, where we dined at 1 P.M." Thus the passage was completed, making " at Trenton " parallel in construction with " at Princeton." [1]

Heflin argued plausibly that " the *o k* of the manuscript looks like *O.K.*", that " it does not stand for anything scratched out in the manuscript," and that " it makes sense if interpreted *all well*," and concluded that it should be accepted as a genuine appearance of the term, earlier than any other that has been authenticated. I was inclined to the same conclusion myself at the time he wrote, though not altogether convinced,[2] but on reflection I began to develop doubts. They revolved around the possibility that Richardson, who survived until 1867, may have revised his manuscript after the appearance of *O.K.*[3] in New York in 1840, as recorded by Read. To my eye, at least, the letters *ok* show a certain difference in handwriting from the rest of the diary. Somehow, they look more mature. Moreover, even if they are accepted as the equivalent of the printer's *stet*, as Heflin suggests, they leave the entry in confusion, for what it then shows is " Arrived & at Trenton, where we dined." There is likewise the possibility that what seems to be *ok* may actually be two other letters. This was suggested in an editorial note in *American Speech* in April, 1941, appended to the Wait paper lately cited: [4]

1 *O.K.* – But What Do We Know About It?, before cited, p. 94.
2 My view was quoted in Richardson's *O.K.* of 1815, by William Bell Wait, *American Speech*, April, 1941, p. 85.
3 He was keeping diaries so late as 1844, and recorded his observations on a trip to Europe in one headed Notes For Myself. He also kept one of a trip overland from New Orleans in the days after the appearance of railroads. (Private communication from Mr. Wait, Sept. 11, 1939).
4 P. 86. The note was written by Read.

After *N. Brunswick*, where the words *& arrived* are crossed out, Richardson started to interpolate *a handsome little village*, as that idea was in his mind, but after getting as far as *a h* he discovered that he had already used that phrase earlier in the sentence with reference to Princeton. He went no farther in the word, and his attention was attracted to something else before he got the letters crossed out. This *o k* is really therefore the first two letters of *a handsome*.[1]

Altogether, the problem of Richardson's *ok* presents difficulties, but it is perfectly conceivable that O.K. may have arisen from some source other than *Old Kinderhook*, and got itself forgotten before the New York Locofocos began to use it. Not a few competent authorities look forward hopefully to its discovery in some unchallengable situation before 1840. One of them is Dr. Louise Pound, who surmises that, at least in academic circles, it may have been borrowed from the first letters of the Greek phrase ὅλα καλά (*ola kala*), long in use among teachers of Greek " to mark the deserving themes of their pupils." [2] Such dual origins are by no means unheard of in philology.

The Read discovery, of course, has not abated the efforts of amateur etymologists to account for O.K., and to the ten guesses at its origin that I listed in AL4, pp. 206 and 207, new ones are being added all the time. I offer a few of the more picturesque or preposterous:

1. That *O.K.* comes from *aux quais*, used " in the American War of Independence by French sailors who made appointments with [American] girls." [3]
2. That it may be derived from *oikea*, a Finnish word signifying correct.[4]
3. That it arose during the Civil War, when " the War Department brought large quantities of crackers from the Orrins-Kendall Company. This company always put their initials on their boxes and as the crackers were of a high quality the initials gradually came to be used as a synonym for *all right*." [5]

1 Some objections to this note were offered in *O.K. a Comment*, by James B. McMillan, *American Speech*, April, 1942, p. 127, but Albert Matthews offered a new and highly persuasive criticism of Heflin's position in A Note on *O.K.*, *American Speech*, Dec., 1941, pp. 256–59.

2 Editor's preface, by John A. Huybers, to When I Was a Boy in Greece, by George Demetrios; Boston, 1913, p. 5. Robert C. McClelland called attention to this passage in the *Classical Journal*, Oct., 1933, p. 69. See A Greek *O.K.*, by Robert Weber, *American Speech*, April, 1942, p. 127, and *O.K. Redivivus*, by Louise Pound, the same, Dec., 1942, p. 249.

3 *Aux Quais*, by Beachcomber, London *Daily Express*, June 28, 1940.

4 *Main Library News Notes*, Cleveland Public Library, July, 1940. I am indebted here to Mr. L. H. Gergely.

5 *O.K.*, by Robert Greenburger, *Linguist* (Horace Mann School for Boys, New York), Vol. IV, 1939, p. 15. This etymology was borrowed by the Dublin (Ireland) *Evening Herald*, Aug. 19, 1941.

4. " Certain bills in the House of Lords must be read and approved by the Lord Chairman of Committees, Lord Onslow, and by his counsel, Lord Kilbracken, and then initialed by them. They are then *O.K.*" [1]

5. " *O.K.* had its origin several hundred years ago in an expression common among Norwegian and Danish sailors: *H.G.* (pronounced *hah gay*), meaning shipshape, ready for action. *H.G.* was short for the Anglo-Saxon *hofgor*, meaning ready for the sea." [2]

6. " Liddell and Scott have an entry, ωχ, ωχ, a magical incantation against fleas. The authority is a work called ' Geoponica,' the date of which is given, with a query, as 920 A.D." [3]

7. " The Prussian general Schliessen, who fought for the American colonies in the War of Independence, endorsed his letters and orders *O.K.* (*Oberst Kommandant*). Consequently the letters *O.K.* came to be applied to anything having the meaning of official assent." [4]

8. That *O.K.* may have some sort of connection with the Scotch *och aye*.[5]

9. " *O.K.* is an abbreviation of *orl korrec*, all correct. It is English, I think Cockney — not an Americanism. I was born in the 60s and remember it when I was a boy." [6]

10. That *O.K.* may come from *O qu-oui*, an emphatic French form of *yes*, to be found in Sterne's " A Sentimental Journey," 1768.[7]

Of all Americanisms, *O.K.* has been the greatest success. It has been borrowed by virtually all civilized tongues, and also by many lower down the scale. Partridge says that it became naturalized in England as an adjective *c.* 1880 and as a verb by 1900, but other authorities put its adoption further back. Sir William Power, for example, has recorded that it was in use by English telegraphers, as a signal that a message had been clearly received, so early as 1873, and has called attention to the fact that it first appeared in an English slang dictionary a year earlier.[8] At some indefinite time before 1888 it was already familiar enough to the patrons of London music-halls to enter

1 *O.K.*, by John Godley, London *Times*, Nov. 2, 1939.
2 Reported but by no means certified by Frank Colby in his newspaper column, Take My Word For It, March 21, 1943.
3 *O.K.* by W. Snow, London *Times*, Oct. 26, 1935. The first edition of the Greek Lexicon of Henry G. Liddell and Robert Scott was published in 1843.
4 *O.K.* by Sir Anthony Palmer, London *Times*, Oct. 28, 1939. *Oberst Kommandant* is German for colonel in command. In *American Speech* for Oct., 1938, p. 234, Gretchen Hochdoerfer Rogers published a translation of an article in the Omaha (Neb.) *Tribune*, a German daily, of Jan. 23, 1938, in which the German officer was changed to Baron F. W. von Steuben, inspector-general of the Continental Army, and *Oberst Kommandant* to *Ober-Kommando*, meaning high command.
5 The Cry of the English: Words That Bless and Burn, Nottingham *Journal*, April 30, 1943.
6 *O.K.*, by Charles A. Christie, London *Times*, Oct. 24, 1939.
7 I am indebted here to Mr. William McDevitt of San Francisco.
8 *O.K.*, London *Times*, Oct. 21, 1939.

into the refrain of a popular song.[1] But it remained for the American movies to make *O.K.* familiar to all Englishmen, low or high. When the young of the land began to use it in place of the English *righto,* there were the usual loud protests from patriots and pedants, but they were without effect. An especially violent war upon it opened in 1935, and Mrs. Nicholas Murray Butler, who was then in London, lent a hand to its opponents by denouncing it in a letter to the London *Daily Telegraph,*[2] but it was then too late to stay the tide, for, as she had to confess, she had heard it " used in an English drawing-room " and had found it " in the Oxford Dictionary." [3] Before the end of the year the London *Times* heaved a bomb into the patriot ranks by giving its awful *O.K.* to *O.K.* The London *Morning Post* and a few die-hards at Oxford and Cambridge held out,[4] but the jig was up, and when H. W. Horwill brought out his " Dictionary of Modern American Usage " [5] he did not think it necessary to explain *O.K.,* or even to list it. During this same *annus mirabilis* the Judicial Committee of the Privy Council decided formally that inscribing *O.K.* upon a legal document " meant that the details contained . . . were correctly given." [6] Some of the lower judges were greatly shocked by this decision, and a few of them continued to forbid the use of *O.K.* in proceedings before them, but they were engaged upon a forlorn hope. On June 22, 1936, the London bureau of the New York *Herald-Tribune* reported:

Rebuking a witness in a Chancery Court suit here who replied " *Okay,*" Justice Sir Albert Charles Clauson [7] said today: " Because you have been to America there is no need to say *okay.* If you want to say *yes,* say *yes.* Speak

1 *O.K.* – The Victorians Used It, by J. W. Lee, *John o' London's Weekly,* Aug. 29, 1936. The song was Walking in the Zoo, by Hugh Willoughby Sweny, with music by Alfred Lee, and it was sung by Alfred Glanville Vance, a popular comic singer of the time, who died in 1888. The refrain was:

Walking in the Zoo, walking in the Zoo,
The *O.K.* thing on Sunday is walking in the Zoo.

See also *O.K.* in History, by M. E. Durham, London *Spectator,* Jan. 14, 1938, p. 57.
2 March 6, 1935.

3 More precisely, in the NED Supplement, published in 1933.
4 Under the heading of Not *O.K.* By Us, the *Morning Post* printed an editorial on Dec. 16, 1936 saying: " It would be as absurd for us to describe anything as *O.K.* by us as it would be for us to describe five o'clock as six bells."
5 Oxford, 1935.
6 *Chemical Trade Journal* (London), quoted in the *New Yorker,* Oct. 19, 1935, p. 70.
7 His Lordship, before he mounted the bench in 1926, was counsel to Oxford University.

English in this court, if you don't mind." The witness assented, but to the next question he replied: " That's quite *okay*."

A year later the Edinburgh *Evening News* [1] was describing *O.K.* as " now universal " in Great Britain, and in 1940 a provincial journalist was reporting that " almost everybody says *O.K.* now instead of *all right.*" [2] The American troops, when they began to arrive in England, found that this was, if anything, an understatement. Finally, on September 30, 1941 Lord Beaverbrook made *O.K.* impeccable by using it at the Moscow Conference in a formal pledge as official representative of the British Commonwealth of Nations. But let him tell his own story:

> It was at that meeting that Stalin's demands were finally formulated. . . . The interpreter began solemnly and anxiously to read out each item. But there was little need for his services. The lists were familiar to us. We had studied them for long. Most things we were ready to supply, and the answers came straight from Harriman [3] or me. He said " Agreed " if the item concerned the United States. I said " *Okay* " when Britain was producing the supplies.[4]

It was seldom, indeed, during World War II that American troops, though they ranged the earth, encountered a people to whom *O.K.* was unknown. Lieut. Col. W. E. Dyess, in his narrative of his captivity by the Japanese after Bataan, recorded that it was known to and used by every guard in their Davao prison-camp.[5] Similarly, it was familiar to the Moslem allies of the Allies in North Africa.[6] Before World War II began the American volunteers in the Spanish civil war found that it had displaced *salud* as a greeting among the village children of Spain.[7] Nor should it be forgotten that the case before the Judicial Committee of the Privy Council, before mentioned, originated in faraway Burma. In several places *O.K.* seems to have encountered congeners which coalesced with it, *e.g., ola kalla* in Greece, meaning all right.[8] In Liberia the local analogue, in the Djabo dialect, is *o-ke.* Says Charles Blooah, a Liberian, in *American Speech:* [9]

1 The Mystery of *O.K.*, June 4.
2 How the Tank Got Its Name, by Sam Bate, *Northern Daily Telegraph* (Blackburn), Aug. 19, 1940.
3 W. Averell Harriman, the American representative.
4 The Moscow Conference, by Lord Beaverbrook, *Listener* (London), Oct. 16, 1941, p. 320.

5 Installment published in the newspapers of Feb. 18, 1944.
6 Amen, *New Yorker*, Aug. 28, 1943.
7 Associated Press dispatch from Madrid, June 24, 1937.
8 *O.K.* Redivivus, by Louise Pound, *American Speech*, Dec., 1942, p. 250.
9 Oct., 1937, p. 240.

An inferior addressed by one superior in age is expected to reply in rather brisk and short accords at the conclusion of each of a series of orders or instructions, in a successive fashion, *o-we, o-we,* etc., to show that he is giving strict attention to all that is being spoken. At the conclusion of the entire series of instructions the inferior must reply with a summarizing *o-ke.* This indicates that there is perfect accord between him and the superior. *O-ke* has something of the force of the German *ja wohl,* when given in reply to the bidding of a superior.

*O.K.* is sometimes spelled *okeh, okay,* or *okey,* and about 1930 an abbreviation, *oke,* appeared,[1] quickly followed by *oke-doke* (more often *oky-doke*), *oky-doky* and *oky-dory.* The forms terminating in *y* were perhaps suggested by *all-righty,* which had a vogue at about the same time, and maybe *oky-dory* was also influenced by *hunky-dory,* an Americanism traced by the DAE to 1868. The late Woodrow Wilson used *okeh* in *O.K.ing* documents, and seems to have subscribed to the theory [2] that the term came from a Choctaw word, *oke, hoke,* signifying yes, it is. This etymology is accepted as " probable " by Webster's New International, 1934, but there is no evidence for it.[3]

Thornton and the DAE establish the approximate dates of the first appearance of large numbers of other political Americanisms. The DAE shows that the familiar American use of *administration* as an adjective began soon after the opening of the Nineteenth Century. It traces *administration paper* (*i.e.,* newspaper) to 1808, *administration man* to 1810, *administration candidate* to 1827, *administration party* to 1837, and *anti-administration* to 1834. *Administration,* as a noun signifying the executive arm of the government, seems to be of American origin also, for it appeared in Samuel Sewall's diary in 1716, whereas the first recorded English use of it is dated 1731. In the sense of the term or terms during which a President holds office, as in *first administration,* etc., it is unquestionably an Americanism, and the DAE's first example is from Washington's Farewell Address, 1796. The English have borrowed more or less, in recent years, all of these terms in *administration,* as they have also borrowed *campaign* in the political sense. Their own word for pre-election political

---

1 The Centennial of *O.K.,* by Eugene Pharo, Washington *Post,* June 9, 1940.
2 See AL4, p. 206.
3 The literature dealing with *O.K.* is enormous, but save for the papers

I have referred to is of small value. An interesting account of its use in German is in *Okeh,* by A. J. Storfer, *Vossische Zeitung* (Berlin), Sept. 3, 1933.

activity is *canvass*, but they know what *campaign* means, and often use it. The DAE traces it in this country to 1809. At the start it was commonly preceded by *electioneering*, but in a little while it was being used without explanation. Most of its derivatives, rather curiously, did not come in until years later. The DAE traces *campaign-document* to 1871, *campaign-speech* to 1880, *campaign-manager* to 1882, *campaign-club* to 1892, *campaign-orator* and *to campaign* to 1896, *campaign-button* to 1900, and *campaign-fund* to 1905. All of them are undoubtedly measurably older than these dates indicate, but they do not seem to have been in use before the Civil War. *Affiliation* and *to affiliate*, in the political sense, are traced by Thornton to 1852, and *anxious-seat* to 1842. The latter, in the meaning of the bleachers provided for converts at revivals, goes back to the great Methodist campaigns of the 20s and 30s, as does *anxious-bench*, but it did not come into political use until later. *Mourner's bench* is traced by the DAE, in the revival sense, to 1845. Like *anxious-bench* and *amen-corner* it was borrowed by the politicians somewhat later.

*To back and fill*, a phrase taken from the terminology of sailors, began to be used of elusive candidates for office in the 50s. *Ballot-box stuffer* is traced by the DAE to 1856, *bluff* (as a political device) to 1854, *to bolt* to 1833 and *bolter* to 1858, *bugaboo* (in the political sense) to 1835, *in cahoots* to 1829, *to crawfish* to 1848, *to demagogue* to 1850,[1] *to dodge the issue* to 1846, *dyed-in-the-wool* to 1830, *to electioneer* to 1806 (*electioneering* goes back to 1787), *exposé* to 1830,[2] *fat salary* to 1817, *fat office* to 1833 and *fat job* to c. 1861, *favorite son* to 1825, *floater* to 1847, *grand and lofty tumbling* (by a

1 *Demagogue*, of course, is not an Americanism, and neither is *to demagogue*. But *demagoguery* is, and the DAE traces it to 1855. The English seem to prefer *demagogy*. See Letter-Saving, New York *Times* (editorial), Feb. 18, 1942. Says Richard Chenevix Trench in English Past and Present; eleventh edition, revised; London, 1881, p. 109, footnote: "*Démagogue* was first hazarded by Bossuet, and counted so bold a novelty that for long none ventured to follow him in its use." Jacques Bénigne Bossuet, a famous French preacher and sometime Bishop of Condom, died in 1704.

2 The author of an anonymous article in the New York *Times*, Twisting the Dictionary to Pad Political Vocabulary, Dec. 16, 1923, ascribed the introduction of *exposé* to an Ohio congressman named Duncan, and said that he also launched *in cahoots* and *blowing* in the sense of bragging, and popularized *up Salt river*. The DAE quotes the *Virginia Literary Museum*, 1829, to the effect that *exposé* was already "very common" at that time, and had been borrowed from the French. It was apparently first used in the political sense in 1830.

politician) to 1839, *to knife* to 1888, *landslide* to 1895, *lobby* to 1808, *lobbying* to 1832 and *lobbyist* to 1863 (it was preceded by *lobbyer*, 1841),[1] *log-rolling* to 1820, *mass-meeting* to 1842, *office-hunter* to 1806, *office-seeker* to 1813 and *office-holder* to 1818, *party question* to 1803, *party machinery* to 1829, *party ticket* to 1843, *party vote* to 1846 and *party hack* to 1848, *platform* (in the sense of a formal document) to 1848, *plank* to the same year, *on the fence* to 1828, *to mend fences* to 1879,[2] *pap* to 1841, *peanut politics* to 1887, *picayune* (in the political sense) to 1837, *pie* to 1879 and *pie-counter* to 1912, *plum* to 1887,[3] *plunder* (in the political sense) to 1870,[4] *love-feast* to 1893, *pollywog* (a professional politician; now obsolete) to 1854, *pow-wow* (a meeting of politicians) to 1812, *pull* to 1887, *reformer* (nearly always in a derogatory sense) to 1848, *ring* to 1862, *safe* (meaning not radical) to 1862, *scattering* (of votes) to 1766, *to scratch a ticket* to 1841,[5] *to see* (to bribe) to 1869, *slangwhanger* (a political ranter) to 1807, *solid South* to 1878,[6] *slate* to 1865, *to be snowed under* to 1880, *sorehead* to 1855, *spellbinder* to 1888,[7] *split ticket* to 1836, *standard-bearer* to 1848, *straight ticket* to 1860, *straw-vote* to 1891, *to swing*

1 In England a *lobbyist* is a reporter assigned to pick up news in the lobby of the House of Commons. What we call a *lobbyist* is there a *lobby-agent*.

2 In that year Senator John Sherman of Ohio made a visit home, ostensibly to look after his farm but actually to see to his political interests. When tackled by reporters he alleged that he had made the trip "only to repair my fences." The usual form is now *to look after*. The English use *to nurse a constituency*.

3 *Plum* seems to have been launched by Matthew S. Quay, who, on being elected Senator from Pennsylvania in 1887, promised his followers that he would "shake the plum tree."

4 *Plunderbund* came later. It was used by the cartoonist, Frederick B. Opper, and probably invented by him, after he joined the Hearst staff in 1899.

5 *Ticket*, in the sense of "the group of party candidates selected for a given set of officers," is traced by the DAE to 1764, but it seems to have been known long before that, for *to carry a ticket* is traced to 1711. *To run ahead of the ticket* goes back to 1846, *the head of the ticket* to 1884 and *to put a ticket in the field* to 1891.

6 Edward Clark in The *Solid South*, *Century Magazine*, April, 1885, p. 955: "The *Solid South* . . . came into vogue during the Hayes-Tilden canvass of 1876. The Democratic tidal wave in the elections of 1874 had shown a powerful, if not irresistible, drift toward Democracy in all the then lately reconstructed States, as well as in their sisters on the old borderline which had also maintained slavery, but which had not gone into the rebellion. The alliterative term commended itself to the Republican stump speakers and newspaper organs as a happy catchword, and the idea which underlay it was impressive enough to arrest the attention of the whole country."

7 The invention of *spellbinder* is ascribed to the New York *World* in Twisting the Dictionary to Pad Political Vocabulary, New York *Times*, Dec. 16, 1932, but the DAE's first example is from the New York *Tribune*, Nov. 15, 1888.

*round the circle* to 1877, *third party* to 1801, *tidal wave* to 1877,[1]
*timber* (*e.g.*, presidential, gubernatorial) to 1831, *propaganda* (in the
evil sense) to 1880 and *propagandist* to 1824, *rabble-rouser* (perhaps
borrowed from England) to 1843, *repeater* to 1861, *to go* (or *row*)
*up Salt River* to 1832,[2] *stalwart* to 1879, *spoils* to 1812, *spoils system*
to 1838 and *spoilsman* to 1846, *stump* to 1816, *to stump* to 1838, *to
take to the stump* to 1852, *stumping-excursion* to 1844 and *stumping-
tour* to 1900, *to whitewash* to 1800 and *wirepuller* to 1833. *Fat cat*,
a wealthy contributor to campaign funds, was coined by Frank R.
Kent of the Baltimore *Sun*, and was first used in his book, " Political
Behavior," 1928.

It will be noted that most of these terms are opprobrious. Ever
since the first great battle between Federalists and anti-Federalists the
American people have viewed politicians with suspicion, and the word
itself has a derogatory significance in the United States which it lacks
in England. From Shakespeare onward, to be sure, there have been
Englishmen who have sneered at the *politician*, but the term is still
used across the water in a perfectly respectful manner to indicate a
more or less dignified statesmen. In this country it means only a
party manipulator, a member of a professionally dishonest and dis-
honorable class. An *honest politician* is regarded as a sort of marvel,
comparable to a calf with five legs, and the news that one has appeared is commonly received with derision. Thus Walt Whitman

---

1 " The other day, after the election," said S. S. Cox in Why We Laugh; New York, 1877, p. 75, " a New York editor saluted the writer as a *tidal waver*."

2 Carl Scherf, in Slang, Slogan and Song in American Politics, *Social Studies*, Dec., 1934, p. 429, says: " The expression *up Salt river*, often used to describe political defeat, owes its origin to a river of that name. It is a branch of the Ohio running through Kentucky. Clay was opposing Jackson in 1832. He employed a boatman to row him up the Ohio toward Louisville, where he was to make an important speech. The boatman was a Jackson man. He played a dirty trick. 'Acci-dentally or on purpose' he missed his way and rowed Clay up Salt river. Clay did not reach Louisville

in time to make a speech. Clay was defeated. In the campaign of 1840 this phrase was used in a song:
" Our vessel is ready, we cannot delay,
For Harrisons' coming, and we must away —
*Up Salt river, up Salt river,
Up Salt river, oh high-oh*."
The DAE'S first quotation is from Frances M. Trollope's Domestic Manners of the Americans; Lon-don, 1832, Vol. II, p. 117; and Thornton's is from J. K. Paulding's Banks of the Ohio; London, 1833, Vol. I, p. 133. It seems rather strange that the phrase should have gone into circulation quickly enough to get into Mrs. Trollope's book, if Scherf's etymology is to be credited.

described the men who constituted the fateful Democratic conventions of the years just before the Civil War, when problems of the first magnitude were pressing for solution:

[They] were, seven-eighths of them, the meanest kind of bawling and blowing office-holders, office-seekers, pimps, malignants, conspirators, murderers, fancy-men, custom-house clerks, contractors, kept-editors, spaniels well trained to carry and fetch, jobbers, infidels, disunionists, terrorists, mail-riflers, slave-catchers, pushers of slavery, creatures of the President, creatures of would-be Presidents, spies, bribers, compromisers, lobbyers, spongers, ruined sports, expelled gamblers, policy-backers, monte-dealers, duellists, carriers of concealed weapons, deaf men, pimpled men, scarred inside with vile disease, gaudy outside with gold chains made from the people's money and harlots' money, twisted together; crawling, serpentine men; the lousy combings and born freedom-sellers of the earth.[1]

The public attitude reveals itself in a common definition of *politics*, to wit, " Who gets what, when, how? " It is assumed as a matter of course that a professional politician will do anything, say anything or endure anything for votes, and that assumption is seldom controverted by plausible evidence. From the earliest days of the Republic its politics have consisted mainly of a continuing auction sale, with pressure groups of voters offering their votes and gangs of politicians bidding for them with public money. Nearly all the campaign slogans in American history, from the pledges to the veterans of the Revolution down through the " Vote yourself a farm " of 1846 and the " Share the wealth " of Huey Long to the grandiose promises of the New Deal have voiced engagements to loot A for the use and benefit of B.[2] And in the popular proverbs aimed at or ascribed to politicians there is a matter-of-fact acceptance of the theory that they are wholly vicious, *e.g.*, " In politics a man must learn to rise *above* principle," " Root, hog, or die," " You tickle me and I'll tickle you," " To the victor belongs the spoils," " Few die and none resign," " When the water reaches the upper deck, follow the rats," and " Why not me? " These blistering sayings, like American proverbs in general, still lack scholarly investigation. There is an exhaustive and extremely valuable study of English proverbs,[3] and there are others of the prov-

1 Origins of Attempted Secession, *c.* 1880.

2 The historian will recall *forty acres and a mule*, used to inflame the slaves toward the end of the Civil War; the more modest *three acres and a cow*

launched by Jesse Collings in 1886, and the *car in every garage* of the unfortunate Hoover, *c.* 1928.

3 English Proverbs and Proverbial Phrases, by G. L. Apperson; London, 1929.

erbs of other nations, including several useful catch-alls,[1] but American proverbs continue to be neglected, though some of them are extraordinarily pungent, *e.g.*, " Don't monkey with the buzz-saw," [2] " I'd rather have them say ' There he goes ' than ' Here he lies,' " " It will never get well if you pick it," " No check-ee, no shirt-ee," " Cheer up; the worst is yet to come," and " Life is one damn thing after another." [3]

Some of the older political Americanisms have long engaged etymologists, *e.g.*, *caucus, buncombe, mugwump, gerrymander, roorback, scalawag* and *filibuster. Caucus* was first discussed by the Rev. William Gordon, an English clergyman who immigrated to Massachusetts in 1770, took the side of the colonists in the Revolution, and on his return to England in 1786 wrote a four-volume " History of the Rise and Independence of the United States, Including the Late War." [4] In the first volume of this work he printed the following note on the term:

> The word *caucus* and its derivative, *caucusing,* are often used in Boston. The last answers much to what we style *parliamenteering* or *electioneering.* All

1 For example, Racial Proverbs, by Selwyn Gurney Champion; New York, 1938, and Proverbs, Maxims and Phrases of All Ages, by Robert Christy; New York, 1905. Neither contains any mention of American proverbs.

2 The DAE does not list this, though it is undoubtedly American. The verb phrase to *monkey with* is also probably American, for the NED's first English example is dated 1886, whereas the DAE's first American example is dated 1881. Thornton calls it an Americanism. *Monkeyshines* is so listed by the DAE and traced to 1847, and *monkey-business* to 1883.

3 I listed a few of these in The American Language, first ed.; New York, 1919, pp. 301–03, and in all subsequent printings before the fourth edition, 1936. Many go back to Franklin's Poor Richard's Almanac, and new ones are coming in all the time, *e.g.*, " Nobody loves a fat man," " The Lord is my shepherd: I should worry," " Don't spit: remember the Johnstown Flood," " Kick him again; he's down," " Ain't it hell to

be poor? ", " The first hundred years are the hardest," " It's a great life if you don't weaken," " Tell your troubles to a policeman," and " Smile, damn you, smile." The provenance of only a few has been determined. " War is hell," commonly ascribed to W. T. Sherman, is a misreporting of a phrase in a speech he made at Columbus, O., Aug. 11, 1880. See my New Dictionary of Quotations; New York, 1942, p. 1267. " To the victor belongs the spoils (of the enemy) " is from a speech in the United States Senate by William L. Marcy, Jan. 21, 1832. " Life is one damn thing after another " has been ascribed to Frank Ward O'Malley and to Elbert Hubbard, but there is no evidence that either really invented it. " Few die and none resign " is an abridgment of a saying by Thomas Jefferson in a letter to Elias Shipman, July 12, 1801. " I'd rather have them say," etc., was given popularity by Jack Johnson, the colored pugilist, *c.* 1910, but he did not invent it.

4 Published in London in 1788.

my repeated applications to different gentlemen have not furnished me with a satisfactory account of *caucus*. It seems to mean a number of persons, whether more or less, met together to consult upon adopting and prosecuting some scheme of policy for carrying a favorite point. The word is not of novel invention. More than fifty years ago [1] Mr. Samuel Adams's father and twenty others, one or two from the north end of town, where all the ship-business is carried on, used to meet, make a *caucus*, and lay their plan for introducing certain persons into places of trust and power. When they had settled it they separated, and used each their particular influence within his own circle. He and his friends would furnish themselves with ballots, including the names of the parties fixed upon, which they distributed on the days of election. By acting in concert, together with a careful and extensive distribution of ballots, they generally carried the elections to their own mind. In like manner it was that Mr. Samuel Adams first became a representative for Boston.[2]

" From the above remarks of Dr. Gordon," said John Pickering in his Vocabulary of 1816, " it should seem that these meetings were first held in a part of Boston where ' all the ship-business was carried on,' and I had therefore thought it not improbable that *caucus* might be a corruption of *caulkers*, the word *meetings* being understood. I was afterward informed by a friend in Salem that the late Judge Oliver [3] often mentioned this as the origin of the word; and upon further inquiry I find other gentlemen have heard the same in Boston, where the word was first used. I think I have sometimes heard the expression, a *caucus meeting*, i.e., a *caulkers' meeting*. It need hardly be remarked that this cant word and its derivatives are never used in good writing." This etymology was cited without dissent by Robley Dunglison in the vocabulary of Americanisms that he contributed to the *Virginia Literary Museum* in 1829, and Bartlett apparently accepted it in his Glossary, 1848, but the Webster American Dictionary of 1852, edited by the lexicographer's son-in-law, Chauncey A. Goodrich, said that " the origin of the word is not ascertained." In 1872 Dr. J. Hammond Trumbull, an early authority on the Indian languages, suggested in the *Proceedings of the American Philological Association* that *caucus* may have been derived from an Algonquin

1 Which is to say, before 1736.
2 Adams was elected a member of the Massachusetts House of Representatives in 1765. He became a member of the Continental Congress in 1774, and as such was a strong supporter of the committee system of administration, suggesting the *caucus* system. After the Revolution he was Governor of Massachusetts. He died in 1803, aged 81. His father, likewise

Samuel (1689–1748), was also a politico.
3 Peter Oliver (1713–91) was made a justice of the Superior Court of Massachusetts in 1756, though he was not a lawyer, and in 1771 became chief justice. He was a Loyalist during the Revolution, and in 1776 went to England, where he remained for the rest of his life.

word, *caucauasu*, meaning one who advises. This surmise was adopted by the later Webster Dictionaries [1] and, as we have seen in Chapter III, Section 1, by Dr. Alexander F. Chamberlain, a high authority upon loans from the Indian languages, but the NED, the C volume of which came out in 1893, was content to mark the word " origin obscure." The DAE says that the Indian etymology is " more plausible " than Pickering's, but calls attention to the possibility that the word may be derived from the name of a forgotten Boston neighborhood, and cites in evidence thereof a notice in the Boston *Evening Post* of August 19, 1745, to the effect that a " general meeting " of " lay brethren, to take into serious consideration the conduct of those reverend clergymen who have encouraged the itineration of Mr. George Whitefield " was to be held " at West-*Corcus* in Boston." Finally, the Standard Dictionary, 1906, notes that there was a Latin word, *caucus*, signifying a drinking vessel, and observes darkly that " the *caucus* club perhaps had convivial features."

Thus the matter stood when, in 1943, Dr. LeRoy C. Barret, of Trinity College, Hartford, Conn., announced an interesting discovery.[2] Let him tell it in his own words:

> In looking over some old documents in the library of the American Oriental Society I found among the papers of John Pickering [3] an explanation of the origin of *caucus* to the effect that it consists of the initials of the names of six men, *viz.*: Cooper (Wm.), Adams, Urann (Joyce, Jr.), Coulson, Urann, Symmes. The words are in a vertical column with the initial letters spaced a little bit away from the second letters. Below the column of names is written (in Pickering's handwriting): "From B. Russell, who had it from Sam'l Adams and Paul Revere."

The library of the American Oriental Society, of which Pickering was a founder and the first president (1842), is housed in the building of the Yale library. The name *Urann* seemed strange and could not be found in any American reference book, but Barret made a diligent search for it and soon unearthed it. His report on it follows:

> In the *New England Genealogical Register*, Vol. 64, pp. 7–17, I found an account of a family named *Urann* (sometimes spelled *Urine*, et al). On p. 16 is entered the record that Thomas *Urann*, born in Boston, February 3, 1723, was a

---

1 Webster's New International, 1934, inserts a saving *probably*, but seeks to relate the word to *cockarouse*, the designation of an Indian chief in Virginia, applied by extension to a white colonist of wealth and consequence. In the former sense John Smith reported the word in 1624, spelling it *caucorouse*.

2 *Caucus, American Speech*, April, 1943, p. 130.

3 The author of the Vocabulary lately cited.

ship-joiner and prominent in town affairs, and held offices. He was a captain of artificers in Col. Richard Gridley's artificers. He was a Mason, was one of the Sons of Liberty, and was at the Tea Party.[1]

The B. Russell mentioned by Pickering was apparently Benjamin Russell (1761–1845), an early American journalist who, after service in the Revolution, established a semi-weekly journal, the *Columbian Centinel*, which he continued to edit for forty years.[2] One of the frequent contributors to it was Pickering, and the two were on close terms, for both were ardent Federalists.[3] But journalists are notoriously unreliable as philologians, and Russell may have reported as horse's-mouth information what he got from Adams and Revere only at second-hand. There is, furthermore, an unhappy tendency among amateur etymologists to derive words from the initials of proper names, often without justification. The case of *cabal* is in point. It is often said to come from the names of the five ministers of Charles II who made an alliance with France for war against Holland in 1672, to wit, Clifford, Arlington, Buckingham, Ashley and Lauderdale, but the NED shows that the word was in use so early as 1646–7, and was actually borrowed from the French *cabale*, of precisely the same meaning. The Russell memorandum could not have reached Pickering before 1816, for he does not mention it in his Vocabulary of that year. By that time, if Gordon is to be believed, *caucus* was nearly a century old. Also, his evidence conflicts with the fact that the Thomas Urann unearthed by Barret was not born until 1723, which would have made him much too young to be a member of the first *caucus*. The etymology of the word thus remains in doubt. It was spelled variously down to the Revolutionary era, but afterward the present spelling seems to have been agreed upon.

In the United States *caucus* has always meant a meeting of politicians to pick candidates, agree upon plans of action, and so on. The *congressional caucuses* of the major parties dictated the nominations of presidential and vice-presidential candidates from 1804 to 1824, and were finally overthrown only by the adoption of the revolutionary

---

1 Private communication, Oct. 11, 1943. I am also indebted to Dr. Barret for a photostat of Pickering's note.

2 Russell ran away from school to see the battle of Lexington. He supported the Constitution, was a great admirer of Washington, and denounced the War of 1812. There is an account of him in American Journalism, by Frank Luther Mott; New York, 1941, pp. 133 ff.

3 Russell was the author of the phrase *Era of Good Feeling*.

national convention system in 1831.[1] *Caucuses* are still held by congressmen whenever a pending question calls for united party action, but they now deal with measures predominantly, and only occasionally with men. So in the State legislatures and in other theoretically deliberative bodies. The early English commentators on American speechways denounced *caucus* as a low and uncouth word, and their view of it was reflected, as we have seen, by the subservient Pickering, but it was already in respectable usage by 1762, and John Adams was using it soon afterward. The English, after a century of resistance, adopted the word in the 1870s, and, as the NED shows, perverted its meaning. " In American use," says the NED, " a *caucus* is a meeting; English newspapers apply *the caucus* to an organization or system. Such organizations have been, in one form or another, adopted by all parties; and *caucus* is now a term which partisans fling at the organizations of their opponents, and disclaim for their own." In other words, the English use *caucus* in the sense of what we call a *party organization* or *machine*.[2] But in late years they have also begun to use it, albeit somewhat gingerly, in the original American sense. Indeed, they were so using it more than a decade before the date of the first English example cited by the NED. It had appeared in " Alice in Wonderland " in 1865,[3] and in 1867 *Every Saturday* of Boston [4] reprinted a note from *Notes and Queries* (London) saying that the London *Times* had twice used it to designate a palaver of politicians at the home of W. E. Gladstone, then Chancellor of the Exchequer and just turned Liberal. The *Notes and Queries* correspondent objected to the use of the term on the ground that the meeting was not secret, but only showed thereby a misunderstanding of its meaning, for an American *caucus*, though it usually goes on behind closed doors, is not necessarily secret. " *Caucus*," added this

1 An *anti-caucus* movement is traced by the DAE to 1824.
2 " The *caucus* system," said W. E. H. Lecky in Democracy and Liberty; London, 1896, Vol. I, p. 149, " is but another name for the American *machine*." Somewhat similarly, the English have preserved the meaning of an American election term that is now obsolete at home. It is the noun *electioneer*, signifying a political campaigner. It was used by Lowell in the first series of The Biglow Papers, 1848, and may have been

launched by him. The DAE cites no later American example. But I find the following in the London *Times Literary Supplement*, Sept. 9, 1944, p. 444: " Besides being a politician, the author of this pamphlet is a Fellow of All Souls, and it is in that capacity rather than as a Conservative *electioneer* that he has written it."
3 I am indebted here to Mr. Granville Toogood of Philadelphia.
4 May 18, p. 637.

Englishman, " is by no means a pretty, much less a desirable word, to be added to our national vocabulary," but it was already on its way into English usage.

The date of the introduction of *buncombe* remains undetermined. A writer in *Niles' Register* in 1827 [1] said that " talking to *Bunkum* " was already " an old and common saying at Washington," but neither *bunkum* or *buncombe* has been found at an earlier date and neither is recorded again until 1841. *Bunkum*, in its early days, seems to have had the additional meaning, as an adjective, of excellent.[2] The origin of the noun is thus given in John H. Wheeler's " Historical Sketches of North Carolina," [3] quoted by Bartlett (second edition, 1859):

> Several years ago, in Congress, the member from this district [i.e., the one including *Buncombe* county, of which Asheville is the county-seat] arose to address the House, without any extraordinary powers, in manner or matter, to interest the audience. Many members left the hall. Very naïvely he told those who remained that they might go too: he should speak for some time, but " he was only talking for *Buncombe*." [4]

The New International Encyclopedia [5] says that this occurred during the Sixteenth Congress, 1819–21 and that the hon. gentleman's theme was the Missouri question.[6] Why the spelling *Bunkum* should have arisen I do not know. It is possible, of course, that the name of the North Carolina county was originally spelled *Bunkum*, but on that point I am aware of no evidence. The English, who prefer *bunkum* to *buncombe*, began to use the term about 1850, but they have stoutly resisted *bunk*, and *to debunk* arouses their indignation.[7]

1 Sept. 27, p. 66. I take this from Thornton.
2 That meaning still survives in dialect. See *Bunkum*, by Louise Pound, *American Speech*, Feb., 1941, p. 74.
3 Philadelphia, 1851; Vol. II, p. 52.
4 *Buncombe* county was named after a pioneer named Colonel *Buncombe* in 1791.
5 Second ed.; New York, 1917, Vol. IV, p. 155.
6 In *American Speech*, Feb., 1930, p. 222, Thomas Perrin Harrison, Sr., reports, on the authority of Samuel à Court Ashe, a North Carolina historian (1840–1938), that the speaker was Felix Walker, who represented the Buncombe district from 1817 to 1823.
7 One of the not infrequent newspaper wars upon it went on in 1935. It was provoked by its use in the title of a book, Art Debunked, by Hubert Furst. See the letter columns of the London *Daily Telegraph*, March 2, 4 and 9, 1935. One correspondent, A. E. Sullivan, declared that it originated in " the inability of an ill-educated and unintelligent democracy to assimilate long words. Its intrusion into our own tongue," he went on, " is due partly to the odious novelty of the word itself, and partly to the prevailing fear that to write exact English nowadays is to be put down as a pedant and a prig." The NED Supplement traces it in English use (though quoted as an Americanism) to 1927. Who invented it I do not know. It is com-

The American comic poet, John G. Saxe (1816-87), used *bunkum* in his poem, " Progress," in 1846. The verb *to buncombe* appeared in 1855, but it seems to have been assimilated in the course of time to *to bunco*, an entirely different word. *To bunco* is traced by the DAE to 1875 and *bunco-steerer* to the same year. The modern short form *to bunk*, and its derivative *to debunk*, are not listed, though *bunk*, a bed, and a number of its derivatives are.

*Gerrymander*, as a noun, is traced by the DAE to 1812, and as a verb, to 1813. The origin of the term was thus recorded in " A Memorial History of Boston ": [1]

> In 1812, while Elbridge Gerry was Governor of Massachusetts,[2] the Democratic Legislature, in order to secure an increased representation of their party in the State Senate, districted the State in such a way that the shape of the towns forming . . . a district in Essex county brought out a territory of regular outline. This was indicated on a map which Russell, the editor of the *Continent*,[3] hung in his office. Stuart the painter,[4] observing it, added a head, wings and claws, and exclaimed " That will do for a salamander! " " Gerrymander! " said Russell, and the word became a proverb.

Bartlett says that this first *gerrymandering* occurred in 1811, not 1812. He goes on:

> In Massachusetts, for several years previous, the Federal and Democratic parties stood nearly equal. In that year the Democratic party, having a majority in the Legislature, determined to so district the State anew that those sections which gave a large number of Federal votes might be brought into one district. The result was that the Democratic party carried everything before them at the following election, and filled every office in the State, although it appeared by the votes returned that nearly two-thirds of the voters were Federalists.

Pickering overlooked *gerrymander* when he brought out his Vocabulary in 1816, but it was already in wide circulation by that time,

---

monly ascribed to W. E. Woodward, who published a novel called *Bunk* in 1923 and a *debunking* life of George Washington in 1926, but he has disclaimed its paternity.

1 Edited by Justin Winsor; four vols.; Boston, 1880-81, Vol. III, p. 222.

2 Gerry (1744-1814) was one of the early champions of democratic rule and a vigorous opponent of the Federalists. He was a member of the Massachusetts Legislature before the Revolution, and in 1776 he was elected to the Continental Congress. He resigned his seat in 1780 but re-

sumed it in 1783. He was a delegate to the Constitutional Convention in 1787, but refused to sign the Constitution as drafted. After two terms in Congress he was elected Governor of Massachusetts in 1810. He became Vice-President of the United States in the second Madison administration, and died in office.

3 If this was the Russell before noted, his paper was actually the *Columbian Centinel*, not the *Continent*.

4 Gilbert Stuart (1755-1828) specialized in portraits of Washington, and dozens of them still survive.

and the Boston *Gazette* said so early as April 5, 1813 that it was being
" used throughout the United States as synonymous with *deception*." [1]
The Russell map, headed " The *Gerrymander* " and described by a
contemporary diarist as a *caricatura*, was printed in large numbers,
and the copies propagated the term. The verb *to gerrymander* appeared in 1813, and has been in use ever since. The English did not
adopt it until the 80s, but they now employ it as we do. It is commonly given a soft g, though *Gerry* has a hard one.

*Mugwump* is derived from an Algonquin word, *mugquomp*, signifying a chief, and was used by John Eliot in his famous Indian
Bible, 1663, as an equivalent of the *duke* which appears forty-three
times in the Authorized Version of Genesis XXXVI. It seems to have
been used only seldom down to 1884. On June 15 of that year the
ribald New York *Sun* applied it derisively to the Republicans who
refused to support James G. Blaine for the Presidency — many of them
men of means and consequence.[2] The epithet became popular instantly, and on June 20 the New York *Evening Post* reported that all
the Blaine organs were speaking of the Republican independents as
" Pharisees, hypocrites, dudes, *mugwumps*, transcendentalists, or
something of that sort." Some of the independents, far from resenting
the term, boldly adopted it, and on September 13 William Everett,
the son of Edward Everett, made a speech at Quincy, Mass., in which
he said:

I am an independent — a *mugwump*. I beg to state that *mugwump* is the best
of American. It belongs to the language of the Delaware Indians; it occurs many
times in Eliot's Indian Bible; and it means a great man.

---

1 It is possible that Pickering omitted
it in delicate consideration for the
feelings of the Gerry family. Some
years ago Dr. Atcheson L. Hench
found among the papers of M. Schele
de Vere at the University of Virginia an undated and unplaced newspaper clipping saying, on the authority of " Professor Porter of Yale,"
that it was omitted from Webster
1828 for the same reason. The widow
of Gerry lived in New Haven opposite Chauncey A. Goodrich, who
had married Webster's daughter
Julia in 1816, and the two families
were on intimate terms. *Gerrymander* in fact did not appear in
Webster until 1864, fifteen years
after Mrs. Gerry's death. The 1864
edition was edited by Noah Porter,
obviously the Professor Porter aforesaid. He was professor of metaphysics at Yale from 1846 to 1892 and
president of the university from 1871
to 1886. Born in 1811, he lived until
1892. Dr. Hench reported his find
in a paper read before the Present-
Day English section of the Modern
Language Association at Philadelphia, Dec. 29, 1934. I am indebted to
him for access to it.

2 In AL4, p. 107, I say that Theodore
Roosevelt was one of them. This is
an error. He voted for Blaine.

Since the campaign of 1884 *mugwump* has been in general use to indicate a political bolter, but it still carries the special significance of one professing to a certain undemocratic superiority. Soon after it came in General Horace Porter defined it as meaning " a person educated beyond his intellect," and years later another wit defined it as " one of those boys who always has his *mug* on one side of the political fence and his *wump* on the other." [1] The DAE traces *mugwumpery* and *mugwumpian* to 1885, *mugwumpism* to 1886, *mugwumpcy* to 1887 and *to mugwump* to 1889. The English adopted *mugwump* promptly, and Partridge says that it is now fully naturalized. The London *Saturday Review* used it so early as November 22, 1884, and by 1918 it had produced an adjective in England, *mugwumpish*, which is not reported in the United States by the DAE. It is still, however, regarded as a somewhat uncouth term by the English. In 1925 Sir Henry Hadow, then vice-chancellor of Sheffield University, delivered an address to the Royal Microscopic Society in which he said:

> I am always coming across those occasions of controversy in which some amazing person is either too superior or too unstable minded to join in with either side. I have hitherto thought and wanted to call him a *mugwump*, and have refrained from doing so because it is not a word of academic dignity; but in the future I shall know exactly how to deal with him. I shall call him a *neutrophil polymorphonuclear leucocyte*.[2]

*Filibuster* is an old word that has undergone a change of meaning in the United States. The NED says that it was derived originally from the Dutch *vrijbuiter*, a freebooter, and traces its use in that sense to *c.* 1587. In the 50s of the last century it began to be used in this country to designate the adventurers who were running arms to the revolutionists in Cuba and the Central American republics, and in that sense it is still a living term. But in 1853 a member of Congress termed the tactics of his opponents " *filibustering* against the United States," and by 1863 *to filibuster* had come to have the meaning of a delaying action on the floor. In this latter sense, however, it did not come into wide use until the 80s. The DAE traces *filibuster*, in the former sense, to 1851, *to filibuster* and *filibustering* to 1853, *filibusterism* to 1854, and *filibusterer* to 1855. The English know the meaning

---

1 Albert J. Engel: Speech in the House of Representatives, April 23, 1936.

2 *Mugwump* Denatured, New York *Times* (editorial), May 10, 1925.

of the term in its political sense, but seldom use it,[1] and the NED marks it " U. S.".

*Roorback,* signifying a political canard, is traced by Thornton to 1844. In that year the Ithaca (N. Y.) *Chronicle* printed some alleged extracts from an imaginary book entitled " Roorback's Tour Through the Western and Southern States," containing grotesque charges against James K. Polk, then the Democratic candidate for the Presidency, and they were promptly copied by the Albany *Journal* and other Whig newspapers. This hoax, there is reason to believe, was perpetrated by an Ithaca man named Linn, later described by the Philadelphia *Spirit of the Times* as " a violent Abolitionist and an intemperate man." [2] The author of the book was supposed to be a visiting German named Baron von *Roorback.* In part, his adventures were suggested by those of Baron Münchhausen, but there were also borrowings from " An Excursion Through the Slave States," by an Englishman named George William Featherstonehaugh,[3] who had spent many years in the United States but had never quite overcome his dislike of the country. One of the stories was to the effect that Roorback, in traveling through the South in 1836, had encountered an encampment of Negroes on the banks of a mythical Duck river, and had found that every one was branded with the letters J.K.P. The inference was that they were the property of Polk and had been shipped South for sale. *Roorback* was overlooked by Bartlett when he compiled his Glossary in 1848, and by Schele de Vere in 1872, but it survived in the American political vocabulary for many years and is still occasionally encountered.[4] *Scalawag* belongs to the same period. Bartlett says that it originated in Western New York and at first meant " a mean fellow, a scapegrace." After the Civil War era it was applied to the Northern carpet-baggers who invaded the South, and to the white Southerners who trained with them, and since then it has

1 An example of its use occurred in Joe Westwood Does a *Filibuster,* by Hector McNeil, M.P., London *Daily Express,* March 14, 1942. Westwood, a supporter of the government, made a delaying speech until the hour fixed for adjournment in order to choke off the threat of a motion of lack of confidence. He was on his legs less than half an hour.

2 Oct. 3, 1844. I take this from Thornton.
3 Two vols.; London, 1844.
4 See Abraham Lincoln: The Prairie Years, by Carl Sandburg; New York, 1926, Vol. I, pp. 343–44; and Something About Polk, *New Yorker,* Aug. 8, 1936, p. 13.

been used to designate any low-down politician. In the 50s it had variants, *e.g., scallywag, scallaway* and *scatterway*, but they have disappeared. I have encountered suggestions that it was derived from the Greek, but the DAE says that its origin is " obscure " and ventures upon no etymology. Inasmuch as it was also used, at one time, to designate small, runty horses and cattle, Webster's New International, 1934, surmises that it may come from *Scalloway*, the name of a district in the Shetland Islands in which such animals are bred, but for this there is no direct evidence.

Of the political terms not already discussed or listed, *mileage*, signifying a legislator's allowance for traveling expenses, is probably the oldest, for the DAE traces it to 1754, when it was used by Benjamin Franklin. The DAE does not call it an Americanism, but it apparently did not come into use in England until a century later. *Machine*, in the political sense, is traced to 1866, *machine-politician* to 1879, and *anti-machine* to 1881. *Machine-rule* and *machine-politics* followed in 1882, *machine-ticket* in 1887, and *machine-managers* in 1896. *Ballot-box*, of course, is not an Americanism, but *ballot-box stuffer* is, traced by the DAE to 1856. *Band-wagon*, an Americanism first thrown to the world in 1855, does not appear to have been taken into the political vocabulary until after 1900. *Banner State*, in the sense of the State which, in a Presidential election, gives the winning (or losing) candidate the largest majority (or plurality, or vote), was first used by the Whigs in the Harrison campaign of 1840. *Banner county* appeared at the same time, and *banner-district* soon afterward. *Barrel*, in the sense of a political fund (often *bar'l*), is traced by the DAE to 1880, but it notes that the term " is said to have originated in a dispatch to the St. Louis *Globe-Democrat* from Jefferson City [Mo.] about two weeks before the meeting of the Democratic [National] Convention in 1876, in St. Louis." Thornton traces *barrel-campaign* to 1884, and the DAE finds *barrell-candidate* in use in the same year. The DAE does not list *bee*, as in *presidential bee*, but it must be relatively old. *Presidential* itself came in before 1800, and was denounced by the *Monthly Anthology* (London) as a " barbarism," but in a little while the other English reviews were using it and it is now in good usage on both sides of the ocean. *Presidency* appeared at about the same time, and has since elbowed out the earlier English *presidentship*. The DAE does not list *bell-ringer*, in the sense of a bill introduced in a legislative body to extort money from those

whose interest it threatens, nor is there any listing of the analogous
*hold-up* and *shake-down*, at least as political terms. *Strike*, meaning
" a form of legislative blackmail," is traced to 1885, and Thornton,
in his supplement,[1] traces *fat-frying* to 1890. The DAE omits *ripper*,
in the sense of a bill designed to legislate members of the opposition
party out of office, but Webster's New International lists it, and it
has probably been in use since the 90s.[2]

In the days of heavy Irish immigration the ward-heelers of the
Eastern cities were often called *b'hoys*, but it has gone out. *Heeler*
is traced by the DAE to *c.* 1877, *ward-heeler* to 1888, *ward-politics*
to 1883 and *ward-politician* to 1860. *Wheel-horse* goes back to 1867.
*Boss*, from the Dutch *baas*, has been in common use in the United
States since *c.* 1800, but it did not acquire its special political significance until *c.* 1875. The DAE traces *bossism* to 1881 and *boss-rule* to
1882. *Boodle*, from the Dutch *boedel*, meaning property, goods, came
into use in the New York region so early as 1699, but it did not acquire the meaning of money until the 1850s, and was apparently not
used to signify political bribes and loot until after 1880. The DAE
traces *to boodleize* to 1886, *boodler* and *boodlerism* to 1887 and
*boodleism* to 1894. *Carpetbagger*, in the sense of a politico operating
outside his home territory, did not come into general use until the era
of Reconstruction, when the South was invaded by thousands of political adventurers from the North, but it was used to indicate a dubious
stranger so early as 1846. *Carpetbag* itself goes back to 1830 and
*carpet-sack* to 1855. The first political use of *dark horse*, borrowed
from racing, was in 1876, when it was applied to Rutherford B. Hayes.
*Dicker* and *divvy* are old words, but the former did not appear in the
political vocabulary until 1888 and the latter not until *c.* 1900. *To
engineer* became a political term toward the end of the 50s. The
*black-horse cavalry*, which *engineers bell-ringers*, *strikes* and *shake-
downs*, was first heard of in 1893. *Boom*, in the political sense, is
traced by the DAE to 1879, and with it came *to boom* and *boomster*.
*Boomlet* followed in 1887. *Brave*, in the sense of a Tammany man,
does not appear to have come in until 1871. It was borrowed, of course,
from the common designation of an Indian warrior, traced by the
DAE to 1819. Some of the other Indian terms used by or of Tammany

1 *Dialect Notes*, Dec., 1932, p. 287.
2 *Ripper* Bills, by J. R. Schultz, *American Speech*, Dec., 1937, p. 319.

are older. *Sachem* goes back to 1622 and has been used by Tammany since 1786. *Wigwam* came into the general speech in 1628 and was adopted by Tammany in 1787. Another political term of Indian origin that deserves greater popularity than it enjoys is *wikinski* or *wiskinski*, signifying a functionary told off to collect campaign assessments from officeholders.

*Graft*, in the political sense, is said to have been introduced by Joseph W. Folk, at that time circuit attorney in St. Louis. The publication of Josiah Flynt's " Tramping With Tramps " in 1899 had made Americans familiar with the significance of the term in the argot of criminals, and it was a natural thing to transfer it to the operations of the political scoundrels that Folk was called upon to prosecute. Just when this transfer was made has not been determined. The DAE's first example is dated 1903, but the word was undoubtedly in use before then. On the strength of his war upon *grafters* Folk was elected Governor of Missouri in 1904, and eight years later he was spoken of for the Democratic presidential nomination, but withdrew in favor of Champ Clark. He died in 1923. Since *graft* began to denote the thieving of crooked politicians the more elegant of the regular or dirt crooks have abandoned it for *grift*.[1] Partridge says that *graft* is now naturalized in England and the NED gives English examples from 1905 onward. Various verb phrases based on *to go* have been long in use in American politics. The DAE traces *to go for* to 1830, *to go with the party* to 1829 and *to go Democratic* to 1877, and Thornton traces *to go the whole hog*, in the political sense of to swallow the whole party programme, to 1832. *To groom* is found in the 70s, *gumshoe-campaign* in 1904, *to gumshoe* in 1912,[2] *to hornswoggle* (in political use) in 1856, and *to honeyfogle* (now obsolete) in 1855. Rather curiously, the DAE's first example of *job-holder* goes back no further than 1904 and it does not list *job-seeker* at all. Both, I am inclined to believe, must have come into use long before the turn of the century, though I am not too sure. *Contested election*, though not American in origin, is now virtually an Americanism, for in our sense of an election whose returns are challenged

1 According to a correspondent of the New York *Post*, June 2, 1923, signing himself H.P.S., the beautiful term *honest graft* was invented by " ex-Senator Plunkett of New York." The date was not given.

2 The Hon. *Gumshoe* Bill Stone, a distinguished Missouri statesman (1848–1918), was in Congress from 1885 to 1891 and a United States Senator from 1903 until his death.

the English do not use it. When they say *contested election* they mean one in which there is more than one candidate, and hence a contest. *Freeze-out* and *to freeze out*, in the political sense, are traced by Thornton to 1882. *Has-been, immunity-bath, keynote-speech, keynoter, mud-slinger, public-teat, public-trough, rake-off, steam-roller, third-house* and *to view with alarm* are all omitted by the DAE, which is sad, indeed, to see. *Public-crib*, however, is listed, and traced to 1853. *Third-party*, an Americanism, goes back to 1801, and *third-term* to 1833. *Steam-roller* was invented by Oswald F. Schuette, then Washington correspondent of the Chicago *Inter-Ocean*, to designate the rough devices used to force through the nomination of William H. Taft as the Republican presidential candidate in 1908. It has produced the inevitable verb, *to steam-roller*, and the adjective, *steam-rollered*. When *bloc* came in I have been unable to determine, but it was probably not long ago. The *farm-bloc* was not heard of as such until after World War I, though it had been in existence for a century. *To carry an election*, an Americanism, is traced by the DAE to 1848, *to crowd the mourners* to 1859, and *crowd*, in the sense of a political group, usually nefarious, to 1840. *To deliver the vote* is not recorded before 1893, but *to deliver the goods* was used in 1879. A number of terms embodying *election* are peculiarly American and relatively ancient. *Election-district* was in use before 1800, and *election-time* is traced to 1807. The DAE's first example of *election-fraud* is dated 1883, and of *election-bet*, 1925. Both, on further investigation, will no doubt turn out to be much older. In the early days it was customary for the victors in an election to celebrate with a party called an *election-ball*, but it survived into our own time only in the form of the now obsolete *inaugural-ball* or *inauguration-ball*, which the DAE traces to 1817. *Inaugural-address* goes back to 1805, and *to inaugurate* to 1789. *Grass-roots* has not yet got into the dictionaries: it seems to have been brought in by the Farmer-Labor party in 1920 or thereabout,[1] along with *dirt-farmer*.

The trade argot of Congress contains a number of relatively ancient Americanisms. *To get the floor* has been traced by the DAE to 1816, *to yield the floor* to 1835, *to obtain the floor* to 1842, *to take the*

---

1 The late Dr. Frank H. Vizetelly told me in 1935 that he had been informed that *grass-roots*, in the verb-phrase, *to get down to grass-roots*, was in use in Ohio *c.* 1885, but he could never track down a printed record of it, and neither could I. See *American Speech*, April, 1936, p. 186; Oct., 1936, p. 231; and Dec., 1936, p. 376.

*floor* to 1846, *to have the floor* to 1848 and *floor-leader* to 1899. *Gag-rule* goes back to 1810, *lame-duck* to 1863, *omnibus bill* to 1850, *non-committal* (an Americanism once denounced by English purists as barbarous) to 1829, *junket* to 1886, *joker* (inserted in a bill) to 1904, *insurgent* to 1904,[1] *cloakroom gossip* (the congressional equivalent of soldiers' *latrine gossip*) to 1920 (it must be much older), *pork* to 1879 and *pork-barrel* to 1913, *salary-grab* to 1873,[2] *senatorial courtesy* (whereby a Senator may veto a presidential nomination for office of anyone from his own State) to 1884, *slush-fund* to 1864, *straddler* and *to straddle* to 1884, *to stand pat* (from the terminology of poker) to 1896 and *standpatter, standpattism* and the adjective *standpat* to 1904, *smelling committee* to 1877,[3] *steering committee* to 1887, *sectional* to 1806 and *sectionalism* to 1855, and *calamity-howler* to 1892. Thornton's first example of *on the fence* is from the Richmond *Whig* of August 13, 1828, and the DAE's first is from *Niles' Register* of the same year. The DAE does not list either *closure* or *clôture*. The latter was borrowed from the French by the English in 1871 or thereabout, but when the House of Commons adopted rules for the limitation of debate in 1882 *clôture* was dropped for *closure*. Both have been used in this country, but *clôture* the more often.

The business of congressmen, like that of all other politicians, consists largely of the discovery, pursuit and laying of hobgoblins; this, indeed, is the chief phenomenon of the democratic process. Since the earliest days the two Houses have devoted immense amounts of time and wind to pursuing such wicked men and things as *Bourbons, slavocrats, embargoroons,*[4] *gold-bugs, plutocrats, nullifiers, war-hawks,*

---

1 The first *insurgents* to attract general attention were the congressmen who revolted against the iron rule of Speaker Joseph G. Cannon in 1909. In 1912 the term was applied to the followers of Theodore Roosevelt. It was obviously suggested by memories of the Cuban *insurgents*.

2 By an act of March 3, 1873, Congress raised the President's salary from $25,000 a year to $50,000, and the salaries of its own members from $5,000 to $7,500, both retroactive to March 4, 1871. There was such an uproar that the latter provision was repealed a little while later. Congressmen were paid $6 a day until

1856, when they raised their emolument to $3,000, where it stood until after the Civil War. An act of March 4, 1925 lifted their pay to $10,000. In 1909 the salary of the President was raised to $75,000, with a large expense account.

3 Bartlett, quoted by the DAE, says that the term originated "in the examination of a convent in Massachusetts by legislative order."

4 The *embargoroons* were those who favored the Embargo Act of 1807. They were as infamous for a while as *nullifiers, isolationists* and *economic royalists* became in later years.

*embalmed beef, imperialism, isolationists, nigger-lovers, muckrakers, rotten rich, pacifists,* the *trusts,* the *Interests, Wall Street, hell-hounds, tories, reactionaries, reds, fascists, money-sharps, European pauper labor,* the *whiskey-ring, pro-Germans, Japanese spies,* the *white-slave trade, economic royalists, princes of pelf, land-grabbers, land-sharks, mossbacks,*[1] the *open shop,* the *closed shop,* and *labor* and other *racketeers.* Even Washington made a contribution to the menagerie with *foreign entanglements;* as for Jefferson, he produced two of the best bugaboos of all time in his *war-hawks* and *monocrats.* From 1875 onward until the late 80s *waving the bloody shirt* was the chief industry of Republican congressmen, and from the early 90s onward *the crime of '73* engaged the Democrats. *Bourbon,* borrowed from the name of the French royal family, the members of which were said to never learn anything and never forget anything, has been traced to 1859, but it did not come into general use until after the Civil War, when it was applied to the unreconstructed Southern Democrats. *Tory,* of course, has been a term of opprobrium since the Revolution, when it was applied to one loyal to England; *loyalist* was a synonym, but not quite so offensive. *Tory* served so well that it was revived in 1812 to designate New England opponents of the second war with England, in 1861 for Southerners who favored the Union, in 1896 for advocates of the gold standard, and in 1933 for persons who refused to accept the New Deal.[2] *Gold-bug,* always employed in a contemptuous spirit, is traced by the DAE to 1878. *Reactionary* was used by J. A. Froude in his " History of England " so long ago as 1858, but it did not begin to appear in the American political vocabulary until the Bryan era, and it had begun to drop out when the New Dealers revived it in 1933. *Plutocrats* were first heard of in the late 70s [3] and the *trusts* at about the same time.[4] Since 1880, at least forty

1 *Mossback* was first used in 1885 to designate an Ohio Democrat of the conservative wing. Soon afterward it began to be used for any conservative.

2 *Tory* comes from an Irish word, *toraidhe,* meaning an outlaw, and was first used in 1646 to designate the dispossessed Irish who took to the bush against their English overlords. It began to be used as the name of the English conservative party in 1689. In England, as in this country, it has a derogatory signifi-

cance, and has been much used by demagogues.

3 The word was not an American invention. The NED traces it in English use to 1850, and *plutocracy* to 1652.

4 That is, in the sense of large industrial organizations, approaching or alleged to be approaching monopolistic proportions. In the common legal sense *trust* is traced by the DAE to 1700, and in the titles of *trust companies* to 1834.

different *trusts*, real and imaginary, have had the attention of Congress, *e.g.*, the *Coal, Whiskey, Oil, Gas*,[1] *Lumber, Railroad, Fertilizer, Gold, Meat, Telephone, Elevator, Money, Shipping, Steel, Beer, Flour*, and even *Baseball, Civil Service* and *Vice Trusts*. The first *trust-buster* appeared in 1877. *Imperialism* became so infamous under Democratic attack after the Spanish-American War that its Republican defenders sought to disguise it under the milder name of *expansion*. The *Interests*, not listed by the DAE, were first heard of during the Bryan saturnalia of vituperation at the end of the Nineteenth Century, but *Wall Street* had been under fire since the Civil War era, and *money-sharks* were denounced on the floor of the House so early as 1844. The Bryanists invented *hell-hounds of plutocracy*, but *economic royalist, prince of pelf* and *rotten rich* had to wait for the New Deal to born them. The DAE omits *vice-crusade, white-slave trade* and *Vice Trust*, which, in a vocabulary of Americanisms, is almost as sad an oversight as omitting *buffalo, home-run* or *Rotary*. The legend that *white-slave traders* infested the primitive movie-parlors of the land, and fetched their recruits by injecting morphine into their arms, was set afloat *c.* 1910, and soon won millions of believers. For a few years a young woman of any pulchritude, real or imaginary, was afraid to go into a crowd alone. There ensued furious *vice crusades* in all the larger cities, led by *vice-hounds* who were partly psychopaths but mainly frauds, and in a little while most of the old-time tolerated brothels were closed and their inmates were turned loose upon the poorer decent neighborhoods. The culmination of the frenzy came with the passage of the *Mann Act* in 1910.[2] In the ensuing test-case of Caminetti *vs.* the United States[3] Mr. Justice McKenna (with Chief Justice White and Justice Clarke agreeing) denounced the law as an incitement to blackmail, but it was upheld by a four to three vote, with one justice not voting, and a reign of blackmail duly followed.

Virtually all the more eminent politicoes in American history, including especially the Presidents, have made contributions to the roster of American political terms and slogans. I have mentioned some of those of Washington and Jefferson. Lincoln is chiefly remembered

1 It first appeared in 1888 as the *Coal-oil Trust*.

2 Named after its sponsor in the House, the Hon. James R. Mann, of Illinois (1856–1922). He lived to be ashamed of it.

3 Supreme Court of the United States, Oct. term, 1916.

for his more sonorous phrases, *e.g., government of the people, by the people and for the people,*[1] but he also invented or introduced many more homely things, *e.g., yellow dog* as a general indicator of inferiority. He was also probably the author of *the great masses of the plain people,* later worked so hard by Bryan. The heroes between Lincoln and Cleveland were not phrase-makers, but some of them were the beneficiaries or victims of phrases made by others, *e.g., plumed knight,* applied to Blaine by Robert Ingersoll in 1876,[2] and the *rum, Romanism and rebellion* of the Rev. S. D. Burchard in 1884.[3] With the advent of Cleveland came a revival of word and phrase making: he was responsible for *innocuous desuetude*[4] and not a few others, and was falsely credited with " Public office is a public trust."[5] McKinley, who succeeded him, was likewise credited with *manifest destiny,* but the DAE shows that it had been used so early as 1858 and I have found at least one example even earlier.[6] He seems to have actually coined *benevolent assimilation:* this was in 1898 and he used it to describe the annexation of the Philippines. His followers revived and propagated *honest dollar* and *full dinner-pail,* neither of them new. They also called him the *advance-agent of prosperity,* 1897. Bryan's masterpiece was *cross-of-gold-and-crown-of-thorns,* launched at the Democratic national convention in Chicago, July 9, 1896, but he also made many other phrases, including *deserving*

---

1 This was in his Gettysburg address, Nov. 19, 1863. It was by no means original with him. It has been traced, in substance, to Some Information Respecting America, by Thomas Cooper; Dublin, 1794; and it was used almost in Lincoln's words by Theodore Parker in a speech in Boston, May 29, 1850. It was also used in a slightly different form by Daniel Webster in a speech in the Senate, Jan. 26, 1830. See my New Dictionary of Quotations; New York, 1942, p. 902.

2 Speech at the Republican National Convention, June 5. " Like a *plumed knight,* James G. Blaine marched down the halls of the American Congress."

3 Speech as chairman of a delegation calling upon Blaine, Oct. 29: " We are Republicans, and don't propose to leave our party and identity ourselves with the party whose antecedents have been *rum, Romanism and Rebellion.*"

4 Message to Congress, March 1, 1886.

5 The idea was not original: it had been voiced by John C. Calhoun in a speech in the Senate, July 13, 1835. Moreover, Cleveland did not mention *public office.* What he actually said in his inaugural address, March 4, 1885, was: " Your every voter, as surely as your chief magistrate, under the same high sanction, though in a different sphere, exercises a public trust." " Public office is a public trust " first appeared in the Democratic national platform of 1892, but it is almost always credited to Cleveland.

6 *Harper's Magazine,* Feb., 1854, p. 414.

*Democrat.*[1] Theodore Roosevelt made or revived scores, *e.g., big stick,*[2] *malefactors of great wealth,*[3] *Ananias Club, preparedness* (1915), *mollycoddle,*[4] *weasel word,*[5] *nature-faker,*[6] *to pussyfoot,*[7] *strenuous life,*[8] *one hundred percent American, Armageddon, muckraker,*[9] *square deal,*[10] and *lunatic fringe.*[11] Woodrow Wilson was also fertile in neologisms; some of his inventions were *little group of wilful men, new freedom, peace without victory,*[12] *too proud to fight,*[13] *watchful waiting,*[14] *to make the world safe for democracy, open covenants openly arrived at,*[15] and *pitiless publicity.*[16] Then came Harding, with *normalcy* [17] followed by Coolidge with " Well, they *hired* the *money,*[18] didn't they? " and " I do not *choose* to run." Both of these

1 Letter to Walker W. Vick, receiver-general of the Dominican Republic, Aug. 20, 1913. Bryan was then Secretary of State in Wilson's Cabinet, but kept a watchful eye on the party fences.

2 Speech at the Minnesota State Fair, Sept. 2, 1901.

3 Speech at Provincetown, Mass., Aug. 20, 1907.

4 Traced by the NED to 1833.

5 Speech in St. Louis, May 31, 1916.

6 Apparently first used in an article in *Everybody's Magazine*, Sept., 1907.

7 The DAE traces *pussy-footed* to 1893. A distinguished dry of the Prohibition era was the Rev. *Pussyfoot* Johnson.

8 Speech in Chicago, April 10, 1899.

9 *Muckrake* is an old word, traced by the NED to 1684, but Roosevelt seems to have invented *muckraker*. He first used it in a speech in Washington, April 14, 1906.

10 Campaign speech, Nov. 4, 1904. This term, of course, was not invented by Roosevelt. Mark Twain used it in *Life on the Mississippi* in 1883.

11 Letter to Henry Cabot Lodge, Feb. 27, 1913.

12 Address to the Senate, Jan. 22, 1917.

13 Speech in Philadelphia, May 10, 1915. Wilson's right to the invention of this phrase is disputed by Oswald G. Villard.

14 Message to Congress, Dec. 2, 1913.

15 Address to Congress, Jan. 8, 1918.

16 This phrase is to be found in R. W. Emerson's The Conduct of Life, ch. VI, 1860. But Wilson made it generally known.

17 A word much derided by American intellectuals, but of respectable ancestry. The NED quotes its use in a mathematical treatise of 1857, as follows: " If we denote the co-ordinates of the point of attack, and *normalcy,* by $x''$ and $y''$. . ." *Abnormalcy* has also appeared. It was used twice (p. 4) by Dr. A. N. Holcombe in Hearing of the New York Newspapers . . . in Protest to [sic] the Grant of Newsprint Made to the New York *Mirror* in Docket No. R–628; War Production Board, Verbatim Transcript Reported by Office for Emergency Management, Division of Central Administration; Services, Minutes and Reports Section; Washington, 1944. Dr. Holcombe, who is a Harvard Ph. D. who pursued further studies in Berlin, Munich, Paris and London, is professor of government at his *alma mater* and was borrowed by the New Deal in 1942 to be chairman of the Appeals Board, War Production Board.

18 Coolidge, of course, did not invent *to hire* in this sense: he was simply speaking his native Vermont patois. " In recent usage," says the DAE, " few Americans would *hire* land or a house; they would *rent* them. A car would be *rented* but a moving-van would probably be *hired,* the difference seeming to be that things

were sound old American terms. The DAE traces *to hire,* in the sense of to borrow, to 1782, and *to choose,* in the general sense of to elect, must be quite as old. Al Smith, in the period after Coolidge, introduced *baloney* (dollar), *alphabet soup, off the record,*[1] and various other pungent terms. Also, during this period, many other publicists made contributions, *e.g.,* Senator George H. Moses of New Hampshire, with *sons of the wild jackass* to designate the insurgent Republicans of the Western wilds. Hoover will be remembered chiefly, I suppose, for *rugged individualism*[2] and *noble experiment,*[3] the latter of which aroused the implacable dudgeon of the wets and so helped to ruin him. So did *Hooverville,* which he certainly did not invent.

With the Depression[4] and the New Deal came a great flood of novelties — the greatest since the days of Roosevelt I, *e.g., forgotten man,*[5] *economic royalist,*[6] *prince of pelf, horse-and-buggy days, to prime the pump, yardstick, rendezvous with destiny,*[7] *coördinator, directive, ceiling-price, rotten rich, underprivileged, boondoggling,*[8] *more abundant life, court-packing, death-sentence, client* (for bene-

---

are *rented* if no service or labor goes along with them, but are *hired* if a person is employed with them." I doubt that this distinction is valid: one might either *rent* or *hire* a typewriter. *Hired-man, hired-girl* and their like are discussed elsewhere: see the List of Words and Phrases. The American sign, *For Rent,* usually becomes *To Let* in England. In recent years there has been some American imitation of *To Let.*

1 The DAE traces *on record* to 1900, but does not list *off record* or *off the record.*

2 Speech in New York, Oct. 22, 1928. See Coiner, *News-Week,* April 10, 1937, p. 3.

3 Letter to William E. Borah, Feb. 28, 1928. His exact words were: " a great social and economic experiment, noble in motive."

4 Language of the Depression, by Charles Carpenter, *American Speech,* Dec., 1933, pp. 76–77.

5 Borrowed from the title of a speech by William Graham Sumner, delivered in 1883. This speech was reprinted in The *Forgotten Man* and

Other Essays; New Haven, 1919, and again as a pamphlet. The *forgotten man* of Sumner was the hard-working, self-supporting fellow who pays his own way in the world and asks for no favors from anyone. Roosevelt converted him, by a curious perversion, into a mendicant beneficiary of the New Deal doles.

6 Second speech of acceptance, June 27, 1936.

7 The same speech. Obviously suggested by Alan Seeger's poem, I Have a *Rendezvous* With Death, 1916.

8 Said an anonymous contributor to *Word Study,* Sept., 1935, p. 2: " *Boondoggle* was coined for another purpose by Robert H. Link of Rochester. Through his connection with scouting the word later came into general use as a name given to the braided leather lanyard made and worn by Boy Scouts." When the New Deal got under way the term was transferred to the innumerable useless tasks performed by recipients of its doles.

ficiary), *bottle-neck, isolationist, moral climate* [1] and *good neighbor policy. New Deal* was launched in Roosevelt's speech of acceptance, July 2, 1932. It was apparently an amalgam of the *square deal* of Roosevelt I and the *new freedom* of Woodrow Wilson, and is said to have been devised by Samuel I. Rosenman, the candidate's private counsel and intimate adviser and later a judge of the New York Supreme Court.[2] On December 21, 1943 Roosevelt told Delworth Lupton of the Cleveland *Press* that he had tired of it and hoped it would be abandoned for *Win the War* or something of the sort,[3] but it continued in use. *Brain Trust* has been ascribed to Dr. James M. Kieran, president of Hunter College, New York, but it was actually invented by another James M. Kieran, a reporter for the New York *Times.* This was at Hyde Park, N. Y., where Roosevelt was preparing campaign speeches with the aid of three Columbia University professors, Raymond Moley, Rexford G. Tugwell and Adolf A. Berle, Jr. When informed at a press conference that they were in residence Kieran exclaimed, " *The Brains Trust!* ", and soon afterward he used the phrase in a dispatch to the *Times.*[4] He has recorded that he " kept writing it in stories for some time, and some inspired *Times* copy-reader kept cutting it out before it finally sneaked by and got into actual print." [5] It was then adopted by other reporters,

1 Second inaugural address, Jan. 20, 1937.
2 The Roosevelt Revolution, First Phase, by Ernest K. Lindley; New York, 1933, pp. 26 and 27. The *New Freedom* was the title of a book by Wilson; New York, 1913. A large part of it was written by William Bayard Hale. Roosevelt's own somewhat vague account of the origin of *New Deal* was printed in *Liberty,* March 12, 1938, as follows: " On the occasion of the all-night session of the Democratic National Convention in Chicago, in 1932, I was at the Executive Mansion in Albany with my family and a few friends. While I had not yet been nominated, my name was still in the lead among the various candidates. Because I intended, if nominated, to make an immediate speech of acceptance at the convention itself in order to get the campaign quickly under way, we discussed what I should say in such

a speech. From that discussion and our desire to epitomize the immediate needs of the nation came the phrase 'A *New Deal*' which was used first in that acceptance speech and which has very aptly become the popular expression to describe the major objectives of the administration."
3 Associated Press dispatch from Washington, Dec. 23, 1943. In Feb., 1944 Vice-President Henry A. Wallace explained that " to some the definition of *New Deal*" has come to be " Washington bureaucrats and red tape." Wallace himself seems to have launched *century of the common man.* Whether *four freedoms* was invented by Roosevelt, by Churchill or by some anonymous ghost I do not know.
4 Associated Press dispatch from Albany, June 28, 1933.
5 Letter to *American Speech,* Dec.,

and soon *Brains* was reduced to the singular, and Louis McHenry Howe, General Hugh S. Johnson, Lewis W. Douglas, Hermann Oliphant, Arthur E. Morgan, Charles W. Taussig and others were added to the original personnel.[1] Some of the Roosevelt advisers did not like the term, but Roosevelt himself favored it. Johnson later testified that *Brain Trust* had been " used by the line of the Army as a sort of sour grapes crack at the first American general staff established by Elihu Root in 1901." [2] The coiner of *That Man* I do not know. *Globaloney* was the invention of the Hon. Clare Boothe Luce.[3] Many other words and phrases of a derisive sort are in local political use.[4]

Prohibition, which raged from 1920 to 1933, brought in a number of terms that threaten to be remembered, *e.g., home-brew, law enforcement, bathtub gin, highjacker* (or *hijacker*), *rum-runner* and *rum-row. Wet* is traced by the DAE to 1888 and *dry* to 1870. *To go dry* has been found in 1888 and *to vote dry* in 1904, and both are probably older. *Wet-goods* goes back to 1779. *Bone-dry* is not listed by the DAE, but it was probably in use before 1890. *Local option* is first recorded in 1884. During the thirteen theoretically dry years the *wets* invented *dry-dry* to designate a legislator who voted with the Anti-Saloon League and was yet dry personally; such prodigies were not numerous.[5] The *reds* who emerged from hiding on the establishment of the *entente* cordiale with Russia in 1940 have given us *fellow-*

1939, p. 247. The Hunter College Kieran died in 1936.

1 The English still use the plural. *Cf.* The *Brains Trust*, headline in the London *Times Literary Supplement*, April 22, 1944, p. 203.

2 Letter to *American Speech*, Feb., 1940, p. 79. The general's own chief contribution to the terminology of the era was *to crack down*. This was launched upon the country in 1933, when he was administrator of the N.R.A.

3 La Luce has coined or launched a number of other terms that have caught the public fancy, *e.g., snit*, meaning a fit of temper, which she introduced in her play, Kiss the Boys Good-bye, 1939. See Playwright Boothe Adds New Terms to her Mother Tongue, Philadelphia *Evening Public Ledger*, Nov. 13, 1939. In 1944 she used *to ramsquaddle,*

and a few days later explained that it meant " confused, muddled, or mixed up." She applied it to the bureaucrats of the New Deal, and said that it was " an old American word, used by the Missourians in particular." See Associated Press dispatch from Greenwich, Conn., Aug. 10, 1944.

4 See, for example, New Epithets Helped Put Skids Under Officials, by George W. Healy, Jr., *Editor and Publisher*, March 30, 1940, p. 7, dealing with pejoratives used in Louisiana in the war against the last survivors of the Huey Long machine.

5 For many years the ranking souses in both Senate and House were officially Prohibitionists. I hope to print a list of them in my confidential memoirs, to be published *post mortem.*

*traveler,*[1] *cell,*[2] *to follow the party line, people's* (or *popular*) *front, to bore from within* and *transmission belt,* have revived and propagated *left, left-wing, leftist,*[3] the corresponding forms of *right* and *center, to indoctrinate,*[4] *underground,*[5] *class struggle,*[6] *reactionary,*[7] *counter-revolutionary,*[8] *proletarian* and its derivatives,[9] and *Trojan horse,*[10] and have helped to make *fascist* and *bourgeois*[11] general terms of abuse.[12]

1 Max Lerner, in Mr. Roosevelt and His Fellow-travelers, *Nation,* Oct. 24, 1936: "The term has a Russian background and means someone who does not accept all your aims but has enough in common with you to accompany you in a comradely fashion part of the way."

2 The NED Supplement traces *cell* in English use, in the sense of "a center or nucleus of propaganda," to 1930. It is probably a borrowing from the Russian.

3 See Right and Left Words, by George P. Wilson, *Words,* May, 1937, pp. 102–05. *Left,* in the sense of a radical faction, was introduced by Carlyle in his French Revolution in 1837. It comes from the French *côté gauche* (left side). In the French Assembly of 1789 the conservative nobles sat to the presiding officer's right, the radicals of the Third Estate to his left, and the moderates directly before him, in the center. The NED traces *left-wing* (of an army) to 1707. *Centrist* first appeared in English use in 1872.

4 *To indoctrinate,* in the sense of to teach, has been used in England since the early Seventeenth Century, but in the sense of to fill with a chosen doctrine it is not traced beyond 1832.

5 In the sense of secret, surreptitious, *underground* is traced in English use by the NED to 1632. *Underground-railroad* was used in the United States, from *c.* 1840 to the Civil War, to designate a chain of hiding-places for the use of slaves escaping from the South.

6 A borrowing from the early Socialist writers, listed by neither the NED nor the DAE. *Class* was used

in England to designate one of the levels of human society so early as 1656, but the current compounds all came much later and show Socialist influence. Dickens used *class-griev-ance* in 1852, Emerson used *class-legislation* in 1856, the London *Times* spoke of *class-prejudice* in 1861, and Buckle wrote of the *war of the classes* a year or so later. But the NED Supplement's first example of *class-consciousness* is dated 1887, its first of *class-conflict* 1919, and its first of *class-hatred* 1928. The whole *class*-vocabulary was adopted by advocates of the New Deal after 1933.

7 In the current sense of a political conservative *reactionary* was used by Froude in 1858. It is now used to designate any opponent of a new device to save humanity.

8 Gouverneur Morris used *counter-revolutionary* in 1791 and *counter-revolution* in 1793, and may have invented them, for the NED offers no earlier examples.

9 *Proletarian* comes from the Latin *proletarius,* a member of the lowest class in Roman society. The NED traces it in English use as a noun to 1658 and as an adjective to 1663. The derivatives are all later. *Proletariat* is traced to 1853, *proletarianism* to 1851, *proletarianization* to 1918 and *proletarianized* to 1921.

10 From the large wooden horse built by Epeus for Ulysses, in which the Greeks gained entrance to Troy, and then emerged to take the town. It was applied to Wendell L. Willkie during the campaign of 1940. Willkie himself popularized *American way of life* in that campaign, but did not invent it. It had been used

Since the earliest days the chief statesmen of the United States have rated eulogistic nicknames, and some of them are familiar to every schoolboy, *e.g.*, the *Father of His Country* for Washington, *Honest Abe* for Lincoln, *Old Hickory* for Jackson, the *Little Giant* for Stephen A. Douglas, the *Great Commoner* for Clay, and the *Commoner* for Bryan. But respectable schoolboys are not informed that Washington, in his lifetime, was often spoken of by his critics as the *Stepfather of His Country* and the *Old Fox*. Nor have they heard, unless they live in the darker areas of the South, that the sainted Lincoln, now exalted to a place scarcely below Washington's in the American hagiology, was derided by Confederates and Northern Democrats alike as the *Baboon*, a brilliant but indelicate reference to his aspect.[1] Grant, because he was always the soldier more than the politician, escaped with nothing worse than the *Butcher*, but his successors got it hot and heavy. Hayes was the *Fraud* and *Granny*,

---

by Roosevelt II in his second speech of acceptance at Philadelphia, June 27, 1936, and by others before him. See The *American Way, American Notes and Queries*, May, 1941, p. 23.

11 *Bourgeois* is French, but has been in English use since the latter part of the Seventeenth Century. Said a writer in the London *Observer*, Dec. 11, 1938: "How did the word *bourgeois* come to be a term of abuse? No one ever laughed at 'Les Bourgeois de Calais' either in history or art. Yet when, at the time of the French Revolution, the question arose of finding a name for the ordinary man, the word chosen was *citoyen*, not *bourgeois*. It was the rise of Continental Socialism, with its glossary of regrettable words like *proletariat*, that gave *bourgeois* its Aunt Sally reputation. Perhaps it has become too tainted ever to be fit for non-controversial use again." *Bourgeois* simply means citizen, but is commonly used in France to designate the middle class. The *bourgeois* of Calais were six citizens who risked their lives against the English during the siege of the town by Edward III in 1347, and were saved from his vengeance by the pleas of his queen, Philippa of

Hainaut. *Aunt Sally*, traced by the NED to 1861, is the name of a game played at English fairs, analogous to the American *hit-the-nigger-baby-and-get-a-cigar*. Aunt Sally, a grotesque figure smoking a pipe, has become the symbol of dowdy unpleasantness. Partridge says that the term is used jocularly to designate a wicket-keeper in cricket.

12 There is a bibliography of books and papers on American political terminology in Burke, pp. 104 and 105. To it may be added More Political Lingo, by Charles Lindsay, *American Speech*, July, 1927, p. 443; A Dictionary of American Politics, by Everit Brown and Albert Strauss; New York, 1888 (revised and enlarged under the same title by Edward Conrad Smith; New York, 1924); Twisting the Dictionary to Pad Political Vocabulary, New York *Times*, Dec. 16, 1923; and A Political Dictionary, by Eugene Whitmore; Chicago, 1940. See also American Variations, by H. W. Horwill, *S.P.E. Tract No. XLV*, 1936, p. 187.

1 He was also called the *Ape*, probably influenced by *Abe*. The members of the White House secretariat called him the *Tycoon*.

Arthur was the *Dude*, Cleveland was the *Stuffed Prophet* and the *Hangman*,[1] Roosevelt I was the *Bull Moose*, the *Man on Horseback* and *Teddy the Meddler*, Wilson was the *Phrasemaker* and the *Schoolmaster*, Coolidge was *Silent Cal* (always with a sneer), and Hoover had nicknames that had better be forgotten. So with many of those who, after years of ardent membership in the Why-not-me? Club, failed of the capital prize. Calhoun was the *Great Nullifier*, Samuel J. Tilden was *Slippery Sam*, Webster was *Black Dan*, Blaine was the *Tattooed Man*,[2] Charles Sumner was the *Bull of the Woods*, Charles Curtis was the *Indian*, Charles G. Dawes was *Hell and Maria*, W. R. Hearst was the *Yellow Kid*, Charles E. Hughes was the *Feather-Duster*, and John Nance Garner was *Cactus Jack*, *Poker Face* and the *Owl*.[3] Even Mrs. Lincoln had a nickname, to wit, the *She-wolf*. In every campaign since Jefferson's first attack upon the Federalists there has been a vast emission of billingsgate,[4] and more than one figure in American politics is remembered for his prodigies of invective, *e.g.*, the two Roosevelts and Wilson. In our own time one of the most gifted and industrious practitioners has been the Hon. Harold L. Ickes. Some of his masterpieces were assembled in 1940 by Fon W. Boardman, Jr.,[5] *e.g.*, *Trilby* for Alfred M. Landon and *Svengali* for W. R. Hearst, *condittieri* for the newspaper columnists hostile to the New Deal, *jeer leader* for one of them, *vestal virgins* for the members of the unfortunate Liberty League, and *intellectual Dillingers* [6] for other persons he disliked. In return Ickes was given the appellation of *Donald Duck* by Westbrook Pegler. The late General Hugh S. Johnson was both in and out of the New Deal corral and did some loud howling on both sides of the barbed wire. While he was running the NRA he denounced its Republican critics as *intel-*

1 A reference to the fact that, as sheriff of Erie county, N. Y., he hanged a murderer.

2 Suggested by a cartoon of that title by Bernhard Gillam, in which he was depicted as clad in a robe inscribed with the names of the numerous scandals with which his name had been connected. It appeared in *Puck*, April 16, 1884.

3 Many other such nicknames are listed in American Nicknames by George Earle Shankle; New York, 1937, a very useful book, carefully documented.

4 Many amusing examples are assembled in Insults: A Practical Anthology of Scathing Remarks and Acid Portraits, by Max J. Herzberg; New York, 1941.

5 Political Name Calling, *American Speech*, Dec., 1940, pp. 353–56.

6 From the name of *John Dillinger*, an eminent bandit of the early 30s, butchered by FBI agents on July 22, 1934. He was the first *Public Enemy No 1*, a phrase apparently invented by Homer S. Cummings, then Attorney-General.

*lectual prostitutes, academic mercenaries, kippered herring* and *hip-popotami,* and after he became debamboozled he flayed his late colleagues in the salvation of humanity in the same ferocious manner, calling them *breast-beaters, wand-waving wizards, janissaries,* and *Adullamites.*[1] He is also said to have invented the pungent *third termite.* The series of nicknames that began with *Tommy the Cork* for Thomas G. Corcoran is said to have been launched by Mr. Roosevelt himself. Other hands contributed to it, and it presently included *Henry the Morgue* for Henry Morgenthau, Jr., *Leon the Hen* for Leon Henderson, *Benny the Cone* for Benjamin V. Cohen, and *Harold the Ick* for Ickes. According to Boardman, before cited, Gerald L. K. Smith changed the last to *the Itch.* Other critics have denominated Ickes the *gorilla,* the *night-striking cobra,* and the *blunderbuss.*[2]

### 3. LOAN-WORDS AND NON-ENGLISH INFLUENCES

150. [The Indians of the Far West, it would seem, had little to add to the contributions already made to the American vocabulary by the Algonquins of the Northeast. Most of the new loan-words that were picked up west of the Mississippi came in either through the Spanish, *e.g., coyote,* or through the Chinook trade-jargon of the Columbia river region, *e.g., cayuse.*] Harold W. Bentley, in his excellent " Dictionary of Spanish Terms in English," [3] is content to mark *coyote* " from American Indian *coyotl,*" but the DAE and Webster 1934 ascribe it particularly to the Nahuatl language of Mexico, which was spoken, in various dialects, by tribes scattered from Panama to Idaho, and is still the mother-tongue of a large group of Mexican Indians. The DAE's first example of *coyote* is from Albert Pike's " Prose Sketches and Poems," 1834.[4] Pike spelled the word

1 I Samuel XXII, 1 and 2.
2 See also Electionisms, by Robert T. Oliver, *American Speech,* Feb., 1933, pp. 20–22.
3 New York, 1932, p. 129.
4 Pike is not to be confused with Zebulon M. Pike (1779–1813), the explorer after whom *Pike's Peak* was named. Zebulon was an Army officer who became a brigadier-general and was killed during the assault on York, Canada, in the War of 1812. Albert Pike was a Bostonian who went West in 1832, explored the headwaters of the Red and Brazos rivers, settled in Arkansas, was a cavalry commander in the Mexican War, rose to be a brigadier-general in the Confederate Army, and devoted most of the rest of his life to writing about Freemasonry. He was born in 1809 and died in 1891.

*collote*, and other early writers spelled it *coyotl, koyott* and *ciote*. It designates a prairie wolf, *Canis latrans*, never encountered in the East, but Western fiction and the movies have made its meaning familiar to all Americans. That *cayuse* came into American from the Chinook jargon is not certain, though there is a Chinook word, *kiuatan*, signifying a horse: both Webster 1934 and the DAE prefer to find its origin in the name of a tribe of Oregon Indians. The DAE's first example is from the Oregon *Weekly Times* of 1857, which used it in connection with a genuine Chinook word, *cultus*, meaning inferior. There is a strong tendency to ascribe all otherwise unidentified Indian loans to Chinook, but the actual borrowings of the pioneers seem to have been relatively few. Among them are *potlatch*, a gift, or, by extension, a party marked by lavish hospitality and gift-giving, traced by the DAE to *c.* 1861; *skookum*, large or powerful, traced to 1844; and *siwash*, a generic term for Indian, borrowed by the Chinook from the French *sauvage*, and first recorded in American use in 1852. Efforts have been made to derive *hooch* from the Chinook, but without much success. It apparently comes, in fact, from *hoochino* (or *hoocheno*), a name of unknown origin originally applied to a crude fire-water made by the Indians of Alaska.[1] On the advent of Prohibition this *hoochino* began to appear in the Northwestern coast towns, and soon its name was shortened to *hooch*, which quickly penetrated to all parts of the country.[2] *Hike* has been ascribed to the Chinook

---

[1] Dearborn (Mich.) *Independent*, March 3, 1923: "In 1869, when American troops were stationed in Alaska, they were forbidden to have any spirituous liquors. The soldiers took to making their own and concocted liquor noted for its power and vileness. The natives called it *hoocheno* and soon learned to make it."

[2] Chinook arose in the late Eighteenth Century, on the appearance of American fur-traders on the Oregon coast. Its original basis seems to have been the language of the Nootka, but the neighboring Chinooks soon learned enough of it for trading purposes. It is a jargon of very limited vocabulary, with no inflections. It includes French and English words, and also a few formed by onomatopoeia. There

have been many dictionaries of it, but most of them are of small value. Among the latest are The Chinook Jargon and How To Use It, by George C. Shaw; Seattle, 1909 (with a bibliography); Dictionary of the Chinook Jargon, by Frederic J. Long; Seattle, 1909; and Gill's Dictionary of the Chinook Jargon; 15th ed.: Portland, Ore., 1909. Useful discussions of the jargon are in The Chinook Jargon, by Douglas Leechman; *American Speech*, July, 1926, pp. 531–34; The Chinook Jargon, by Edward Harper Thomas, *American Speech*, June, 1927, pp. 377–84; Chinook Dictionaries, by Edward Harper Thomas, *American Speech*, Feb., 1928, pp. 182–85; and Note on the Chinook Jargon, by Franz Boas, *Language*, June, 1933, pp. 208–13. There are three additional titles in

*hyak,* to hurry, but in that sense it did not come into common American use until after Chinook influence had died out.[1] The jargon is still spoken more or less by ancients in the Oregon country, both white and Indian, and a number of its terms, unknown elsewhere save in fiction, are familiar locally, *e.g., klootchman,* a woman; *wawa,* talk, *muckamuck,* food; *tenas,* small; *hyas,* big; *cheechako,* a stranger; *keekwilly,* a house, and *kla-how-ya?,* how are you? [2]

In the same way borrowings from the Indians of the Southwest are current in that region, though not in general use elsewhere, *e.g., hogán,* an Indian house; *mesquite,* a shrub; *peyote,* an intoxicant made of cactus; *sapote,* a persimmon; *pinole,* a dish of parched corn, sweetened; *tequila* or *mescal,* an intoxicant distilled from agave bulbs; and *wickiup,* a brush hut, now used to designate any mean habitation. *Wickiup* is derived by the DAE from an Algonquian language, but all the rest come from the Nahuatl, usually by way of the Spanish. This is true also of a number of words that have got into general circulation in the United States, *e.g., chili* and *tamale.* The word *Mexico* is likewise of Nahuatl origin, as are *tomato, cocoa, copal* (varnish), *chicle* (the gum of which chewing-gum is made), *chocolate, avocado* (pear) and *jalap.*[3] Some of these terms got into English in the days of the early explorations, and are hardly to be classed as Americanisms today, but others had to wait until the great movement into the West began. The DAE traces *tamale* to 1854, *mesquite* to 1838, *peyote* to 1849 and *mescal* to 1831. There were relatively few additions across the Mississippi to the translated Indian terms (or supposed Indian terms) listed in Chapter III, Section 1. The forest Indians of the East applied *father* to a friendly white in the

---

Burke, p. 150. Two other Indian jargons arose in the Eighteenth Century — in New Jersey and along the Gulf coast. The former, based on Lenape, is discussed in The Pequots' Language, by J. Dyneley Prince, *American Anthropologist,* April–June 1902, and the latter, called the Mobilian trade language, in Reminiscences of the Creek or Muscogee Indians, by Thomas S. Woodward, 1859. Both are now extinct.

1 It seems much more likely that it comes from *heik,* an English dialect verb signifying to swing. The DAE's first example of *hiking,* in the sense

of tramping, is spelled *heiking* and dated 1868. In the same era it seems to have had the sense of to hoist, still preserved in *to hike prices.* The NED Supplement traces *to hike* in English use, in the sense of to tramp, to 1809. This first example is from a letter by Samuel Wesley (1766–1837), son of Charles and nephew of John.

2 I am indebted here to Mr. William E. Ricker, of Vancouver, B. C.

3 Nahuatl Words in American English, by George Watson, *American Speech,* April, 1938, pp. 108–21.

Eighteenth Century, but it was not until the reservation Indians of the West began trooping to Washington with their grievances that *Great White Father* was heard of. *Snake-dance* is traced by the DAE to 1772, but it remained rare in American use until nearly a century later. *Squaw-man* is traced to 1866, but is probably older. *Happy hunting grounds* first appeared in Cooper's " The Pathfinder," 1840, and *Father of Waters* (for the Mississippi) is first recorded in 1812. That all Indians used *heap* and *heap big* as general intensives, and *how* as a greeting, and loosed frequently a grunt represented by *ugh* was believed firmly by the American boys of my generation, but the evidence is not too impressive.[1] The DAE traces *how* to 1817 and *heap* to 1850, but does not list *ugh*. What was supposed to be the universal Indian war-cry was produced in my youth by crying *wah* as loud as possible, and breaking it into a sort of trill by slapping the open palm against the lips.

As I have noted in Chapter III, Section 1, direct loans from the Spanish were relatively rare in American speech before 1800, but during the half century following they appeared in large number, and many additions have been made in our own time. Indeed, it is highly probable that American English has borrowed more terms from the Spanish than from any other language. " In some instances," says Bentley, " words have been adopted because there existed no adequate words in English. More often Spanish elements are taken over for local color effects, for their richness of connotation, including humor, for picturesqueness, or for descriptive contribution of some kind." He gives *siesta* as an example of the first class, and *savvy* and *juzgado* (corrupted to *hoosegow*) as examples of the second. Of loans that every American is familiar with the DAE traces *adobe* to 1821, *alfalfa* (usually called *lucern* in England) to 1855, *bonanza* to 1844, *bronco* to 1850, *burro* to 1844, *calaboose* (taken in by way of Louisiana French) to 1792, *canyon* (*cañon*) to 1834, *chapparel* to 1845, *cinch* (originally a saddle girth) to 1859, *corral* to 1839, *fiesta* to 1844, *frijole* to 1838,[2] *hombre* to 1846, *lariat* to 1835, *lasso* to

---

1 The analogous (and perhaps identical) *wagh* is said to have been used as a " greeting between Taos and Apache" in the early days of the Southwest. It is stated in The Southwestern Word Box, by T. M. P., *New Mexico Quarterly*, Nov., 1932, p. 344, that among the white trap-pers the term "substituted for most of the fill-in terms of present-day speech, such as *sure, that's right, O.K. by me, I'll say,* etc."

2 I am indebted to Dr. J. N. Tidwell, of Ohio State University, a native of Texas, for a reminder that *frijole* (pronounced *freeholay*) is the Span-

*1833, mesa* to *1844, mosey* (from *vamose*) to *1829, mustang* to *1808, padre* to *1844, patio* to *1827, peon* to *1826, placer* to *1842, plaza* to *1836, pronto* to *1850, ranch* to *1808, rodeo* to *1851, sabe* (or *savvy*) to *1875, señorita* to *1823, sierra* to *1844, sombrero* to *1836, stampede* to *1844, tortilla* to *1831,* and *vigilante* to *1867.* The Mexican War brought in a large number of Spanish terms [1] and the California gold rush brought in more. The Spanish-American War did not introduce *insurrecto, incommunicado, machete, junta* and *rurale,* but it made all Americans familiar with them. Others filter in more or less steadily. The DAE finds no example of the use of *loco* before 1883, or of *mañana* before 1889, or of *marihuana* before 1894, or of *chili con carne* before 1895, or of *wrangler* (as in *horse-wrangler*) before 1896, and its first example of *rodeo* in the sense of a traveling show is dated 1914. *Hoosegow,* from *juzgado,* is so recent that the DAE does not list it. As in the case of Indian loans, the vocabulary of Spanish words taken into the everyday speech of the West is very extensive. More than fifty years ago Professor H. Tallichet listed nearly 450 in a series of papers contributed to *Dialect Notes,*[2] and many other observers have added to the record since.[3]

Next to Spanish, German has probably made the heaviest donations to the American vocabulary. They range all the way from such

ish plural. But Americans insist on regarding *frijole* as singular, and add an *s* in the plural. So with *tamal* (*e*), borrowed from the Nahuatl by way of the Spanish.

1 One of them was *staked plains,* now obsolete. It came from the Spanish *llano estacado.* The DAE's first example is dated 1848.

2 A Contribution Towards a Vocabulary of Spanish and Mexican Words Used in Texas, Part V, 1892, pp. 185–96; Part V, 1893, pp. 243–53; Part VII, 1894, pp. 324–26. Tallichet's death, on April 16, 1894, probably prevented a considerable extension of the list.

3 The English Language in the Southwest, by Thomas Matthews Pearce, *New Mexico Historical Review,* July, 1932, pp. 210–32; Geographical Terms in the Far West, by Edward E. Hales, *Dialect Notes,* Vol. VI, Part IV, July, 1932, pp. 217–34; Geographical Terms From the Spanish

by Mary Austin, *American Speech,* Oct., 1933, pp. 7–10; Californese, by José Rodriguez, *Words,* Feb., 1936, pp. 16–17; Terms From the Spanish, by Stuart A. Northrup, *American Speech,* Feb., 1937, pp. 79–81; Trader Terms in Southwestern English, by Thomas M. Pearce, *American Speech,* Oct., 1941, pp. 179–86; Two Spanish Word-Lists From California in 1857, by George R. Stewart, *American Speech,* Dec., 1941, pp. 260–69. Bentley's Dictionary of Spanish Terms in English, already cited, lists about 430 words and phrases, including a number of American derivatives from Spanish loans, *e.g., doby, bronco-buster, burro-load, loco-weed, rancher* and *ranching.* An interesting discussion of *ten-gallon hat,* from the Spanish *sombrero galón,* by A. L. Campa, is in *American Speech,* Oct., 1939, p. 201.

familiar words as *sauerkraut, hamburger, frankfurter, noodle, gesundheit,*[1] *delicatessen, kindergarten, pretzel, nixy* and *ouch* to such phrases as *so long, wie geht's* and *rous mit 'im.* Unhappily, there has never been any really scientific investigation of their history, and only too often, especially since 1916, their discussion has been incommoded by partisan heat. The NED's first example of *sauerkraut* is from the " Itinerary " of Fynes Moryson, 1617, but Moryson recorded it as the foreign name of a foreign comestible, and both name and comestible retain a foreign smack in England to this day.[2] The thing itself seems to have been introduced to Americans by the Pennsylvania Germans, but the date is unknown, even approximately. The first occurrence of the word recorded by the DAE is in Alexander Wilson's poem " The Foresters," published in 1818 but probably written in 1813. There is then a hiatus until 1863, but *sauerkraut* must have been in frequent use in the interval,[3] and was familiar to many Americans, in all probability, long before 1813. The word is sometimes spelled *saurkraut, sourkraut, sourkrout* or *sourcrout,* but both the DAE and Webster 1934 prefer *sauerkraut,* which is the correct German form. It is hardly likely that it was taken into American from the Dutch, for the Dutch form is *zuurkool.* There has been a considerable controversy over *shyster,* formerly assumed to be a German loan but now in dispute. The DAE marks it " origin uncertain," as does Webster 1934. It has been traced to 1849. Webster 1909 suggested that it may have come from the Gaelic *siostair,* meaning a vexatious litigant, and the late Dr. Frank H. Vizetelly, editor of the Standard Dictionary, once proposed a Gipsy origin, but the matter remains undetermined.[4] The American *bum,* a shortened form of an earlier *bummer,* is commonly believed to have been suggested by the German verb *bummeln,* meaning to waste time, but the connection has not been established.[5] The DAE, whose first example of *bummer* is dated 1856, says that " in early use " the term

1 *Gesundheit* was used in Walt Disney's Pinocchio, 1940.

2 The English apparently prefer *pickled cabbage.*

3 An example from the Shippensburg (Pa.) *Herald* was reprinted in the Baltimore *Sun,* in June, 1838. The spelling was *sour crout* (two words). There is another in *Sartain's Magazine* (Philadelphia), Jan., 1852, p. 74, with the spelling *sauer-kraut.*

4 I am indebted here to Mr. Donald Powell of Washington.

5 David P. Marvin suggested in *Word Study,* Sept., 1935, that the original may have been the German *böhm,* "a Bohemian, a foot-loose wanderer," but for this I know no evidence.

was "confined to San Francisco," but it offers no etymology. During the Civil War *bummer* was used to designate a soldier who went foraging on his own. *Bumming*, in the sense of going on a carouse, is traced to 1860, but the DAE's first example of *bum* to designate such a carouse, is from 1871. *To bum* in the sense of to loaf or wander about is traced to 1863. *On the bum* and *to bum a ride* apparently did not come in until the last decades of the century. To the English *bum* means the backside, and is hence an inelegant term, but they use it without blushes in such pejorative compounds as *bum-bailiff* and *bum-boat*. The NED traces *bum* to 1387, *bum-bailiff* (used by Shakespeare) to 1601, and *bum-boat* to 1671. There is no evidence that the American permutations of *bum* owe anything to the English *bum*. *Loafer* is another possible German loan that remains in dispute. It is apparently derived from the German *landläufer*, meaning a vagabond, and on its first appearance in print, in the 30s, was sometimes *landloafer* and sometimes simple *loafer*. The DAE traces the verb form, *to loaf*, to 1837. The following early discussion of the term [1] is offered for what it is worth:

> *Loafer* . . . only found its way into writing about the year 1830, but it had been in use long before, especially in the vicinity of the [New York] markets. It is equivalent to *vagabond* intensified, and its personal application is one of the greatest insults that can be offered to an American — something like calling a Frenchman *canaille*. It is singular that the verb (of later formation) has not necessarily a bad meaning; a man will say of himself, "have been *loafing* about" — that is, "I have been lounging or idling." We must seek the root in Dutch. It *may* be from *loof*, primarily weary, tired, thence faint-hearted, lazy, cowardly; but it more probably comes from *loopen* ( = German *laufen;* compare in English *inter-loper*). The term *loper*, applied to deserters from South Sea whalers, and Jack-tar's familiar *land-lubber*, are probably connected. *Looper* in old Dutch, such Dutch as honest old Peter Stuyvesant may have used, meant a running footman, so that perhaps the idea of lackey or flunkey was mixed up with the term of contempt.

The DAE is anything but strong in the department of German loans, and passes over many of them without mention, *e.g.*, *zwieback*, *pumpernickel, sauerbraten, stein* (as in the Maine *Stein* Song), *gesundheit* (as a toast), *spieler, maennerchor, wanderlust, hausfrau, katzenjammer* and *Schweizer-cheese*. It traces *dumb*, in the American sense of stupid (a borrowing from the German *dumm*) to 1825; [2] *smearcase*

1 The English Language in America, by Charles Astor Bristed, in Cambridge Essays, Contributed by Members of the University; London, 1855, p. 68.

2 Its first example of *dumb-head* (*dummkopf*) is dated 1887. It does not list *dumbbell* or *dumb Dora* or *rum-dumb*.

to 1829; lifts *fresh* (from *frech*), in the sense of impertinent, from Bartlett, 1848;[1] and runs *ouch* (from *autsch*) back to 1837,[2] *bower* (in cards, from *bauer*) to 1844, *lager* to 1855, and *turnverein* to 1856, but its first example of *pretzel* is dated 1874, of *beer-garden* 1870, of *bock-beer* 1883,[3] of *delicatessen* 1893, of *wienerwurst* and *frankfurter* 1899, of *rathskeller* 1900, and of *hamburger* 1901. *Check*, in the sense of a restaurant bill, is traced to 1868, but there is no mention of its probable relation to the German *zeche*. *To dunk*, from the Pennsylvania German *dunke*, a dialect form of the German *tunken*, is not listed.[4] *So long* is traced to 1860 (when Whitman used it in a revision of " Leaves of Grass "), but there is no mention of its possible borrowing from the German *so lange*, a shortened form of *adieu so lange*.[5] *Nix, nixie* and *nixy* are recorded, but their relation to the German *nichts* is not noted, nor is there any mention of *aber nit* and *nitwit*.[6] It is noted, however, that the American *bub*, used as " a playful form of address to boys," is probably related to the German *bub(e)*, and its American history is traced to 1846, with a hint that it was probably known in 1837. It is also noted that *bushelman*, meaning a repairer of men's clothes, is probably related to the German *böscheln*. Scattered in the etymological literature, professional and lay, are discussions of various other possible American loans from the German. It has been suggested, for example, that *and how* may be

1 How America Got *Fresh*: Bits of a New Language Made in Germany, by Edward Shanks, London *Evening Standard*, Nov. 16, 1927: "An American, when he uses the word *fresh* of a person, means what in England we used to express by the word *saucy*. He has obviously appropriated the German word *frech*, which has almost exactly that meaning, but he has assimilated it to the English pronunciation."

2 Not infrequently it is abbreviated to *au*. See Interjections of Pain, by Steven T. Byington, *American Speech*, Dec., 1942, p. 278.

3 The term appears as *buck-beer* in The American Language, *Putnam's Magazine*, Nov., 1870, p. 523. Along with it is *shenk-beer*, which has passed out of the American vocabulary.

4 *To dunk* is discussed by Atcheson

L. Hench in *American Speech*, June, 1931, pp. 388–89.

5 *So-long* . . . , by H. Z. Kip, *Philological Quarterly*, Oct., 1927, pp. 400–05. Efforts have been made to connect it with the Arabic *salaam* and the Hebrew *sholom*, but without plausibility.

6 Nor of the *Sag Nichts* who opposed the Know Nothings before the Civil War. See Prenticeana, by George D. Prentice; New York, 1860, p. 211. *Nix*, in various senses, appeared in the cant of English rogues in the Eighteenth Century, though it is not recorded by Grose. It has never come into general use in England. In American Postal Laws and Regulations for 1879 *nixes* was defined as " misdirected second-class matter." The term is still in use in the Postoffice to designate undeliverable mail.

a translation of the German *und wie;* [1] that *cant-hook*, first recorded in 1848, may be from the German *kanthaken;* [2] that *it listens well* may be from *es hört sich gut an;* [3] that *hold on* may be an imitation of *halt an;* that the substitution of the American *shoe* for the English *boot* may have been helped by the German *schuh;* [4] that *to cut a face* may be from *er schneidet ein gesicht;* [5] that *bake-oven* may come from the German *backofen;* [6] that *slim* (as in *slim chance*) may be the German *schlimm;* [7] that such shortened and characteristically American forms as *cook-book, barber-shop* and *sail-boat* (for the preferred English *cookery-book, barber's shop* and *sailing-boat*, etc.) may have been promoted by German example; [8] and that the numerous American terms in *ker-* may owe something to the German *ge-*. [9]

In some of these suggestions, of course, there are signs of folk-etymology, [10] and all of them are to be received with extreme caution, but they at least reveal the lack of a scientific investigation of the subject. The number of German words and phrases that have been completely assimilated into American is quite large, and there is in addition a formidable number that are generally understood, though not altogether assimilated, *e.g., eins, zwei, drei, hofbrau, knackwurst, leberwurst, hoch, wie geht's, ganz* (or *sehr*) *gut, auf wiedersehen,*

1 *And how* and *und wie*, by E. E. Ericson, *Beiblatt zur Anglia*, June, 1937, p. 186; *And how*, by J. R. Schultz, *American Speech*, Dec., 1933, p. 80. Schultz offers the following quotation from a letter of Bayard Taylor to Edmund Clarence Stedman, June 16, 1865: "*And how?* as the Germans say; Americanicé — you'd better believe it."

2 Deutscher und englischer Sprachgebrauch in gegenseitiger Erhellung, by Friedrich Thiele, *German Quarterly*, Nov. 1938, pp. 185–90.

3 German Influences on the American Language, by Andreas Dorpalen, *American-German Review*, Aug., 1941, p. 14.

4 German Influences Upon English, by Ruth M. Stone, *American Speech*, April, 1933, p. 77.

5 Private communication; Herbert M. Schueller, Tracy, Minn.

6 The DAE suggests that its source was more likely the Dutch *bakoven*. It is traced to 1777 and is marked an Americanism.

7 H. Philipps in the *Gentleman's Magazine*, 1832, Part II, p. 414.

8 German Influences on the American Language, by Andreas Dorpalen, before cited, p. 14. See also American Variations, by H. W. Horwill, *S.P.E. Tract No. XLV*, 1936, p. 176.

9 A number are listed and discussed in American Intensives in *ka-, ke-* and *ker-*, by Exha Akins Sadilek, *American Speech*, Dec., 1931, p. 142. The DAE traces *kerslush* to 1843, *kawallup* to 1848, *kerwhop* and *kerflummux* to c. 1849, *kerchunk* to 1850, *kerplumpus* and *kerbim* to 1851, and *kasouse, kerswop* and *kerswollop* to c. 1859. Many more have appeared during the years since.

10 The classical example of folk-etymology is in Sir John Davies's Orchestra, 1596, quoted in Robert Southey's Commonplace Book, Fourth Series; London, 1851, p. 431:

Behold the *world*, how it is *whirled* round,
And for it is so *whirled* is named so

*gemütlichkeit* and *seidel*. The vocabulary of the latter class is greatest in the big cities of the Middle Atlantic and Middle Western States, and smallest in the South. In the regions heavily settled by Germans, *e.g.*, Pennsylvania and Wisconsin, the common stock is largely augmented, and many German phrases are understood.[1] A diligent inquiry would probably develop the fact that not a few German loans, once flourishing in American, have since passed out. *Shenk-beer* has been noted, and *schützenfest* suggests itself at once. In *Harper's Magazine*, 1861,[2] I find *cylinder* for a plug hat, probably from the German *zylinder*, but it is not listed in any dictionary and is now quite extinct. Many nonce-words have gone the same way, *e.g.*, *kindergraph*, meaning a photograph of a child.[3]

The influence of Irish English upon American also awaits investigation. The before-mentioned Bristed, in 1855, declared that the only Irish mark upon the speech of New York at that time was the general abandonment of *shall* for *will*, but this was a palpable underestimate. It is highly likely, in fact, that the speechways of the Irish immigrants who swarmed in after 1847 really had a powerful effect upon the general language of the country, at least above the Potomac; indeed, not a few Irish observers detect that effect in both the American phonology and the American vocabulary of today.[4] I have given

---

1 See Some Iowa Locations, by Katherine Buxbaum, *American Speech*, April, 1929, pp. 302–04; English in the Pennsylvania German Area, by Eugene R. Page, *American Speech*, Oct., 1937, pp. 203–06; Pennsylvania-German English, by W. L. Werner, *American Speech*, Dec., 1937, pp. 323–24; Linguistic Substrata in Pennsylvania and Elsewhere, by R. Whitney Tucker, *Language*, March, 1934, pp. 1–5; Some German-Americanisms From the Middle West, by A. W. Meyer, *American Speech*, Dec., 1926, p. 134; The English of the Pennsylvania Germans, by George G. Struble, *American Speech*, Oct., 1935, pp. 163–72. At the Dec., 1940 meeting of the Linguistic Society of America Hans Kurath and Guy S. Lowman, Jr., presented a paper on Pennsylvania English, and for the 1943 meeting of the Modern Language Association (cancelled on account of the war)

Leo L. Rockwell prepared one on The Earlier German Loan-Word in American English. So far as I know, both these papers remain unpublished. Meanwhile, A. M. Aurand of Harrisburg, Pa., has been collecting an extensive vocabulary of German words and phrases current in Pennsylvania English. In Pittsburgh, which is outside the Pennsylvania German area, the official remover of animal carcasses is called the *fallmaster*, apparently a translation of the German *fallmeister*, of the same meaning. I am indebted here to Mr. Charles C. Arensberg of Pittsburgh.

2 The Man in the Rocking-Chair, Aug., p. 429.

3 It appeared in an advertisement of Weller-Lewis *Kindergraphs* in the rotogravure section of the Baltimore *Sun*, May 31, 1925.

4 For example, H. S. Skeffington, in Irishing the American Language, *Irish Press* (Dublin), Dec. 10, 1936.

some of the evidence in AL4, pp. 160 ff. The American liking for intensives, especially marked during the pre-Civil War period, undoubtedly got a lift from the Irish newcomers. The DAE traces *no sir-ee* to 1851 and *yes sir-ee* to 1852.

The Dutch, after the opening of the Nineteenth Century, contributed few additions to the American vocabulary. The DAE traces *to snoop* (Dutch *snoepen*) to 1832, and *bedspread* (probably from the Dutch *beddesprei*) to *c.* 1845, but offers no example of *dope* (apparently from the Dutch *doop*, a sauce) before 1872. At the start *dope* meant a harmless drug, but by the end of the century it had taken on the special meaning of a narcotic, especially opium. It has, in late years, come to signify any composition of unknown ingredients, and since the turn of the century it has also signified information. Like German, Dutch has provided many additions to the local vocabulary in regions where immigrants speaking the original language have settled.[1] After the Louisiana Purchase and the settlement of the Mississippi valley and the Great Lakes region there was a considerable accession of new French terms, not a few of them geographic. The D.A. traces *butte* to 1805, *chute* to 1806, *coulee* to 1807, *sault* to 1809 and *crevasse* to 1814. *Cache* and *picayune* are first recorded in 1805, *shanty* in 1822, *depot* (railroad) in 1832, *shivaree* in 1843, *lagniappe* in 1849, and *to sashay* in 1860. There have been bitter etymological battles over *shanty*. P. W. Joyce, in " English As We Speak It in Ireland," [2] claims it for his native land and says that it is " probably from Irish *sean*, old, and *tigh*, house," but the DAE and Webster 1934 both derive it from the Canadian French *chantier*. *Shivaree* is described by the DAE as " a corruption of *charivari*," which appeared in American simultaneously.[3] *Lagniappe* came into American from the French, but is not actually a French word. William

---

1 See Dutch Survivals in Holland, Michigan, by Peter Veltman, *American Speech*, Feb., 1940, pp. 80–83, and *Sloughter*, by Nathan van Patten, *American Speech*, Aug., 1931, p. 464.

2 Second ed.; Dublin, 1910, p. 319.

3 Both are traced by the DAE to 1843. *Shivaree* is defined as " a noisy demonstration, especially a serenade for a newly wedded couple; a racket; a confused noise." In some parts of the country *callithumpian*, which Bartlett traces to 1848, is used,

and there are also other synonyms. See *Charivari*, by Mamie Meredith and Miles L. Hanley, *American Speech*, April, 1933, pp. 22–26; A Note on *Shivaree*, by John T. Flanagan, *American Speech*, Feb., 1940, pp. 109–10, and *Shivaree* or *Charivari*, by Walter C. Lawrence, *American Notes and Queries*, Jan., 1943, p. 159. The history of the *charivari* in Europe is set forth in Ueber den Ursprung der Katzenmusiken, by G. Phillips; Freiburg im Breisgau 1849.

A. Read in "Louisiana-French,"[1] defines it as meaning "a trifling gift presented to a customer by a merchant," and says of it:

> *Lagniappe* is composed of the French *la*, the, and a French adaptation of Spanish *ñapa*, which is taken in turn from Kechuan *yapa*, a present made to a customer. From Peru the word was carried to other parts of South and Central America, appearing as *ñapa* in Venezuela, Costa Rica and Colombia, but maintaining the form *yapa* in Ecuador. *Ñapa* is heard in the eastern part of Cuba, but this word is replaced by *contra*[2] in the rest of the island.

Kechuan (usually spelled Quichuan) is the name of one of the South American Indian language stocks. Its principal dialect was the tongue of the Incas of Peru, and thus became the common speech of a large area. It is still spoken by 3,000,000 or more Indians in Peru and Ecuador. "As an English word," says Read, "*lagniappe* is pronounced *lanyap*, with the stress usually on the second syllable, but sometimes on the first. The first *a* has the value of that in *land*, and the second of the vowel in *gap*. As a French word *lagniappe* is pronounced in French fashion, save that the palatal *gn* is often replaced by the sound of *ny*." The DAE traces it in American use to 1849, but it is probably older. It is one of a large number of French or pseudo-French loans that survive in the speech of the lower Mississippi region, but are seldom heard elsewhere.[3] Similar loans are to be encountered in the English of the French-speaking sections of Canada.[4] *To sashay*, from the French *chassé*, is defined by the DAE as "to glide or move around, to go about, to go." The first example quoted is from Oliver Wendell Holmes's "Elsie Venner," 1860. Mark Twain used the verb in "Sketches Old and New," 1865.

1 Baton Rouge, 1931, p. 142.
2 A pamphlet called Mexicanismos en los Estados Unidos, published in the City of Mexico, c. 1920, says that *la ñapa* originated in Bolivia, and was carried to Cuba, where it means the thirteenth biscuit of a baker's dozen. I am indebted here to Mr. H. L. Davis. I am also in debt for information about *lagniappe* to Mr. Roark Bradford.
3 See Terms From Louisiana, by James Routh, E. O. Becker, Stanley Clisby Archer and S. C. Arthur, *Dialect Notes*, Vol. IV, Part VI, 1917, pp. 420–31; Louisiana, by James Routh, *Dialect Notes*, Vol. IV, Part V, 1916,

pp. 346–47; New Orleans Word-List, by E. Riedel, *Dialect Notes*, Vol. IV, Part IV, 1916, pp. 268–70, and Louisiana Gleanings, by James Routh, *Dialect Notes*, Vol. V, Part VI, 1923, pp. 243–44. The name of the author of the last-named article is given as Rontt at the head of it and as Rouse on the cover of *Dialect Notes*, but he seems to be identical with the James Routh before mentioned.
4 Canadian French has been studied extensively, but not Canadian English. See Dialect Research in Canada, by A. F. Chamberlain, *Dialect Notes*, Vol. I, Part II, 1890, pp. 43–56, for a bibliography up to that year.

# V

# THE LANGUAGE TODAY

## I. AFTER THE CIVIL WAR

164. [There was a formidable movement to bring American into greater accord with English precept and example during the years following the Civil War. This movement was led by such purists as Edward S. Gould, William D. Whitney and Richard Grant White, and seems to have got its chief support from schoolma'ams, male and female, on the one hand, and from Anglomaniacs on the other.] It was at its height in the 70s and 80s and has been ebbing steadily since 1900, but there is still a certain amount of energy in its backwash, as is evidenced by the continuing prosperity of handbooks of " correct English," most of them humorless cribs from White. There is little reason, however, to believe that what is left of this old innocent belief in authority is having any serious effect upon the development of the national speech. The schoolma'am's victims forget her hortations the moment they escape her classroom, and she is herself increasingly frustrated and demoralized by the treason of the grammarians, most of whom, being only pedagogues of a larger growth themselves, are highly susceptible to the winds of doctrine, and thus accept without much resistance the current teaching that one man's " grammar " is as good as another's, and maybe a damned sight better. Even Anglomania exerts a great deal less influence than aforetime. It remains enormously potent, to be sure, in the twin fields of national policy and moral theology, but it certainly cuts much less figure than it used to in the field of language. Only an inch or so below the level of Harvard and Groton, English speechways are regarded as preposterous, and even as a shade indecent. Back in 1882, when Charles Dudley Warner spoke of the Standard English of that time as " the English dialect," complained that it had " more and more diverged from the language as it was at the time of the separation," and concluded that " we must expect a continual divergence in our litera-

ture," [1] there was a vast lifting of eyebrows, [2] but today such notions pass unnoticed, for no one can think of anything to say against them. Even in 1882 Warner's description of the American novelist under the English hoof had to be thrown into the past tense:

We compared every new aspirant in letters to some English writer. We were patted on the back if we resembled the English models; we were stared at or sneered at if we did not. When we began to produce something that was the product of our own soil and our own social conditions, it was still judged by the old standards, or, if it was too original for that, it was only accepted because it was curious or bizarre, interesting for its oddity.

Whether Warner realized how powerful an influence Mark Twain was to exert on American writing I do not know, but probably he did, for the two had done a book in collaboration only nine years before. [3] Whether he did or he didn't, that influence was already in the making, and by the turn of the century, eighteen years ahead, it was to produce a wholly new style of writing — a new and freer choice of words, a new way of putting them together — that was to be as clearly American as the style of Hawthorne, dead eighteen years before, had been clearly English. Even the prissy Howells was to yield to it, though he could never get over the uneasy feeling that Mark went too far. On lower levels the revolution proceeded quite as slowly, but was even more complete. The American journalist of today has forgotten altogether the banal clichés of the Horace Greeley era, and devotes himself joyously to embellishing and glorifying the national vulgate. Here it was Charles A. Dana's bright young men of the old New York *Sun* who showed the way, but the thing has gone a great deal further since the *Sun* went into Frank A. Munsey's cannibal pot, and there are now signs that the journalese of tomorrow may be indistinguishable from the barbaric (but thoroughly

1 England, *Century Magazine*, Nov., 1882, p. 141.
2 Accompanied, apparently, by protests, for in Feb., 1883, p. 616, the editors of the *Century* were constrained to go to Warner's defense. "We are willing to submit to any fairly constituted international Peace Congress," they wrote, "whether Mr. Warner's article . . . is not a good-natured, frank, mainly serious, partly humorous, literary essay. Along with its earnestness of statement is the dry humor and exag-

geration of the same author's 'My Summer in a Garden' and 'Back-log Studies.' The fact is that Mr. Warner was principally moved to write this essay on England by a cordial friendship for English people and a hearty admiration of the country. But he wrote judicially, not gushingly, not sycophantishly." Whether or not this somewhat fawning disclaimer allayed the current indignation I do not know.
3 The Gilded Age; Hartford, 1873.

American) jargon of *Variety* and *Time*. Even the politicoes of the country no longer try to write like Junius and the Samuel Johnson of the *Rambler*. They still, of course, write badly, but they at least try to write in the actual language of the people they address.[1] It was Abraham Lincoln, fresh from the Western wilds, who first broke away from the bow-wow style of the classical school of American statesmen, and made a deliberate effort (far more artful than most of his admirers seem to think) to speak and write in the simple terms of everyday Americans. He did not succeed altogether, as Mark Twain was to succeed, but he at any rate made the effort, and it had a long-reaching influence.[2] " The new words of the American language," says Carl Sandburg, " streamed across the Lincoln addresses, letters, daily speech. The Boston *Transcript* noted old Abe's use of ' the plain homespun language ' of a man of the people who was accustomed to talk with the ' folks,' and ' the language of a man of vital common sense, whose words exactly fitted his facts and thoughts.' That ex-President John Tyler should protest his grammar was natural. W. O. Stoddard wrote that the President knew how some of his plainer phrasing would sound in the ears of millions over the country and did not ' care a cornhusk for the literary critics.' "[3]

Today it is no longer necessary for an American writer to apologize for writing American. He is not only forgiven if he seeks to set forth his notions in the plainest and least pedantic manner possible; he is also sure of escaping blame (save, of course, by an Old Guard of English reviewers) if he makes liberal dips into the vocabulary of everyday, including its most plausible neologisms. Indeed, he seems a bit stiff and academic if he doesn't make some attempt, how-

---

1 This is true even when they tackle what they conceive to be a high-toned audience. I point, for example, to a speech made by the then Chief Justice, the Hon. Charles Evans Hughes, at a meeting of the American Law Institute in Washington, May 7, 1936. In less than 2000 words he managed to use *yes-man, joy-ride*, and *human* as a noun. See also AL4, p. 203.

2 The Gettysburg Address, so much esteemed, was not a specimen of his new style, but an evidence of literary stagefright on a great occasion. Many of its phrases — *four score and seven years ago, final rest-*

*ing-place, honored dead*, etc. — belonged to the age of Daniel Webster. But, as the anthologists are beginning to see, the address was poetry, not prose, and so criticism must stand silent before its astounding declaration that the Union soldiers killed at Gettysburg were fighting for self-determination. That, in fact, is precisely what they were fighting against. Poetry is not to be judged by the laws of evidence. It is always, at bottom, a sonorous statement of the obviously *not* true.

3 Abraham Lincoln: The War Years, II; New York, 1939, p. 305.

ever unhappy, to add to the stock of such neologisms himself. How many are launched in this great Republic every year I do not know, but the number must be formidable. So long ago as 1926 a lexicographer of experience was reporting that " the accepted language grows at the rate of 3000 words a year — of sufficient currency to be inserted in the dictionary." " In days of stress, in times of war, in an era of discovery and invention," he continued, " 5000 or more words will win the favor of the public so that their inclusion in the dictionary is demanded by scholar and layman." [1] This estimate may have been too high, for during the same year the late Dr. Frank H. Vizetelly put the number of new words submitted for inclusion in the Standard Dictionary at but seven or eight a day, and reported that " relatively few " were accepted,[2] but it must be obvious that words thus submitted do not include the whole crop, nor indeed any substantial part of it. In 1944 Dr. Charles E. Funk, successor to Dr. Vizetelly as editor of the Standard, testified, without venturing upon statistics, that the production of new words and phrases was still at a high mark. " The art of neology," he said, " is by no means dead or even decadent. It is distinctly alive and flourishing. Personally, I have no doubt that it is more robust than in the days of Shakespeare and Bacon, and that inventiveness of phrase is even more ingenious and delectable than in their day." [3] So many novelties swarm in that it is quite impossible for the dictionaries to keep up with them; indeed, a large number come and go without the lexicographers so much as hearing of them. The present book and its predecessors were written in vain if it is not obvious that at least four-fifths of those which get any sort of toe-hold in the language originate in the United States, and that most of the four-fifths remain here. We Americans live in an age and society given over to enormous and perhaps even excessive word-making — the most riotous seen in the world since the break-up of Latin. It is an extremely wasteful process,

1 Let's Look It Up In the Dictionary, by Spencer Armstrong, *Saturday Evening Post*, March 6, 1926, p. 16.
2 Daily Coinage of Words, *American Speech*, Sept., 1926, pp. 687–88.
3 Our Tongue Stabilized? New York *Herald Tribune* (editorial page), March 31, 1944. Interesting discussions of neologisms are in Word-Coinage, by Leon Mead; New York,

1902; New Words Self-Defined, by C. Alphonso Smith; Garden City, 1919; and Nature and Art in Language, by Otto Jespersen, *American Speech*, Dec., 1929, pp. 89–103. Dr. Louise Pound and her colleagues report a large number of current novelties in every issue of *American Speech*.

for with so many newcomers to choose from it is inevitable that large numbers of pungent and useful words and phrases must be discarded and in the end forgotten by all save linguistic paleontologists.[1] But we must not complain about that, for all the great processes of nature are wasteful, and it is by no means assured that the fittest always survive.

## 2. THE MAKING OF NEW NOUNS

168. [All the processes for the formation of new words that are distinguished by philologians have been in operation in the United States since Jackson's time, and after the Civil War their workings took on a new impetus.] These processes are numerous, and are best described by examples. In the following classified list of nouns I have added the year of first recording whenever the term appears in Bartlett, Thornton or the DAE:

*Clippings or back-formations: gas* from *gasoline,*[2] *photo* from *photograph* (1863), *auto* from *automobile* (1899), *phone* from *telephone, movie* from *moving-picture, facial* from *facial-treatment, flat* from *flat-tire, lube* from *lubricating-oil, smoker* from *smoking-car* (1882), *sleeper* from *sleeping-car* (1875), *bronc* from *bronco* (1893), *knicker* from *knickerbocker, co-ed* from *co-educational, coke* from *coca-cola, frat* from *fraternity* (1899), *ad* from *advertisement* (1868), *Y.* from *Y.M.C.A., high-brow* from *high-browed,*[3] *bunk* from *buncombe.*[4]

1 For example, *scorcher, in the neck, upper ten, over the left, shad-bellied, hired girl* and *plug-ugly.* The chief cause of the obsolescence of nouns, of course, is the disappearance of the things they designate, *e.g., antimacassar, lambrequin, ear-pick, pulse-warmer, scholar's-companion.* An interesting discussion of the subject is in Obsolete Words, by Edwin Berck Dike, *Philological Quarterly,* April, 1933, pp. 207–19. A bibliography is in the footnotes thereof.

2 The *New Yorker* noted on May 23, 1942 that the New York *Times* and *Sun* were still putting *gas* in discreet quotes, but that all the other New York papers had accepted it as established. The English *petrol* is also a back-formation, from *petroleum.* The London *Daily Express,* April 24, 1944, reported that it was coined by F. R. Simms, a pioneer English motorist, who is also credited with *motor-car.* I am indebted here to H. W. Seaman.

3 *High-brow* was coined by Will Irwin, *c.* 1905, and first used in the New York *Sun.* It was suggested by *low-brow,* which had been in student use at Leland Stanford, Jr., University, *c.* 1895. I am indebted here to Samuel Hopkins Adams. Both *high-brow* and *low-brow* had been preceded by the corresponding adjectives. *High-browed* is traced by the NED Supplement to 1875 and *low-browed* to 1855. The search for a term to designate persons neither *high-brows* nor *low-brows* has led to the suggestion of *mizzen-brow* and *mezzo-brow* (the latter by the

*Blends:* [1] *Hobohemia* (*hobo* and *Bohemia*), *Aframerican* (*Africa* and *American*), *Hoovercrat* (*Hoover* and *Democrat*), *radiotrician* (*radio* and *electrician*), *sportcast* (*sport* and *broadcast*), *swellelegant* (*swell* and *elegant*), *Chicagorilla* (*Chicago* and *gorilla*), *refugew* (*refugee* and *Jew*), *sneet* (*snow* and *sleet*),[2] *guestar* ( *guest* and *star*), *travelogue* (*travel* and *monologue*), *cablegram* (*cable* and *telegram*, 1868), *radiogram* (*radio* and *telegram*), *insinuendo* (*insinuation* and *innuendo*, 1885).

*Compounds:* *sack-suit* (1895), *sales-lady* (1870), *schedule-time* (1881), *glamor-girl*, *iron-lung*, *barb-wire* (1880),[3] *share-cropper*, *trouble-shooter*, *scrub-woman* (1885), *section-hand* (1873), *bargain-counter* (1888), *shanty-town* (1898), *shawl-strap* (1873), *sheep-grower* (1868), *shirt-waist* (1887), *shore-dinner* (1895), *four-hundred* (1888),[4] *cafe-society*,[5] *storm-door* (1878), *Summer-kitchen* (1875), *sweat-shop* (1867), *milk-shed*, *chewing-gum* (1864), *monkey-business* (1883), *fox-trot* (1915).[6]

*Nouns made of verbs and verb-phrases:* *know-how*,[7] *hideaway*, *kick-back*, *eats*, *build-up*, *hair-do*, *come-down*, *send-off* (1856), *show-down* (1884), *strike-out*, *consist*,[8] *shake-up* (1887), *shoot-the-chutes* (1895), *yes-man*, *hand-out* (1882),

---

*Literary Supplement* of the London *Times*, Nov. 12, 1925, p. 751), but they have not caught on. One R.W.H. reported in *S.P.E. Tract No. XXVII*, 1927, p. 218, that the pedagogues of Harvard then divided students into *highbrows, low highbrows, high lowbrows, lowbrows* and *solid ivories.*

4 *Flu* for *influenza* is not an Americanism. In the earlier form of *flue* it was used by Southey in 1839.

1 Also called *portmanteau-words, telescope-words, amalgams*, etc. See Twenty-nine Synonyms for *Portmanteau-word*, by Harold Wentworth, *American Speech*, Dec., 1933, p. 78. See also More *Portmanteau* Coinages, by Robert Withington, *American Speech*, Feb., 1932, pp. 200–03 (with a brief bibliography), and AL4, p. 172, n. 2.

2 Reported in *American Speech*, Dec., 1940, p. 371, where it is credited to *Kalends*, house-organ of the Waverly Press, Baltimore, Sept., 1940, p. 12.

3 The date here is from New Evidence on Americanisms, by Woodford Heflin, *American Speech*, Feb., 1942, p. 65. The DAE's first example is dated 1882.

4 Coined by Ward McAllister. He said to Cecil Jerome Allen, a society reporter, " There are only 400 peo-

ple in New York that one really knows," and Allen gave the term currency. See Cecil Allen, N. Y. *Sun* Society Editor, Dies, *Editor and Publisher*, Dec. 18, 1937. McAllister died in 1895.

5 *American Notes and Queries*, Dec., 1943, p. 134, says on the authority of the New York *Times*, July 18, 1942, that *cafe-society* was coined by the late Maury Paul (Cholly Knickerbocker) of the New York *Journal American*.

6 *Fox-trot* is really much older. It appeared so early as 1900 in an article on the once-famous Cherry Sisters in the Des Moines *Leader*. The sisters sued for libel, but lost the case. See Cherry Sister's Death Recalls Libel Decision, *Editor and Publisher*, Aug. 12, 1944, p. 48.

7 In *Know-How, American Speech*, Feb., 1944, pp. 65–66, Louise Pound presents a discussion of this term by Clifton P. Williamson. It includes a definition by the U. S. District Court for the District of New Jersey, March, 1942.

8 A railroad term signifying the make-up of a train of cars, extended in recent years to mean the make-up of a meal on a dining-car. See *Consist*, Noun, by Philip M. Wagner, *American Speech*, Oct., 1940, p. 342.

*hang-over* (1894), *set-down*,[1] *stand-off* (1888), *stand-in* (1870), *get-up-and-get* (1888), *shut-down* (1884), *shut-in*.[2]

*Nouns made of other parts of speech: pink*,[3] *married*,[4] *whodunit*,[5] *trusty* (1889), *what-is-it* (c. 1882), *smarty* (1874), *am*,[6] *prominental*,[7] *sissy* (1891), *once-over, hello-girl* (1889), *what-have-you*,[8] *high, low*.[9]

*Nouns made with agent-suffixes: spotter* (1876), *sooner* (1890), *jokesmith, saloonkeeper* (1873), *sandbagger* (1882), *sand-lotter* (1887), *scalper* (ticket; 1874), *sinker* (doughnut; 1870), *kibitzer, all-outer, do-gooder*,[10] *uplifter, spell-binder* (1888), *go-getter, standpatter* (1903), *gangster, trust-buster, racketeer.*

*Nouns made with other suffixes: shortage* (1868), *stick-to-it-ive-ness* (1867), *professoriat, kitchenette, motorcade, socialite, conventionitis, come-at-ability, walkathon, jazz-fiend, gold-bug, chickenburger, dognapper, trainee, receptionist, trailerite, talkfest.*

*Nouns made with prefixes: near-silk, pro-German, super-film.*

*Extensions or narrowings of meaning: taxpayer* (a building erected to pay the taxes on the lot),[11] *drive* (to raise money; 1890),[12] *public enemy* (criminal),[13]

1 Said to be used by Tammany as a folksy equivalent of the tattered *conference.*
2 *Shut-in*, meaning a person confined to the house by illness or infirmity, is not listed by the DAE, but the NED marks it " U.S." The NED's first example is dated 1904; it is actually much older.
3 In the sense of a Socialist less radical than a *red*. The DAE does not list *pink*, but the first example of the NED Supplement, dated 1924, is from the United States.
4 Usually, *young marrieds. Vogue*, quoted in New Words for Old, Baltimore *Evening Sun*, (editorial page), March 8, 1939: " *Young marrieds* are building."
5 A mystery story or film. In Who Done *Whodunit, Publishers' Weekly*, April 11, 1942, pp. 1405–06, C. B. Boutell presented evidence that *whodunit* was launched by Donald Gordon in *American News of Books*, July, 1930. I am indebted here to Mr. Jacob Blanck.
6 Apparently a shortened form of *great I-am*. Inside Stuff — Legit, *Variety*, Jan. 12, 1944: " People who saw the *ams* then attended the professional show to see the difference with Karloff in action."
7 Julia Bumry Jones in Pittsburgh *Courier*, Feb. 5, 1938: " Many *prominentals* visited with us last week."
8 See A Contribution to the Study of the Conversion of Adjectives Into Nouns in English, by Carl Bergener; Lund (Sweden), 1928.
9 The use of *high* and *low* as meteorological and stock-market terms seems to be American. Neither is listed by the DAE, but the NED Supplement's first example of *low* (weather) is from the *Popular Science Monthly*, July, 1878, p. 310, and its first of *high* (stock market), from the London *Weekly Dispatch*, June 3, 1928, was long antedated in the United States. Its first of *low* (stock market), from the London *Observer*, 1929, was also antedated in this country. Said a writer in *John o' London's Weekly*, 1938, " An American does not turn a hair when he reads that ' American Can [*i.e.*, Tin] was nearly twenty points below its *high* of the year,' or ' What the fate of psychology will be now that it has hit its new *low* is difficult to predict.' " Both terms are used in numerous figurative senses.
10 The *Do-gooder* Defined, St. Louis *Post-Dispatch* (editorial), Jan. 18, 1927.
11 *American Speech*, April, 1930, p. 328.
12 The American *Drive*, by C. D. P., *American Speech*, Oct., 1929, p. 51.
13 In the *New Yorker*, Jan. 10, 1942, W. E. Farbstein ascribed the introduction of this term to H. B. Chamberlin of Chicago, but without hazarding the date.

*dude*,[1] *blueprint* (any plan, of anything), *cinch* (originally, 1859, a saddle-girth; later, 1888, any strong or sure hold; still later, 1898, a certainty), *outfit* (originally, 1809, equipment and supplies; later, 1869, a group or company of any kind).

*Nouns formed by the devices of metaphor: rubber-neck*,[2] *bar-fly, dirt-farmer*,[3] *grass-roots* (in the political sense),[4] *dog-house* (place of imaginary incarceration for persons out of favor), *tight-wad, stuffed-shirt, tenderfoot* (1875), *bulldozer*,[5] *hay-seed* (1892), *shuttle-train* (1891), *Atlantic-grayhound*,[6] *skin-game* (1868), *sky-scraper* (1883), *square-deal* (1883), *straw-bid* (1872), *coffee-pot* (a lunchroom), *hot-dog*,[7] *cow-puncher* (1879), *bonehead, road-agent, screw-ball, steam-roller* (political), *lounge-lizard, bromide*,[8] *dust-bowl*,[9] *road-hog* (1898).

1 *Dude* is an Americanism of unknown origin, traced by the DAE to 1883. Originally it meant a dandy, but now it is used in the West to indicate any tourist. See *Dude, Dudine, Duding*, by J. D., *American Speech*, April, 1935, p. 158.

2 Not listed by the DAE. The NED Supplement traces it to 1896, and Partridge says that it had reached England by 1902.

3 The antonym of *dirt-farmer* is *suit-case-* or *sidewalk-farmer*. Says Robert Diller in Farm Ownership, Tenancy, and Land Use in a Nebraska Community; Chicago, 1941 (quoted in *American Speech*, Oct., 1941, p. 239): "*Suitcase-farmer* is used of farmers on the Great Plains who put in a crop of wheat in the Fall and come back to harvest it the next Summer, after having spent the Winter in their permanent homes elsewhere. A *sidewalk-farmer* . . . seems to be merely a farmer who lives in town and goes out to farm his fields in the neighboring countryside." The prefix *dirt-* has been attached metaphorically to other nouns, *e.g., dirt-lawyer, dirt-musician, dirt-sailor*.

4 The DAE traces *grass-roots*, in the sense of "the soil immediately below the surface of the ground," to 1880. The Republican *grass-roots* conference was held at Springfield, Ill., early in June, 1935. See *Grass-Roots*, by Atcheson L. Hench, *American Speech*, Oct., 1936, p. 231, and *Grass-Roots*, by James Rorty, *American Speech*, Dec., 1936, p. 376.

5 First applied, *c.* 1876, to Louisiana *vigilantes* who specialized in flogging Negroes seeking to vote; later, 1881, applied to a revolver; still later to any persons applying duress to another; finally to a machine for pushing earth.

6 First applied to the Guion Line steamer *Arizona*, which crossed the Atlantic in 1870 at an average speed of 17.3 knots an hour. I am indebted here to my brother, August Mencken.

7 Said to have been named by T. A. Dorgan, *c.* 1900. See Harry Stevens, Park Caterer, is Dead at 78, New York *Herald Tribune*, May 4, 1934. In an editorial, The *Hot-Dog* Mystery, June 2, 1931, the *Herald Tribune* reported that the Coney Island Chamber of Commerce, in 1913, "passed a resolution forbidding the use of the derogatory term *dog*" by concessionaires on the boardwalk. It added that *hot-dog* had reached England by that year.

8 Proposed by Gelett Burgess in The Sulphitic Theory, *Smart Set*, April, 1906. This essay was reprinted as a book, under the title of Are You a Bromide? or, The Sulphitic Theory; New York, 1907. It was dedicated "to Gertrude McCall, chatelaine of Mac Manor and discoverer of the Sulphitic Theory." A *bromide* was defined as one who "does his thinking by syndicate, follows the main-traveled roads, goes with the crowd"; his marks were his use of such clichés as "I don't know much about art, but I know what I like" and "It's bad enough to see a man

*Nouns from proper names: tuxedo* (1894), *panama* (1873).

*Proper nouns from the initials or other parts of a series of words: socony* from *Standard Oil Company of New York, dokkie* from *Dramatic Order Knights of Khorassen,*[1] *nabisco* from *National Biscuit Company.*[2]

*Nouns made by onomatopoeia: oomph,*[3] *zow, biff,*[4] *ki-yi* (dog and its bark).[5]

*Arbitrary coinages: blurb,*[6] *thobbing,*[7] *googal* (1 followed by 100 zeros),

drunk — but, oh! a woman! " A *sulphite* was defined as " a person who does his own thinking, a person who has surprises up his sleeve." *Sulphite* gained but little vogue, but *bromide* had an immediate success, and now appears in most dictionaries. The NED Supplement shows that it was in use in England — by the professor of English literature at Oxford! — by 1909.

9 On Oct. 13, 1941, Albert Law, editor of the Dalhart (Texas) *Texan,* broadcasting from Station KGNG at Amarillo, offered a reward of $50 for information as to who first used *dust-bowl* in print. There were various claimants, but the man whose claim seemed most valid to Mr. Law was nominated by others and refused to take the money. He was Robert Geiger, an Associated Press staff writer, who used the term in the introductory matter to a dispatch from Guymon, Okla., April 15, 1935. His disinclination to accept credit for originating it was due to fear that he might have picked it up from some one else. But the evidence seems to be clear that it was new in 1935. The money was handed to the Last Man's Club of Dalhart, which gave it to the Boys' Ranch at Old Tascosa, nearby. I am indebted here to Mr. Law.

1 A fraternal order. See Over 100 Take Part in *Dokkie* Gathering, Greensboro (N. C.) *News,* Aug. 16, 1939, p. 12.

2 Such words are called *acronyms.* See Initials Into Words, by Basil Davenport, *American Notes and Queries,* Feb., 1943, p. 167.

3 *Oomph* is defined by Peter Tamony, in Origin of Words, San Francisco *News Letter and Wasp,* Aug. 11, 1939, as " an articulation of a common male appraisal of a personable girl." He says that " Walter Win-

chell used the present spelling in 1936, but changed to *umph.*" The word apparently originated in Hollywood, and Tamony says that the first " *oomph* girl of America " was Ann Sheridan, who was awarded the honor in 1937.

4 *Biff,* as an interjection, is traced by the DAE to 1847, but it did not take on the sense of a blow until *c.* 1890.

5 The DAE traces *ki-yi* as a verb to 1850, but its first example of the noun is dated 1883.

6 Signifying an encomium of a book on the slip-cover. Coined by Gelett Burgess in 1907. The story was thus told in Footnotes to a Publisher's Life, by B. W. Huebsch, in the *Colophon,* quoted in *Word Study,* May, 1938, pp. 5–6: " Burgess had come to me with a copy of an essay of his that had appeared in the *Smart Set,* entitled, ' The Sulphitic Theory,' and suggested my issuing it in book form. . . . Under the name of ' Are You a Bromide? ' it was published. . . . It is the custom of publishers to present copies of a conspicuous current book to booksellers attending the annual dinner of their trade association, and as this little book was in its heyday when the meeting took place I gave it to 500 guests. These copies were differentiated from the regular edition by the addition of a comic bookplate drawn by the author and by a special jacket which he devised. It was the common practise to print the picture of a damsel — languishing, heroic, or coquettish — anyhow, a damsel, on the jacket of every novel, so Burgess lifted from a Lydia Pinkham or tooth-powder advertisement the portrait of a sickly sweet young woman, painted in some gleaming teeth, and otherwise enhanced her pulchritude, and placed her in the center of the jacket. His accom-

*wobbie,*[1] *dingle-doo,*[2] *goof* (1920), *dingus* (1882), *dingbat* (1861), *doodad.*[3]

During the quarter century following the Civil War, as during the same period preceding it, the West was the chief source of American neologisms; down to *c.* 1885, in fact, they were commonly called *Westernisms*. But as the pioneer movement lost momentum, the industrialization of the country proceeded, and immigration reached a high tide, the center of language-making moving back to eastward of the great plains, and there it has remained ever since, with a sort of outpost at Chicago [4] and another at Hollywood. It is new objects and new procedures that make the largest share of new words, and both are now much more numerous in the big cities than they are on the land. *Tenderfoot* (1875) was redolent of the old West, and *trust-buster*, which appeared toward the end of the 80s, still suggested the great open spaces, but *rubber-neck, hair-do, kitchenette, mortician, socialite, go-getter, kibitzer* and *racketeer* are unmistakably urban, if very far from urbane.

Two classes of professional word-makers have appeared in the national Gomorrahs since the turn of the century and between them they produce a majority of all the new words that come and go. The first is composed of sub-saline literati, *e.g.,* gossip-column journalists, writers of movie and radio scripts, song writers, comic-strip artists, and theatrical, movie and radio press-agents. The second is composed of the persons who invent names for the new products and services that constantly bid for patronage, and the advertising agents who

panying text was some nonsense about 'Miss Blinda *Blurb*,' and thus the term supplied a real need and became a fixture in our language." Partridge says that *blurb* reached England in 1924. On Jan. 9, 1942, Lord Dunedin, an aged Scots peer, upbraided the Edinburgh *Scotsman* for using it, and demanded to know its meaning. He said he could not find it "in the Bible or in Macaulay or in Walter Scott." The *Scotsman* printed a definition of it the same day, and various correspondents spoke of it favorably, but Lord Dunedin would have none of it, and on Jan. 12 denounced it as "a monstrosity imported, like so many others, from America."

7 Title of a book by Henshaw Ward; Indianapolis, 1926.

1 Defined in *American Notes and Queries*, Aug., 1943, p. 71, as "a new root vegetable — a cross between a carrot and a beet."

2 Suggested by Maury Maverick as a substitute for *hors d'oeuvres*, which most Americans find unpronounceable.

3 For a long list of such forms see American Indefinite Names, by Louise Pound, *American Speech*, April, 1931, pp. 257–59. In *American Speech*, April, 1940, p. 135, James McCune Harrison made some additions.

4 Chicago and American Slanguage, by John Drury, Chicago *Topics*, Feb., 1926, pp. 12–36.

distort and torture the language in whooping them up. The mortality among the inventions of these innovators is almost as great as that among the fry of the oyster, but now and then one of them contributes a word or phrase that is pungent and really needed, and at all times they keep the fires of transient slang burning. The work of one of them, Walter Winchell of the New York *Mirror*, is noticed in AL4, pp. 560–61. He runs largely to verbs and verb-phrases, *e.g.,* *to be Reno-vated,*[1] *to infanticipate, to middle aisle,* and *to blessed event,* but he is also fertile in new nouns, many of them blends, *e.g., revusical* (a musical revue), *profanuage* (profane language), *Chicagorilla* (Chicago and gorilla), *go-Ghetto,* and *terpsichorine* (a chorus girl). He is not averse to puns, *e.g., merry Magdalen* and *messer of ceremonies,* and does not hesitate to stoop to phonetic spellings in the manner of the newspaper humorists of the Civil War era, *e.g., Joosh* (Jewish), *phlicker* and *moompitcher* (a movie), *dotter* (daughter), *Hahlim* (Harlem) and *phewd* (feud). Inasmuch as he is chiefly concerned with the life of Broadway and its circumambient nightclubs, his inventions have largely to do with the technics and hazards of its ethnology, *e.g., on the merge* (engaged), *on fire, that way* and *uh-huh* (in love), *welded* and *sealed* (married), *phfft, soured* and *curdled* (separated), *baby-bound* and *storked* (pregnant), and *melted* (divorced). Some of his phrases are old ones to which he has imparted an ironical significance, *e.g., bundle from Heaven* (a child) and *blessed event* (the birth thereof), and he has made a number of ingenious contributions to the roster of Broadway place-names, *e.g., Two-Time Square* and *Hard-Times Square* (Times Square), *Hardened Artery, Bulb Belt* and *Baloney Boulevard* (Broadway), and *Heart-Acre Square* (Longacre Square). Many of his contributions to the current vocabulary are apparently not original with him, but he may be credited with giving them vogue, *e.g., pash* (passion), *phooie,*[2] *squaw* (wife), *giggle-water,* and *whoopee.*[3] He is not only an as-

---

1 A correspondent reports that *Renovated* was used in 1921 in a book by Lillyan Corbin, but I have been unable to verify this.

2 A borrowing from the Yiddish (and German) *pfui.*

3 Winchell did not invent *whoopee,* but the verb-phrase, *to make whoopee,* seems to be his. See Walter Winchell on Broadway, New York *Mirror,* Jan. 17, 1935.

*Whoopee,* as an interjection, is traced by the DAE to 1862. It was used as a noun by Mark Twain in *A Tramp Abroad,* 1880, p. 80. Discussions of the term are in *American Speech,* April, 1930, p. 327; Feb., 1931, p. 234 and June, 1931, pp. 394–95, and in Delver in Dictionaries Believes That *Whoopee* Has Ancestors, New York *Herald Tribune,* Sept. 21, 1930.

siduous inventor and popularizer of new words and phrases, but also no mean student of them, and has printed some interesting discussions of them,[1] though his attempts at etymologies are often open to question.

No other living newspaper columnist has launched so many neologisms, but he has a respectable rival in Arthur (Bugs) Baer, a master of buffoonery who never yields to Winchell's weakness for throwing off the jester's motley and putting on the evangelist's shroud. Both had a forerunner in Jack Conway, who died in 1928. He was a baseball player who took to vaudeville, and ended his career on *Variety*, the theatrical weekly.[2] He is credited with having launched *baloney*, though it was the Hon. Alfred E. Smith who, by using it in *balony-dollar* in 1934, made the country *baloney*-conscious.[3] It is possible that Conway borrowed the term from the argot of the Chicago stockyards, where an old and tough bull, fit only for making sausage, has long had the name of a *bologna*. The DAE traces *bologna*, in American use, to 1758, and says that it has been reduced colloquially to *balony*. The English commonly make it *polony*. Conway's other contributions to the vocabulary of his era included *S.A.* (sex appeal), *Arab* (a Jew), *to click* (to succeed), *high-hat*, *pushover*, *pay-off*, *headache* (a wife), *belly-laugh*, *palooka* and *to scram*.[4] The sports

1 For example, in A Primer of Broadway Slang, *Vanity Fair*, Nov., 1927, pp. 67–134, and in his column in the New York *Mirror*, June 20, 1936. He has been the frequent subject of other students of the subject, as in Winchellese, by Paul Robert Beath, *American Speech*, Oct., 1931, pp. 44–46; Portrait of Walter Winchell, by Henry F. Pringle, *American Mercury*, Feb., 1937, pp. 137–44; The Vocabulary of Columnists, by P. R. Beath, *American Speech*, April 1932, pp. 312–13; Walter Winchell, *American Speech*, Oct., 1937, p. 194; More Winchellisms, *American Speech*, April, 1942, p. 105, and Newly-Wedded Words, by Lester V. Berrey, *American Speech*, Feb., 1939, pp. 3–10.

2 Winchell hailed him as " my tutor of the slanguage he helped me perfect " in an obituary notice in the New York *Graphic*, Oct. 4, 1928.

3 The decree reducing the gold-con-

tent of the dollar from 25 8/10 grains to 15 5/21 was issued on Jan. 31, 1934. See A Note on *Baloney*, by Macklin Thomas, *American Speech*, Dec., 1935, pp. 318–19. There is some uncertainty about the spelling, and Berry and Van den Bark in their American Thesaurus of Slang record *bolony*, *balony*, *bologna* and *ba-log-na*. Al Smith apparently preferred *baloney*.

4 The provenance of *to scram* is disputed, and Conway may have borrowed it from the cant of criminals, with which he was well acquainted. See *Scram* — " a Swell Five-Letter Woid," by V. Royce West, *American Speech*, Oct., 1937, pp. 195–202. Partridge lists it as an Americanism and says that it reached England through the movies by 1930, but suggests that it may be related to an English dialect verb, *to scramble*, meaning " to get away with, with a notion of fear or stealth."

writers, as everyone knows, are diligent coiners of neologisms, and not a few of their inventions have been taken into the common speech, but on the whole they contribute only nonce-words, here today and gone tomorrow.[1] They are surpassed in ingenuity and success by some of the comic-strip artists, of whom Thomas A. (Tad) Dorgan, Elzie Crisler Segar and Billy De Beck are examples. Dorgan, who died in 1929, is said to have invented or introduced *skiddoo, twenty-three, drug-store cowboy, nobody home* and the series of superlatives beginning with *cat's pajamas*, and to have launched such once popular phrases as " You tell him," " Yes, we have no bananas," and " You said it." [2] Segar, who died in 1940, is credited with *goon, jeep* and various other terms that, at the hands of others, took on wide extensions of meaning, and with starting the vogue for the words in *-burger*.[3] To De Beck, who died in 1942, are ascribed *heebie-jeebies, hot-mama, hotsy-totsy* and *horse-feathers*.[4] Damon Runyon's name is always included when lists of word-coiners are published,[5] but he has himself protested that he is only a popularizer of the inventions of others.[6] George Ade, who died in 1944, is likewise often mentioned

1 Some examples of their hard effort are given in Varying the Football Jargon, by Willis Stork, *American Speech*, Oct., 1934, pp. 237–39, and Color Stuff, by Harold E. Rockwell, *American Speech*, Oct., 1927, pp. 28–30.

2 See AL4, p. 561; Cartoon Cavalcade, by Thomas Craven; New York, 1943, p. 18, and Tad, by Peter Tamony, San Francisco *News Letter and Wasp*, May 26, 1938.

3 A Word-Creator, by Jeffrey Fleece, *American Speech*, Feb., 1943, pp. 68–69, and *Hamburger* Progeny, by Arnold Williams, *American Speech*, April, 1939, p. 154.

4 Billy De Beck Dies, *Editor and Publisher*, Nov. 14, 1942. See also How Snuffy Smith Became a Yard Bird, by Joseph Willicombe, Jr., Washington *Times-Herald*, Nov. 16, 1941. There are interesting discussions of the comic-strip vocabulary in Character Names in the Comic Strips, by Helen Tysell, *American Speech*, April, 1934, pp. 158–60, and The English of the Comic Cartoons, by the same, Feb., 1935, pp. 43–55. In

the second of these papers Miss Tysell calls attention to the fondness of comic-strip artists for onomatopes, e.g., *whap, zam, sputtt, tsk-tsk, urr-r-ruff, bam, yazunk* and *wham-bo*. The effects of comic strips upon the vocabulary and thinking of American school children have been discussed by George E. Hill in Children's Interest in Comic Strips, *Educational Trends*, March–April, 1939, pp. 11–14; Relation of Children's Interests in Comic Strips to the Vocabulary of These Comics, *Journal of Educational Psychology*, Jan., 1943, pp. 48–87; Word Distortion in Comic Strips, *Elementary School Journal*, May, 1943, pp. 520–25, and The Vocabulary of Comic Strips, *Journal of Educational Psychology*, Feb., 1943, pp. 77–87. Dr. Hill's conclusions were summarized in Comic-Strip Language, *Time*, June 21, 1943, p. 96.

5 See AL4, p. 560.

6 The Brighter Side, New York *Mirror*, Dec. 30, 1937, p. 10: " We never invent slang in fiction, or anywhere else. We merely report the language

as an introducer of novelties, but as a matter of fact his long series of " Fables in Slang," begun *c.* 1900, borrowed from the slang of the day much oftener than they contributed to it.

The strange vocabulary of the American newspaper headline is discussed in AL4, pp. 181–85. Its distinguishing mark is its excessive use of very short words — a necessity forced on it by the fact that newspaper columns are narrow. That necessity was not felt as pressing down to 1885 or thereabout, for it was then the custom to arrange headlines in a free-and-easy manner, with each section (or bank) thereof consisting of two lines, the second line of each bank centered under the first, and sentences running on from one bank to the next. The choice of type was left to the printer, and he was esteemed in proportion to the number of different faces and sizes he got into a given head. Not infrequently one filling half a column was a single sentence. When the custom arose of setting headlines in more or less uniform type, according to a relatively few fixed patterns, and with each bank self-contained, the copy-reader took over the job of making them fit, and he soon found that he was greatly incommoded by long words, for if one of them filled a whole line it looked somewhat awkward, and if it was too long for a line it could not be used at all. Thus the search for shorter synonyms began, and whenever an effective one was unearthed it was quickly endowed with extended and sometimes very strained meanings. Today *probe* is used to signify any sort of quest or inquiry, however little it may suggest a surgeon's probing of a wound,[1] and *hint* is a synonym-of-all-work that may mean anything from rumor to accusation. Other favorite nouns of the headline writers are *ace, aid, balm, ban, blast, bloc, blow, bout, chief, cleric, crash, deal, drive, edict, fete, gain, grip, head, hop, job, try, meet, net, pact, plea, quiz, slate, snag, span, talk* and *toll.* Many of

---

of our characters." Runyon is very popular in England, and on Jan. 22, 1938, p. 59, the London *Times Literary Supplement* praised him as it has seldom praised an American author. " The capital interest in his stories," it said, " lies in his use of words, particularly in his use of cant terms which, by allusion or analogy, are given fresh or vivid meaning."

1 It was admitted to Webster 1934 in the headline sense of " an investigation or inquiry directed to the discovery of evidence of wrongdoing." See Recent Developments in Usage Evident From a Comparison of the First and Second Editions of Webster's New International Dictionary, by W. Paul Jones, summarized in *Word Study Suggestion Leaflet,* issued by the publishers of the dictionary, May, 1938.

these are converted freely into verbs,[1] and in addition there is a large repertoire of midget verbs proper, *e.g.*, *to back, balk, ban, bar, bare, best, cite, comb, cry, curb, cut, face, flay, hit, ire, lure, map, nab, name, net, oust, quash, quit, rap, raze, rule, score, see,*[2] *slate, slay, speed, spike, stage, vie* and *void*. Clipped forms are naturally much used, *e.g.*, *ad, auto, confab, gas, isle, mart, photo* and *quake*. Even the compounds in use are commonly made up of very short words, *e.g.*, *clean-up, come-back* and *pre-Yule*.[3] A constant search goes on for short forms of proper names frequently in the news, *e.g.*, *F. D. R.* for Roosevelt, *Bruno* for Richard Hauptmann, and *Wally* for Wallis Warfield.[4] It was probably not moral indignation so much as the effort to conserve space that made the Germans *Huns* in World War I; in World War II they escaped with the inoffensive but happily short appellation of *Nazis*. *Norse, Dons* (Spaniards), *Japs, Reds* and the like are godsends to copy-readers, and I have encountered *Liths* for Lithuanians.[5]

Nor is it only in vocabulary that liberties are taken with the language. There is also a strong tendency to juggle the parts of speech, and to indulge in syntactical devices that dismay orthodox grammarians. A few examples: Galento *Has* $10,000 *He'll Stop* Louis,[6]

1 "Headline idiom," says Frederick Bodmer in The Loom of Language; New York, 1944, p. 118, "breaks through all the functional fences which schoolbooks put up round the parts of speech."

2 As in Dewey *Sees* Victory, Accord with Britain *Seen*, *See* Realty Gains in New Parkway, etc.

3 I take most of these examples from Scribes Seek Snappy Synonyms, by Maurice Hicklin, *American Speech*, Dec., 1930, pp. 110–22. There are others in Headline Words, by Harold E. Rockwell, *American Speech*, Dec., 1926, pp. 140–41; The Invading Goth of Literature, by William N. Brigance, *North American Review*, Sept., 1928, pp. 316–20; Newspaper Balladry, by Winifred Johnston, *American Speech*, April, 1935, pp. 119–21; Headline Pep in America, London *Morning Post*, Dec. 29, 1936, and Motley Notes, by Alan Kamp, *Sketch* (London), Nov. 3, 1937, p. 2.

See also Head Writing Made Easy, by Lucien Kellogg; Salt Lake City, 1944.

4 What's In a Name?, by Floyd Olds, Omaha *World-Herald*, Sept. 15, 1943: "Sometimes the answer is too many letters, when it comes to getting the name in a newspaper headline. The fellows we're thinking about are Bill *Dellastatious* of Missouri and Bob *Hoernschemeyer* of Indiana. For headline purposes they're likely to become *Della* and *Hunchy*, for the same reason Coach Adolph *Lewandowski* is known intimately as *Lew* to the boys on copydesks." See also Shop Talk at Thirty, by Jack Lait, *Editor and Publisher*, Sept. 9, 1944, p. 72.

5 *Liths* Here in Toast to Homeland, Chicago *Sunday Times*, Feb. 18, 1940, p. 5.

6 Oakland (Calif.) *Tribune*, quoted in the Martinez (Calif.) *Gazette*, Feb. 16, 1940.

Gob Crabs Gal's *F. D. R.* Love Plea,[1] Woman *Critical* After Night-gown Is Set Afire,[2] *Smock Day* All Over, Girls Say,[3] Byrd Shushes "Why" of White House Trip,[4] "In the process of doing things to formal English," said the St. Louis *Star-Times* in 1937, "the press has been helping to develop a homegrown grammar."[5] In this revolution there is some ingenuity and also some daring, but another of its principal constituents is simply Philistinism. The average American copy-reader shows his disdain of verbal niceties in many other ways, *e.g.*, by his disregard for the correct forms of foreign words, and especially of foreign titles. He makes no distinction between *résumé* and *to resume*, and it is one of his fondest beliefs that an English knight is a peer.[6] Similarly, his columnist colleague frequently insists on using the editorial *we* under or over his signature, or, as the brethren choose to call it, *by-line*.[7]

1 New York *Daily News*. The meaning is that a sailor's sweetheart petitioned President Roosevelt to order his release from the Navy, but that the sailor refused to acquiesce. I am indebted here to Mr. Albert K. Dawson.

2 New Haven *Journal-Courier*, noted by the Ansonia (Conn.) *Sentinel*, Jan. 24, 1938.

3 Boston *Post*, quoted in The Attributive Noun Becomes Cancerous, by Steven T. Byington, *American Speech*, Oct., 1926, p. 35. The meaning is that the vogue for wearing smocks in offices is passing. It should be noted that Mr. Byington's diatribe against such forms was itself denounced by George O. Curme, one of the most influential of American grammarians, in Newspaper Headlines, *American Speech*, April, 1929, p. 306. "They are," he said, "as old as our language and very much older in fact." In The Attributive Noun Again, *American Speech*, Dec., 1929, pp. 173–75 Byington made another attack, and under the same title, Aug., 1930, pp. 490–92, Curme took another hack at him.

4 Baltimore *Evening Sun*, Jan. 12, 1938.

5 Newspaper-Made Language, editorial page, Dec. 30. Some of the headline-writers' rhetorical devices are discussed in Alliteration on the Sports Page, by Eugene S. McCartney, *American Speech*, Feb., 1938, pp. 30–34, and The Cliché Expert Tells All, by Frank Sullivan, *New Yorker*, June 20, 1936, pp. 16–17. In 1942 John W. Harden, news editor of the Salisbury (N. C.) *Post*, collected from other North Carolina editors a list of prevailing newspaper clichés, and it was printed in the *Editor and Publisher*, Jan. 2, 1943, p. 12. See also Where is Usage Bred?, by Robert Withington, *Commonweal*, Dec. 17, 1937, pp. 208–11.

6 See Newspapers Err in Use of Foreign Titles, *Editor and Publisher*, Oct. 8, 1938, and Accents Wild, by Charles Fitzhugh Talman, *Atlantic Monthly*, Dec. 1915, pp. 807 ff.

7 This banality was constantly affected by the late Heywood Broun. See The Phoenix Nest, by William Rose Benét, *Saturday Review of Literature*, Feb. 13 and March 13, 1943, and The Talk of the Town, *New Yorker*, March 4, 1944, p. 15. In From the Oak to the Olive; Boston, 1868, p. 1, Julia Ward Howe undertook to account for the origin of the editorial *we* as follows: "[It] is essential for newspaper writing because people are liable to be horsewhipped for what they put in the

But the writing of American newspaper columnists, at its most advanced, is as the writing of Walter Pater compared to that of the two weeklies, *Variety* and *Time*. Each has developed a dialect that is all its own, and both are heavily imitated, the former by newspaper writers on the theatre, the movies and the radio, and the latter by a large following of young reporters, and not only by young reporters, but also by editorial writers and other such more austere varieties of journalists, and even by authors of presumably elegant kidney. The vocabulary and syntax of both are so bizarre that they have attracted much attention from students of the national language, and the literature of the subject is already formidable.[1] *Variety* bangs away at the language in an innocent, hearty and insatiable manner. It invents and uses a great variety of back-formations, *e.g.*, *pix* for *moving pictures*, *vaude* for *vaudeville*, *nabe* for *neighborhood*, *intro* for *introduction*, *preem* for *premier*, *admish* for *admission*, *biog* for *biography*, *to collab* for *to collaborate*, *orch* or *ork* for *orchestra*, *concesh* for *concession*, *juve* for *juvenile*, *crick* for *critic*, *fave* for *favorite*, *mat* for *matinee*, *situash* for *situation* and *sked* for *schedule*; and it launches many new and tortured blends, *e.g.*, *filmusical* (a movie with music), *newscaster* and *thespsmitten*, and bold compounds, *e.g.*, *chin-fest* (a conference), *bell-ringer* (a success), *pic-parlor*, *show-shop*, *hand-patter*, *spine-chiller*, *straw-hat* and *cow-shed* (a Summer theatre), *cliff-hanger* (a serial melodrama), *splinter-bug* (a shoeless dancer) and *oats-opera* (a Western film). It puts old and new suffixes to use in a free and spacious manner, *e.g.*, *hoofologist* (a dancer), *flopperoo* (a failure), *socko* and *clicko* (a success), *nitery* (a *night-club*), *twinner* (a double-feature bill), *vox-popper*, *ball-*

---

sacred columns of a daily journal. *We* may represent a vague number of individuals, less inviting to, and safer from, the cowhide than the provoking *egomet ipse*." The bastard *ourself*, archaic in English save as a poetic term, survives among American columnists. The DAE does not list it but I find an example as early as 1852 in *Harper's Magazine*, Nov., p. 849.

1 For *Variety* see, for example, *Variety*, by Hugh Kent, *American Mercury*, Dec., 1926, pp. 462–66; *Variety*, by Raymond Tyson, *American Speech*, Dec., 1937, pp. 317–18;

A Guide to *Variety*, by the same, April, 1940, pp. 204–05; Lord Broadway, by Dayton Stoddart; New York, 1941, pp. 268 *ff*, and The Story of *Variety*, by Bennett Cerf, *Saturday Review of Literature*, April 17, 1943, pp. 32–34. Two *Variety muggs* (the name used by the staff to designate its members) have contributed to the discussion in Veteran *Variety Mugg* Gives Some Inside Stuff on Sime's Starting *V*, by Epes W. Sargent, *Variety*, Sept. 26, 1933, p. 3, and The *Variety Mugg*, by Abel Green, *Esquire*, Sept., 1936.

*roomology, pianology, legmania, peelery* (a burlesque show), *10%ery* (the office of an actor's agent), *payola* (bribery), *ghostitis, invitee, pixite, Coastie, oldie, cinamaestro, microphonist, blurbist* and *lackage;* it makes verbs of nouns, e.g., *to author, to ink* (to sign), *to lens, to emcee* (to act as master of ceremonies), *to preem* and *to terp,* and it converts all the other parts of speech into nouns, e.g., *rave* (an enthusiastic review), *de luxer, personaling* (making personal appearances), *tie-in, pink* (a sexy picture), *clicky* (a picture making money), *cheapie, biggie, brush-off* and *vocal* (a song). It also borrows freely from the argots of sports, of the circus, of hobos and of criminals, e.g., *to beef* (to complain), *eight-ball* (a failure), *G* ($1,000), *to gander* (to go sightseeing), *handle* (a title), *spieler* (an announcer) and *on the lam. Variety's* headlines are done in such a jargon that only the initiated can fathom them. One of the most famous, *Hicks Nix Sticks Pix,* attracted so much attention that it was discussed solemnly in far-away Egypt.[1] Its meaning, it turned out, was that bucolic movie audiences did not like pictures with rustic settings. Once, challenged for reporting that the Minneapolis *Star,* by promoting a boxing carnival with Joe Louis as its principal figure, was diverting patronage from the local movie parlors, it refused to recant but explained sententiously: " Story recounted show biz squawks against opposish from newspaper ballyhoo showmanship stunts." [2] Soon after this *Variety* was moved to poke fun at its own style by calling attention to a news item sent in by its Philadelphia correspondent, whom it described as " an otherwise lucid newspaper man." This item was headed " Contagious " and was as follows:

Philly Orch on Thursday (11) night will preem composition of 23-year-old Omaha college soph. Cleffer, titled " Mystic Pool," is by John S. Hefti, who is studying theory at Municipal University of Omaha. Kid's b.r.ing his higher educash by playing in collegiate dance band. " Pool " originally composed for his terp orch.[3]

The jargon of *Time* has been imitated by American newspaper men much more extensively than that of *Variety,* but it is measurably less interesting, mainly because most of its neologisms are more or less obvious blends, e.g., *shamateur, cinemactress, franchiseler, boxofficially, bookritic, charitarian* and *powerphobe,* but also be-

1 Headlines, *Egyptian Gazette* (Alexandria), May 12, 1937.

2 *Variety,* May 5, 1937, p. 63. I am indebted here to Mr. George Weller.

3 *Variety,* Nov. 10, 1937. The meaning of *b.r.ing* I can only guess.

cause its assaults upon orthodox syntax are not carried on, like those of *Variety*, in an atmosphere frankly raffish, but under cover of a pretension to information and even learning. Among its gifts to American English are the heavy use of attributive nouns, sometimes in the possessive case, *e.g.*, *Hearsteditor* Jones, *Harvardman* Brown and *Columbia's* Nicholas Murray Butler, and the suppression of the definite article, *e.g.*, " *Report* was circulated today," etc. It also likes to begin sentences with adjectives, and it deals heavily in compounds of the Homeric variety, *e.g.*, *hot-eyed, kinky-bearded, smudge-moustached, Maine-born, moon-placid, plush-plum, legacy-stalking, strike-badgered* and *Yankee-shrewd*.[1] Some of these idiosyncrasies have had a powerful influence upon current newspaper writing, both in the United States and in England. Conservative journalists in both countries have denounced them bitterly,[2] but they are still widely imitated. These have also made some inroads on presumably higher levels, to the consternation of purists.[3] For several years the

[1] I take these from *Time* Makes a Word For It, *Reader's Digest*, March, 1936, and The Vocabulary of *Time* Magazine, by Joseph J. Firebaugh, *American Speech*, Oct., 1940, pp. 232–42. There are other discussions of the *Time* vocabulary and syntax in A Guide to the Pronunciation of Words in *Time*, by E. B. White, *New Yorker*, March 14, 1936, p. 16 (reprinted in his Quo Vadimus?; New York, 1939); Observations on American Prose, by J. Howard Wellard, *Nineteenth Century and After*, Jan., 1937, pp. 66 *ff*; Some Neologisms From Recent Magazines, by Robert Withington, *American Speech*, April, 1931, pp. 277–89; Coinages, by the same, April, 1940, pp. 216–18, and Profiles: *Time, Fortune, Life*, Luce, by Wolcott Gibbs, *New Yorker*, Nov. 28, 1936, pp. 20–25. The last is a merciless parody of the *Time* style.

[2] In England S. K. R[atcliffe], in *Everyman* (London), Sept. 19, 1929, belabored the omission of the article as " a parsimony such as used to be thought of as natural only to the natives of Bengal " (reprinted in *American Speech*, Aug., 1930, p. 481), and in this country Westbrook

Peglar let go as follows in the New York *World-Telegram*, May 29, 1943: " I have no quarrel with Mr. Luce's nervous weekly news review. The *Time*-style is original with *Time* and may be called an honest affectation, although I should think any normal writer, joining the *Time* staff fresh from the outside world, would be driven nuts the first few weeks by the office rule which makes it necessary to back into sentences, telescope certain sets of words into such combinations as *GOPsters* and *OPAdministrator*, throw in the correct proportion of *tycoons* and avoid use of the definite article. If *Time* wants to gibber, that's *Time's* privilege in a free country. But, for gossakes, what has come over our city editors and our press association desk men, particularly in Washington, that they accept this as correct American journalese and harass the undeserving reader with something that may be gullah and may be geechee but certainly isn't newspaper language? "

[3] I find the following, for example, in a release of the National Geographic Society, Jan. 12, 1939: " Busiest trade artery is the railroad from

*Reader's Digest* gave space every month to imitations of the *Time* neologisms by various hopeful apes, but it was seldom that they showed any ingenuity or humor, or any sign of entering the common stock.[1] Indeed, I have seen the statement somewhere that the only invention of *Time* itself to lodge in the language is *socialite*. In 1930 or thereabouts there appeared a magazine called *Ken* which undertook to carry out the *Time* formula to half a dozen more places of decimals, with borrowings from *Variety*, the comic strip and the Cossacks of the Don, but it blew up before it could work its wicked will upon the style of American journalism.

The concocters of trade names have contributed many familiar terms to the American vocabulary, and some of them have circled the world, e.g., *kodak, vaseline, coca-cola* and *linotype*. Many others are so well known at home that it surprises most persons to hear that they are, or ever were, registered or claimed as private trademarks, e.g., *linoleum, tabasco-sauce, celluloid, radiogram, caterpillar-*

---

France," etc. And the following in an editorial in the *Journal of the American Medical Association*, Aug. 9, 1941, p. 453: "Desirable therefore was separation chemically, if possible, of the addiction property of morphine from its analgesic attributes." And the following in Death and Dentistry by Martin H. Fischer, professor of physiology in the University of Cincinnati; Springfield, Ill., 1940, p. 52: "Grossest error lies in the nonrecognition of obviously infected tonsils." And the following in a statement by the Australian News and Information Bureau in London, *Literary Supplement* of the London *Times*, June 10, 1944, p. 288: "Virtual cessation of book importing has caused public demand for local work." In The Oxford Cockneys, London *Observer*, Feb. 13, 1938, St. John Ervine had this to say of a book review in an Oxford undergraduate magazine: "The reviewer, who seems ambitious to join the staff of an American tabloid, an ambition which scarcely justifies his presence at a university, is possessed of the New Style in which articles are omitted, adjectives are used as verbs, and nouns are telescoped to

such an extent that a sentence looks like a railway accident. This is not, as you may imagine, the idiosyncrasy of an undergraduate whose brains have recently received a good hard knock, but is the style that is becoming commoner in our popular press. . . . Cub reporters undergo an intensive training in cinemas and the contents of American ragtime magazines, and are then let loose on the British public. . . . Having learnt in *Time* and magazines of that sort to foreshorten every sentence, they join the staff of a popular print and start zipping the language."

1 In *American Speech*, April, 1940, p. 217, Robert Withington gave these specimens: *tantrumental, snoopidity, cosmeticulous, to make-belove* and *intoxicateer*. Among the *Reader's Digest* gleanings from *Time* itself I find *AAAdministrator, ballyhooligan, dramateur, franchiseler, GOPossibility, intelligentiac, microphonie* and *vitalics*. See *Word Study*, Sept., 1936, p. 4. *Time* once protested that "there is no such thing as *Time* style, but only *Time* tempo and attitude." See the *Reader's Digest*, March, 1938.

tractor, carborundum, dictaphone, neutrodyne, thermos, *menthol* and *Waterbury* (watch).[1] Dr. Louise Pound published a study of such names so long ago as 1913,[2] but since then the subject has been neglected by students of American speech, and in consequence its later literature is meagre. The laws lay down conditions which make the choice of a really effective trade-name far from easy. To become one, legally speaking, it must be a word that does not really name or describe the article to which it is affixed, and it must be sufficiently unlike the trade-names of other articles of the same general type to prevent the buyer mistaking one for the other. If it is applied to an entirely new article, having no other name, it may become that article's common name, and so lose its validity in law by becoming descriptive. The inventor of a new article, to be sure, may patent it, and so acquire a monopoly of its manufacture and sale under whatever name, but a patent is good for but seventeen years, whereas a trade-mark may go on so long as the article is offered for general sale. The Swiss inventor of *cellophane*, Brandenberger, or rather his American assignee, E. I. du Pont de Nemours & Company, lost the exclusive right to the name when the courts decided, on the expiration of his patent, that the article had no other general name, and that *cellophane* was thus descriptive. Much the same thing happened in the cases of *aspirin*, *linoleum*, *kerosene* and *featherbone*. In the case of *dry ice* the name was clearly descriptive from the start.[3] Even *nylon* is not, in the eye of the law, a trade-mark, for the du Pont chemists coined it to designate a whole group of synthetic polyamides that they had developed, and today it is applied to dozens of different substances.[4] But most of the more familiar American trade-names are not common designations for a new article, but special designations for some special brand of a new or old article, and in consequence they are protected by the laws. In the early days of a new

---

1 A number are listed in Pillaging the Dictionary, by Frank H. Vizetelly, *Atlantic Monthly*, Aug., 1932, pp. 228–34. An English list is in Trade Terms Adopted in Standard English, by Edward J. G. Forse, *Notes and Queries*, Oct. 25, 1911, p. 238.

2 Word-Coinage and Modern Trade-Names, *Dialect Notes*, Vol. IV, Part I, pp. 29–41.

3 The subject is intricate, and I do not pretend to be a patent lawyer:

my *Fach* is moral theology. There is an excellent exposition in Lost Monopolies of Names and Things, by E. W. Leavenworth, *Industrial and Engineering Chemistry*, Sept., 1937, pp. 1006–08. See also Surname or Trade Name, the Purpose is the Same, by Edward S. Rogers, *American Druggist*, March, 1944.

4 I am indebted here to Mr. James K. Hunt, of the du Pont public relations department.

article its manufacturers are usually eager to get its name entered in the dictionaries, but when they discover that so entering it tends to give it the significance of a common word, and thus imperils their trade-mark, they are just as eager to have it expunged. The late Frank H. Vizetelly, in the *Atlantic Monthly* paper lately cited, complained bitterly that this shift of interest and desire produces one of the commonest and most racking headaches of a lexicographer's life. The wise inventor, if he has something really new in the world, first patents it and then devises two names for it — one a common and more or less descriptive name, and the other a name so wholly undescriptive that it qualifies as a trade-mark. If he is lucky the trade-mark will have become so firmly established by the time his patent runs out that other persons essaying to market the article will have hard going.

The history of some of the more familiar American trade-names is interesting and deserves the professional attention of etymologists. That of *kodak* and that of *vaseline* are recounted briefly in AL4, p. 172, n. 3 and n. 5. Both meet the requirements of the law precisely and are thus still protected, though *kodak* has been in use since 1888 and *vaseline* since 1870.[1] *Nylon,* just mentioned, has no etymological

---

1 To the history of *kodak* may be added the following extract from a letter from its inventor, George Eastman (1854-1932) to John M. Manly, Dec. 15, 1906: "It was a purely arbitrary combination of letters, not derived in whole or in part from any existing word, arrived at after considerable search for a word that would answer all requirements for a trade-mark name. The principal of these were that it must be short, incapable of being misspelled so as to destroy its identity, must have a vigorous and distinctive personality, and must meet the requirements of the various foreign trade-mark laws, the English being the one most difficult to satisfy owing to the very narrow interpretation that was being given to their law at that time." I take this from George Eastman, by Carl W. Ackerman; New York, 1930, p. 76n. Ackerman himself says: "Eastman was determined that this product should have a name that could not be misspelled or mispronounced, or infringed or copied by anyone. He wanted a strong word that could be registered as a trade-mark, something that everyone would remember and associate only with the product which he proposed to manufacture. *K* attracted him. It was the first letter of his mother's family name. It was 'firm and unyielding.' It was unlike any other letter and easily pronounced. Two *k*'s appealed to him more than one, and by a process of association and elimination he originated *kodak* and gave a new name to a new commercial product. The trade-mark was registered in the United States Sept. 4, 1888." The first *kodak* had been offered for sale in June, 1888. Eastman also originated the slogan, "You press the button and we do the rest." In the early days owners of *kodaks* did not do their own developing and printing.

significance. When the du Pont chemists began making synthetic polyamides some simple and easily remembered name for them was needed, and about 250 were proposed and considered. *Nylon* was finally chosen because it seemed the best of the lot. It is now applied, as I have said, to dozens of different substances, and also to the yarns, filaments and flakes made of them. It is protected, not as a trade-mark, but by the du Pont patents on the manufacturing processes. *Nabisco*, the name of a sugar wafer made by the National Biscuit Company, is composed, as I have noted, of the first syllables of the company's name, and was adopted June 28, 1901 and registered as a trade-mark on November 12, 1901. It is not descriptive, and under the terms of its registration may be used on "biscuits, crackers, bread, wafers, sugar wafers, cakes, snaps, jumbles, hard and soft boiled confectionary, including grainwork, creamwork, panwork, chocolatework, lozenges, and medicated candies." *Uneeda*, owned by the same company, has been in use since September 6, 1898 and was registered on December 27, 1898. It covers the same products as *nabisco*, but may be used by others, I gather, on anything so unlike them as to preclude fraud or confusion. The name of the *kelvinator* was coined by Major Nathaniel B. Wales, who began experimenting with a domestic refrigerating unit (at first a heating unit) in 1907 or 1908, and joined in the incorporation of the first company to make the present *kelvinator* in 1914. The name was derived from that of Lord *Kelvin* (1824–1907), the English physicist whose theoretical studies paved the way for the development of the appliance. *Mazda*, as a name distinguishing electric lamps, was suggested to the General Electric Company by the late Frederick P. Fish, a Boston lawyer and one-time president of the American Telephone and Telegraph Company. He thus described its genesis:

I had long been of the opinion that an ideal trade-name might well be made up of two syllables, both long. For example, I had always regarded *kodak* as a most effective name. While a trade-name need not [1] be descriptive it is advantageous to have it in some way remotely reflect some of the characteristics of the article to which it is applied. In this case it seemed to me that a suggestion of the light-giving property of the lamp might well be indirectly involved. I naturally thought of *Apollo*, *Jupiter* and *Jove*, but these names were relatively commonplace and none of them had the two long syllables that I thought desirable. But I knew, of course, of the Zoroastrian god of the ancient Persians, who stood for the firmament with its light-giving characteristics and whose name

1 No doubt Mr. Fish intended to say *may* not.

was *Ahura Mazda*. It seemed to me that *mazda*, with its two long syllables and its suggestion of the light-giving firmament, might prove an attractive trade-name for the new tungsten incandescent lamps. A long list of other words was suggested, some of them based on proper names, some more or less artificial in character. The name *mazda* was adopted by the General Electric Company.[1]

*Kewpie*, the name of a once very popular doll, was invented by Rose Cecil O'Neill Wilson in 1912, and was first used in the decoration accompanying some verses that she contributed to the *Ladies Home Journal*. Her *kewpies* were almost as successful as Palmer Cox's *brownies* had been in the 8os, and the first dolls bearing the name were made by George Borgfeldt & Company, of New York, in 1913.[2] *Zipper*, as the name of a slide fastener, was coined by the B. F. Goodrich Company, the rubber manufacturers, in 1913, and was registered as a trade-mark on April 7, 1925. It was first used on an overshoe but its great success suggested the use of the slide fastener on other articles, and by 1928, as the NED Supplement shows, *zipper* was taking on the aspect of a common noun. The Goodrich Company thereupon appealed to the courts and its rights were sustained.[3] I gather, however, from a recent statement that its claim is now directed especially to footwear.[4] *Ivory* as the name of a soap was launched in October, 1879. The soap itself, popular because it floats, was invented by accident. One day a workman in the plant of Procter & Gamble at Cincinnati let a machine called a crutcher run during his lunch-hour and it introduced minute bubbles of air into the batch of soap being made. No one suspected that a great revolution had been

1 I take this from Scientific Terms in American Speech, by P. B. McDonald, *American Speech*, Nov., 1926, p. 70. *Mazda* was first used Dec. 21, 1909; its registration as a trade-mark is dated May 3, 1910. I am informed by Mr. C. W. Maedje, of the General Electric Company's lamp department, that the term is "not the name of a thing but rather the mark of a research service."

2 I am indebted here to an anonymous writer in *American Notes and Queries*, April, 1944, p. 9. Mrs. Wilson died in 1944.

3 Goodrich *vs.* Hockmeyer, 40 Fed. 2nd 99.

4 The statement, sent to me by the company on April 27, 1944, said: "The trade-mark 'Zipper' . . . re-

mains today the exclusive trade-mark of B. F. Goodrich for footwear just as it was when adopted by B. F. Goodrich in 1923. No other has the right to use the trade-mark for footwear or in connection with a business in footwear, nor has any other, to the knowledge of B. F. Goodrich so used it." On Jan. 3, 1938, Philip Handerson, then director of advertising and publicity for the company, printed in *Life*, p. 6, a letter protesting against an article published on Nov. 8, 1937, in which *zipper* was treated as a common noun. The editors replied: "*Life's* apologies, but the Goodrich Company must be aware that its trade-mark has passed into the English language."

effected until the soap reached the firm's customers and they began writing in demanding more of the same. " Few of the towns along the [Ohio] river," said a booklet published by the company in 1944, " had filtration plants. For long periods of the year water was a tawny brown. When a bar of soap sank in a sink or bathtub it was lost to view. But floating soap . . ." [1] Unhappily, it still lacked a name. One Sunday morning soon afterward Harley Procter, the senior partner in the company, went to church and heard a sermon on Psalms XLV, 8: " All thy garments smell of myrrh and aloes and, cassia, out of the ivory palaces whereby they have made thee glad." The new floating soap was a dead white, so *Ivory* it became.

*Rayon* is not a trade-mark, but a generic name: the manufacturers of the different brands distinguish them by special names, usually embodying their own names. *Rayon* was chosen by the National Retail Drygoods Association in 1924 after various other names had been proposed, *e.g., glos*. It has been defined by the Federal Trade Commission as " the generic name for manufactured textile fiber or yarn produced chemically from cellulose or with a cellulose base, and for thread, strands or fabric made therefrom, regardless of whether such fiber or yarn be made under the viscose, acetate, cuprammonium, nitrocellulose or other processes." [2] *Bakelite*, on the contrary, is a trade-mark suggested by the name of the inventor, Leo Hendrik *Baekeland*. The substance is synthesized from formaldehyde and carbolic acid, and is generally described as a *vinyl resin*.[3] Many trade-names have fanciful and even romantic origins. An example is afforded by *veronal*, which is of German genesis, though it is familiar in the United States. *Veronal* was invented by Emil Fischer and Freiherr von Mering, two distinguished chemists. After long work upon the project Mering took a holiday and went to Italy. One day, at *Verona*, he received a telegram from Fischer saying that the synthesis of the substance had been effected, and the name *veronal* immediately suggested itself.[4] *Aspirin*, another German invention,

---

1 Into a Second Century With Procter & Gamble; Cincinnati, 1944.
2 Labeling, *National Consumer News*, Nov., 1937, p. 8.
3 War Calls the Tune; Industry Supplies the Words, *American Speech*, April, 1941, p. 160. Dr. Baekeland is a Belgian who came to the United States in 1889, and founded in 1893 a business for the manufacture of photographic papers. He sold out to the Eastman Kodak Company in 1899 and devoted himself to chemical research. The Bakelite Corporation was launched in 1910.
4 Genesis of the Word *Veronal*, by Kurt F. Behne, *Journal of the American Medical Association*, July 18, 1931, p. 198.

had a more prosaic origin. The name is simply a blend of *acetyl* and *spiraeic acid,* the latter an old name for salicylic acid. *Coca-cola,* a compound based on the names of two of the drink's constituents, was first used by J. S. Pemberton, an Atlanta druggist, in 1886, and was registered as a trade-mark on January 31, 1893. The Coca-Cola Company has been much plagued by imitations, some of them borrowing the word *cola* and others playing on *coke,* a common abbreviation for thirty years. The courts have been loath to prohibit others from using *cola,* for it is descriptive, but in 1930 the Supreme Court of the United States decided that *coke* is the exclusive property of the Company.[1] There was a time when it discouraged the use of *coke,* for the term was also a name for cocaine, then present in *coca-cola* in microscopic amount, and the uplifters responsible for the Harrison Act had convinced the country that cocaine was an extremely dangerous drug. But after cocaine was eliminated altogether from the formula, and the alarms about it began to subside, the company found the abbreviation *coke* a good advertisement, and has since stressed it in its advertising.[2] *Coke,* of course, is a common word in other significances, and is traced by the NED to 1669 in the sense of the product remaining after coal is distilled, but in the sense of a non-alcoholic drink made of vegetable extractives it is now the property of the Coca-Cola Company.

---

1 The *Coca-Cola* Company *vs.* The *Koke* Company of America *et al,* 254 U. S. 143; 65 L. Ed. 189.

2 As, for example: "*Coke = Coca-Cola.* It's natural for popular names to acquire friendly abbreviations. That's why you hear Coca-Cola called '*Coke*'." The following is from the decision of the Supreme Court in *Coca-Cola* Company *vs. Koke* Company of America, just cited: "Before 1900 the beginning of the good will [of Coca-Cola] was more or less helped by the presence of cocaine, a drug that, like alcohol or caffein or opium, may be described as a deadly poison or as a valuable item of the pharmacopoeia according to the rhetorical purposes in view. The amount seems to have been very small, but it may have been enough to begin a bad habit, and after the Food and Drug Act of June 30, 1906, if not earlier, long before this suit was brought, it was eliminated from the plaintiff's compound. Coca leaves still are used, to be sure, but after they have been subjected to a drastic process that removes from them every characteristic substance except a little tannin and still less chlorophyl. The cola nut, at best, on its side furnishes but a very small portion of caffein, which now is the only element that has appreciable effect." This decision is printed in full, along with many decisions of lower courts, in Opinions and Decrees Involving *Coke,* the Abbreviation of the Trade-Mark *Coca-Cola;* Atlanta, 1943. I am indebted to Messrs. William J. Hobbs and Ralph Hayes, vice-presidents of the company, for a copy of the book.

Dr. Pound, in her pioneer study, already cited, attempted a classification of trade-names by methods of coinage, as follows:

*Derivatives of proper names: listerine* from that of Sir Joseph *Lister, maxim* (gun) from that of Hiram *Maxim,* postum from that of C. F. *Post.*

*Shortenings or extensions of descriptive words: jell-o, alabastine, resinol, protectograph, shinola, wooltex, reflecto, wheatena.*

*Diminutives: wheatlet, toasterette, chiclet.*

*Compounds: palmolive, willowcraft, waxit, malt-nutrine.*

*Disguised spellings: prest-o-lite, uneeda, rubifoam, porosknit, holsum, shure-on, pro-phy-lac-tic, pil-o-rest, taystee, klingtite.*

*Blends: jap-a-lac,*[1] *locomobile, tweeduroy, triscuit, vaporub, eversharp, damaskeene, cuticura* (from *cuticle* and *cure*), *valspar* (from *Valentine* & Company and *spar*), *philco.*

*Terms made from initials or other parts of proper names: pebeco* from *P. Beirsdorf & Company, reo* from *R. E. Olds.*

*Arbitrary coinages: kotex, zu-zu, tiz, kryptok.*

A lucky hit in coining trade-names establishes a fashion and brings in a host of imitators. *Kodak* was followed by a great many other terms beginning or ending or both beginning and ending with *k*, and *uneeda* had a long progeny, e.g., *uwanta, ibuya.* In the 20s there was a craze for the *-ex* ending in arbitrary coinages, and it produced scores of examples, e.g., *lux, celotex, pyrex, kleenex, kotex, simplex, laminex, cutex,* etc.[2] Ten years later *master* came into fashion as both suffix and prefix, e.g., *toastmaster, mixmaster, masterart, masterlite.*[3]

Some of the current coinages show a considerable ingenuity, e.g., *klim,* the name of a powered milk, which is simply *milk* backward; *flit,* a spray for obnoxious insects, suggesting very forcibly their precipitate departure; *rem,* a cough cure, obviously based on *remedy;*[4] *jonteel,* a perfume, from the French *gentile; toncan,* a brand of sheet-iron, produced by reversing the syllables of *Canton,* the town in Ohio where it is made; and *gunk,* "a self-emulsifying colloidal detergent solvent."[5] Many trade-names embody efforts to state claims for the product without colliding with the legal prohibition of descriptive terms, e.g., *holeproof, eversharp, interwoven, softee,* and *klingtite.*[6] The number of new ones registered in the United

1 See AL4, p. 172.
2 Trade-Name Suffixes, by Walter E. Myers, *American Speech,* July 1927, p. 448, and X-ploiting the La-z-y Letters, by Mabel E. Strong, *Words,* Dec. 1938, pp. 136–37.
3 The Word *Master* in Trade Names, by G. H. Reese, *American Speech,* Dec., 1937, pp. 262–66.

4 *Rem* was invented by Joseph Katz, a Baltimore advertising man.
5 Launched by the Curran Corporation, Malden, Mass., in 1932.
6 An interesting discussion of the qualities required in such names, dividing them into categories, is in 33 Check Points for Finding a Name for That New Product, by P. H.

States in a normal year is about 10,000. Between 1939 and 1943, because of the impact of World War II upon private enterprise, it declined almost a half.[1]

The copious imitation of new suffixes noted among trade-names is matched in the general speech of the Republic. *Printery*, traced by the DAE to 1638 in America and not found in England until 1657, seems to have stood alone for a century and a half, but after *grocery* came in in 1791 it was quickly followed by other forms in *-ery*, and their coinage continues briskly to this day. The DAE traces *bindery* to 1810, *groggery* to 1822, *bakery* to 1827, *creamery* to 1858, and *cannery* to 1870, and marks them all Americanisms. It suggests that Dutch forms in *-ij*, e.g., *bakkerij* and *binderij*, may have produced the earlier examples, and a correspondent suggests that the later ones may owe something to German forms in *-ei*, e.g., *bäckerei* and *konditorei*,[2] but the suffix *-ery* and its attendant *-ory* are really old in English,[3] and *buttery*, never in general use in the United States, goes back to the Fourteenth Century.[4] It is, however, on this side of the water that they have been hardest worked, and that hard working has been frequently noted by both English travelers and native students of language. In the United States, reported one of the former in 1833, " shops are termed *stores*, and these again figure under the respective designations of John Tomkins's *grocery*, *bakery*, *bindery* or even *wiggery*, as the case may be." [5] Bartlett, in the first edition of his Glossary, 1848, listed *stemmery* as the designation of " a building in which tobacco is stemmed," and also all the terms just noted save

---

Erbes, Jr., *Printers Ink*, Oct. 1, 1943, pp. 28–97. An account of the method, frequently used, of finding a new name by means of a prize competition, is in $1,000 a Word, by Homer A. Parsons, *Writers' Digest*, Feb., 1927, pp. 102–03. The names in a special field are dealt with in Trade-Names in the Petroleum Industry, by Dora Lee Brauer, *American Speech*, April, 1935, pp. 122–28.

1 Patent Office Report for 1943, p. 8.
2 Mrs. William W. Elder, Jr., of Idaho City, Idaho.
3 *Carriage-repository*, now obsolete, was apparently an Americanism, though the DAE does not list it.
4 It survives more or less in New England. Up to within recent times

it had an elegant smack there and was thought to be better than *pantry*. (I am indebted here to Mrs. Isaac Gerson Swope of Wayne, Pa., and Mr. J. F. Malley of Boston.) At Oxford and Cambridge the term is used to designate a pantry. It was borrowed by Harvard and Yale to designate a room in which food and drink for sale to the students was stored. The Yale *buttery* was abolished in 1817.
5 Notes of a Tour of the United States, by A. Fergusson. I am indebted for this to the DAE. Fergusson's book is not listed in the bibliographies of English travelers' books by Nevins, Brooks and Mesick.

*wiggery*, which is likewise omitted by the DAE. So is *drygoodsery*, used by *Putnam's Monthly* in 1853 to describe the new A. T. Stewart store in Broadway.[1] Since 1900 many additions to the ever-growing list have been reported by lexicographical explorers, *e.g.*, *cobblery*, *renewry* (a hat-cleaning shop),[2] *shoe-renewry* or *shu-renury*,[3] *shoe-fixery*,[4] *juicery* (apparently a stand for the sale of fruit juices),[5] *cattery*,[6] *rabbitry*,[7] *cyclery*, *condensery* (a milk condensing plant), *chickery*,[8] *bowlery*,[9] *sweetery*,[10] *beanery*,[11] *eggery*,[12] *refreshery*,[13] *henry*,[14] *eatery*, *cakery*, *car-washery*, *doughnutery*, *lunchery*, *mendery*, *stitchery*,[15] *nuttery*, *chowmeinery*, *drinkery*, *dancery*, *hattery*, *cleanery*, *drillery* (a civil-service cramming school),[16] *squabery*, *snackery*, *breakfastry*,[17] *smeltery* and *skunkery* (a place where skunks are bred for their fur).[18] Some of these, of course, show an effort to be waggish, and there is more of that conscious humor in *ham-and-eggery*, *hashery*, *boozery*, *nitery* (a night-club), *hoofery*, *cocktailery*, *praisery* (a press-agent's den), *sickery* (for hospital), *learnery* (for a girls' boarding-school) and *stompery* (a dancing-school).[19] Now and then a learned man takes a hand in the business, as when Dr. Franklin H. Giddings launched *taboobery* and *tomtomery*, which do not, of course, fall precisely within the pattern, for they designate abstrac-

1 New York Daguerreotyped, April, 1853, p. 358, col. 1.
2 Observed in Atlanta, Ga., by Mr. C. Mertzanoff of New York: private communication, Feb. 11, 1938.
3 *New Yorker*, June 11, 1938, p. 8.
4 Advertisement of Filene's department-store, Boston *Herald*, Dec. 18, 1935.
5 *American Speech*, April, 1941, p. 120.
6 *American Speech*, just cited.
7 Notes of a Peninsula Commuter, by Joseph Burton Vasché, *American Speech*, Feb., 1940, p. 54.
8 *American Speech*, March, 1927, p. 296.
9 Sign on a bowling alley in North Charles street, Baltimore, 1944: "*Most Modern Bowleries*."
10 The Second Visitor, by Timothy Fuller, *American Magazine*, Sept., 1937.
11 Not listed by the DAE, but it must go back to the 80s, at least.
12 The Living Language, by Dwight L. Bolinger, *Words*, May, 1938, p. 69.

13 Some Odd Names, by Manuel Prenner, *American Speech*, Oct., 1931, p. 80.
14 *Atlantic Monthly*, May, 1935, p. 38: "Fresh Eggs from our Own *Henry*" —a sign encountered at Tannersville, N. Y.
15 The examples from *eatery* to *stitchery* come from Irradiation of Certain Suffixes, by E. C. Hills, *American Speech*, Oct., 1925, p. 38.
16 Vogue Affixes in Present Day Word-Coinage, by Louise Pound, *Dialect Notes*, Vol. V, Part I, 1918, p. 10.
17 The last two were reported by Ethel M. Head, *Better Homes and Gardens*, Dec., 1938.
18 *Stock Grower and Farmer*, June 21, 1890, quoted by the DAE.
19 The last three are credited to Barney Oldfield, of the Lincoln (Neb.) *Journal and Star*, by *American Speech*, Oct., 1941, p. 207.

tions.[1] Neither does *toiletry*, which is in very wide use, usually in the plural. The English employ one *-ery* word that is seldom, if ever, encountered in the United States, to wit, *farmery*, which is defined by the NED as " the buildings, yards, etc., belonging to a farm," and traced to 1656. It has never got any lodgment in the United States.[2] Neither has *servery*, which is defined by the NED as " a room from which meals are served " and traced to 1893.[3] *Booterie* and *snackerie* [4] show pseudo-English influence, but are not often encountered. An archaic term, *beefery*, signifying a packing-plant for beef, is reported by Woodford Heflin.[5]

Perhaps the most fertile of the latter-day American suffixes is *-eria*, borrowed from *cafeteria*. All the lexicographers agree that *cafeteria* is of Spanish origin,[6] but they are vague about the time and place of its entrance into American English, and about its acquirement of a special American meaning. When, in 1927, Phillips Barry discovered it in an obscure dictionary of Cuban Spanish, defined as *la tienda en que se vende café por menor*, the shop where coffee is sold at retail,[7] the problem appeared to be moving toward solution,

---

1 They are in his The Mighty Medicine; New York, 1929. *Comstockery* is said to have been contributed to American by George Bernard Shaw. In 1905 the New York Public Library, in response to the uproar over his play, Mrs. Warren's Profession, put his Man and Superman on its reserved list. Shaw thereupon cabled a statement to the New York *Times*, Sept. 1, 1905, in which he said: "*Comstockery* is the world's standing joke at the expense of the United States. Europe likes to hear of such things. It confirms the deep-seated conviction of the Old World that America is a provincial place, a second-rate town civilization, after all." *Comstockery*, of course, was derived from the name of Anthony Comstock (1844–1915), chief smeller for the New York Society for the Suppression of Vice from 1873 until his death.
2 From an advertisement for the sale of Levishaw Manor, Norfolk, in the London *Observer*, May 31, 1936: "Four receptions, 8 bedrooms, 2 bathrooms. Mains electricity. Ga-

rage for 4 cars. Small *farmery*. Cottage, Grass tennis court." I am indebted here to the collectanea of the late F. H. Tyson, of Hong Kong.
3 Welfare Work for L.P.T.B. Men, London *Times*, June 17, 1938: " The canteen and *servery* have been so designed that each girl can serve eight lunches a minute."
4 *American Speech*, Dec., 1936, p. 374.
5 New Evidence on Americanisms, *American Speech*, Feb., 1942, p. 65. The only example given is from the *Stock Grower and Farmer*, April 12, 1890.
6 An early effort to derive it from the Turkish has come to nothing. See *Cafeteria*, by Charles E. Edgerton, *American Speech*, Jan., 1927, pp. 214–15, and *Cafeteria* — a Correction, by the same, April, 1927, p. 331.
7 Diccionario Provincial Cuasi Razonado de Voces i Frases Cubanas, by Esteban Pichardo y Tapia; third ed.; Havana, 1862. The first edition of this work was published at Matanzas in 1836, and there was a second at Havana in 1849.

but it is still to be shown precisely how, when and where *cafeteria* reached the United States and how it came to acquire the meaning of a self-help eating-place. Says Mr. Barry:

> Outside of Cuba and Porto Rico the word is not quoted for American Spanish in lexicons. This [Cuban] *cafetería* has no connection with Spanish *cafetera*, a coffee-pot, but is explained as a new formation on the analogy of Cuban-Spanish *bisutería*, which Rubio [1] correctly calls a loan-word from the French *bijouterie*. Other words in Cuban Spanish formed in the same manner are *platería* and *joyería*, the last an alleged purist substitute for *bisutería*.[2]

In a later dictionary of American Spanish, compiled long after Pichardo's and published after Barry's paper,[3] *cafetería* is credited, not only to Cuba and Porto Rico, but also to Mexico, and defined as an *establecimento donde se sirva esta bebida*. This ascription shows some gain in plausibility, for there has been little if any infiltration of Cuban Spanish into the United States, save in the Key West area, and all the available evidence indicates that *cafeteria* came into American English west of the Alleghanies, where the only Spanish prevailing is of the Mexican variety. The exact place of its birth is in dispute, for though California claims it there is reason to believe that it actually made its first appearance in Chicago at the time of the World's Fair of 1893. The DAE cites an authority who says that it was in use in California *c.* 1853, but he adds that it then signified " rather a place for drinking than for eating," as in the Mexican example just cited. The DAE's first example in the American sense is from the Chicago Directory for 1894, which listed a *Cafetiria* Catering Company (note the spelling) at 45 Lake Street. The names and addresses for this directory, in all probability, were gathered in 1893. By 1895 it was listing four *cafetirias*, and by 1896 one of them (with its name changed to *caféteria*) had become so prosperous that Chicago gunmen were inspired to crack its safe.[4] Meanwhile, the *cafeteria* had begun to spread,

1 Estudios Lexicográficos: La Anarquía del Lenguaje en la América Española, by Darío Rubio; two vols.; City of Mexico, 1925.

2 Cafeteria, American Speech, Oct., 1927, p. 37. Nearly a year before this, in The Pronunciation of Cafeteria, American Speech, Nov., 1926, p. 114, E. C. Hills reported finding the word in two Spanish dictionaries, and surmised that it was a Cubanism, but he did not run down the evidence unearthed by Barry.

3 Diccionario General de Americanismos, by Francisco J. Santamaria; City of Mexico, 1942, Vol. I, p. 264.

4 Chicago Tribune, June 28, 1898, quoted by the DAE. Mr. W. K. Hale, of Montreal, tells me that he has a definite recollection of a cafeteria in Chicago during the Summer of 1893. His memory, of course, may err as to the spelling.

and before the end of 1893 there was at least one in St. Louis. A witness to its existence is Mr. George F. Longdorf, of Oakland, Calif., who says:

> I have personal knowledge and positive recollection of the word *cafetiria,* as it was then spelled, over a self-help restaurant on Pine street, St. Louis, opposite the Merchants' Exchange, in 1893. Some of my schoolmates patronized it, and Alec Blair, son of Frank P. Blair, called it " the conscience joint " because each patron appraised his own tray and paid the amount without any check or ticket. I have always fancied that it came up the river — from New Orleans, possibly. One person suggested to me that it may have been derived from *café* and the French verb *tirer,* to draw, to pull, to reach for. When I saw it the Spanish form *cafeteria* was not used, and the pronunciation was *caf-e-ti'r-i-a.*[1]

*Cafetera,* in standard Spanish, means a coffee-pot, not a coffee-house. The Italian *caffetiere* is of precisely the same meaning, and it is not at all impossible that it, and not the Cuban-Spanish word, suggested *cafeteria.* There were, in fact, a great many more Italians than Cubans in Chicago in the World's Fair era. Meanwhile, California continues to claim its origin, and it may be admitted that that great State, if not actually responsible for the word itself, is at least largely responsible for the proliferation of the *cafeteria*'s progeny. In the early days the *-teria* ending was always used as an indicator of self-service, but as J. M. Steadman, Jr., has shown,[2] its scope began to widen by 1930, and it is now used in many terms signifying establishments in which the customer is waited on by others. Steadman distinguishes three meanings, to wit:

> 1. " A place where articles are sold on the self-service plan." Examples: *caketeria, candyteria, drugteria, pastreria, cleaneteria* (" a place furnishing hot water, soap, cleaning fluids, brushes "), *groceteria* (*grocerteria, groceryteria*), *healtheteria, drygoodsteria, luncheteria, marketeria, basketeria, mototeria* (" a *groceteria* on wheels "), *restauranteria, shaveteria* (" a place where one finds all the things needed for shaving oneself "), *shoeteria* (" a place where one examines the stock of shoes and selects a pair to one's liking "), *resteteria, casketeria.*
> 2. " A place where certain articles are sold without the self-service plan." Examples: *chocolateria, sodateria, fruiteria, hatateria, kalfateria* (" a shoe store "), *radioteria, smoketeria.*
> 3. " A place where certain services are rendered — by others, not by the customer himself." Examples: *bobateria* (" where hair is bobbed "), *valeteria, wrecketeria* (" a place where old cars are wrecked and parts sold ").

The majority of such terms, of course, are hardly more than nonce-words, but some of them show signs of sticking as *cafeteria* itself has

---

1 Private communication, Oct. 18, 1939.
2 *Basketeria* and the Meaning of the

Suffix *-teria, American Speech,* June, 1930, pp. 417 and 418.

stuck. Since Steadman published his list there have been many additions to it, for example, *gasteria*,[1] *buffeteria*,[2] *caveteria* (a basement
restaurant),[3] *camerateria*,[4] *scarfeteria* (a necktie shop),[5] *danceteria*,[6]
*honeyteria*,[7] *sweeteria*,[8] *washerteria* (a laundry), *icerteria*,[9] *movie-
teria*,[10] *furnitureteria*,[11] *bootblackateria*,[12] *typewriteria*,[13] *roadateria*,[14]
and *garmenteria*.[15] Others, antedating the Steadman list but omitted
from it, are *healthateria*, *millinteria*, *bargainteria*,[16] *farmateria*, *cleaniteria*, *spaghetteria*,[17] *accomateria* (a small truck from which vegetables
are sold),[18] and *smoketeria*.[19]

The literature of *-teria* is extensive, and there have been many contributions to it in *American Speech*. The pioneer investigator of the
suffix was the before-mentioned E. C. Hills (1867–1932), professor of
Spanish and later of Romance philology at the University of California.[20] There is an extensive article on the *cafeteria* in the Encyclopedia

1 Reported from Louisville, 1936, by
Mr. Verne Salyards, of New Albany, Ind., and from Indianapolis,
1937, by Mr. P. H. Long.
2 In Chicago. *American Speech*, April,
1940, p. 131.
3 In the Baker Hotel, Dallas, Texas.
4 Reported by the Indianapolis *Star*,
Aug. 18, 1940, to have opened in
New York. " Camera fans may use
its dark rooms and equipment upon
the payment of a small fee. The
chemicals are on the house. Print
paper may be bought in quantities as
small as one sheet."
5 Found by a correspondent in Randolph street, near Dearborn, Chicago, 1941.
6 *New Yorker*, Dec. 16, 1939. " It is
advertised as the world's first self-
service night club and is located over
the Rialto Theatre on Times
square."
7 Reported from Benton Lake, Minn.,
in *American Speech*, April, 1933, p.
80.
8 Found by a correspondent in Los
Angeles.
9 The last two were reported from
Fort Worth, Texas, by Miss M. L.
Hudson, 1937.
10 Reported from San Francisco by
Ethel S. Mitchell in *American
Speech*, Feb., 1932, p. 233.
11 Reported from Lincoln, Neb., in

*American Speech*, April, 1931, p.
304.
12 Reported from the Bowery, New
York, in *American Speech*, Dec.,
1930, p. 159.
13 Found at 5216 Wilshire boulevard,
Los Angeles, by Victor T. Reno,
1944.
14 Reported from New Haven, Conn.,
by Manuel Prenner in *American
Speech*, June, 1930, p. 438.
15 Reported from North Carolina by
George W. Snyder of Charlotte,
April 20, 1939.
16 All three reported by C. N. Nelson
in *American Speech*, Dec., 1929, p.
177.
17 *Farmateria* and *cleaniteria* were reported from Toronto and *spaghetteria* from New York City in *American Speech*, April, 1929, p. 333.
18 Reported from a Philadelphia sub-
urb by M. A. Shaaber in *American
Speech*, Oct., 1927, p. 67.
19 Reported from Santa Ana, Calif., by
E. C. Hills in *American Speech*, Jan.,
1926, p. 246.
20 His early publications on the subject were New Words in California,
*Modern Language Notes*, March,
1923; and Irradiation of Certain Suffixes, *American Speech*, Oct., 1925.
They were followed by The Pronunciation of *Cafeteria*, already
cited. In the last-named paper he

Britannica,[1] which records that a self-service restaurant for men only was established in New York in 1885, and another for both sexes in Chicago in 1891. But neither was called a *cafeteria.* In July, 1925 the *Journal of Home Economics* reported an investigation which indicated that the first real *cafeteria* was set up in Chicago. Phillips Barry, in the paper that I have quoted, shows that the idea of self-service was familiar in the coffee-shops of the Eastern Mediterranean region more than a century ago. In 1941 the *American Mercury* printed an article [2] in which a Los Angeles *cafeteria* magnate, Clifford E. Clinton by name, was quoted as claiming that his father, Edmund J. Clinton, " once a missionary to China for the Salvation Army," established in Los Angeles, in 1900, " the world's first serve-yourself eaterie," and that " for it the term *cafeteria* was coined." As we have seen, there were *cafeterias* in Chicago and St. Louis at least seven years before this. In *American Speech,* October, 1940, p. 335 M. C. McPhee reported that *cafeterian* had come into use (apparently at the University of Nebraska) to signify " a student who visits classes for a week or two before registering in some of them," but it does not seem to have spread elsewhere.

Among the other American suffixes that have produced notable progeny are *-orium* and *-cade.* Of words made of the former I listed the following in AL4, p. 179: *beautorium, healthatorium, preventorium, barberatorium, bobatorium, lubritorium, infantorium, hatatorium, motortorium, odditorium, pantorium* or *pantatorium, printorium, restatorium* or *restorium, shavatorium, suitatorium* and *pastorium.* To these may be added *corsetorium,*[3] *hot-dogatorium,*[4] *parentorium,*[5] *furnituorium* (a furniture store), *hairitorium* (a store dealing in wigs and hair goods), *puritorium* (a Jewish ritual bath),[6]

---

showed that the Spanish pronunciation of the word, with the accent on the penultimate, was still heard in California in 1925. In April, 1928, p. 352, *American Speech* reported that the movie magazine, *Picture Play,* was giving it an accent and making it *cafétéria,* apparently on the theory that it was related to the French *café.*

[1] Fourteenth Edition, Vol. IV; New York, 1929.

[2] A New Boss Takes Los Angeles, by Rena M. Vale, March, pp. 299 ff.

[3] I am indebted here to Mrs. Isaac Goldberg of Boston.

[4] Title of an article by Robert Littell, *Today,* June 6, 1936.

[5] *Survey Midmonthly,* Oct., 1940: " The unique Welles *Parentorium,* parent guidance center of the National Hospital for Speech Disorders, New York, has a new director."

[6] For the last three I am indebted to More Notes on Neo-Suffixes, by Manuel Prenner, *American Speech,* Feb., 1943, p. 71.

*shoetorium*,[1] *theatorium*,[2] *sonotorium*,[3] *eatatorium* and *servitorium*.[4] The analogous *-arium* has meanwhile produced *vocarium* (a collection of gramophone records of the human voice),[5] *oceanarium* (an underwater zoo),[6] *abortarium* (a hospital specializing in abortions),[7] *ritualarium* (a Jewish ritual bath, identical with a *puritorium*, just noted),[8] and *terrarium* ("a covered glass globe or fish-tank containing flowers and plants to be grown indoors during the Winter").[9] *Preventorium*, which is listed by the NED Supplement, was coined by the late Nathan Straus in the early 90s as a euphemism for *sanitorium* to designate a hospital for the early treatment of consumptives.[10] *Odditorium* was launched by Robert L. Ripley to designate an exhibition of oddities at the Chicago World's Fair of 1933–34, but his claim to its invention has been challenged by Allen Walker Read, who reports that there was an *odditorium* in Kingston-on-Thames, a village near London, before World War I.[11] Latinate suffixes in *-ium* and *-ory* have also been put to use by the English. Grose noted *nicknackatory*, in the sense of a toy-shop, in his "Classical Dictionary of the Vulgar Tongue," 1785, and Robert Southey recorded in his Commonplace Book [12] that an *opificium* for the sale of "the celebrated Belleish Convent soap" was maintained in his time at 116 Pall Mall, London.[13] *Planetarium*, to designate a machine for exhibiting the motion of the heavenly bodies, is probably an Americanism, though the DAE does

---

1 Notes, by Louise Pound, *American Speech*, Oct., 1936, p. 274.
2 The designation of a movie-theatre in Uniontown, Ala. I am indebted here to Mr. Sigmund Sameth of New York: private communication (with a photograph of the marquee), July 1, 1939.
3 A building equipped with loudspeakers. Reported in *American Speech*, Oct., 1939, p. 236, to have been coined by McClure and Walker, Kearney, Neb., architects.
4 Reported as a euphemism for *grease-pit* by Robert W. Meader in the *Classical Outlook*, Feb., 1942, p. 46, noted in *American Speech*, Dec., 1942, p. 284.
5 Profile of George Robert Vincent, *New Yorker*, May 17, 1941.
6 The Marine Studios *Oceanarium* at Marineland, Fla., was reported by the Baltimore *Sun*, Dec. 10, 1939.

7 What Everyone Should Know About Abortion, by Jane Ward, *American Mercury*, Aug., 1941, p. 196.
8 I am indebted here to Mr. Lewis Bertrand of the Language Service Center, New York.
9 *American Speech*, Dec., 1942, p. 284.
10 At his death on Jan. 11, 1931 the Associated Press reported, on the authority of his son, that he regarded this invention as one of the three greatest achievements of his life. See *American Speech*, Feb., 1933, p. 74.
11 *Odditorium* – Believe It or Not, *American Speech*, Dec., 1940, p. 442.
12 Vol. IV, p. 421.
13 The NED does not list *opificium*, but it traces *opifice*, in the sense of a fabric, a work, to 1616, and *opificer*, in the sense of a fabricator, to 1548.

not so mark it. The first example of its use offered by both the DAE
and the NED comes from John Adams's diary, 1774. The University
of Chicago has lately revived a medieval monkish term to designate
its Ricketts *Scriptorium*, " the only establishment in the United States
engaged exclusively in manuscript lettering and illumination." When,
in 1938, the first volume of the DAE was published, the lay brothers
of the *scriptorium* prepared illuminated copies for King George of
England, for President Roosevelt, for Sir William A. Craigie, the chief
editor of the dictionary, and for Dr. James R. Hulbert, his chief
associate.

All the words in *-cade* seem to have been suggested by *cavalcade*,
which is a loan from the French and is traced by the NED, in English use, to 1591. Its true suffix is not *-cade* but *-ade*. The latter got
into French in loan-words from the Southwestern Romance languages,
and many of the words embodying it subsequently passed into English, *e.g., accolade, ambuscade, arcade, balustrade, brigade, cannonade,
esplanade, marmalade, parade* and *serenade*. But *lemonade*, which the
NED traces to 1663, was apparently taken into English direct from
the Spanish; in fact, it seems to have been preceded by *lemonado*, a
plain imitation of the Spanish *limonada*. *Motorcade* was first reported in *Notes and Queries* in 1924.[1] A year later it was noted by
*Modern Language Notes*,[2] but for a while it seems to have made
progress only slowly. By 1930, however, an anonymous correspondent of *American Speech* was sending in word that the pedagogues
of the University of North Carolina had adopted it.[3] This correspondent denounced it as "a monstrosity" and argued that *-cade* was
"not by any chance a philological entity, like a root or suffix," and
thus could not be "lifted from one companionship and thrust into
another." But no one paid any attention to him, and soon afterward
W. L. Werner reported to *American Speech* that it had been used
in an Associated Press dispatch from Jamestown, N. D., on June 9,
1928, when a party of North Dakota politicians, headed by Governor
A. G. Sorlie, started from Jamestown in a *motorcade* for the Republi-

1 The Earliest *Motorcade*, by W. L.
Werner, *American Speech*, June,
1932, p. 388.
2 March, 1925, p. 189. I take this from
*Motorcade*, by Robert Withington,
*American Speech*, April, 1931, p. 313.
3 *Motorcade*, Aug., 1930, pp. 495 and

496. It was used in a bulletin of the
extension division of the university
announcing that two *motorcades*
would set out from Chapel Hill on
June 7, 1930 to carry the enlightenment to Tar Heel share-croppers.

can national convention at Kansas City.[1] A few months later Dr. Atcheson L. Hench, of the University of Virginia, reported that " despite legitimate protest, *motorcade,* like John Brown's body, goes marching on," and added two more examples of its use to the growing stock.[2] On November 1, 1929, he said, the Baltimore *Sun* printed an Associated Press dispatch from Thomas, W. Va., announcing the departure of a *motorcade* of 500 cars from that town, and on October 1, 1930 the Charlottesville (Va.) *Progress* printed another from Cartersville, Ga., saying that " a *motorcade* of 45 or 50 masked men " had taken a colored brother named John Will Clark from the local calaboose " and hanged him to the cross-beam of a telephone pole on the fair grounds a mile away." In the note before cited Werner reported that the invention of *motorcade* was ascribed by a contributor to F. P. Adams's column in the New York *Herald Tribune* [3] to Lyle Abbott, automobile editor of the Arizona *Republican* of Phoenix. Abbott used it for the first time, according to this contributor, " in 1912 or 1913 to describe the procession of motor-cars which took part in a Sociability Run from Phoenix to Prescott." He continued:

There was some comment on the word, and the *Republican's* editor, Uncle Billy Spear, the outstanding classicist and pundit among Western editors, came to Abbott's defense with so much charm and fervor that *motorcade* was soon in general use in that community. It should not be used in referring to a string of cars that has formed by chance in traffic, but does properly apply to cars that have come together for a trip, parade, or demonstration with a common destination or purpose.[4]

Despite its success, *motorcade* has produced only a meagre progeny. I have encountered, indeed, none save *autocade,*[5] *aquacade,*[6] *icecapade,*[7] *communicade,*[8] *camelcade* and *areocade.*[9] The more cor-

---

1 *Motorcade* and *to demagogue, American Speech,* Dec., 1930, p. 155.
2 *Cavalcade's Daughters, Motorcade* and *Aerocade, American Speech,* April, 1931, p. 254.
3 Garth Cate, June 29, 1931.
4 I take this from Werner's article, just cited.
5 In an Associated Press dispatch from Chicago, May 9, 1931. Reported in *Autocade,* by Atcheson L. Hench, *American Speech,* Aug. 1931, pp. 463–64.
6 The Living Language, by Dwight L. Bolinger, *Words,* April, 1940, 54.

Bolinger reported it occurring in Chesterfield cigarette advertisements, Oct., 1939.
7 Washington *Times-Herald,* Jan. 18, 1941, reported in Free Wheeling, *American Speech,* April, 1941, p. 158.
8 *Gardens, Houses and People* (Baltimore), Jan., 1944, p. 8. Apparently a display of war equipment.
9 The Talk of the Town, *New Yorker,* June 24, 1939. I find among my notes a newspaper clipping reprinting an editorial from *Life,* in which *aerocade* is offered as a novelty, along with two alternatives.

rectly formed *lemonade* has begotten *orangeade, fruitade, pineapple-ade, gingerade, limeade* and a number of others.[1] "*Lemonade* is never written as two words, *lemon ade,* but its suffix sometimes detaches itself in the names of other fruit drinks. Signs advertising *orange ade, grapefruit ade, wild cherry ade* are not unusual. Drug stores and groceries sometimes announce lines of *ades.*" [2]

A number of the suffixes in continued use in both England and the United States show considerably more life in this country, *e.g.,* -*dom,* -*ster,* -*eer* and -*ette.* In 1912 Logan Pearsall Smith was complaining [3] that -*dom* was being displaced in England by -*ness,* and that the effort of Thomas Carlyle and others to revive it during the Nineteenth Century had produced only one generally accepted word, *boredom,* which the NED traces to 1864. But this statement was far too sweeping, for though it is true that some of Carlyle's inventions had but short lives, *e.g., duncedom,* 1829, *rascaldom* and *scoundreldom,* 1837, and *dupedom,* 1843, it is also true that various other novelties of his era have survived, *e.g., officialdom,* 1863, *serfdom,* 1850, and *stardom,* 1865. In the United States the old suffix, which goes back to Anglo-Saxon days, is still very much alive. In 1918 Louise Pound published in *Dialect Notes* [4] a list of twenty-three new words embodying it, *e.g., fandom, filmdom, moviedom, screendom.* She made the suggestion that the influence of the analogous German -*thum* probably had something to do with its current popularity, and no doubt this was true, but the suffix had been in constant use long before the outbreak of World War I made Americans aware of *deutschtum, kaisertum* and their like.[5] In 1927 Josephine M. Burnham printed a longer list,[6] and showed that *dom* had acquired four distinguishable

*avicade* and *aircade.* Unhappily, I have been unable to determine the date of this editorial, but it seems to have been printed before *Life* became a picture paper.

1 *Apple-ade* appeared in an advertisement of the British Ministry of Food, London *Daily Express,* Dec. 3, 1940. The advertisement said: "Never waste the peel and cores of your apples. Boil them in a little water, and you'll have a delicious and very health-giving drink."

2 *American Speech,* Oct., 1933, p. 76.

3 The English Language: New York, 1912, p. 93.

4 Vogue Affixes in Present-Day Word-Coinage, Vol. V, Part I, 1918, pp. 6 and 7.

5 In one column of *Putnam's Monthly,* Dec., 1854, p. 624, I find *waiterdom* and *Cuffeydom.* On Feb. 2, 1887, as the NED notes, the St. Louis *Globe-Democrat* used *blizzardom.*

6 Three Hard-Worked Suffixes, *American Speech,* Feb., 1927, pp. 244–46.

significances: (1) realm or jurisdiction, *e.g., filmdom, fraternitydom, motordom;* (2) state or condition, *e.g., pauperdom, stardom, hickdom;* (3) type or character, *e.g., crookdom, loaferdom, thugdom;* and (4) common interest, *e.g., cattledom, footballdom, puzzledom.* Finally, in 1941, Dr. Harold Wentworth rounded up more than 200 dated examples of *-dom* words introduced since 1800, both in this country and in England, and so provided a refutation of the theory of Smith (and of various other authorities) that the suffix is obsolescent.[1] Many of his earlier examples were English, but for the later years the American inventions were numerous, *e.g., authordom* (traced to 1925), *bookdom* (1918), *crackerdom* (1934), *crossword-puzzledom* (1939), *dictatordom* (1939), *editorialdom* (1939), *folkdom* (1939), *freckledom* (1940), *gangsterdom* (1934), *grouchdom* (1939), *lawn-mowerdom* (1933), *Nazidom* (1933), *newsdom* (1931), *ringdom* (1940), *slumdom* (1927), *sovietdom* (1927). To Wentworth's list a large number of other American examples might be added, for new words in *-dom* are being coined all the time, *e.g., retaildom.*[2]

The suffix *-ster*, in the early days of English, was mainly used in the formation of feminine agent-nouns, but since the Middle Ages it has lost its suggestion of gender. At the beginning of the Eighteenth Century it began to take on a disparaging significance, apparently because of its frequent appearance in the designations of the humbler sort of workmen. The NED traces *rhymester* to 1719, *trickster* to 1711 and *punster* to 1700. The late O. F. Emerson, in his " Outline History of the English Language," 1906, expressed the opinion that it was going out of use, but since then it has enjoyed a considerable revival in both England and the United States, but especially in the United States. In 1918 Dr. Pound, in the paper lately cited, listed *clubster, funster, hopster, mobster,* and *speedster* as recent American inventions, and *hymnster* and *wordster* as novelties in England, and in 1927 Miss Burnham added *gangster, gridster, dopester, roadster, prankster, playster* and *workster.* Since then various contributors to *American Speech* have reported *netster* ( a tennis-player), *thug-*

1 The Allegedly Dead Suffix *-dom* in Modern English, *Publications of the Modern Language Association,* March, 1941, pp. 280–306. The other authorities, four in number, are named and quoted, pp. 280 and 281, along with eight dissenters.

2 *Women's Wear* (New York), 1938, quoted in the Baltimore *Evening Sun* (editorial page), Oct. 6.

*ster, pinster* (a bowler), *stuntster, pollster* (a taker of polls), *mobster, campster, puckster* (a hockey player), *exoduster,*[1] and *grownster.* Some of these deserve to be dismissed as nonce-words, but *roadster, gangster, ringster, speedster* and *mobster* have become firmly imbedded in American speech.

Another suffix that carries a disparaging significance is *-eer*. This is visible in *sonneteer*, which the NED traces to *c.* 1665, in *pulpiteer*, which goes back to 1642, and in *racketeer*. The NED says that *eer* is an anglicized form of the French *-ier*, which was derived from the Latin *-iarius*. *American Speech* has recorded a large number of new words based on it in recent years, *e.g., conventioneer, junketeer, fountaineer* (a soda-jerker, said to be with " no suggestion of a derogatory flavor "), *vacationeer, fictioneer, motorneer* (a trolley motorman), *questioneer* (a disseminator of questionnaires), *budgeteer,*[2] *batoneer, chariteer* (a professional charity-monger), *concerteer, unioneer, gardeneer, mustangeer, aeroneer* (a fancier of model airplanes), *oilateer* (a gas-station attendant), *balladeer, basketeer* (a basketball player), *gadgeteer, black-marketeer* or *blackteer, buckateer* (from *bucketshop* and *racketeer*), *upper-bracketeer, ubiquiteer, swingateer, cabineteer, pigeoneer, picketeer, revolutioneer,* and *sloganeer.*[3] *Profiteer* is traced by the NED Supplement to 1913, but it had existed in the verbal form of *profiteering* since 1814. The latter was popularized by a speech made by David Lloyd-George in July, 1917. " I believe," he said, " that the word is rather a good one. It is *profit-eer-ing* as distinguished from *profiting*. Profiting is fair recompense for services rendered; *profit-eer-ing* is an extravagant recompense, unfair in peace, and during war-time an outrage." *Patrioteer* is also English. It was reintroduced to the United States in 1939 by *Time*, which defined it as " the professional patriot, the kind of refuge-seeking scoundrel who waves a red-white-&-blue handkerchief when he should be

---

1 First used *c.* 1880 to designate a Southern Negro moving northward; revived by the Topeka *Daily Capital*, Nov. 25, 1938, to designate a fugitive from the Dust Bowl. See The Revival of *Exoduster*, by Dwight L. Bolinger, *American Speech*, Dec., 1941, pp. 317–18.

2 Cf. Better Houses For *Budgeteers*, by Royal Barry Wills; New York, 1941.

3 *Sloganeer* was used by President F. D. Roosevelt in a speech at Columbus, O., Aug. 20, 1932. It was apparently invented by Richard Connell, who used it in the titles of three short stories contributed to the *Saturday Evening Post*, 1921–22. See The Invention of *Sloganeer*, *Word Study*, Jan., 1933, p. 6.

wiping his own nose (not, it may be hoped, with that handkerchief)." [1]

178. [*Cellarette* has been in English for more than a century, but *kitchenette* is American, and so are *farmerette, conductorette, officerette* and a number of other analogous words.] Rather curiously, the English make the first of these words *cellaret*, not *cellarette*, though they are slow to follow American example in such forms as *cigaret* and *etiquet*. The NED's first example of *cellaret*, which it defines as " a case of cabinet-work made to hold wine-bottles, etc." or " a sideboard with compartments for the same purpose," is dated 1806–07, and comes, with excessive inappropriateness, from a book called " The Miseries of Human Life." There are later quotations from Thackeray and Benjamin Disraeli. *Suffragette* also originated in England and is said to have been invented by Charles Eustace Hand, a reporter for the London *Daily Mail*.[2] The NED's example is from the *Daily Mail* of January 10, 1906. The DAE omits *kitchenette*, but the NED Supplement, 1933, marks it " orig. U. S.." The thing itself was invented by Andrew J. Kerwin, a New York real-estate operator, in 1901, and he gave it its name a little while later. Thus the story has been told:

> He called one evening on a young couple living in an apartment-hotel, and was touched by their effort to serve him a midnight supper of beer cooled under a bathroom tap and Welsh rabbit cooked over a gas ring. He decided then and there that even in an apartment-hotel there ought to be a place to toss together a light meal. If he hadn't been a real-estate operator he would probably have forgotten the idea the next morning; as it was, he incorporated it into the plans of a hotel he was building.[3]

This hotel was the Carleton (not to be confused with the Ritz-Carlton). The *kitchenette* was quickly imitated by other builders of apartment-houses, and after a while it acquired a brother (or sister) in the *dinette*. Presently someone called a small lunch-room a *luncheonette*, later reduced to *lunchette*, and a numerous progeny followed. But it was World War I that really gave the *-ette* ending a start in the United States. It was first applied, I believe, to the *yeomanettes* who did clerical work for the Navy and were the *Stammütter* of the multitudinous WACS, WAVES and so on of World War II. The function of *-ette* as a diminutive began to recede, and in nearly all the new words ending with it it served to indicate the

1 Feb. 27, 1939, p. 9. Quoted in *American Speech*, April, 1940, p. 217.
2 See the obituary of Hand, who died on Nov. 2, 1937, in the *Editor and Publisher*, Nov. 6.
3 *New Yorker*, Aug. 21, 1937, p. 11.

feminine gender. The scouts of *American Speech*, especially Dwight L. Bolinger, have unearthed and recorded a great many, including *usherette*,[1] *sailorette*, *tractorette* (a lady tractor operator), *coppette* (a policewoman), *coxwainette*, *firette* (a firewoman), *bachelorette*, *glamorette*, *laughette*, *Latin Quarterette*, *greeterette*, *welcomette*,[2] *centaurette*, *legionette*, *dudette* (a female patron of a dude-ranch), *drum-majorette*, *chaufferette*, *tanksterette* (a woman swimmer), *stagette* (the feminine equivalent of *stag*), *rockette* (a chorus girl, apparently from *Roxy*, the name of a New York theatre), and *realty-ette* (a female realtor).[3] In Hollywood, for some reason unknown, a larval movie queen is not a *starlette*, but a *starlet*, and one full of malicious animal magnetism is an *oomphlet*. Despite this effeminization of the suffix it is still sometimes used as a diminutive, as in *blous-ette*, *orderette*, *featurette*, *bookette* (" a 6000-word condensation of a best-seller "),[4] *chambrette* (a new-fangled sleeping-compartment on trains), *bathinette* (a portable bath for babies), and *inette* (a combination of bath and table). The English contributions include *sermonette*, *flannelette*, *wagonette* and *leatherette*. The NED says of *wagonette* that it is " well established " and of *leatherette* that it has " come into general use." There is also the later *censorette*, applied to female " members of the Imperial Censorship staff which war brought to Bermuda." [5] Mr. Harry Leon Wilson, Jr., tells me that, in the San Francisco region, the Italianate suffix *-etta* has also made some progress; he reports *cafetta* (a small cafe) and *tavetta* (a small tavern). He also reports *waffelet* (a small waffle).[6]

Many other suffixes, new and old, have produced a plentiful offspring in the Republic, *e.g.*, *-ite*, *-ist*, *-itis*, *-ogist*, *-or*, *-ator*, *-age*, *-ism*, *-ian*, *-ation*, *-atics*, *-ee*, *-ine*, *-ization*, *-craft*, *-ology* and *-ography*. The hideous *-ite* has been put to most frequent use in the concoction of names to indicate residence or citizenship, *e.g.*, *Camdenite*, *Yon-*

---

1 Listed in the Dictionary of Occupational Titles; Part I: Definitions of Titles, issued by the United States Employment Office; Washington, 1939, p. 987.
2 *New Yorker*, Nov. 11, 1939: " The girls employed to annoy visitors to some kind of Chamber of Commerce festival in Southern California will be called *welcomettes*."

3 *Realtyettes* to Instal, Portland *Oregonian*, April 16, 1944. I am indebted here to Mr. Leo C. Dean of Portland.
4 *American Speech*, Feb., 1943, p. 42.
5 Now War Adds *Censorettes*, *Life*, Aug. 18, 1941.
6 Private communication, Dec. 2, 1939.

*kersite* and *Englewoodite;* in that field, indeed, it shows a tendency to drive out all other suffixes.[1] But it has also been heavily employed to indicate other sorts of membership or allegiance, as in *Hicksite,*[2] *socialite,*[3] *suburbanite, laborite, trailerite, third-termite.* The analogous *-ist* is rather more euphonious, and many of the terms embalming it are relatively respectable, *e.g., impossibilist, manicurist,*[4] *behaviorist,*[5] *feminist, hygienist, monopolist,* and *alarmist. Receptionist,* not listed by the DAE, has also gathered a certain amount of dignity, for there is no other word that clearly and conveniently designates the person referred to.[6] But there are also such uncouth examples as *swimmist, knittist, doggist,*[7] *duopolist, oligopolist,*[8] *cigarist, misterogynist* (a man-hater),[9] *hoofologist, truckologist,*[10] *emotionologist* (a voice trainer),[11] *mentalist* (a crystal-gazer),[12] *editorialist* (an editorial writer),[13] *cosmetist, tennist,*[14] *vaudevillist, neotrist,*[15] *chalkologist,* and *hygiologist.*[16] Among public performers of various sorts there has been a tendency for years to use the French termination *-iste* as an

1 See AL4, p. 549.
2 A member of a sect of Quakers, traced by the DAE to 1832, and still in use.
3 Defined by Alva Johnston in Public Relations, III, *New Yorker,* Sept. 2, 1944, p. 27, as "a technical tabloid term meaning a member of the human race."
4 Apparently an Americanism, traced by the DAE to 1889, a year before its first recorded appearance in England.
5 Coined by John B. Watson in 1913.
6 What's a *Receptionist?*, New York *Times,* Oct. 5, 1924, indicated that the term was then a novelty. It was first used by photographers, but the doctors and dentists soon borrowed it, and now it is in very wide use.
7 I am indebted to Mr. Paul Palmer for a *Doggist's* Code, issued by a dog dealer named Will Judy.
8 The last two are from an article by John Chamberlain in the *New Republic,* quoted by the Baltimore *Evening Sun* (editorial page), June 21, 1938. No doubt Mr. Chamberlain used them sportively.
9 Girls with Ideals Have Hard Sledding When Elders Are Lax, by

Doris Blake, Chicago *Tribune,* Feb. 18, 1926, p. 28.
10 Reported by the *Engineering News-Record,* April 21, 1927.
11 Advertisement of Alcide Felix Cormier in the New York *Herald Tribune,* June 12, 1941. I am indebted here to Mr. John C. Sullivan of New York.
12 Advertisement of the Shoreham Hotel, Washington, June, 1938: "The Country's Outstanding *Mentalist.* Prince Mogul, the Shoreham Seer, will answer your questions with the aid of his crystal. Shoreham Cocktail Lounge."
13 Used by the *Editor and Publisher* Aug. 19, 1944, p. 26, in the heading on a notice of the death of "Joseph Cookman, chief editorial writer of the New York *Post.*"
14 New Words For Old, Baltimore *Evening Sun* (editorial page), July 3, 1940.
15 The invention of this new word for an inventor of new words was ascribed to Dr. Charles E. Funk by the *New Yorker,* April 3, 1937, p. 15.
16 From a letter in the *Atlantic Monthly* by E. C. Alling, March, 1932, p. 429.

indicator of femininity, as in *violiniste, pianiste, saxophoniste* [1] and so on, to which *cosmetiste* may be added. The new words in *-itis* no doubt stem from the multitudinous medical terms showing the same suffix, and not a few of them show a suggestion of pathology, *e.g.*, *radioitis, headlineitis* and *golfitis*. Miss Josephine M. Burnham says, in fact, that " *-itis* is always disparaging." [2] She lists some grotesque examples, *e.g.*, *crosswordpuzzleitis, let-George-do-it-itis* and *Phi-Beta-Kappa-itis*. Others on her list are rather more seemly, *e.g.*, *convention-itis, danceitis, flapperitis, motoritis, Americanitis*,[3] *committeeitis* and *Philippinitis*.[4] The suffix *-ism*, of course, is old in English, and has produced a huge list of words. New ones are coming in all the time, and not infrequently an old one enjoys a vigorous revival, as when *ab-senteeism* in the war plants began to attract notice in 1942. The miracle-working Henry J. Kaiser tried to get rid of it in 1943, along with it its embarrassing connotations, by introducing *presentee-ism*.[5] The English make words in *-ism* almost as busily as we do. Now and then a purist denounces the suffix, as when one W. P. G., wrote to *John o' London's Weekly* in 1938 to condemn *pianism*. The editor, however, defended it stoutly, showing that " the scholarly *Athen-aeum* " had used it so long ago as 1889.[6] But he admitted that some of its possible analogues were dubious. " I would not advise anyone," he said, " to write of a performer that his *trombonism* was weak, or of a recital at the Albert Hall that the *organism* was superb." [7]

Examples of words embodying some of the other suffixes I have listed are given by Dr. Pound in the paper already cited. Among those ending in *-ee* are the familiar *draftee* of World War I (supplanted in World War II by *selectee* and *trainee*), and *honoree*, used widely in the South and Middle West to indicate the person for whom a party is given. Some fantastic forms have been recorded, *e.g.*, *holdupee* (the victim of a hold-up), *tryoutee* (one who tries for a position on a

---

1 Reported from Washington, D. C., by J. Foster Hagan in *American Speech*, March, 1927, p. 293.
2 Three Hard-Worked Suffixes, *American Speech*, Feb., 1927, p. 245.
3 The title of a book by Dr. W. S. Sadler, a psychiatrist; New York, 1925. The sub-title is " Blood Pressure and Nerves." Dr. Louise Pound, in the paper lately cited, traces *Americanitis* to 1915.
4 Mr. Hartford Beaumont of New

York tells me that this term was in wide use in the Philippines before the late unpleasantness. It was employed to designate the mental state of an American who had "missed too many boats" for home.
5 *National Liquor Review*, July, 1943, p. 4. I am indebted here to Mr. Fred Hamann.
6 The NED traces it to 1844.
7 *John o' London's Weekly*, March 18, 1938.

competitive basis),[1] *bombee, purgee, pollee* (one polled in a public opinion poll), *rushee, crack-upee, quizee, squeezee,*[2] and *parolee.*[3] *Jamboree* is listed as an Americanism by the NED, and traced to 1872. When, in 1908, General Robert Baden-Powell organized the Boy Scouts in England, he borrowed the term to designate a scout festivity, and when, two years later, the scout movement was taken up in the United States it returned to the land of its birth. It has produced a number of derivatives, *e.g., yamboree* (a festival honoring the *yam,* or sweet potato) [4] and *camporee* (from camp).[5] It has also, I gather, revived the word *corroboree,* which came into English from a native Australian dialect (now extinct) during the Nineteenth Century, but had died out by 1900.[6] Other curious words in *-ee* are *beateree* (person or thing that " beats all "),[7] *tutoree* and *biographee.*[8] The old suffix *-er* is also put to frequent use in American word-coinage, as in *soap-boxer,* which is not listed by the DAE but seems to be an Americanism. The following more recent coinages are noted by Dwight L. Bolinger: [9] *first-termer, party-liner, inner-circler, low-incomer, rank-and-filer, underworlder, bottlenecker, WPAer, dust-bowler, guilder* and *midnighter.* Another ancient, *-ism,* has also produced a long list of American terms, *e.g., greenbackism, populism, know-nothingism, red-tapeism, bossism, hoodlumism, rowdyism.*[10] Other old suffixes in continued request are *-age,* as in *teacherage* (a teacher's residence, obviously suggested by *parsonage*),[11] *outage,*[12] *up-*

---

1 I am indebted here to Mr. Alan F. Blair, of Pasadena, Calif.

2 For the last seven I am indebted to Among the New Words, by Dwight L. Bolinger, *American Speech,* Dec., 1941, p. 306.

3 I find the euphemistic *incarceree* in an article by a lady convict in *Viewpoint,* published by the prisoners in the New Jersey State Prison, Trenton, June–July, 1944, p. 42.

4 *Jamboree* Has Two Children, by Atcheson L. Hench, *American Speech,* April, 1937, p. 99. A *yamboree* was held at Gilmer, Texas, in Oct., 1935.

5 Reported from Nebraska in *American Speech,* Oct., 1940, p. 261.

6 It was used in the Baltimore *Sun,* May 25, 1935, by Folger McKinsey (the Bentztown Bard).

7 *Beateree, American Speech,* Oct.,

1942, p. 181. The DAE traces the term to 1861. It apparently dropped out of use in the early 80s.

8 *Biographee* is in Federal Trade Commission: Complaint against Julius C. Schwartz *et al;* Docket No. 5108, Dec. 29, 1943. The history of *-ee* is recounted in The Fate of French *-é* in English, by C. T. Onions, *S.P.E. Tract No. LXI,* 1943.

9 Among the New Words, *American Speech,* April, 1941, p. 144.

10 *Greenbackism* is traced by the DAE to 1882, *populism* to 1893, *know-nothingism* to 1854, *bossism* to 1881, *hoodlumism* to 1872, and *rowdyism* to 1842.

11 *Teacherage,* by Hugh Sebastien, *American Speech,* Oct., 1936, p. 271.

12 The street lighting engineer of Los Angeles in the *Record* of that city, date undetermined: " I have re-

*page, readerage,*[1] *coverage* [2] and *overage* (a bank term: the opposite of a *shortage*); *-arian*, as in *Rotarian* and *charitarian;* [3] *-ability*, as in *grindability,*[4] *buyability,*[5] *cleanability,*[6] *come-atability, get-ability* and *clubability; -ography*, as in *leicography* [7] (from the name of the German *Leica* camera); and *-ization*, as in *filmization.*

But of more interest, though many of them are strained and silly, are the words showing recent vogue-affixes, *e.g., -athon*, as in *walkathon, speedathon, danceathon, swimathon, talkathon, readathon,* and *superwalkathon;* [8] *-eroo* or *aroo*, as in *floppero, kickeroo, smackeroo,* and *stinkaroo; -dor* or *tor*, as in *beerador* and *radiotor;* [9] *-legger*, as in *bootlegger* and *meatlegger; -caster*, as in *newscaster* and *sportscaster; -crat*, as in *Hoovercrat, Willkiecrat* [10] and *popocrat; -hog*, as in *endseat-hog, roadhog* and *gashog; -mobile*, as in *bookmobile;* [11] *-buster,* as in *trustbuster* and *gangbuster; -fiend*, as in *dopefiend* and *autografiend;* and *-baloney*, as in *globaloney* and *verbaloney.* All the *-thon*

---

ported the light *outage* at Ninth and Los Angeles streets." I am indebted here to Mr. Charles J. Lovell.

1 Office advertisement in the Oklahoma City *Times*, Oct. 27, 1924: " These want-ads reach 114,000 subscribers daily, 84,000 on Sunday. You cannot find a greater Oklahoma newspaper *readerage*." I am indebted here to Monsignor J. B. Dudek.

2 *Coverage* means the extent of a newspaper's treatment of a matter of news. I first heard it in Chattanooga, Tenn., in 1926. It has since come into wide use among newspaper men.

3 Seattle *Times*, Feb. 16, 1937: " Mrs. Harry Fargo Ostrander, well-known *charitarian* and society leader, today was named president of the Seattle Visiting Nurse Service."

4 In 1938 the Bureau of Mines, Department of the Interior, issued a publication called *Grindability* of Alabama Coals. The NED traces the adjective *grindable* to 1652, but does not list *grindability*, nor does it appear in the NED Supplement, 1933.

5 The Detroit *News:* " Congress does not propose to use its power to enlarge the *buyability* of the dollar." Quoted in the Baltimore Evening *Sun* (editorial page), July 10, 1939.

6 The NED traces *cleanable* in English use to 1882, but does not list *cleanability*. I am indebted here to Mr. Fred Hamann, who reports *cleanability* in an advertisement of the Holyoke Card and Paper Company, Springfield, Mass., *Paper Progress*, Aug., 1943.

7 *Canadian Stage*, 1936, p. 1: " Miniature camera fans have coined a new word." I am again indebted here to Mr. Hamann.

8 Reported by *American Speech*, Feb., 1934, p. 76.

9 *Radiorator* (*radio* and *orator*) was used by *Time* in 1936, but has been abandoned. I am indebted here to Mr. Winslow Ames, of New London, Conn.

10 *Hoovercrat* appeared in 1928, when many Southern Democrats, unable to tolerate the introduction of the Pope into the White House, voted for the Republican Hoover and against the candidate of their own party, Alfred E. Smith. According to the *Editor and Publisher*, Aug. 7, 1940, *Willkiecrat* was coined by James L. Verhoeff, assistant city editor of the *Arkansas Democrat* of Little Rock, in 1940, and used for the first time in a headline.

11 *American Speech*, Feb., 1937, p. 30.

words derive from *marathon*, which came into general cognizance in 1896, when the first of the series of revived Olympic games was held at Athens, and rules were laid down for the famous *marathon-race*. Twenty-one years later, when enterprising entrepreneurs began staging dance endurance contests in the United States, they borrowed the term. The first dance contests were actually continuous, but in 1930 a manager at Des Moines, Iowa, introduced rest periods, during which the contestants walked about the floor. This new form of a *marathon* was called a *walkathon*, and in a little while the other derivatives followed.[1] *Readathon* usually appears as *Bible-readathon;* it designates a relay reading of the Bible by a series of pious persons, usually led by their pastor.[2] The history of *-eroo* has been investigated by Dr. Harold Wentworth.[3] He suggests that it may have been borrowed from *buckaroo*, a corruption of the Spanish *vaquero*, a cowboy, traced by the DAE, through the various forms of *buckeroo*, *buckayro*, *bucchro*, *buckhara* and *buckharer*, to *c.* 1861.[4] He says:

In certain circles — notably radio, sports, advertising, and motion pictures — one often does not pay the check, take a dive, tell a joke, or listen to swing music. Instead he pays the *checkeroo*, takes a *diveroo*, tells a *jokeroo*, and listens to *swingeroo*. Do such terms as these merely end with meaningless extra syllables? Sometimes they do, but not always. There is a perceptible semantic variation between the new forms with tails and the old acaudate ones. That is, it may not be quite so jarring to the playwright's sensibilities to read that his work is a *flopperoo* as to read that it is — tersely, bluntly, rudely — a *flop*. And the hapless *sapperoo* or *bummaroo* seems somehow less so than he used to be before the suffixion.[5]

1 I am indebted here to Mr. Don King, endurance shows editor of the *Billboard*, and to Mr. Hal J. Ross of St. Louis. From the *Billboard*, Aug. 18, 1934, p. 26: "Washington, Aug. 11. — The Ray C. Alvis *walkathon*, which started in the Washington Auditorium on July 30 with 73 couples, is down to 30 couples and four solos at the 100-hour mark."

2 A dispatch to the Detroit *Free Press* from Ponca City, Okla., dated Jan. 4, 1936, reported that at a *Bible-readathon* in Tabernacle Baptist Church there 359 volunteers read both Testaments in 69 hours, 4 minutes and 10 seconds. M. E. Powell, an advertising man, won "a de luxe edition of the Bible for guessing within an hour and 39 minutes when the reading would end." I am indebted here to Mr. Vernon Arthur Lucas of Detroit.

3 The Neo-Pseudo-Suffix *-eroo, American Speech*, Feb., 1942, pp. 10–15.

4 Wentworth calls my attention to the fact that *jackaroo*, perhaps also a corruption of *vaquero*, has been in use in Australia for a long while, and may have worked its way to the United States. It is listed in Sidney J. Baker's Popular Dictionary of Australian Slang; second ed.; Melbourne, 1943, and defined as "a station hand." There is also, says Baker, an Australian verb, *to jackeroo*, meaning to work on a sheep station.

5 Dwight L. Bolinger, in *American Speech*, Dec., 1941, p. 306, adds that "much of the success of the suffix is undoubtedly due to the coincidental support of *kangaroo*, the im-

*Jiggeroo*, used by tramps as a warning of the approach of police, was reported by F. H. Sidney in *Dialect Notes* in 1919,[1] and again in the same sense by another observer in 1927,[2] and *gazaroo*, meaning a boy, and *gozaroo*, meaning a fellow, were reported from Newfoundland in 1925,[3] but it was not until 1939 that *-eroo* and its congeners, *-aroo*, *-roo*, *-oo* and *-amaroo*, began to flourish in a large way. Wentworth, in his paper, presented nearly fifty examples, all of them dated. They included *antseroo* (ants in his pants), *bounceroo* (the grand bounce), *brusheroo* (the brush-off), *bummaroo* (a loafer), *checkeroo* (a night-club check), *crusheroo* (a love affair), *flopperoo* (a failure), *gaggeroo* (a poor joke), *jitteroo* (a jazz song), *kickeroo* (a mule), *kissaroo* (a kiss), *scooteroo* (a ski-jumper), *smackeroo* (a dollar), *sockeroo* (a success), *stinkaroo* (a bad play, movie or other show), and *ziparoo* (energy). To them, in 1942 and 1943, Bolinger [4] and Manuel Prenner [5] added *jugaroo* (a jail), *congaroo* (a dancer of the conga), *pepperoo* (a peppy story), *switcheroo*, *whackeroo*, *chickeroo* (a great success), *howleroo* (the same) and *payeroo* (the pay-off). The *-ador* suffix was probably suggested by *humidor*, which the NED Supplement traces to 1903, and most of the words embodying it show analogous meanings, *e.g.*, *beerador*.[6] Whether or not *warmolator* belongs to this group I do not know.[7] The various words in *-legger* are all children of *bootlegger*, a term that was much in the consciousness of Americans from 1920 to 1933. During the middle 20s, when there was a great upsurge of comstockery and simultaneously a large flood of obscene books, *booklegger* came in to designate a person who either sold them or let them out for reading. Most of the *bookleggers* flourished in the college towns. *Votelegger* appeared in 1940, and in 1941 *Time* began to use *foodlegger* to designate the illicit foodsellers of rationed England. When rationing was

age of the animal's antics contributing to the festive tone of the *-aroo* words."

1 Vol. V, Part II, p. 41.
2 The Jargon of the Underworld, by Elisha K. Kane, *Dialect Notes*, Vol. V, Part X, 1927, p. 452.
3 Newfoundland Dialect Items, by George Allan England, *Dialect Notes*, Vol. V, Part VIII, 1925, pp. 332 and 333. England's observations were made in 1920 and 1922.
4 Among the New Words, *American Speech*, Dec., 1942, p. 269.

5 More Notes on Neo-Suffixes, *American Speech*, Feb., 1943, p. 71.
6 Melvin M. Desser advertised for sale, in the Baltimore *Sun*, May 29, 1941, a *beerador* of "23-case capacity."
7 An advertisement in the Los Angeles *Times*, Oct. 19, 1937, ran: "For quality heating use Williams *Warmolator*. For large or small spaces. Standard for motion picture industry." I am indebted here to Mrs. Emma Sarepta Yule of Los Angeles.

set up in the United States *meatlegger* and *tirelegger* followed.¹ *Gas-leggers, coalleggers* and *duckleggers* have also been reported.² *Broad-caster* apparently arose in England,³ but it is in the United States that it has produced its chief derivatives, *e.g., newscaster, gridcaster* (an announcer of football combats), *dogcaster, smearcaster,*⁴ and *game-caster,* and the verbs *to telecast, to radiocast, to sportcast* and *to news-cast. Sportscaster* also appears as *sportcaster.*⁵

The use of *-ocrat* and *-ocracy* is by no means new. The NED traces *mobocrat* in English use to 1798 and *mobocracy* to 1754. *Monocrat* (a partisan of monarchy) was launched by Thomas Jefferson in 1792. *Shamocrat* (from *sham* and *aristocrat*) was listed by Bartlett in the fourth edition of his Glossary, 1877, but it apparently had only a short life, for it does not appear in Thornton, in the DAE, in Webster 1934, or in the NED Supplement. *Technocracy,* which had a great vogue in the closing years of the Hoover era, is also now obsolete. The term was coined in 1919 by William H. Smyth, an inventer of Berkeley, Calif., but was given popularity by Howard Scott, of New York. In its brief heyday *technocracy* produced many derivatives, *e.g., flapperocracy, sexnocracy, pianocracy* and *healthocracy,* but they have vanished with *technocracy* itself.⁶ *Pluto-crat* was borrowed from England, but *popocrat* made its first appearance in the Bryan campaign of 1896. The English are partial to *-crat* and have produced some forms so fantastic as to suggest American provenance, *e.g., shopocrat, millocrat, chromatocrat, poshocrat* and *demoplutocrat.*⁷ The words in *-buster* seem to be the children of

---

1 Among the New Words, by Dwight L. Bolinger, *American Speech*, Feb., 1943, p. 63, and Dec., 1943, p. 303.

2 Yes! We All Talk, by Marcus H. Boulware, Pittsburgh *Courier*, July 11, 1942.

3 The NED Supplement traces it to 1922. On Nov. 30 of that year the London *Daily Mail* reported that the Prince of Wales, later King Edward VIII and still later Duke of Windsor, "made a great hit as a 'broadcaster' when he delivered a message by wireless to the Boy Scouts." The word was quoted, indicating that it was then still a novelty.

4 *Guild Reporter*, Aug. 15, 1944, p. 16.

5 Among the New Words, by Dwight L. Bolinger, *American Speech*, April, 1943, pp. 147 and 148.

6 Some Word-Products of *Technocracy*, by Harold Wentworth, *American Speech*, April, 1933, pp. 68–70. Said *American Speech*, Dec., 1933, p. 47: "The combining form *-ocracy*, which showed such life less than a year ago, has now returned to a state of suspended animation."

7 I am indebted here to Mr. Arthur D. Jacobs, of Manchester, England. He says that *chronatocracy*, to designate the government of British Southwest Africa, was launched by Lancelot Hogben in the London *New Statesman and Nation* in 1939. *Poshocrat* made its debut in Lions and Shadows, a novel by Christo-

*trustbuster. Gangbuster* appeared during the days of Thomas E. Dewey as a prosecutor of racketeers in New York, *c.* 1935. *Unionbuster* seems to be the invention of the *Nation.*[1] The first of the words in *-fiend* was probably *opium-fiend*, which goes back to the early 80s, and maybe to the 70s. It was followed, *c.* 1890, by *cigarette-fiend*,[2] and a little later by *absinthe-fiend, dope-fiend*,[3] and *cocaine-fiend*. Then came *baseball-fiend, camera-fiend, kodak-fiend, movie-fiend, dance-fiend, radio-fiend, marathon-fiend, golf-fiend, jazz-fiend* and the like. The best known of all the children of Al Smith's *baloney*, of course, is *globalony*, launched by the Hon. Clare Boothe Luce in her maiden speech in Congress, February, 1943. Another is *verbaloney*, which was thrown to the world by the *New Yorker* on March 27, 1943. There was a time, *c.* 1925, when aviators of unusual daring (including Charles A. Lindbergh) were called *flying -fools*, and from the term flowed *riding-fool, writing-fool* and so on, but they have apparently gone out.[4] Many other words have produced, from time to time, a small and transient progeny, but these derivatives are of hardly more than curious interest, *e.g., book-mobile* and *club-mobile* from *automobile;*[5] *booboisie* and *joboisie* from *bourgeoisie;*[6] *elegantsia* from *intelligensia;*[7] *janissariat* from *proletariat; aquatennial* from *centennial;*[8] *hustlerati* from *literati;*[9] *carnapper, dognapper* and

pher Isherwood. *Demoplutocracy*, according to Mr. Jacobs, was borrowed by the English from Mussolini.

1 June 22, 1940, p. 746. I am indebted here to Bolinger, before cited.

2 During the 90s Kansas and a few other advanced-thinking States passed statutes forbidding the sale of cigarettes on the ground that they were poisonous. It was widely taught by the moralists of the period that they contained opium. These statutes were repealed on the return of the soldiers from World War I. They had seen even the Y.M.C.A. selling cigarettes, and had ceased to believe that smoking them was either dangerous or sinful.

3 In The Argot of the Underworld Narcotic Addict, Part II, *American Speech*, Oct., 1938, p. 189, D. W. Maurer says that *dope-fiend* "is practically taboo among underworld addicts." Two analogues, *pipe-fiend*

and *needle-fiend*, have been likewise displaced by "more modern synonyms."

4 I am indebted here to Mr. Carl Zeisberg, of Glenside, Pa.

5 *American Speech*, Feb., 1937, p. 30, and Feb., 1944, p. 78.

6 In 1934, at the time of the Russian and German purges, Simeon Strunsky launched *purgeoisie* in the New York *Times* (Topics of the Times), and it was noted in *Word Study*, Feb., 1935, p. 2. but it did not flourish.

7 *American Speech*, Oct., 1939, p. 237.

8 *American Speech*, Dec., 1940, p. 371.

9 Defined by Reinzi B. Lemus in the Washington *Tribune*, Dec. 26, 1925, as "that type which will write and print anything for money, particularly if it be detrimental to the black man." Most of these enemies to the Negro, I gather, are themselves black.

*pupnapper* from *kidnapper;* [1] *strippeuse* (a stripteaser) from *danseuse; bookvertising* from *book* and *advertising;* [2] *turkeywich* from *turkey* and *sandwich;* [3] *labor-baiter, red-baiter,* and *Jew-baiter* from some earlier *-baiter;* [4] *typistry* from *artistry;* [5] *motel* and *airtel* from *hotel;* [6] *trainasium* from *gymnasium;* [7] and numerous forms in *-ology* e.g., *boyology, oilology, bagology.* [8]

The suffix *-ie* was far from new when it appeared in the back-formation *movie,* but its resurrection gave it fresh fertility and *movie* was soon followed by *speakie, talkie, quickie, okie,* and a host of other forms. Nor was *-bug* new when it appeared in *jitterbug,* for the DAE traces *tariff-bug* to 1841 and *gold-bug* to 1878, but *shutterbug* and various like terms seem to have flowed from it. Sometimes an old suffix, revived, undergoes a change in significance — for example, *-ana,* which dates from 1666 in the sense of things said or written *by* a person, and to 1741 in the sense of things written *about* him, or about any other subject. [9] In American usage I have encountered it in the strange sense of a trading region. [10] " English," says Edwin Bercke Dike, " has picked up her affixes everywhere, and people have used them freely, and given them strange vogues " [11] — especially American people. Prefixes are used much more sparingly. Indeed, I

1 *American Speech,* Oct., 1941, p. 239; *Words,* May, 1940, p. 73.

2 *Bookvertising,* said the *Publisher's Weekly,* Feb. 7, 1942, " was coined by H. J. Stoeckel to apply to the use of hardbound or flexible bound books for commercial and institutional advertising."

3 The last three are reported in Among the New Words, by Dwight L. Bolinger, *American Speech,* Dec., 1943, pp. 301–02.

4 The NED traces *bear-baiting* to c. 1475, but it has been obsolete since the disappearance of the sport. *Jew-baiter's* first recorded appearance was in the New York *Evening Post,* April 21, 1883. Six months later it appeared in England. The NED suggests that it may have been borrowed from the German *Judenhetzer.*

5 Used by Bruce Rogers in the preface to Fra Lucca Pacioli, 1935. I am indebted here to Mr. Philip C. Duschnes of New York.

6 *Notes and Queries,* May 24, 1941, p. 370. I am indebted here to Mr. Lincoln S. Ferris of Portland, Ore.

7 Used at the Army Parachute School in World War II. See Typical Parachute Injuries, by C. Donald Lord and James W. Coutts, *Journal of the American Medical Association,* Aug. 26, 1944, p. 1182.

8 *Bagology* is the name of the house-organ of the Chase Bag Company of Chicago.

9 On the Suffix *-ana,* by Joseph Jones, *American Speech,* April, 1933, p. 71.

10 Advertisement of the Louisville *Courier-Journal* and *Times* in the *Editor and Publisher,* July 4, 1936, p. 1: " They alone give complete coverage, not only of Greater Louisville, but also of practically every important trading center in *kentuckiana,* . . . which includes practically all of Kentucky and a score of Southern Indiana counties."

11 Obsolete Words, *Philological Quarterly,* April, 1933, p. 214.

can think of but three that have had any great popularity in recent years, to wit, *near-*, *super-* and *pro-*. The first is discussed in AL4, p. 181. The DAE ignores it, but the NED Supplement traces *near-seal* (fur) to 1902, *near-beer* to 1909, *near-smile* to 1911 and *near-engagement* to 1926.[1] *Super-* has been used mainly by Hollywood press-agents, to give oomph and zowie to adjectives, as in *super-colossal*, but it has also appeared in the general vocabulary, as in *super-service*, *super-criminal* and *super-junket*.[2] *Pro-*, which goes back to 1645 in English, usually carries a hostile significance, as in *pro-slavery*, 1856, *pro-rebel*, 1868, and *pro-German*, 1914.

American English is rich in blends, and some of them have been taken into the English of England, *e.g.,* *gerrymander*. There are authorities who include *boost* among them, holding that it is made up of *boom* and *hoist*, but the evidence seems to be very dubious, for *boom* in the sense of sudden activity did not come in until the 70s,[3] whereas *boost* as a verb was included in David Humphreys' Glossary of 1815. Whatever its origin and history, the great vogue of the word was delayed until the last years of the Nineteenth Century, when *boosters* began to infest the land, and the American proverb, " Every knock is a *boost*," was invented by some forgotten Solomon.[4] Extensive studies of blends have been made by Louise Pound,[5] Harold Wentworth,[6] Lester V. Berrey [7] and Robert Withington,[8] and there have been many smaller contributions to the subject in *American Speech*. Novelties are produced in great number by *Time* and the newspaper columnists, but many of them involve puns, most are banal, and only a few have got into general circulation. Wentworth's doctoral thesis lists 3,600, and includes examples long standard in

1 A floating newspaper paragraph says that *near-accident* was used by the *Federal Gazette*, Baltimore, in May, 1803. The precise date is not given.
2 *American Speech*, Oct., 1939, p. 237.
3 See *Boom*, by Rex Forrest, *American Speech*, Oct., 1941, p. 237.
4 See *Boost*, by Klara H. Collitz, *American Speech*, Sept., 1926, pp. 661–72.
5 Blends: Their Relation to English Word Formation, *Anglistische Forschungen*, Vol. XLII; Heidelberg, 1914.
6 Blend Words in English: an Ab-

stract of a Thesis Presented to the Faculty of the Graduate School of Cornell University for the Degree of Doctor of Philosophy; Ithaca, 1933.
7 Newly-Wedded Words, *American Speech*, Feb., 1939, pp. 3–10.
8 Some New Portmanteau Words, *Philological Quarterly*, April, 1930; More Portmanteau Coinages, *American Speech*, Feb., 1932; Dickensian and Other Blends, the same, Oct., 1933; Verbal Pungencies, the same, Dec., 1939; Coinage, the same, April, 1940; and various shorter notes.

English, *e.g.*, *tragicomedy*, *squirearchy*, *luncheon* and *aniseed;* others slowly making their way into good usage, *e.g.*, *anecdotage;* and a large number of American inventions, *e.g.*, *pulmotor* and *japalac*. The English, perhaps because they are a good deal less inventive in the philological field than Americans, devote themselves diligently to such simple forms, and some of their less painful inventions have crossed the ocean, *e.g.*, Lewis Carroll's *chortle*, and the later *brunch* (*breakfast* and *lunch*) and *smog* (*smoke* and *fog*). The NED Supplement presents evidence that *smog* was invented by an English medical man named Des Voeux in 1905, but on February 7, 1926 the Associated Press sent out a dispatch from Indianapolis saying:

> The United States Weather Bureau has given a new word, *smog*, to the American language. It is used to describe a combination of smoke and fog which occurs chiefly over the cities of the Central States.

It is possible, of course, that this was really an independent invention, but it is hardly likely, for *smog* had been occurring in English discussions of the weather for more than twenty years, and the American weather prophets must have encountered it.

Back-formations such as *gas* for *gasoline* are constantly coming in, and some of them last only a short while, but *photo* for *photograph* is now of respectable antiquity, for the DAE traces it to 1863. *Auto* was apparently launched in 1899, when the Boston *Herald* printed an editorial saying, " If we must Americanize and shorten the word [*automobile*] why not call them *autos?* " [1] *Movie*, *phone* and *gas* are not listed by the DAE, but the NED Supplement calls two of them, *movie* and *gas*, Americanisms, and it is probable that *phone* is another. Terry Ramsaye, author of the standard history of the *movie*, thus sets forth the genesis of its name:

> The word appears to have come into the folk-tongue out of the gamin life of either New York or Chicago about 1906–1907. The motion picture arrived at the status of an independent narrative art in the Autumn of 1903 with " The Great Train Robbery," a dime novel in 800 feet of film, leading directly to the flowering of the motion picture theatre. It had its beginning in Smithfield street, near Diamond alley, in Pittsburgh during Thanksgiving week, 1905. By 1908 *movie* began to appear in the reports of social workers and contemporary newspaper accounts. It attained wide circulation shortly through the distribution of the cartoon and comic strip in the daily press. [2]

1 July 4. Quoted by the DAE, from which I take it.

2 *Movie* Jargon, *American Speech,* April, 1926, p. 357.

*Bike*, for *bicycle*, is traced by the DAE to 1882.[1] *Pep*, which seems a characteristic Americanism to the English, though it is not listed by the DAE, is traced by the NED Supplement to 1915, marked " U. S.," and called " an abbreviation of *pepper*." The same etymology is given by Webster 1934, by H. W. Fowler and F. G. Fowler in the Concise Oxford Dictionary, and by Partridge, and I favored it myself in AL4, p. 169, but I have begun to suspect that it may be erroneous. Mr. E. H. Peabody suggests, rather more plausibly, that *pep* is really a shortened form of *pepsin*.[2] I first heard the term in 1890 or thereabouts, at which time there was a rash of popular confidence in the prophylactic virtues of pepsin, comparable to the latter faith in vitamins. One of the most widely-selling chewing-gums of the time contained it, and millions believed that taking frequent doses of it would improve the digestion and stimulate the energies. So far as I know there has never been any similar belief, in the United States, about pepper: it is thought of as a flavor, not as a metabolic booster. Thus there is reason for making *pepsin* the father of *pep*, and I shall embrace that etymology provisionally, with thanks to Mr. Peabody, until the dirt lexicographers apply themselves to and solve the problem.

In *Dialect Notes*, more than thirty years ago, Miss Elizabeth Wittman printed a long list of similar American shortenings, with a valuable commentary.[3] Many of them are still in current use, *e.g.*, *ad* for *advertisement*, *beaut* for *beauty*, *boob* for *booby*, *bronc* for *bronco* and *Yank* for *Yankee*. Others have come in in later years, *e.g.*, *mum* for *chrysanthemum*, *pash* for *passion*, *bunk* for *buncombe*, and so on. The origin of *buncombe*, which produced not only *bunk* (through *bunkum*) but also *to debunk*, and probably helped to promote the popularity of *bunco* (which really comes from the Spanish *banca*, a card game), has been discussed in Chapter IV, Section 2. The American advertising men, in the glorious days when the more forward-looking of them hoped to lift their art and mystery to the level of dogmatic theology, astronomy, ophthalmology and military science,

1 I am informed by Miss Jane D. Shenton of Philadelphia that a family legend credits the invention of *bike* to her mother's brother, W. I. Wilhelm, who was a bicycle racer in the early 80s and later became a bicycle manufacturer.
2 Private communication, June 8, 1936. Mr. Peabody is a mechanical engineer, and president of the Peabody Engineering Corporation, New York.
3 Clipped Words: A Study of Back-Formations and Curtailments in Present-Day English, Vol. IV, part II, 1914, pp. 115-45.

carried on a crusade against the clipped form *ad,* but it came, alas, to nothing. This crusade was launched by one of the most eminent of them, William C. D'Arcy, in a speech before a convention of advertising savants holden at San Francisco in 1918, and it roared on through the hopeful 20s. When, in 1925, the brethren met at Houston, Texas, their executive secretary, Robert H. Cornell, asked " the local advertisers and all local organizations that have anything whatever to do with the convention to avoid use of *ad* in all printed matter and letters going out in connection with the convention." [1] The advertising men of England, it was pointed out, never used it, not even in such convenient forms as *ad-writer* and *want-ad.* But though many high-toned and eloquent men took part in this holy war, and Mr. D'Arcy, the pioneer, denounced *ad* as " the language of bootblacks, and beneath the dignity of men of the advertising profession," it survived unscathed and is still in almost universal use. To most Americans *want-advertisement* would sound quite as affected as *taximeter-cabrolet;* the term is *want-ad.* When the Great Depression overtook the *ad-men,* and they began to be harried and sweated by the New Deal, they forgot all about their philological reform, and nothing has been heard from them on the subject since March 4, 1933.

Miss Wittman, in the paper before quoted, called attention to the fact that it is not only nouns that are clipped by apocope. From adjectives, for example, there come *fed* (usually used as a noun) for *federal,* *gat* for *gatling-gun,* *met* for *metropolitan,* *mex* for *Mexican,* *co-ed* (also become a noun) for *co-educational,* and *legit* for *legitimate,* not to mention such borrowings from England as *zoo.*[2] There are also many short forms of verbs, but most of them are cognate with nouns, *e.g., to phone, to gas, to photo, to auto, to bike* and *to con.* Finally, there is an apparently growing tendency to shorten a phrase made up of an adjective and a noun to the adjective alone, and then to convert it into a noun, *e.g., flat* for *flat tire,* and *permanent* for *permanent wave.*[3]

American English is rich in deliberate coinages, some of which have gone into standard English, *e.g., appendicitis, moron* and *sundae.*

---

1 Cornell Scores Use of Word *Ad, Associated Advertising,* Jan., 1925.
2 *Zoo,* from *zoölogical* (garden), is traced by the NED to *c.* 1847. A writer in the London *Times Literary Supplement,* March 28, 1936, p. 273, said that it was invented by " the great Vance in the 60s," but this was an error.
3 Words, by Clifford Howard, *Your Life,* Aug., 1939, p. 99.

The DAE lists *sundae* under *Sunday*, but adds "usually *sundae*." It is marked "of obscure origin, but usually regarded as related to *Sunday*." The DAE's first example, taken from the New York *Evening Post* of May 21, 1904, spells the word *sundi*, and in an abridged dictionary issued by the Consolidated Book Publishers of Chicago in 1925 it is spelled *sondhi*, with *sundae* and *sunday* as variants.[1] The amateur etymologists have had some desperate struggles with it, but without establishing its origin beyond cavil. Perhaps the most plausible of their theories ascribes the introduction of the *sundae* itself to George Hallauer, of Marshall, Ill., and the invention of its name to George Giffy, of Manitowoc, Wis. This was in the early 90s. At that time Hallauer, who died in 1939, was living in Two Rivers, Wis., and one of his places of call was an ice-cream parlor kept by E. C. Berners. "One night," related Berners years afterward, "Hallauer dropped in and ordered a dish of ice-cream. As I was serving it he spied a bottle of chocolate syrup on the back bar, which I used for making sodas. 'Why don't you put some of that chocolate on the ice-cream?' he asked. 'You don't want to ruin the flavor of the ice-cream,' I protested, but Hallauer answered 'I'll try anything once,' and I poured on the chocolate. Hallauer liked it, and the ice-cream *sundae* was born." News of the novelty soon reached the nearby town of Manitowoc, and presently George Giffy, who operated an ice-cream parlor there, was offering it to his customers. The addition of chocolate, of course, increased its cost, and in order to cut down the demand Giffy sold it on Sundays only. One day, a week-day, a little girl came in and asked for a dish of it. "I serve it only on Sundays," said Giffy. "Why, then," she replied, "this must be Sunday, for it's the kind of ice-cream I want." Giffy gave it to her and simultaneously was seized with the inspiration to call the new concoction a *Sunday*. How the spelling came to be changed to *sundae* deponent saith not.[2]

News of the novelty spread rapidly, and it was soon popular in the

---

1 For this I am indebted to Mr. Valdemar Viking of Red Bank, N. J.

2 Two Rivers the Birthplace of Ice-Cream *Sundae*, by Mary Seidl, Two Rivers *Reporter*, May 28, 1941. In this article the essential parts were reprinted from an article in the centennial edition of the *Reporter*, July 25, 1936. I am indebted here to the courtesy of Mr. Seymour S. Althen, managing editor of the paper; of Miss Sarah Corcoran, of Mitchell, S. D.; and of Mrs. A. Pilon, of Fond du Lac, Wis., a sister to Berners. He died at Mrs. Pilon's home July 1, 1939. See also Man Who Made the First Ice-Cream *Sundae* Is Dead, Chicago *Tribune*, July 2, 1939, p. 1.

college towns. Mr. Charles P. Davis tells me that in the 90s "one Tuttle, who kept a restaurant at State and William streets, Ann Arbor, used to serve a slab of ice-cream topped with strawberries which he termed a *sunday*, not a *sundae*," [1] and Mr. Robert Follansbee that at Ithaca in 1898 "*sundaes* were being served at the soda-fountain of Christiance and Dofflemyer." [2] Mr. Follansbee adds that he was told that the *sundae* had originated in the Christiance and Dofflemyer laboratories a year or two before this time. That claim for its birth in Ithaca was supported by the late Gilbert M. Tucker in his "American English," [3] but Tucker held that it was thrown to the world by the Red Cross Pharmacy, in State street, in 1897. There are also claimants for Norfolk, Va., for Washington, and for Evanston, Ill. [4] From Mrs. Rho Fisk Zueblin, of Lugano-Cassarate, Switzerland, a former resident of Chicago, I have received the interesting suggestion that the *sundae* may have been named, not after the Christian Sabbath, but after William A. (Billy) *Sunday*, the baseball evangelist. Before he took to good works he served for a while as coach of the baseball nine of Northwestern University, and Mrs. Zueblin believes that when the new sweet came in the students may have named it after him. [5] But this suggestion makes it all the harder to account for the shift from *Sunday* to *sundae*. It is rather astonishing that the *-ae* ending has produced so little progeny. The only child of the *sundae* that I have ever encountered is the *mondae*, a mixture of *sundae* and soda-water, offered for sale in Des Moines, Iowa, in 1937. [6]

The history of *moron* is told briefly in AL4, pp. 174–75. There are more details in the following letter from Dr. Henry H. Goddard, who coined it:

In 1909 the American Association for the Study of the Feeble-minded met at Chippewa Falls, Wis. As the result of some discussion of the various terms used to designate the mental defective, a committee was appointed to report

1 Private communication, Jan. 7, 1938.
2 Private communication, Sept. 7, 1937.
3 New York, 1921, p. 306. Mr. Tucker, editor of the *Country Gentleman* from 1867 to 1911, was a pioneer writer on American speechways. He died in 1932.
4 The case of the first is set forth briefly in AL4, p. 190, that of the second in Washington Wayside Tales, Washington *Evening Star*, Dec. 1, 1936; and that of the third in the Autobiography of William Lyon Phelps; New York, 1939, p. 920.
5 Private communication, June 18, 1937. Sunday was a Y.M.C.A. secretary in Chicago from 1891 to 1895. He died in 1935.
6 The *ice-cream soda*, the forerunner of the *sundae*, made its first appearance in Philadelphia in 1874. See The Story of the Franklin Institute, by Sydney L. Wright; Philadelphia, 1938, p. 49.

the next year on the classification of the feebleminded. The committee consisted of Dr. Walter Fernald, chairman, another member whose name I forget,
and myself.

When I returned to Vineland,[1] I set to work on the classification so as to
have something ready when Dr. Fernald should call for suggestions. The matter
must have slipped his mind because he never called for anything on the subject.

At that time I was enthusiastic over the results of the Binet tests. We had
classified all our cases at Vineland in accordance with the tests and it worked
wonderfully. It was therefore an easy matter to classify our lowest grade as
*idiots* with a mental age of from birth to 2 years; the next group as *imbeciles*
ranging from mental age 3 years to 7. The highest group would include mental
ages from 8 years to 12. I thought first to call them *feebleminded*, as is the
English custom, but when I recalled that practically every institution for mental
defectives in the United States was called an Institution for the *Feebleminded*,
it was evident the word was already established as a generic term for the
entire group.

Therefore it became necessary to discover a new term. *Idiot* and *imbecile*
are both Greek. A Greek word would make it uniform. But I could think of
none. I appealed to my friends and got many suggestions, all the way from
*deviates* to *the almosts!* One day there dropped into my mind a relic of my college days in the form of the rhetorical term *oxymoron*, with its interesting
etymology, "sharp-foolish"; then I thought of *sophomore* — the "wise fool."
Turning to my Greek lexicon, I found *moros — mora — moron*, "dull, stupid,
silly, foolish" a perfect description of our 8-12 year-group.

When the Association met the next year — May, 1910 — at Lincoln, Ill., I
happened to be the only member of the classification committee present. When
this was discovered and it was learned that I had a plan which I had intended
to offer to Dr. Fernald, I was asked to present it to the association for their
information and to show that the committee had done something. To my surprise the meeting voted to accept the proposed classification.

The new word was accepted rather quickly by students of and workers
with the feebleminded and very quickly by the public. Writers and the general
public seem to have stretched its meaning somewhat to cover any case of mental
dullness, whether such person would be technically feebleminded or not.
That of course is not unusual in our language and is not particularly objectionable.[2]

The extension of meaning mentioned by Dr. Goddard has been accompanied by a change of meaning, especially in the Chicago area.
There a *moron* has come to mean a sexual pervert, and its use in its

1 *i.e.*, the Training School for Feeble
Minded Children at Vineland, N. J.,
where Dr. Goddard served as director of research from 1906 to 1918.
In the latter year he became director
of the State Bureau of Juvenile Research at Columbus, O. In 1922 he
became professor of abnormal and
clinical psychology at Ohio State
University, retiring as professor
emeritus in 1938. He is best known,
perhaps, as the author of The Kal-
likak Family, 1912, but he has also
written other important books in
his field. Dr. Walter E. Fernald
(1859-1924) was superintendent of
the Massachusetts School for Feeble
Minded.

2 The report of the committee on
classification of the feebleminded
was printed in the *Journal of Psy-
cho-Asthenics*, 1910, p. 61.

correct sense has overtones of libel.[1] *Moron* is the name of a character in Molière's play, " La Princesse d'Elide," first played May 8, 1664, and this *Moron*, by a happy coincidence, is a fool, but his name was not in Dr. Goddard's mind when *moron* was coined.[2] Nor was he aware, I take it, that *Moroni* figures in the Book of Mormon as the son of Mormon and the author of about half of the text thereof, and that his name is not infrequently bestowed upon Mormon boys — or was, at least, until the entrance of *moron* into the language gave it an embarrassing significance. *Moron* has been taken into English, and begins to show itself in other languages. The English *ament*, used to designate all three classes of the feeble-minded, is seldom used in America.[3]

Not many other deliberate inventions have had the success of *moron* and *sundae*, but new ones are coming in all the time, and some of them are supported by ardent advocacy, *e.g.*, *americanity*, coined by Dr. F. M. Kercheville, head of the department of modern languages at the University of New Mexico, to designate " the broad but none the less profound concept of the genuine spirit — the fundamental elements and characteristics — common to all the Americas." [4] In such matters, as in kissing, success goes by favor, and the overwhelming majority of the new words thrown out by ingenious neologists do not catch on. Gelett Burgess, whose launching of *bromide* and *blurb* has been noted, proposed many others in " Burgess Unabridged," 1914, but they failed to make their way into the language. *Gwibit*, dedicated to the nation by Congressman Karl E. Mundt, of South Dakota in 1943 to designate " the guild of Washington incompetent bureaucratic idea throat-cutters," seemed to meet a need, but it nevertheless died the death.[5] When Dr. Charles H. Grandgent offered *osteocephic* as an elegant substitute for *bone-*

1 See Miscellaneous Notes, *American Speech*, Dec., 1925, p. 188; *Moron* — A Misconception, by Eston Everett Ericson, *American Speech*, Dec., 1937, p. 323; and The Natural History of a Delinquent Career, by Clifford R. Shaw; Chicago, 1931, p. 4.

2 I am indebted here to Mr. Francis M. Currier of Winchester, Mass. He says: " This was the last appearance of the fool or jester upon the French stage until the romantic outburst of Hugo *et al.*"

3 Brightness and Dullness in Children, by Herbert Woodrow, second ed.; Philadelphia, 1923, p. 45.

4 *Americanity*, by F. M. Kercheville, *American Speech*, Feb., 1939, pp. 71–73, reprinted in the *Congressional Record*, March 31, 1939, pp. 5091–92. Dr. Kercheville proposes that the Spanish equivalent be *americanidad*. See his Dialogues of Don Placido, *New Mexico* (Albuquerque), Nov., 1938, p. 5.

5 *Congressional Record*, Dec. 15, 1943, p. 10835, and Dec. 18, 1943, p. A5999; *American Notes and Queries*, Jan., 1944. p. 149.

*head* he seemed to be performing a public service, but it went unrequited by acceptance,[1] and the same fate befell my own less couth *osseocaput*, launched in 1913, along with *lithocaput*, *ferrocaput* and various other analogues. Will *coolant* make its way? It seems to be an excellent and necessary word, but its fate is hidden in the bosoms of the gods.[2] Nor is there any certainty about what is in store for *lapkin*, the name of a newly-invented napkin with a button-hole in one corner, to anchor it to coat or waistcoat and prevent it sliding to the floor.[3] Nor about the destiny of *homancing*, meaning house-hunting, and *homancier*, meaning " one skilled in home financing." [4] At not infrequent intervals some newspaper or magazine editor, struck with the thought that the vocabulary of the American language, despite its unparalleled richness, still has gaps in it, calls upon his readers to apply themselves to the invention of new words. Such an inspiration seized C. K. Ogden, then science editor of the *Forum*, in 1927, and he invited contributions to " the language of tomorrow," either original or dredged up from the current stream.[5] There was a hearty response, and a great many new words were suggested, *e.g.*, *souprano* (a noisy eater of soup), to *vacueat* (to eat spaghetti by suction), *crool* (the wind in a forest), *pneumocrat* (a man of great spiritual influence), *megaphonia* (the habit of talking too loud), *wildcraft*, *fieldsome*, *hallusion* (*hallucination* and *illusion*) and *schemestress*, but though some of them were ingenious and amusing they all failed to survive. Deliberate efforts to resuscitate obsolete words are also made from time to time, but they seldom succeed.[6]

There was a transient craze in the second lustrum of the 30s for nouns on the order of *maker-upper*, compounded of a verb and an adverb, with *-er* added to each. A somewhat similar fashion, in the days before the Civil War, had produced such forms as *come-outer*,

1 Some Neologisms From Recent Magazines, by Robert Withington, *American Speech*, April, 1931, p. 284.
2 It appears in an advertisement of S. F. Bowser & Company, of Fort Wayne, Ind., *Chemical Equipment Review*, July–Aug., 1942, p. 25. I am indebted here to Mr. Fred Hamann.
3 This invention is said to have been made in Boston, but I get news of it from The Non-Slip *Lapkin*, London *Daily Express*, April 29, 1944.
4 Both launched by the First Federal Savings and Loan Association of Lima, O., in 1938, along with an explanatory poem by C. L. Mumaugh.
5 The New American Language, *Forum*, Feb., 1927, p. 265 *ff*.
6 In the New York *World*, Oct. 6, 1930, Richard Connell proposed the revival of *gomeral* (a fool), *nugacity* (frivolity), *appetent* (eagerly desirous), *docity* (quick comprehension), and *gestion* (management), but there were no seconds.

traced by the DAE to 1840, and *come-uppance*, traced to 1859, but this new one was wilder and woolier, and some of the examples reported by Louise Pound and other contributors to *American Speech* were curious indeed, *e.g.*, *fighter-backer; passer-byer; caller-, jotter-,* (shirt) *holder-, sitter-,* and *tearer-downer; dropper-, filler-* and *taker-inner; putter-* and *topper-offer; diner-, finder-, holder-, putter-* and *worker-outer;* and *bracer-, breaker-, checker-, freshener-, giver-,* (sock) *holder-, maker-, pepper-, putter-, setter-, snapper-, stayer-, summer-, waker-* and *warmer-upper.*[1] A round-up of some of the most picturesque examples was attempted by Harold Wentworth in *American Speech* in 1936,[2] and he assembled a number of genuine monstrosities, *e.g.*, *lobby-drifter-througher, dance-mixer-upper, home-breaker-upper, haircut-putter-offer,* and *builder-upper-tearer-downer.* He said:

> Newspaper columnists' and college students' language furnished more than half of the data adduced. . . . Of the six adverbs involved, *up* occurs about twice as often as *out, in, off, down* and *through* combined. . . . Why the evil genius of slang permits *-er,* but not *-ing* or *-ed,* to be so misused is puzzling. Forms like *calling-downing, thinking-upping, dropped-inned* and *walked-upped* have not been observed.

In 1940 Dr. Pound reported[3] that " the vogue of locutions of the *picker-upper, filler-inner* type has now mostly subsided."[4] *Hair-do* came in during their heyday and was followed by *up-do*. A series of terms in *walk-* is older: *walk-around* is traced by the DAE to 1869 and *walk-out* to 1888, and *walk-up*, an apartment without elevator service, is traced by the NED Supplement to 1919, but probably goes back to the late years of the last century. The contagion spread to the adjectives, and some bizarre superlatives were concocted, *e.g.*, *getting-aroundest, datingest, most-workingest,*[5] and *homer-lessest* (of a baseball pitcher who held down the opposing clubs to eight home-runs in a season).[6] But like the parent fashion, this one soon died away.

---

1 General Hugh S. Johnson launched *fire-putter-outer* in his newspaper column, Dec. 13, 1939.
2 On Adding the Suffix of Agency, *-er*, to Adverbs, Dec., 1936, pp. 369 and 370.
3 News, *American Speech*, April, 1940, p. 213.
4 Notes dating many of the forms listed are in *American Speech*, April, 1936, pp. 179 and 182; Oct., 1936, pp. 274 and 280; Feb., 1937, pp. 18 and 82; Oct., 1937, p. 243; and April, 1940, p. 213.
5 All three were reported in *American Speech*, Oct., 1937, p. 242.
6 *American Speech*, April, 1940, p. 131.

### 3. VERBS

Verbs made of nouns unchanged are numerous in American English, and hundreds of new ones seem to be made every year, but they are by no means new to the language. Since the early Middle English period, indeed, they have constituted one of the chief evidences of that almost complete abandonment of inflections which separates English from the other principal languages of the Indo-European family. Its nouns, save for the addition of *s* in the plural and of *'s* in the genitive, are the same in all situations, and many of them may be turned into verbs without any modification whatever, *e.g., place* and *to place*. To be sure, a number of suffixes are still in use to notify the change — *e.g., -ize* and *-fy,* as in *carbon, to carbonize; beauty, to beautify* —, but often they are not necessary, and when they are used to make new verbs it is usually only because (at any rate in the opinion of the verb-maker) they promote euphony. Many of the most common English verbs are borrowed nouns, and go back to a very early time, *e.g., to ground.* The thing also runs the other way, and such verbs are matched by large numbers of common nouns that began as verbs, *e.g., sleep* and *walk.* The process is going on constantly, and in both directions, but it is naturally most active at times when the language is in one of its recurrent stages of vigorous growth and radical change, and in circles wherein there is least respect for established forms and hence least resistance to innovation. One can hardly ask an Oxford don to accept complacently such a novelty as *to contact,* for it offends all his notions of linguistic order and decorum, but the average American, having only the faintest concept of order and decorum in that field, takes it almost as a matter of course. As we have seen, the same thing was true, in the age of Shakespeare, of the average Englishman, and even of the superior Englishman, and in consequence it was a time of bold and often barbaric experiment in language, and some of the novelties it produced were so extravagant that even the American of today finds them somewhat excessive, or as he would probably say, ultra. You will find a large number of them listed in E. A. Abott's " Shakespearean Grammar," [1] many falling into the class of verbs made of nouns. Shakespeare did not hesitate to use *to happy, to barn, to child, to climate, to disaster,*

1 New ed.; London, 1879.

*to fame, to furnace, to lesson, to malice, to property* and *to verse.*
Some of his innovations, *e.g., to fever* and *to fool,* made their way
into the language and are questioned by no one today, but others died
quickly, for there is a large turnover in such novelties, and no one
can ever predict the ultimate fate of a given example.

One of the newcomers that seems destined to stick is *to contact.*
The DAE does not list it, no doubt because it did not appear until
after 1900, but the NED Supplement traces it to 1929 and marks it
" U.S." It was preceded by the addition of a new sense to the old
noun *contact,* given by Partridge as " an acquaintance(ship), a connection, both with a view to business or self-interest." This new sense,
he says, appeared in the United States at some time before 1925, and
is (1938) " fast verging on Standard English, at least the Standard
English of trade." The verb came in soon afterward, and on September 8, 1928 the *Editor and Publisher* was noting its employment by
an advertising executive. It apparently made relatively slow progress
at the start, but after a couple of years it was in wide and indeed
almost general use,[1] and soon afterward got to England. There it met
with a hostile reception from purists, and so recently as 1939 the
London *Times Literary Supplement* was bracketing it with *to peeve*
and declaring the two " do not exist in reputable English," [2] but this
was hardly more than whistling in the dark, for the London *News
Review,* which specializes in introducing Americanisms to England,
had used it in a headline three years before,[3] and a year later Ivor
Brown, writing in the Manchester *Guardian,*[4] was throwing up his
hands. " The war," he said,

through the power it gives to bureaucracy and to the industrialist turned administrator, will certainly add to our language — or rather inflate it. The tendency
of such people is always to prefer a new and heavy word to an old and short
one. Instead of bidding us *meet* their Mr. Smith in Birmingham, they would
have us *contact* him. In doing this they are following a habit particularly dear
to the American — that is, to take a noun belonging to a verb and then turn
that noun into another and longer verb. The most absurd and offensive example
of this is the use of the word *to decision. Decide* is not nearly swollen enough
for the swollen-headed Napoleon of a film corporation. " Have you *decisioned*
this? " he inquires with a happy illusion of appearing the educated man.

1 Now it is *Contacting,* Reno (Nev.)
Gazette, (editorial page), July 7,
1931. This was apparently a syndi-
cated editorial. It noted that *to intrigue,* which had been borrowed, *c.*
1915, from the English, who had borrowed it, *c.* 1890, from the French.

was beginning to lose popularity as
a counter-word.
2 Jill the Ripper?, April 15, 1939.
3 Anthony Eden Will Not *Contact*
Adolf Hitler, April 30, 1936, p. 8.
4 Verbs and Verbiage, July 20, 1940.

Mr. Brown's contention that in all the situations where *to contact* was being used the ancient *to meet* would suffice was not shared by other English observers. In 1941, an anonymous writer in the *Cheshire Observer*,[1] in noting its adoption by British Army headquarters in Greece, lamented that there was "no precise one-word substitute for it." It was attacked, in the 30s, in the United States as well as in England, and in 1931, as I have recorded in AL4,[2] one of the high officials of the Western Union denounced it as a "hideous vulgarism" and forbade its use by employés of the company. But they continued to use it, and are still using it today, and so are multitudes of other Americans. Early in 1937 there was a brief, inglorious war upon it in the correspondence columns of the New York *Times*, but its opponents were put to rout under date of February 13 by Jacques W. Redway, of Mount Vernon, N. Y., who pointed out sensibly that every attack upon *to contact* was also an attack upon *to harness, to bridle, to saddle* and even *to rain, to hail, to snow* and *to thunder.* More than a year later the *New Republic* called it "dreadful,"[3] but Westbrook Pegler and others replied at once that *to implement*, then a counter-word among Liberals, including especially the editors of the *New Republic*, had no more support in logic.[4] To this the editors made the fatuous reply that *to implement* was "perfectly good English," and had been so "since the days of Walter Scott." In other words, they set up the tests of age and general acceptance, which would have barred out *to implement* itself when it was first launched. Finally, they crowned their confusion by advising their critics to "consult Webster's or the Concise Oxford Dictionary," apparently unaware that the verb had been listed in Webster's New International since 1934, in the NED Supplement, the big sister of the Concise Oxford, since 1933, and in the Standard Dictionary since 1931.[5]

Not a few of the more recent verbs-from-nouns meet genuine

1 *Contact* as Noun or Verb?, April 19, 1941.
2 p. 195, n. 1.
3 *Contact* as a Verb, June 1, 1938, p. 87.
4 Philologically Fastidious, by Arthur Loesser, *New Republic*, June 22, 1938.
5 In Oct., 1938, p. 205, the editors of *American Speech* rebuked the editor of Macmillan's Modern Dictionary; New York, 1938, for omitting it. "Any smart, forward-looking, modern dictionary-maker," they said, "would call attention to the word as a verb. He might wish to label it as *colloquial* or *slang* but he would be sure to list it, knowing that shortly it will be respectable."

needs, and deserve to be treated with more seriousness than they usually get, *e.g., to thumb* (a ride), *to audition,*[1] *to co-star,*[2] *to curb* (take a dog to the curb),[3] *to secretary,*[4] *to cystoscope* (and its numerous medical analogues), *to stench,*[5] *to debut,*[6] *to deadhead, to highlight, to intern,*[7] *to model,*[8] *to service,*[9] *to alert,*[10] *to message,*[11] *to vaca-*

1 Here the only alternative would be something on the order of *to give a hearing to* or *to grant an audition,* both long and clumsy. The term seems to be picking up meanings outside the realm of the ears. On March 17, 1937 *Variety* printed a heading reading: Ice-Skater *Auditions* in Rockefeller Plaza to Agcy 14 Floors Up.

2 Neologisms, by Dwight L. Bolinger, *American Speech,* Feb., 1941, p. 65.

3 *American Speech,* Oct., 1940, p. 242.

4 Middleburg (Va.) *Chronicle,* quoted by the Baltimore *Evening Sun* (editorial page), April 23, 1940. If *to valet,* traced by the NED to 1840, and *to doctor,* traced to 1737, why not *to secretary?*

5 *i.e.,* to empty a theatre (or other place) by liberating ill-smelling fumes. The only alternative I can think of is *to stink up.* Newburgh, N. Y., dispatch in *Variety:* "Cameo, Strand and Academy Theatres here were *stenched* Friday while shows were in progress. Houses were all being picketed by Local 45 MPOU."

6 Apparently the English have begun to use it. Amateur Hour Is Here to Stay, London *Daily Express,* Sept. 10, 1936: "The BBC decided yesterday that the Amateur Hour which *debuted* on Tuesday is to stay put." The *Daily Express* specializes in Americanisms, and its wireless correspondent is called its *radio reporter.*

7 Young Woman Licensed to Practise Medicine, Los Angeles *Times,* Sept. 5, 1934: "For the past year she has been *interning* at the Glendale Sanatorium."

8 In the sense of to display garments by wearing them. Winston-Salem (N. C.) *Journal and Sentinel,* Sept. 23, 1934: "During the broadcast the little artists will *model* garments

from the Anchor Company's children's department."

9 Mr. Justice Owen J. Roberts, decision in N. Y., N. H. and H. R. R. Co. *vs.* Bezue, Jan. 25, 1932: "These facilities are used for *servicing* and repairing locomotives." R. L. Stevenson used the verb (in dialect speech) in Catriona, 1893, but it did not come into general use. It was reborn in the United States, *c.* 1926. See *Service,* by B. M. Peebles, *American Speech,* Jan., 1927, p. 214. Webster's New International marked it "rare" in the edition of 1927, but omitted the "rare" in that of 1934. The English sometimes use *to vet* (from *veterinarian*) where Americans would use *to service.* On May 22, 1938 the London *Sunday Express* announced that "Miss Phyllis Haylor, Britain's first dancing ambassadress," had left for Australia and New Zealand to "*vet* the Empire's dancing." On July 25, 1936 *John o' London's Weekly* printed an advertisement by an author's agent which included the following testimonial from a client: "I have spent £5 with you, and have taken over £50 now in stories sold immediately after you had *vetted* them."

10 *To alert* is to be found in Section IX of the report of the committee appointed to investigate the Pearl Harbor incident. One of the members of the committee was Mr. Justice Owen J. Roberts. The report was submitted to the President Jan. 24, 1942. The verb was then new, and James J. Butler said in Capital Press Corps Quickly Mobilized On War News, *Editor and Publisher,* Dec. 13, 1941, p. 8, that it had been first used in a War Department communiqué following Pearl Harbor. The noun *alert* may have been borrowed from England. It was appar-

*tion,*[1] *to special,*[2] *to package, to press-agent, to research, to pressure,*[3] *to accession,*[4] *to sabotage, to remainder* (unsalable books), *to panic,*[5] *to recess,*[6] *to wastebasket,*[7] *to grand-marshal,*[8] *to momentum,*[9] *to referee,*[10] *to chairman,*[11] *to alibi, to baton,*[12] *to onion,*[13] *to gavel,*[14] *to*

ently new there on Oct. 12, 1940, when the London *Times Literary Supplement* announced magisterially that "it will pass muster."

11 United Press dispatch from Eureka, Calif., Feb. 23, 1931: "The Standard Oil tanker El Segundo *messaged* today that it was standing by the distressed Muleleon, lumber schooner."

1 Los Angeles *Times*, Sept. 5, 1934: "Mrs. Williams *vacationed* for a month at Hotel Laguna." The DAE does not list *to vacation*, but traces *vacationing* to 1896.

2 Used by trained nurses in the sense of *to go on special duty*, *i.e.*, to have the care of one or more special patients. Also used generally in the sense of *to send by special delivery*. See New Words for Old, Baltimore *Evening Sun* (editorial page), June 14, 1939.

3 *Newsweek*, quoted in New Words for Old, Baltimore *Evening Sun* (editorial page), May 16, 1938: "Influential men who enjoy John L. Lewis's confidence have been *pressuring* him to agree to temporary wage cuts."

4 A librarian's term. We Do Odd Things to Words, by J. W. B., New York *Times*, March 27, 1932: "A few years ago the late Melvil Dewey wrote that a certain book had been *accessioned* to a library. Thereupon librarians all over the State ceased to *add* books to their libraries; they preferred to *accession* them. The use of the word as a verb was severely criticized by many editors, but it filled a technical use and it has remained."

5 Used by Thomas Hood in 1827, but apparently by no one else in England afterward. Reinvented in the United States *c.* 1910, and since adopted in England. Denounced by the Manchester *Guardian* Nov. 24, 1939 as one of "our nastier newcomers."

6 In the sense of *to take a recess*. List-

ed as an Americanism by the NED and traced to 1893. The English seldom use *recess* in the American sense of a hiatus in proceedings.

7 And Here's Another, by H. H. Williams, Philadelphia *Record*, Nov. 7, 1930: "If you refuse to publish letters as they are written, have the common manhood to *wastebasket* them."

8 Mayor Won't Ride Horse, New York *World-Telegram*, Nov. 3, 1932: "He saw Paddy Collins *grand-marshalling* a St. Patrick's Day parade."

9 A Seeming Injustice, Ottawa *Journal*, March 7, 1934: "Its sale is no longer *momentumed* by advertising."

10 The DAE does not list this word, but it is probably an Americanism. The NED's first English example is dated 1889. Five years before this the New York *Sun* was denouncing the Intercollegiate Football Association for using it in a pronunciamento regarding a dispute in a Princeton game. See *Referee* as a Verb, by W. L. Werner, *American Speech*, Feb., 1933, p. 81.

11 *Capitol Daily* (Washington), quoted in New Words for Old, Baltimore *Evening Sun*, June 2, 1938: "Ohio's Senator Donahey *chairmans* the joint congressional committee investigating the Tennessee Valley Authority."

12 Headline in Los Angeles *Daily News*, July 22, 1937, quoted in *Words*, Oct., 1937, p. 154: "Alfred Hertz Again *Batons* Symphony."

13 *American Speech*, April, 1935, p. 154: "'Do you wish your hamburger *onioned*?' is a query heard at lunch-stands."

14 Associated Press dispatch from Washington, Feb. 25, 1926: "The Vice President *gaveled* through a motion." The DAE lists the noun, *gavel*, in the sense of a mallet or

*bombshell,*[1] *to submarine,*[2] *to architect,*[3] *to solo, to pancake, to jim-crow, to belly-ache, to pussy-foot, to sidetrack* (traced by the DAE to 1881), *to headquarter, to patrioteer, to loudspeaker,*[4] *to chamoise,*[5] *to first-name, to night-club, to sherlock,*[6] *to clearance,*[7] *to Book-of-the-Month,*[8] *to mastermind,*[9] *to blueprint,*[10] *to needle,*[11] *to cold deck,*[12] *to night-raid,*[13] and *to gift-price.*[14]

This list might be extended almost indefinitely, especially if I included citations from the iconoclastic vocabulary of *Variety*, some of which have gone into the common stock. A few of its characteristic inventions will suffice: *to ash-can, to angel, to showcase, to baritone, to background, to questionnaire, to music, to guest, to pact, to biography, to bankroll, to clipper,*[15] *to premier* (often shortened to *to*

---

hammer used by a presiding officer, as an Americanism, and traces it to 1860. It seems to be borrowed from the name of a hammer used by stonemasons, traced to 1805 and also marked an Americanism. The origin of the term is said by the DAE to be "obscure."

1 Used by Mark Twain in Life on the Mississippi, 1883, p. 379. Ramsay and Emberson call attention in their Mark Twain Lexicon: Columbia, Mo., 1938, p. lxxxii, to his delight in "turning nouns, adjectives or interjections into verbs; verbs, adjectives or adverbs into nouns; adjectives into adverbs; adverbs into adjectives; transitive verbs into intransitive or vice versa." They list, among verbs made of nouns unchanged, *to argument, to chain-mail, to Christian-missionary, to deficit, to discretion, to foreground, to grail, to Jew's-harp, to majesty, to paregoric, to sarcasm, to stove-polish* and *to tadpole.*

2 Harry L. Hopkins at a press-conference in Washington, quoted in New Words for Old, Baltimore *Evening Sun*, Aug. 26, 1938: "I do not appoint those who would *submarine* the program."

3 Advertisement in *Architectural Forum*, May, 1937, p. 8: "*Architected* by A. N. Rebori." I am indebted here to Mr. Winslow Ames. See also The Erteguns Serve a Dinner Worthy of Diplomatic Dean, by

Evelyn Peyton Gordon, Washington *Daily News*, April 26, 1944.

4 The last two are noted in *American Speech*, Oct., 1933, p. 76.

5 *American Speech*, Oct., 1934, p. 236.

6 From the name of *Sherlock* Holmes. *American Speech*, July, 1927, p. 449, reported that the Germans had adopted it in the form of *sherlockieren.*

7 Advertisement in the Los Angeles *Times*, Aug. 8, 1926, noted in *American Speech*, Dec., 1926, p. 163. The verb has since appeared frequently in department-store advertising.

8 *Saturday Review of Literature*, Dec. 26, 1936, noted in *American Speech*, Oct., 1937, p. 239.

9 *True Detective*, June, 1941, noted in Among the New Words, by Dwight L. Bolinger, *American Speech*, April, 1942, p. 123.

10 *Common Sense*, Sept., 1941, noted by Bolinger, just cited.

11 Used in various metaphorical senses, all suggesting penetration. See Bolinger, just cited, p. 123.

12 First noted in 1884. See New Evidence on Americanisms, *American Speech*, April, 1942, p. 125.

13 New York *Post*, Sept. 12, 1939, noted by Dr. Louise Pound in Miscellany, *American Speech*, Dec., 1939, p. 316.

14 Advertisement in the New York *Times*, Sept. 24, 1939, noted by Dr. Pound, just cited.

15 *i.e.*, to travel by a *Clipper* airship.

*preem*), *to option, to commentator* and *to barnum. Variety* frequently reduces verb phrases to simple verbs, *e.g., to ready* for *to make ready*,[1] *to siesta* for *to take a siesta, to train* for *to go by train,* and *to outlet* for *to serve as an outlet.* Rather curiously, it also affects a number of new and clumsy verbs, made from nouns, that are not nearly so vivid as the old verbs they displace, *e.g., to decision* for *to decide*,[2] *to author* for *to write*,[3] *to signature* for *to sign*,[4] *to theft*

1 *To ready* is actually very old in English, and the NED traces it to *c.* 1350. In 1831 Thomas Carlyle used it in Sartor Resartus (what a swell *Variety* reporter he would have made!), but after that it apparently dropped out of use save in racing slang, and I believe that the *Variety* brethren invented it all over again. It seems to be creeping back into use in England.

2 Whether or not its revolutionary literati invented *to decision* I do not know, for the verb is also much used by sports writers. It was defended by Ira Seebacher in the New York *Telegraph*, May 30, 1940, as follows: "*To decision* fills a need. . . . If a man wins a prizefight by knocking out his opponent he is said to have won by a *knockout* or a *kayo*, in fact, *kayo* is used often as a verb — he *kayoed* his man. Similarly, if a fighter wins by a *decision*, it isn't clear enough to say Joe Doaks won over John Doe. That wouldn't explain whether he was the winner by a knockout, by a technical knockout or by a decision. But if you were to say Joe Doaks *decisioned* John Doe, that would make it fairly evident just what you meant. . . . There is no other solution than to give each play, each position, and each situation a name. When you have names, you must correspondingly have verbs that describe the action that takes place. There is no way to circumvent it. The best one can hope for is a terse word that takes care of the matter completely."

3 *To author*, I believe, is authentically a *Variety* coinage, but it has been in general use for some years, and seems to be a favorite among the pseudo-literati. 1927 Sees Decrease

in Number of Syndicates, by Philip Schuyler, *Editor and Publisher,* Aug. 27, 1927, p. 7: "Patten *authors* the text of the strip." Bobbs-Merrill Company circular to book reviewers, Aug. 17, 1937, signed D. A. Cameron: "Lawrence Greene *authored* 'America Goes to Press.'" Washington Is Indignant Over Farr Convoy Story, *Editor and Publisher,* March 14, 1942, p. 16: "The *Mail* story was *authored* by that newspaper's representative with the United States fleet." Bennett Cerf in the *Saturday Review of Literature,* Feb. 19, 1944, p. 19: "Hammerstein *authored* 'Carmen Jones.'" *Journal of the American Medical Association,* April 15, 1944, p. 1151: "Radley once *authored* an article in a chiropractic journal." Louis J. Halle, Sr., in the *Saturday Review of Literature,* June 10, 1944, p. 20: "The article should have appeared not as *authored* by me but by my son." *To author* was defended by James Gray in Critics Extreme in Attempt to Enrich Speech, St. Paul *Pioneer Press,* July 14, 1929. It was once, he said, "a perfectly good word, meaning to create or originate. The dictionaries now list it as obsolete. But if Broadway in its devotion to vigor and directness wishes to take a short cut back to the early habits before our tongue became fussily refined, the professors themselves should be the ones to clear the way." *To author* was used by Chapman in 1596, but apparently did not last long. The NED's last example is dated 1632. When the thing written is a movie script *Variety* uses *to script.*

4 This is apparently not one of *Variety's* inventions. I find "It is never

for *to steal*,[1] *to gift* for *to give*,[2] *to guest* for *to entertain*,[3] and *to destruct* for *to destroy*. Such forms are by no means confined to the vocabulary of *Variety*. Walter Winchell and his disciples produce them in large number, and they are also plentiful in presumably more decorous circles. I have encountered *to teacher* in a learned journal of Florida [4] and it seems to have countenance in other parts of the South. Indeed, the manufacture of such new verbs goes on on all levels. *To letter*, probably suggested by *to major*, is used in the colleges to indicate a choice in physical training, *e.g.*, " He *lettered* in wrestling," [5] and I cherish " a town poised on the borderland between North and South, *sourced* by French and Swedish and German and plain English stock," found in an advertisement of " Jordanstown," by Josephine Johnson, published in 1937 by Simon and Schuster. I reach into my collectanea and bring forth *to air* (to disseminate by radio), *to wax* (to record for the phonograph), *to postcard, to canary* (to sing), *to doghouse, to true-bill* (to indict), *to blurb, to statistic* (and *to outstatistic*), *to bum's rush*,[6] *to lumberwagon, to landslide, to dead-heat, to picture-peddle, to front-page, to hostess, to by-line, to conquest, to roadster, to cafe, to highwayman, to trailer, to lyric* (to write the lyrics for a musical piece), *to brain-trust*, and *to third-degree*.[7] Nor are the English altogether out of the running, though the wild exuberance of fancy that marked them in the age of Elizabeth has now been transferred to the United States. I find *to stonewall* in no less decorous a London journal than

*signatured* by the Postmaster General or his assistants " in Observations On the Duties of Contact Men as Applied to Post Office Department Organization, by John H. Bartlett, First Assistant Postmaster General; Cleveland, 1924, p. 1. Instead of *to signature, Variety* and its imitators sometimes use *to ink*.

1 New Words for Old, Baltimore *Evening Sun*, May 21, 1938, quoted from *Variety:* " Clancy claimed the plot of the film was *thefted* from his play."

2 Cole Porter's Gift, *Variety*, Sept. 16, 1942: " Porter's ' Glide, Glider, Glide ' was *gifted* to the fliers without any strings." *To gift* is very old in English, but *Variety* seems to have revived it. It has produced a

number of derivatives, *e.g.*, *to Christmas-gift* and *to gift-price*, already noted.

3 I find *to luncheon-guest* in the *Goldfish Bowl*, house organ of the National Press Club, Washington, March, 1937, p. 2. Along with it is *to luncheon-hear*, *i.e.*, to listen to a speaker invited to unburden himself at lunch.

4 *Florida Review*, Spring, 1938, p. 2.

5 I am indebted here to Mr. R. Balfour Daniels of Pittsburg, Kansas.

6 Used by the late General Hugh S. Johnson; New Words For Old, Baltimore *Evening Sun*, July 11, 1938.

7 Many more are in The Current Tendency Toward Denominative Verbs, by Manuel Prenner, *American Speech*, Oct., 1938, pp. 193–96.

the *Morning Post*,[1] *to partner* in a highly respectable provincial paper,[2] *to town-plan* in the austere Edinburgh *Scotsman*,[3] and a revival of the archaic *to servant* in the *Countryman*.[4] Whether *to park*, in its current senses, originated in England or in the United States is in dispute. It was borrowed from the French early in the Nineteenth Century to indicate the storing of artillery, and was taken into the vocabulary of automobilists *c.* 1910. Since then it has been extended in meaning to indicate any deposit of an object that must be kept safely, and Americans *park* not only their automobiles but also their dogs, their children and their consciences.[5] Another verb whose provenance is uncertain is *to streamline*. The NED Supplement traces it in English use to 1913, but it was probably in use in the United States earlier, though the DAE does not list it. It came into popularity *c.* 1937,[6] and was greatly extended in meaning, so that it now designates any attempt at simplification. On January 10, 1944 it appeared in H. J. Res. 211, introduced in the House of Representatives by the Hon. Frank Carlson of Kansas, and so became official.[7]

One of the most mysterious American verbs is *to goose*. Its meaning is known to every schoolboy, but the dictionaries do not list it, and so far as I know no lexicographer has ever worked out its etymology. The corresponding adjective, *goosey*, was noted in *American Speech* in 1933 as meaning " nervous, touchy," [8] and the diligent Bolinger has recorded that *to goose* itself has been taken over by truck-drivers and aviators to signify feeding gasoline to an engine in irregular spurts,[9] but beyond this the philological literature is a blank.

---

1 Now absorbed by the *Daily Telegraph*. Mr. Eden as *Stonewaller*, Dec. 17, 1935: " Mr. Anthony Eden *stonewalled* persistent attacks."

2 *Western Morning News*, Nov. 27, 1937: " He is again *partnered* by Miss Joan Blondell."

3 March 1, 1937: " ' In many cases,' declared one speaker, ' county councils neither want themselves *to town plan* nor will they allow the small burghs *to town plan*.' "

4 July–Sept., 1938.

5 *Park*, by Louise Pound, *American Speech*, May, 1927, p. 346. I am informed by a correspondent that the French use *stationner* of automobiles, and that the Germans use *parken* or *stationieren*.

6 The Living Language, by Dwight L. Bolinger, *Words*, Sept. 1937, p. 135.

7 " It is hereby declared to be the policy of Congress . . . to establish a *streamlined*, long range, integrated Federal tax policy." On Feb. 16, 1944 it appeared again in the preamble of H. J. Res. 236, introduced by the Hon. Henry O. Talle of Iowa. I am indebted here to Mr. H. R. Bishop of Washington.

8 Ranch Diction of the Texas Panhandle, by Mary Dale Buckner, Feb., 1933, p. 31.

9 Among the New Words, *American Speech*, Feb., 1943, p. 64.

The preponderance of medical opinion, I find, inclines to the theory that the verb was suggested by the fact that geese, which are pugnacious birds, sometimes attack human beings, and especially children, by biting at their fundaments.[1] There is also the possibility that the term may be derived from the old custom of examining a goose before turning it out to feed in the fields by feeling of its rear parts: if an egg could be felt it was kept in its pen for the day.[2] This method of exploration is still used by some housewives in order to estimate the fatness of a dressed goose. The question remains why one person is *goosey* and another is not. Some resent *goosing* no more than they resent a touch on the arm, whereas others leap into the air, emit loud cries, and are thrown into a panic. One of my medical informants suggests that susceptibility is mainly psychic, and may have its origin in an obscure fear (and perhaps an infantile memory) of a sexual attack, but other authorities believe that it is caused by physical sensitiveness and is psychic only by association. Meanwhile, every American knows what *to goose* means, though the term appears to be unknown in England, and there are no analogues in the other European languages. The practice is the source of many serious accidents in industry and the National Safety Council has issued a number of posters warning against its dangerous and sometimes even fatal consequences.[3] It is also frowned upon by the various State industrial accident commissions,[4] and by the Army and Navy. The

---

1 I am indebted here to the late Admiral Charles S. Butler, M.C., U.S.N., (1875–1944), to Dr. Logan Clendening, author of Modern Methods of Treatment, The Human Body, Source Book of Medical History, etc., and to Dr. Morris Fishbein, editor of the *Journal of the American Medical Association.* In some of the countries of Europe, where geese are plentiful, they are also said to attack women by striking at the pudenda. An illustration of both methods of attack is in Illustrierte Sittengeschichte, by Eduard Fuchs; München, 1912, p. 86.

2 I am indebted here to Dr. Carey P. McCord, medical director of the Industrial Health Conservancy Laboratories, Detroit.

3 One of them reads: "*Goosey*. A *goosey* man is one who is nervous.

When you touch him he jumps. There is nothing funny about it. One *goosey* man jumped off a scaffold and broke both legs when a fellow worker touched him. Another almost jumped into a pot of molten slag. To intentionally startle a nervous person while at work is more than a mean trick – IT IS CRIMINAL." Another poster warns especially against *goosing* with an air hose: "you might kill him." I am indebted here to Fred Hamann.

4 It is denounced, for example, along with horseplay and scuffling, on p. B of General Safety Manual Applicable to All Hazardous Industries, issued by the State Industrial Accident Commission of Oregon, Jan. 1, 1937. I am indebted here to Mr. Robert W. Evenden, director of the commission.

Army also discourages the old soldiers' game of *hot-foot*, which consists in inserting matches between the soles and uppers of a sleeping comrade's shoes, and then lighting them.[1] There was a time when a craze for *goosing* arose on the Hollywood movie lots, to the consternation not only of its victims but also of their directors, who saw many a scene spoiled. One of its most assiduous practitioners was the late Douglas Fairbanks, Sr. When the other performers in his company became so wary of him that he was constantly watched, he took to hiding behind scenery and properties and operating stealthily with a long fishing-rod. He was finally put down by threats of heavy fines from the front office.[2]

American English has been producing a great many pungent verb-phrases since the Revolutionary era, and some of them are now firmly imbedded in the national speech, *e.g.*, *to stay put* (traced by the DAE to 1848), *to stand from under* (1857), *to do the square thing* (1860), *to face the music* (1850), *to spread it on thick* (1865), *to knock the spots off* (1861), *to slip up* (1854), *to slop over* (1861), *to clear one's skirts* (1854), *to sit in* (1868), *to keep one's shirt on* (1854), *to shinny on one's own side* (1866), *to cut a shine* (1819), *to take a shine to* (1840), *to skin out* (1869), *to shell out* (1833), *to shoot off one's mouth* (1880), *to paint the town red* (1884),[3] *to go in for* (1835), *to go him one better* (1845), *to rope in* (1840), *to go it blind* (1846), *to go it alone* (1855), *to fork over* (1839), *to go for* (1835), *to go under* (1848), *to go the whole hog* (1829), *to snow under* (1880), *to be solid with* (1882), *to go to the spot* (1868), *to make a stake* (1873), *to size up* (1877), *to sell short* (1861), *to scare up* (1841), *to step lively* (1891), *to stand off* (1878), *to stand for* (1896), *to put on style* (1864), *to shoot up* (1890), *to be stuck on* (1886), *to strike it rich* (1852), *to take stock in* (1870), *to stop off* (1855), *to stop over* (1857), *to win out* (1896), *to get back at* (1888), *to get*

1 Art and the Soldier, by Paul May-riel; Biloxi, Miss., 1943, p. 42. I am indebted here to Captain A. M. Klum, Special Service, Keesler Field, Miss.

2 The phrase, *the goose hangs high*, is an Americanism, so marked by the DAE and traced to 1870. The DAE says that there is "no convincing evidence" that it is "a corruption of *the goose honks high*." There was a discussion of it by various folk-etymologists in Trade Winds, *Saturday Review of Literature*, Sept. 4, 1943.

3 The DAE's first example is from the Boston *Journal*, Sept. 13, 1884. In *Painting the Town Red*, by T. F. Crane, *Scientific Monthly*, June, 1924, p. 605, it is shown that the phrase reached England (in *Punch*) by Jan. 24, 1885. Dr. Crane's paper is a learned discussion of the underlying idea.

*away with* (1878), *to make a stab at,* and *to play up* (or *down*). English commentators often mark the American fondness for hooking adverbs or prepositions to verbs, and note sadly the spread of the practice to England.[1] It is, in many situations, quite irrational: there is no logical difference between *to lose* and *to lose out.* But in other situations important differences are easily discernible, as between *to play* and *to play up* (or *down*), *to try* and *to try out.*[2] New verb-phrases of a more elaborate sort are coming in all the time, *e.g.,* *to go Hollywood,*[3] *to get it off one's chest, to tell him where to get off, to go places, to go into a burn,*[4] *to slip one's trolley,*[5] *to pull a fast one, to do a Corrigan,*[6] *to pitch a woo* (to make love), and *to eat a little higher on the hog.*[7] *To go haywire,* familiar to every American, is not listed in the DAE, but Stewart H. Holbrook says in " Holy Old Mackinaw "[8] that it originated in the Maine logging camps and thus discusses it:

No camp could operate without haywire. This wire was the stuff with which hay for the oxen and horses was bound into bales, for compact toting into the distant camps. Teamsters shaking out a bale to feed the animals took to saving the wire strands, throwing them over an oxbow nailed to the side of the hovel. They would do to mend a busted hame strap, or to put a link in a

1 Adjectives — and Other Words, by Ernest Weekley; London, 1930, p. 182; The American Language, by S. K. Ratcliffe, *New Statesman and Nation,* July 27, 1935, p. 131. Says Ratcliffe: "There is no doubt at all that American influence is fast changing our usage. Twenty years ago no one in England *started in, started out* or *checked up;* we did not *stand for* or *fall for,* as we do today. . . . We have learned from the American how *to try out,* but not as yet *to curse out,* and when we *make out* we are still deciphering something and not, as the American is, doing something fairly well. We may sometimes *call down* an offender, but we still refrain from *bawling him out.* Nor do we have things *salted down.*"

2 In Studies in Stylistics, V, *American Speech,* Feb., 1929, p. 233, Mildred E. Lambert calls attention to the fact that when a verb-adverb combination is used the ensuing object appears in a prepositional phrase.

*Cf.* " He can't *win* his bet," and " He can't *win out on* his bet."

3 *Neologisms,* by Dwight L. Bolinger, *American Speech,* Feb., 1941, p. 66.

4 Apparently a *Variety* invention. New Words For Old, Baltimore *Evening Sun* (editorial page), May 11, 1938.

5 Brought in by the trolley-car and now obsolescent. See *American Speech,* Dec., 1940, p. 363.

6 Suggested by an historic wrong-direction flight by an aviator named Corrigan, *c.* 1938. See As We Stroll Around, New Rochelle (N. Y.) *Standard-Star,* Sept. 1, 1938.

7 I heard this masterpiece at a meeting of Negro Democrats in Chicago in 1940, just before the opening of the Democratic National Convention. They met to formulate their demands and grievances, and one of their speakers summarized the former as a desire *to eat a little higher on the hog.*

8 New York, 1938, p. 49.

broken chain. And loggers used the strands to strengthen an ax helve **or to** wind the split handle of a peavey. Cooks strung haywire above the stove **over** which to dry clothes and to hang ladles; and often to bind the very stove together. A camp that was notoriously poor in its equipment came to be known as a *haywire camp;* and from this usage it spread to mean broken, busted, sick, crazy, no-good, and a score of other things, none of them praiseworthy. It is possibly the only authentic logger word the lay public has accepted.

I have a high respect for Holbrook's philological parts, but it seems to me that in this case he has got entangled in haywire himself. No one who has ever opened a bale of hay with a hatchet, and had the leaping wire whirl about him and its sharp ends poniard him, will ever have any doubt as to how *to go haywire* originated. I should add, however, that the Holbrook etymology is supported by Wayne Shirley, librarian of the Pratt Institute, Brooklyn, who spent some time in a Wisconsin lumber-camp in his early days.[1] *To feeze* is another verb that deserves more attention from philologians than it has got. In the sense of to put to flight it is very old in English, but in the sense of to disconcert it seems to be American. It is spelled variously, *e.g., faze, faeze, feaze, phase* and even *pheeze* and *pheese.* Thornton tracks it, in its usual American sense, to 1843, and the DAE to 1830. In those early days it had a corresponding noun, signifying perturbation, and that noun is traced by the DAE to 1647. It is now obsolete. But the verb *to faze,* hough it is seldom used in England, is very familiar in the United States. The preterite *fazed* is recorded for 1830, but the negative form *unfazed* is not listed by the DAE, though it is in common use.[2] *To interview* is unquestionably an Americanism, though the cautious DAE does not so mark it. The first example listed is from the *Nation* (New York) of January 28, 1869, and the quotation is: "*Interviewing* is confined to American journalism." The NED's first English example is from the London *Daily News* of December 17 of the same year: "The *Sun interviews* Corbin, Fisk . . . and whoever else has any story to tell or axe to grind." Obviously, the *Sun* referred to here was the New York *Sun.* The DAE's first example of the noun *interview* is from the issue of the *Nation* just quoted; the NED's first English example is from the *Pall Mall Gazette* of December 31, 1884, which said: "Among the permanent gains of the year the acclimatization of the *interview* in English jour-

---

1 Private communication, Aug. 17, 1943.
2 I find *unphased* in Remembrances of

the Mississippi, by T. B. Thorpe, *Harper's Magazine,* Dec., 1855, p. 35.

nalism certainly should be reckoned." There is a newspaper tradition that the *interview* was invented by James Redpath, a Scotsman who followed Sherman's and Thomas's armies for the New York *Tribune* during the latter part of the Civil War.

Verbs produced by back formation are usually challenged by high octane purists, and sometimes denounced with great bitterness: as a result many linger in the Alsatia of slang. But others have won their way into more or less decorous American usage, *e.g.*, *to phone* and *to commute*. The DAE does not list *to phone*, but it has an American smack, and the NED's first English example is dated 1900, some years after the term had become commonplace in the United States. The DAE traces *to commute* to 1865, the date, also, of its first example of *commuter*. *To enthuse* first appeared in the *Congressional Globe* on February 16, 1859. For years thereafter it was derided as fit only for bad newspaper reporters, worse politicians and other such *Simiidae*, but in recent years it seems to be gathering respectability, and I encountered it not long ago in a serious paper by an American scholar.[1] At the start it was a transitive verb only, but it began to be used as an intransitive in the 70s. Richard Grant White denounced it as " ridiculous " and said that he had never heard it used " by any person born and bred north of the Potomac," [2] but he was constrained to admit that it might be derived logically from the Greek root in *enthusiasm*. By 1929 J. Y. T. Greig was listing it as an Americanism that had forced its way into English,[3] and by 1944 John B. Opdycke was reporting that, though still " a low colloquialism," it was prevailing " in spite of all efforts made by grammarians and lexicographers to discourage its use." [4]

Various other American verbs of the same non-Euclidian sort are listed in AL4, pp. 191 and 192, *e.g.*, *to insurge*, *to vamp* and *to inno-*

---

1 *Publications of the Modern Language Association*, March, 1944, p. 91. " The devotees of *to enthuse*," wrote Dr. Louise Pound in *American Speech*, Jan., 1926, p. 247, " believe in the word as firmly as they do in the feeling it denotes, and employ it in their most serious writing or speaking. It is one of their greatly cherished words. Condemn it and you hurt their feelings. It would be impossible to persuade them to discard it."

2 Words and Their Uses; new ed.; New York, 1876, p. 207.
3 Breaking Priscian's Head; New York, 1929, p. 80.
4 Say What You Mean; New York, 1944, p. 250. *To enthuse*, in its turn, has produced a shortened noun, *thuse*, in use at the University of West Virginia to designate a pepmeeting. *American Speech*, Feb., 1935, p. 35.

*vate.* To them may be added *to propagand,*[1] *to galack,*[2] *to stenog,*[3] *to chiropract,*[4] *to garrul,*[5] *to sanitate,*[6] *to glam,*[7] *to auth,*[8] *to hoke,*[9] *to liase,*[10] *to mart,*[11] *to junk,*[12] *to bootleg,*[13] *to bish,*[14] *to emote, to elocute, to ghost-write, to bookkeep, to televise,*[15] *to collab,*[16] *to referend,*[17] *to reluct,*[18] and *to best sell.*[19] Some of the verbs of this class are already of respectable antiquity. The DAE's first example of *to jell* comes from Louisa M. Alcott's " Little Women," 1869, and it traces *to resolute* to 1860, *to bach* to 1878, *to ush* to 1890, *to burgle* to 1870, and *to dressmake* to 1884. Mr. R. P. Whitmer, secretary of the American Foundry and Furnace Company, tells me that the noble verb *to combust* apparently originated in Bloomington, Ill., where the first oil-burner heating plants for private houses were made. It is universally used, he says, by the workmen engaged in the industry. To them, " to properly *combust* the oil means to so shatter it into minute particles as to achieve complete burning." Thus *to combust* may owe almost as much to *to bust* as *to combustion.*[20] *To sculp* is not

1 *Left News*, March, 1939.

2 Omaha *World-Herald*, Oct. 6, 1940: " *Galacking* is the business of collecting decorative greens, the term being derived from *galax* leaves." I take this from *American Speech*, Feb., 1941, p. 31.

3 O. Henry: The Four Million; New York, 1906, Ch. XIV.

4 Philadelphia *Evening Bulletin*, March 10, 1926.

5 From *garrulous*. Proposed in 1942 by Dr. James Francis Cooke, editor of the *Étude*.

6 Ask Aesculapius, *Forum*, Jan., 1926, p. 9.

7 From *glamor*. *American Speech*, Oct., 1937, p. 242.

8 From *author*. *American Speech*, Dec., 1936, p. 374.

9 From *hokum*. Associated Press dispatch, Oct. 30, 1938, reported in *American Speech*, Dec., 1939, p. 318. *Saturday Review of Literature*, June 15, 1940, reported in *American Speech*, Feb., 1941, p. 31.

10 This lovely verb may be English. *American Notes and Queries*, Dec., 1941, p. 141, reports its appearance in a Home Guard instruction sheet. But I am told by Mr. Paul W. Kesten of the Columbia Broadcasting System that it is also used in the American Army.

11 From *martyr*.

12 From *junction*. *American Speech*, Feb., 1941, p. 31.

13 Some Neologisms From Recent Magazines, by Robert Withington, *American Speech*, April, 1931, p. 280.

14 From *bishop*. *Outlook and Independent*, Oct. 29, 1930, p. 328, recorded by Withington, just cited.

15 Suggested by Dr. Milton Harris of New York in Book Marks For Today, New York *World-Telegram*, Dec. 17, 1931, and since often used, especially as *televising*.

16 Often used by *Variety* and imitated by many newspaper writers on the movies.

17 Candidates Queried, *Oregon Daily Journal* (Portland), May 1, 1942, p. 10.

18 Used in Dr. William A. Brady's newspaper health column, Nov. 20, 1935, and recorded by *American Speech*, Dec., 1935, p. 315.

19 Collectanea, *American Speech*, Oct., 1938, p. 236.

20 For an interesting discussion of verbs of this class see Slipped Words: A Study of Back-Forma-

American but English. Dr. Johnson listed it in his Dictionary of 1755, but dismissed it loftily as " a word not in use." But the NED shows that it dates from *c*. 1535 and that both Stevenson and Kipling used it.

The American fondness for shortened forms is shown by the prevalence of transferred verbs of the *to sleep* class, as in " A Pullman sleeper *sleeps* forty passengers." Such forms are by no means rare in Standard English, *e.g.*, " He *walked* his horse," traced by the NED to the Fifteenth Century; but in late years the chief reservoir of new ones has been the United States. They serve a very real need, for without them the only recourse is to long and sometimes unclear circumlocutions. Bartlett, in his first edition of 1848, recorded of a landlady that " she could *eat* fifty people in her house, although she could not *sleep* half the number." *To meal, to room* and *to fly* (in the sense of to convey by airship) have been noted and embalmed by the scouts of *American Speech*.[1] *To subsist* occurs in an article by an American admiral, and is apparently official in the Navy.[2] *To go* has arisen by analogy with *to stop*, as in " We'll see traffic cops *stopping* and *going* the entrants." [3] *To dance*, as in " I was *danced* by a sailor," I have not encountered in the United States, but it is recorded in England.[4] The medical men seem to have not only adopted *to sleep*,[5] but also to have invented a verb of their own, *to belch*.[6] So far, at least to my knowledge, no saloon or night-club has been described as *drinking* so many clients an evening, but I suppose it is on its way. An ingenious correspondent, Mr. Julian T. Bentley of Chicago, suggests that the verbs of this class may owe something to the old

tions and Curtailments in Present-Day English, by Elisabeth Wittmann, *Dialect Notes*, Vol. IV, Part II, 1914, pp. 115-45.

1 For *to meal* see the issue for June, 1928, p. 434; for *to room* that for Oct., 1927, p. 25, and for *to fly* that for Feb., 1928, p. 258.

2 Rear Admiral W. A. Moffett in Flying Boats and Seaplanes, *Liberty*, Aug. 18, 1928, p. 46: " We could have the most efficient naval aviation service in the world, and still be helpless if there were no surface ships to transport, fuel and *subsist* them." The verb, in fact, is old in this sense, and is traced by the DAE in American use to 1835, when it was used of Indians on reservations.

3 Baltimore *Post*, Sept. 1, 1925. I am indebted here to Mr. Lewis George Lederer of Baltimore.

4 He *Danced* Me, *John o' London's Weekly*, Nov. 5, 1937.

5 I find the following in a review of a book called Life With Baby in the *Journal of the American Medical Association*, May 8, 1943: " The photographs portray various stages in bathing, dressing, feeding and *sleeping* a new baby."

6 As in " Do you *belch* the baby after giving it a bottle? " I am indebted here to Mr. R. Balfour Daniels of Edinburg, Texas.

Greek first aorist, " which carried a sense of causing or forcing action upon the object." [1] Analogous forms are to be found in various terms which, so Mr. Dayton Stoddart tells me, are in common use among American farmers, *e.g.*, *to barn*, in the sense of to drive cattle to a barn, *to grain*, in the sense of to feed them grain, and *to bug*, in the sense of to spray potatoes with insecticides; and in *to dessert*, in the sense of to serve a dessert.[2] Also, there are the verbs *to sell*, meaning to snare a customer, and, by extension, to propagate an idea; *to shave*, as in " I *shave* at the Terminal barber-shop "; and *to graduate*, in the room of *to be graduated*.[3]

To the list of verbs made of nouns, already given, should be added some specimens of verbs made of other parts of speech. *To up* offers a good example. It has had a twilight sort of life in English for many years, but it did not flower in American until *Variety* began to use it. Nothing whatever can be said against it, for its brother, *to down*, has been accepted since Shakespeare's time, and it is obviously just as legitimate. It is now in very respectable usage.[4] *Variety* has also used *to in* and *to out*, but only with apparent timidity, and not often. I suppose they will be followed soon or late by *to on* and *to off*, and perhaps by *to with*, *to at*, *to by* and *to to*. To the same general category belong *to ad lib* and *to yes* and the verbs made of interjections, *e.g.*, *to shush, to oomph, to whump,*[5] and *to wow*, all of which have

1 Mr. Bentley points for authority to Homeric Greek, by Clyde Pharr, third ed.; Boston, 1924, p. 277.

2 *Printer's Ink*, Feb. 18, 1944: " Current Borden Company advertisements urge housewives to ' *dessert* your family with Borden's Black Raspberry Rocky Road Ice Cream.' This seems to be the first recorded use of this familiar term as a verb. Might be that the idea is worth extending to cover suggestions that the homemaker *soup* or *cereal* or *meat* or *vegetable* the folks. There are limitations though. For example, Borden might well hesitate — in view of the sensitiveness on the part of many husbands toward the little woman's financial demands — to suggest publicly that the housewife *milk* her family."

3 This was formerly looked on as an Americanism, though Southey used it in 1807. In late years the English

have taken to it. See, for example, the obituary of the Rev. A. N. Campbell in the London *Times*, July 13, 1934.

4 In *American Speech*, Feb., 1934, p. 76, Louise Pound reported the following from a speech in Birmingham, Ala., Sept. 17, 1933, by Dr. Sterling J. Foster, chairman of an association opposed to municipal ownership: " Taxes will be *upped* on every house in the city." I add the following from a pamphlet entitled Taxes and Estates, published by the Equitable Trust Company, Baltimore, in Jan., 1944, p. 1: " A tremendous *upping* of the rates of death taxes." And this from an Associated Press dispatch from Washington, Oct. 1, 1941: " The excess profits tax on corporations has been *upped*."

5 Apparently invented by *Life*. See *American Speech*, Feb., 1941, p. 31.

a reputable forerunner in *to hem and haw,* which goes back, in various forms, to the Fifteenth Century. Also, the pathologist of speech must not overlook the verbs made of adjectives, *e.g., to obsolete* [1] and *to à-la-mode, i.e.,* to spread ice-cream on a slice of fruit-pie, thus converting it into *pie à la mode.* [2]

New verbs are frequently formed by adding prefixes or suffixes to old ones, or to nouns or adjectives. Of the prefixes *de-* seems to be the most popular, with *un-* as its only serious competitor. *To debunk,* which appeared *c.* 1923, was denounced not only on the ground that it was an uncouth word but also on the ground that the activity it described was immoral and against God, but it has survived. [3] It was made popular by William E. Woodward, and may have been suggested by *to delouse,* which appeared during World War I, probably in imitation of the German *entlausen.* [4] Before it came in the English used *to disinfest.* The DAE records but three American verbs in *de-* before 1900, to wit, *to demoralize* (1806), *to dehorn* (1888) and *to demote* (*c.* 1891). Even *to derail* seems to have been borrowed from England, which also produced *to detrain.* [5] But the crop has been larger in recent years, and in my collectanea I find *to dewax, to dejell,* [6] *to degerm,* [7] *to dewater,* [8] *to debulk,* [9] *to deoomph,* [10] *to detooth, to*

1 *American Speech,* Dec., 1939, p. 286.
2 New Verbs, by Mabel E. Strong, *American Speech,* Feb., 1926, p. 292. In an Associated Press dispatch from Cambridge, N. Y., May 20, 1939 the invention of *pie à la mode* was claimed for Charles Watson Townsend, who had died there that day. The inspiration seized him, it was said, while dining at a local hotel, *c.* 1887, and soon afterward he introduced the dessert to Delmonico in New York.
3 In the Manchester *Guardian,* April 5, 1929, Harold Brighouse hinted that *to debunk* was my private property, with the inference that I had invented it. I did not invent it, and have never, so far as I can recall, made more than occasional use of it.
4 *Debunk, American Speech,* May, 1927, p. 374.
5 *To detrain* was originally a military term, and is traced by the NED in Army usage to 1881. It came into general use soon afterward and was borrowed in this country. American

purists sought to dispose of it by concocting satirical analogues, *e.g., to deomnibus, to dehack, to dehorsecar* and *to decanalboat.* See New Words in the New World, by C. B. A., *American Speech,* Feb., 1933, p. 78. In recent years the English have toyed with some new words in *em-,* imitated from *to embark, e.g., to embus.* See A Spectator's Notebook, London *Spectator,* Aug. 9, 1940, p. 137 and Aug. 16, p. 161.
6 Both used in automobile service-stations. See *American Speech,* April, 1935, p. 154.
7 Defined as follows in the *Journal of Infectious Diseases,* Nov.–Dec., 1938, p. 301: "To *degerm* an object is to reduce, by any means, the number of microbes, pathogenic or nonpathogenic, in or on it. . . . *To disinfect* an object (successfully) means fully to eliminate its infectious quality. Likewise, *to sterilize* means to carry through destruction of the germs to completion. The word *degerm,* how-

*deflea*,[1] and *to derat*.[2] The new verbs in *un-* are not numerous. *To unquote*, meaning to finish a quotation, has been borrowed from the cablese of newspaper correspondents, who must indicate when a quoted passage ends and are forced by high cable tolls to avoid any words of two syllables when they can find or invent one of one.[3] *To unstink*, as in " The American reds have attempted to *unstink* themselves," seems to have been coined by Westbrook Pegler. Walter Winchell and *Variety* have launched a number of analogues, but they have not come into general use.

The suffix *-ize* has been used to make verbs in English for many centuries. It was reinforced in the Seventeenth Century by the French *-iser*, and there is still a fashion in England for spelling such words in *-ise*, as in *to advertise*, but the NED says that *-ize*, the common American form, is correct. A large number of examples are listed in " Lexicological Evolution and Conceptual Progress," by John Taggart Clark,[4] the earliest dating from the 1351–1400 period. *To apologize* and *to latinize* came in before 1600, and *to barbarize*, *to criticize* and *to sermonize* in the age of Shakespeare. The DAE traces *to burglarize* to 1871 and marks it an Americanism. When August Kemmler, the first murderer to be put to death by electricity, was waiting to be executed at Sing Sing [5] many of the newspapers re-

---

ever, refers simply to the act of reduction, and not to the bacteriological state at its termination." I take this from Use of the Term *Degerm*, by Philip B. Price, *Journal of the American Medical Association*, May 6, 1944, p. 82.

8 Advertisement of the Simplicity Engineering Company, Durand, Mich., in the *Chemical Equipment Review*, May–June, 1942, p. 11. I am indebted here to Mr. Fred Hamann.

9 *American Speech*, Oct., 1943, p. 237.

10 Apparently coined by Barney Oldfield, " a newspaper writer on film topics," Jan. 14, 1940. *American Speech*, April, 1940, p. 131.

1 The last two are reported in Two More *De-* Words, by Atcheson L. Hench, *American Speech*, Feb. 1935, p. 78.

2 The English have heard *to derat*, but buck at it. See a note on it in the London *Observer*, Nov. 13, 1938. They accept, however, *deratization*, which the NED Supplement traces to 1914, when it appeared in a circular of the Board of Trade. *To deskill* was recorded by *Country Life* (London), Feb. 1, 1941, but not hailed with joy. " Civil servants," said the editor gloomily, " are adepts at the creation of new words, and soldiers are not without a certain merit in the same hideous art; so when a war comes and the two are on the same side we must expect something out of the common. One of the latest examples is the verb *to deskill*, which is, we believe, applied to factories and refers to the increasing use of unskilled labor in them."

3 The Living Language, by Dwight L. Bolinger, *Words*, Oct., 1937, p. 155.

4 *University of California Publications in Modern Philology*, Sept. 21, 1918, pp. 175–200.

5 He went to the chair Aug. 3, 1890.

ported that he was to be *electrized*, and it was some time before they abandoned *to electrize* for *to electrocute*.[1] But it is in recent years that the coinage of such verbs has been most active, and putting together anything approaching a comprehensive list of those that have been launched would be impossible. I must content myself with some specimens:

*Verbs made of proper nouns, including trade-names: to hooverize, to fletcherize,*[2] *to oslerize,*[3] *to peglerize,*[4] *to broadwayize,*[5] *to winterize,*[6] *to texanize,*[7] *to sanforize,*[8] *to TVAize,*[9] *to websterize,*[10] *to sovietize, to bolshevize, to simonize.*

*Verbs made of common nouns: to accessorize,*[11] *to partnerize,*[12] *to pressurize,*[13] *to funeralize,*[14] *to glamorize,*[15] *to filmize,*[16] *to peopleize,*[17] *to publicize,*[18] *to sea-*

1 The DAE's first example of *to electrocute* is dated Aug. 1, 1889. It does not list *to electrize*. Kemmler's crime was committed March 29, 1889. The act establishing electrocution as the means of inflicting the death penalty in New York went into effect Jan. 1, 1889. See The First Electrocution, by Tom Mahone, *Real Detective*, May, 1935, p. 27.

2 From Horace *Fletcher* (1849–1919), a fanatic who advocated chewing food until all its taste was lost. He had a large following in the early years of the century, but his cure-all is now forgotten. F. H. Garrison says in An Introduction to the History of Medicine; fourth ed.; Philadelphia, 1929, p. 737, that he "really cultivated constipation and suffered from chronic toxemia and decayed teeth."

3 See AL4, p. 193.

4 New Words For Old, Baltimore *Evening Sun* (editorial page), April 29, 1940.

5 *Gardens, Houses and People* (Baltimore), Jan., 1944, p. 24.

6 Among the New Words, by Dwight L. Bolinger, *American Speech*, April, 1941, p. 148. Defined as "to equip or prepare for Winter use."

7 Motto of the Texas centennial celebration at Corsicana, 1936: Let's *Texanize* Texas.

8 To pre-shrink cloth, from the first name of *Sanford* Lockwood Cluett, inventor of the process. *American Speech*, Feb., 1942, p. 24.

9 Down the Spillway, by John O'Ren, Baltimore *Sun*, June 9, 1937, p. 12.

10 *American Speech*, Dec., 1939, p. 316.

11 *Cue*, Sept. 9, p. 7.

12 *Women's Wear Daily*, recorded in New Words For Old, Baltimore *Evening Sun* (editorial page), Oct. 25, 1938. Example: "The trade is *partnerizing* the consumer."

13 *American Speech*, Dec., 1943, p. 303. It is there defined in the sense of "to provide with air under pressure, as in an aircraft for breathing purposes to compensate for low natural pressure at high altitudes." But it is also used, like *to pressure*, to indicate any sort of persistence or duress, whether physical or psychic.

14 Recorded by Bartlett in his second edition of 1859 and marked an Americanism by the DAE. The English do not seem to know it, but they use the even more hideous *to obituarize*. See the *Literary Supplement* of the London *Times*, June 7, 1934, p. 407.

15 A Hollywood coinage, borrowed by the *News of the World* (London), June 12, 1938. To *deglamorize* is recorded by Dwight L. Bolinger in Among the New Words, *American Speech*, April, 1943, p. 149.

16 A *Variety* coinage, recorded in New Words For Old, Baltimore *Evening Sun* (editorial page), July 1, 1939.

17 Graham Taylor in the Chicago *Daily News*, Oct. 17, 1936, recorded by *American Speech*, Dec., 1936, p. 373.

18 Traced by the NED Supplement to 1928 in English use, but older in American. Used by Mr. Justice Murphy in the opinion of the Su-

*sonize, to picturize,*[1] *to forumize,*[2] *to routinize, to rapturize, to machinize,*[3] *to powerize,*[4] *to moronize, to ovenize, to durationize, to moistureize, to posturize, to satinize,*[5] *to expertize.*[6]

· *Verbs made of adjectives or adverbs: to customize,*[7] *to socialize* (in the sense of *to go into society*),[8] *to slenderize,*[9] *to tenderize,*[10] *to backwardize,*[11] *to permanentize, to finalize.*[12]

*Verbs made of other verbs: to prosperize,*[13] *to renovize,*[14] *to flavorize,*[15] *to featurize.*

Not infrequently, of course, such verbs are used with humorous intent. Thus when the Hon. Tom Connally of Texas used *to intellegenceize* during a Senate debate on May 9, 1944, the reporters for the *Congressional Record* dutifully inserted [*laughter*] after it.

It is often noted by English observers that Americans neglect the distinction between *will* and *shall;* in fact, many Englishmen show a certain pride in the fact, as they allege, that only a Briton of superior capacity, schooled from birth in Oxford English, ever uses them properly. " The grammatical rules for [their] right use," said H. W. Fowler with prissy complacency in 1921, " are very elaborate, and anyone who studies them must see that a complete understanding of

---

preme Court of the United States in Thornhill *vs.* State of Alabama, April 2, 1940: " No clear and present danger . . . can be thought to be inherent in the activities of every person who approaches the premises of an employer and *publicizes* the facts of a labor dispute involving the latter."

1 Madison (Wis.) *State Journal*, Dec. 18, 1925, recorded in English as She is Wrote, by Charles Forster Smith, *American Speech*, June, 1926, p. 507.

2 *Forumize*, by Charles P. Greene, *American Speech*, June, 1928, p. 432.

3 The last three are recorded in New Verbs in *-ize*, by Anne E. Perkins, *American Speech*, June, 1928, p. 434.

4 *American Speech*, Oct., 1934, p. 236.

5 The last five are recorded in The New Language, Chicago *Journal of Commerce*, Aug. 18, 1943.

6 *To expertize* is not listed by the DAE, but the NED's first (and only) example is from *Harper's Magazine*, Feb. 1889. The noun *expertise*, borrowed from the French, is traced in England to 1869.

7 From *custom-made*, which is traced

by the DAE to 1855 and marked an Americanism.

8 *American Speech*, Feb., 1934, p. 76.

9 *American Speech*, Sept., 1927, p. 515.

10 *American Speech*, Dec., 1936, p. 374.

11 Used in the *Farm Journal*, March, 1926. I am indebted here to Mr. Thomas M. Sloane of Washington. Noted by Wilson Follett in The State of the Language, *Atlantic Monthly*, Oct. 1939.

12 This verb, now in wide use to designate the winding-up of any matter of business, especially in official circles at Washington, may have been coined in Australia. A New South Wales correspondent of *John o'London's Weekly*, April 18, 1936, reported that it was used there at the end of World War I.

13 *American Speech*, Oct., 1937, p. 236. The meaning, however, is not to prosper, but to make to look prosperous.

14 Described in *American Speech*, Oct., 1933, p. 76 as " a popular novelty of the year." It has since made inroads on *to renovate*.

15 *American Speech*, Oct., 1940, p. 261.

them cannot be expected from ordinary writers and speakers." [1]
This same Fowler, in his "Dictionary of Modern English Usage,"
1926, took nearly seven columns to expound them as he understood
them, but his exposition was a great deal more learned than lucid,
and most English schoolmasters, I suppose, prefer the easier device
of teaching by an old and familiar example:

> I *shall* drown: nobody *will* save me.
> I *will* drown: nobody *shall* save me.

But the simplicity of this is deceptive, for like most of the other
rules of grammar, those governing *will* and *shall* are subject to many
exceptions. Moreover, they are often ignored, even by the dons of
Oxford, and some of the greatest of English writers have flouted them
habitually. Dr. Charles C. Fries, in his "American English Grammar," [2] shows that, as they are now taught, they were not formulated
until the pedantic Eighteenth Century, and that the grammarians who
launched them did not try to derive them from " the practice of the
language as it actually was " but " definitely repudiated usage, even
that of ' our most approved authors,' " and sought light in a purely
imaginary " rational grammar." In a review of some preliminary
papers by Fries, the late Sterling Andrus Leonard [3] pointed out that,
in the United States at least, the endless pother over the correct use
of the two verbs is largely moot, for most Americans have replaced
them " by the . . . contraction *'ll* and by the forms *is to go, about
to go, is going to,* and the whole range of auxiliary verbs which mean
both past and future." This point was developed at length, and with
great plausibility, by Dr. John Whyte in a paper published in 1944. [4]
He sent out a questionnaire to 139 teachers and students in four colleges asking them how they would translate the German " Spielen
Sie morgen? " Only 2% reported that they would use " *Shall* you
play tomorrow? ": it seemed to the rest to be of " hopelessly schoolmarm quality." But not many more declared in favor of " *Will* you
play tomorrow?, for " all felt the modal quality of *will you;* in other
words, they understood the *will you* question to be in invitation to
play, *with me* being understood." The overwhelming majority replied that they would translate the German by " *Are you going* to

1 *Shall* and *Will, Should* and *Would*
in the Newspapers of Today, *S.P.E.
Tract No. VI,* 1921, p. 14.
2 New York, 1940, pp. 150 *ff.*

3 *Shall* and *Will, American Speech,*
Aug., 1929, pp. 497–98.
4 The Future Tense in English, *College English,* March, pp. 333–37.

play tomorrow? ", and that, precisely, is what nine out of ten Americans, whether educated or not, would use. " Just as ' *Are you going to play?* ' is the indispensable question in the second person for pure futurity," said Whyte, " so ' *Are we going* to play tomorrow? ' is the only unambiguous and currently used pure future question in the first person." In the second and third person imperative, of course, *shall* is often used, as in " You *shall* listen to me " and " They *shall* not pass," [1] but in other situations it is largely confined to conscious imitation of English usage.[2]

The schoolma'am has begun to be wary of *shall* and *will*, for she finds the rules laid down for their use by the textbooks contradictory and unintelligible, and it is easy for a bright and wicked pupil to frame problems that leave her blushing and sweating. But she still makes a gallant, if vain effort to put down *ain't*. This war upon it has been going on in the American public schools for half a century, and Harry R. Warfel estimates [3] that at least 12,500,000 teacher-hours have been spent in seeking to eradicate it. He continues:

> With what result? The word is more widely used today than ever before. It is to be heard in almost every circle or level of society; in popular speech it has been accepted — indeed, it never was rejected — as a perfectly useful, necessary and correct locution.

The grammarians are somewhat uncertain about the origin of *ain't*. The NED defines it as " a contracted form of *are not*, used also for *am not, is not* in the popular dialect of London and elsewhere," and Jespersen agrees,[4] but Harold H. Bender suggests that its apparent forerunner, *an't*, " arose almost simultaneously from two sources: (a) contraction of *am not* (through *amn't*, which still survives in

1 British-American Differentiations in Syntax and Idiom, by Stuart Robertson, *American Speech*, Dec., 1939, p. 252.

2 It is not uncommon, when *shall* and *will* are used by an American in what is taken to be in accord with English practise, for him to be derided for pedantry or worse. This happened, for example, in July 1944, when President Roosevelt used " If the convention *should* . . . nominate me for the presidency I *shall* accept; if the people elect me I *will* serve " in his letter to the chairman of the Democratic national committee. On July 13 the Boston *Herald* sneered at him in an editorial headed *Willy-Shallying*. He was defended in the *Herald* two days later by E. K. Rand of Cambridge, who argued that he wrote " like a cultivated gentleman." The English themselves are shaky about *will* and *shall*, and there are frequent discussions of the verbs in their newspapers.

3 Fire in Our Ears, *English Journal* (College Edition), May 1932, p. 412.

4 A Modern English Grammar on Historical Principles, by Otto Jespersen; Part I, Sounds and Spellings; third ed.; Heidelberg, 1922, p. 228.

England and, especially, Ireland); (b) contraction of *are not.*" [1] *An't*
is traced by the DAE to 1706, but its first example of *ain't* is from
Fanny Burney's " Evelina," 1778. Curme surmises that *an't* may have
arisen from *aren't* by reason of the English habit of dropping *r* before
consonants.[2] It was denounced by Witherspoon in 1781 as a vulgarism prevailing in both England and America, along with *can't, han't*
(now *haven't*), *don't, shouldn't* and *wouldn't,* but he did not mention
*ain't.*[3] Nor was *ain't* listed by Pickering in his Vocabulary of 1816. In
1837, however, it was included by Sherwood among his Southern
provincialisms, and defined as a substitute for both *is not* and *am not.*
The DAE, whose first American example is dated 1779, defines it as a
" contracted form of *airn't, are not,*" and traces *air* for *are,* in American use, to 1777. The DAE shows that *an't* was used in American for
*are not* so early as 1723. There are logical objections to the use of
*ain't* for *are not* and *is not,* but when used for *am not* it is certainly
better than the clumsy English *aren't.*[4] Says H. W. Fowler in his
" Dictionary of Modern English Usage ": [5]

*A*(*i*)*n't,* . . . as used for *isn't,* is an uneducated blunder and serves no useful
purpose. But it is a pity that *a*(*i*)*n't* for *am not,* being a natural contraction and
supplying a real want, should shock us as though tarred with the same brush.
Though *I'm not* serves well enough in statements, there is no abbreviation but
*a*(*i*)*n't I?* for *am I not?* or *am not I?;* and the shamefaced reluctance with which
these full forms are often brought out betrays the speaker's sneaking affection
for the *ain't I* that he (or still more she) fears will convict him of low breeding. (" *Well, I'm doing it already, ain't I? Yes, ain't I a lucky man? I'm next,
ain't I?* ")

This from a very high English authority. The American, Warfel,
goes further:

[1] The Origin of *Ain't, Word Study,*
March, 1936, p. 3. In the same issue,
p. 2, E. Payson Willard suggests that
*ain't* " has come from the verb *have*
rather than from the verb *be.*" His
reasons: " 1. It is used in all three
persons and is not confined to the
first person singular. 2. As an auxiliary it has the meaning of *have* much
more than that of *be.* 3. Short forms
of *have* can be found in the older
English and in dialect English (*e.g.,
han* in Chaucer and *ha'* in Burns).
4. It is sometimes aspirated. 5. *Ha*
has the long *a*-sound in the word

*halfpenny* (which is pronounced by
Englishmen as if the first syllable
were *hay*); hence the *ha* of *have*
may have been given this sound
also."
[2] A Grammar of the English Language, by George O. Curme; II.
Parts of Speech and Accidence; Boston, 1935, p. 248.
[3] See p. 8.
[4] Wallace Rice says in *Ain't, American Mercury,* Aug., 1927, p. 450, that
" this Briticism began only with the
present century."
[5] Oxford, 1926, p. 45.

I suggest a moratorium on the abuse showered upon this innocent word. Let us recognize it as a proper form in speech of the colloquial level, and let us denounce it no more than we denounce other contractions. If *ain't* is a valuable tool, its usefulness will increasingly be demonstrated. If it is an affected form, used merely to shock pedants, inattention will lead to a cessation of its use. In any case it is folly to legislate concerning colloquial language.[1]

To which Rice adds:

In self-defense let us form an *Ain't I Society*. With those who want to use it, backed by the millions who do, a constitutional amendment is already in sight.[2]

The last word, perhaps, was said by the late Will Rogers, to wit: " Maybe *ain't ain't* so correct, but I notice that lots of folks who *ain't* usin' *ain't ain't* eatin'." [3]

### 4. OTHER PARTS OF SPEECH

Most of the process that we have seen at work in the coinage of new nouns and verbs also produce other words, especially adjectives. There are adjectives made of nouns unchanged, *e.g.*, *bum, one-horse* [4] and *bogus*,[5] or from verbs or verb-phrases, *e.g.*, *sit-down, gimme* (as in *gimme farmer*), *back-to-work* and *cash-and-carry*, or from pronouns, *e.g.*, *she-gal* and *he-man*, or by telescoping, *e.g.*, *radiopaque*

1 Fire in Our Ears, already cited, p. 416. In a paper read before the National Council of Teachers of English at Milwaukee (reported in *Shall and Will Yield to Present-Day Usage*, New York *Herald Tribune*, Dec. 6, 1931) Dr. J. C. Tressler suggested that the only way for the schoolma'am to make headway against *ain't* would be for her to set her pupils to " chanting in unison for five minutes a day for a month: 'I *ain't* going, you *ain't* going, we *ain't* going, they *ain't* going; in fact, nobody *ain't* going.'" Whether or not this suggestion was ever adopted does not appear in the record.

2 *Ain't*, already cited, p. 450.

3 There is frequent discussion of *ain't* in the lay press, but not often to any profit. Some specimens: We're Right, *Ain't We?*, Cleveland *Press* (editorial), March 11, 1937; *Ain't* Wins Promotion (editorial), Syracuse *Post-Standard*, same date; Kind

Words for *Ain't*, New York *World-Telegram*, same date; *Ain't* It the Truth, by Milton Ellis, *Saturday Review of Literature*, April 3, 1943. In The Grammarian's Corner, *Writer*, March, 1937, p. 94, an anonymous writer suggested the substitution of *'m I not*, pronounced *my not*, in such forms as "I am to speak ten minutes, *'m I not?*" A more learned discussion is in *Ain't I* and *Aren't I*, by R. I. McDavid, *Language*, Jan.–March, 1941, pp. 57–59. The English objection to *ain't* is stated in The Owlglass, by Mark Over, London *Outlook*, Aug. 13, 1927.

4 Traced by the DAE, in the figurative sense of small or petty, as in *one-horse town*, to the middle 50s, and marked an Americanism.

5 The etymology of *bogus* remains undetermined, but the DAE's examples show it appearing as a noun in 1826, sixteen years before its appearance as an adjective.

(*x-ray* and *opaque*) [1] and *sophomoronic*,[2] or by the use of prefixes or suffixes, *e.g.*, *super-colossal, overniggered, underbibled, untaxpaid, non-skid, air-minded, food-conscious, cosmogenic, plushy, news-worthy* and *bosomatic*.[3] Of these devices, the last is the most productive. The *super-* prefix, of course, is old in English (the NED traces it to the middle of the Fifteenth Century), but the movie press-agents of Hollywood have given it a new lease on life, and their inventions include not only *super-colossal* but also *super-modern, super-maximum, super-superlative, super-ultra* and even *super-super*.[4] Who launched the vogue for *-minded* and *-conscious* I do not know, but his inspiration prospered beyond most mayhems upon the language. It is my impression that *social-minded* was the first of the former class to make its way, so perhaps the offender was an uplifter: if I am right he will reach Hell with two life-sentences. *Social-minded* was early followed by *civic-minded* and has since produced a long progeny, *e.g.*, *hospital-minded*,[5] *spa-minded*,[6] *air-minded, fire-works-minded* [7] and the like, not to forget a child by the left hand, *presence-of-minded*.[8] The related *-conscious* has been even more fecund, *e.g.*, *insurance-conscious*,[9] *America-conscious, cow-conscious, radio-conscious, constitution-conscious, cosmetic-conscious* and *college-conscious;* moreover, it has also had offspring in England, *e.g.*, *herb-conscious*,[10] *food-conscious*,[11] and *big-ship-conscious*.[12] Sir Oswald

1 *Journal of the American Medical Association*, Aug. 26, 1944, p. 1188, col. 1.
2 Coined by Willard Houghland of Albuquerque, N. Mex.
3 Used by Rudolph Justice Watson, in the *Capitol Daily* (Washington), to describe the dames of the D.A.R., and noted in New Words For Old, Baltimore *Evening Sun*, June 18, 1938.
4 Mamie Meredith says in *Super-power, American Speech*, Feb., 1939, p. 79, that *ultra-* was a favorite prefix in the Civil War era, but the DAE lists only a few examples. So far as I know, the Greek prefix *pan*, meaning all, has produced but one Americanism, to wit, *pan-American*. The DAE traces it to Sept. 27, 1889, when it appeared in the New York *Evening Post*, but on April 11, 1940 the *Post* laid claim to having used it so early as June 27, 1882.
5 *Journal of the American Medical Association* (editorial) Aug. 19, 1939, p. 682.
6 Want-ad in the same journal, May 11, 1940.
7 Advertisement of Thearle-Duffield Fireworks, Ltd., in the *Billboard*, Dec. 29, 1934, p. 158.
8 Sired by Westbrook Pegler, and recorded in New Words For Old, Baltimore *Evening Sun* (editorial page), July 17, 1939.
9 *Journal of the American Medical Association*, Feb. 26, 1944, p. 572.
10 London *Morning Post*, Feb. 24, 1936.
11 Used twice in Woman and Her World, by H. Pearl Adam, London *Observer*, Jan. 5, 1936.
12 Peterborough's column in the London *Daily Telegraph*, May 20, 1936.

Mosley, in the days of his glory as boss of the English Fascists, took some nasty hacks at such evidences of democratic contamination of the language. On August 19, 1939, for example, he launched two burlesques of them, *bamboozle-conscious* and *hocus-pocus-minded*, in his weekly paper, *Action*.[1] Whenever a new suffix appears in the United States, it is put to use. An example is provided by *-genic*, which seems to have been borrowed from the *pathogenic* of the medical men: I have encountered *photogenic, radiogenic, telegenic* [2] and *cosmogenic*.[3] Another is *-phobia*, borrowed from the psychiatrists, and made to do heavy duty in a multitude of nouns designating violent aversions, *e.g. radiophobia, New Dealophobia, negrophobia, ergophobia* [4] and *sexophobia*,[5] all of them with attendant adjectives in *-phobic*. A third is *-worthy*, old in English but recently revived in this great Republic, as in *newsworthy, creditworthy, earworthy, gaspworthy* and *prizeworthy*.[6] A fourth is *-matic* (from *automatic*), as in *traffomatic, adjustomatic* and *geomatic*.[7] All the traditional adjectival suffixes are used for new words, *e.g.*, *-y*, as in *plushy*,[8] *drapy*,[9] *contrasty*,[10] *Ritzy* and *corny*, to which may be added *nifty*,[11] and *iffy*.[12] But American word-makers show little liking for the English *-ish*, as in *fairish, liverish* and *biggish*. I throw in a few miscellaneous

1 In a paper on Conditions in the United States of America, read before the Insurance Institute of London on March 30, 1936, Lord Knollys, managing director of the Employers' Liability Assurance Corporation, reported that American holders of automobile accident policies were becoming increasingly *claim-minded*.

2 Among the New Words, by Dwight L. Bolinger, *American Speech*, Dec. 1943, p. 301.

3 *American Speech*, Dec., 1940, p. 360.

4 I am indebted here to Mr. K. P. McElroy of Washington.

5 I find *chronophobia* in the title of an article by Salvatore Russo in *Viewpoint*, the house-organ of the convicts locked up in the New Jersey State Prison at Trenton. He defines it " a fear of time " and says of it: " It is a neurotic disorder from which almost all inmates suffer sooner or later, although it is more pronounced in individuals with long

sentences. . . . It may be characterized as prison panic."

6 Among the New Words, by Dwight L. Bolinger, *American Speech*, April, 1941, p. 144.

7 *American Speech*, Feb., 1935, p. 35.

8 Atcheson L. Hench reported in *American Speech*, Dec., 1942, p. 250, that it came in during that year.

9 Coined by *Women's Wear Daily*.

10 Used in Methods Help *Tribune* Reader, South Bend (Ind.) *Tribune*, March 22, 1944.

11 *Nifty* is traced by the DAE to 1865 and marked an Americanism. It is discussed at length in *Nifty, Hefty, Natty, Snappy*, by Klara Hechtenberg Collitz, *American Speech*, Dec., 1927, pp. 119–28, and Observations on *Nifty, Hefty, Natty* and *Snappy*, by Henry J. Heck, *American Speech*, Oct., 1928, pp. 80–81.

12 Used by President Roosevelt at a White House press conference. 1941. See *American Speech*, April, 1941, p. 158.

marvels and pass on: *slap-happy*,[1] *alco-joyed*,[2] *fishful* (favorable to fishing),[3] *cosmeticulous, glitterous*,[4] *sexotic*,[5] *snazzy* (elegant), *must* (as an adjective),[6] *stumble-bum*,[7] *teen-age*,[8] *hard-boiled* [9] and *untouristed*. Rather curiously, the suffix *-oid*, certainly full of possibilities in a country swarming with imitations, is not in American use, and the excellent English *bungaloid* has not been borrowed.[10] The comparison of adjectives, on the levels where most new words are made, is not incommoded by linguistic prudery. The field agents of *American Speech* report *disappearingest, actorest*,[11] *getting aroundest, most workingest*,[12] *homer-lessest* [13] and *he-est*,[14] nearly all of them from Hollywood, and I have encountered *keyest*,[15] *thrillinger, superer, uniquer, uniquest*,[16] and *more ultra* elsewhere. Adverbs, of course, are made with the same freedom, *e.g.*, *ritzily* [17] *productionally* [18] and *clas-*

1 Defined as "a synonym of *punch-drunk*" by Dwight L. Bolinger, in *American Speech*, Feb., 1944, p. 60. He lists *sap-happy, scrap-happy, snap-happy* and *tap-happy* as congeners.

2 Associated Press dispatch from Omaha, noted in New Words For Old, Baltimore *Evening Sun*, Oct. 27, 1939.

3 Chapel Hill (N. C.) *Weekly*, noted in New Words For Old, just cited, June 10, 1940.

4 *Modern Screen*, noted in New Words For Old, just cited, May 6, 1938.

5 Program of the National Theatre, Detroit, for the week of Aug. 9, 1940, p. 1.

6 As in *must legislation*. The usage is borrowed from the argot of newspaper men, to whom a *must story* is one that must be published at all hazards, often because the owner is interested in it.

7 Neologisms, by Dwight L. Bolinger, *American Speech*, Feb., 1941, p. 66.

8 *American Speech*, Feb., 1942, p. 41.

9 *Hard-boiled* apparently originated before 1900, but it did not have much popularity until T. A. Dorgan began using it in the noun form, *hard-boiled egg*, in 1915. The vogue of the adjective followed during World War I. See The Origin of

*Hard-Boiled*, by Peter Tamony, *American Speech*, Dec., 1937, pp. 258–61.

10 The NED Supplement's first example is from Dean W. R. Inge, writing in the London *Daily Express*, Nov. 22, 1927: "Hideous allotments and *bungaloid* growths make the approach to any city repulsive."

11 April, 1941, p. 156.

12 Oct., 1937, p. 242.

13 Oct., 1941, p. 207.

14 Oct., 1941, p. 207.

15 Drew Pearson in Washington Merry-Go-Round, Washington *Post*, May 9, 1944: "California is going to be one of the *keyest* States in the Union." I am indebted here to Mr. Lester Hargrett of Washington.

16 A newspaper paragraph, widely printed in 1944, accused Winston Churchill of using *uniquest* in his speech to the House of Commons on the German robot bombs, July 6, 1944. The Associated Press report shows that what he actually said was: ["London] . . . is the *unique* target for the use of a weapon of such proved inaccuracy."

17 *American Speech*, April, 1928, p. 349.

18 Coined by *Variety*, and recorded in New Words For Old, Baltimore *Evening Sun*, June 19, 1939.

*sically.* But in most cases the flat adverb is used, as in *run slow,* or, more often, *run slo.*[1]

The American fondness for abbreviations was given a tremendous stimulus by the advent of the multitudinous New Deal agencies, many of them with names too long to be used in full, but its origins lie in the past. *O.K.,* the most successful abbreviation ever coined, whether in the United States or elsewhere, has been discussed at length in Chapter V, Section 2. The DAE does not list *P.D.Q.*[2] or *on the Q.T.,* but it traces *N.G.* to 1840, *F.F.V.* (first families of Virginia) to 1847, *C.O.D.* to 1863, *G.A.R.* to 1867, *L* (elevated) to 1879, *G.B.* (grand bounce) to 1880, and *G.O.P.* to 1887. World War I brought in or made popular a few that have survived, *e.g., a.w.o.l.,*[3] and the example of the English, later reinforced enormously by that of the Russians, introduced the forms converted into words, *e.g., Dora* (Defence of the Realm Act), *anzac, cheka* and *gestapo.*[4] A few made on this plan have come into wide use in the United States, *e.g., Nazi, Wac* and

1 It does not concern adverbs, but this may be a good place to mention that the sign at railroad grade-crossings, *Stop! Look! Listen!,* is said to have been devised by Ralph R. Upton, safety lecturer for the Puget Sound Power Company of Seattle, in 1912. He was killed in an automobile accident at La Porte, Ind., Aug. 4, 1935. See his obituary in the New York *Herald Tribune,* Aug. 5. Also, *platinum-blonde* is said to have been invented by Charles Washburn, publicity engineer for Jean Harlow. See Public Relations, II, by Alva Johnston, *New Yorker,* Aug. 26, 1944, p. 30.

2 Said to have been coined by Dan Maguinnis, one of the comedians of the Boston Stock Company from 1867 to his death. There is an account of him in Dan Maguinnis, 1834–1889, a Biographical Sketch With Ancestral Notes on His Mac-Kenna Line, by Ella Lane Mielziner; Provincetown, Mass., 1935. I am indebted here to Mrs. Mielziner and to Mr. Paul North Rice, chief of the reference department of the New York Public Library.

3 This abbreviation, which quickly became a verb, is generally assumed to have been coined during World

War I, but Elbridge Colby indicates in Army Talk; second edition; Princeton, N. J., 1943, p. 16, that it is old in Army use, and I find the following in The Plain People of the Confederacy, by Bell Irvin Wiley, Baton Rouge, La., 1944, p. 31: " [In the Confederate Army] unwarranted absences of short duration were often unpunished and in many other cases offenders received such trivial sentences as reprimand by a company officer, digging a stump, carrying a rail for an hour or two, wearing a placard inscribed with the letters AWOL. . . ."

4 A List of Abbreviations Commonly Used in the U.S.S.R., by George Z. Patrick; revised ed.: Berkeley, Calif., 1937. This pamphlet runs to 124 pp. and lists nearly 1,500 terms. The Russian alphabet is used for both abbreviations and definitions, but there are also explanations in English. The first of the Russian abbreviations to come into use in either England or America seems to have been *cadet,* made of *konstitutsionalnyie demokrati* — constitutional democratic, or liberal party. It was formed *c.* 1905. The NED Supplement's first example of *cadet* in English use is dated 1906.

*Wave*, but the majority that are commonly employed are either un-pronounceable as words, or not so pronounced, *e.g., I.Q.* (intelligence quotient), *T.V.A.* (Tennessee Valley Authority), *R.F.C.* (Reconstruction Finance Corporation), and *C.I.O.* (Congress of Industrial Organizations). There was a vast accretion of abbreviations on the advent of the New Deal, *e.g.*, for *Board of Investigation and Research: Transportation* and *Office of Bituminous Coal Consumers Council*, and there was an even vaster reinforcement on the outbreak of World War II. In 1943 E. M. Biggers of Houston, Texas, circulated an alarm to taxpayers listing more than 100, most of them in everyday use, *e.g., A.A.A., H.O.L.C., N.L.R.B., S.E.C., O.P.A.* and *F.C.C.* He reported that as of June 11, 1943 there were 2,241 Federal agencies, bureaus and commissions in being, including 96 authorized to "undertake real estate transactions."[1] Nearly all of them were known by their initials. This *alphabet soup*, as Al Smith called it, provided sustenance for millions of job-holders, and some of them acquired bizarre designations. In 1943 the Associated Press reported from Minneapolis that a Mrs. Frank J. Boulger, living there, had inquired of a daughter working in Washington just what her position was. The daughter replied:

> I work in the Data Analysis Group of the Aptitude Test Sub-unit of the Worker Analysis Section of the Division of Occupational Analysis and Manning Tables of the Bureau of Labor Utilization of the War Manpower Commission.[2]

The American newspapers quickly dropped the periods in such forms as *N.R.A.* and *A.A.A.* and they became *NRA, AAA*, etc. In 1944 the New York *Times* undertook to argue that this use of simple initials was better than the totalitarian custom of making articulate words of abbreviations, and that it proved anew the moral superiority of the American way of life. In reply a reader in Vallejo, Calif., pointed out that the Navy was using *BuAer* for Bureau of Aeronautics, *BuOrd* for Bureau of Ordnance, *ComSubRon* for commander submarine squadron, *NavTorpSta* for naval torpedo station, *ComAir SoPa* for commander aircraft, South Pacific force, and so on. The *Times*, caught on a barb, wriggled off in the following somewhat unpersuasive manner:

[1] I am indebted here to Mr. Robert F. Hicks of Baltimore.
[2] Tonics and Sedatives, *Journal of the American Medical Association*, June 17, 1944.

We trust it is not quibbling to say that this naval nomenclature, if it is indeed as represented, is not quite the sausage and hash etymology of the totalitarians. The vital difference is in our own striking usage of capital letters in the middle of a word. This at once gives the story away. A person who sees *BuOrd* will never attempt to pronounce it that way; he will say at once Bureau of Ordnance. And when his eyes light on a combination like *ComSubRon* he will automatically start in to say commander of submarine something, even if the *Ron* will have him puzzled. But in the unfree countries they would write it *Consubron*, which looks plausible if not exactly intelligible at first sight.[1]

A great many abbreviations occur in the argot of various crafts and professions, *e.g.*, the common medical terms: *T.B.* (tuberculosis), *G.Y.N.* (gynecology), *G.P.* (grateful patient or general practitioner) and *T.P.R.* (temperature, pulse, respiration),[2] and not a few of them are intended to be unintelligible to the outsider. Others of the same quasi-esoteric sort are in more or less general use, *e.g.*, *f.h.b.* (family hold back, *i.e.*, with a guest present at table), *m.i.k.* (more in the kitchen),[3] and *P.D.* (plain drunk).[4]

Public jobholders, taking one with another, are anything but masters of prose: their writing, indeed, is predominantly pretentious and shabby, and they are greatly given to counter-words and clichés. This is true equally of the British and American species. So long ago as 1916 the official English style was denounced bitterly by the late Sir Arthur Quiller-Couch, then professor of English literature at Cambridge, and in recent years it has been given constant but far from loving attention by A. P. Herbert, M.P. Sir Arthur defined it as the jargon that " has become the medium through which boards of government, county councils, syndicates, committees, commercial firms, express the processes as well as the conclusions of their thoughts, and so voice the reason of their being." [5] In the United States syndicates and commercial firms are not often practitioners of it, but it has attained to a truly appalling development among sucklers at the public teat. Both Quiller-Couch and Herbert tackled it in England

---

1 Topics of the Times, April 6, 1944.
2 Hospital Talk, by Dorothy Barkley, *American Speech*, April, 1927, pp. 312–14.
3 Semi-Secret Abbreviations, by Percy W. Long, *Dialect Notes*, Vol. IV, Part III, 1915, pp. 245–46.
4 Nearly 5,000 English abbreviations (with a few American specimens included) are listed in A Dictionary of Abbreviations, by Eric Partridge;

London, 1942. They show some juicy coinages, *e.g.*, *D.A.D.D.S.* (deputy assistant director of dental services), *L.R.F.P.S.G.* (licentiate of the Royal Faculty of Physicians and Surgeons of Glasgow), and *U.G.S.S.S.* (Union of Girls' Schools for Social Service).
5 Interlude on Jargon in On the Art of Writing; New York, 1916.

with the weapon of parody. The former, for example, thus translated Hamlet's soliloquy into British officialese:

To be or the contrary? Whether the former or the latter be preferable would seem to admit of some difference of opinion, the answer in the present case being of an affirmative character according as to whether one elects on the one hand to mentally suffer the disfavor of fortune, albeit in extreme degree, or, on the other hand, to boldly envisage adverse conditions in the prospect of eventually bringing them to a conclusion.[1]

Herbert, in his turn, offered the following version of Lord Nelson's " England expects every man to do his duty ":

England anticipates that as regards the current emergency personnel will face up to the issues and exercise appropriately the functions allocated to their respective occupation groups.[2]

This bombastic style has marked all English official utterance for many years, and there is evidence that it antedates even the great upsurge of pedantry in the Eighteenth Century.[3] Some of its masterpieces are famous — for example, the sign reading " These basins are for casual ablutions only," formerly hanging in the men's washroom of the British Museum. In the same place the following, for all I know, is still displayed:

Stoppages having been caused in the drainage through the pipes having been used in order to dispose of miscellaneous objects, it is notified that the provision for public accommodation must be dependent on only proper use being made of it.[4]

1 Quoted in Ponderous English, Manchester *Guardian Weekly*, Aug. 30, 1940, p. 149.

2 Associated Press dispatch from London, Aug. 3, 1939. One of Herbert's targets is the verb *to explore*. When, early in 1936, *to explore every avenue* appeared in a House of Commons order paper he moved an amendment, backed by twenty other members, to substitute *to leave no stone unturned*. (Closed to Explorers, *John o' London's Weekly*, April 4, 1936). But hardly more than a month later, in a letter to the London *Telegraph* (Parliament and Divorce, May 22, 1936), he used it himself: " The government might, at least, *explore* opinion among leading churchmen and lawyers." In Political Jargon the London *Morning Post*, March 18, 1936, said that *to explore every avenue* was " invented by the Marquis of Lansdowne when he was Foreign Secretary at the beginning of the century." " It exercised," said the *Post*, " a mortal fascination over politicians, . . . and it has done menial duty for them ever since. The *exploring of avenues* has become one of the main preoccupations of political life."

3 The Jacobean Age, by David Matthews; London, 1938, p. 8.

4 Simple English, by Cornelia Craigie, *Commonweal*, Jan. 7, 1938, p. 295. An example from the standing orders of the House of Commons was cited in Week-End Puzzle, London *Sunday Times*, Nov. 13, 1938: " Government business shall have precedence on as many Wednesdays im-

Quiller-Couch and Herbert are not the only Britons who have protested against this sonorous rubbish. It was denounced by the late Lord Tweedsmuir, Governor-General of Canada,[1] and in 1940 Winston Churchill had at it in an official memorandum to the members of his government and the heads of the civil service, begging them to order their subordinates to write more simply. In the United States its chief critic in office has been the Hon. Maury Maverick, chairman of the Smaller War Plants Corporation, who boiled over on March 30, 1944 with a formal prohibition of what he called *gobbledygook language* by the tax-eaters under his command. Thus his order:

> Be short and say what you're talking about. Let's stop *pointing up* programs, *finalizing* contracts that *stem from* district, regional or Washington *levels*. No more *patterns, effectuating, dynamics*. Anyone using the words *activation* or *implementation* will be shot.[2]

In defense of the jobholders it should be said that many of the ideas they have to deal with are probably unstatable in plain American, or even in literary English. Perhaps this must be the excuse for such masterpieces as the following, taken from an OPA directive defining fruit-cake:

> "Fruit cake of a comparable type sold by the producer in the period October 1st to December 31st, 1941, inclusive," means a fruit cake (1) the ingredients of which would have had the same approximate total cost if such ingredients had been purchased in March, 1942, as the total cost of ingredients used in making the fruit cake for which a maximum price is to be determined if such ingredients

mediately before Good Friday as the number of Wednesdays before Christmas on which it has not had precedence, and on as many Fridays immediately before Good Friday as the number of Fridays (reduced by three) on which it had not precedence before Christmas." The subject is often discussed in the English newspapers, *e.g.,* in M.P.s Pass Clause They Cannot Fathom, by William Barkley, London *Daily Express,* June 17, 1936; A Journey in Jargantua, by Ivor Brown, Manchester *Guardian Weekly,* March 14, 1941, and Official Jargon, Manchester *Guardian Weekly,* Sept. 12, 1941.
1 Jargon a Danger, Tweedsmuir Says, New York *Times,* Jan. 18, 1936.
2 In the New York *Times Magazine,*

May 21, 1944, p. 11, Maverick explained that he was driven to action at a committee meeting "at which the chairman spoke at length of 'maladjustments co-extensive with problem areas, . . . alternative but nevertheless meaningful minimae, . . . utilization of factors which in a dynamic democracy can be channelized into both quantitative and qualitative phases.'" "People ask me," he said, "where I got *gobbledygook*. I do not know. It must have come in a vision. Perhaps I was thinking of the old bearded turkey gobbler back in Texas who was always gobbledy-gobbling and strutting with ludicrous pomposity. At the end of this gobble there was a sort of gook."

had also been purchased in March, 1942, and (2) of the same weight when completed and ready for packaging as the fruit cake for which a maximum price is to be determined.[1]

And this from a directive to internal revenue agents, expounding the inwardness of a proposed amendment to the famous Income Tax Act of 1944:

> The effect of the amendment, as explained on the floor of the Senate, if finally enacted into law, would be to permit, after having made an adjustment in an item affecting the excess profits tax, in a year to which the amendment is made applicable, which has an effect on the normal or surtax for the year, any resulting adjustment necessary in the normal or surtaxes may be accomplished although the statute of limitations for assessment of any deficiency or making any refund of such taxes, has expired.[2]

Complaints about the unintelligibility of OPA directives became so bitter during the Spring of 1944 that an expert was employed to attempt their translation into English. Characteristically, the savant selected was an Austrian who arrived in the United States so recently as 1938. He undertook an elaborate analysis of the American vocabulary, separating it into seven categories, the first and easiest embracing the simple words used in radio soap-operas and the seventh and worst the hard words used by the *Scientific Monthly*. Applying these categories to the directives, he found that some of them, *e.g.*, OPA regulation MPR 496, amended section 5 [D] [1], dealing with the price of beet, carrot, onion and turnip seeds, included terms running far beyond the hardest in the *Scientific Monthly* répertoire.[3] Whether or not he managed to effect a reform I do not know: there is no mention of it in the record. Meanwhile, the Army and Navy also succumbed to the new official style. The Army, in the days before World War II, was largely staffed by West Pointers and they used the plain and excellent American taught at that great seminary, but the entrance of large numbers of officers from civil life brought in a taste and a

1 I borrow this from Surname or Trade Name, the Purpose is the Same, by Edward S. Rogers, *American Druggist*, March, 1944, p. 95.

2 *New Yorker*, March 4, 1944, p. 62. "Income-tax prose," said Simeon Strunsky in Topics of the Times, New York *Times*, Sept. 22, 1943, " is also a favorite literary style with the men who compose the text on the back of express baggage receipts in which are set down the conditions on which you may expect to get your trunk delivered to the house without yourself landing in jail."

3 I take this from The OPA and the Common Tongue, by Marcia Winn, printed in the Chicago *Tribune* during June, 1944.

talent for jargon, and by the end of 1943 such monstrosities as the following were appearing in official handbooks:

Proper application of prescribed preventative maintenance measures must be a prime consideration in order to minimize replacements. Vehicle equipment of tactical organizations and that of administrative units and reserve pools should be interchangeable wherever possible in order that needed replacements for forward areas be secured by interorganization transfers to meet emergencies in which normal channels of supply would introduce delays.[1]

Among the favorites of the New Deal wizards between 1933 and 1944 were *coördinator*,[2] *expediter, priority, pool*,[3] *duration, bottle-neck*,[4] *roll-back, gradualism, over-all*,[5] *rationale*,[6] *directive*,[7] *pattern*,[8] *objective, plateau*,[9] *level*,[10] *clearance*,[11] *long-range, to stem from, to*

1 This is from a field manual for quartermasters. The officer who sends it to me suggests that it should have been translated as follows: "Replacements must be kept at a low level by a rigid system of truck servicing. When emergencies cut off the normal flow of supply, all trucks in the unit, plus those in reserve pools, should be pressed into service by making transfers within the organization."

2 *Coördinator* was invented by Herbert Spencer in 1864 to describe the cephalic ganglion in primitive animals. It was used by the New Deal bureaucracy to designate a functionary told off to adjust differences between different agencies. Sometimes a given *coördinator* had as many as a dozen to deal with.

3 Used to designate a common store, whether of persons or of materials. In Dear Washington, Washington *Times-Herald*, March 9, 1943, Helen Essary expounded its meaning in the following dialogue:
"Where is your daughter now?"
"Oh, she's in the *pool* at the OPM. She's a secretary, you know."
"And your husband, where is he?"
"Why, didn't you know? He's in the doctors' *pool* at Walter Reed Hospital."
"How did you get downtown this morning?"
"It was very simple. We have the loveliest motor *pool*. And it's great

fun. We have a sign, 'Motor *Pool*,' on the back of our car. We do pick up some interesting people."

4 *Bottleneck* may have been borrowed from England. It was denounced by a contributor to the Bristol *Evening Post*, April 3, 1943, as causing "a tedium merging on nausea" there.

5 "Of all Washington words," said James D. White in an Associated Press dispatch from Washington Sept. 18, 1943, "*over-all* is the most habit-forming. Talk long enough to enough government officials, and you'll find yourself telling the little woman that she overcooked the Brussels sprouts, but that the *over-all* impact of the dinner was not bad."

6 White, just cited: "Potomac medicine men say a *rationale* is an OPA explanation of an OPA order."

7 *Directives* are defined in Washington Is What We Make It, by Paul Grabbe, *Harper's Magazine*, June, 1944, as "instructions about policy, procedure or conduct, aimed at no one in particular, therefore at everybody."

8 *Pattern* also had a vogue in England. It was attacked as "truly monstrous" by A. R. Cripps in the London *Times Literary Supplement*, July 1, 1944, and defended by Herbert Furst in the same, July 15.

9 White, before cited: "*Plateaus* are the thing now. War production is on a *plateau*, meaning that it is way up and has been up long enough to

*point up, to finalize, to explore, to implement, to gear in, to spell out,
to be severed,*[1] *to process,* and the sentencious saying " Time is *of the
essence.*" Few if any of these were their inventions, but they gave
all of them wide currency, and one of them, *to process,* now threatens
to take its place in the language alongside *to contact.* It is old as a law
term, but in the sense of to subject to a mechanical or chemical process
it seems to be an Americanism, first recorded by the NED in the
New York *Evening Post* of January 28, 1884, where it was described
as " a new verb invented to fit a new thing," to wit, the process of
making photo-engravings. Webster 1934 lists it in the general sense
of to convert a raw material into marketable form by some form of
manipulation, *e.g.,* to process milk by pasteurizing it, or beets by
extracting the sugar, or rancid butter by getting rid of the products
of decomposition. But the New Dealers gave it a much wider range
by using it for purely ideational operations, and widening it to include human beings among its objects. It has since been adopted by
the pre-Roosevelt or dirt jobholders of the Old Guard in Washington,[2] by the Army and Navy,[3] and by large groups, mostly of learned

---

establish a *plateau* in the curve of production figures."

10 White: " *Level* is a trusted, war-essential word, almost as inescapable as *overall.* Four *levels* have been discovered publicly. Biggest distinction is between *operational* and *policy levels.* On the *operational level* you do things. On the *policy level* you tell others how and why. Bureaucrats on the *operational level* get their ears pinned back if they speak publicly of things on the *policy level.*"

11 Grabbe, before cited: " The policy-makers must be consulted on every-thing that is not part of the estab-lished routine. Getting their okay is known as *clearing on policy,* or *clearance.*" It will be recalled that " *Clear* it with Sidney " was a fa-miliar slogan during the 1944 presi-dential campaign. Sidney was Sid-ney Hillman, chairman of the CIO's political action committee. The phrase was apparently first used by President Roosevelt at the time of the Democratic national convention, at which Hillman was told off to act as moderator in the struggle for the

vice-presidential nomination. Later the Republican campaign orators sought to make it appear that he was the President's representative and spokesman in various other fields.

1 White: " Small fry are said to be *severed.* Not *severed* from anything, just *severed.* The big shots *with-draw* or *return* to private jobs."

2 The division of the Bureau of In-ternal Revenue which sorts out re-ports from employers of payments to employés is now called the *Proc-essing* Division.

3 Letter from the Hon. Henry L. Stimson, Secretary of War, to the Hon. Louis Ludlow, congressman from Indiana, *Congressional Record,* April 17, 1944, p. A1937: " In a re-cent study of all men *processed* at reception centers . . . 20% of the Negroes and 74% of the whites were rated in grades I, II and III." Memo-randum of the War Department Service of Supply, Officer Procure-ment Service, Feb. 27, 1943, *Journal of the American Medical Associa-tion,* March 13, p. 843: " This mem-orandum states the procedure . . . in *processing* physicians, dentists

pretensions, outside the ranks of officialdom, both in its older sense of doing something to inanimate materials and its new sense of mauling and manipulating God's creatures.[1]

There was no need for most of these groups to borrow it, for they all have plenty of counter-words and clichés of their own. The medical brethren here come to mind at once, for they are notorious for their muggy writing. In part its defects are produced by mere garrulity, but in other part they flow out of a fondness for irrational and misleading terms, *e.g.*, the shortenings, *to operate* (a patient) for *to operate on* and *temperature* for *elevation of temperature*.[2] Not a few of them use *case* for *patient*,[3] and some even lean toward such bizarre forms as *to diagnosticate*,[4] *to do a urine, rectal* and *basal* (as nouns), *pathology* for *pathological condition, to clinic, to wassermann, to obstetricate, to cystoscope, to blood count*, and so on.[5] The psychiatrists,

and veterinarians for appointment as officers." Headline on an article in the same *Journal*, June 17, 1944, p. 499: "*Processing* of Physicians," *i.e.*, for the Veterans Administration. Female Physicians, same *Journal*, May 8, 1943: "The procedure for the *processing* of male physicians [in the Army] will apply to the *processing* of female physicians."    .

1 Headline on an article by Dr. Fred B. Wishard, medical director of the Delco Remy Division of the General Motors Corporation, *Journal of the American Medical Association*, March 13, 1943, p. 810: "*Processing* Technics in Physical Examination." AP Starts Service to Sweden, Finland, *Editor and Publisher*, April 8, 1944, p. 9: "The Associated Press this week began . . . the first AP news report *processed* in a language other than English in the Eastern Hemisphere." Daily Penalized for Exceeding Paper Quota, *Editor and Publisher*, Aug. 19, 1944, p. 24: "With two publishing companies already penalized for unauthorized consumption of print paper, the compliance section of the War Production Board is *processing* several other cases." Report of the Manuscript Division, New York Public Library, for 1943, p. 53: "The staff at the Central Building has kept up well with current accessions. . . . In

addition to the *processing* of single items . . . it put through a collection of personal papers."

2 Both are flogged in Suggestions to Medical Authors and A[merican] M[edical] A[ssociation] Style Book; Chicago, 1919, p. 9, but in vain. See also The Verb *Operate*, by Marion L. Morse, *American Speech*, April, 1930, pp. 287–89. Another shortening, apparently invented by the Army Medical Corps, is *to survey out of the service*, used in the sense of to retire from the service after a medical survey. It is used twice in Peptic Ulcer, Gastritis and Psychoneurosis, by Hugh Montgomery and others, *Journal of the American Medical Association*, July 29, 1944, p. 893.

3 This may have been borrowed from the undertakers. The undertakers, become *morticians*, now use *patient* themselves.

4 Headline in the *Weekly Bulletin* of the New York City Department of Health, May 22, 1926, p. 81. Unhappily, *to diagnosticate* is traced by the NED to 1846 and the more seemly *to diagnose* no further back than 1861, so the former has seniority, if not beauty.

5 I take most of these from Medical Jargon, by Hobart A. Reimann, *Journal of the American Medical Association*, May 17, 1941, p. 2335.

especially those of the psychoanalytical faction, have concocted a vast vocabulary of new words,[1] and some of them have got into the common speech, *e.g., complex (inferiority, Oedipus,* etc.), *libido, inhibition, repression, introvert, extrovert, fixation, subconscious, psychopathic personality,* and various derivatives of *schizophrenia.*[2] From the répertoire of the internists has come the adjective *allergic,* now in wide use as a general indicator of aversion, whether physical or psychic.[3] The orthodox psychologists have also made contributions, *e.g., reaction,*[4] *conditioned, to stultify,*[5] and *psychological moment.* But of all the bands of learned men who devote themselves to inventing new terms, and then to hugging them until the last drop of juice is squeezed out of them, the most assiduous are the pedagogues. A few of their favorites, *e.g., outstanding,* have got into the common stock,[6] but on the whole their jargon remains esoteric, *e.g.,*

---

Dr. Reimann lists many others, and includes a brief bibliography of papers by distinguished medical men protesting against such forms. See also The Decay of Medical Language (editorial), New Zealand *Medical Journal,* Dec., 1942.

1 *Psychoanalysis,* in the German form of *psychoanalyse,* was coined by Sigmund Freud *c.* 1900. It first appeared in English in 1907. The first International Congress of Psychoanalysis was held in 1907. The popular craze for the new revelation struck the United States in 1912 or thereabout, in succession to Couéism, the Emmanuel Movement and paper-bag cookery.

2 In *American Speech,* Nov., 1926, p. 95, Edna Heidbreder printed a sheaf of sapphics made up entirely of psychoneurotic terms. See the Jargon of Psychology, by W. Béran Wolfe, *Forum,* Feb. 1932, pp. 81–85.

3 Some examples of its use are assembled in The Living Language, by Dwight L. Bolinger, *Words,* Oct., 1937, p. 154, and Jan., 1938, p. 11. The parent noun, *allergy,* is traced by the NED Supplement to 1913, and *allergic* to 1925.

4 Weare Holbrook, writing in *This Week,* quoted in *American Speech,* Dec., 1936, p. 297, says that *reaction* became a counter-word in 1935. See

also The Jargon of Psychology, by W. Béran Wolfe, *Forum,* Feb., 1932, pp. 81–85. Lord Tweedsmuir, then Governor-General of Canada, denounced *reaction* in 1936, but it laughed at him.

5 Used in the sense of to diminish in mental power, to become dull, stale or stagnant. As a legal term *to stultify* means to escape responsibility by pleading one's own insanity. In the sense of to make one's self appear foolish or absurd it is traced by the NED to 1809, and in that of to render nugatory to 1865. The sense in which psychologists use it seems to be peculiar to them. I am indebted here to Miss Nina Ridenour of New York.

6 The NED traces *outstanding,* in the sense of conspicuous, important, superior, to 1830, but it was little heard in the United States until the gogues began to labor it. In AL4, p. 211, n. 1, I recorded the case of an American superintendent of schools who managed to use it five times on a single page of a book. On Nov. 25, 1940, when Columbia University gave honorary degrees to Bela Bartok, the Hungarian composer; Sir Cecil Thomas Carr, an English lawyer; Dr. Karl T. Compton, president of the Massachusetts Institute of Technology, and Paul Hazard, a member

*stimulus-response bond, mind-set, creativity, differentia, overview, overall* (adjective), *factor, integration, implication, essentialism, function, core-curriculum, challenge, emphases,*[1] *orthogenic, purposeful, control of the learning situation, dynamic, to motivate, educationist,*[2] *to evaluate, to vitalize* and *to socialize.* The so-called progressive gogues, in the days of their glory, had a large and bristling vocabulary of their own, much of it lifted from the lingo of the psychoanalysts, the various warring wings of psychologists, the Rotarians and the Boy Scouts. One of its favorite terms was *creative:*[3] The progressives are now in the dog-house, and the generality of public-school gogues are going back to what they call *essentialism, i.e.,* the teaching of such once-scorned subjects as reading, writing and ciphering. They have, in both their thinking and their talk, made liberal drafts from the more advanced and idealistic sociologists,[4] and especially from that faction of soaring pseudo-sociologists known as social workers.[5] " Newer sciences like sociology and pedagogy," said William Allen Neilson in 1938,

of the French Academy, Dr. Harry Morgan Ayres, who presented the candidates to Dr. Nicholas Murray Butler, read citations describing Bartok as " a truly *outstanding* artist," Compton as " chief administrator of an *outstanding* institution of scientific training," and Hazard as the author of " works of *outstanding* importance." A derivative noun, *standout,* made its debut in the *Jackson Hole Courier* (Jackson, Wyo.), Jan. 28, 1943, p. 1. In the *Congressional Record,* Sept. 15, 1943, p. 7654, col. 1, the variant *upstanding* appeared. In the literal sense the NED traces it to *c.* 1000.

1 The plural alone is swagger: the singular does not mark the supergogue.

2 " *Educator,*" said *American Speech,* Oct., 1938, p. 235, " has lost vogue." But *educationist* has a rival in *educationalist.*

3 In *Word Study,* Feb., 1937, p. 3, an anonymous writer (probably the editor, Dr. Max J. Herzberg) reported that the use of *creative* in such combinations as *creative listening* and *creative janitorial service* was launched by a schoolma'am

sweating for credits (and a lift in salary) at Teachers College, Columbia, the Vatican of American pedagogy. " She claimed," says this writer, " that she was entitled to a copyright fee on every employment of it made in educational circles, . . . and was prepared to collect $173,677 for the use made of the word in Teachers College alone."

4 There is a long list in Educational Lingo, by Olivia Pound, *American Speech,* Feb., 1926, pp. 311–14, but many of the terms cited have now been supplanted by later inventions. See also The Language of Modern Education, by Lester K. Ade; Harrisburg (Pa.), 1939, which defines the more seemly pedagogical terms and pays little attention to the trade argot.

5 Some of the euphemisms devised by the latter are listed in AL4, pp. 292–93. More are in The Terminology of Social Workers, by LeRoy E. Bowman, *American Speech,* June, 1926, pp. 478–80. For the vocabulary of sociologists see Sociological Nomenclature, by Maurice Greer Smith, *American Speech,* Sept., 1927, pp. 507–08; Jargon, *Bulletin of the Asso-*

which aren't quite certain of their place in the academic hierarchy, are anxious to establish themselves as real sciences, and naturally but stupidly what they do is to imitate real sciences by being unintelligible. Students of pedagogy and sociologists have already invented the worst English that any class of scholars write, as far as I know. Take up one of their books and you will find no ideas, once you have penetrated the shell, that are not perfectly capable of being expounded in good English.[1]

The prevalence of counter-words in everyday speech is familiar to everyone. There is a constant accretion of new ones, and some have come into such wide use that they are read or heard every hour, and indeed every minute. Not a few are adjectives or adverbs, *e.g.*, *awful(ly)*, *grand* and *swell*. So long ago as September 27, 1749 Lord Chesterfield was noting (and denouncing), in a letter to his son, the vogue for *vastly* in England. *Jolly*, still in use in England, is traced by the NED in English use, sometimes followed by *well*, to 1548, but it has never had a run in the United States, though the verb *to jolly* was adopted years ago. The DAE marks *awful* and *awfully* Americanisms. The first is traced to 1809, more than sixty years before it appeared in England. " In New England," said Pickering in his Vocabulary of 1816, " many people would call a disagreeable medicine *awful*, an ugly woman an *awful*-looking woman; a perverse, ill-natured child that disobeys his parents would be said to behave *awfully*, etc." Pickering seemed to believe that *awful* and *awfully* were on their way out, but they still survive. He also noted *grand*, in the general sense of superior or noteworthy, and it is apparently an Americanism, though the DAE overlooks it. *Swell*, as a noun signifying a person of fashion, seems to have been borrowed from the cant of thieves in England, *c.* 1800. In 1804 a number of young English officers were dismissed from the Army for forming what they called the *Swell* Club, but soon afterward the term was in general use, and the adjective seems to have followed almost immediately. *Swell* had a revival in the United States *c.* 1910, and acquired an antonym in *lousy*. Both became counter-words of the first virulence, and there is an illustrative story about an Eastern literatus who said

*ciates in the Science of Society at Yale University*, May, 1940, pp. 4 and 5; and A Student's Dictionary of Sociological Terms, by Constantine Panunzio; Berkeley (Calif.), 1941.

1 Speech at the annual meeting of the American Association for Adult Education in New York. See Neilson Condemns Academic " Jargon," New York *Times*, May 22, 1938. An assault directed especially at teachers of English is in The Faculty Style, *Saturday Review of Literature*, Dec. 18, 1937, p. 8.

to a movie-queen: " The only words used in Hollywood are *swell* and *lousy*." Her reply was: " What words are they? " Many other counter-words of recent years will occur to the reader, *e.g., constructive* (beloved of Rotarians), *angle*,[1] *consistent*,[2] *gesture*,[3] *shambles*,[4] *stream-lined, alibi*,[5] *definitely*,[6] *flair*,[7] *proposition*,[8] *plus*,[9] *lurid, re-*

[1] For long a favorite with bad newspaper reporters, in the general sense of aspect or point of view. *Editor and Publisher*, Sept. 2, 1944: " Betty has been writing sports from the feminine *angle*. . . . She knows the feature *angle* as well." Peter Tamony says, in *Angle*, San Francisco *News Letter and Wasp*, June 16, 1939, p. 5, that *angle* was borrowed from the vocabulary of billiards, along with *good break* and *bad break*. It has reached England, and I find the following in The Commoner's New Forest, by F. E. Kenchington; London, 1943 (reviewed in the London *Times Literary Supplement*, Jan. 22, 1944). " My *angle* . . . is that in any part of England's green and pleasant land the rights of the folk," etc. See The Supplement to O.E.D., by George G. Loane, London *Times Literary Supplement*, March 8, 1934, p. 162.

[2] Another journalistic pet, used in the sense of continuous, regular, habitual, persistent, etc. *Editor and Publisher*, March 25, 1944: " *Hygeia* has been a *consistent* advertiser in women's, medical and baby magazines." Counting in *consistently*, the term is here used four times in one column. Associated Press dispatch from Mauch Chunk, Pa., June 12, 1939: " To clear up certain *consistent* rumors," etc. In such senses *consistent* is old in England, but it fell out of use in the Seventeenth Century. Who revived it in the United States, and when, I do not know.

[3] Described as recent in *Beau Geste*, by J. M. Steadman, Jr., *American Speech*, June, 1928, p. 416. George Philip Krapp, in his Comprehensive Guide to Good English; New York, 1927, suggested that it came from the French *beau geste*. Steadman listed many examples of its use.

[4] *Shambles* is a very old word in Eng-

lish. The NED traces it to *c.* 825 in the sense of a stool, to 971 in that of a counter for exposing goods for sale, to *c.* 1305 in that of a stall for the sale of meat, and to 1548 in that of a slaughtering-place. In Notes on American Usage, *American Speech*, Feb., 1941, p. 19. I. Willis Russell says that, in American usage, it has now come to signify any sort of " very great, perhaps complete disorder, confusion or destruction." He gives nine examples from current books, newspapers and magazines. In *Shambles* (editorial), Aug. 9, 1939, the Norfolk *Ledger-Dispatch* said that the word had come in " within the last year."

[5] In AL4, p. 210, I expressed the opinion that *alibi* was going out. In *American Speech*, Oct., 1937, p. 186, the late Stuart Robertson described this as " overoptimistic," and he was right. *Alibi* is still in wide use to indicate any sort of excuse. In the legal sense it is confined to a plea on the part of a person accused of crime that he was somewhere else when it was committed. See Speech Degeneracy, by M. V. P. Yeaman, *American Speech*, Nov., 1925, p. 93.

[6] *Definitely* seems to have been borrowed from the English. Partridge says that it came into use in England during the present century, and has been a counter-word since *c.* 1920, confined to " non-proletarian " circles. Wilson Follett says in Words Across the Sea, *Atlantic Monthly*, March, 1938, p. 365, that it was introduced in the United States by an English best-seller, Busman's Honeymoon, by Dorothy L. Sayers. Weare Holbrook, quoted in *American Speech*, Dec., 1936, p. 297, says that it came in in that year. Dwight L. Bolinger, in The Living Language, *Words*, May, 1938, p. 67 calls it a favorite of the " tricky-

*action, conference* and *to intrigue*.[1] *Strenuous* should not be forgotten,[2] nor the counter-words that occupy the intelligentsia without ever descending to lower levels, *e.g., meticulous,*[3] *chemurgic* [4] and *podium*.[5] The English have many counter-words that fail to make the Atlantic journey, *e.g., knowledgeable,* which had a great run in the 1935–38 era,[6] *unilateral,*[7] and the fashionable intensives of the *foul*

speech crowd." In 1937 it was denounced by Wilfred J. Funk, the lexicographer, as one of the ten most overworked words of the time, the others being *O.K., terrific, lousy, to contact, gal, racket, swell, impact* and *honey*. In *Okay* and *Lousy* Terrific to Funk, the New York *Times,* March 27, 1937, reported him as saying that " American débutantes evidently thought they were imitating the English by saying ' Yes, *definitely,' definitely so* and just *definitely*." He declared that " the word in England is used excessively by the lower classes." In 1940 (*Definitely:* I Don't Like It, by Man in the Street, London *Star,* Aug. 30) Mr. Justice Humphreys, an English judge, protested against its use by witnesses before him.

7 *Flair:* A Recent Semanic Development, by Albert H. Marckwardt, *American Speech,* April, 1935, pp. 104–06, and *Flair,* by Joseph E. Gillet, *American Speech,* Dec., 1937, pp. 247–57. Gillet presents a long list of examples, the earliest dated 1927.

8 Some examples from the *Congressional Record,* ranging from 1917 to 1921, are in The American Language, third ed.: New York, 1921, p. 136, n. 22.

9 *Plus,* by Mamie Meredith, *American Speech,* Dec., 1927, p. 161.

1 Used by Chaucer in The Romaunt of the Rose in its old sense of to deceive. It now means to interest, to inveigle, to enchant, and a host of other things.

2 Popularized by Theodore Roosevelt by a speech at Chicago, April 10, 1899, and in vogue for a quarter of a century.

3 In its original meaning, traced by the NED to 1535, fearful, timid; by extension, traced to 1827, over-scru-

pulous, over-cautious; now used in the general sense of careful, painstaking. I am indebted here to Dr. Sherman Kent of Yale.

4 I am indebted here to Mr. Stephen E. Billings of the Rutland (Vt.) *Herald.*

5 In heavy counter-use to designate the stand of an orchestra-conductor. It is an architectural term indicating, *inter alia,* a raised platform in an ancient ampitheatre. In that sense it was recorded so long ago as 1848, but in the sense of a perch for a musical gymnast it did not come into vogue until *c.* 1935. I am indebted here to Mr. John Irwin Bright of Ardmore, Pa.

6 Advertisement in the London *Telegraph,* Sept. 27, 1935: " Lagonda will appeal particularly to *knowledgeable* motorists." London *Morning Post,* Oct. 5, 1935: " The author has fulfilled his commission very *knowledgeably*." The same, July 2, 1936: " *Knowledgeable* gardeners will now have *Iris juncea* abloom." *News of the World,* June 21, 1936: " The locale of the play is the home of an amusing, *knowledgeable* matriarch." London *Telegraph,* June 17, 1937: " *Parisians* ... wish to appear *knowledgeable* about international affairs." Autolycus, in London *Sunday Times,* Feb. 20, 1938: " If the steps of any *knowledgeable* Londonlover chanced to carry him to Soho Square on Friday afternoon he would surely have blinked with astonishment." For all these examples I am indebted to the collectanea of the late F. H. Tyson.

7 Denounced by A. P. Herbert, with many horrible examples, in WordSkirmish, *Punch,* March 17, 1937, pp. 288–89.

and *putrid* order.[1] Whether or not the *and/or* combination originated in England I have been unable to determine. Like *alibi*, it comes from the argot of the law. It has been denounced in both England and America, even by judges,[2] but it continues to flourish.[3]

To the notes in AL4, pp. 201 *ff*, on various peculiarities of American usage little need be added. *Whom* is now almost obsolete, save as a conscious affectation usually employed incorrectly. " *Who* are you talking to? " has come into well-nigh universal use, and may be called sound American; indeed, the late Dr. Stuart Robertson argued that it was also sound English.[4] He also argued for the validity of the

---

1 There are some examples in All For Love, by Joseph Wood Krutch, *New Republic*, June 3, 1936, p. 714.

2 In Re *Quisling* and Others, the Manchester *Evening News*, July 8, 1940, reported that a High Court judge had " refused to look at any document with *and/or* in it." In 1935 Justice Chester A. Fowler, of the Supreme Court of Wisconsin (*Word Study*, Feb., 1936, p. 3), described it from the bench as " that befuddling nameless thing, that Janus-faced verbal monstrosity, neither word nor phrase, the child of a brain of someone too lazy or too dull to know what he did mean, now commonly used by lawyers in drafting legal documents, through carelessness or ignorance or as a cunning device to conceal rather than express a meaning, with a view to furthering the interest of their clients." On Jan. 21, 1938, at a meeting of the New York City Board of Estimates, Acting Mayor Henry H. Curran ordered *and/or* expunged from all documents brought before the board, and *x or y or both* substituted.

3 The linguistic pathologist eager to pursue the subject will find more material in A Dictionary of Clichés, by Eric Partridge; New York, 1940; the various parades and exemplifications of clichés by Frank Sullivan in the *New Yorker* (for example, The Cliché Expert Testifies on Literary Criticism, July 24, 1937, pp. 15–16, and The Cliché Expert Testifies on Vacations, Aug. 21, 1937, pp. 15–16); How Copy Desks Treat Hot Days,

by H. I. Phillips, *American Press*, Aug., 1930, p. 7; The State of the Language, by Wilson Follett, *Atlantic Monthly*, Oct., 1939, pp. 549–50; The Cry of the English, Nottingham *Journal*, April 30, 1943; Experiments in Words, London *Times Literary Supplement*, June 24, 1944; Bad Words, London *Observer*, Nov. 27, 1938; and *Attractive* Is Too, Too Attractive, London *Morning Post*, April 9, 1937. The argot of revivalists is dealt with by John D. M'Inerny in *American Speech*, Dec., 1935, p. 316; that of Jewish uplifters in Definitions From a Demagogue's Dictionary, *Jewish Standard* (Toronto), July 9, 1934; that of book reviewers in The Book Reviewer's Vocabulary, by Wilson O. Clough, *American Speech*, Feb., 1931, pp. 180–86; that of radio announcers in Clichés on the Air, by Frank Sullivan, *Atlantic Monthly*, Aug., 1941, pp. 220–22; and that of business men in Business English, Coming and Going, by Maurice H. Weseen, *American Speech*, May, 1926, pp. 447–49; The Business Letter, Old Style and New, by F. Walter Pollock, *American Speech*, July, 1926, pp. 539–40; On Commercial Correspondence, by the same, *American Speech*, Nov., 1926, pp. 96–99; Re: Business English, by Herbert B. Bernstein, *American Speech*, April, 1927, pp. 319–21; and Business English, by William Feather, *American Speech*, July 1927, pp. 447–48.

4 Notes on the American Language, *American Speech*, Oct. 1937, p. 186.

terminal preposition, as in " Where are we *at?* " The split infinitive has even more impressive support. Dr. George O. Curme defended it at length in *American Speech* in 1927,[1] and gave over nearly eight pages of his monumental grammar of 1931 to detailing its history and proving its utility.[2] Other eminent authorities have taken the same line, including H. W. Fowler, author of " A Dictionary of Modern English Usage." [3] I see no sign that academic dubieties are making any impression on other popular American forms, *e.g.*, the *one-he* combination,[4] *but that*,[5] and the intrusion of *of* between *question* and *whether*.[6] There are many others of the same sort.[7]

The familiar use of *whom* in Matthew XVI, 13 (Authorized Version) — " *Whom* do men say that I, the Son of man, am? " — has long engaged grammarians. For the following note on it I am indebted to Mr. Sydney J. Mehlman of Brooklyn: " The Greek simply means ' Who do men say that the Son of God is? ' The rest is dogmatical interpolation. The Latin version would be: ' Quem dicunt homines esse Dei Filium? '. In this construction both Latin and Greek employ the accusative (objective), whereas good English uses the nominative. So I guess it should be *who*."

1 The Split Infinitive, May, 1927, pp. 341–42.

2 A Grammar of the English Language; III. Syntax; Boston, 1931, pp. 458–67.

3 Fowler devotes six columns to the subject in this book. This discussion was first published as The Split Infinitive, along with an essay on The Position of the Adverb, in *S.P.E. Tract No. XV*, 1923. The Dictionary of Modern English Usage was first published in 1926. The other defenders of the split infinitive include Dr. Kemp Malone (To Split or Not to Split, *American Speech*, Feb., 1932, p. 223), Wallace Rice (The Split Infinitive, *English Journal*, College Ed., March, 1937, pp. 238–40), and the late Frank H. Vizetelly (Our Much-Criticized Language, New York *Times*, Dec. 20,

1931). Intelligent lay discussions of the subject are in The Pardonable Sin, by Jackdaw, *John o' London's Weekly*, Nov. 12, 1937, and Split Infinitives (editorial), Mobile (Ala.) *Press*, Feb. 4, 1937.

4 I find the following beautiful variation in H. P. Blavatsky, by Caroline Hoering, New York *Herald Tribune Books*, Jan. 9, 1938: " It is my belief that one should acquaint *themselves* first with the subject."

5 Calvin Coolidge: Message to Congress, Dec. 9, 1929: " There is no question *but that* Federal contributions have materially added to the State expenditures of State funds." The Hon. George W. Norris, *Congressional Record*, June 12, 1939, p. 9923, col. 2: " There is no doubt *but that* the Sherman Act was not intended to apply." The English also use *but that* occasionally. I find the following in Two More Days of Pilgrimage (editorial), London *Times*, July 13, 1934: " There seems to be no question *but that* the pilgrimage," etc.

6 Described in the *Literary Digest*, Jan. 17, 1935, as " grammatically incorrect" but " a familiar colloquialism." It was used by Shelley, but is not common in English.

7 See American Variations, by H. W. Horwill, *S.P.E. Tract No. XLV*, 1936, and British-American Differentiations in Syntax and Idiom, by Stuart Robertson, *American Speech*, Dec., 1938, pp. 243–54.

## 5. FOREIGN INFLUENCES TODAY

218. [Since the Civil War the chief contribution of German has been the domestication of the suffix *-fest*.] In 1916 Louise Pound rounded up twenty-three specimens from the current vocabulary, to wit: *Ananiasfest, batfest, blarneyfest, bloodfest, crabfest,*[1] *eatfest, gabfest, gabblefest, gadfest, grubfest, jawfest, olymphest,*[2] *singfest, slugfest, smilefest, smokefest, sobfest, songfest, spooffest, stuntfest, swatfest, talkfest* and *walkfest.*[3] Many others appeared during the years following, e.g., *hoochfest, lovefest, bullfest, boozefest, bookfest* and *applefest,*[4] and in 1918 Dr. Pound herself added *chatfest, egofest, funfest* and *gossipfest.*[5] Since then the scouts of *American Speech* and other linguistic explorers have unearthed *beerfest, hymnfest,*[6] *gagfest,*[7] *hamfest,*[8] *suitfest,*[9] *blabfest, chatfest, chawfest, chinfest, gasfest, hashfest, pipefest, joshfest, laughfest, nudefest, stripfest, pepfest* and *henfest.*[10] On April 9, 1927 the Pittsburgh *Courier* announced that the Northside Community Club of that city, a colored organization, was about to hold a *sangerfest* (no umlaut). The Spanish *fiesta* seems to have reinforced *fest* in the West, and *funfesta,*[11] *jubilesta, mulesta, goldesta* and *hallowesta* have been recorded.[12] The DAE does not list *sängerfest*, but its meaning has been familiar to all Americans interested in music since the 70s. It also omits *schützenfest*, which was likewise familiar in the 1850–90 era. Webster 1934 lists both, along with *sängerbund*. There was a fashion *c.* 1900 for words in *-bund*, and for a while *moneybund* and *plunderbund* were

1 This was apparently picked up in the Middle West. In the Chesapeake Bay country *crabfeast* has never yielded to *crabfest*.
2 Coined at Hays, Kansas, to designate a series of contests at the normal school there, not only in athletics but also in spelling, cookery, drawing, music and handicrafts.
3 Domestication of the Suffix *-fest*, *Dialect Notes*, Vol. IV, Part V, 1916, pp. 353 and 354.
4 There are notes on *gabfest, bookfest* and *applefest* in AL4, p. 218, notes 4 and 5.
5 Vogue Affixes in Present-Day Word-Coinage, *Dialect Notes*, Vol. V, Part I, 1918, p. 11.
6 *American Speech*, April, 1914, p. 149.

7 The Living Language, by Dwight L. Bolinger, *Words*, March, 1940, p. 41.
8 Defined by William White in Radio Jargon, *Words*, Dec., 1941, p. 99, as "a convention of amateur radio broadcasters."
9 Defined by Maurice H. Weseen in A Dictionary of American Slang; New York, 1934, p. 405, as "a mess of lawsuits."
10 The last fourteen are listed by Berry and Van den Bark.
11 *American Speech*, April, 1938, p. 157.
12 For the last four I am indebted to Dwight L. Bolinger, *Words*, March, 1940, p. 41.

in wide use. Both are omitted by the DAE, but Webster lists them. The suffix early acquired a pejorative significance, accentuated when the F.B.I. began running down *bundists, i.e.,* members of a *bund* of Nazis. The latest word in *-bund* seems to be *smearbund,* signifying a band of defamers, *e.g.,* of the Jews.[1] Other German suffixes that have produced progeny in American are *-lust, -heimer* and *-burger.* The first-named was introduced by *wanderlust,* which was in wide use for some years, *c.* 1930, and produced the derivatives *wanderluster* (Eng. *rambler*), *wanderlust-club* (Eng. *rambling-club*), *wanderlusting* and *wanderlustful.* The DAE omits all of them, but Webster lists *wanderlust, wanderlusting* and *wanderlustful.* In 1933 the Hon. Louis Ludlow, a member of Congress from Indiana, launched *squanderlust* in a book, " America Go Bust," but it did not catch on.[2] The suffix *-heimer* begat *wiseheimer* and various other terms. It was probably helped into American English by Yiddish influence. Along with it came *-sky* or *-ski,* as in *allrightsky, hurryupsky, youbetsky, buttinski* and *damfoolski,* but of these only *buttinski* shows any sign of surviving.[3] All the American words in *-burger* appear to be derived from *hamburger.* In its early days in the United States the chopped beef now known as a *hamburger* was called a *hamburg-steak,* and was served like any other steak, not in the form of a sandwich. The DAE traces *hamburg-steak* to 1884 and it is probably older. By the turn of the century it had become *hamburger-steak,* and soon afterward it degenerated from the estate of a steak to that of a sandwich and became a simple *hamburger.* It began to produce numerous offspring after World War I. Says Arnold Williams:

> Like *lemonade* it has, at least in the vulgate, added a new suffix to the language. To the proprietors and clientèle of thousands of roadside inns, diners and eat-and-run lunch-counters *-burger* has come to mean almost any meat or meat-substitute ground or chopped and, fried or grilled, made into sandwiches.[4]

Williams lists *chickenburger, cheeseburger, clamburger, lamburger* (made of ground " lamb," and tasting, he notes, like ram), *rabbitburger, nutburger, porkburger* and *wimpyburger.* He says:

1 *Editor and Publisher,* April 8, 1944, p. 16, col. 3.
2 Miscellany, by Louise Pound, *American Speech,* April, 1935, p. 155.
3 Domestication of a Suffix, by Louise Pound, *Dialect Notes,* Vol. IV, Part IV, 1916, p. 304; Addenda to IV, 4,

304, by the same, *Dialect Notes,* Vol. IV, Part V, 1916; Vogue Affixes in Present-Day Word-Coinage, by the same, *Dialect Notes,* Vol. V, Part I, 1918, p. 11.
4 *Hamburger* Progeny, *American Speech,* April, 1939, p. 154.

*Wimpyburger* suggests to the student of etymology a clue to the popularity of *-burger* as a suffix. Popeye, the popular comic strip of the late Segar, though it cannot be credited with the popularity of the *hamburger* sandwich, did, in the character of Wimpy, endow *hamburger* with a *mythos*. Like all of Segar's characters, Wimpy is an inveterate coiner of new words. Several years ago he created *goonburger*. More recently *demonburger* has appeared.

In 1940 Louise Pound reported *beefburger* from New York City, *kirschburger* from Lincoln, Neb., and *shrimpburger* from New Orleans.[1] Three years later Dwight L. Bolinger followed with *glutenburger, barbecueburger, Spamburger* (made of a proprietary ground-meat preparation called *Spam*), *huskiburger, Bar-B-burger, sausageburger, pickleburger* and *Meet-the-People-burger*, named after a musical comedy called "Meet the People."[2] In 1937 a correspondent reported a *tomatoburger* from Minneapolis,[3] and another a *liverwurstburger* from Washington.[4] In 1940 the austere sausage-engineers of the Institute of American Meat Packers converted the latter into a *liver-sausage-burger*.[5] Other searchers have unearthed the *horsemeatburger,*[6] *Mexiburger, chuckburger, dogburger, seaburger, fishburger,*[7] *whinneyburger* (a euphemism for *horsemeatburger*)[8] *oomphburger*[9] and *griddleburger*.[10]

The DAE's first examples of *frankfurter* and *wienerwurst* are both dated 1899, but the two sausages were well known in the United States long before. The former is the variety commonly used in the hot-dog: the latter is smaller. But the terms are frequently interchanged, even by Germans. Two clipped forms of *wienerwurst*, to wit, *wiener* and *wienie*, are in wide use. Webster 1934 lists *wiener* but not *wienie:* the DAE ignores both. *Liver-pudding*, corresponding

1 More Progeny of *Hamburger*, American Speech, Dec., 1940, p. 452.
2 Among the New Words, *American Speech*, April, 1943, p. 148.
3 Mr. L. Clark Keating; private communication, June 20, 1937.
4 Mrs. Frederick H. Goldman; private communication, June 1, 1937.
5 Advertisement in *Life*, April 29, 1940. The recipe for it follows: "Brown slices of *liver-sausage* slowly in butter. Turn and continue cooking until well browned. Split buns. Toast if desired. Serve hot *liver-sausage* slices between buttered halves of buns. Add onion, pickle, relish or chili sauce as desired."
6 *American Speech*, Feb., 1944, p. 78.

7 The last five are reported by Mamie Meredith in *American Speech*, April, 1942, p. 132. She adds *jamburgo*, "a Mexican spelling of *hamburger* found by Dr. A. H. Marckwardt across the Rio Grande."
8 *American Speech*, Oct., 1943, p. 237.
9 The Living Language, by Dwight L. Bolinger, *Words*, March, 1940, p. 41. It is defined as "a *hamburger* served with *oomph*."
10 A concoction of ground beef, flour, eggs, milk and spices, browned on a griddle and described by Louella G. Shouer in Main Dishes On Your Budget, *Ladies' Home Journal*, Sept., 1943, as a "point saver."

to the German *leberwurst*, may be an Americanism, though the DAE does not list it, for neither is it recorded by the NED. In the Baltimore of my childhood *leberwurst* was in frequent use, though *liverwurst, liver-pudding* and *liver-sausage* were also heard. In 1930 Swift & Company, the Chicago packers, began calling the sausage *braunschweiger* — the adjective often prefixed to *leberwurst* by the Germans, for the variety most esteemed in their homeland comes from Braunschweig (Brunswick).[1] The other Chicago packers seem to prefer *liver-sausage*. Swift has also reduced *frankfurter* to *frankfurt*, and put on the market a preparation of liver called *liver cheese*.[2] *Frankfurter* has produced at least one derivative, *turkeyfurter*.[3] Sometimes these German borrowings are sadly misspelled in American use. I have encountered *brownswoger, weanerwust*, and even *wienna shitzel* (for *wiener schnitzel*).[4]

During World War I an effort was made by super-patriots to drive all German loans from the American vocabulary. *Sauerkraut* became *liberty cabbage, hamburger steak* became *Salisbury steak, hamburger* became *liberty sandwich*, and a few extremists even changed *German measles* to *liberty measles*.[5] A similar movement got under way during World War II, but it does not seem to have prospered, for so late as the end of 1942 the Army's model menu included spareribs and *sauer-*

---

1 In Nebraska, according to *American Speech*, Dec., 1934, "a *braunschweiger* is a sandwich made of bread and ground meat."

2 All three are listed in the Swift & Company Yearbook for 1943, issued Dec. 20, 1943. It also lists *hamburger patties, dried beef, head cheese, bologna, cervelat, salami* and *genoa*. The DAE traces *dried*, applied to beef, to 1661, but shows that the adjective was usually applied to buffalo meat. The more familiar *chipped beef* is an Americanism, traced to 1833. The DAE also marks *head cheese* an Americanism, and traces it to 1841, but H. W. Seaman tells me that it is also in use in the Northern counties of England. *Brawn*, however, is the usual English word, and *pork cheese* is used in Norfolk. In the Baltimore of my youth *hogs'-head cheese* was in common use, and the German *schwartenmagen* (pro. *schwattermagen*) was not unknown. *Salami*, from the

Italian, is traced by the NED to 1852, and *cervelat*, from the Italian through the French, to 1708. I can't find *genoa* in any dictionary.

3 Reported by Dwight L. Bolinger in *Words*, Jan., 1940, p. 11, and described, on the authority of an unnamed newspaper of Nov. 5, 1939, as "turkey on a roll with cranberry sauce." In *American Speech*, Dec., 1943, p. 302, Bolinger also reported *turkeymally*, from *tamale* (1940), *turkeywich* and *duckwich* (both 1941).

4 This last appeared on a restaurant bill-of-fare in Reading, Pa., and may have been due to Pennsylvania-German influence.

5 In 1917 a theatre manager in Cleveland complained to the United Booking Office of the Keith Circuit against a vaudevillian who used the word *gesundheit* in his act. See Reporting the Acts, *Variety*, Jan. 12, 1944.

*kraut.*[1] But attacks were made from time to time on *hamburger,*[2] *kindergarten,*[3] and even *crème vichyssoise.*[4] I also heard a suggestion, perhaps not altogether serious, that the reminder of things German, and hence abhorrent, in *Bismarck herring* be got rid of by substituting *Eisenhower herring.* The farthest leap of this movement was led by Lee Elmaker, publisher of the Philadelphia *Daily News,* who announced in August, 1942, that all German and Japanese proper names, including *German* and *Jap,* would be spelled thereafter, in his paper, with lower-case initial letters.[5] This was done even when such a word began a sentence. After Pearl Harbor it was proposed in Washington that the name of the *Japanese* cherry-trees in a local park be changed to something less obscene, but nothing more seemly could be thought of. On March 29, 1943 the Hon. John E. Rankin of Mississippi allayed public feeling by announcing in the House that they were " not *Japanese* cherry-trees but *Korean* cherry-trees, . . . stolen by the Japanese from Korea just as she is now stealing everything that China has." [6] The Nazis, meanwhile, had staged a wholesale purge of foreign words in German. All the common grammatical terms, for example, were translated into German, so that *grammatik* itself became *sprachlehre,*[7] and there were similar changes in most of the other arts and sciences, including especially medicine.[8] World War II, of course, introduced Americans to a great many new German terms, and a few of them promise to linger on to naturalization, and even to produce derivatives,[9] but most of them were also borrowed by the English, and hence do not concern us as Americanisms.[10]

1 *Consumer Reports,* Oct., 1942, p. 273. The information here was supplied by the Army Information Service, 90 Church street, New York.

2 In August, 1941, the National Association of Meat Merchants, meeting in Detroit, considered a proposal to adopt *defense steak,* but it did not prevail.

3 The proponent here was a radio orator calling himself Uncle Robert. He offered a prize for the best substitute suggested. Among them were *pastime-class* and *juvenile-class,* but no satisfactory proposal seems to have been received. See an editorial in the *Nation,* Jan. 9, 1943, and the *New Yorker,* Nov. 14, 1942, p. 11. *Kindergarten* has been traced in

English use to 1855 and in American use to 1862.

4 *New Yorker,* Jan. 23, 1943, p. 8.

5 Drops Caps on Japs, *Editor and Publisher,* Aug. 15, 1942, p. 16.

6 *Congressional Record,* March 29, 1943, p. A1589.

7 Nationalism in Grammar, London *Times,* Jan. 25, 1938.

8 This last patriotic reform long ante-dated the Nazis. See Medical Terminology in Germany, by A. N. Tasker, *Journal of the American Medical Association,* July 1, 1922.

9 *Hairsatz,* from *ersatz,* was launched by *Time,* Feb. 16, 1942.

10 A long list is in Borrowings From the German (1930–1941), by Karl F. Koenig, *Modern Language Journal,* Nov., 1943, pp. 486–93. Another is

Two undoubted Americanisms that have puzzled etymologists may also be loans from the German, to wit, *to scram* and *hoodlum*. The origins of the latter have been sought in Spanish and in various Indian languages, but in vain. The DAE says that it came into use in San Francisco *c.* 1872, but that its source is unknown. In a paper published in *Modern Language Notes* in 1935 [1] Dr. John T. Krumpelmann suggested that it may come from a Bavarian dialect term, *hodalump*, of the same meaning precisely. In the San Francisco of those days, he said, " the Germans constituted the largest foreign-language " group, and many of them were Bavarians.[2] The theory that *to scram* may be of German origin was set forth in *American Speech* in 1938 by Dr. G. Kirchner of Jena,[3] who argued that it probably comes from " the German slang word *schrammen*, of exactly the same meaning." Partridge suggests, alas only lamely, that it may come from a South Cheshire dialect word, *to scramble*, meaning " to get away with, with a notion of fear or stealth," but he admits that it originated in the United States, and that the English were unaware of it until American movies introduced them to it, *c.* 1930. *Yes-man* is another Americanism that may be of German origin. The equivalent German *jaherr* is defined by Cassell's New German and English Dictionary as " a compliant person, one unable to say no," and the aforesaid Krumpelmann has shown that it was used in that sense by a German writer on America, Charles Sealsfield (Karl Postl), in ' Die Vereinigten Staaten von Nordamerika " in 1827.[4] H. W. Horwill is of the opinion

---

in Recent American Loan Words From German, by Harold G. Carlson, *American Speech*, April, 1940, pp. 205–08. It is rather astonishing (and perhaps also lamentable) that Prohibition did not bring in the magnificent German word *saufschwester*.

1 Feb., pp. 93–95.

2 Bartlett, in the fourth edition of his Dictionary of Americanisms, 1877, ventured upon the following hearsay etymology: " A newspaper man in San Francisco, in attempting to coin a word to designate a gang of young street Arabs under the beck of one named Muldoon, hit upon the idea of dubbing them *noodlums* — that is, simply reversing the leader's name. In writing the word, the strokes of the *n* did not correspond

in height, and the compositor, taking the *n* for an *h*, printed it *hoodlum*." But this is only too plainly fanciful. Barrère and Leland, in their Dictionary of Slang, Jargon and Cant; London, 1889, described the word as " probably of Spanish origin," but then added: " It may possibly be the Pidgin English *hood lahnt*, good, *i.e.*, very lazy; *lahnt'o*, mandarin." This is also incredible.

3 *Scram*, April, 1938, pp. 152–53.

4 Charles Sealsfield's Americanisms, *American Speech*, Feb., 1941, p. 27. I am told by Dr. M. J. Bach, for many years London correspondent of the *Wiener Neue Freie Presse*, that in the years before 1848 *Ja-Ja-Manderl* was Viennese slang for docile marchers in political parades.

that the influence of German on American English has been rather underestimated. It shows itself, he says, not only in vocabulary but also in idiom. He adds:

> It is doubtful, however, whether such influence as German has exercised over American idiom is wholly, or even mainly, to be attributed to immigration from Germany. It is more likely to be a by-product of the fact that, for more than a single generation, the only Americans who studied abroad studied in Germany.[1] Accordingly, the literary style of many American scholars, teachers and writers came to be affected by German rather than English practice.[2]

A number of German terms are still in common use among Americans of the learned faculties, *e.g.*, *arbeit*, designating a scientific enterprise, and *fach*, meaning a specialty. The influence of German is also shown in the vocabulary of American musicians, *e.g.*, in *concert-master*, from *konzertmeister*. This term is not listed by the DAE, but the NED Supplement's first example, dated 1889, is from an American source. The English commonly use *leader*.[3] The use of *German* as an adjective has made Americanisms since the Eighteenth Century. The DAE traces *German corn* (rye) to 1741, *German Lutheran* to 1799, *German Reformed* (church) to 1812, *German cotillion* to 1839, *German Methodist* to 1849, *German* (from *German cotillion*) to 1863, *German Jew* to 1865, and *German-American* to 1880.[4]

1 The first to do so was Edward Everett (1794–1865), who entered Göttingen in 1815. He was followed by many others, and the stream ran high until 1914. Even those Americans who did not study in Germany were strongly influenced by German ideas, *e.g.*, Emerson. See George Bancroft, Brahmin Rebel, by Russel B. Nye; New York, 1944, pp. 33 ff.
2 American Variations, *S.P.E. Tract No. XLV*, 1936, pp. 176–77.
3 The influence of Germans on the musical life of the United States has been recounted more than once. I take the following from Editorial Notes, *Putnam's Monthly*, May, 1854, p. 564: "We do not regard the Ethiopian opera [*i.e.*, the minstrel show] and the popularity of Old Folks at Home as proof of a general musical taste. At the concerts of the Philharmonic Society at least half of the audience is German."

4 Beside the works already cited, the bibliography includes The German Influence on the English Vocabulary, by Charles T. Carr, *S.P.E. Tract No. XXLII*, 1934; Germany's Contribution to the English Vocabulary, by Harold G. Carlson, *Words*, May, 1937, pp. 114–16; Some Notes on German Loan Words in English, by Charles T. Carr, *Modern Language Review*, Jan., 1940, pp. 69–71; and German Influence on the English Vocabulary of the Nineteenth Century, by Edward Taube, *Journal of English and Germanic Philology*, Oct., 1940, pp. 486–93. In Feb., 1935, p. 69, *American Speech* noticed Studien über den deutschen Einfluss auf das amerikanische Englisch, by R. M. Stone, a dissertation submitted for the doctorate at Marburg in 1934. So far as I know, it has not been translated.

The influence of Yiddish upon American has been felt mainly in the New York area, and many of its contributions to the vocabulary are of German origin, *e.g., gefilte-fish, phooey (pfui), kibitzer,*[1] *schul* (the German word for school, but used to designate a synagogue in Yiddish), *dreck* (garment-workers' term for an inferior dress), *schlag* (of the same general meaning),[2] *schnorrer* (a beggar), and perhaps also the phrases *so what?, for why?,*[3] and *something else again.* Contrariwise, German brought in a number of Yiddish terms before Yiddish became one of the principal languages of New York, *e.g., ganov* (a thief), *kosher, mashuggah, mazuma,*[4] and *tochos.*[5] I heard all of them used by German schoolmasters in Baltimore, *c.* 1888. In the early days of Hitler the Nazis made some effort to purge German of these words, but apparently it was a failure. Dr. A. A. Roback, in an interesting survey of the Yiddishisms current in New

1 For the following I am indebted to Dr. M. J. Bach, before cited: "*Kibitzer* was born, not amongst the Jews, but in the old Austrian Army. Count Karl Schoenfeld (1828–66) left a manuscript of reminiscences, the first part of which, Ein Ordonnanzoffizier Radetskys, was published in 1909. In this he tells how, during the Italian campaign of 1848–49, he was a member of the *Adjutantenkorps* under General Haizinger, and how the latter had a little dog called *Kiebitz*, meaning a plover, and how the officers of the line jocularly called those of the *Adjutantenkorps Kiebitze*. *Kiebitz* soon became a slang word for anyone who merely looks on at the game, and from the army it spread to the cafés of Vienna." The connection, of course, arose from the fact that, to line officers, staff officers seem to be mere onlookers. In a newspaper article, Feb. 13, 1935, noted in *American Speech*, April, 1935, p. 128, Ely Culbertson reported two variations of *kibitizer – dorbitzer*, signifying "one who has asked and received the permission of the *kibitzers* to join them," and *tsitser*, meaning "one who has asked permission of no one" and whose rights "are restricted to hovering in the background and expressing himself by *Ts! ts! ts!*" In *Lighting Fixtures and*

*Lighting*, Feb., 1927, p. 70, I find *kibitzee*, designating a player *kibitzed*. *Kibitzer* has passed to England, as witness Bridge, by A. E. Manning Foster, London *Observer*, Aug. 2, 1936: "It was decided to allow *kibitzers* who pay for admission."

2 For the last two see Consumer Vocabulary, *American Speech*, Feb., 1933, p. 80.

3 Both *so what?* and *for why?* are also in use in England. I find the latter, for example, in Peter Howard's column in the London *Sunday Express*, May 1, 1938, and in an office ad of the *Daily Express*, June 25, 1936. *So What?* was the title of a book by an Englishman, Charles Landery, published in London in 1938. In *Saturday Night* (Toronto), Feb. 5, 1944, p. 9, it appears in an advertisement of the National Trust Company, Ltd., over the signature of J. M. MacDonnell, the president thereof, who is a member of the bar and a former Rhodes scholar. I am indebted here to Mr. J. Ragnar Johnson of Calgary.

4 *Mazuma*, by H. Heshin, *American Speech*, May, 1926, p. 456.

5 Sometimes written, incorrectly, *tokos, tokus, tochus* or *dokus*. The *ch* should have the sound in the German *ich*. I am indebted here to Dr. C. A. Rubenstein of Baltimore.

York, points out that most of them have come in on the lower levels of speech. He says:

> The majority of such locutions are slang, and quite a few find a place in the underworld vocabularies. Numerous expressions derived from the Yiddish constitute the backbone of commercial lingo. There is an auction jewelry jargon as well as a furniture jargon and a shoe business cant. . . . [Yiddish] has not been able to influence literary English yet, simply because, as a rule, Yiddish-speaking people do not move in higher society, and if they do they find no need to resort to foreign phrases or expressions.[1]

Most of the Yiddishisms in the cant of criminals were not introduced by Jewish immigrants to the United States: they go back to the Europe of the Middle Ages, and Martin Luther called attention to them so long ago as 1528 in his introduction to a reprint of Gerold Edilbach's " Liber Vagatorum," the first dictionary of thieves' jargon ever compiled.[2] The first such compilation in English, published in 1698,[3] contained several, *e.g., gelt*, and there were more in Grose's " Classical Dictionary of the Vulgar Tongue," 1785. Partridge says that variations of *ganov* have been current among English criminals since *c.* 1835. The contributions of Yiddish to trade argots have been mainly in the trades dominated by Jews. That of the retail furniture salesmen, for example, contains the following terms, most of them originally German:

> Macher (from *machen*, to make, to effect, to perform). A boaster.
> Momser (bastard). A general term of opprobrium.
> Schlepp (from *schleppen*, to move, to drag). To move furniture about on the sales floor.
> Schmeer (from *schmieren*, to smear, to grease). To flatter a customer.
> Schmiss (a blow). To break off a sale.
> Tzorris. Trouble caused by a complaining customer, or one in default on his instalment payments.[4]

Shoe salesmen have a similar lingo, and it includes a number of the terms used by the furniture salesman. One of its gems is *T.L.*, from *tochos lekker* (backside kisser), signifying a salesman who tries to

---

1 You Speak Yiddish, Too! *Better English*, Feb., 1938, p. 50.
2 The first edition was published at Augsburg in 1512 or thereabout. Luther's edition was published at Wittenberg. The material in the book was mainly derived from the records of a series of trials of rogues and vagabonds at Basel in 1475.

3 The Dictionary of the Canting Crew. The author signed himself B. E., and his identity has not been established.
4 I take these from Furniture Lingo, by Charles Miller, *American Speech*, Dec., 1930, pp. 125–28.

ingratiate himself with the boss.[1] Other argots showing Yiddish influence are those of department-store salesmen and grind-shop auctioneers.[2] Julius G. Rothenberg has called attention to the fact [3] that not a few of the words and phrases thus borrowed have, in the original, a more or less obscene significance, *e.g.*, *to futz around, A.K.* (from *alte kacker*), *yentzer* and *pisher*. He says that *canary*, often heard in New York in such phrases as " He's giving me a *canary*," is derived from the German *kein* (no) and the Hebrew *ayin* (eye) and *harrah* (evil), and that it thus alludes to the evil eye. Dr. Roback, in the paper lately cited, argues for the Yiddish origin of a number of familiar American phrases, *e.g.*, *I should worry, give me a ring, I'm telling you* and *it's all right by me*.[4] A number of Yiddishisms in use in the New York area are understood by a great many non-Jews, *e.g.*, *mazuma* (money), *kosher* (ritually clean), *trefa* (ritually unclean), *goy* (a non-Jew), *shadchen* (a marriage-broker), *shmus* (idle talk), *bar-mitsva* (the Jewish confirmation ceremony for boys), *ganov* (a thief), *mashuggah* (crazy), *blintzes* (a savory dish), *matzoth* (unleavened bread), *schnozzle* (a large nose), *shochet* (a ritual butcher), *shofar* (a ram's horn blown in the synagogue on solemn holidays), *mohel* (one licensed to perform circumcision), *tochos* (the backside), *yentser* (a cheat), *mazzaltov* (good luck), *momser* (a bastard), *shikse* (a Christian woman), *sheitel* (a woman's wig), *kishkes* (the intestines), *borshtsh* (sour beet soup), *minyan* (the synagogue quorum of ten men), *gefilte fish* (stuffed fish), *lokschen* (noodles), *mechulle* (bankrupt), *menora* (a candlestick), *schnorrer* (a beggar or chisler), *schlemihl* (a ne'er-do-well), *shabbath* (Sabbath), *shalom alechem* (peace be with you), and *yehudi* (a Jew). Some of them have become so far naturalized that they are often given the English *-s* in the plural instead of the Hebrew *-im*, *e.g.*, *shochets* instead of *shochtim*.[5]

1 See Lingo of the Shoe Salesman, by David Geller, *American Speech*, Dec., 1934, pp. 283–86. This paper includes a glossary compiled by J. S. Fox. See also Shoe-store Terms, by Erik I. Bromberg, *American Speech*, April, 1938, p. 150, and Shoe-store Shop-talk Language of Its Own, New York *Herald Tribune*, July 3, 1936, p. 6.

2 For the former see Department-store Technical Expressions, *American Speech*, Dec., 1938, pp. 312–13.

For the latter see Jewelry Auction Jargon, by Fred Witman, *American Speech*, June, 1928, pp. 375–76.

3 Some American Idioms From the Yiddish, *American Speech*, Feb., 1943, pp. 43–48.

4 A Yiddish popular song often sung in 1938 was Bei Mir Bist Du Scheen (By Me You Are Beautiful).

5 I am indebted for help with this Yiddish section to the late Dr. Isaac Goldberg, Dr. Carl Manello of Youngstown, O., Mr. Harry B.

"We may take it as a fixed rule," said Engelbrecht Kaempfer in his "History of Japan,"[1] "that the settlement of foreigners in a country will bring a corresponding proportion of foreign words into the language; these will be naturalized by degrees, and become as familiar as the native words themselves." The truth of this is well demonstrated by the foregoing record. Every fresh wave of immigrants has brought in new loan-words, and some of them have become so thoroughly imbedded in the language that they have lost their air of foreignness, and are used to make derivatives as freely as native words, *e.g.*, *peonage* (from the Spanish *peon*, traced by the DAE to 1849), *spaghetti-joint*, the *turkeymallie* lately noticed, and *to stevedore*, from the noun (Spanish *estivador*, a stower of cargo). Not infrequently naturalization brings in a change in meaning, as when the Spanish *silo*, signifying an underground chamber for the storage of grain, came to mean, in the United States, an aboveground structure in which green crops are fermented, and *rodeo*, originally a cattle round-up, was transferred to an exhibition of cowboy tricks. *Alfalfa*, also from the Spanish, is not an Americanism, but only in the United States has it picked up such connotations as are to be seen in *Alfalfa Bill*.[2] As I have noted in Chapter IV, Section 3, American has probably made more loans from the Spanish than from any other language. They are, indeed, coming in all the time, *e.g.*, *hoosegow*, which was unheard of in 1900; *politico*, which has come into vogue within the past twenty years,[3] and *wah-wah*, first reported in 1941.[4] There are other belated loans from other immigrant languages,

Winkeler of St. Louis, Mrs. Louis Silverman of Baltimore, the late Dr. William A. Rosenau of Baltimore, Mr. B. G. Kayfetz of Toronto, Mr. Garrett Oppenheim of New York, Mr. Charles Lam Markmann of New York, Mr. Harry G. Green of Chicago, Dr. John Whyte of Brooklyn, and Dr. J. S. Slotkin of Madison, Wis. The best vocabulary of Yiddishisms that I know of is in Wonder Words, by Benjamin L. Winfield; New York, 1933. A briefer glossary is in So Help Me, by George Jessel; New York, 1943, pp. 228–29. Yidische Oisdrukn in Amerikaner English, by M. Hurvitz, *Yivo Bleter* (New York), 1934, pp. 187–88, is a discussion of Yiddish loans in American, written in Yiddish.

1 Kaempfer (1651–1716) was a German doctor who entered the Dutch service and traveled extensively in the Far East. The MS. of his History of Japan was translated into English by J. G. Scheuchzer and published in London in 1727. The original German was not published until 1777.

2 The nickname of William H. Murray, Governor of Oklahoma, 1931–35. He gives it in parentheses in his autobiography in Who's Who in America. *Alfalfa*, up to *c.* 1850, was usually called *lucern*.

3 The Living Language, by Dwight L. Bolinger, *Words*, Jan., 1938, p. 14.

4 The Spelling of *wa-wa* or *wah-wah*, by Mary Elizabeth Fox, *American Speech*, Oct., 1941, p. 240.

notably the Swedish *smörgåsbord,* which has been taken in since World War I, with the loss of its diacritical marks.[1] Even the Indian languages have not ceased to yield tribute, as the case of *chautauqua* shows.[2] From French there is a continual borrowing, *e.g., brassière,* which did not appear until *c.* 1910. The DAE traces the Italian *macaroni* in American use to 1802, and *spaghetti* has been familiar since the 80s, but *ravioli* is so recent that it is not listed. *Policy* (from Italian *polizza*) is traced to 1851, and apparently first appeared in England. It is now obsolete, having been supplanted by *numbers.* The DAE first records *policy-ticket* in 1872, *policy-dealer* in 1875, *policy-backer* and *to play policy* in 1882 and *policy-shop* in 1899.[3]

The contributions of Chinese to the American vocabulary are few in number, and most of them are confined to the Pacific Coast and its immediate hinterland. *Chow* is not listed by the DAE, and the NED Supplement traces it no farther back than 1886. It is Pidgin English and was probably brought to the United States by Chinese immigrants at the time of the gold rush, for *chow-chow* (the condiment) is recorded for 1852. *Chow* has never got above the status of slang, but *chow-chow* is in perfectly respectable usage. It reached England by 1857. *Chow-mein, chop-suey* and *yok-a-mi* are all overlooked by the DAE, but most Americans are familiar with them. Webster 1934 says that *chow-mein* means, primarily, a fried noodle, and is derived from the Chinese words *ch'ao,* to fry, and *mien,* flour. It has come to designate a thick stew of chicken, mushrooms and savories, with fried noodles added. *Chop-suey* is described by Webster as " a mélange . . . consisting typically of bean sprouts, onions, mushrooms, etc., and sliced meats, fried and flavored with sesame oil." The term represents a Cantonese pronunciation of the standard Chinese *tsa-sui,* meaning miscellaneous pieces. The NED Supplement traces *chop-suey* in American use to 1904, but it is probably older. Regarding *yok-a-mi* I can find nothing in the authorities. *Fan-tan* is not listed by the DAE, but the first English example given by the NED Supplement is dated 1878, and the game was well known in California at least twenty years before. *Joss* and its derivations got

1 *Smorgasbord, lutfisk, lefse,* by E. G. Johnson, *Saturday Review of Literature,* July 20, 1940, p. 9.
2 As a proper noun, designating a lake in New York, it goes back to 1749, but as a common noun it is not recorded before 1884. See The Word

*Chautauqua,* by J. R. Schultz, *American Speech,* Oct., 1934, pp. 232-33.
3 Why Should Not This *Policy* as Well be Called Spinach?, by Charles Wyer, New York *Sun,* Sept. 3, 1938.

into English in the Eighteenth Century, but they seem to have been taken into American independently. The DAE traces *joss* in American use to 1873, and *joss-house* and *joss-stick* to 1871. *Tong*, which is marked an Americanism by the DAE, came in in the early 80s and was soon followed by *tong-war*. *Highbinder* is not a loan from the Chinese. It was first used in 1806 to designate a variety of gangster then in practise in New York, and was not applied to Chinese until the late 70s. Two of the Chinese loans in use only in California and thereabout are *yuen*, a vegetable garden, and *egg-fuyong*, a popular dish.[1] The Chinese, it should not be forgotten, also contributed one of the most pungent American proverbs: *No checkee, no shirtee*.

The other immigrant languages have contributed very little to the American vocabulary, save in areas of high immigration density. It is the custom on the Pacific Coast to ascribe to Japanese any strange word that cannot be ascribed to Chinook, but it is seldom that plausible evidence is forthcoming. The Japanese etymologies proposed, for example, for *hobo* and *hunky-dory* are far from persuasive. *Tycoon* was brought in by the Perry expedition of 1852–54 and seems to have come into use in the United States before the English became aware of it. It was used as an affectionate nickname for Abraham Lincoln by the members of his secretariat, and has been worked to death in recent years by *Time*. *Hara-kiri* first appeared in *Harper's Magazine* in 1856,[2] and *jiu-jitsu* seems to have been introduced by Lafcadio Hearn in 1891, but *geisha* (1887), *jinricksha* (1874), followed by *rickshaw* (1886), *kimono* (1887) and *soy-bean* (1802) came to the United States by way of England.[3] In the Scandinavian regions of the Middle West a number of Swedish and Dano-Norwegian terms have come into wide use, but most of them show no sign of entering the general

1 The *Idaho Statesman* (Boise), July 23, 1939, described *yuen* as "an important word in the history of Boise Valley and Southern Idaho. . . . Chinese gardeners began feeding the miners more than half a century ago. They're still feeding the miners, the bankers, and the general public. . . . *Yuens* of the present day are, for the most part, operated by the children, grandchildren and great-grandchildren of the original gardeners."

2 It is often turned into *hari-kari*. For its etymology and true spelling see A Distorted Japanese Word, by

Eston Everett Ericson, *American Speech*, Dec., 1936, pp. 371–72.

3 A long list of Japanese words that are more or less understood in England and the United States is in The Influence of Japanese on English, by E. V. Gatenby, *Studies in English Literature* (Tokyo), Vol. XI, 1931, pp. 508–20, and in Additions to Japanese Words in English, by the same, Oct. 1934, pp. 595–609. The loans used to designate Japanese in California are discussed in Chapter VI, Section 6.

vocabulary. Some Swedish examples are given in AL4, p. 215. Dano-Norwegian examples are *gubbefest,* which is used in Minnesota to designate a men's party,[1] and *lefsi,* " a mixture of white flour, salt, water and baking-powder," served with unsweetened coffee as a " mid-morning, mid-afternoon and midnight refreshment." [2] The Czech *koláč,* in the transliterated form of *kolach,* has got into Webster: it means " a kind of small tart usually round (*kolo,* a wheel or circle), made with a variant of bread dough, and filled or topped, before baking, with jam or preserve." [3] Similar loans have been made from the Finnish in North Dakota, the Portuguese in Massachusetts,[4] the Polish in Chicago and Buffalo,[5] and the Russian in the parts of Kansas settled by Russian-Germans.[6]

---

1 I am indebted here to Mr. Carl B. Costello of Duluth, Minn.

2 Norsk Novelties by M. Mattison, *American Speech,* April, 1934, p. 152.

3 I take this from Czech Influence Upon the American Vocabulary, by J. B. Dudek, *Czecho-Slovak Student Life* (Lisle, Ill.), June, 1928, p. 12. Monsignor Dudek goes on: " The favorite filling is a typical Czech marmalade made of dried prunes and known as *povidla.* Sometimes curd, sweetened and flavored, or a cinnamon and sugar mixture, is used; another filling, which however has not proved acceptable to the American palate, is boiled poppy seeds,

highly sweetened." See also AL4, p. 216.

4 AL4, p. 216.

5 Poland Is Not Yet Lost, by Ralph Lane, *American Speech,* April, 1940, pp. 209–10.

6 Russian Words in Kansas, by G. D. C., *Dialect Notes,* Vol. IV, Part II, 1914, pp. 161–62. The Indian loans used by anthropologists in describing Indian artifacts and cultural patterns are listed in Some Anthropological Terms Used in the Southwest, by T. M. Pearce, *El Palachio* (Santa Fe, N. Mex.), June, 1943, pp. 130–41.

# VI

# AMERICAN AND ENGLISH

## 1. THE INFILTRATION OF ENGLISH BY AMERICANISMS

223. Sir William Craigie, editor of the Dictionary of American English and one of the editors of the New English Dictionary, is authority for the statement that the infiltration of English by Americanisms began on a large scale more than a hundred years ago. He says:

> For some two centuries, roughly down to 1820, the passage of new words or senses across the Atlantic was regularly westward; practically the only exceptions were terms which denoted articles or products peculiar to the new country. With the Nineteenth Century, however, the contrary current begins to set in, bearing with it many a piece of driftwood to the shores of Britain, there to be picked up and incorporated in the structure of the language. The variety of these contributions is no less notable than their number.[1]

Sir William then proceeds to list some of the principal categories of these adopted Americanisms, as follows:

> 1. "There are terms which owe their origin to the fresh conditions and experiences of the new country," *e.g.*, *backwoods, blizzard, bluff, canyon, dug-out, Indian-file, prairie, squatter.*
> 2. "There are terms of politics and public activity," *e.g.*, *carpet-bagger, caucus, gerrymander, indignation-meeting, lynch-law.*
> 3. "There are words and phrases connected with business pursuits, trades, and manufactures," *e.g.*, *cross-cut saw, elevator, snow-plow, to corner, to strike oil.*
> 4. There is "a large residue of miscellaneous examples," *e.g.*, *at that, to take a back seat, boss, to cave in, cold snap, to face the music, grave-yard, to go back on, half-breed, lengthy, loafer, law-abiding, whole-souled.*

How many such Americanisms have actually got into accepted English it would be impossible to say, for on that point there is sharp disagreement among Englishmen. But a large number have become so thoroughly naturalized that the English dictionaries no longer mark

[1] The Study of American English, *S.P.E. Tract No. XXVII;* 1927, p. 208.

them aliens, and even the most intransigent Englishmen have ceased to denounce them, *e.g.*, *reliable, lengthy, prairie, caucus* and *bluff.* Others still have the sharp tang of novelty and are avoided by all persons careful of their speech, and in the middle between these two extremes there is a vast twilight zone of Americanisms that have more or less current popularity but may or may not find lodgment in the vocabulary hereafter. In the early days the chief exchanges in both directions were on the upper levels of usage, and most of the Americanisms adopted in England were sponsored on this side of the ocean by such men as Jefferson, John Adams, J. Fenimore Cooper and Noah Webster, but since the beginning of the present century the chief English borrowings have been from American slang. It is generally agreed by English observers that American movies have been mainly responsible for this shift, but it is not to be forgotten that the American comic-strip and American pulp-magazines have also had a powerful influence, and that the American popular humorists of the post-Civil War era opened the way long before movies, comic-strips or pulp-magazines were thought of.[1] When the silent movies began to be supplanted by talkies many hopeful Englishmen rejoiced, for they believed that the American accent would be unendurable to their countrymen, that English-made talkies would thus prevail over those from Hollywood, and that the inundation of Americanisms would be stayed at last. But this hope turned out to be in vain, for the Hollywood producers quickly trained their performers to speak what passed sufficiently as English, and in a little while they were deluging the English plain people with even more and much worse Americanisms than had ever appeared in the legends on the silent films.[2] The battle

1 See AL4, p. 224. Says H. W. Seaman (private communication, May 9, 1944): "Hard-boiled fiction from America has influenced English speech and writing. The boys' papers have heroes who speak as nearly American as the authors can manage to make them."

2 At the start they were upset more or less by the objurgations in the English newspapers, and made some effort to placate English prejudices. When a talkie called No! No! Napoleon was under way in 1929 *Variety* reported (July 10, p. 15) that it was being done in both an "American version" and an "English translation." The sentence, "A *nut-factory*, eh?," was translated into "A *madhouse*, eh?," and "I've been *framed*" was converted into "This is a *put-up job*." This spirit of concession was well received by the English cinema magnates, and one of them contributed an article to the London *Star* on Feb. 4, 1930 in which he expressed the opinion that the day of American slang in England was over. "English actors of both sexes," he reported, "are being employed in ever increasing number, and a superior type of American

between English and American talkies that ensued came to highly significant issues in both countries. In England the commonalty rejoiced in the new influx of American neologisms and soon adopted large numbers of them, but in America the movie fans refused to tolerate the pseudo-Oxford accent and frequent Briticisms of the English actors,[1] and in consequence the English films, with relatively few exceptions, failed dismally. Simultaneously, the educated classes in England resented and resisted the American talkies, and the Anglomaniacs of the United States welcomed the English talkies with colonial enthusiasm. The educated Englishmen, always powerful in their government, procured the enactment of laws limiting the importation of American films,[2] and carried on a violent war upon them in the newspapers, but the English middle and lower classes found them perfectly satisfying, and soon the Americanisms they introduced in such large number were in wide use, and many began to penetrate to the higher levels of speech.[3] In the linguistic interchanges between England and the United States this curious dichotomy has been witnessed for a long while. Americanisms get into

---

artist is being engaged who has the culture and ability to acquire English cadences and intonations." But Hollywood's reform did not last long. In a little while its producers discovered that the English fans, at least on the lower orders, really enjoyed and esteemed American slang, so *nut-factory, to frame* and many congeners were restored to use, and the "superior type of American artist" was displaced by the traditional recruits from the ten-cent stores and barbecue-stands.

1 Hollywood *Reporter*, quoted in Language Trouble, by Stephen Watts, London *Sunday Express*, Nov. 20, 1938: "It's next to impossible for Americans to understand an English accent on the screen." A very typical American's difficulties with the speech of actors on the London stage will be recalled by readers of Sinclair Lewis's Dodsworth. See Dodsworth's Dilemma, *Nation* (New York), May 29, 1929, p. 638.

2 See AL4, p. 38, n. 1.

3 "If half the members of a talkie audience," said a contributor to the Liverpool *Daily Courier*, signing himself H. W. S., on Sept. 4, 1929, "shudder every time a character on the screen says 'Get a *load* of this' or 'It's *in the bag*,' the other half make a mental note of the expression for future use. I can offer no hope to the professors who think that talkies in pure English prose and verse would stem the American tide; for every such professor there are a thousand talkie-goers to whom American has become almost as intelligible as English, and more attractive because of its novelty. There has never been a talkie in pure English prose and verse, and there never will be. American has made such headway, even among its opponents, that there is hardly a modern English play that does not contain half a dozen phrases of American origin, and it is almost impossible to write a defense of English without using a locution or two that ten years ago would have been recognizable as American but now has become common English usage."

English use on the lower levels and then work their way upward, but nearly all the Briticisms that reach the United States first appear on the levels of cultural pretension, and most of them stay there, for the common people will have none of them.

As we have already seen in Chapter I, Section 4, the old English battle against the American invasion, which began violently in the closing years of the Eighteenth Century and raged on with frequent bursts of fury for more than a hundred years, has now begun to abate, and a considerable number of Englishmen appear to be convinced that the American tail is destined to wag the English dog hereafter; indeed, there are plenty who try to convince themselves that the inevitable is also the agreeable, and had better be enjoyed as much as possible. It seems to be generally agreed that nothing can be done, short of pumping up a war with the United States, to shut off the flow of Americanisms, at all events on the lower levels of the population. Nor has anyone devised any plausible scheme to keep them from penetrating upward. English newspapers, even the most stiff-necked, admit them constantly and in large number, they are eagerly seized upon by native imitators of the American comic-strips,[1] advertisement writers make eager use of them, and it becomes the sign of *bonhomie* for politicians and other public entertainers to play with them, albeit they usually do so somewhat ponderously, as will appear. Such familiar Americanisms as *chain-store, can* (for *tin*), *to rattle, to put across, back number, boom, crook, to feature, filling-station, O.K., mass-meeting, up against* and *up to* have now become so familiar in England too that it is no longer necessary to interpret them, and many others, perhaps to the number of thousands, seem destined to make the grade hereafter. So late as 1932 the New York correspondent of the London *Observer*[2] was at pains to explain that *hot-dogs* were "broiled sausages in split rolls," but since then the austere London *Times* has given its countenance to *high-brow*, the *Daily Express* has quite nonchalantly characterized the chaplain to a bishop as a *fence-sitter*,[3] the eminent *News of the World* has adopted *gate-crasher*,[4] the Birkenhead *Advertiser* has given its imprimatur to

1 For example, I find *all set* in the caption of a drawing in *John Bull*, and *to knock his block off* in a cartoon in the Glasgow *Record*.

2 The Democratic "Vaudeville," July 3, 1932.

3 The Wrath of the Church, July 14, 1936.

4 Precautions Against *Gate-Crashers* at Ascot, June 12, 1938.

*to scram*,[1] the Air Ministry has used *hooch* in a warning to the gentlemen of the R.A.F.,[2] Gilbert Frankau has printed a moving defense of *lousy*,[3] and Edward Shanks has gone earnestly to the bat for *alibi*, in the American sense of any dubious excuse.[4] The list of such yieldings and embracings might be lengthened greatly. New Americanisms are being taken in all the time, sometimes with a time lag, sometimes with a change (or, more accurately, a misunderstanding) of meaning, but usually very promptly and in their native sense. The English newspapers frequently report and philosophize upon a recent novelty, and usually they advise their readers to avoid it, but most of them seem to be convinced that stemming the influx has now become hopeless. In 1935 a contributor to a sedate provincial paper attempted a round-up of the Americanisms " that we constantly employ," including some " that we hardly recognize as of American origin, so rooted in standard English have they become." [5] Under the letters from H to O his list showed the following:

| | |
|---|---|
| half-baked | happy hunting-ground [11] |
| halfbreed [6] | hash, to settle his [12] |
| hand it to him (verb) [7] | have the floor (verb) |
| hang out (verb) [8] | have the goods on [13] |
| handy [9] | hayseed [14] |
| happen in (verb) [10] | |

1 Brevity and Punch, Oct. 10, 1942.
2 R.A.F. Check on *Hooch* Drinking, London *Daily Mail*, Jan. 21, 1942.
3 London *Daily Mail*, July 21, 1938. The *Mail's* headline on his article was Gilbert Frankau *Puts One Over*.
4 *Alibi*, London *Sunday Times*, Oct. 23, 1938. On March 9, 1940 the Manchester *Guardian* condemned the use of the term in " a well known paper," but had to admit that it was " being more and more used to cover any sort of explanation." " The meanings of words," it observed sadly, " sometimes become distorted because newspapers look for lively terms that will mean much and be short enough for headlines."
5 Later American Word-Imports, by A. H. C., IV, Forres *Gazette*, Nov. 6, 1935.
6 Traced by the DAE to 1761 and marked an Americanism.
7 Partridge says that this phrase was naturalized in England by 1930.
8 The DAE does not list this verb-phrase, but it traces *to hang around* (or *round*) to 1847.
9 *Handy* is to be found in Thomas Fuller's once-famous book, A Pisgah-Sight of Palestine, 1650, but it fell out of use in England and was reintroduced from America.
10 First used by J. Fenimore Cooper in Homeward Bound, 1838. *To happen along* is also an Americanism.
11 Apparently introduced by J. Fenimore Cooper in The Pathfinder, 1840.
12 Traced by the DAE to 1809. Thornton says that the phrase " may have been learned by the English in the War of 1812."
13 Partridge credits this verb-phrase to New Zealand, but offers no evidence.
14 In the sense of a yokel. The DAE's first example is dated 1892, but the term must be much older. *To get the hayseed out of one's hair* is traced to 1840.

| | |
|---|---|
| headed for disaster [1] | hold-up [11] |
| headlight [2] | home-folks |
| head off (verb) [3] | homely |
| head-on (collision) | homesick [12] |
| help (servant) | homespun [13] |
| he-man [4] | honk (verb) [14] |
| hike, hiker | hook, one's own [15] |
| hard-boiled (in the figurative sense) | hoot, to care a [16] |
| highfalutin [5] | horse-sense [17] |
| high old time [6] | house-keep (verb) |
| hitch (verb, usually with *up*) [7] | house-clean (verb) |
| hitched (married) [8] | hunch [18] |
| hobble (verb) [9] | hurry up |
| holding company | hustler, to hustle [19] |
| hold on (imperative) [10] | |

1 The DAE traces *to head for* to 1835 and marks it an Americanism.

2 The DAE's first example is dated 1864.

3 The DAE traces *to head off* to 1841 and marks it an Americanism.

4 This excellent term is not listed by the DAE. Partridge says that it came into general use in England *c.* 1930.

5 Recorded by Bartlett in 1848. "This word," he said, "is in common use in the West, and bids fair to spread over the country. There can be little doubt of its derivation from *high-flinging*." Webster 1934 suggests that *highflown* may have had some influence on it.

6 The DAE does not list this phrase, but Partridge says that it originated in the United States before 1869, and began to be used in England in 1883.

7 Traced by the DAE to 1817 and marked an Americanism.

8 *Hitched* is traced by the DAE to 1847. It has never been used save humorously in the United States.

9 Not of American origin, but in much more frequent use in the United States than in England.

10 Traced to 1835 in the United States and to 1867 in England.

11 In the sense of a check or obstruction the DAE traces *hold-up* to 1837, and in the sense of a robbery at the point of a gun to 1878. In both senses the term is an Americanism, as are the corresponding adjective and verb.

12 The writer says: "The earliest recorded use of this adjective is American." That is not true. It appeared in England in 1756 as a translation of the German *heimweh*. It is often stated that English is the only language having a word of the meaning of *home*. This is nonsense. The German *heim* is its exact equivalent, and both come from the same Old Germanic root. The NED traces *home* to *c.* 950.

13 An old English word that went out in England but survived in America.

14 Originally, the sound made by a wild goose, noted by Boucher in 1800, but apparently not in general use until *c.* 1850. It was first applied to the sound of an automobile horn in 1906.

15 The DAE traces *on one's own hook* to 1812 and marks it an Americanism. It was used by Thackeray in Pendennis, 1849, and Partridge says that it is now naturalized in England.

16 Partridge says that this phrase came into English use *c.* 1905.

17 The DAE traces *horse-sense* to 1832 and marks it an Americanism.

18 This is not an Americanism, but after long desuetude it seems to have been reintroduced to England from America. Partridge says that the Canadian soldiers made it popular in 1916.

19 These terms are old in English, but they came to their present vogue in the United States, and returned to England as Americanisms. **Partridge**

Indian Summer
influential
inside [1]
interview
iron out (verb)
it [2]
jack-knife [3]
jam [4]
jay-walker
jazz
jell (verb) [5]
jeopardize [6]
jiggered [7]
joker (in card games) [8]
jolly (verb) [9]

joy-ride
jugged (jailed) [10]
jumping-off place [11]
jump on with both feet
junk (in the sense of refuse) [12]
just [13]
keep company with [14]
keep tabs on [15]
keep your shirt on [16]
key man
kick (as in " something with a *kick* in it ")
kick the bucket [17]
kid (verb) [18]
kitchenette
knickers

says that they became naturalized *c.* 1905 and are now " almost Standard English."

[1] As in *inside twenty-four hours.* Traced by the DAE to 1877.

[2] In the sense of a person of the first importance. Partridge says that the English borrowed the term from the United States *c.* 1910. The use of *it* in group games also seems to be American. An authority on games, cited by the DAE, says that in England the player who is *it* " is sometimes called *he.*" See Toys and Games, by W. Macqueen-Pope, London *Times Literary Supplement,* March 25, 1944, p. 151.

[3] Traced by the DAE to 1711 and marked an Americanism.

[4] In such phrases as *to be jam up against.* Traced by the DAE to 1842 and marked an Americanism.

[5] The DAE traces this back-formation to 1869 and marks it an Americanism.

[6] See AL4, pp. 121, 141 and 165.

[7] The writer lists *jiggered* as meaning " put in order." Where he picked it up I do not know: it is certainly not American. *Jigger,* in the sense of a measure of strong drink, is an Americanism, traced by the DAE to 1836.

[8] The DAE's earliest example is dated 1885, but the term must be considerably older.

[9] The DAE traces *to jolly,* in the sense of to chaff ingratiatingly, to 1890, and marks it an Americanism.

[10] The DAE traces *jug* for jail to 1815, but does not mark it an Americanism, though it probably is.

[11] Traced by the DAE to 1826 and marked an Americanism.

[12] In the sense of old rope or cable *junk* has been in nautical use in England since the Fifteenth Century, but in the American sense the DAE traces it no further back than 1842. There was a time when dealers in marine stores were called *junk-dealers* in this country.

[13] As a general intensive, as in *time just flew.*

[14] Whether or not this is an Americanism remains to be established. Partridge says that it was used in England before 1861, but indicates that it then began to go out. It has always been in much more frequent use in the United States. In England the common phrase is *to walk out with.*

[15] This verb-phrase is old in English, but it seems to have been forgotten, and Partridge says that it was reintroduced from the United States *c.* 1905.

[16] Traced by the DAE to 1854 and marked an Americanism.

[17] This verb-phrase is probably not an Americanism. Grose listed it as English slang in 1785. But it seems to have come into much wider use in the United States than in England, and to most Englishmen it sounds American.

[18] In the sense of to deceive.

knife (verb) [1]
knock about (to wander) [2]
know him like a book
know the ropes [3]
kodak
kow-tow [4]
landslide (political) [5]
laugh in one's sleeve
laugh on me
law-abiding [6]
lemon, to hand him a [7]
lengthy
let it slide [8]
level best [9]
level-headedness [10]
lid on, to put the
limelight, in the
limit ("the last stage of endurance")
lip, to keep a stiff upper [11]

loaf (verb), loafer
lobby (verb)
lounge-lizard
lynch (verb)
machine (political)
mad (angry)
make a get-away [12]
make oneself scarce [13]
make the fur fly [14]
make tracks [15]
mark, easy
mark up (verb)
mass-meeting [16]
medicine, to take your [17]
melon [18]
mending [19]
mileage
mixer (in the social sense) [20]

[1] In the political sense *to knife* is traced by the DAE to 1888 and marked an Americanism.

[2] In the more usual form of *to knock around* this verb-phrase is traced by the DAE to 1877 and marked an Americanism.

[3] The DAE traces *to know the ropes* to 1840 and *to learn the ropes* to 1850, and marks them Americanisms. They apparently come from the language of the sea. Partridge says that *to know the ropes* was accepted as Standard English after 1900.

[4] A loan from the Chinese. See AL4, p. 162.

[5] The DAE's first example is dated 1895, but the term must be older.

[6] The earliest English example of *law-abiding* is dated 1867. The DAE traces it in American use to 1834.

[7] *Lemon*, in the sense of something unattractive, *e.g.*, a homely woman, is not listed by the DAE. Partridge says that it was adopted by the English *c.* 1921.

[8] *To let slide* is old English, but it dropped out in the Seventeenth Century. The DAE shows that it was revived or reinvented in the United States *c.* 1845, and reappeared in England in 1885.

[9] Traced by the DAE to 1851 and marked an Americanism. Partridge

says that it was accepted in England *c.* 1870.

[10] Traced by the DAE to 1888. The adjective *levelheaded* is traced to 1879.

[11] The DAE traces this verb-phrase to 1815 and marks it an Americanism. Partridge says it was not naturalized in Standard English until the Twentieth Century.

[12] Partridge says that this phrase was adopted by the English *c.* 1895.

[13] *To make myself scarce* was used by Smollett in 1749 and by Scott in 1821, but it seems to have dropped out, and Englishmen apparently think of it as an Americanism.

[14] Partridge says that this Americanism, traced by the DAE to 1834, was taken into English *c.* 1860.

[15] The DAE's first example is from J. P. Kennedy's Swallow Barn, 1832. Partridge says that the term was naturalized in England *c.* 1860.

[16] The DAE traces *mass-meeting* to 1842 and marks it an Americanism.

[17] The DAE's first example is dated 1896, but the phrase must be older.

[18] In the sense of a large extra dividend.

[19] In the sense of garments needing mending.

[20] The DAE's first example is from George Ade's Artie, 1896.

| | |
|---|---|
| monkey with (verb) | O.K. |
| mossback | old-timer [5] |
| mutt [1] | one-horse [6] |
| nearby (close at hand) [2] | on the job |
| N.G. [3] | on the level [7] |
| nigger in the woodpile [4] | on the q.t. |
| nothing doing | out for [8] |
| not on your life | overcoat [9] |

This list, obviously, was by no means exhaustive. It might have been doubled in length, or tripled, or even quadrupled without putting any strain on the record. Most of the borrowings of the 1930s were probably on the level of slang, but even on that level many of them were so pungent and useful that they quickly found lodgment. "It is difficult to imagine," wrote Professor Ernest Weekley of Nottingham in 1930,[10] "how we got on so long without the word *stunt*, how we expressed the characters so conveniently summed up in *dope-fiend* and *high-brow*, or any other possible way of describing that mixture of the cheap pathetic and the ludicrous which is now universally labeled *sob-stuff*."[11] Other English philologues of the era were a good deal less hospitable. In 1931 Dr. C. T. Onions, one of the editors of the NED, described it as a "grievance" that English was being "invaded — and degraded — by the current idiom from the United States,"[12] and so late as 1936 he was trying to get rid of that grievance by arguing stoutly that the extent of the invasion was "much exaggerated."[13] But even Dr. Onions had to admit that "a

1 Not listed by the DAE. It has been suggested that it is a clipped form of *muttonhead*, but for this I know no evidence.

2 Marked "chiefly U.S." by the NED.

3 The DAE traces *N.G.* to 1840 and Partridge says that it was naturalized in England by 1890.

4 Traced by the DAE to 1861.

5 *Old-timer* seems to have come in during or immediately after the Civil War.

6 The DAE traces *one-horse*, in the figurative sense of petty or unimportant, to 1854, and *one-horse town* to 1855. Both are marked Americanisms.

7 Traced by the DAE to 1875. Partridge says it was adopted in England by 1905.

8 Traced by the DAE to 1892.

9 Traced by the DAE to 1807 and

marked an Americanism. Until they began to use *overcoat* the English used *greatcoat* or *topcoat*. Both, of course, survive.

10 Adjectives — and Other Words; New York, 1930, p. 182.

11 Of these terms the DAE traces *dope-fiend* to 1896, *stunt* to 1895, but omits *sob-stuff* and *high-brow*. The NED Supplement traces *sob-stuff* to 1920, *sob-story* to the same year, and *sob-sister* to 1927. All are actually older. The NED's first example of *stunt* in the wide sense of any spectacular effort or enterprise is from the United States.

12 Is English Becoming Too American?, London *Evening News*, Nov. 19, 1931.

13 Oxford correspondence of the Hong Kong *Telegraph*, Oct. 6, 1936.

certain proportion of the American language of the film caption "
would " *catch on* [1] and become permanent." He noted that *to put it
across, to get it across,* and *to put it over* [2] were already " firmly
domiciled " in England and apparently " entered upon a large career
of metaphorical use." Other Americanisms that he spoke of politely,
if not enthusiastically, were *bedspread,* [3] *to make good,* [4] *grape-fruit,* [5]
*dope,* [6] *mass-meeting, best girl,* [7] *to fire* (an employé) [8] and *to fizzle
out.* [9] But he refused to have any truck with *to stand for, glad rags*
or *hot squat,* and he described *to spill a bibful* as " tinged with vulgarity." Sir William Craigie made it plain in 1936 that he did not
agree with Dr. Onions that the number of Americanisms taken into
English was " much exaggerated." To the contrary, he told a correspondent of the London *Morning Post* [10] that " current English
contains many more real Americanisms than most people imagine."
Many other authorities, high and low, agreed with him, then and
afterward. " England," wrote Alistair Cooke in 1935, [11] " has been absorbing American words at an unbelievable rate. . . . There are thousands of these borrowings — debts which I am afraid we are never
going to pay back to America. . . . Every Englishman . . . uncon-
sciously uses thirty or forty Americanisms a day, however much he is
opposed to American idiom on principle." In 1936 H. W. Horwill
reported from London in the New York *Times* [12] that the sales of
American books were increasing in England, and ascribed it to the

1 " Is that," he asked in parenthesis,
" an Americanism? "

2 Dr. Onions described all these verb-
phrases as " idioms derived from the
stage footlights." This is possible,
but it seems much more likely that
they really got their vogue in the
United States as baseball terms.

3 Traced by the DAE to *c.* 1845 and
marked an Americanism. It did not
reach England until the late 80s.

4 An old English phrase, revived by
the game of poker in the United
States, traced by the DAE to 1882,
and adopted in England, according
to Partridge, *c.* 1913.

5 First recorded by Bartlett in his second edition, 1859.

6 " The American applications of the
word *dope*," said Onions, " have
generally commended themselves
and have obtained a wide currency."

7 Partridge says that *best girl* appeared in English use *c.* 1890. The
DAE does not list it.

8 Traced by the DAE in this sense to
1887 and marked an Americanism.
*To fire out,* in the sense of to throw
out, is also an Americanism, traced
by the DAE to 1871 and first used in
England, according to J. Redding
Ware, in 1896, though Partridge says
that it did not become naturalized
until *c.* 1905.

9 Traced by the DAE to *c.* 1848 and
marked an Americanism.

10 Americanisms Now Used in English, Aug. 26, 1936.

11 English on Both Sides of the Atlantic, *Listener* (London), April 3,
1935, p. 572.

12 News and Views of Literary London, Oct. 4, 1936.

ever wider English familiarity with and use of Americanisms. " However much the pedants may rail and the grammarians quake," wrote an observant Englishman in 1939,[1] " American is steadily entering more and more into the Englishman's written and spoken language. Nobody now would jibe at *governmental, hold-up* or *junk,* and the use in conversation of such a phrase as ' an idea *resurrected*[2] from the Nineteenth Century ' breaks no one's heart except the ultrapurist's, while the *Times Educational Supplement* (of all papers), has used *to enthuse* in its book reviews." " The English language," added a resigned Scotswoman in 1944, " is probably unique in being a blend of two languages — not counting Latin and Greek — and is rapidly absorbing a third — American."[3]

The English newspapers frequently print anecdotes designed to show the extent to which American slang has been absorbed from the movies by English children, especially on the lower levels. One tells of a schoolboy who was asked to put the following sentences into his own words: " I see a cow. The cow is pretty. The cow can run." His reply was: " Boy, *lamp* de cow. Ain't she a *honey?* An' *I ask you,* kin she take it *on de lam!* "[4] Another has to do with a boy arrested at Southend for riding a bicycle without lights. His defense was that someone had pinched his *dynamo, i.e.,* his *generator.*

> The Magistrate. You mean *stolen* it.
> The Prisoner. That's right — *pinched* it.
> The Magistrate. *Stolen.*
> The Prisoner. Yes. *Pinched* it. *Pinched* it at the railway-station.[5]

The arrival of American troops in England and Northern Ireland in 1942 helped along the process that American movies and comic-strips had started. A correspondent of the Belfast *News-Letter,* early in 1943,[6] reported that the erstwhile *sonsy wee lassies* of the Scotch-Irish North had become *swell dames,* and that " farmers' children deep in the heart of Ulster " had learned " Aw, *lay off.*" A month or so later a correspondent of the Belfast *Telegraph*[7] reported that

---

1 Mr. Arthur D. Jacobs of Manchester; private communication, July 19, 1939.
2 *To resurrect* has been found in English use in the Eighteenth Century, but it came to flower in pre-Civil War America, and to the English of today it seems an Americanism.
3 A Scot Can Always Find the Words,

by Lady Sinclair, Dundee *Evening Telegraph and Post,* April 12, 1944.
4 A Wow. Liverpool *Echo,* Dec. 6, 1943.
5 *Pinched* or *Stolen.* London *Evening Standard,* Nov. 1, 1943.
6 Sticking Out, April 6, 1943.
7 Fair Exchange, May 20, 1943.

*truck* for *lorry* had come into universal use in Ulster, and that the American *guy*, meaning simply anybody, had begun to displace the English *guy*, meaning a grotesque and ridiculous person. Says H. W. Horwill: [1]

> The naturalization of American usage in England . . . is a process that never slackens. . . . (1) The use of adverbs to intensify the meaning of verbs, *e.g., to close down, to test out,* has made rapid headway among English writers and speakers since the beginning of the present century. (2) There is an increasing tendency to adopt those combinations of verb and adverb which Americans prefer to a single verb or a more roundabout expression, *e.g., to turn down* rather than to reject, and *to put across* rather than to secure the adoption of. (3) Those sections of the English daily press which have been becoming more and more Americanized in other respects are following the American example in the choice of short words for headlines. (4) Certain uses of familiar words, which at the beginning of the century (or, at the outside, fifty years ago) were peculiar to the United States, are now either completely naturalized . . . or evidently on their way to naturalization. (5) . . . Many words and locutions invented in America . . . have become so thoroughly incorporated in the language that few of us are aware that they are actually American coinages. Every one recognizes, of course, that such terms as *banjo, blizzard, bogus, bunkum* and *lynch law* came to us from across the Atlantic, but it would surprise most Englishmen to be told that they owe to American *to belittle, boarding-house, business man, governmental, graveyard, hurricane-deck, law-abiding, lengthy, overcoat, telegram* and *whole-souled.*[2]

Horwill, after discussing the influence of the movies and talkies in this Americanization of English, adds that two other factors have had an important effect: " the increasing attention . . . paid in England to American books and magazines," and " the fact that . . . many members of the staffs of English newspapers are either Americans or English journalists who have spent several years in the practice of their profession in the United States." [3] An example of this class is provided by H. W. Seaman. His ten years of American experience made him a master of the American language, and since his

1 American Variations, *S.P.E. Tract No. XLV,* 1936, pp. 196–97. See also his Modern American Usage; Oxford, 1935, p. ix.

2 The DAE traces *to belittle* to 1781–2, *boarding-house* to 1787, *business man* to 1832, *governmental* to 1744, *graveyard* to 1773, *hurricane-deck* to 1833, *law-abiding* to 1834, *lengthy* to 1689, *overcoat* to 1807, *telegram* to 1852 and *whole-souled* to 1834.

3 In The American Impact on Great Britain, 1898–1914; Philadelphia, 1940, p. 310, Richard Heathcote Heindel says that *Punch* noted the influence of American on the English press so early as the 90s. He also says that many terms " in the category of business . . . came into English usage before 1914." " Such invasion of the language as has taken place," he concludes, " proves the power of the cinema, press and business, not the connivance of British literary masters."

return to England he has recorded a large number of observations of its influence upon English. I leave the subject by offering some of his notes: ¹

*To stop*, meaning to stay, has not been adopted in England, but the railways issued *stopover* tickets.

*Peanut* has completely ousted *monkey-nut*.

*Chain-store* is heard much more often than *multiple-shop*.² A *stores* is almost obsolete. Woolworth's is a *store*, not a *stores*, or even a *shop*. The corner grocery, however, remains a *shop*. We speak of the Army and Navy *Stores* and the Civil Service *Stores*, but of Selfridge's *store* or Gamage's *store*: these are *department-stores*.³ A *department-stores* sounds old-fashioned.

*Cooler*, meaning a jail, is now fairly current in England, and even *calaboose* is understood, thanks to a popular song.

No English dramatic critic would shrink from writing of a *flop*.

*Snag* is much used here of late, but only in its figurative sense. Few Englishmen have any idea that it means a sunken or half sunken log in a river.⁴

Headline in *Daily Express*, May 16, 1944: Russia *Puts Heat* on Sweden. No quotes or explanation now necessary.

I came across *hamburger*, in Roman, with no quotes, in the *Times* the other day. No eating-place here serves *hamburgers*, but everybody knows what they are, or nearly. All same *hot-dogs*. But *barbecue*, word and thing, is still unknown.

The *Daily Chronicle* recently explained that a *baloney* was a sort of breakfast sausage, but all movie-goers know the use of the word.

Kids now say *choo-choo* instead of *puff-puff*.⁵

Boys write " So-and-so is a *sap*," or a *sis*, on walls.

These are now used without a thought of their American origin: *bat, to bawl out, blowhard, bunk, darn, golly, gosh, grouch, hick* (old English, but apparently reintroduced from America), *ice-cream soda, to knock, lid, once-over, peach* (of a), *pull* (influence), *roughneck, simp* and *wop*.

These are used as conscious Americanisms: *to beat it, bootlegging, dumb-bell, to fall for, to fix, four-flusher, go-getter, good mixer, graft, hunch, nut, room-mate, whale of a.*

*Tuxedo* was used without quotes in the head and body of a story on the sports page of the London *Sunday Chronicle*, May 14, 1944.⁶

1 Private communications at different times in 1944.
2 The NED Supplement traces *multiple-shop*, in English use, to 1903. It marks *chain-store* an Americanism, but when it came in I do not know. The DAE does not list it.
3 *Department-store* is traced to 1893 by the DAE and marked an Americanism. The NED Supplement's first English example of its use is dated 1928.
4 The DAE traces *snag*, in its literal sense, to 1804 and marks it an Americanism. In the figurative sense of

any impediment or difficulty it is traced to 1829. Apparently it first appeared in this sense in England a year later. *To snag* goes back to 1807.
5 To designate a locomotive. See AL4, p. 240.
6 In Do You Speak American?, London *Daily Mail*, Aug. 17, 1932, John Blunt included *tuxedo* in a list of Americanisms " positively incomprehensible without the context " to an Englishman. Others on his list were *commuter, rare* (of meat), *interne, truck-farming, realtor, mean* (nas-

*Bathing-suit* is now heard far more often than *swim-suit*.[1]

*Through*, meaning finished, is now respectable English. This has come to pass within ten years or less.[2]

London *Daily Express*, May 20, 1944: "The Abbey is an *ashcan*." *Ashcan* is now preferred to *dustbin*.

*Radio* has driven *wireless* virtually out of use. Even the London *Times*, which clings to *aether*, has surrendered to *radio*.

*Stag-party* is understood, but has not been widely adopted. *Stag* alone, as an adjective or noun in the American sense, is unknown.

*Punch's* theatre article used to be headed "Our *Booking Office*." Today everybody speaks and writes of the *box-office* of a theatre. Only a railway ticket-office is a *booking-office*.

*What it takes* is now used freely. Few Englishmen realize that the idiom in "Britain *can take it*" is American.

*Double-cross* and *four-flush* are now respectable English, though poker is not an English popular game.

*Good-looker* is now fairly common in England, but not *good buy* for a bargain.

*Pin-up girl* is in wide use.

*To lay off*, meaning to desist from, is used editorially in the London *Sunday Times*, June 11, 1944.

*Racket*, for a swindling conspiracy, is well known and much used, but so is its English equivalent, *ramp*.[3]

## 2. SURVIVING DIFFERENCES

Despite the evidence offered in the preceding section that American has had a heavy influence upon English in recent years, it remains

ty), *dumb* (stupid), *enlisted man, sea-food, living-room, dirt-road, roomer, scrubwoman, mortician* and *hired-girl*. Four years later, on April 19, 1936, "Are You '*Dumb*'?" appeared as the heading of an advertisement of Sandeman sherry in the London *Sunday Dispatch*.

1 The DAE's first example of *bathing-suit* is dated 1886.

2 *Through* was still so far from acceptance in 1939 that a correspondent of the London *Times* was arguing for it formally. He said: "If, say, a film is billed for Monday to Thursday I would probably not go to see it on the Thursday without 'phoning to make sure that *to* meant *on* as well. 'Our lease goes on *till* September': what does that mean? Till the end of September, the middle or the beginning? In America they say

the film is on from Monday *through* Thursday. The lease is from January *through* September (if it meant the end of September; if September 1 it would be *through* August). And so on. We could use that *through* in English." I take this from On American Speech, Baltimore *Evening Sun* (editorial), Jan. 27, 1940.

3 There are earlier examples in Seaman's article, Ninety-nine Percent British, *American Mercury*, Sept., 1937, pp. 46–53. See also Some Recent Americanisms in Standard English, by Helen McM. Buckhurst, *American Speech*, Dec., 1925, pp. 159–60; The Talkies and English Speech, by Beatrice White, *American Speech*, April, 1932, pp. 314–15, and Say It in American, London *Morning Post*, Sept. 11, 1936.

a fact that the two languages still show many differences, not only in vocabulary but also in idiom, accent and intonation. When an untraveled American finds himself among Englishmen for the first time these dissimilarities inevitably puzzle him. The English in many cases use different words for the same common objects, they give to common words quite different meanings, they make frequent use of words and phrases that are seldom or never heard in America, they have different répertoires of everyday intensives and cuss-words, they pronounce many words differently and their talk is based upon different speech-tunes.[1] The same thing, of course, runs the other way, but I believe that Englishmen, talking one with another, find American considerably less difficult than Americans find English, if only because they have become so familiar with large numbers of American terms and idioms. Unhappily, not a few of them, especially on the more literate levels, resent the notion that English and American are different quite as much as they resent the notion that American is influencing their speech, and anyone who undertakes to investigate either subject is pretty sure to be denounced for his pains. In each of the four editions of " The American Language " I have printed lists of the surviving differences between the current vocabularies of American and English, and each time I have been belabored by such chauvinists as a false prophet, and, indeed, an idiot. More than one of them has added the suggestion that my real motive in undertaking such cruel labors was to drive a wedge between the two great branches of the Anglo-Saxon peoples, and thus prosper the enemies of democracy and Christianity, and more than one American Anglomaniac has played with the same idea. There is in each country, in fact, a highly articulate group which holds that any notice of linguistic disparities between them, however academic, is seditious, immoral and against God. Fortunately, this doctrine does not seem to be shared by their official spokesmen, for when World War II brought American and British troops into contact for the second time in a generation, the General Staffs of both armies, recalling the unpleasantness that had followed misunderstandings in World War I, proceeded at once to issue what amounted, in substance, to American-English dictionaries.[2]

---

1 See AL4, pp. 322 *ff.*

2 Such dictionaries, of course, were nothing new. Many are to be found in works of travel by both English-men and Americans, and not infrequently glossaries have been added to English editions of American books or offered as programme notes

That of the American Army was included in a pamphlet entitled " A Short Guide to Great Britain," prepared by the Special Service Division, Service of Supply, and first published in 1942. It did not pretend to be exhaustive, but nevertheless it managed to present a list of no less than 183 everyday American terms, unknown or unfamiliar in England, that are represented in English by equivalents similarly strange in the United States. Soon afterward the Special Service Division prepared like pocket-guides to Northern Ireland, Australia and New Zealand, each containing notes on language differences, and all three were issued jointly by the Army and Navy. On June 15, 1943 there followed a dictionary for American supply men, published in the various editions of the Army paper, the *Stars and Stripes*,[1] and at other times yet other vocabularies were published for other special purposes.[2] Meanwhile, the English brought out various pamphlets of the same general tenor, the most widely circulated of which was " Meet the U. S. Army," written by Louis MacNeice and issued on July 22, 1943. This was put on sale at the low price of fourpence, and had a large circulation in England, Scotland and Northern Ireland, not only among British troops but also among civilians. It was not the first thing of its sort to appear in England under official auspices. Early in 1942, when R.A.F. cadets began coming to the United States for training, the Air Ministry prepared a little pamphlet for them under the title of " Notes For Your Guidance," and soon afterward the Ministry of Information issued a wordlist for the information of British artists invited to exhibit at an Anglo-

to English productions of American plays. Most of these English-American word lists have been designed to interpret Americanisms to Englishmen, but there have also been a few efforts in the other direction. Allen Walker Read, for some years past, has been engaged upon what will be a comprehensive and scientific Dictionary of Briticisms. He has accumulated nearly 35,000 illustrative quotations, and his skill and experience are such that the work is awaited eagerly. Unhappily, his service with the Army interrupted his labors upon it. See Plans For a Historical Dictionary of Briticisms, *American Oxonian*, July, 1938, pp. 186-90.

1 The headline on this vocabulary, in the edition of the *Stars and Stripes* before me, is British Names Headache to Supply Men: *GI Can* is *Dust Bin, Hot Water Bottle* a *Stomach Warmer*. I am indebted here to Mr. J. F. Burke.

2 One showing differences in the American and English names for various maintenance items was prepared for the Staff Officers' School, and another on the same subject was published in the *Quartermaster Review*, March–April, 1943, by Col. Wayne Allen of the Quartermaster Corps. Dave Breger, the Army cartoonist, did one for the troops in general in the form of an illustrated alphabet beginning with *absorbent cotton — cotton wool* and running down to *zee — zed.*

American show at the Metropolitan Museum of Art. In January, 1943 the N.A.A.F.I.[1] brought out a pamphlet for the guidance of its staff in dealing with American soldiers, and later a number of other such treatises were published by other organizations. The pamphlet for air cadets contained this:

> What can we say about studying the American people as a whole? . . . The best key to a nation's mind is its language. That, you will say, is English. Not at all. It may be called English, but it is American.

The guide for N.A.A.F.I. girls warned them not to be shocked if American soldiers opened a conversation with " How-ya, baby? " If this, it said, seemed saucy, let them remember that it was just as normal to a lad from Iowa as " Lovely day, isn't it? "[2] To these English guides to speech differences the New Zealanders presently added a glossary headed " How We Talk " in a pamphlet entitled " Meet New Zealand." It explained for the information of American soldiers sent to the Dominion the meaning of such characteristic New Zealanderisms as *to argue the toss, benzine* (for *gasoline*), *to feel crook, dinkum, jakealoo, lollies, pommie, to shout, to right* and *up the pole*.[3]

So far as I know, the English foes of the notion that American and English differ have not complained of any of these official lists, but they are sure to denounce any list less authoritatively supported, so I have sought to baffle them by basing the one that follows on the vocabulary in the War Department's " Short Guide to Great Britain," and by offering printed evidence, usually English, for most of the other differences noted. In not a few cases it is genuinely difficult to establish the facts, for a great many Americanisms, as we saw in the last section, have got into English use in recent years, and not a few terms that seem distinctively American today are actually English archaisms. It is easy for the English guardians of the language to produce evidence that these archaisms were used, say, by Chaucer or Shakespeare, and to argue thereby that they are not Americanisms at all. In case after case the attitude of such earnest but humorless men toward a

1 The Navy, Army and Air Forces Institutes. Partridge, in his Dictionary of Abbreviations; London, 1942, says that it conducts canteens and other service centers for soldiers and sailors. The name is often abbreviated to *naafi*, pronounced *narfy* or *naffy*.

2 I have not seen the pamphlet, but take this from a notice of it in the London *Evening Standard*, Jan. 4, 1943.

3 I am indebted here to Mr. J. W. Heenan, Under-Secretary for Internal Affairs in the New Zealand government, and to Mrs. Frances Trimble, of the New Zealand Legation at Washington.

given Americanism recalls that of Holy Church toward embarrassing scientific discoveries, as described by Andrew D. White, *viz.*, they first denounce it violently, then admit it quietly, and then end by denying that they were ever against it. This, in brief, has been the history in England of the early *reliable* and *caucus*, and no doubt many an Americanism that is still below the salt will follow the pattern. That there are still wide divergences between American and English usage on the level of everyday speech, despite the powerful influence upon the English vocabulary of American movies, was demonstrated beyond cavil by Horwill in his " Dictionary of Modern American Usage " and again in his " Anglo-American Interpreter." [1] There are slips and misunderstandings in both books, and inevitably so,[2] but on the whole Horwill is well-informed and painstaking, and I am glad to acknowledge a debt to him. In the following list [3] all doublets taken from the Army's " Short Guide to Great Britain " are indicated by an asterisk (*).

| American | English |
|---|---|
| A.B. (bachelor of arts) | B.A.[4] |
| *absorbent cotton | cotton wool [5] |
| ad (advertisement) | advert [6] |

1 Both published by the Clarendon Press, Oxford, 1935 and 1939. This press, which is owned and operated by the university, is also the publisher of the New English Dictionary.

2 Some of those in A Dictionary of Modern American Usage are noted in reviews of it in the *Nation* (New York), Oct. 9, 1935, p. 418; the *Oxford Magazine*, Oct. 17, 1935, pp. 10–14; *American Speech*, Dec., 1936, pp. 302–06; and *Publications of the Modern Language Association*, Jan., 1938, pp. 35–37. I have noted others myself. Horwill says that *blind baggage* means baggage carried in a *blind car*. He says that *cleanse* " is often preferred in America where *clean* would be used in England," and cites *street-cleansing* department in support thereof. He says that *Gentile*, in America, " more commonly indicates " a non-Mormon than a non-Jew. He mistakes an *accommodation train* for one carrying both passengers and freight. He seems to be unaware that American freight-

trains have *conductors*. He confuses *hand-me-down* and *ready-made* He neglects to give the chief meaning of *hangover*. He says that, in America, " *home* denotes a house inhabited by a single family." He confuses *trunk-line* with *main-line*. And so on, and so on. But in a book of 360 double-column pages these errors are relatively rare, and not many of them are important.

3 Some of the terms listed are discussed at greater length in other places. See the List of Words and Phrases.

4 The NED says: ' *Artium baccalaureus* . . . , *artium magister* . . . in England are now written *B.A., M.A.*"

5 U. S. and British Staff Officers Overcome Language Difficulties, by Milton Bracker, London correspondent of the New York *Times*, July 1, 1943.

6 Advertisement in *News of the World* (London), Jan. 23, 1938: " Why are you publishing this *advert?* "

| American | English |
|---|---|
| admit to the bar (law) | call to the bar [1] |
| advertising manager (or director) | advertisement manager [2] |
| *aisle (theatre) | gangway [3] |
| *alcohol-lamp | spirit-lamp |
| *ale | beer, or bitter |
| almshouse | workhouse [4] |
| alumnus (of a college) | graduate [5] |
| A.M. (master of arts) | M.A. [6] |
| ambulance-chaser | accident tout [7] |
| anxious-bench, or -seat, or mourners-bench, or -seat | penitent-form [8] |
| *apartment | flat [9] |
| apartment-hotel | service-flats [10] |
| *apartment-house | block of flats [11] |
| appropriation (legislative) | vote [12] |

1 The DAE traces *to admit to the bar* to 1768 and marks it an Americanism.

2 So used by the London *Times* in its daily announcements of advertising rates.

3 Horwill says: " *Aisle* is used in England, except in a few dialects, only of a division of a church or of a passage between rows of pews. In America it may denote almost any kind of gangway, whether in a train (where it corresponds to the English *corridor*), or a theatre, or a shop."

4 The DAE traces *almshouse* in American use to 1662. Its forthright harshness early bred euphemisms, *e.g.*, *county-farm* and *infirmary*. *Poorhouse* is traced to 1785 and *poorfarm* to 1859. In England, according to Horwill, *workhouse* is being displaced by *public assistance institution*. It came in *c.* 1650 and was preceded by *house of work*, traced to 1552, and *working-house*, traced to 1597. Since 1653 *workhouse* has been used in America to designate a house of correction for minor offenders.

5 The NED marks *alumnus* " U. S.", and the DAE, which traces it to 1696, calls it an Americanism, but it seems to be making progress in the English colonies, if not in England. The Hong Kong University *Alumni* Association flourished before World War II, and issued an *alumni* maga-

zine. (*South China Morning Post*, May 5, 1938). *Alumna* is widely used in the United States to designate a female college graduate. The DAE traces it to 1882.

6 See *A.B.*

7 *Accident Touts* May Be Penalized, London *Daily Express*, Sept. 28, 1936: " Another name for the *accident tout* business is *ambulance-chasing*."

8 The DAE traces *anxious-bench* to 1832, *anxious-seat* to 1835, *mourners'-seat* to 1845 and *mourners'-bench* to 1848, and marks them all Americanisms. The NED's first example of *penitent-form* is from Hall Caine's The Deemster, 1887.

9 Americans Bound Coronationwards Should Read This Alphabet, London *Daily Express*, April 28, 1937: " *Apartments* are what you call rooms."

10 The DAE's first example of *apartment-hotel* is dated 1902, and marked an Americanism.

11 The DAE's first example of *apartment-house* is dated 1876 and marked an Americanism. *Block* seems to be an Americanism also, but the English have been using it in the sense of a group of buildings since *c.* 1850.

12 The DAE traces *appropriation* in this sense to 1761 and marks it an Americanism. *Appropriation-bill* is traced to 1789.

| American | English |
|---|---|
| *ash-can | dust-bin [1] |
| ash-cart, or -truck | dust-cart [2] |
| *ashman | dustman [3] |
| *atomizer | scent-spray [4] |
| *automobile | motor-car [5] |
| baby-carriage | perambulator (pram), or baby-coach [6] |
| *baggage | luggage [7] |
| *baggage-car | luggage-van [8] |
| *bakery | baker's shop |
| banked (curve in a road) | superelevated [9] |

[1] Also commonly applied to what Americans call a *garbage-can*. *Stars and Stripes*, June 15, 1943: "A mess sergeant wanting a *GI can* wouldn't find his *swill-bucket* listed in those words on a British maintenance list, but if he were well versed in British nomenclature he'd ask for a *bin, dust*." Further on the *Stars and Stripes* listed: "*Can, garbage — bin, dust*." I am indebted here to Mr. J. F. Burke. But see the Seaman list at the end of the last section.

[2] Mr. P. E. Cleator, of Wallasey, Cheshire: private communication, Sept. 28, 1936: "The name remains with us, but the *cart* is now an electrically-propelled vehicle. I venture that the old name will inevitably suffer a change."

[3] Mr. Cleator tells me that *binman* is often used. See *garbage-man*.

[4] There are Englishmen willing to swear that *scent-spray* is archaic in England.

[5] An interesting account of the other terms in use in the early days of the automobile is in The Automobile and American English, by Theodore Hornberger, *American Speech*, April, 1930, pp. 271–78. This paper also discusses the names for parts and models. London *Morning Post*, Dec. 10, 1935: "Mr. Justice Bennett, in the Chancery Division, yesterday, criticised a man who described himself in an affidavit as an *automobile engineer*. Counsel said that he did not know what an *automobile* was. Mr. Justice Bennett: Nor do I, and nor does he, I expect."

[6] Americans, of course, know the meaning of *perambulator*, and even of *pram*. *Baby-carriage* is not listed by the NED; its Supplement marks the term U. S., along with *baby-coach*. The DAE traces *baby-carriage* to 1882, and *perambulator*, in American use, to 1893. It does not list *baby-coach*. Before *baby-carriage* came in the American term was *baby-wagon*, traced by the DAE to 1853. The NED traces *perambulator* to 1857 and *pram* to 1884.

[7] Horwill says that in the United States *luggage* means empty *baggage*. But the term is often used in the English sense, and *baggage* is certainly not unknown in England. See AL4, p. 254. Also, see *baggage-car*, below. Also see The Growth of American English, by Sir William Craigie, *S.P.E. Tract No. LVII*; Oxford, 1940, p. 233.

[8] Mournful Numbers, by Colin Ellis; London, 1932:

I'm certain we shall miss the train!
Is all the luggage in the van?
Oh, George, you've dropped that box *again*!
I'm certain we shall miss the train —
Well, don't swear, if you *are* in pain —
Oh, how I wish I were a man!
I'm certain we shall miss the train!
Is all the luggage in the van? "

(Note the use of *miss* for the former English term, *lose*.)

[9] Regulations of the English Ministry of Transport, 1938: "All curves of less than 1,000 feet radius should be *superelevated*."

| American | English |
|---|---|
| *bartender | barman, or potman [1] |
| baseboard (of a wall) | skirting [2] |
| bath (sea) | bathe [3] |
| *bathrobe | dressing-gown [4] |
| *bathtub | bath [5] |
| *battery (automobile) | accumulator [6] |
| *beach | seaside |
| bed-bug, or chinch | bug [7] |
| *beer | lager |
| beet | beetroot |
| bellboy, or bellhop | page, or buttons [8] |
| *bill (money) | banknote, or note [9] |
| *billboard | hoarding [10] |
| bill-fold | wallet [11] |

1 More often, of course, *barmaid*.

2 I am indebted here to the late Sir E. Denison Ross: private communication, May 16, 1939.

3 H. W. Seaman: "We go for a *bathe* in the sea or a river or a swimming-pool. We take a *bath* in the bathtub. *Bathe*, verb or noun, always rhymes with *lathe* and *bath* with *lath*." London *Daily Mirror*, Nov. 21, 1938: "Lady Morris, wherever she is, gets home in time to *bath* her babies." Headlines in *News of the World* (London), June 12, 1936: "Doctor's Last *Bathe*. Lost His Life After Disregarding Advice at Seaside."

4 This is disputed by many Englishmen, who say that a *bath-robe* and a *dressing-gown* differ in meaning, as with us. The NED's first example of *bathrobe* is from the American *Smart Set*, 1895. Its first English example is dated 1924.

5 London *Daily Telegraph*, March 26, 1936: "Beryl Mary Shelton Parker . . . was found with her head under water in the *bath*." The DAE traces *bathtub* to 1870 and marks it an Americanism.

6 *Battery* is also used in England.

7 See *bug*. Bed-bug is traced by the DAE to 1808. *Chinch* is old in English, but has been mainly American for many years. *As crazy as a bed-bug* is an Americanism, traced to 1832.

8 *Learn English Before You Go*, by Frank Loxley Griffin, *Atlantic*

*Monthly*, June, 1932, p. 775: "A *bellhop* will never bring you a *pitcher* of *ice water*, but a *page* can usually fetch a *jug* of *iced water*." See *pitcher*.

9 *As She Is Spoke in the United States*, by J. H. M., Glasgow *Evening Citizen*, Aug. 29, 1936: "Don't embarrass the *booking-clerk* by asking him if he can change a fifty-dollar *note* for you; you mean a *bill*." See *ticket-agent*.

10 The DAE traces *billboard* to 1851 and marks it an Americanism. *Hoarding* is traced by the NED, as a builders' term for a fence around a building under construction or repair, to 1823, but it apparently did not come into common use to designate a billboard until the 60s. It was apparently preceded by *show-board*, traced by the NED to 1806, and by *posting-board*. See Stolen Flowers, *Harper's Magazine*, Sept., 1871.

11 Oxford *Mail*, Oct. 14, 1942: "Seeing one of our soldiers unable to understand what a U. S. A. sergeant was asking him, I offered my services. It appeared that the American required a *bill-folder* [sic]. This stumped me for a minute or so, but at last I suggested it might be a *wallet* he required. This proved to be correct when I displayed my own." The learned Englishman's use of *to stump* will be noted. It is an Americanism and is traced by the DAE to 1812.

| American | English |
|---|---|
| billion | milliard [1] |
| bingo | house, or housey-housey [2] |
| *biscuit | scone, or tea-cake [3] |
| blackjack | life-preserver [4] |
| blank | form [5] |
| blow-torch | brazing lamp [6] |
| boards | deals [7] |
| boot | Wellington, or Wellington boot [8] |
| boulevard, or main road | arterial road, or trunk road [9] |
| *bouncer | chucker-out [10] |
| *bowling-alley | skittle-alley [11] |
| box-car | covered waggon [12] |
| brief-case | portfolio [13] |
| *broiled (meat) | grilled [14] |
| bucket | pail [15] |

[1] Chicago *Tribune*, Aug. 13, 1923: " A *milliard*, in the American language, is a *billion*."

[2] *Chinese Mail* (Hong Kong), Dec. 19, 1938: " The game so popular in army circles in Hong Kong under the name of *tombola* is now sweeping South London as a craze called *housey-housey*. It is played for the most part by housewives who are attracted to open-door booths by a glittering display of cutlery and chromium-plated clocks." The article then proceeds to describe the method of playing what Americans call *bingo*. Bingo is a form of *lotto*, traced by the NED to 1778. *Bingo* is listed by Grose, 1785, as thieves' cant for " brandy or other spirituous liquor " and " a dram drinker."

[3] See *soda-biscuit*.

[4] Headline in London *Daily Telegraph*, Oct. 12, 1936: " *Life Preserver* For ' Self-Defence.' " The DAE traces *blackjack* to 1895 and marks it an Americanism.

[5] As She Is Spoke in the United States, by J. H. M., Glasgow *Evening Citizen*, Aug. 29, 1936: " During the voyage the purser will send out at least one *form* to be *filled in*, but to the Americans it will be a *blank* to be *filled out*."

[6] The King's English, by Wayne Allen, *Quartermaster Review* (Washington), March–April, 1943, p. 58: " A *torch, blow*, is a *lamp, brazing*."

[7] The NED says that *deals* now commonly means fir or pine cut in planks not more than three inches thick.

[8] Mr. P. E. Cleator tells me that both terms are commonly used in the plural. See *shoe*.

[9] Aids To the Talkies, by D. W. B (rogan), *Oxford Magazine*, Oct. 17, 1935: " *Boulevard*, for *arterial road*, can be illustrated from North Britain." London *Times Literary Supplement*, Aug. 23, 1934, p. 570: " Milton described in ' Paradise Lost ' the modern ideal of an *arterial road* — ' a passage broad, smooth, easy.' "

[10] London *Leader*, March 27, 1943: " We have yet to call . . . a *chucker-out* a *bouncer*."

[11] H. W. Seaman: " Your game of *bowls*, played in an alley, is called *skittles* here, and is played in a *skittle-alley*. Our game of *bowls* is played on a *green*, which is a *lawn*." In the United States *bowling* is commonly used, not *bowls*.

[12] Industrial Coinage, *Nation's Business*, June, 1942, quoting This Fascinating Railroad Business, by Robert S. Henry; New York, 1942.

[13] I am indebted here to Mrs. Pieter Juiliter of Scotia, N. Y.

[14] *Grilled*, of course, is known in the United States.

[15] *Pail* is also used in the United States.

| American | English |
|---|---|
| bug | insect [1] |
| building (in a proper name) | house [2] |
| bulletin-board | notice-board [3] |
| bureau | chest of drawers [4] |
| business suit | lounge suit [5] |
| caboose (railroad) | brake-van [6] |
| cab-stand | cab-rank [7] |
| calendar (of a court) | cause-list [8] |
| call-boy (railroad) | knocker-up [9] |
| can (vessel) | tin [10] |
| candy | sweets [11] |
| *candy (hard) | boiled sweets |
| *candy-store | sweet-shop [12] |

1 *Bug* in England, has acquired the special meaning of *bed-bug*, and is thus avoided. See AL4, p. 310. American As She Is Spoke, by Eric Partridge, London *Observer*, Sept. 8, 1935: "Citizens of the United States have often offended English ears with their use of *bug*."

2 The *Al Smith Building*, in England, would be *Smith House*. "In America," says Horwill, "a structure bearing the name of *house* would be understood to be a hotel." But this use of *house* for hotel is going out.

3 I am indebted here to Mr. P. A. Browne.

4 *Bureau*, in this sense, is traced by the DAE to 1751 and marked an Americanism. It is also used in the United States in the sense of what the English call a government *office*, as in *Weather Bureau*. In this sense the DAE traces it to 1831. *Chest of drawers* has some vogue in the United States, but is used chiefly of an antique.

5 London *Leader*, March 27, 1943: "Our *lounge suits* are their *sack suits*." *Sack suit*, seldom used, is traced by the DAE to 1895, and marked an Americanism. *Business suit* is traced to 1880.

6 The DAE traces *caboose* to 1862, but it must be older. The term, which comes from the Dutch *kabuis*, has been used for many years to designate a cooking galley on the deck of a merchant ship.

7 Please Speak English, by Dale Warren, *Seven Seas*, Spring, 1939, p. 26: "You go to a *rank*, not a *stand*, to get a taxi."

8 But Horwill says that *calendar* is used in England in the criminal courts. It is used in Congress to designate the official agenda — what is known in Parliament as the *order paper*.

9 Industrial Coinage, *Nation's Business*, June, 1942, quoting This Fascinating Railroad Business, by Robert S. Henry; New York, 1942.

10 In England, says Horwill, *can* means a vessel for holding liquids, but it seems to be ousting *tin* for other purposes. A Truck by Any Other Name, by Robert Lynd; London *News Chronicle*, May 22, 1943: "I hate to see the Food Ministry constantly using the word *canned* where the traditional English word is *tinned*."

11 As She Is Spoke in the United States, by J. H. M., Glasgow *Evening Citizen*, Aug. 29, 1936: "All *sweets*, even chocolates, are *candy* or *candies*." But the English use *sugar-candy* to designate what Americans call *rock-candy*, and Mr. James E. Walker, chief librarian of the London Public Libraries, tells me that *candy*, in its American sense, is "in common use in Durham and Northumberland."

12 Or, *confectioner's*.

| American | English |
|---|---|
| *cane | stick [1] |
| *can-opener | tin-opener, or key |
| *car (railway passenger) | carriage |
| carnival | fun-fair [2] |
| *carom (billiards) | cannon |
| carrousel | merry-go-round, or roundabout [3] |
| catalogue (school or college) | calendar [4] |
| catnip | catmint [5] |
| *chain-store | multiple-shop, or -stores [6] |
| check (restaurant) | bill [7] |
| *check baggage (verb) | register luggage |
| *checkers (game) | draughts [8] |
| check-room | left-luggage office, or -room [9] |
| cheese-cloth | butter-muslin [10] |
| *chicken-yard | fowl-run, or chicken-run [11] |

1 In England *cane* is used for a very slender stick.

2 Lord Harewood in the London *Daily Telegraph*, July 2, 1936: "We should like to see these *fun-fairs* run in such a manner that they are not eye-sores to the neighbourhood."

3 *Carrousel*, which is a loan from the French, has nothing to do with the word *carousal*, meaning a drinking-bout or other orgy.

4 The DAE shows that Harvard issued a *catalogue* so early as 1682.

5 The DAE traces *catnip* to 1712 and marks it an Americanism. French: *herbe du chat;* German: *katzen-münze.* H. W. Seaman: "Our movie-trained smarties write glibly of *poison-ivy* and *catnip* without knowing what the words mean. *Catnip* has no commercial value here. I have asked several druggists and none has heard of its use as a kitten's hooch."

6 *News of the World* (London), Oct. 23, 1938: "Mrs. Maude Booth, of Ipswich, has been forbidden ever again to enter 'a shop known as a *stores*'. The ban was placed on her when she was put on probation for two years on a conviction for stealing two bars of soap from a *multiple stores*." But since *c.* 1930 *chain-store* has been in increasing use in Eng-

land. Headline in the Sunderland *Echo*, Jan. 15, 1940: "Mammoth R.A.F. *Chain-Store*." See *five-and-ten*. Also, see the Seaman list at the end of the last section.

7 Do You Speak American?, by John Blunt, London *Daily Mail*, Aug. 17, 1932: "When you want to pay your *bill* you ask for a *check*."

8 The DAE finds *checkers* in the letter-book of Samuel Sewall for 1712. The NED traces *draughts* to *c.* 1300. Mr. James E. Walker, before cited, tells me that *checkers* is in use in the north of England.

9 Please Speak English, by Dale Warren, *Seven Seas*, Spring, 1939, p. 26: "A *left-luggage office* is simply a place where you check your bag."

10 The NED traces *cheese-cloth*, in English use, to 1741, but it had appeared in America, as the DAE shows, in 1657. *Butter-muslin* seems to be relatively recent in England.

11 *Chicken* is an old word in English, traced by the NED to *c.* 950, and Apperson reports an early form of the proverb, "Don't count your *chickens* before they are hatched," in 1577. But the English, in general, use the term only to indicate very young fowl. In the United States it may designate an old rooster or hen. The DAE traces *chicken-pie* to 1733.

| American | English |
|---|---|
| cigar-store | tobacconist's shop |
| *cigarette-butt | cigarette-end |
| city hall | town hall, or guildhall [1] |
| clapboard | shiplap [2] |
| clean-up campaign | cleansing campaign [3] |
| clipping (newspaper) | cutting [4] |
| clipping-bureau | press-cutting agency [5] |
| 'closed season (for game) | close season |
| *closet | cupboard |
| clothespin | clothespeg [6] |
| *coal oil [7] | paraffin |
| *collar-button | collar-stud, or back-stud [8] |
| commencement (school) | speech day, or prize-day [9] |

chicken-soup to 1816, chicken-house and -yard to 1853, chicken-feed to 1865, chicken-salad to 1888 and chicken-dinner to 1896. All are Americanisms.

1 American and English, by Claude de Crespigny, *American Speech*, June, 1926, p. 492: " The *City Hall*, to an Englishman, is a *town hall*, a *guild hall*, or in the case of the London County Council, a *Spring Gardens*."

2 Advertisement in the London *Morning Post*, May 21, 1938, with a picture of a *clapboarded* house: " Walls: cedar *shiplap*." The DAE marks *clapboard* an Americanism and traces it to 1637.

3 *News of the World* (London) June 12, 1938: " There is to be an office slum clearance — a mass attack on the thousands of insanitary and overcrowded offices which abound in London. . . . Every local authority [must make] returns showing the extent of the *cleansing campaign*." In Dublin the street-cleaning department is called the *cleansing* department. (Cleanliness, *Irish Times*, Dec. 30, 1939).

4 The DAE traces *clipping* in this sense to 1838 and marks it an Americanism.

5 Durrant, the Romeike of England, calls his business *Durrant's Press Cuttings*.

6 New York *Times Magazine*, quoted in *Writer's Monthly*, Oct., 1927, p. 337: " Garments flap in the breeze . . . attached to the line with a *peg* instead of a *pin*."

7 Or *kerosene*. Kerosene is traced by the DAE to 1855 and *coal-oil* to 1858, and both are marked Americanisms. See *paraffin*.

8 " I have received a clipping from an American paper," wrote G. K. Chesterton in 1934, " stating on the authority of Professor Howard Wilson that America's greatest contributions to civilization are plumbers, dentists and the *collar-button.* . . . My ignorance may horrify the world — but what is a *collar-button?* " I take this from Prams, Trams and *Collar-Buttons*, by Frank Sullivan, New York *American*, May 26, 1934. It is hard to believe that Chesterton wrote *clipping*: the English term is *cutting*; but I let it go. The DAE marks *collar-button* an Americanism, and traces it to 1886. It must be older.

9 *Commencement* was in use in the English universities in the Fourteenth Century, and was apparently borrowed from the French. At Oxford, two centuries later, *act* was substituted but Oxford has returned to it. When it began to be used in the United States to designate the closing orgies of lesser schools I do not know. The NED's first example of *speech-day* is from Thackeray's Vanity Fair, 1848. It is used only in the so-called *public-schools*, corresponding to the American prep schools.

| American | English |
|---|---|
| common stock | ordinary shares |
| commutation ticket | season ticket [1] |
| commuter | season-ticket holder [2] |
| *conductor (railroad) | guard [3] |
| cone (ice-cream) | cornet [4] |
| confidence game | confidence trick [5] |
| consent decree (courts) | agreed verdict |
| cook-book | cookery-book [6] |
| *cop | bobby |
| copy-reader (newspaper) | sub-editor |
| *corn | maize, or Indian corn |
| corner (street) | turning [7] |
| *cornmeal | Indian meal |
| cornstarch | cornflour [8] |
| corporation | limited liability company [9] |
| councilman (municipal) | councillor [10] |
| *cracker | biscuit |
| cruising (taxi) | crawling [11] |
| crystal (watch) | watch-glass [12] |

1 The DAE traces *commutation ticket* to 1849 and marks it an Americanism.

2 London *Times Literary Supplement*, Aug. 19, 1939: "The *commuters* of America . . . are brothers and sisters under the skin to our own suburban *season-ticket holders*." *Commuter* is traced by the DAE to 1863, and *to commute* to 1865.

3 As She Is Spoke in the United States, by J. H. M., Glasgow *Evening Citizen*, Aug. 29, 1936: "There will be no *guard* on the train, but an official with exactly the same duties whom you call *conductor*." The English use *bus-conductor* and *tram-conductor*. *Conductor* was used in America, in the sense of a man in charge of a stage-coach, so early as 1790.

4 Advertisement in the London *Morning Post*, July 24, 1936, under a picture showing a small girl eating a banana and a boy holding an *ice-cream cone*: "A banana for the lady, a *cornet* for the gent." In Baltimore I have encountered a sign reading *ice-cream cohens*.

5 *Confidence game* is traced by the DAE to 1867 and marked an Americanism.

6 The authority here is Horwill. He says also that a *cook-stove* is a *cooking-stove* in England.

7 New York *Times Magazine*, quoted in *Writer's Monthly*, Oct., 1927, p. 335: "A street does not have *corners* in England, but *turnings*; neither does it have a *head* or *foot*. English thoroughfares possess *tops* and *bottoms*."

8 Anglo-American Equations, by William Feather, *American Speech*, Dec., 1940, p. 444. The DAE traces *cornstarch* to 1857. Before then it seems to have been called *cornflour* in the United States also.

9 *Corporation law* is *company law* in England. The English, of course, know the meaning of *corporation* in the American sense, but they tend to restrict the word to municipal corporations. See Horwill, p. 85. See *president* and *Inc*.

10 *Councilman* is old in English, but it is seldom used. The DAE traces the American *councilmanic* to 1861.

11 Taxicabs and Tips, by E. R. Thackwell, London *Observer*, May 24, 1936: "The prohibition of the *crawling* taxi is long overdue."

12 In England, says Horwill, "*crystal* is used in this sense by watchmakers only." I Discover America, by Kenneth Adam, London *Star*, Nov. 30,

| American | English |
|---|---|
| custom-made | bespoke [1] |
| cut (railroad) | cutting [2] |
| daylight-house | sun-trap [3] |
| *daylight-saving time | Summer time [4] |
| *deck (of cards) | pack [5] |
| delegation | deputation |
| deliveryman (say of milk or bread) | roundsman [6] |
| *derby (hat) | bowler, or hard hat [7] |
| *dessert | sweet course [8] |
| denatured alcohol | methylated spirit |
| detour (road) | road diversion, or loopway [9] |
| dime-novel | penny-dreadful [10] |
| dining-car, or diner | restaurant-car [11] |
| dipper (water) | pannikin [12] |
| *dishpan | washing-up bowl, or washer [13] |

1937: "I broke my *watch-glass* yesterday. The jeweller to whom I took it could not make head or tail of what I wanted until I held out the watch dumbly. 'Ah,' he nodded. 'You want a new *crystal.*' "

1 *Custom-made* is an Americanism, traced by the DAE to 1855.

2 In this sense the DAE traces *cut* to 1862 and marks it an Americanism.

3 London *Mirror*, Sept. 19, 1935: "I'd like to build a *sun-trap* house, designed to catch each ray of golden sunlight."

4 E. O. Cutler in the New York *Times*, Feb. 14, 1937: "I suggest the use of *Summer time* instead of the more cumbersome *daylight-saving time. Summer time* seems to be in general use in Europe and South America." I am indebted here to Mr. Edgar Gahan, of Westmount, Quebec.

5 In this sense the DAE traces *deck* to 1853. *Cold deck* followed in the 60s.

6 An assault upon a *baker's roundsman* was reported in the London *Morning Post*, Nov. 25, 1935.

7 Americans Bound Coronationwards Should Read This Alphabet, London *Daily Express*, April 28, 1937: "In England it is a horserace, not a hat. If you want to bet call it the *Darby;* if you want headgear call it a *bowler.*" In Australia it is a *boxer*.

8 In England, says Horwill, *dessert*

means only "uncooked fruit, nuts, etc." In America it includes "pies, puddings, etc."

9 Mr. Maurice Walshe of London; private communication, Feb. 22, 1937: "A road *detour* is, according to the Automobile Association, a *loopway.*" The commoner English term used to be *road diversion*, but Mr. P. E. Cleator tells me that *detour* is coming in.

10 The DAE traces *dime-novel* to 1865. It is now obsolete, save historically, as *penny-dreadful* is in England.

11 The DAE traces *dining-car* to 1839 and *diner* to 1890, and marks both Americanisms.

12 U. S. and British Staff Officers Overcome Language Difficulties, by Milton Bracker, New York *Times*, July 1, 1943. The NED traces *pannikin* to 1823. It marks *dipper* "chiefly U. S." The DAE traces *dipper* to 1783 in American use and marks it an Americanism.

13 *Washer* was given as the English name for a *dishpan* in a chapter entitled Selling American Goods in Great Britain, in a handbook, The United Kingdom, issued by the Department of Commerce in 1930. I am indebted here to Mr. R. M. Stephenson, chief of the European section of the division of regional information.

| American | English |
|----------|---------|
| distributor (of merchandise) | stockist [1] |
| district (legislative) | division, or constituency [2] |
| district attorney, or State's attorney | public prosecutor [3] |
| dock | wharf [4] |
| domestic mails | inland mails [5] |
| down-town | the City [6] |
| *drawers (men's) [7] | pants |
| dredge | dredger [8] |
| *druggist | chemist [9] |
| *drug-store | chemist's shop [10] |
| *drygoods-store | draper's shop [11] |
| dumbwaiter | service lift [12] |
| dump | refuse tip [13] |
| editorial (noun) | leading article, or leader [14] |

1 Advertisement in the *Countryman*, Oct., 1937, p. 41: "Write for samples and prices, and the name of the nearest *stockist*." Advertisement in the London *News Observer*, June 18, 1936: "Post this coupon for . . . the name of the nearest *stockist*."

2 *District*, in this sense, is traced by the DAE to 1712 and marked an Americanism.

3 Though every criminal offense is prosecuted in England in the name of the crown, the actual prosecution was left, until 1879, to persons aggrieved. Under the Prosecution of Offenses Act of that year, followed by others in 1884 and 1908, something like the American system was set up, but even today the director of public prosecutions and his staff do not intervene invariably.

4 Topics of the Times, *New York Times*, Sept. 29, 1943: "With us a *dock* is what the British call a *wharf*. With them a *dock* is the body of water enclosed within wharves, the thing we call a *basin*. They say East India *Docks* and we say Erie *Basin*. If an American on furlough in London were to tell his English buddy in fun to go and *jump off the dock* the English soldier would reply, 'But, I say, a chap can't jump off a hole in the water, you know.'" See also What is a *Dock? P. L. A. Monthly*, Nov., 1943, p. 306.

5 In England the *domestic* postal rates are *inland* also.

6 American and English, by Claude de Crespigny, *American Speech*, June, 1926, p. 491: "*Downtown* districts in England are called the *City* because the metropolitan areas take their cue from London."

7 Now commonly called *shorts*. Long *drawers* for men are obsolescent.

8 Encyclopaedia Britannica, 14th ed., 1929, Vol. VII, p. 641: "Dredging . . . deals with the process of removing materials lying under water. . . . The machines employed by engineers to that end are termed *dredgers* (*dredges* in America)."

9 *Druggist* is old in English, but is seldom used today.

10 *Pharmacy* is known in England, but is seldom used. *Drug-store* is traced by the DAE to 1819 and marked an Americanism.

11 The DAE traces *drygoods-store* to 1789 and marks it an Americanism.

12 Says Mr. A. D. Jacobs of Manchester: "We use *dumb-waiter* to mean a small table on wheels for transporting food from one room to another."

13 London *Daily Telegraph*, Sept. 4, 1937: "At the Weymouth inquest yesterday on a newly-born unidentified male child found on Monday on a municipal *refuse tip* it was revealed that death was caused by a blow on the head."

14 The DAE traces *editorial* to 1830. It was denounced by Richard Grant

| American | English |
|---|---|
| electric heater | radiator [1] |
| *elevator | lift [2] |
| engineer (locomotive) | engine-driver [3] |
| eraser | Indian-rubber [4] |
| espantoon, or night-stick (policeman's) | truncheon |
| excelsior | wood wool [5] |
| expelled (from college) | sent down |
| express company | carrier [6] |
| extension (university) | extra-mural studies |
| extension-wire | flex [7] |
| faculty (school or college) | staff [8] |
| Fall | Autumn [9] |
| farm-hand | agricultural laborer [10] |
| *fender (automobile) | wing, or mudguard [11] |

White in Words and Their Uses, 1870, but has survived.

1 So denominated, with pictures of *electric heaters*, in various English newspaper advertisements.

2 The DAE marks *elevator* an Americanism and traces it to 1787, but it was not used to indicate a machine for lifting human beings until the 50s. *Elevator-boy* is first recorded in 1882, *elevator-shaft* in 1885, and *elevator-man* in 1890. The English *lift* also dates from the 50s. It is one of the few Briticisms that are more pungent and succinct than the corresponding Americanisms. *Elevator* in the American sense of a building for storing grain is traced by the DAE to 1858.

3 But the union of the English *engine-drivers* is called the Associated Society of Locomotive *Engineers* and Firemen.

4 Says Mr. A. D. Jacobs of Manchester: "*Eraser* is also used, but to English ears sounds more pedantic and official than the other term, which is commonly abbreviated to *rubber*."

5 U. S. and British Staff Officers Overcome Language Difficulties, by Milton Bracker, New York *Times*, July 1, 1943. The DAE traces *excelsior* to 1869 and marks it an Americanism.

6 The first *express company* unearthed by the DAE was Harnden's, which began to operate between New York and Boston March 4, 1839. *Express-age, express agent, express business, express car, express charges, express company, expressman, express office, express wagon* and *to express* are all Americanisms, but *express train* seems to have been used in England a few years before it appeared in the United States. London *Times Literary Supplement*, May 31, 1934: "The *express*, or, as we should say, *carrier* or *parcels delivery* companies."

7 London *Daily Telegraph*, May 11, 1936: "She was lying on her bed, and had apparently been strangled with a piece of electric *flex*." London *Morning Post*, Dec. 4, 1936: "The [telephone] subscriber wanted 8 feet of *flex* for his hand telephone." The English call an *outlet* a *point*.

8 But the English use *faculty* to designate a department in a university; *e.g.*, *faculty of medicine*.

9 Americans Bound Coronationwards Should Read This Alphabet, London *Daily Express*, April 28, 1937: "*Fall*. Say *Autumn*. There's poetry in your word, but Keats . . . knew his London climate when he wrote about the season of mists and yellow frightfulness."

10 Americanisms and Briticisms, by Brander Matthews; New York, 1892, p. 19.

11 The English-Speaking Peoples, by Alistair Cooke, London *Evening Standard*, Dec. 1, 1936: "They ask

| American | English |
|---|---|
| filling-station | petrol-pump [1] |
| fire-bug | fire-raiser [2] |
| fire department | fire-brigade [3] |
| first floor | ground floor [4] |
| *fish-dealer | fishmonger |
| *five-and-ten (store) | bazaar [5] |
| flashlight | torch [6] |
| floor-space | carpet-area [7] |
| *floorwalker | shopwalker [8] |
| flophouse | doss house |
| *frame house | wooden house [9] |
| fraternal order | friendly society |
| *freight-car | goods-waggon [10] |
| *fruitseller (or -dealer) | fruiterer [11] |
| *fruit-store, or -stand | fruiterer's [12] |
| full time (adverb) | full out [13] |

to have the *fender* (the *mudguard*) and the *windshield* (the *windscreen*) wiped." Seaman says that *wing* is usually used.

1 The English-Speaking Peoples, by Alistair Cooke, London *Evening Standard*, Dec. 1, 1936: " Their *filling-station* is now ousting our *petrol-pump*."

2 The DAE's first example of *fire-bug* is from a poem by Oliver Wendell Holmes, 1872. *Fire-raising*, in English use, is traced by the NED to 1685, but its first example of *fire-raiser* is dated 1891.

3 Rather curiously, *fire brigade* was used in the official programme of the Oriole Pageant in Baltimore, Oct. 10, 11 and 12, 1881. It is never heard in the town today. The DAE traces *fire department* to 1825.

4 " The *first floor* of an American building," says Horwill, " is what would be called the *ground floor* in England, and the numbering of the higher floors follows according to the same reckoning," *e.g.*, the American *second floor* is the English *first floor*, or *storey* — always given the *e*.

5 Or, rather, *sixpenny-store*. Headline in London *Telegraph and Post*, March 19, 1938: "Duchess of Kent at *Sixpenny Store*." It was at Slough and she bought " a pair of quoits, a kite and a toy windmill." *Bazaar* is now obsolescent, and *Woolworth's* is often heard.

6 The King's English, by Wayne Allen, *Quartermaster Review* (Washington), March–April, 1943, p. 57: " You are all familiar, I am sure, with the British expression *torch* as compared with the American *flashlight*." I am indebted here to Dr. George W. Corner.

7 Advertisement in the London *Sunday Times*, March 8, 1936: " A distinguished Modern Office Building. *Carpet-Area*, 11,000 Square Feet."

8 *Floorwalker* is now virtually extinct in America. He is either an *aisle-manager* or a *section-manager*. The DAE traces the term to 1876.

9 *Wooden Houses*, by N. Newnham Davis, London *Times*, July 1, 1935: " The chief disadvantage of *wooden* (called *frame* in U. S. A.) *houses* has always been the difficulty of maintaining an equable temperature."

10 Or *goods-van*. The English also use *goods-train* for *freight-train*, *goods-station* for *freight-station* or *-depot*, and *goods-yard* for *freight-yard*, but of late they have shown some tendency to adopt *freight*. American Journey, by J. A. Russell, *Scottish Educational Journal*, Nov. 9, 1934: " We should be prepared for *freight-car* for *goods-van*."

11 The DAE traces *fruit-dealer* to 1874.

12 The DAE traces *fruit-store* to 1872.

13 London *Sunday Express*, Nov. 13, 1938: " Alvis are working *full out* to supply the demand."

| American | English |
|----------|---------|
| fusion (political) | coalition |
| game (*e.g.*, football) | match |
| garbage can | dust-bin [1] |
| garbage man | dustman [2] |
| *garter (men's) | sock-suspender [3] |
| *gasoline, or gas | petrol [4] |
| *gear-shift (automobile) | gear-lever |
| general delivery (post office) | poste restante [5] |
| *generator (automobile) | dynamo [6] |
| ginger-snap | ginger-nut [7] |
| given name, or first name | Christian name [8] |
| gondola (railroad) | mineral-waggon [9] |
| grab-bag | lucky-dip [10] |
| grade (road) | gradient [11] |
| grade (school) | form, standard or class [12] |
| grade-crossing (railroad) | level crossing [13] |

1 See *ash-can.*

2 Where the Pavements Become Sidewalks, by Alex Faulkner, London *Telegraph and Post*, May 8, 1939: " The *dustman* (*garbage man*) going about his work with an opulent-looking five-cent cigar in his mouth, the *milk-carts* on rubber-*tyred* wheels, and the *armoured-car* guards standing outside the banks with drawn pistols all make their distinctive contribution to the New York scene."

3 Or simply *suspender. Garter,* of course, is an old word in English, and the *Knights of the Garter* go back to April 23, 1349. The term was not used to indicate an article of men's wear until the 1880s. Before that time American men held up their socks with strings attached to the lower ends of their long drawers. Short drawers were brought in by the bicycle craze. See *suspenders.*

4 American Journey, by J. A. Russell, *Scottish Educational Journal*, Nov. 9, 1934: " *Gas* for *petrol* we are — or should be —prepared for."

5 This French phrase, meaning remaining at the postoffice, is traced by the NED, in English use, to 1768.

6 The English-Speaking Peoples, by Alistair Cooke, London *Evening Standard*, Dec. 1, 1936: " [The

Americans] talk with the [English] mechanic about the *generator,* which he calls a *dynamo,* and admire the shape of the *hood,* which he knows only as a *bonnet.*"

7 Advertisement in the London *Telegraph and Post*, Feb. 22, 1938, with a picture of *ginger-snaps:* " Romary's *ginger-nuts* just melt! " *Ginger-snap* is not unknown in England, but the NED's first English example is dated 1868. The DAE traces it in American use to 1805.

8 As She Is Spoke in the United States, by J. H. M., Glasgow *Evening Citizen*, Aug. 29, 1936: "Even if he is a Christian he may not know that he has a *Christian name;* you ask him what his *given-name* is."

9 New York *Times Magazine*, quoted in *Writer's Monthly*, Oct., 1927, p. 335: " *Mineral-waggons* take the place of coal *gondolas.*"

10 The DAE traces *grab-bag* to 1855 and marks it an Americanism.

11 The DAE traces *grade* in this sense to 1808 and marks it an Americanism.

12 In *American Speech*, Oct., 1942, p. 208, Dwight L. Bolinger traces *grade* in this sense to 1835.

13 *Level crossing* has been in use in England since 1841. The DAE traces *grade crossing* to 1890, but it must be much older.

| American | English |
|---|---|
| graduate (of a school)[1] | old boy |
| grocery | grocer's shop, or grocer's [2] |
| *ground-wire (radio) | earth-wire |
| guard, or deputy warden (prison) | warder |
| hall, or hallway (in a private house) | passage [3] |
| *hardware | ironmongery [4] |
| hardware-dealer | ironmonger |
| hash | shepherd's pie [5] |
| *headliner (theatre, and figuratively) | topliner |
| *highball | whiskey and soda |
| hike (verb) | tramp |
| hitch-hike | lorry-jump or -hop [6] |
| hockey | ice-hockey [7] |
| hog-pen | pig-sty [8] |
| hog-raiser, or -grower | pig-breeder [9] |
| holdup man, or stickup man, or highjacker | raider [10] |

1 Sometimes *alumnus* is used. America Revisited, by Cyril Alington, London *Sunday Times*, Feb. 14, 1937: "They [Americans] have leisure to speak of *alumni* when we speak of *boys*."

2 *Grocery* is traced by the DAE to 1791, and marked an Americanism.

3 I am indebted here to the late Sir E. Denison Ross. *Hall*, in England, ordinarily means a large apartment, e.g., *music-hall* or the *hall* of a castle. It is also used in special senses at the universities. *Servants' hall* likewise shows a special British use. But *hall-bedroom*, *hallroom*, *hall-boy* and *hallway* are all Americanisms.

4 Learn English Before You Go, by Frank Loxley Griffin, *Atlantic Monthly*, June, 1932, p. 75: "In the *ironmongery* department one can purchase what Americans ignorantly call *hardware*." *Hardware* is not an Americanism, but *hardware-store* is, and the DAE traces it to 1789.

5 The Spoken Word That May Occasionally Baffle, by Joyce M. Horner, Yorkshire *Evening Post* (Leeds) Sept. 1, 1933: "The [American] *hash* is near to being *shepherd's pie*."

*Hash* is mentioned in Pepys' Diary, Jan. 13, 1662/63, but it seems to be but little used in England. The DAE traces *hash-house* to 1875, *hashery* to 1872, *hash-slinger* to 1868, and *to settle one's hash* to 1809; all are Americanisms.

6 Fell In Love With Prison, *News of the World* (London), June 7, 1936: "I have *lorry-jumped* my way from Manchester to London." Partridge says that the British soldiers began to use *lorry-hop* in 1915.

7 Dos and Don'ts For Doughboys, by H. W. Seaman, Manchester *Sunday Chronicle*, March 22, 1942: "*Hockey* is here called *ice-hockey*. The game the British call *hockey* is played on the ground with a ball."

8 *Hog*, says Horwill, "is rarely used in England nowadays except figuratively, e.g., *road-hog*." Partridge says that *road-hog* is an Americanism, adopted by the English c. 1898.

9 The DAE traces *hog-grower* to 1869.

10 London *Daily Sketch*, July 14, 1938: "A woman shopkeeper at Knockholt was threatened by two men, armed with what appeared to be a

| American | English |
|---|---|
| *hood (automobile) | bonnet [1] |
| hook-and-ladder | fire-escape [2] |
| hope-chest | bottom-drawer [3] |
| horn (automobile) or siren | hooter [4] |
| *hospital (private) | nursing-home |
| hot-water bag | stomach-warmer [5] |
| house-wrecker | housebreaker or house-demolisher [6] |
| *huckster [7] | coster, or hawker |
| *hunting | shooting [8] |
| ice-cream | ice [9] |
| identification-tag | identity disk [10] |
| Inc. | Ltd. [11] |

revolver, in her shop yesterday and robbed of about £5 in cash. The *raiders* also visited her cottage nearby and took about £2."

1 See *generator*.

2 On May 14, 1936 the London *Daily Telegraph* printed a picture of a *hook-and-ladder* in action, captioned " A *Fire-Escape* Used by Painters." The DAE traces *hook-and-ladder company* to 1821 and *hook-and-ladder truck* to 1882, and marks them both Americanisms.

3 A Bristol correspondent of an unidentified English newspaper, *c.* 1936: " English girls who have thoughts of getting married collect things to that end in what they call their *bottom drawer*. A Canadian girl who married my nephew always spoke of her *hope chest*."

4 London *News-Chronicle*, Oct. 31, 1936: " The Ministry of Transport has failed to convince the local authorities that . . . electric *hooters* should be silenced day and night." Advertisement in the *Cape Times* (Cape Town), June 18, 1938: " Nash Sedans have Twin *Hooters*."

5 U. S. and British Staff Officers Overcome Language Difficulties, by Milton Bracker, New York *Times*, July 1, 1943. On July 5 the *Times* printed a letter from David Allan Ross of Budd Lake, N. J., saying " I have never heard a *hot-water bottle* or *bag* called anything but that in England. *Stomach-warmer*, at least in army circles, would be a euphemism

for bellyband." But Col. Wayne Allen, U.S.A., listed *stomach-warmer* as the English equivalent of *hot-water bag* in the *Quartermaster Review* (Washington), March–April, 1943, p. 58. So did the *Stars and Stripes*, June 15, 1943.

6 London *Daily Telegraph*, Nov. 1, 1935: " *Housebreaker's* Fate. After over 50 years as a *house-demolisher* Henry Elbury was killed yesterday." London *Times*, April 5, 1936: " The School of Oriental Studies, in Finsbury Circus, is now in the hands of the *housebreakers*." In the United States a *housebreaker* is a burglar.

7 *Huckster* is not an Americanism, but it is used much oftener in the United States than in England.

8 " An Englishman," says Horwill, " *hunts* foxes, stags, otter(s) and even hares. When he pursues grouse or partridge he does not go *hunting* but *shooting*." In the United States *gunning* is often used. See Notes on " The American Language," by Stuart Robertson, *American Speech*, Oct., 1937, p. 187.

9 Please Speak English, by Dale Warren, *Seven Seas*, Spring, 1939, p. 26: " [In England] *ice-cream* is always an *ice*."

10 The King's English, by Wayne Allen, *Quartermaster Review* (Washington), March–April, 1943, p. 58: " A *tag, identification*, is an *identity disk*."

11 *i.e., limited*, from *limited liability company*. See *corporation*.

| American | English |
|---|---|
| information-bureau | inquiry-office [1] |
| inning | innings [2] |
| *instalment plan | hire-purchase system, or hire system [3] |
| insurance (life) | assurance [4] |
| *intermission (theatre) | interval |
| internal revenue | inland revenue [5] |
| *janitor | caretaker, or porter [6] |
| jimmy (burglar's) | jemmy [7] |
| *junk | rubbish |
| landscape architect | landscape gardener [8] |
| landslide | landslip [9] |
| lease | let [10] |
| *legal holiday | bank holiday [11] |
| letter-man (college) | blue [12] |
| life-guard | life-saver [13] |

1 Aids to the Talkies, by D. W. B(rogan), *Oxford Magazine*, Oct. 17, 1935: "The difference in attitude involved in the American for *inquiry-office* being *bureau of information* is left to the reader to appraise."

2 The plural is used in the United States when more than one *inning* is spoken of.

3 *News of the World* (London), July 31, 1938: "*Hire-purchase agreement* means an agreement under which the goods become the property of the hirer upon the payment of all the agreed instalments. *Credit-sale agreement* means an agreement for the sale of goods under which the purchase-price is payable by five or more instalments." Mr. P. E. Cleator tells me that *instalment plan* is now often used in England.

4 D. Cameron-Forrester, author of A Dictionary of Life Assurance, explained in *John o' London's Weekly*, Sept. 3, 1937, that *assurance* is used because the insured, if he keeps up his payments, is *assured* of benefits soon or late, whereas the holder of, say, a fire *insurance* policy may pay for years and never have a fire.

5 See *domestic mails*. The DAE traces *internal revenue* to 1796.

6 Sometimes *doorkeeper*. The Trial of Professor John White Webster, by George Dilnot; London, 1928, p. 5: "This was the college *caretaker*,

or, in American terminology, the *janitor*."

7 The DAE traces *jimmy* to 1854. It does not list *to jimmy*.

8 See Encyclopaedia Britannica, 14th ed.: New York, 1929, Vol. XIII, p. 659.

9 The DAE traces *landslide* to 1838 and marks it an Americanism.

10 London *Daily Telegraph*, Feb. 1, 1936: "Major Courtauld claims damages for alleged breach of agreement relating to a *let* to him for five years." *Lease*, of course, is used in England, and the NED traces it to 1292, but *let* seems to be common in advertisements and law reports.

11 London *Leader*, March 27, 1943: "Other Yankee words that come to mind are *legal holiday* for *bank holiday*, and *union suits* for *combinations*."

12 A Guide to British Educational Terms, by Herbert B. Grimsditch, *Wilson Bulletin* (New York), May, 1936, p. 578: "Men of both the ancient universities wear blue shirts for athletics, Oxford dark and Cambridge light. *To be a blue* is to be chosen to represent one's university in a team. Football, cricket, rowing and other consecrated sports carry *full blues;* while less popular games, like hockey and lacrosse, give only *half-blues*."

13 In England a *life-guard* is a member of the Household Cavalry. In

| American | English |
|---|---|
| life-preserver | life-belt [1] |
| limited (in the name of a train) | express [2] |
| *line up (verb) | queue up [3] |
| *living-room | sitting-room [4] |
| *long-distance (telephone) [5] | trunk |
| *low gear (automobile) | first speed |
| lumber | timber [6] |
| lunch | snack [7] |
| machine-tender, or -operator | machine-minder [8] |
| mad | angry |
| mail | post, or letters [9] |
| *mail a letter | post a letter |
| mail-box | letter-box, or pillar-box [10] |

the United States, a *life-saver* is a member of the former Life-saving Service of the Coast Guard, now the Beach Patrol Division. *Life-guard* in the American sense is traced by the DAE to 1896, *life-saver* to 1887, and *life-saving station* to 1858.

1 London *Times Literary Supplement*, Nov. 16, 1935: " By *life-preservers* are clearly meant what we call *life-belts*." See *blackjack*.

2 *Limited* is traced by the DAE, in American use, to 1879. The first English example is dated 1883. See *express*.

3 " A row of persons waiting their turn," says Horwill, "is in England a *queue*. In America it is a *line*." *Queue* seems to have been introduced by Carlyle in his French Revolution, 1837. *To queue up* is traced by the NED Supplement to 1927.

4 *Living-room* is not exclusively American and *sitting-room* is certainly not exclusively English.

5 The first recorded English example of *long-distance* is from American usage.

6 In England *lumber* usually means discarded objects, as in *lumber-room*.

7 Horwill says that *lunch*, in England, always means a midday meal; in America it may designate a light repast at any time. A *lunch-counter* is a *snack-bar* to the English.

8 The English call a *sewing-machine operator* a *machinist*. Want-ad in London *News-Chronicle* May 4, 1936: " *Machinists* required for ladies' gowns."

9 Americans Bound Coronationwards Should Read This Alphabet, London *Daily Express*, April 28, 1937: " Ask at your hotel for your *post* or your *letters*, and you'll get your mail safely." A Truck By Any Other Name, by Robert Lynd, London *News-Chronicle*, May 22, 1943: " The English traveler in America gets all the happier sensation of being a traveller when in a hotel he has to ask for his *mail* instead of his *letters*." Horwill says that the English use *mail* very little, though *mail-train*, *mail-bag* and *mail-van* occur.

10 Learn English Before You Go, by Frank Loxley Griffin, *Atlantic Monthly*, June, 1932, p. 775: " There are no *mail-boxes* from which *mail* is collected. The lack of them is not a serious inconvenience since there are a number of *letter-boxes*, which are cleared frequently." A *letter-box* is attached to a wall; a *pillar-box* is on a stand. The NED traces *pillar-box* to 1858 and *letter-box* to 1849. *Mail-box* is not an Americanism, but *to mail*, *mailability*, *mailable*, *mail-carrier*, *mail-day*, *mail-matter*, *mail-order*, *mail-pouch*, *mail-robber* and *mail-wagon* are.

| American | English |
|---|---|
| mail-car, or railway-postoffice | postal van [1] |
| *marriage certificate | marriage lines [2] |
| master of ceremonies (of a show) | compère [3] |
| maybe | perhaps [4] |
| *molasses | treacle [5] |
| *monkey-wrench | spanner, adjustable spanner, or screw-spanner [6] |
| motorman | driver [7] |
| *movie | cinema [8] |
| moving | moving house [9] |
| *mucilage | gum [10] |
| *muffler (automobile) | silencer |
| napkin (table) | serviette [11] |

1 The DAE traces *railway-postoffice* to 1874, and *mail-car* to 1855.

2 *Marriage lines* is confined to the vulgar. On higher levels *marriage certificate* is used.

3 Heard and Overheard, *P.M.* (New York), Nov. 24, 1943: "[In England] an *emcee* is a *compère*." New York Studies, London *Daily Telegraph*, May 12, 1936: "Naunton Wayne is the witty *compère* this week, and he has some clever acts to introduce."

4 Horwill says that *maybe* has "almost become an archaism and a dialect word" in England.

5 "In the United States," says the DAE, "*molasses* has entirely supplanted *treacle*." *Molasses* is not an Americanism: the NED traces it in English use to 1582. But it is now supplanted by *treacle*, first recorded in 1694. The DAE traces *molasses* in American use to 1666, *molasses-candy* to 1809, *molasses-cake* to 1836, *molasses-jug* to 1839, and *molasses-barrel* to 1846. All the latter are Americanisms. *Molasses* is still used in England to designate a heavy, crude syrup, mainly used in cattle feeds.

6 London *Daily Mail*, June 17, 1936: "Life is complicated enough without any help from outside in the way of throwing *spanners* into the works."

7 As She Is Spoke in the United States, by J. H. M., Glasgow *Eve-ning Citizen*, Aug. 29, 1936: "You may take the *trolley*, also called the *street-car* or *surface-car*, but never the *tram*. In any case the *driver* is the *motorma.*"

8 These terms, of course, are for the house, not the film. The film, in both countries, is the *pictures;* in the United States it may also be the *movies* or *film* (or *fillum*), and in England the *flicker* or *flick*. All the terms for pictures are usually heard in the plural. In 1927 the London *Mercury* dropped the *Cinema* title on its film article and substituted *Movies*, and since then various other English publications have followed suit.

9 London *Morning Post*, Aug. 25, 1936: "Take, for instance, the question of *moving house*. Every woman in her heart rejoices in the event, as in a festival. It stirs her to the depths of her being, as if it were a translation to another and a better world."

10 The DAE traces *mucilage* in this sense to 1859 and makes it an Americanism.

11 Please Speak English, by Dale Warren, *Seven Seas*, Spring, 1939, p. 26: "I presume that in some of the smarter places they know what a *napkin* is, but many's the apple-cheeked lass who responds more readily if you let it be known that a *serviette* is what you desire." The NED defines *napkin* as "a square

| American | English |
|---|---|
| *necktie | tie [1] |
| newsdealer | news-agent |
| *newsstand | kiosk [2] |
| notions | fancy goods, or novelties, or haberdashery [3] |
| oarlock | rowlock [4] |
| *oatmeal (boiled) | porridge [5] |
| occupant (of a building) | occupier [6] |
| office (doctor's or dentist's) | surgery [7] |
| office (lawyer's) | chambers [8] |
| *oil-pan (automobile) | sump |
| on (a street) | in [9] |
| one-way ticket | single ticket |
| operating cost | running, or working expense [10] |
| *orchestra seat (theatre) | stall [11] |

piece of linen, used at meals to wipe the fingers and lips, . . . a *serviette*," and traces it in English use to *c.* 1489. It traces *serviette* to 1420. There are Englishmen who deny indignantly that *serviette* is ever used by respectable people in their country. Vandalism?, *John o' London's Weekly*, March 18, 1938: "To plant palm trees and pampas grass on the Devon hills is like calling a *table napkin* in an Englishman's dining-room a *serviette*."

1 *Tie*, in fact, is in common use in America. *Black tie*, on an invitation, means that *dinner-coats* (or *tuxedos*) are to be worn.

2 A railway-station *newsstand*, in England, is a *bookstall*. The DAE traces *newsstand* to 1871 and marks it an Americanism.

3 The DAE traces *notions* to 1796 and marks it an Americanism. At the start it included anything sold by a peddler, *e.g.*, clocks and wooden ware, but it began to be restricted to its present meaning after the Civil War. The English-Speaking Peoples, by Alistair Cooke, London *Evening Standard*, Dec. 1, 1936: "He asks for the *notion* counter and a bright girl assistant, who has heard that it is the American name for *haberdashery*, directs him there."

4 Horwill says that *oarlock* is "seldom heard" in England.

5 The DAE does not list *breakfast-food*, but it traces *cereal* to 1900.

6 Learn English Before You Go, by Frank Loxley Griffin, *Atlantic Monthly*, June, 1932, p. 775: "A tenant is not the *occupant*, but the *occupier* of the building, and he does not *rent* his quarters — he *hires* them, or they are *let* to him."

7 London *Daily Telegraph*, July 11, 1936: "Mr. G. W. Simpson, a dentist, was attacked in his *surgery* in the Broadway, Southall, last night." The *Mr.* before the name and the *the* before Broadway will be noted.

8 T. L. Nichols: Forty Years of American Life; London, 1864, Vol. I, p. 344: "In the *office*, as the American lawyer's *chambers* are called." I take this from the DAE.

9 Please Speak English, by Dale Warren, *Seven Seas*, Spring, 1939, p. 26: "In England you invariably . . . live *in* a street." A Guide to British Educational Terms, by Herbert B. Grimsditch, *Wilson Bulletin* (New York), May, 1936, p. 576: "*On the street* pulls the Englishman up a little queerly, for he thinks of a street (not a *road*) as a canyon, and says *in*, only using *on the street* for daughters of joy."

10 The authority here is Horwill.

11 The DAE traces *orchestra*, in this sense, to 1856 and marks it an Americanism.

| American | English |
|---|---|
| ordinance (municipal) | by-law [1] |
| overcoat | greatcoat [2] |
| *package | parcel [3] |
| pantry | larder [4] |
| paraffin | white wax [5] |
| parking-lot | car-park [6] |
| parlor-car | saloon-carriage [7] |
| parole (for a criminal) | ticket-of-leave [8] |
| patrolman (police) | constable [9] |
| peanut | monkey-nut [10] |
| *pebbly beach [11] | shingle |
| penitentiary | prison [12] |
| pen-point | nib [13] |

1 In the United States *by-law* designates only the rules and regulations of private associations.

2 British Names Headache to Supply Men, *Stars and Stripes*, June 15, 1943: "The British list . . . an *overcoat* as a *greatcoat*." But *overcoat* is also used in England.

3 *Package* is by no means exclusively American, and *parcel* is often used in the United States, as in *parcels-post*.

4 New York Speaking, by T. Kerr Ritchie, *Northern Daily Telegraph* (Blackburn) May 20, 1939: "[In America] the *larder* is a *pantry*." *Pantry* is not an Americanism.

5 Letter from a Canadian in the Manchester *Guardian*, reprinted in the Baltimore *Evening Sun*, Oct. 5, 1937: "What those quaint folk in Britain call *paraffin* the United States Americans call *kerosene* and we Canadians call *coal-oil*. What we call *paraffin* you poetically acclaim as *white wax*." See *coal-oil*.

6 An unidentified London paper: "Many of the large houses were pulled down and the sites converted into *car-parks*."

7 Both terms are now obsolescent: *Pullman* is already in wide use in England, and *chair-car* in the United States. The DAE traces *parlor-car* to 1868 and marks it an Americanism. *Chair-car*, also so marked, is traced to 1895. *Pullman-car* goes back to 1870. In the United States *Pullman* usually signifies a sleeper.

8 Horwill says that in England *parole* "is used in relation to prisoners of war only."

9 Officially, *police constable*, usually abbreviated by the English newspapers to *P.C.* The DAE marks *patrolman* an Americanism. *Patrol-wagon* is another.

10 But see the Seaman list at the end of the last chapter. *Peanut* is traced by the DAE to 1807. It was preceded by *ground-nut*, 1622, and *ground-pea*, 1769. *Goober* apparently did not come in until the 40s of the last century. The NED traces *monkey-nut* to 1880 in England; apparently the English were not familiar with *Arachis hypogaea* before that time. The DAE traces *peanut-politics* to 1887, but *peanut* was used as an adjective of disparagement so early as 1836. *Peanut-candy* is traced to 1856, *peanut-stand* to 1866, *peanut-gallery* to 1897, and *peanut-brittle* and *-butter* to 1903.

11 I have never heard *pebbly beach*.

12 *Penitentiary* is used in England to designate a reformatory. It began to be used for a prison in the United States early in the Nineteenth Century. The DAE traces *penitentiary-offense* to 1855.

13 New York Speaking, by T. Kerr Ritchie, *Northern Daily Telegraph* (Blackburn), May 20, 1939: "[In America] *nibs* are *pen points*."

| American | English |
|---|---|
| period (punctuation) | full stop [1] |
| personal (business) | private [2] |
| *phonograph | gramophone [3] |
| *pie (fruit) | tart [4] |
| pin-boy (bowling) | thrower-up [5] |
| *pitcher | jug [6] |
| plumbing, or sewerage (house) | drains |
| porch-climber | cat-burglar |
| porterhouse (steak) | sirloin [7] |
| postpaid | post-free [8] |
| *poolroom | billiards-saloon [9] |
| *potato-chip | crisp [10] |
| pot-pie | meat-pie [11] |
| preferred stock | preference shares [12] |
| president (of a corporation) | chairman [13] |
| pry (to raise or separate) | prise [14] |

1 Do You Speak American?, by John Blunt, London *Daily Mail*, Aug. 17, 1932: "A *full stop* is a *period*."

2 In 1935, when Rudyard Kipling's The Light That Failed was being done as a movie in Hollywood, the author made a number of changes in the script, seeking to substitute English locutions for Americanisms. Associated Press dispatch from Hollywood, July 31: "Where Torpenhow says: 'He had some very important *personal* business,' Kipling's question is, 'What does this word *personal* mean?' He substitutes *private*." So, in English usage, before *letter*, etc.

3 As She Is Spoke in the United States, by J. H. M., Glasgow *Evening Citizen*, Aug. 29, 1936: "What's that in that window? *Gramophones*? No, *phonographs*, or *victrolas*."

4 Dos and Don'ts for Doughboys, by H. W. Seaman, Manchester *Sunday Chronicle*, March 22, 1942: "What you call an *apple pie* we should have to call an *apple tart* with a lid on it."

5 Hong Kong *Sunday Herald*, Aug. 7, 1938: "Just as the ball crashed past the pins for a broken leg [the *thrower-up*] side-stepped with the easy grace of a matador." The DAE does not list *pin-boy*.

6 Horwill says that *pitcher* is "nowa-

days an archaic or poetical word in England."

7 See *sirloin*.

8 *Postpaid* is not an Americanism, but it is used much oftener in the United States than in England.

9 *Poolroom*, in the United States, also means a room in which bets on horse-races, etc., are taken.

10 Dos and Don'ts For Doughboys, by H. W. Seaman, Manchester *Sunday Chronicle*, March 22, 1942: "If you want *French-fried* [*potatoes*] you must ask for *chips*. If you want *chips* you must ask for *crisps*."

11 The DAE traces *pot-pie* in American use to 1824. Mr. James E. Walker, before cited, tells me that it is in use in the North of England.

12 The DAE traces *preferred stock* to 1850 and marks it an Americanism.

13 Do You Speak American?, by John Blunt, London *Daily Mail*, Aug. 17, 1932: "The *chairman* of a company is its *president*." The American *chairman of the board* is a different functionary. The DAE traces *president*, in this sense, to 1781, and marks it an Americanism.

14 H. W. Horwill in the London *Times Literary Supplement*, April 16, 1938, p. 264: "Your . . . reviewer of an American work on landslides notes, among errors that

| American | English |
|---|---|
| public comfort station | public convenience |
| public-school | council-school [1] |
| publisher (newspaper) | proprietor [2] |
| pumps | court-shoes [3] |
| puncture (tire) | flat |
| *pushcart | barrow |
| *race-track | race-course [4] |
| *radio | wireless [5] |
| railroad | railway [6] |
| *raincoat | mackintosh, or mac, or waterproof |
| *raise (in pay) | rise [7] |
| rare (of meat) | underdone [8] |

demand correction in a future edition, the author's use of *prying* in the sense of *prising*. I am afraid it is unlikely that this correction will ever be made, for this use of the word was not due to a slip of the pen but was intentional. It is an Americanism. One of the definitions of *pry* given in the New Webster is 'to raise or move, or pull (apart) or attempt to do so, with a *pry* or lever; to prize' . . . In his 'Three Centuries of Harvard,' Professor S. E. Morison writes: 'Two years later he was found to be lodging with various undergraduates, and was only *pried* loose from the college by the faculty's forbidding the students to feed or lodge him.'"

1 Formerly *board-school*. A *public-school*, in England, is an establishment for the sons of the rich, usually endowed. It corresponds to the more fashionable sort of American *prep-school*. The DAE traces *prep-school* to 1895. *Public-school*, in the American sense, is traced to *c.* 1669.

2 In England *publisher* means a book-publisher. . . . An English newspaper may have a *publisher;* he is not, however, the owner, but corresponds roughly to what Americans call a *business manager*.

3 *Pumps* is old in English, traced by the NED to 1555, but it seems to have gone out in the 80s. The DAE's first American example is dated 1726. The Spoken Word That May Occasionally Baffle, by Joyce M. Horner, *Yorkshire Evening Post*

(Leeds), Sept. 1, 1933: "In the [American] shoe department confusion can arise if one asks for *court-shoes*, for which the American is *pumps*."

4 The English-Speaking Peoples, by Alistair Cooke, London *Evening Standard*, Dec. 1, 1936: "The *race-course* they call *race-track*."

5 King Edward VIII used *radio* in a speech soon after his accession, and was denounced for the Americanism, but the official organ of the B.B.C. is the *Radio Times* (Robert Lynd, London *News-Chronicle*, May 22, 1943).

6 Learn English Before You Go, by Frank Loxley Griffin, *Atlantic Monthly*, June, 1932, p. 775: "There are no *railroads* in England, and the *railway* trains do not have *engineers*." But see engineer. Railway is by no means unknown in the United States. On Oct. 4, 1940, p. 14, the Chicago *Tribune* printed an article showing that of the 137 Class I *railroads* of the country, 69 use *railroad* in their names, 65 use *railway*, and three use neither. But an American always speaks of *the railroads*, not *the railways*. Street-railways are always so called in the United States.

7 The DAE's first example of *raise* in the sense of an increase in pay is marked an Americanism and dated 1898. The word must be much older. See *Raise or Rise?*, by Helen C. Munroe, *American Speech*, Aug., 1931, pp. 407-10.

8 I Discover America, by Kenneth

| American | English |
|---|---|
| recess (school) | break [1] |
| *roadster (automobile) | two-seater [2] |
| *roast (of meat) | joint [3] |
| *roller-coaster | switchback-railway or scenic-railway [4] |
| roll of bills | sheaf of notes |
| room-clerk (hotel) | reception-clerk |
| *roomer | lodger [5] |
| rooster | cock [6] |
| rotogravure | intaglio [7] |
| roundhouse (railroad) | running shed [8] |
| *round trip | return trip [9] |
| rubber-check | stumer-cheque [10] |
| *rubberneck-wagon, or car, or bus | char-a-banc [11] |
| *rubbers | galoshes |
| *rumble-seat | dickey |
| *run (in a stocking) | ladder [12] |

Adam, London *Star*, Nov. 30, 1937: "*Underdone* beef is, of all things, *rare*." Aids to the Talkies, by D. W. B(rogan), *Oxford Magazine*, Oct. 17, 1935: "Applied to *underdone* meat, *rare* . . . can easily be heard in Scotland."

1 The DAE traces *recess*, in this sense, to 1860, and marks it an Americanism.

2 The DAE traces *roadster* for an automobile to 1908, and marks it an Americanism.

3 Horwill says that "in England *joint* is preferred."

4 *Switchback* is in use in the United States.

5 The DAE traces *roomer* to 1871, *rooming-house* to 1893 and *room-mate* to 1789, and marks them all Americanisms.

6 *Rooster* is marked "chiefly U. S. and dialect" by the NED. Its first example, dated 1822, is of American origin. The DAE says that the use of the term "has been ascribed to . . . squeamishness about using the word *cock*." Mr. Percy Marks reminds me that chicken-breeders use *cockerel*.

7 *Cape Times* (Cape Town), July 16, 1938: "In the *intaglio* section of to-day's magazine supplement you will find more high-level photographs."

8 The DAE marks *roundhouse* an Americanism and traces it to 1870. The word exists in other senses in English usage.

9 As She Is Spoke in the United States, by J. H. M., Glasgow *Evening Citizen*, Aug. 29, 1936: "If you want a *return ticket* you ask for a *round-trip*."

10 From the cross-examination of a bankrupt in the London Bankruptcy Court, 1938:

Q. You know the expression *stumer cheques*?

A. Too well.

Q. I have some which you have passed at home and abroad.

Partridge says that *stumer* originally meant "a horse against which money may be laid without risk," and suggests that it may come from the Yiddish. In the sense of a *rubber-check* he traces it to 1890.

11 H. W. Seaman informs me that *char-a-banc* is dying in England, but that some of the English roadside pubs still exhibit signs reading *Char-a-banc* Parties Not Accommodated. The term is pronounced *sharabang* or *sharrybang*.

12 Mr. A. D. Jacobs of Manchester tells me that *run* "is making headway" in England.

| American | English |
|---|---|
| run (political verb) | stand |
| rutabaga | Swede [1] |
| *saloon | public-house, or pub [2] |
| saloon-keeper | publican |
| scab (labor) | blackleg [3] |
| *scallion | Spring onion [4] |
| schedule (railroad) | time-table [5] |
| scholarship | studentship [6] |
| school-ma'am | school-mistress |
| *scrambled eggs | buttered eggs |
| scratch-pad | scribbling-block |
| scrimmage (football) | scrum [7] |
| *second floor | first floor [8] |
| *sedan (automobile) | saloon-car [9] |
| sell out (verb) | sell up [10] |
| *shade (window) | blind [11] |
| shingle (sign) | brass plate [12] |
| shoe | boot [13] |

1 London *Morning Post*, Jan. 1, 1936: "*Rutabaga* . . . is a perfectly good English word (spelled *ruta-baga*), though not much in use now. *Brassica rutabaga* is the Latin name for the *Swede* or (as we used to call it in the army) *horse* turnip." The *rutabaga* was introduced into England from Sweden *c.* 1800 and into the United States soon afterward.

2 Dos and Don'ts For Doughboys, by H. W. Seaman, Manchester *Sunday Chronicle*, March 22, 1942: "A *pub* is not a *saloon*, but a group of bars of different social ranks. The *saloon-bar* is the swellest and the *public-bar* is the lowest."

3 British and American, by Josiah Combs, *American Speech*, April, 1941, p. 153: "William Feather reports that the British magazines that use copy prepared in his Cleveland office [substitute] *blackleg* for *scab*."

4 *Scallion* is by no means unknown to the English. The NED traces it to the Fourteenth Century, and Mr. A. T. Grime of London tells me (private communication, Aug. 8, 1940) that it was in constant use in Northeastern Lancashire in his youth. He says that *scally-onion* was also used.

5 When the English use *schedule* they make the first syllable *shed*, not *sked*.

6 London *Observer*, Feb. 9, 1936: "University College will award a Sir William Meyer *studentship*, of the value of about £120, for two years." But *scholarship* is also used in England.

7 Headline in the London *Morning Post*, Sept. 25, 1935: Rugby *Scrum* Fatality.

8 See *first floor*.

9 The English-Speaking Peoples, by Alistair Cooke, London *Evening Standard*, Dec. 1, 1936: "They ask for a *sedan*, and with a little difficulty get what we call a *saloon-car* (a phrase that to an American means nothing, but in a vision might mean a rowdy bar on wheels, attached to a train)."

10 London *Daily Express*, Sept. 2, 1936: "He *sold up* practically all of his home."

11 But *Venetian blind* is familiar in the United States. The DAE traces *shade* to 1867 and marks it an Americanism.

12 The First Reader, by Harry Hansen, New Bedford (Mass.) *Mercury*, July 27, 1935: "In America the professional man *hangs out his shingle*, meaning a signboard. In England he *puts up his brass plate*."

13 See AL4, p. 122. Efforts have been made to introduce the English *boot* in the United States, but in vain, for the term still indicates, to an American, a foot-covering reaching to the

| American | English |
|---|---|
| shoe-clerk | bootmaker's assistant [1] |
| *shoestring | bootlace, or shoelace [2] |
| *shot (athletics) | weight |
| *shoulder (of road) | verge |
| sidewalk | pavement [3] |
| silent partner | sleeping partner [4] |
| *silverware | plate [5] |
| sirloin | rump [6] |
| *slacks | bags |
| slingshot | catapult [7] |
| *smoked herring | kipper [8] |
| snap (a bargain, a sure thing) | snip [9] |
| *soda-biscuit, or -cracker | cream-cracker [10] |

knee. "Inconsistently enough," says Horwill, "an American calls the boy who *shines* his *shoes* a *bootblack*, while an Englishman calls the boy who *blacks* his *boots* a *shoeblack*." See *boot*.

1 American and English, by Claude de Crespigny, *American Speech*, June, 1926, p. 492.

2 *Shoestring* is not an Americanism, but it is used in the United States much oftener than in England, mainly because of the influence of *shoe. On a shoestring* is traced by the DAE to 1882.

3 Do You Speak English?, by John Blunt, London *Daily Mail*, Aug. 17, 1932: "*Sidewalk* for *pavement* is logical, as very few American *sidewalks* were paved in the olden time." A correspondent of the Liverpool *Daily Post*, Nov. 9, 1939, called attention to the fact that the Liverpool Corporation uses *pavement* to indicate the roadway, not the *sidewalk*. A clipping from the *Industrial Daily News*, Sept. 22, 1936, sent to me by Mr. P. E. Cleator, indicates that it also uses *sidewalk* as Americans do.

4 The DAE traces *silent partner* to 1828 and marks it an Americanism.

5 *Silverware* is not unknown in England, but it apparently did not come in there until *c.* 1860, whereas it was used in America in the Eighteenth Century. *Flat-silver* and *flat-ware* seem to be Americanisms.

6 The English-Speaking Peoples, by

Alistair Cooke, London *Evening Standard*, Dec. 1, 1936: "What they call *sirloin* is what we call *rump*, and our *sirloin* is their *porterhouse*."

7 In Australia a *slingshot* is a *shanghai*. The *slingshot* is becoming obsolete in America, for American boys have begun to forget their old sports and games. The DAE traces the term to 1849 and marks it an Americanism.

8 But *kippered herring* is used in America. *Kipper* is an old English name for the male salmon in the spawning season. But its relation to *to kipper*, which the NED traces to 1773, is not clear.

9 Advertisement in the London *Morning Post*, Nov. 30, 1935: "A *snip*! 2 magnificent Python Skins, 18 ft. and 21 ft.; EXTREMELY moderate, for disposal privately." The NED traces *snip* to 1894. The DAE does not list *snap* in the sense here indicated, but traces it in that of a brief, sudden spell of weather to 1740, in that of a string-bean to 1844, and in that of vim and dash to 1865. It is an Americanism in all these senses. So are *snap judgment, to snap the whip, snapping turtle*, and *to snap into it*.

10 The old difference between the English and American meanings of *biscuit* and *cracker* seem to be breaking down. The English begin to use both words in our senses, and *biscuit* is often used in America for what was formerly a *cracker*, e.g., the *Uneeda biscuit*.

| American | English |
|---|---|
| soda-fountain | soda-bar [1] |
| *soft drinks | minerals [2] |
| *spark-plug | sparking-plug |
| special delivery (post-office) | express delivery, or express post [3] |
| speed-cop | mobile police [4] |
| *spigot (or faucet) | tap [5] |
| spool (of thread) | reel [6] |
| sports goods | sporting requisites [7] |
| *squash | vegetable marrow [8] |
| *stairway | staircase, or stairs [9] |
| stenographer | shorthand-writer [10] |
| *store | shop [11] |
| straight (of a drink) | neat [12] |

1 New York *Times Magazine,* quoted in *Writer's Monthly,* Oct., 1927, p. 335: " Soda fountains are *soda bars* tucked away in *sweet shops,* never at the *chemist's.*"

2 London *Leader,* March 27, 1943; " Lord Woolton's Ministry of Food has adopted Uncle Sam's *soft drinks* in the place of *minerals* — few of which were made from mineral waters, anyway."

3 London *Daily Express,* Sept. 22, 1936: " I have just got an *express delivery* letter with the South Kensington postmark of 11.30 A.M. the previous day."

4 *Mobile Police,* London *Times,* Feb. 22, 1937: " There has been a friendly reception for last week's announcement in the House of Commons that the number of *mobile police* is to be greatly increased. It has been taken as a further and a proper acknowledgment that the duty of the police towards road-users must be educative as well as punitive." But see AL4, p. 226, n. 1.

5 Aids to the Talkies, by D. W. B(rogan), *Oxford Magazine,* Oct. 17, 1935: " Many Americanisms are also Scoticisms, *e.g., faucet* for *tap.*" Mr. L. Clark Keating of Minneapolis (private communication, June 30, 1937) says that *spigot* seems to be confined to the Philadelphia-Baltimore area. He says that *tap* is used in up-State New York.

6 The English-Speaking Peoples, by Alistair Cooke, London *Evening*

*Standard,* Dec. 1, 1936: " At the next counter he tries to come to the rescue of an American girl who wants a *spool of thread* and can make nobody understand. They go into a dumb show and begin to thread imaginary needles for the benefit of the girl behind the counter, who suddenly knows that what they've wanted all the time was a *reel of cotton.*"

7 The authority here is Horwill.

8 *Squash* is one of the oldest of Americanisms. It was borrowed from the Indians and is traced by the DAE to 1643.

9 *Stairs* is now common in the United States. The DAE traces *stairway* in American use to 1708, more than a century before it is first recorded in England.

10 Law Society and Legal Delays, London *Daily Telegraph,* Sept. 25, 1935: " The obvious remedy is to have a *shorthand-writer.*" *Stenography* is traced to 1602, in English use, by the NED, but all its examples of *stenographer* are American. The DAE traces *stenographer* to 1796 and marks it an Americanism. It is, of course, known to the English, but they seem to prefer *shorthand-writer,* especially when referring to court *stenographers.*

11 See Chapter III, Section 3.

12 The DAE marks *straight,* in this sense, an Americanism, and traces it to 1862.

| American | English |
|---|---|
| straw hat | boater [1] |
| stream-lined | swept-out [2] |
| street-cleaner | road-sweeper [3] |
| *string-bean | French bean [4] |
| student (school) | schoolboy, or -girl [5] |
| *subway | underground [6] |
| *sugar-bowl | sugar-basin |
| surplus (corporation) | reserve [7] |
| *suspenders | braces [8] |
| *sweater | pull-over [9] |
| sweet (of butter) | fresh [10] |
| *syrup | treacle [11] |
| *taffy | toffee |
| taxes (local) | rates |
| *taxi-stand | cab-rank |
| telephone-booth | call-box [12] |
| *tenderloin (of beef) | undercut, or fillet |
| *tenpins | ninepins [13] |

1 London correspondence of the *South China Morning Post*, June 11, 1936: "The Prince of Wales, who for years wore a *boater*, could not make *boaters* fashionable."

2 London *Daily Telegraph*, Sept. 4, 1936: "A new model 22 h.p. Ford V8 car . . is offered only as a four-door *saloon* with a *swept-out* tail." See *sedan*. But *stream-lined* is often used in England.

3 I am indebted here to Mr. P. H. Muir of London.

4 The DAE traces *string-bean* to 1759 and marks it an Americanism.

5 As She Is Spoke in the United States, by J. H. M., Glasgow *Evening Citizen*, Aug. 29, 1936: "Even *schoolboys* and *schoolgirls* are *students*."

6 Or *tube*. In England *subway* means an underground passage for persons on foot.

7 London *Morning Post*, May 6, 1936: "The Viscose Company . . . dividends were . . . maintained for the year by drawing upon *surplus* — or, as we should probably call it, *reserve*."

8 *Suspenders* is traced by the DAE to 1810, and *suspenders-button* to 1833. See *garter*. Aids to the Talkies, by D. W. B(rogan), *Oxford Magazine*, Oct. 17, 1935: "A striking example was afforded by the puzzlement of a visiting English professor at Har-

vard who read that [William Jennings] Bryan, at the [Dayton, Tenn.] monkey trial, spoke ' with his thumbs in his *suspenders*,' this appearing to be an acrobatic feat to which all others were (as Americans used to say) ' not a circumstance.' "

9 Or *cardigan*, or *jumper*. The Spoken Word That May Occasionally Baffle, by Joyce M. Horner, *Yorkshire Evening Post* (Leeds), Sept. 1, 1933: "Your Englishwoman in America . . . may cause some puzzlement by demanding to be shown *jumpers*, and will learn that all *jumpers* are *sweaters*, that *cardigans*, too, are *sweaters*, and *sweaters* are somewhat unhappily termed *sweat-shirts*."

10 As She Is Spoke in the United States, by J. H. M., Glasgow *Evening Citizen*, Aug. 29, 1936: "You insult the *grocer* by asking for *fresh* butter. What you wanted was *sweet* butter."

11 See *molasses*.

12 *Call Box*, by Taylor Scott Hardin, *New Yorker*, Dec. 7, 1935: " ' Where's the *telephone booth?* ' I interrupted. ' *Telephone booth?* ' ' Yes. Isn't there any place I can telephone from? ' ' Oh, a *call box*.' "

13 The NED says that *tenpins* is called *American bowls* in England. It is not, however, an American inven-

| American | English |
|---|---|
| thriller | shocker [1] |
| *thumb-tack, or push-pin | drawing-pin [2] |
| ticket-agent (railroad) | booking-clerk [3] |
| ticket-broker (or speculator) | library [4] |
| *ticket-office (railway) | booking office [5] |
| ticket-seller | booking-clerk [6] |
| tie (railroad) | sleeper [7] |
| tie-up (traffic) | hold-up [8] |
| *toilet | lavatory, or closet [9] |
| *top (automobile) | hood |
| touchdown (football) | try |
| tracklayer (railroad) | platelayer |
| trained nurse | hospital nurse [10] |
| *transom (door) | fanlight [11] |
| transport (Army ship) | troopship, or trooper |
| *trolley, or street car [12] | tram, or tram-car |

tion, and the traditional etymology given in AL4, p. 248, n. 1, is probably unsound. The DAE traces *tenpins* in American use to 1830 and *tenpin-alley* to 1835. A variant called *duckpins* originated in Baltimore in 1903. See Baltimore *Duckpins*, by Martin S. Day, *American Speech*, Dec., 1940, pp. 361–63.

1 Murder For Pleasure, by Howard Haycraft; New York, 1941: "In America the term *thriller* is usually employed to indicate the sensational crime story, as distinctive from the police novel proper. In England it has come increasingly to mean the bona fide detective story. When the English wish to signify the sensational novel they say *shocker*." I take this from *American Speech*, Feb., 1942, p. 70.

2 Please Speak English, by Dale Warren, *Seven Seas*, Spring, 1939, p. 26: "I seldom have a need for *thumbtacks*, but if I did I would have to explain to the stationer that I'd be pleased to have a package of *drawing-pins*."

3 Please Speak English, by Dale Warren, *Seven Seas*, Spring, 1939, p. 26: "A *booking-clerk* is just our old friend the *ticket-agent*."

4 London *Observer*, Feb. 9, 1936: "The *libraries* have bought a lot of seats."

5 The DAE traces *ticket-office* to 1835 and marks it an Americanism.

6 The DAE traces *ticket-seller* to 1857.

7 *Tie* is marked an Americanism by the DAE and traced to 1853. *Sleeper* was probably driven out of American use by the hazard of confusing it with the common American term for a *sleeping-car*, introduced c. 1875.

8 London *Daily Telegraph*, May 11, 1936: "Southern Railway *Hold-up*." It was achieved, not by train-robbers, but by "a *point* failure outside Waterloo Station," i.e., some trouble with switches.

9 Or *W.C. Toilet* is not unknown in England, but it is not common. *Restroom* is apparently never used.

10 In the United States she is addressed as *Miss* ——; in England as *Nurse* or *Sister*.

11 Mr. R. Raven-Hart tells me that in England a *transom* is still the bar below the *fanlight*, as it once was in America. See Americanisms and Briticisms, by Brander Matthews; New York, 1892, p. 21.

12 Or, in New York, *surface-car*. The DAE traces *trolley-car* to 1891, *street-car* to 1862, and *surface-car* to 1889. All are Americanisms, as is *you're off your trolley. Trolley-ride*, now obsolete, was in use c. 1900. *Electric-car*, now also obsolete, is traced to 1888. See *motorman*.

| American | English |
|---|---|
| trolley-line | tramway |
| *truck | lorry [1] |
| truck-farmer | market-gardener [2] |
| truck-line | road-haulier [3] |
| trunk | box [4] |
| tube (radio) | wireless valve [5] |
| *undershirt | vest, or singlet [6] |
| union station | joint station [7] |
| *union-suit | combinations [8] |
| vacationist [9] | holiday-maker |
| *vaudeville | variety [10] |
| *vaudeville-theatre | music-hall |
| *vest | waistcoat [11] |
| *vomit (verb) | to be sick |
| warden (prison) [12] | governor |
| *washbowl [13] | washbasin |
| wash-day | washing-day [14] |
| *wash-rag | face-cloth [15] |

1 *Truck* was used in America, before the automobile, to designate any heavy wagon, and in that sense is traced by the DAE to 1701.

2 Do You Speak American?, by John Blunt, London *Daily Mail*, Aug. 17, 1932: "Who could tell that *truck-farming* is *market-gardening*?" The DAE traces *truck-farm* to 1866, *truck-farming* to 1870 and *truck-farmer* to 1877, and marks them all Americanisms.

3 *Road Hauliers* Win Test Case, London *Daily Telegraph*, Feb. 16, 1937: "If there were good foundation for the suggestion of the railway companies that goods were carried by road at rates economic to the *haulier* and lower than the rates at which the railways could carry the same goods, the railway companies must seek their remedy elsewhere."

4 See *baggage-car*. *Trunk* is not an Americanism, but it is seldom encountered in England.

5 When a Doughboy Goes Shopping in Britain, by Jack Brooks, *Chain Store Age* (New York), Nov., 1943: "A radio *tube*, in England, is a *wireless valve*." As She Is Spoke in the United States, by J. H. M., Glasgow *Evening Citizen*, Aug. 29, 1936: "Your room may have a *radio* (with *tubes*); it will not have a *wireless* (with *valves*)."

6 See *vest*.

7 The DAE does not list *union station*, but it traces *union depot* to 1862.

8 See *legal holiday*.

9 The DAE traces *vacationist* to 1888 and *vacationer* to 1890, and marks them Americanisms.

10 H. W. Seaman: "*Vaudeville* has an exotic flavour in England."

11 A Truck By Any Other Name, by Robert Lynd, London *News-Chronicle*, May 22, 1943: "In England your tailor talks of a *coat and vest*, and by the *vest* he means a *waistcoat*. Outside a tailor's shop, however, a *vest* nowadays almost always means, not a *waistcoat* but an *undershirt*." See *undershirt*.

12 *Warden*, an old English word, was apparently first applied to the officer in charge of a prison early in the last century.

13 The DAE traces *washbowl* to 1816 and marks it an Americanism.

14 The DAE traces *wash-day* to 1846. It is not marked an Americanism, but is not recorded in England until 1864. *Washing-day* is still preferred there.

15 Several English correspondents say that the English for *wash-rag* is really *flannel*, but others deny it. The NED does not list *flannel* in this sense, and its definition of *face-*

| American | English |
|---|---|
| *washstand | wash-hand stand [1] |
| wastebasket | waste-paper basket [2] |
| *water-heater | geyser [3] |
| weather bureau | meteorological office [4] |
| weather man | clerk of the weather |
| white-collar (worker) | black-coat [5] |
| windshield (automobile) | wind-screen [6] |
| witness-stand | witness-box [7] |
| wrecking-crew | breakdown gang [8] |

A list similar to the foregoing, made up of words which occur in both American and English, but in quite different senses, would run to like length. *Overalls*, to an Englishman, means " tight trousers which fit over the boots," [9] *corn* means any kind of grain for human consumption, *lumber* means disused articles of furniture, a *longshoreman* may mean a man who takes oysters along the seashore, a *prep-school* does not train for college but for what we call *prep-schools*,[10] a *cranberry* is a fruit about half the size

*cloth* is " a cloth laid over the face of a corpse," but its Supplement, 1933, adds *face-cloth* in the sense of " a cloth for washing the face," and traces it to 1930. The *Stars and Stripes*, June 15, 1943, says that *flannel* is the English term.

1 I am informed by Mr. Maurice Walshe of London that *washstand* is in common conversational use.

2 In the London *Sunday Express*, July 10, 1938, I encountered an advertisement of *wastepaper-tubs* made of " *papier maché* finished in light walnut, with nautical designs in low relief."

3 Don't Take My Word For It, by Frank Colby, San Bernardino (Calif.) *Sun*, Nov. 8, 1940: " The Briton takes a bath in water heated in a *geyser;* the American's bath water comes from a *water-heater*, usually referred to redundantly as a *hot-water-heater*." A *water-heater* for kitchen use is called a *copper* in England.

4 The *Weather Bureau* was operated by the Signal Corps of the Army from Feb. 9, 1870 to July 1, 1891, when it was transferred to the Department of Agriculture. Later it was transferred to the Department

of Commerce. The English *Meteorological Office* was established in 1854. See *bureau*.

5 London *Sunday Times*, July 26, 1936: " The Minister of Health expressed the hope that soon the bill providing for the contributory persons scheme for *blackcoated* workers, too often neglected in social efforts, would be introduced in Parliament."

6 Title of an article in *Motor News*, organ of the Chicago Motor Club, April, 1939, p. 2: " *Windshield* is *Windscreen* to the Britisher." See *fender*.

7 The DAE's first example of *witness-stand* is dated 1885, but it must be much older.

8 *News of the World* (London), unidentified date: " *Breakdown gangs* with a crane and axes went out from Melton Mowbray, while villagers, motorists and police did their best to get at the men, pinned in the *cabin* of the *lorry*."

9 Right Dress, London *Daily Express*, June 27, 1936.

10 Our *prep-school* is a *public-school* in England, and is almost exclusively for the sons of the rich. The best known are Eton and Harrow. In re-

of ours, *partridge* never means grouse or quail, a *dodger* is always a
rascal and never an advertising leaflet or a corn-cake, a *frontier* is
always a boundary between two countries, an *orchestra* is always a
band of music and never a section of seats in a theatre, a *check*
(always spelled *cheque*) is never a *bar-check* or *rain-check*, and so on
and so on.[1] Horwill gives many other examples in his excellent " Dictionary of Modern American Usage." He explains, for example, that
*precinct*, to an Englishman, means an enclosed space, especially one
including a church, and that the American sense of a political sub-
division is unknown to him. The type called *ruby* in England is
*agate* in America, and the American *ruby* is *brilliant* in England, but
these old names are going out, for the printers of both countries
now designate type-sizes by the point system, in which the English
*ruby* is 5½ and the American 3½. The American use of *brotherhood*
to designate a railroad trades union is unknown in England. So is
*dues* used for what the English call a *subscription* to a club or other
such organization. They know, of course, the word *senior*, but they
never use it to designate a last-year college student. *Homestead*, they
know too, but not in our special sense of a grant of free land. They
never use *to fit* in the sense of to prepare for college. They distinguish between *hunting* foxes or stags and *shooting* birds. They never
call a judge a *jurist*, but reserve the term for " one versed in the science
of law," *i.e.*, a legal writer or professor. They do not regard *politics*
as an opprobrious word, they know nothing of *office politics*, or
*campus politics*, or *church politics*, nor do they *play politics*. What
we call a *citizen* they commonly call a *subject*. They seldom use
*to conclude* in the sense of to decide, and they think of *tardy* as
meaning slow-moving rather than behind time. *Thrifty*, in the sense

---

cent years a number of a less expensive sort have been opened, but they
are still below the salt. An English
*prep-school* prepares boys for these
*public-schools* and also for the Royal
Navy. Its pupils seldom remain beyond the age of fourteen. An official
document published in 1900 — Preparatory Schools For Boys: Their
Place in English Secondary Education, by C. C. Cotterill — said that
the first English *prep-school* was
opened on the Isle of Wight in 1837,
but this is disputed by old boys of
various schools now operating as

such, though they may have been
something else in earlier times. See
The First *Prep-school*, London *Sunday Times*, Jan. 12, 1935.

1 As She Is Spoke in the United States,
by J. H. M., Glasgow *Evening Citizen*, Aug. 29, 1936: " It is not a question of slang but of the astonishing
number of everyday words used
predominantly in one sense by the
British and in another by the neph-
ews of Uncle Sam. It is in the use
of these that the stranger is detected
— and perplexed."

of a *thrifty* plant, is confined to a few English dialects, and *town* is never used in the New England sense of a rural area. A football *gridiron*, to them, is simply a football *field*, and they know nothing of *to knife* and *pork* in the political senses. We have many words in *blue* that they do not use, *e.g.*, *blue laws*, *blue-sky laws*, *blue grass* and *blue-nose*. They know nothing of the policeman's *night-stick*, nor of *night-riders*, nor of *scratch-pads*.

Even the common measures differ in England and the United States, sometimes in name but more often in value. When, in 1942, World War II took officers and men of the Quartermaster Corps, U.S.A., to England, they were greatly puzzled by these differences until Colonel Wayne Allen prepared his bilingual glossary, already mentioned, for the *Quartermaster Review*.[1] I quote the following from his accompanying discourse:

> Goods or produce usually sold in the United States by capacity, such as bushels, are here sold by weight, sometimes expressed in *stones* or *scores*. A *stone* is equivalent to 14 pounds, and a *score* is equal to 20 pounds. Packaging of articles in *half-stone* (7 lbs.) or *quarter-stone* (3½ lbs.) weights is customary. . . .
>
> We refer to nails in terms of *pennyweights*, which is a vestige of the past and originally meant the weight of a silver penny, equivalent approximately to 1/20 ounce. The British describe nails by their length. We had a great deal of difficulty in correlating these two methods, because our people never knew how long a *six-penny* nail was, but after getting together with the British and inspecting samples of our nails and samples of theirs we were able to arrive at a common understanding. . . .
>
> We describe rope in measurements of the diameter and the weight in pounds, whereas the British describe it in measurement of circumference and the length in fathoms. . . . *Rope, manila, 5/16" diameter* is, in British terminology, *cordage, sisal, white, 1" circumference*.[2]

Colonel Allen seems to have been in error about the value of a *stone*, which is actually a variable quantity. Said a writer in the London *Observer* in 1935: [3]

> Whilst a *stone-weight* of a living man is 14 lb., that of a dead ox is 8 lb. A *stone* of cheese is 16 lb., of glass 5 lb., of iron 14 lb., of hemp 32 lb., of wool sold by growers and woolstaplers 14 lb., but sold to each other 15 lb.

The same writer offered the following notes upon other English weights and measures:

1 The King's English, March–April, 1943, pp. 57–134.
2 I am indebted for Col. Allen's paper to Dr. George W. Corner of the Carnegie Institution.
3 Weights and Measures, Oct. 27.

A *barrel* of beef is 200 lb., butter 224 lb., flour 196 lb., gunpowder 100 lb., soft soap 256 lb., beer 36 gallons, and tar 26½ gallons, while a *barrel* of herrings is 500 fish.

Butter in England is sold by the *pound* of 16 oz., by the *roll* of 24 oz., by the *stone* and by the *hundredweight*, which is not 100 lb., as in Canada and the United States, but 112 lb.

Even the English *gallon* differs from the American *gallon*. In 1937, when large numbers of Americans went to London for the coronation of King George VI, some of them taking their automobiles, a writer in the London *Daily Express* thus sought to enlighten them: [1]

*Gallon:* you will receive 277½ cubic inches of *petrol*. In the States you would have to be content with 231 cubic inches of *gas*.
*Pint:* English, 20 fluid ounces; American, 16 ditto.[2]

One of the most striking differences between even nearly related languages is their varying use of fundamentally identical prepositions: it is almost unheard of for both members of an apparent pair to be used similarly in all situations. The German *über*, for example, may serve for *above, over, across* or *about* (concerning) in English, and the English *to* may call for *zu, nach* or *um zu* in German.[3] A few examples will show how, in this field, English usage sometimes differs from American:

Helstonleigh, Emsworth, Hants . . . will be offered *to* auction in October.[4]
Since the sale of the property it has been offered for resale *by* auction.[5]
He knows everything it contains *off by heart*.[6]
Strube . . . was entertained *to* dinner by his colleagues of the *Express*.[7]
" What is the use of waving a red flag *to* a bull? " he asked.[8]
31 ft. 6 in. frontage *to* Curzon St.[9]

Many other examples might be cited. An Englishman, as we have seen, does not live *on* a street, but *in* it, though he lives *on* a road. He does not get *on* a train or *aboard* it, but *in* it, and when he leaves

1 Americans Bound Coronationwards Should Read This Alphabet, April 28, 1937.
2 Some curious English weights and measures, unknown in the United States, are listed in *American Speech*, April, 1930, p. 330.
3 The Loom of Language, by Frederick Bodmer; New York, 1944, pp. 126 and 127. Bodmer's discussion of the subject is exhaustive and excellent.

4 Advertisement of Wm. Whiteley, Ltd., London *Daily Telegraph*, Sept. 25, 1935.
5 Houses and Estates, same paper, same date.
6 *John o' London's Weekly*, June 20, 1936.
7 London *Daily Express*, Dec. 12, 1937.
8 Socialist Repartee, London *Daily Telegraph*, Oct. 5, 1935.
9 Advertisement in the London *Telegraph and Post*, May 10, 1938.

it he does not *get off* it but *out of* it.[1] There are also curious differences in the use of *up* and *down*. Says R. Howard Claudius: [2]

> Our general rule is to say *up* when we are going north and *down* when we go south; with the English, in most of their goings about, a quite different idea underlies their feeling of direction. It is an idea they inherit, through their railroads, from old stagecoach days, that of one end of the run being of more importance than the other, and, consequently, being the *up* end. London is *up* for points lying around it for many miles in all directions, and every other city enjoys the same prerogative. Every railroad running into a city has its *up-line* and its *down-line*, and every Englishman knows which is which — as long as he is in that particular city. But how far can he go from that city, toward the city at the other end of the run, before the *up-line* becomes the *down-line* and the *down-line* the *up-line*? When in London he may freely speak of going *down* to Liverpool, but in Liverpool that would be patronizing.[3]

In the United States *up* and *down* tracks are not unknown, but it is much more common to use *eastbound, westbound, northbound,* and *southbound*. The latter terms are also used in the London underground, but otherwise they are foreign to English practise. The DAE, rather curiously, marks *eastbound, westbound* and *southbound,* in railroad use, Americanisms, but not *northbound;* that, however, may be only one more proof that lexicography is not yet an exact science. It traces all four to the early 80s, but I suspect that they are actually much older. There are some other peculiarities, in American, in the use of indicators of geographical direction. Our *downtown* and *uptown* are seldom, if ever, encountered in England: the DAE records both in American use in the early part of the last century.[4]

1 Mr. Theodore Spencer, of Cambridge, Mass., suggests that this is probably because " the English station platforms are always level with the door of the *carriage*. With us there is usually a difference of level between platform and *car;* hence *on* and *off*, with their suggestion of ascent and descent. . . ."

2 *Up* and *Down, American Speech,* Oct., 1926, p. 19.

3 The whole English railroad terminology differs radically from that prevailing in the United States, though there have been some interchanges. See AL4, pp. 146 and 147. The following is from an advertisement of the Associated British Railways in the New York *Times Magazine,* May 17, 1936: " What! No *cowcatchers?* It's quite true that our railway engines have no *cowcatchers*, no *headlights* — no, not even a *bell*. But they're modern, and they draw luxurious trains at 80 miles an hour." The same advertisement warned American tourists that there were " no familiar *hot-dog stands, tourist-camps* or *one-arm lunchrooms* along the route." Why railroad travelers should look for such things was not explained.

4 Anne-Laurence Dodge reports in *American Notes and Queries,* March, 1944, p. 188, that in Newburyport, Mass., *up-along* and *down-along* are used instead of *uptown* and *downtown*. There are probably other local variations elsewhere.

*Down East*, as noun, adjective and adverb, dates from the same period, and so does *down-country*, but *up-country* seems to have been in English use, at all events in the colonies, for many years. The DAE does not list *up-State*, but it shows that *up-boat* is recorded in 1857, *upbound* in 1884, and *up-river* in 1848. *Up-south* and *up-east* are also to be found, but only, apparently, as nonce-words. *Down* is in common use in New England when the journey is to Boston or to Maine. Says Claudius:

> *Out to the coast* is to the Pacific what *down to the shore* is to the Atlantic except that you must not be too near the Pacific when you say the former nor too far from the Atlantic when you say the latter. This *out* seems to be a survival from frontier days; its opposite is *back*. In Denver we say we are going *back* to Omaha. *Up* applies to altitude as well as to latitude; in Colorado Springs we go *up* to Cripple Creek. *Over* very obviously applies where some water must be crossed by bridge or ferry; New Yorkers go *over* to Jersey City or Brooklyn. But, not so obviously, Philadelphians go *over* to New York, and New Yorkers return the compliment, if that is what it is.

The use of *at* before points of the compass, as in *at the North*, is an Americanism, and Bartlett, in his second edition of 1859, recorded that it then " offended an English ear." The DAE traces *at the East* in American use to 1636, *at the southward* to 1697, *at the South* to 1835, *at the West* to 1839 and *at the North* to 1841. The form seems to be going out, though Atcheson L. Hench has recorded its use so recently as 1910.[1] The English *West End*, which the NED traces to 1807, is in common use in the United States, but *West Side* seems to be preferred, and *East End*, traced to 1883 in England, is almost unknown. *East Side* is traced by the DAE to 1894, but is probably much older, for *West Side* is traced to 1858. *North Side* and *South Side* are also in use in the United States, though the DAE lists neither of them.

In 1939 the late Dr. Stuart Robertson of Temple University published in *American Speech*[2] an interesting discussion of other differences in American and British usage in dealing with the minor coins of speech — a subject not often studied, for most observers seem to be chiefly interested in disparities in vocabulary. For example, the English rule[3] that *to* may be omitted when the accusative object is a

---

1 *At the South, At the North, American Speech*, Dec., 1931, pp. 154–56. All of Hench's examples came from the writings of George Carey Eggleston (1839–1911).

2 British-American Differentiations in Syntax and Idiom, Dec., 1939, pp. 243–54.

3 Cited by Jespersen, Sonnenschein and other grammarians.

pronoun, *e.g.*, " Give it me " instead of the usual American " Give it *to* me." There are also some curious differences in the use of the definite article. The English commonly insert it before *High street*, and use it in situations wherein Americans would use *a*, *e.g.*, " ten shillings *the bushel*." Contrariwise, they omit it altogether before *government* and *out of window*. Robertson called attention to the fact that this last struck Mark Twain as one of the salient differences between American and English usage.[1] In late years there has been a war upon the article in American journalistic writing, chiefly, as I have recorded, under the influence of *Time*, and the English have begun to join in it. They have also imitated the American present subjunctive, as in " It was moved that the meeting stand adjourned," where orthodox English usage would ordain " *should* stand adjourned." [2] The English plural verb following collective nouns seems to be holding out better, though even here there are some signs of yielding. Nearly all the English newspapers still use the plural after *government, committee, company, ministry* and *vestry*, and even after proper names designating groups or institutions.[3] In 1938 a Tasmanian journalist specializing in cricket and football news wrote to the lexicographer of *John o' London's Weekly* asking for advice about the use of the plural after, say, *Eton* and *Harrow*, and was told that he should use the singular when referring to " the team as a whole " and the plural when speaking of " the individual players in that team." " As a matter of literary grace," said the *John o' London* expert, " it is going too far to attach a plural verb to the *name* of the team." [4] Nevertheless, plenty of English sports writers still do it, and such headlines as " Jesus Outplay All Souls " are still common in the newspapers.[5] " The real proof for the existence of an American lan-

1 Concerning the American Language, in The Stolen White Elephant, Etc.; New York, 1888, p. 269.
2 " Our journalists," said Ernest Weekley, in Words, American and English, London *Observer*, Oct. 9, 1938, " are gradually ejecting the English *should* in favor of the revived American subjunctive."
3 From the London *Times Literary Supplement*, Sept. 16, 1944, p. 456: " The Bodleian *do* not regard it as a pseudonym."
4 Cricket English, July 22, 1938.
5 I take an example from the London

*Times*, Feb. 20, 1939: " New College retained *their* position at the head of the river, but St. Edmund Hall gained rapidly on *them* over the second half of the course." A little further on in the same article: " Much confusion was caused in the Second Division when Jesus claimed to have bumped Queen's at the boathouse. The Queen's cox failed to acknowledge it and Wadham then bumped Jesus at the Cherwell. The matter will come before the committee for decision."

guage," said the New York *Times* less than two months after the Tasmanian called for help, " is not that we say *suspenders* and *elevator* and the British say *braces* and *lift*. These are mere dialectical differences. The rub comes when the British newspapers say that their government *have* been exploring all possible channels, whereas we say our government *has* been exploring. The British say that Kent *face* an emergency, by which they mean that the Kent county cricket team *faces* an emergency. Reporting one of our own boat races, the British papers would say that Harvard *have* a big advantage over Yale." [1] The English are also fond of using *are* after United States. This was also the American custom in the early days, but *is* was substituted before the War of 1812. In 1942 a magazine called *Philippines*, published by the Philippine resident commission at Washington, protested against the use of *are* after Philippines. It said:

> The constitution of the Philippines, formulated in English and approved by the President of the United States, employs a singular verb to predicate the Philippines. For the phrase *Philippine Islands*, however, the plural verb is used. Thus, the Philippines *is*, and the Philippine Islands *are*.[2]

The House of Lords has a watchman, Lord Bertie of Thame, who devotes himself to seeing that consistency in number is maintained in drawing up government bills. He does not object to the singular verb *per se*, but insists that when a bill starts off with a plural verb, which is usually, it must so continue to the end. In 1936, when the National Health Insurance bill was before a joint committee of Lords and Commons, he kicked up such a pother on the subject that the newspapers took notice.[3] Lord Bertie also insists that *who* instead of *which* shall be used in referring to the government. The majority of Englishmen, in fact, seem to prefer *who* after all collective nouns, and there are some curious specimens in my collections, *e.g.*, " Many

1 New York *Times* (editorial page), Aug. 3, 1938.
2 Aug., 1942, p. 23. I take this from A Protest From the Philippines, by M. J. M., *American Speech*, April, 1944, pp. 147–48.
3 London *Daily Telegraph*, Aug. 8, 1936. In 1937 he had the temerity to tackle A. P. Herbert, the linguistic expert of the House of Commons, and suffered in consequence a bad fall. (Lord Bertie Meets His Match, London *Daily Telegraph*, July 11, 1937). The dispute this time was not

over the plural verb after collective nouns, but over *amongst*, which many Englishmen apparently prefer to *among*, as they prefer *whilst* to *while*. Herbert came out strongly for the American forms and managed to convince the Lords. This defeat so crushed Lord Bertie that he withdrew a motion to substitute " petition *for* divorce " for " petition *of* divorce " and " decree *of* divorce " for " decree *for* divorce " in a pending Marriage bill.

big concerns *who* are excellent employers," [1] and " The Bank of France, *who* today lowered the bank rate." [2] But, with that dogged inconsistency which is one of their chief national glories, they use *which* in reference to God in their official version of the Lord's Prayer, and in 1944 the London *Times* actually dismissed the use of *who* therein as " American idiom." [3]

Two common words that differ widely in meaning in England and the United States are *guy* and *homely*. The English *guy*, which signifies a grotesque and ludicrous person, owes its origin to the effigies of *Guy* Fawkes, leader of the Gunpowder Plot of 1605, which used to be burned by English schoolboys on November 5; the American word, which may designate anyone and is not necessarily opprobrious, seems to be derived from the *guy-rope* of a circus tent, and first appeared in the forms of *main-guy* and *head-guy*. This etymology was first suggested by Thomas P. Beyer in *American Speech* in 1926,[4] and though the DAE casts doubts upon it I am inclined to cling to it. The effort to connect the word with the English *guy* has always come to grief; they are too far apart in meaning to be the same.[5] The English word was in some use in the United States before the American *guy* was born, and it survives today in the verb *to guy*. That verb gave birth to the verb-phrase *to guy the life out of* not later than 1880, and by 1890 *to guy* itself was being used by American actors in the sense of to trifle with a part. But the noun *guy*, in the simple sense of a man, a fellow, with no derogatory significance, seems to have come in a bit later and the DAE's first example is from George Ade's " Artie," 1896. Partridge says that it began to be heard in England *c.* 1910, and soon afterward it was made familiar by American movies, but it still strikes the more elegant sort of Englishman as rather strange. In 1931 Dr. Walther Fischer of Giessen suggested in *Anglia* [6] that it may have come from the Yiddish *goy*, meaning a heathen and hence a Christian, but this etymology seems to me to be improbable, for *goy* always carries a disparaging significance.

1 8 More Hours — for 6s., London *Daily Mirror*, Sept. 20, 1935.
2 London *Daily Express*, Oct. 3, 1936. I am indebted here to Mr. James R. Barbour of London.
3 American Idiom, London *Times Literary Supplement*, Feb. 26, 1944, p. 103.
4 *Guy*, April, p. 400: " It is doubtful if the word would ever have obtained its present currency in America if it had not been for the telescoped meaning of *guy-rope* or *guy-pole* in the circus tent. ' Who's the main *guy* around here? ' carries to an American no unpleasant associations; it is just the vulgate for ' Who is the main support of this institution? ' "
5 See AL4, p. 254.
6 Band XLIII, Heft 4, Oct., 1931.

The essence of the American *guy* is that it is not necessarily opprobrious.

*Homely,* in the United States, always means ill-favored, but in England its principal meaning is simple, friendly, home-loving, folksy. The American meaning was formerly familiar to the English, and in 1590 Shakespeare wrote:

> Hath *homely* age th' alluring beauty took
> From my poor cheek? [1]

The NED offers other English examples from 1634 (Milton), 1669 (William Penn), 1706 (John Phillips, nephew of Milton), 1797 (Horace Walpole), 1873 (Ouida) and 1886 (Mrs. Linn Lynton), but the use of *homely* in this sense of " commonplace in appearance or features, not beautiful, plain, uncomely " has been rare in England since the Eighteenth Century, and the Englishman of today always understands the word to be complimentary rather than otherwise. The following from the London *News Review,* an imitator of the American *Time,* no doubt seemed patriotic and felicitous on its home-grounds, but must have struck American readers, if any, as in very bad taste:

> *Homely* Queen Elizabeth, First Lady of England, spends much time planning the deft touches which take the formal austerity out of state visits paid by European rulers to the court of St. James.[2]

The English meaning may be discerned in certain phrases that have survived in America, *e.g., homely fare* and *homely charm,*[3] but no American, without hostile intent, would apply *homely* to a woman. Its opprobrious significance seems to go back a long way, for on October 19, 1709 William Byrd of Westover wrote in his diary:

> About ten o'clock we went to court, where a man was tried for ravishing a very *homely* woman.[4]

A number of very common American words, entering into many compounds and idioms in the United States, are known in England only as exoticisms, for example, *swamp.* The NED suggests that *swamp* may have been in use in some English dialect before it was

1 The Comedy of Errors, II.
2 Woman's Touch, June 16, 1938.
3 I am indebted here to Mr. Percy Marks.
4 A Shorthand Diary of William Byrd of Westover, by Louis B. Wright, *Huntington Library Quarterly,* July, 1939, p. 494, later reissued as a reprint.

adopted in this country, but the first example so far unearthed is from Captain John Smith's " General History of Virginia," 1624, a mine of early Americanisms. The word is old in English as an adjective meaning lean, unthriving, and it is possible that the American noun was derived from this adjective, but Weekley prefers to connect it with the German noun *sumpf*, which means precisely what Americans call a *swamp*. The late George Philip Krapp, in " The English Language in America," [1] suggested that the word, to the early colonists, was occasionally used to designate quite dry ground, and in support of this he cited various passages in the town records of Dedham, Mass. But a careful study of those records by Miss Martha Jane Gibson [2] has demonstrated that Dr. Krapp was in error. The word was invariably used, she says,

to mark off a certain condition of soil — not inundated intermittently, as were meadows; not extremely boggy, as were marshes; and yet a soil too wet for easy going on foot, or for actual cultivation with the plow, but one at the same time rich and productive of either trees, underwood, or grass for pasturage.

*Swamp* has produced many derivatives in the United States, *e.g.*, *to be swamped* in the sense of to be overwhelmed, traced by NED to 1646; *swamp-angel* and *swamper*, a dweller in a swamp, traced to 1857 and 1840 respectively; [3] *swamp-apple*, a gall growing on the wild azalea, 1805; *swamp ash*, any one of various ashes growing in swamps, 1815; *swamp-blackbird*, 1794; *swamp-chestnut-oak*, 1801; *swamp-grass*, 1845; *swamp-hickory*, 1805; *swamp-honeysuckle*, 1814; *swamp-huckleberry*, 1800; *swamp-land*, 1663; *swamp-laurel*, 1743; *swamp-lily*, 1737; *swamp-lot*, 1677; *swamp-maple*, 1810; *swamp-milkweed*, 1857; *swamp-oak*, 1681; *swamp-pine*, 1731; *swamp-pink*, an azalea, 1784; *swamp-prairie*, 1791; *swamp-rabbit*, 1845; *swamp-rose*, 1785; *swamp-sassafras*, 1785; *swamp-sparrow*, 1811; *swamp-warbler*, 1865; *swamp-willow*, 1795; and *swamp-wood*, 1666. During the Revolution the South Carolina leader, Francis Marion, was called the *Swamp Fox*. *Swampoodle*, after the Civil War, came to be the designation of a city slum.

I have recorded in AL4, pp. 26 *ff*, the fact that *to fix* is used in the

1 New York, 1925, Vol. I, p. 81.
2 *Swamp* in Early American Usage, *American Speech*, Feb., 1935, pp. 30–35.
3 *Swamp-angel* was the nickname of a big gun used at the siege of Charleston in the early part of the Civil War; it was later used to designate a member of one of the bands of ruffians allied with the Ku Klux Klan.

United States in many senses unknown to the English, and that this large use of the verb has attracted the notice of English travelers for many years. A number of American observers, in the early days, called *to fix* a Southernism or Westernism,[1] but the DAE's examples come from all parts, including Canada. The verb, of course, was not invented in America, but its meanings became greatly extended here, and the DAE marks it an Americanism in such sentences as " He stopped to *fix* the lock of his rifle," " Clarence will *fix* you all right," " You *fix* my pillow," " *Fix* the table," " The politicians *fix* primaries," " The race was *fixed*," " I'll *fix* you," and " We had better *fix* the fire." The DAE devotes more than three pages to it, as verb, as noun and in various compounds; indeed, it gives more space to *fix* than to any other word. The meanings of the verb are divided into fourteen categories, five of them further subdivided into sub-categories, and one into no less than eight. Of the fourteen, twelve are marked American, and in addition there are eight different definitions of the noun, all of them marked American. In the sense of to repair or mend the DAE traces *to fix* to 1737, in that of to accommodate wants to 1779, in that of to arrange to 1796, in that of to tidy or make trim to 1820, in that of to clean up to 1836, in that of to adjust in any manner and in that of to repair a fire to the same year, in that of to prepare a meal to 1839, in that of to influence a jury to 1882, and in that of to tamper with a race-horse to 1881.[2] " In England," says Horwill, " it is commonly restricted to the meaning of to establish, make stable, place in a permanent position, but in America it is a word-of-all-work which saves the trouble of finding the specific term to describe almost any kind of adjustment or repair." Like many other American verbs, *to fix* is frequently coupled with adverbs. *To fix out* is traced to 1725, *to fix down* to 1787, and *to fix up* to 1817. As a noun the word seems to be wholly an Americanism; the DAE traces it, as such, to 1809. There are numerous derivatory nouns and adjectives, *e.g.*, *fixer*, traced to 1889; *fix-up*, to 1843; *well-fixed*, to 1822; *fixings*, to 1820; and *Mr. Fix-It*.

English observers have frequently remarked, in recent years, a

1 See Mathews's The Beginnings of American English, pp. 106 and 119.
2 James Macaulay, in Across the Ferry: First Impressions of America and Its People; fourth ed.; London, 1887, p. 93, reported that he had even found it used in the sense of getting right with God. " It represents expressively," he said, " the vain attempt of the sinner to make himself more worthy of receiving divine mercy and grace."

like heavy use, in the United States, of *to get*.[1] Some of the American significances of the unadorned verb are relatively old — for example, the sense of to track down and kill, traced by the DAE to 1853, the sense of to depart, traced to 1869, the sense of to vex or annoy, traced to 1867 —, but most of them have come in within recent years — for example, the sense of to grasp or comprehend, traced only to 1907. So with the verb compounds. The DAE traces *to get around* to 1848, *to get away with* to 1878, *to get back at* to 1888, *to get behind* (in the sense of to support) to 1903, *to get down on* to 1898, *to get into* (in the sense of to get a hold on) to 1876, *to get on to* to 1889, *to get through* (say a bill in Congress) to 1873, *to get together* to 1904, *to get up and get* to 1877, *to get busy* to 1904, *to get off* (a joke) to 1849, *to get one's back up* to 1854, *to get even with* to 1845, *to get one's goat* to 1912, *to get the hang of* to 1840, *to get one's mad up* to 1867, *to get a move on* to 1893, and *to get one dead* to 1891. All these verb phrases are Americanisms. So are *to get going, to get wise, to get religion, to get right with God, to get back at, to get by with, to get on the right side of, to get next to, to get by, to get there, to get the bulge on, to get the drop on, to get ahead of, to get solid with,* and *to get sore*.[2] So also, are *get out*, an exclamation of incredulity, *all get-out, it gets me, get-rich-quick* and the lovely *go-getter*. Some of these Americanisms have become more or less familiar in English, but the rest strike an Englishman as strange, and Horwill is at pains to explain the meaning of a number of them. From *go-getter*, he says, a new verb, *to go get*, has been produced by back formation.[3] *Right* is also in much more frequent use in the United

---

1 For example, Ernest Weekley in Adjectives — and Other Words; New York, 1930, p. 174.

2 The English purists frequently discuss this American habit of reinforcing verbs with adverbs. Sometimes they denounce it as ignorant and naughty, as when *to try out*, for example, was belabored by Dr. Terrot Reavley Glover, Public Orator at Cambridge, in 1933. The London *Times Weekly Edition* (Feb. 16, 1933) agreed with him in principle, but argued that it was too late to attempt a reform, and testified to its humorous despair by using *to get away with, to face up, to stand up for, to slip up, to blow up, to catch*

*on, to play out, to tick off, to haul up, to let off, to stick it out, to hand up, to check up, to shoot up, to bump off, to speed up* and *to listen in* in its comment. At other times the question is dealt with by dredging up proofs that this or that verb-adverb is really ancient in English. See, for example, American Prepositions, by L. Pearsall Smith, London *Times Literary Supplement*, Feb. 12, 1933.

3 A learned discussion of *to get*, including some consideration of the American *gotten*, is in *Get* and *Got*, by Wallace Rice, *American Speech*, April, 1932, pp. 280–96.

States than in England, and Charles Dickens marvelled upon some of its combinations so long ago as 1840.[1] Thornton traces *right away* to 1818 and hazards the guess that it may have been brought in by Irish immigrants. The DAE lists it along with *right about, right along, right in, right down, right off* and *right smart* as an Americanism, and the NED marks *right there* and *right here* " now chiefly U.S." Other forms in *right* are old in English, *e.g., right now, right from, right on, right at, right then* and *right round*. Sometimes American phrases in *right* are used strangely by Englishmen. I find the following use of *right away* in a colonial paper: [2] " In a studio *right away* from his home . . . Low does his work."

On the English side there are many words and idioms which puzzle an American, for, as I have noted, the exchanges in vocabulary run mainly eastward, and Americans have nothing to help them toward an understanding of English comparable to the American movies which introduce Englishmen to all the latest Americanisms. In several areas of speech the English make daily use of terms that have never penetrated to the United States — for example, in that of ecclesiastical activity. No American ever makes natural use of such words as *dissenter* and *nonconformist*, and to most Americans they are quite meaningless. As for such common English terms as *vicar, canon, verger, primate, curate, chapter, locum tenens, suffragan, dean, lay-reader, holy orders* and *churchman*, they are seldom used in the United States, at least in their English senses, save by members of the Protestant Episcopal Church, the crown colony of the Church of England. To the average American outside that loyal fold a *curate* must seem as puzzling a mammal as an *archimandrite*, and a *locum tenens* must suggest inevitably what, in the vulgate, is known as *jim-jams*. The NED traces *dissenter* to 1663, and says that " in early use " it included Roman Catholics, but is " now usually restricted to those legally styled *Protestant dissenters*." Jews, like Catholics, are excluded. *Nonconformist*, of the same meaning, is traced to 1672, but *nonconformist conscience* is not listed, though every civilized Englishman is its goat. Many of the English *dissenters* are harmless sectarians analogous to our Dunkers and Jehovah's Witnesses, but among them are also nearly all the more violent wowsers [3] of the land. In

1 See AL4, p. 253.
2 *Cape Times* (Cape Town), Nov. 12, 1938.
3 An English *dissenter* is free to carry

on his gloomy croaking as much as he pleases and is often extremely influential, but his social position is alway inferior. Up to a few years

Scotland one who refuses to swallow the national Presbyterianism is likewise a *dissenter*. The term was in use in America in colonial days, but disappeared when the battered fragment of the Church of England among us became converted into the Protestant Episcopal Church. In 1928 the New York *Times* began to use *nonconformist* to designate Protestant churches outside the Protestant Episcopal fold, *e.g.*, the Congregational, but this imitation of English usage did not take and was presently abandoned.[1] In their " Mark Twain Lexicon "[2] Robert L. Ramsay and Frances Guthrie Emberson take me somewhat waspishly to task for saying that *dissenters* are unknown in the United States, and cite the use of *dissentering* in " Huckleberry Finn,"[3] but a brief inspection is enough to show that *dissentering* is here used as a quoted Briticism. The English have a number of *dissenting* sects whose very names are unknown in the United States, but the American crop is much larger and considerably more bizarre. The Census Bureau's official list of American denominations omits, unaccountably and to my personal regret, the *Holy Rollers* and the *Footwash* and *Hardshell Baptists*, but includes the *General Six Principle Baptists*, the *Two-Seed-in-the-Spirit Predestinarian Baptists*, the *Progressive Dunkers*, the *United Zion's Children*, the *Christadelphians*, the *Hutterian Brethren*, the *Schwenkfelders*, the *Social Brethren* and the members of the *Apostolic Overcoming Holy Church of God, Christ's Sanctified Holy Church*, the *Church of the Full Gospel*, the *Church of Daniel's Band*, the *Pillar of Fire*, the *House of David*, the *Church of Illumination*, the *Italian Pentacostal Assembly of God*, the *Kodesh Church of Immanuel*, the *Mennonite Kleine Gemeinde*, the *African*

---

ago the B.B.C., the official English radio, refused to describe a service in a noncomformist tabernacle as a *religious* service, but always used *Wesleyan* service, *Baptist* service, etc. *Religious* was reserved for the orgies of the Church of England. Once a broadcaster, having inadvertently called a Baptist service at Folkestone a *religious* service, apologized at once. But this prejudice seems to be abating. So is the feeling that *dissenters* are presuming beyond their station when they call one of their meeting houses a *church*. The old name was *chapel*, and the customers were commonly spoken of as *chapel-goers*, to distinguish them from Church of England *church-goers*. Even Catholic churches were called *chapels*. But in late years that old invidious distinction tends to disappear, and there are now plenty of Methodist *churches* in England, some of them free of debt.

1 *Sectarian* and *Nonconformist*, by C. P. Mason, *American Speech*, Feb., 1929, p. 202.
2 *University of Missouri Studies*, Jan. 1, 1938, pp. cxi and 64.
3 Chapter XXIV. Ramsay and Emberson give 241 as the page number in the first edition of 1884. In my edition of 1886, apparently printed from the original plates, it is 208.

*Methodist Episcopal Zion Church*, the *Evangelical Unity of Bohemian and Moravian Churches*, the *Pentecostal Assemblies of Jesus Christ*, and the *United Holy Church of America*, not to mention more than a dozen cubicles and cell-blocks of the *Church of God*.

The English educational terminology also differs from our own, and on all levels from that of the universities to that of what we would call the *public-schools*. I attempted, in AL4, pp. 240 *ff*, to list and define some of the English terms unknown in the United States, but fell, I fear, into sundry errors. For the following illuminating gloss upon my exposition I am indebted to Mr. P. A. Browne, an inspector of the English Board of Education: [1]

> *Council-schools* are those schools in the public elementary system that are "provided" by the Local Education Authority. Nearly half, if not more than half, of the schools that are run by these Authorities are "non-provided," *i.e.*, they were built by other bodies (*e.g.*, the Church of England, the Wesleyans); [2] except for certain regulations about the appointment of teachers, the management of religious instruction, and the upkeep and use of the buildings outside school hours, they are run by the Authorities on a par with *council-schools, i.e.*, the Authorities pay the teachers, provide books and equipment, and make such improvements to the premises internally as are required by "fair wear and tear.". . .
>
> After the *babies class* a child moves into *class four, class three, class two* and *class one, i.e.*, the nomenclature goes backwards, the top class of infants being *class one*. It is by no means universal that the sexes should be separate above the *infants' school;* I fancy that more than half of the public *elementary schools* of England that deal with children of seven or more are still "mixed." Nor will a boy always be put under a male teacher at the *third* or *fourth standard*. Sometimes he will meet one in *Standard I*, while in small schools he may be under a woman teacher until he leaves. . . .
>
> The time at which children go from *elementary school* to *secondary school* in England is now pretty universally at the age of eleven. The *standard* system is being gradually replaced by a *class* system in *elementary schools* other than *infants' schools*. These are called *forms* in *secondary schools*, and I have met with them occasionally in the swaggerer *elementary schools*, though they are still not frequent there.
>
> *Head-mistresses* are found in mixed schools as well as girls' schools, though not usually if there are men on the staff. The lower pedagogues used to be called *ushers* in the so-called *public schools*,[3] and still are at Harrow (at Winchester they are called *dons*), but are now *masters* or *assistant masters* (or *mistresses*) at *public-schools* and *secondary schools*, though far more usually *teachers* at *elementary schools*.[4]

1 Private communication, Jan. 12, 1938.

2 The English *Wesleyans* are the American *Methodists*.

3 *i.e.*, the endowed schools, for sons of the upper classes, *e.g.*, Eton and Harrow.

4 The seeker after further light on this difficult subject is referred to As the English Twig is Bent, by William Oliver Stevens, *Saturday Evening Post*, May 9, 1936, pp. 14 *ff*; The School Question in England, by S. J. Gosling, *Commonweal*, Aug. 13,

245. [The English keep up most of the old distinctions between *barristers* and *solicitors*. A *barrister* is greatly superior to a *solicitor*. He alone can address the higher courts and the parliamentary committees; a *solicitor* must keep to office work and the inferior courts.] In part, the distinction is like that between the American trial-lawyer and office-lawyer, but only in part, for an American may function as both, whereas an English lawyer must stick to his class. In the London *Sunday Express*, in 1938,[1] Viscount Castlerosse described eloquently the pains and costs of becoming a *barrister*. First, the candidate must be entered at one of the Inns of Court, the English equivalent of our law-schools, and there he must prove his diligence by eating thirty-six dinners with its resident bigwigs, or, if he is not a university man, seventy-two. Said Castlerosse:

This is rather the same as at a university, where there is no obligation to swallow the food, but a man must check in. At the university he waves his hat at the marker, but for legal purposes a student must stay there from " the grace before dinner until the concluding grace should have been said." Dinners cost 3s. 6d. each, and some diners consider they do not get much value for the money. Joining an Inn is expensive. The admission documents cost £1 1s., government stamp £25, admission fees £20, lecture fees £12 12s. — in all £58 13s. Also, unless the student can get two householders to put up a bond for him, he has to deposit £50. Next come the examinations, and then, if successful, the business of being *called*,[2] which costs £100, of which £50 is bagged by the government.

Finally, there is the outfit. A wig costs £8 8s. Second-hand wigs are half-price, but it is not everybody who likes to wear second-hand wigs, and, besides, they have a way of going to bits. The tin box to keep the wig in costs 6s. 6d.; the gown costs £4 4s., — why I cannot imagine; white bands 2s. a pair, and the blue bag 10s. 6d.

Even though our friend has got through the sacred portals he still has to go on paying out. He reads in *chambers* for twelve months, during which period he *devils* for some junior counsel.[3] Instead of getting paid he has to shell out 100 guineas plus five guineas to the *clerk of the chambers*. When the year is out he has to get chambers of his own, and he is now taken over by a clerk.

A *barrister's* clerk is a truly remarkable man, and requires qualities not found in any other profession. The perfect *barrister's* clerk must be able to imbibe endless quantities of alcohol without feeling it. He must be on friendly

---

1943, pp. 422 *ff*; and A Guide to British Educational Terms, by Herbert B. Grimsditch, *Wilson Bulletin* (New York), May, 1936, pp. 576 *ff*.
1 March 20.
2 *i.e.*, to the bar — the equivalent of the American *admitted*.

3 An English lawyer, whether *barrister* or *solicitor*, never has an *office*, but always *chambers*. To devil is defined by the NED as " to do professional work for another without fee, or without recognition."

terms with every *solicitor's* clerk, and, as all wise men know, there's only one way to do that. Further, he must know how to put his man over.

At the beginning the young *barrister* pays his clerk a pound a week. After that the clerk collects about 7 per cent. on the earnings of the *barrister*, who, by the way, loses about another 7 per cent. through bad debts. Eventually work will come to a *barrister*, probably in the shape of inquests in the suburbs at £1 3s. 6d. a time, which works out at £1 1s. net to the *barrister*.

The American visitor to England is often brought up by Briticisms so seldom heard in the United States, even as quotations, that they have the effect on him of foreign words. When, on passing a butcher's shop, he sees a sign offering *offals*, he is unpleasantly affected until someone tells him that, to an Englishman, the word simply means liver, kidneys, tongue, heart, etc. Nor can he grasp without aid the meaning of the *silversides*, *gigots* and *stewing steak* offered at the same place, nor of the *brill*, *raker*, *monkfish*, *coalfish*, *periwinkles*, *prawns*, *ling*, *doreys* and *witches* announced by the nearest fish-monger, nor of the *Forfar bridies*, *Scotch baps* and *treacle scones* on the list of the adjacent pastry-cook,[1] nor of the *fireside-suites* and *surrounds* advertised by the dealers in house-furnishings, nor of the *judge's kettles*, *secateurs*, *coal-cauldrons* and *spark-guards* to be had of the same. He is puzzled by the rubric *Au Pair* in the want-ad columns of the newspapers — until he reads the ads and finds that it simply indicates an offer of services for board and lodging. In their news columns he finds that the police are on the hunt for *smash-and-grab raiders* and *gutter-crawling motorists:* the meaning of the first he readily penetrates, but it takes him some time to discover that *gutter-crawling* is practised by mashers who run close to the sidewalk, hoping to pick up light-headed girls. *To tout*, he finds after a while, may have the harmless meaning of to collect party funds, and making a *whip-round* is only passing the hat. But what is a *tomasha*, and what are *gold-sticks*, *crocodiles*, *satellite towns*, *navvies*, *hydros*, *tied houses*, *hooroosh*, *tarmac*? How can there be such a thing as a *proper* bungalow? What, precisely, is *good form*?[2] This Ameri-

---

1 Contrariwise, many American names for comestibles puzzle the English. In I Discover America, by Kenneth Adam, London *Star*, Nov. 30, 1937, the author, writing from Richmond, Ind., found it advisable to supply definitions of *sauerkraut-juice*, *clam-chowder*, *squabs with yams*, *succotash*, *cole-slaw*, *caraway-roll* and *pie*

*à la mode*. He defined *sauerkraut-juice* as "a kind of bitter apertif," and *squabs* as "small chickens."

2 A Thing Called Not Done, London *Morning Post*, Aug. 4, 1936: "*Good form* — that mysterious ideal of schools — was the subject of pointed comment by Mr. W. B. Curry, head-master of Dartington Hall, Devon,

can finds it hard, sometimes, to claw the news out of the English newspapers. To be sure, most of them are full of Americanisms or pseudo-Americanisms, but they are also full, and to much nearer the brim, of Briticisms, and some of those Briticisms, when he guesses at their meaning, turn out to mean something quite different. Nor is he helped, in reading the papers, by the archaic and murky past perfect tense in which they commonly report the speeches of the national haruspices. A sample:

> Good pictures could only be made by building up writers, directors, and stars and keeping them in this country. This could only be done with money, and Mr. Rank was the only man who rightly had attempted to do so. He (Lord Grantley) was the last person to wish to see any monopoly in the film industry, but so far from worrying about the so-called Rank monopoly and the fact that Mr. Rank would become a Colossus in the industry, striding over it, he would like one or two more colossi like him to help them, because money was the only thing that put pictures on the celluloid. Mr. Rank had done a tremendous lot to improve the quality of the pictures manufactured in this country, and to achieve good marketing.[1]

Contrariwise, there are many familiar and characteristic Americanisms that have not been adopted in England, and are little known there, *e.g.*, *snarl* (tangle), *lye* (household), *to hospitalize*, *truck-garden*, *immortelles* (the English call them *everlasting flowers*), *to shuck* (oysters), *gum* for chewing-gum (in England it always means mucilage), *in back of* (though the English use *in front of*), *dirt* (for earth, though *dirt-track* is coming into use), *jigger*, *bung-starter*, *powder-room* (though it is occasionally used), *stein*, *to sashay*, *scallion*, *waist* and *shirtwaist* (the English always use *blouse*), *lima-bean*, *pipe-dream*, *goose-pimple* (the English use *chicken-flesh*) and *badger-game*. Some of these are old English terms that have become obsolete in England, *e.g.*, *scallion*, which the NED traces to the Fourteenth Century. " An Englishman," says Seaman, " never

yesterday. ' *Good form*, so far as I understand it,' he told the New Education Fellowship at Cheltenham, ' is a way of making important things seem trivial and trivial things seem important. It is concerned with manners and behaviour and a thing called *not done*. In schools where *good form* is thought important, it is much more serious to violate the canons of *good form* than to violate the Ten Commandments. Serious worship of *good form* among the young seems inevitably to lead to inflexibility of temper, because the essence of *good form* is that you do not question it."

1 Parliament, London *Times*, Feb. 24, 1944, p. 8. I am indebted here to Dr. John Whyte of Brooklyn College. An amusing note on the difficulties encountered by Americans in English novels is in Mrs. Miniver's Briticisms, by Marian and George Hibbitt, *American Speech*, April, 1941, pp. 149–51.

calls his car his *machine*. His *machine* would be his *bicycle*. . . . *Closet*, for cupboard or wardrobe, always rouses a titter in an English cinema. Here it means a W. C. . . . We still speak of having our teeth *stopped*, but the American *filled* is coming in." [1]

### 3. ENGLISH DIFFICULTIES WITH AMERICAN

255. [Very few English authors, even those who have made lengthy visits to the United States, ever manage to write American in a realistic manner.] In the earlier days their attempts were usually upon the so-called Yankee or Down East dialect. The pioneer was apparently the anonymous author of " The Adventures of Jonathan Corncob," brought out in London in 1787. He had his Americans use *I snore* and *I snort* as expletives,[2] and stretched their vowels out into such forms as *blaaze away like daavils, get aloong* and *let me alo-one*.[3] By 1866, when Charles Dickens published " Mugsby Junction," this Yankee dialect had developed, in English hands, into the following: [4]

> I tell Yew what 't is, ma'arm. I la'af. Theer! I la'af. I Dew. I oughter ha' seen most things, for I hail from the Onlimited side of the Atlantic Ocean, and I haive travelled right slick over the Limited, head on through Jee-rusalemm and the East, and likeways France and Italy, Europe, Old World, and am now upon the track to the Chief European Village; but such an Institution as Yew, and Yewer young ladies, and Yewer fixin's solid and liquid, afore the glorious Tarnal I never did see yet! And if I hain't found the eighth wonder of monarchical Creation, in finding Yew, and Yewer young ladies, and Yewer fixin's solid and liquid, all as aforesaid, established in a country where the people air not absolute Loonaticks, I am Extra Double Darned with a Nip and Frizzle to the innermostest grit! Wheerfur — Theer! — I la'af! I Dew, ma'arm, I la'af!

This was supposed to be addressed by a traveling American to a strange Englishwoman at a railway refreshment-counter. I should add that there were English critics who recognized that it was excessively bad reporting, and denounced it accordingly. One of them

1 Private communications, May 25 and June 4, 1944.
2 The DAE's first example of the former is dated 1790. Its first example of *corncob* is dated 1793. Obviously, its searchers overlooked The Adventures of Jonathan Corncob.
3 America in English Fiction, 1760–1800, by Robert Bechtold Heilman.

Baton Rouge (La.), 1937, p. 368. " The author's use of italics," says Heilman, " makes doubly sure that the reader will notice what the Americans are doing with the language."
4 I preserve the capitals he used for emphasis.

was Edward Dicey, who declared that "you might travel through the United States for years and never hear such a speech uttered out of a lunatic asylum." [1] But there was often more than bad reporting in such stuff; there was also (and preëminently in Dickens's case) a bitter dislike of all things American. "How can we wonder Americans do not love us," added Dicey, "when, as Hawthorne said, with too much truth, ' not an Englishman of them all ever spared America for courtesy's sake or kindness '? " In the years since 1866 there have appeared English authors whose loathing of the United States and its people is less apparent than Dickens's, but even the most friendly of them runs into difficulties when he tries to report American colloquial speech. The only latter-day English novelist, said an American correspondent of the Manchester *Guardian* in 1937, " who can speak American " is P. G. Wodehouse.[2] John Galsworthy's difficulties with it were discussed by the late Dr. Stuart Robertson in *American Speech* in 1932,[3] and some specimen blunders are given in AL4, p. 257. Many of them arose from Galsworthy's apparent belief that Americans use *gotten* instead of *got* in *all* situations, instead of only in the sense of *acquired* or *become*. Said Robertson:

> The following sentence from "Maid in Waiting": "I fear you've *gotten* a grouch against me, Miss Cherrell," is wrong unless Hallorsen means "You've *acquired* a grouch." The context shows, however, that he does not; what he means is "You *have* (or *cherish*) a grouch." In the following instances there can be no manner of doubt as to the error: "You've lost the spirit of inquiry; or if you've still *gotten* it, you have a dandy way of hiding it up.". . . "We haven't *gotten* your roots and your old things." [4]

Arnold Bennett, E. Phillips Oppenheim, Edgar Wallace and Bram Stoker were other English novelists, popular in the United States, who had distressing difficulties with American speech.[5] Here is a specimen of the curious jargon that Stoker put into the mouth of an American supposed to hail from "Isthmian City, Bleeding Gulch, Maple Tree county, Nebraska ":

1 *Every Saturday* (Boston), March 30, 1867, p. 397.
2 American Slang in England, by D. B. Whitman, of Winthrop, Mass., May 4, 1937. His letter was reprinted in various American newspapers, *e.g.*, the Milwaukee *Journal*, Oct. 9, 1937.
3 American Speech According to Galsworthy, April, pp. 297–301.

4 Dr. Robertson had noted this misuse of *gotten* by another English novelist, Rose Macaulay, in A British Misconception, *American Speech*, April, 1931, pp. 314–16.
5 Cockney American, by Mildred Wasson, *American Speech*, April, 1932, pp. 255–56.

Not me, ma'am. Why, I'm as tender as a Maine cherry-tree. Lor' bless me, I wouldn't hurt the poor pooty little critter more'n I'd scalp a baby. An' you may bet your variegated socks on that.[1]

The whole tribe, for some occult reason, seems to be convinced that all Americans give a *u*-sound to the *er* in such words as *very* and *American*, and usually they double the *r*.[2] At other times American-isms are used in senses and situations that must inevitably give every actual American a start. In 1942, for example, the lady novelist, Margaret Louise Allingham, in a book review in the English edition of *Time and Tide*, described two quite respectable American girl characters as *floosies*.[3] During the same year another lady novelist, Elizabeth Bowen, used Americanisms in an amazing (if usually correct) manner in a serious historical work, "Bowen's Court." Some examples:

> The Stuarts gestured, flattered and *double-crossed* (p. 47).
> Lord Muskerry was *putting something across* (p. 55).
> On the claim of having discovered a papist plot (which they *faked*), etc. (p. 58).[4]

Again in 1942 a third lady novelist, Dorothy Sayers, got into hot water by introducing indecorous Americanisms into a serial radio life of Christ, *e.g.*, *to hop it*. She was flayed for the sacrilege in the London *Star* by the Rev. James Colville, pastor of St. Peter's Presbyterian Church, Balham,[5] and the *Star* announced primly that "M.P.'s have been told that a number of alterations to the original script are being considered." A fourth lady novelist, Rosamund Lehmann, did measurably better, and one of her American reviewers was moved to exclaim at her correct (and frequent) use of *boy friend*, *bunk* and *kidding*.[6] But to counterbalance this a he-novelist, Bruce Graeme, brought out a crime shocker, reprinted in the United States, in which American gangsters were made to use *blimey* and *ruddy*.[7] "There

1 I am indebted here to Miss Miriam Allen deFord of San Francisco.
2 American Speech in English Fiction, by Francis Hayes, *American Notes and Queries*, Jan., 1942, p. 156.
3 Oct. 10, 1942. She was brought to book in *Time and Tide*, Oct. 17, by D. W. Brogan.
4 The page numbers are those of the American edition; New York, 1942.

5 Your Radio Life of Christ is an Affront, Jan. 22, 1942.
6 All of Us, by Marshall Maslin, South Bend. (Ind.) *Tribune*, June 27, 1936.
7 Gangsters, British Type, Detroit *Times*, May 5, 1935. The book was called Public Enemy No. 1 in England and John Jenkin, Public Enemy, in the United States.

are very few English writers," concluded a resigned London journalist in 1937, "who can employ American slang correctly." [1]

Errors in its use made by English statesmen and other such more austere characters are not infrequently reported in the American newspapers, *e.g.*, the late Neville Chamberlain's extension of *jitterbug* to indicate an alarmist.[2] At about the same time the Opposition Leader, the Right Hon. C. R. Attlee, accused Chamberlain of trying *to put sob stuff over the House*, forgetting the *on* that, by American rules, should have followed *over*.[3] Chamberlain replied by describing himself as a *go-getter for peace*. He was very fond of Americanisms, and occasionally used them more or less correctly. One of his favoiites was *in the neighborhood of*. His predecessor, Stanley Baldwin (created an earl in 1937), had a formidable répertoire, and made precise use of *to try out, to deliver the goods,*[4] *rattled, more to it,*[5] *best-seller,*[6] and party *dog-fight*.[7] Sometimes he was accused by purists of mouthing Americanisms when he was actually using ancient English terms, as when he adorned a debate with *backslider*, which the NED traces to 1581. Winston Churchill, who is half American, clings to the Oxford accent but lards his discourses with many American terms, *e.g.*, *proposition* and *cold feet*. Nevertheless, he once rebuked a Conservative M.P., Arthur Hugh Elsdale Molson, for using *stooge* in a question asked in the House of Commons. "I am not prepared," he

---

1 War Between US and U. S. A.— Over Language, by Collinson Owen, London *Sunday Pictorial*, April 11, 1937.

2 Chamberlain seems to have been misled by Sir Samuel Hoare, then Home Secretary, who, in a speech in the House of Commons on Jan. 26, 1939, said: "I am told that in the United States of America there is a class of people who sit listening in hysterical excitement to what is called *hot music* and waiting for the final crash. Americans, in their forcible language, call them the *jitterbugs*. There are many people in Europe today that seem to be behaving in much the same way. They sit, listening to all the hot music of the scares and alarms, waiting helplessly for the crash that, according to them, will destroy us all." This was a correct enough definition of *jitter-*

*bug*, but Chamberlain's subsequent use of it in the extended sense suggested by Hoare puzzled Englishmen who were familiar only with the original American sense.

3 British Americanisms, *Newsweek*, March 13, 1939.

4 Oh! What Slanguage!, by A. Whitcomb Jenkins, *Answers*, July 23, 1938.

5 The Correspondence of an Easy Gentle Essayist, by Geoffrey Grigson, London *Morning Post*, Jan. 21, 1936.

6 *Best-seller* is marked "orig. U. S." by the NED Supplement and traced in English use to 1912. The DAE does not list it, but I believe it was in use in the United States not later than 1895.

7 Fie, Fie, Right Honourable Member!, Sunderland *Echo*, Oct. 31, 1934.

said primly, " to answer a question couched in such very unseemly terms." [1] Other M.P.'s have shocked patriotic Englishmen in recent years with Americanisms that, in some cases, are not indecorous to American ears. In 1943, for example, Lord Morris got into the newspapers by using *skullduggery* in a debate in the House of Lords; [2] in 1937 the Commons was thrown upon its haunches by *to debunk;* [3] and in 1940 Capt. Harold Harington Balfour caused a raising of eyebrows by saying to a Labor member, Emanuel Shinwell, " I apologize if I *got you wrong.*" [4] Even higher dignitaries have occasionally sinned. In 1936 no less a character than the Archbishop of Canterbury used *up against* in a public pronunciamento, and during the same year King Edward VIII used both *radio* and *to broadcast* in his first fireside chat to his lieges. [5] As Prince of Wales he had employed Americanisms in a number of speeches — a fact hailed by a few advanced Englishmen as " evidence of a charming disposition to speak the democratic language of a democratic age, to speak to genial Englishmen, not in the trappings of princely oratory, but as another genial Englishman like themselves," but frowned upon by old-timers on the ground that it was " the duty of the king's son to defend the king's English against the undesirable aliens of speech." [6] The former king's cousin, Admiral Lord Louis Mountbatten (*geb.* Battenberg), speaks American fluently, for in the interval between the two wars he made intensive linguistic and other studies at Hollywood. On September 24, 1943, he told the scholars assembled at a luncheon of the Royal Naval Film Corporation in London that he thought he was fully qualified to act as an interpreter between the British and American forces in Southeastern Asia. [7] Three years before this Sir Eric Phipps, then British ambassador to France, had warned a luncheon meeting of the American Club in Paris that World War II was not a

1 I am indebted here to Mr. John A. Tillinghast, of Providence, R. I.

2 London *Daily Express,* June 17, 1943. This beautiful word was first listed by Bartlett in the late 70s; he said that it originated in Missouri. The DAE marks it an Americanism.

3 English Undefiled?, Barbados *Advocate,* Sept. 11, 1937. I am indebted here to Mr. R. C. Hackett, of Balboa, C. Z.

4 London *Daily Express,* Nov. 14, 1940.

5 London *Morning Post,* March 2, 1936; King's English, Manchester *Guardian Weekly,* March 6, 1936.

6 The King's English and the President's American, by Robert Lynd, *New Statesman* (London), Feb. 4, 1930.

7 Lord Louis Learns American, London *Evening Standard,* Sept. 24 1943.

*phony* war.[1] Some of the earlier American political terms, *e.g.*, *caucus*, *gerrymander* and *carpet-bagger*, have been taken over, as we have seen in Chapter IV, Section 2, by the English politicos. According to the political correspondent of the *Eastern Evening News* (Norwich),[2] *carpet-bagger* was first used in the parliamentary campaign of 1880. How the meaning of *caucus* has been perverted in England has been described. The English have done almost as badly with *gerrymander*, which they employ to indicate any "method whereby one political party obtains an unfair advantage over another."[3] The New Deal *boondoggling*, when it reached England, was converted into *boonwiggling*,[4] and the London *Times*, until 1939, was still calling the *Brain Trust* the *brains trust*, and spelling it with small letters.[5] Even the English newspapers on levels where American neologisms may be presumed to be more familiar often make shining blunders. In the *News of the World*, for example, I once encountered *sawn-down* for *sawed-off* in a description of fire-arms.[6] Some of the interpretations of Americanisms in English editions of American books are far from illuminating. When Marjorie Hillis's "Live Alone and Like It" was published in London in 1936 *Junior Leaguers* was changed to *Girl Guides*.[7]

## 4. BRITICISMS IN THE UNITED STATES

264. As has been noted in Section 1 of the present chapter, a large proportion of the Americanisms that get into English use enter upon

1 This is Not a *Phony* War: Paris Envoy, London *News-Chronicle*, Jan. 19, 1940. The *News-Chronicle* explained that *phony* was "American slang, anglicized about 1920." Early in 1940 Lord Willingdon, in an interview in the London papers on the progress of World War II, said "the Empire is *all in*." He meant, of course, that it was pledged to fight to the last gasp. The American correspondents in London were warned to explain this meaning if they transmitted his speech to the United States, lest Americans assume that he had said that the Empire was done for. *Phony* was also used by Paul Reynaud, then premier of France, in a radio speech to Americans on April 3, 1940: "'Il faut en

finir'; tel fut, dès le début, le refrain qu'on entendit. Et cela signifie qu'il aura pas de 'phoney peace' après une guerre qui n'est nullement une 'phoney war'." I am indebted here to Mr. Howard C. Rice of Cambridge, Mass.
2 Election Expenses, 1880, April 24, 1935.
3 Premier's *Gerrymandering* Rebuked, London *Morning Advertiser*, Nov. 21, 1941.
4 London *Daily Mirror*, quoted in the *New Yorker*, Oct. 17, 1936.
5 Obituary of Thomas Gilbert White, Feb. 20, 1939.
6 Shot Man's Legacy to Woman Friend, Aug. 2, 1936.
7 *New Yorker*, Dec. 19, 1936.

the lower levels of culture, among the intellectually underprivileged patrons of American movies and comic strips. Some of them afterward penetrate to more austere circles, including even the academic, but while they are still new they are commonly scorned as vulgarisms. In the United States the thing runs the other way. That is to say, Briticisms are nearly always first adopted by persons of some pretension to culture, and on that level they commonly remain, for to the plain people most of them seem affected and even sissified. It would be hard to imagine any male American of the plain people using such terms as *rotter*, *braces* (for *suspenders*), *boot-shop*, *fed up*, *tube* (for *subway*), *pram* (for *baby-carriage*), *nursing-home* or *master's bedroom*.[1] A number of Briticisms, to be sure, have got and are still getting into his vocabulary, *e.g.*, *tabloid* and *bungalow*, but by the time they reach him he has no awareness of their provenance, and in consequence they do not collide with his conviction that everything English has a pansy cast. England, however, is still the fount of honor and mold of fashion to all Americans of social aspiration, including the tonier sort of pedagogues, and they make diligent efforts to imitate English cultural patterns, including the linguistic. That fact, I suspect, is responsible for the change of the old American sequence of *breakfast*, *dinner* and *supper*, surviving even among the rich until the Ward McAllister era, to *breakfast*, *luncheon* (often shortened to *lunch*) and *dinner*, with *supper* left hanging in the air as a designation for a nonce meal in the late evening. But that change has never been adopted by the great masses of Americans, nor, for that matter, by their opposite numbers in the British Isles, among whom the sequence is *breakfast*, *dinner* and *tea*.

There seems to be some tendency, in late years, to substitute the English *postman* for the older American *letter-carrier* (traced by the DAE to 1825), and it was apparently given a lift by the great success of James M. Cain's novel, " The *Postman* Always Rings Twice," in 1934, but *postman*, as the DAE shows, was actually in use in the

---

1 When, in 1937, J. M. Steadman, Jr., of Emory University, Atlanta, Ga., polled the students of that seminary, seeking to find out what terms they avoided as beneath their dignity, his returns included *chap*, *cheerio*, *cinema*, *jolly* (swell, fine), *mater* (mother), *pater* (father), *petrol*, *righto*, *stunning* and *top-hole*, all of them recognized as Briticisms. See his Affected and Effeminate Words, *American Speech*, Feb., 1938, pp. 13–18. " Americans," said the London *Times* in an editorial, Two Peoples and One Tongue, June 29, 1943, " have always been rather shy of drawing upon what they believe to be un-American English. This phrase, that accent, t'other manner remain a joke."

United States long before *letter-carrier*, and it has always been favored in large parts of the country. The American telephone salutation, " Hello," has never been supplanted by the English " Are you there?, " even among Anglomaniacs who affected the English *secret'ry* and pronounce *been* to rhyme with *seen*, and any American telephone-operator who said " You are through " to a subscriber in the sense of " There is your party " would get an unpleasant earful. So would a Federal jobholder who ventured to describe himself as a *civil servant*,[1] or an investment banker who attempted to float an issue of *preference-shares*,[2] or a *baggage-smasher* who began to talk of *luggage vans*, or a Greek lunchroom man who hung out a sign announcing *brunch*, or a farmer who called his hired-man an *agricultural laborer*, or a public school principal who let it be known that he had become a *headmaster*,[3] or a filling-station attendant who spoke of gas as *petrol*,[4] or the hood of a car as the *bonnet*, or an elevator-starter who (outside a few fashionable shops and hotels) called his goons *liftmen*, or a candidate for any office of public honor or trust who dared to turn secretary into *secret'ry* or *been* into *bean*.

World War II made all Americans familiar with a few Briticisms, *e.g.*, *commando*, but they were not numerous, even on official levels. When, on March 3, 1942, the word *rating* was used to describe enlisted men in a Navy communiqué, and I made alarmed inquiries at Washington, I was assured at once by Captain Leland P. Lovette, then head of the Navy's literary and philological bureau, that the word had slipped in advertently, by the hand of a patriotic officer whose resistance had been broken down by the incessant reading of

1 The title of a paper on Walt Whitman's adventures as a Washington jobholder, by Dixon Wecter, in *Publications of the Modern Language Association*, Dec., 1943, pp. 1094 ff, called him a *civil servant*, but I suspect that Dr. Wecter may have intended the term to be satirical rather than swanky.

2 Indeed, such an investment banker might run some risk of getting into Sing Sing or Atlanta prematurely, and even unjustly.

3 In England there is a distinction between *headmaster* and *head master*. The former is reserved for the chief pedagogues of so-called *public-schools* (see p. 502); the latter may be applied to the head of what we would call a *public-school* in the United States. The learned will find an illuminating discussion of this orthographical distinction in the eminent *News of the World*, Dec. 26, 1937.

4 In his speech to Congress on May 19, 1943, Winston Churchill announced that the British troops in North Africa had begun to drop the English *lorry* for the American *truck*, and that the Americans as a return courtesy, had agreed to use *petrol*. The second part of this was not supported, so far as I know, by any American authority.

communiqués from England.[1] Other English military and naval terms that appeared during the war were *alert*, *quisling* and *paratroops*, and the German loans, *flak*, *panzer* and *lebensraum*, but they did not penetrate to the common speech. *Blitz* and its derivatives were apparently in use in the United States before they got into general circulation in England. Some of the phrases launched by English politicians of the war era, such as Neville Chamberlain's *to miss the bus* and Winston Churchill's *blood, sweat and tears*, were heavily labored by the American newspapers, just as King Edward VIII's *at long last* had been labored before them, but the vulgar were no more than dimly aware of them. *Blood, sweat and tears*, in fact, was not Churchill's invention, though he had employed it even before it appeared in his speech of May 13, 1940. Nor was *at long last* original with Edward's anonymous ghost, for the NED traces it to 1523.[2]

Some of the Briticisms that actually come into use in America, whether in wide or narrow circles, have rather curious histories, *e.g.*, *flapper*. This excellent term, now obsolescent in both countries, is not listed by the DAE, for it was not borrowed from England until after 1900, the last year the DAE pretends to cover. It is also missing, in the sense here meant, from the NED, whose F–G volume was published in 1901, but it appears in the NED Supplement, 1933. Its history in England, however, goes back at least to 1892, for in that year there was a discussion of it in *Notes and Queries*, summed up by an anonymous writer in the London *Evening News* on August 20. A year later Farmer and Henley listed it in their " Slang and Its Analogues " as meaning both " a very young prostitute " and " a little girl." In the latter sense it had not been listed in " A Dictionary of Slang, Jargon and Cant," by Barrère and Leland, published in 1889, though they had noted it in the sense of " a very young girl trained to vice, generally for the amusement of elderly men." Thus it seems to have come into respectable significance in England at some time between 1889 and 1892. The anonymous writer in the London *Evening News*, just mentioned, inclined to believe that it represented a figurative borrowing of an earlier *flapper* meaning " a young wild duck, unable to fly," which has been traced by the NED to 1773.

---

1 *Rating* has been used in the English Navy to designate the rank or station a man holds on a ship's books since the early Eighteenth Century, but it has been applied to the man himself only since the closing years of the Nineteenth.

2 *At Long Last*, by Marie Drennan, *American Speech*, April 1939, p. 156.

That etymology is also favored by other authorities, but the NED Supplement suggests the contrary possibility that the term may really come from a dialect word, *flap*, meaning any unsteady young woman, not necessarily a prostitute. Partridge says that in the English society slang of the early Nineteenth Century *flapper* meant " a very immoral young girl in her early teens " ( a definition borrowed from J. Redding Ware's " Passing English of the Victorian Era," 1900), and that World War I " firmly established the meaning (already pretty general by 1905) of *any* young girl with her hair not yet up (or, in the late 1920s and the 30s, not yet cut short)." I am inclined to believe, as I have indicated, that this transformation occurred at least a decade before the time set by Partridge. *Flapper* began to be heard in the United States not later than 1910, and it had, from the start, the perfectly unopprobrious signification of the German *backfisch*. It is one of a long series of jocular terms used to designate a young and somewhat foolish girl, full of wild surmises and inclined to revolt against the precepts and admonitions of her elders. The *filly* of the Eighteenth Century was of that general type, and so was the *chicken* of the pre-1900 era. The NED Supplement traces *flapperhood* to 1905, *flapperdom* to 1907, *flapperism* to 1909, *flapper-age* to 1917, *flapperish* to 1920 and *flapper-vote* to 1928. All save the last reached America, but they survived only until *flapper* itself succumbed to various home-brewed terms, *e.g.*, *sub-deb*, which, so far as I can find, has never been in use in England.[1]

Some of the Briticisms taken into American have got in only after long delays, and others have been changed in meaning or otherwise modified. *Bungalow*, from *bangla*, a Hindustani word meaning belonging to Bengal, appeared in English use in the sense of a one-story house so long ago as 1676, but was not adopted in this country until *c.* 1900, though it now seems almost as native as *rubberneck*. In England, as we have seen, it has produced the excellent derivative *bungaloid*, not yet in use in the United States.[2] *Tabloid* was invented

1 Mr. Harold M. Tovell of Toronto calls my attention to the fact that *flapper* occurs in the English translation of the diary of Mme. d'Arblay, published in London in 1846, Vol. VII, p. 253, as follows: " Alex is my companion, or rather I am Alex's *flapper*." But this does not seem to be a use of the word in the modern sense.

2 The following is from Mournful Numbers, by Colin Ellis; London, 1932, p. 15:
*Bungaloid Growth*
When England's multitudes observed with frowns
That those who came before had spoiled the towns,
" This can no longer be endured! " they cried,

by Sir Henry Wellcome in 1884, and was registered as a trade-mark in England by his pharmaceutical firm, Burroughs, Wellcome & Company, on March 14 of that year. But the rights of the firm extend only to its use in marketing what in this country are commonly called *tablets,* and it began to be used to designate newspapers smaller than the usual size in 1901. At some undetermined time afterward it reached the United States in both this new sense and in its original sense. Since then its meaning has been greatly extended in this country, and it is now used to designate anything small, from a prize-fighter to an automobile. The familiar *cop* is an American shortening of the English *copper,* and has been renaturalized in England.[1] All the slang authorities derive *copper* from an old cant verb, *to cop,* meaning to capture or catch, which is traced by the NED to 1704. It has, however, become one of the favorite marks of amateur etymologists, and their speculations about its origin often get into the newspapers.[2] *Copper* was in use in England by the early 50s, and soon afterward made its way to New York, where it was presently reduced to *cop.* The English police of the time greatly disliked *copper,* and the street boys badgered them by yelling the word after them. When this contumacy began to be punished by the magistrates the boys resorted to holding up a copper coin as they passed a policeman.

Many Briticisms have not only been long delayed in getting into American, but have continued on levels of affectation after coming in. Examples are *swagger* and *swank.* *Swank* first appeared in English, as university slang, at the beginning of the Nineteenth Century, but it was not heard in the United States until near the century's end. In England *swank* is the noun and verb and *swanky* is the adjective, but in the United States *swank* has been used as an adjective also.[3] The English attach the meaning of over-swagger to it, and hence it would hardly persuade them in an advertisement,[4] but in the United States it has become virtually synonymous with *fashionable* and *chic.*

---

And set to work to spoil the countryside.

1 See AL4, pp. 40 and 226, n. 1.

2 One is to the effect that it is from C.O.P. (*constable of police*) which the English police used to write under their names on reports. Another is that it is a telegraphers' abbreviation for *chief of police.* A third is that it derives from the fact that early English *cops* wore brass buttons, mistaken for *copper* by the street boys. These etymologies are discussed in Calling All Cars, by Malcolm W. Bingay, Detroit *Free Press,* Feb. 2, 1939.

3 I am indebted here to Mr. Douglas Leechman, of the National Museum of Canada.

4 I am indebted here to Mr. R. Raven-Hill.

*Brunch,* designating a combination of breakfast and lunch, eaten about noon, appeared in England about 1900, but it was thirty years later before it began to make any headway on this side of the water.[1] *Snack-bar* began to be used by some of the swagger American drinking-places after the repeal of the Eighteenth Amendment, but, like *brunch,* it survived only in a narrow circle.[2] The Federal Reserve System set up by the Act of December 23, 1913 has *governors* in imitation of the Bank of England, but all other American banks continue to be operated by *directors.*[3] In the National Bank Act stock is designated by the English *shares* and stockholder by *shareholder,* but the New York Banking Act sticks to *stock* and *stockholder,* and so do virtually all American corporations.[4] The introduction of golf to the United States in 1888 naturally brought with it the vocabulary of the game, and most Americans are now familiar with many of its terms, e.g., *to tee off, to putt, hole in one, long drive, hazard* and *bunker,* and even with *cleek, mashie* and *niblick.* But the American players have discharged this debt by inventing some terms of their own, e.g., *birdie, eagle* and *nineteenth hole,* nearly all of which have passed to the British Isles. " There is nothing an Englishman could object to in any of these words," said Charles Ambrose in the London *Morning Post* in 1931,[5] " except the fact that they are used by American golfers and now by ourselves in an unaccustomed sense." It was probably golfers who brought in the English *sorry* for the American *excuse me:* it is now in wide use among Americans pretending to elegance.

The advertisement writers, especially for firms catering to the rich, show a considerable liking for Briticisms, and to them, I believe, we owe the appearance of *master's bedroom, swim-suit* and the various terms in *-shop. Swim-suit,* as a matter of fact, is seldom used in England, and I see no sign that it will ever oust *bathing-suit* in this country. The DAE traces *bathing-suit* to 1886. The earlier American term

1 On April 10, 1941, the Fifth Avenue Hotel in New York was advertising a " Sunday strollers' *brunch,* $1 per person, served from 11 A.M. to 3 P.M.," in the *Villager,* p. 8.

2 The Savoy-Plaza Hotel was advertising a *snack-bar* in the *New Yorker* July 25, 1936, but apparently it had changed the English meaning, which is virtually identical with that of our *lunch-counter,* for its *snack-bar* of-

fered " luncheon and dinner daily and Sunday."

3 *Governor* was used in colonial America to indicate the college dignitary now known as a *trustee,* or, at Harvard, an *overseer.*

4 I am indebted here to Mr. Hartford Beaumont of New York.

5 Reprinted in the Baltimore *Sun* as Our Golf Terms Get British O.K. (editorial page), Aug. 8, 1931.

seems to have been *bathing-dress*.[1] The American Postoffice still makes a distinction between a *postal-card*, on sale at every postoffice, with the stamp printed on it, and a *post-card*, which means something supplied by the sender himself and to which he must affix a stamp, or print, by arrangement with the postoffice, a notice that the postage has been otherwise paid for, but in everyday American usage that distinction seems to be breaking down. The first American *postal-card* was issued in 1873.[2] The English always use *post-card*: they saw their first in 1870. It had been invented in 1865, under the name of *offene postblatt* (now *postkarte*), by Heinrich von Stephan, later postmaster-general of the German Empire and founder of the International Postal Union, and Austria adopted it in 1869.[3] It may be that the increasing use of *post-card* in America is due to English influence, but on that point, of course, it is difficult to find evidence. *Parcel-post* was undoubtedly borrowed, for *parcel*, save in the legal sense, is a word but seldom used in the United States: *package-mail* would have sounded more American. The English *parcels-post* was set up in 1859, and the plural form continued in use until 1884, when *parcel-post* was adopted. In the United States *parcels-post* was used during the congressional discussion of plans for such a service, but when the project was at last executed, in 1912, *parcel-post* appeared in the statute, and it has been *parcel-post*, officially, ever since, though many Americans continue to say *parcels-post*. A number of other familiar terms may be borrowings from England, *e.g.*, *gadget* and *exchange* (telephone). The history of *gadget* is obscure, but it appears to have come into the argot of British sailors about the middle of the Nineteenth Century, perhaps suggested by the French *gâchette*, meaning a piece of machinery. It seems thoroughly and even typically American today, but the DAE does not list it, and the NED and Partridge show that it was in English use a good while before it began to rage in the United States. So with *exchange*. The original American word was apparently *central*, though the DAE's first example is dated 1889, two years after its first example of *exchange*. The latter has been in use in England since 1879. Just when the American *scrub-*

---

1 Traced by the DAE to 1864, but to be found in *Harper's Magazine*, Aug., 1855, p. 429.

2 Stamp Notes, by R. A. Barry, New York *Herald Tribune Books*, July 12, 1936, p. 20–VII.

3 *Post-Cards*, by Florence S. Hellman and Erna R. Stech, *American Notes and Queries*, June, 1941, p. 44.

*woman* began to yield to the English *charwoman* I do not know, but it was probably toward the end of the last century. The NED traces *charwoman* in English use to *c.* 1596.

269. [Fashionable American mothers teach their children to call them *Mummy*.] This most hideous and irrational of Briticisms was not imported into the United States until the Twentieth Century; indeed, the NED reported in 1908 that it had come into vogue in England itself only " in recent years." It has been traced to 1839 and its short form *Mum* to 1823, but the earlier examples of both are all from low life. In my boyhood American children called their mothers *Mamma*, and it was not until the turn of the century that any effort was made to displace it with the more formal and adult *Mother*. The latter showed good progress for a while but was presently challenged by *Mummy*. *Mamma* is ancient in English and has congeners in many other languages. It is, says the NED, " a reduplicated syllable often uttered instinctively by young children." It was reinforced early in the Seventeenth Century by the French *maman*, and in the course of the next hundred years became so fashionable that even adults used it. But it was confined to the upper classes, and it was not until the Nineteenth Century that the English lower orders began to adopt it. By the end of the century it had become so unfashionable that the way was open for *Mummy*. In England *Mamma* usually had the accent on the last syllable, but in the United States it more often fell upon the first. The first *a*, in this country, gradually became indistinguishable from *o*. The NED does not list *Mom* as in English use, but the Supplement thereof, 1933, records it as a " U.S. abbreviation of *Mamma*." I observed during World War II that it frequently occurred in published letters from American soldiers, greeting the folks at home. *Mammy*, for a colored woman and especially for a child's nurse, apparently did not appear until the 1830s. It was preceded by *momma*, *mauma* and *maum*, and was apparently pronounced at the start so that its first syllable had the vowel of either *comma* or *dawn* rather than that of *slam*, as now. *Ma* is recorded as a Suffolk dialect form in 1823 by the DAE, and as in general use soon afterward. *Maw* is not listed by either the NED or the DAE.

The history of *Papa* is much like that of *Mamma*. It, too, is based upon sounds uttered by babies, and it too got reinforced in England by French example in the Seventeenth Century. Again, it too became fashionable during the century following, and began to fall out of vogue in the Nineteenth. The accent, at the start, was sometimes on the first syllable and sometimes on the second, but the latter form finally prevailed in England and the former in America. In America the *a* gradually acquired the sound of *o*, and by 1840, as the DAE shows, a shortened form, *Pop,* had developed. In England *Pop* was not used, perhaps because, in the Eighteenth Century, it had become there a general term of endearment for a woman or girl, and had later taken on the narrower significance of a kept woman. *Pa* is traced by the NED to 1811, but it and *Paw* were not much favored by the English, since they were in nursery use (the former spelled *pah*) as euphemisms for nasty, indecent. *Pa* seems to have been popular in America before its first reported appearance in England, for Parson Mason L. Weems, in his original telling of the cherry-tree story, 1800, made Washington say to his father: " I can't tell a lie, *Pa;* you know I can't tell a lie. I did cut it with my hatchet." *Pappy* is traced by the NED in English use to 1763 but is marked " now rare." Like *Mammy,* it is still heard among the whites of Appalachia, and does not denote that a colored person is being addressed or spoken of.

In my boyhood in Maryland *Dad* and *Daddy* were in use, but not extensively, for *Dad* was a familiar American euphemism for *God* and appeared in many words and phrases that were considered more or less profane, e.g., *dad-blamed, dad-blasted, dad burn me, dad fetch it* and *dad gum.* But *daddy-longlegs* for a spider-like creature with long, slender legs was in common and unquestioned use, though it had rivals in *granddaddy-longlegs* and *grandfather-longlegs. Grandpa* and *Grandma* were in almost universal use as vocatives, with *Grandfather* and *Grandmother* heard only rarely, save of course in the third person. *Grandpappy* and *Grandmammy* were confined to Appalachia and the South, but *Grandpop* and *Grandpaw* were tolerated variants of *Grandpa. Dad* is traced by the NED to c. 1500, as is *daddy.* They became fashionable in England toward the end of the Nineteenth Century and were soon afterward adopted widely in the United States. An American boy of today, at least above the age of five, would blush to call his father *Papa,* though in my boyhood the term was used even by grown men. The effort to substitute *Father* arose simultaneously with the effort to substitute *Mother* for *Mamma,* but was presently challenged by *Dad.*[1] In England, I gather, *Mummy* and

---

1 *Aunt* (or *Aunty*) and *Uncle,* as terms used in addressing aged colored people, are traced by the DAE to 1830. Both were in use before this for addressing whites. *Granny* and *Goody* are old in English. The

*Daddy* are a shade more elegant than *Mum* and *Dad*.[1] *Mater* and *pater*, nearly always used in the third person and with the definite article, have never made any headway in the United States. The NED marks them both " chiefly schoolboys' slang," and it is obvious that they must have arisen among boys more or less familiar with Latin. *Pater* is traced to 1728, but there is a long gap afterward until 1880; *mater* is traced to 1864. *Governor* as a designation for father is traced by the NED to 1847. It is not unknown in the United States, but has never been in wide use.[2]

In AL4, p. 268, I ascribed to Dr. J. Milnor Coit, physician to St. Paul's School at Concord, N. H., the introduction to America of the terminology of the swagger English *public-schools, e.g., form* and *headmaster*. I am informed by various correspondents that I thereby confused Dr. Coit with his kinsman, the Rev. Dr. Henry Augustus Coit, the first *rector* of St. Paul's, who, on his death in 1895, was succeeded by his brother, the Rev. Joseph Howland Coit, who died in turn in 1906. Dr. J. Milnor Coit was not physician to the school, but its *master* in natural sciences from 1876 onward, its *vice-rector* in 1904 and 1906, and its *acting rector* a short while after the death of Dr. Joseph Howland Coit. He was not a medical man, but held the degree of Ph.D. from Dartmouth and that of Sc.D. from Hobart. Born at Harrisburg, Pa., in 1845, he was manager of the Cleveland Tube Works before taking to the birch. On his withdrawal from St. Paul's he went to Munich and there operated the Coit School for American boys.[3] The true begetter of St. Paul's excessive Anglicism was Dr. Henry Augustus Coit. It still

---

former, about 1790, acquired the special American significance of a midwife. The latter, in early use in the colonies to designate any married woman, survives at Harvard as the designation of a woman who cares for students' rooms. The DAE traces it, in that sense, to 1819.

1 Lost *Mum* and *Dad:* headline in the *News of the World,* April 19, 1936, referring to two working-class orphans. "I lost my *Mummy* and *Daddy*": caption in an appeal for funds by the Shaftesbury Homes and *Arethusa* Training Ship in the London *Times Literary Supplement,* Jan. 1, 1914, p. 10. On Nov. 12, 1939 the Baltimore *Sun* published an ar-

ticle by Mrs. L. Baring-Wilson, recently returned from England, in which evacuated English children were represented as addressing their fathers and mothers, in letters home, as *Pop* and *Mom,* but I have never encountered either term in an English newspaper.

2 I am indebted for help here to Miss Margaret Butcher and H. W. Seaman.

3 The statement in AL4, p. 268, n. 1, that he was a native of Harrisburg caused the antiquaries of the town to inquire into his early history, but they could find no record of him. See Mirrors of Harrisburg, Harrisburg *Sunday Courier,* Feb. 18, 1940.

has *forms, removes, evensong* and other parrotings of Eton and Harrow, and also an annual cricket holiday, though the game is no longer played by the boys. Its chief rivals in the emulation of the English public schools are Groton, St. Mark's and Choate, but virtually all American prep schools of any pretensions show the same influence. Dixon Wecter notes in " The Saga of American Society,"[1] that " the introduction of *fives*[2] at Groton and a modified *fag* system at St. Mark's are richly significant of social Anglophilia."

There are plenty of Briticisms, especially on the level of slang, that deserve American adoption better than any of these shaky borrowings from the English upper classes, *e.g., pub-crawl* (a tour of saloons). Many more are to be found in the extraordinarily rich and pungent slang of Australia, *e.g., donk* (a fool), *fork* (a jockey), *hunk* (a large man), *to mizzle* (to complain), *rest* (a year in jail), *smoodger* (a flatterer) and *wowser* (" a drab-souled Philistine haunted by the mockery of others' happiness "[3]). During the hurricane of moral endeavor that beset the United States after the first World War I tried to introduce *wowser* in the Republic, but without success. It gained, however, at least one recruit who was worth a host, to wit, the late Dr. William Morton Wheeler (1865–1937), professor of entomology at Harvard from 1908 onward, dean of the Bussey Institution, and the world's greatest authority on ants and their kindred. Dr. Wheeler was not only an eminent man of science; he was also a highly adroit and pungent satirist, and it was in both capacities that he introduced *wowser* into a paper contributed to the *Scientific Monthly* in 1920.[4] Not long after this the term was also used by his and my friend, the late Dr. Raymond Pearl, (1879–1940), professor of biology at the Johns Hopkins, but my memorandum of the time and place is unhappily mislaid. Every Puritan is not necessarily a *wowser*: to be one he must devote himself zealously to reforming the morals of his neighbors, and, in particular, to throwing obstacles in the way of their enjoyment of what they choose to regard as pleasures. The Prohibitionist of the thirteen dark years was an archetypical example. The word was invented by an Australian named John Norton, editor of a somewhat saucy and even ribald weekly paper called *John Norton's Truth,* published simultaneously in Sydney, Melbourne and

---

1 New York, 1937, p. 241.
2 A somewhat tame English ball game, traced by the DAE to 1636.

3 I take this definition from Baker.
4 Termitodoxa, Feb., p. 116.

Wellington, N. Z.[1] *Truth* had, in its heyday, a style as characteristic and individual as the style of the American *Time,* and all its contributors were trained to write like Norton himself. He invented many other spicy terms, including *stink-chariot* for automobile, but only *wowser* has survived. Partridge says that it was launched *c.* 1895 and had become domiciled in England by 1930. " If Australia," said the London *Daily Telegraph* in 1937, " had given nothing more to civilization than that magnificent label for one of its most melancholy products it would not have been discovered in vain." There have been several guesses at the etymology of *wowser* but I have encountered none that is convincing, and the Shorter Oxford marks it " origin obscure." My own surmise is that Norton simply invented it, just as Lewis Carroll (C. L. Dodgson) invented *to chortle* in 1872. Such masterpieces are inspired by the powers and principalities of the air.[2]

The English *opposite number,* signifying a person in corresponding office or position, *e.g.,* the American Secretary of State with respect to the English Foreign Secretary, has made some progress in the United States in recent years, but only on relatively lofty levels: the common people know nothing of it. It has come in in England since World War I, and probably had a military origin. The most hard-worked of all the English counter-words of recent years, to wit, *amenities,* is seldom if ever encountered in the United States. *Amenity* is the French word *amenité,* borrowed in the Fifteenth Century. To an American it is very similar in meaning, in the plural, to *civilities,* as in " the *amenities* of the occasion," but the English have widened it, since *c.* 1916, to mean almost anything agreeable, from a beautiful view to a sound system of drains, and from the chance to hear a band of music to law and order. There is an *Amenities* Society in Norwich which devoted itself, before the late unpleasantness, to restoring the antiquities of the town,[3] there is an *Amenities* Group in the House of Commons which keeps an eye on public monuments and memorials,[4] and there is a Bath Preservation Trust which seeks " to preserve for the benefit of the public the *amenities* of Bath and its sur-

---

1 Norton was often in court. Once he was asked on the stand to define *wowser.* " It means," he said, " a fellow who is too niggardly of joy to allow the other fellow any time to do anything but pray." I am indebted here to Mr. J. A. B. Foster, of Hobart, Tasmania.

2 I am indebted for information about Norton to Mr. Alan Tytheridge, late of Tokyo.

3 Tudor Architecture Restored, London *Times,* June 17, 1938.

4 Memorial to George V, London *Times,* June 17, 1938.

roundings." [1] I have in my collectanea clippings from English papers applying the term, *inter alia*, to public parks, bandstands, piers at the seaside, improved water supply, public health services, bathing accommodations, parking lots,[2] meal service in jails,[3] playing fields,[4] housing developments, public comfort stations,[5] telephones, public washrooms,[6] libraries, swimming-pools, air-raid shelters, inspiring outlooks on land or river [7] and town-planning.[8] The English realtors have seized upon the term with violent affection, and it is seldom that an advertisement of a country estate for sale or flats in a new apartment house for rent appears in the London papers without a long catalogue of the *amenities* offered with it, *e.g.*, central heating, electric clocks, elevator service, refrigerators, radio installation, fireproof doors, open fireplaces, tiled bathrooms, garages, roof gardens, " constant hot-water," kitchen-cabinets, shower-baths, " box-room accommodations " (storage space), softened drinking water, " pet's parlour," wall safes, separate tradesmen's entrances and built-in beauty-shoppes.[9] " Every modern *amenity* " or " Every possible up-to-date *amenity* " appears in fully half of these offers.[10] In 1937 Lord Horder, physician-in-ordinary to the king, went about the country explaining the meaning of the term as he understood it. In November he defined it thus:

> By the *amenities* I mean clear air to breathe, contact with the earth in our games and hobbies, quiet and leisure, time to stand and stare — over a gate in the country, or, if Scotland Yard would allow it, on the kerb in the city.[11]

A couple of weeks later he had revised his definition as follows:

1 *Amenities* of Bath, London *Times*, June 24, 1938.
2 For all the foregoing see Holiday Resorts Spend Money, Manchester *Guardian Commercial*, June 24, 1938.
3 Everything But Haggis, Hong Kong *Daily Press*, June 12, 1936.
4 Famous Pottery Firm to Move, London *Telegraph*, May 15, 1936.
5 Macao *Amenities*, *South China Morning Post*, April 20, 1936.
6 Railway *Amenities*, London *Telegraph*, Sept. 4, 1937.
7 Thames For M.P.'s, London *Telegraph*, May 16, 1936: " Sir Nicholas Grattan-Doyle likes to see the Thames. He is asking Mr. Ormsby-Gore on Monday whether, in the interests of members [of Parliament] 'whose sole outlook at present is a

blank wall,' he will provide a view of the river's *amenities* by restoring some of the raised seats on the terrace [of the House of Commons]."
8 Small Burghs Handicapped, Edinburgh *Scotsman*, March 1, 1937.
9 I am indebted for most of these examples to the collection of the late F. H. Tyson.
10 But sometimes the American influence conquers even *amenities*, for example, in Rebuilding of Wellington Barracks, London *Sunday Times*, Dec. 11, 1938: " Barracks are now being built as homes where *every modern convenience* is obtainable."
11 Lord Horder, London *Sunday Times*, Nov. 26, 1937.

What do I mean by *amenities*? Clean air to breathe. Close contact with the earth and sky and sun. The sight of beautiful things. The hearing of beautiful sounds. Quiet and leisure to enjoy all these.[1]

It is a wonder that this noble word has not migrated to America. It has an elegant smack.

### 5. HONORIFICS

274. [The American fondness for hollow titles goes back to colonial days.] In the Eighteenth Century, says Allen Walker Read, " anyone could become a *colonel* or a *doctor* if he impressed his fellows as deserving some mark of distinction." [2] The DAE traces *colonel*, as a mere title of esteem, to 1744, *captain* and *major* to 1746, *professor* to 1774, *judge* to 1800 and *general* to 1805, and all are probably older. In 1723 a writer in the *New England Courant* noted that " sow-gelders and farriers " were already calling themselves *doctor*. The English give the courtesy title of *doctor* to medical men who are only M.B.'s. (bachelors of medicine) but the fact that it is only a courtesy title is borne in mind. In America all who pretend to leechcraft have been *doctors* since the early Nineteenth Century, and the degree of *M.B.* has disappeared.[3] Druggists and dentists are not *doctors* in England,[4] and even surgeons insist on being called *Mr.*,[5] but in this country all three classes are *doctors*, unanimously, and so are a great variety of other healers, including osteopaths, chiropractors, optometrists, chiropodists and veterinarians. Most of these have

1 At Last We Know What the *Amenities* Really Are, London *Daily Express*, Dec. 5, 1937.
2 Words Indicating Social Status in America in the Eighteenth Century, *American Speech*, Oct., 1934, p. 208.
3 I am informed by Mr. Milton Halsey Thomas, curator of Columbiana at Columbia University, that the *M.B.* was given by Columbia (then King's College) from 1769 to 1774, by Harvard from 1788 to 1811, and by Dartmouth from 1798 to 1812. At King's College a further year of study and a thesis were required for the *M.D.* In 1811 Harvard granted complimentary *M.D.* degrees to all previous *M.B.'s* who had not proceeded to the doctorate.

4 Dr. William Brady, who has conducted a health column in American newspapers since 1918, has tried to induce American dentists to put *Dentor* instead of *Dr.* on their signs, but in vain. I am indebted here to Mr. Fred Hamann.
5 Says an English correspondent: " Until he begins to specialize in surgery he is *Dr.* like any other medical man, though his degrees may be only those of *M.B.* and *Ch.B.* (bachelor of surgery). It is a sign of rising in the world, proof that he has made the grade, *i.e.*, has become the surgeon in a great hospital or teacher of surgery in a medical school, when he can be content with the title of *Mr.*"

set up doctorates of their own, and that of the veterinarians, like that of the dentists, really represents advanced professional training, but those of some of the others are often highly dubious. Thus the state of affairs among the optometrists,[1] as described by Dr. Frederick Juchhoff in the *Journal of the American Medical Association:* [2]

> Optometric education may be divided into two distinct types of institutions. The first type includes Columbia, Ohio State and California universities. These offer a standard four-years course, based on a high-school training, which course leads to the degree of *B.S.* or *B.A.* None of these standard institutions recognizes the " doctorate " in optometry either by granting the degree or by indicating that the degree is held by a member of the faculty. On the other hand, the second type of schools, privately owned and actually conducted for profit (although frequently chartered "not for profit"), grants the doctorate on less work than is required for graduation from a good junior college. An official of one of the Chicago optometric colleges recently boasted that the Chicago schools receive a good many students from California because they give the " doctorate " while the students' own State university grants merely a bachelor's degree.

Dr. Juchhoff added that some of the schools of chiropody [3] are almost as bad as the worst of those of optometry. In both fields, he reported, there is a tendency among the more ambitious schools to extend their courses to include " practically all the subjects in the regular medical curriculum," with the aim of permitting graduates to prescribe for disease — something which is now forbidden, as I note below, by the State licensing acts. " The plan," he said, " appears to be to convert these schools into medical schools granting the *M.D.* degree, first by calling it *M.D. in Optometry* or *M.D. in Chiropody*, and then making it straight *M.D.*" He went on:

> It is probably only a question of time until some bright mind will conceive the idea of purchasing from the State of Illinois a charter for a college of barbering and beauty culture and of granting a " doctorate " to its graduates.

1 Webster 1934 defines *optometry* as " scientific examination of the eyes for the purpose of prescribing glasses, etc., to correct defects, without the use of drugs." In most States *optometrists* are licensed, and their license forbids them to treat actual diseases. Such treatment is the function of the *ophthalmologist*, who is a regular *M.D.*

2 The Degree of Doctor, Aug. 26, 1939, p. 876.

3 Webster defines *chiropody* as " originally, the art of treating diseases of the hands and feet; as now restricted, the treatment of ailments of the feet, especially minor ailments." The State licensing acts for *chiropodists*, like those for optometrists, usually define the bounds past which a practitioner may not go. When his patient presents a condition beyond his science he is supposed to call in an *orthopedist*, who is a regular *M.D.* The more high-toned chiropodists now call themselves *podiatrists*, a term based on the Greek word for *foot*.

That such a plan would be quite profitable seems certain. The barbers would have in their favor, at least, some historical basis. The various functions of the beauty culturist, such as massage, application of electricity to the hair and face, the puncturing and squeezing of pimples and extraction of blackheads, certainly are as much "doctoring" as removing corns, extracting ingrown toe nails and massaging fallen arches.

The colleges of osteopathy and chiropractic all offer doctorates to their graduates, and in addition some of them also offer other degrees. An *osteopath* [1] on taking his diploma becomes a *D.O.* (*doctor of osteopathy*), but may advance to the degrees of *D.O.S.* (*doctor of osteopathic science*) and D.L.O. (*doctor of laws in osteopathy*).[2] A chiropractor becomes a *D.C.* (*doctor of chiropractic*) and then advances to *Ph.C.* (*philosopher of chiropractic*).[3] All the other non-Euclidian healers have similar degrees.[4] Graduates in *naturopathy* [5] become *D.N.'s*, and those in " divine science," which seems to be a variety of faith healing, may choose between the degrees of *Ps.D.* (*doctor of psychology*), *Psy.D.* (*doctor of psychotherapy*), and *D.S.D.* (*doctor of divine science*).[6] The tendency to multiply degrees has been marked in the United States since the turn of the century.

1 *Osteopathy* is a system of healing based on the theory that most disease is caused by structural derangements which interfere with either the circulation of the blood or the free functioning of nerves. It was launched by Dr. A. T. Still (1828–1917), of Kirksville, Mo., in 1874. *Osteopaths* are now licensed in nearly all States. The course of instruction in their schools is much more comprehensive than that enjoyed by other irregular practitioners, and they have of late made a campaign for full recognition, including the right of admission to the medical corps of the Army and Navy. A statement of their doctrine as they understand it is in the Encyclopedia Americana; New York, 1932, Vol. XXI, pp. 28–34.

2 The Higher Degrees, in Tonics and Sedatives, *Journal of the American Medical Association*, April 1, 1939.

3 *Chiropractic* was introduced by D. D. Palmer in 1895. It is based upon osteopathy, but finds nearly all the lesions responsible for disease in the spinal column. It also adds a curative principle called *innate intellec-*

*tuality*, which seems to be identical with the *vis medicatrix naturae* of the regular faculty. *Chiropractors* are licensed in nearly all American States. They have invented a number of fancy names to designate specialists within their fold, *e.g., radionist*, meaning one who operates " a calbro-mago wave *radionic* machine," which " deals with disease vibrations . . . just as the radio registers vibrations of sound."

4 Some of the varieties of quacks in practise in New York in 1926, with the doctorates they pretended to, are listed in AL4, p. 271, n. 1. Many others have appeared since.

5 *Naturopathy* is defined by Webster as " a system of physical culture and drugless treatment of diseases by methods supposed to stimulate or assist nature." It has become, in the United States, a catch-all for every system of healing not embraced in the other schools. In not a few States *naturopaths* are licensed.

6 Advertisement of the University of Divine Science, Los Angeles, in the London (Ont.) *Evening Lamp*, Nov. 15, 1938.

The degrees of bachelor, master and doctor are now often followed by designations of particularity, *e.g.*, *in Ed.* (education), *in Eng.* (engineering), *in Mus.* (music), etc. These distinctions are needed, lest the sheer multitudinousness of new bachelors, masters and doctors reduce them to an undifferentiated horde.[1] Columbia University and its various outhouses, during the academic year 1943–44, conferred no less than 3455 degrees, certificates and diplomas on 3442 individuals,[2] and all the other great rolling-mills of learning followed suit. How many *Ph.D.'s* are turned out in the United States every year I do not know, but the number must run to thousands.[3] This degree was borrowed from the Germans, and was almost unheard of in American colleges before the great influx of German ideas in the 70s and 80s. The English universities did not adopt it until after World War I. They are much less liberal than the American universities with honorary degrees, which are distributed lavishly in the United States, especially the *LL.D.* The champion degree-bearer of all times seems to be the Hon. Herbert C. Hoover, who got his *A.B. in Eng.* at Leland Stanford in 1895 by the sweat of his brow and has since accumulated 49 honorary degrees of various sorts, chiefly *LL.D.'s.* His runner up is Dr. Nicholas Murray Butler, president of Columbia, who is *A.B.*, *A.M.* and *Ph.D.* by honest toil and has received 37 degrees *honoris causa.* There are few members of Congress without at least one *LL.D.*, and few other politicos of any puissance. It is also conferred wholesale upon the presidents and other high officers of rich corporations, newspaper editors and columnists, eminent radio crooners, college presidents who may be trusted to re-

---

1 There is already, in fact, a considerable confusion, as witness *M.D.* — Not *Dr.*, by D. H. McCarter of Washington, *Journal of the American Medical Association*, March 11, 1944. "The physicians of the country," said Mr. McCarter, "in connection with the preparation of many millions of forms required by various government activities, frequently neglect to have their degrees following their signatures and at times prefix their names with the word *Dr.*, providing no other evidence that they are doctors of medicine. This occasionally works a hardship on us bureaucrats because, in order to assure proper distribution of certain types of materials,

supplies, equipment and services, we must determine that the applicant is a physician rather than a doctor of science, of divinity, philosophy, naturopathy, chiropractic, podiatry, chiropody or whatever."
2 Report of the President for the Year 1944, p. 55.
3 In Doctor's Degrees in Modern Foreign Languages, 1940–41, *Modern Language Journal*, Nov., 1941, pp. 804–12, Henry Grattan Doyle listed more than 130 *Ph.D.'s* in the non-English modern languages for one academic year. This was the crop in 31 colleges only. Dr. Doyle confessed that his list was incomplete, and asked for additions.

ciprocate, and a miscellaneous rabble of contributors or potential contributors to college funds.

The misuse of *professor* began in America at an early date, and still prevails. The DAE records a *professor of book-auctioneering* in 1774, and Bartlett, in 1859, noted the use of the term to designate " dancing-masters, conjurors, banjo-players, etc." It has been applied, first and last, to a really immense range of virtuosi, mainly frauds. Said an anonymous contributor to *American Speech* in 1927: [1]

> Most of those who insist on being given the title of *professor* are quacks or fakers of some kind, or they are chiropractors, or chiropodists, or tonsorial experts, or boxing instructors, or they are men teachers in secondary schools. In the United States the word has no aura of dignity, whatever standing it may retain across the Atlantic Ocean. I have an official right to the title myself, but like other academic bearers of it I much prefer to be termed merely *Mr.*

Two years before this the professors at the University of Virginia organized a society " for the encouragement of the use of *Mister* to all men, professional or otherwise," and during the years since then its crusade has made such progress that most genuine professors now prefer to be called *Mister*, and that term is in wide use in the larger colleges.[2] But *Professor* is still cherished by pedagogues on the lower levels, and not long ago, according to a writer in *American Speech*, " a man who taught the fifth and sixth grades in Byers, Kansas, threatened to lick the children if they did not call him *professor*." [3] There was a time when every county superintendent of schools and high-school principal was a *professor* by unanimous local consent, but of late years so many of these birchmen have been made *Ph.D.'s* that they are now usually called *doctor*, even when they are not.[4] In the Baltimore of my boyhood, *c.* 1890, the following, *inter alia*, were

---

1 The Title *Professor*, by N. R. L., Oct., p. 27.

2 *Professor* is thus defined in The Language of Modern Education, by Lester K. Ade; Harrisburg (Pa.), 1939, p. 29: " Basically, one who professes and pursues an academic subject. The term is applied to the highest academic rank of college and university teachers. It is incongruous to designate as *professor* a teacher or administrator of any institution below collegiate level, or anyone not actually holding a pro-

fessional [possibly a misprint for *professorial*] rank in a college."

3 Auctioneer *Colonels* Again, by E. L. Jacobs, Oct. 1935, p. 232.

4 Other discussions of *professor* are in *Professor Again*, by Charles L. Hanson, *American Speech*, Feb., 1928, pp. 256 and 257; *Professor Again*, by C. D. P., *American Speech*, June, 1929, pp. 422–23, and *Professor or Professional?*, by Mamie Meredith, the same, Feb., 1934, pp. 71 and 72. Miss Meredith reprints the protest of a Nebraska

called *professors:* colored hostlers who bit off the tails of puppies, bootblacks serving in barber-shops, rubbers of baseball-players, tattooers, Indian-club swingers, painters of black eyes, owners and operators of rat terriers, and distinguished crab-soup and oyster-flitter cooks. During Prohibition days the functionary who went about reinforcing near-beer with shots of alcohol or ether was first called a *professor,* but after a while, for some reason unknown, his designation was changed to *doctor. Professor* is not altogether unknown in England in the extended American sense. The NED records a protest, dated 1864, against its use " in connection with dancing schools, jugglers' booths, and veterinary surgeries," and shows that it was used in 1893 by a champion high-diver. An English correspondent tells me that he has observed its use by the proprietor of a Punch-and-Judy show, and adds that in the *New Statesman and Nation,* in 1939,[1] G. W. Stonier spoke of " *Professor* Morley's select bathing-tents " at Brighton. But the English treat genuine professors much more politely than we do. In writing, the title takes precedence of all other titles, but in conversation it may be dropped, *e.g., Professor* Sir Alfred Zimmern and Sir Alfred Zimmern.[2] The following additional notes on British university degrees and dignities come from an academic correspondent:

At Oxford the degree of *D.D.* used to be given to any divine of the Church of England who published three sermons at his own expense and paid a fee. But some years ago, when the Faculty of Divinity was made non-Anglican, *i.e.,* when any Christian clergyman was admitted to degrees, the regulations for the grant of the *D.D.* were tightened, and a candidate must now take a serious examination.

Every university in the British Isles has a *chancellor* who is its nominal head, but in nearly all of them the real head, corresponding to the American university *president,* is the *vice-chancellor.* In the Scottish universities the office of *vice-chancellor* is combined with that of *principal,* a permanent official of lower rank, in actual charge of the administration. At the University of London there is a *vice-chancellor* as well as a *principal,* and at Dublin there is a *provost* as well as a *vice-chancellor.* The *vice-chancellor,* at Oxford, Cambridge and London, is a head of one of the constituent colleges, and commonly serves for three years.

At St. Andrews, Glasgow and Aberdeen the *principal* is appointed by the Crown; at Edinburgh, which was originally a municipal foundation, he is elected by a committee representing the City Council and the university. At

---

editor of 1869 who had been called *professor* by a colleague. She shows that in his own paper he permitted the term to be applied to a horse-trainer, a barber, the manager of a roller-skating rink, and a dancing-master.

1 May 27.

2 I am indebted here to Professor D. W. Brogan.

Dublin the *provost* is appointed by the heir of the Crown, *i.e.*, the president of the Irish Free State. In all other universities the *chancellors, vice-chancellors,* etc., are elected by the alumni. At Oxford there is a system of rotation, whereby the head of Beelzebub College is sure to be *chancellor* when his college's turn comes. At Cambridge there is slightly more choice, but not much. At the Scotch universities there is, in addition to the *chancellor*, another honorary head, the *lord rector*. He is elected by the students, who lose their right to vote when they are graduated.

A *regius professor* is appointed by the Crown, *i.e.*, in England by the Prime Minister and in Scotland by the Secretary of State for Scotland, but it does not necessarily follow that the Crown has endowed his chair. All *B.A.'s* of a university have the right to vote in parliamentary elections; if they have residence elsewhere they may vote twice. But at Oxford and Cambridge only *M.A.'s* have any voice in university affairs. Both grant the degree as a matter of course after a lapse of time and the payment of a fee, but at the other universities it is given only after an examination or the submission of a thesis.

At Oxford and Cambridge the faculty is called the *dons;* elsewhere it is the *staff*. Dons are the *fellows* of colleges, and are their own employers, for there are no outside trustees. There are many junior teachers at Oxford and Cambridge who are not *fellows*, but they all hope to be elected. At both universities all *professors* are attached to colleges, and at Oxford a college must accept as a *fellow* anyone appointed to a chair. At Cambridge this is not necessary, and some *professors* are thus not *fellows*. There are *fellows* who do not aspire to professorships, for if they become *heads* of their colleges they may have more power and more money than if they became *professors*.

The introduction of the *Ph.D.* degree into Great Britain has caused some perturbation in the older universities, the statutes of which give all *doctors* precedence of *M.A.'s*, no matter what the college or university rank of the latter. In the old days this did not matter, for the *doctors* were bound to be senior people anyway, and most heads of colleges were *D.Litt.'s* or *D.D.'s*. But nowadays hardly any clerics are *heads* of colleges, and many of the *heads* are not *doctors*. (As in American colleges they tend to be administrators rather than scholars.) Meanwhile, a good many younger *dons* have become *Ph.D.'s*, and they take great pleasure in asserting their doctoral rights. Sooner or later the heads of colleges will have to be treated like bishops and made *doctors* regardless of their academic claims.[1]

Read, in the paper before cited, and the DAE, under the appropriate rubrics, assemble many comments of early English travelers upon the fondness for military titles in America. " Whenever you

[1] There are *deans* in the English and Scottish universities, but they are heard of much less than their opposite numbers in the United States. To the average Englishman a *dean* is an ecclesiastical functionary, *e.g.*, *Dean* Inge. He may be either the head canon of a collegiate or cathedral church or a sort of assistant to an archdeacon. The English seldom use *dean* in our sense of any senior. What we would call the *dean* of the House of Commons is its *father* to them. For discussions of the heavy American use of the term see What is a *Dean?*, by J. R. Schultz, *American Speech*, Dec. 1935, pp. 319-20, and Why *Dean?*, by Z. S., *American Speech*, Feb., 1926, pp. 292-93.

travel in Maryland (as also in Virginia and Carolina)," wrote Edward Kimber in 1746,[1] " your ears are constantly astonished by the number of *colonels, majors* and *captains* that you hear mentioned; in short, the whole country seems at first to you a retreat of heroes." Two years before this a Scottish physician, Alexander Hamilton, found *colonels* so thick along the Hudson that he recorded a common saying that any man who had killed a rattlesnake was entitled to the title.[2] After the Revolution there was a great increase in these titles, for any veteran of respectable position — say, an innkeeper — was commonly called *captain*, and all actual officers continued to use their titles, usually with an informal promotion of a rank or two. Every other American war, even the most trivial, brought in a horde of other such brevet holders of imaginary commissions, and during the great movement into the West they were multiplied enormously. " Every man who comes from Georgia," said a writer in the *Southern Literary Messenger* in 1852, " is a *major!* " But *major* was never as popular as *captain* and *colonel*. The former got a great lift when, on the coming of railways, it began to be applied to conductors, and the latter was assisted when the Governors of the States began appointing large and glittering staffs, some of whom were made *generals* but most of whom were *colonels*.[3] How many such bogus colonels were commissioned first and last I do not know, but the number must have run to many thousands. The late Ruby Laffoon, during his glorious reign as Governor of Kentucky (1931–35),[4] bestowed the silver eagle on whole brigades, divisions and army corps of them, and so helped to give the term *Kentucky colonel* a reinforced validity.[5] Some of the Governors

1 *London Magazine*, July, p. 324.
2 Hamilton's Itinerarium. . . . From May to September, 1744, edited by Albert Bushnell Hart; St. Louis, 1907, p. 94. See also Rattlesnake *Colonel*, by Albert Matthews, *New England Quarterly*, June, 1937, pp. 341–45.
3 Not infrequently a notable who started out as *captain* was gradually promoted, by public acclamation, to *colonel*. " When we first came here," says Mulberry Sellers in The Gilded Age, by Mark Twain and Charles Dudley Warner; Hartford, 1873, p. 515, " I was *Mr.* Sellers, and *Major* Sellers, and *Captain* Sellers, . . . but the minute our bill went through the

House I was *Colonel* Sellers every time. And nobody could do enough for me, and whatever I said was wonderful." " I wonder," says Washington Hawkins, " what you will be tomorrow, after the President signs the bill." " *General*, sir! " answers Sellers. " *General*, without a doubt."

4 It should be explained for the benefit of English readers that Ruby, despite his given-name, was male, not female. He was born in 1869 and died in 1941.
5 For some reason unfathomable and greatly to be lamented, the DAE does not mention *Kentucky colonel*. It lists *Kentucky bite* (or *Indian*

of other militaristic States, despairing of beating him at this game, turned to other titles, and one of them actually began making *admirals*. One of the most conspicuous Kentucky *colonels* of the between-war era, Colonel Patrick H. Callahan of Louisville (1866–1940), who had served in that rank on the staffs of two Kentucky Governors, was a stout defender of the title. In 1934 or thereabout he thus wrote to John A. Doyle, of River Forest, Ill., who had criticized Governor Laffoon's great spate of *colonels:*

> *Colonel* [in Kentucky] is not much more than a nickname, like *Tom, Dick* or *Harry*, and is used and appreciated mostly on that account. It is often applied to all Kentuckians without the formality of an appointment, just as *major* is used in Georgia. Nine out of ten people who call me *colonel* otherwise would be saying *Mr.* Callahan. It is a handle that breaks down formality.

To another correspondent, John D. Moore, of Brooklyn, N. Y., he wrote in 1935:

> The names of *Pat* and *Mike* were used so much by slapstick comedians and bum story-tellers that my friends and even chums had some hesitancy in addressing me as *Pat*, although when I played ball as a young fellow I was addressed in no other way. . . . When one is given a title like *colonel* or *judge* it is a middle ground, and where people would hesitate to call one by his given name it is just the thing to use the title.[1]

When the late Milton McRae was offered an appointment on the staff of William McKinley, then Governor of Ohio, and refused it, it was bestowed upon him nevertheless by his fellow journalists, and in the end he bore it proudly.[2] In all probability he would have got

---

*hug*, traced to 1830), *Kentucky fence* (1837), *Kentucky leggins* (1817), *Kentucky reel* (1832), *Kentucky yell* (1845), *Kentucky coffee* (1859), *Kentucky mahogany* (1847), *Kentucky ark* (1824), *Kentucky boat* (1785), *Kentucky jean* (1835), *Kentucky rifle* (1839), and *Kentucky Derby* (1875), but not *Kentucky colonel*. It had become a byword so early as 1825, when John Marshall, then Chief Justice of the United States, wrote a quatrain that still survives:

> In the Blue Grass region
> A paradox was born:
> The corn was full of kernels
> And the *colonels* full of corn.

1 Colonel Callahan sent me copies of these letters. He maintained a mimeographed service that he called

the Callahan Correspondence, and whenever he wrote a letter to one acquaintance that seemed to him to be interesting — which was very often — all the other persons on his list got copies of it. The colonel had been a professional baseball player in his youth, but lived to be president of the Louisville Varnish Company and a man of substance. He was very active in all lay movements among Catholics, and was the only Catholic I ever knew who professed to be a Prohibitionist.

2 The authority for this is the *Dictionary of American Biography*, quoted by Horwill, p. 73. McRae (1858–1930) was one of the founders of the Scripps-McRae (now Scripps-Howard) chain of newspapers.

it soon or late, even without the suggestion of McKinley, for it is often bestowed on American newspaper editors by common consent, as a sort of occupational honorific, especially in the South. In the Middle West it is similarly given to auctioneers. Said E. L. Jacobs in *American Speech* in 1935:

> The title of *colonel* is as punctiliously accorded all auctioneers in small towns and in the country as the title of *professor* is given to all principals of high-schools.[1]

A number of American Governors, in order to put down the pestilence of *colonels*, have declined to appoint honorary military staffs: in this reform, I believe, the late Albert Cabell Ritchie (1876–1936), Governor of Maryland from 1920 to 1935, was the pioneer. In Virginia, in 1942, a member of the Legislature named Pilcher lent a hand by introducing a bill providing that upon the payment of one dollar any adult white citizen of the State should become a *colonel*.[2] The English historian, Edward A. Freeman, who made a lecture tour of the United States in 1881–82, reported when he got home that at that time, at least in parts of the United States, any stranger not obviously of inferior status was " commonly addressed as *colonel* or *judge*." [3] Another English visitor of the 80s, W. G. Marshall, thus reported his own adventures: [4]

> The hotel runners at Ogden called me *Boss*, and my friend they called *Cap'n*. Hitherto I had generally been known as *Colonel*, particularly among the Negroes. I rather approved of being called by this latter appellation. "To call a man *Colonel*," says the Philadelphia *Post*, "is to convey the idea that he is of a mild, meek and benevolent disposition.". . . But it is another matter altogether, indeed it is beyond a joke, when a letter comes addressed to you with some bogus title appended to your name on the envelope, or when the newspapers take you up and proclaim your name with a like spurious title attached to it, thereby causing you to become a laughing-stock to your friends. During my visit to the United States I was twice dubbed a *Right Hon.* (by letter), thrice was I knighted (in the newspapers), and once I was addressed (by letter) as *colonel*. In the arrival-list of guests staying at the Massasoit House, Narragansett

1 Auctioneer *Colonels* Again, Oct., p. 232. Mr. Jacobs wrote from rural Missouri. In Auctioneer *Colonels*, *American Speech*, April, 1935, Dr. Louise Pound had reported the same usage prevailing in Nebraska. Mr. Jacobs reported encountering in Missouri a young man "of perhaps twenty-two or three" who "had assumed the title upon his graduation from some institution, probably calling itself a college, which taught auctioneering."

2 Add Kurneliana, Norfolk *Virginian-Pilot*, April 11, 1942, editorial page.

3 Some Impressions of the United States; New York, 1883.

4 Through America; London, 1882, pp. 239-40.

Pier (a seaside resort on Rhode Island), on August 10, 1879, I found myself figuring prominently as *the Right Honorable,* etc.[1]

*Judge* seems to have come into courtesy use relatively late, for the first example given by Read, in the paper before cited, is from John Maud's diary for July 27, 1800.[2] Before this the lawyers of the colonies and the new Republic were apparently content with *esquire.* But when the great march to the West got under way *judges* began to proliferate in a dizzy manner, and by 1869 John Ross Browne was reporting in his " Adventures in the Apache Country "[3] that " all popular lawyers are *judges* in Nevada, whether they practise at the bar or sit upon the bench." This is true in large parts of the South and Southwest to the present day. In the South most lawyers of any skill at hullabaloo actually become judges soon or late, for there is rotation in the petty judgeships, and once a judge always a judge.[4] In England there are no judges at the bar, for a lawyer who has once been upon the bench is not permitted to practise thereafter. But in the United States there is no such squeamishness, and even retired Federal judges are free to plead and beat their breasts before their late colleagues. Justices of the peace and police magistrates are also called *judge. Squire* survives in the rural areas, but is disappearing from the towns, and is now almost unheard of in the cities. The DAE traces it to 1743. Horwill says that " the *squire* in an English country district is usually both a landowner and a magistrate, but it is in the former rather than the latter capacity that he is given the name; in America the *squire* is primarily a justice of the peace, but the name is loosely given, most commonly as a title, to any prominent resident in a village." In Webster's American Dictionary of 1852, revised by the lexicographer's son-in-law, Chauncey A. Goodrich, it was noted that the New Englanders then used the word to designate not only a justice of the peace but also a judge; to this was added: " in Pennsylvania, justices of the peace only."

275. [In the United States *the Hon.* is applied to all public officials of any apparent respectability, and with some show of official sanc-

---

1 I am indebted to my brother, August Mencken, for this reference.
2 Visit to the Falls of Niagara in 1800; London, 1826, p. 74.
3 New York, 1869, p. 394.
4 From time to time there are protests against this rule, as, for example, in Question of Title, by Lee

Casey, Denver *Rocky Mountain News,* Dec. 5, 1941: " A *judge* is properly a *judge* only so long as he occupies a bench — for that matter, only so long as he is physically sitting on the bench. The title ought to expire with the term of office." But it never does.

tion, but it is questionable whether this application has any actual legal standing, same perhaps in the case of certain judges.] Nevertheless, the Style Manual of the Department of State, which is the highest American authority upon epistolary etiquette,[1] grants it to a long list of functionaries,[2] as follows:

> American ambassadors.
> American and foreign ministers plenipotentiary.
> Ministers resident.[3]
> Governors of States, Territories and island possessions of the United States.
> High commissioners.
> Cabinet officers.
> Senators.
> Members of Congress.
> The secretary to the President, and his assistant secretaries.
> Under and assistant secretaries of executive departments.
> Judges.[4]
> Heads of independent Federal boards, commissions and other establishments.[5]
> State senators and representatives.
> The secretary of the United States Senate.
> The clerk of the House of Representatives.
> The commissioners of the District of Columbia.
> The mayors of large cities.[6]

In addition, the Style Manual grants *the Hon.*, if not by precept then at least by example, to various other persons, including the secretary of the Smithsonian Institution (p. 33), the archivist of the United States (p. 35), the director-general of the Pan-American Union (p. 48), all members of international commissions (who apparently rank as diplomats; pp. 47 and 48), and the acting heads of boards, commissions and other such bodies whose actual heads are

1 The latest edition was "prepared under the direction of the Secretary of State by Margaret M. Hanna, chief of the Office of Coördination and Review, and Alice M. Ball, chief of the Special Documents Section, Division of Research and Publication"; Washington, 1937.
2 p. 8.
3 In the case of foreign diplomats, of course, their native titles take precedence, if they have any.
4 The justices of the Supreme Court of the United States are excepted. On the envelope of a letter addressed to the Chief Justice is to be written simply *The Chief Justice*, without his surname. Letters to his colleagues are to be addressed *Mr. Justice ——*.

But the *Supreme Court Reporter*, a quasi-official publication, makes an associate justice *Honorable*, with the word spelled out and no *the* before it. See Proceedings in Memory of *Honorable* Pierce Butler, *Supreme Court Reporter*, May 1, 1940, p. xix.
5 If such a functionary has "a military, naval or scholastic title" it is to be used (p. 31) instead of *the Hon.*
6 The Style Manual does not specify how large a city has to be for its mayor to rate *the Hon.* It ordains (p. 8) that the mayors of small cities shall be addressed John Jones, *Esquire*, and notes that it is American usage to spell out the *Esquire*, whereas the English make it *Esq.*

entitled to it (p. 35).[1] But it is denied, *inter alia*, to all diplomatic officers under the rank of minister (p. 27), to consuls (p. 27), to the librarian of Congress (p. 31), and to the president of the American Federation of Labor (p. 38). All these puissant men are merely *Esquires*. Congress is very much more liberal with *the Hon*. It is bestowed in the *Congressional Record* upon a vast and miscellaneous congeries of dignitaries, and to the examples given in AL4, p. 276, n. 1, may be added the following from more recent issues:

Thomas J. Curran, chairman of the New York Republican County Committee, Dec. 9, 1943, p. A5791.[2]

Joseph P. Tumulty, secretary to President Woodrow Wilson (1913–21), April 2, 1940, p. 6126.[3]

M. H. McLean, " attorney at law, of Covington, Ky.," Dec. 14, 1943, p. A5880.

Augustus E. Giegengack, public printer, Dec. 18, 1943, p. A5996.

Guy T. Helvering, commissioner of internal revenue, Dec. 18, 1943, p. A5996.

Alfred H. Stone, editor of the *Staple Cotton Review*, Dec. 17, 1943, p. A5954.

Sumner Welles, former Under Secretary of State, Dec. 17, 1943, p. A5963.

Leander H. Perez, district attorney for the parishes of St. Bernard and Plaquemines, La., Dec. 21, 1943, p. A6063.

Alfred M. Landon, of Kansas, Jan. 14, 1944, p. A175; Jan. 11, 1944, p. A58.

J. B. McLaughlin, commissioner of agriculture for West Virginia, Jan. 12, 1944, p. A143.

G. Mason Owlett, Republican national committeeman from Pennsylvania, Jan. 13, 1944, p. A161.

Sergio Osmeña, vice-president of the Philippines, Jan. 17, 1944, p. A203.

M. J. Caldwell, member of the Parliament of Canada, Jan. 24, 1944, p. A364.

Harold N. Graves, acting commissioner of internal revenue, Jan. 26, 1944, p. A422.

Charles E. Dierker, United States district attorney for the western district of Oklahoma, Jan. 31, 1944, p. A507.

Peter Zimmerman, " of Yamhill, Ore.," Feb. 3, 1944, p. A591.

Thomas E. Lyons, executive secretary of the Foreign Trade Zones Board, Feb. 7, 1944, p. A657.

G. Seals Aiken, " a practising attorney of the capital city of Atlanta," Ga., Feb. 7, 1944, p. A652.

George P. Money, editor of the Gulfport-Biloxi (Miss.) *Daily Herald*, Feb. 7, 1944, p. A665.

Roland J. Steinle, " the great jurist of Wisconsin," Feb. 17, 1944, p. A839.

1 The Style Manual warns all concerned (p. 10) that the form *the Honorable* Morgenthau, without a given-name, is not to be tolerated. In all cases it prefers *the Honorable* to *the Hon*.

2 The letter *A* in a page number indicates that it is in the Appendix to the *Record*.

3 He was entitled to *the Hon.*, according to the Style Manual, while he was in service as secretary to the President. All persons so entitled to it continue in enjoyment of it, by congressional usage, for life.

Chauncey Tramutolo, special assistant to the Postmaster General, March 14, 1944, p. A1391.

W. M. Garrad, general manager of the Staple Cotton Coöperative Association, March 14, 1944, p. 2604.

Paul Scharrenberg, director of the California state department of industrial relations, March 14, 1944, p. A1393.

Mike Holm, secretary of state of Minnesota, March 22, 1944, p. A1545.

Charles M. Hay, general counsel for the War Manpower Commission, April 24, 1944, p. A2082.

Thomas C. Buchanan, public utilities commissioner in Pennsylvania, April 27, 1944, p. A2150.

J. Edgar Hoover, director of the FBI, May 2, 1944, p. A2241.

Marion E. Martin, assistant chairman of the Republican National Committee, May 8, 1944, p. A2365.

Peter V. Cacchione, city councilman in Brooklyn, May 19, 1944, p. 4777.

David Diamond, former Supreme Court justice in New York, May 19, 1944, p. 4777.

Richard P. Freeman, "who represented the second congressional district of Connecticut [in the House of Representatives] from 1914 to 1932," Aug. 17, 1944, p. 7121.

Ezequiel Padilla, Secretary of Foreign Affairs of Mexico, Aug. 18, 1944, p. A3934.

J. C. Nance, "an able legislator and one of the leading newspaper men of Oklahoma," Sept. 1, 1944, p. A4146.

Edward N. Scheiberling, national commander of the American Legion, Nov. 16, 1944, p. A4757.

Maurice F. Lyons, "secretary to William F. McCombs during the 1911–12 prenomination and presidential campaigns," Nov. 16, 1944, p. A4756.

Helen Gahagan Douglas, "national committeewoman from the State of California," Nov. 22, 1944, p. A4815.

James E. Chinn, a Washington *Post* reporter, Nov. 24, 1944, p. A4835.

In the *Congressional Record* proper, which is devoted mainly to a stenographic report of the previous day's debates in the two Houses, all members are designated *Mr.*, including even Senators, but excluding, of course, females, who are *Miss* or *Mrs.*, as the case may be.[1] Even members lawfully bearing other titles, *e.g.*, *Dr.*, *Col.* or *Bishop*,[2] are denied them. But in the Appendix to the *Record*, wherein members embalm speeches that they have made elsewhere and reprint

---

[1] Even the Vice-President of the United States, who is *ex-officio* president of the Senate, appears in its actual proceedings without *the Hon.* See *Congressional Record*, Sept. 14, 1943, p. 7599, top of col. 1.

[2] The Hon. Reed Smoot (1862–1941), who was a Senator from Utah from 1903 to 1933, had been a Mormon bishop before he got into politics,

and was promoted to the awful rank of *apostle* before his election to the Senate. Many other members of the two houses hold military rank, whether real or bogus, and almost all of those above the grade of big-city ward heelers have learned degrees, whether earned or honorary. Even the females have such degrees.

all sorts of other memorabilia, they are called *Hon.*, without a preceding *the*, and in writing about themselves in state papers they often use the term, even in the first person.[1] In recent years, however, there has been some faltering in this department, chiefly as a result of a war upon *Hon.* launched by the Hon. Jerry Voorhis, M.A., Representative of the Twelfth California district.[2] When he began his first term in 1937 he asked the reporters for the *Record* to cease calling him *Hon.* in its Appendix, but they resisted him stoutly, apparently on the ground of ancient custom, and it was not until October 28, 1940 that they finally yielded. Since then he has been plain Jerry Voorhis. No other congressman followed him until the Spring of 1944, when the Hon. Clare E. Hoffman induced the reporters for the *Record* to drop the *Hon.* from in front of his name also. Mr. Voorhis is a violent New Dealer, and Mr. Hoffman is perhaps the most earnest enemy the New Deal has ever had, so his imitation of so radical an opponent was not without its piquancy. Now and then the reporters put one over on Mr. Voorhis, as for instance on May 31, 1944, when they described him as *Hon.* in the programme of the memorial service in honor of dead members, holden that day.[3] No congressman save Mr. Hoffman has ventured to jump aboard his bandwagon, and the lady members also hold aloof. But there has been visible, since he began his revolution, a certain wobbling in usage.

1 See, for example, the *Congressional Record* for May 6, 1938, p. 8467, wherein the Hon. Mrs. Norton, a congresswoman from New Jersey, describes herself in a motion to discharge a committee as "I, *Hon.* Mary T. Norton." Again, on Jan. 19, 1938 (*Record*, p. 194) Congressman Ditter of Pennsylvania introduced a privileged resolution in which he referred to himself as *Honorable* J. William Ditter. Yet again, on May 11, 1943, three congressmen printed in the *Record*, p. A2474, a letter they had sent to the *Hon.* Carter Glass, signed *Hon.* Walt Horan, *Hon.* Hal Holmes, and *Hon.* Fred Norman. In the applications for war bonds sent out in 1943 the Secretary of the Treasury had himself addressed as *Hon.* Henry Morgenthau, Jr. See *A. L. P. Digest,* May, 1943, p. 250.

2 The hon. gentleman was born in Kansas in 1901 and has had a varied career. He says in his autobiography in the Congressional Directory, 78th Congress, 2nd Session; Washington, 1944, that he was "educated in public schools," though "graduated from Yale College in 1923." Subsequently he was a factory worker, a freight handler and a ranch hand and for a time had a job in an automobile assembly plant. He then "traveled in Germany for the Y.M. C.A." and was a teacher in a farmschool in Illinois, director of the Dray Cottage Episcopal Home for Boys in Wyoming, and headmaster of the Voorhis School for Boys at San Dimas, Calif., which his family owned and eventually gave to the State, which now operates it as a vocational unit of the State university. The latter office, I assume, gave him the local rank and title of *professor*, but he does not use it.

3 *Congressional Record*, May 31, 1944, p. 5228.

Even such austere dignitaries as the Hon. Josephus Daniels, Sidney Hillman, Mayor LaGuardia of New York, the late Wendell Willkie and Bernard M. Baruch have appeared in the *Record* as non-*Hons*.[1] Moreover, there has been irresolution in other cases. The eminent O.P.A. administrator, the Hon. Chester Bowles, B.Sc. (Yale), was mentioned in the *Record* during 1944 as *Hon*.,[2] as *the Honorable*[3] and as plain *Mr*.;[4] the Hon. James A. Farley has appeared as *the Hon*.,[5] as *the Honorable*,[6] and as plain James A. Farley, without even *Mr*.;[7] and the Hon. James F. Byrnes, director of war mobilization and reconversion and "assistant President," has been both *the Hon*.[8] and James F. Byrnes unadorned.[9] There even seems to be some uncertainty about the Vice-President, who, as we have seen, appears in the actual proceedings of the Senate without the *Hon*. In the Appendix to the *Record*, during 1944, he was listed as the *Honorable*,[10] as *Mr*.[11] and as *Vice-President of the United States*, without any mention of his name.[12] State Governors are sometimes *Hons*.,[13] but more often mere *Govs*., always abbreviated.[14]

Most American newspapers refrain from calling a politico *the Hon*., even when writing about him formally and favorably: when the term appears in them at all, it is usually used satirically.[15] When, in 1935, I printed a magazine article[16] making fun of its overuse by all sorts of dubious persons, a number of newspapers printed editorials in agreement.[17] But many other American publications tend to be more

1 For Daniels see the issue for Sept. 1, 1944, p. A4160; for Hillman, Aug. 24, 1944, p. A4036; for LaGuardia, Aug. 23, 194, p. A4011; for Willkie, June 13, 1944, p. A3215; and for Baruch, May 23, 1944, p. A2760.
2 April 24, p. A2088.
3 April 12, p. A1873.
4 Nov. 22, 1944, p. A4808.
5 Nov. 21, 1944, p. A4795.
6 Nov. 20, 1944, p. A4787.
7 Nov. 16, 1944, p. A4763.
8 Nov. 16, 1944, p. 8303.
9 April 12, p. A1883, and April 24, p. A2099.
10 Nov. 24, p. A4831.
11 Feb. 18, p. 876, and Sept. 13, p. A4341.
12 Feb. 17, p. A837.
13 Jan. 31, 1944, p. A539.
14 Jan. 31, 1944, p. A530; April 28, p. A2163; April 28, p. A2165; Sept. 29, p. A4577.

15 The old New York *Sun*, in the days before Frank A. Munsey bought it, always accorded *the Hon*. to the mountebanks it excoriated daily in its editorial pages. A great admirer of the *Sun* of that era, I borrowed the custom as a young journalist, and stuck to it throughout my days of writing on politics.
16 The Advance of Honorifics, *New Yorker*, Aug. 17.
17 For example, the Charlottesville, Va., *Progress*, Aug. 19, 1935. "Of all the titles abroad in the land," it said, "none is so absurd or meaningless as that of *the Hon*. Even a *Kentucky colonel* has to get a commission from Governor Ruby Laffoon and to pay a fee for being registered, but the title *honorable* is one that a man simply gives himself. It is enjoyed by all mayors, all district attorneys, all governors, all congress-

tolerant of the pretensions of bogus *Hons.*, and I have some curious specimens of their misuse of the honorific in my collectanea.[1]

During the colonial era in America it seems to have been in rather restricted use, probably following the English pattern. The DAE shows that it was sometimes added to the titles of men in high office, as in *the Honble. Governor Winthrop* (1704), and also used to dignify the names of official bodies, as in *the right Honble. Counsell* [*i.e.,* Council] *for New England* (1640) and *the Honourable House* (1721) Hugh Jones, writing in 1724, recorded that the *Honourable the Council* was then in use in Virginia,[2] and the inference is that each member was also *the Honourable*, but this is by no means clear. By the time of the Revolution, however, the honorific was being applied to the members of at least some of the colonial legislatures. William Maclay, who served in the first Federal Senate as one of the two Senators from Pennsylvania, noted in his spicy journal[3] that the members debated, in 1789, the question whether they should be styled *the Hon.* in their minutes. What the result of this discussion was he doesn't say, but despite the qualms of those Senators who argued for the negative the issue was already decided, for members had been called *the Hon.* in the journals of the Continental Congress (1777). In 1791, as the DAE shows, the honorific was used in a post-mortem panegyric on James Bowdoin the elder (1726–90), who had been Governor of Massachusetts and a member of the Constitutional Convention.[4] A number of English travelers of the first part of the Nineteenth Century noted its wide use. Henry Bradshaw Fearon, in 1818,[5] quoted

---

men, and practically every ward-heeling politician in the country."

1 In the issue of *True Detective* for May, 1935, p. 5, for example, it is accorded to Eugene W. Biscailuz, sheriff of Los Angeles county, California. In the issue of *Bolivia* for Jan.–Feb., 1942, it is accorded to all Bolivian consuls in the United States, including honorary consuls, and under the flagstaff of the magazine the consul-general in New York, who publishes it, is mentioned as *the Hon.* T. Hartmann.

2 The Present State of Virginia; London, 1724; reprinted, New York, 1865. I am indebted for this reference to Words Indicating Social Status in America in the Eighteenth

Century, by Allen Walker Read; *American Speech*, Oct., 1934, p. 205.

3 This invaluable record was first published in 1890, edited by Edgar Stanton Maclay.

4 Said the *American Museum* (Philadelphia) in Oct. of the same year, p. 202: "Nothing shows the propensity of Americans to monarchy more than their disposition to give titles to all our officers of government. *Honorable* and *esquire* have become as common in America as *captain* in France, *count* in Germany or *my lord* in Italy."

5 A Narrative of a Journey of 5,000 Miles Through the Eastern and Western States of America; London, 1818.

with proper British horror the following news item printed in the Boston *Sentinel* in August, 1817:

*Dinner to Mr. Adams.* — Yesterday a public dinner was given to the *Hon.* John Q. Adams, in the Exchange Coffee-House, by his fellow-citizens of Boston. The *Hon.* Wm. Gray presided, assisted by the *Hon.* Harrison Gray Otis, George Blake, Esq., and the *Hon.* Jonathan Mason, vice-president. Of the guests were the *Hon.* Mr. Adams, late president of the United States, his *Excellency* Governor Brooks, his *Honour* Lt. Gov. Phillips,[1] Chief Justice Parker, Judge Story, President Kirkland, Gen. Dearborn, Com. Hull, Gen. Miller, several of the reverend clergy, and many public officers, and strangers of eminence.

Sixteen years later, in 1833, another British traveler, Thomas Hamilton, said in his " Men and Manners in America ": [2]

The members of the Federal Senate are addressed generally in the Northern States with the prefixture of *Honorable,* but the New Englanders go further and extend the same distinction to the whole body of representatives, a practise followed in no other part of the Union.

But this was bad reporting, for the real stamping-ground of *the Hon.* was in the South and West. There were, indeed, few politicos beyond the Alleghanies or below the Potomac, after the beginning of the Jacksonian Century of the Common Man, who did not wear it proudly, and it was there that the custom arose of bestowing it indiscriminately upon all notables lacking other titles, whether real or imaginary. On March 24 and August 22, 1862, for example, Abraham Lincoln, whose English, despite its mellifluousness, always showed frontier influences, sent letters to Horace Greeley which addressed him as *Hon.* Lincoln, in fact, was very fond of the prefix, and not infrequently used it without a name, as in *Hon. Secretary of the Treasury*. It was also applied, in that genteel era, to distinguished foreigners. Bartlett, in the second edition of his Glossary, 1859, noted that Americans who had once attained to *the Hon.* by office-holding retained the honorific after they had been retired to private life, for " once an *honorable,* always an *honorable.*" This, as I have recorded, is still the American rule.

The English are much more careful in the use of *the Hon.* The title belongs as of right, in the British Isles, only to the younger sons of earls, to all the sons and daughters of viscounts and barons, to the

---

1 A writer in *Harper's Weekly,* Jan. 9, 1892, quoted by the DAE, said: " It is only permissible in the United States to place before the name of one man the prefix *Honorable,* and that man is the Lieutenant-Governor of Massachusetts, upon whom the title is conferred by law."

2 Two vols.; Philadelphia, 1833, Vol. I, p. 241.

wives of these sons, to justices of the High Court, if not ranked as peers, during their terms of office, and to the Scotch Lords of Session. If the son of a peer entitled to bear it happens to be made a baronet in his own right he becomes *the Hon. Sir John Smith, Bt.*, and his wife becomes *the Hon. Lady*. The chief English authority, " Titles and Forms of Address," [1] notes that " it is *never* used in speech, even by a servant," nor " in letter-writing, excepting on the envelope." The English prefer *the Honble.* to *the Hon.* A maid of honor must be addressed as *the Honble. Miss* (or *Mrs.*) So-and-So, and that is the rule also for addressing a female *Honble.* whose title comes from her husband, but if she is an *Honble.* in her own right the *Miss* or *Mrs.* is to be omitted. The daughter of a peer, however, on marrying a man of no title, becomes *the Honble. Mrs.* A judge of the High Court is *the Honble. Mr. Justice* ——, but a judge of a county court is only *His Honor Judge* ——.[2] In the case of the former, *Mr. Justice* may be omitted on the envelopes of personal letters, making the recipient simply *the Honble. John Smith*. All peers from baron up to and including earl are *Right Honble.*, and so are all members of the Privy Council, the Lord Chief Justice and various other higher judges, and the Lord Mayors of London, Manchester, Norwick, York, Belfast, Dublin, Melbourne, Sydney and Adelaide, and with them their wives.[3] A marquis is *Most Honble.* and so is his marchioness. A member of the Cabinet is not *Right Hon.* as such, but only because he is a member of the Privy Council. His wife does not share his title, but he keeps it himself for life. An ordinary member of Parliament is neither *Right Hon.* nor *Hon.*, but simply *Esq.*, with *M.P.* following the *Esq.*[4]

On the floor of the House of Commons, however, every member

---

1 Second ed.; London, 1929, p. 35. See also Whitaker's Titled Persons; London, 1898.

2 A county judge's *His Honor* is retained after he retires.

3 The NED traces *Right Hon.* in English use to the Paston letters, *c.* 1450. It was used by Shakespeare in his dedication of Venus and Adonis to " the *Right Hon.* Henrie Wriothesley, Earle of Southampton and Baron of Titchfield." The NED's first example of *Hon.* preceding a given name is dated 1674. It was then applied to Robert Boyle the

chemist, who was a son of the Earl of Cork. *Hon.* has been accorded, in England, to corporations as well as individuals, *e.g.*, *the Hon.* East India Company.

4 The Style Manual of the Department of State, p. 58, gives the form *the Right Honorable* for a member of Parliament, but that is an error — unless, of course, he is entitled to the honorific on some other ground. See Titles and Forms of Address, before cited, p. 116, and A Dictionary of Modern American Usage, by H. W. Horwill, p. 169.

is at least *the honorable member* (or *gentleman*), and may be much more. If he is a legal officer — say, Attorney-General or Solicitor-General — , or a practising lawyer he is *the honorable and learned gentleman*,[1] if he holds a commission in the armed forces he is the *honorable and gallant gentleman*, and if he is a member of the Privy Council he is *the right honorable gentleman*. "Technically speaking," said Paul Ward, London correspondent of the Baltimore *Sun* in a dispatch to his paper in 1939,[2] "if a member is a privy councillor, a barrister and a commissioned officer all rolled into one he should be *the right honorable, learned and gallant gentleman*, but that is too much of a mouthful for even M.P.'s and is not used."[3] Mr. Ward noted that, when the member spoken of happens to be a member of the party of the member speaking, it is usual to substitute *friend* for *gentleman*, and that when he is not it is permissible to substitute *member*, adding or not adding *for* —— (the name of his constituency). If he happens to hold a courtesy title or is an Irish or Scotch peer without a seat in the House of Lords he is *the noble gentleman*. In the case of a female member *lady* is substituted for *gentleman*.[4] But when she asks a question and the answer is a simple yes or no it takes the form of *Yes, sir*, or *No, sir*, for in theory all remarks are addressed to the Speaker, who is always male. In the American Senate a Senator refers to another as *the Senator from* ——, whether male or female, or simply as *the Senator*. In the case of a Senator from his own State he may use *my colleague*. Sometimes he refers to himself as *the Senator from* ——. In the House a member mentioned in debate is *the gentleman from* ——, or simply *the gentleman*. When the first female representatives appeared *the lady from* —— was used in referring to them, but after a while (apparently at the suggestion of the sportive Nicholas Longworth, then Speaker) this was changed to *the gentlewoman*. Neither word was a snug fit for some of the stateswomen who have adorned the House.

The British dominions and colonies follow, in general, the usage of the Motherland, but with extensions suggested by their more

---

1 But not if he is actually a learned man. A Ph.D. would be simply *the honorable gentleman*. Only lawyers, by House of Commons rules, can be *learned*.

2 Dec. 24.

3 The NED's first example of *honorable gentleman* is dated 1783 and comes from a speech in the House of Commons by Richard Brinsley Sheridan.

4 Winston Churchill referred to Lady Astor as *the noble lady* in a debate in the House of Commons in Sept., 1938. See The Astors, by Harvey O'Connor; New York, 1941, p. 453.

democratic way of life. The following "Table of Titles to be Used in Canada" is official:

1. The Governor-General of Canada to be styled *His Excellency* and his wife *Her Excellency*.
2. The Lieutenant Governors of the Provinces to be styled *His Honour*.
3. Privy Councillors of Canada [1] to be styled *Honourable*, and for life.
4. The Solicitor General to be styled *Honourable* while in office.
5. Senators of Canada to be styled *Honourable*, but only during office and the title not to be continued afterwards.
6. The Speaker of the House of Commons to be styled *Honourable* during tenure of office.
7. The Chief Justice of Canada, the Judges of the Supreme and Exchequer Courts of Canada, and the Chief Justices and Judges of the undermentioned Courts in the several Provinces of Canada: —
Ontario. — The Supreme Court of Ontario;
Quebec. — The Court of King's Bench, the Superior Court and the Circuit Court of the District of Montreal;
Nova Scotia. — The Supreme Court of Nova Scotia;
New Brunswick. — The Supreme Court of New Brunswick;
Manitoba. — The Court of King's Bench and the Court of Appeal;
British Columbia. — The Court of Appeal and the Supreme Court of British Columbia;
Prince Edward Island. — The Supreme Court of Prince Edward Island and the Chancery Court;
Saskatchewan. — The Supreme Court of Saskatchewan;
Alberta. — The Supreme Court of Alberta, — to be styled *Honourable* during tenure of office.
8. The Presidents and Speakers of the Legislatures of the Provinces to be styled *Honourable* during tenure of office.
9. Executive Councillors of the Provinces to be styled *Honourable* while in office.
10. Gentlemen who were Legislative Councillors in the Provinces at the time of the Union (1st July, 1867), to retain their title of *Honourable* for life.
The following to be eligible to be personally recommended by the Governor-General for His Majesty's permission to retain the title of *Honourable:* —
(*a*) Speakers of the Senate and of the House of Commons on retirement after three years of office not necessarily continuous;
(*b*) The above-mentioned Chief Justices and Judges on retirement.[2]

In the other English dominions and colonies and in India *the Hon.* is commonly accorded to all important members of the government,

---

1 Not to be confused with Privy Councillors of Great Britain.
2 It will be noted that this official list shows the English spelling of *honourable*, though the American *honorable* is used by virtually all Canadian newspapers. The French of Canada use *l'honorable*. See Études sur les parlers de France au Canada, by Adjutor Rivard; Québec, 1914, p. 256

including the Executive Council, and when there is a Legislative Council the members commonly assume it, sometimes with warrant of law and sometimes without. In the Crown colony of Hong Kong, before the unhappy events of 1942, the curious custom prevailed of inserting *Mr.* after *Hon.* in the style of members of the Legislative Council, even when their given-names were used. This custom was established by the fiat of Lieut. Col. the Right Hon. Sir Matthew Nathan, P.C., G.C.M.G., K.C.M.G., C.M.G., LL.D.,[1] during his term as Governor of the colony, 1903–07. There was considerable opposition to the innovation in Hong Kong, and the people of the other Far Eastern colonies snickered, but Sir Matthew stuck to his mandate, and it was obeyed ever after.[2] When a member of the Council happened to be knighted he became *the Hon. Sir.*[3]

The American tendency to drop the *the* before *hon.*, and likewise before *rev.*, *right rev.*, *very rev.*, etc., is noted in AL4, pp. 279–82. Dr. Edward C. Ehrensperger has shown that, in the case of *rev.*, the omission of the article preceded its use in England, and that American usage has thus an archaic foundation.[4] The English, even today, sometimes drop it, but not as often as Americans. Episcopalians often use it, but members of the other Protestant denominations commonly omit it, and so do Catholics. Rather curiously, its use seems to be more frequently in the West than in the East. The use of *Reverend* as a vocative (usually pronounced *revrun*), with no name or title following it, seems to be American. The DAE does not list this form, but it goes back to 1877 at least, for in that year Mark Twain used it.[5] It has been denounced frequently, usually on the ground that *reverend*

1 It is thus, precisely, that he described himself in Who's Who.
2 I am indebted here to the late F. H. Tyson of Hong Kong. The matter is dealt with in Marriage at 6 A.M., by Tom Clarke; London, 1934.
3 There was, in the old days, a Chinese member of the Legislative Council named Chow Shou-son, who had become *the Hon. Mr.* on his appointment in 1921. When, five years later, he was knighted, he became *the Hon. Sir* Shouson Chow, for Chow was his surname, and it was necessary, in order to avoid a solecism, to take it out of its Chinese position in front and put it in the English position behind. See the

*South China Morning Post* (Hong Kong), July 23, 1936.
4 The Use of the Abbreviation *Rev.* in Modern English, *American Speech*, Oct., 1931, pp. 40–43.
5 On Aug. 3, 1944, Lieut. Gen. Mark W. Clark, in a letter of thanks to the Rev. Frederick Brown Harris, D.D., B.D., LL.D., chaplain of the United States Senate, thanking him for a rousing prayer delivered from the Senate rostrum on June 6, addressed him as "Dear *Reverend* Harris." General Clark is a native of New York State, but Dr. Brown is an Englishman and the salutation must have struck him as somewhat strange. It is not, however, wholly

is an adjective, but Ehrensperger argues that this objection is not valid. " No doubt," he says, " *Rev.* is an adjective historically, but it is certainly not used as an adjective in modern English, for adjectives are not abbreviated before nouns, nor are they capitalized as is always the case with *Rev.*"[1] Its use " immediately before a surname, especially in conversation," he concludes, " is, in my opinion, certainly growing. The assaults of purists and grammarians may stop the practice temporarily, but I doubt very much if they can do anything permanent." Not a few clergymen, revolting against being addressed as *Reverend*, and lacking the dignity of *divinitatis doctor*, have tried to induce their patients to call them *Mr.*, but not often with success, for many Americans have a feeling that *Mr.* is rather too worldly and familiar for use in addressing a man of God.[2] The Catholics get around the difficulty by using *Father*, and the High Church Episcopalians imitate them. In the South *Reverend* is used in addressing colored clergymen for the purpose of avoiding calling them *Mr.*[3] The Style Manual of the Department of State bans it, and also insists that *the* precede *Rev.* Incidentally, it prefers *Reverend* to the abbreviation, just as it prefers *the Honorable* to *the Hon.*

It devotes nine pages to ecclesiastical titles, followed by a blank page for further notes. It begins with the Pope and runs down to the superiors of Catholic and Episcopal brotherhoods. There is no informal style, it says, for addressing the Pope: he is always *His Holiness the Pope* or *His Holiness Pius XI* on the envelope of a letter, and *Your Holiness* in the salutation thereof. A patriarch in the Eastern Orthodox Church is also usually *Your Holiness*, but there are exceptions which it does not list. A cardinal is *His Eminence* outside and *Your Eminence* inside. A Catholic bishop or archbishop is the *Most Reverend* outside and *Your Excellency* inside, an English arch-

---

unknown in England, 'for a correspondent writes: " The chaplain of my college at Oxford was always referred to by the servants as the *Reverend* Ridley, and occasionally as *Reverend* Ridley, but he had married an American."

1 Neither part of this is invariably true. *The rev. clergy* is often encountered.

2 *Mr.* for *Rev.*, *Time*, Nov. 27, 1939, p. 50.

3 The amusing rhymed protest against *Reverend* in AL4, p. 280, was written by the Right Rev. Douglas H. Atwill, now Protestant Episcopal missionary bishop of North Dakota. He was at that time rector of St. Clement's Memorial Church, St. Paul, Minn., and the verses made their first appearance in his parish paper, *St. Clement's Chimes*, on July 25, 1925. I am indebted here to the Rev. E. H. Eckels, Jr., of Tulsa, Okla., and to Bishop Atwill himself.

bishop is *Your Grace*, and an English bishop is *My Lord Bishop*, with *My dear Bishop* sufficing if you know him.[1] All Episcopal bishops in the United States are *the Right Reverend*, save the presiding bishop, who is *the Most Reverend*. An archdeacon is *the Venerable*. The Style Book says that a Methodist bishop should be addressed as *the Very Reverend*, but this is an error, for the Methodists use *Rev.* for bishops and clergy alike.[2] They address a bishop simply as *Bishop*. A Mormon bishop, as the Style Book notes, has no ecclesiastical title at all: he is plain *Mr.* The vexed question of the proper titles for different classes of monsignori is not tackled, but there is a note on it in AL4, pp. 282–83. On this head there is still some difference of opinion among Catholic experts. The bishops and archbishops of the United States have monopolized *the Most Rev.* for themselves, but there is no apparent authority for this in canon law. Nor is there any authority for the distinction made in America between monsignori who are *Very Rev.* and those who are *Right Rev.* The Style Book is vague about the proper form of address to the superior of a Catholic sister-hood: she may be, it says, either the *Reverend Mother Superior*, *Mother Superior*, or *Sister Superior*, according to the rules of her order. An interesting short article on addressing the members of such sisterhoods was printed in *American Speech* in 1940 by Sister Mir-iam, R.S.M.[3] She said that *Dear Sister* is a proper salutation to a nun not a superior, save in the case of three orders which "give their members, after either final profession or an assigned number of years as professed members, the title of *Mother*." Many American teaching nuns, in recent years, have become *Ph.D.'s*, but they are not to be addressed as *doctor*, though it is permissible to use such a form as

---

1 An English archbishop or bishop drops his surname when he is con-secrated and uses the name of his see instead. Thus the Archbishop of York signs himself William *Ebor* — *Ebor* being an abbreviation of *Ebo-racum*, the ancient Latin name of York. So far as I know, only one American bishop has ever ventured to adopt this style. He was William Croswell Doane (1832–1913), bishop of Albany from 1869 until his death. He subscribed himself *William of Albany*. When an English bishop re-signs his bishopric he becomes sim-ply *Bishop* ——. See Inconsistency or Convenience?, *John o' London's*

*Weekly*, Oct. 8, 1937. The rules of the American Postoffice require that, in sending an international money order, one must give "the surname and the initial letters" of the payee's name, unless he be "a peer or a bishop, in which case his ordinary title is sufficient."

2 I am indebted here to Dr. George McCracken of Otterbein College. But the Pittsburgh *Courier*, a leading colored paper, uses *Right Rev.* to designate a bishop of the A.M.E. Zion or C.M.E. Church.

3 Saluting Nuns, Oct., 1940, pp. 338–39.

*Sister M.* (*i.e.*, Mary) *Genevieve*, followed by the initials of the sister's order and *Ph.D.* " Usually nuns," said Sister Miriam, " regardless of the number of degrees awarded them, confine the initials after their names to those of the order to which they belong."

The Style Manual of the Department of State clings to the doctrine that *Mr.* is good enough to be put on an envelope addressed to an ordinary American (p. 39), but it allows the use of *Esquire* (always spelled out) in addressing certain dignitaries who fall a little short of rating *the Hon.*, *e.g.*, consuls (p. 27), the mayors of small cities (p. 30) and court clerks (p. 36), and hastens to add that *Esquire* had better be used in addressing all Englishmen, " except in business communications." My impression is that this position is somewhat outmoded: certainly there has been an increasing use of *Esq.* in the United States of late, no doubt under English influence.[1] The NED devotes a column to a discussion of the honorific's history and significance. In its original sense it meant a young aspirant to knighthood who carried a knight's shield and gave him other service, but it was soon confused with *equerry*, which meant, properly speaking, a groom, and also with *armiger*, which first meant an armor-bearer and was then gradually extended to a man entitled to bear arms himself, in the heraldic sense. Since the Fifteenth Century *esquire* has been used in England to designate any gentleman below the rank of knight. Says the NED:

> The designation is now commonly understood to be due by courtesy to all persons (not in clerical orders or having any higher title of rank) who are regarded as *gentlemen* by birth, position or education. It is used only on occasions of more or less ceremonious mention, and in the addresses of letters, etc.; on other occasions the prefix *Mr.* is employed instead. When *Esq.* is appended to a name, no prefixed title (such as *Mr.*, *Doctor*, *Captain*, etc.) is used.

To which may be added the following from " Titles and Forms of Address," the chief English authority:

> The almost universal use of this title for every man who cannot claim a higher one persists in spite of protests and objections from those who are really entitled to it.[2] The rule has established itself that it is positively rude to address an envelope to anyone above the rank of working man as *Mr.*

1 *Mr.* is also preferred for American men by Frank O. Colby, author of Your Speech, and How to Improve It, and the conductor of a newspaper column on speechways. In a pamphlet entitled Forms of Address and Precedence; Houston, Tex., 1942, p. 3, he says that *Esq.*, in America, is still " rare." But I doubt it.

2 The nature of this right is not defined, but I suppose that it is identical with the right to use a coat-of-arms.

The NED says that " in the United States the title belongs officially to lawyers and public officers," but this is an error. There is, so far as I know, no Federal or State statute which confers it upon anyone, and appending it to the name of a lawyer, or even of a judge, is a mere courtesy. In colonial America it seems to have belonged, as of accepted right, only to justices of the peace, but virtually every lawyer in good standing, at least in New England, was a J.P., so it gradually became extended to all lawyers.[1] It was in his character as lawyer, no doubt, that Noah Webster described himself as *Esquire* on the title-page of his " Dissertations on the English Language," in 1789. During the Seventeenth Century it was applied not only to magistrates, but also to all functionaries of higher rank, provided they had no other titles. The following is from a Massachusetts document of 1646, showing the seating of the principal dignitaries in the Boston meeting-house:

John Winthrop, Sen., *Esqr.*, Gou'nr.
Thomas Dudley, *Esqr.*, Dept. Gou'nr.
John Endecott, *Esqr.*, Assistant.
Herbert Pelham, *Esqr.*, Assistant.
Increase Nowell, *gent.*, Assistant and Secretary.
William Pinchon, *gent.*, Assistant.
*Mr.* Rich. Russell, Treasurer.[2]

Seats in the meeting-house were allotted according to rank, with the hot shots getting the best spots. This was called *seating* the *meeting.* It will be noticed that *Esq.*, in those days, was regarded as superior to *gent.* The latter came into use in England as an indicator of rank, at first spelled out and then often abbreviated, early in the Fifteenth Century, and was brought to America by the English colonists. The DAE's first American example is dated 1637. It ceased to have any legal significance after the Revolution, and gradually abandoned.[3] The NED says that the use of *gent* in common speech passed out about 1840, when " its use came to be regarded as a mark of low breeding." [4]

---

1 I am indebted here to Dr. S. E. Morison.
2 I take this from Curiosities of Puritan History, *Putnam's Monthly*, Aug., 1853, p. 136.
3 Charles Edgar Gilliam says in *Mr.* in Virginia Records Before 1776, *William and Mary College Quarterly Historical Magazine*, April, 1939, p. 144, that it appears in the early Virginia records " after the names of the following classes of public servants without regard to their right to it by birth: vestrymen, wardens, sheriffs, justices, trustees of towns, etc."
4 It seems to have moved to the United States after this. Said *Harper's Magazine* in July, 1852: " There is a certain London cockneyism that begins

Early in the Nineteenth Century, as the examples offered by the DAE show, *Esq.* began to be used very loosely, and presently came to signify only a male of respectable social position.[1] J. H. Ingraham reported, in " The Southwest by a Yankee," 1836, that the New Englanders in the new territories called themselves *esquires* as a sort of symbol of their superiority to the common run of immigrants, and in 1844 the *Knickerbocker Magazine* discovered that "a broker may be called a gentleman, visit in the first circles, and have those mysterious letters, *E.S.Q.*, written after his name." [2] Sometimes *Esq.* was put before instead of after a surname.[3] The NED says that it is the custom in England, when a man's name is followed by a territorial designation preceded by *of*, to write *Esq.* after that designation, whereas in Scotland it goes before it and immediately after his surname. In England, again, *Esq.* follows any abbreviation for *junior* (usually *Jun.*, not *Jr.*, as in the United States), but in Scotland it precedes the abbreviation. In the British colonies *Esq.* is cherished by those who, on any plausible ground, believe they are entitled to bear it. In Hong Kong, before World War II, the chairman and chief manager of the Hong Kong and Shanghai Banking Corporation — always called, in the Far East, simply the Bank — added *Esq.* to their names in its advertisements, and also to those of such directors as did not rate, by virtue of membership in the colonial Legislative Council, the prefix of *Hon. Mr.*[4]

*Mr.*, an abbreviation of *master*, is traced by the NED to *c.* 1524. It originally indicated a certain social status, but, as the NED says, " the inferior limit for its application has been continually lowered," and " at the present time [in England] any man, however low in station,

---

to obtain among some persons even here — and that is the substitution of the word *gent* for *gentleman*. It is a gross vulgarism."

1 Pickering said that it was frequently coupled with *Honorable* as in *the Honorable A. B., Esq.* "In Massachusetts," he added, *c.* 1816, "they say in their proclamations, 'By his Excellency Caleb Strong, *Esquire*,' which must seem a perfect solecism among the English. . . . In the British West Indies they use *Esquire* with *Honorable*, as we do."

2 Schele de Vere said in his Americanisms, 1872, p. 467: " *Esquire* is a title in England still given only to

certain classes of men, and long reserved in the United States also to lawyers and other privileged persons [but it is] now, with republican uniformity, given alike to the highest and the lowest who does not boast of a military or other title, the result being that it is strictly limited to the two extremes of society."

3 The NED shows that this was done in England in the Eighteenth Century, apparently in an effort to dignify *Squire*. The DAE's only American example is dated 1845.

4 Hong Kong *Daily Press*, Sept. 25. 1935.

would be styled *Mr.* on certain occasions, *e.g.*, in the address of a letter." In colonial America, as we have seen, it ranked in the hierarchy of honorifics below *Esq.* and *gent.* Gilliam, lately cited, says that in early Virginia " it would not have been improper to honor any free-man in the colony with the title of *Mr.*" and that it was applied in fact to " every member of the House of Burgesses who had no special colonial military title," and then to all jurymen, and finally to " almost any property-owner, merchant or tradesman." It became, he says, " a recognition of the right of the average citizen to attain a higher and freer dignity of individual personality than past emphasis on birth rather than personal worth had allowed it. It was one of the earli-est colonial whispers of the democracy to come." In parts of the South it is still customary for a married woman to address her hus-band as *Mr.*, often followed by his first name instead of his surname. It is possible that this custom owes something to French influence.[1]

Such forms as *Mr. President, Mr. Justice, Mr. Mayor* and so on are traced by the NED, in English use, to *c.* 1524. They were brought to the United States by the early colonists, and the DAE traces *Mr. Sheriff* to 1703. The Style Manual of the Department of State or-dains that letters to the President of United States shall bear the simple inscription, *The President, the White House*, on the envelope, and that he shall be addressed inside as *The President* (very formal; official), *Mr. President* (formal) or *My dear Mr. President* (informal). The First Congress debated his style and appellation at great length. John Adams put the question before the Senate by inquiring if Wash-ington, on coming to New York to be inaugurated, should be ad-dressed as *Mr. Washington, Mr. President, Sir*, or *May it please your Excellency*. A committee of both Houses was appointed to consider the matter, and it reported that his title should be simply *The Presi-dent of the United States*. The House of Representatives agreed to this, but the Senate disagreed and a new committee advocated *His Highness the President of the United States and Protector of Their*

1 Says Mr. Gordon Gunter of Rock-port, Tex., who was brought up in Louisiana: " My wife's grandmother, now ninety years old, always called her husband to his face or in speak-ing of him *M'sieu* Hilaire, which was his first name. The old lady can't speak English. The French or at least the older set often called a man by his first name preceded by *Mister* or *M'sieu*. In small communities, as a matter of fact, they must have for-got what the man's last name was in some instances, for his wife was also called by his first name, decorously preceded by *Madam*. My grand-father Gunter's first name was Miles and to all of her French-speaking friends my grandmother was known as *Madam* Miles."

*Liberties.* The Senate was willing, but the House objected, and the recommendation of the first committee finally prevailed. Adams, who was Vice-President, was strongly in favor of a more sonorous title, and had the active backing of Richard Henry Lee of Virginia. " Is it not strange," wrote the other Virginia Senator, William Grayson, to Patrick Henry on June 2, 1789, " that John Adams, the son of a tinker and the creature of the people, should be for title and dignities and preeminences, and should despise the herd and the ill-born? . . . He was *primum mobile* in the Senate for the titles for the President, in hopes that in the scramble he might get a slice for himself." On April 7, 1789 John Armstrong, a Representative from Pennsylvania, wrote to General Horatio Gates that " even Roger Sherman [then a Representative from Connecticut] has set his head to work to devise some style of address more novel and dignified than *Excellency*." In all probability it was the influence of Washington himself that induced Congress to abandon all such follies.[1]

The English, in their newspapers, commonly withhold *Mr.* from professional players of such games as cricket and football, but are careful to use it in referring to amateurs. The former are called *players* and the latter *gentlemen*.[2] No Englishman would put *Esq.* on his visiting-card: the proper title for all commoners is *Mr.* Any Englishman of condition, whether real or imaginary, would be offended, however, by receiving a letter addressed *Mr:* in that use it is reserved for tradesmen and the like. But it is considered correct, in enclosing an addressed reply-envelope, to describe one's self on it as *Mr.*, not as *Esq.* The English, though they are careful to use all titles according to the mode when they must be used at all, avoid them as much as possible in conversation between presumed equals. The simple surname is employed by friends of any intimacy, even in addressing peers, and the excessive mistering that goes on on certain levels in the United States is unknown. An Englishman, in speaking of his wife, commonly uses the formal *Mrs. Smith* only when he is addressing strangers or inferiors. To his friends she is *my wife* and to his intimates *Mary*. The American overuse of *Mrs. Smith* has been attacked for many years by reformers, but without much effect.[3] Nor has the frequent

1 I take this from The Inauguration of Washington, by Clarence Winthrop Bowen, *Century Magazine*, April, 1889, p. 823.

2 *Mr.*, New Statesman and Nation (London), May 8, 1937, pp. 766-67.

3 I denounced it myself so long ago as 1911, to wit, in the Baltimore *Evening Sun*, Dec. 26. *Mrs.*, an abbreviation of *mistress*, is traced by

belaboring of the mistering madness abated it appreciably. Nor has much success attended the occasional effort to establish the simple surname in the gap between *Mr.* and the given-names and nicknames of Rotary. Of this last William Feather said in 1942: [1]

If the University of Chicago Round Table, broadcast on Sunday afternoons, had no other merit I would have a friendly feeling for it because the participants are required to address each other by surname, thus eliminating handles like *Mister, Doctor,* and *Professor,* and familiarities like *Bob, Dutch, Doc,* and *T. V.* The American idea is that you address a man as *Mister* or you call him by his given name or a corruption thereof. The University of Chicago is doing its part to correct the custom. Personally, I like the homely tags, but there are innumerable situations that have passed the *Mister* stage but have not and properly never should reach the *Bob* stage. . . . Once, when I called a professional man by his last name, he told me that he was either *Mr.* or he was *Rudolph,* to me.

Not many American newspaper editors seem to agree with Feather. They are, in large part, assiduous members of Rotary and the other clubs of organized lovey-dovey, and they profess to see a useful and even a noble purpose in the somewhat strained bonhommie enforced by the rules thereof. Thus the Dayton *News* on those of Rotary: [2]

One of the oddities of that once much laughed-at order was a rule that members must know each other by their first names. The minister member was *John* or *Bill;* the eminent merchant or manufacturer was *George* or *Jake.* The dignified doctor was *Henry* or *Mike.* It all seemed artificial and funny and helped the Henry Menckens mightily in their efforts to make the movement a joke. Yet the idea stuck and the habit grew. New organizations, seeing that something subtly friendly followed the practice, adopted the rule for themselves. From these or whatever beginnings there has come a nearly universal vogue of the first name. Members of the United States Senate largely address each other, in private at least, by their first names. The President of the United States to hundreds of his friends is simply *Frank.* Daniel Webster would have frozen stiff the person, however near, who called him *Dan.* . . . Let the psychologist say whether or not this first-name movement isn't the most

---

the NED to 1615. It is a curious fact that neither it nor *Mr.* has an English plural. To designate more than one *Mr.* the French *messieurs* is used, commonly abbreviated in writing to *Messrs.,* and to designate more than one *Mrs.* there is *mesdames.* The NED traces *Messrs.* to 1793 and *mesdames* to 1792. The former is commonly pronounced *messers* in the United States. Down to the end of the Eighteenth Century *Mrs.* was applied to both married and single women. Until that time *Miss,* which goes back to c. 1660, was reserved for very young girls. In 1940 *Motion Picture* launched *mrandmrs* as an (unpronounceable) designation for a married couple, but it did not catch on. See *American Speech,* April, 1940, p. 131.

1 *William Feather Magazine,* June, p. 6.

2 First Name Land (editorial), Jan. 5, 1934.

democratizing and humanizing force that has come to bless this country in fifty years.

When Rotary began to spread over the world, taking the great boons and usufructs of American *Kultur* with it, the given-name habit went along, and no doubt it was as influential as any other Rotarian idea in preventing World War II. But it must have caused, at least at the start, some quiet grinding of teeth among English converts, and I suspect that the German, French, Italian and Japanese Rotarians may have also found it somewhat disconcerting. The English often remark another American habit that strikes them as strange, to wit, the frequent use of *Sir*. They seldom use it save in addressing indubitable superiors, especially royalty, but in this country, more particularly in the South, it is heard very frequently in the palaver of equals. It was thus defended by the Lynchburg (Va.) *News* in 1939: [1]

> *Sir* is a word of importance and of diversified application. We use it, especially here in the South — where we are said to pronounce it *suh* — in a number of different ways and yet without greatly disturbing its fundamental status. Eliminating its baronial and knightly references, which mean nothing in these provincial precincts, the word finds a place in the American language in the following instances, and perhaps many others:
>
> As a definite courtesy to one's superior in age, attainments or authority.
>
> As a customary "compellation" to one's equal not yet placed upon the plane of informal acquaintanceship or intimacy.
>
> Strictly formal address or in the meeting of strangers.
>
> Addressing an inferior to whom a sharp order is given, as "Do this or that, *sir!*"
>
> In speaking to animals to emphasize the weight of discipline. . . .
>
> Virginians and most other Southerners use the word with such changes and variations as we only seem perfectly to understand, but can not quite explain. . . . It has been with us through the generations and the prospect is that it will survive at least a few others. [2]

In the South the question whether members of the Negro race should or should not be accorded the ordinary American honorifics constantly agitates publicists. When, in 1940, the colored teachers in the Durham (N. C.) public schools received notices of reappointment bearing *Miss, Mrs.* or *Mr.* before their names there was loud rejoicing in Aframerica. It seemed, indeed, to be almost too good to

1 Yes, *Sir* (editorial), reprinted in the Norfolk *Virginian-Pilot*, July 21, 1939.

2 The DAE traces *Sir* as "a respectful term of address" to 1805, and as a mere intensive, as in *No, sir* (or *siree*) and *Yes, sir*, to 1799. The latter is marked an Americanism.

be true, but investigation showed that the female teachers had been called by telephone before the notices were sent out and asked if they were *Miss* or *Mrs.*[1] In an article in *Ken* in 1939 R. E. Wolseley told the sad story of a young Northern journalist who went South and began describing blackamoors in a paper of the Bible Belt as *Mr., Mrs.* and *Miss.* When protests poured in from local guardians of the Caucasian hegemony he sought for light and leading in his paper's Southern exchanges. Said Mr. Wolseley: [2]

> He found out that some eight or ten devices have been invented by Southern journalists to avoid using *Mr., Mrs.* and *Miss* in front of the names of Negroes. They are:
>
> *Mademoiselle*
> *Madame*
> *Professor*
> *Doctor*
> *Reverend*
> *Uncle*
> *Aunt*
>
> Another variation, he learned, is not to include any title whatsoever, making it impossible, therefore, to distinguish a married from an unmarried woman. Still one more is to phrase it " The wife of *Prof.* Dodie Barnes will sing a soprano solo next Sunday at the A.M.E.Church." Or, " The daughter of *Rev.* Mank Arter will teach grammar, etc." Another is to use first names on second references.
>
> One Mississippi editor, being somewhat more courageous or at least original than his fellows, solved it by printing an explanation in a box at the head of a column of news of Negro residents:
>
> " The publisher of this paper assumes no responsibility for the manner in which the writer of this column addresses members of his own race."
>
> Still another plan now in use down South is to replate or make over (substitute a new page in) the paper and send the special edition containing Negro news only to the Negro neighborhoods. . . . A large star on the front page identifies it.

*Aunt* (or *auntie*) and *uncle* are greatly disliked by the now emancipated colored folk, who see in them a contemptuous sort of patronage. As the DAE shows, both were formerly used in addressing white persons. A writer in the *Gentleman's Magazine* reported in 1793 [3] that elderly persons were so called on the island of Nantucket, and the DAE confirms this with a quotation dated 1801. But by the 30s of the last century *aunt* and *uncle* had begun to be confined to Negroes, and the latter got a great boost in 1851, when Harriet Beecher

---

1 Pittsburgh *Courier*, April 27, 1940.    3 Part II, p. 1083.
2 Journalistic Headache, *Ken*, March 9, 1939, pp. 62 and 63.

Stowe started the serial publication of " *Uncle* Tom's Cabin." But both terms now seem to be going out, and the more advanced Aframericans use *Uncle Tom* to signify a subservient and pusillanimous member of their race.

Few Englishmen of title settled in America in the early days, though some of the transitory colonial Governors and other high officials were knights, baronets and even peers. Thus the English scheme of honorifics soon passed out of common knowledge, and Dr. S. E. Morison has suggested that the disappearance of its sonorous handles for the names of notables may have had something to do with the proliferation of more or less dubious military titles. With the pre-revolutionary rise of feeling against English institutions even Americans who, by English law, had a right to something better than *Mr.* tended to forget the fact, and this tendency was increased in the first days of the new Republic. The case of the Fairfax family is in point. When Thomas, the sixth Baron Fairfax, took possession of his estate of 6,000,000 acres in Virginia in 1748 his Scottish title was universally recognized, and after his death as a bachelor in 1782 it passed to Bryan Fairfax, the son of his cousin William, who had married a daughter of George Washington's elder brother Lawrence. Bryan's claim was admitted by the House of Lords in 1800, but his heirs soon dropped the title and it remained under cover until 1908, when one of them, Albert Kirby Fairfax, born in the United States in 1870, resumed it, becoming the twelfth Baron Fairfax of Cameron. Thomas Fairfax, so far as I know, was the only English peer ever to settle and die in colonial America; even baronets were scarce, and a British traveler reported in 1724 that there was only one in Cavalier Virginia, to wit, Sir William Skipwith.[1] The Skipwith title, says Allen Walker Read, " was kept up even after the establishment of the independent government," [2] but apparently not for long. Despite Article I, Section 9 of the Constitution, which provides that " no title of nobility shall be granted by the United States," there is no statute, so far as I am aware, forbidding an American to accept one from a foreign state, or even to assume one on his own motion. A Federal jobholder is forbidden by the same section to accept one without the consent of Congress, but the inference is that that consent may be granted constitutionally — and even after half a generation of the New Deal there

[1] The Present State of Virginia; London, 1724; reprinted, New York, 1865, p. 63.

[2] Words Indicating Social Status in America in the Eighteenth Century, *American Speech*, Oct., 1934, p. 205.

are still plenty of Americans who are not Federal jobholders. Not a few, in fact, are counts, marquises and so on by creation of the Pope, and no one objects to their bearing these titles, though when they register for voting purposes they have to give their dirt names.[1]

American newspapers, in dealing with foreign titles, often use them ignorantly, to the horror of visiting Englishmen. When Sir William Craigie landed at the University of Chicago in 1925 to take charge of the Dictionary of American English the campus newspaper, the *Maroon*, noted his arrival under the heading, " Chicago Welcomes Sir Craigie and Lady Sadie " — a triple error, for it should have been *Sir William* and *Lady Craigie*, and the lady's name was not Sadie but Jessie.[2] It is almost an everyday occurrence for some paper to speak of a knight or a baronet as a peer, or of a duke as *Lord* So-and-so.[3] The intricacies of English nomenclature as they are set forth in such an authority as " Titles and Forms of Address " lie far beyond the professional equipment of the average American copy-reader.[4] Even the official experts who compiled the Style Manual of the Department of State show a certain ignorance of accepted English usages.[5] When,

1 General John J. Pershing, who was made a G.C.B. (Knight Grand Cross of the Most Honorable Order of the Bath) in 1918 thereby became *Sir John Pershing* by English law and custom. See Titles and Forms of Address, p. 75. But he never used the honorific.

2 In his account of himself in Who's Who (English) Sir William does not mention his service as editor (jointly with Dr. James R. Hulbert) of the DAE, though he notes that he is professor emeritus of English at the University of Chicago. Even in Who's Who in America there is no mention of the DAE. There was none of his knighthood in Who's Who in America until the 1942–43 volume, which put (*Sir*) before his name.

3 Said William Hickey in the London *Daily Express*, June 15, 1939: " From a New York paper: ' *Lord* Sassoon, Briton, dies,' meaning *Sir* Philip. From a New York paper: An open letter to the King and Queen of England: ' *Your royal highnesses*,' meaning *majesties*."

4 Continental usages are also unfath-

omable to him. So long ago as 1880 Wendell Phillips wrote to *Harper's Magazine* (Dec., p. 149) protesting against the current treatment of the name of the author of Démocratie en Amérique, not only by journalists, but also by such bigwigs as William Graham Sumner, Francis Bowen of Harvard, and the editor of *Harper's*. " The rules of the French language," he wrote, " require that when we omit the *Alexis* or the *Monsieur*, and give only the family name, it should be simply *Tocqueville*. There are a few exceptions to this rule. Names of one syllable, like *De Thou*, retain the *de*, and names beginning with a vowel." American copy-readers refuse, however, to drop the *de*, or the *von* in German names.

5 For example, they ordain (p. 50) that a formal letter to a duke may begin either *My Lord Duke* or *Your Grace*, whereas Titles and Forms of Address gives only *My Lord Duke*, reserving *His Grace the Duke*, etc., for the envelope. Again, they pass up altogether, as apparently beyond

in 1942, the copy-readers of the Chicago *Tribune* began to find their nightly struggle with the titles of English statesmen and war heroes " as tedious as picking birdshot out of a prairie chicken," Colonel Robert R. McCormick, the iconoclastic editor and publisher of the paper, proposed that all such fripperies be dropped by the American newspapers. This proposal, which was couched in somewhat contumacious terms, was denounced as subversive by many of the English papers, and especially by the London *Daily Telegraph*, whose proprietor, originally William Ewert Berry, was made a baronet in 1921 and Baron Camrose of Long Cross in 1929. The *Editor and Publisher*, the trade journal of the American Press, also protested,[1] mainly on the ground that the change might cause confusion, but Colonel McCormick stood his ground, and presently let fly with the following:

> Obviously there would be no confusion in any one's mind if we omitted the *Sir* from *Gen. Sir* Bernard Montgomery. Nor would any one be in doubt about the identity of the person described as *Gov.* Windsor of the Bahamas. These changes in style would promote the idea in American minds that our allies, like us, are fighting for democracy. . . .
> We appear to be undermining something. We hope we are. Lincoln said this nation could not exist half slave and half free, and his words could not have been much weightier if they had been uttered by an earl. Likewise, a nation cannot survive half democratic and half aristocratic. So far as this country is concerned it will make considerable sacrifices to preserve a British democracy, but it doesn't find any great satisfaction in fighting for an aristocratic Britain.
> In deference to American opinion we should expect the British to abolish their titles and the privileges that go with them. After all, the deprivation wouldn't amount to much; it isn't as if Camrose didn't have another name that sounds less like soap to fall back on.[2]

The old English title of *dame* was revived in 1917 to adorn female members of the new Order of the British Empire. There are two

American grasp, the complicated and baffling rules for addressing such personages as dowager marchionesses and earls' daughters who have married commoners.

1 A Step Toward Democracy?, Nov. 26, 1942, p. 26.

2 Every Man a *Mr.* (editorial), Dec. 3, 1942. That Colonel McCormick found some supporters in England is probable, but if so they were kept silent by the censorship. So long ago as Oct. 5, 1935 Lord Camrose's *Daily Telegraph* reported that the Socialist Party Conference, in session at Brighton, debated a resolution saying: " This conference deprecates the acceptance by members of the party of titles or honours other than those which a Labour Government finds necessary for the furtherance of its own business in Parliament " — in other words, for packing the House of Lords. This resolution was carried with an amendment instructing the National Executive Committee of the party " to frame rules setting forth the conditions, if any, under which members of the party should accept honours from capitalist governments."

divisions of the order, military and civil, and five classes in each. Women gazetted to the first class become *dames grand cross;* those in the second class are *dames commander;* those in the remaining classes are not *dames* at all, but simply *commanders, officers* or *members.* The order is conferred upon eminent women writers, actresses, politicos, uplifters and so on, and the members of the first class wear gaudy decorations, including a star, a badge, a sash and a collar, and have the right to put *G.B.E.* after their names. A *dame* is dealt with precisely like a *knight;* that is, she is to be addressed as *Dame Mary Smith* in writing, with her given-name always inserted, and as *Dame Mary* in speech. American reporters, when they have to mention a *dame,* commonly call her *Lady Smith,* for the word *dame,* in this great Republic, has a rather contemptuous significance, but that is an error which upsets an Englishman. *Dame* was a generic name for any Englishwoman of position in the Middle Ages, and in the early Seventeenth Century it became the legal title of the wife of a knight. But in the Eighteenth Century the wives of knights began to call themselves *Lady* So-and-so (never with either their own or their husbands' given-names), and that is their usual style today. The wife of a *knight grand cross* or *knight commander* of the British Empire is probably also a *dame,* legally speaking, but it is usual to call her *Lady,* for her husband is *Sir.* The husband of a female *dame* does not gain any reflected title from his wife.

During the mid-Nineteenth Century it was usual for American wives to borrow the honorifics of their husbands — a custom long prevailing in Germany and the Scandinavian countries, but never popular in England, save, of course, in the case of wives of peers. I find *Mrs. Captain* Voorhees in the diary of Isaac Van Bibber of Maryland, 1844,[1] and so late as 1883 the English historian, Edward A. Freeman,[2] reported that he had seen *Mrs. Professor* on an American woman's visiting card, and that " the newspapers sometimes tell one how *Mrs. ex-Senator* A went somewhere with her daughter, *Mrs. Senator* B." Mark Twain, in his famous appendix on " The Awful German Language " in " A Tramp Abroad," 1879, recorded *Mrs. Assistant District Attorney* Johnson, and there are other amusing ex-

---

[1] March 18. *Maryland Historical Magazine,* Sept., 1944, p. 252.
[2] Some Impressions of the United States; New York, 1883. His remarks on American honorifics are reprinted in American Social History as Recorded by British Travelers, by Allan Nevins; New York, 1923, pp. 481–82.

amples in Carl Sandburg's "Abraham Lincoln: The War Years." [1] Sandburg reproduces fashion drawings from *Leslie's Weekly* showing frocks worn at the White House by *Mrs. Commodore* Levy, *Mrs. Senator* Weller, *Mrs. Senator* Ames, and *Mrs. Senator* Crittenden,[2] and records that in a pass permitting Mrs. Lincoln's stepmother, Mrs. Robert S. Todd, to go through the lines to bring her daughter, Mrs. B. Hardin Helm, northward, Lincoln described Mrs. Helm as *Mrs. General.*[3] General McClellan, in letters referring to Mrs. Lincoln, spoke of her as *Mrs. President.*[4] This transfer of husbands' titles to wives is now virtually obsolete in the United States, but another barbarism that seems to have arisen in Civil War days, to wit, the habit of prefixing long and cumbersome titles to names, still flourishes. The latter was first noted, so far as I know, in the appendix to " A Tramp Abroad " lately cited: the example offered was: " *Clerk of the County and District Court* Simmons was in town yesterday." The style of *Life* and *Time* promotes the creation of such monstrosities, and they are imitated by the newspapers. I could fill pages with them, but content myself with two magnificent specimens. The first is from *Life:* " *Episcopal Bishop in Japan's brother* J. C. Reifsnider." [5] The second is from an Associated Press dispatch: " *Vice-President in Charge of Sales of Evaporated, Condensed and Malted Milk, Cheese, Mince-Meat and Caramels* Arthur W. Ramsdell, and *Vice-President in Charge of Casein, Adhesives and Prescription Products* William Callan were elected to those offices today by the board of directors of the Borden Company." [6] Not infrequently such thunderous titles are preceded by *ex-* or *former. Former,* in this situation, is an Americanism, and the DAE traces it to 1885. I am told by Mr. Charles Honce, of the Associated Press, that it is now preferred to *ex-* by many American newspapers. *Ex-* is not an Americanism. The DAE unearths *ex-President* in 1798 and *ex-Special Agent of the Government* in 1869, but the NED counters with *ex-Bishop of Autun* in English use in 1793. In late years the English columnists who imitate American columnists have gone in heavily for such mild forms as *leading amateur jockey* Ivor House,[7] and *Soviet Ambassador* Ivan Maisky,[8] but their use is pretty

1 New York, 1939.
2 Vol. II, pp. 251 and 257.
3 Her husband, who was in the Confederate Army, was killed at Chickamauga.
4 Sandburg, Vol. II, p. 260.
5 New Words for Old, Baltimore

*Evening Sun,* editorial page, June 3, 1938.
6 How's That Again? Department, *New Yorker,* Jan. 6, 1940.
7 William Hickey, in the London *Daily Express,* July 7, 1939.
8 Henry Bean, in the London *News-*

well confined to gossip columns and the cheap cinema and radio journals. Both the Style Manual of the Department of State and the Style Manual of the United States Government Printing Office seem to prefer *ex-* (with a hyphen) to *former*.[1]

The first female politicians to whom *Ma* was applied seem to have been the Hon. Nellie Tayloe Ross, who became Governor of Wyoming in January, 1925, and the Hon. Miriam A. Ferguson, who became Governor of Texas at the same time. La Ross succeeded her husband, the Hon. William B. Ross, who died October 2, 1924, and La Ferguson followed hers, the Hon. James E. Ferguson, who was impeached and removed from office in 1917. Another stateswoman who was commonly called *Ma* was the Hon. Mabel Walker Willebrandt, who was assistant Attorney-General of the United States from 1921 to 1929, in charge of Prohibition enforcement. The term was applied to many other lady jobholders, chiefly of the more bosomy moiety, but began to drop out of use in the 30s. The Hon. Frances Perkins, who became Secretary of Labor in 1933, was often called *Ma* during her early days in that great office, but after a while it became a custom in Washington to speak of her, and even to address her, as *Madam*. In 1937 the Style Manual of the Department of State [2] ordained that she be called *Madam Secretary* in the salutation of informal letters, and that her style and appellation upon the envelopes of all communications be *the Hon.* Perhaps it was this official lead that led to the general custom of calling her *Madam* instead of *Mrs.* in all situations. In the *Congressional Record* she almost always appears under that title.[3] The Style Manual gives similar forms for addressing a female diplomat, though it permits *My dear Mrs.* (if she has or has had a husband), with her surname following.[4] But it does not accord the honorific of *Madam* to congresswomen, who are to be addressed as *My dear Mrs.* ——, nor even to lady Senators, who rate only *My dear Senator* —— or *My dear Mrs.* ——. The reasons for

---

*Chronicle,* July 11, 1939. I am indebted for both examples to an English correspondent, but his name has unhappily vanished from my notes.

1 For the first; Washington, 1937, see p. 120; for the latter; Washington, 1935, p. 53.
2 p. 28.
3 On Oct. 25, 1939, for example, a

congressman of the name of D'Alesandro described her as *Madame Frances Perkins* in the superscription of a letter on official business, and addressed her as *Dear Madame Perkins* in the salutation thereof. See the *Congressional Record,* April 9, 1940, p. 6396.
4 p. 26.

these distinctions I do not know: they lie concealed in the secret dungeons of the State Department.

In the Eighteenth Century in both England and America *Madam(e)* was the common designation of any woman of dignified position. During the Nineteenth Century it began to be restricted, on this side of the ocean, to a widow with a married son, leaving *Mrs.* for the latter's wife. This usage was noted as prevailing in both New England and the South by Sir Charles Lyell, the English geologist, who visited the United States in 1845 and again in 1849.[1] The title was also given *post mortem,* at a somewhat earlier day, to the deceased wives of men of any mark.[2] In this last sense it was an Americanism, but in the other senses noted it was borrowed from England, where it had been in use since Chaucer's time. *Mistress* is almost as old, but at the start it was always fully pronounced, and not reduced to *missus* or *missez.* Until the beginning of the Seventeenth Century the common abbreviation was not *Mrs.,* but *Mis.* or *Mris.* " Originally distinctive of gentlewomen," says the NED, " the use of the prefix has gradually extended downwards; at the present time every married woman who has no superior title is styled *Mrs.,* even though her husband is of so humble a position as not ordinarily to be referred to as *Mr.*" In England, adds the NED, it is uncommon to use *Mrs.* before a given-name save in legal documents, but in the United States both *Mrs. Smith* and *Mrs. Mary Smith* are in everyday use. The Style Manual of the Department of State [3] advises the use of the form *Mrs. John Smith* in addressing even a widow, though it allows *Mrs. Mary Smith.*[4] It ordains the use of *Madam* as the salutation in all formal letters. In writing to Frenchwomen, it says, the spelling

1 His remark upon it was in his Travels in The United States: Second Visit; London, 1849, Vol. I, p. 129. I borrow this from the DAE. A revival of the use of *Madam* to indicate a dowager was reported in *American Speech,* Dec., 1936, p. 376. Apparently it was confined to the East. I am informed by a correspondent that the aged widow of Sidney Lanier was so spoken of by her Connecticut neighbors.

2 Edward Augustus Kendall reported in his Travels Through the Northern Parts of the United States in 1806–08; New York, 1809, Vol. II, p. 44, that in Plymouth, Mass., and "some of the neighboring places," it was prefixed to "the name of a deceased female of some consideration, as the parson's, the deacon's, or the doctor's wife." Here I am again indebted to the DAE.

3 p. 39.

4 It delicately evades the case of a divorced woman. Frank O. Colby, in Forms of Address and Precedence; Houston, Tex., 1942, p. 3, advises the retention of her late husband's given-name, but adds that the substitution of her own "is seen more and more in common use."

*Madame* should be used. The English authority, " Titles and Forms of Address," advises that envelopes be addressed either *Mrs. Smith* or *Mrs. John Smith,* and recommends *Madam* as the salutation for formal letters. The editor of an 1828 edition of John Walker's " Critical Pronouncing Dictionary and Expositor of the English Language " (1791) noted that to pronounce *Mrs. mistress* would " appear quaint and pedantick," and Noah Webster, in his " American Dictionary " of the same year, gave its " colloquial " pronunciation as *mis-ses.* But Schele de Vere reported in 1872 [1] that " in the South " it was still " very frequently heard pronounced fully, without the usual contraction into *misses.*" This full pronunciation continues to be heard occasionally from the lips of old-fashioned Southerners.[2]

The NED says that *madam* early acquired a derogatory significance in England, " more or less " because of " prejudice against foreign women." Grose, in 1785, defined it as " a kept *madam* [*sic*], a kept mistress." In the United States, probably in the Civil War era, it acquired the special meaning of a brothel-keeper, and so went definitely below the salt.[3] The colored folk, however, still retain it as a label for a conspicuous woman of their race, say, a popular singer or the proprietor of a successful business. In the early days of the Republic *Lady* was in common use to designate the wife of the President. *Lady Washington,* indeed, was heard much oftener than *Mrs. Washington,* and the honorific remained popular until the days of *Lady Jackson.* During the years before the Civil War *Lady of the White House* became the usual designation of any woman serving as the President's chatelaine, not being his wife. In 1861, as the DAE shows, General George B. McClellan was speaking of Mrs. Lincoln as the *Lady President,* but that designation seems to have passed out quickly. When *First Lady* arose I do not know, but it goes back at least to the time of Grover Cleveland's marriage in the White House in 1885. At the start the usual form was *First Lady of the Land,* but in the course of time the second element dropped off.

1 Americanism: The English of the New World, p. 507.
2 All old speechways seem to linger longer in the South than elsewhere, just as old theological doctrines and political hallucinations linger. It is also common there for colored servants to address their mistress as *Miss Mary* instead of as *Mrs. Smith.* The *Miss* is always heard in this combination, never *Mrs.*
3 The DAE does not list this meaning. I judge by its absence from Partridge's Dictionary of Slang and Unconventional English that it is unknown in England. Nor is it listed in Sidney J. Baker's Popular Dictionary of Australian Slang; Melbourne, 1942.

## 6. EUPHEMISMS

285. [*Realtor.*] The history of this elegant term, which was invented by Charles N. Chadbourn of Minneapolis in 1915 and adopted formally in 1916, is given in AL4, pp. 285–87. Its use is restricted to members of the constituent boards of the National Association of Real Estate Boards, now numbering more than 16,000 ethical and advanced-thinking real-estate agents organized into nearly 500 boards.[1] In its early days it was frequently assumed without authority by non-members, but a series of legal battles that began in 1925 and ended triumphantly in 1936 disposed of this effrontery, and rump *realtors* have now pretty well disappeared. The insigne of the association, an oval design showing both a suburban home and a sky-scraper in silhouette, with the words " *Realtors* Are Active Members of Constituent Boards " across it, has been registered as a trade-mark, and fifteen different courts have held that the association is seized and possessed of " the exclusive property right to the term *realtor.*" In addition, " numerous State commissions which issue real-estate licenses have ruled that the unauthorized use of . . . *realtor* constitutes misrepresentation to the public." These quotations are from a pamphlet entitled " *Realtor:* Its Meaning and Use," issued by the association for the information and inspiration of members. From the same pamphlet I take the following " Word to Editors ":

> The term or symbol *realtor* should never be used in any publication, or in any other manner, in connection with the name of any person, firm, corporation or any other organization not affiliated with the National Association of Real Estate Boards. The term is not a word of the common language and should not be used as a synonym for *real estate agent.*[2]

The rules of the association forbid its use in the corporate name of any company qualified for membership, but it may be used in the name of a constituent real-estate board. All persons interested are advised that " it should always be capitalized in order to manifest its

1 I am indebted here and below to Miss Georgia Dickerman, assistant librarian of the association, whose headquarters are in Chicago.

2 On Oct. 4, 1941 the Baltimore *Sun* fell into the error of describing as a *realtor* a real-estate agent who had got into the hands of the police on a charge of fraud. It was promptly brought to book by the Real Estate Board of Baltimore, and apologized handsomely on Oct. 7, citing Webster 1934, as authority for the fact that only a member of a body affiliated with the National Association could properly use the name.

distinctive character and because of its inclusion in various registrations." In the conduct of his business a *realtor* is bound by much stricter rules than incommode an ordinary business man; in fact, he is cribbed, cabined and confined in a way that almost suggests the harsh working conditions of a justice of the Supreme Court or an archbishop. Thus the preamble to the *Realtor's* Code of Ethics adopted at a convention of the association on June 6, 1924:

> Under all is the land. Upon its wise utilization and widely allocated ownership depend the survival and growth of free institutions and of our civilization. The *Realtor* is the instrumentality through which the land resource of the nation reaches its highest use and through which land ownership attains its widest distributions. He is a creator of homes, a builder of cities, a developer of industries, and productive farms.
>
> Such functions impose obligations beyond those of ordinary commerce; they impose grave social responsibility and a patriotic duty to which the *Realtor* should dedicate himself, and for which he should be diligent in preparing himself. The *Realtor*, therefore, is zealous to maintain and improve the standards of his calling and shares with his fellow-*Realtors* a common responsibility for its integrity and honor.
>
> In the interpretation of his obligation, he can take no safer guide than that which has been handed down through twenty centuries, embodied in the Golden Rule:
>
> " Whatsoever ye would that men should do unto you, do ye also unto them."
>
> Accepting this standard as his own, every *Realtor* pledges himself to observe its spirit in all his dealings.

The suggestion that *realtor* is derived from two Spanish words, *real*, meaning royal, and *toro*, a bull, and that it thus connotes *royal bull*, is spurned by the bearers of the name. Mr. Chadbourn's own account of its etymology is as follows:

> *Real estate* originally meant royal grant. It is so connected with land in the public mind that *realtor* is easily understood, even at a first hearing. *Or* is a suffix meaning a doer, one who performs an act, as *grantor, executor, sponsor, administrator. Realtor:* a doer in real estate.[1]

The official pronunciation is not real*tor*, but *reel*-tor.[2] The agent suffix -*or* has always conveyed a more dignified suggestion in English than the allied -*er*, perhaps because it often represents the Latin -*ator* or the French -*eur*. *Professor*, to most persons who use the language, is not only superior in meaning to *teacher*, but also in aspect and atmosphere, and in the same way *author* stands above *writer*. When, in 1865, the male hairdressers of England formed a British Hair-

---

1 Private communication, Sept. 28, 1935.

2 *Realtor:* Its meaning and Use; Chicago, 1925, p. 3, footnote.

dressers' Academy and began giving demonstrations of their art at the Hanover Square Rooms in London, they let it be known that they desired to be called *expositors*. Unhappily, the newspaper wits of the time poked fun at this pretension, and in a little while they were reduced to the estate of *dressers*, and their effort to glorify their science came such a cropper that they had to abandon their demonstrations.[1] In this great free republic there is less hostility to human aspiration, and in consequence there have been a number of imitations of *realtor*, e.g., *insuror* (an insurance agent),[2] *furnitor* (a furniture dealer),[3] *merchantor* (a member of the merchants' bureau of a chamber of commerce), *avigator* (an airplane pilot),[4] *publicator* (a press-agent),[5] and *weldor*.[6] In 1924, inflamed by the vast success of *realtor* in the United States, some of the more idealistic English real-estate men, members of the Institute of Estate Agents and Auctioneers, began calling themselves *estators*, but the term never came into general use. *Realtor* has also bred *realtress*, but it does not seem to be in wide use, though there are many lady realtors.[7] The radio trade has a long list of terms in *-or*, but they are applied to mechanical contrivances, not to God's children, e.g., *resistor, inductor, capacitator* and *arrestor*, the last an elegant substitute for the earlier *lightning-arrester*, which is traced by the DAE to 1860 and is probably an Americanism.[8]

287. [*Mortician* was suggested by *physician*, for undertakers nat-

1 *Every Saturday* (Boston), Feb. 17, 1866, p. 196.
2 *Insurors*, by G. P. Krapp, *American Speech*, June, 1928, p. 432.
3 San Francisco *Examiner*, Nov. 2, 1930, Section 1, p. 11.
4 *Avigation* and *Avigator*, by Mamie Meredith, *American Speech*, Aug. 1928, p. 450. *Avigator* was apparently invented by Lieut. Albert J. Hegenberger. The Cleveland *Plain Dealer* reported him as saying: "When we become familiar with it we shall not confuse it with *alligator*." But it did not catch on, and is not listed in Nomenclature for Aeronautics, issued by the National Advisory Committee for Aeronautics; Washington, 1933.
5 *American Speech*, Oct., 1942, p. 212.
6 *Weldor* was launched as the result of a labor squabble. In 1941 the *weld-*ers in the shipyards and on building construction petitioned the American Federation of Labor for a charter of their own. When it was refused they left the Federation and formed the Brotherhood of *Weldors*, Cutters and Helpers of America. Who thought of substituting the *o* for the *e*, and so giving the trade a more dignified smack, I do not know. See *Weldors, American Speech*, Oct., 1942, p. 214, and An *O* Creates a New Profession, Des Moines *Register* (editorial), Dec. 27, 1941.
7 Washington Signs, by J. Foster Hagan, *American Speech*, March, 1927, p. 293.
8 More Words in *-or*, by C. P. Mason, *American Speech*, April, 1929, p. 329.

urally admire and like to pal with the resurrection men.] [1] From the earliest days they have sought to bedizen their hocus-pocus with mellifluous euphemisms, but it was during the Civil War that they undertook their first really radical reform of its terms. It was then, I believe, that the term *casket* was first substituted for *coffin*, which the NED traces to 1525. Many purists did not like it, and one of them was Nathaniel Hawthorne, who thus denounced it in "Our Old Home," 1863:

> *Caskets!* — a vile modern phrase [*sic*] which compels a person of sense and good taste to shrink more disgustfully than ever before from the idea of being buried at all.

But *casket* quickly made its way, and since the early 80s it is highly improbable that *coffin* has ever appeared in an American undertaker's advertisement or in a newspaper account of the funeral of anyone above the dignity of an executed murderer. There were nascent *morticians*, in the Civil War era, who preferred *case*, especially for a metallic coffin,[2] but *casket* gradually prevailed, and it remains in almost universal use to this day, though there are poetic morticians who root for *slumber-cot*. Before the Civil War the embalming of the dead was not much practised in the United States,[3] but in the course of that struggle the job of bringing home dead soldiers from distant battlefields, perhaps in warm weather, forced its introduction. All the pioneer embalmers of the time called themselves *Dr.*, but for some reason unknown (maybe the opposition of the medical men) that title was soon dropped, and today even the most high-toned picklers of the departed are content to be *sanitarians*. Dr. Charles Mayo, an English physician who made a tour of the United States in 1862 and 1863, thus recorded his observations in Washington:

> The streets bristled with great placards informing you that *Dr.* A. or *Dr.* B. would embalm you better than anybody else, and moreover that the *Drs.* would undertake to make you comfortable in a patent metallic burial *case*, or contract for your coffin and fixings in any style. Those who had been lucky published a list of their distinguished patrons; a dead general was a great catch, and was

1 Various correspondents write in to say that I used this term inaccurately. A *resurrection man*, they point out, was one who robbed graves for the doctors in the days before the Anatomy Acts gave them a lawful supply of cadavers. Nevertheless, I continue to think of them as *resurrection men* themselves, for the frequent (if not always beneficial, socially speaking) effect of their labor is cheating the grave.

2 The DAE traces *burial-case* to 1851, and defines it as "a coffin made of metal."

3 The common substitute, when a body had to be kept more than a day or two, was to put it on ice.

immediately announced in the newspapers. I often saw the process: it consisted simply of the injection of a common antiseptic fluid into the femoral artery. Touters in the employ of these harpies followed the rear of the army, and their notices were stuck up at every steamboat wharf, railway station, or other available place near the camp. The effect of these announcements can hardly have been encouraging to the men at first; fortunately for them, however, they soon got accustomed to anything.[1]

The newspapers of all the towns near battle-fronts were full of the advertisements of these *Drs*. Here, for example, is one that appeared in the Nashville *Press and Times* on October 21, 1865, after the war was over and bereaved relatives from the North were flocking into the area in the hope of recovering the bodies of fallen soldiers:

Disinterring Deceased Soldiers
Dr. Prunk

has established reliable agents at Chattanooga, Tenn., Atlanta, Macon, Andersonville, Ga., and Huntsville, Ala., who have access to all the burial records to enable them to establish the identity of bodies, in order that they may be able to forward the remains of deceased soldiers there, as well as all intermediate points, with promptness.

As the time is short, in this warm climate, in which bodies can be removed, and the probability of the head-boards being defaced, policy dictates to you to attend to the removal of your friends this Winter.

Headquarters: Nashville, Tenn., Cherry street, five doors south of the postoffice.

Metallic *cases* and fine coffins on hand.

D. H. Prunk
Licensed Embalmer.

The DAE's earliest example of *mortician* comes from an advertisement in the Columbus (O.) *Dispatch* of August 14, 1895, which was only six months after the term was launched by the *Embalmer's Monthly*.[2] But it was not until September 17, 1917 that 200 of the most eminent American undertakers banded themselves into an organization called the National Selected *Morticians*,[3] and began to strike out for a general reform of necrophoric nomenclature.[4] Some

1 Vacation Tourists and Notes of Travel; London, 1864, p. 387.
2 Feb., 1895. According to Elmer Davis (The Mortician, *American Mercury*, May, 1927, p. 33) "it owes its origin chiefly to Frank Fairchild of Brooklyn and Harry Samson of Pittsburgh, distinguished members of the profession." He does not give the date.
3 For this date I am indebted to Mr.

W. M. Krieger, executive secretary of the National Selected Morticians, with headquarters in Chicago.
4 A *mortician*, said D. W. Brogan in Our Uncle's Tongue, *Oxford Magazine*, June 10, 1937, p. 731, "was once defined by a wit as 'the man who buries a *realtor*.'" It is highly probable that Brogan invented this saying himself.

of their inventions are now familiar — *patient* or *case* for *body*; *funeral-car, casket-coach* or *ambulance* for *hearse; negligée, slumber-robe* or *slumber-shirt* for *shroud; slumber-room, reposing-room, chapel, funeral-home* or *funeral-residence* for *funeral-parlor* or *undertaking establishment; operating-parlor, operating-room, preparing-room* or *preparation-room* for the cellar in which the embalmer does his work; *service-car* for *dead-wagon; limousine* for *mourners'-coach*,[1] and so on. In September, 1935, a Washington mortician was advertising by cards in the local trolley-cars that the *reposing-rooms* in his *funeral-home* were " *Autumn-breezed* by the finest air-conditioning equipment." [2] Four years later the term *mortician* got official recognition in a report of the Bureau of the Census,[3] and three years after that the more elegant members of the profession in the District of Columbia tried to induce Congress to pass an act providing for the examination and licensing of its practitioners. This proposal was energetically opposed by the common run of Washington undertakers, who alleged that it was inspired by an effort of " a small minority of *morticians* to gain control of the profession in the District." [4] At least one *mortician* has promoted himself to the estate and dignity of a *mortuary consultant*,[5] and another has become a *funeral counselor*,[6] but so far I have heard of none who calls himself a *mortuary, obituary* or *obsequial engineer*. No doubt it will come. Meanwhile, the owners and press-agents of places of sepulchre have followed their associates into the flowery fields of euphemism. Graveyards, in all the more progressive parts of the United States, are graveyards no longer, nor even cemeteries, but *memorial-parks, burial-abbeys* or *-cloisters*, or *mortaria*.[7] " Before long," said the before cited Elmer Davis in 1927, " they will probably be calling them *memorial-cathedrals*. . . . Ground burial, one learns, is out of date and barbarous;

1 In the early days of the automobile *limousine* was in wide use to designate a closed car, but it survives only in the vocabulary of morticians.

2 I am indebted for this to Mr. H. D. FitzGerald.

3 Manufactures, 1939. *Caskets, Coffins, Burial-Cases*, and Other *Morticians'* Goods. Prepared under the supervision of Thomas J. Fitzgerald, chief statistician for manufactures; Washington, 1941.

4 *Morticians* Protest Proposal to Require $20 License Fee, Washington *Times-Herald*, Oct. 15, 1942.

5 He is reported by Mr. Dudley Fitts of Boston: private communication, Aug. 30, 1935.

6 Euphemistic Classifications, by Wayland D. Hand, *American Notes and Queries*, June, 1944, p. 48.

7 In Houston, Tex., there is a cemetery called the Garden of Memories. See the *Billboard*, Oct. 2, 1943, p. 31, and Forest Lawn, *Life*, Jan. 5, 1944, pp. 65–75.

mausoleum entombment is modern, progressive and humanitarian —
' as sanitary as cremation and as sentimental as a churchyard.' " Some
of the new mausoleums are structures of great pretentiousness, usually either Gothic or Byzantine in style and as gorgeous as a first-
rate filling-station. They flourish especially in Southern California,[1]
and those of Los Angeles are heavily patronized, for one of the in-
ducements they offer is the chance to store the beloved dead cheek
by jowl with a Valentino or a Jean Harlow.

A correspondent assures me that he saw the sign of a *mortician* in
the town of Driffield in Yorkshire (pop. 6,000) in 1925, but the term
has made very little progress among the hunkerous English, who
prefer *undertaker*.[2] *Funeral director* is not listed in the NED, but an
older term, *funeral undertaker*, is traced to 1707. *Undertaker* itself
goes back to 1698. It once had a formidable rival in *upholder*, the
original meaning of which was a dealer in and repairer of old furniture. In that sense *upholder* is traced by the NED to 1333, but it does
not seem to have come into use to designate a funeral contractor until
the beginning of the Eighteenth Century. It still survives in England,
though it is not in common use; there was a firm of *funeral upholders*
in the Kensington district of London in 1938.[3] The art of the undertaker and the trade of the furniture-dealer were often associated in
the United States in the Nineteenth Century; in fact, they are still
so associated in many small towns. *Morgue*, to designate a dead-house,
was borrowed from the French less than a century ago, and *mortuary*
is even more recent. The NED's first example of *mortuary* is dated
1865. Three years later a writer in the London *Spectator* was sneering
at it as the invention of newspaper reporters.[4] *Crematory* is traced

1 The ceremony of depositing ashes
in one of these basilicas is called
*inurnment*. See *Inurnment*, by C.
Douglas Chrétien, *American Speech*,
Dec., 1934, p. 317. In the early days
of California the Spanish term
*campo santo* was often used to designate a graveyard, but it seems to
have gone out, save, of course,
among the Mexicans.

2 They also cling to the old-fashioned
lozenge-shaped coffin. Says H. W.
Seaman: " The rectangular casket is
unknown. Stiffs are rarely embalmed, and never exhibited in fu-
neral-parlors. Funeral fashions in
England are simpler than they used
to be. Hearses are plainer and plumes
are out. Black is but little worn by
the bereaved. But the shroud is still
*à la mode*." The coffin in which the
bones of George Washington lie at
Mount Vernon is lozenge-shaped.
There is a drawing of it in Mount
Vernon As It Is, *Harper's Magazine*,
March, 1850, p. 435.

3 The Undertaker's Trade, by C.
Wise, London *Telegraph and Post*,
Feb. 17, 1938.

4 His sneer was reprinted in *Every
Saturday* (Boston), May 16, 1868,
p. 636.

by the DAE, in American use, to 1885; the NED traces it to 1876 in England. It is now pretty well supplanted in the United States by the more mellifluous *crematorium*, which borrows elegance from *pastorium, healthatorium, lubritorium*, and their congeners.

The resounding success of *mortician* brought in many other words in *-ician, e.g., beautician, cosmetician, shoetrician, radiotrician, fizzician, locktician, whooptician, linguistician, strategician*. They were preceded by *stereoptician*, a tony name for the operator of a stereopticon, recorded by the DAE in 1887. Who invented *beautician* I do not know, nor the precise time of its invention, but the owner of a beauty salon by the name of Miss Kathryn Ann, at 214 Seventy-first Euclid Building, Cleveland, O., was advertising in the November, 1924 issue of the Cleveland telephone directory that she had a staff of " very efficient *beauticians*." [1] By 1926 Dr. Morris Fishbein, editor of the *Journal of the American Medical Association*, was reporting in the *American Mercury* [2] that *beauticians, cosmeticians* and *cosmetologists* were in practise from end to end of the country, and that nine States had already passed acts providing for their examination, licensing and regulation. Other States followed soon afterward, but it was not until May 5, 1938 that Congress took cognizance of the new art and mystery by passing H.R. 6869, which created " a District of Columbia Board of *Cosmetology* . . . to regulate the occupation and practise," and laid down the following definition:

The word *cosmetology*, as used in this act, shall be defined and construed to mean any one or any combination of practices generally and usually, heretofore and hereafter, performed by, and known as the occupation of beauty culturists or *cosmeticians*, or *cosmetologists*, or hairdressers, or of any other persons holding him or herself out as practicing *cosmetology* by whatever designation and within the meaning of this act and in and upon whatever place or premises; and in particular *cosmetology* shall be defined and shall include, but otherwise not be limited thereby, the following or any one or a combination of practices, to wit: Arranging, dressing, styling, curling, waving, cleansing, cutting, removing, singeing, bleaching, coloring, or similar work upon the hair of any person by any means, and with hands or mechanical or electrical apparatus or appliances, or by the use of cosmetic preparations, antiseptics, tonics, lotions, or creams, massaging, cleansing, stimulating, exercising, beautifying, or similar work, the scalp, face, neck, arms, bust, or upper part of the body, or manicuring the nails of any person, exclusive of such of the foregoing practices as come within the scope of the Healing Arts Practice Act in force in the District of Columbia at the time of the passage of this act.

1 I am indebted for this to Miss Lucile    2 The Cult of Beauty, Feb., 1926, pp.
Dvorak of Cleveland.                          161–68.

*Beautician* reached England by 1937, but it was apparently collared there by beauty-preparation manufacturers, who also tried to lay hands on *cosmetician*.[1] In the United States both seem to be yielding to *cosmetologist*, and the chief organization of the beauty-shop operators is called the National Hairdressers and *Cosmetologists* Association. In Boston, in 1935, a lady specializing in "tinting hair for Boston's most discriminating women" began to call herself a *canitist*,[2] and in Australia there is a tony *beautician* who uses the Frenchy designation of *cosmetiste*,[3] but neither term has swept the American profession. In my youth the dens of lady hairdressers were called simply *hairdressing-parlors*, but *beauty-parlor* began to appear before World War I, and soon afterward it was displaced by *beauty-shop*. Sometimes the latter is spelled *beauty-shoppe*, or even *beauté-shoppe*. The girls have produced a considerable vocabulary of elegant terms to designate their operations, *e.g.*, *to youthify*, and some of their literati begin to talk of such metaphysical things as *beauty characterology*.[4]

*Radiotrician*, perhaps suggested by *electrician* rather than by *mortician*, was adopted by the radio repairmen in the late 1920s,[5] a little while after the regular electrical jobbers began to call themselves *electragists*.[6] The *shoetricians*, who appear in reactionary dictionaries as *cobblers*, dallied with *shoe-rebuilder* before they hit upon *shoetrician*. There was a *Shoe-Rebuilders'* Association in Baltimore so early as October 17, 1935, as I record for posterity in AL4, p. 288, n. 5. But on Sunday, February 25, 1940, the directors of the Texas Master *Shoe-Rebuilders'* Association met at the Hotel Texas, Fort Worth, and "decided that their service included more than rebuilding, . . . so the organization's name was changed to the Texas-

---

1 William Hickey in the London *Daily Express*, July 20, 1937. I am indebted here to Mr. P. E. Cleator.
2 Apparently from the Latin *canitudo* or *canus*, signifying grey. I am indebted here to the late Dr. Isaac Goldberg.
3 Sydney *Herald*, Nov. 1, 1935.
4 Beauty and You, by Patricia Lindsay, Baltimore *Sun*, March 10, 1943.
5 It first appeared in print, so far as my records show, in Feb., 1930, when the *Rota Monica*, organ of the Rotary Club of Santa Monica, Calif., announced that C. C. Hopkirk, " our own *radiotrician*," would address the members on Experiences in Korea, Feb. 7.
6 *Electragist*, like *realtor*, is withheld from the public domain. It may be used only by members of the Association of *Electragists* International, which seems to have been organized *c.* 1925. See *Electragist*, by Cornell Ridderhof, *American Speech*, Aug., 1927, p. 477.

Southwestern Association of *Shoetricians.*"[1] When news of this decision permeated the country there was mocking in the newspapers. The New York *Times* led off with an editorial sneer in which it was assumed idiotically that the customs shoemakers had begun to call themselves *booticians,* and that the cobblers were simply trying to leap aboard their bandwagon.[2] It may seem incredible that even an editorial writer could have been unaware of the fact that *bootician* was the designation of a high-toned bootlegger, but there is the fact. During the months following a great many other papers took hacks at the *shoetricians,*[3] but the more idealistic of them stuck to their new and lovely name. *Fizzician,* a second stage (the first being *fountaineer*) in the advance from *soda-jerk,* was reported by *PM* in 1938. *Strategician,* applied to a master of lawn-tennis, seems to have been invented in 1937 by John Lardner, son of the immortal Ring. *Linguistician* has been ascribed to a lady pedagogue of Lincoln, Neb.[4] *Locktician* was noted in *American Speech* in 1937,[5] and many other such marvels have been recorded in the same learned journal, *e.g., whooptician,*[6] *fermentician,*[7] *bootblackitician,*[8] *scholastician,*[9] *dramatitian.*[10] *Ecstatician* (" one who studies, or is versed in, ecstasies ") turned up in the *Atlantic Monthly* in 1936,[11] and *jazzician* in England in 1938.[12] *Bootician* was my own invention, launched in the *American Mercury* in 1925.[13] It was followed five years later by *super-bootician.*[14] It came too late to be included in the DAE, but is listed by Berrey and Van

1 Exit the *Cobblers* — Enter *Shoetricians,* Fort Worth *Star-Telegram,* Feb. 26, 1940. I am indebted here to Mr. Warren Agee of Fort Worth. I am informed that there was a *shoetrician* in Omaha in 1936, but if so he must have been a lonely pioneer. In 1938 *Women's Wear* (New York) reported that *shoeist* was being " applied to the proprietor of a shoe store," but it did not survive. *Shoe-rebuilder* is by no means extinct. In Jan., 1942, the *Bulletin* of the New York Public Library announced the appearance in Boston of a monthly called the Master *Shoe-Rebuilder.*

2 Topics of the Times, March 13, 1940.

3 A canned editorial headed The *Icians,* appeared in the Indianapolis *News* and other papers, March 15, 1940, and was widely copied. Another, headed Why Not? They're All Doing It, originated in the Des Moines *Register* and then made the rounds.

4 For the last two see Verbal Novelties, *American Speech,* Oct., 1937, p. 237.

5 April, p. 162.

6 Aug., 1929, p. 500.

7 Dec., 1934, p. 318.

8 Feb., 1938, p. 258.

9 April, 1928, p. 350.

10 Jottings in Gotham, Dec., 1930, p. 159.

11 *Words,* Feb., 1938, p. 30.

12 *Jazzicians* Voluntarily Join Discharged Colleagues, *Cavalcade* (London), Aug. 13.

13 Philological Notes, April, p. 450.

14 Some Neologisms From Recent Magazines, by Robert Withington, *American Speech,* April, 1931, p. 287.

den Bark, who define it as "a high-class bootlegger." It enjoyed a considerable vogue during the last half dozen of the thirteen years of Prohibition, and reached England by 1931.[1] The parent *bootlegger* is not as old as most Americans are apt to assume. The DAE's first example is dated 1889. The term apparently originated in what is now Oklahoma in the days before the region was opened to white settlement, when the sale of liquor to the Indians was prohibited.

The tendency to engaud lowly vocations with names presumed to be dignified goes back to the earliest days of the Republic, and has been frequently noted by English travelers, beginning with Thomas Anburey in 1779.[2] In 1784 John Ferdinand Dalziel Smyth observed that the smallest American shopkeepers were calling their establishments *stores*, which indicated a large place to an Englishman. "The different distinct branches of manufacturers," he said, "such as *hosiers, haberdashers, clothiers, linen-drapers, grocers, stationers*, etc., are not known here; they are all comprehended in the single name and occupation of *merchant* or *storekeeper*."[3] A dozen years later Francis Baily was reporting from Tennessee that *storekeeper* was "the general denomination" there for "everyone who buys and sells."[4] By 1846, as the DAE shows, the American barber-shop had begun to be a *shaving-saloon*, and by 1850 a photographer was a *daguerreian artist*. By the end of the 70s barbers were *tonsorial artists*,[5] and in the early 80s presentable saloon-keepers became *restauranters* or *restauranteurs*.[6] By 1901 the *Police Gazette* was carrying on a campaign

1 One-Way Glass in Chicago, by Tom Rylands, Manchester *Guardian Weekly*, Dec. 4.
2 His Travels Through the Interior Parts of American, embodying his diary in the 1879 period, was published in London in 1780. For this reference and several following I am indebted to Words 'Indicating Social Status in America in the Eighteenth Century, by Allen Walker Read, *American Speech*, Oct., 1934, pp. 204–08.
3 A Tour in the United States of America; London, 1788, Vol. I, pp. 98 and 99.
4 Journal of a Tour in Unsettled Parts of America in 1796–1797; London, 1856, p. 414.
5 In 1924 3,000 of the more aspiring of them met in Chicago and resolved

to become *chirotonsors*, but a loud chorus of newspaper ribaldry wrecked the term, and it did not stick. See the *Commonweal*, Nov. 26, 1924, p. 58. The *tonsor* part was not new. It is recorded as a name for a barber in Thomas Blount's Glossographia, 1656.
6 Always with the *n*; never in the French form, *restaurateur*. See my Newspaper Days; New York, 1941, pp. 215–16. When jitney-busses came in they brought the *jitneur*, but when they departed so did he. *Confectauranteur* for a confectioner, *scripteur* for a Hollywood scriptwriter and *camerateur* for an amateur photographer have also been reported, and likewise *scripteuse* for a female script-writer and *strippeuse* and *stripteuse* for a strip-teaser. See

for the abandonment of the lowly *bartender* and the adoption of either *bar-clerk* or *mixologist,* which last had been proposed sportively by the *Knickerbocker Magazine* in 1856, and had come into more or less use in the West by 1870.[1] The early American photographers called their working-places *studios,* and in the course of time the term was adopted by the operators of billiard-rooms, barber-shops, and even various sorts of stores.[2] A contributor to *American Speech,* in 1926,[3] reported encountering *tonsorial studio, food studio* and *shoe studio.* In 1940 the makers of Fanny Farmer candies were advertising that they maintained " *studios* in which these candies are made in Rochester, N. Y., Brooklyn, Minneapolis, Cleveland, Cambridge, Mass., and Milwaukee," and at about the same time a candy-factory in Canada was inviting patrons to " pay us a visit and see the absolute cleanliness of our *studios.*" [4] Welker Cockran, at last accounts, was operating a *billiard studio* in Hollywood, Calif., but it should be added that most of his colleagues seem to still prefer *parlor* or *academy.* Dr. A. G. Keller tells me that he once heard a chiropodist refer to his *studio.*

The list of such euphemisms might be lengthened almost endlessly. A correspondent sends in the advertisement of a bill-collector who describes himself as a *collection correspondent,*[5] another reports a tapeworn specialist who operates a *Helminthological Institute,*[6] and a third turns in *section manager* (formerly *aisle manager*) for a *floor-*

---

Among the New Words, by Dwight L. Bolinger, *American Speech,* Dec., 1943, p. 301.

1 The DAE records that an effort was made in Jersey City in 1910 to outlaw *bartender* and substitute *server.* On Oct. 15, 1936 the *Berkshire Evening Eagle* (Pittsfield, Mass.) recorded that a Pittsfield bartender, on presenting himself to the local registers of voters for registration, insisted upon being put down a *mixologist,* and that they let him have his way. (I am indebted here to Mr. Robert G. Newman.) *Bartender* is an Americanism, traced by the DAE to 1855. The English use *barman* or *barmaid. Barroom* is also an Americanism, traced to 1807. So, indeed, is *bar,* at least in the sense of the room. In the sense of the counter on which drinks are served it has been in English use since the latter part of the Sixteenth Century.

2 John T. Krumpelmann suggests in *Studio, American Speech,* Dec., 1926, p. 158, that this craze, at least in the Central West, may have been influenced by the German partiality for *atelier.*

3 May, p. 460.

4 I am indebted here to Mr. Edgar Gahan, of Westmount, Quebec.

5 In the *Saturday Review of Literature,* Jan. 20, 1934, Christopher Morley reported one who called himself an *arrears negotiator.*

6 *Institute* is in wide use to designate trade organizations formed to resist legislative attacks upon the larger industries. See Among the New Words, by Dwight L. Bolinger, *American Speech,* April, 1942, p. 120.

*walker*. From North Carolina comes *over-the-counter salesperson* for *store-clerk*,[1] from Philadelphia comes a demand for a more elegant name for the airline *stewardess* or *hostess*,[2] Chicago contributes *trolley-pilot* for *motorman*,[3] Peoria, Ill., follows with *gemmologist* (a lady jeweler),[4] and New York bands its *soda-jerks* into a Cooks, Countermen, *Soda Dispensers* and Assistants Union. *Tree-surgeon* is too familiar to need notice: Webster lists it without comment, and in 1934 the man who coined it, Martin L. Davey, was elected Governor of Ohio. The old-time newsboy is now a *newspaper-boy*, which seems to be regarded as somehow more dignified; [5] a dog-catcher is a *canine control officer* in Peoria, Ill.,[6] and a *humane officer* in Tulsa, Okla.; [7] an iceman, in Denver, is an *ice-attendant;* [8] a janitor is an *engineer-custodian* or a *custodial engineer;* and a grocer is a *provisioner* or *victualer*.[9] So long ago as 1928 President E. L. Robins, of the National *Fertilizer* Association, started a campaign to drop its name and substitute either the National Association of *Plant Food* Manufacturers or the American *Plant Food* Association,[10] and in 1940 the International Brotherhood of *Red Caps* changed its name to the United *Transport Service Employees* of America.[11] In 1939, when the surviving customers' men in the offices of the New York stockbrokers formed an Association of *Customers' Men*, there was a considerable debate among them about the designation of their craft, which had been made somewhat dubious by the jibes of the town wits. Sixty-seven per cent. of them turned out to be in favor of changing it, with *associate broker* and *broker's representative* polling the most votes as substitutes.[12] But when the members met at their first annual convention on June 5 they decided to adopt *customers' broker*.[13] Three years

1 Euphemistic Classifications, by Francis H. Hayes, *American Notes and Queries*, July, 1944, p. 64.

2 Wanted: A Better Name For Those Queens of the Airlines, by Herb Graffis, Philadelphia *Record*, May 9, 1940.

3 W. L. McAtee in *American Notes and Queries*, June, 1944, p. 48.

4 Word of the Week, *Printers' Ink*, June, 1923.

5 President's Greeting on *Newspaper-Boy* Day, *Editor and Publisher*, Oct. 9, 1943.

6 In Other Words, by W. E. Farbstein, *New Yorker*, Aug. 8. 1942.

7 Workers, Arise!, by W. E. Farbstein, *New Yorker*, Sept. 16, 1939.

8 Farbstein, just cited.

9 Euphemisms for *Grocer*, by Elsie Pokrantz, *American Speech*, Feb., 1942, p. 73.

10 United Press dispatch from Atlanta, Ga., Nov. 13, 1928.

11 For New Dignity, Boston *Transcript* (editorial), Jan. 23, 1940. I am indebted here to Mr. David Sanders Clark, of Cambridge, Mass.

12 *Customers' Men*, *Newsweek*, May 8, 1939.

13 *Brokerettes*, *Newsweek*, June 19, 1939.

before this the hod-carriers of Milwaukee, acting through the Milwaukee Building Trades Council, had resolved to be hod-carriers no more, but *mason-laborers*,[1] and only a few months later the Long Island Federation of Women's Clubs decreed that housewives should cease to be *housewives* and become *homemakers*. In 1942 some reformer in Kansas City launched a crusade to make it *household executive*.[2] In 1943 the more solvent spiritualists of the country, fretting under a name that had acquired discreditable connotations, resolved to be *psychists* thenceforth, and organized *Psychists, Inc.*, with John Myers of New York, " a non-professional medium of varied and remarkable powers," as its first president.[3]

Gardeners posturing as *landscape architects* and laborers posturing as *gardeners* are too numerous to be remarked. So are lobbyists under the guise of *industrial consultants*, press-agents disguised as *publicity directors, public relations counsel* or *publicists*, detectives as *investigators* or *operatives*, and messenger boys as *communications carriers*.[4] *Public relations counsel* was launched by Edward L. Bernays of New York, one of the most distinguished members of the fraternity. It had been preceded by *councillor in* (or *on*) *public relations*, occasionally used by Ivy L. Lee (1878–1934), another eminent publicist. The history and true meaning of *public relations counsel* were thus expounded in a memorandum issued from the Bernays office on February 18, 1944:

In 1919, Mr. Bernays returned to this country from the Peace Conference, at which he was present as a member of the United States Committee on Public Information. On September 27, 1919, he unlocked the door of offices at 19 East 48th street. In Paris Mr. Bernays had been impressed with the effectiveness of the work carried on by the Committee on Public Information. For want of a better name, he called his new activities *publicity direction* and it was under this name that they were announced in a folder at the time. Ivy Lee at this time had already set up offices in downtown New York. He was calling himself an *advisor on public relations*. Sometimes he called himself a *councillor in* (or *on*) *public relations*.

Mr. Bernays, and Doris E. Fleischman, a young woman working with him in his office at the time, whom he later married and who is now his partner, were semantically minded. They were dissatisfied with the term *publicity direc-*

1 Associated Press dispatch from Milwaukee, July 31, 1936.
2 I am indebted here to the two Farbstein articles, before cited.
3 *Psychists* Incorporated, *Psychic Observer* (Lily Dale, N. Y.), Nov. 10, 1943.

4 The Western Union advertised for them in the New York *Times*, Aug. 16, 1943, p. 29. " Men 50 years or over," it said, " can help during the war by serving as temporary *communications carriers*." I am indebted here to Major R. D. Heinl, Jr.

*tor* and searched for terminology that would come to mean the functions they were performing and no others. In casting about for a term, the two hit upon an expression that seemed to them to fit the need. They took the word *counsel* from legal nomenclature and added to it *on public relations*. To them, at the time, this phrase was the nearest approach to indicating just what they felt they were doing, that is, giving professional advice on relationships with the public to their clients, regardless of whether such advice resulted in publicity or not.

Mr. Bernays then wrote a book, "Crystallizing Public Opinion," published in 1923. Its purpose was to outline the scope and function of the new work. All the reviewers did not regard the new term as simply a euphemism for an old one. The New York *Herald Tribune* opined that, "individuals and nations may find equal profit in Mr. Bernays' exposition of the new profession of *public relations counsel*." The Baltimore *Sun* saw in the *public relations counsel* "a man who performs for the commercial, industrial, financial or governmental interests which retain him, the methods of both journalism and advertising, and embracing the use of all established mediums of communication." In 1923 the New York Telephone Company's Red Book was persuaded by Mr. Bernays to use the title in one of its listings and from this the practice became nationwide. Every large city today has *counsels on public relations*.

Mr. Bernays then attempted to get universities and colleges to adopt the new term. Today there are courses in *public relations* in many universities. Mr. Bernays himself gave the first at New York University in 1923. In 1928 he wrote "Propaganda" and further currency was given to the term. In 1944 the Dictionary of Sociology described *public relations* as:

" (1) Relations of an individual, association, government, or corporation with the publics which it must take into consideration in carrying on its social functions. These publics can include voters, customers, employees, potential employees, past employees, stockholders, members of antagonistic pressure groups, neighbors, etc.

" (2) The body of theory and technique utilized in adjusting the relationships of a subject with its publics. These theories and techniques represent applications of sociology, social psychology, economics, and political science as well as of the special skills of journalists, artists, organizational experts, advertising men, etc., to the specific problems involved in this field of activity."
and *public relations counsel* as:

"Specialist in public relations. Specifically, an expert in (*a*) analyzing public relations maladjustments, (*b*) locating probable causes of such maladjustments in the social behavior of the client and in the sentiments and opinions of publics, and (*c*) advising the client on suitable corrective measures. The latter requires "bedside" techniques as delicate and complex as those utilized by the psychiatrist in many cases. The public relations counselor has a field of competence that overlaps somewhat those of press agents, public opinion analysts, lobbyists, organizational experts, etc., and requires him to be in a broad sense a societal technician, proficient in the application of scientific social theories and tested publicity techniques.

The lowly garbage-man and ash-man (English: *dustman*) have begun to disappear from the American fauna: they are now becoming *sanitary officers,* and the bureau under which the former works (at all events in heavenly Pasadena) has become the *table waste dis-*

*posal department.*[1] Street-sweeps are also becoming *sanitary officers* or *sanitation men.* The United States Postoffice now calls its male sweepers and cleaners *charmen,* and may be trusted on some near tomorrow to give a lift to its *charwomen.*[2] The junkmen, by their own resolve, are now *waste-material dealers.*[3]

This American aversion to designations indicating a servile or ignominious status goes back to the first days of the Republic, and in Chapter 1, Section 6 we have encountered J. Fenimore Cooper's discussion of it. *Help* is traced by the DAE to 1630, and *hired-men* to 1694, but before the Revolution both terms seem to have been descriptive merely, with no hint of euphemism. Albert Matthews maintains with his accustomed great learning that this was certainly true of *hired-man.*[4] Before 1776, he says, there was not " the slightest indication of its having been employed in a euphemistic sense." But after 1776 it began to be employed to distinguish a freeman from a slave, and after 1863 it became a general substitute for *servant,* a " hated appellation." It was not noted as an Americanism by any of the early writers on the subject, but Webster listed it in his American Dictionary of 1828. The NED does not mark it an Americanism, but *hired-girl, hired-hand* and *hired-help* are so designated. *Hired-girl* is traced to 1818, *hired-hand* to the same year, and *hired-help* to 1815. *Help* is also marked an Americanism. At the start it appears to have designated a person giving occasional assistance only, as opposed to a regular servant. Just when it became a euphemism is not clear, but it was probably after the Revolution, when the servant problem became acute. In the closing years of the Eighteenth Century Hugh Jones reported from New York in his " Travels in the United States, 1793–1797," p. 24,[5] that " if you want to hire a maid-servant in this city

---

1 I am indebted here to Mr. Charles J. Lovell of Pasadena.

2 *Charwoman* is a borrowing from England, where the NED traces it to 1596. Under date of Oct. 28, 1937 David Shulman was complaining in the New York *Times* that the American *scrubwoman* was not listed in any dictionary, but this has since been remedied by the DAE, which traces it to 1885. " The *scrubwoman,*" said Mr. Shulman, " should not be confused with the *charwoman.* The former scrubs, whereas the latter does other chores besides."

The NED Supplement lists *scrubman* as an Americanism, and traces it to 1905.

3 *Waste Dealers* to Meet March 17, New York *Times,* March 10, 1941. They call their trade organization the National Association of *Waste-Material Dealers.*

4 The Terms *Hired-man* and *Help,* *Publications of the Colonial Society of Massachusetts,* Vol. V, 1900.

5 Words Indicating Social Status in America in the Eighteenth Century, by Allen Walker Read, *American Speech,* Oct., 1934, p. 207.

she will not allow you the title of *master*, or herself to be called *servant*." In 1807 Charles William Janson reported in " the Stranger in America," pp. 87 and 88, the following dialogue with a maid-servant at the door of a friend's house:

Q. Is your *master* at home?
A. I have no *master*.
Q. Don't you live here?
A. I *stay* here.
Q. And who are you then?
A. Why, I am Mr. ——'s *help*. I'd have you know, *man*, that I am no *sarvent*. None but *negers* are *sarvents*.[1]

By the end of the Civil War, when the servant problem again became acute, it was impossible to placate these rambunctious females with euphemistic words, with the result described by another English observer, George Augustus Sala: [2]

Goaded to desperation by *young-lady helps*, who *will* wear jewelry, crino-line, and ringlets, the employers of female labor advertise every day for foreign domestics. " A willing German girl," " A hard-working Irish girl just arrived! " and so forth. They get hold of raw emigrants, simple and uncouth young ladies from the middle states of Germany or the wilds of southern Ireland. For a time they do very well. Accustomed to toil from their infancy, they will sweep and scrub, wash and iron, from early in the morning to late at night. They are too unsophisticated not to be obedient. They are temporarily grateful for abundant food and comfortable lodging, and make capital servants. But there comes a time when three meals a day, and unstinted meals too, bring about their inevitable consequences. They have more money than they know how to spend; they learn to talk American-English; they have their beaux and their female gossips; they awaken at last to the conviction that they are as good as you, and a great deal better.

*Help* and *hired-girl* are now both abandoned, and *maid* is the al-most universal designation of a female servant.

289. [The *Engineering News-Record*, the organ of the engineers, used to devote a column every week to uninvited invaders of the

1 Here again I am indebted to Read. He says that the same dislike of the word *servant* was noted by J.F.D. Smyth in Tour in the United States of America; London, 1784, Vol. I, p. 356, and by John Harriott in Struggles Through Life; second ed.; London, 1808, Vol. II, p. 41. Picker-ing, in his Vocabulary, 1816, said that *help* was then used only in " some parts of New England," and Dunglison, in 1829, also marked it " New England," but we have seen, on the evidence of Jones, that both were in error. For more about *help* see Schele de Vere, p. 487, Horwill, p. 163, and *Hyppo, Blue Devils*, etc., by Atcheson L. Hench, *American Speech*, Oct., 1941, p. 234.
2 The Streets of New York, *Eclectic Magazine* (New York), Aug., 1865, p. 163.

craft. . . . One of its favorite exhibits was a bedding manufacturer who became the first *mattress-engineer* and then promoted himself to the lofty dignity of *sleep-engineer*.] This hatching of bogus engineers still goes on. The following specimens from my collectanea, with examples of their use, include a few from the files of the *Engineering News-Record*, not listed in AL4:

Civilization-engineer. A scientist.

1927. Philadelphia *Evening Bulletin* (editorial), quoted in *Engineering News-Record*, Feb. 17. This is the only fitting term for the representatives of forty-five learned societies who gather under the auspices of the American Association for the Advancement of Science.

Custodian-engineer. A janitor.

1939. Richard C. Hottelet, private communication, March 7. In New York City the janitors of the public schools are called *custodian-engineers*.[1]

Educational-engineer. A pedagogue.

1937. P. W. L. Cox and R. E. Langfitt in *High School Administration and Supervision*. As an *educational-engineer* the [high-school] principal functions in three rôles.[2]

Equipment-engineer.

1941. Private communication from Robert H. Quinn of Brooklyn, July 24. Sign observed on the truck of a firm of office-furniture dealers.

Esthetic-engineer. A painter.

1942. *Life*, Aug. 17. Because his artists [of the Federal Art Project] work to exact specifications Supervisor Seitelson refers to them proudly as *esthetic-engineers*.

Newspaper-engineer. A reorganizer of newspapers.

1940. *Editor and Publisher*, April 20. Mrs. Ackley was formerly associated with Guy T. Viskniski & Associates, *newspaper-engineers*.

Odor-engineer. A perfumery manufacturer.

1940. Ray Giles in the *Reader's Digest*, July, p. 81, (condensed from *Advertising and Selling*). *Odor-engineers* frequently have to caution enthusiastic clients against overdoing the use of scent.

1941. *American Magazine*, Feb. An *odor-engineer's* business is creating sweet-smelling scents to counteract all sorts of unpleasant odors.

Pediatric-engineer. A chiropodist.

1926. *New Yorker* (quoted in *Engineering News-Record*, May 27). Dr. M——, Pediatric Engineer; Certificate of Merit for Relieving Foot Trouble. (Sign in a window in Third avenue, New York.)

Sales-engineer. See the quotation.

1939. Terre Haute *Star*, Jan. 10. John Wesley Coates, nationally known *sales-engineer*, will instruct sales staffs of Terre Haute stores.

Social-engineer. An uplifter.

1937. P. W. L. Cox and R. E. Langfitt in *High School Administration and*

---

1 W. E. Farbstein reported in the *New Yorker*, Sept. 16, 1939, that a Janitors' Institute in session at Mt. Pleasant, Mich., had lately proposed that its fellows be called *engineer-custodians*.

2 Reported in *American Speech*, Oct., 1937, p. 238, by Mary Mielenz.

*Supervision.* The *social-engineer* appreciates that one important function of education is the release of the potential energies in human nature.[1]

1942. Joseph N. Ulman in *Journal of Criminal Law and Criminology*, May-June, p. 8. These are problems for the *social-engineer* rather than for the penologist.

Terminix-engineer. See the quotation.

1937. Louise Pound in *American Speech*, April, p. 163. *Terminix-engineers* sell Bonded Terminix in Richmond, Va. (*Terminix* is an insulation against termites.)

Touchdown-engineer. A football coach.

1939. Title of an article by Fred Russell, *Saturday Evening Post*, Dec. 30.

The Dictionary of Occupational Titles prepared by the Job Analysis and Information Section of the Division of Standards and Research of the Department of Labor [2] lists many curious varieties of engineers. including the *rigging-up-engineer*, the *yarder-engineer* and the *roader-engineer*, but all of them appear to have to do with some form of actual engineering or engine-operation, however lowly, and so their titles, while perhaps rather florid, do not qualify as euphemisms. In this list a *sanitary-engineer* appears, not as a plumber but as " a civil engineer who designs and supervises the construction and operation of sewers, sewage disposal plants, garbage disposal plants, ventilation tunnels, and other sanitary facilities," and such savants as the *termite-engineer*, the *social-engineer* and the *human-engineer* are *non est*. Neither do any of these latter-day wizards appear on the list of engineers employed by the Tennessee Valley Authority, though it has room for *cost-engineers*, *erosion-engineers* and *material engineers*.[3] The alert *Engineering News-Record* reported so long ago as October 2, 1924, that the master-bakers of the United States, in convention assembled at Atlantic City, had resolved to organize a Society of *Baking-engineers*, but if it was ever actually launched it seems to have perished. In the United States Forest Service, according to the *News-Record*, there is a functionary known as a *recreation-engineer*, but what his duties are I do not know. The rat, cockroach and bedbug eradicators of the country have had for years an organization called the American Society of *Exterminating Engineers*. On November 8, 1923 the *News-Record* reported that one of its members followed the

1 Reported in *American Speech*, Oct., 1937, p. 238, by Mary Mielenz.
2 Washington, 1939. I quote the title page of this formidable volume of 1287 pp. In the preface signed by the Hon. Frances Perkins its preparation is ascribed to the Research Division of the Employment Service.
3 *Congressional Record*, March 15, 1938, p. 4556.

sideline of a mortician in Bristol, Pa., and suggested sportively: " That's service for you. Kill 'em and bury 'em for the same fee." But the title of *engineer* seems to be reserved with some plausibility for the head men of the profession: its lowlier representatives are apparently content to call themselves *exterminators*, for their union in New York is the *Exterminators* and Fumigators, Local No. 155. On April 19, 1923, the *News-Record* reported that the private-car chauffeurs of New York had organized the Society of Professional *Automobile Engineers* (not to be confused with the Society of *Automotive Engineers*) and opened a clubhouse, but if that clubhouse still exists it must have a silent telephone, for it is not listed in the Manhattan telephone-book (1944). Perhaps *imagineering*, which appeared in an advertisement of the Aluminum Company of America in November, 1943, should be noted here. It designates the art and mystery of an engineer who serves the customers of the company by thinking up swell ideas for using aluminum.

My invention of *bootician* in 1925 strained and indeed exhausted my onomatological faculties, and it was not for fifteen years that I hatched another neologism of the same high tone. Then I was inspired by the following letter from a lady subscribing herself Georgia Sothern and giving her address as Room 408, 745 Fifth Avenue, New York:

I am writing this letter to you because I have read and admired your book on the American language and believe that semantics can be of some help to me.

It happens that I am a practitioner of the fine art of strip-teasing. Strip-teasing is a formal and rhythmic disrobing of the body in public. In recent years there has been a great deal of uninformed criticism levelled against my profession.

Most of it is without foundation and arises because of the unfortunate word *strip-teasing*, which creates the wrong connotations in the mind of the public.

I feel sure that if you could coin a new and more palatable word to describe this art, the objections to it would vanish and I and my colleagues would have easier going. I hope that the science of semantics can find time to help the verbally underprivileged members of my profession. Thank you.

I say this charming note inspired me, but as a matter of fact, it also filled me with certain doubts, for I have been long familiar, as a practicing journalist, with the flattering wiles and literary style of public relations counsel.[1] But I always answer letters of working-girls po-

---

[1] I learn from How It Happened, Philadelphia *Record*, March 27, 1944, that the counsel in the woodpile was one Maurice Zolotov, described as " Broadway's Boswell and author of that fascinating series of biographi-

litely, however suspicious I may be of their purpose, so I replied to La Sothern as follows on April 5, 1940:

> I need not tell you that I sympathize with you in your affliction, and wish that I could help you. Unfortunately, no really persuasive new name suggests itself. It might be a good idea to relate strip-teasing in some way or other to the associated zoölogical phenomenon of molting. Thus the word *moltician* comes to mind, but it must be rejected because of its likeness to *mortician*.
>
> A resort to the scientific name for molting, which is *ecdysis*, produces both *ecdysist* and *ecdysiast*. Then there are suggestions in the names of some of the creatures which practise molting. The scientific name for the common crab is *Callinectes hastastus*, which produces *callinectian*. Again, there is a family of lizards called the *Geckonidae*, and their name produces *gecko*. Perhaps your advisers may be able to find other suggestions in this same general direction.

I heard nothing further from the lady, but in a little while I learned by articles in the public prints that she (or her press-agent) had decided to adopt *ecdysiast*. It appeared by these articles that two other savants had been consulted — Dr. S. I. Hayakawa, assistant professor of English in the Illinois Institute of Technology and author of " Language in Action," and Stuart Chase, S.B. *cum laude* (Harvard), author of " The Economy of Abundance," " A Honeymoon Experiment," " Your Money's Worth," " The Tyranny of Words," " Idle Money, Idle Men " and other scientific works. Hayakawa, I gathered, gave La Sothern (or her press-agent) to understand that he had never seen a strip-teaser in action and hence had nothing to offer, and Chase, busy with the salvation of humanity on a dozen fronts, made no reply at all, so I won by a sort of forfeit, and within a few weeks *ecdysiast* was on its way.[1] Soon the British United Press correspondent cabled news of its invention to London, and it was discussed gravely in many of the great English organs of opinion, though strip-teasing itself was prohibited in the British Isles,[2] even in Sunday-school entertainments. Meanwhile, La Sothern (or her press-agent) had written to the English Lord Chamberlain, the official censor of stage performances, suggesting that the adoption of *ecdysiast* might perchance open the way for lifting the ban, and in due course the following reply came from his secretary:

cal sketches titled 'Never Whistle in a Dressing-room.' " A portrait of this social-minded literatus is in *Esquire*, Dec., 1944, p. 58.

1 Strip Teasing Alters Name; Same Exposure, by Robert M. Yoder,

Chicago *Daily News*, April 19, 1940.

2 What's In a Name, Manchester *Evening News*, May 25, 1940; Do You Know What an *Ecdysiast* Is?, Birmingham *Evening Dispatch*, May 25, 1940.

I am desired by the Lord Chamberlain to acknowledge the receipt of your letter on the subject of *strip-tease* displays, and to inform you that its contents are noted.[1]

But though Lord Chamberlain's secretary was thus cagey, the moral element among the English took alarm, and on July 25 the London *Reformer* printed the following under the heading, " Rose by Any Other Name — ":

> Since conjurors have often been referred to as *prestidigiteurs* and the classical Greek word *terpsichore* has been revived for dancing, it was inevitable that someone at some time would glorify the " art? " of strip-tease by a high-sounding name. Now novelist [*sic*] H. L. Mencken has coined the name of *ecdysiast*, from the Greek *ekdysis* (literal translation: a getting out; or, as *ecdysis*, a zoölogical term for the act of molting) for the strippers. So much has the term caught on that there has already been established — in America, of course — a Society of *Ecdysiasts*.[2]

The society, which by 1942 had changed its name (perhaps as the result of a change of press-agents) to the Association of *Ecdysiasts*, Parade and Specialty Dancers, played an heroic rôle when bands of wowsers in various parts of the United States launched local campaigns to put down strip-teasing as indecent. In Los Angeles, for example, its members undertook to picket the police commissioners when orders were issued prohibiting their art and mystery in the movie Holy Land. Carrying placards reading " L. A. Censors Unfair to Streamlined *Ecdysiasts* " and " They Got Me Covered & It Ain't Fair," a band of them led by a lovely creature by the name of Miss Marie Wilson stormed a session of the commissioners on October 13, 1942, and made headlines in newspapers from Oregon to Maine.[3] The police commissioners, fearing that the ladies were about to strip in their audience-chamber, took to the woods, leaving them to a functionary named the Hon. H. F. Lorensen. " We're not strip-teasers," they chanted. " We're *ecdysiasts* — something that molts or sheds. *Ecdysiast* comes from the Greek." [4] " Gee! " exclaimed Lorensen, and

1 Mainly About Manhattan, by John Chapman, New York *News*, May 25, 1940.

2 This indignant item went the round of the English press, and even reached the great moral organs of the colonies — for example, the Johannesburg *Sunday Times*, Nov. 24, 1940.

3 Both the Associated Press and the United Press, under date of Oct. 13, sent out sympathetic accounts of this demonstration, and photographs of La Wilson and her associates were disseminated by the Wire Photo and other photographic agencies.

4 Police Board Put to Flight by Irrepressible *Ecdysiasts*, Los Angeles *Times*, Oct. 14, 1942. I am indebted here to Mr. James M. Cain

then departed also, with the commissioner's studio abandoned to the *ecdysiasts*, their press-agent, and forty head of reporters and photographers. Most of the newspaper comment upon this uprising was favorable to the ladies. I introduce a specimen from the Middle West:

Here in America, land of the free, a small and persecuted minority cries out for justice. People talk about rehabilitating the okies and the sharecroppers, but do they worry their heads about the *ecdysiasts*, those hard-working and long-suffering souls? Like other artists, the *ecdysiast* is highly sensitive and proud. Compensation means less to her than the simple joy of work. Yet society refuses to consider her problem. True, she is not "one-third of a nation." She is not ill-fed. She is not ill-housed. But she is certainly ill-clothed. What is the New Deal doing about it? [1]

Rather curiously, the most eminent of all the *ecdysiasts*, Miss Gypsy Rose Lee, refused to adopt the new name. Interviewed for the New York *World-Telegram* by H. Allen Smith,[2] she let go with the following harsh words:

*Ecdysiast*, he calls me! Why the man is an intellectual slob. He has been reading books. Dictionaries. We don't wear feathers and molt them off. . . . What does he know about stripping? [3]

Englishmen are a good deal less ashamed of their trades than Americans, and in consequence there is less exuberance of occupational euphemism among them than in this country. But this is certainly not to say that it is lacking altogether. So long ago as the Seventeenth Century some of the more advanced English dressers of female coiffures were calling themselves *woman-surgeons*,[4] and before the end of that century there were English men's tailors who claimed to be *master-fashioners*. At this moment many of the buyers and sellers of old clothes in London pass as *wardrobe-dealers*, and from time to time

1 *Ecdysiastic* Woe, Youngstown *Vindicator*, Oct. 16, 1942.
2 Gypsy Rose Lee Indignantly Strips Herself of a Definition, May 2, 1940. The substance of the interview was reprinted in Mr. Smith's anthropological work, Low Man on a Totem Pole; Garden City, N. Y., 1941, p. 92.
3 Despite her professed scorn of the intelligentsia, La Lee is an author herself. Her thriller, The G-String Murders, published in England as The Strip-Tease Murders, got friendly notices in both countries. See, for example, the London *News*

*Review*, March 4, 1943. She soon followed it with another, Mother Finds a Body, and on Oct. 21, 1943 her play, The Naked Genius, was presented at the Plymouth Theatre, New York. Also, she contributed some amusing reminiscences of her early days on the stage to the *New Yorker* in 1943. There is a sympathetic account of her in Gypsy Rose Lee, Strip-tease Intellectual, by John Richmond, *American Mercury*, Jan., 1941.
4 The term appears in John Ford's The Lover's Melancholy, II, 1628.

there are proposals that street-sweeps be outfitted with some more delicate name. When this last matter was under debate in 1934 a provincial borough councillor proposed that *highwayman* be adopted, but his council turned him down.[1] In 1944 the rat-catcher employed by the Westminster County Council was actually turned into a *rodent officer*, and simultaneously his pay was raised, in keeping with his new dignity, from £4 17s. to £5 10s. a week.[2] Later in the year it was announced that the charwomen working in the government offices in London had been organized into a union bearing the sonorous title of the Government Minor and Manipulative Grades Association of *Office Cleaners*,[3] and that the Glasgow *dustmen* (American: *garbagemen*) would be known thereafter as the *cleansing personnel*.[4] Meanwhile, the rat-catching department of the Ministry of Food had become the *directorate of infestation control*. The English butchers, fishmongers and fish-and-chips-shop keepers have long panted for more romantic designations. Many of the butchers already call themselves *purveyors*, usually in the form of *purveyors of quality*,[5] and those of Birmingham use *meat-traders*, and have set up a Birmingham *Meat-Traders' Diploma Society* which issues diplomas to its members, and calls its meat cutters *meat-salesmen*,[6] just as American milk-wagon drivers are called *milk-salesmen* and bakers' deliverymen *bread-salesmen*.[7] The fishmongers still vacillate between *fish specialist* and *sea-food caterer*, the latter borrowed from America,[8] but they have a committee at work that will no doubt solve the problem soon or late, and so get rid of what they describe as " an undignified and unpopular " name. Meanwhile, the English used car dealers and other such idealists are also showing signs of unrest, and P. E. Cleator sends

1 Niminy Piminy, *Bystander*, Dec. 18, 1934.
2 Promoted, Liverpool *Echo*, Jan. 31, 1944. I am indebted here to Mr. P. E. Cleator and Mr. Edward L. Bernays.
3 London *Times*, June 7, 1944. I am indebted here to H. W. Seaman.
4 London *Daily Express*, April 29, 1944.
5 Butchers or *Purveyors?*, by S. W. Corley, London *Times*, Aug. 23, 1936.
6 Random Thoughts on Education, by Adelantemnos, *Knife and Steel* (the organ of the society), Dec., 1936, p. 6. This article was an eloquent plea for more vision in the retail meat trade. " It is not my job," said the author, " to educate you; I only wish to stir the smouldering fire of your intellect into a living flame. . . . You may be tempted to describe these words as bovine excreta. I shall not mind."
7 Ada S. Kellogg reported in *American Notes and Queries*, April, 1944, p. 10, that " a transportation company in New Jersey now refers to its drivers and motormen as *salesmen*, and gives this new name official sanction on placards, etc."
8 William Hickey in the London *Daily Express*, Oct. 4, 1943.

me a sworn statement, attested by the finger-prints of the vicar of his parish, that he encountered a *car-clinic* at Wrexham, in North Wales, so long ago as 1937. Finally, from *Punch* comes news that a Cheshire cobbler, disdaining both *shoe-rebuilder* and *shoetrician,* calls himself a *practipedist.*[1]

293. [The English euphemism-of-all-work used to be *lady,* . . . and even today the English newspapers frequently refer to *lady-secretaries, lady-doctors, lady-inspectors, lady-golfers* and *lady-champions.*] This was written in 1936, and during the years that have passed *lady* seems to have gone into something of a decline. But the vocative form hooked to *Lord* and *Sir* naturally survives, and there is no sign of an abandonment of *lady-mayoress.* On May 7, 1937 the New York *Herald Tribune* printed a London dispatch saying that "the retiring-rooms specially erected at Westminster Abbey for Coronation Day will be severally marked as follows: *Peers, Gentlemen, Men,* and *Peeresses, Ladies, Women,*" but this seems to have been a rather unusual reversion to ancient forms. A correspondent informs me that in the signs on the public lavatories of London *ladies* and *women* appear to be varied without rule. " Usage," he says, " does not follow a social distinction: very shady neighborhoods put up *Ladies;* very swanky ones *Women.*" A review of the decay of *lady* in the United States was published by Robert Withington in 1937.[2] The DAE traces *saleslady* to 1870 and *forelady* to 1889, and marks both Americanisms. They are now virtually obsolete, but now and then a new congener appears, *e.g., flag-lady,* which began to be used by the Union Pacific Railroad in 1944 to designate female watchers at grade-crossings.[3] But the women at work in the shipyards and other war plants were seldom if ever called *ladies,* and the Pennsylvania Railroad, when it put female trainmen to work in 1943, marked their caps, not *train-lady* or even *train-woman,* but simply *trainman.* The English still cling to the suffix *-ess,* and use it much oftener than Americans. Such of these common forms as *mayoress* or *managress*[4] would strike most Americans as very odd, and so would *conductress* (of a street-

---

1 Word-Skirmish, April 7, 1937, p. 370.
2 *Lady, Woman* and *Person, American Speech,* April, 1937, pp. 117-21. Withington returned to the subject in *Woman — Lady, American Speech,* Oct., 1937, p. 235. But the *Ladies' Home Journal,* founded in 1883, survives and flourishes.
3 I am indebted here to Mr. Vernon L. Hoyt of Columbus, Neb. Female heads of shop committees in the International *Ladies* Garment Workers Union are called *chairladies.*
4 London *Telegraph and Post,* May 20, 1938.

car).[1] But the older forms in -*ess* are still alive in the United States, e.g., *deaconess, patroness, actress, poetess* and *songstress*, and now and then a novelty appears, as when a contributor to the Chicago *Tribune*, in 1943, described Mrs. Roosevelt as " our *commandress-in-chief*." [2] During the era of elegance straddling the Civil War the termination was considered to be rather swagger, and some grotesque examples came into use. In a survey published in 1930 Mamie Meredith assembled *doctress, lecturess, nabobess, rebeless, traderess, astronomess, editress* and *mulatress*: the comic writers of the time contributed *championess, Mormoness* and *prestidigitateuress*.[3] In 1865 *Godey's Lady's Book* printed a resounding plea for -*ess*,[4] based upon the authority of the learned Archbishop Richard Chenevix Trench of Dublin, who had discovered some affecting specimens in the Wycliffe Bible.[5] Said the fair authoress:

> It is not an innovation, inventing a new way of writing or speech, when we desire to see these terminations revived whenever the two sexes are, to any considerable extent, employed in the same pursuit. For instance, in teaching; as our system of public schools now recognizes young women as its most efficient agents, while yet men are employed, both sexes often in the same school. If the title *teacher* were confined to men and *teacheress* to the women (as the titles *actor* and *actress* are to the sexes) the language would be rendered more direct and definite, and this adds dignity to speech. We have sought out and arranged a catalogue of words ending in *ess* now in use in our dictionaries as feminine terminations. We have introduced a few never before used, because the professions, or offices, were never, till within this century, held or exercised by women. For instance, *professoress;* no lady in England or America has held this important office. But in Vassar College [6] ladies are eligible to this dignity. We hope they will not usurp the man's title; but, following the analogies of our language, assume their own womanly style — *professoress*.

1 And How! Liverpool *Echo*, Dec. 10, 1942. I am indebted here to Mr. P. E. Cleator.
2 Editorial page, Dec. 3.
3 *Doctresses, Authoresses* and *Others, American Speech*, Aug., 1930, pp. 476–81. See also The Suffix -*ess*, by Edwin B. Dike, *Journal of English and Germanic Philology*, Jan., 1937, pp. 29–34.
4 Diminutions of the English Language, May, 1865, p. 464. I am indebted for this to Dr. Joseph M. Carrière of the University of Virginia.
5 English Past and Present; London, 1855. They included *teacheress, singeress, servantess, neighboress* and *sinneress*. He added *pedleress, victoress, ministress, flatteress, discipless, auditress, cateress, detractress, huckstress, tutoress* and *farmeress* from Chaucer, Spenser, Shakespeare, Milton, Addison and lesser authors.
6 Vassar had been opened in 1861 as Vassar Female Seminary, but its designation was changed to Vassar College in 1867. Its founder was Matthew Vassar, a rich and eminent brewer of Poughkeepsie.

### Titles of Professions [1]

| | | | |
|---|---|---|---|
| actor | actress | professor | professoress * |
| adulterer | adulteress [2] | scholar | scholaress |
| arbiter | arbitress | sculptor | sculptress * |
| author | authoress | songster | songstress |
| doctor | doctress | shepherd | shepherdess |
| hunter | huntress | sorcerer | sorceress |
| instructor | instructress | steward | stewardess |
| janitor | janitress | tailor | tailoress |
| monitor | monitress | teacher | teacheress |
| painter | paintress * | traitor | traitress |
| postmaster | postmistress | tutor | governess |
| porter | portress | waiter | waitress |
| preceptor | preceptress | | |

### Titles of Office, Rank, Respect

| | | | |
|---|---|---|---|
| abbot | abbess | inheritor | inheritress |
| ambassador | ambassadress | Jew | Jewess |
| American | Americaness * | marquis | marchioness |
| ancestor | ancestress | mayor | mayoress |
| baron | baroness | Mister, or Mr. | Mistress, or Mrs. |
| benefactor | benefactress | patron | patroness |
| Briton | Britoness | protector | protectress |
| canon | canoness | president | presidentess * |
| chieftain | chieftainess | priest | priestess |
| deacon | deaconess | prince | princess |
| director | directress | prior | prioress |
| druid | druidess | prophet | prophetess |
| earl | countess | python | pythoness |
| enchanter | enchantress | seer | seeress |
| emperor | empress | sultan | sultaness |
| giant | giantess | viscount | viscountess |
| god (heathen) | goddess | | |

Unhappily, some of the lady's novelties were really not new, though she may have thought them up on her own. The NED traces *sculptress*, in English use, to 1662, and the DAE traces *presidentess*, in English use, to 1782, and, in American use, to 1819. James Fenimore Cooper used *Americaness* in his " Home as Found," 1838. But it never caught on, and neither did *paintress, professoress, scholaress* or *teacheress*.

In AL4, p. 293, I listed a number of familiar substitutes for the harsh *second-hand, e.g., used, rebuilt, reconditioned* and *repossessed*.

---

1 The authoress notes that those marked * are her own inventions.
2 The judicious will note that this term is listed under Titles of Professions, not under Titles of Office, Rank, Respect.

All of them are in the vocabulary of dealers in second-hand automobiles, and one of the latest that I have encountered comes from the same source. It is *experienced*, which was reported in use in Los Angeles, in the form of *experienced tires*, in 1942. In New York a second-hand store is now often called a *buy-and-sell shop*. There is also a continuous flow of euphemisms for *damaged* or *shop-worn*, e.g., *seconds, slightly-seconds, slightly hurt,*[1] *store-used*, and *sub-standard*. The last had got to England by 1938.[2] The department-stores run heavily to like euphemisms, e.g., *simulated* for artificial pearls, and many more have been launched by advertisement writers, e.g., *halitosis*[3] and *B.O.* In 1942 the flood of *ersatz* articles that came in with rationing and priorities brought with it a demand for a word for them, less offensive to the refined mind than *substitute*. In the April, 1943 issue of the *Rotarian*, an English contributor suggested *superstute* as a name " to designate materials, originally substitutes, which later supplement and supplant the original." At about the same time *syntute* was offered by a Missouri neologist " as a word to embody the ideas of *synthetic* and *substitute*, without their connotations of makeshift," and *supplantitude* was proposed by a North Carolinian.[4] Meanwhile, materials used as substitutes for tin in the canning industry were being called *alternates*.[5] The appearance of horse-meat for human consumption in 1943 started a search for euphemisms to designate it. Various sportive readers of *Life*, engaging in this aesthetic quest, suggested *filly, stallion, cheval* and *centaur*. One submitted a list of names for dishes designed to " tempt the most ticklish palates," including *braised fetlocks* and *fillet of Pegasus*.[6] But sometimes there is a transient revulsion against euphemism, and a bold advertiser resolves to tell the truth. Thus, from a correspondent in California comes a clipping of an advertisement of a Carmel restaurant, announcing *pseudo-mint-juleps*, and in Baltimore there is a department-store that has more than once advertised *fake pearls*.

The uplifters in their almost innumerable incarnations are naturally

---

1 Used by a book-store in Fifth avenue, New York.
2 Advertisement of Selfridge's (American-owned) in the London *Daily Express*, March 13, 1938. It was applied to women's hose.
3 I am told by H. W. Seaman that *oral offense* has been used instead of *halitosis* in England.

4 In England *art-silk* is used to designate artificial silk, and *effects* to designate an imitation, as in *tweed effects*.
5 I am indebted here to Substitutes for Substitute, by M. J. M., *American Speech*, Oct., 1943, p. 207.
6 Names for Horse-Meat, *Life*, Aug. 2, 1943.

heavy users of ameliorative and disarming words, and some of their more juicy inventions are listed in AL4, pp. 292 and 293. One of the best of recent coinage is *doorkey children*, a humane designation for the youngsters who are turned loose on the city streets at night to shift for themselves.[1] In the lunatic asylums (now *state hospitals*), a guard is an *attendant*, a violent patient is *assaultive*, and one whose aberration is not all-out is *maladjusted*.[2] In the Federal prisons a guard is a *custodial officer*,[3] among social workers *case work* has become *personal service*,[4] and every surviving orphan asylum has become an *infant home* or something equally mellifluous. In many American cities what used to be the office of the overseers of the poor is now the *community welfare department*. The English, in this field of gilding the unpleasant facts of life, yield nothing to Americans. Their reform-schools for wayward boys, which had been *Borstal institutions* [5] since 1902, are now called *approved schools* [6] and there is talk of a further change to *hostels*.[7] *Slum* has almost gone out of use in England: the reigning term is *depressed area*, obviously suggested by *depressed classes*, a euphemism long in use to designate the members of the lowest caste in India. The English prisons have also undergone a cleaning up of terminology, and the old-time *warder* is now a *prison officer*.[8] Simultaneously, there has been a relaxation in prison discipline, once extremely harsh, and even the incorrigible convicts at Dartmoor, the Alcatraz of England, are now entertained at lectures and concerts, have the use of a library, go to night-school, no longer wear uniforms marked with broad arrows (the English equivalent of the former American stripes, now also abolished), are permitted to shave with safety-razors, and have a weekly paper to tell them what

1 Reported by Max Lerner, *PM*, April 2, 1943, p. 2. I am indebted here to *American Notes and Queries*, April, 1943, p. 7.
2 Straight Talk About Sick Minds, by Edith M. Stern, *Hygeia*, March, 1944, p. 195.
3 I am indebted here to Mr. W. T. Hammack, assistant director of the Bureau of Prisons, Department of Justice. He says, May 12, 1937: " Very few officers in the *custodial service* bear arms. They are intended as leaders for groups of men and instructors in various activities undertaken for the utilization of prison labor."
4 Counselling as Social Case Work, by Gordon Hamilton, *Social Service Review*, June, 1943.
5 From the name of the first such establishment, at Borstal, a village near Rochester in Kent.
6 Basil L. Q. Henriques said in The Word *Borstal*, London *Times*, Dec. 7, 1938, that " music-hall jokes about the old school tie " had brought the name into " general disrepute."
7 Young Offenders: *Hostels* Instead of *Approved* Schools, *News of the World* (London), July 17, 1938.
8 Jottings by a Man About Town, Dublin *Evening Mail*, July 22, 1935.

is going on outside.[1] I add a couple of other characteristic English euphemisms and pass on. In 1936 the British United Press, in a dispatch to colonial newspapers describing the booing of Cabinet ministers in Downing Street, called it *counter-cheering*,[2] and in 1937 the London *Telegraph* described the goods found upon a smuggler as *uncustomed*.

The American *movie-cathedral* must not be forgotten, though the DAE ignores it, as it does, in fact, *movie*. The first *movie-cathedral* to bedazzle and enchant the fans was the Paramount Theatre in New York. Unhappily, the newspaper wits began to poke fun at it by writing about *movie-mosques, movie-synagogues* and *movie-filling-stations*, and so it did not prosper. But so late as 1941 a *news-cathedral* was opened in Poughkeepsie, N. Y.,[3] and in Pittsburgh the huge sky-scraper used to house the multitudinous departments of the town university is called the *Cathedral of Learning*. For many years there has been a quiet effort to find a substitute for *mother-in-law*, which has been cursed with unpleasant connotations by the cheaper humor of the press and stage, and also, perhaps, by personal experience. Gene Howe, editor of the Amarillo (Texas) *News-Globe*, a son of the cynical E. W. Howe, but himself a man of heart, began a magnificent effort to rehabilitate and glorify the lady in 1930 or thereabout, but did not invent a new and softer name for her. In 1942, however, the Mother-in-Law Association that flowed from his campaign adopted *kin-mother*, which had been proposed by Mrs. E. M. Sullivan. Other suggestions were *our-ma, lawma, assistant mother, ersatz-mother*, and *motherette*, but *kin-mother* won.[4]

Substitutes for *death* and *to die*, both euphemistic and facetious, have been numerous in America since the earliest days. Many of the latter class are heritages from England, *e.g., to croak, to kick the bucket* and *to peg out*, but others are of American origin, *e.g., to pass in one's checks, to go under* (traced by the DAE to 1848), and the short form *to kick*. *To go West* may be American also, though the DAE does not list it and it was used by the British soldiers in World War I. The same may be said with more certainty of *to blow*

1 Dartmoor's 600 Empty Cells to be Filled Up, *News of the World*, April 26, 1936.

2 Dec. 6, 1936. This was at the time the Cabinet was considering a plan to force King Edward to abdicate, and public opinion was with His Majesty.

3 Beautiful Home of Poughkeepsie Newspapers to be *News-Cathedral, Editor and Publisher*, July 12, 1941. The newspapers were the Poughkeepsie *Evening Star-Enterprise* and *Morning Eagle-News* and the *Hudson Valley Sunday Courier*.

4 In Other Words, by W. E. Farbstein, *New Yorker*, Aug. 8, 1942.

*off, to fade out, to kick off, to bite the dust, to fan out, to flunk out, to fold, to get the ax, to hop off, to go off the deep end, to lose the decision, to pass out, to pass out of the picture, to poop out, to pop off, to shove off, to shuffle off, to shoot the works* and *to slough off*.[1] Similarly, for *death* there are *the blow-off, the one-way ticket, the wind-up, the fade-out, the finish, the last call* and *the pay-off,* and for *dead, checked out, done for, finished, gone under, down and out* and *washed up.* In the days of Prohibition the racketeers invented (or had invented for them by newspaper reporters) a number of picturesque terms for *to kill,* e.g., *to take for a ride, to put on the spot, to put the finger on, to bump off, to wipe out* and *to rub out,* and at other times ordinary criminals have launched synonyms for *to be executed,* e.g., *to fry, to take a hot squat* and *to walk the last mile* (electrocution), *to be topped* (hanging), and *to be gassed* (lethal gas). There are also many more decorous terms in the field of mortality, and Dr. Louise Pound has made a study of them in " American Euphemisms for *Dying, Death* and *Burial.*" [2] The following elegant specimens are seldom encountered of late in city newspapers, but the country weeklies still use them:

For *dead: breathed his last, gathered to his fathers, laid down his burdens, gone to rest, called home, sleeping the long sleep, passed to his reward, gone ahead, gone to his reward* (or *account*).
For *buried: laid to rest, consigned to earth, resting in peace, gone to join his fathers.*
For *grave: narrow home, long home.*
For *death: the Grim Reaper, the Destroying Angel, the Pale Horseman.*

Along with euphemisms go terms of opprobrium, of which the American language boasts a large stock, chiefly directed at aliens. The English have fewer strangers within their gates, and hence their native armanentarium is smaller, and not a few of the achthronyms [3] they use come from the United States. But there has also been some traffic in the other direction, *e.g., frog* for a Frenchman. It was borrowed by the American troops in World War I, and subsequently got into wide circulation at home, but it had been in sporadic use before.

1 Berrey and Van den Bark print a long list in The American Thesaurus of Slang, pp. 117 and 118, but do not attempt to distinguish between American and English phrases.
2 *American Speech,* Oct., 1936, pp. 195–202. Some Western terms are in Cowboy Euphemisms for *Dying,* by Mamie J. Meredith, the same, Oct., 1942, p. 213.
3 I lift this word from E. E. Ericson, who used it in the title of an article, *Acthronyms;* Derisive Names for Various Peoples, in *Words,* Oct., 1939.

Its history in its present sense in England, according to Partridge, goes back only to *c.* 1870. In the Seventeenth Century it was used to designate a Dutchman (sometimes in the variant form of *froglander*), and also a Jesuit. At some time before 1870 a Frenchman came to be called a *frog-eater* in England [1] — the NED's first example is dated 1863 —, and in the era of the Franco-Prussian War this was shortened to *frog*. It has been suggested by various etymologists that *frog* embodies a reference to the formerly quaggy state of the streets of Paris and also to the presence of toads on the coat-of-arms of the city, but it seems to be much more reasonable to believe that the eating of frogs by the French, a custom regarded with loathing by the English, is at the bottom of it, as *frog-eater* indicates. *Frog* has a derivative in *froggy*, which is used by the lower classes of Londoners to designate any man with a French-sounding name. They also use *frog* in the sense of policeman, but Partridge says that this use is so low as to verge upon thieves' cant. *Froggy* is in common use in the British Army to designate a French soldier. I am informed by Mr. Edgar Gahan, of Westmount, Quebec, that *frog* is not applied in Canada to a French-Canadian. The common name for him is *Joe*, but it is not used often. Mr. Gahan says that in Quebec a drink made by dumping some oysters into a glass of beer is called a *frog*. In general the Canadians use American terms, in this as in other fields. In the days of the California gold rush the few Frenchmen who turned up were called *parleyvoos* (*parlez vous*) or *keskydees* (*qu'est-ce qu'il dit?*) by the 49ers.[2] Both terms were revived by the American and British troops during World War I. Neither is American. The NED traces *parleyvoo* in English use to 1815, and in the sense of the French language to 1754. *Frencher* was used by Cooper in " The Last of the Mohicans " in 1826, but seems to have passed out. The DAE traces *cajan* (from *Acadian*), the common term in Louisiana for a rustic of French descent, to 1880, but it is undoubtedly older. The word carries a deroga-

---

1 It is possible that this was a loan from the German. The German traveler, Charles Sealsfield (Karl Postl), in Der Virey und die Aristokraten, oder Mexico in 1812, published in 1834, used *froschesser*. It was his habit to quote Americanisms in their original form, but this time he used German. I therefore surmise that he may have brought the term in in-stead of picking it up. I am indebted here to Charles Sealsfield's Americanisms, II, by John T. Krumpelmann, *American Speech*, April, 1941, p. 110.

2 Three Years in California, by J. D. Borthwick; 1857, p. 252. I take this from California Gold-Rush English, by Marian Hamilton, *American Speech*, Aug., 1932, p. 424.

tory significance, and is never applied to the high-toned French of New Orleans, who are *creoles*. The common American assumption that *creole* connotes Negro blood is bitterly resented. In 1926 Lyle Saxon published the following disquisition upon the term:

> The *creole* is one who is born away from his country — whatever that country may be. The New Orleans *creole* is our finest product. The women are lovely. The men are brave. They have charming manners. They are exclusive. They are clannish. They have their own language, their own society, their own customs. They still speak a pure French. The reason the word *creole* has been so often misunderstood is that their slaves spoke a *creole* dialect, bearing about the same relation to pure French as our Southern Negro talk does to English purely spoken. Then, of course, there was the Acadian French, or *cajan* French, as spoken in the outlying districts of Louisiana. And *gumbo* French — that simply means French incorrectly spoken.[1]

The DAE says that *creole* is a French borrowing from the Spanish *criollo*. This has been challenged by E. C. Hills, who prefers a Portuguese origin. " In the Spanish and Portuguese colonies," he says, " it referred to any person, animal or plant of European stock that was born or grown in any part of the Americas." [2]

From the first appearance of syphilis in England it was labelled *French* — first, the *French pox* (1503), then the *French marbles* (1592),[3] and then the *French disease* (1598), which remained in common English use for more than two centuries. Various sportive synonyms arose from time to time, all of them now forgotten, *e.g.*, the *French mole* (1607), the *French measles* (1612), the *French cannibal* (1614), the *French goods* (1678). The adjective *French-sick* survived from 1598 to the end of the Eighteenth Century.[4] When, in 1776 or thereabout, a certain contraband device for the limitation of offspring was invented, the English gave it the name of *French letter*, and the French retaliated by calling it a *capote anglaise*. This last was changed to *capote allemande* during World War I, as a gesture in furtherance of the entente cordiale, but the English did not reciprocate, and *capote anglaise* was restored. To them, any-

---

1 New Orleans *Times-Picayune*, Feb. 11, 1926, quoted in *Creole and Cajan*, by William A. Read, *American Speech*, June, 1926, p. 483.
2 *Creole and West Indies, American Speech*, March, 1927, pp. 293–94.
3 A corruption of the archaic French *morbilles*, pox.

4 The use of *French* was not confined, of course, to the English. Sebastian Brant in De Scorra Pestilenta, (1496) called syphilis *mala de Franzos*, and other writers of the time called it *morbus Gallicas*.

thing French is likely to be suspicious, and their language embalms the fact in many common words and phrases, *e.g., French leave.* The simple word *French,* to them as to Americans, connotes sexual perversion. The Germans, Spanish and Italians also have forms of *French leave.* Rather curiously, the French and German belabor one another with opprobrious phrases rather sparingly, despite their long enmity. In Prussia lice are called *Franzosen,* but in other parts of Germany they are commonly called *Schwaben* (Swabians) — and cockroaches are *Preussen* (Prussians). The French call a louse an *espagnol* (Spaniard) and a flea an *espagnole*: the difference in gender I do not attempt to account for.[1] The chief butts of the French seem to be the Spaniards, the Swiss and the Greeks; of the Spaniards, the Moors; of the Danes and Norwegians, the Swedes; and of the Germans, the Poles.

The origin of *gu-gu* for a Filipino is mysterious, but it may have some analogy to that of *greaser* for Mexico, to be discussed presently. *Goo,* in the vulgar speech, means anything of a syrupy or oleaginous nature, and *goo-goo* or *gugu* is a common derivative, as is *gook.* *Gook* is also applied to a Filipino, and sometimes *gook* or *gugu* is applied to any native of the Pacific Islands, but the more usual term in the latter case is *kanaka,* a loan from the Hawaiian signifying simply man, or, in a more general sense, the people.[2] At the turn of the century, when the Filipinos were in armed revolt against their first salvation by the United States, *Filipino* came into use in the Boston area to signify an opponent of a regularly-nominated candidate for office.[3] The older term *mugwump* was retained to designate a *Filipino* of high tone, and *Filipino* meant especially a *mugwump* of low tone. During World War II Col. Carlos P. Romulo, aide to General Douglas MacArthur, used *Filamericans* to designate his people, but the term apparently made no headway.[4]

*Squarehead* is applied, not only to Germans, but also to Scandinavians. A correspondent calls my attention to the fact that it is used

1 I am indebted here to Call'ng Names in Any Language, by Joachim Joesten, *American Mercury,* Dec., 1935, pp. 483–87.

2 The Hawaiian Language, by Henry P. Judd; Honolulu, 1940, p. 99. Judd says that it is also used by the Hawaiians as an adjective, in the sense of manly, strong, stable.

3 Alexander F. Chamberlain, *Journal of American Folk-Lore,* Oct.-Dec., 1902, p. 293.

4 A Protest From the Philippines, by M. J. M., *American Speech,* April, 1944, p. 148.

in Germany to designate a Holsteiner. In Gustav Frennsen's novel, "Jörn Uhl,"[1] Prussian Army officers are made to speak of recruits from Schleswig-Holstein as *die vierkantigen* [four-cornered] *Holsteiner*. Berrey and Van den Bark hint that it was originally applied to Scandinavians only, and say that it has been transferred to Germans "since the World War [I]." The other opprobrious names for a German that they list include *boche, dutchie, heinie, hun, kraut, limberger, sauerkraut* and *sausage*. In June, 1861, *Harper's Magazine* printed a series of caricatures of various American types of the time under the heading of "Modern Idolatry." The German immigrant was depicted as wearing a beer-barrel as a coat, smoking a porcelain pipe with a long stem, and carrying a long sausage and a sheet of music under his arm. Henry Bradshaw Fearon said in his "Sketches of America," 1819, that General Joseph Heister, when a candidate for Governor of Pennsylvania, was called *Old Sauerkraut* by supporters and opponents alike. In those days Germans were also called *cabbageheads*, but that term was apparently likewise applied to the Dutch.[2]

How the early German immigrants acquired the name of *Dutch* is well known: it was their use of *Deutsch* (pronounced *Deitsch*) to designate themselves that misled the English-speaking Americans. The DAE's first example of *Pennsylvania Dutch* is dated 1868, but the term must be very much older. The use of *Dutch* in the sense of Germans in general is traced to 1742. In the California of gold-rush days it was applied indiscriminately to Germans, Hollanders and Scandinavians.[3] In Missouri, during the Civil War, all Northern sympathizers were called *Dutch*, no doubt because many of them were Germans. Three familiar American phrases, *to beat the Dutch, that's all Dutch to me*, and *in Dutch*, may allude to the actual Dutch of New York, but it seems more likely that they allude to the Germans. The first is traced by the DAE to 1775, the second to 1899, and the third to 1920. *To talk like a Dutch uncle* is also probably American, and so is *Dutch supper*. Both apparently allude to Germans, not Dutchmen. In Ontario, where there has been some immigration of Pennsylvania Germans, they are called *hickories*.[4] The use of *Hessian*

1 Berlin, 1901.
2 On this point I am not sure. See *Harper's Magazine*, Jan., 1854, p. 269, col. 2.
3 California Gold-Rush English, by

Marian Hamilton, *American Speech*, Aug., 1932, p. 424.
4 Says W. J. Wintemberg in the *Journal of American Folk-Lore*, Vol. XVI, 1903, p. 128: "I am informed

in Indiana folk-speech to designate " anyone who is rough, uncouth, boorish, or, more particularly, an individual whose moral character is of the lowest," was noted in *American Speech* in 1943 by Paul G. Brewster,[1] and no doubt it is to be found elsewhere. It apparently came into American English in Revolutionary times, but Brewster shows that it is also in use on the Isle of Man and in Ireland. It was used by the Confederates during the Civil War as a term of opprobrium for Northerners, and by 1877, according to Bartlett, had gained some currency as a designation for " a hireling, a mercenary politician, a fighter for pay." *Hessian* is used in England to designate what we call burlap. *Prushun*, apparently from *Prussian*, is the American hobo's term for a boy who travels with an older tramp and is usually a homosexual.

The old naval rivalry between England and Holland, at its peak in the Seventeenth Century, brought in a great many compounds in which *Dutch* appeared as a derisory adjective. The NED shows that in 1608 a *Dutch widow* meant a prostitute, and that in 1678 a *Dutch bargain* meant one made in drink. Not a few of the more familiar terms in Dutch originated in America, and had their genesis in hostility between the English and the Dutch in early New York, or between the Germans (almost always called *Dutch*) and the other stocks in Pennsylvania and elsewhere. *Dutch courage*, meaning a false courage produced by alcohol, is probably an Americanism (though the DAE does not so mark it), for the earliest known American example of its use, dated 1812, precedes the earliest English example by fourteen years. *To beat the Dutch* may also be American, for the NED's first example, dated 1775, is from an American song of the Revolution. *Dutch route*, signifying suicide, is almost certainly American, though the DAE does not list it. So, I suspect, is *Dutch auction*, signifying one beginning with a high bid and then working downward, for though it is not recorded in America earlier than in England, *Dutch auctioneer* is. Other opprobrious terms based on *Dutch*, either English or American, are *Dutch concert*, meaning one full of discord; *Dutch feast*, at which the host gets drunk before his guests; *Dutch*

---

that the name was first applied in Pennsylvania, and that it owes its origin to the fact that most of the Pennsylvania Dutch voted for Andrew Jackson (*Old Hickory*) for President. . . . It is in general use as a derisive epithet." Mr. Wintemberg adds that it appeared, in 1903, to be passing out.

1 A Note on the Epithet *Hessian*, Feb., p. 72.

*drink*, one that empties the pot at a gulp; *Dutch treat* (unquestionably an Americanism), one requiring each drinker to pay for himself; *Dutch uncle*, a brutally frank adviser (I'll talk to you like a *Dutch uncle*); *Dutch wife*, a bolster; *Dutch reckoning*, a bill not itemized;[1] *Dutch comfort*, meaning the kind that does not comfort;[2] *Dutch consolation*, meaning the same; *to talk Dutch* (or *double-Dutch*), to speak gibberish; *to do a Dutch*, to take to one's heels; *Dutch nightingale*, a frog; *Dutch barn*, one without side-walls; *Dutch defense*, no defense at all; and *in Dutch*, in disfavor. In truth, there are so many such terms that Farmer and Henley, in "Slang and Its Analogues," define *Dutch* itself as "an epithet of inferiority." It is significant that it serves no such purpose in any other language. The Netherlands government, in 1934, tried to pull the teeth of the English pejoratives by ordering all its officials to drop *Dutch* and use *Netherlands* instead,[3] but apparently the device did not succeed. In the 80s, as Theodore Roosevelt once recorded in a magazine article,[4] "anything foreign and un-English" was called *Dutch*. "It was in this sense," he said, "that a West Virginian member of the last Congress used the term when, in speaking in favor of a tariff on works of art, he told of the reluctance with which he saw the productions of native artists exposed to competition 'with *Dutch* daubs from Italy.'"

*Hunk* and *hunkie* (or *hunky* or *hunkey*), I suppose, are properly applicable to Hungarians only, but they have been extended in meaning to include all Europeans coming from the region east of the German lands and west of Russia, save only the Greeks. In Canada, so I am informed by a correspondent,[5] *hunkie* is used to designate Poles, Ukrainians and miscellaneous Slavs, maybe because actual Hungarians are scarce. Berrey and Van den Bark report extensions, in the United States, signifying a country bumpkin, a numskull, a common laborer, and a foreign-born miner of any nationality. There are also other meanings of *hunky*, but they derive from the American *hunky-dory*, signifying all right, safe, first-rate. It is possible that *bohunk* (sometimes abbreviated to *boho* or *bo*) is a blend of *Bohemian* and

1 "As brought," says Grose, "at sponging or bawdy houses."
2 Grose, in his third edition, 1785, illustrates this term with "Thank God it is no worse."
3 The Dutch Government *Beats the Dutch*, by J. F. Bense, *English Studies* (Amsterdam), Dec., 1934, pp. 215 and 216.
4 Phases of State Legislation, *Century Magazine*, April, 1885, p. 827.
5 Mr. B. G. Kayfetz of West Toronto.

*Hungarian*, and may thus be applied with plausibility to both races. In 1938 a writer in *American Speech* [1] recorded it in use to designate any unskilled laborer, "more specifically a Bohemian, Magyar, Slovak or Croatian." In 1926 Helen L. Moore reported that it was used in the mining-camps of the Northwest for any foreign miner save a Cornishman, who was called *Cousin Jack*.[2] In 1937 a book reviewer in the Manchester *Guardian Weekly* [3] made a characteristically English error by extending it to a Jew, the hero of the American book of sketches, "Hyman Kaplan." In 1937 one Anak Singapura, of Singapore, writing in the *Straits Times* of Penang, made the even more egregious blunder of using it to designate a German.[4] In regions where Czech immigrants are numerous *cheskey* is frequently heard. Monsignor Dudek says that it is "an attempted transliteration of the Bohemian adjective *český* (Czech)." [5] He adds: "This spelling, in view of the Czech value of *ch*, is rather inconsistent. If the word ever gets into the written American language I would suggest *czesky*." *Bootchkey* is also sometimes applied to a *Czech*. It comes from the Czech word *počkej*, meaning wait, hold, which is often used by Czech boys in playing games.

*Mick, harp* and *Turk* are listed in AL4, p. 295, as achthronyms for Irishman. To these *flannel-mouth, shamrock, spud* and *terrier* may be added, and *biddy* for an Irishwoman, though they are no longer in wide use. The DAE omits all save *biddy*, which it traces to 1858, though it lists *flannel-mouth* as the name of various fishes, and *spud* in two senses, neither relating to Irishmen. *Flannel-mouth*, in England, designates any well-spoken person, and *spud* means not only a potato but also a baby's hand. A discussion of *Mick, harp* and *Turk*, by W. A. McLaughlin, was printed in *Dialect Notes* in 1914.[6] Of the latter two the author said:

1 Oct., p. 236.
2 The Lingo of the Mining Camp, Nov., 1926, p. 88.
3 Dec. 3.
4 Informed of his error, he apologized in the *Times* on May 8. "On the authority of Mencken's 'American Language,'" he said, "a reader assures me that the slang expression for a German in the United States is *squarehead* or *dutchman*, not (as I said) *bohunk*, which euphonious name is applied to Hungarians and usually shortened to *hunky*. Fortunately, there is no *hunky* community in Singapore, so I need say no more than express the hope that, as between the local *limeys* and *squareheads*, my mistake has caused no ill-feeling."
5 Czech Influence Upon the American Vocabulary, by J. B. Dudek, *Czecho-Slovak Student Life* (Lisle, Ill.), June, 1928, p. 16.
6 Some Current Substitutes For *Irish*, Vol. IV, Part II, pp. 146–48.

The use of *harp* is not unreasonable when we recall that this instrument appears on the Irish standard as its one great feature. *Turk* is a trifle harder to explain. Though *wild* may appear synonymous with *terrible*, it would take more than that to establish the identity of the expressions, *the wild Irish*[1] and *the terrible Turk*. It seems more than likely that all attempts to connect the word with *Turk*, a native of Turkey, must be abandoned. May not *Turk*, Irish, be simply the Gaelic word *torc* in disguise? The pejorative *pig* has been long in many tongues the supreme but inadequate expression of absolute disgust, anger and disdain, and *torc* signifies, among other things, boar, pig.[2] Its Welsh equivalent, *twrch*, is equally depreciatory.[3]

May it not be that this word, often in the mouth of the Irish-speaking person, came to be used by his English-speaking neighbors, at first with some notion of its original force and with certain knowledge that the speaker of Irish would grasp the meaning as he himself had? Later, addressed, perhaps, by the English-speaking Irish to the Gaelic-speaking members of the community, may it not have come to be looked upon as a mere tag meaning simply Irish, the more restricted became the use of Gaelic? In any case its use today, without malice, with no touch of contempt as a mere substitute for *Irish*, is attested by the following sentence from the speech of an Irish candidate for office addressing a meeting of Irish and Italian voters: "You Italians have the votes, but it takes us *Turks* to run the government."

*Turk* is used among Roman Catholic priests in the United States to designate a colleague of Irish birth: it is assumed that every such immigrant has a special talent for ecclesiastical politics, and hence gets on in the church. *Irish* has been an element in many English compounds, chiefly of a derogatory or satirical significance. *Irish-evidence*, perjury, and *Irish-apricots*, potatoes, and *Irish-legs*, thick ones, were listed by Grose in the first edition of his "Classical Dictionary of the Vulgar Tongue," 1785, and *Irish-beauty*, a woman with two black eyes, was added in his third edition of 1796. The NED traces *Irish-diamond*, a rock crystal, to 1796; *Irish-blunder*, defined by Swift as "to take the noise of brass for thunder," to 1725; and *Irish-bull* to 1802. The DAE adds *Irish-dividend*, an assessment on stock, 1881; *Irish spoon*, a spade, 1862, and *Irish-pennant*, a loose end of rope, 1840. Berrey and Van den Bark add many others, *e.g.*, *Irish-apple*, a potato; *Irish-cherry*, a carrot; *Irish-clubhouse*, a police sta-

---

1 The NED traces *wild Irish* to 1399.
2 In A Pronouncing Gaelic-English Dictionary, by Neil MacAlphine; Glasgow, 1942, it is defined as "a castrated boar."
3 To this McLaughlin appended the following note: "Professor George L. Hamilton of Cornell suggests that *torc*, originally meaning boar, may have been at first specifically applied to a coarse, brutal fellow, for he feels that there is a great difference between calling a person a *pig* and calling him a *boar*. However, Professor C. P. Wagner calls my attention to the French-Canadian use of *verrat*, boar, with no other significance than that implied in *cochon*."

tion; *Irish confetti*, bricks; *Irish-fan*, a shovel; *Irish-turkey*, corned beef; *Irish-nightingale*, a bullfrog; *Irish-promotion*, a demotion, and *Irishman's dinner*, a fast. In the United States, in the days of the great Irish immigration, the designation of almost anything unpleasant was hung with the adjective, and it was converted into a noun to signify quick temper. A wheelbarrow was an *Irish chariot* or *buggy*, and there was a stock witticism to the effect that it was the greatest of human inventions, since it had taught the Irish to walk on their hind legs. Also, *No Irish Need Apply* was a sign as common as *Juden sind nicht erwünscht* was to become in Nazi Germany.[1] Farmer and Henley list *Irish arms*, thick legs; *Irish apricot*, a potato; *Irish beauty*, a woman with her eyes blacked; *Irish dinner*, a fast; *Irish evidence*, perjury; *Irish hurricane*, a dead calm; *Irish rifle*, a fine-toothed comb; *Irish promotion*, a reduction in pay; and *Irish theatre*, a military lock-up; and the NED adds *Irish trick* and *Irish bull*. "References to Ireland," says Joesten in the article lately cited, "appear in no other language than English, and hardly favorably there." Among the Jews of New York an Irishman is sometimes called a *baytzimer*, from the Hebrew *baytzim*, egg.[2] Why this designation is used I do not know. It has been suggested that it is because the first Jewish immigrants found the sale of eggs monopolized by Irishmen, but this seems far-fetched and incredible. In Yiddish the word for egg is the German *ei*.

The etymology of *wop* has been heavily debated, but there seems to be an increasing agreement to derive it from *guappo*, a term in the Neapolitan dialect signifying a showy, pretentious fellow. Says an Italian authority:[3]

> The origin of *wop* . . . takes us back to the Latin *vappa*, which, in its figurative sense, means a spoiled fellow, a good for nothing. From the analogously formed masculine *vappus* there developed . . . the Neapolitan *guappo*, with the added meaning of blusterer, and then, by natural extension, a *fop*. . . . This word, which is also familiarly used adjectively in Spanish with like meaning, later became current as a term of greeting among Neapolitans. Overhearing the word so frequently in cities where the Italian population is large, those with linguistic background other than Latin naturally applied to the

1 In Hanover, which was annexed by Prussia on Sept. 20, 1866, it was the custom, for several years after, for cards of invitation to bear the words *Ohne Preussen* (No Prussians). *Every Saturday* (Boston), Jan. 4, 1868, p. 30.

2 I am indebted here to Mr. Michael Gross of New York.

3 Camillo P. Merlino, associate professor of Italian in the University of Michigan, in Word Vagaries, *Words*, Sept., 1936, p. 7.

Italians the epithet *wop*. "Naturally" because the *gu* in Romance words of Latin or Germanic derivation is generally written and pronounced *w* in English, *e.g.*, *guerra, war; guastere, waste; Guillaume, William. Wop* from *guappo* thus represents a regular phonological development.

Webster 1934 suggests that *guappo* may have got into the Neapolitan dialect by way of the Spanish adjective *guapo*, meaning bold, elegant, gay, but for this the evidence seems to be meagre. *Guapo* has produced a number of derivatives in Spanish, *e.g.*, *guapazo*, truculent; *guapear*, to boast; *guapeton*, a braggart; and *guapeza*, meaning both courage and showy dress.[1] The early immigrants from Southern Italy, *c.* 1885, brought *guappo* with them, and used it frequently in referring to one another, usually in a sportive sense and without offence.[2] It was picked up by the Americans among whom they labored in ditch and tunnel, and by 1895 or thereabout had come to signify any Italian.

*Wop* has produced a number of derivatives in the United States, *e.g.*, *wop-house*, an Italian restaurant; *wop-special*, spaghetti; and *Wopland*, Italy. In *wop-jawed* it has been assimilated with *wap-jawed*, a dialect term meaning askew.[3] Partridge says that it got into English use by way of the talkies, *c.* 1931. During the first years of World War II it appeared often in the English newspapers, always in a derogatory significance, but after the surrender of Italy it was used less. Incidentally, and rather curiously, it was adopted by the Royal Air Force to signify a wireless operator, and also seems to have been applied occasionally to an air gunner.[4] Its derivation and meaning were often discussed in the English press before and during the war.[5]

1 I am informed by a correspondent that *guapo* is used in Latin America as an adjective signifying strong.

2 Editorial Notes, *American Mercury*, Oct., 1926, p. lviii.

3 *Wap-jawed* is listed in A Second Word-List from Nebraska, by Louise Pound, *Dialect Notes*, Vol. III, Part IV, 1911, p. 548, and its use is illustrated in "That skirt hangs *wap-jawed*." Berrey and Van den Bark give the variants *wapper-jawed, wabble-jawed, wocker-jawed, whomper-jawed, whopper-jawed, wobble-jawed, womper-jawed, wop-jawed* and *wopper-jawed*. Thomas Wright, in his Dictionary of Obsolete and Provincial English; London, 1857, lists *wap* in eight senses and *wapper* in two, but none of them shows any connection with *wap-jawed*, which may possibly be an Americanism, though it is not listed by the DAE.

4 It's a Piece of Cake: R.A.F. Slang Made Easy, by C. H. Ward-Jackson; London, n. d., p. 63.

5 For example, *Wop*, by John Fairweather, London *Sunday Times*, June 9, 1929; *Wop*, by Harold Lamb, the same, June 23, 1929; *Wop: Derivation*, by Robert S. Forsythe, *Notes and Queries*, Jan. 2, 1937; *Wops*, by William Poulton, Newcastle *Journal*, Dec. 3 and 4, 1940; Why the *Wops*, Edinburgh *Scots-*

Various extensions of meaning are listed by Berrey and Van den Bark. *Wop* is sometimes used to designate any European of dark complexion,[1] and like *hunky* may even be applied to any man of uncertain nationality. In railroad slang it is sometimes used for a section hand, and among criminals it means a sentence of less than a month. It has also appeared as a slang word for a motor knock. During the discussion of the term in England the curious fact turned up that the students who gave aid to Sir Wilfred Grenfell, the arctic missionary, in vacation time " were known affectionately as *wops*." [2] *Woppage* appeared in England as a designation for the retreating Italian Army in North Africa,[3] but it was only a nonce-word and did not survive.

*Dago*, which preceded *wop* in American favor, is traced by the DAE to 1832. It comes from the Spanish *Diego*, James, and was first used to designate a Spaniard. When it began to be transferred to Italians it is not clear, but it was probably during the 80s. In 1891 it appeared in the form of *Daigos* as the name of a secret organization,[4] and in 1900 E. H. Babbitt listed it in his " College Words and Phrases " [5] as signifying (*a*) the Italian language, (*b*) a professor of Italian, (*c*) a student studying Italian, and (*d*) any uncouth person, and reported it as in use in one or more of these senses in twenty American colleges, including Harvard, Princeton and Smith. Its derivative, *dago red*, meaning a cheap red wine, is in wide use. *Guinea* is probably another term of changed meaning. In the sense of a Negro from Guinea the DAE traces it to 1823; when it came to signify an Italian I do not know. *Ginzo*, which is seldom heard, is probably a derivative. Berrey and Van den Bark also list *dino, duke, gin, macaroni* and various proper names, but most of the former are heard but rarely, and of the latter only *Tony* seems to be in general use. The DAE shows that in the middle 90s, at least in the Pennsylvania mining

---

man, Dec. 7, 1940; *Wops*, Belfast *News-Letter*, Jan. 1, 1941; *Wop-Italian*, *Notes and Queries*, Jan. 18, 1941.

1 The following is in The Conquest of New England by the Immigrant, by Daniel Chauncey Brewer; New York, 1926, pp. 323–24: " Up to the beginning of the Twentieth Century the alien was an alien. . . . The bosses had their own vernacular. . . . To some of these the Jew was a *sheeney*, the Pole a *wop*, and the

Italian a *dago*." I am indebted for this reference to Mr. Alexander Kadison.

2 William Poulton in the Newcastle *Journal*, just cited.

3 London *Daily Express*, Jan. 20, 1943. I am indebted here to Mr. P. E. Cleator.

4 Baltimore *Sun* Almanac, 1891, p. 100. I am indebted here to my brother, August Mencken.

5 *Dialect Notes*, Vol. II, Part I, 1900, p. 31.

region, Italians were called *hikes*.[1] Among the Eastern Jews in New York and Chicago, and perhaps elsewhere, they are called *lukschen*, from a Yiddish word meaning a noodle.[2] There is here, I presume, a reference to spaghetti. In Louisiana *gi-gi* has been recorded; it is also a contemptuous term there for a creole, " especially from the country." [3] The NED Supplement's first example of the use of *wop* in England is from a story by P. G. Wodehouse, published in 1915. The term does not seem to be known in Australia, and neither is *dago*. Nor is it recorded for New Zealand. Baker reports that the Australians call Italians *eyetos* or *skies*. In Chicago, during the era of Al Capone, the high-toned Italians of the town set up a clamour against the constant use of *Italian* by the newspapers to designate a gunman. The newspapers thereupon switched to *Sicilian*, which was more accurate, for nine-tenths of the gunmen were actually either Sicilians or Neapolitans. The terms *mafia* (or *maffia*), *black-hand* (from the Spanish *mano Negra*) and *camorra*, which had come into frequent use in the early days of the great Italian immigration, began to die out before the butcheries of Prohibition got under way. All three designated Italian secret organizations which preyed, in the main, not on Americans but on Italian immigrants. In 1890, when the New Orleans *mafia* was accused of having a hand in the murder of a chief of police, a mob took eleven Italian suspects out of jail and lynched them. There was a violent protest from the Italian government, but nothing came of it, and thirty-two years later the unfortunate Benito Mussolini began the extermination of all such organizations in Southern Italy. *Black-hand* had a derivative, *black-hander*, and *camorra* produced *camorrist*. None of these terms is listed in the DAE.

*Skibby*, which is used to designate Japanese on the Pacific Coast, is extremely offensive to them, for it was applied originally to a loose woman, though it now means, at least in California, any Japanese, male or female. It seems to have been borrowed from a Japanese word, though what that word was is uncertain. In the British Navy *skivvy*

1 Its first quotation is from the New York *Herald*, Jan. 13, 1896: " The average Pennsylvanian contemptuously refers to these immigrants as *hikes* and *hunks*. The *hikes* are Italians and Sicilians." A second quotation is from the *Century Magazine*, 1898: " The Italians are termed *hikes*."

2 I am indebted for this to Mr. Harry G. Green of Chicago and Mr. Michael Gross of New York. *Lukschen* also means extremely elongated in Yiddish and is applied to any tall man.

3 Louisiana Gleanings, *Dialect Notes*, Vol. V, Part VI, 1923, p. 243.

is an interjection of greeting, and is commonly believed to have come from the Japanese: perhaps it was encountered as a salutation of Japanese prostitutes. Since 1905 or thereabout, according to Partridge, it has been used in English slang to designate an English maid-servant of the rougher sort, and a correspondent in Canada informs me that it is used in the same sense there, and carries a suggestion of defective virtue. In 1942 Damon Runyon printed a treatise on the word in the New York *Mirror*,[1] from which I take the following:

> The fact that the Japanese consider *skibby* particularly odious naturally increased the popularity of the word among the Jap-hating Californians. The kids in the street used to yell it at the Japs as an invitation to a chase. As the years wore on, common usage brought *skibby* into the local language as a handy term without reference to its origin. . . . [It] is what the Jap is called to this day by most Californians, even in polite circles, and it is unlikely that the California soldiers will dismiss it for the more polite *Charlie* and *Tojo* that the dispatches from the Far East would have us believe are now terms for the enemy.

*Skibby* is listed in Webster 1934, but there is no attempt at an etymology. It does not appear in the DAE. In " A Word-List from the Northwest," in *Dialect Notes*, 1920,[2] it was dealt with thus:

> A rough name for a Japanese. Common nowadays for Japanese without distinction. It is said to have been used ten years ago only for Japanese women of ill repute.

The designation *nisei* (pro. *ne-say*) for Japanese of American birth was seldom heard, before Pearl Harbor, save on the Pacific Coast, nor was *kibei*, the name for those American-born Japanese who were sent to Japan for their schooling, and so presumably underwent Japanese indoctrination. *Nisei* is sometimes spelled *nissei*.[3] It is simply the Japanese term for second generation.[4] In the days before they lost their civil rights the American-born Japanese objected frequently and vigorously to the use of *Jap* to designate their people, and sometimes Americans went to their assistance.[5] Their crusade made

1 Feb. 11, p. 30.
2 By Robert Max Garrett of Seattle; Vol. V, Part III, p. 84.
3 Our Stakes in the Japanese Exodus, by Paul S. Taylor, *Survey Graphic*, Sept., 1942.
4 I am indebted here to Mr. Masami Nakachi of Manzanar, Calif. " Twenty years hence," he says, " we may hear of *san-sei*, third generation."

5 For example, Dr. C. Walter Young, of the Johns Hopkins University, who addressed the Baltimore *Evening Sun* on the subject under date of May 5, 1931. (His letter was published on the editorial page, May 7.) He said that he had induced the Paris edition of the Chicago *Tribune* to abandon *Jap* "three years ago."

but little progress, for *Jap*, as a very short word, was irresistibly tempting to headline writers, and during the electric days preceding and following Pearl Harbor it appeared on almost every first page in the United States almost every day.[1] The related *Nip*, from *Nipponese*, was reported in *American Speech* by Dwight L. Bolinger in April, 1943.[2] He said that it had been used in an NBC broadcast on January 12, 1942, and by *Time* on February 23 of the year. After Pearl Harbor many American Jews began calling the Japanese *gelber momzayrim* (yellow bastards). The English use *chink* for a Chinese, as we do, but Partridge says that it did not come in until *c.* 1890, and hints that it was probably borrowed from Australia.[3] The Australians, according to Baker, call a Chinese, not only a *chink*, but also a *chow*, a *dink*, a *dingbat*, a *Johnnie* and a *pong*. The DAE's earliest example of *chink* in American use is dated 1901, but it is unquestionably older, and may go back to the days of the gold-rush to California. The Chinese greatly dislike the term *Chinaman* and *Chinee*, just as the Japanese dislike *Jap*. The DAE traces *Chinaman* to 1849 and marks it an Americanism. *Chinee* is traced to 1870 and *chinawoman* to 1872, when it was used by Mark Twain in " Roughing It." *Chinatown* is traced to 1877.

Bartlett defines *greaser* as " a term vulgarly applied to the Mexicans and other Spanish Americans " and says that " it first became common during the war with Mexico." The DAE's earliest example is from the *Spirit of the Times*, July 11, 1846. Two years later George F. Ruxton explained in his " Life in the Far West " (published in 1849) that Mexicans were so called " by the Western people " on account of " their greasy appearance." In August, 1861, a writer in the *Knickerbocker Magazine*, quoted by Thornton, opined that a *greaser* " would not be seriously injured if held under a pump for half an hour." The Mexicans in the Southwest resent all this, and have concocted a number of more seemly etymologies. One holds that the term was first applied to a Mexican who set up a studio for greasing the ox-carts of early settlers at the top of the Raton Pass, and that

1 The NED reports it in colloquial use in England, *c.* 1880.
2 p. 151.
3 Its use is forbidden to broadcasters for the B.B.C. Albert Deutsch in Minorities, *PM*, Sept. 17, 1942: " Who but the very meanest among us can ever again refer to the great and valiant Chinese as *chinks*? The spectacle of the sturdy, heroic people pouring out their life-blood for freedom forever blots out the pat caricature of the wily, tricky heathen *Chinee* portrayed by Bret Harte."

his designation, the *Mexican greaser*, was gradually extended to all his countrymen.[1] Its application has been further extended to include any Latin-American, but it is still used mainly to denote a Mexican. It has had, at different times, various rivals, *e.g.*, *pepper-belly* (sometimes shortened to *pepper*), which embodies an obvious allusion to the Mexican cuisine, as do *chili-eater* and *frijole-eater*. When Italian laborers began to appear in California, in the middle 80s, they were at first called *greasers* like the Mexicans whom they appeared to resemble, but after a little while their superiority was recognized and they were elevated to the estate of *lubricators*.[2] In the Colorado sugar-beet fields the Mexican laborers are spoken of by the euphemism of *Spaniards;* they are also called *primos*. In New Mexico they are often called *natives*. In the same State Americans are *Angles* and Indians are *pueblos*.[3] The Marines who occupied Nicaragua in 1912 took to calling the natives *gooks,* one of their names for Filipinos, and it and *goo-goo* have survived, though both are regarded as very offensive. *Goo-goo* is also used to designate a Costa Rican, but a more common term is *tica*. In Brazil many Americans call the natives *Brazzies*,[4] probably a borrowing from the English. The use of *spiggoty* and *spick* for any Latin American, but especially for a native of Panama, is discussed in AL4, p. 296, n. 1.

*Grease-ball* is most often applied in the United States to Greeks, but it is also used to designate any foreigner of dark complexion. In the argot of Sing-Sing, and perhaps of other American prisons, it designates an Italian.[5] In the general slang of the country it means any dirty person, and in various occupational argots it has various special significances, all having to do with some notion of unkemptness. So far as I know, the Greeks in the United States have never undertaken a crusade against it, but some of the more hopeful of them endeavor to persuade Americans to use *Hellas* or *Hellade* instead of Greece in speaking of their country. This is in line with the movement toward native names which has converted *Ireland* into *Eire, Persia* into *Iran*, and *Siam* into *Thai*.

1 This tale is quoted in The Southwestern Word Box, by T. M. P., *New Mexico Quarterly* (Albuquerque), Aug., 1932, p. 267, but the author does not vouch for it.
2 Popular Tribunals, by Hubert H. Bancroft; New York, 1887; Vol. I, p. 151.

3 *American Speech*, Oct., 1937, p. 241.
4 I am indebted here to Mr. C. H. Calhoun, of Balboa Heights, C. Z.
5 The Psychology of Prison Language, by James Hargan, *Journal of Abnormal and Social Psychology*, Oct.–Dec., 1935, p. 362.

*Herring-choker*, listed in AL4, p. 296, as a designation for a Scandinavian, is also used by the New England fishermen to mean a Newfoundlander, and sometimes also a Nova Scotian or a Canadian in general.¹ The more common name for a Nova Scotian is *bluenose*, which the DAE defines as " a native of Nova Scotia or New Brunswick " and traces to 1837. Before this it had apparently been used to designate a New Englander. Bartlett defines it as " the slang name for a native of Nova Scotia," but Thornton says " of Nova Scotia or New Brunswick." Bartlett quotes the following from " Sam Slick," by T. R. Haliburton:

[*Blue-nose*] . . . is the name of a potato which they [the Nova Scotians] produce in great perfection, and boast to be the best in the world. The Americans have, in consequence, given them the nickname of *blue-noses*.¹

During the days of Prohibition *bluenose* was widely used to designate a Prohibitionist, and before that it had been applied to reformers in general, especially those of the sort called *wowsers* by the Australians. Berrey and Van den Bark say that American sailors also call a Nova Scotian a *novy* and a Newfoundlander a *newfy* or *cod-hauler*. Mr. Theodore Irwin, who used *scoovy* in his novel, " Strange Passage," in 1935, tells me that it means " more particularly a Swede." ³ Other names for Swede, in addition to those listed in AL4, p. 296, under Scandinavian, are *roundhead* and *swensky*. Danes and Norwegians are usually called *squareheads*. *Polack*, for a Pole, is old in English, and the NED traces it to 1599. It is to be found in " Hamlet," Act II, Scene I, spoken by Horatio.⁴ A correspondent calls my attention to the fact that in conversation the *a* is often changed to *o*.

297. [The English . . . are free to laugh at stage Irishmen without bringing down the dudgeon of the Knights of Columbus, and they continue to use the word *Jew* freely, and even retain the verb *to jew* in their vocabulary.] *To jew*, in the original sense, now obsolete, of to cheat, may be an Americanism, and in the sense of to

1 I am indebted here to Messrs. George Weller and C. V. L. Smith.
2 The DAE, in borrowing part of this, dates it *c.* 1840. Haliburton began his Sam Slick sketches in the *Nova Scotian* of Halifax in 1835. They appeared in book form in three series, 1837, 1838 and 1840.
3 An extract from the novel was printed in the *New Masses*, Aug. 6,

1935, under the title of Deportation Special. From it I take this: " Then out with you, go back where you came from, you dago, you hunky, you *scoovy*, you heinie, you mick, you sheenie, you limey! Get out and stay out! "
4 For this I am indebted to Mr. William H. Davenport, of New Haven, Conn.

bargain for a lower price (usually *to jew down*) it certainly is. The NED's first example of the former is dated *c.* 1845, and the latter is not listed at all. The DAE's first example of the former is dated *c.* 1834 and of the latter 1870.[1] The Jews of the United States have been carrying on a campaign against the use of the verb for many years, and with such success that it seldom appears in any save frankly anti-Semitic writings, though it is still heard by word of mouth. This campaign began so long ago as the 70s, when they petitioned the publishers of Webster's and Worcester's Dictionaries to omit it. The publisher of Worcester's complied, but it still appears in Webster 1934, as likewise in the DAE. Webster throws a sop to the protestants by appending to its definition of the word, in the first sense, " originally used opprobriously in allusion to practises imputed to the Jews *by those who dislike them*," but its definition of *to jew down* is accompanied by no such plea in confession and avoidance. In 1939, after the publication of AL4, I received a letter from an apparently intelligent Jewish woman in Brookline, Mass., demanding that I expunge all discussion of the word from the book. Three years before this another vigilant Jew, this time a male and hailing from Chicago, undertook a jehad against the publishers of a new edition of Roget's Thesaurus because it listed *Jew* as a synonym for lender.[2]

The very word *Jew* appears to be offensive to many American Jews, and they commonly avoid it by using *Jewish* with a noun. This is noticeable in " Who's Who in America," where the majority of Jews who mention their faith at all use *Jewish religion*, not *Jew.* In New York, *Jewish boy, girl, man, woman* or *people* is often used as a sort of euphemism. In 1927 a statistician at Yale examined the replies made by 91 Jewish candidates for admission as freshman there to the question " Church affiliation? " Nineteen answered by

1 The first two examples of *to jew down* are from the proceedings of Congress. Mark Twain used it in Life on the Mississippi, 1883, p. 473, and Frank Norris in Vandover and the Brute, *c.* 1895 (published 1914), p. 259.
2 His circular letter, addressed to " leading literary men, persons and organizations of national importance, and deans of principal universities," was dated July 21, 1936. One of the definitions of *Jew* in the College Standard Dictionary, 1941, is " any usurious money-lender; an opprobrious use applied irrespective of race." This is marked slang. The Winston Simplified Dictionary; Advanced Edition; 1926, defines *Jew, inter alia*, as " any one who deals craftily, or drives hard bargains." In these senses the word is seldom used in the United States. The English still say of a spendthrift borrower that he is *in the hands of the Jews*, but the American term is *loan-sharks*.

giving the names of the congregations to which they belonged; of the rest, forty-eight answered *Jewish*, fourteen answered *Hebrew*, two answered *Jewish orthodox*, one each answered *Judaism, reformed Judaism, Jewish temple* or *synagogue, Jewish faith* or the like; not one answered simply *Jew*. There is apparently no objection to *Jews* in the plural to designate the whole body of Israel, but in the singular it is avoided. Not infrequently *Hebrew* is used instead, though it is inaccurate.[1] *Variety*, which is owned and mainly staffed by Jews, reduces *Hebrew* to *Hebe*, obviously with jocose intent. Other sportive Jews use *Arab* or *Mexican* to designate a member of their nation.

The deliberately offensive names for a Jew — *sheeny, kike, mockie* and so on — are of mysterious etymology. Webster 1934 dismisses *kike* as " derogatory," with the sententious (and misleading) definition, " a Jew; Yid," and omits *sheeny* altogether. The DAE ignores both, though both were in use before its upset date, 1900. *Sheeny* is listed in the NED and in the English-Yiddish Dictionary of Alexander Harkavy.[2] The NED marks it " of obscure origin," and traces it to 1824. Ernest Weekley, in his " Etymological Dictionary of Modern English " calls it " East End slang " and hazards the guess that it may have arisen from a " Yiddish pronunciation of the German *schön*, beautiful, used in praising wares." Partridge says: " Very tentatively, I suggest that it arose from the *sheeny*, *i.e.*, glossy or brightly shiny hair of the average ' English ' Jew." Maurice Samuel, in " The World of Sholom Aleichem,"[3] suggests that it may be derived from the Hebrew phrase, *meeseh meshineh*, but enters upon no particulars. Barrère and Leland mark it Yiddish and say: " It is probably taken from *scheina — scheina, jaudea lischkol —*, a stupid fellow who does not know enough to ask or inquire." They add: " *Schien*, a policeman, and *schiener*, a house-thief, may have contributed to form this rather obscure word." They say also that " in America a pawnbroker is sometimes called a *sheeney*," but this seems to be an error, for the word in that sense occurs in none of the American glossaries of slang. But Farmer and Henley note its use in English. They also list it as an adjective meaning " base, Jewish, fraudulent." Thackeray used

---

1 A discussion of the historical difference between *Hebrew* and *Jew*, by Dr. Solomon Solis Cohen, is in AL4, pp. 298–99.

2 Twenty-second ed.; New York, n. d., p. 562.

3 New York, 1943, p. 200.

*Sheeney* in " The Book of Snobs," 1847, as a generic name for a Jew, along with *Moses.* Partridge says that the word was apparently inoffensive so late as the 70s, but by the 80s it had become very obnoxious to the Jews of both England and the United States. He notes that it is used by English tramps to designate a tramp of dark complexion, and Edward Fraser and John Gibbons say in " Soldier and Sailor Words and Phrases " [1] that it is English soldiers' slang for " a careful, extra economical man."

The most commonly accepted etymology for *kike* was thus stated in *American Speech* in 1926 by J. H. A. Lacher, of Waukesha, Wis.:

> In Russia there began some forty years ago a fierce persecution of the Jews. . . . Many found their way to the United States. . . . Here they offered keen competition to their brethren of German origin, who soon insisted that the business ethics and standards of living and culture of these Russians were far lower than theirs. Since the names of so many of these Eastern Jews ended in -*ki* or -*ky*, German-American Jewish traveling men designated them contemptuously as *kikis,* a term which, naturally, was soon contracted to *kikes.* When I heard the term *kikis* for the first time at Winona, Minn., about forty years ago, it was a Jewish salesman of German descent who used it and explained it to me; but in the course of a few years it disappeared, *kike* being used instead.
>
> A traveling salesman myself twenty-five to forty-five years ago, I know from personal experience that, soon after the Russian invasion, the credit men of that period were greatly prejudiced against firms whose names ended in -*ki* or -*ky.* . . . Hence it was not long before -*ki* and -*ky* disappeared as tails to their names, and *Gordensky* became *Gordon,* and *Levinski* became *Levin.* I have even known them to drop their Slavic-Jewish patronymics and to assume German names so as to disarm the credit man and escape the odium of being *kikes.* There are still plenty of surnames to be found in the city directories terminating in  -*ki* or -*ky*, but almost invariably they are owned by Christians. The word *kike* remains, however, to designate a low type of merchant.

As I have said, this etymology, or something resembling it, seems to be widely accepted, but it by no means goes unchallenged. In 1937 Rabbi Jacob Tarlau, of Flushing, L. I., argued for a different one as follows: [2]

> The German Jews, from time immemorial, have had the habit of calling an Eastern European Jew, no matter where he came from, a *Pollak.* The word *Ostjude* [Eastern Jew], as used today officially but with no less sneering contempt, is of comparatively recent date. Even the Jews of the then German province of Posen were nothing but *Pollaken,* in spite of their rather pitiful efforts to be more German than the Kaiser. This habit of using *Pollak* had grown to such a degree that it came very near being a synonym for alien or

stranger. . . . Why these German Jews should suddenly forget an almost innate habit and overthrow the time-honored *Pollak* and *Pollaken* for *kiki* and *kikis* seems to me to be far more of a puzzle than the origin of the word *kike* itself, especially as they had ample opportunity to do so while they lived in Germany, where they had, in proportion, met at least as many -*kis* and -*kys* as they did later in America, and where the people bearing those supposedly objectionable names did not even make an attempt to hide or change them. . . .

The objectionable endings are not even -*ki* and -*ky;* they are -*ski* and -*sky*. More attractive seems to me the suggestion hinted at in Webster's New International Dictionary [to the effect that *kike* may be related to *keek*, which is defined as, "in the clothing trade, one employed by a manufacturer to spy out the latest designs of rivals"]. But if we consider the fact that the clothing trade, until long after the influx of Russian immigrants, was almost entirely in the hands of Germans, Jews and non-Jews alike, we can perhaps imagine that *keek*, as used in the trade, might have become *kuck* or *kucker*, but hardly *kike*.

I like to think that the first one nicknamed *kike* was some Polish or Galician Jew who had the misfortune to be overheard by some objector when he called a *cake*, in true Yiddish, a *kike*. This same objector might have met others committing the same offense, and might have started the ball rolling by saying, either indignantly or in joke, "There is another *kike*." Naturally, this is nothing but a mere suggestion. However, it is based upon a well-known and undeniable fact — that the Polish, and especially the Galician Jew almost invariably turns the long German vowel *e* [as in *kek*, cake, a loan from English] into *ei*. The same fate befalls the diphthongs *oe* and *ae*, which, unpronounceable to the Yiddish tongue, first become long *e* and then also *ei*.

Thus they would not say *er geht*, but *er geit*; not *er steht*, but *er steit*. *Legen* becomes *leigen*, *schön* is *schein*, and *nötig* is *neitig*. A very pretty girl is a *schein meidel*. Even *der melech*, the king, cannot escape from becoming *meilech*.

Dr. A. A. Roback, in "Curiosities of Yiddish Literature," [1] agrees that *kike* is "of Yiddish origin," but does not attempt its etymology. In another place [2] he quotes the opinion of the late Dr. Gotthard Deutsch (1859–1921), professor of history in the Hebrew Union College, Cincinnati, that the word may be derived from the Yiddish *kikel*, a circle. He says:

According to him a certain new arrival from Russia became a drummer as soon as he set foot in this country. He could neither read nor write, but his profession required that he enter certain facts in a notebook, so he began jotting down names and figures by using a system of circles. His acquaintances would sometimes ask him how he could get along without knowing English but he produced those circles and said that his *kikels* were quite sufficient for the work he was doing. He came to be known as a *kike*, and the term was later applied to all similar persons. Most probably that particular case was known to Prof. Deutsch, else we cannot see how a story would be invented to prove a fantastic etymology.

1 Cambridge, Mass.; 1933, p. 33.
2 You Speak Yiddish, Too!, *Better English*, Feb., 1938, p. 52.

Despite Dr. Roback's confidence in Professor Deutsch, it is a sad fact that preposterous folk-etymologies have been known to deceive learned men, and this case seems to offer an example. *Kike* has acquired a somewhat extended meaning since World War I, and now designates, not only an Eastern Jew, but any Jew who happens to be in ill favor. This extension is shown by a familiar witticism: " A *kike* is a Jew who has left the room." [1] A correspondent calls my attention to the fact that in the heyday of the Ku Klux Klan, the term was used to designate a Jew who opposed the ideals of that great Methodist-Baptist organization.[2] " There are good Jews, and there are *kikes* " is still frequently heard, and not only in the Bible country. *Mockie* seems to be confined to the New York area. Its etymology I do not know, but it may have some sort of relation to the word *mock*. *Goose*, I suppose, embodies a reference to the tailor's smoothing-iron, which has been called a *goose* since Shakespeare's time.

There are several English names for Jew, all of them more or less opprobrious, that have never flourished in the United States, *e.g.,* *shonk* and *smous(e)*. A. F. Hubbell suggests in *American Speech* [3] that *shonk* may be a recent invention: it does not appear in any of the standard vocabularies of English slang. *Smous(e)* has a longer history. It was listed by Grose in 1785, and defined as meaning a German Jew. It is traced to 1705 by the NED, which suggests that it is probably derived from the Yiddish *schmus*, which in turn is derived from the Hebrew *sh'muoth*, meaning tales or news, " the reference being to the persuasive eloquence of Jewish pedlars." It seems rather more likely, if this etymology is sound, that the reference is to the chatter of Jews among themselves, for in the DAE's first example, from " A Description of the Coast of Guinea," a translation of a Dutch work by W. Bosman, published in 1705, the word is introduced in a simile running " as . . . noisy as the *smouse* of German Jews at their synagogue at Amsterdam." Partridge says that *smous* and *smouse*

---

1 In the course of a speech in the House of Representatives on Jan. 26, 1944 (*Congressional Record*, p. A446) the Hon. John E. Rankin of Mississippi reported that he had been given the following definition by " a Jewish friend ": " A *kike* is a Jew that is so detestable that the other Jews are ashamed of him, the Gentiles despise him, and the intelligent Negroes have contempt for him."

2 In the South many prudent Jews joined it. This course offered them their only means of escape from its afflictions.

3 A List of Briticisms, Feb., 1942, p. 8.

are now archaic in England, but that *smouch* and *smoutch*, which he thinks are variants, survive. The NED lists *smouch* as signifying a Jew, and traces it to 1765. *To smouch*, in the sense of to kiss, is old in English, and seems to have come originally from a German dialect use of *schmutzen*, which means to dirty in standard German. In the sense of to pilfer, *to smouch* may be an Americanism. I am informed by an English correspondent that *shmog* is sometimes used to designate a Jew in England, and that it is regarded as obscene, but it is not listed in any dictionary of English slang. In the days of the British Fascist party, which was strongly anti-Semitic, *yid* was used. This is also encountered in the United States: apparently it is not regarded as offensive by the Jews, who use it themselves, often in the form of *yiddisher*, and sometimes as a plural, *yidden*. The use of *nose* for a Jew is reported in the student slang of Ohio State University, but it is very rare elsewhere. The use of *jew* to designate a ship's tailor is noted by Partridge. *Christ-killer*, which is not recorded in any of the dictionaries (though Berrey and Van den Bark list *Christ-killer* as " a Socialistic soap-box speech "), was familiar in my boyhood, but has passed out with the decay of Bible searching. *Creole of Jerusalem*, used in *Harper's Magazine* in 1858,[1] may have been only a nonce-term, for I have found no trace of it elsewhere. *Galitzianer* (Galician) is sometimes used by Jews of other origin as a term of opprobrium, along with the *Polack* already noted.

The American Jews have succeeded in putting down two newspaper practises that formerly worked against the dignity of their people — first, the designation of Jewish criminals as *Jewish*, and second, the use of anti-Semitic phrases in advertising, especially of hotels. The former practise is now virtually obsolete, and the latter is under such heavy fire that it is fast going out. There was a time when hotels and apartment-houses refusing Jewish patronage advertised that refusal in terms almost as frank as the Nazi *Juden sind nicht erwünscht*, but the protests of Jews gradually reduced them to such equivocal (but well understood) phrases as *restricted* (or *selected*) *clientele*, and eventually to the single word *restricted*. In 1942 the newspaper *PM*, which has a large circulation among Jews, undertook to put down even *restricted*, and a year or so later, apparently under some pressure from District Attorney Frank S. Hogan, all the

1 Editor's Drawer, May, p. 854.

dailies of New York agreed to ban it from their classified advertising.[1]

Whether or not *Bronx cheer* embodies an allusion to the Jews who swarm in the Bronx I do not know. *Bronx vanilla,* for garlic, obviously does.[2] *Jewish engineering* is used in some of the colleges to designate the course in business administration, and *Jewish cavalry* is an old term for the quartermaster's corps of the Army.

299. [The Negroes carry on a double campaign — first, against the use of *nigger,* and secondly, for the capitalization of *Negro.* On March 7, 1930, when the New York *Times* announced that it would capitalize *Negro* thereafter, there was jubilation in the Negro press.] This decision of the *Times* was brought about by representations from Major Robert Russa Moton, LL.D., Litt.D., then principal of Tuskegee Institute,[3] but the movement had been launched seventeen years before by Lester Aglar Walton, a colored journalist who, in 1935, was made envoy extraordinary and minister plenipotentiary to

---

1 Resort Ads Reformed, *Editor and Publisher,* Aug. 7, 1943. The *Editor and Publisher* was not altogether in favor of this censorship. It said: "The religious observances and dietary laws which make it difficult for orthodox Jews to share accommodations with those of other creeds were the base upon which the now out-ruled practices stood. That base has not changed, and instead of the words that offended tender sensibilities, the advertisers have found others to indicate the character of their enterprises. The *Editor and Publisher* does not believe that racial or religious discrimination is indicated when a hotel advertises that it is prepared to cater to either a preponderantly Christian or Jewish clientele. A good part of vacation joys are based upon association with congenial people, and that is true for people of every religious faith. If the elimination of words which imply inferiority of one racial group to others can be accomplished without limiting the advertisers' right to choose their patronage groups it is a job worth doing."

2 *American Speech,* Dec., 1936, p. 374.

3 He succeeded Booker T. Washington in 1915, retired in 1935, and died in 1940. The origin of his military

title I do not know. The *Times*' announcement of its conversion at his hands was embodied in the following editorial:

"The tendency in typography is generally toward a lessened use of capital letters, yet reverence for things held sacred by many, a regard for the fundamental law of the land, a respect for the offices of men in high authority, and certain popular and social traditions have resisted this tendency.

"Races have their capitalized distinction, as have nationalities, sects and cults, tribes and clans. It therefore seems reasonable that a people who had once a proud designation such as Ethiopians, reaching back into the dawn of history, having come up out of the slavery to which men of English speech subjected them, should now have such recognition as the lifting of the name from the lower case to the upper can give them.

"Maj. Robert R. Moton of Tuskegee, the foremost representative of the race in America, has written the *Times* that his people universally wish to see the word *Negro* capitalized. It is a little thing mechanically to grant, but it is not a small thing in its implications."

Liberia. " In 1913," Mr. Walton says of himself in " Who's Who in America," " with coöperation of Associated Press, started movement for capitalization of *N* in *Negro*." The *Times*, in fact, was rather behind the procession, and on March 9, 1930, two days after its own surrender, it printed a list prepared by the National Association for the Advancement of Colored People, showing that the following other newspapers were already using *Negro:* the New York *World, Herald Tribune* and *Telegram,* the Brooklyn *Eagle,* the Springfield (Mass.) *Republican* and *News,* the *Christian Science Monitor* of Boston, the Portland (Maine) *Press-Herald,* the Chicago *Herald-Examiner,* the Newark *News,* the Montgomery (Ala.) *Advertiser,* the Durham (N. C.) *Sun,* the Sacramento *Bee,* the Raleigh (N. C.) *News,* the Omaha *Bee,* the Waterbury (Conn.) *Republican,* the Indianapolis *Times,* the Trenton *Gazette,* the Oakland (Calif.) *Tribune,* and the Columbus (Ga.) *Enquirer-Sun.* In addition, these weeklies and monthlies had also fallen into line: the *Atlantic Monthly,* the *American Mercury,* the *Nation,* the *New Republic,* the *Virginia Quarterly Review,* the *Living Church,* and *Time.* Finally, *Negro* was being used in the Encyclopedia of the Social Sciences, then in progress, in all books published by the Macmillan Company, Duffield & Company, Harcourt, Brace & Company, Alfred A. Knopf, and Doubleday, Doran & Company, and by the United States Census Bureau, the Bureau of Education, and the whole Department of Commerce. In March, 1933, the Style Manual of the Government Printing Office was revised to make *Negro* and *Negress* begin with capitals in all official publications of the United States, including the *Congressional Record.* The Pittsburgh *Courier,* the most widely circulated of Negro newspapers, hailed the conversion of the *Times* with an exultant editorial on March 15, 1930, but its star columnist, the sardonic George S. Schuyler,[1] refused to agree that the colored folk " universally wished " to become *Negroes,* and on the same day printed the following:

It really doesn't matter a tinker's damn whether *Negro* is spelled with a small or large *N*, so far as the Negro's economic, political and cultural status is concerned. The gabble, mostly senseless, to the contrary has vastly amused me; for, if anything, it is worse to spell *Negro* with a large *N* than with a small one, and if I had my way I would discontinue it. . . .

The truth is that the American Negro is an amalgam of Caucasian, Amerin-

[1] Mr. Schuyler is the most competent journalist that his race has produced in America. There are few white columnists, in fact, who can match him for information, intelligence, independence and courage.

dian and African, there being but 20 per cent "pure," and those are the only ones entitled to the term Negro when used as a descriptive adjective. Geographically, we are neither Ethiopians or Africans, but Americans. Culturally, we are Anglo-Saxons.

Used as a noun, the term is therefore a designation of a definite social caste, an under-dog, semi-serf class which believes it is dignifying its status by a capitalization of the term by which it is called and recognized. This is the same thing as arguing that an imbecile is somewhat ennobled by spelling the word with a capital *I* or that a convict has his status improved by spelling the word with a capital *C*. Lifting *Negro* from the lower case to the upper typographically does not in the least elevate him socially. As a matter of fact, it fits right in with the program of racial segregation. As *negroes* we are about 3,000,000 strong, as *Negroes* we are 12,000,000 strong; as *negroes* we are a definite physical type, as *Negroes* we are a definite social class. It is significant that Southern newspapers and magazines were more ready and willing to make the change in *Negro* than the Northern publications. The former are ever eager to make the Negro satisfied with his place; the latter based their objections on etymological and grammatical grounds. . . .

The possession of physical characteristics or ancestry different from other people by any citizen should not be constantly emphasized and brought to the attention of newspaper readers, especially in this country. The interests of interracial peace demand the abolition of such references and we ought to fight for that and lose no time trying to get white folks to "dignify" a sociochromatic caste system established and maintained by them for their own convenience and economic advantage. There is something ridiculous about a so-called *Negro* bellowing against color discrimination and segregation while wearing out his larynx whining for a glorification of his Jim Crow status in society through capitalization of the *N* in *Negro*.

Mr. Schuyler returned to the subject many times afterward. Thus on July 17, 1937:

*Negro* clearly belongs with *blonde, brunette, ruddy, mulatto, octoroon* and such descriptive terms, and has no stronger claim on capitalization. . . . Capitalized, it tends to bolster the *status quo,* and thus is at best conservative and at worst reactionary, for it discourages differentiation and strengthens the superstition that "all coons are alike."

And again on March 20, 1943:

*Negro* is either an adjective meaning black or it is a caste name like *Sudra.*[1] When we eagerly accept it as a group designation, regardless of our skin tint, we are accepting all the "racial" nonsense of Hitler, Bilbo, and the myriads who believe as they do — at least in the day time.

Mr. Schuyler's ideas, of course, got but little support from the general run of American colored folk, or from their accepted fuglemen and haruspices. Even so intelligent and independent a leader of the

[1] A member of the lowest of the four Hindu castes.

race as Dr. Kelly Miller [1] was moved to dissent. In 1937 Dr. Miller contributed a thoughtful article, under the title of " *Negroes or Colored People?* " to *Opportunity*, the organ of the National Urban League,[2] and in it said:

A printed list consisting of Englishmen, Germans, Italians, Jews and *negroes* would evidently be a case of unexplained typographical discrimination. If it be said that *Negro* is not derived from a country or geographical division, as other racial designations are, an adequate rejoinder would be that neither is *Jew*.[3]

In this article Dr. Miller rehearsed the history of the common American designations of persons of his race. In the first days of slavery, he said, they were called simply *blacks*, and even after interbreeding lightened their color the term continued in use " in a generic sense." Then came *African*, which was accepted by the race " in the early years, after it first came to self-consciousness," and still survives in the titles of some of its religious organizations, *e.g.*, the *African* Methodist Episcopal Zion Church. (This, according to the DAE, was during the first half of the Eighteenth Century.) A bit later *darky* or *darkey* began to be used, and " at first it carried no invidious implication." (The DAE's first example is dated 1775.) Then came *Africo-American* (1835 or thereabout), but it was too clumsy to be adopted.[4] After the Civil War *freedman* was in wide use, but it began to die out before the end of the 70s.[5] In 1880 *Afro-American* was invented by T. Thomas Fortune, editor of the New York *Age*, and it still survives, but only in rather formal usage.[6] " Mr. Fortune," said

1 Dr. Miller was dean of the College of Arts and Sciences, at Howard University, Washington, and a recognized Negro publicist.

2 May, 1937, pp. 142–46.

3 Here Dr. Miller slipped. The NED says that *Jew* was " originally a Hebrew of the Kingdom of *Judah*."

4 It survives, however, in the name of the *Africo-American Presbyterian*, a weekly published since 1879 by the Negro Presbyterian Church at Charlotte, N. C.

5 Carl Sandburg says in his Abraham Lincoln: the War Years; New York, 1939, Vol. II, p. 137: " Demurrings arose to Lincoln's progressions in styling the Negroes, in 1859, *negroes;* in 1860, *colored men;* in 1861, *intelligent contrabands;* in 1862, *free*

*Americans of African descent.*" *Contraband* came into use in 1861, when General Benjamin F. Butler issued a proclamation declaring slaves owned by Confederates contraband of war, but it was obsolete by 1870.

6 It is the name of a Negro newspaper of wide circulation and influence, published in Baltimore with local editions in other places. The readers of the paper in Baltimore call it the *Afro*, and it so refers to itself. " It is interesting to note," said Dr. Miller, " that the *Africo-American Presbyterian* and the *Afro-American*, which stress their names in heavy type at the head of their papers, rarely use these terms in their news service or editorial columns."

Dr. Miller, "repudiated the word *Negro* because of the historical degradation and humiliation attached to it." At some undetermined time after 1900 Sir Harry Johnston, the English African explorer and colonial administrator,[1] shortened *Afro-American* to *Aframerican*, but the latter has had but little vogue.[2] After rehearsing, in his article, the history of all these appellations, Dr. Miller turned to *Negro* and *colored*, and proceeded to discuss their respective claims to general adoption. The latter, he concluded, could not qualify, for it was properly applicable to any person not white, including Chinese, Japanese, Indians and Mexicans, and had been so applied in various State laws, and even, at least by inference, in Federal population statistics.[3] Thus his reasoning:

> Try, if you will, to express the idea involved in *Negro* art, *Negro* music, *Negro* poetry, *Negro* genius, the *Journal of Negro History*, the *Journal of Negro Education* and the *Negro Handbook* in terms of the word *colored* and see what a lamentable weakness would result from this substitution. . . . The

1 Johnston (1858–1927) spent nearly his whole adult life in Africa, and was the author of a number of authoritative books about its peoples. He also wrote a popular novel, The Gay Dombeys, 1919, with characters descended from those of Dickens's Dombey & Son.

2 It was preceded, and probably suggested, by *Amerindian*, a name for the American Indian coined by Major J. W. Powell, of the Bureau of American Ethnology, in 1899. *Amerindian* was quickly displaced by *Amerind*, which is still in use. See AL4, p. 171, n. 2. In South Africa a similar quest for a sonorous designation for themselves has been carried on by the natives. "Their latest choice," said J. A. Rogers in Sex and Race; New York, 1941, p. 131, "is *Eur-African*." But this is objected to by the whites, who say that they are the only real *Eur-Africans*. The term *Afrikander*, which might well designate the blacks, is already monopolized by the whites. In Liberia the descendants of returned American slaves who constitute the ruling caste of the country used to call themselves *Americo-Liberians* to distinguish their group from the general mass

of blacks. But I am informed by Mr. Ben Hamilton, Jr., of the Liberian consulate in Los Angeles, that this compound is now out of favor. He says: "Because of the great amount of intermarriage between the descendants of the colonists to Liberia from America with aborigines of the Negro republic, and because of a wave of nationalism that is sweeping the country, Liberians consider the term *Americo-Liberian* opprobrious as reflecting upon their [ancestors'] condition of servitude in the States. Hence they prefer to be called *civilized* or *Monrovian Liberians* to distinguish them from the natives of the hinterland, who are generally called by their tribal names." Monrovia is the capital of Liberia, and the home of virtually all its *noblesse*.

3 Mexicans were not formally classified as white until the 1940 Census. Before that they were lumped with "other races." Very few of them, of course, are actually white, even in part. The change was made in furtherance of the Good Neighbor policy, and presumably produced a favorable impression below the Rio Grande.

term *Negro* is far superior to the term *colored* in grammatical inflection, for it may be used either as a noun or as an adjective, whereas *colored* has no nominal equivalent. Unlike the words *black* and *white* it does not pluralize into a noun. . . . The word *people, race* or *persons* must be added to give collective or plural effect. . . . This handicap is seen in the possessive case. . . . Again, the word *Negro* may be easily inflected into *Negroid* by adding the Greek ending *-oid*, which implies likeness or resemblance to. This term may be used either as a noun or an adjective, and forms an apt designation of the derivatives of African blood now scattered through the world.

Dr. Miller admitted that " such terms as *colored lady, colored gentleman* and *colored society* " sounded " more polite than the corresponding *Negro* equivalents," but argued that the preference for them probably grew out of " that to which the ear is accustomed." He went on:

Many of the off-colored group object to the term *Negro* because it serves as a reminder of the humiliation and degradation through which the race has passed. The fact that *Negro* is now used to describe the group does not indicate any lesser degree of appreciation or esteem. . . . Any race or group, in the long run, will derive its reputation from its character and worth, and not from the appellation by which it is known. . . . Sensitiveness about a name is always a sign of the inferiority complex.

Dr. Miller, going further than most other advocates of *Negro*, was also willing to accept *Negress*, which is intolerably offensive to most high-toned colored folk. Here the iconoclastic Schuyler agreed with him, saying,

If we accept the term *Negro* there is no sound reason for spurning *Negress*, and yet its use is discouraged and condemned without, of course, any sensible argument being advanced for this position. I understand Jews are similarly unreasonable about the term *Jewess*.[1]

But despite this agreement of two high Negro authorities the *Atlantic Monthly* got into hot water when, in October, 1935, it used *Negress* in an editorial reference to a colored contributor, Miss Juanita Harrison, author of a serial entitled " My Great, Wide, Beautiful World." Moreover, it added to its offense by speaking of the lady by her given name alone, without the honorific *Miss*. Protests came in promptly, and one of them, from Isadore Cecelia Williams, of Washington, was printed in the issue for December, along with an editorial explanation. I take the following from Miss (or Mrs.?) Williams's letter:

[1] Views and Reviews, Pittsburgh *Courier*, July 17, 1937.

*Negress* . . . is obnoxious to Negroes chiefly because of the sordid, loose, and often degrading connotations it has been forced to carry. From the standpoint of etymology I believe I am right in saying that the use of *ess* as a suffix to designate the women of any race is practically obsolete. Out of courtesy to a race and a sex I suggest that you hereafter discard the offensive term *Negress*.

It was petty, to say the least, to refer to Miss Harrison as *Juanita* in the editorial preface to her letters. Perhaps it is mere class distinction, but class distinction should be beneath the dignity of your pages. A witness in a recent kidnapping case, though only a nursemaid, was referred to as *Miss* Betty Gow. Certainly Miss Harrison, whose honesty you commend and whose native intelligence merited a place in your pages, deserves at least common courtesy at your hands.

To this the editor of the *Atlantic* replied somewhat lamely that he " really did not know that the word *Negress* carried a derogatory connotation." " I suppose," he went on, " that the feeling must come from the analogy of the suffix -*ess* being used throughout the animal kingdom." In further confession and avoidance he cited the parallel terms, *Jewess* and *Quakeress*, conveniently overlooking the fact (maybe also unknown to him) that the former is vastly disliked by Jews. As to the use of her simple given-name in referring to Miss Harrison he said:

In the correspondence regarding her which came from a former employer she was continually referred to as *Juanita*, and it was natural to transfer this designation to the *Atlantic*. We certainly meant no disrespect, for as you surmise, we thought her an honest, interesting and able character.

Other Negro publicists have proposed various substitutes for any designation pointing directly to color, among them *race* and *group*. According to Dr. Miller, *racemen* was suggested in 1936 or thereabout by Robert S. Abbott, editor of the Chicago *Defender*. Dr. Miller himself rejected it as equally applicable to a white man or an Indian and predicted that it would " fall under the weight of its own ineptness." It has, however, survived more or less, and *group* is really flourishing. Many of the Negro newspapers use *our group, group man, group leader*, etc. At present the objection to *Negro*, now capitalized by nearly all American publications, takes two forms. First, there is a campaign against using it whenever a person of color comes into the news, on the ground that calling attention to his race is gratuitous, and usually damaging to the other members of it. Thus an anonymous Negro quoted by R. E. Wolseley:

Why is it necessary to differentiate us so clearly? We don't see newspaper reporters identifying a man in a newspaper story as a *Catholic* or a *Methodist* or a *Brazilian* or a *Frenchman*. Why go to so much pains to explain that his color is black? [1]

In this objection, of course, there is a certain falsetto, for the question whether a certain person in the news is white or black is often of interest and even of importance, especially in the South. Very few Negroes object when a newspaper describes Paul Robeson as an eminent *Negro* singer or reminds its readers that Joe Lewis is a *Negro* who has slaughtered a long line of whites; they are heard from principally when it is recorded that *Negro* pickpockets have been at work or that *Negro* soldiers have staged a riot. Only Schuyler, so far as I am aware, has ever argued for " the doing away entirely of the word." " There is no more reason why we should say *Negro educator* or *Negro criminal*," he once wrote, " than we should say *white educator* or *white criminal*." [2] But this will remain a feeble argument so long as Negro educators are differentiated in function from their white colleagues, and Negro criminals, at least in some areas, constitute a specialized faculty. In more logical moments Schuyler argues plausibly that all such verbal reforms and ameliorations are in vain — that the race conflict in the United States will never be abated until the overwhelming majority of whites are induced to look at *Negroes* with more tolerant eyes, and with less than their present uneasiness.[3]

The other objection to *Negro* has to do with the fact that the word is frequently mispronounced, and tends to slide into the hated *nigger*. In the South it is commonly heard as *nigrah*, and not only from white

1 Journalistic Headache, *Ken*, March 9, 1939.
2 Views and Reviews, Pittsburgh *Courier*, Nov. 7, 1936.
3 " Whenever two distinguishable groups," said Dr. Miller in the article before cited, " are thrown together in close juxtaposition and association, there is always imperative necessity of some mark by which the individual is tied to his classification. Sex constitutes the deepest division of the human race. The individuals of the two sexes are separated by dress as well as by name, so as to relieve the embarrassment of mistaken identity across the sex line. A mistaken identity of race in Mississippi or Alabama might cause as much embarrassment as a similar mistake in sex. . . . Wherever significant group distinction exists, whether based on race, religion or culture, such terms as *Jew* and *Gentile*, *Greek* and *barbarian*, *Christian* and *heathen* have been universally applied for the purpose of identification." When Dr. Miller wrote, in 1937, there were 29 American States with laws setting up legal distinctions on account of race, *e.g.*, in such matters as separate schools, separate accommodations for travel, and bans on interracial marriages. But in none of them had the courts ever attempted a precise definition of *Negro*, nor had the Supreme Court of the United States undertaken that difficult, and maybe even impossible task.

lips.[1] Indeed, *nigrah* is also used by Northern Negroes, including some of the most eminent, as witness the following protest from a reader of the Pittsburgh *Courier:*

A great many professional Negro orators, prominent speakers, leaders and so on are speaking on the radio all over the country — on forums, "March of Time" programs, etc. Nearly all make the one big noticeable error of pronouncing *Negro* as if it were spelled *nigro* [2] or *nigrah.* . . . It is all the more noticeable when white people are on the same program. They pronounce *Negro* correctly, with the emphasis on *ne* and not *nig.*[3]

Worse, even the abhorred *nigger* is in wide use among the colored people themselves, at least upon the lower levels. Said Lucius Harper, managing editor of the Chicago *Defender,* in 1939:

It is a common expression among the ordinary Negroes and is used frequently in conversation between them. It carries no odium or sting when used by themselves, but they object keenly to whites using it because it conveys the spirit of hate, discrimination and prejudice.[4]

*Nigger* is so bitterly resented by the more elegant blackamoors that they object to it even in quotations, and not a few of their papers spell it *n——r* when necessity forces them to use it.[5] On March 4, 1936, Garnet C. Wilkinson, first assistant superintendent of schools of Washington, in charge of the Negro public schools of the District

---

1 In a paper entitled Our Flouted Heritage, by Frank Foster, of Seattle, Wash., not published but sent to me by the politeness of the author, it is suggested that what the Southern cracker really says is *nigrer.* But the upper classes, unless my ears deceive me, commonly use *nigra.* I have also heard *niggero,* but it was used sportively.

2 In The Field, the Dungeon and the Escape; Hartford, Conn., 1865, p. 101, Albert D. Richardson said that the Southerners of that time usually made it *nigro,* "never *negro,* and very rarely *nigger."*

3 This protest appeared May 15, 1943, in Yes! We All Talk, a philological column conducted by Marcus H. Boulware. Mr. Boulware, in a note appended to the letter, said that " *ne* in *Negro* should rime with *see,* and *gro* with *grow."*

4 Quoted in Journalistic Headache, by R. E. Wolseley, *Ken,* March 9, 1939.

Perhaps the interracial tolerance of the term is helped along by recollection of the fact that in the Old South it often had, on white lips, a ring of genuine affection, though at best it was patronizing, and that it carried something of that character even into the new South. There is never any hint of affection in *Negro* (or *nigrah*). It is grudging and hostile.

5 For example, I find the following on p. 1 of the Pittsburgh *Courier,* Nov. 1, 1941, in a dispatch from Due West, S. C., reporting the beating of a colored pastor, the Rev. B. J. Glover, Jr., "because law officers of this prejudice-ridden town thought he was too uppity for a *N——r."* Here, it will be noted, the offending word was given a capital *N.* In the same dispatch occurred the following: "Another officer said, 'Let's teach that *D—— N——* a lesson,' and struck Rev. Glover."

of Columbia, actually recommended to Superintendent F. W. Ballou that *Opportunity*, organ of the National Urban League and for years a recognized leader among Negro magazines, be barred from the schools of the District on the ground that it used " the opprobrious term *N——* in its publications on Negro life." When news of this recommendation reached Elmer A. Carter, editor of *Opportunity*, he naturally protested, and under date of March 11 received the following from Dr. Wilkinson:

It is contrary to a long established administrative policy, initiated and fostered by the school teachers and officers of Divisions 10–13 of the public schools of the District,[1] to recommend to the Board of Education the adoption of any textbook, basic or supplementary, magazine, or periodical known to make use of the term *N——* in its publication.

Textbooks published by white authors and making use of such material have been refused for adoption in our public schools. Textbooks have been withdrawn from the approved list for the same reason. Obviously, a textbook, magazine, or periodical published by a Negro should be subject to the same administrative policy. There can be no double standard of evaluating such school materials — one standard for white authors, another standard for Negro authors.

You are now advised that this office would be willing to recommend the placing of *Opportunity* on the approved list of magazines and periodicals for the public schools of the District if you, as editor, will give us the assurance that *Opportunity* will discontinue the policy of using any opprobrious term or terms in referring to the Negro.

Mr. Carter replied to this curious communication under date of March 17, as follows:

Even a casual examination of the magazine will reveal that your recommendation has been based on a total misconception of the use of the term *nigger* when it appears in *Opportunity*. That use is limited to quotations from other writers or is the reproduction in poem or story of the speech and conversation of characters who commonly use this term, and in both cases the word or the line in which it occurs is always set off by quotation marks, italics, or other literary and printing insignia.

It should not be necessary for me to direct your attention to the fact that there is a vast and obvious difference in the use of a word or phrase in quotation and its use as a definitive term in the editorial contents of a publication, nor to affirm that *Opportunity* never employs any epithet of opprobrium in its columns except under the limitations mentioned above.

If impartially applied, the ruling of the Board of Education will achieve astonishing if not fantastic results. For by the same standards the *Nation*, the *New Republic, Harper's, Time*, the *Literary Digest*, the *Forum*, in fact, almost every magazine which on occasion publishes stories or articles involving the

[1] These divisions are made up of Negro elementary and high schools.

Negro must likewise be removed from the list of magazines approved for the children in the Negro schools of Washington. By the same token the most authoritative books on the Negroes' status in America must of necessity fail of approval as suitable reading matter for Negro children in the District of Columbia. For this incredible decision would refuse approval to " The Souls of Black Folk " and " Black Reconstruction," by DuBois; " The Black Worker," by Harris; " Shadow of the Plantation," by Johnston; the autobiography of Frederick Douglass; " The Life and Works of Booker T. Washington," the novels of Walter White, Chesnutt and Dunbar, and the poetry of Countee Cullen, Sterling Brown, Langston Hughes, to mention only a few.[1]

Five years later there was an uproar in the Negro newspapers because the manufacturers of Noxzema, a lotion popular among Negroes as among whites, had sent out a dunning letter to delinquent druggists headed by the words " *N——r* in the Woodpile." [2] In 1943 there was another over the belated discovery that the American Tobacco Company was making a brand of tobacco called *Nigger Head*. In the latter case the crusade for redress was carried on by the *Amsterdam Star-News* of New York, and in a little while the company announced that the brand was being withdrawn.[3] *Nigger in the woodpile* is traced by the DAE to 1861, and is defined by it as " a concealed or inconspicuous but highly important fact, factor or ' catch ' in an account, proposal, etc." Of the six examples that it gives, two are from the *Congressional Record*. *Niggerhead*, in the more refined form of *negrohead*, is traced to 1833, and defined as " a low grade of strong, dark-colored tobacco." It was used by Huckleberry Finn in contradistinction to *store-tobacco*. *Niggerhead*, in the sense of a piece of extraordinarily hard rock, goes back to 1847, and has been used in a report of the Smithsonian; it also appears in " Chicago Poems " by Carl Sandburg, 1916.

*Negro* is not, of course, an Americanism. It is simply the Spanish and Portuguese word for black, and was borrowed by the English

1 This correspondence was published in full in *Opportunity*, April, 1936, pp. 126 and 127.
2 The offense was tracked by eager Negro G-men to G. T. Brian, credit manager of the company, which has headquarters in Baltimore. He protested that he had merely quoted an old phrase and meant no harm, and added that he was a graduate of Cornell, where he had Negro fellow-students, and was on the board of the Baltimore Y.M.C.A., where he " worked with an inter-racial committee whose job it has been to aid Negro boys." But professional saviors of the Negro saw in the episode a chance to make hay, and the company was presently visited by a delegation of them which made a long list of demands, including the employment of Negroes in the manufacturing plant, and threatened a boycott in case of non-compliance. The company refused to be intimidated and nothing came of the boycott.
3 *Nation*, March 20, 1943.

during the Sixteenth Century. By 1587 a Northern English form, *neger*, had appeared, and it was from this that both the Irish *naygur* and the English-American *nigger* were derived. The NED's first example of *nigger* comes from a poem of Robert Burns, published in 1786. In the United States, in the spelling of *niger*, the DAE traces it to Samuel Sewall's diary, 1700. But after that the DAE offers no example until the Nineteenth Century. *Nigger-boy* is traced to 1825, *nigger-wench* to 1837,[1] *nigger-regiment* to 1863, *nigger-talk* to 1866 (*nigger* alone, meaning the manner of speech of Negroes, goes back to 1825), *niggerish* to 1825, *nigger-killer* to 1856, *nigger-luck* (meaning good luck) to 1851, and *nigger-heaven* (the top gallery in a theatre) to 1878. There are many other derivatives. I have mentioned *niggerhead* in the sense of a lump of hard rock, and in that of coarse chewing and smoking tobacco. It is also used to designate the common black-eyed Susan, a variety of greenbrier, one of cactus, and a recalcitrant clay soil.[2] After the Civil War it was used to designate a person in favor of full political equality for Negroes. There are a *nigger-duck*, a *nigger-goose*, a *nigger-weed*, and several kinds of *nigger-fish*. *To nigger off* means to divide a log into convenient lengths by burning through it, *to nigger out* means to exhaust the soil by working it without fertilizer, and *to nigger it* means to live meagerly. A *nigger* is a device used in sawmills to turn a heavy log, and also a defect in an electrical conductor, causing a short circuit. *Niggertoe* is a dialect name, in rural New York, Ohio and Pennsylvania for the Brazil nut, and was once used to designate a variety of potato. *To nigger lip* is " to moisten the tip of one's cigarette," [3] and *niggertone* is " a buzzing tone produced in the lower register of a wind instrument by constricting the throat muscles." [4] *To work like a nigger* is traced by the DAE to 1836, and *to let off a little nigger* to

---

1 *Negro-wench* is much older: the DAE traces it (in Boston!) to 1715, and simple *wench* (in North Carolina) to 1717. In 1807 Charles William Janson reported in The Stranger in America; London, p. 309 (quoted in Words Indicating Social Status in America in the Eighteenth Century, by Allen Walker Read, *American Speech*, Oct., 1934, p. 208) that female slaves were " uniformly called *wenches*." The term remained in general use until the Civil War and is still used in the South. A male slave was called a *buck*, and that term also survives in the South.

2 Topographical Terms in Virginia, III, by George Davis McJimsey, *American Speech*, Oct., 1940, p. 289.

3 Smokers' Slang, by Robert H. Weber, *American Speech*, Oct., 1940, p. 335.

4 A Musician's Word List, by Russel B. Nye, *American Speech*, Feb. 1937, p. 47.

1828. It lists many other derivatives, but omits *nigger-gal*, *nigger-job*, *nigger-lover*,[1] *nigger-stealer* and *nigger-mammy*. The use of *niggerhead* to signify a hard stone was no doubt suggested by the old American belief that the skull of the Negro is extraordinarily thick, and hence able to stand hard blows without cracking. That superstition is accompanied by one to the effect that the shins of the colored folk are extremely tender. The notion that they have an inordinate fondness for watermelon belongs to the same category. This last is so far resented by high-toned Negroes that they commonly avoid *Citrullus vulgaris* in their diet as diligently as the more elegant sort of German-Americans used to avoid Limburger cheese.[2]

Before 1890, according to Dr. Miller, the Census Bureau " sought to sub-divide the Negro group into *blacks*, *mulattoes*, *quadroons* and *octoroons*," but found it " impossible to make such sharp discriminations, since these divisions ran imperceptibly into one another." It was upon the advice of Booker T. Washington that it began calling all colored persons of African blood *Negroes*. *Mulatto*, *quadroon* and *octoroon* have now almost disappeared from American speech. Of them, only *octoroon* seems to be an Americanism. *Mulatto*, which comes from the Spanish and Portuguese *mulato*, signifying a young mule, and hence a halfbreed, is traced by the NED in English use to 1595, but the DAE's first American example is dated 1658. Originally, the word meant the immediate offspring of a Negro and a white person, but by the beginning of the Eighteenth Century it was being applied to anyone of mixed white and Negro blood.[3] In the early

1 *Nigger-lover* and its congener, *nigger-worshipper*, were bitterly resented by the Abolitionists to whom they were applied in the days before the Civil War. Max Herzberg says in Insults: A Practical Anthology of Scathing Remarks and Acid Portraits, quoted in *Encore*, March, 1944, p. 322, that after Stephen A. Douglas had used the latter in a speech in the Senate William H. Seward said to him: " Douglas, no man will ever be President of the United States who spells *Negro* with two g's."

2 From Journalistic Headache, by R. E. Wolseley, already cited, I take the following: " The sports editor of a small Midwestern daily learned

this unforgetably one Fall when he jokingly suggested that a good way to stop Ozzie Simmons, the great Negro football star from Iowa, was to roll a number of big juicy watermelons out on the field. . . . Telephone calls, letters and personal visits from the Negroes of the city made him realize he had hurt some feelings. A formal protest — a petition — from the local Inter-Racial Council brought the matter to the attention of the newspaper's managing editor."

3 Hugh Jones reported in The Present State of Virginia; London, 1724, p. 35 (quoted by Read, before cited, p. 208) that *mulattoes* were " born of a Negro and an European." Per-

chronicles and travel-books it was spelled in a dozen different ways, some of them quite fantastic, *e.g.*, *malatta, melatto, molatto, muletto* and *mulattoé. Quadroon* is a loan from the *quateron* of the Louisiana French, who borrowed it in turn from the Spanish *cuarteron*. The NED's first example of *quarteron* is dated 1707; Thomas Jefferson used it in that form in 1793. In the form of *quatroon* it goes back to 1748 in English usage and to 1808 in American, and in the form of *quadroon* to 1796 and 1832 respectively. *Octoroon* is apparently more recent. There is no trace of it before 1861, when Dion Boucicault used it in the title of a play. *Griffe*, another loan from the French of Louisiana, is now obsolete. It signified, according to Miss Grace E. King, quoted by the DAE,[1] a mixed breed one degree lighter than an *octoroon*, the series being *mulatto, quadroon, octoroon, griffe*.[2]

---

sons born of a Negro and an Indian, he said, were called *mustees*. The DAE says that *mustee* was at first applied to what were later to be called *quadroons*. The word was borrowed from England, where the NED traces it to 1699. It meant there, originally, the offspring of a quadroon and a white, but came to signify any half-caste. It was derived from the Spanish *mestizo*.

1 New Orleans: The Place and the People; New York, 1895, p. 333.
2 The Swiss naturalist and traveler, Johann Jakob Tschudi (1818-89), in his Peru, Reiseskizzen (translated by Thomasina Ross as Travels in Peru; London, 1847, p. 114) gave the following list of designations for mixed bloods prevailing in Lima:

| PARENTS | CHILDREN |
|---|---|
| White father and Negro mother | *mulatto* |
| White father and Indian mother | *mestizo* |
| Indian father and Negro mother | *chino* |
| White father and *mulatta* mother | *quarteron* |
| White father and *mestiza* mother | *creole* (only distinguished from the white by a pale-brownish complexion) |
| White father and Chinese mother | *chino-blanco* |
| White father and *cuarterona* mother | *quintero* |
| White father and *quintera* mother | *white* |
| Negro father and Indian mother | *zambo* |
| Negro father and *mulatta* mother | *zambo-negro* |
| Negro father and *mestiza* mother | *mulatto-oscuro* |
| Negro father and Chinese mother | *zambo-chino* |
| Negro father and *zamba* mother | *zambo-negro* (perfectly black) |
| Negro father and *cuarterona* or *quintera* mother | *mulatto* (rather dark) |
| Indian father and *mulatta* mother | *chino-oscuro* |
| Indian father and *mestiza* mother | *mestizo-claro* (frequently very beautiful) |
| Indian father and Chinese mother | *chino-cholo* |
| Indian father and *zamba* mother | *zambo-claro* |
| Indian father and *china-chola* mother | *Indian* (with rather short frizzy hair) |

The irreverent Schuyler, who does not hesitate to refer to the members of his race, in his column in the Pittsburgh *Courier*, as *dark brethren, Senegambians, tarbrushed folk* and so on, frequently discusses the opprobrious names that have been applied to them, *e.g.*, *darkey, coon, shine, smoke, dinge* and *boogie*. In 1936, when the Baltimore *Afro-American* started a crusade against " My Old Kentucky Home " because *darkey* occurs in it, and the National Association for the Advancement of Colored People denounced the Rev. Charles E. Coughlin for using it in a radio speech, he said:

> Will someone who has the gift of logic and intelligence tell me what is the difference between *darkey* and *Negro*? . . . There can be no more real objection to *darkey* than there can be to *blondie*. It is a far more acceptable term than *wop* or *kike*. As my friend J. A. Rogers [1] once profoundly remarked, the difference between *Negro* and *nigger* is the difference between *sir* and *sah*. Granted that the overwhelming majority of Negroes are opposed to the use of these terms, I can see no point in constantly making a wailing protest against their use.

*Coon*, though it is now one of the most familiar designations for a Negro, did not come into general use in that sense until the 80s; the DAE's first example is dated 1887.[2] For many years before that it had been used in the sense of a loutish white man, and in Henry Clay's time it had designated a member of the Whig party. It is generally assumed to have come from the name of the animal,[3] *Procyon lotor*, which was borrowed from the Algonquian early in the Seventeenth Century, and was shortened from *racoon* to *coon* before 1750. It

---

Indian father and *cuarterona* or *quintera* mother — *mestizo* (rather brown)

Mulatto father and *zamba* mother — *zambo* (a miserable race)

Mulatto father and *mestiza* mother — *chino* (of rather clear complexion)

Mulatto father and Chinese mother — *chino* (rather dark)

I retain Tschudi's comments, and also his use of the Spanish feminine forms.

1 A Negro historian. He has published a number of valuable books on the history of his people, and accumulated an enormous store of illustrative material.

2 Walter D. Edmonds says in *American Notes and Queries*, May, 1941, p. 23, that " Zip *Coon*, the blackface song, was being sung in 1834," but it apparently did not lead to the application of *coon* to Negroes.

3 I should add that this etymology was doubted by the late Dr. George Philip Krapp, who inclined to the theory that it came from *barracoon*, a word of Spanish origin designating slave quarters. See his letter in the *American Mercury*, June, 1926, p. 240.

appears variously in the early American chronicles as *rarowcun,
raugroughcun, rackoone, rockoon, arocoun, racoun, rahaugcum* and
*rattoon,* but the spelling *raccoon,* sometimes with one *c,* began to be
settled by 1700.[1] The use of *coon* to designate a Negro apparently
got its great vogue from the success of Ernest Hogan's song, " All
*Coons* Look Alike to Me," in 1896. Hogan, himself a colored man,
used the term without opprobrious intent, and was amazed and
crushed by the resentment it aroused among his people. Says Edward
B. Marks in " They All Sang ": [2]

> The refrain became a fighting phrase all over New York. Whistled by a
> white man, it was construed as a personal insult. Rosamond Johnson [3] relates
> that he once saw two men thrown off a ferry-boat in a row over the tune.
> Hogan became an object of censure among all the Civil Service intelligentsia,
> and died haunted by the awful crime he had unwittingly committed against
> his race.

" All *Coons* Look Alike to Me " was followed in 1899 by " Every
Race Has a Flag But the *Coon,*" by Heelan and Helf, two white men,
and in 1900 by " *Coon, Coon, Coon,*" by two others, Jefferson and
Friedman, and from that time forward *coon* was firmly established
in the American vocabulary.[4] The history of the other more or less
opprobrious synonyms for *Negro* is mainly obscure. The DAE does
not list *boogie* and its congeners, but reports that *booger* is an Americanism, traced to 1866, for a bogy. In 1891 a writer in *Harper's Magazine,*[5] quoted by the DAE, defined *boogah-hole* as " the hiding place
of cats and of children fleeing from justice " and of *boogars* or

1 Cf. AL4, p. 104.
2 New York, 1935, p. 91.
3 The colored composer of Under the
Bamboo Tree; Oh, Didn't He Ram-
ble; Lazy Moon; Li'l Gal; Mandy,
Won't You Let Me be Your Beau?;
Nobody's Looking But the Owl and
the Moon, and other great successes
of the 90s, and also of the Negro
anthem, Lift Every Voice and Sing.
He was the partner for many years
of Bob Cole, and the words of some
of his songs were written by his
brother, James Weldon Johnson,
one of the best writers the race has
yet produced.
4 In South Africa *coon* is sometimes
used by the newspapers to designate
a black native, apparently without

derogatory intent. The following is
from Stilt-Walker of Serowe, by
Normal Howell, *Cape Times* (Cape-
town), Aug. 22, 1936 " Why is stilt-
walking a common thing among the
*coons* of the Cape? " In the Virgin
Islands, formerly under the Danish
flag, the blacks are called *goons* or
*goonies.* In Lady Islands Come to
Life, Baltimore *Sunday Sun,* March
22, 1942, Lawrence H. Baker suggested that the *g* may be " a gut-
turalizing of the *c* in *coon,* arising
out of the Danes' attempt to pronounce the latter word." *Coon's
age,* traced by the DAE to 1845, and
*gone coon,* traced to 1839, had no
reference to Negroes.
5 Oct., p. 825.

*boogahs,* whatever these mysterious beings may be. It is possible that the suggestion of darkness developed *boogie* from *booger* or *boogah.* The latter form hints at a Southern variant of *bogy* or *bogey,* which has been traced in England by the NED, in the sense of the devil, to 1836, in the sense of a goblin to 1857, and in that of a bugbear to 1865. In Baltimore, in my childhood, *boogie-man* was one of the names of the devil. *Buffalo* as a designation for a Negro is not listed by the DAE, but it gives the word as used to designate a North Carolina Unionist during the Civil War; it has also been applied to the people of seaboard North Carolina in general. From the early Eighteenth Century down to 1880 or thereabout *Cuffy* was a generic name for a Negro, comparable to *Pat* for an Irishman. George Philip Krapp says in " The English Language in America " [1] that " it is said to be derived from Dutch *Koffi,* in Guiana a common name for Negroes and by custom applied to anyone born on Friday." The DAE calls it " of African origin " and traces it to 1713. It had a rival in *Sambo,* which apparently arose, not in the United States, but in England. The DAE traces it to 1748 there and to 1806 here. In my boyhood *Cuffy* had disappeared and *Sambo* was being supplanted by *Rastus.* [2] During the same era *Liza* or *Lize* was the common name for a colored girl, apparently a reminiscence of " Uncle Tom's Cabin."

The DAE omits *dinge* and lists *dinkey* only in the adjectival sense of small, trifling. *Dinkey,* in the Baltimore of my nonage, meant a colored child. Webster's New International, 1934, lists *dinge,* but omits *dinkey* in the sense here considered. *Kink* shows an obvious allusion to the Negro's hair; the DAE says that *kinky,* as applied to it, is an Americanism, and traces it to 1844. When, in 1936, Cab Calloway, the Negro musician, used *kinky-head* in a broadcast, he was violently belabored by the radio critic of one of the Negro weeklies.[3] *Moke* is traced by the DAE to 1856, but the word was used in England before this in the sense of a donkey. An amateur lexicog-

1 New York; 1925, Vol. I, p. 256.
2 The once very popular song, *Rastus on Parade,* by Kerry Mills, was published in 1896. The DAE traces *Sambo* to 1806. Schele de Vere says that it comes from the Spanish *Zambo,* " originally meaning bandy-legged," first applied " to the offspring of a Negro and a mulatto, and afterward, in the South American colonies, to the child of a Negro and an Indian woman." Bartlett says that in the middle of the last century it was used in the United States " more specifically to mean the offspring of a Negro and mulatto."
3 The episode is recorded by Schuyler in the Pittsburgh *Courier,* Nov. 7, 1936. *Woollyhead* is traced by the DAE to 1827.

rapher calling himself Socrates Hyacinth, writing in 1869,[1] sought
to derive it " from Icelandic *möckvi*, darkness "; and called it " a word
chiefly in use among the Regulars stationed in Texas and in the Territories." He added that it also had " Cymric affinities, and was probably brought into currency by Welsh recruits who have occasionally
drifted into the Army from New York City." This suggestion of a
possible Welsh origin was supported by an anonymous writer in the
London *Daily Mirror* in 1938,[2] who said that the etymology " which
receives the greatest expert support derives *moke* from the Welsh
gipsy *moxio* or *moxia*, a donkey." " *Moxio*," he continued, " existed
some fifty years before the first recorded instance, in 1848, of *moke*.
Moreover, about 1839 somebody of the name of Brandon records
*moak* as a cant word of gipsy origin, and, at that time, mainly gipsy
use." The NED calls *moke* " of unknown origin " and Webster's New
International marks it " origin uncertain." Weekley suggests that it
is " perhaps from some proper name (? *Moggy*) applied to the ass,"
and says that *Mocke*, *Mok*, *Mog* and *Mug* " all occur as personal
names in the Thirteenth Century and survive in the surnames *Mokes*
and *Moxon*." *Moke* was thrown into competition with *coon* in 1899
by the success of " Smokey *Mokes*," a popular song by Holzmann
and Lind, but is now heard only seldom. *Pickaninny*, in the sense of
a Negro child, is not an Americanism. It was in use in England so
long ago as 1657, whereas the DAE's first American example is dated
1800. The English prefer the spelling *piccaniny;* the word in the
past was variously spelled *piccanini*, *pickoninnie*, *pick-ny*, *piccanin*
and *picannin*. It appears to be derived from the Cuban Spanish *piqui-
nini*, meaning a small child. It was taken into English in the British
West Indies. It is used in South Africa precisely as we use it, but it is
commonly spelled *piccanin*. In Australia it designates a child of the
aborigines, and has there produced a derivative, *piccaninny-daylight*,
signifying dawn.[3] In the Baltimore of my youth *pickaninny* was not
used invidiously, but rather affectionately. So, indeed, was *tar-pot*,
also signifying a Negro child.

1 South-Western Slang, *Overland
Monthly*, Aug., 1869. His article is
reprinted in full in The Beginnings
of American English, by M. M.
Mathews; Chicago, 1931, pp. 151–63.
2 Nov. 28.

3 A Popular Dictionary of Australian
Slang, by Sidney J. Baker; second
ed. Melbourne, 1943, p. 58. See also
Australian English, by Edward E.
Morris; London, 1898, p. 350.

The DAE does not list such vulgar synonyms for *Negro* as *ape, eight-ball, jazzbo, jigabo* (with the variants, *jibagoo, jig, zigabo, zigaboo, zig*), *jit, seal, shine, skunk, smoke, snowball, spade, squasho* and *Zulu*.[1] *Crow* is traced to 1823, when it was used by J. Fenimore Cooper in " The Pioneers," the first of his Leatherstocking tales. Whether it suggested *Jim Crow* or was suggested by *Jim Crow* I do not know. The DAE's first example of *Jim Crow* is dated 1838, but that example includes the statement that " ' *Zip Coon* ' and ' *Jim Crow* ' are hymns of great antiquity." The DAE says, however, that Thomas D. Rice's song and dance, " *Jim Crow*," was written in 1832.[2] The verb phrase, *to jump Jim Crow*, appeared a year later. By 1838 *Jim Crow* had become an adjective and was so used by Harriet Beecher Stowe in " Uncle Tom's Cabin," 1852; of late it has also become a verb. The DAE's first example of *Jim Crow car* is dated 1861; of *Jim Crow school*, 1903; of *Jim Crow bill*, 1904; of *Jim Crow law*, 1904, and of *Jim Crow regulations*, 1910. All are probably older. Mr. Valdemar Viking, of Red Bank, N. J., suggests that *eight-ball* is derived from the game of pool, which is played with fifteen numbered and vari-colored balls, No. 8 being black. The DAE lists *blueskin* as an early synonym for Negro. It occurs in Cooper's " The Spy," 1821, but had become obsolete before the Civil War. In Baltimore, in the 80s of the last century, the German-speaking householders, when they had occasion to speak of Negro servants in their presence, called them *die blaue* (blues). In the 70s *die schwarze* (blacks) had been used, but it was believed that the Negroes had fathomed it. They had also, I am sure, fathomed *die blaue*, for they always penetrate the stratagems of white folk. The New York Jews formerly

---

1 James Hargan, in The Psychology of Prison Language, *Journal of Abnormal and Social Psychology*, Oct.–Dec., 1935, p. 36, says that the inmates of Sing-Sing call a Negro a *jig* or *buggy*, and use *gee-chee* to designate one from Charleston, S. C. J. Louis Kuethe, in Prison Parlance, *American Speech*, Feb., 1934, pp. 25–28, says that the inmates of one of the Maryland prisons use *head-light* for a light-skinned Negro, *spade* for a very dark one, and *three-quarters Kelt* for a very light one. Raven I. McDavid, Jr., says in Miscellaneous Notes on Recent Articles, *Ameri-*

*can Speech*, April, 1943, p. 152, that *brass ankle* is used by the older Tennesseans for a mulatto. Dorothy Bentz says in American English as Spoken by the Barbadians, *American Speech*, Dec., 1938, p. 310, that in the Canal Zone all West Indians are called *jigs*.

2 Rice (1808–1860) was a comedian, playwright and songwriter, and *Jim Crow* was only one of his songs that became popular. He is not to be confused with Dan Rice (1822–1900), an acrobat, circus clown and temperance orator.

used *schwarze* also, but in recent years they have abandoned it for *gelbe* (*yellow*), which without doubt is likewise penetrated.[1] There is a brief list of the terms Negroes use in speaking of themselves, especially to distinguish between different skin-colors, in AL4, p. 296, n. 3. On p. 214, n. 2, thereof there is a discussion of *ofay*, which the sophisticates among them use to designate a white person. It is usually derived from the French *au fait*, but without any evidence that I am aware of. Mr. William V. Glenn, of Harrisburg, Pa., suggests [2] that it may be a pig-Latin form of *foe*, but that also seems unlikely. The Negroes use various other sportive terms for whites, *e.g.*, *pale-face*, *chalk* and *milk*. A few of a militantly race-conscious kidney call Africa the *mother country*.[3] Unhappily, most of the ideas and all of the cultural criteria of the American blacks are so thoroughly American that such gestures always smack of affectation. Even their norms of personal beauty are white. " As Negroes," said a colored lady journalist in 1944,[4] " we usually say that a person is beautiful if they closely approach white standards, for we think of beauty as we have been taught since we have lived in this country. Straight noses, thin lips and skin that is not black come in for our share of admiration. Whether we like to admit it or not, this is true." A curious euphemism for *Negro*, apparently originating in the South, deserves a line. It is *nonpromotable*, and it designates primarily a locomotive fireman who is ineligible to promotion to engineer because of his color.[5] It has come into use to signify any Negro in a like unfortunate position.

The English have many derisive terms embodying references to Scotland and the Scots, *e.g.*, *Scotch mist*, a driving rain; *Scotch fiddle*, the itch; and *Scotch warming-pan*, a loose girl; but they are not in use in the United States. " I have heard the term *Scots greys*," said a recent Scots writer, " used in an entomological connection." [6] He might have added *Itchland*, *Scratchland* and *Louseland*, all of them derisive English names for Scotland. Also, he might have recalled the Scotch-hating Samuel Johnson's definition of propinquity: " In close juxtaposition, as a Scotchman and a louse." The inhabitants of the

1 I am informed by Mr. Harry G. Green of Chicago that *gelbe* is not used in the Chicago region.
2 Private communication, July 20, 1937.
3 America's Mother Country, by Rex Forrest, *American Speech*, Feb., 1941, p. 74.
4 New Yorker's Album, by Constance Curtis, *Amsterdam News*, March 4.
5 *Congressional Record*, Dec. 17, 1943, p. A5942, col. 3.
6 International Libels, by William Power, Glasgow *Record*, April 10, 1929.

Northern kingdom greatly prefer *Scot* or *Scotsman* to *Scotchman*. *Scot* is traced by the NED to 1338, *Scotsman* to *c.* 1375, and *Scotchman* to 1570. The NED notes that, from the Seventeenth Century onward to recent times, *Scot* was " chiefly historical except in jocular or rhetorical use," but now it is dominant. Says an English correspondent: " *Scotchman* is now barred from most English newspapers. To call a Scot a *Scotchman* is like calling a Negro a *coon*. This tenderness is quite modern, and I have been told that it was propagated by Robert Louis Stevenson. James M. Barrie ignored it, and all the older Scotch authors, *e.g.,* Burns and Scott, used *Scotch* and *Scotchman* without apology. But now even the adjective is *Scots*." Nearly all the English words and phrases based on *Scotch* embody references to the traditional penuriousness of the Scots, *e.g., Scotch coffee*, hot water flavored with burnt biscuit; *to play the Scotch organ*, to put money in a cash-register; *Scotch pint*, a two-quart bottle; *Scotch sixpence*, a threepence, and the *Scotchman's cinema*, Piccadilly Circus, because it offers many free attractions.[1]

In the interchange of international objurgations the United States gets off very lightly, for only the Spanish-speaking nations appear to have any opprobrious names for Americans, and these are few in number.[2] I can find, indeed, only two, *Yanqui-blofero* (in Cuba, *blofista*), and *gringo*. The latter is traced by the DAE to 1853, but it is probably much older. In 1929 the late Dr. Frank H. Vizetelly printed its history in the New York *Times*.[3] He said:

> *Gringo* dates back to 1787. It is explained in P. Esteban de Terreros y Pando's Diccionario Castellano, in volume 2, page 240, column 1 of that work, published in Madrid in that year: " Gringos — Llaman en Malaga a los estranjeros, que tienen cierta especie de acento, que los priva de una locucion facil y natural Castellana; y en Madrid dan el mismo, y por la misma causa con particularidad a los Irlandeses." Roughly translated, this means: " Gringos — The name given

---

1 I take these from A Dictionary of International Slurs, by A. A. Roback; Cambridge, Mass., 1944, pp. 61–63. So far as I know, this is the only book in print listing what the compiler calls *ethnophaulisms*. It is not exhaustive, but it contains a great deal of amusing and instructive stuff.

2 But Roback, just cited, lists several words and phrases that reflect unfavorably upon what are thought to be American traits, *e.g.,* the Hungarian verb *amerikázni*, to loaf on the job; the Italian noun *americanata*, an advertising stunt; and the French *oeillade américaine*, goo-goo eyes. Says Roback in his preface: " Undoubtedly some lay person will interpose the question: Why confine oneself to slurs and not include also the complimentary allusions? The answer is simple. There are practically none of the latter."

3 The Origin of *Gringo*, editorial page, Sept. 29.

in Malaga to those foreigners who have a certain accent which prevents them from speaking Spanish fluently and naturally; and in Madrid the same term is used for the same reason, especially with reference to the Irish." The word may be found also in Melchior Emmanuel Nunez de Taboada's Dictionnaire Espagnol-Francais, issued in Paris in 1838, where one may read, sub verbo: " *Gringo, ga,* adj. (figuré et familier) Grec., hébreu. On le dit d'une chose unintelligible."

Various other etymologies for the term have been proposed, but they are all fanciful.[1] In New Mexico an American is called an *Anglo.*[2] Rather curiously, no pejorative for *Indian* has ever appeared in American speech. The DAE's first example of *injun* is dated 1825, but *indjon, ingen* and *engiane* preceded it: these forms are hardly to be called derogatory. *Lo,* borrowed from Alexander Pope's line, " Lo, the poor Indian " [3] is merely sportive. It seems to have been a long time coming in, for the DAE's first example is dated 1871. *Buck* has been applied to a male Indian since the middle of the last century, but it was used to designate a male Negro somewhat earlier. The use of *Siwash* to designate any Indian seems to be confined to the Northwest. The English use *wog* for a native of India, and it has been extended to indicate any native of the Red Sea and Indian Ocean country. It was borrowed by the American troops serving in Egypt during World War II from the argot of the British troops. It is supposed to be an abbreviation of *wily oriental gentleman.*[4]

### 7. FORBIDDEN WORDS

304. [We yet use *toilet, retiring-room, wash-room* and *public comfort station* in place of franker terms.] The list of such euphemisms is long, especially for women's rooms. In the high days of euphemy in the United States they were not called anything at all, but simply marked *For Ladies Only*. Later this was reduced to *Ladies Only*, then

1 See also The Southwestern Word Box, by T. M. P., *New Mexico Quarterly*, Aug., 1932, pp. 263–68, and Nicknames for Americans Abroad, by R. G. W., *American Notes and Queries*, Dec., 1943, pp. 139–40. The latter quotes Katharine Ward Parmelee (*Romanic Review*, Vol. IX, pp. 108–10) to the effect that *gringo* is applied in Mexico and Honduras to Americans, in Chile and Peru to Englishmen, in Guatemala to Englishmen and Germans, and in Venezuela to anyone who speaks Spanish badly or not at all.
2 Among the New Words, by Dwight L. Bolinger, *American Speech*, Dec., 1943, p. 302.
3 An Essay on Man, I, 1732.
4 I am indebted here to Mrs. W. W. Elmer, Jr., of Idaho City, Idaho, and to Mr. Peter V. Chew of Berryville, Va.

to *Ladies,* and finally to *Women.* Simultaneously, *For Gents Only* went through the stages of *Gents Only, Gents, Gentlemen* and *Men.* During the days of Prohibition some learned speak-easy proprietor in New York hit upon the happy device of calling his retiring-room for female boozers a *powder-room,* and meanwhile various other euphemists had borrowed or invented *rest-room, dressing-room, ladies'-room, cloak-room* and *lavatory. Lavatory* and *toilet* are in use in England, but the NED, which traces the latter to 1819, marks it " in U. S. esp." Various other designations, sometimes very fanciful, have been recorded from time to time, *e.g., boudoir,* which appears on the ladies' room at the Casa Italiana, Columbia University, and *Egypt,* in use in the phrase *to go to Egypt* at Wabash College, Crawfordsville, Ind.[1] In the American women's colleges, in the 30s, there arose a fashion for calling the retiring-place the *John* or *Johnnie.* In July, 1941, Louis Untermeyer asked the readers of *American Notes and Queries* for light on its etymology, and during the months following received a number of replies. One signing himself E.F.W. suggested in August, 1941, p. 79, that the term may have come from the old English *jakes,* which the NED traces to 1530 or thereabout.[2] When, in 1596, Sir John Harington, one of Queen Elizabeth's courtiers, invented the modern indoor toilet, with its flushing arrangement, he announced it in a work with the punning title of " The Metamorphosis of *Ajax.*" [3] In the September, 1941 issue of *American Notes and Queries,* pp. 95 and 96, H. E. Allen reported that " the use of *John .* . . . goes back to the second half of the Seventeenth Century, at least," but offered no documentary evidence. In November, 1941, p. 125, J.D.W. noted that at Vassar, during the early 20s, the *John* was known as *Fred.* The usual term among male students is *can,* which is also a common American word for jail. The outdoor latrine that still survives in country districts is often called a *Chick Sale,* in compliment to an entertainer whose amusing account of the

1 An American Euphuism, by Ted Robinson, *American Notes and Queries,* Aug., 1943, p. 78.
2 Veiled Language, by Otto Jespersen, *S. P. E. Tract No. XXXIII,* 1929, p. 424.
3 *Ajax* was then pronounced *a-jakes.* Harington was Elizabeth's godson, and is best remembered as the translator of Orlando Furioso. In 1605

he applied for appointment as Archbishop of Dublin, though he was not in holy orders. The Metamorphosis of *Ajax* included working drawings of his invention. It was republished in London in 1927. He followed it with An Anatomie of the Metamorphosed *Ajax,* and Ulysses Upon *Ajax.*

building of one was widely circulated, *c.* 1920.[1] Other terms recorded by philologians are *boggard, bog-house* and *bog-shop.*[2] Some of the soldiers in the South Seas, in 1944, used *Shangri-la.*[3]

The inventor of *public comfort station* remains unknown. The DAE's first example of the term comes from a news item in the New York *Evening Post,* June 30, 1904, announcing that excavations had been begun for New York's first such station, in Chatham square. The French *pissoir,* either as public convenience or as a word, has never got any lodgment in the United States. The French themselves sometimes substitute *vespasienne,* apparently in memory of the Roman emperor who forced the Romans to pay fees for the use of the city latrines. The same designation is recorded in the French sections of Canada, but it is seldom used. Instead, the Canadians say *toilette,* which is short for *chambre de toilette.*[4] *Water-closet,* which is commonly abbreviated to *W.C.* in England, is traced by the NED to 1755. It was preceded by *closet of ease,* which is traced to 1662. The shortened form *closet* is not found before 1869. It has long been in wide use in the United States, though the DAE does not list it. The old English term *necessary-house,* traced by the NED to 1611, has dropped out of use. So have its congeners, *necessary-vault,* 1609; *necessary-place,* 1697 and *necessary-stool,* 1761, and the shortened form *necessary,* 1756. When the American newspapers have to mention a privy-vault, say when a child falls into it or a murderer hides his victim's body in it, they call it a *cesspool.*

305. [Hollywood, always under heavy pressure from official and volunteer censors, has its own *Index,* augmented from time to time.] This *Index* was first adumbrated on December 8, 1921, when the Motion Picture Producers and Distributors of America, Inc., was organized, and Elder Will H. Hays, an eminent Presbyterian quasi-ecclesiastic, who had been Postmaster General in the Cabinet of President Harding, was offered the post of president and moral dictator. The situation awaiting him on his consecration was thus described in 1943 by a movie magnate, Samuel Goldwyn:

1 This work was reprinted in England, but H. W. Seaman tells me that it was a failure there. " Its only sales," he says, " were among the extremely up-to-date."

2 Aliases for the Latrine, *American Notes and Queries,* Oct., 1941, p. 103.

3 The Physiology of War, *Journal of the American Medical Association* (Tonics and Sedatives section), Jan. 29, 1944.

4 I am indebted here to Mr. S. H. Abrahamson of Montreal.

If people were cynical, the movies were more so. If people talked about loose morals, the movies pictured it for them. If you want a clue to those times look at these movie titles: " Loving Lips," " Mad Love," " Temptation," " Passion Flame," " Twin Beds," " Flaming Youth," " Children Not Wanted," " On to Reno," " Trifling Women," " Why Be Good? "

You can guess the result. In one year — 1921 — indignant groups saw to it that State legislators introduced nearly 100 censorship bills in 37 States. Most of them were defeated and, fortunately, the industry took the hint and set up a code of its own with the Will Hays office to administer it.[1]

The elder laid about him vigorously, preventing the completion of a number of bawdy films already in progress, and in the course of the next eight years gradually evolved a so-called Production Code by which all save a few outlaw producers are still bound. Its text, promulgated on March 31, 1930, and since revised from time to time, is as follows:

General Principles.

1. No picture shall be produced which will lower the moral standards of those who see it. Hence the sympathy of the audience shall never be thrown to the side of crime, wrongdoing, evil or sin.

2. Correct standards of life, subject only to the requirements of drama and entertainment, shall be presented.

3. Law, natural or human, shall not be ridiculed, nor shall sympathy be created for its violation.

Particular Applications.

I. Crimes Against the Law.

These shall never be presented in such a way as to throw sympathy with the crime as against law and justice or to inspire others with a desire for imitation.

1. Murder

*a.* The technique of murder must be presented in a way that will not inspire imitation.

*b.* Brutal killings are not to be presented in detail.

*c.* Revenge in modern times shall not be justified.

2. Methods of crime should not be explicitly presented.

*a.* Theft, robbery, safe-cracking, and dynamiting of trains, mines, buildings, etc., should not be detailed in method.

*b.* Arson must be subject to the same safeguards.

*c.* The use of firearms should be restricted to essentials.

*d.* Methods of smuggling should not be presented.

3. Illegal drug traffic must never be presented.

4. The use of liquor in American life, when not required by the plot or for proper characterization, will not be shown.

II. Sex.

The sanctity of the institution of marriage and the home shall be upheld.

1 No New Jazz Age, *This Week,* Dec.     *Congressional Record,* Dec. 14, p.
12, 1943; reprinted in full in the     A5857.

Pictures shall not infer that low forms of sex relationship are the accepted or common thing.

1. Adultery, sometimes necessary plot material, must not be explicitly treated, or justified, or presented attractively.

2. Scenes of Passion.

*a.* They should not be introduced when not essential to the plot.

*b.* Excessive and lustful kissing, lustful embraces, suggestive postures and gestures, are not to be shown.

*c.* In general, passion should so be treated that these scenes do not stimulate the lower and baser element.

3. Seduction or Rape.

*a.* They should never be more than suggested, and only when essential for the plot, and even then never shown by explicit method.

*b.* They are never the proper subject for comedy.

4. Sex perversion or any reference to it is forbidden.

5. White slavery shall not be treated.

6. Miscegenation (sex relationship between the white and black races) is forbidden.

7. Sex hygiene and venereal diseases are not subjects for motion pictures.

8. Scenes of actual child birth, in fact or in silhouette, are never to be presented.

9. Children's sex organs are never to be exposed.

III. Vulgarity.

The treatment of low, disgusting, unpleasant, though not necessarily evil, subjects should be subject always to the dictate of good taste and a regard for the sensibilities of the audience.

IV. Obscenity.

Obscenity in word, gesture, reference, song, joke, or by suggestion (even when likely to be understood only by part of the audience) is forbidden.

V. Profanity.

Pointed profanity (this includes the words, *God, Lord, Jesus, Christ* — unless used reverently — *Hell, S.O.B., damn, Gawd*), or every other profane or vulgar expression, however used, is forbidden.

VI. Costume.

1. Complete nudity is never permitted. This includes nudity in fact or in silhouette, or any lecherous or licentious notice thereof by other characters in the picture.

2. Undressing scenes should be avoided, and never used save where essential to the plot.

3. Indecent or undue exposure is forbidden.

4. Dancing costumes intended to permit undue exposure or indecent movements in the dance are forbidden.

VII. Dances.

1. Dances suggesting or representing sexual actions or indecent passion are forbidden.

2. Dances which emphasize indecent movements are to be regarded as obscene.

VIII. Religion.

1. No film or episode may throw ridicule on any religious faith.

2. Ministers of religion in their character as ministers of religion should not be used as comic characters or as villains.

3. Ceremonies of any definite religion should be carefully and respectfully handled.

IX. Locations.

The treatment of bedrooms must be governed by good taste and delicacy.

X. National Feelings.

1. The use of the Flag shall be consistently respectful.

2. The history, institutions, prominent people and citizenry of other nations shall be represented fairly.

XI. Titles. Salacious, indecent, or obscene titles shall not be used.

XII. Repellent Subjects.

The following subjects must be treated within the careful limits of good taste:

1. Actual hangings or electrocutions as legal punishments for crime.

2. Third Degree methods.

3. Brutality and possible gruesomeness.

4. Branding of people or animals.

5. Apparent cruelty to children or animals.

6. The sale of women, or a woman selling her virtue.

7. Surgical operations.[1]

The Hays office is very watchful, and not only profanity and indecency, but also what it chooses to regard as vulgarity, are prohibited. Late in 1942, for example, the New York *Times*[2] reported that it had ordered a producer to delete the word *louse* from a film lambasting the Japanese, and had suggested *stinkbug* as a substitute. It even frowns on such relatively harmless words as *belch*. Also, it serves as a listening-post for the British Board of Film Censors, and prohibits the use of terms that are offensive in England but innocuous here, *e.g.*, *bum*, *shyster* and *sissy*.[3] Nor is the Hays office the only

1 I am indebted for this text to Mr. Alfred J. Croft, of the Hays office in New York. During the heyday of kidnappers and Prohibition gangsters special regulations were drawn up for the making of films dealing with crime, but they are now rather obsolete. In 1940, under pressure from the American Humane Association, pictures showing cruelty to animals were forbidden. The producers also subscribe to an Advertising Code prohibiting " profanity and vulgarity " in their advertising.

2 Quoted in the *New Republic*, Jan. 4, 1943.

3 *Look*, Aug. 2, 1938, p. 16. Censors' Bans, *News Review* (London), Feb.

7, 1938. When Al Jolson's Hallelujah, I'm a *Bum* was shown in England the title had to be changed to Hallelujah, I'm a *Tramp*, for *bum*, over there, designates the backside. *Sissy* is even worse to English ears, for it means a homosexual. Why *shyster* is objected to I do not know. Partridge says that the English borrowed it from America, in the sense of a disreputable lawyer, *c.* 1890. In 1938 the British Board of Film Censors forbade Walt Disney's Snow White for showing to children on the ground that it might frighten them. At that time all the children in London were being taught how to wear gas-masks.

bugaboo in the movie zoo. The producers must also submit to censorship by a committee of Catholics, frequently very drastic in its demands, and there are State boards of censorship in Maryland, New York, Ohio, Pennsylvania, Virginia and Kansas, and city boards in Boston, Chicago, Detroit and elsewhere. In the days when the Motion Picture Producers and Distributors of America was organized the speaking stage, and especially the vaudeville stage, was heavily beset by censors,[1] but it has since thrown most of them off, and save in Boston, New York and a few other cities, is virtually free. Thus it can indulge in a vocabulary almost approaching that of Ernest Hemingway, James Joyce, *et al.*,[2] and exhibit the female form in nearly complete nudity, whereas the movies are cribbed, cabined and confined by regulations that would now seem oppressive in a Baptist female seminary. The radio, in the department of speech, is policed quite as rigorously, and its boss, the Federal Communications Commission, has the power to deprive an offending station of its license. This fact makes station and network directors very skittish, and some of them go to extreme lengths to avoid trouble. The following from *Radioland*[3] illustrates their fears:

Networks don't always agree on just what is offensive. A Negro spiritual which the NBC deemed harmless failed to pass the Columbia censors because they considered its title, " *Satan*, I Give You My Children," sacrilegious. Even a revision which made the title " O *Lord*, I Give You My Children" failed to pass muster.

But not even the radio is under such oppressive censorship as the magazines and newspapers, which may be barred from the mails, and

---

1 Under the heading of Verbotens of 1929, compiled by Joe Laurie, Jr., *Variety*, the theatrical weekly, once printed a list of the words and phrases forbidden to vaudevillains in that year. It included *to ʰell with*, *cockeyed*, *wop*, *Arab* (signifying a Jew), *pushover*, *dammit*, *belly*, *fanny* and *lousy*. It should be added that these prohibitions were imposed by the Keith booking-office, not by any official censorship. See also Lefty's Notebook, by the aforesaid Laurie, *Variety*, June 14, 1944.

2 The result in one case was described by Wolcott Gibbs in a review of Storm Operation, by Maxwell Anderson, *New Yorker*, Jan. 22, 1944,

p. 34, as follows: " The humor is hard to discuss in a magazine that is distributed by a moral Postoffice. For purposes of verisimilitude (to give him the benefit of a considerable doubt), Mr. Anderson has found it necessary to use a good many Anglo-Saxon monosyllables; for obvious reasons he has had to rearrange them a little, which he does by changing their initial letters. Obviously nothing is disguised by this clever trick and there is even a certain amount of emphasis gained by forcing the ear to adjust itself to a variation; it is almost as if the original had been underlined."

3 You Can't Sing That, March, 1935.

hence subjected to ruinous loss, at the fiat of a Postmaster General who maintains a bureau of snoopers and smut-snufflers for harassing them. In the proceeding against *Esquire* in 1943–44 these Dogberries actually objected to its use of such perfectly harmless words as *backside, behind* and *bawdy-house*.[1] It is thus no wonder that American newspapers, with few exceptions, continue to use the euphemisms inherited from the Victorian age, *e.g., criminal operation, house of ill repute, statutory offense, intimate relations*, and *felonious assault*. Sometimes the result is extremely amusing. Not long ago, for example, a New York paper reported that a *fiend* had knocked a girl down, " dragged her down the cellar-steps, beat her with an iron pipe, and *then* assaulted her." [2] In 1943, when a wealthy lady of café society named Lonergan was murdered in New York by her husband, all the local papers avoided mention of the fact that the accused claimed to be a homosexual, and in fact had made it an essential part of his defense. Finally *PM* broke the ice by referring prissily to " indications of an abnormal psychological nature," and a few days later " every paper, as if by common agreement, came right out with the word *homosexual*." [3] *Romance* is constantly used to designate an illicit love-affair,[4] and *love-nest* has been widened in meaning to include the more elegant varieties of houses of prostitution. In 1931 a Chattanooga paper made journalistic history by reporting that a man in that town had been arrested for " walking the streets accompanied by a woman." [5] It was generally recognized by the brethren that this was a euphemism for something else, but precisely what that something was did not appear, and they speculated in vain. It is in England, however, that this fear of plain terms produces the most absurd extravagances. In AL4, p. 311, I give some specimens from the *News of the World*. Others that have accumulated since are *a certain illness* (syphilis), *mode of living* (prostitution), *certain suggestions* (a proposal that women go on the street), *a certain result* (abortion), *improper assault* (rape), *to interfere with* (to rape), and *associating* (living in adultery). In 1936, when a female lunatic stripped off her clothes in St. Paul's Cathedral, " the *Daily Telegraph* described her

---

1 The NED traces *backside* to *c.* 1500 and shows that it was used by Addison. *Bawdy-house* is traced to 1552, and *behind* to 1786.

2 I am indebted here to Mr. William McNulty, of Bedford Village, N. Y.

3 Five Days Wonder, *New Yorker*, Nov. 6, 1943, pp. 70 *ff.*

4 *Romance*, by Mary Mielenz, *American Speech*, Oct., 1937, p. 237.

5 Euphemism, Monroe (Mich.) *Evening News* (editorial), Nov. 21, 1931.

as *unclothed*, as did the *Daily Mail* and the *Daily Express*. The *Daily Herald* went so far as to call her *nude* in a heading but used *unclothed* elsewhere. The *News-Chronicle* favored *unclothed* and *unclad*. Not one was able to face the horror of the word *naked*." [1]

306. [Ever since the beginning of the Sex Hygiene movement, *c.* 1910, *syphilis* and *gonorrhea* have been struggling for recognition.] Since this was written, in 1935, they have forced their way into general newspaper use, and promise to shoulder out such former euphemisms as *social disease* and *vice disease*. In 1934 the New York *Times* Index indexed no reference whatever to either *syphilis* or *venereal disease*, but in the 1935 volume there were six references, in that for 1936, 18; in that for 1937, 72; and in that for 1938, 92; and since then the old ban has been definitely off. [2] The Chicago *Tribune* claims credit for having been the first American newspaper to print *syphilis* and *gonorrhea*. [3] This was in 1913, and the claim may be valid, though I printed both words during the same year in the Baltimore *Evening Sun*. The other newspapers followed only slowly. In 1918 the editors of the Scripps Northwest League decided to stick to *vice diseases*, and in 1933, twenty years after the *Tribune's* revolt, the New York *Times* was still using *blood disease*. But soon afterward came the break, and today all save a few of the prissier papers use *syphilis*, and large numbers also use *gonorrhea*, which, for some mysterious reason, seems to be regarded as a shade more offensive. [4] On the entrance of the United States into World War II the surgeons of the Army and Navy began to discuss both *syphilis* and *gonorrhea* with the utmost freedom, and the plain people became weathered to placards and circulars telling the soldiers and sailors how to avoid both. The only surviving opposition to such plain speaking seems to come from Catholics, who hold that any open discussion of prevention breaks down moral restraints and so inspires to sin. When, in the Summer of 1944, a body of altruistic advertising agents called the War Advertising Council prepared a series of advertisements couched in realistic terms and proposed that the newspapers sell them to patriotic advertisers, there was an

1 Vancouver (B. C.) *Daily Province*, June 9, 1936.
2 Syphilis Sive Morbus Humanus, by Charles S. Butler, rear admiral, M.C., U.S.N., ret.; Washington, 1939, p. xii.
3 Shadow on the Land (editorial), Feb. 2, 1938.

4 Perhaps because what even medical men used to conceal under the euphemism of *Neisserian infection* is more frequently the subject of folk ribaldry. Albert L. S. Neisser (1855–1916) discovered the gonococcus in 1879.

earnest protest from the national commander of the Catholic War Veterans, Inc. Such advertisements, he argued, would " weaken the sense of decency in the American people, . . . increase immorality by promising to make promiscuity safe,". . . and " ignore a fundamental fact in human conduct, that shame and embarrassment are among the strongest deterrents to the sins that spread VD." The campaign of the advertising agents was backed by the Public Health Service and the OWI, but that of the Catholic war heroes had the support of the Knights of Columbus and many of the Catholic diocesan weeklies, and when the latter began to hint at a boycott of both the sponsoring advertisers and the beneficiary newspapers there was some abatement of the initial enthusiasm.[1]

In England, the opposition to free discourse on venereal disease seems to come, not from religious bodies, but from the newspapers. When, in 1937, Sir William Wilson Jameson, a distinguished health officer there, demanded " Let us get rid of this taboo," and the Ministry of Health followed a year later by preparing the first of a series of very frank advertisements for insertion in the newspapers, the copy committee of the Newspaper Proprietors' Association, of which Leonard Raftery, advertisement manager of the London *Daily Mail*, was chairman, objected to some of the terms used, and the ministry was forced to modify them. Here, for example, is a paragraph from the advertisement:

> The two principal venereal diseases are *syphilis* and *gonorrhoea*[2] (vulgarly known as *pox* and *clap*). Both are caused by tiny living organisms or germs, but the germ of *syphilis* is quite different from that of *gonorrhoea*.

And here is what the prudish copy committee made of it:

> The two principal venereal diseases are *syphilis* and *gonorrhoea*. They are caused by quite different living organisms or germs.

In another paragraph the sentence " Professional prostitutes are not the only source of infection " was struck out, and in yet another the phrase *sex organs* was twice eliminated. The *Lancet*, the principal organ of the English medical men, protested against this bowdlerization with great vigor, saying:

[1] The record of this episode is to be found in the *Editor and Publisher — Catholic News* Protests VD Ad Campaign, Sept. 2, 1944; CWV Continues Protest Against Anti-VD Ads, Sept. 16, and U. S. Agencies Prepare Guides on VD Ads, Sept. 23 — and in the *Congressional Record*, Sept. 18, 1944, p. A4413.

[2] *Gonorrhoea* is the English spelling.

This is the second occasion on which prudery has been allowed to hinder health education: it will be recalled that about a year ago advice to the public about washing the hands after evacuation of the bowel had to be withdrawn because the papers could not bring themselves to print *water-closet*. In the present instance the precision of the original advertisement has had to give place to vaguer general statements. . . . It would be well to bear in mind that this advertisement has been designed to reach the simplest people; a barricade of unfamiliar terms may seem almost as impenetrable to them as a barricade of silence.

This protest had some effect, but not much. The *Times*, after some hesitation, accepted the original advertisement with a few minor changes, but the *Daily Telegraph* and other papers insisted on substituting *reproductive organs* for *sex organs*, and the *Daily Express*, the *Evening Standard* and a group of Scotch papers did not print it at all.[1]

The rage for euphemisms arose in England in Puritan times, and was quickly transferred to the American colonies. The Restoration naturally brought some abatement at home, but there was never any real return to the free utterance of the Elizabethan era, and during the Eighteenth Century prissiness enjoyed a considerable revival. The Puritans not only made war upon all the old expletives and all the immemorial names for physiological processes; they also strove to put down the abhorrent vocabulary of Holy Church, which they described elegantly as the Whore of Babylon. Zachary Grey records in his notes to Samuel Butler's " Hudibras," 1744, that the word *saint* was actually deleted from the titles of the principal London churches, and that some of the more fanatical Puritans began substituting an ironical *sir* for *saint* in the designations of the saints themselves, *e.g.*, *Sir* Peter, *Sir* Paul and even *Sir* Mary. Some of them, going further, tried to substitute *Christ-tide* for *Christmas* in order to get rid of the reminder of the outlawed mass in the latter, but this effort seems to have failed. The nasty revival of prudery associated with the name of Victoria in England went to extreme lengths in the United States, and proceeded so far that it was frequently remarked and deplored by visiting Englishmen. Said Captain Frederick Marryat in 1839:

[The Americans] object to everything nude in statuary. When I was at the house of Governor Everett, at Boston, I observed a fine cast of the Apollo

1 Hush-Hush Over V.D., *News-Review*, London, March 11, 1943, p. 19

Belvidere; but in compliance with general opinion it hung with drapery, although Governor Everett himself is a gentleman of refined mind and high classical attainments, and quite above such ridiculous sensitiveness.[1] In language it is the same thing. There are certain words which are never used in America, but an absurd substitute is employed. I cannot particularize them, lest I should be accused of indelicacy myself. I may, however, state one little circumstance which will fully prove the correctness of what I say.

When at Niagara Falls I was escorting a young lady with whom I was on friendly terms. She had been standing on a piece of rock, the better to view the scene, when she slipped down, and was evidently hurt by the fall: she had, in fact, grazed her shin. As she limped a little in walking home, I said, "Did you hurt your *leg* much? " She turned from me, evidently much shocked, or much offended, — and not being aware that I had committed any very heinous offence, I begged to know what was the reason of her displeasure. After some hesitation, she said that as she knew me well, she would tell me that the word *leg* was never mentioned before ladies. I apologized for my want of refinement, which was attributable to having been accustomed only to *English* society; and added, that as such articles must occasionally be referred to, even in the most polite circles in America, perhaps she would inform me by what name I might mention them without shocking the company. Her reply was, that the word *limb* was used; "nay," continued she, "I am not so particular as some people are, for I know those who always say *limb* of a table, or *limb* of a piano-forte."

There the conversation dropped; but a few months afterwards I was obliged to acknowledge that the young lady was correct when she asserted that some people were more particular than even she was. I was requested by a lady to escort her to a seminary for young ladies, and on being ushered into the reception-room, conceive my astonishment at beholding a square piano-forte with four *limbs*. However, that the ladies who visited their daughters might feel in its full force the extreme delicacy of the mistress of the establishment, and her care to preserve in their utmost purity the ideas of the young ladies under her charge, she had dressed all these four limbs in modest little trousers, with frills at the bottom of them! [2]

Marryat then quoted the following from the book of a fellow traveler, Mrs. Trollope:

An English lady, who had long kept a fashionable boarding-school in one of the Atlantic cities, told me that one of her earliest cares with every new-comer, was to endeavour to substitute real delicacy for that affected precision of manner. Among many anecdotes, she told me of a young lady about four-

[1] The history of the war upon nudity in America remains to be written. It had its forgotten heroes, and they deserve to be resurrected. One of them, apparently, was Dr. Josiah Gilbert Holland (1819–81), editor of *Scribner's Monthly* and author of "God Give Us Men! ", a favorite school declamation of the Gilded Age. At a time when the art mu- seums of the country were still hesi- tating to take the drawers off their statuary he printed in *Scribner's* (Nov., 1879, p. 24), a shameless woodcut of Raphael's "Apollo and Marsyas," showing anatomical de- tails that must have shocked many a reader.

[2] A Diary in America; New York, 1839, p. 153.

teen, who, on entering the receiving-room, where she only expected to see a lady who had inquired for her, and finding a young man with her, put her hands before her eyes and ran out of the room again, screaming, "A man, a man, a man!" On another occasion, one of the young ladies, in going upstairs to the drawing-room, unfortunately met a boy of fourteen coming down, and her feelings were so violently agitated that she stopped, panting and sobbing, nor would pass on till the boy had swung himself up on the upper bannisters, to leave the passage free.[1]

Mrs. Trollope recorded that, to the more delicate Americans of that day, Shakespeare was obscene and unendurable, and that the very mention of Pope's "The Rape of the Lock" made them shrink in horror. It is worth noting here, as one of the ironies of literary history, that Pope himself, in his edition of Shakespeare, brought out in 1725, heavily bowdlerized the Bard. In the masquerade scene of "Romeo and Juliet," for example, he changed the word *toes* in the lines:

> Gentlemen, welcome! Ladies that have their *toes*
> Unplagued with corns will have a bout with you.

to *feet*, though letting *corns* stand.[2] A century later, in the United States, *feet* was also under the ban. The palmy days of euphemism ran from the 20s to the 80s. Bulls became *male cows*, cocks became *roosters*,[3] the breast became the *bosom*,[4] both a chair and the backside became *seats*, harlots became *fallen women*, cockroaches became *roaches*,[5] trousers became *inexpressibles, unmentionables, unwhisperables, nether garments*,[6] or *conveniences*,[7] stockings (female) became

1 Domestic Manners of the Americans, by Frances M. Trollope; London, 1832.
2 Mr. Collier's Corrected Folio of 1632, by Richard Grant White, *Putnam's Monthly*, Oct., 1853, p. 401, footnote. Two years later, in March, 1855, *Putnam's* turned *ass*, the name of the animal, into *a—*.
3 The NED's first example is from James Flint's Letters from America; Edinburgh, 1822, p. 264. Its first example in English use is dated 1882. The DAE traces *rooster* in American use to 1772, but it does not seem to have become general until the 30s. At the start it was regarded as somewhat advanced, and an anonymous writer in *Bentley's Miscellany*, 1838, p. 581, records that a New York landlady preferred *barndoor he-biddy*.
4 In the sense of the front of a shirt, *bosom* is traced by the DAE to 1852. Shirts themselves became *linen*.
5 Traced by the DAE to 1837 and marked an Americanism.
6 *Inexpressibles, Unmentionables, Unwhisperables* and Other Verbal Delicacies of Mid-Nineteenth Century Americans, by Mamie Meredith, *American Speech*, April, 1930, pp. 285-87.
7 Charles Sealsfield's Americanisms, II, by John T. Krumpelmann, *American Speech*, April, 1941, p. 109, and Lexical Evidence from Charles Sealsfield, by James B. McMillan, *American Speech*, April, 1943, p. 122.

*hose* [1] and such ancient words as *bitch, sow, boar, stallion, ram* **and buck** disappeared from the vocabulary. How, in the midst of this excess of delicacy, the harsh and forthright *female* should have come into general use as a noun I simply can't tell you. It was old in English and had been used by Steele in the *Guardian* in 1713, but it seems to have carried a suggestion of scorn in early Nineteenth Century England. In the United States, however, it was used perfectly seriously, and was apparently a special favorite of clergymen, reformers and other such patterns of propriety. The DAE shows that there were *female* seminaries, boarding-schools, institutes, orphan-asylums and missionary societies in the 1820–70 era. The term did not go unchallenged, but it took a long while to put it down, for there was a span of nearly thirty years between the time the Legislature of Maryland expunged it from the title of a bill on the ground that it was " an Americanism " and the time Mrs. Sarah Josepha Hale, editor of *Godey's Lady's Book* succeeded in persuading the trustees of Vassar to drop it from the name of that great institution. Thus her argument:

> Where used to discriminate between the sexes the word *female* is an adjective; but many writers employ the word as a noun, which, when applied to women, is improper, and sounds unpleasantly, as referring to an animal. To illustrate: almost every newspaper we open, or book we read, will have sentences like these: " A man and two *females* were seen," etc., . . . " The *females* were much alarmed." . . . It is inelegant as well as absurd. Expressed correctly, thus, " A man and two *women*. . . . The *women* were alarmed.". . . who does not see and *feel* that these last sentences are in better taste, more correct in language, and more definite in meaning? [2]

The Maryland Legislature substituted *women* for *females*, in the bill just mentioned, but *woman* was felt to be somewhat rough, and the true rival of *female*, for many years, was the English favorite, *lady*. Says Dixon Wecter in " The Saga of American Society ": [3]

> Harriet Martineau, visiting the United States from 1834 to 1836, quotes the rhetorical question of a preacher: " Who were last at the Cross? *Ladies.* Who were first at the Sepulchre? *Ladies.*" When she asked the warden of the Nashville prison whether she might visit the women's cells he replied: " We have no *ladies* here at present, madam. We have never had but two *ladies*, who were convicted for stealing a steak; but, as it appeared that they were deserted by their husbands, and in want, they were pardoned." By 1845 New York boasted a *Ladies'* Oyster Shop, a *Ladies'* Reading Room, and a *Ladies'* Bowling Alley elegantly equipped with carpets and ottomans and girls to set up the pins.

1 Bartlett, 1859, listed *hose* as a Western term. " *Stockings*," he said, " is considered extremely indelicate, al-  though *long socks* is pardonable."
2 I take this from Bartlett, 1859.
3 New York, 1937, p. 316.

Banks and post-offices afforded a *ladies'* window where the fair sex would be untouched by greasy elbows and tobacco-laden breath. Mrs. A. J. Graves in her book, Woman in America (New York, 1855) reported that our cities were crowded with "*females* in their ambition to be considered *ladies*" who employed their lily hands only "in playing with their ringlets, or touching the piano or guitar." We are told that a poor Irish prospector, John H. Gregory, who struck the fabulous lode of gold near Central City, Col., on May 19, 1859, flung down his pick and exclaimed with instant fervor: "Thank God, *now* my wife can be a *lady!*"

The word *woman* had become a term of depreciation if not downright abuse; it was however sufficient for that foundation in Philadelphia named the Lying-In Charity for Attending Indigent *Women* in their Homes, and in such a euphemism as the phrase *fallen women*. Female was at least noncommittal as to the financial, social and moral standing of the person designated; this nice distinction appears in the title of a charity organization started in 1833 in the frontier town of Jacksonville, Ill.: the *Ladies'* Association for Educating *Females*. Yet for the lady *in excelsis* a term of even higher praise was reserved. Of Mrs. Paulding, wife of Van Buren's Secretary of the Navy, we read in Mrs. Ellet's Court Circles of the Republic, 1869: "The word *lady* hardly defined her; she was a perfect *gentlewoman*."

The DAE notes that *gentleman* was used, so early as 1804, as " a courteous appellative regardless of social standing," and offers " *gentleman tailor* from 1838. So far as I am aware, *gentleman* never had any rival save *masculine*, which was reported in use at the fashionable resorts of New York in 1856,[1] but is not listed by Bartlett, Schele de Vere or the DAE. In those days no American *lady* was permitted to use slang, even the most decorous. Said a famous *female* writer of the time: [2]

Men can talk slang. *Dry up* is nowhere forbidden in the Decalogue. Neither the law nor the prophets frown on *a thousand of brick*. The Sermon on the Mount does not discountenance *knuckling to*.[3] But between women and these minor immoralities stands an invisible barrier of propriety — waves an abstract flaming sword in the hand of Mrs. Grundy. . . . Who can reckon up the loss we sustain? . . . I should like to call my luggage *traps*, and my curiosities *truck and dicker*,[4] and my weariness being *knocked up*,[5] as well as Halicarnassus, but

1 Sulphur Springs of New York, *Harper's Magazine*, June, 1856, p. 4.
2 Mary A. Dodge (Gail Hamilton): Country Living and Country Thinking; Boston, 1864, pp. 94–96.
3 The DAE traces *like a thousand of brick* to 1842, *to dry up* to 1854, and *to knuckle to* to 1864.
4 The DAE traces *truck*, in the sense here indicated, to 1822 and marks it an Americanism. Its first example of *dicker* is from the book here

quoted. It does not list *traps* in the sense of luggage.
5 Apparently *knocked up* had not yet acquired its American sense of pregnant — or maybe La Dodge was too refined to be aware of it. On p. 4 of the same book she thus described herself: "Representing the gentler half of humanity, of respectable birth, tolerable parts, and good education, as tender-hearted as most women, not unfamiliar with the best

I might as well rob a bank. Ah! high-handed Mrs. Grundy, little you reck of the sinewy giants that you banish from your table! Little you see the nuggets of gold that lie on the lips of our brown-faced, shaggy-haired newsboys and cabmen! . . . Translate them into civilized dialect — make them presentable at your fireside, and immediately the virtue is gone out of them.[1]

As we have seen, there is still a strong tendency in the United States to deprecate plain words, but the war upon them has become official rather than popular, and though the movies and the radio still submit, the majority of newspapers and magazines make some show of resistance. One of the first rebels against the delicacy of the era we have been reviewing was the elder James Gordon Bennett (1795–1872), founder of the New York *Herald*. Says Frank Luther Mott: "He flouted the prudery of the times which prescribed the use of the word *limbs* for legs, of *linen* for shirt, of *unmentionables* for trousers." [2] As we have also seen, it took a long while to break down even the most irrational and preposterous of the taboos, but in the end they succumbed. They survive today, save in the obscene fancies of Post-office wowsers, only in the back-waters of American speech, *e.g.*, dialects of such regions as the Ozarks. Vance Randolph, whose studies of the Ozark vocabulary have been numerous and valuable, has devoted one of them to its forbidden words.[3] In it he says:

> The names of male animals must not be mentioned when women are present; such words as *bull, boar, buck, ram, jack* and *stallion* are absolutely taboo. . . . It was only a few years ago that two women in Scott county, Arkansas, raised a great clamor for the arrest of a man who had mentioned a *bull-calf* in their presence. Even such words as *bull-frog, bull-fiddle* and *bull-snake* must be used with considerable caution, and a preacher at Pineville, Mo., recently told his flock that Pharaoh's daughter found the infant Moses in the *flags:* he didn't like to say *bull-rushes*. . . . The hillman sometimes refers to animals merely as the *he* or the *she*, and I have heard grown men use such childish terms as *girl-birds* and *boy-birds*.

society, mingling, to some extent, with those who understand and practise the minor moralities, you would at once infer from my circumstances that I was a very fair specimen of the better class of Americans, — and so I am. For one that stands higher than I in the moral, social, and intellectual scale, you will undoubtedly find ten that stand lower."

1 Mary Abigail Dodge (*c.* 1830–96) is not to be confused with the Mary E. Mapes Dodge (1838–1905) who for many years edited *St. Nicholas*. Mary Abigail was born at Hamilton, Mass., and got her pen-name from the last syllable of her middle name and the name of her native town. She wrote many books and was editor of *Our Young Folks* for a short time in the 60s.

2 American Journalism; New York, 1941, p. 232.

3 Verbal Modesty in the Ozarks, *Dialect Notes*, Vol. VI, Part I, 1928, pp. 57–64.

A stallion is sometimes called a *stable-horse*, and very rarely a *stone-horse*, the latter term being considered unfit for respectable feminine ears. Such words as *stud* and *stud-horse* are quite out of the question, and a tourist's casual reference to *shirt-studs* once caused considerable embarrassment to some very estimable hill-women of my acquaintance. The male members of most species of domestic animals are designated simply as *male*. *Cow, mare, sow, doe* and *ewe* are used freely enough, but *bitch* is taboo, since this last term is often applied to loose women.

The male fowl is usually called a *crower;* the word *cock* is quite out of the question, since it is used to designate the genitals. . . . I have myself seen grown men, when women were present, blush and stammer at the mere mention of such commonplace bits of hardware as *stop-cocks* or *pet-cocks*, and avoid describing a gun as *cocked* by some clumsy circumlocution, such as *she's ready t' go* or *th' hammer's back*. . . . Even *cock-eyed, cock-sure* and *coxcomb* are considered too suggestive for general conversation, and many natives shy at such surnames as *Cox, Leacock, Hitchcock* and the like. . . .

The Ozarker very seldom uses *virgin* or *maiden*, since these terms carry a too direct reference to sex. A teacher of botany tells me that he is actually afraid to mention the *maidenhair* fern in his high-school classes.

The word *bed* is seldom used before strangers, and the Ozark women do not *go to bed;* they *lay down*. . . .

The innocent verb *alter* is never used in the presence of women, because *alter* in the Ozarks means to castrate, and is never used in any other sense. . . . A paper bag is always a *sack* or *poke*, since *bag* means the scrotum in the hill country. . . . The sex organs in general are known as the *prides*, and the word *pride* has thus acquired an obscene significance. . . . A midwife is always called a *granny-woman*, and *granny* is often used as a verb, designating the actual delivery of the child. It is sometimes employed with reference to the lower animals. . . .

Many of the hill people still shy at the word *leg*, and usually say *limb*, particularly if the speaker is a woman. . . . *Love* is considered more or less indecent, and the mountain people seldom use the term in its ordinary sense, but nearly always with some degrading or jocular connotation. The noun *ass* must be avoided because it sounds exactly like the Southern pronunciation of *arse*, and even *aster* is sometimes considered suggestive.

Along with this extreme delicacy there goes an innocent freedom in the use of words ordinarily frowned upon as vulgar outside the mountains. Says Randolph:

A woman who would be highly insulted if *bull* was used in her presence will employ *God-a-mighty* and *Jesus Christ* freely. . . . Women of the best families *give tittie* to their babies in public, even in church. . . . Such inelegant terms as *spit* and *belch* are used freely, and I have heard the wife of a prominent professional man tell her daughter to *git a rag an' snot that young 'un*, meaning to wipe the child's nose.

The movement, apparently originating in Hollywood, to reintroduce the old four-letter words to polite society by inserting a euphemistic *r* into them — the substitution of *nerts* for *nuts* offers a relatively decorous example — [1] has made but little progress. On one level they have come back unchanged, and on another they are still under the ban. The first effort to treat them scientifically and without moral prepossession, made by Allen Walker Read in 1934,[2] has been followed up by Read himself,[3] by Partridge [4] and by others.[5] Such words, says Read,

are not cant or slang or dialect, but belong to the oldest and best established element in the English vocabulary. They are not even substandard, for they form part of the linguistic equipment of speakers of standard English. Yet they bear such a stigma that they are not even listed in the leading dictionaries of the language. But although they are in such marked disrepute it does not follow that they should be ignored by the student of the language. A sociologist does not refuse to study certain criminals on the ground that they are too perverted or too dastardly; surely a student of the language is even less warranted in refusing to consider certain four-letter words because they are too "nasty" or too "dirty." For the scientific linguist the propriety or respectability of a word is merely one aspect of its history.

To which the impeccable Henry Seidel Canby added in 1944: [6]

The question is whether the time has not come to end the bootlegging of the so-called four-letter words. . . . They belong to the honest speech of our Puritan [7] forefathers, who, when they were morally aroused, did not make the rhetorical error of calling a whore [8] a *prostitute*. They are certainly not evil, nor wrong in themselves, although, since they have to do with bodily functions, a pornographer can always make wrong, and often evil, use of them.[9]

1 See AL4, p. 301. A Study of Verbal Taboos, by J. M. Steadman, Jr., *American Speech*, April, 1935, p. 95, shows that *nerts* itself is considered "coarse, obscene" by not a few college students.

2 An Obscenity Symbol, *American Speech*, Dec., pp. 264–78.

3 Lexical Evidence From Folk Epigraphy in Western North America; Paris, 1935.

4 In A Dictionary of Slang and Unconventional English; New York, 1938. See also his revised and enlarged edition of Grose's Classical Dictionary of the Vulgar Tongue; London, 1931.

5 There is a useful bibliography of the earlier literature of the subject in Read's An Obscenity Symbol, just cited.

6 Strange Fruit, *Saturday Review of Literature*, April 1, p. 14.

7 Probably a slip of the pen for *pre-Puritan*.

8 The original spelling was *hore*. This is traced by the NED to *c.* 1100. *Hure* was an early variant. The NED's first example of *whore* is from the Coverdale Bible of 1535. The word occurs 16 times in the King James Version. *Whoredom* occurs 26 times, *whore-monger* 5 times, and *whorish* 3 times. Dr. Leonard Bloomfield suggests in Language; New York, 1933, p. 401, that *whore* "must have been at one time a polite substitute for some word now lost."

9 Edwin M. (Ted) Robinson printed an intelligent discussion of the subject in his Philosopher of Folly's Column, Cleveland *Plain Dealer*, Aug. 19, 1944. He called attention to the anomalous fact that the current taboo applies only to the words themselves, not to the ideas behind them. "All the matters referred to by these awful words," he said, "may

Some of these words are in Shakespeare, and others are in the King James Version of the Bible. All of them are old in English, and nearly all were at one time quite respectable. There are many euphemistic substitutes for them, ranging in repute from terms scarcely more decorous than they are themselves to terms acceptable in any society which does not deny altogether that sexual and excremental functions exist in *Homo sapiens*. There are also euphemisms for a number of terms that are measurably less shocking to the delicate, but still highly indecorous, *e.g.*, the familiar derivatives of *bull* and *horse*, and the common names for flatulence and eructation. The first-named is usually reduced, in the United States, to either *bull* or *b.s.*; in Australia it is turned into *bullsh* or *boolsh*.[1] There are many other substitutes in American use, *e.g.*, *bushwah*,[2] *oxiline*, *pastureine* and *prairie mayonnaise*,[3] but they are not tolerated in refined circles, and even *bull*, on account of its suggestion of the missing second element, is looked upon as somewhat indecorous.[4] In 1936–37 Edwin R. Hunter and Bernice E. Gaines inquired into its use among 280 freshmen, 48 seniors and 48 members of the faculty of " a coeducational college in East Tennessee." They found that about 20% of the males avoided it, and about 40% of the females.[5] Other words under the ban of these teachers and students, usually to a much greater extent, were *ass*, *bastard*, *belch*, *belly*, *bitch*, *bugger*, *drawers*, *guts*, *pregnant*, *sex*, *stink* and *whore*. The progress of frankness since the Golden Age of euphemism in America was shown by the fact that 72.3% of the men and 54.6% of the women reported that they saw no impropriety in *garter*, that 88.6% of the men and 72.8% of the women used *sex*,

---

be discussed in print by the use of synonyms."

1 The former is listed by Baker. A derivative, *boolshevik*, signifying an active trader in *boolsh*, was coined by C. R. Bradish of Melbourne.
2 Webster 1934 derives *bushwa(h)* from *bodewash*, a Western American mispronunciation of the French *bois de vache*, cow's wood, *i.e.*, the bits of dried buffalo dung used as fuel on the prairies in the early days. In *Bushwah*, San Francisco *News Letter and Wasp*, July 14, 1939, Peter Tamony argues that it is rather derived from *bourgeois*. But it is commonly used as a euphemism

for *bullshit*, and I incline to think that it represents a deliberate mispronunciation of that term.
3 The last three are used in a poem called *Oxiline*, by a Tulsa, Okla., poet who conceals himself behind the initials R. M. H. His work was published at Tulsa in 1939.
4 *Bull — Bunk*, by P. G. Perrin, *American Speech*, April, 1940, p. 216. See also *Bull*, by Joseph E. Gillet, *American Speech*, April, 1939, pp. 97–98, and *Bull*, *American Speech*, Dec., 1939, pp. 303–04.
5 Verbal Taboo in a College Community, *American Speech*, April, 1938, pp. 96–107.

that 95.2% and 92.4% respectively used *leg*, and that 97% and 93.3% used *sick*. The word most abhorred by the men was *puke*, and by the women *bitch*. *Bitch* was the pet abomination of both sexes taken together, with *puke* as its runner-up. Only 47.4% reported that they used *vomit:* what terms the others resorted to to indicate emesis was not indicated.

The number of euphemisms for forbidden words in use in the United States is still large, but so far as I know they have never been investigated at length. Various correspondents inform me that *single child* is used by colored people in Baltimore to designate a bastard, that *bastrich* is used in the Duluth region as a happy compound of *bastard* and *son-of-a-bitch*, that the older rustics of Virginia use *Durham* for bull, that to castrate is *to cut* in the Middle West and *to make a Baptist minister of him* in Georgia, that to be pregnant is *to walk uphill* in Southern Illinois, that *male-cow* serves for bull in Tennessee, *top-cow* in Missouri and simple *male* in Texas, and that *she* is a derogatory prefix in many parts of the country and is felt to be more or less indecent.[1] Many disarming names for a house of prostitution are in common use, *e.g., sporting-house, cat-house,*[2] *fancy-house, crib,* and *call-house.*[3] There are even more for prostitute.[4] Euphemisms are by no means confined to slang and dialect: they also exist on the highest levels, *e.g., intestinal fortitude* for guts, *to burp* for to belch,[5] *derrière* for the female backside,[6] *to make, to lay,* and so on. *Derrière,* borrowed from the French, is one of many such loans in the argot of fashion writers, *e.g., brassière;* [7] other familiar euphe-

---

1 In my boyhood in Baltimore a loose paving brick was called a *she-brick.* On wet days it discharged a stream of dirty water on anyone who stepped on it.

2 In the Middle West, in the days when harlots were itinerants, the conveyances they used were called *cat-wagons.*

3 *Call-house* especially indicates a house whose inmates go out to parties on call. See Among the New Words, by Dwight L. Bolinger, *American Speech,* Oct., 1942, p. 204.

4 One of the earliest of these, indicating a woman infected with venereal disease, is *fire-ship.* The NED traces it in English use to 1672, but it is to be found in the archives of Mary-

land (Vol. LVII, pp. xxxv–vi; Baltimore, 1940) three years earlier. I am indebted here to Dr. J. Hall Pleasants of Baltimore, editor of the archives.

5 Among the New Words, by Dwight L. Bolinger, *American Speech,* April, 1941, p. 145.

6 Advertisement of Bonwit Teller in the New York *Times,* Oct. 2, 1935: "What can I wear that will make me flat enough for the new suits? This question is most frequently asked by women who have large *derrières.*"

7 When, in 1943, the WPB allotted some synthetic rubber to the makers of *brassières* it designated them *breast forms* and *breast shields.* I take this

misms are thoroughly American, *e.g.*, *step-in* and *undie*.[1] But the general tendency, as I have noted, is toward ever plainer speech, and many words that were under the ban only a few years ago are now used freely. I have encountered an impassioned defense of *bastard* in the Washington *Post*,[2] and seen *womb* in a two-column head in the Baltimore *Sun*.[3] Rupert Hughes, in an amusing essay on the relative respectability of the various organs and regions of the body,[4] calls attention to the fact that a few such words as *womb* have been " sanctified when used metaphorically," but are still frowned upon in " literal usage." He finds that " so long as you speak of the north and south ends of the human machine you may go pretty nearly as far as you like," but that " when you enter the intermediate region you must watch your every step." The reason, of course, is obvious. When such areas must be discussed willy nilly, the common device of decorum is to resort to Latin or Greek names, usually polysyllabic. " A long word," says Hughes, " is considered nice and a short word nasty." And as with terms for organs and functions, so with terms for voluntary acts. " You can refer to anything under the sun if you will call it *illicit relations, soliciting, perversion, contributing to juvenile delinquency*. But the police will be after you if you print the short words." I myself published a somewhat similar study in 1915.[5] In it I undertook to arrange the parts of the body in eight classes, beginning with the highly respectable and ending with the unmentionable. Into the highest class I put the heart, brain, hair, eyes and vermiform appendix; into Class II, the collar-bone, stomach (American), liver (English), bronchial tubes, arms (excluding elbows), tonsils, ears, etc.; into Class III, the elbows, ankles, teeth (if natural), shoulders, lungs,

---

from an article in the New York *Post* by Earl Wilson, reprinted in Tonics and Sedatives, *Journal of the American Medical Association*, Jan. 1, 1944, p. 30. *Brassière* is usually reduced to *bra*.

1 A list of euphemistic brand-names invented by American manufacturers of such things is in Glamour Words, by Charles E. Bess, *American Speech*, April, 1941, pp. 96–99, among them, *undikins, roll-ons, campus briefs* and *cup-forms*.

2 Much Ado (editorial), Dec. 14, 1942.

3 One of Twins Delivered Here Was Never in Mother's *Womb*, Aug. 25,

1944. This was one of the words expunged from the Bible by Noah Webster in his expurgated version of 1833. It occurs in the King James Version 40 times.

4 The Latin Quarter in Language, Dutch Treat Club banquet book, 1937. I have not seen this book, but have had access to the manuscript of the essay through the courtesy of Mr. Hughes.

5 The Interior Hierarchy, *Smart Set*, Jan., pp. 413–15. It was reprinted in A Book of Burlesques; New York, 1916, pp. 190–98.

neck, etc., and so on. My Class VI included the thighs, paunch, esophagus, spleen, pancreas, gall-bladder and caecum, and there I had to stop, for the inmates of Classes VII and VIII could not be listed in print in those high days of comstockery.

The difference between English and American ideas of propriety, noted in this buffoonery, have caused embarrassment to unwarned travelers since the earliest days. As I have noted elsewhere in this book, many words that are quite innocuous in the United States have a flavor of impropriety, sometimes marked, in England, *e.g.*, *bum*, *bug* [1] and *bloody*. The English aversion to *bug* has been breaking down of late, however, probably under the influence of such naturalized Americanisms as *jitterbug*,[2] but it yet lingers in ultra-squeamish circles, and a *lady-bird* is never called a *lady-bug*. So, to a more limited extent, with *bum*. Contrariwise, there are many English words and phrases that have indecent significances in the United States, quite lacking in England, *e.g.*, *to be knocked up* (to be tired),[3] *to stay with* (to be the guest of),[4] *screw* (as a noun, in the sense of salary or pay),[5] *to keep one's pecker up*,[6] *douche* (shower-bath), and *cock* (a male chicken). The English use *bitch* a great deal more freely than Americans, mainly, I suppose, because they are in more frequent contact with animals.[7] Now and then an American, reading an English newspaper, is brought up with a start by a word or phrase that would never be used in the same way in the United States. I offer two examples. The first is from an advertisement of a popular brand of smoking-tobacco in the *News of the World*. " Want a good *shag*? " [8] The second is from the *Literary Supplement* of the London *Times:* " On the

1 On *Bugs*, by Steven T. Byington, *American Speech*, Feb., 1938, p. 41.
2 I am told by H. W. Seaman that *squanderbug* was used in official advertisements during 1944 as a symbol for waste. Also, that a song called The Love-*Bug* Will Bite You was popular *c*. 1938.
3 Mark Twain (to an Englishman) in Concerning the American Language, in The Stolen White Elephant, 1882: " When you are exhausted you say you are *knocked up*. We don't."
4 The DAE shows that, in 1833, *to stay with*, in American usage, had the meaning of to marry.

5 Mr. Alistair Cooke tells me that as a verb it is banned from refined discourse in England as in America.
6 In the sense of to keep up one's courage or resolution the NED traces this verb-phrase to 1853. It was used by Dickens in 1857. In W. S. Gilbert's Trial by Jury, 1875, is: " Be firm, my moral *pecker*! "
7 Its use among American dog breeders is discussed in Dog Pups and Horse Colts, by Louise M. Ackerman, *American Speech*, Dec., 1942, p. 238, and Dog Terminology, by Elrick B. Davis, *American Speech*, Oct., 1943, pp. 235–36.
8 June 19, 1938, p. 15.

whole we may congratulate ourselves on having chosen not to be born in that excellent and indispensable century when an infant of six could be hanged . . . and schoolboys were encouraged to match *cocks*." [1]

## 8. EXPLETIVES

313. [In 1931, writing in *American Speech*, L. W. Merryweather observed that " *hell* fills so large a part in the American vulgate that it will probably be worn out in a few years."] [2] Merryweather regarded this deterioration as so likely that he proposed that " clerical circles should take it upon themselves, as a public duty, to invest some other theological term with a shuddering fearsomeness that will qualify it as the successor to *hell*, when the lamentable decease of the latter actually takes place." Fortunately, his fears have not been borne out by the event. *Hell* still flourishes in the Republic, in so far as profanity flourishes at all, and every one of the combinations and permutations of it that he listed remains in use. I borrow his grand divisions:

1. *Hell* as "the equivalent of negative adverbs," or as an intensifier thereof, as in *the hell you say* and *like hell I will*.

2. As a super-superlative, as in *colder than hell*.

3. As an adverb of all work, as in *run like hell* and *hate like hell*.

4. As an intensifier of questions, as in *what the hell,? who the hell?, where in hell?*, etc.[3]

5. As an intensifier of asseverations, as in *hell, yes!*

6. As an intensifier of qualities, as in *to be hell on*, and *hell of a price*.[4]

7. As an indicator of intensified experience, as in *hell of a time*,[5] *get the hell*, and *to play hell with*.

8. In a more or less literal sense, as in *wouldn't it be hell?*, *go to hell*, *the hell with*, *hell on wheels*, *hell to pay*, *like a snowball in hell*, *till hell freezes over*, and *to beat hell*.

9. As a synonym for uproar or turmoil, as in *to raise hell, to give him hell*, and *hell is loose*.

10. As a verb, as in *to hell around*.

1 Children of a Harsh Age (a review of The English Child in the Eighteenth Century, by Rosamond Bayne-Powell; London, 1939), June 24, 1939, p. 303.

2 *Hell* in American Speech, Aug., 1931, pp. 433–35.

3 The choice between *the* and *in* is determined by euphony and the taste of the speaker. Sometimes, as Merryweather notes, both are used, as in *how in the hell?* Occasionally, *hell* is reinforced with another intensifier, as in *what the goddam hell?*

4 Sometimes used in a negative sense, as in George Ade's *hell of a Baptist*.

5 Merryweather notes that *hell of a time* may indicate either the intensely agreeable or the intensely disagreeable.

11. As an adjective, as in *in a hellish hurry* and *hell-bent*.

12. In combination with other nouns, as in *hell's bells, hell and red niggers, hell and high-water, hell and Maria, hell-raiser, hell-diver, hell-bender,* and *hell-to-breakfast*.

13. In derivatives, as in *hellion, hell-cat* and *heller*.

14. As a simple expletive, as in *Oh, hell.*[1]

Nearly all the examples I have cited are of American origin: the English have a much less inspiring répertoire of terms in *hell*. The DAE traces *to give him hell* to 1851, *to be hell on* to 1850, *hellion* to 1845, *hell-diver* (a bird) [2] to 1839, *hell-bent* to 1835, and *hell of a* to 1776, and marks them all Americanisms. It records a number of forms that have since become obsolete, *e.g., hell-face* and *hell-to-split* (1871), *to smell hell* and *hellabaloo* (1840), *hell-sweat* (1832) and *hell-kicking* (1796). It also records some forms that have flourished only in relatively restricted areas, *e.g., hell-rotter* and *hell-west*. Merryweather says that *hellion* seems to have been invented by the Mormons, along with *by hell* and *son of hell*. He adds that the use of these terms by the saints is apparently grounded on the theory that " if it is evil to use celestial names profanely, it must be good to take infernal names in vain. *Hellion* and *son of hell* are obvious substitutes for a pair of common obscene epithets, and *by hell* takes the place of *by God*." [3] New combinations embracing *hell* are being launched all the time, and old and forgotten ones are frequently revived. In 1944, for example, a United States Senator got a flattering editorial notice in the New York *Times* for springing " The hardtack was *as hard as the hubs of hell* " in the course of a Senate debate on the Army K ration. It was, said the *Times*, " a striking number." A few days later a correspondent wrote in to say that the simile was used by the soldiers during the Spanish-American War, and that *hubs* should have been *hobs*.[4]

Dwight L. Bolinger has called attention to the fact that *hell* and its derivatives make much milder oaths in English [5] than in other

---

1 This, says Merryweather, is the " most common " use of *hell*, " and the most soul-felt. With proper variations of voice it may be made to express resignation, weariness, boredom, exasperation, consternation, rage, and probably other emotions." Certainly surprise, disappointment, alarm, and even mere disagreement might be added.

2 Transferred to airmen, *c.* 1935.

3 See also *Hellion*, by Willa Roberts, *American Speech*, Feb., 1932, p. 240, and *Hell* in American Speech, by J. R. Schultz, the same, Feb., 1933, p. 81.

4 It's Hard Enough, Anyway (editorial page), March 10, 1944.

5 Especially, I should add, in American English.

languages. They are not as innocuous as the terms in *heaven*, but nevertheless they fall below those in God, *e.g.*, *goddam*.[1] It would be an exaggeration, however, to say that they have lost altogether the character of profanity. The contrary is proved by the continued use of euphemisms, *e.g.*, *heck*, *blazes* and *thunder*. *By heck* is not listed as an Americanism by the DAE, but the NED Supplement calls it " dial. and U. S." and traces it in American use to 1865, more than twenty years before the date of the first English dialect example.[2] The provenance of *blazes* is uncertain, for though the DAE's earliest example is dated 1837 it appeared in England only a year later. Among the phrases embodying it that are recorded are *by blazes*, *as blue as blazes*, *as black as blazes*, *as hot as blazes*, *as cool as blazes* (*cf. as cold as hell*), *like blazes*, *oh blazes*, *where in blazes* and *what in blazes*. *Thunder* is undoubtedly an Americanism and the DAE traces it to 1841. It seems to have been preceded by *thunderation*, which was obviously a euphemism for *damnation*, but it had taken on the definite sense of *hell* by 1848. Some of the *thunder*-phrases recorded by the DAE are *by thunder*, *go to thunder*, *why* (*how* or *what*) *in thunder*, and *to give him thunder*. There is also *thundering*, which James Russell Lowell defines waggishly, in the vocabulary attached to the second series of " The Biglow Papers," as " a euphemism common in New England for the profane English *devilish*." He adds: " Perhaps derived from the belief, common formerly, that thunder was caused by the Prince of the Air, for some of whose accomplishments consult Cotton Mather." *Go to Halifax* and *go to Guinea* are not Americanisms; they belong to an English series of which *go to Jericho* is perhaps the most familiar example. An anonymous correspondent of *American Speech*, in August, 1927, p. 478, sought to connect the former with the name of the Nova Scotian capital, which had an evil reputation in the Eighteenth Century, but the NED traces it in English use to 1669, more than a century before the first recorded Ameri-

---

1 Profanity and Social Sanction, *American Speech*, April, 1938, p. 153.

2 The NED Supplement calls *heck* a " euphemistic alteration of *hell*," but for this there is no evidence, though in such forms as *what the heck*, *heck of a time* and *by heck* it is undoubtedly used in place of *hell*. Dr. L. G. Van Loon of Reading, Pa., suggests that it may be a Dutch loan. The rural Dutch, he says, often put *bai je gek?*, meaning are you crazy? at the end of a sentence, and heck may represent an American attempt to pronounce *gek*. The use of the phrase, he says, in no way reflects upon the sanity of the listener, but is intended to be merely intensive, like *do you understand?*

can example. It apparently owes its origin to the fact that there was a famous gibbet at Halifax, England, in the Seventeenth Century. Thornton and the DAE indicate that *Jesse*, as in *give him Jesse*, is a euphemism for *hell*. It has had, from time to time, many congeners, now mainly obsolete, *e.g.*, *Zachy*, *Moses*, *Israel*, *Peter*, and *saltpetre*. Sometimes it is preceded by *particular*, as is *hell* itself. Its origin is unknown. Bartlett and Thornton call *all-fired* a softened form of *hell-fired*. It is traced by the DAE to 1835 and marked an Americanism. Thornton also lists *jo-fired* and traces it to 1824. It has been obsolete since the Civil War era.

The only comprehensive collection of American swear-words is in "A Dictionary of Profanity and Its Substitutes," by M. R. Walter, of Dalton, Pa. It has not been published, but a typescript is in the Princeton University Library and may be consulted there by learned men of reasonable respectability.[1] Walter's list is especially rich in euphemisms. Some of them follow, along with a few from other sources:[2]

For *damn*: *drat, bang, blame, blast, bother, darn, cuss, dang, ding, bean, bang.*

For *damned*: *all-fired, blamed, blasted, blowed, confounded, darned, dashed, cursed, cussed, danged, deuced, dinged, switched, swiggered.*

For *damnation*: *botheration, thunderation, perdition, tarnation.*

For *goddam*: *goldarn, doggone, consarn, goldast, goshdarn,* and various terms in *dad-*, *e.g.*, *dad-blame, dad-blast, dad-burn, dad-shame, dad-sizzle, dad-rat, dad-seize, dad-swamp, dad-snatch, dad-rot, dad-fetch, dad-gum, dad-gast.*

For *hell*: *Sam Hill,*[3] *blazes.*

For *Lord*: *land, law, lawks, lawdy, lawsy.*

For *God*: *gosh, golly, (great) guns, (great) Scott, (great) horn spoon, (great) snakes, (good) grief, gum, Godfrey.*

For *God Almighty*: *goshamighty, gorramity.*

For *Jesus*: *gee,*[4] *jeez, jiminy* (or *jeminy*) or *gimini,*[5] *Jemima, Jerusalem, Jehosaphat, jiminy-whizz, gee-whizz, gee-whillikins,*[6] *gee-whittaker.*

1 I have had access to it by the grace of Dr. Julian P. Boyd, the librarian.

2 Mainly, Exclamations in American English, by E. C. Hills, *Dialect Notes*, Vol. V, Part VII, 1924, pp. 253–84.

3 The DAE agrees that *Sam Hill* is a euphemism for *hell*, marks it an Americanism, and traces it to 1839, but in *What the Sam Hill?*, *American Speech*, Feb., 1940, pp. 106–09, A. E. Sokol argued that it really represents *devil*, and that it was probably suggested by *Samiel*, the devil in Carl Maria von Weber's opera, Der Freischütz, first performed in New York in 1825.

4 *Hully gee* (for *holy Jesus*) was introduced by Edward W. Townsend's Chimmie Fadden and Major Max; New York, 1895, but it disappeared with the decay of the Bowery boy as an American comic type.

5 Sometimes *jiminetty* or *jiminetties*. See College Words and Phrases, by B. S. Monroe and C. S. Northrup, *Dialect Notes*, Vol. II, Part III, 1901, p. 142.

6 Traced by the DAE to 1857 and marked an Americanism. There are

For *Christ:* cripes, crickey, Christmas, cracky, Christopher.

For *Jesus Christ:* jiminy-crickets, jiminy-crackers, Judas priest, Judas Christopher.[1]

Many of these are Americanisms, but not all. The DAE traces *blasted* in the sense of damnably to 1854, *blamed* to 1863, *consarn* to 1825, *cussed* to 1840,[2] *cracky* to 1851, *dinged* to 1843, *dad-blamed* to 1884, *dad-burn* to *c.* 1845, *dad-shamed* to 1834, *dad-seized* to 1844, *dad-blasted* to 1890, *dad-sizzled* to 1898, *dad-swamped* to 1866, *switched* to 1838, *goldarn* to 1853, *gum* to *c.* 1815, *goldast* to 1888, *great snakes* to 1862, *great guns* to 1884, *gee-whizz* to 1888, *Jemima* to 1887, *land* (in *land's sake*) to 1834, *good land* to 1845, *law* (in *law sakes*) to 1846, *Jerusalem* to 1861 and *gosh* to 1857.[3] Walter notes some Irish euphemisms, familiar to all Americans, but now obsolete, *e.g.*, *bedad*, *faith*, *bejabers* and *begorrah*. He also notes some extensions of *Jesus* and *Jesus Christ*, *e.g.*, *ke-rist*, *Jesus H. Christ*, *Jesus H. Particular Christ*, *Jesus Nelly*, *holy jumping Jesus*, *Jesus Christ and his brother Harry*, *Jesus Christ and John Jacob Astor*, and *G. Rover Cripes*. He lists nearly 400 picturesque oaths in the *by* form, *e.g.*, *by hell's peekhole*, *by all the ten legions of divils of Killooly*, *by Amerigo Vespucci*, *by hatchet-heads and hammer-handles*, *by St. Boogar and all the saints at the backside of the door of Purgatory*, *by the devil and Tom Walker*, *by the double-barreled jumping jiminetty*, *by the high heels of St. Patrick*, *by the holy cinders*, *by the holy St. Mackerel*, *by the piper that played before Moses*, and *by the ripping*,

---

many spellings, *e.g.*, *gewhilikins*, *gheewhillikins* and *geewhilikins*. Bartlett also lists *jewillikins*. He calls it "a Western exclamation of surprise," and does not indicate any relationship to *Jew*.

1 *Judas priest* is listed by Wayland D. Hand, in his Dictionary of Words and Idioms Associated with Judas Iscariot, *University of California Publications in Modern Philology*, Jan. 30, 1942, p. 342, but he does not mention *Judas Christopher*. He also lists *jumping Judas* and *great jumping Judas*, both of them, I take it, euphemisms for *holy jumping Jesus*.

2 *Cuss*, in the sense of a worthless fellow, often used good-naturedly, is traced to 1775, *don't care a cuss* to 1850, *not worth a cuss* to 1826, *to cuss* to 1815, *to cuss out* to 1881,

*cussed* to 1840, *cussedest* to 1845, *cussedness* to 1857 and *cussing* to 1841. In all these situations, of course, *cuss* is a euphemism for *curse*, which is itself a euphemism for *damn*, very old in English.

3 Since the appearance of the DAE's second volume in 1940 James B. Mc-Millan has found *gosh* in an English translation of the German works (all dealing with the United States) of Charles Sealsfield, 1842 (Lexical Evidence From Charles Sealsfield, *American Speech*, April, 1943, p. 124). The DAE's first example, 1857, is in the form of *gosh-all-Potomac*, now obsolete. *Gosh* also appears in *gosh-all-hemlock* (1865), *goshdang* (1871), and *gosh-durned* (1884), not to mention *gosh-awful*, from *god-awful* (1883).

*roaring, jumping Jerusalem.* Finally, he notes that the Old Testament makes Jahveh Himself swear gently on occasion, as the pious will discover in Ezekiel XVIII, 3.

Regarding the etymology of the euphemism *darn*, with its variants *dern* and *durn*, there is a difference of opinion among lexicographers. Noah Webster, in his "Dissertations on the English Language,"[1] sought to identify it with the Old English word *dern* or *derne*, meaning secret. He said:

> For many years I had supposed the word *dern*, in the sense of great or severe, was local in New England. Perhaps it may not now be used anywhere else, but it was once a common English word. Chaucer used it in the sense of secret, earnest, etc.
>
> > This clerk was cleped Hende Nicholas,
> > Of *derne* love he could and of solas.
> > *The Miller's Tale*, 1. 3200.
> > Ye mosten be full *derne*, as in this case.
> > do.         1. 3297.
>
> The word is in common use in New England and pronounced *darn*. It has not, however, the sense it had formerly; it is now used as an adverb to qualify an adjective, as *darn sweet*, denoting a degree of the quality.

This etymology was accepted by the late George Philip Krapp, and argued for with great learning in his excellent work, "The English Language in America,"[2] and it is adopted by the DAE and mentioned favorably by the NED Supplement. Nevertheless, it seems to me that there is considerably more plausibility in Dr. Louise Pound's theory, launched in 1927,[3] that *darn* and its congeners, *dern* and *durn*, are really derived from *tarnal*, an American contraction of *eternal* that arose during the Eighteenth Century and was in wide use as an intensive by the time of the Revolution. There are, to be sure, some difficulties in this theory, but they are not as great as those which confront the Webster-Krapp etymology. *Tarnal*, at the start, was a mere intensive, but it quickly gave rise to *tarnation* as a euphemism for *damnation*, and in a very short while *tarnation* was in use as an expletive. By 1798 it had assimilated the initial *d* of *damnation*, and in the course of time *tarnal* and its direct derivatives in *t* dropped out of use, and only *darn* remained. The evidence against the Webster-

1 Boston, 1789, p. 385.
2 New York, 1924; Vol. I, pp. 118–26.
3 The Etymology of an English Intensive, *Language*, June, 1927, pp.

96–99. See also *Darn*, by Dr. Pound, *Saturday Review of Literature*, Sept. 7, 1940, p. 19.

Krapp etymology and in favor of that of Dr. Pound is somewhat complicated and rather too technical to be summarized easily; it may be found in the Pound article before mentioned, and in a later discussion by Woodford A. Heflin in *American Speech*.[1]

*Darn* as a mere intensive, as in Webster's *darn sweet*, is traced by the DAE no further back than his mention of it in his " Dissertations on the English Language," but it must have been in use in America for some time before that. *Tarnal*, as an intensive, is traced to 1775. Both words took on the special sense of *damned* very soon afterward. The DAE's first example of *darnation* is dated 1825, but Thornton, cited by Heflin, traced the word to 1798. *Tarnal* and all its derivatives, whether in *t* or in *d*, are Americanisms. Visiting Englishmen found them piquant, and took them home. Dickens reported *darn* as an expletive in his " American Notes," 1842, and made one of his Americans use it in " Martin Chuzzlewit," 1843. But it never really took hold in England. *Not by a darned sight* is traced by the DAE to 1834 and marked an Americanism. It was preceded by *not by a jugful*, 1833, and has been followed by various euphemisms of the second degree, *e.g., not by a considerable sight*, used by Mark Twain in " Huckleberry Finn," 1884, and *not by a long sight*, used by Joel Chandler Harris in " Sister Jane, Her Friends and Acquaintances," 1896. *Darn* seems quite innocuous to most Americans today, but so recently as 1941 a Federal judge sitting in New York was objecting to its use in his courtroom, and threatening a lawyer who used it with punishment for contempt of court.[2] Rather curiously, Webster 1934 does not list either *darn* as an expletive or its variants, *dern* and *durn*. *Damn* is listed, and also *goddam* (the latter in the French sense of an Englishman), but not *darn*. The verb *to darn*, meaning to repair a hole in a fabric, may come from the old English *derne* or *dierne* to which Webster and Krapp sought to lay the expletive, but it is much more probable that it is derived from *derner*, a French dialect verb which likewise means to repair.

*Dog-gone* is marked an Americanism by the DAE and traced to the middle of the last century. Its origin is said to be uncertain, but there seems to be reasonable ground for believing that it is simply the Scotch *dagone*, of exactly the same significance and use, changed in spelling and pronunciation by some vague association with going

1 *Darn* Again, Dec., 1942, pp. 276 and 277.    2 *Darn* Upsets Court, New York *Times*, July 15, 1941.

to the dogs.[1] In the common speech, indeed, it is often *dag-gone*, with the first syllable rhyming with *drag*. As adjectives both it and *darn* have produced superlatives by analogy with *damndest*, to wit, *doggondest* and *darndest* (*derndest, durndest*). As we have seen, they are by no means the only American euphemisms for *damn*. The Linguistic Atlas of New England [2] lists many others in use in that region, *e.g.*, *dem, dum, dim, dean, dan, dang, ding, dash, dast, dag, dad, drat, blame, blast, bust, burn, bother, bugger, butter, confound, condemn, consarn, condarn, curse, cuss, crump, gast, gum, hang, rat, ram, rabbit, shuck, torment, plague, dunder* and *tarn*. *Dem* was brought from England, where it is recorded in the Seventeenth Century; it has produced, in its turn, several derivatives, *e.g.*, *demme, demmy* and *demmition*, the last of which may have been invented by Charles Dickens. *Dum* is traced to 1787 by the DAE and marked an Americanism. *Ding*, first recorded in America in 1834, did not appear in England until twelve years later, and then only in dialect use. *Dad*, usually combined, as in *dad-fetch* and *dad-gum*, is also apparently of American origin. The DAE suggests that *blame*, which is traced to 1829, is " probably a substitute for *blast*," but this seems improbable, for *blast* itself is not recorded before 1854. *Consarn* is traced to 1825. *Curse the fellow* is in " Tristram Shandy," 1761, but the NED's first example of *to give a curse* is from a letter of Thomas Jefferson, 1763. *Gum*, which is also a euphemism for *God*, as in *by gum,* is traced by the DAE, in the latter use, to *c*. 1815 in the United States; it did not appear in England until 1832. *Shuck*, in the plural, is commonly used as an exclamation of disgust or regret without any reference to *damn*, and in that use the DAE traces it to 1847, but it is also apparently employed in the form of *shucked* as a euphemism for *damned*. *Tormented* is traced by the DAE to 1825.

*Damn* is a borrowing from the Old French *dampner*, which in turn was a borrowing from the Latin *damnare*. It goes back to the Ages of

1 Dr. Josiah Combs suggests the possibility that *dagone* was borrowed from the name of *Dagon*, the god of the Philistines and a formidable early rival to Jahveh. When Delilah delivered Samson to the Philistines they took him to their town, Gaza, and there made thankful sacrifices to Dagon. How Samson, given supernatural strength by Jahveh, pulled down the temple of Dagon upon their heads is told in Judges XVI, 26-31. Later on Jahveh took on Dagon for a battle to a finish, with the result described in I Samuel V, 2-5.

2 Vol. III, Part I, Map 599; Providence, R. I., 1943.

Faith, but it did not come into use in England as an expletive until just before Shakespeare's time. As a noun it is traced to 1619. The NED says that it is " now very often printed *d——n* or *d——*; in pa. pple. *d——d*." From this reluctance to spell it out, I suppose, arose the English *dashed* and *dash it*, which sound effeminate to most Americans and have never had any vogue here. *Goddam* is first recorded in English use in 1633, and soon afterward the French were using it to designate an Englishman, apparently because it was often on the lips of English soldiers and travelers. The once celebrated Baron Amable Guillaume Prosper Brugière de Barante put it into the mouth of Joan of Arc in his " Histoire des ducs de Bourgoyne," 1824, which won him membership in the French Academy. Her use of it, if authentic, would be a fit match for Jahveh's oath to Ezekiel, already mentioned, for she has been a canonized saint of Holy Church since 1919, but there is no evidence in support of Barante. Toward the middle of the Seventeenth Century the Puritans began calling the Cavaliers *goddammes*, but the term seems to have passed out at the Restoration. Many euphemisms for *goddam* have flourished in America, *e.g.*, *goshdarn*, *goldarn*, *goshdad* and *goshdang*.[1] *Gosh* itself was borrowed from England, but all these combinations are Americanisms, and so are *goshamighty*, *goshwalader* and *goshawful*. The DAE records the astonishing *goy blame it* as in use in 1829, long before the influx of European Jews had converted Christian Americans into *goyim*. *Golly* is not an Americanism, but *gravy*, as in *by gravy*, is, and the DAE traces it to 1851. *I swan* (for I swear) and *I vum* (for I vow) are now obsolete save in a few remote country districts. The former is traced to 1823 and the latter to 1785. Both are apparently of American origin. The DAE's first example of *by the great horn spoon*, also an Americanism, is from " The Biglow Papers " I, 1848, but Miss Mamie Meredith has traced it to " The American National Song Book," 1842.[2] Its

1 Neither Thornton nor the DAE lists *goddam*. *Time* caused a painful sensation in Nov., 1944, by reporting that President Roosevelt, finding the voting-machine at Hyde Park, N. Y., out of order when he went to vote on Nov. 7, called out " The *goddammed* thing won't work." On Nov. 16 the Glendale Ministerial Association of Glendale, Calif., demanded that he apologize for this " shocking profanity." On Nov. 21 he told the reporters at a White House press conference that what he had really said was " The *damn* thing won't work." This explanation apparently placated both clergy and laity, for nothing more was heard of the matter.

2 *The Great Horn Spoon*, *American Speech*, Aug., 1929, pp. 499–500.

original meaning has been discussed by contributors to *American Speech*, but remains a mystery.[1]

Profanity has never had a scientific historian, though the literature on the subject is not inconsiderable.[2] The ancient Jews, like any other levantine people, must have had a large armamentarium of cuss-words, but the admonitions and threats of the Old Testament seem to be directed principally to perjury, which was regarded by the early sages as a kind of blasphemy. The more orthodox Quakers, in our own time, forbade all oaths, even on the witness-stand, as savoring of blasphemy. This prohibition was based upon the words of Jesus as reported in Matthew V, 34: "I say unto you, Swear not at all; neither by heaven; for it is God's throne." Profanity, like any other art, has had its ups and downs — its golden ages of proliferation and efflorescence and its dark ages of decay and desuetude. Medieval England appears to have had a large répertoire of foul language, much of it obscene and the rest highly blasphemous to modern ears. The Puritans, when they began to make themselves heard and felt in the 1560s, opened a bitter war upon this vocabulary, and with considerable success. By 1611 the somewhat prissy Thomas Coryat, in his "Crudities," the first English book of travel, was denouncing the French postillions for their "most diabolical custom" of urging on their horses with the cry of *Allons, diable!* The fact that so mild a phrase could strike an Englishman as profane shows how far the Puritan crusade had gone at home, though the hard-swearing Elizabeth

---

1 *The Great Horn Spoon*, by D. L. Chambers, Aug., 1928, p. 459; *The Great Horn Spoon*, by N. R. L., Feb., 1929, pp. 255–56.

2 There is a brief bibliography in The Literature of Slang, by W. J. Burke; New York, 1939, pp. 152 and 153. To it may be added Children of Linguistic Fashion, by Robert Withington, *American Speech*, Dec., 1934, pp. 255–59; The Psychology of Profanity, by G. T. W. Patrick, *Psychological Review*, 1901, pp. 113–27; Profanity, by Henry Woodward Hulbert, *Biblical World* (Chicago), 1920, pp. 69–75; The Art of Swearing, by H. L. Mencken, Baltimore *Evening Sun*, May 24, 1937; Eighteenth Century Conversation, by William Matthews, Manchester *Guardian Weekly*, Jan. 14, 1938, p. 36; Hard Swearing on a Church Steeple, by A Quiet Man, *Putnam's Monthly*, Jan., 1855, pp. 41–50; and A Cursory History of Swearing, by Julian Sharman; London, 1884. The article on Profanity in Hastings' Encyclopedia of Religion and Ethics; New York, 1928, Vol. X, pp. 378 *ff.*, is worth consulting. There is a brief section headed Exclamations, Expletives, Oaths, Etc., in A History of Modern Colloquial English, by Henry Cecil Wyld; London, 1920, pp. 386 *ff.* In The World of Sholom Aleichem, by Maurice Samuel; New York, 1943, Chapter XXIII is mainly devoted to Yiddish billingsgate, and in English As We Speak It In Ireland, by P. W. Joyce; second ed.; Dublin, 1910, Chapter VI is on Swearing.

had been dead only eight years. Two years after her death Parliament passed an act providing a fine of £10 for anyone who should " in any stage play, interlude, show, etc., jestingly or profanely speak or use the holy Name of God, or of Christ Jesus, or of the Holy Ghost, or of the Trinity." This law greatly cramped the style of the playwrights of the Bankside, including Shakespeare. The quartos of his plays had been full of oaths and objurgations, but when his friends Heming and Condell assembled the First Folio in 1623 they undertook a prudent bowdlerization, and the editors of the bard in later years had the exhilarating job of restoring the denaturized expletives.

At the Restoration there was naturally a revival of profanity, but it was apparently confined within rather cautious metes and bounds. The NED shows that the forthright *God's wounds* of 1535 became the euphemistic *zounds* by the beginning of the next century and then vanished altogether, and that the numerous old oaths naming the Virgin Mary were diluted down to the innocuous *marry*. Wyld[1] lists a number of the fashionable oaths of the 1650–1700 period: they run to such banal forms as *strike me dumb, rat me, split my windpipe, by the universe, gadzooks, gads my life* and *dag take me*. *Lord* was reduced to *lard*, *devil* to *Harry*, *Jesus* to *Jeminy* and various resounding appeals to God to *dear me*.

It is highly probable that, during the Seventeenth Century, English swearing really moved from England to America. Even in the heart of Puritan New England there was a large population of non-Puritans, some of them sailors come ashore and others wastrels and fugitives of a dozen varieties, and it was hard for the magistrates and clergy to dissuade them from sulphurous utterance, just as it was hard to dissuade them from drunkenness and fornication. The frequency of prosecutions for profane cursing and swearing, as reported in the town records, shows that the offense must have been a common one. Allen Walker Read has exhumed some interesting contemporary evidence to that effect.[2] Ned Ward, an English visitor in 1699, reported of the New Englanders that " notwithstanding their sanctity, they are very profane in their common dialect." Sixty years later the Rev. Jonathan Boucher, writing from Maryland, said that " obscene conceits and broad expressions " were heard constantly there, and

---

1 Lately cited, pp. 389 and 390.
2 British Recognition of American Speech in the Eighteenth Century, *Dialect Notes*, Vol. VI, Part VI, July, 1933, p. 328.

that " no sex, no rank, no conduct " could save a visitor from them. The Revolution, like any other general war, greatly prospered both obscenity and profanity. In 1775 John Adams, assigned by the Continental Congress to draw up " rules for the regulation of the Navy of the United Colonies," was moved to authorize commanders to punish profane and blasphemous sailors " by causing them to wear a wooden collar or some shameful badge," and a year later George Washington issued a general order to the Army deploring the growth of " the wicked practise of profane cursing and swearing." But these admonitions had no effect, and at the end of the century an English visitor named Richard Parkinson was recording that " the word *damned* " was " a very familiar phrase " in the new Republic, and that even the clergy used language that was " extremely vulgar and profane." Washington himself, despite his order to his men, used both *damn* and *hell* with considerable freedom, as have several other American officers since.

All recent writers upon the subject seem to be agreed that profanity is now in one of its periods of waning. This is the melancholy thesis, for example, of " Lars Porsena, or, The Future of Swearing and Improper Language," by Robert Graves.[1] Graves believes that there has been a steady decline in England, marked by ameliorations in war time, since the age of Elizabeth.[2] In 1920 H. W. Seaman had come to the same conclusion. " True oaths," he said, " are rare among the English. There are a number of ugly words, probably descendants of true religious oaths, and a few that are merely dirty, and beyond that practically nothing." Ten years later, returning to the theme, Seaman reiterated this judgment, and added that all the surviving English expletives, save only *bloody*, had been reduced to a pansy-like insignificance, and were quite devoid of either zip or wow. He said:

> Most of us, even experts at the art of imprecation, find some difficulty nowadays in distinguishing between forbidden and permitted words. The social rule is to wait for the cue from your hostess. If she says what the captain of the *Pinafore* did not say,[3] you are at liberty to go a little farther.[4]

1 London, 1927; revised ed.; 1936.
2 P. W. Joyce, before cited, makes a similar report with respect to Ireland. " The general run of our people," he says in English As We Speak It In Ireland; second ed.; Dublin, 1910, p. 66, " do not swear much; and those that do commonly limit themselves to the name of the devil either straight out or in some of its disguised forms, or to some harmless imitation of a curse."
3 He never used a big, big *d——*.
4 Let's Stick to Our Own Bad Language, London *Sunday Chronicle*, Jan. 26, 1930.

Six years later, in 1936, the London *Sunday Dispatch* reported that swearing had gone altogther out of fashion in London, at least in circles pretending to any elegance. " Instead of full-blooded expletives," it said, " young bloods of Berkeley square and Belgravia use the names of flower, fish or plant. . . . Conversations run like this: ' Hullo, you old baked *walnut*. How goes the *mackerel-footed flea*? ' " To this the *Dispatch* added a speech by a youth in training for the R.A.F.:

> Did fifty *blue-belled* miles on Monday, but had to come down to *turbotting* terra firma as some *sweet-williamed* wallah had pinched my *mistletoe* maps, and I was afraid of getting lost in the *wallflowered* wilds.[1]

Seaman, as a patriotic Englishman, warned his countrymen against adopting American profanity, but he must have known that it was almost as feeble as their own, despite the continued prosperity of *hell* and its derivatives, for he had but recently returned from a visit to the United States, and while here had traveled widely. All American treatises on the subject agree that there has been a marked decline in the Republic since the Civil War, with only faint revivals during the two World Wars. Writing in the *North American Review* in 1934, Burges Johnson declared that American profanity was fast losing its punch. He said:

> When man began to lose his belief in a petty-minded interfering God, then oaths and curses began to lose their true value. . . . At their worst, when they were made up of words which were socially ostracized, they became maledictions, or bad words. A malediction is an invocation of evil from no omnipotent source, but a sort of homemade defilement. . . . [Now] even the surviving cuss-words, maledictions and execrations of ancient and half-forgotten lineage are dying of anemia, sharing the fate of *zounds* and *gramercy* and *odsblood*. There seems to be little left that a man might use against his adversary except logic, and that of course is out of the question.[2]

Johnson noted that a number of intrinsically innocuous words, *e.g.*, *plutocrat, capitalist, bolshevik, communist, fascist, pacifist, radical, Rotarian* and *bourgeoisie*, were coming into use for purposes of invective, and predicted that they would gradually take on the dignity of general expletives. This prediction has been borne out by the event, and to them have been added many other terms, *e.g.*, *isolationist* and

---

1 Mayfair Gives Up Swearing, London *Sunday Dispatch*, April 19, 1936. I am indebted for this to the late F. H. Tyson, of Hong Kong.

2 Modern Maledictions, Execrations and Cuss-Words, *North American Review*, Nov., 1934, pp. 467-71.

*Nazi.* But this process, of course, is old in English, and does not lead to the production of true profanity. Another American observer, writing in 1935,[1] reported the results of a thirty-day " campaign of listening," carried on with the aid of " a small clique of men and women who live anything but cloistered lives." His conclusion was that Americans had become " a trifle disgusted with their one-time penchant for cursing," and were turning to such puerile words and phrases as *dad-gummed, dad-slapped, fathead, for the love of Mike,* and *go climb a tree.* This tendency, I have no doubt, has been helped by the extraordinary prudishness of the American newspapers, which always hesitate to report genuine profanity in full, or even any harmless discourse quoting its more familiar terms. I had a curious personal experience of this in 1939, when, in the course of a lecture delivered at Cooper Union, New York, I ventured to observe: " American grammar is fast going to *hell,* which is where all grammars will land, I hope and pray, soon or late." In the New York *Journal-American's* report of the lecture the next morning hell was printed *h——l.*[2] Some American newspapers even hesitated to use such euphemistic forms as *damfino, damphool* and *helluva.*[3] Hollywood is still more prudish. As we have already seen, Article V of its official code of morals prohibits the use of " pointed profanity (this includes the use of *God, Lord, Jesus Christ,* unless used reverently, *hell, s.o.b., damn, Gawd*), or every other profane or vulgar expression, however used."

The Holy Name Society carries on a crusade against the use of the more forthright forms of profanity by American Catholics, apparently with some success among its actual members, who are all males. But many Catholics do not belong to it, and numbers of those who are enrolled have apparently got wind of the fact that *hell* and *damn,* if unaccompanied by sacred names, are not, in the judgment of moral theologians, blasphemous, and hence do not involve mortal sin.[4] The society, despite its late appearance in this country, is very ancient, for the cult upon which it is founded, to wit, devotion to the Holy Name of Jesus, was prescribed by the Council of Lyons in 1274. In its early days, that devotion seems to have been wholly of a positive char-

1 An Anthology of Printable Profanity, by Oren Arnold, Los Angeles *Times Sunday Magazine,* Jan. 13, 1935, p. 4.

2 The lecture was on Dec. 1, 1939. I should add that the Boston *Evening Globe,* in an editorial on it on Dec. 4, spelled out the word.

3 The elegant *swelluva* was reported in *American Speech,* Dec., 1939, p. 318.

4 I am reminded of this by a learned Dominican.

acter, and there was no emphasis upon the negative virtue of avoiding profane language. The latter object seems to have come forward in the Fifteenth Century, when a Spanish Dominican named Didacus of Victoria founded a confraternity to oppose the extravagant and often blasphemous swearing that marked the age. This confraternity was approved by Pope Pius IV on April 13, 1564, and soon afterward it absorbed the earlier cult, and became the Holy Name Society that flourishes today. How and by whom it was introduced in the United States seems to be unknown. By 1882 it was already sufficiently well established in the archdiocese of New York for a diocesan union to be formed there, but it was not until 1900, when a Dominican missionary priest, Father Charles H. McKenna, was appointed its director, that it began to reach its present proportions. In its early American days it seems to have been thought of mainly as a league against blasphemy, but since then its devotional purposes have been emphasized, and it has a wider programme. The obligations of members have been thus set forth officially:

1. To labor individually for the glory of God's Name, and to make it known to those who are ignorant of it.

2. Never to pronounce disrespectfully the Name of Jesus.

3. To avoid blasphemy, perjury, profane and indecent language.

4. To induce their neighbors to refrain from all insults against God and His saints, and from profane and unbecoming language.

5. To remonstrate with those who blaspheme or use profane language in their presence. This must be governed by zeal, prudence and common sense.

6. Never to work or carry on business unnecessarily on Sunday.

7. To do all they can to induce their dependents to sanctify Sunday.

8. To attend regularly the meetings and devotional exercises of the society.

9. To communicate in a body on the feast of the Holy Name of Jesus,— the second Sunday of January—and on the regular Communion Sunday of the society.

10. To have a requiem mass said each year, some time after the feast of the Holy Name, for all the deceased members. All who can attend the anniversary mass should do so.

11. To assemble at an hour convenient to the society every second Sunday of the month for devotional exercises, and for the transaction of business.

Every member, on being enrolled in the society, signs the following pledge:

> Blessed be God.
> Blessed be His Holy Name.
> Blessed be Jesus Christ true God and true Man.
> Blessed be the Name of Jesus.
> **I believe O Jesus**

That Thou art the Christ
The Son of the Living God.
I proclaim my love
For the Vicar of Christ on Earth.
I believe all the sacred truths
Which the Holy Catholic Church
Believes and teaches.
I promise to give good example
By the regular practice
Of my faith.
In honor of His Divine Name
I pledge myself against perjury
Blasphemy, profanity and obscene speech.
I pledge my loyalty
To the flag of my country.
And to the God given principles
Of freedom, justice and happiness
For which it stands.
I pledge my support
To all lawful authority
Both civil and religious.
I dedicate my manhood
To the honor of the Sacred Name of Jesus
And beg that He will keep me faithful
To these pledges
Until death.[1]

This pledge is recited by the members after the mass they are supposed to attend every month, and at all meetings of the society. In each diocese it has a spiritual director, appointed by the ordinary, but all the other officers are laymen. There is also a junior society for boys twelve years old or older. At eighteen or thereabout they pass into the society proper. It is apparently the theory of the spiritual directors that Catholic women do not swear, for they are not solicited to join.

Of the non-profane pejoratives in common American use *son-of-a-bitch* is the hardest worked, and by far. It rose to popularity in the United States during the decade before the Civil War,[2] and at the

---

1 I am indebted for the history of the society in the United States to Mr. Vincent dePaul Fitzpatrick, managing editor of the Baltimore *Catholic Review*. For its principles and practices see In His Name: Official Holy Name Manual; New York, 1941.

2 Partridge traces it in English use to 1712, but Mr. Eric Sandquist of Boston has pointed out "son and

heir of a mongrel bitch" in Shakespeare's *King Lear*, Act II, scene 2 (1605-6). There is evidence in the journal of Captain Thomas Morris, of the British Army, that the American Indians, if not the American whites, had picked it up by 1764. He says: "There was an alarm in the night, a drunken Indian having been seen at the skirt of the wood. One of the Delaware nation, who

start was considered extremely offensive. A German traveler, Theodor Griesinger, reported in 1858 [1] that it was " der ärgeste Schimpfname, dessen sich der Amerikaner bedient." He added, however, that " man hört es von Tausenden tausendmal täglich," and that " nirgends in der Welt wird mehr geflucht and geschimpft als in Amerika, and besonders in Newyork." He noted its identity with *hurensohn*, a fighting word among Germans.[2] *Son-of-a-bitch* is likewise supposed to be a fighting-word among Americans, but I am inclined to think that many other terms, including the simple *liar*, are more apt to provoke actual blows. Not infrequently, indeed, it is used almost affectionately, and when accompanied by a smile does not necessarily offer offense. It was so used in " The Virginian," a novel and movie by Owen Wister, wherein one character said to another, " You *son-of-a* ——," and the other interrupted with " When you call me that, smile." [3] But, as we have seen, it is now forbidden by the movie code of morals, along with its abbreviation, *s.o.b.*[4] The American newspapers avoid it diligently. When, on October 4, 1939, the tabloid New York *Daily News*, which is bolder than common, ventured to use it in a cartoon caption in the denatured form of *son-of-a* ——, the *Editor and Publisher*, the trade journal of the daily press, expressed indignation. The offending cartoon, which was by Ray Bailey, showed Stalin, Hitler and Mussolini standing at a bar. Mussolini seemed to be sulking, and Hitler, with one hand on a bottle of vodka and the other on Mussolini's shoulder, addressed him thus: " Come, Benito, I want you to shake hands with this *son-of-a* ——." The caveat of the *Editor and Publisher* was as follows:

No newspaper outside of New York City could get by with it, and we doubt that any other newspaper than the *News* would try to. Our own opinion is that they don't need to. The *News* editorial page is abundant proof every day that forcefulness can be attained without vulgarity or the introduction of corner-loafer vernacular. The undeniable fact that the four-word epithet has

---

happened to be with Pontiac's army, passing by the cabin where I lay, called out in broken English: 'D—d *son of a b—ch!* '" Morris, who served with the Seventeenth Regiment of Infantry, published his journal in Miscellanies in Prose and Verse; London, 1791. It was republished in the first volume of Early Western Travels, 1748–1846, edited by the late R. G. Thwaites; 33 vols.; Cleveland, 1904–07. For this I am in-

debted to Roy Harvey Pearce of the Johns Hopkins University.

1 Lebende Bilder aus Amerika; Stuttgart, 1858, p. 292.

2 So is *hijo de puta* in the Spanish-speaking countries.

3 I am indebted here to Mr. Edgar Gahan, of Westmount, Quebec.

4 The cognate *s.o.a.b.* is embalmed in the name of *Soab* creek on a map issued by the Canadian Geological Survey.

become one of the most common in the American language does not, we think, warrant its use in print before millions of people who still regard it as offensive. It isn't a word that a father would care to hear from the mouth of his young son, and its appearance in a *Daily News* editorial cartoon is about all the approval many young sons would ask for its inclusion in their own vocabularies. Editors can't afford to forget that phase of their responsibility.[1]

The English *bloody* continues to seem innocuous to Americans. The NED's first example of its use as foul language is from " Two Years Before the Mast," by the American Richard Henry Dana, 1840. After that it seems to have gone into hiding until the turn of the 8os, when John Ruskin denounced its use as " a deep corruption, not altering the form of the word, but defiling the thought in it." There has been some lessening of the English horror of it since George Bernard Shaw shocked the British Isles, in 1914, by putting it into the mouth of the elegant Mrs. Patrick Campbell, playing Eliza Doolittle in his play, " Pygmalion," but it is still regarded as somewhat advanced, though every male Englishman from 4 to 90 uses it more or less, and it is not unrecorded on the lips of females, at least below the rank of royal duchesses. Perhaps one may best explain its position by saying that it is still frowned upon officially, but is gradually losing its offensiveness to public opinion. Indeed, there is even some doubt about it officially, and that doubt shows itself in irresolution and lack of consistency. The Lord Chamberlain's Examiner of Plays, who censors all stage plays, allowed it to pass in " Pygmalion," but six years later, in 1920, he deleted it from a play dealing with labor.[2] In 1936 he winked at it when Noel Coward used it three or four times in a one-acter,[3] but before the end of the year the magistrates at Bath were fining a Fascist soap-boxer for uttering it in a speech.[4] During this period there was some discussion in the London newspapers of an order issued by Lord Beatty to Captain Sir Ernle Chatfield at the battle of Jutland — to wit: " There must be something wrong with our

1 Oct. 7, 1939. The worldly *New Yorker* used it in the collision form of *sonofabitch* on Feb. 26, 1944, p. 20.

2 It was likewise deleted when Pygmalion became a film, but the Lord Chamberlain had nothing to do with that. Films are policed by the Film Censor, who is even more watchful. But nothing comparable to our Postoffice censorship of books and magazines exists in England, so

there was no official action when John Masefield used *bloody* in The Everlasting Mercy in 1911, and the fact was not brought up against him when he was made Poet Laureate in 1930.

3 What Stage May Say, London *Daily Telegraph*, Jan. 15, 1936. I am indebted here to the late F. H. Tyson, of Hong Kong.

4 —— But Unbowed, London *Morning Post*, Sept. 25, 1936.

*bloody* ships, Chatfield. Turn two points to port " — but all the papers represented *bloody* by a dash.[1] They were still doing so in 1939,[2] but soon afterward the decline of prudery which came in with World War II emboldened some of them to spell it out. In 1941 even the London *Times* went overboard, as D. B. Wyndham Lewis recorded maliciously in the *Tatler*.[3] " Clashing her wiry old ringlets in a kind of palsied glee at her own audacity," he wrote, " Auntie *Times* has printed a little poem containing the line, ' I really loathe the *bloody* Hun,' and all Fleet Street stands aghast. . . . Don't say we didn't warn you if Auntie is seen dancing down Fleet Street ere long in her red flannel undies, bawling little French songs."

By 1942 the consternation of the journalists had begun to wear off, and before the end of that year a respectable provincial paper was printing *bloody* boldly — in a report of a speech before a Rotary Club by a rev. canon! [4] Simultaneously, the British Ministry of Information was employing Eric Knight to prepare a handbook for the use of American troops in England, in which it was explained that while *bloody* had still better be avoided in mixed company it was not forbidden to soldiers in the field. But this change of front was naturally accompanied by aberrations. So late as December, 1939, a Labor M.P., William Dobbie of Rotherham, was forced to apologize to the House of Commons for using *bloody* in debate.[5] There is, as I have said, no general objection to it in the United States, but it is not often heard save as a conscious Anglicism, and there are tender persons who profess to shiver when it is used, apparently on the ground that it has not yet come into full repute in England. In 1938 the Boston *Globe*, a highly decorous paper, shocked the Anglomaniacs of its territory by reporting that a six-year-old American girl, asked on her return from a trip to England how she had liked the country, replied that

1 For example, in Beatty's Immortal Phrase, London *Daily Telegraph*, March 12, 1936.
2 For example, Do You Know?, by Edward Shanks, London *Sunday Times*, Jan. 1, 1939.
3 Standing By, May 21, 1941.
4 Changing Language, Gorton *Reporter* (Ashton-under-Lyne), Oct. 30, 1942. The canon was the Rev. T. W. Taylor and the Rotary Club was that of Rochdale. The speech was quite iconoclastic in doctrine. The canon came out strongly against

Thomas Bowdler (1754–1825), who published an expurgated Family Shakespeare in 1818 and so gave the language the verb *to bowdlerize*. "He doubted," said the *Reporter's* report of the speech, "whether a severe expurgation was on the right lines, and questioned whether to-day we were lowering our standards."
5 British Decorum's Heavy Hand, by Paul W. Ward, London dispatch in the Baltimore *Sun*, Dec. 24, 1939.

she had liked it *bloody* well, and the *Globe* was forced to get out of the resulting unpleasantness by putting the blame upon an abandoned telegraph operator, who, so it alleged, had substituted *bloody* for *very*.[1]

There are frequent discussions of the origin of the term in the English philological literature, and even in the newspapers, but no general agreement has been reached. Most Englishmen, asked to account for its lingering disrepute, will tell you either that it is a shortened form of *by Our Lady*, and is hence blasphemous, or that it embodies a reference to catamenia, and is hence indecent. The first theory, of course, is obviously nonsense, for the English, taking one with another, do not object to blasphemy, and some of their common expressions are much worse. Nor does the known history of the term show any relation to any physiological process.[2] It apparently arose as a mere intensive in Restoration days, when there was a mild revival of strong language in England, and by the first quarter of the Eighteenth Century it had become quite innocuous. The NED suggests that it may have been related, at the start, to the noun *blood*, signifying a roistering young man of the upper class, but Partridge rejects this derivation as bookish and unwarranted. " There is no need," he says, " of ingenious etymologies; the idea of blood suffices." " The root-idea of blood as something vivid and/or distressing," he adds in his edition of Grose's " Classical Dictionary of the Vulgar Tongue," [3] " is never absent in the adjective." In the early days of its popularity in England *bloody* often appeared in the adverbial form of *bloodily*, and it is still used as an adverb quite as often as it is used as a verb, but the *-ly* ending long ago disappeared — a phenomenon frequently encountered in English, especially when the corresponding adjective ends with *y* and is in constant use, *e.g., very, jolly* and *pretty*. Says Ernest Weekley in " Words Ancient and Modern ": [4]

If we compare the use of Fr. *sanglant*, Ger. *blutig*, and Dutch *bloedig*, we see that we merely have to do with an expletive instinctively chosen for its grisly and repellent sound and sense. In Dutch *een bloedige hoon* is a bitter insult, what would be called in French *un sanglant outrage*. . . . [In French]

1 Retracts Slang, *Editor and Publisher*, May 14, 1938.
2 A third popular theory occasionally bobs up, but it is heard much less often than the two I have mentioned. It is to the effect that *bloody* refers to the blood shed at the Crucifixion, and is thus related to the archaic *God's blood*, which later became *'sblood*. See The Origin of *Bloody*, by P. A. Waldron, *John o' London's Weekly*, Oct. 29, 1937.
3 London, 1931, p. 42.
4 New York, 1926, p. 17.

the word is used with *injure, reproche, outrage,* etc. . . . German *blut* is still used as an intensive prefix, *e.g., blutarm* means miserably poor,[1] and the archaic *blutdieb* might be rendered in robust English by *bloody thief.* " *Das ist mein blutiger ernst* " is fairly polite German for " I seriously (Shavian *bloody-well*) mean what I say." Less polite is " Ich habe keinen *blutigen* heller " as a declaration of impecuniosity. Here *blutig* is a decorative substitute for *rot,* red. From all this it appears that there is no need to build up fantastic theories in order to account for the word with which we are dealing.[2]

The question as to how *bloody* came to be so disreputable in England remains. In 1942 Walter Duranty suggested that it may have suffered that change at the time of the Crimean War (1854–56), when the British soldiers probably encountered the Russian word *bliudi,* pronounced *blewdy* and meaning dirty, improper, obscene.[3] Unhappily for this theory *bloody* apparently aroused no indignation among English prudes until long after the middle of the Nineteenth Century, and I have been unable to find any evidence that the British soldiers in the Crimea ever actually became aware of *bliudi.* It is much easier to believe that the opposition to *bloody* was originally merely a squeamish Victorian objection to its reference to blood, and that its later extreme disrepute arose from the folk etymologies I have mentioned, and especially from the effort to relate it to catamenia. Such imbecile afterthoughts are common in the history of language, and it is not unusual for a term once perfectly harmless to acquire an aura of the forbidding with the passage of the years.

The English have produced a number of euphemisms for *bloody,* *e.g., bleeding, ruddy* and *sanguinary.* Of these, says an English correspondent,[4] *bleeding* and *ruddy* have become " swear-words in their

1 Several correspondents suggest that Weekley erred here. *Blutarm,* in German, is most often used to designate anemic, and when it is used in the sense he gives it is usually spelled as two words, *blut arm.* But *blutarm* as one word is given in Cassell's New German and English Dictionary, edited by Professor Karl Breul of Cambridge; London, 1909, as also meaning " poor as a church-mouse."

2 Of this Robert Withington says in A Note on *Bloody, American Speech,* Oct., 1930, p. 33: " It is, however, to be remarked that both the French and the German ' equivalents' of *bloody* are distinctly lit-

erary words." Weekley's examples of *sanglant* are from Molière and Voltaire. When Shaw's Pygmalion was translated into German and presented at the austere Lessing Theatre in Berlin an equivalent for the *bloody* in Eliza Doolittle's speech, " Not *bloody* likely," was found in the banal exclamation *quatsch,* meaning twaddle. In German, London *Morning Post,* Sept. 9, 1935.

3 Private communication, Dec. 4, 1942. Duranty later recorded this surmise in his book, Search For a Key; New York, 1943, p. 18.

4 Mr. Arthur D. Jacobs, of Manchester.

own right, as strong as *bloody* itself," and *sanguinary* is used " only facetiously." For a while the more prissy English newspapers used *the Shavian adjective*, and, for the adverb, *pygmalionly*, but these somewhat arch and roguish forms did not last long. *Blooming*, which the NED traces to 1882, has also been used, but it is regarded as so feeble that the British Broadcasting Corporation allows message-bringers and crooners to moan it upon the ether.[1] When, on January 22, 1887, a new operetta, " *Ruddygore*," by Gilbert and Sullivan, was presented at the Savoy Theatre, London, the title caused a considerable raising of eyebrows. It was exactly descriptive, for the piece was a burlesque on the gory melodramas of the time, but the more queasy Savoyards raised such a pother against it that it was changed to " *Ruddi*gore " after the fourth performance. Even then, there were murmurs, and letters of protest flowed in on the authors. To one (and perhaps to more than one) of these letters Gilbert made the following characteristic reply:

> I do not know what there is to complain of. *Bloodigore* would have been offensive, but there can be no offense about *Ruddygore*. *Ruddi* is perfectly harmless; if, for example, I were to talk of your *ruddy* cheek you could not be angry with me, but if I were to speak, as well I might, about your – well —— [2]

The Australians, who are much more spacious in their speech than the English, use *bloody* with great freedom, and do not seem to regard it as especially shocking. They call it, somewhat proudly, *the great Australian adjective*,[3] and have embodied it in some of their folk-poetry — for example, the following refrain of a song sung by Australian troops stationed in Newfoundland in 1942:

1 Here I am again indebted to Mr. Jacobs, who says that *blooming* bears " exactly the same relation to *bloody* as *dash* does to *damn*."

2 The record here is taken from a series of letters in the London *Sunday Times*, May 24, May 31, June 7 and June 14, 1936. I am indebted for clippings of them to the late F. H. Tyson, of Hong Kong.

3 A contributor signing himself R. G. H. reports in the Sydney (N. S. W.) *Morning Herald* (A Word of Fear, Feb. 11, 1939) that this phrase originated at the University of Melbourne in 1898. The university, at that time, conferred the degree of doctor of letters on Edward E. Morris, author of Austral English: A Dictionary of Australian Words, Phrases and Usages; London, 1898, and the students staged a burlesque of the ceremony. Morris had omitted *bloody* from his book. The students, apparently resenting this prudery, presented a solemnly-gowned candidate who carried under his arm a huge tome inscribed The Great Australian Adjective. Other Australian discussions of *bloody* are in Australian or Shavian?, by George Mackaness, Sydney *Morning Herald*, March 1, 1941, and After Business Hours, by Wallace Nelson, *Australian Manufacturer* (Sydney), Jan. 28, 1939.

No *bloody* sports; no *bloody* games;
No *bloody* fun with *bloody* dames;
Won't even tell their *bloody* names;
Oh, *bloody, bloody, bloody!* [1]

The Australians (like the English, but to a larger extent) use *bloody* as an inserted intensive in various other words, just as Americans use *goddam,* e.g., *imma-bloody-material, umber-bloody-ella, inde-bloody-pendent, hippo-bloody-crite, abso-bloody-lutely, hoo-bloody-rah.*[2] It will be noted that the *ma* in the first example is duplicated, no doubt for euphony. There is also a common abbreviation, *N.B.G.,* i.e., *no bloody good.*[3]

1 Robert Graves says in his Lars Porsena, or, The Future of Swearing; New York, 1927, p. 34, that this song originated during World War I and is called simply The Australian Poem. New stanzas are added from time to time.

2 I am indebted here to Messrs. P. E. Cleator, Norman Anning, David H. Dodge and G. S. Leach. An interesting note on such forms is in Sandwich Words, by Harold Wentworth, *Philological Studies,* Sept., 1939, pp. 65–67. Wentworth lists some curious forms, *e.g., abso-one-hundred-percent-lutely, abso-god-* *dam-lutely, West-by-God-Virginia,* and Sinclair Lewis's "I'll *by thunder* make you artistic." The late Irving Babbitt of Harvard (1865–1933), the foe of the Romantic movement, is said to have been fond of *son-of-a-Romantic-bitch.* Joseph Pulitzer's invention of *inde-god-dam-pendent* and *obli-goddam-nation* is noted in AL4, p. 315.

3 A long essay on *bloody* is in Words, Words, Words!, by Eric Partridge; London, 1934. See also Words Ancient and Modern, by Ernest Weekley; New York, 1926, pp. 16–19.

# LIST OF WORDS AND PHRASES

bilk, to, 11
bill, 460
bill, to, 463
billboard, 460
billdad, 250
bill-fold, 460
billiard-academy, 576
billiard-parlor, 576
billiards-saloon, 478
billiard studio, 576
billion, 168, 461
bimbam, 251
bindery, 348
bingo, 461
biog, 337
biographee, 365
biography, to, 387
birdie, 517
biscuit, 68, 79, 220, 461,
    465, 482
bish, to, 396
bishop, 260, 538, 548
Bismarck herring, 430
bitch, 652, 657, 658, 660
bite, to, 11
bite the dust, to, 67, 68,
    595
bite the ground, to, 68
bite the sand, to, 68
bitter, 268, 458
bitter-beer, 268
blabfest, 426
black, 168, 201, 621, 630;
    -alder, 168; -bass, 168;
    -bear, 168; -coat, 487
black as blazes, as, 663
Blackberry Winter, 184
black boots, to, 481
Black Dan, 308
black-hand, 607
black-hander, 607
black-horse cavalry, 295
black-jack, 261, 461
blackleg, 481
black-marketeer, 360
blackteer, 360
black tie, 476
black velvet, 269
blades, 38
blame, 664, 668
blamed, 664, 665
blank, 461
blarneyfest, 426
blast, 334, 664, 668
blasted, 664, 665
blather, 94

blaue, 636
blazes, 663, 664
bleeding, 681
blessed event, 331
blessed event, to, 331
blewdy, 681
blickie, 191
blimey, 508
blind, 481
blind baggage, 457
blind-pig, 265
blind-tiger, 265
blintzes, 435
blitz, 245, 514
blizzard, 93, 244, 245, 440,
    451
blizzardom, 358
bloc, 297, 334
block, 75, 217, 220, 458
block of flats, 458
block of shops, 220
bloedig, 680
blofista, 638
blonde, 620
blondie, 632
blood and thunder, 243
blood count, to, 418
blood disease, 647
bloodfrst, 426
bloodily, 680
blood, sweat and tears, 514
bloody, 111, 660, 678, 679,
    680, 681, 682, 683
bloody-well, 681
blooming, 682
blouse, 505
blousette, 362
blow, 334
blowed, 664
blowhard, 452
blowing, 280
blow-off, 595
blow off, to, 594
blow-torch, 461
blow up, to, 499
blow up like a steamboat,
    to, 229
blud, 78
blue, 201, 473; -belled,
    673; -blazer, 260; -grass,
    489; -law, 200, 489;
    -nose, 489, 611
blue as blazes, as, 663
blueprint, 328, 387
blue-sky law, 489
blue, to be as, 473

bluff, 68, 217, 223, 224,
    280, 440, 441
bluff, to, 67
Bluff City, 223
bluffer, 224
bluffing, 224
blummie, 191
Blunderbuss, the, 309
blurb, 110, 329, 330, 379
blurb, to, 389
blurbist, 338
blustiferous, 231
blutarm, 681
blutdieb, 681
blutig, 680, 681
blutiger, ernst, 681
bo, 601
B.O., 592
boar, 603, 652, 654
boarding-house, 451
boards, 461
board-school, 479
boatable, 39
boater, 484
bobateria, 352
bobatorium, 354
bobby, 465
bobolink, 210
boche, 599
bock-beer, 316
bodaciously, 94, 230, 231
bodewash, 657
body, 570
bogey, 634
boggard, 641
bog-house, 641
bog-shop, 641
bogue, to, 232
bogus, 73, 122, 232, 406,
    451
bogy, 634
Bohemian, 601
bohunk, 601, 602
boiled sweets, 462
bologna, 332, 429
bolshevik, 673
bolshevize, to, 401
bolt, to, 280
bolter, 280
bombee, 365
bombshell, to, 386
bonanza, 312
bone-dry, 264, 305
bonehead, 328, 379
bonnet, 470, 472, 513
bony-fidely, 13

by hatchet-heads and hammer-handles, 665
by heck, 663
by hell, 662
by hell's peekhole, 665
by-law, 477
by-line, 336
by-line, to, 389
by me, 127
by Our Lady, 680
by St. Boogar and all the saints at the backside of the door of Purgatory, 665
by the devil and Tom Walker, 665
by the double-barreled jumping jiminetty, 665
by the great horn spoon, 669
by the high heels of St. Patrick, 665
by the holy cinders, 665
by the holy St. Mackerel, 665
by the piper that played before Moses, 665
by the ripping, roaring, jumping Jerusalem, 665
by the universe, 671
by thunder, 663
cabal, 287
cabbage-head, 599
cabin, 150, 487
cabineteer, 360
cablegram, 243, 326
caboodle, 244
caboose, 244, 462
cab-rank, 462, 484
cab-stand, 462
cache, 319
cactus-cat, 250
Cactus Jack, 308
-cade, 354, 356
cadet, 410
caecum, 660
Caesar-or-nobody-dom, 127
cafe, to, 389
cafe-society, 326
cafeteria, 350–354
cafetiria, 351
cafetta, 362
cajan, 596
cajan French, 597
cakery, 349

caketeria, 352
calaboose, 151, 197, 312
calamity-howler, 298
calculate, to, 44, 45, 47, 52, 77, 78
calendar, 462, 463
calf's neck, 259
calico-corn, 220
call-box, 484
call-boy, 462
call down, to, 393
called home, 595
called to the bar, 503
caller-downer, 381
call-house, 658
callithumpian, 233, 319
call to the bar, to, 458
call you back, to, 70
calumet, 1, 197
Camdenite, 362
camelcade, 357
camera-fiend, 370
camerado, 125
camerateria, 353
camerateur, 575
camorra, 607
camorrist, 607
campaign, 279, 280; -button, 280; -club, 280; -fund, 280; -document, 280; -manager, 280; -orator, 280; -speech, 280
campaign, to, 280
camporee, 365
campo santo, 571
campster, 360
campus, 215
campus briefs, 659
campus politics, 488
can, 268, 443, 462, 640
canary, 435
canary, to, 389
Candelmas Day, 177
candidacy, 168
candidature, 168
candy, 64, 462
candy-store, 73, 462
candyteria, 352
cane, 150, 463
canine control officer, 577
canitist, 573
canned, 462
cannery, 348
cannon, 463
cannonade, 356

canoe, 177, 178, 180; -club, 179; -fleet, 179; -man, 180; -place, 180; racing, 180; -tree, 180; -wood, 180
canoeing, 179
canoeist, 179, 180
canoer, 180
canon, 500, 591
cañon, 312
canoness, 591
can-opener, 463
can't, 8, 405
cantabile, 126
can take it, 453
cant-hook, 317
cantico, 170
canvasback, 201
canvass, 280
canyon, 198, 312, 440
capacitator, 567
capitalist, 673
capote allemande, 597
capote anglaise, 597
captain, 525, 532, 541, 549
car, 463
caraway-roll, 504
carborundum, 341
carcajou, 170
car-clinic, 589
cardigan, 484
careless, 155
caretaker, 473
caribou, 169, 171, 197
car in every garage, 283
carnapper, 370
carnival, 463
car-park, 477
carom, 463
carousal, 463
carpet-area, 469
carpetbag, 295
carpetbagger, 295, 440, 511
carpet-sack, 295
carriage, 463
carriage-repository, 348
carrier, 468
carrousel, 463
carryall, 197
carry an election, to, 297
carry a ticket, to, 281
cart, 459
car-washery, 349
case, 418, 568, 569, 570
case work, 593

crematory, 571
crème vichyssoise, 430
creole, 597, 607, 631
creole of Jerusalem, 617
crevasse, 197, 319
crib, 658
crick, 337
crickey, 665
crime of '73, 299
criminal operation, 646
criollo, 597
cripes, 665
crisp, 478
critic, 154
criticize, to, 400
crittur, 45
croak, to, 594
crocodile, 504
crone, 160
crook, 443
crookdom, 359
crool, 380
cross-cut, 440
cross-of-gold-and-crown-
  of-thorns, 301
cross the path, to, 185
crosswordpuzzledom, 359
crosswordpuzzleitis, 364
crow, 636
crowd, 297
crowd the mourners, to,
  297
crower, 655
crowing-cock, 259
cruising, 465
cruller, 186, 189
crump, 668
crusheroo, 368
crystal, 465, 466
cucumber, 119
Cuffey, 634
Cuffeydom, 358
culheag, 170
cultus, 310
cumfort, 78
cupboard, 464
cup-form, 659
cup-towel, 113
cup-wiper, 113
curate, 500
curb, to, 335, 385
curdled, 331
curl up, to, 53
curse, 665, 668
cursed, 664
curse out, to, 393

Curtis creek, 221
curved, 266
cushaw, 170
cuspidor, 192
cuss, 77, 664, 668
cuss, to, 665
cussed, 77, 228, 664, 665
cussedest, 665
cussedness, 665
cussing, 665
cuss out, to, 665
custodial engineer, 577
custodial officer, 593
custodian-engineer, 582
customable, 23, 24
customers' broker, 577
customers' man, 577
customize, to, 402
custom-made, 402, 466
cut, 466
cut, to, 335, 658
cut a face, to, 317
cut a shindy, to, 239
cut a shine, to, 392
cute, 78
cute-cuss, 246
cuter-cuss, 246
cutex, 347
cuticura, 347
cutting, 464, 466
cyclery, 349
cylinder, 318
cystoscope, to, 385, 418
dad, 520, 521, 668
dad-, 664
dad-blame, to, 664
dad-blamed, 520, 665
dad-blast, to, 664
dad-blasted, 520, 665
dad burn, to, 520, 664, 665
D.A.D.D.S., 412
daddy, 520, 521
dad-fetch, to, 520, 664, 668
dad-gast, to, 664
dad-gum, to, 520, 664, 668
dad-gummed, 674
dad-rat, to, 664
dad-rot, to, 664
dad-seize, to, 664
dad-seized, 665
dad-shame, to, 664
dad-shamed, 665
dad-sizzle, to, 664
dad-sizzled, 665
dad-slapped, 674
dad-snatch, to, 664

dad-swamp, to, 664
dad-swamped, 665
dag, 668
dag-gone, 668
dago, 606, 607
dagone, 667
dago red, 262, 606
dag take me, 671
daguerreian artist, 575
Daiquiri cocktail, 260
daisy, 255, 256
damaged, 592
damaskeene, 347
dame, 559
dame commander, 560
dame grand cross, 560
Dame Mary, 560
damfino, 674
damfoolski, 427
dammit, 645
damn, 643, 664, 665, 667,
  668, 672, 674, 682
damnation, 663, 664, 666
damndest, 668
damned, 664, 667, 668, 672
damphool, 674
damyankee, 193
dan, 668
dance, to, 397
danceathon, 366
dance-fiend, 370
danceitis, 364
dance-mixer-upper, 381
dancery, 349
danceteria, 353
dander, 53
dang, 664, 668
danged, 664
danseuse, 371
Darby, 466
dark brethren, 632
dark-brown taste, 263
darkey, 621, 632
dark horse, 295
darling, 73
darn, 13, 14, 67, 452, 664,
  666, 668
darn, to, 667
darnation, 667
darndest, 668
darned, 77, 664
darn sweet, 666, 667
darter, 78
dash, 668, 682
dashed, 664, 669
dash it, 669

sician, 328; -road, 453;
-sailor, 328; -track, 505
dis-, 155
disappearingest, 409
disarray, 160
disaster, to, 382
discipless, 590
discombobberate, 244
discomboberate, 244
discomboborate, 244
discombobulate, 244
discretion, to, 387
disgraceful, 154, 155
disguised, 267
dish-cloth, 113
dishpan, 466
dish-towel, 113
dish-wiper, 113
disinfect, to, 399
disinfest, to, 399
dissenter, 500, 501
dissentering, 501
distingué, 125
distributor, 467
district, 467
district attorney, 467
diveroo, 367
divide, 223
division, 467
divvy, 295
D. Litt., 531
D. L. O., 527
D. O., 527
do a Corrigan, to, 393
do a Dutch, to, 601
do a urine, to, 418
doby, 313
docity, 85, 86, 380
dock, 467
doctor, 525, 529, 531, 548,
554, 556, 591
doctor, to, 385
doctress, 590, 591
dodger, 488
dodge the issue, to, 280
doe, 655
dogburger, 428
dogcaster, 369
dog-catcher, 577
dog-fight, 509
doggist, 363
doggondest, 668
doggone, 664, 667
dog-house, 328
doghouse, to, 389
dognapper, 327, 370

do-gooder, 327
Dogwood Winter, 184
dokkie, 329
-dom, 358, 359
domestic mails, 467
domestic servant, 120
dominie, 191
Don, 335
don, 502, 531
Donald Duck, 308
donate, to, 122, 244
done did, 94
done for, 595
done said, 94
donk, 522
don't, 8, 405
don't care a cuss, 665
doodad, 330
doorkey children, 593
dope, 186, 189, 319, 449;
-fiend, 189, 366, 370,
448; -peddler, 189;
-sheet, 189
dope, to, 189
dope out, to, 189
dopester, 189, 359
-dor, 366
Dora, 410
dorey, 504
D.O.S., 527
doshdang, 669
doss house, 469
do the handsome thing,
to, 50
do the square thing, 392
dotter, 331
double-cross, 453
double-cross, to, 508
double-Dutch, 601
double-house, 201, 202
douceur, 125
douche, 660
doughnutery, 349
Dow City, 222
down, 491, 492
down, to, 228, 398
down-along, 491
down and out, 595
down cellar, 228
down country, 228, 492
down East, 228, 492
down grade, 228
down-line, 491
down on, 228
down river, 228
down sick, to be, 228

down South, 228
down to the shore, 492
downtown, 228, 467, 491
doxologize, to, 85
doxology, 240
Dr., 525, 528, 538, 568
draftee, 364
dragon, 246
drains, 478
dramateur, 340
dramatician, 574
draper's shop, 467
drapy, 408
drat, 664, 668
draughts, 86, 463
drawers, 467, 657
drawing-pin, 485
dreadful, 46
dreck, 433
dredge, 467
dredger, 467
drei, 317
dresser, 567
dressing-gown, 460
dressing-room, 640
dressmake, to, 396
drew, 8
dried beef, 429
drillery, 349
drink, to, 397
drinkery, 349
drive, 327, 334
driver, 475
dropper-inner, 381
drownded, 8
drugeria, 352
druggist, 225, 467
drug-store, 90, 467
drug-store cowboy, 333
druidess, 591
drum-majorette, 362
drunk, 266
dry, 305
dry-dry, 305
dry-goods, 201, 202
drygoodsery, 349
drygoodsteria, 352
drygoods-store, 217, 467
dry ice, 341
dry Martini, 268
dry, to go, 305
dry up, to, 653
D.S.D., 527
dubble, 78
Dubonnet cocktail, 260
ducklegger; 369

# INDEX

It would burden this Index unduly, and serve no useful purpose, to enter all the references to *American Speech, Dialect Notes*, the New English Dictionary and the Dictionary of American English. The entries are therefore confined to those which go beyond the mere citing of these indispensable authorities.

## A NOTE ON THE TYPE

*This book was set on the Linotype in Janson, a recutting made direct from the type cast from matrices (now in possession of the Stempel foundry, Frankfurt am Main) made by Anton Janson some time between 1660 and 1687.*

*Of Janson's origin nothing is known. He may have been a relative of Justus Janson, a printer of Danish birth who practised in Leipzig from 1614 to 1635. Some time between 1657 and 1668 Anton Janson, a punch-cutter and type-founder, bought from the Leipzig printer Johann Erich Hahn the type-foundry which had formerly been a part of the printing house of M. Friedrich Lankisch. Janson's types were first shown in a specimen sheet issued at Leipzig about 1675. Janson's successor, and perhaps his son-in-law, Johann Karl Edling, issued a specimen sheet of Janson types in 1689. His heirs sold the Janson matrices in Holland to Wolffgang Dietrich Erhardt.*